ELBRIDGE THOMAS GERRY

Commodore Elbridge Thomas Gerry
1837-1927

ELBRIDGE THOMAS GERRY

AN EXCEPTIONAL LIFE IN GILDED GOTHAM

SHELLEY L. DOWLING

TALBOT
PUBLISHING
Clark, New Jersey

ISBN 978-1-61619-387-4 (hardcover)
ISBN 978-1-61619-569-4 (paperback)

TALBOT PUBLISHING

AN IMPRINT OF

THE LAWBOOK EXCHANGE, LTD.
33 Terminal Avenue
Clark, New Jersey 07066-1321

Please see our website for a selection of our other publications and fine facsimile reprints of classic works of legal history:
www.lawbookexchange.com

Frontispiece: Elbridge T. Gerry wearing NYSPCC badge and holding book. Source: Gerry estate at Lake Delaware, photograph by Notman Photographic Company, Boston (no date). Digital copy by author.
Cover: *Top left:* Gerry mansion exterior photograph. Source: Byron Company (New York, N.Y.) Museum of the City of New York, Street Scene, 1899, 5th Ave. & 61st St. (Gerry House), 93.1.1.18049, licensed for book publishing. *Top right:* Supreme Court Building in Washington, D.C. Source: Office of the Archivist, Architect of the Capitol of the United States, Item # AOC image #356372, Exterior of the Supreme Court Building, Michael Dunn, Chief of Photography, Architect of the Capitol. *Bottom right:* New York Society for the Prevention of Cruelty to Children carriage. Source: Archives of the New York Society for the Prevention of Cruelty to Children, 61 Williams Street, New York City. Courtesy of Joseph Gleason, Archivist. *Bottom left:* "Annual Cruise of the New York Yacht Club – 1911: Grand Illuminations at Station 4 – New London," oil on linen, 26" x 48." Copyright 2011 Russ Kramer Fine Art. All rights reserved. www.russkramer.com. *Center:* Elbridge T. Gerry portrait. Source: Author's digital photograph of unsigned oil painting hanging in the General Morgan Lewis, Lake Delaware estate, New York, no date.

Library of Congress Cataloging-in-Publication Data

Names: Dowling, Shelley L., author.
Title: Elbridge Thomas Gerry : an exceptional life in gilded Gotham / Shelley L. Dowling.
Description: Clark, New Jersey : Talbot Publishing, An Imprint of The Lawbook Exchange, Ltd., 2017. | Includes bibliographical references and index.
Identifiers: LCCN 2017023926| ISBN 9781616193874 (hardcover : alk. paper) | ISBN 9781616195694 (pbk. : alk. paper)
Subjects: LCSH: Gerry, Elbridge T. (Elbridge Thomas), 1837-1927. | Gerry family. | Lawyers--United States--Biography. | Lawyers--New York (State)--New York--Biography. | Reformers--United States--Biography. | Reformers--New York (State)--New York--Biography. | Social reformers--United States--Biography. | Social reformers--New York (State)--New York--Biography.
Classification: LCC KF373.G466 D69 2017 | DDC 340.092 [B] --dc23
LC record available at https://lccn.loc.gov/2017023926

Printed in the United States of America on acid-free paper

Dedication

The Supreme Court Library Family

To honor the Library's eternal commitment to the preservation of legal history through the care, organization and daily use of the Library's *Gerry Collection* in support of the essential and enduring case work of the Justices of the Supreme Court who analyze, interpret and infuse life into the *Rule of Law* from generation to generation in America.

The Gerry Family

To honor the Gerry family's commitment to the faith, principles, and civic duty of their forefathers through the continued personal contributions of each generation to the living legacies of the Gerry family. To thank the Gerry family for their preservation of documents and artifacts that tell the story of the founding period and the evolutionary decades that followed in New York and throughout the United States of America.

Also, to honor the related Gallatin, Goelet, and Livingston families for their philanthropic commitment and contributions made from generation to generation in New York City and New York State; and most especially to recognize their generous and continued preservation of historic documents and artifacts in their homes, archives, libraries and museums.

My Family

To thank and honor my family without whom this book could not have been completed. The enthusiastic support of my husband, Patrick, and my daughter, Kathleen, who provided the wind beneath my wings over several years of research and writing. They have been my fun travel companions, assistant photographers and the extra pair of hands that I needed to help search through many city directories and local records, a true labor of love. For my daughter Aaren and granddaughters Lauren and Ashely for whom this story may light a candle of inspiration.

TABLE OF CONTENTS

	Foreword by Elbridge T. Gerry III	ix
	Acknowledgments	xi
	Introduction	xv
1	The Early Years	1
2	Education and Apprenticeship	35
3	Passing the Torch	67
4	Father, Lawyer, Leader	91
5	Gerry's Society	115
6	Gilded Gotham: The 1880's Part I	153
7	Gilded Gotham: The 1880's Part II	197
8	Gilded Gotham: The 1880's Part III	249
9	Gilded Gotham: The 1890's Part I	277
10	Gilded Gotham: The 1890's Part II	321
11	The Twentieth Century: Part I 1900 to 1909	403
12	The Twentieth Century: Part II 1910 to 1930	465
	APPENDIX	533
A	Goelet, Gerry, Livingston, Gallatin Family Tree	534
B	New York City Locations	536
C	Commodore Elbridge T. Gerry's Children	539
	C-1 Mabel Gerry Drury 1872–1930	540
	C-2 Angelica Livingston Gerry 1871–1960	548
	C-3 Senator Peter Goelet Gerry 1879–1957	558
	C-4 Robert Livingston Gerry 1877–1957	566
D	Commodore Elbridge T. Gerry's Grandsons	579
E	American Family Legacies	595
F	European Family Origins	605
	F-1 Emigration Map	606
	F-2 Albert Gallatin and his Descendants	607
	F-3 The Gallatin Family Ancestry	608
	F-4 Goelet Family Tree	615

F-5 The Goelet Family Ancestry 616
F-6 Succession of Family Titles to Lake Delaware 623
F-7 Livingston Family Tree 624
F-8 The Livingston Family Ancestry 625

List of Illustrations 633
Notes 653
Table of Cases 673
Index 679

FOREWORD

After more than 275 years in America our family story has been brought together into one cohesive narrative by the diligent research and writing of the author. During her several years of work on this project we were glad to share the artifacts, photographs, family papers and anecdotes that have been collected and treasured through the generations at our Lake Delaware home built by our ancestors, General Morgan Lewis and his wife, Gertrude Livingston.

While none of our generation, unfortunately, are old enough to have known the Commodore, the author's research has given us a better understanding of his and the family's contribution to the history of our country. We are therefore indebted to the author for bringing it all together in one important story that we can share with present generations of our extensive family.

Importantly, our family stories, memories and the many contributions of our ancestors over generations have been resurrected and a new level of detail and connectedness has been produced. We are most pleased that our story has the added benefit of shedding light on the cultural, political and social history of our country, our state and our city for the enjoyment of the American people.

With gratitude,

Elbridge Thomas Gerry, Jr.

[referred to as Elbridge T. Gerry III in the book]

Acknowledgments

Individuals

The following individuals have generously contributed their knowledge, their friendship, and their unqualified support during my many years of research and writing for this historical biography. I could not have done it without them and I thank each of you here for sharing in this journey that has been a labor of love for the subject matter, the Gerry family and for the Supreme Court of the United States and its Library.

Elbridge T. Gerry III. *My trusted advisor, editor, and source of encouragement, and now, dear friend.*

Justice Ruth Bader Ginsburg. *A treasured mentor, reference, and friend at the Supreme Court.*

Diane Simpson, Associate Librarian, Rare Book & Tech Services, USSC. *My partner in crime during the early years of research, I could not have done it without you.*

Patricia Evans, Senior Reference Library, USSC. *Friend, advisor, and generous reference.*

Patti Hummel, Manager, Lake Delaware Estate. *Friend, guide, and keeper of all things Gerry.*

John Goelet. *Charming host, creative vintner, and valued storyteller.*

Tom Antoshack, Goelet LLC. *Generous liason with the Goelet family.*

Robert Manice and family. *Brilliant, artistic siblings who shared their historic Newport home, Southside, with me.*

Ann Puckett. *Dear friend, colleague and generous reference.*

Shelley Waite, Gerry Archives. *Patient, skilled, keeper of the Gerry family papers.*

Joseph Gleason, NYSPCC. *Archivist, dedicated and kind historian who shared the Gerry Society archives in New York City with me, as well as insightful stories.*

Stephanie Latimer, William & Mary Grad Assist 2009-2010. *I could not have done it without her steadfast support with her work on the 7 reels of Gerry family papers.*

Charles Dodson Walker. *Charlie, famous organist and wonderful Gerry family friend, a story teller and friend.*

Neal Campbell. *Organist, liason in New York who is now a family friend.*
Russ Kramer. *Artist, amazing painter who captured the vibrancy of the Gilded Aged life on the yacht* Electra.

Special Thanks

Gilder Lehrman Foundation, for awarding me a 2012-2013 *Gilder Lehrman fellowship* to complete my New York research.
Deb Cyprych, Editor, *National Genealogical Society Magazine,* for her professional editing of the book and her kind words of support.
Valerie Horowitz, Managing Editor, Publications, Talbot Publishing and The Lawbook Exchange Reprints. Thank you for your expert advice and collaborative improvements throughout the design and production of this book. You are a welcome new friend in legal publishing and law librarianship.
Doris Kappes, manuscript reviewer and friend whose editorial skill and suggestions improved the initial draft of the manuscript and affirmed by efforts.
Gregory Talbot, President, Talbot Publishing /The Lawbook Exchange, Ltd. I am most grateful for your interest and confidence in publishing the Gerry biography and your dedication to rare and historical legal materials.

Churches

Cathedral of Saint John the Divine, NYC, Wayne Kempton, Archivist
Church of the Transfiguration, NYC
Saint Edward the Martyr, NYC, Father Derby, Pastor
Saint James, Bovina, NY
Saint James, Hyde Park, NY

Colleges and Universities

Columbia University, New York City
Avery Architectural & Fine Arts Library, Jason Escalante, Drawings & Archives Assistant

Butler Library, Jocelyn K. Wilk, Public Services Archivist, Rare Book & Manuscript Library
Hartwick College, Shelley Waite, Archivist of the Gerry Family Papers
New York University, Bobst Library, Special Collections & Archives, Lisa Darms, Senior Archivist
Salve Regina College, Goelet Family Papers
Stanford University, microfilm loan of the Gerry Family Papers
Yale University, Sterling Memorial Library, research access to collections.
William & Mary College, for graduate student assistance for one year and encouragement.

Historical Societies and Libraries

Delaware County Historical Association, H. Fletcher Davidson Library Archives
City of New York Department of Records
City of New York Municipal Library, Christine Bruzzese
Library of Congress, Prints and Photographs Division
Marblehead Museum and Historical Society
Museum of the City of New York, Lindsay Turley, Archivist
Mystic Seaport Museum
New Haven Museum & Historical Society
New York Historical Society
Gilder Lehrman Collection at the New York Historical Society
National Portrait Gallery, London
New York Local History Library
New York Public Library
Prints & Photographs, Meredith Friedman
New York Society for the Prevention of Cruelty to Children,
Mary L. Pulido, Ph.D., Executive Director
New York Yacht Club Library, Vanessa Cameron, Librarian & Archivist
Newport Preservation Society
Newport Local History Library
Roosevelt Library, Hyde Park
Staatsburgh-on-Hudson Historical Site
Supreme Court Historical Society, Publications Committee, and Clare Cushman, Director of Publications
United States Supreme Court Library, entire staff.

Introduction

The idea for this epic biography came about through a happy accident over twenty-five years ago in the Library of the *United States Supreme Court.* As the newly appointed Librarian of the Court I was exploring the special 30,000 volume *Gerry Collection* which occupied the beautiful Rare Book Room. One set of small books caught my eye, a rare 1765 Dublin Edition of *Blackstone's Commentaries,* the bible of English law for students and lawyers in the eighteenth century. It was a four volume miniature edition, one a lawyer or law student might carry with him while traveling. As I opened the soft brown leather cover of volume one a letter slipped out from between the pages and fell on the table before me. It was a small, single sheet of paper, a note from Elbridge Gerry, Jr., the son of the Founding Father, Vice President Elbridge Gerry, to his nephew Elbridge *Thomas* Gerry, on his twenty second birthday, December 25, 1859. After young Elbridge safely tucked the note inside the small leather book in 1859 it was not discovered until 80 years later when the Court Librarian restored the book's leather cover in 1940 and returned the note to its hiding place inside the cover. Another 50 years passed until I curiously opened the little set of brown leather books in the Rare Book Room. The note read:

> New York December 25, 1859
> Mr. Elbridge T. Gerry,
>
> My dear nephew, allow me to wish you a very merry Christmas and to present a copy of Blackstone's Commentaries which my father gave me from his library when I commenced the study of law.
>
> May you live in health and happiness, to transmit it to <u>your</u> grandson personally, and if he shall possess the virtues, talent, and merit of <u>his</u> grandfather, he will be an ornament to society and his name will be honored by his posterity.
>
> Truly your affectionate Uncle, Elbridge Gerry, Jr.

After catching my breath I began to wonder about these three Gerry men, each successively named *Elbridge* and how and why did the Supreme Court obtain this collection. Indeed which of the Elbridge Gerrys was the book collector and which was the donor of the collection? Ultimately these simple questions led to an epic story of the fascinating lives and legacies of the extended Gerry family from the founding era of America to the present day.

To my surprise, after a lengthy preliminary investigation, the only information the *Supreme Court* records or the *National Archives* possessed was the fact that the collection was donated in 1928 by Senator Peter Gerry of Rhode Island, the son of Elbridge Thomas Gerry, and that legislation was passed in Congress to authorize the Court to accept the gift. The library administrative records held little more than a letter from Senator Peter Gerry with a general offer of a book collection and a list of the 30,000 books typed on old onion skin paper which included the designated" box number" followed by a list of the books that were packed into that numbered storage box. The books were packed in no particular order so the box list told us nothing about where the books were located before or how they might have been organized by the previous owner in the Gerry family. When the gift was made it was understood that the Gerrys were in a hurry to wisely dispose of the collection, however, the *Supreme Court of the United States* had no building of its own in which to place the several hundred boxes of books. In fact, as late as 1928 the Supreme Court still heard oral arguments for their cases in the old court room in the Old Senate Chamber on the second floor of the Capitol building. Most of the Justices had their offices at home and had to use law books from the *Library of Congress* collection, some of which were moved to rooms adjacent to the courtroom. As a result, the entire 30,000 volume gift was shipped from New York City to Washington D.C. in 1928 where it sat in the shipping boxes in various closets and storage rooms in the sub-basement of the Capitol for nearly eight years. It was not until a magnificent building, designed and built by Architect Cass Gilbert for the *Supreme Court of the United States,* was opened for occupancy in 1935 that the boxed Gerry books were moved out of storage in the Capitol and relocated to the new Court building across the street. The collection was inventoried against the 1928 "box list" and placed on the shelves after which the books were progressively catalogued over the next few decades to make them accessible for research on behalf of the Justices.

Essentially, for the next seventy-five years only the library staff who were responsible for the care, preservation and use of the gift books, knew the Gerry collection existed. Although the Court library contains over half a million volumes today it was the Elbridge T. Gerry Collection that was the foundation of the Court's first library, separate from the shared books in the Chamber of the Capitol. Indeed, Elbridge T. Gerry is to the *Supreme Court Library* what Thomas Jefferson is to the *Library of Congress,* their founding benefactors. The Gerry collection contains an exceptional array of rare titles plus the laws of each state in America up to 1927, as well as several unique subject collections, including canon law, dreams and insanity, torture, the health of women, and other equally intriguing topics.

Thus began, in the midst of a professional job and raising a family my twenty-five year investigation into the epic history of the extended Gerry family, which ultimately answered the simple question of who, when, and why such a comprehensive personal law library was accumulated, with its diverse, eccentric tastes in subject matter. Indeed, was it possible that all three "Elbridges" in the Gerry family contributed to the collection? And why, among many possible institutions, was the Supreme Court chosen to receive the gift? Eventually I discovered that the man at the center of my crusade was Commodore Elbridge Thomas Gerry (1837-1927), the grandson of the Founding Father, Vice-President Elbridge Gerry (1744-1814), and a man whose life story compelled me to travel to Connecticut, Massachusetts, New York and Rhode Island to visit the family homesteads, holiday retreats, places of work, and the institutions where family papers and artifacts are held. I walked in the footsteps of the Gerry family and discovered the untold story of one of America's greatest lawyers, humanitarians, bibliophiles and family patriarchs, whose legacy has endured from the Founding Father to the present generation. The Gerry family legacy is part of the fabric of the evolving story of America which has captured the imagination of the world since the seventeenth century. The people who individually and collectively moved thirteen colonies from a loosely- affiliated extension of the mother-land, Great Britain, to revolution and into an independent nation are the subjects of countless books. Some of the most cherished stories about America are the biographies of courageous and fascinating individuals and their families, such as colonists John and Abigail Adams, George and Martha Washington, and others like Benjamin Franklin and Thomas Jefferson. After the revolution, stories were written about the developing new nation; stories about the building of railroads by the Vanderbilt family, the establishment of the private banking industry by the Morgan family, the development of the steel industry and the building of beautiful libraries by the Carnegie family. Untold, yet significant stories continue to be discovered that shine a bright and welcome light on what might be called America's family history.

This is the story of one such family, the Gerry family of New York state, and most especially, New York City. The name Gerry is pronounced with a hard G like the male name Gary, not the soft G sound of the male name Jerry. The Gerry family originates in Devonshire, England, with Thomas Gerry arriving in Massachusetts in 1730 as the Captain of a merchant ship from London. His son, Elbridge Gerry, became Vice-President of the United States under James Madison, and his son, Thomas Russell Gerry, was appointed a United States Naval officer at the death of his father in 1814. It is Captain Thomas Russell Gerry's son, Elbridge Thomas Gerry, a lawyer and humanitarian in New York City's *Gilded Age* who is the focus of this biography, indeed he is the key to understanding the fascinating history of the Gerry family and is "the bridge" between the founding era and the modern era of this great American family. There is a dynamic historical context both across generations and amongst related families that colors, explains, and enriches the story of the Elbridge T. Gerry family. This story introduces four great American families that have shared their destinies through business, marriage, politics and social interaction for over two hundred years with the focus on the *Gilded Age* life of Elbridge T. Gerry.

The strongest and most lasting bonds are through marriage and the earliest family of significance to our story is the lineage of Robert Livingston of Albany, New York. They were the Lords of *Clermont Manor* and the heirs to part of the two-million acre *Hardenburgh Patent,* the largest British land grant in Colonial New York's history. Part of that Patent remains in the Gerry family to this day through the marriage of Elbridge T. Gerry to Louisa M. Livingston in 1867. The next significant family tie is the mother of Elbridge T. Gerry, Hannah Greene Goelet, the sibling of Robert and Peter Goelet, the children of Peter P. Goelet of Dutch extraction, a founder of the *Chemical Bank* of New York. Another family of great distinction is the Gallatin family into which Elbridge T. Gerry's sister, Almy Buchanan Gerry, married Frederick Gallatin. Both the Gerry and Goelet families are descendants of the great pre-Revolutionary New York merchant, Jacob Walton, upon whose *Bellevue* mansion's old foundation now stands *Gracie Mansion* the official residence of the Mayor of New York City. Other proud American families inter-married along the way and will find their worthy places in this extended story. The ancestral origins of the Gallatin, Goelet and Livingston families are found in the appendix so that readers can appreciate the epic sweep of their lives beginning in their country of origin and ending with their journey across the Atlantic to the new world in America.

The historical context of this biography lifts the veil that has hidden the daily family life of wealthy families in the *Gilded Age* and shows not only their extravagance but also their contributions to significant social change in the *Progressive Era.* Indeed, New York City is a major "character" in this story; it is a hometown that became the cultural and financial center of the world.

To my great satisfaction this long and dedicated research journey allowed me to discover both the lost story behind the history of the Supreme Court Library and the long over-looked story and legacy of the warm and vibrant Gerry family of

New York and Massachusetts. Every great American family has a worthy story to tell and through historical biography we capture those stories so that we might understand and appreciate why and who we are today, indeed, we look back in history so that we might look forward more enlightened, even inspired.

Author's Note

Italics are used more than usual to make it easier for the reader to find the names of institutions, organizations or places of significance in the midst of a long and complicated story. Chapter illustrations are placed at the end of each chapter for the reader's convenience.

The Appendices include an *integrated family tree* (Appendix A) across four families and a *map of Manhattan* (Appendix B) identifying the locations of family homes, businesses and schools across the decades. There are essays on the remainder of the lives of *Commodore Gerry's four children* (Appendix C) and his four grandsons (Appendix D), plus *American Family Legacies* (Appendix E). Appendix F provides a brief description of the *origins* of the related Gallatin, Goelet and Livingston families before they arrived in America with their individual family trees.

We are fortunate to be able to include hundreds of illustrations in this biography. Most of them are in photo collages following each chapter or section. Please note that, as is often the case with historic images, the quality of the images vary. We have optimized them to the best possible quality given the nature of the original images.

1

THE EARLY YEARS

It is the duty of every citizen, though he may have but one day to live, to devote that day to the good of his country.

Elbridge Gerry

The story of every American family begins in another place, in a country that was home before they sailed to the new world in search of opportunity and adventure. The epic story of Elbridge Thomas Gerry's remarkable life in New York City's glamorous *Gilded Age* began with the courageous choices his great-grandfather, a "Sea Captain," made in early eighteenth century England. The British soul is tied to the sea so it was inevitable that the love of sailing was inherited by Captain Gerry's sons who were merchant mariners in colonial Massachusetts, and by his grandsons who were naval officers in the *War of 1812,* and by his great-grandson, Elbridge Thomas Gerry, who became the Commodore of the *New York Yacht Club* in 1886. The Gerry ancestors were as passionate about the sea as they were about the politics of freedom in Europe and Colonial America. Elbridge Thomas Gerry was the proud grandson of an American Founding Father from Massachusetts and England, and he fell in love with the relative of a Founding Father from New York and Scotland, and not to be out done, his sister married the grandson of a Founding Father from Pennsylvania and Switzerland.

The British ancestors of the Gerry family in America were Captain Thomas Gerry's parents, Daniel and Lydia Gerry, of Newton Abbot, Devonshire in southwestern England. Their personal history is obscure except for the record of the character and success of their "Sea Captain" son. They raised three boys, Daniel Jr., John, and Thomas in a small and bustling market town situated on the north side of the narrow River Lemon which then flowed into the nearby navigable River Teign. Because the town was just fifteen miles south of the city of Exeter and five miles from the seaport of Teignmouth, it was the perfect location for the distribution of goods. The area known as Newton Abbot comprises two adjoining boroughs or villages which are separate civil and ecclesiastical parishes, Newton Abbot and Newton Bushel. Traces of Neolithic people and a Roman fort have been found in the area as well as a mid-thirteenth century Norman Castle which stood on the high ground, and a Catholic Abbey which stood on the low ground near the River Lemon. By 1300 the "high ground" had been re-named Newton Bushel, and the "low ground" had been renamed Newton Abbot where the monks had initiated weekly markets near the river bank. By 1700 when Daniel and Lydia Gerry were starting their family the weekly markets were supplemented with three annual "fairs." In June the cattle fair was held, in September the cheese and onion fair was held, and in November the cloth fair was held which included leather and woolen goods. Daniel and Lydia had steady work opportunities in Newton Abbot as did their three sons. Nevertheless, there had always been stories of local adventurers who went in search of distant places to establish new markets. One such adventurer was Humphrey Gilbert who landed in Newfoundland in 1583 and claimed the area as a British Colony. Between 1600 and 1850 there was a steady trade of cod fish from Newfoundland to the Newton Abbot markets. The Gerry boys were no less intrigued by these local adventurer stories than were their school and work friends. Of the three sons, Daniel, Jr. and John remained in England for their lifetimes while Thomas felt compelled to explore life beyond the rural Devonshire village of his childhood.

Daniel and Lydia's adventurous son, Thomas Gerry, was born March 15, 1702 in the parish of Newton Abbot just down the hill from rural Newton Bushel where he was actually raised. As a young man Thomas traveled to London, fifty miles to the east, where he joined the lucrative and exciting shipping trade that did business with his own market town, Newton Abbott. He had hopes of becoming a "local adventurer" like Humphrey Gilbert of his childhood stories. He too wanted to travel the world. In the early eighteenth century, colonial America was becoming a well-established trade route, not yet involved in the disruptions of revolutionary discord between England and America. It is difficult to imagine the hardships endured by those who ventured forth on the high seas in the eighteenth and nineteenth centuries. As Edward King observed on a voyage to China in 1835, "I find no one on board who likes the sea – it is truly no home for man. A catalogue of the hazards of sea life would have included boredom, fever and dysentery, drowning, pirates, hurricanes, mutiny and desertion, frostbite, icebergs, leaks, vermin, seasickness, contrary winds and currents, shoals, rocks and shortages of food and water."[1] Nonetheless, the heartiest of men, courageous and fearless, found traveling the seas the most exciting and surest way to see beyond their own shores or simply a way to make a living when times were difficult and work was scarce.

In this world of adventure and certain profit, Thomas Gerry was fearless and he was eventually hired to captain trans-Atlantic trading vessels on consignment, passing his early adult life sailing between Europe and the colonies exchanging goods needed to support both the evolving social life in the colonies and also, to provide necessities for their safety. In turn, goods produced in the colonies were sold in England making for years of a bachelor's life traversing the Atlantic Ocean. Eventually, being familiar with the ports in America and skilled in the business of merchant shipping he decided in 1730 to re-establish himself in America. The multinational character of colonial America was well suited to Captain Thomas Gerry who had sailed to every known port of Europe and the colonies where he honed his trade and shipping skills in the world market place. At the port of Boston, Massachusetts he was hired by the prominent businessman, Enoch Greenleaf, to Captain one of his merchant ships on consignment. He soon became a well-respected and successful merchant seaman and decided to establish his own business at Marblehead, just fourteen miles east of Boston. His business involved the local retail sale of imported merchandise and cod fish to colonists from his own store/warehouse located at the end of *Gerry's Wharf,* which stands today, converted into a private residence on the waterfront. With his success came ownership of his own merchant ships, whereby he could decide where to sail to obtain the most sought-after goods, including the West Indies for raisins, lemons and sugar, and where, in turn, to ship colonial goods, especially cod fish, to sell in England and other valued ports of call. Thomas Gerry's fleet included a fifty-ton schooner, the *Makepeace,* a forty-five ton schooner the *Pretty Betsey,* and two sixty-ton schooners named the *Success* and the *Rockingham.*[2] This was a sizeable fleet making Thomas Gerry a member of the economic elite in Massachusetts.

Over time, Captain Thomas Gerry became both wealthy and politically active, was elected selectman in the 1740s and 1750s and served as a justice of the peace in 1764. During the period leading up to the *Revolutionary War* he led the people of Marblehead as moderator of their town meetings. Thomas Gerry's active role in the community reflected his standing as an influential member of the town's business leaders known as the "codfish aristocracy."[3] Letters home to Daniel and Lydia Gerry reassured them of their son's success which resonated with their own "codfish aristocracy" in Newton Abbot, England. When the Massachusetts legislature granted Marblehead 550 pounds sterling in 1742 to fortify the town harbor, Thomas was appointed one of the three treasurers for the fund and once Fort Sewell was built, Captain Thomas Gerry was placed in charge by the Governor. Fort Sewell stands today proudly overlooking Marblehead Bay.

The town of Marblehead, Massachusetts, seat of the Gerry family business in colonial America, had commercial dealings throughout the region particularly with Boston, just 14 miles away. It was during Thomas's early work in Boston that he fell in love with Rebecca Russell Greenleaf, the daughter of the prosperous Boston merchant, Enoch Greenleaf, who had first hired Thomas in 1730 to captain one of his merchant ships. Rebecca's great-great-grandfather, Edmund Greenleaf, was born in Malden, England, and came to America in 1635, fully one hundred years before Captain Gerry arrived. One of the family descendants was the famous New England poet, John Greenleaf Whittier. The Greenleafs originally settled in Newbury, Massachusetts with a company of colonists. When British subjects joined a *Company* to travel to America to establish a settlement in one of the colonies, they all signed an agreement that outlined the expectations of the settlement by the British Crown, as well as how the colonists would individually contribute to the finances of the expedition, including how colonists would be compensated. One point of the agreement was that an individual or family gave some or all of their own land in Britain to the Crown, and in turn, they were given a proportionate share of land in the new settlement. Based on the Greenleaf contribution of land to the Crown in England, an allotment of 122 acres was given to Captain Edmund Greenleaf as his share of the settlement lands in Newbury. After a short period of establishing the settlement Captain Greenleaf was appointed overseer of business in the village. By 1650 the next generation of Greenleafs had moved to Boston where the family of merchants and silk dyers continued to prosper, and where the third generation, Joseph Greenleaf and wife Sarah, established a successful Boston printing business. They had three children, including a son Enoch born September 2, 1686, who married Elizabeth Russell the daughter of Samuel and Rebecca (Elbridge) Russell. Elizabeth Russell Gerry's great uncle, John Elbridge, Esq. was the Collector of Customs at Bristol, England, a wealthy and respected businessman. Enoch and Elizabeth Greenleaf's daughter, Rebecca Russell Greenleaf, named after her grandmother, was born in 1716 and grew up in Boston, a large and vibrant market town like Newton Abbot where Thomas Gerry had grown up. Her family did business with adventurous merchant mariners and Rebecca was raised with stories about faraway places, pirates and shipwrecks. She first met the self-assured Captain Thomas Gerry in 1730 when she was just 14 and he was the 28 year-old Captain of her father's ship. After Thomas moved to Marblehead, Massachusetts just fourteen miles away to establish his own business, Rebecca saw him many times when he returned to Boston to do business with her family. His adventure stories would have been some of the best Rebecca Greenleaf had heard. Soon enough Thomas and

Rebecca fell in love and were married in Boston on December 16, 1734 just four years after Captain Gerry arrived in America. This is the first among several historic and lasting family connections through business and marriage that strengthened the Gerry family as colonial America grew and evolved into the United States of America. Rebecca Russell Greenleaf introduced the now honored names of *Elbridge* and *Russell* into the Gerry lineage from her side of the family. This is the origin of Commodore Elbridge Thomas Gerry's name and that of his father, Captain Thomas Russell Gerry. Her silver baptismal cup from 1653 has been handed down in the Gerry family along with a portrait of Rebecca Russell Greenleaf Gerry that once hung over the fireplace in her great-grandson, Elbridge T. Gerry's bedroom in his New York City mansion until his death in 1927.

Capt. Thomas Gerry returned with his bride to the seaside village of Marblehead to his large and welcoming home just up the road from Gerry's Wharf. The marriage happily produced six surviving children out of nine births: 1735 Thomas Gerry Jr., 1737- Samuel Gerry (lived 1 year), 1741 John Gerry, 1744 Elbridge Gerry, 1746 Samuel Gerry 2nd (lived 4 years) 1750 Samuel Russell Gerry 3rd, 1748 Elizabeth Gerry Austin, 1752 Rebecca Gerry, 1754 Daniel Gerry (died same year). The family prospered through their growing merchant shipping business as did the entire colony of Massachusetts. An inheritance from Rebecca Greenleaf Gerry's side of the family made their domestic life comfortable. Rebecca looked forward to visits with her Greenleaf family which gave her an opportunity to shop in bustling Boston, her hometown, a welcome change from the quiet seaside village she now called home. The Gerrys were steadfast members of the First Congregational Church in Marblehead and avoided pretentious displays of wealth. "The only crime associated with the Gerry family was that of their third son, Samuel Russell Gerry (1750-1807) who on April 24, 1771, along with Francis Abbot, came before the Justice of the Peace and confessed that they were severally guilty of unnecessarily walking on the Sabbath Day in Marblehead contrary to law. Whereupon it was ordered that they do each of them pay a fine to the poor of the town of Five Shillings and costs."[4] Captain Gerry would not regret the choice to emigrate from England to America, a choice which, unbeknownst to him, was the founding of a great American family. Between 1740 and 1940 Marblehead would honor the name of Gerry: by 1745 the busy wharf in Marblehead became known as *Gerry's Wharf*, by 1845 there was the *Gerry Fire Association* and a *Gerry* engine, then in 1861 the name of the great patriot Elbridge Gerry (Capt. Thomas Gerry's son), was invoked to inspire young men to join the militia to fight the Civil War; and today, there is the *Gerry Elementary School* in Marblehead. Captain Thomas Gerry's eighteenth century home still stands just down the lane from his son Elbridge Gerry's home which is now a designated *Historic Landmark* in Marblehead, Massachusetts.

Three of the four sons of Captain Thomas Gerry, Samuel Russell, Thomas Jr., and John all remained in Marblehead and worked in the family merchant shipping business, just as Captain Thomas Gerry's brothers had done in Newton Abbot, England. They actively participated in local politics with their father over many years until 1774 when Captain Thomas Gerry died at the beginning of the *American Revolution.* His four sons emerged as the next generation of Marblehead leaders both politically and as part of the mercantile elite. Indeed during the Revolution the Gerrys turned their vessels into warships and the major trading routes became military supply lines. The Gerrys fully and successfully participated in the government sanctioned trading of cod fish for ammunition and supplies through trade with the West Indies and France.[5]

Captain Thomas Gerry's third child, Elbridge Gerry, brought great distinction to the family eventually becoming Vice President of the United States under President James Madison. Like most young boys in Marblehead Elbridge was educated as a child in the local common school. At age fourteen he was admitted to Harvard College in Cambridge, Massachusetts. Harvard College in the 1760's was given less to training ministers than it had been in the seventeenth century; its graduates were now more inclined to become lawyers, doctors, and merchants. The Harvard College library of nearly 5,000 volumes still mirrored the interests of an earlier age with most of the books devoted to Holy Scriptures, scriptural commentaries, and theological treatises. Geographies, gazetteers, and travel books were also included, as they were in most personal libraries during this period of colonization, world exploration, and trade. But there were also many volumes of the Greek and Roman classics, writings on political theory, ancient and modern history, and numerous biographies. It was these books that attracted Gerry. The impression that the classical writers made on him was later reflected in his political career, when he frequently cited the fall of the Roman republic as an example of what might happen to America, invoked Latin maxims in correspondence and speeches, and relied on the writers of antiquity to bolster his political arguments. At the time of his death, Gerry's personal library included the writings of Virgil, Pliny, and Cicero; works of Pufendorf, Grotius, and Vattel; copies of Montesquieu, Rousseau, and Voltaire; editions of Locke's *Two Treatises on Government* and Gibbins' *Decline and Fall of the Roman Empire*; and histories of England by Rapin, Hume, and Smollett, in addition to volumes by Paine, John Adams, and Mercy Otis Warren (Adams and Warren being life-long personal friends of Gerry).[6] Gerry's personal library was offered at auction upon his death to raise money to support his family. Not all his books were lost to this sale because the family retained the law and history books requested by the Vice President's son, Elbridge Jr. for use in his law office.

During his studies at Harvard Elbridge was concerned about the political and economic crisis growing between mother England and her colonies. In fact he focused the research and writing of his Master's thesis on the proposition that the colonists were justified in their resistance to the new prohibitory duties that made it impossible for the people of America and his own family to profitably engage in commerce.[7] After graduation Elbridge returned home to join his father and brothers in the merchant shipping trade in the thriving port town of Marblehead, which had also emerged as a center of anti-British activity during the 1760's and 1770's. In 1769 Elbridge Gerry became a Master Mason in the Philanthropic Lodge in Marblehead. As an educated local businessman Elbridge served on the town committee to enforce the ban on the sale and consumption of tea in 1770. On December 1, 1771 Elbridge along with his brother Thomas, Jr. joined the town meeting in Marblehead that was moderated by their father Captain Thomas Gerry. The meeting was prompted by the circular letter to the colonies and the resolves of Samuel Adam's *Boston Committee on Correspondence.* All three Gerrys were on the committee that drafted the fiery resolves which were adopted by Massachusetts. The committee also resolved to build a hospital on nearby *Gerry Island* for citizens in the town who were stricken with small pox. The wealthy merchants funded the hospital for the welfare of the town to prevent the spread of the contagious disease.

Like his sea captain father, twenty-eight-year-old Elbridge Gerry felt compelled to pursue a career that would take him beyond the limits of the family business in Marblehead. Eager to enlarge his role in Revolutionary politics he decided to run for office. Elbridge Gerry was elected to the state legislature and Provincial Congress in 1772 and served as chairman of the *Committee on Supplies* during the fall and winter of 1774-75, coordinating in effect the procurement and distribution of arms and provisions. This was considered treasonous work by the British and placed Elbridge in some danger. During these tense times Gerry's seventy-two-year old father was ill and progressively left the day-to-day business at *Gerry's Wharf* to his sons. He still took an active interest in local politics and advised his sons and the town elders. In mid-1774 shortly before Captain Gerry's death a mob of townspeople burned the 3-year old smallpox isolation hospital to the ground believing that their families should not be sent away. Captain Gerry and his sons, joined by the entire town council, resigned in disgust because the hospital was built at their own expense on private Gerry property. Public opinion in Marblehead protected the culprits from punishment because they did not or could not understand the council's explanation that isolation would help prevent the spread of smallpox.[8]

In 1775 Elbridge Gerry was elected to the *Continental Congress* where he served until 1780 and again from 1783-1785. As the revolution was in a most intense period in 1775 members of the *Continental Congress*, whether at home or assembled, were in as much danger as the colonial militia being themselves targets of the British infantry. One such incident involved Elbridge Gerry. In the spring of 1775 the prospect of open war increased every day and the British expedition to Concord and the bloody scenes which occurred there and at Lexington, Massachusetts, ushered in the long expected war. Among the objects of this spring expedition by the British was to seize some of the influential members of Congress and to hold them as hostages for the moderation of their colleagues, or send them to England for trial as traitors and thus strike dismay and terror into the minds of their associates and friends. British spies had learned that the Americans had amassed ammunition which they wanted to confiscate. They also wanted to capture Adams and Hancock and those allied with them. On the night of April 18, 1775 a Committee of Congress, including Mr. Gerry, Colonel Azor Orne, and Colonel John Hancock, had been in session in a village in Cambridge on the road to Lexington on the day preceding the march of British troops. After the committee adjourned all left the village except Mr. Gerry and Colonel Azor Orne who remained in the Wetherby's Black Horse Tavern for the night. Without taking the least precaution against personal exposure, they rested quietly in their beds, even as Paul Revere made his famous ride down the road to Lexington.[9]

When the center of the British troop arrived in front of the Tavern/Inn occupied by the two committee members an officer and contingent of soldiers were detached and marched toward it. It was not until this moment that Mr. Gerry and Col. Orne entertained any apprehension of danger. The gentlemen found means by their better knowledge of the tavern to escape half-dressed into an adjoining cornfield where they remained concealed for more than an hour until the troops were withdrawn. Every room in the tavern was searched by the British soldiers for members of the rebel congress, even the beds in which Mr. Gerry and Colonel Orne had slept were examined. Nonetheless, their property, including a valuable and much loved watch of Mr. Gerrys that was under his pillow, were all secure and undisturbed.[10]

Unfortunately Colonel Orne, the wealthiest leading citizen in Marblehead, caught pneumonia from his overnight stay in the corn field and died three weeks later, a shocking loss to his family and the community. Colonel Orne's magnificent house still stands proudly on the town square of Marblehead as an historic site and a tribute to the colonial era in Massachusetts.

Fortunately Elbridge Gerry survived the night hidden in the cornfield unharmed and was more determined than ever to obtain and protect the munitions of the colonial patriots. Hiding behind the house in a wooded area has been a successful ploy for the Gerrys even in the twentieth century as told with a wry smile by Bill Oles the former manager of the Gerry estate, Elbridge T. Gerry II slipped out the back door of his Aknusti mansion and hid in the nearby woods until a persistent and pestering real estate investor finally gave up and left the hilltop estate.[11] This latter flight from the house was of course a more humorous adventure than that of fleeing for one's life, as was the case for Mr. Gerry's great-great-great grandfather that fateful night in 1775.

Just seven months after the Tavern escape on November 15, 1775, the Legislature of Massachusetts passed the first Act written by Elbridge Gerry to authorize the fitting-out of armed vessels "to protect the sea-coast" and to cut off supplies intended for the enemy. [12] This legislative act is considered to be the beginning of the official United States Navy as we know it today.

In the summer of 1776 Elbridge Gerry's dear friend John Adams praised him saying, "If every man here was a Gerry, the liberties of America would be safe against the Gates of Earth and Hell." Gerry's biographer, George Billias, reminds us that the Revolution was Gerry's defining moment and the future vice-president considered "the signing of the Declaration of Independence the greatest single act of his entire life."[13] Gerry recalled that after the Secretary of the *Continental Congress,* Charles Thompson, announced that the *Declaration of Independence* was ready to be signed, a deep silence pervaded the historic assembly. Tradition says that the silence was broken by Benjamin Franklin who then remarked, "Gentlemen, we must now hang together, or we shall surely hang separately."[14] All of Gerry's subsequent actions, inconsistent and idiosyncratic as they may have appeared to others, were driven by his single-minded goal of preserving the hard-won gains of the Revolution.[15] Elbridge Gerry remained a bachelor until age forty-two when he married Ann Thompson in 1786. She was the well-educated daughter of James Thompson, a wealthy New York City merchant who was born in County Derry, Ireland in 1727. During the Revolution James Thompson, along with most successful merchants in major port cities, continued to trade with France during the Seven Years' War when England prohibited colonial trade with the enemy. In June 1760 his brig *Achilles* was seized coming out of the Cape and the crew was tried in the Jamaican Court of Vice-Admiralty where his ship and cargo were condemned and confiscated. In dire financial trouble James Thompson turned to his wife's uncle, who had raised her, William Walton, Sr. who advanced him enough money against his wife's inheritance to survive the ordeal. Catharine Walton Thompson was the daughter of Jacob Walton, one of the wealthiest merchants in New York City who built his summer home *Bellevue* at Horn's Hook on 11 acres of land on the East River at 87th Street. Although the mansion was destroyed by the British, Archibald Gracie rebuilt the mansion in 1799, and today it is the official home of the Mayor of New York City, *Gracie Mansion*.

Ann Thompson was educated in Dublin, Ireland while at the same time her two brothers were students at Edinburgh University in Scotland. They entered the English army after college but did not fight with the British against America. Ann returned to New York City after college and was considered one of the most beautiful women in the Colonies. Her father did business with other merchants who competed for goods arriving in port and who also exported local goods on their own ships. The Gerry family business in Marblehead did business with Boston, New York, Philadelphia and other major cities along the eastern seaboard. These merchants were well acquainted and as leaders in their communities were now working together as elected representatives to the *Continental Congress*. Ann Thompson, 21 in 1786, was a hostess with her mother Catharine Walton Thompson when a few of the representatives stayed in their home during Congressional Assemblies in New York. Ann's brother was William Walton III whose daughter, Sara, married Jonathan Ogden, another wealthy merchant who lived next door to the Goelet family on State Street across from the Battery. The Goelets, Ogdens, Thompsons and Waltons were the leading merchant families that hosted members of the *Continental Congress* when they met in the City. The next two generations of the Gerry, Goelet and Ogden families also inter-married which joined the wealthiest merchant families of New York City during the Revolutionary Era, and these extended families remain in New York City to this day.

Due to the demands of Revolutionary life Elbridge Gerry was already forty when he first met young Ann Thompson during one of many stays in New York City among the wealthy merchant families for business and political meetings. He was 42 when he finally asked for her hand in marriage. She had already discovered over the previous year or two that Elbridge traveled a great deal and was committed to his political career. Indeed, they were separated for much of their married life due to the political intensity of the founding period in America. They first lived in a lovely small salt-box style house in Marblehead just three blocks up the road from Captain Thomas and Rebecca Gerry's large family home. However, it was never Elbridge or Ann's desire to live in a small town and they decided that Boston would suit them if they could find the right house.

In May, 1787 the Gerry's purchased a beautiful estate in Cambridge, Massachusetts; a property which had been confiscated from a loyalist. The estate was named *Elmwood* and it is where the nine Gerry children were born and raised. Ann Thompson Gerry was well-respected, known as a fitting helpmate to her husband, and cheerfully and gracefully met the demands of their political and social life. She possessed considerable force of character and a dignified, gentle manner. Although somewhat an invalid she personally superintended the education and religious training of her children and inspired them with a strong affection and reverence for herself, which was evidenced by their devotion to her in her later years in New Haven, Connecticut.[16] The couple and their many children regularly corresponded throughout their collective life-times. The family correspondence held in the *Massachusetts Historical Society* described Ann and Elbridge as clearly missing the affection and company of their intimate relationship, and most especially of Gerry missing his children. In a letter to James Monroe on affairs of state written by Mr. Gerry in 1787 he states, "Your sentiments are perfectly correspondent with my own respecting domestic Happiness; it is the only Happiness in this life which in my opinion is worth pursuit. Our little pet is named Catherine after its Grand Mama (Catharine Walton), and is our Mutual delight."[17] Gerry's older daughters Catherine, Elizabeth, and Ann were in fact his confidants throughout his life on political issues as well as conveyors of news about family and life back home in Boston as documented in their faithful correspondence. A letter typical of the family's exchanges was written by Elbridge Gerry while in New York, June 13, 1801, where he wrote to his daughter Ann:

> Your letter, my lovely affectionate child, to your sister, has given us all great pleasure; to hear that you all harmonize with each other, that the only objects of contention were, who should please your Aunt Skinner most, and who give the best satisfaction to your instructors, and who by these means should make Mamma, Papa, and sister Catharine, most happy, I say to learn these things could not but make us completely so. Desire Aunt Skinner to direct the gardener, when the cherries are ripe, not to gather the blackhearts until they are quite black. They are often gathered half ripe, and are then unwholesome. The English beans should be top'd, that is, have a small part of the top plucked, which is good to eat, when the lower blossoms begin to fall.... Mamma sends a French book, the only one we have met with, for yourself and dear Elizabeth, two small books for your brothers Elbridge and Thomas, a horse for James, and a silk pincase for Helen, and a rattle with a whistle to it for the dear baby. Elbridge is to have his choice of the books.... Be assured, my dear child, I am ever your affectionate papa.
>
> E. Gerry[18]

As a member of a favored class he considered public service a responsibility not an opportunity for personal gain. Oftentimes during the Revolution when Elbridge Gerry was responsible for obtaining arms and supplies for Massachusetts he quietly used his own money to ensure the success of the colonial militia. He eventually reduced the family wealth by a considerable measure. One of four delegates chosen by the Massachusetts legislature to attend the 1787 Constitutional Convention, Gerry was one of the most active participants during the entire convention. The definitive biography of Elbridge Gerry by George Billias notes that "despite his speech impediment" Gerry talked a great deal and much of what he had to say has relevance to our own age.[19] While there is another reference in 1800 by Benjamin Rush to Gerry's manner of speaking, he referred to Elbridge Gerry as stammering in his speech, it must have been minor because his insightful words captured the attention of his many and varied audiences.[20] His power of persuasion through speech is exemplified in Elbridge Gerry's role as chair of the committee to resolve the impasse between the large and small states over representation in the national legislature. Gerry made several impassioned speeches in support of the great compromise, which provided for equal representation of the states in the Senate and proportional representation in the House of Representatives.[21] Gerry had some reservations about the balance of power in the draft language of the constitution and some of his proposals to redress his concerns were adopted, such as the prohibition against bills of attainder (a legislative act that singles out an individual or group for punishment without a trial) and ex post facto laws (laws intended to apply to crimes or events that took place before their passage, thereby punishing an act which was not illegal when committed). However, even these limitations did not soothe Gerry's deeper concerns and so he made a bold proposal in a motion to include a bill of rights to safeguard popular liberties. Unlike the *Declaration of Independence* Elbridge Gerry did not sign the final draft of the *U.S. Constitution* because the convention defeated his call for a bill of rights. As history often bears out, one small flame of an idea once thought extinguished will be re-ignited into a bright fire of passion, which was the case with Elbridge Gerry's proposal for a bill of rights. Congress later drafted, as an addendum to the final constitutional document, the *Bill of Rights* as we know it today. This addendum was the only way to convince all of the states to vote favorably for the final ratification of the *U.S. Constitution* because the states recognized, as did Gerry, that the people's popular liberties were not clearly enumerated in the text of the official constitutional document.

There was yet another bright flame that flickered in the mind of Elbridge Gerry in 1789, which Congress snuffed out by again refusing to pass the proposed measure, but this idea too was re-ignited years later in 1832, and again in 1925.

Representative Elbridge Gerry while at the temporary seat of the new government in Philadelphia, was the author in 1789 of the first legislative proposal to establish a library for Congress that would be shared with the Supreme Court Justices when the new Capitol city of Washington was finished. President George Washington asked Rep. Gerry to chair a committee and prepare a recommendation of titles and a budget for such a library. Unfortunately, the measure was "laid on the table" by Congress, with no interest in taking up the matter until the seat of government moved to Washington. In 1812 not long after the seat of government moved to Washington, D.C, the Library of Congress was finally established but the Supreme Court was not permitted to use it. The justices had to use personal libraries they had in their private homes. Years later in 1832 the Justices were given limited access to the legal materials in the Library of Congress and not until 1860 did Congress allow a few of those books, as a convenience, to be moved to the Capitol's second floor Chamber of the Supreme Court. Legislation was finally passed in 1925 to build a stately Supreme Court building with a magnificent library. It was completed and occupied in 1937 when the private law library of the Founding Father's grandson, Commodore Elbridge T. Gerry was donated to the Court to be the foundation collection of the Supreme Court Library.[22]

Elbridge Gerry was always a deeply principled man who stood by his convictions in the political arena, often appearing as uncompromising. However, Gerry's major positions during the Continental Congress and the Constitutional Convention, more often than not, withstood the test of time when evaluated historically by scholars. Generally, Gerry supported resolutions in Congress against theatrical entertainment, horse racing and other such diversions. In a letter shortly before his death he wrote to his daughter Eleanor about his "amusements" in Washington saying, "I had cards [tickets] for three days successively to the horse races; but these are amusements which are to me painful, on account of the suffering of such noble animals, to gratify jockeys in their swindling practices."[23] It is interesting to note here that his grandson, Commodore Elbridge T. Gerry, also fought some aspects of the theatre, specifically the exploitative appearance of children on the stage. Additionally, his great-great grandsons would become the leading horsemen in the state of New York at the turn of the twentieth century, both exceeding in the sport of polo and in thoroughbred and harness racing.

Elbridge Gerry served in the United States House of Representatives during the first and second Congresses (1789-1793) under the newly established Constitution. Gerry retired at the end of his second term and returned to Elmwood, his Cambridge, Massachusetts farm estate. Today Elmwood is the President's House at Harvard University, continuing its role as a home of leading men in America. Gerry's return home was to attend to his business affairs which continued to be merchant sales, real estate, shipping, and cultivating the estate. Of equal importance Gerry was home to care for his large and growing family. Ann Gerry's frequent pregnancies — nine children arrived between 1787 and 1801 placed a severe strain on her health. It was clear Elbridge was needed at home. His brief retirement ended in 1796 when he served as a presidential elector, supporting his friend and former colleague, John Adams. In 1797, with relations between the United States and France quickly deteriorating before the adoption of the Jay Treaty which normalized trade and resolved disputes with England, President John Adams appointed a commission to France consisting of Charles Pinckney, John Marshall, and Elbridge Gerry to establish peaceful relations and normalize trade. However, before the negotiations began the French foreign minister, Charles Maurice de Talleyrand, sent three French agents to meet with the commission members. The agents suggested that Talleyrand would agree to the treaty if he received from the United States a $250,000 bribe and France received a $10 million loan. The American commission refused and sent a report to President Adams who inserted the letters X, Y, and Z in place of the French agents' names and forwarded the report to Congress. Gerry's fellow commissioners left Paris, but Gerry, who had been meeting privately with the French in an effort to facilitate negotiations, remained behind believing that accommodation was possible. Although he left France unsuccessful, Gerry was convinced that the extended negotiations averted war. He was later supported in that belief by President John Adams who wrote, "He [Gerry] finally saved the nation for he alone discovered and furnished the evidence that X., Y. and Z. were employed by Talleyrand and he alone brought home the direct, formal, and official assurances upon which the subsequent commission proceeded and peace was made in 1800."[24] However, attacks on American shipping continued and so Gerry was still widely criticized at the time for the failure of the mission to France. In the midst of the ship attacks Gerry once again appeared at the State House in Boston where he was asked to speak. His words at the State House became his most famous and memorable expression of patriotism when he said to his fellow patriots, "It is the duty of every citizen, though he may have but one day to live, to devote that day to the good of his country."[25] This now famous speech overshadowed the criticism of his friend from the *Continental Congress* days, Rufus King, Minister to England at the time of the XYZ Affair, when he said that Elbridge Gerry's efforts in Paris were "Folly." This is the first but not the last time that a Gerry's singular determination in a principled enterprise would be deemed "Gerry's Folly."[26] Years later the Founder's grandson, Commodore Elbridge T. Gerry, would be known for his own

"Gerry's Folly" in New York City, where he successfully negotiated real estate acquisitions in the mid-nineteenth century, similar to the diligent efforts of his name-sake, Vice President Elbridge Gerry in his extended negotiations to acquire a treaty with France nearly 75 years earlier. In both cases such "Folly" contributed substantially to the establishment of the nation and the growth of the great city of New York, known affectionately as Gotham.

Elbridge Gerry left politics for five years between 1804 and 1809 when he spent time in a philosophic, yet active retirement, following politics, caring for family and engaged in agricultural pursuits at his Cambridge farm estate, Elmwood. In a letter dated November 19, 1803, at the outset of his retirement, Elbridge wrote to William Eustis, "Mrs. Gerry has been exceedingly sick of late. She is now, God be praised, much better and with the family writes in compliments to you." Other letters suggest the breadth of his interests. One dated April 4, 1805 discussed a real estate matter where Gerry was attempting to lease property, and later on February 19, 1806 he wrote an eight page letter to James Madison discussing many issues facing the new republic. Then, in February 1807 his brother, Samuel Russell Gerry, died in Marblehead, Massachusetts. He traveled to Marblehead for the funeral and to visit with his family and assist his niece in any way he could. Later that year a letter from Gerry to Mercy Otis Warren, a life-long mutual family friend and correspondent of John Adams and Elbridge Gerry, responded to a plea for assistance from Mrs. Warren. She was a noted author of the time who wrote poetry, dramas and essays throughout the Revolutionary period. She had in fact written to every colonial leader she knew, including her dear friends Elbridge Gerry and John Adams, asking for their reminiscences of the Colonial and Revolutionary periods for her book, *History of the American Revolution*, published in 1805.[27] Unfortunately, she wrote rather critically about many of the things John Adams wrote to her in his letters. He became very angry with Mrs. Warren and broke off their friendship of many years. She wrote to Elbridge Gerry in mid-1807 asking him to intercede with Adams to reconcile the friendship. Gerry's response on September 15, 1807 was:

> The subject of your letter of yesterday has astonished me. I cannot judge of it without seeing the letters; but am already of opinion, that of but one dignified line of civility on the part of a lady is that of silence. This giving an opportunity to the offended party to cool and reflect, often itself cures the evil, which volumes of recrimination, or justification would but serve to increase. I will soon communicate to you my sentiments on that part of your history [her book], which relates to this matter".... closing the letter immediately with affectionate regards from the Gerry family to the Warren family. *He notes too in this letter that*

> *he* "has been severely afflicted by the influenza, which for ten days so prostrated me, as to render me incapable of attention of any kind; but it is now abating, and I hope will depart, never to return again.[28]

After this brief, second retirement Gerry was elected governor of Massachusetts in 1810. During his second term as governor in his frustrating attempts to mediate Federalists and Republicans in their irreconcilable disagreements over President Madison's foreign policy, Gerry approved a controversial redistricting plan designed to give Republicans an advantage in the state Senatorial elections. The Federalist press responded to this plan with a broadside (one page) article with a cartoon map of a salamander-shaped election district dubbed the "Gerry-Mander" in January 1812; thus adding to the American political lexicon a term that is still used to describe an irregularly shaped district created by legislative design to benefit a particular party, politician, or other group.

This negative publicity and highly partisan proposal led to Gerry's defeat in the spring 1812 election. Heavily in debt and saddled with the expenses of a large family, Gerry asked President James Madison to appoint him Collector of Customs in Boston.[29] However, with the fall 1812 presidential election approaching and the vice-presidency vacant since George Clinton's death in April, Madison was more anxious to find a suitable running mate than concerned about filling a local customs post in Boston. The Republican caucus turned to the sixty-seven-year-old Gerry, a choice Madison approved despite Secretary of the Treasury Albert Gallatin's prediction that the Massachusetts patriot "would give us as much trouble as our late Vice-President."[30] Albert Gallatin's grandson, Frederick Gallatin, eventually married Elbridge Gerry's grand-daughter, Almy Gerry Gallatin in 1865 forging another lasting family alliance of friendship and wealth well into the twentieth century.

In the fall of 1812, by a margin of 39 electoral votes, Madison defeated opposition candidate De Witt Clinton and Gerry triumphed over Jared Ingersoll of Pennsylvania.[31] The new administration did not convene in Washington until May 24, 1813 which allowed Vice-President Elbridge Gerry to remain with his family for a few precious months, taking the oath of office in Boston from the local U.S. District Judge, John Davis. In the Spring of 1813 about the same time that the newly elected Vice President left home for Washington, his eldest son and name-sake, Elbridge Gerry, Jr. set out on horseback for a two month journey through the states of Massachusetts, Connecticut, New York, New Jersey, Pennsylvania, Ohio, and then back through Virginia and Maryland, ending in Washington, D.C.. Elbridge Jr. kept a journal or diary of this trip that was later published by his great, great niece, Annette Townsend who inherited the diary. Elbridge Jr. was introduced to Washington society by his father, the Vice President, after which he returned home to Boston. His journal was not published for one hundred years after it was first written.[32]

After arriving for the opening of the Thirteenth Congress in late May, Vice President Elbridge Gerry's early hopes that the Senate would resolve their bitter differences and support President Madison quickly faded as the war deepened the divisions between the parties and split the Republican coalition. President Madison's health was weakening and he was not up to the leadership required of his role as Commander in Chief. Elbridge Gerry himself was in poor health and old age had so withered his slight physique that the press often commented on his advanced age. The summer session of Congress ran from May through August 1813.

President Madison's health improved by August, allowing Vice-President Gerry to return home to Boston for several months until January 1814, a month before the second session began. He was immediately busy with Washington affairs and noted in a letter to his wife on February 8, 1814,

> I have but a moment, my dearest Life, to express the high degree of pleasure which your letter produced of the 29th of January. The day after my arrival being the 4th, I received between twenty and thirty letters, not one of which was from either of my families. [33]

As busy and often unpleasant as his Senate duties had become with the endless political squabbling, Gerry still enjoyed the seasonal round of dinners, receptions and entertainments that crowded his spring calendar. With his elegant manners and personal charm, the vice president was a favorite guest of Washington's Republican hostesses, including first lady Dolly Madison. Gerry remained in Washington through the second session of Congress which adjourned on April 18, 1814; he had hoped to return home to Cambridge immediately thereafter but he would instead, remain in Washington for most of the hot, humid summer. On April 20 Elbridge wrote in a letter to his wife Ann about a minor accident traveling on bad roads between Alexandria, Virginia and Washington:

> Arrived at Gadsby's Tavern in the evening ... and was fortunate in making it; for it rained and the roads are very bad. By a sudden plunge of the carriage, and a sudden swerving, I received a blow above my eye, which was made by the top corner of my hat striking against the top of the carriage, and communicating the strike to my forehead, which almost stunned me. No other injury is the result, than a *mouse* as seamen call it, raised on my forehead by the contusion.[34]

Elbridge Gerry spent the last part of the summer of 1814 in Massachusetts awaiting news of the war effort from Madison and enjoyed the company of his family and tended to personal business.[35] Gerry returned to Washington in the fall and was shocked to see that the British troops had burned the Capitol in his absence, and had ransacked the city. Despite resuming his duties in the Patent Office Building, the temporary Capitol, Vice President Gerry carried-on with resolve as was his nature, and returned to the exhausting rounds of Washington socializing. Elbridge wrote on November 10, 1814 that one of their family friends, Colonel Morgan Lewis, had been to Washington and called on the Vice President but the Colonel had left town before Gerry could return his visit. Colonel Morgan Lewis was a prominent New Yorker, indeed he was the third Governor of New York from 1804-1807. He was a lawyer and a military commander whose father, Francis Lewis signed the *Declaration of Independence* along with Elbridge Gerry. Col. Morgan married Gertrude Livingston of the historic Albany family to whom King George granted the *Hardenburgh Patent* of land, the largest in colonial America. Col. Morgan Lewis's great-grand-daughter, Louisa M. Livingston, married Elbridge Gerry's grandson, Commodore Elbridge T. Gerry in 1867, joining two of the greatest New York and Massachusetts families in America.

Vice President Elbridge Gerry's letters home from Washington were always affectionate with each member of his family, especially his daughters. In fact he had an intimate correspondence with his daughters Catherine, Ann and Eleanor over several years, sharing political gossip and exchanging ideas and advice on issues of the day, not unlike the correspondence between John and Abigail Adams throughout his political life. Mrs. Gerry was the consummate mother, certainly well educated, but she was never in the best of health in these later years, having borne nine children; nevertheless, she and Elbridge wrote faithfully and with great affection.

In 1814, Elbridge Gerry was seventy years old and most of his daughters were adults and ranged in age from Catharine 26, Elizabeth 24, and Ann 23, to Helen 18, Eleanor 14, and Emily 12. In late October and early November Elbridge wrote frequently to family members to give directions about farm chores, studying, and requests for books and papers to be sent to him in Washington. Except for the blow to the head in April during a bumpy carriage ride, his letters made no mention of ill health in the 10 months prior to November 1814. However, contemporary observers and colleagues in Washington described the Vice President as weak and not in good health. It was on the morning of November 23, 1814, that after breakfast at the common table of his boarding house and in apparent good health, except for a transient complaint of pressure in his chest, he left for a day in the Senate. Elbridge Gerry was approaching the temporary capitol building, anticipating a full day presiding over the Senate when he fell ill. The Vice President asked his coachman to take him back to his boarding house but he died before he could receive medical assistance. It is believed he died of a lung hemorrhage within 20 minutes of taking ill. His biographer relates that shortly before he breathed his last, "he drew from his bosom a miniature which he always wore when the original was absent (portrait of his wife Ann). He spoke of it to show that although the surpassing beauty delineated in the picture might have first charmed the imagination, more enduring qualities had left the impress of affection on his heart."[36] Just thirteen days before his death, Elbridge wrote to his daughter Eleanor, clearly responding to an observation she had made to her father about the keepsake: "The original and miniature are too much; send dear mama to me, and you shall all be welcome to the miniature."[37] This miniature portrait and its twin, the miniature of Elbridge held by his wife in his absence, are both in the possession of the Gerry family today, symbols of family fidelity and loving bonds across the miles and through time in the extended Gerry family.

Members of the Senate adjourned for the day upon hearing the news, and the following day had a black shroud draped over Vice President Elbridge Gerry's empty chair in the Senate, where it remained covered until the end of the first session of the Fourteenth Congress. Indeed, members of the Senate wore black cloth mourning bands on their left-arms for the next thirty days to honor the fallen patriot. A monument in the Congressional Cemetery would not be erected to honorably mark the grave of Vice President Elbridge Gerry until 1823 when, by an act of Congress, $1,000 was appropriated toward the costs of design and construction. The monument was made of white marble from the state of Massachusetts. The monument was designed and executed by Messrs. W. and J. Frazee of New York. Vice President Gerry's monument was a pyramid in style with leaf ornamentation with the top crowned by a sculpted flame. The inscription reads:

> The Tomb of Elbridge Gerry, Vice President of the United States, who died suddenly in this City, November 23, 1814, on his way to the Capitol, as President of the Senate, aged 70. Thus fulfilling his own memorable injunction, "It is the duty of every citizen, though he may have but one day to live, to devote that day to the good of his country.

While a proposal was made in Congress to continue the Vice President's salary for the remainder of the congressional session, to assist his widow and children, it was not passed for fear of setting a precedent. Although Elbridge Gerry had inherited a large business fortune from his father, it was found after his death that the fortune had been, to a great extent, sacrificed in the cause of his country during the

Revolution. President Madison did step-in to ensure the security of the family by having the Secretary of State, James Monroe, promise to appoint the eldest son of the Vice President, his name-sake Elbridge Gerry, Jr., age 21, to the post of Inspector of Revenue in Boston (not effective until 1817). Monroe also appointed the second eldest son, Thomas Russell Gerry, age 20, a Navy Cadet, midshipman in December 1814. One year later, on his eighteenth birthday, the third son, James T. Gerry, was also appointed a Cadet, midshipman in the Navy.[38] These appointments, facilitated by the President, placed all three sons in a position to indefinitely contribute to the support of their mother and sisters, who immediately sold the large Cambridge family home and relocated to a smaller house in New Haven, Connecticut, where the unmarried ladies quietly lived out their lives. The youngest daughter Emily, twelve at the time of her father's death, lived to age 92 in 1894 and was the last surviving child of a signer of the *Declaration of Independence.* All three sons, Elbridge, Thomas and James supported their mother and unmarried sisters for the next 40 years. Thomas Russell Gerry drafted his will to include trusts for the benefit of his four sisters. In 1895 the remainder of each trust was inherited by Thomas Gerry's wife, Hannah Goelet Gerry, after the death of his last surviving sister.

Elbridge Gerry, Jr. (1793-1867) graduated from Harvard College in 1813. In the year before his death, Vice President Elbridge Gerry had a correspondence with Alexander J. Dallas about placing his son Elbridge Jr. in his office. Dallas was the sixth Secretary of the Treasury from 1814–1815, and prior to that he was the first Reporter of Decisions for the United States Supreme Court for four years (1790-1800). In a letter dated October 1814, just one month before his death, the Vice President wrote to his wife Ann:

> Mr. Dallas informed me he had written to me and proposed an arrangement to take Elbridge into his office. Pray desire Ms. Ann to look into my trunk of papers in the entry to find the files of letters for 1813-1814 and to send me the letters which passed between Mr. Dallas and myself on this subject.[39]

Because the War of 1812 continued, Alexander Dallas was called upon in mid-1814 by Albert Gallatin, Secretary of the Treasury, to assist in raising money for the war effort; Dallas immediately left his office work and was still raising money for the war effort at the time of Gerry's death so the Vice President had no time to reconnect with Dallas to pursue a placement in his office for his son, Elbridge Jr. However, the effort may not have succeeded in any event because Dallas retired in late 1815, returned home to Pennsylvania and died the next year.

Elbridge Jr. likely apprenticed in a law office from 1815 to 1817 until he was appointed the *Inspector of Revenue* at the Port of Boston by James Monroe as promised in December 1814. Four months after his father's death, Elbridge Jr. wrote from Washington to his sister Ann:

> The first week of my temporary residence in this City was devoted solely to business, which being finished as far as possible at present, more leisure moments were offered. But pleasure is fleet.... And this week I embark, partly in becoming acquainted with persons, who, at some future opportunity, may be useful friends to me, and the remainder is listening to the first orators at the U.S. Bar [likely arguments before the Supreme Court] .... As well-read lawyers ... they convinced me of the indefatigable research they had made..... I expect by today or tomorrow to hear from Mr. Austin [*brother-in-law and attorney*] in respect to my placement and am very anxious. If it succeeded, pray keep the library [*Vice President Gerry's*] until I return, or remove all the law, the journals, and history books. If you wish to save money, I will save you the trouble, as I shall have to buy a library, and this is a good one. If I have succeeded we will all live together, I will turn into the bank. If it has not succeeded, I have another plan that will do.[40]

There are no further letters of explanation, and what letters Elbridge Jr. subsequently wrote were posted from Boston. He was compelled to implement his "other plan" which most likely was to return home to the Boston area to seek work with a local law office. Throughout his life letters addressed to Elbridge Gerry, Jr. add Esq. after his name, indicating "attorney." Further evidence is that Elbridge did indeed save his father's law books from the auction block in 1815 so he might have his own law library as discussed in his letter in November 1814 to his sister. Also, at least one of those original books survives today. Vice President Gerry's personal copy of one of the most important legal treatises ever written, *Blackstone's Commentaries,* was handed down by Elbridge Gerry, Jr. to his nephew, Commodore Elbridge Thomas Gerry in 1857; in turn, after his death, the Commodore's large law library, including the *Blackstone's Commentaries,* was gifted by his son Senator Peter G. Gerry in 1928, to the *United States Supreme Court Library,* in Washington, D.C.[41]

On November 12, 1817, Elbridge Gerry Jr. was sworn-in as the *Inspector of Revenue* for the Port of Boston, a position he held until January, 1830, when he was removed with some controversy. Letters suggest that President Jackson had assured Mr. Gerry that he would be reappointed to his position, but subsequently a newspaper article publicly announced the appointment of someone else. Elbridge Gerry traveled to Washington to meet with the President to discuss how he had "relied" on the President's earlier commitment to him. Witnesses state that it was President Jackson who was unwilling to explain his arbitrariness and asked Gerry to leave his office; he left but immediately returned to demand an explanation, doing so in a courteous but steadfast manner. Indeed, it was noted in the *Boston Courier* that, "Mr. Gerry, of whom we stated in our last paper, it was rumored he had conducted himself very "ungentlemanly" toward the President, assures us that nothing that could be distorted into a violation of decorum transpired during his interview with General Jackson. We are authorized by Mr. Gerry to say, that the above paragraph from the Statesman of this morning is ambiguous, he having expressly said to the Editor of the Statesman, there was nothing "ungentlemanly" on his part during his interview with the President."[42] After leaving the position of *Inspector of Revenue,* Elbridge Gerry, Jr. opened a store in Boston at Number 53 Kilby Street, establishing himself as a commission merchant for selling American packaged goods. The store eventually moved to Liberty Square, Boston.[43]

In his youth, Elbridge lived at the family home, Elmwood, in Cambridge, and despite not having experience with the historic Gerry merchant shipping business in Marblehead, as had his father and uncles, he eventually succeeded with his business. His first adventure after graduating from Harvard in 1813 was his road trip through several states, documented in his later published diary. Elbridge worked hard for the next twenty seven years establishing and developing a stable business. Regular and plentiful advertisements can be found in the Boston *Atlas* newspaper for fabric, gloves, foreign goods, wool, cotton, sheets, and shirts, "received and for sale" by Elbridge Gerry, 10 Liberty Square, Boston. Oftentimes, Elbridge was doing business with, and on behalf of his brothers, Thomas and James. He remained, as the eldest son, the steadfast father-figure to his sisters and with his brother Thomas, the constant advisors and protectors of their invalid mother, managing the extended Gerry family business affairs among Boston, Marblehead and New York City.

James Thompson Gerry, in 1815, a year after the death of his father, was appointed a naval cadet at the age of eighteen, and would serve the United States Navy throughout his life. In 1824 he was assigned to the sloop *Concord* while, at the same time, his older brother Thomas Russell was assigned to the sloop *John Adams.* When at port in America for any length of time, James spent his furloughs with family, often in New Haven, Connecticut with his mother and sisters. Correspondence with his brother Thomas Russell Gerry was faithful over the years and the letters make it clear that Thomas procured incidentals and personal items for his brother James to retrieve whenever he was in port. James in turn would write his family to let them know he had procured cigars for his brother Thomas and sweets or other gifts for his mother and sisters. James wrote from Havana, Cuba in December, 1839, a three page letter to his youngest sister Emily, which read in part:

> My Dear Emily,
>
> Your very charming letter of October 25th has been acknowledged, but not answered and as it is Sunday evening and all my messmates are on shore, I cannot pass it more agreeably than writing to and thinking of those who constitute the principle attachment I have for this world. The many little family incidents you so kindly collect for my amusement, fill up a vacuum which no one can realize until deprived of all such society as affords pleasure to associate with, and I have nothing in return to offer, but my warmest gratitude.... *He mentions his sisters Kitty (Catharine), Eleanor and other friends...then James mentions his brother Thomas Russell's wife's family, the Goelets....* What a queer set those Goelets are! I do verily believe that when the old lady dies, she will make a request that the event shall be kept a perfect mystery until they are all ready to put her right under the sod, and then it must appear in some obscure part of the paper to avoid all excitement in the world.... *and in the post script James adds ...* I wrote to dear mother by the New York packet, and think it very likely this will be sent by the same vessel. The sweet meats I shall send from Pensacola, Florida to save duties. We are all ready to sail at a moment's notice upon some extra service on a short cruise and have our Boats ready for a frolic, but tis all mystery and would delight old Mrs. Goelet.
>
> James T. Gerry[44]

The playful intimacy in James T. Gerry's reference to "old Mrs. Goelet" may have its genesis in mid-1830 when his brother married her daughter, Hannah G. Goelet, but old Mrs. Goelet did not formally announce the marriage and the marriage was done in haste. It would seem a mystery at the time for such a prominent New York family to not have a formal announcement and formal wedding for their daughter. Apparently the Goelet family was still in mourning, perhaps for Hannah's father who had died less than two years earlier.

James T. Gerry was assigned to the *U.S.S. Concord* in 1824, and again in 1831, then the *U.S.S. Constellation* in 1829. During the year 1836 Gerry is listed as excused from naval service due to bad health, and is stationed at the Navy Yard in Boston. He was later assigned to the *U.S.S. Warren* in 1839, the *U.S.S. Franklin* 1850-1851, the *U.S.S. Albany* in 1853-1854, among other assignments spanning a thirty-nine year naval career. A collection of letters spanning his duty at sea on these naval sloops were at auction in 2006. A sampling of their content provides some insight into navy life in the early nineteenth century, and specifically, into the life of James T. Gerry. He talks much about family and current affairs, plant life (a shared interest with his sisters), and gives advice to his teenage nephew, Elbridge Thomas Gerry (whose father, Thomas Russell died in 1845). James also wrote in detail about what he had seen during his world travels. Quotes from a few undated letters:

> Pensacola is a very uninteresting, poor miserable place. It was built many years ago by the Spanish government and then extended one mile length less than half a mile width, in form a regular parallelogram, with a population of eight to ten thousand, of all shades and colors. *Another*, We anchored in the harbor of St. Thomas, one of the Virgin Islands, and found the Flag Ship Columbia (15 days from New York) and Steamer Fulton, the former with small pox among her crew... This evening we first heard that some 20 cases of Cholera were reported in the city and the next day 65 deaths were reported. It is now certain that my ship must proceed north for a new main mast and other necessary repairs, as it is impossible to hire the requisite workmen for the Navy Yard, either here or in New Orleans, wages at the North being exorbitantly high, that ships carpenters did not migrate south. *Another*, "we made sail for Matanzas being required to visit that port... that is a noble harbor and very easy to access, and had many merchant vessels in it waiting for Sugar and Molasses, mostly Americans...."

Captain Gerry's description of a slave ship and his anger at what he observed spoke to his principled sense of outrage at the illegal and cruel practice.

> A Slaver run in just before us, having landed 280 Africans 15 leagues from the harbor, the same morning, and a steamboat was sent after them which also went into port at the same time, and landed the slaves in open day although against the laws of Spain, but the Governor here, as in Havana, receives a handsome bribe for closing his eyes. An English schooner chased this and another with 550 aboard and succeeded in capturing the latter, on the south side of Cuba. The Slaver, to induce the cruiser to give up his chase, threw over several of his Cargo (slaves), thinking while they were picking-up these poor wretches he could make his escape. But John Bull pushed on for the whole (being worth five pounds a head to him paid by his own Government) and caught them; now he has the whole crew, I trust every rascal will be hung for murder.[45]

James Thompson Gerry often wrote letters between six and eight pages in length, describing every port of call from Europe and the Mediterranean to the West Indies, Cuba and the Caribbean. Included in his letters are brawls, weddings of crew members, deaths, and the discovery of new plants and cultures that clearly inspire him. James, the consummate navy captain, described himself perfectly when he shared his need to be at sea in a letter home in September 1830:

> My dear family,
>
> My health continues very good and could we be more actively employed I should feel perfectly contented, but such is my moving disposition, that I am never satisfied unless actively employed and on the move somewhere. I am in excellent health, good spirits, happy, but vexed to think that we are so much of our time in a port like this, where nothing is to be seen and left to be learnt.[46]

After years of dedicated service as a true and happy man of the sea, James T. Gerry was lost at sea while Captain of the twenty-gun sloop of war, the *U.S.S. Albany,* in 1854 during a hurricane in the Gulf of Mexico. Third Lieutenant John Quincy Adams, Jr., the grandson of President John Adams, also died with James and his crew on the *U.S.S. Albany.*[47] The navy searched for over a month for the *Albany.*

Thomas Russell Gerry, the second eldest son, continued his career in the Navy for nineteen years, from his December 1814 appointment until 1833. There is only one period of note during these nineteen years that Thomas was on extended leave from his naval duties. There was an announcement in 1817 of gentlemen admitted to the degree of Master of Arts from Harvard University in Cambridge, Massachusetts on August 17 of that year, and Thomas Russell Gerry was one of the gentlemen listed.[48] His undergraduate degree was from Harvard College in 1814, the year of his father's death. The Harvard commencement ceremony included orations from several of the graduates. Thomas Russell Gerry was listed as presenting an oration in English Composition, and all of the performances were described as judiciously selected and they added honor to the Institution of Harvard College. Except for the untimely death of his father, Vice President Elbridge Gerry, just three months after graduation, it was expected that Thomas Russell Gerry would immediately engage in the practice of law. However, many who knew Thomas at the time speculated that he accepted the naval appointment from President Madison so quickly because that was his preferred calling; indeed, young men in 1814 were eager to join in the defense of their country in the continuing War of 1812, no doubt inspired by the highly publicized battles of the famous U.S.S. Constitution, "Old Ironsides," which was stationed in the Boston Harbor in 1816. During his eighteen years of service in the United States Navy, Thomas R. Gerry was assigned to the *U.S.S. Congress,* the *U.S.S. Constellation, the U.S.S. Erie,* and the *U.S.S. John Adams,* among other assignments.

Thomas Russell Gerry did not marry until age 36. He was married quietly on Wednesday, June 30, 1830 to Hannah Green Goelet, age 25, the daughter of Peter

P. Goelet and Almy Buchanan, a wealthy mercantile and banking family in New York City.[49] As mentioned earlier, in James T. Gerry's 1839 letter to his sister Emily, it is Thomas's mother-in-law who James referred to as "old Mrs. Goelet." This marriage took place just one month after Thomas's brother Elbridge Gerry Jr. was unexpectedly removed from his position as *Inspector of Revenue* in Boston by the President of the United States. The forced resignation was surrounded by unwanted publicity in the papers. The disappointed older brother, Elbridge Gerry, Jr., with little experience, was at this time, embarking upon a store-front business venture in Boston which exchanged goods with the Peter P. Goelet business in New York City and his brother Samuel Gerry in Marblehead, Massachusetts. Because Elbridge, Jr. and Samuel Gerry's brother, Thomas Russell Gerry, represented their commercial interests with Peter P. Goelet, the publicity of President Jackson's slight to Elbridge in Boston may have presented some embarrassment for the Goelets, a well-known and highly respected business family in New York City. Also, Peter P. Goelet had died just a year and a half earlier, leaving Mrs. Goelet a widow who was naturally very concerned about the welfare of her daughter, Hannah. Mrs. Goelet came to know Thomas R. Gerry and his affection for her daughter when he visited her husband Peter P. Goelet on business in the years before his death. Thomas had also done business for years with his mother's New York City paternal-side family, the Thompsons, and on her maternal-side, the Walton family: both leading merchants who did business with the Goelet family for generations. In fact, as early as 1750, just twenty years after Captain Thomas Gerry had established the family in Marblehead, Massachusetts, the famous Captain Francis Goelet had sailed into Marblehead and described the town in his diary as not only prosperous in the fishing industry but also "smelling of fish," completely unaware that his family would one day be closely associated with Marblehead's famous Gerry family. Today, the *Diary of Francis Goelet* is held in the archives of the New York Historical Society.

By the time Peter P. Goelet was near death, he had given his blessing to Thomas's courtship of his daughter, Hannah. Under the cloak of a family in mourning, Mrs. Goelet declined to send out wedding announcements or invitations for Thomas R. Gerry and Hannah Goelet's marriage. Thomas sent letters on June 22, 1830, from New York City, to his sister Elizabeth and her husband, Major David S. Townsend, in New London, Connecticut, inviting them to join him in New York City to witness his marriage:

My Dear Sister,

By the express desire of Mrs. Goelet, I am requested to invite you and your husband to witness the marriage of myself and her daughter on the 30th of June – and I most ardently solicit the pleasure of your presence myself. In consequence of our being married in the most private manner, Mrs. Goelet has avoided sending any written invitations to her own relations, and begs therefore you will not consider this form of invitation as indicative of any other than the most sincere wish to have you present. I need not say how gratifying it will be to me to have you present. – though I can offer you no inducements in the line of gayety or pleasure, as we are in deep mourning and shall not go into company, nor entertain any.

Most affectionately your fond brother
Thomas R. Gerry

On the same day, Thomas sends a nearly identical letter to Elizabeth's husband, also in New London, Connecticut:

My Dear David,

I have just sent an invitation to you and sister Eliza – at the express desire of Mrs. Goelet and my own earnest wish – to have you present at my wedding on the 30th June. Having but a few moments to write, I invited you both in one letter, but to convince you I did so only because I wished to give you all the time I could, and not because I intentionally omitted a proper attention. I again repeat Mrs. Goelet's and my own urgent request that you would favor me with your presence – and rest assured it will be gratefully remembered by your most sincere

Thomas R Gerry[50]

Perhaps from a record of the civil registration of the marriage, a public announcement of the marriage was published on July 2, 1830 in the *New York Morning Herald* along with other marriages of the day.[51] In September, just three months after their wedding, while Thomas and Hannah shared a cordial and satisfying visit with his mother and sisters in New London, Connecticut, James T. Gerry sent a letter to his family that confirms that both Thomas's mother and one of his sisters traveled to New York with Elizabeth and David Townsend for the private wedding at the Goelet mansion:

My dear Family,

A package of July 14 from our dear Thomas has given me much satisfaction and a lively account of his wedding; also yours and Helen's visit upon the occasion. He relates all the particulars in a style so totally different from that of some of his former letters, that it did my very heart good to re-peruse it, and I think if there is

> any happiness in this world, his chance for a goodly portion of it is as fair as any young man with whom I am acquainted.[52]

Captain Thomas R. Gerry remained in the Navy for three years after his marriage. It is not clear what profession, if any, Thomas pursued after 1833. There are suggestions through family letters, his navy record, and his early death at age 51, that Thomas may have had health problems his entire adult life, or perhaps he simply did not have the physical constitution to continue such a rigorous military career. His navy record was uneven compared with that of his brother James, who would rise to Captain his own ship and thrived on his life at sea. Navy records show that Thomas was on furlough more often than his younger brother James and he is not listed for any assignment in 1818 or 1819; however, he had been accepted to Harvard for a Master of Arts program in the summer of 1817 and was likely studying in Cambridge. In 1825-26, the Navy took advantage of his education by assigning Thomas to the recruiting service rather than to a ship. Most ships, whether commercial or navy, have designated home ports, where they are said to be in "ordinary" when stationed in the home port for a long period of time. Port towns, small or large, center many of their routines around the arrival and departure of ships carrying, not only trade goods, but more importantly, their husbands, fathers, brothers and friends. The local newspapers report all activity regarding the movement of ships, important events in the life of the town. The *Boston Courier* reported on December 10, 1832, that " the United States sloop of war *Concord* arrived in Boston Harbor on Wednesday afternoon, 48 days from Mahon; officers and crew all well; experienced bad weather. The list of the officers included lieutenants Thomas R. Gerry and James T. Gerry."[53] This is the only recorded time when the brothers, Thomas and James, were at sea together, assigned to the same ship, the *Concord*. This was Thomas R. Gerry's last voyage; he would retire on August 27, 1833. His retirement from navy life would come as no surprise to his family, and would certainly have been understood by his seafaring bachelor brother James, since Thomas and Hannah's first child, Peter Goelet Gerry, was born just seven months later in March 1834. One year after resigning from the Navy, Thomas wrote to his sister Elizabeth Townsend on March 29, 1834 announcing,

> I was blessed today with the birth of a fine large boy, with the Gerry crest upon his visage – viz – an aquiline nose, dark hair and eyes, and dimple in his chin, and I should say about 12 lbs. in weight. Hannah had a tedious time of 12 hours but got through her troubles like a true Christian and is wonderfully well after them. It feels queer to be called Father, and I can't yet realize that this is <u>my son</u>,
>
> Your fond brother, Thomas.[54]

Three months later, on May 22, 1834, Thomas writes once again to his sister Elizabeth from New York City, asking if her husband Major Townsend was reappointed to his commission, and further, he writes:

> My Dear Elizabeth,
>
> Gerry Austin and his young bride passed through this city last Friday on their way to Washington. Dear Hannah (always anxious to do everything she can towards a good feeling with the branches of my family) insisted on calling upon Mrs. Austin – tho' I remonstrated against it, as she was very delicate and had only rode out twice in warm weather. My little boy has been vaccinated and it has taken very well. He is still suffering from it tho' otherwise perfectly healthy. ... Hannah sends her love to you and your children and best respects to the Major – with which receive the unaltered attachment of your affectionate brother, T.R. Gerry[55]

Thomas Russell Gerry occupied his time from 1834 until 1845, managing his mother's affairs; coordinating business in New York on behalf of his brother Elbridge, Jr. in Boston; dabbling in politics, and taking care of his growing family. Assisting his mother involved routine business matters plus a complicated property settlement of an uncle's estate over several years. Ann's brother Jacob wrote from Bath, England on October 18, 1821:

> My dear Sister,
>
> Since I wrote to you last I have received your letters of June and July last, containing the particulars of Uncle Garrand's property which fails to be divided amongst his next of kin... I have written to the Executor to pay to you my share of the estate.... I only wish that the amount were much larger.
>
> Always your affectionate brother, J. Thompson[56]

Letters between Great Britain and America were exchanged for years between the executors of the estate to coordinate endless problems with currency conversion, powers of attorney, and many other issues that plagued the extended Thompson family and Thomas R. Gerry as his mother's representative.

Elbridge Gerry, Jr. also relied on his brother Thomas to deliver documents and packages to New York clients to expedite business between Boston and New York. When Elbridge invested in a cotton and wool spinning mill in Mansfield, Massachusetts, Thomas had to represent the interests of his brother James who was at sea, and his mother Ann, who understood the need to invest. After several years of moderate success the Gerrys sold the mill in the 1840's and reinvested elsewhere.

As a Gerry, Thomas was raised in the home of a Founding Father and politics was a regular topic of conversation, a topic for college papers, and a topic to include in correspondence involving the entire family throughout their life-times. In a letter to his sister Elizabeth in May 1834, Thomas acknowledged he was somehow involved in politics, without being specific:

> My Dear Sister,
>
> I hope next fall…(pardon the opinion of a Wig) to send some strong friends of ours to the House & (tho' opposed in Politics to you & your husband) I hope to aid in getting more Wigs into the house, as I think they add to the respectability of an August Body.

In the same letter, Thomas continues:

> Hannah sends her love and says she regrets that she will be deprived the pleasure of meeting you at the Point as we have made our arrangements to visit mother the last of June or 1st July and shall proceed from New Haven direct to Rockaway, preferring to go down the Sound early rather than late in the Season, on account of the weather and baby" T R Gerry[57]

Three months later, on August 15, 1834 Thomas wrote to his mother about the recent appearance of cholera in New York City and therefore he and Hannah and the baby would remain in Rockaway for the indefinite future, until the danger passed. He did mention that his son Peter had been ill due to the change of weather but was doing well and was growing fast. Thomas and Hannah's life was quiet and unremarkable on the public stage, as described by a newspaper editor who knew the Goelet/Gerrys in New York City, "When young Tom Gerry, as I have no doubt he was called in his day, married Hannah Goelet he succeeded in securing one of the best catches then in the matrimonial market. Beyond the fact of his marriage I have never seen any account of him."[58] Thomas Gerry's political life was low-key but nonetheless, effective. In April, 1839 he was elected as the Assistant Alderman of the Common Council, New York City representing the 12th Ward. He was listed as a member of the Whig party, which Thomas referenced in his letters to his mother when discussing his efforts to un-seat political opponents.[59]

Tragedy struck at the heart of Thomas and Hannah's little family. While she was 3 months pregnant with their second son, their beloved three-year old Peter died unexpectedly on June 30, 1837. The sorrow expressed in the letters of Thomas to family and friends over the next several months was heartbreaking. The blessing in the midst of the loss was the birth of Elbridge Thomas Gerry, on December 25 of that same year, a cherished Christmas gift for Hannah and

Thomas. The Gerrys continued to live in New York City most of the year and spent summers and early fall at Rockaway. Hannah and her brothers spent most of their childhood summers at West Point or Rockaway, favorite "watering places" for the wealthy. That is perhaps why Thomas brought Hannah and young Peter to Rockaway for "the season." However, he wrote in July, 1837 that Hannah could no longer bear to go any place that held memories of her lost son. Happily, the following summer, August 1838, found Thomas writing more cheerful letters, and indeed, writing from Rockaway which suggested that Hannah had recovered from her time of mourning. He wrote to his mother Ann, that he was leaving Rockaway on business for his brother James and noted that baby Elbridge and his wife's family, the Goelets, were doing well. By June 1840 the Gerrys found a renewed sense of life with the birth of their first daughter, Almy Goelet Gerry. Elbridge had a playmate and Hannah and Thomas felt like the family was whole once again. In August 1841, Thomas wrote his usual end-of-season letter to his mother, noting that he was leaving his summer holiday in Rockaway to deliver a draft deposit to New York City on behalf of his brother Elbridge, Jr., continuing the pattern of a simple yet happy life dedicated to his immediate and extended family. In the spring of 1842 their second daughter Jean Buchanan Gerry was born solidifying the contentment of the family. The baby remained healthy and grew strong over the next three years, no doubt spending lots of time with her brother Elbridge and sister Almy at the Goelet mansion on Broadway with their aunt Jean, and uncles Peter and Robert. The last summer of Thomas Russell Gerry's life was not spent at Rockaway, but at the Huguenot settlement of New Rochelle in West Chester County, eighteen miles from New York City on Long Island Sound. By the 1840's New Rochelle was considered the most fashionable suburb and *Neptune House* was the summer residence of many persons of wealth and prominence.[60] In late September, 1845 Thomas wrote to his mother from New Rochelle and described the beautiful views of *Hunter's Island* from his window, a yacht ride to Oyster Bay for a picnic with friends, and stated that they would return to New York City in another week. In less than ten days, Thomas Russell Gerry died at New Rochelle, New York from what is described as a sudden illness of just a few days. He left behind his forty-one-year old wife Hannah, his eight year-old son Elbridge Thomas Gerry, his five year-old daughter Almy Goelet Gerry, and three-year-old daughter Jean Buchanan Gerry. Hannah returned to New York City to stay with her siblings in the Goelet family mansion on Broadway, where she and Thomas had been married fifteen years earlier. That same year on February 28, Thomas's mother, Ann Thompson Gerry, lost her brother Jacob Thompson in England. Elbridge, Jr. and his brother Thomas had worked with their uncle for many years to resolve the disputed Thompson estate held in probate in England, and now, four months before Thomas Russell Gerry died the entire Thompson estate was finally settled at the death of Jacob Thompson in London.

> We learn today that the venerable widow of the late Hon. Elbridge Gerry, now a resident of this city, has become the legatee or inheritor of a handsome fortune, by the death of a brother in England. The amount is said to be 50,000 dollars.[61]

There are no letters in the *Gerry Family Papers* discussing either the death of Thomas R. Gerry in 1845, or the death of his brother James T. Gerry nearly ten years later in 1854. Ann Thompson Gerry lived just four more years, and she died in 1849, the last living wife of a Signer of the *Declaration of Independence.* Hannah Goelet Gerry survived her beloved husband, Thomas Russell Gerry for another fifty years, she died in 1895 in the old Broadway Farm mansion of her brother Peter Goelet at Nineteenth and Broadway in New York City.

Gerry Home, Marblehead, MA
Built in 1730, the year Captain Thomas Gerry arrived in America. Elbridge Gerry was born and lived here until married.

Rebecca Russell Greenleaf
1720–1771
Daughter of wealthy Boston merchant with whom Thomas Gerry worked.

Captain Thomas Gerry
1702–1774
Son of Daniel & Lydia Gerry Newton-Abbot, Devonshire, UK.

Ann Thompson Gerry
Daughter of NYC merchant, educated in Dublin. Granddaughter of NYC merchant Jacob Walton.

nine children

Vice-President Elbridge Gerry
Signed Declaration of Independence.
Proposed first Supreme Court Library.

Gerry's Massachusetts re-districting map that originated the term GERRYMANDERING in the United States

Historic Town Hall, Marblehead, MA

Wall Street, NYC, 1798

ELMWOOD
Gerry mansion in Cambridge, MA where all nine children were born and raised.
Today, the *President's House*, Harvard University.

Elbridge Gerry, Jr.
1793–1867
Boston merchant,
father figure to his sisters.

Thomas Russell Gerry
1794–1848
Married Hannah Greene
Goelet.

four children

Hannah Goelet Gerry
1802–1895
Survived her husband
by 50 years.

Sloop of War sank
in a storm in 1854.
All were lost,
including John
Quincy Adams, Jr.

Captain James Thomas
Gerry
1791–1854
Wrote to his siblings
his entire life.

Emily Gerry
1802–1893
Youngest of nine Gerry
children and the last child
of any signer of
the *Declaration of Independence* to die.

Helen Gerry
1796–1864

Ann Gerry
1793–1883

No photographs
of three sisters:

Eleanor (unmarried)
1800–1871

Elizabeth Gerry Townsend
1792–1882

Catherine Gerry Austin
1790–1850

Gerry home in New Haven, CT at the corner of Temple and Church streets where Ann Thompson Gerry, widow of Vice-President Elbridge Gerry, lives with her four unmarried daughters until their successive deaths — the last, Emily Gerry in 1893. Their sea captain brother, James T. Gerry, lived with them when on leave from duty on his assigned ship.

2

Education and Apprenticeship

Education begins the gentleman, but reading,
good company and reflection must finish him.
John Locke, 1693

Commodore Elbridge Thomas Gerry was just eight years old when he lost his father in the fall of 1845 while on holiday at New Rochelle, New York. The next three years he, his five-year-old sister Almy, and three-year-old sister Jean lived, with their mother, Hannah Goelet Gerry at 48 Broadway in New York City, a block from the Peter P. Goelet family home, a Georgian Mansion at 54 Broadway where she had been raised, and where she was privately married to Thomas Russell Gerry in 1830. Mrs. Almy Buchanan Goelet, the widow of Peter P. Goelet (*pronounced* guh-LETT) and mother of Hannah Gerry, died in 1848 the year before Hannah's mother-in-law, Ann Thompson Gerry, died in New Haven, Connecticut. Elbridge Gerry, Jr. continued as head of the Gerry family in Massachusetts until his death in 1867 and his brother's widow, Hannah Goelet Gerry, was the head of the Gerry family in New York until her death in 1895.

The four Goelet siblings, Peter, Robert, Hannah and Jean, inherited the family fortune jointly and the brothers managed the New York City real estate on behalf of their sisters. Their father and grandfather had been the most successful merchants in the city and over their successive life-times they invested considerable sums of money in real estate, purchasing farm and pasture land located just ahead of the fast growing metropolis. After the death of their mother, the Goelet family moved to a large four-story house situated on family farmland on the outskirts of the city at Nineteenth and Broadway. Peter Goelet, the oldest of the four Goelet siblings, was born in 1800 nine years older than his brother Robert who was born in 1809 the youngest of the four. They were not only brothers but companions in the truest sense of the word. It was their life-long custom to go as a family to the popular watering place "West Point" or to "Saratoga Springs" both situated on the Hudson River north of New York City.

The Goelet brothers remained especially close in business and in their personal life and actually died in the same year just four months apart in 1879. Curiously, their namesakes, Peter G. Gerry and Robert L. Gerry, Commodore Elbridge T. Gerry's sons, likewise remained close during their lifetimes and died within four hours of each other on the same day in 1957.

At the time of Almy Buchanan Goelet's death in 1848 it was impossible to accurately estimate the wealth of the Goelets. Like their father before them, Peter and Robert Goelet were both actively associated with the *Chemical Bank* of New York, with Peter being one of the largest stock holders. Peter remained a bachelor his entire life while Robert married his State Street "next door" neighbor, Sarah Ogden, in 1839. Robert and Sarah's son, named for his father, Robert Goelet, Jr., also became a Director of the *Chemical Bank* in New York in 1878, and he was one of the original stockholders at the founding of the New York City *Metropolitan Opera Company*. Three generations of Goelets continued to support the opera. Their sisters, Hannah a widow and Jean a spinster lived with their bachelor brother, Peter Goelet, in the same house at Nineteenth and Broadway until their deaths. Hannah was the last surviving sibling when she died in 1895. This close-knit, wealthy family raised Thomas Russell Gerry's children, Almy, Jean, and Elbridge, as their own.

It was Peter Goelet, *Uncle Peter*, who became the father-figure in young Elbridge Thomas Gerry's life and that of his sisters Almy and Jean. Peter was forty-eight when he relinquished full-time work to move his new family circle to the outskirts of the city. The children had fresh air, room to play and were surrounded with animals of every sort. There were pheasants, chickens, guinea pigs, proud peacocks, handsome horses and a large cow. Even as the city grew around the "Broadway Farm" leaving it the only residential structure amid towering businesses in 1895, the cow was the last animal to wander the grounds long after the children had grown-up and married.[1] About the time the Gerrys moved into the brick and brownstone house at 19th Street, a beautiful doll house, a miniature of the original was constructed, depicting every detail, inside and out. Peter Goelet made the lovely replica for the entertainment of his nieces Almy and Jean Gerry who were eight and five at the time the little house was made. Today the doll house and all the miniature furnishings are in the archive collections of the *Museum of the City of New York* on Fifth Avenue.[2]

The house at Nineteenth and Broadway was large enough at the time to be called a mansion, but was actually very plain in style with a dark brownstone and brick façade. The interior had painted, solid mahogany woodwork throughout except for the floors, which were most likely oak. The property included a barn and stable which suited Peter Goelets fondness for fine horses, usually housing upward of six horses. Although Peter could have rode a horse or driven his own carriage into town, he usually walked or took a public carriage. His nephew, Elbridge, also developed a fondness for horses and years later built his own stables on East Sixty-Second Street. Indeed, Elbridge's own children shared the Goelet and Gerry passion for horses, owning, riding and breeding thoroughbred horses into the twentieth century.

Although retired in 1848 and no longer employed by the *Chemical Bank* Peter Goelet was still the largest stockholder in the bank. He was a valued banker and he continued to advise the bank's Board of Directors. Peter was often found in the Board Room reviewing documents and consulting with board members at their leisure. Peter Goelet was also charitable without ostentation and during the Civil War he took a special interest in the New York regiments, expending money freely to relieve the suffering of veterans who returned home sick or disabled and to assist the families of soldiers killed in the war.[3] Elbridge T. Gerry grew up happily sharing the somewhat reclusive life style of his Uncle Peter, who was known to mend his own clothes, saved the backs of envelopes for his stationery, and with his own hands, milked his prize cow.[4]

Just as his grandfather Goelet was an ironmonger who owned an expansive hardware store on Hanover Square in earlier days, Peter Goelet, the banker by day, had a blacksmiths forge in the basement of the house at Nineteenth and Broadway, where he manufactured various sorts of locks in curious and intricate patterns using specialized machinery.[5] Peter was by nature intellectual, curious, and private, and those who didn't know how busy he was with a variety of endeavors would call him reclusive.

Peter Goelet was indeed thrifty as was the custom of his father and grandfather before him, but he also continued the policy of investing in land and buildings, mainly in those parts of the growing city where in a few years there was certain to be a dense aggregation of buildings of the highest class. There was considerable power in the hands of real estate owners, especially when so much property was held by one family in the heart of the business district of New York City. Of note, it was Peter Goelet who blocked the attempt of Boss Tweed to extend Madison Avenue through to Broadway.[6] Peter invested in land, he did not sell land. He refused to sell the land now occupied by the *Grand Central Station* to Commodore Cornelius Vanderbilt, so the Commodore acquired the property for the railroad by invoking eminent domain, a legal taking of the Goelet land for public use.[7] Edith Vanderbilt, the widow of Cornelius's grandson, George Vanderbilt, later married Elbridge T.

Gerry's son, Senator Peter Goelet Gerry in 1925, once again joining two great American families through the bond of marriage.

Peter Goelet was an influential role model in young Elbridge Thomas Gerry's life. The attention to detail and the pursuit of passionate interests were Goelet traits that became deeply impressed on young Elbridge. There were several significant passions that Elbridge developed and pursued throughout his lifetime, all of which had their genesis during his childhood at the Broadway Farm and his associations with the extended Goelet family.

Foremost was a deep faith and steadfast commitment to the Episcopal Church. His parents, Thomas and Hannah, expressed their spirituality in all of their correspondence, turning to God for guidance, consolation and a sense of meaning in their lives. With Uncle Peter young Elbridge found that same devotion and continued example. As an adult, Elbridge would also develop a professional relationship with the Episcopal Church of New York that would demand much of his time and attention.

The love of reading and books was a very personal connection between Peter and his nephew. During Elbridge's nineteen years at the Broadway Farm from age eleven until he married in 1867, he collected books of every kind with the guidance and shared passion of his Uncle Peter. He became a bibliophile, collecting books up until his death in 1927 at which time Elbridge had amassed a library collection of 30,000 volumes.

Elbridge discovered the love of music from his uncles who co-founded the *Metropolitan Opera House* in New York City, which was built on Goelet land. While at Columbia College Elbridge followed the Goelet example and organized music programs staged at the *Academy of Music.*

From his early youth Elbridge Gerry was an enthusiastic yachtsman, whose last memory of his father, Captain Thomas Russell Gerry in 1845, was a yachting trip to Oyster Bay for a picnic just several days before his father's death in New Rochelle. Young Elbridge taught himself sailing, practicing at every opportunity, and learning the skillful details of the sport from his cousins, Robert Jr. and Ogden, who owned luxurious yachts as adults, sailing from America to many ports in Europe during their summer holidays. Often at sea from one to three months, Robert Jr., Ogden and cousin Elbridge were cut from the same cloth as his uncle, Captain James T. Gerry, who sailed the same oceans and docked at similar ports over a lifetime in the navy. The sea clearly flowed through the Goelet and Gerry bloodlines. Peter Goelet's brother Robert Goelet joined the *New York Yacht Club* at its founding in 1844, and his son Ogden later engaged Tiffany & Company to design and produce most of the *Goelet Cups* to award at annual American yacht races at Newport, Rhode

Island. Elbridge became Commodore of the *New York Yacht Club* and had the first steam yacht in America built to his own specifications in 1884 with a generator that powered electric lights designed by Thomas Alva Edison.

Elbridge Thomas Gerry was educated at *Columbia College* as were his Goelet uncles and cousins, unlike the Harvard educated Gerrys of Massachusetts before him. He became a well-known, highly respected, and very busy practicing lawyer, a profession he employed in all aspects of his life, from church affairs and yachting, to representing those in need: a duty and sensibility Elbridge experienced with his Uncle Peter when he cared for the Civil War regiment's sick, wounded, and their fatherless families. The legal profession suited Elbridge's strong character and principled way of thinking, very much like his grandfather, Vice President Elbridge Gerry, the Founding Father. Given the circumstances of his family, both wealthy and deeply committed to the Episcopal Church, Elbridge T. Gerry was educated at the elementary level by private tutors and by attendance at the Episcopal *Columbia Grammar School.* The family's local parish was Trinity Church, not only the grammar school's location but also the Church where Elbridge would eventually be married.

Columbia Grammar School was founded in 1764, just ten years after the founding in colonial New York City of the *Kings College* by Great Britain. Originally established as a boys' preparatory school for the college, it functioned for twelve years under the direct auspices of Oxford's Kings College and the Episcopal Church. In July 1754, Samuel Johnson held the first classes in a new schoolhouse adjoining Trinity Church, located on what is now lower Broadway in Manhattan. There were only eight students in the class. One of the most illustrious headmasters during the school's history was Dr. Charles Anthon, one of America's earliest and most distinguished classical scholars. During his tenure the Grammar School provided over half the students to Kings College and eventually, to Columbia College's freshman class.[8] Elbridge T. Gerry was a student of Professor Anthon and Gerry's handwritten notes from his classes are in the *Rare Book Room* at Columbia University's *Butler Library,* along with many other documents from Elbridge's school days, from grammar school through college years at Columbia.[9] Notebooks include translations at age 12 of *Euripides* and *Terrenes* under the guidance of Prof. Anthon, as well as Elbridge's 98 pages of handwritten translations of Homer's *The Iliad* Books I and II, and the rough translations of Books V and VI, and part of Book VII. The translation notes of *The Iliad* are dated 1853, placing Elbridge at the end of grammar school and only 13 years old as he pursued an intense classical education.[10]

During the Revolutionary War the British dismantled Kings College in New York. Almost immediately after colonial independence, Columbia College rose from the remnants of Kings College into one of the most academically selective and intensive college programs in early America. The *Columbia Grammar School,* first established under the auspices of Kings College, continued to function on the Trinity Church property through the American Revolution but eventually it too came under the auspices of the new Columbia College. After two hundred years the school continues to this day as a rigorous college preparatory school in New York City.

In 1853, at the age of fourteen, Elbridge Thomas Gerry entered *Columbia College* to begin four years of study to earn a Bachelor's degree in 1857 followed by two years of part-time study at *Columbia College* to earn a Master's degree in 1860. These were significant years of development both intellectually and socially for Elbridge and he made good use of his time. He gained a reputation as an epicure, an athlete and a scholar who graduated with honors.[11] The summer between his freshman and sophomore years of college Elbridge had the adventure of a lifetime. His uncles, Peter and Robert Goelet, held stock in the Illinois Central Railroad and in Western Union Telegraph Company.[12] In June 1854 invitations were sent to railroad bond and stock holders, as well as the press, bankers, financiers, historians, even the United States President Millard Fillmore to join the Grand Excursion by train and steamboat from Chicago to Saint Paul, Minnesota. Uncle Peter no doubt gave his invitation to his nephew to expand his experiences beyond the limits of New York City.

This excursion celebrated the completion of the first train line running from the East coast to the Mississippi River, cutting the last leg of the trip from Chicago to Rock Island from weeks to days. Two trains of nine coaches each left Chicago on June 5 with nearly a thousand passengers, who then transferred to seven steam boats to continue up the Mississippi River to St. Paul, Minnesota.[13]

The trip was described by the press as elaborate with fireworks and speeches at every stop, multi-course gourmet meals, dancing to small orchestras, and always surrounded with beautiful scenery. The ten day round-trip Grand Excursion introduced the West to the East and initiated a surge in holiday travel westward. It not only stimulated enormous investment in the railroads. It also led to dangerous over-expansion.

As a college student Elbridge Thomas Gerry took thorough and meticulous notes, progressing over four years from his first notebook in 1853, which he indexed, to later notebooks in 1857 in which he adorned topic sections with gold and color illuminated designs, just like ancient illuminated manuscripts.

Coursework included Ancient Geography, Literature and Writing, Mathematics, Chemistry, Music, and Classical Languages, including Greek and Latin, hence the many translation notebooks across all four years of college. In 1855, his sophomore year of college, Elbridge wrote an essay on *Curiosity*. In his junior year he wrote an essay on *Energy*, a thirty-six page essay on *The Revolt of the Netherlands*, and one titled *An Essay on the Neglect of Classical Studies*. In his senior year in 1857 Elbridge wrote short essays of seven pages, such as *Brief Essay on Night*, and lengthy papers, such as his forty-one page *German Oration* presented at Graduation as an honors student.[14]

In a graduating class of twenty-six Elbridge Thomas Gerry was a leader by nature. He progressed from committee member, to Vice President, to President of the Philolexian Society for Literature and Music. He prepared the seating chart for the Fifty-fifth Anniversary dinner at the New York Academy of Music and presented a paper entitled *Talent Without Principle*. An undated newspaper clipping in Gerry's notebook provided the following review:

> Notwithstanding the inclemency of the weather, a numerous highly respectable audience was present. The exercises were literary and musical. The pieces were interspersed with operatic selections and waltzes. The entertainment was pleasing and instructive, and was fully appreciated by the audience. The orations displayed great ability on the part of the authors.[15]

Elbridge Thomas Gerry was elected *Secretary of the Class* of 1857, a role he played while at Columbia and for the rest of his life. He prepared the class treasury report, had invitations and pamphlets printed as needed, coordinated the copying and distribution of course lecture notes, and organized graduation lectures. After graduation Elbridge coordinated class reunion dinners, drafted resolutions to honor deceased faculty and classmates, and had personal custody of the *Class Papers* (documents) his entire life, all of which were donated to Columbia College after his death. The collection includes Gerry's white satin graduation ribbon, as perfect as the day he received it.

The close friendships among the class of 1857 could be characterized as a brotherhood whose commitment to civic duty extended to philanthropic projects as well as assisting, as appropriate, classmates down on their luck. Correspondence with one classmate over the years, Rev. Mytton Maury, involved requesting financial assistance from Gerry to recover from bad property investments. Reverend Maury writes of a $1,000.00 New Jersey land deal gone bad and another investment in an onion farm with his itinerant brother, placing him in debt for $3,000.00, a very large sum of money at the time. Gerry's response letters to these requests are not included in the Columbia files, but one would expect Elbridge T. Gerry to take a lawyers perspective, perhaps advising his old friend rather than facilitating bad judgment. In 1880 Elbridge gave his classmate and friend, Rev. D.S. Tuttle a donation of $500 to build a mission church.

Elbridge continued part-time at *Columbia College* for another two years to earn a Master's degree in German in 1860. His facility with languages held him in good stead throughout his life; he taught his own children the classic languages and regularly traveled throughout Europe with his family. While earning his Master's degree (1858-1860) Elbridge T. Gerry began his preparation for the practice of law. Columbia College did not establish a law school until the year after Elbridge graduated from college so he apprenticed in a law office which was the common practice. The tradition of *office apprenticeship* as the only "right way" to become a lawyer was an established belief if not bias of the legal profession since the founding of America. In fact, there was a pervasive prejudice against formal schooling that was rooted in the colonial cult of the self-made man. The first instance of law being "taught" as a subject occurred in England at *Oxford University* in 1753, when lawyer William Blackstone prepared and gave lectures on the common law for several years. He then published the lectures as *Blackstone's Commentaries on the Laws of England,* ultimately re-issued in seventeen editions over the years. His lectures were so successful that in 1758 he was unanimously elected to the new post of Regius Professor of Civil Law, the first professorship of the English common law in the world.[16] To apprentice in a law office Elbridge T. Gerry had to pass four or five years in the performance of tasks that required him to copy pleadings, draft briefs, file papers in court, research land titles, and collect payments from clients. In return his mentor gave him advice, information, and instruction as his time permitted. Nonetheless, learning the substance of the law in all its varied topics, from property and criminal law, to corporate and constitutional law was done on his own by reading classic law books. Elbridge had a distinct advantage in his private library at the Broadway Farm. If he needed *Blackstone's Commentaries*, or *Coke Upon Littleton*, or even Rapin's *Dissertation on the Laws and Customs of the Anglo Saxons,* or any of the many required treatises, Elbridge would simply purchase the title and add it to his library. With a voracious appetite for learning, an exceptional intellect, and his growing law library, Elbridge T. Gerry began an apprenticeship in the law office of William Curtis Noyes, a man of extensive learning who took a deep interest in public affairs. This was a perfect match for the gifted young Elbridge. Both men had conversational powers of the highest order and both cultivated an interest in beauty, art and literature. Indeed, Mr. Noyes had one of the best law libraries in the country from which Elbridge learned the skill and art of collecting law books. In the courtroom, Elbridge learned from the best. Mr. Noyes was retained in some of the most celebrated cases of the day, masterfully arguing cases on moral insanity, railroad disputes, and estate cases, all marked by his learning, eloquence and close logic. He was a firm advocate of temperance and devoted much time to address this subject. Mr. Noyes' talents were always enlisted on the side of the people among whom he lived, as an equity lawyer he was without parallel, and in cross-examination he had no equal. Few witnesses that went on the stand before Mr. Noyes with the determination to commit perjury ever left the stand without it being exposed. His motto was "better that a man's brain should wear out than rust out."[17]

Elbridge apprenticed two years rather than the usual four, was admitted to the Supreme Court of New York in November 1860, and immediately argued a property case which was won before the end of the year. Less than three months later, on February 13, 1861, Elbridge Thomas Gerry arrived in Washington, D.C. with William Curtis Noyes as his sponsor to be sworn in as a member of the United States Supreme Court Bar.

Beginning in 1857 and continuing during Elbridge's apprenticeship, a financial panic in the fall of 1857 brought on what turned out to be a short-lived but intense depression. Causes of the panic stemmed partly from the international economy and partly from domestic over-expansion of railroads, banks and business. This speculative house of cards came crashing down in September 1857. The failure of one banking house sent a wave of panic through the financial community. Banks suspended specie payments, businesses failed, railroads went bankrupt, construction halted, and factories shut down. Failure of the Ohio Life Insurance and Trust Company in August, 1857, precipitated the panic, which was followed by a depression from which the country did not emerge until 1859.[18] The 1857 financial crisis triggered a run on banks, including Peter Goelet's *Chemical Bank* in New York City. Jacob Cox Parsons, a Vice President of the *Chemical Bank* at his retirement in 1899 fondly recalled how the bank responded to the 1857 panic:

> The position taken by the Chemical Bank at the time of the panic was in keeping with the views entertained by the founders of the institution. On the cornerstone they had inscribed 'public confidence is the best capital,' hence those entrusted with the management could only prove worthy of the confidence reposed in them by being prepared at all times for such an emergency. Well, I remember that day. Reaching the bank long before the hour for business, I waited with anxiety the arrival of the President. He walked in as quiet and undisturbed as usual. In reply to my question, 'What are we going to do, Mr. Jones?' he said, 'We

> will pay all demands on us in gold.' In a few minutes the vault was opened and the clerks commenced carrying out bags, each containing $5,000, which were divided into smaller bags. The tills were filled with gold coins. At ten o'clock every inch of the room was occupied by an anxious crowd. Robert McCoskrey, our watchful Scotch Director, stood by my side to watch the proceedings in his usual position with hands behind him and softly whistling a favorite Scotch tune. No sooner were the demands of one person met than he was pushed aside by another in a hurry to get his money. All demands were paid. An old woman thrust a handful of bills at me. I looked at them and remarked: 'These are not bills of this bank,' 'What's the matter, Mr. Parsons?' asked Mr. McCoskrey, the bank Director, 'If the other banks cannot redeem their promises to pay, we'll do it for them." This remark was received with an outburst of applause and many withdrew satisfied that they could get their money at any time, and in three hours the excitement was over. A large portion of the gold paid out to customers was re-deposited in a day or two. From that time on we were kept busy by the rush of new business from the city and all parts of the country.[19]

The *Chemical Bank* story brings to mind a similar public run on a bank, the *Bailey Savings & Loan* in the classic story, "It's a Wonderful Life," where a business operating on principle and customer good will thrived in the midst of financial crisis. Elbridge Thomas Gerry learned significant economic lessons while living under the guidance of Peter Goelet at home and while working with William Curtis Noyes during his law office apprenticeship.

Elbridge Thomas Gerry entered manhood in the 1860s as the first generation of Gerrys to be raised in New York City rather than Massachusetts. Through the Goelet family Elbridge met another historic family in New York City, in fact the second most important family in Elbridge's life, the well-respected and very wealthy Livingston family. During the 1860's Elbridge became associated with Robert James Livingston, the great-great-great grandson of Robert Livingston (1654-1728), the family patriarch in America who was born in Ancrum, Scotland. Known affectionately as the First Lord of the Manor, Robert Livingston obtained through a series of land purchases approximately half a million acres of New York property that was part of Johannes Hardenburgh's (on behalf of several investors) land Patent, a royal grant in 1708 from Queen Anne in England. The Great Hardenburgh Patent totaled two-million acres. Due to land squabbles and sometimes dangerous encounters among the several investors, the state of New York had the *Great Patent,* as it was known, surveyed and divided into forty-three enormous lots (areas). At his death in 1729, Robert Livingston's three sons inherited designated lots of the half million acres allotted to their father. Two generations later, in 1779 Robert C. Livingston divided his share among his several brothers and sisters. His sister Janet Livingston married Gen. Richard Montgomery. His sister Gertrude Livingston married General Morgan Lewis and they settled on the 20,000 acres deeded to her in Delaware County, New York. Gertrude's older brother, also a Robert Livingston (1743-1828) would, through state legislation, be granted a monopoly to navigate steamboats on the Hudson River "if" he could build a steam boat within one year. Robert Livingston financed Robert Fulton to procure a steam engine of the most approved pattern from Messrs. Watt & Boulton in England, the inventors and greatest manufacturers of steam engines. Fulton then proceeded to build a boat driven by the British steam engine. On August 7-9, 1807, Fulton's steamboat, called the "Clermont" after Livingston Manor, made a successful trip from New York to Albany and back at the average rate of 5 miles an hour. Livingston acquired the monopoly from the state of New York for steam navigation of the Hudson River, the first incorporated steam-navigation company in America.[20] Gertrude Livingston Lewis's niece, Harriet Livingston (1783-1815) married Robert Fulton. Gertrude's niece Margaret Alida Rebecca Livingston Armstrong (1800-1872) married William Backhouse Astor, the son of John Jacob Astor. Although William B. Astor's fortunes grew with his father's company, he became a truly wealthy man when he inherited the $500,000 estate of his uncle Henry Astor who died without children. When his father John Jacob Astor died in 1848 William and his wife Alida Livingston Armstrong, Louisa Livingston Gerry's great-aunt, became the richest couple in America. Elbridge T. Gerry and his wife Louisa Livingston were joined by marriage to the Astors.

Gertrude Livingston's husband, General Morgan Lewis, was born in New York City in 1754, graduated Princeton in 1773 and began to study law. As a Revolutionary patriot he abandoned his studies, joined the army in 1774 and was made captain of a New York militia regiment. In 1776 Major Lewis served as Aide to General Horatio Gates up to the battle of Saratoga. In 1783 he resumed his legal studies, was admitted to the bar of New York and soon thereafter was elected a member of the assembly. In 1790 his brilliant legal career began when he was appointed Judge of the Court of Common Pleas. In 1791 he became the Attorney General of New York State and in 1792 he was appointed Chief Justice of the state Supreme Court. Finally in 1804 General Morgan Lewis was elected Governor of the state. While governor he urged the necessity of national education, and under his administration a permanent fund for common schools was established. General Morgan Lewis returned to duty in the War of 1812 and at the war's end he advanced funds that were necessary for the discharge of American prisoners in Canada. He remitted all arrears of rents that were due from those of his own tenants in Delaware County that had either gone or sent a son to war, and by his good management avoided on his own estates later anti-rent difficulties that troubled land-owners in pre-Civil War New York. Similar charitable caring of the post-war soldiers was undertaken by Peter Goelet in New York City, and it was the generosity of these and other great American colonial families that ensured the survival of a new nation.

In 1794 Morgan Lewis surveyed the Delaware County land that his wife Gertrude Livingston had inherited, had it subdivided into farms, and then settled the farms with tenants who paid their rent in labor and crops. Lewis and his wife Gertrude built a large pillared house and traveled each year to spend the hot summer months in their home by Lake Delaware on the well-accepted theory that living in healthy mountain air avoided illness like cholera and yellow fever, so prevalent in the cities. The local town of Margaretville was named after their daughter, Margaret, whose granddaughter, Louisa M. Livingston, married Elbridge T. Gerry in 1867. The current Gerry family like all the generations before them spend their summers at the Delaware Lake house, continuing the tradition started over two hundred years ago. Colonel Morgan Lewis also purchased 1,600 acres in Staatsburg, New York on the Hudson River, north of Poughkeepsie and south of Clermont, the patriarchal Livingston Manor. General Lewis and his wife, Gertrude Livingston, built a mansion on this property where their daughter Margaret and her husband, Maturin Livingston, a distant cousin, later raised their children, including Commodore Elbridge T. Gerry's father-in-law, Robert James Livingston. Robert J. Livingston had twin nieces, Elizabeth married the MP of the British Museum, George Cavendish Bentnick, and her twin Ruth married Ogden Mills a California gold rush millionaire. The Staatsburg estate was inherited by Ruth Livingston where she and Ogden Mills lived and raised their family. The historic Livingston (Morgan Lewis) Hudson River home was remodeled and enlarged in 1895 by the Mills family, who employed architects McKim, Mead and White to transform it into a Gilded Age Beaux Arts mansion of sixty-five rooms. Thereafter Staatsburg has mainly been associated with the Mills family and is on the National Register of Historic Places.

In 1769 at Albany, New York, the Livingston family patriarch, Robert Livingston, first Lord of the Manor married Alida Schuyler, the sister of the Albany, New York leader, Peter Schuyler (1657-1748) of Dutch descent. In fact, Peter Schuyler's daughter, Margaret (1682-1725) married Robert Livingston's nephew, also named Robert Livingston (1663-1725), who came from Scotland to join his uncle in Albany. Robert and Margaret's grandson, Maturin Livingston (1769-1847), was born at Staatsburg and graduated with high honors from

Princeton University in New Jersey. He was appointed a member of the 1801 *Constitutional Convention* and was appointed Recorder of New York City in 1804. Later he was appointed Judge of the Court of Common Pleas for Dutchess County, New York. The Schuyler family of Albany was connected with the Livingston and Gerry families in business, marriage and friendship though many generations, indeed Peter Schuyler's great-grandson, George L. Schuyler, the co-founder of the *New York Yacht Club* and owner of the famous yacht *America,* died onboard Elbridge T. Gerry's yacht in 1890. Schuyler was the winner of the first *America's Cup* trophy in 1851 and he donated it to the *New York Yacht Club* for all of the club's future international yacht races.

The wealth of both the Goelet and Livingston families, based on their banking and business interests, was most famously increased by the wise purchase of land in New York City. Nineteenth century newspapers not only chronicled the property purchases of New York's leading citizens, they also chronicled the scourges of New York City which included poverty, poor housing, crime, and epidemics. All of these dark and dismal conditions led writers to nick name New York City, *Gotham.* It was not until the Batman comic book serial that the name *Gotham* became iconic and was then celebrated by New Yorkers as a glamorous rather than a pejorative nick-name. Another adjective favored by writers of the day was *folly,* used to describe an unwise investment or a costly and foolish undertaking such as short-term real estate speculation and over-expansion in any of a number of industries. The often unwise speculation in large cities resulted in the lack of investment in housing for the poor and little or no construction of needed sanitation infrastructure to stem disease. In the midst of the prevalent scourges of nineteenth century American cities any kind of speculation was viewed as absurd. Newspapers reported on the darker side of New York City and began to criticize the rapid expansion of business, railroads, and land speculation as unwise, indeed as *folly*. Between 1825 and 1857 speculation of every kind was rampant and led to the panic of 1857. One New York newspaper characterized the general view of the economic folly of financial speculation in New York City:

> The evils originally set on foot by the real estate speculation of 1836 as by the cotton speculation of 1825, have been aggravated by the folly of the government and the banks, one half of which are utterly ignorant of the principles of commerce ...[21]

The Goelet purchase of land in lower Manhattan, as well as that of the Astor family and the Livingstons, among others, was specifically viewed as folly by observers. However, not all land purchases were short term speculations; indeed, many developers incorporated renewal projects into their plans to resolve some of the city scourges, like the need for sewer systems. The Goelet and Livingston families were historically interested in advancing both business and residential building investments to ensure the steady, healthy growth of New York City. Their land investments stabilized the future of New York with a solid tax base and made the city's growth methodical and productive. What was initially called "folly" or foolish, eventually was hailed as "wise" and "welcome" by the public. An added benefit to the city was the generous philanthropy of the families who became wealthy from their endeavors. The Goelet, Gerry, and Livingston families were advocates for the beautification of New York City and sought to improve the well-being of its citizens. They actively worked to protect the children of the streets. The phrase "Gerry's Folly" emerged in the press when writers covered Elbridge T. Gerry's defense or prosecution of landmark property cases that represented the wealthy Goelets and Livingstons, land-owners to whom he was a son of one family and was married into the other family. In the 1957 obituaries for Elbridge's sons, Peter G. Gerry and Robert L. Gerry who died the same day, was the following excerpt:

> A member of a family that made a fortune in New York City real estate, he was born there on September 18, 1879, a son of Commodore Elbridge T. Gerry and Louisa Matilda Livingston Gerry. His great-grandfather was signer of Declaration of Independence and Vice President in the second administration of President James Madison. His grandfather bought Manhattan farmland in a venture that in its day was known as *Gerry's Folly*. The land lay between Fifth Avenue and Broadway.[22]

And again, nearly fifty years later in 2003 a newspaper article described the Gerry family connection to Delaware County, New York:

> Descendants of Elbridge Gerry went on to make a fortune for the family in early New York City real estate. One bought property in Manhattan that was nicknamed "Gerry's Folly" at the time. As things turned out, the land lay between what is now Broadway and Fifth Avenue.[23]

The misperception by the press that Elbridge T. Gerry was the central figure in early nineteenth century speculative property investments in lower Manhattan led newspaper's to arbitrarily assign his professional work the nick name *Gerry's Folly*. This misperception would be compounded later in Gerry's life when he inherited city property from the Goelets and Livingstons, further encouraging newspaper articles to recall the phrase *Gerry's Folly* as part of the family lore.

The Goelet-Gerry family continued their summer holidays together even as Elbridge transitioned from his college life to his busy professional life. In the summer of 1858 Uncle Peter took his family, sisters Jean and Hannah, along with Hannah's adult children, Elbridge, Almy and Jean, up the picturesque Hudson River Valley by steamer to Saratoga Springs, north of Albany. In a few years, both Almy and Elbridge would marry. Almy spent future summers in Long Island with her husband's family, while Elbridge and his Goelet cousins and their families began to summer in Newport, Rhode Island.

After a restful summer in upstate New York the Goelet family returned to a busy fall in New York City where Elbridge's apprenticeship filled his days with legal case work, book collecting, and private study for the bar examination. The Christmas holidays found the Goelet household preparing for family celebrations. On December 25, 1859 Elbridge T. Gerry's twenty-second birthday, he received a very special gift from his Uncle Elbridge Gerry, Jr. who at the time was a businessman living in Boston, Massachusetts. It was a four-volume set of *Blackstone's Commentaries* with leather binding and of small size, perfect for traveling. The enclosed letter from his uncle reads:

> New York, December 25th 1859
>
> Mr. Elbridge T. Gerry,
>
> My dear nephew, allow me to wish you a very merry Christmas and to present a copy of Blackstone's Commentaries, which my father gave me from his library when I commenced the study of law. May you live in health and happiness, to transmit it to your grandson personally, and if he shall possess the virtues, talent, and merit of his grandfather, he will be an ornament to society and his name will be honored by his posterity.
>
> Truly your affectionate uncle
> Elbridge Gerry [24]

The discovery of this letter in 1990, which Elbridge had tucked inside the first volume of this rare set of Blackstone's in 1859, was made by the author of this biography. That letter set in motion twenty years of research to discover the story of the Gerry family.

Elbridge Thomas Gerry began his professional life as a lawyer in 1860 while also beginning his public service to society. He participated in professional associations and joined gentlemen's clubs. Typical of the brilliant and driven twenty-three year old Elbridge, he charged head-long into a full and busy life style. Just twelve days before his June 27, 1860 commencement ceremony at Columbia University where Elbridge was awarded his *Master's Degree* in German alongside his cousin Robert Goelet, Jr. who graduated with a *Bachelor of Arts* degree (J.D. Columbia 1860), Elbridge accompanied his law firm associate John McKeon, to a hearing with their client, New York City Comptroller Robert T. Haws. They appeared before a referee on June 19, 1860 to arbitrate the final settlement of the *West Washington Market Controversy*. The large and busy market area, now known as Tribeca, was located on State-owned land which had been illegally occupied by the City of New York for business. The State leases had been assigned to Mr. James B. Taylor and Mr. Owen Brennan, who were owed back rent due from the City. Anticipating the complexity of the case, the State of New York passed legislation in the fall of 1859 that authorized and directed the Comptroller of New York City to compromise and settle all claims on the best terms possible to avoid similar entanglements with regard to other property along both rivers that was situated in precisely the same way. Newspapers of the day, *The Express* and the *Tribune*, took partisan sides on whether to blame the Republican or Democratic parties for the mess. The *New York Times* suggested that both parties were equally culpable. The Democrats ran the Land Office Commission in 1858, when the lease was granted, and the Republicans ran it in 1859, when the lease was renewed. Further, the newspaper reported that Mr. Taylor sued the City for six months back rent, in response the City contested the claim and retained several of the most eminent lawyers in the City to fight it, including the William Curtis Noyes law firm, for whom Elbridge had just completed his apprenticeship. The law case was elaborately argued and a jury composed exclusively of city tax-payers returned a verdict that the State owned the property. Other suits which Mr. Taylor commenced for other portions of the back rent were sent to referees, not to decide the title, but to determine the amounts due.[25] Elbridge T. Gerry was 23 when he participated with his law firm in the Referee Hearings representing the City of New York, an enviable experience for any young, untested lawyer. The State ordered the property to be surveyed and with proper knowledge of the boundaries the negotiations continued until January 29, 1861 when the City settled all claims with Mr. Taylor and Mr. Brennan by payment of three hundred thousand dollars in stocks, authorized by the 1859 Act to be issued for that purpose and the release by the State of the property to the City of New York. One month later in February 1861 Elbridge Thomas Gerry was in Washington, D.C. to be sworn in and admitted to practice before the Supreme Court of the United States. In just a few years, Elbridge would discover that his future wife Louisa M. Livingston had inherited the successful grocery business of her wealthy grandfather, Garritt Storm, located at No. 9 Coenties Slip in the *West Washington Market.*

Perhaps one of the most important social tasks that Elbridge T. Gerry accepted in 1860 was to participate on the large Committee of gentlemen that managed preparations for the great ball in honor of Albert Edward, Prince of Wales, who at the age of nineteen was the first member of the British Royal Family to visit the United States since it declared independence from England just eighty-four years earlier. Another member of the *Grand Ball* planning committee was Robert James Livingston whose twenty-four year old daughter Louisa Matilda was undoubtedly one of many lovely young ladies who attended the Ball with their fathers. It was on this special occasion that Elbridge was introduced to his future bride by her father, a fellow committee member. The Ball was held at the Academy of Music at Irving Place and Fourteenth Street where Elbridge had organized musical programs for Columbia College as the President of the Philolexian Society. He felt right at home assisting with management of the Ball. An astonishing three thousand invitations were issued and when the Prince arrived in New York City he was greeted by nearly half a million people on Fifth Avenue. The Prince and his escorts had first arrived in Canada to visit Niagara Falls; he then traveled to Detroit and on to Washington for a five-day stay at the White House. From Washington the Prince traveled by train to Philadelphia and finally ended his trip in New York City. The *Great Ball* was the climax of his month-long trip and it was also one he would not soon forget. So great was the crush at the ball that part of the flooring gave way in view of the Prince. Only two people were hurt but newspaper articles made for great reading during the royal visit.[26] The Prince left New York and passed through Boston with just an overnight stay. While in Boston the young Prince had the pleasure of meeting poet Henry Wadsworth Longfellow, and the writer/philosopher Ralph Waldo Emerson among other famous Americans. He visited Bunker Hill and was introduced to Ralph Farnham, the last survivor of the Battle of Bunker Hill, who remarked that the enthusiastic reception to the Prince made him fear that the country was turning royalist again. The Prince and Mr. Farnham exchanged autographs after which the old man observed that he wished to show the "boy" that he bore no anger for old times. A correspondent wrote from Boston that one of the Prince's escorts asked where the soldiers who formed the party's guard at Boston got their red coats. "They took them in 1776" was the reply which drew a welcome laugh. From Boston the Prince went to Portland, Maine where he sailed for home on the British ship *Hero.* Several days out a storm drove the *Hero* away from the British coast and caused her to be long overdue in port. There was great anxiety in England when the navy sent their warships out in search of the royal vessel. Provisions ran low and the Prince was reduced to salt fare, but the storm abated and on November 15, 1860 he set foot again on English soil amid great rejoicing.[27]

Elbridge T. Gerry and his future father-in-law Robert James Livingston shared a passionate interest in the well-being of children abandoned on the streets as well as an interest in the care of the mentally ill in New York City. The sensitivity to the needs of others was engendered in Elbridge by the example of his uncle Peter Goelet while growing up on the Broadway farm. This set the stage for Elbridge to develop close association with kindred minds in his church and social circles, especially with Robert J. Livingston who would be his father figure after the death of his uncle Peter Goelet in 1879.

Born December 11, 1811 on his grandfather General Morgan Lewis's 1,600 acre estate in Staatsburg, New York, Robert J. Livingston was one of ten children born to Maturin and Margaret Livingston. He entered Yale College at age seventeen in 1828 and left in 1830 to study civil engineering. He then worked with the Coast Guard Survey Team under Ferdinand R. Hassler on a project to survey and triangulate the East Coast of the United States.[28] Had not revolution in Europe brought him to America in 1805, Ferdinand Rudolph Hassler might have found his place in the scientific community abroad. He was born in the town of Aarau, in the northern German part of Switzerland on October 7, 1770. Educated in law, mathematics, astronomy and geodetic science, he began mapping the area around Berne in 1791. Between field expeditions, Hassler traveled to Paris and the university towns of Germany to attend courses, collect books for his growing library, and acquire better instruments and standards for the survey work. He became a member of the *Academy of Science* in Berlin in 1804. He fled political oppression after the French Revolution, sailing to Philadelphia, then the seat of America's new government. He was met by his compatriot, Albert Gallatin (the grandfather of Frederic Gallatin, the future husband of Elbridge T. Gerry's sister, Almy), then Secretary of State. Gallatin introduced Hassler to President Thomas Jefferson. He soon applied for citizenship and through Gallatin and Jefferson he became a member of the *American Philosophical Society* in 1807. To the Society he later sold some of his instruments and standards in order to maintain his family, and to the *Library of Congress* part of his scientific library of about 3,000 volumes. His new friends in the Philosophical Society wrote to President Jefferson recommending Hassler's employment to head the geodetic survey of the coast, then under consideration. In 1812, Congress appointed Hassler the superintendent of the first United States Coast survey. They sent him to France and England to collect supplies for his endeavor. The English, however, detained Hassler, thinking him an enemy spy. He returned to the United States in 1815, at which time the survey formally began. Two years later, dissatisfied with his work, Congress suspended the survey.

He started teaching and writing textbooks which included Analytical Trigonometry, Elements of Geometry, Systems of the Universe, and Elements of Arithmetic. In 1828 he composed an article for the journal *Transactions,* a publication of the *American Philosophical Society*. In that piece he defended his methods for the 1815 *Coastal Survey.* Many respected scientists read the article and approved of his methods and wrote to express their support for his leadership of the project. In 1832 President Andrew Jackson reappointed Hassler Superintendent of a new Coastal survey.[29] On April 13, 1833 Hassler arrived in New York to begin preparations for the field work. He also hired civilian assistants, one being Robert James Livingston, the grandson of Morgan Lewis. On April 26 Hassler headed to Staten Island to begin survey operations. He stayed in the field along the Northeast coastline until December 11, 1833. While surveying in Connecticut on July 24 Hassler wrote about an incident:

> At half past 2:00 pm a threatening storm approached, I took the theodolite and secured in a bed in a tent. It took the strength of all of us, assistants and men, to hold the tent and instrument against the severest gale, rain and hail. With difficulty I brought the theodolite out of the tent into the open storm, leaving the tent, the instrument stand and all else, which were blown off. All our tents except one were fully blown away, partly broken; and the three barometers that were in one of them were entirely broken, so they have been sent to New York for repair.[30]

The 1833 survey was more than just training in civil engineering for Robert James Livingston, it was a welcome adventure for such a young man. He discovered the coastline of the northeastern colonies and camped with a troop of intelligent and skilled men who endured the whims of nature, great fun indeed.

In October 1833 Robert James Livingston married Louisa Matilda Storm, the daughter of the wealthy New York merchant Garrit Storm (1878-1851) who inherited his father's successful grocery business at No. 9 Coenties Slip in the *West Washington Market.* Through smart investments, he left his two daughters property valued at over a million dollars at his death. Louisa Storm's grandfather, Thomas Storm, was Lieutenant Governor when General Morgan Lewis was Governor of New York state. Louisa's daughter was her name-sake, Louisa Matilda Livingston who married Elbridge T. Gerry in 1867.

Robert James Livingston was described by those who knew him as a man of a social and genial nature, warm hearted and philanthropic, with a large circle of friends. In politics he was a war democrat, but he never held political office. He was one of the oldest members of the Union Club, the Century Club, and the Knickerbocker Club. In 1834 Robert J. Livingston entered into business at 44 Wall Street with Charles Christmas, considered by contemporaries as one of the best brokers and bankers in the City of New York. Mr. Christmas was a close associate of August Belmont (1816-1890) who had his business training in European branches of the Rothschilds' banking empire. August Belmont came to America as the foreign representative of the Rothschilds' and found a first class partner in Charles Christmas. In 1835 Robert J. Livingston and Charles Christmas added two more partners to their Banking/Brokerage house, Rufus Prime and Washington Coster, who died in 1846.[31] The banking partnership was established just three years prior to the 1837 financial panic in America which adversely affected the investment business, indeed many banks closed. By 1843 after ten years of business the brokerage firm amicably dissolved allowing the four partners to individually pursue other options. Robert James Livingston took this opportunity to retire from the business world and focus on managing the property and investments of his wealthy wife, Louisa Matilda Storm Livingston. As recorded in the Middlesex County, New Jersey, deed office, on April 7, 1843 Louisa M. Livingston purchased a ninety-six acre tract on which the Livingstons built a grand two and one-half story Greek Revival style house. Similar to Gertrude Livingston's Lake Delaware estate in Delhi, New York, most of Robert and Louisa's land remained productive with tenant farmers producing crops and tending livestock. The Livingstons had left New York City with their children, Warren, nine years old, and Louisa, seven years old for a pastoral life-style, similar to the Broadway farm in New York City. The children were raised in Highland Park with Warren attending Burlington College, graduating in 1852. Warren distinguished himself as one of three students at Burlington College who established a Delta Chapter of Saint Anthony Hall or The Order of St. Anthony, the national college literary society formerly known as the Fraternity of Delta Psi (ΔΨ) at American colleges. The Delta Chapter activities fostered the social and intellectual development of its undergraduate members by encouraging individual expression, promoting the exchange of ideas by providing a forum for discussion, presentations, and public lecture series. The first Chapter was founded at Columbia University on January 17, 1847, which is the feast day of St. Anthony. The Burlington College chapter was the second in the United States, established in 1849 just two years after Columbia. Warren Livingston also gave the honorary English Oration *Milestones of*

Ages at his 1852 graduation ceremony, about which the Dean said "we cannot forebear to express our entire admiration of the fluent and graceful delivery of the eloquent *Milestones of Ages* in English oration."[32] Warren's class of fourteen was only the third class to graduate from the new college.

After college, Warren went on to study at Oxford University in England, finishing his graduate studies with honors and earned a Master of Arts degree. Sadly, not long after his return home to America Warren Livingston died in New Brunswick, New Jersey at the early age of twenty-three before entering a profession or marrying. There is no record of the cause of Warren's death after his return from Oxford. However, there was an inspiring Baccalaureate address by Bishop William Doane, the Dean of Burlington College, given at the 1857 Burlington College graduation in honor of Warren Livingston. He was the first alumnus of the college to die and the Bishop titled the address *A Christian Scholar and a Christian Gentleman.* Three years later in 1860 the Livingstons left the Highland Park farm estate to resume their life in New York City. During his years in New Jersey Robert J. Livingston did participate in local initiatives, particularly the reconstruction of the Albany Street Bridge between east and west New Brunswick that traversed the Raritan River and the railroad tracks. Between 1836 and 1837 the railroad built a wooden double decker bridge that carried rail traffic on its upper deck and highway traffic below. The controversy over this new bridge waged on for ten years including the period when the Livingstons moved to the New Brunswick area in the mid 1840's. The old Albany Street Bridge was built in 1795 and, while in continuous disrepair it remained standing not far from the new double decker railroad bridge. The competition for money to maintain the two bridges triggered the controversy. In April 1849 the Albany Street Bridge was finally dismantled, six years after the Livingstons had arrived. Although pedestrian and vehicular traffic could cross the Raritan on the lower level of the double-decker railroad bridge, it was an arduous and frightful passage with noisy trains lumbering overhead. In May 1851 a small group of wealthy New Brunswick and Highland Park residents, including Robert J. Livingston, met with the intention of forming a new company to rebuild the Albany Street Bridge. The corporation was established, the remains of old stone piers were assessed, and a Philadelphia architect, Daniel Stone, drew up the architectural plans. The bridge was rebuilt by 1853 and a toll was charged in sufficient amount to pay the annual expenses plus an annual dividend to stockholders with a surplus for repairs. The success of the new bridge was attributed to corporate partners, Robert J. Livingston and his brother-in-law Samuel V. Hoffman. Both men were given life-time free passage for themselves and their families. Samuel Hoffman was married to Glorvina Storm,

Louisa Storm Livingston's sister. The Hoffmans owned an estate just north of Mill Brook, very near the Livingston's estate on River Road.[33] The Hoffman's son, the Rev. Eugene Augustus Hoffman, was appointed the Head of the General Theological Seminary in New York City in 1879. He led the Episcopal Church's revision of Canon Law, a project which included the legal skills of Elbridge T. Gerry in the early 1890's.

The Livingstons returned to New York City in 1860 not long after the death of their beloved son Warren. They retained ownership of the Highland Park, New Jersey estate through 1891 where they returned for summer holidays. The Livingstons daughter, Louisa Matilda, was a young woman of twenty-four in 1860 and ready to be introduced to New York society; indeed just eight months after arriving in New York Louisa and her parents attended the great *Metropolitan Ball* for the Prince of Wales at the Academy of Music where she met her future husband Elbridge T. Gerry. The first record of Robert J. Livingston's activity upon his return to New York City was March 1, 1860 when he was elected to the Board of Trustees of the *Children's Aid Society*. He participated as one of the leaders of the society for the next thirty-one years; his last meeting was in November 1890 just three months before his death at age eighty. The 1899 forty-seventh Annual Report of the *Children's Aid Society*, published in the New York Times, described the goals, activities and sources of support that sustained its work for nearly fifty years:

> Few can fail to be aroused by the story of thousands of infants and half-grown children raised from the lowest pits of vice and transferred from the curse of poverty into an existence leading to useful citizenship. It is in such a work of transformation that this society has been engaged for almost half a century. Full inspection reports based on site visits are made each year by the *Inspector of the State Board of Charities*. Annual evaluations of the different industrial schools, kindergartens, lodging houses, and six summer vacation schools conclude that the *Societies* programs are of excellent quality and character in both management and teaching, indeed teachers are required to be licensed. Reports on each of the Societies establishments are also submitted each year to the *Board of Education* and an exhaustive examination into all the organizations records and accounts is made by the New York City *Commissioner of Accounts.*. The annual report shows how many of the best people of New York are voluntarily giving their time and means to support the charitable work of the Children's Aid Society. A subscription of $5,000 from Mrs. William Astor was designated for the construction of an enlarged dining room and pavilion at the Bath Beach Home. Two thousand dollars was given in 1899 in memory of Robert J. Livingston, who died in 1891.[34]

Mrs. William B. Astor II was a relative by marriage to Robert J. Livingston whose sister Alida Livingston Armstrong's daughter, Margaret, married William Backhouse Astor Sr., the richest man in America. Mrs. Astor II led New York City's *Gilded Age* society, making her the focus of contemporary newspaper articles across America. Nonetheless, the philanthropy of these great American families during the *Progressive Era* of a maturing nation was the saving grace for the poor and forgotten children of New York City.

One of the most progressive yet somewhat controversial programs initiated by the founder of the *Children's Aid Society*, Charles L. Brace, was the removal of orphaned or poor children from New York City for permanent placement with families in western states. Popularly known even to this day as the *Orphan Trains;* the first train departed New York City in 1854 carrying fifty-four children. In his own words in the 1860 annual report of the *Children's Aid Society,* the year Robert J. Livingston was first elected a Trustee, Charles L. Brace wrote:

> The *Children's Aid Society* takes its children from City officials, when offered, from the *Newsboy's Lodging House,* from the streets, the wharves, the cellars, and the garrets; from scenes of temptation, poverty, and misery. Such of them as are fit subjects for the public schools are placed there, others are placed in our Industrial Schools, and still others receive a good bath and a decent suit of clothes for their move to the great West. In a week's time they are no longer orphans (or worse than orphans) but are the well-cared for children of some respectable family. They now have a father, and heaven be praised, a mother too. They have found what all hearts claim, social and domestic relations. Every feature in this sudden transition is calculated to make them happier and better children. They are not indentured, but they are put under a moral bond to themselves not to be unworthy or ungrateful.
>
> They have good wholesome food... they are taught from books. They are no longer idle or tempted to evil and can now appreciate the kindly influences which surround and sustain them. Self-respect is awakened within them. They can grow in usefulness and honor.[35]

Charles L. Brace was a native of Hartford, Connecticut who came to New York City in 1848 to study theology and was horrified both by the hordes of vagrant children and by the way civil authorities treated them. Up through the early nineteenth century there had been no slums in American cities, however immigration in the nineteenth century swelled New York City from a population of 40,000 to 1,500,000 by the end of the century, stimulated by famine, wars and the *Industrial Revolution.* In 1849 New York's first police chief reported that 3,000 children lived on the streets and these vagrant children were sent to juvenile prisons and asylums that were harsh and punitive. Rev. Brace believed that most of these children were not criminals but victims of miserable economic and social conditions and incarceration did nothing but harden them in the ways of crime. What they really needed he maintained, was education, jobs, and good homes. It was in March 1853 when he established an organization to provide them with just such benefits, the *Children's Aid Society*.[36] When Reverend Brace failed to raise enough money he looked beyond New York City for assistance. As a minister he understood the connections among parishes across cities, states, and the nation. Ministers migrated with the rapidly growing westward expansion and farm families needed strong backs and a new generation to carry-on the expansion. All over the country there were men and women who had lost children or were unable to have children of their own, many of them good Christians. Reverend Brace realized that the children needed these families as much as the families needed them. A long-term, stable environment was something even money could not provide these children in New York City. Working with a group of social reformers the program was successfully established. The 1899 annual report of the *Children's Aid Society* noted:

> From the guardians to whom these young people have been entrusted there come frequent letters of commendation and encouragement to the Society in its praiseworthy work. From every source whence proofs are attainable it is being constantly demonstrated that the work done yields a thousand fold, and that the good result is disproportionate to any financial consideration.[37]

What controversy there was or continues to be, focuses on those children who either did not want to go out West, leaving their poor, unstable home-life, or the uncertainty of the well-being of some of the children sent to the west. Not all families followed-up with letters to the society describing the success or indeed the failure of the placement. The failure of a placement might be due to abuse or indenture of the child by the family, some children simply ran away, and still others just could not be rehabilitated, even outside the scourges of the city. Between 1853 and 1929 more than 150,000 abandoned, abused and orphaned children were rescued from the streets and slums of New York City and taken by train to start new lives with families on farms across the country. The positive results of the *Orphan Trains* far out-weigh the failures of the placements with documented stories in the literature on the topic by adults who in fact, were children of Charles L. Brace's family placements.

While Robert James Livingston was generously working with the *Children's Aid Society* and managing the family property, he lost his mother, Margaret Lewis Livingston, who died in October 1860 at his childhood home in Staatsburg, New York. She was the last matriarch of the Livingston Clan up and down the Hudson Valley and her death signaled the transition of the mansion from a Colonial Mansion to the Gilded Age mansion of her daughter Ruth Livingston Mills, the wife of California millionaire Ogden Mills.

Between 1863 and 1891 Robert J Livingston was a member of the *Society of the New York Hospital,* being elected in various years to the Board of Governors or to the Vice-Presidency. The New York Hospital included four distinct facilities: the New York Hospital itself, the House of Relief, the Bloomingdale Hospital for Mental Disease, and the Campbell Convalescent Cottages in White Plains. Of the four institutions, Robert J. Livingston was elected to the Board of Governors' of the *Asylum Committee* which provided oversight for the *Bloomingdale Hospital for Mental Disease.* In the 17th century "Bloomingdale" referred to the territory north of the settled areas on the west side of Manhattan island, then, in the 18th century lower Broadway from 23rd Street was extended to Morningside Heights and the new northern stretch of road was renamed Bloomingdale Road. Later, when the New York Hospital decided to build a facility in Morningside Heights it made sense to name it for the road upon which it would stand. As for that other fashionable New York institution sharing the same name, it appears that the geographic term used to name the asylum pre-dates the arrival of Bavarian immigrant and hoop-skirt peddler Benjamin Bloomingdale in America. Therefore the asylum and the department store are unrelated. The asylum had fruit orchards, fountains, and even a stable for horses, and across the road was the *Orphans Asylum* built on land where Saint John the Divine cathedral stands today. The *Bloomingdale Asylum* stood on the Morningside Heights property until 1890 when most of the buildings were demolished and Columbia University was built on the site where it majestically stands to this day. The hospital was moved to a new location across the Hudson River to White Plains, New York.[38] The move of the hospital was the subject of considerable thought and no little anxiety for the Board and the hospital staff. The New York Times reported:

> The removal was, very fortunately, accomplished without mishap of any kind, and with comparatively little discomfort or inconvenience to anyone. The great majority of the patients, who are quiet and well behaved, were transferred by special cars leaving New York without hurry or confusion. The feeble patients and those liable to violent or disorderly impulses went in small parties by ambulances and carriages all the way, the distance being about twenty miles. The re-

> moval from New York to the country was found by most of the patients to be an agreeable change. It took place in the Fall of the year, when the country is most attractive, and this fact and the cheerful appearance of the new buildings and grounds caused a very perceptible brightening of the faces of the more intelligent patients.[39]

The modern descendant of this asylum is the Westchester division of the New York Hospital in White Plains. In 1878 Elbridge T. Gerry was also elected to the Board of Governors of the *Society of the New York Hospital* on which he served for the next thirty-four years. He shared the Board leadership with his father-in-law Robert J. Livingston between 1878 and 1890, contributing their legal skills and their shared family wealth. The move of the Asylum from Bloomingdale to White Plains was managed during their joint tenure on the Board of Governors.

The other philanthropic institution to which Robert J. Livingston gave his attention was the *New York Home for Incurables* established in 1866 by the Protestant Episcopal Church. The institutions special work was to care for the incurably sick and to furnish a "home" for its patients, who, unlike those in an ordinary hospital remained objects of its nursing care for life. The institution was located at 182nd Street and Third Avenue in Fordham, New York. One third of the patients stayed free of charge, others paid per week, and those with some wealth could pay $5,000 for a free bed in perpetuity. In celebration of the sixteenth anniversary of the Home in 1882, a special car on the Harlem Railroad left Grand Central Station with a party of clergymen and laymen to attend a celebration at Fordham. No doubt Robert J. Livingston was present as he was recognized for his $25,000.00 contribution to the *Home for Incurables* in honor of its anniversary.[40]

Almy, Elbridge Thomas and Jean, the children of Thomas and Hannah Goelet Gerry, just a few years after their father's death, around 1850.

Elbridge T. Gerry graduated from Columbia College with a B.A. and a Master's degree in German.

Blackstone's Commentaries
Given to E.T. Gerry in 1857 for his birthday and college graduation by his Uncle Elbridge Gerry, Jr., of Boston

Elbridge T. Gerry's illuminated class notes at Columbia College.

Goelet doll house

Columbia College, 1865

19th & Broadway Farm
Peter Goelet raised the three Gerry children here, 1848–1865.

Elbridge T. Gerry enjoyed summer adventures on the *Great Western Expedition* by train and boat to the midwest.

William Curtis Noyes accepted Elbridge T. Gerry into a law apprenticeship for two years after which Mr. Noyes sponsored him at his swearing-in to the Supreme Court Bar in November 1860.

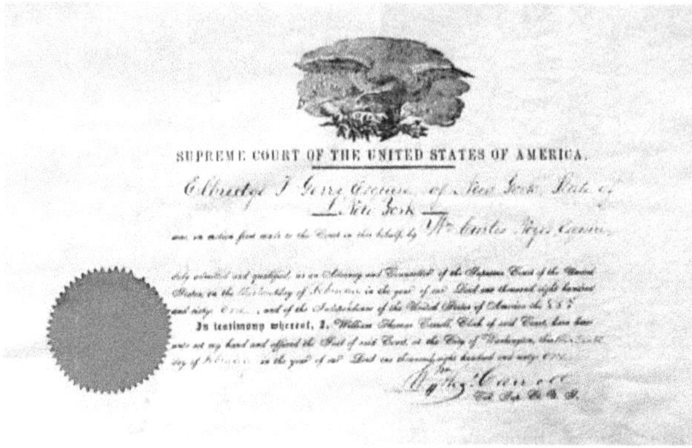

SUPREME COURT OF THE UNITED STATES OF AMERICA.

Elbridge T. Gerry's *Admission Certificate* to the Bar of the United States Supreme Court

One of Elbridge T. Gerry's first cases was to assist with the settlement of the Washington Market land dispute between New York City and New York state.

Family holiday at Saratoga Springs, NY around 1863. Uncle Peter Goelet with his sisters Jean Goelet, left, and Hannah Goelet, *right;* Uncle Peter's nephews Robert Goelet *lower right* and Ogdon Goelet *upper right.* Elbridge T. Gerry on *left side* with sisters Almy and Jean *right.*

In 1860 the nineteen-year-old Prince Edward Albert of England came to America for a grand tour. When the Prince stopped in New York City he attended a Great Ball that was organized by a committee on which young Elbridge T. Gerry was a member and through which he met his future wife, Louisa M. Livingston.

Gertrude Livingston Lewis inherited Lake Delaware with 22,000 acres as her share of the great 1708 Hardenburgh Patent.

General Morgan Lewis married Gertrude and built Lake Delaware House and the Staatsburg Mansion.

Original Lake Delaware House circa 1840

One child

Lake Delaware House in 2000

Margaret Lewis Livingston

Fifth cousins

Maturin Livingston

12 children

Staatsburgh-on-Hudson in 1840

Louisa M. Storm Livingston, wealthy New York City heiress

Robert James Livingston, wealthy banker and surveyor

Staatsburg-on-Hudson in 2000
Enlarged for Ruth Livingston Mills in 1895
by Stanford White

Louisa M. Livingston
1836-1920

Warren Livingston

died age 18

Robert J. Livingston built the Albany Street Bridge, New Brunswick, NJ, near his Highland Park estate in the 1850's.

Children's Aid Society orphan train

Elbridge T. Gerry
Rising young lawyer taking
his place in New York City
charitable endeavors

New York City street boys in need of a home

Original Bloomingdale Hospital for the insane in Morningside Heights where Columbia University now stands.

The Gerry Family Tree

3

Passing the Torch

Each age is a dream that is dying or one that is coming to birth.
Arthur W. E. O'Shaughnessy

By July of 1860 Elbridge T. Gerry had completed his Master's degree at Columbia University and was an exceptionally self-confident young man who eagerly stepped into the professional world of New York City. He had participated in the great *Washington Market* arbitration case between New York State and New York City and had represented his first client. Elbridge's personal life brightened considerably in the fall of 1860 when he began a long and meaningful courtship of his future wife, Louisa M. Livingston, the daughter of one of his mentors, Robert James Livingston.

Elbridge T. Gerry's first case was *Townsend v Goelet* and he represented the defendant, Robert Goelet, his beloved first cousin who had a lien on land that he sold to a Mr. Townsend who in turn had resold the land. The issue was whether the original lien could be held against the second owner. Understanding the intricacies of property law in New York City was a challenge which the young lawyer Elbridge Gerry quickly mastered. This was the first of many property law cases he successfully argued over his professional career, many on behalf of his extended family.

The year 1862 opened with a great "rite of passage" for the young lawyer. Elbridge T. Gerry traveled to Washington, D.C. to be admitted to the Bar of the *United States Supreme Court.* Lawyers often joined the Supreme Court Bar in anticipation of a future case that might involve a federal constitutional issue. Other lawyers joined the Bar simply for the prestige, never intending to bring a case before the high court. Elbridge was practicing with a major New York law firm and it was wise to be prepared for the likelihood that one of his cases might be appealed to the United States Supreme Court.

The next reported case for Elbridge T. Gerry was in March, 1862 when he joined his legal mentor, William Curtis Noyes, as co-counsel in *Chauncey v Arnold and Wife*. This case involved an ante-nuptial agreement, a power of attorney regarding the wife's property and the validity of actions by her trustee in a mortgage transaction with a deed that had no name designating to whom the property was transferred. One of the complexities of the case was whether to decide the issues under property law or commercial paper law. One measure of the significance of a court decision is how often the case has been cited and relied upon to argue subsequent cases. This case has been cited twenty times and as late as 1965. The case is noted in the 2010 standard legal reference, *Tiffany Real Property* and in the 2011 New York legal encyclopedia, *New York Jurisprudence,* 2nd. In October of 1862 Elbridge T. Gerry once again represented his uncle, Robert Goelet, in a property case dealing with the lessee abandoning the property and refusing to pay the remaining rent. Many cases at this level of dispute resolution are never reported in the volumes of case reports. So there were likely other small cases handled by the Noyes and Gerry law firm in between the more high profile cases that kept them busy and gave Elbridge ample opportunity to hone his legal skills.

Elbridge T. Gerry's social calendar was full in December 1862 when he attended the sixteenth anniversary of the *Philolexian Society* of which he was President while a student at Columbia University. He was also invited to take a seat on the stage in Irving Hall at 7:00 p.m. which was an honor for Elbridge as the past president of the Society.[1] His subtle charm and sharp intelligence made Elbridge a natural leader over the course of his career and enhanced his social standing in New York City.

When the Civil War started in 1861 New Yorkers quickly rallied behind the Union cause with 8,000 men volunteering to join the military while prominent men in New York, like Peter Goelet, aided and sponsored the returning wounded soldiers and their families. New York City had more than enough volunteers the first two years of the war, 1861-1862, so Elbridge did not volunteer. Instead he pursued his intensive legal apprenticeship and helped his Uncle Peter serve the families of war veterans. However, by 1863 there were few volunteers from any of the Union states, including New York, thus requiring Congress to pass the *Enrollment Act* in March 1863. The *Act* required single males twenty to forty-five to be drafted first before married men of the same age. Each congressional district had a quota of men to recruit, either as volunteers or as draftees to achieve the required number. If not achieved by volunteers a lottery was held to determine who would be drafted in each district. The Goelet brothers and Elbridge lived in the 8th District of which 2,030 men were required to enlist or be drafted.[2] There were a number of "exemptions" provided in the Act, including a medical exemption, a substitution exemption, and a commutation exemption that required a

$300 payment. In May 1864 the Eighth District was notified that a draft would be held in June which put eligible men on notice to apply for exemptions. The enrollment archive noted:

> On June 18, 1864, "Elbridge T. Gerry was discharged by the Board of Enrollment having furnished John H. Morton as a substitute for the U.S. Navy in anticipation of a draft on June 18, 1864." Further, "his substitute was mustered at the 2nd District to Captain Maddax." This same record book notes that on June 21, 1864, "Robert Goelet of 857 Broadway, was discharged by the Board of Enrollment having furnished Felix Fayer as a substitute in anticipation of a draft on June 25th and said substitute was enlisted by Captain Robert Nugent at Tammany Hall." Recorded next to Robert's name was the entry, "Theodore Roosevelt of 33 East Twentieth Street discharged by the Board of Enrollment having furnished Abraham Graf as a substitute in anticipation of a draft on June 25 and said substitute was enlisted by Captain Robert Nugent at Tammany Hall.[3]

Theodore's son, future President Teddy Roosevelt, never forgave his father for not serving in the *Civil War* and it was one of his motivations for leading the Rough Riders in *the Spanish American War* in the late 1890's. Complicating the nation's opposition to the war in 1862, President Abraham Lincoln issued an *Executive Order* in September, 1862 known as the *Emancipation Proclamation* declaring the freedom of all slaves in every Confederate State. In April of 1863, just one month after passage of the *Enrollment Act,* reaction to the *Proclamation* ignited small labor strikes by the longshoremen of New York City which intensified the fear of labor competition from freed slaves moving north. The predominantly Irish longshoremen had been striking off and on for several years seeking regular work and better pay. In New York the first drafts were held July 11-13, 1863 which triggered a resistance known as the *Draft Riots.* The riots were fueled and intensified when the striking longshoremen joined forces with draft protesters causing thousands of New Yorkers to rush into the streets between July 13 and 16. This was the second largest civil disruption in the history of the United States, second only to the Civil War. Leonard Jerome (1817-1891) the American grandfather of Sir Winston Churchill was in the thick of it too. He was forty-six years old and a Sergeant in the army who was also part owner of the *New York Times* paper. At the height of the draft riots he grabbed the latest in military hardware, a pair of Gatling guns, and mounted them in the Times Building front windows which so terrified the mob that they headed off to harass the *Herald Tribune.*[4] The disturbance was primarily in lower Manhattan where Elbridge T. Gerry was living at the Goelet Broadway Farm. Thousands of people in the loud and angry mob started down Broadway to attack private homes and were headed toward the Goelet mansion at Nineteenth Street. The following anecdote while humorous transpired in the midst of approaching danger and no little panic by Elbridge and Uncle Peter:

> Here in New York, as drunken Irishmen lurched through the streets, decent people locked themselves in their homes. Peter Goelet owned a big house at Broadway and Nineteenth Street. With him lived his twenty-five-year-old nephew, Elbridge Gerry. The old man raised peacocks and pheasants and let them strut about the lawn. In normal times pedestrians stopped to peer at them between iron railings. On this day of peril young Gerry felt that the gorgeous plumage of the birds might attract the attention of rioters. He ordered the coachman to pull out all their colorful tail feathers. Divested of this weight, the peacocks and pheasants, looking like drunken acrobats, lost their balance and toppled over onto their beaks.[5]

The situation in New York City improved the next day when newspapers reported that the draft was suspended and federal troops returned to the city to restore order. The underlying issues of under-employment, a draining war, and the rights of freed slaves would take much longer to resolve for the city and the nation.

In 1864 Elbridge continued to live at the Broadway house with his uncle Peter, his mother Hannah Goelet Gerry and his adult sisters Almy Gerry twenty-four and Jean Gerry twenty-two. Most likely Elbridge escorted both his mother and sisters to the Grand Ball for the Prince in September 1860, which served as Almy and Jean's introduction to Society just as it was for Louisa Livingston. Elbridge remained close to his mother, Hannah Goelet Gerry and she in turn gave her son steadfast encouragement in all his endeavors. Hannah maintained her friendship with the Gerry sisters living in New Haven, having spent extended periods of time in their home when she visited with her husband Thomas R. Gerry before his death. In early April 1864 Elbridge's aunt Helen Maria Gerry died in New Haven, Connecticut, in the house where Elbridge's grandmother had died in 1849. Hannah, Almy and Elbridge traveled to New Haven for the funeral to console the remaining sisters, Ann, Eleanor, and Emily and to assist with settling the estate. The last remaining brother, Elbridge Gerry, Jr. then seventy-one, was living in Boston and also made the trip to New Haven for the funeral of his sister Helen and to visit with family, including his nephew, Elbridge T. Gerry.

Back in New York the next month, Elbridge once again wore the mantle of Secretary of his 1857 college class when he published a *Resolution* in honor of classmate Morgan L. S. Brower who had recently died. The short article closes with the announcement that members of the class would meet at the office of Mr. Haven, No. 67 Wall Street at 2:30 p.m. precisely in order to attend the funeral as a group. The Resolution was signed on behalf of the Class of 1857 by Elbridge T. Gerry, Class Secretary.[3]

Another significant death in 1864 was that of Elbridge T. Gerry's senior law partner and professional mentor, William Curtis Noyes, who died on Christmas day 1864. The Church of the Covenant in New York City installed the *William Curtis Noyes* stone tablet *Faith* to honor him as one of the founding members of the congregation in 1862.[4] In his will Mr. Noyes left his law library of nearly 5,000 volumes to his alma mater Hamilton College in Clinton, New York. When his library was inspected after it reached Hamilton College it was found to contain a copy of *Bracton* on *the Laws and Customs of England* (13th century) along with a complete historical set of the *British Statutes* and a *Stratham's Abridgement* printed in Rouen in 1470, the first printed law book in the English language. Also an original *Cowell's Interpreter* 1637 not the revised edition after the suppression by Sir. Edward Coke and a 1671 copy of *Dugdale's Origines Judiciales* and all the *Doomsday Books*, the earliest English adjudications on the legal calendar (*Doom* = judgment, *Day* = hearing date). These specimens of law library luxury were in a collection with every possible working tool that an active, metropolitan New York City practitioner could desire for his professional workshop.[5] All of the above rare titles were also in Elbridge T. Gerry's personal law library at his Broadway residence, no doubt he was replicating the exceptional library with which he worked in his mentor's law office.

After the death of Mr. Noyes, Elbridge worked with his remaining partner, John McKeon to close Mr. Noyes' active cases. In November 1865 Elbridge joined William F. Allen and Benjamin Vaughan Abbott in the firm *Allen, Abbott and Gerry*. The senior partner William F. Allen was soon appointed a judge of the Court of Appeals, thereby establishing the firm of *Abbott & Gerry,* which continued to practice law at No. 54 Wall Street and afterwards at No. 164 Nassau Street until 1874 when this firm was dissolved at Mr. Abbott's retirement. Elbridge T. Gerry thereafter remained a solo practitioner and devoted more of his time to charitable institutions and state commissions.

After practicing law full-time for five years Elbridge T. Gerry became an established New York City attorney, and in May 1865 he was appointed an *Examiner* for the general term of the New York Supreme Court. Elbridge joined two other appointed attorneys to sit as a committee to examine or test young lawyers applying for membership in the practicing Bar Association of New York City. He enjoyed mentoring younger lawyers which made him feel like a true member of the Bar. Between June and November of 1865, before joining *Allen & Abbott* in November, Elbridge T. Gerry and John McKeon handled three major cases left open at Mr. Noyes' death. The cases dealt with divorce, maritime insurance, and the fraudulent conveyance of property; each lasted several weeks.

The first case *Strong v Strong* resumed in February 1865 with an appeal from the October 1864 lower court verdict against defendant Mrs. Mary Strong. This turbulent case would continue over the next eighteen months and was not resolved until after Elbridge Gerry and John McKeon parted at his retirement and Elbridge had joined the Allen & Abbot law firm. *Strong v Strong* was one of the most notorious divorce cases in nineteenth century New York. The husband was the wealthy Peter R. Strong of Islip, New York, a prominent and wealthy lawyer and the nephew of noted writer George Templeton Strong. His wife was Mary Stevens, the daughter of an influential businessman and the President of the Bank of Commerce. Newspapers printed the testimony of every witness, the motions and arguments of the attorneys, and even printed a detailed description of each of the twelve jurors who spent forty-five hours debating the case before being discharged as a hung jury. Both parties to the divorce accused the other of adultery, of destroying evidence, of confessions obtained under duress, and even the Jurors accused one another of "jury tampering." Elbridge T. Gerry argued several legal issues that were procedural technicalities of significance. His most fascinating argument was that the husband had "forgiven" his wife and therefore could not sue her for divorce. The issues of the husband's guilt and that of "forgiveness" as a defense divided the jury forcing the Judge to discharge the jury. The judge then granted the divorce without a verdict of guilt assigned to either husband or wife, thereby protecting the rights of the wife, including the right to alimony which she refused. In June 1866 one last appeal was made to the Court by Elbridge T. Gerry to direct the wealthy Peter R. Strong to pay his wife's legal fees, which in fact the Judge decreed. Ultimately, the Strongs were divorced and both remarried. Peter continued to live in New York while Mary lived the remainder of her life in Paris, France. The Strong divorce case has been discussed in several journal articles into the twenty-first century.[6]

The second case was *Walsh v Washington Marine Insurance* which was of little interest to New York newspapers but of great interest to the commercial world. The action sought payment of insurance on a policy for the ship *Senator* that sank on a voyage from New York to Liverpool. On the morning of August 22, 1862 the ship *Senator* left the port of New York laden with grain and just four days later the vessel was sinking with nine feet of water in her hold, and the pumps were clogged with grain. The officers and the crew were rescued by a passing ship and within an hour afterwards the *Senator* went down with its cargo, at a distance of 120 miles from the nearest coast. Two witnesses on board the Senator testified falsely at the trial, on behalf of the insurance company, and were found guilty of perjury. It was shown by the testimony of skillful and experienced commanders that the rolling of a ship laden with grain, in heavy sea, with a light wind, has a more straining effect, and is attended with greater peril, than a severe and continued gale. The special hazards which may attend a particular voyage are necessarily unforeseen by both the insured and the insurance company. The import of the case is that all the law requires of the ship owner in this regard is that the ship is seaworthy on leaving port, properly manned with sailors, and equipped and prepared to meet the perils ordinarily incident to ocean navigation. However, if on a particular voyage the perils prove too great to be surmounted by a seaworthy ship, then the loss falls properly on the insurance company who were paid by the ship owners to assume the risk. The *Senator* was loaded for her last voyage under the immediate direction of the surveyor of the board of the underwriters, of which the defendant insurance company were members, and when she left port the *Senator* was well-manned and equipped. This was established by the testimony of disinterested witnesses, former owners and masters, experienced shipwrights and navigators and officers employed by the insurance companies. The evidence and testimony left no doubt that the *Senator* was seaworthy at the inception of the risk when she left port. Elbridge T. Gerry once again won a complex case in a specialized subject area that has since been cited by successive court actions through 1989.

The third case argued in 1865 by Elbridge T. Gerry was *Dunlevy v. Tallmadge* in which a creditor was owed money by a business that was bankrupt, yet the owners nonetheless sold their business before settling the debt. The question was whether the purchaser of the bankrupt company acts as a trustee who holds the business assets of the company on behalf of unpaid creditors and must therefore pay what is owed them. Or was the sale fraudulent where the owners intended to avoid debt payments? If so the Court could choose to cancel the sale and require the original owners to pay their debts. Business owners watched this case carefully because the outcome affected both debtors and creditors in every type of commercial enterprise. Once again, Gerry won the appeal on behalf of the purchaser of the bankrupt company who was deemed by the Court not to be liable for the unpaid debts of the original owners. Further, the Court indicated that the creditor should have sued the original owners, the only individuals he had a right by law to sue, before they sold the company. Like many Gerry cases this case was complex and it set a precedent in the field of Commercial Law.

In September 1865 Elbridge took a well-deserved vacation to West Point as was the tradition of the Goelets while he was growing up on the Broadway Farm. He stayed at the *Cozzens Hotel* which had opened in 1861. It was already a famous resort, not only because it was located on a spectacular bluff above the Hudson River, but because of a visit by President Abraham Lincoln in late June, 1862. The President traveled up the East side of the Hudson River after taking the ferry from Jersey City to New York City. At the town of Garrison he took another ferry west across the river to West Point, likely the same route Elbridge would take a couple of years later to reach West Point. Lincoln visited General Winfield Scott to discuss the military strategy of General George B. McClellan. The conference with Scott lasted about five hours after which Lincoln inspected the apartments, barracks, and West Point Foundry opposite the Academy. A dinner party was held at the *Cozzens Hotel* in the afternoon. That night the President charmed all the ladies with his conversational powers and affability at a reception also held at the hotel. All along the route back to New York City the next day, people gathered to get a glimpse of the president.[7] The *Cozzens Hotel* is well known for the dances, known then as "hops" with the cadets of West Point Academy. During the weekend of September 3-5, 1865 a correspondent for the *New York Times* was at the Cozzens Hotel to report on society activity and wrote:

> Herewith I had an account of a fancy dress hop that was given to the ladies of the hotel on Friday evening, September 1. Admittance to the ballroom was by invitation only. On the occasion of which I write, the assemblage was a curious one of curious people, all sorts of men and women, and here and there a child or two, like a daisy in a field. Everyone has witnessed, at some point in their life that maddest of gay scenes a fancy ball, and everyone knows how exhilarating to the spirits is the consciousness that for once conventionalities of society may be thrown aside, and new characters assumed with a new dress (costumes). This was exemplified in the festive scene in the parlor of *Cozzens Hotel.* Joy illumined every brow, and pleasure ruled supreme until the gray hours, when all retired with aching beans and weary limbs. Two of the managers were Edward H. Harriman and E.T. Gerry.[8]

Perhaps by now it was not surprising to find Elbridge T. Gerry enjoying a vacation that entails more effort in organizing the activities, like the fancy ball, than just relaxing like most vacationers. He was by nature energetic and driven, less in need of a break from work than he was in need of a change of scenery, reinvigorated with the companionship and gaiety of friends, good food and good music. Many years later Elbridge's co-chair, Edward H. Harriman, joined him for the marriage of their children Robert L. Gerry and Cornelia Harriman, when yet another great American family is united with the Gerry clan.

Refreshed and back in New York, Elbridge's legal work continued into 1866, particularly the first six months of the year when he was closing out the Strong divorce case. Elbridge T. Gerry's personal life was also eventful in 1866. His sister Almy Goelet Gerry was twenty-six and engaged to be married to Frederic Gallatin a promising young lawyer. Frederic's grandfather and Elbridge's grandfather worked together under President James Madison, Albert Gallatin as Secretary of the Treasury and Elbridge Gerry as Vice President. The Gallatins were a distinguished New York banking family that worked along side the Goelet family to develop local New York City banks as well as to establish the first national bank in New York. In July 1800 as Secretary of the Treasury, Albert Gallatin prepared a report entitled *Views of the Public Debt, Receipts and Expenditure of the United States,* which is still considered a classic analysis of the fiscal operations of a constitutional government. The *Treaty of Ghent* that ended the War of 1812 was considered largely Gallatin's personal triumph because he was the most effective of the American Commissioners. He served as Minister to both France and England where he concluded his years in the field of diplomacy in 1817 and returned to New York to take up his residence. Albert Gallatin became President of the *National Bank* of the City of New York, later known as the *Gallatin National Bank* of the City of New York.[9] The *Gallatin National Bank* merged and changed names several times over nearly two hundred years; today the banks successor is the federal *JP Morgan Chase Bank* in New York City. Albert Gallatin was a founder of *New York University* from which his son, Frederic Gallatin, would graduate with both his bachelor and law degrees. During the Civil War, Frederic was a Vice Judge-Advocate in the Second Brigade from which he resigned on January 13, 1866 and returned to New York City to join the family banking business as a lawyer.[10] Frederic shared many interests with Elbridge and joined many of the same associations and clubs like the *New York Bar Association* and the *New York Yacht Club.* Almy Goelet Gerry's marriage to Frederic Gallatin was celebrated on November 3, 1866 at Trinity Church in New York City. Their marriage happily joined the Gerry family to yet another distinguished American family, the Gallatins.

Elbridge T. Gerry's life was on the fast track and 1867 was no exception, starting with two cases that were argued early in the year and decided in March and April respectively. The first case *Newell v Wheeler,* was a question of implied agreement where the plaintiff transferred to the defendants the exclusive right to use his patent invention for cleaning coffee in three states, including New York. The consideration for this transfer was the payment of $5,000 in cash and the agreement to pay a certain amount for each and every bag of coffee that should pass through the plaintiff's cylinders or process machine. Elbridge represented the patent owner, the appellant William Newell. Gerry asked whether a failure to keep the machine in full operation was caused by the negligent and fraudulent operations of the defendants or the worthlessness of the machine. Elbridge won the case in the lower level court but the case was appealed on the issue of breach of contract and that the argument about the operation of the machine was irrelevant. Gerry now argued that the defendants were bound to keep the machine in operation and were bound to pay the toll upon the amount of coffee that could have been run through it whether it was actually so run or not. This time, on appeal, Elbridge lost the case with the judge ruling that the defendants were not bound to run the cylinders to their full capacity, and that they were only bound to pay the percentage on what had actually passed through the cylinders or had been subjected to the process. This view was confirmed by the implied meaning of the contract language that both parties had signed.[11] Elbridge handled cases for clients from every walk of life, indeed the publicity from the Strong divorce case quickly expanded Gerry's law practice with his reputation as a brilliant and effective lawyer growing throughout New York City.

The second case Elbridge argued early in 1867, *Osgood v Amidon*, was decided on April 24. Elbridge represented the defendant stockholders of the insolvent *Columbian Insurance Company* against the plaintiff bank receivers who were handling the dissolution of the insurance company and the settlement of its debts. The defendant stockholders were issued a cash dividend by the insurance company when the company knew it was insolvent, had no profits, and therefore used money from capital to pay the dividend. Plaintiffs asked that the stockholders return the dividend payments to which they were not entitled. Elbridge argued that the officers of the company who paid the cash dividends did not know that by doing so the capital would be impaired and there was no allegation that the dividend was paid fraudulently. The Court disagreed with Elbridge, it stated that the issue of fraud was entirely independent of the statutory duty of the stockholders to repay the dividends; which by law can never be paid out of capital and can only be paid out of the profits. This case was closely followed by the New York business community because insolvency was common as a result of the 1857 financial panic that caused banks and businesses to close and the economy had only just started to recover.

In the midst of his active legal practice Elbridge continued to participate in the social life of New York through his growing charity work. The annual *Charity Ball* for the benefit of the *Nursery and Children's Hospital* was held March 4, 1867 at the *Academy of Music.* The announcement in the New York Times listed the patrons and organizers of the event, which included Robert J. Livingston, Albert Gallatin, Jr. (brother of Frederic Gallatin), and Elbridge T. Gerry.[12] As was the custom, it is likely that Robert J. Livingston escorted his wife and daughter, both named Louisa, to the Ball. Elbridge escorted his mother, Hannah Goelet Gerry, while his sister Almy was escorted by her new husband, Frederic Gallatin. Elbridge's intimate family social circle brought relaxation and pleasure to his hectic life.

On March 29, 1867 just three weeks after the *Charity Ball* the New York State Legislature passed *An Act to Provide for a Convention to Revise and Amend the Constitution* to address a variety of problems voiced by the citizens of New York, state agencies, the Judiciary and state business leaders. This would be the fifth such convention since the first constitutional convention held in July 1776 amid the strife and turbulence of the *War of the Revolution.* After five weeks of discussion the first *Constitution of the State of New York* was adopted by the people. The second convention in 1807 was called to straighten out the disturbances that had arisen between the Governor and the Council of Appointments over the question of patronage and to fix the number of members in the Senate and the Assembly. It settled its business in just two weeks. The third convention was called in 1821 and resulted in the abolishment of the Council of Appointments, the reduction in the terms of the Governor and Lieutenant Governor from three to two years, and the franchise to vote was conferred on every white male citizen at the age of twenty-one who had resided in the state for one year preceding any election. The work of the convention was completed in three months and shortly thereafter, the citizens voted to accept the new Constitution. Although the people of New York had once again voted to adopt the revised Constitution, between 1825 and 1846 ten additional amendments were proposed and nine were adopted. The fourth convention was called to order on June 1, 1846 and for the first time the judicial system was reorganized, abolishing some courts, establishing new ones and dividing the state into eight judicial districts. Additionally, the power of the Governor to make appointments was abridged.[13]

The fifth constitutional convention was one of the longest thus far, starting in June 1867 and it continued until the end of February, 1868. The first order of business was to hold an election of delegates on the fourth Tuesday of April to select 128 delegates from the state senatorial districts and to elect 32 delegates chosen for the State at large. In May the election results were announced by the Secretary of State and Elbridge T. Gerry at the young age of 30 was elected a delegate to the New York *Constitutional Convention* to represent the Fifth

Senatorial District. The elected delegates convened on the first Tuesday of June, 1867 in the Assembly chamber of the Capital building in Albany. Each delegate to the convention was entitled to the sum of six dollars per day plus mileage for the duration of the convention, including recess days not to exceed four days at a time. Elbridge T. Gerry was one of six Secretaries to the *Committee on the Pardoning Power.* In addition to committee assignments, the delegates met daily as a committee of the whole to discuss recommendations from committees and to allow each individual delegate to make motions, offer resolutions, or to present petitions. Elbridge T. Gerry made twelve motions, offered seven resolutions, and presented two petitions over the course of four months' participation at the convention. The delegates were in residence in Albany for the entire convention except during recess or excused absences. Rather than select problematic parts of the constitutional document, this convention reviewed it page by page. The newspapers of the day described the delegates assigned to this challenging task as a remarkable body of men of ability and experience and noted that no gathering in the history of the State had brought together so many men of distinction and of national reputation.[14] In addition to Elbridge T. Gerry another young delegate was Smith M. Reed who reminisced years later about his experience, specifically recalling the first day of the convention when Martin Grover, an eminent member of the Court of Appeals left his courtroom in the Capitol that morning:

> Judge Grover went into the gallery of the Assembly and looked the convention over. Upon his return to the courtroom, one of the other judges said, "Well, Grover, what do you think of them?" and he answered, "Those fellows will never make a Constitution that the people will adopt." "Why?" said the other judge. Grover answered: "Too many of them have long hair.[15]

Surprisingly, the people of New York did in fact reject almost the entire revised Constitution by a vote of 223,935 to 200,456 later that year. However, the convention's proposal to reorganize the Judiciary was actually approved in the same election in November 1868.

Elbridge T. Gerry was not listed as having any absences from the convention and his Committee work was finished and the Report submitted to the Assembly by mid-August 1867. By the fall recess Elbridge was back in New York City handling a memorial for a deceased lawyer, Alexander W. Bradford, on behalf of the *Bar Association* in November 1867. This and other activity confirm that Elbridge was excused from the November to February final session of the convention, his work completed.

On May 19, 1867 just as the constitutional convention was electing delegates, the Gerry family once again suffered the loss of a beloved family member. The last son of the founding father, and his namesake, Elbridge Gerry, Jr. died in Boston, Massachusetts on May 19 at the age of seventy-four after a short illness. His nephew, Elbridge T. Gerry attended the funeral which was held at the family residence, 127 Temple Street, New Haven, Connecticut. Elbridge steadfastly kept in touch with the New Haven family and assisted his aunts with the settlement of the estates as he had done three years earlier with his Aunt Helen. Elbridge couldn't stay long because he was expected in court to close a legal case in early June; immediately after which he was expected in Albany for the start of the Convention. The mournful correspondence among the aunts and cousins on the occasion of Elbridge Gerry, Jr.'s death was touching. His nephew George J. Townsend wrote to his aunts in New Haven:

> My Dear Aunts, The sudden death of my dear uncle has taken me entirely by surprise, and yet for some time I have thought that his hermit life might result in his being found dead in his bed with no one to tell us the story. A kinder, more noble hearted friend I never had from my earliest childhood and my house even now is full of little tokens of affection from him, the last being a snuff case. All these I have ever prized above all intrinsic value, fully appreciating the generous heart that sent them. I most deeply regret that I cannot come on to pay the last tribute of respect to his memory, but my present engagements render it impossible for me to leave just now. Lucy joins me in kindest remembrances to you all.
>
> Your affectionate nephew, George J. Townsend[16]

Another letter was sent to New Haven from a cousin of the Gerry sisters, Samuel R. Gerry Jr., the namesake of another son of the Founding father who remained in Marblehead, Massachusetts.

> My dear cousin Ann, In the papers of this last week I saw with great sorrow notice of the death of our dear friend and your most excellent brother Elbridge and I hasten to assure you of our sincere sympathy in your great bereavement. His last visit gave us great pleasure and we had hoped that we should see him again in Marblehead. But God has seen fit that our next meeting should not be in this world. You have indeed been called to part with many of those near and dear to you. At the time of my dear cousin Helen's death I should have written but illness prevented me. I hope you will be able to write and tell me some of the particulars of your two brother's illnesses. My wife sends her sincere sympathy.
>
> I am your affectionate cousin, Samuel R. Gerry[17]

There remained only Ann 75, Eleanor 67, and Emily 65, three of the last four children of the Founding Father who lived together at the New Haven Gerry home. One other sister, Elizabeth Gerry Townsend, 77, was married and living in Boston with her family. Their sister, Catherine Gerry Austin, had died in Boston at age 70 in 1850; she was the eldest of the nine children of the Founding Father.

Early in the winter of 1867 following a year of intense legal case work, the death of his uncle, and participation in the *Constitutional Convention*, Elbridge T. Gerry turned a new page in his life. On December 3, 1867 Louisa M. Livingston married Elbridge T. Gerry at Trinity Chapel in New York City, the church where the year before his sister Almy Goelet Gerry married Frederic Gallatin. Although this was a marriage between two well-known and highly respected families, the Livingstons and Gerrys, there were no articles about the wedding in any of the newspapers nor was there a formally announced engagement. This follows the pattern of Hannah Goelet's marriage to Thomas R. Gerry in 1830. As the only living child of Robert J. Livingston, his daughter Louisa's marriage warranted some kind of celebration among the Livingston, Goelet and Gerry families. It was most likely a catered private affair at the Livingston home. There was an interesting article in *Harper's Bazaar* magazine published November 2, 1867, the month before the Gerry wedding. The article noted that "marriage is in a fair way, just now to become a standard topic for newspaper treatment."[18] The introspective and religious nature of the Gerry, Goelet and Livingston families may well explain the private circumstance of the wedding coupled with what has been described as only an emerging interest by the press to cover weddings as a news topic. Nonetheless, the quiet wedding of Elbridge and Louisa began a warm, intimate, active and happy family life into which six children were born over the next twelve years. The newlyweds moved in with Louisa's parents at 184 Fifth Avenue where they happily remained for the first five years of their marriage. The Gerry-Livingston marriage was perhaps the most historic joining of two American families from the Founding Period and it still remains a strong and lasting family bond. Within the first year of their marriage, on August 28, 1868 Elbridge and Louisa welcomed their first child, a daughter, Margaret Louisa Gerry. No doubt due to this happy event there were no cases reported for Elbridge T. Gerry in 1868, but he may well have handled legal matters in his office that were transactional such as drafting wills and estates, handling property transactions, and managing the financial affairs of his wife Louisa who was wealthy in her own right. That same year, Elbridge's sister Almy Gerry Gallatin gave birth to her first child, Almy Gallatin (her namesake), providing a playmate for the Gerrys' little Margaret. The two girls were the second generation to play with the historic dollhouse built in 1846 by Peter Goelet in his basement workshop at the *Broadway Farm* brownstone. The dollhouse bears the address 890 Broadway over the front door entry. The doll house was donated to the *Museum of the City of New York* by a later generation of the Gallatin family.[19]

Elbridge joined the *American Geographical Society* in 1868, as a life member, known as a Fellow of the *Society*. The object of the *Society* was the advancement of geographical science by encouraging exploration of the world, and by the diffusion of scientific knowledge through lectures and the publication of books, charts and maps. Another major objective of the Society was the permanent establishment in the city of New York of an institution in which geographical and scientific works, voyages and travels, maps, charts, globes, instruments, documents, manuscripts, prints, and engravings could be collected, classified and arranged, so as to be accessible for public use in a great maritime and commercial city.[20] The *Society* continues today, having met both of its objectives, particularly a building that houses a Council Room, Reception and Lecture space, an Exhibition Hall and a Library with a public reading room. Located in Brooklyn, New York, the *Society's* tradition of service to the U.S. government, business community, and the nation-at-large continues unabated.

In February 1869, six months after the birth of his daughter, Margaret, Elbridge T. Gerry resumed trial work, still a partner with Benjamin V. Abbott at No. 164 Nassau Street. On this rare occasion, Elbridge and his brother-in-law Frederic Gallatin joined as co-counsel in their first case together. They represented a British author as the plaintiff in the case of *Reade v Sweetzer*. While not a notorious case the subject matter was libel and slander, and being subject to such charges themselves, New York newspapers took a serious interest in the court's decision. The action was brought by Charles Reade, an Englishman residing in London who was the author of a novel titled *Griffith Gaunt*. He wanted to recover $25,000 damages for an alleged libel published in the *Round Table* a New York weekly newspaper. Mr. Reade charged that the *Round Table* intentionally printed three articles containing false, libelous and defamatory matter about his skill as an author. The three articles had a similar tone:

> It is one of the worst stories that had been printed since Sterne, Fielding and Smollett defiled the literature of the already foul eighteenth century; that the book is not only tainted with this one foul spot, it is replete with impurity, it reeks with allusions that the most prurient scandalmonger would hesitate to make," and further, the article recommended that the "publishers discontinue it, as unfit for circulation to families." The third article was titled, "Did Charles Reade Write Griffith Gaunt.[21]

The defense argued the articles were just "honest criticism" and that the defendant was not the owner or publisher of the *Round Table* and therefore could not be sued. Frederic Gallatin made the opening argument and Elbridge T. Gerry argued the case and gave the closing argument. Gerry and Gallatin won the case when the jury returned a verdict for Mr. Reade, but only assessed damages at six cents. Perhaps it was the partial reading of the novel to the jury during the trial that also convinced them that Mr. Reade's novel was one of the worst stories ever printed.

The next case was a hearing with the formality of a trial, in which Elbridge T. Gerry represented the City of New York. The press coverage was national and international and invited scholarly discussion for years to come. In the midst of a significant *Spiritualist Movement* across America, which began as early as the 1850's, newspapers in New York City began publishing the photographs of William Howard Mumler (1832-1884) that purported to show "spirits" behind the subjects of his photograph. The mayor of the city, A. Oakey Hall, needed a distraction from his own corruption, and sought to find favor with a very public investigation into spiritualist fraud, thereby protecting the good citizens of New York City. Through a sting operation he sent his Chief Marshal Joseph H. Tooker undercover to the *Mumler Photography Studio* to sit for a photograph which could be used as evidence. William H. Mumler first discovered "spirit photographs" while working in a Boston photography studio. He took a photograph of himself, alone in the studio, but as he developed the picture he saw the mysterious figure of a girl, like a spirit standing near him. Mumler actually believed that it was caused by a previously used glass plate from which the prior photographic imprint had not been adequately cleaned and removed. However, having a sense of humor Mumler showed the photograph to a spiritualist friend who had Mumler briefly note on the back that this was a "spirit photograph" and that he should sign it. The rest is history, the friend had numerous newspapers in Boston publish the photograph as proof that spirits existed and to bolster the reputation of the *Spiritualist Movement.* A well-known leader in the movement, Dr. H.F. Gardener, went to Mumler for a "sitting" to see if a spirit of his father-in-law would appear in his portrait photograph. Unfortunately, the shadowy image of a woman appeared, a woman still living and known to Dr. Gardener. The incident was publicized and others came forward with the same complaint. It was then that Mumler was forced to abandon Boston for New York City in 1869.[22]

The mayor's sting operation was also intended to charge Mumler with obtaining money by trickery or device because he charged ten dollars per spirit photograph when a standard photo of the day only cost twenty-five cents for a sitting. The mayor specifically asked prominent lawyer Elbridge T. Gerry to prosecute the case. Although this is called a trial in the press and subsequent literature, it was actually a lengthy preliminary hearing to determine if there was enough evidence to send the case to a Grand Jury. The hearing began March 19, 1869 and ran for three weeks. The hearing had the weight of a full criminal trial, witnesses were called and evidence was introduced. Indeed, Elbridge called the infamous P.T. Barnum to testify for the prosecution because he was the great American showman who had denounced spirit photography in his writings and was an authority on detecting what was then called "humbug."[23]

The defense lawyer, John D. Townsend, took an aggressive position. Rather than deny the involvement of spirits he asserted the legitimacy of Mumler's supernatural images. His opening statement threw down the gauntlet:

> There is no trick, fraud or deception in what are called spirit pictures by the accused. Mumler did not know how the spirits appeared in his photographs; he knew only that they did not result from any manipulations on his part. His first spirit photographs appeared nearly a decade earlier, and in the intervening time they had been investigated thoroughly and repeatedly. No one had been able to discover any deceptions on Mumler's part.[24]

The case was predicated on the existence of spirits and Mumler's lawyer presented evidence for this claim, citing a long list of passages from the Bible which narrated countless episodes in which supernatural beings had appeared to mortals. Implicitly, the defense challenged the prosecution, Elbridge T. Gerry, both to provide direct evidence of Mumler's involvement in studio machinations and to discredit the patron's definitive identification of the vague forms hovering around their portraits.

Chief prosecutor Gerry recognized the traps set in these challenges. One witness for the prosecution, Abraham Bogardus, a photographer and representative of *the National Photographic Association* (an organization committed to protecting photographers from false patents and humbugs,) stated that recognition of a portrait "depends upon the quantity of imagination of the sitter." He recounted occasions when visitors to his gallery recognized Henry Clay's portrait as that of General Jackson, while other visitors had failed to recognize the perfect likeness of their close friends in photographs.[25] Circumstantial evidence was all Elbridge had so he built his case around it, often eliciting detailed discussion of photographic processes. Defense witnesses were asked under cross-examination whether any of the mechanical means could have produced the effects seen in their photographs. Newspaper readers learned from the prosecutor, Elbridge T. Gerry, that the sharpness of the ghost's features was determined by the distance between the two plates used to make the image, and, that a ghost projecting over the sitter probably resulted from a second printing. Those following the compelling courtroom drama in the news learned about the technical procedures that produced subtle differences in photographs even though the source of information was a newspaper account without illustrations.[26] The public also learned about the Spiritualist Movement and developed a healthy mistrust of photographic evidence. Ultimately, Elbridge T. Gerry was unable to prove beyond a reasonable doubt that Mumler's photographs were frauds or that Mumler used any trickery. The defense showed that in the age of P.T. Barnum and Mumler truth was no longer the issue, not even in a court of law.[27] What mattered now was the style of the deception while the business of the court was to determine which styles would be protected by law and which would not. This left much for legal scholars to debate for years to come. Mumler was acquitted. In his release statement for the defendant William H. Mumler the judge said:

> I am morally convinced that there may be fraud and deception practiced by the prisoner, yet I, sitting as a magistrate to determine from the evidence given by the witnesses according to law, am compelled to decide that I would not be justified in sending this complaint to the Grand Jury, as, in my opinion, the prosecution has failed to make out the case.[28]

The decision seemed clear, reasonable, and principled but, as in all civil activities in the time of Boss Tweed and Tammany Hall New York, there was reason to wonder. The public exposure of the trial Judge's own malfeasance began to unfold just a few months after the Mumler hearing ended, when the judge was charged with corruption and removed from office along with several other judges who had been under investigation. Four days after the trial closed in early May *Harper's Weekly* devoted its cover to the case and reproduced nine woodcut illustrations of the photographs, one of which was Mumler's self-portrait where he first noticed the "spirit" in Boston a decade earlier. Mumler returned to Boston after the trial where he established a studio in his mother-in-laws' parlor to resume his photographic work. Some of his most interesting photographs include the widely circulated portrait of first lady Mary Todd Lincoln with the spirit of her dead husband, President Abraham Lincoln, taken by Mumler in 1870 at the White House.[29] When he died in 1884 his obituary referred to Mumler as a well-known inventor. His then famous *Mumler Process* enabled newspapers and book publishers to illustrate their stories using actual photographic images instead of lined wood-cut reproductions.

Elbridge T. Gerry at age 33 was now one of the most prominent lawyers in New York City and experienced first-hand the corruption in the judiciary and the legal community at large. Criticism of the profession grew more unrestrained as offenses of the bar became so notorious that there was little or no use to disguise them. Out of this emergency sprang a leading group of lawyers who took measures in December 1869 to create a Bar Association as evidence of the general high character of the profession in New York City. Two hundred signed to join the Association as did Elbridge T. Gerry, who joined a list of names of such pre-eminently high character that there was no doubt in New York City as to the integrity of the bar membership as a whole. Elbridge was named to the Library Committee of the Bar Association to coordinate the selection and purchase of books by its members. The published history of the Bar Association notes the following:

> The ease with which the Association established itself as an institution with its own house, furniture and librarian, as well as pleasant atmosphere, reflects the wealth of the men who founded it. The leaders of the city bar were rich – and generous. When in May 1871 an unusually fine set of rare books came on the market at a price higher than the library committee was prepared to pay, a committee member, Elbridge T. Gerry, bought the set privately and gave it to the Association. After this manner, many books found their way quietly to the shelves of the library. In much the same fashion pictures blossomed on the walls, and busts of eminent lawyers appeared on the mantels.[30]

The year 1869 closed quietly as the Gerry family enjoyed the company of their 1 ½ year old daughter Margaret. The Gerrys lived with Louisa's parents for the next few years at 184 Fifth Avenue which required Elbridge to leave his beloved but very large book collection at the "Broadway Farm" townhouse where his mother and sister Jean still lived. In December of 1869 Elbridge assisted the Goelets with negotiations on a lease renewal between Cornelius Vanderbilt and Peter, Jean, Hannah, and Robert Goelet for a parcel of land in the 19th Ward between 46th and 47th Streets. Managing Livingston properties and assisting with Goelet property transactions became a parallel career for Elbridge T. Gerry.

Sometime in 1869 just one year after the birth of Almy and Frederic Gallatins first child, they welcomed their second child, a son, Thomas Gerry Gallatin named for Almy and Elbridge's late father, Thomas R. Gerry. Sadly, the Gallatin's first son died within a year on April 25, 1870. Louisa Gerry was able to console her sister-in-law Almy since she had lost her only sibling, her brother Warren when he was just twenty-three. The sisters-in-law found hope in their little girls who were not only cousins just six months apart in age but also happy little playmates. They were raised in an affectionate, close-knit, and growing family circle. Hannah Goelet Gerry, now sixty-five, along with Uncle Peter Goelet and Robert and Louisa Livingston had become proud grandparents, delighted to share the affections of their extended families.

six children

Married 1866. Childhood playmates with Teddy Roosevelt and his siblings; all lived on 19th and 20th Streets just off Broadway.

Grandsons of Albert Gallatin, Secretary of the Treasury, founder of the first federal bank in NYC, *Gallatin National Bank* (absorbed by *Hanover Bank*)

Frederic Gallatin
Judge Advocate

Albert Gallatin
Surgeon

Married Trinity Church, NYC, 1867

Elbridge Thomas Gerry
Lawyer, philanthropist, and founder of the New York Society for the Prevention of Cruelty to Children
Grandson of founding father, Vice-President Elbridge Gerry

Margaret "Pearl" Gerry
(first of six children)

Louisa Mathilda Livingston

Spirit photograph

William Mumler, photographer whose pictures showed ghosts or spirits behind his sitters. His was one of Elbridge T. Gerry's most famous legal cases.

Marry Todd Lincoln
spirit photograph

The Gerry siblings vacationed together from childhood until married, at the Hudson River resort at West Point near the military academy. They stayed at the Cozzens Hotel year year with the extended Goelet family. Sometimes the entire family sailed north of Albany to holiday at Saratoga, NY.

Cozzens Hotel stood on a beautiful bluff overlooking the Hudson River.

View of the Hudson River and West Point Academy from the Cozzens Hotel

Old State Capitol, 1879

Contemporary photograph of Assembly Room
(photo from Elbridge T. Gerry's collection)

Contemporary diagram of the Assembly Room

Delegate Elbridge T. Gerry, seat 33

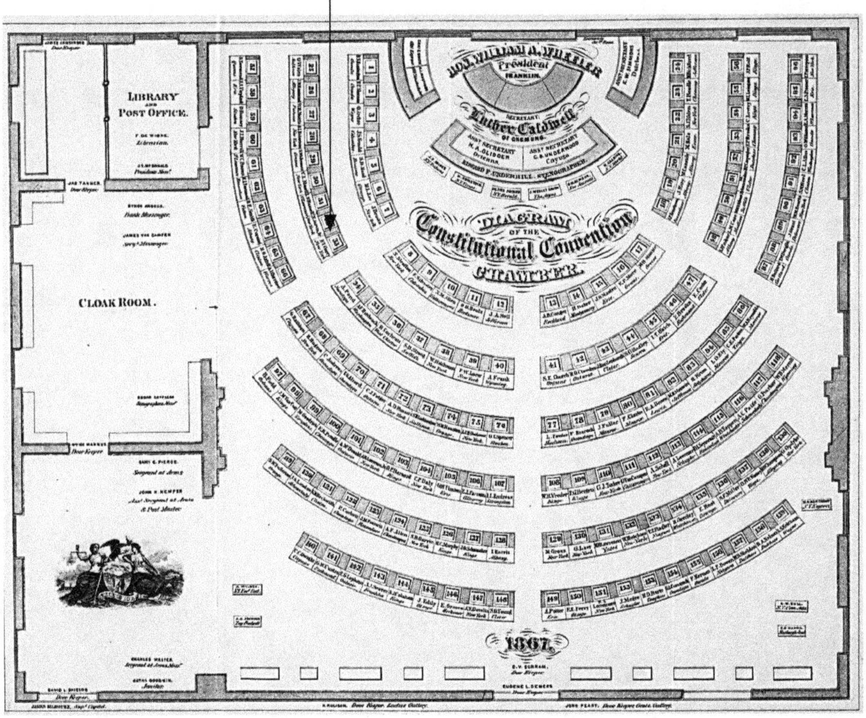

Diagram of the Constitutional Convention Camber, 1867, from *The New York Convention Manual: Prepared in Pursuance of Chapters 194 and 458, of the Laws of 1867, Under the Direction of Francis C. Barlow, Secretary of State, Thomas Hillhouse, Comptroller, and John H. Martindale, Attorney-General, by Franklin B. Hough*. Albany: Weed, Parsons, 1867.

4

FATHER, LAWYER, LEADER

If your actions inspire others to dream more,
learn more, do more and become more, you are a leader.
John Quincy Adams

The early 1870's offered Elbridge T. Gerry new opportunities as well as new challenges in his professional life. He no longer sought clients. Instead he selectively responded to those who sought out his renowned legal expertise. His personal life was enriched by the birth of three daughters who required more space than the shared Livingston brownstone could offer. Elbridge would not only seek out a new home for his growing family, but he would also devote more time to humanitarian causes beginning a notable shift of focus and priorities.

Frederic Gallatin spent the next decade actively yet quietly in the business world of banking and real estate. His social life paralleled his brother-in-law Elbridge's where they continued to socialize through clubs, charity work, and shared family holidays. Although Frederic had a more low-key temperament than the driven Elbridge the birth of their children over the next several years sealed their bond and that of sisters-in-law, Almy Gallatin and Louisa Livingston Gerry.

The Goelet family was similar to the Gallatins during this period, deeply involved in the real estate business. Elbridge's first cousin Robert Goelet, Jr. was 39 and on the Board of the *Chemical Bank* as was his father and Uncle Peter. Although a lawyer, Robert did not practice law except as it applied to the family real estate business. He lived at 591 Fifth Avenue close to his brother who lived at 608 Fifth Avenue. His younger brother Ogden was 34 in 1870 the same age as Elbridge. Unlike his brother who was on the board of the *Chemical Bank,* Ogden was not; rather he was a major real estate investor in New York City, his primary business. The Goelets as a rule were a private, intellectual clan who, while part of New York's high society, were only in the public eye through press coverage of their social engagements and real estate transactions, often affecting significant parcels of New York property. Typical advertisements read:

> To Let: The three-story buildings No. 889 and No. 891 Broadway; also, the five-story marble stores No. 631 and No. 633 Broadway; four-story brick store No. 7 East 18th Street. Apply to Robert Goelet, No. 857 Broadway.[1]

A typical article in the press tracking the real estate activities of the Goelet investments included participation in auctions as well as sales and leasing:

> Yesterday the Exchange Salesrooms were tolerably well attended by those who anticipated the auction of fifty-two lots in Westchester County, on the east side of the Central-Avenue, one and one-half miles above the Macomb's Dam Bridge, between New York City and Jerome Park. *Additionally*, A.J. Bleecker, auctioneer, sold the property known as the Collyer Shipyard, situated between Forty-third and Forty-fourth streets, fronting the East River. Noticeable among the bidders yesterday were Amos R. Eno, Robert Goelet and other prominent dealers in real estate.[2]

It was not unusual to see the Goelet name in the *Law Reports* section of the *New York Times* with short notices about court appearances, motions, and referee decisions. In the normal course of managing large scale real estate holdings in New York City there are many legal disputes such as suing for back rent, title arbitration and contract interpretation, among other procedural and equitable issues. From time to time Elbridge T. Gerry was consulted by the Goelets in more difficult matters that could potentially require a court trial.

Elbridge T. Gerry did start the year 1870 with a legal case, but it was not a family matter. The case was a notorious murder that occurred the prior year in late November 1869. Not since the *Mumler Photographic Spirit* case had Elbridge found himself in the daily papers. This was a newspaper story with all the "who, what, where, when and why" to capture the public eye for seven months. **Who,** Daniel McFarland, an out-of-luck lawyer; his wife, Abby Sage, an actress/writer; the lover, Albert D. Richardson, a *Tribune* newspaper feature writer; the friend Horace Greeley, the *Tribune* newspaper publisher; Abby's friend, Henry Ward Beecher, a prominent preacher; and various *Tribune* staff friends of Abby. **What**, the murder of the newspaper feature writer by the out-of-luck lawyer for having an affair with his wife, the actress. **Where**, the murder took place in broad daylight in the *Tribune* newspaper building in front of a witness. **When**, on Thanksgiving Day 1869. **Why**, love, revenge, insanity. It is clear that by the end of December, 1869 Elbridge and two other lawyers, Mr. Charles Spencer and Mr. John Graham, had already been hired to defend the murderer Daniel McFarland.

By February 7, 1870, the first motion in the case was heard in court requesting the trial be moved to a different court. The motion was denied. Immediately thereafter Mr. Spencer informed the court that he, Mr. Gerry and Mr. Graham, co-counsels for the defense had made the most vigorous preparations for the trial and were confident they would be ready in four or five weeks. In response the Judge noted the busy court calendar and the fact that this case had already gathered intense public interest. He then directed the Clerk of the Court to identify and reserve a secondary room in the courthouse to accommodate the McFarland trial.[3]

A month later on March 5, Elbridge T. Gerry and co-counsel appeared in court to request additional time to prepare for trial:

> These counsel have been working steadily to be ready for trial. They have made many private examinations, and have now a great mass of evidence before them. Commissioners for taking testimony have been sent to distant parts of the United States and Europe. Besides this, many witnesses have been summoned so that the defense would be ready on the second or third Monday of this month. It now appears, however, that they will not be prepared for trial until March 21.[4]

The story had dominated the front pages of New York's many newspapers and when the trial finally opened on Monday, April 4, 1870 reporters, stenographers, and spectators fought for space. Defense lawyers Elbridge T. Gerry, John Graham, and Charles Spencer, sensing the emotional pull of the trial of a man for murdering the alleged seducer of his wife, arranged for 10-year old Percy McFarland to be seen running happily to his father when the defendant was brought to the courtroom. The court permitted the boy to sit beside his father the first day of the trial. The District Attorney, Mr. Samuel B. Garvin, made the opening statement for the prosecution during which the story unfolded.

Daniel McFarland, a Dartmouth educated lawyer who never practiced law or held a job for any length of time, married Abby Sage in 1862 and within five years they had two children. Daniel had become an abusive, drunken husband while Abby had published some poetry and presented dramatic readings to earn money for food and to pursue acting and writing as a career. She was befriended by the owner/editor of the *Tribune* newspaper, Horace Greeley and his wife, among other newspaper columnists who have noticed her talent and welcomed Abby into their social circle. The Associate Editor of the *Tribune* was Whitelaw Reid, the husband of Louisa Gerry's second cousin, Elizabeth Mills, of Staatsburg, New York. The circle of *Tribune* friends grew to include Albert D. Richardson, a feature writer for the *Tribune* who had been sent by Greeley to secretly report on the Civil

War and was subsequently captured and imprisoned in the South until he escaped in 1864. He returned to New York not only working with the *Tribune* but successfully publishing books in his own right. Abby Sage was given an opportunity to act on the New York stage with the help of her friends. She became recognized and loved by her audiences. The more abusive Daniel McFarland became to his successful wife Abby the more she was convinced that a divorce was inevitable. In 1867 she began an affair with Albert Richardson with the approval of their circle of friends, among whom letters were exchanged advising Abby on how to proceed. Abby's husband, Daniel, discovered a letter from Albert to his wife confirming his worst fears. Shortly after this heart-breaking discovery Daniel waited outside the stage door to the theatre where Abby was performing. There, from the shadows he saw Albert arrive and meet Abby at the door; Daniel pulled his gun and shot Albert, wounding him in the leg. Albert did not press charges but Abby made it clear to Daniel that she would leave him and take the children.

From 1868–1869 during their separation, Abby and Albert became a couple while Daniel spiraled into depression, erratic behavior, he no longer took care of himself and appeared to all who encountered him to be very unstable. The divorce was finalized in October of 1869 and seemed to push Daniel over the edge. Just weeks after the divorce, late in the afternoon of November 25, 1869, Albert Richardson walked into the *Tribune* offices in New York's Printing House Square. He went to the first-floor mail room to see if his mail slot held a letter from Abby Sage who was out-of-town visiting friends. As Albert neared the mail desk Daniel McFarland rose from the shadows where he had been lingering just like at the theatre. For the second time he pointed his pistol at Albert who was just five feet away, and in front of the staff mail boy, he fired at Albert and ran out of the building. Albert staggered upstairs to the editorial offices. A doctor administered morphine and friends carried him to the *Astor House Hotel* two blocks down Park Row. Abby was contacted and she returned immediately to be by Albert's side.[5]

Jailed, McFarland denied remembering the shooting but showed no remorse over it. At the *Astor House Hotel* doctors tried to make the victim comfortable. Facing the inevitable, Abby Sage called on her friend the prominent preacher Henry Ward Beecher to perform a death-bed wedding ceremony. *Tribune* editor Horace Greeley was a witness. On December 2 Richardson died in the arms of his bride. On December 8, McFarland was indicted for murder in the first degree and for felonious shooting with malice aforethought.

Prosecutor Samuel Garvin presented a straightforward case while the defense commanded the attention of the courtroom and the newspapers with a defense by reason of insanity. The law regards all men as sane, therefore if a jury cannot say beyond a doubt that the defendant was sane at the time of the commission of the alleged act, or cannot say whether at that time he was sane or insane, they are bound to acquit him. The defense produced forty witnesses and three doctors to testify to the insanity of Daniel McFarland, not only at the time of the murder, but for the previous eighteen months. Indeed he had a cousin who was committed to an institution for the insane. The entire trial was published in the papers every day for several weeks, not just witness testimony but also the letters that were read to the jury.

A sketch of Elbridge T. Gerry reading letters into evidence in court was widely published by the press.[6] Gerry offered the letters to show why Daniel McFarland believed there was a conspiracy which contributed to his mental excitement and insanity. The closing argument for the defense was presented by co-counsel John Graham and it is said that he was weeping upon completion of the statement. On Tuesday, May 10 the jury retired to deliberate. A storm which had been approaching burst forth in a thunderstorm of unusual violence and flash after flash of lightning lighted the gray sky and reflected through the windows of the courtroom. Amid this disturbance of nature and after just two hours of deliberation the jury returned at 4:50 p.m. with a verdict of "not guilty."[7] Under most circumstances proving insanity is difficult at best so this was a major win for Elbridge and his colleagues. As late as 2008 this case was cited in law reviews discussing the insanity defense.

Sadly, on May 8, 1870 a dear uncle in the Massachusetts Gerry family, James Trecothick Austin, died at age 86 in Boston. James T. Austin married Catherine Gerry the eldest daughter of Founding Father, Elbridge Gerry. He was the Attorney General of Massachusetts 1832-1843, and authored the first full biography of his father-in-law, Elbridge Gerry. The Gerry family once again met in Massachusetts for a funeral reunion and the settling of an estate.

With the McFarland trial behind him and back in New York City, Elbridge began to close out his legal work to spend time with his family. On May 19 Elbridge T. Gerry appeared in court one more time before his summer holiday:

> Mr. Elbridge T. Gerry appeared today before Judge Cardozo to ask that the report of a referee be confirmed which forbids the Harlem Railroad Company to take possession of the land of Mr. Elbert S. Kip, situated between Fourth and Lexington avenues and Forty-sixth and Forty-seventh streets, valued at $100,000, for their use as a depot. The referee holds that inasmuch as it does not sufficiently appear that the Company cannot buy land in the same neighborhood, he reports against the appointment of commissioners, notwithstanding they may require the land in question for their accommodation. The decision was reversed.[8]

About the same time, Robert J. Livingston, Elbridge's father-in-law was, elected to the Board of Governors of the *Society of the New York Hospital* on May 18, ten days later after several busy and exhausting months, on May 28, 1870 Elbridge, Louisa and 2-year old daughter Margaret, joined Robert and Louisa Livingston on the steamship *Lafayette* and set sail to Havre, France for a well-deserved holiday in Europe.

While in Europe a disturbing article appeared in the June 19, 1870 *New York Times* titled *Desecration of Mr. Goelet's Retirement, the Nineteenth Street and Broadway House to Come Down.* Unfortunately for 70 year-old Uncle Peter Goelet his *Broadway Farm* stood in the way of the proposed extension of Madison Avenue to Broadway at Nineteenth and it was also included in the proposed widening of Broadway. The legislative bills for extending Madison Avenue to Nineteenth Street, just signed by the Governor, proposed that the improvement include destruction of the old land mark Goelet mansion. The article noted that Mr. Goelet "was not at all pleased with the encroachment by the powers that be and would leave the place of his long seclusion with reluctance."[9] Also living in the house with Uncle Peter Goelet were his sisters Jean Buchannan and Hannah Goelet Gerry (Elbridge T. Gerry's mother) and Elbridge's sister Jean. The large library collection was also in the old house because Elbridge had no other place to store his books. Uncle Peter Goelet refused to sell his property when approached by Boss Tweed. The *New York Times* reported on more than just "street improvements," indeed, the facts showed Boss Tweed's corrupt land speculation was at the center of the scheme. The *New York Times* reported:

> Following on the heels of the Broadway widening scheme comes the extension of Madison Avenue, a maneuver which is intended to benefit a few property owners who hold lots between Nineteenth and Twenty-third streets. The Ring, as usual, have been very extensive buyers hereabouts, and Boss Tweed purchased property lying on the north-east corner of Broadway and Twenty-first street, this valuable tract cost $600,000, an impartial commission considered it somewhat high, although it is less than the figure put down by the Tammany Hall clique, as they estimate the cost at nearly $3,500,000. The extension of Madison Avenue will meet at the corner of Nineteenth and Broadway, where an open square will be made on the present site of Peter Goelet's mansion. It is proposed to purchase this site for $250,000.[10]

In June 1870 a new law was passed that transferred title to the City of New York for all lands "taken" for the Madison Avenue extension. This effectively blocked Madison Avenue land speculation by Boss Tweed and his cohorts, who then abandoned the Madison Avenue "extension" and focused on "widening" Broadway. While litigation by land-owners over the amount of monetary awards for the City "to take" curb-side slices of their property continued until settlement in December 1871, Broadway was successfully widened without tearing down Peter Goelet's *Broadway Farm;* in fact only a curb-side slice of his property was taken for the widening. The *New York Times,* in April, 1874, summed up the corruption of Tweed and Hall:

> The public are beginning to see through the well-worn stock of misrepresentations used by the organs that lived on the bounty of Tweed and Hall. A reform administration found the net amount of the City and County debt on January 1, 1874 to be one hundred and six and one-third millions, or debt accumulated at the rate of three hundred and thirty-thousand per month. It suits the advocates of the municipal plunderers to represent them as the improvers of the City. What they really left us was new debt in the millions for furniture in the Court-house, the leveling and planting of the down-town parks, a section of boulevard, a bit of pier wall, a few big pipes, and streets, the wretchedness of whose paving and sewering could not be matched in the civilized world.[11]

Mid-summer 1870 was an anxious time for the family at the *Broadway Farm* and the Goelets likely left the City for their summer watering place at West Point on the Hudson River. Upon their return from Europe the Gerry family also retreated from the heat of New York City to the Highland Park, New Jersey estate of Robert and Louisa Livingston, the home where Louisa Gerry was raised with her brother Warren. Most New Yorkers abandoned the heat, smells and congestion of the city to seek relief in the countryside or seaside; most would not return to resume the business and social routines of city life until late September or early October.

By October, 1870 the Gerrys were back in New York rested and engaged in new and continuing endeavors. Louisa Gerry was pregnant with their second child and would limit her social calendar until after the baby was born in the spring of 1871. Meanwhile, the court calendar listed Elbridge T. Gerry as appearing at the 11:00 a.m. hearing session on October 10 on behalf of his uncle Peter Goelet who was suing Paul N. Spofford. This is a perfect example of the litigious nature of the real estate business on the scale and complexity of the Goelet holdings throughout New York City. This action was brought by plaintiff landlord Peter Goelet for a quarter of the year's rent accruing after May 1, 1868 on a lease for a term of twenty-one years from May 1, 1867 which was to be mutually terminated. The defendant Spofford wished to surrender the property and end the lease according to provisions of the agreement. This litigation was on the court calendar, on and off, from 1868-1873, with both parties arguing over technicalities, such as a "defective acknowledgement" document, or the document was not "prepared in proper form," or because "time had expired," or the calculation for the "amount of rent due" at the time of surrender was in dispute. Finally, even the court's own "certified Judgment Roll" was challenged because it was not signed by the Clerk of the Court.[12] After six years of litigation over endless technicalities a referee appointed by the court finally settled the case. This case garnered no public interest as it was routine real estate business; yet it exemplifies one of the significant legal strategies used throughout Elbridge T. Gerry's legal career, he was detail oriented almost to the extreme, a personal trait that was apparent to those who knew him or worked with him. Elbridge could nearly overwhelm a court proceeding with technical objections, motions and arguments. None were frivolous, in fact, it was the mind of a brilliant lawyer who left no stone unturned and seemed to relish the thrill of the research, the analysis of the facts, the composing of arguments and, indeed, engaging expert witnesses to testify. Elbridge T. Gerry was a formidable opponent in court, who, at age 33 was one of New York City's best attorneys.

On October 13 three days after the Spofford case was decided Elbridge T. Gerry attended the annual meeting of the *New York Medico-Legal Society* at the College of Physicians and Surgeons and was elected a *Trustee*. The first objective of the *Society* was to research difficult topics facing the courts and lawyers in cases that focused on medical issues, such as morbid impulses to homicide or alcoholism, the insanity defense, the need for a coroner in murder cases. There was a recommendation to research newspapers of the day that published stories of heinous crimes and in the same paper, published advertisements with wicked information as to the place, means and manner of committing just such a crime. The research was presented as a lecture open to the public and the lectures were subsequently published in the *Society's* journal. The second objective was to develop a method to educate medical specialists in the art of appearing as expert witnesses at trial; both doctors and lawyers were trained to ask and answer questions in the most useful and productive manner to a court proceeding. The third objective was to propose new state and local laws based on the research. The *Society's* committee members drafted the proposals into formal legislative language for consideration in the state Capital at Albany or the city's legislative council as appropriate. Elbridge T. Gerry's experience with highly publicized insanity and murder cases made him valuable as a committee member and also as a Trustee of the *New York Medico-Legal Society*.[13]

1870 would close as busy as it began with two cases, involving a commercial dispute over a debt paid by check, and a case of negligence. Elbridge T. Gerry lost both cases. The *Hecker's Bakery* case, an appeal from a lower court decision, was decided November 26, 1870 in favor of Angelina Seabrook who lived in a house with her husband and three children adjacent to the back of a lot owned by John Hecker, a baker. Mr. Hecker was building a stack of brick ovens at the back of the property as the first stage of building a bakery. Before the ovens were finished a violent storm blew them down toppling the bricks and mortar onto the Seabrook home. The damage was devastating with one child killed and Mrs. Seabrook seriously injured. There was considerable damage to the house. The argument on behalf of the Seabrook family was negligence on the part of Mr. Hecker who should have known about any defects in the construction of the ovens and should have taken precautions during the violent storm to protect neighbors. Elbridge T. Gerry argued that the violent storm lasted several days and was an act of God and not negligence. He further argued that even if the ovens were defective when built by Mr. Hecker's hired mechanics, if he was not told of the defects he could not be held liable. After argument the Court affirmed the earlier ruling in favor of the Seabrook family and awarded them $1,400.00 in damages.[14]

The second case was decided December 13, 1870 just twelve days before Christmas and Elbridge's 34th birthday. This is a case where Mr. Smith sold merchandise to Mr. Miller who paid with a draft note to be presented to J.K. Place and Company for a cash payment on the same day of the sale. When presented with the draft the company offered cash but Mr. Smith preferred to receive a check which he did not deposit into his bank until the next day. By the next day the J.K. Place and Company had gone out of business. Mr. Smith then sought payment from Mr. Miller who argued he was no longer liable for the debt. The court held that when a check is taken instead of cash money by one acting for others, as was done by the plaintiff, a delay of presentment of the check for a day is at the peril of the plaintiff. The proof is that the bank account of the Company was in good standing during the business hours of the day on which the check was issued and the cash was offered to Mr. Smith. If the check had been presented to the bank on the day it was received it would have been paid or certified as good, which would have been equivalent to payment. By Mr. Smith's delay and neglect, unless some evidence in explanation or excuse could be given, he made the check his own; the defendant Mr. Miller was discharged of the debt.[15] This small case has taken its place in legal literature for over a hundred years. Gerry's small but complex commercial debt case has been cited fifty-six times by other cases and in the 2011 *New York Jurisprudence* state legal encyclopedia and in New York law journals and legal treatises.

There are moments in one's life that begin an inalterable shift of direction neither foreseen nor understood at the time. For Elbridge T. Gerry the moment was the period from mid-1873 to mid-1874. The story does not begin as Elbridge's own but rather the story of Henry Bergh, who, like Elbridge, was raised with wealth and opportunities. Henry Bergh at age fifty-eight was well known in New York City where newspapers routinely followed his activities and lectures, no doubt Elbridge knew of Bergh and was familiar with his work. In 1871 Bergh found himself in need of legal counsel so he sought the best legal mind in New York City, thirty-four year old Elbridge T. Gerry whose prominent cases Bergh had read about in the papers.

Henry Bergh was born in New York City August 28, 1813 to Christian and Elizabeth Bergh, a wealthy ship building family. Henry attended Columbia College in New York but did not complete a degree. Instead he traveled to Europe, 1831-1836, where he dabbled in the arts and attempted a career in writing. In 1836 he married Catherine Matilda Taylor. Henry and his brother Christian Bergh Jr., took over the family ship business in New York City upon the retirement of their father. After his father's death in 1843, Henry cashed in his inheritance and became a man of privileged leisure and often traveled to Europe with his wife. Bergh's social circle included the political elite of his time. He supported abolitionist positions and shared this conviction with fellow New York resident, William Seward. When Seward joined Abraham Lincoln's cabinet as Secretary of State Bergh gained an appointment as legation secretary for the American delegation to Russia. He traveled about the city of St. Petersburg in his carriage and often observed the cruel mistreatment of horses, something he realized was common not only in European cities but also back home in New York City. After one year in Russia his health failed in the severe climate in St. Petersburg so Henry Bergh resigned his office in 1864 to return home. On his trip back to America Berg visited London, England to meet with the Earl of Harroby, the president of the *Royal Society for the Prevention of Cruelty to Animals.*

Shortly after his return to America from England, Henry Bergh began to make the rounds in New York City to contact friends and allies to whom he explained his plan to form a *Society for the Prevention of Cruelty to Animals.* When Berg felt he had sufficient support for his plan he announced a public lecture series to which there was a ground swell of support. Most of the social and political elite of the city and state signed a legislative petition to form the Society. Shortly thereafter on April 10, 1866 the New York State Assembly granted a Charter for the *American Society for the Prevention of Cruelty to Animals* (ASPCA). Henry Berg was soon on the street with a copy of the Charter in his pocket and a society badge on his coat. Eventually known as "Berghsmen" the Society's agents worked the streets, alleys, docks and numerous unsavory districts of the city. None of them however were able to outdo or outshine their leader. Tall and imposing in his frock coat and top hat Bergh became a familiar figure in the City.

In addition to his work on the street, Henry Bergh took his cause to the people through the mass media of the day Newspapers and magazines that published a flood of correspondence from him. He carried on a high profile dispute with, P.T. Barnum over the treatment of the animals in his shows menagerie. In the end Bergh's persistence and integrity eventually turned Barnum into a friend who would help to form the SPCA in Bridgeport, Connecticut.[16] In November, 1870 Henry Bergh took on a New York gang for illegal animal sporting:

> Fourth Ward police appeared at the Tombs yesterday morning in full force, having in their custody the thirty-four men arrested in Kit Burns' rat pit at No. 338 Water Street on the complaint of Mr. Bergh. The appearance of the prisoners was heralded by a large crowd. (*The Tombs is the colloquial name for the New York Halls of Justice and House of Detention which was designed by John Haveland in 1838 based on an engraving of an Egyptian mausoleum*) A more villainous lot of men and boys than those brought before the Magistrate cannot be imagined. Mr. Bergh stated that the proprietor of the rat pit, Christopher Keybourne, alias Kit Burns, was well known as a man who delighted in such sports, and made his living in the cruel torture of animals. Bergh demanded that Kit Burns and those arrested with him be punished to the full extent of the law as an example to others. The Judge accordingly held Kit Burns and two of his cohorts for trial.[17]

In most cities prior to the ASPCA horses that had fallen sick or had been injured in the streets were left to die in their tracks owing to the lack of a proper vehicle to transport them to hospitals for treatment. This difficulty was remedied by Mr. Bergh who designed and constructed an ambulance for transporting disabled animals.

While progress was being made in the treatment of city animals many horse owners, particularly commercial enterprises like horse-drawn delivery and taxi services, found Berg and his men to be over zealous and interfered with their business. The city newspapers had a great time with Henry Bergh and he became known as the "Great Meddler" based on cartoons published during his many years as president of the ASPCA. However, even bad publicity was good publicity if it kept Bergh's campaign in the public eye as a topic of conversation. Articles and cartoons became a regular means of opening the eyes of citizens who, while traversing the streets of New York, would now notice and pay attention to animal cruelty in the daily life of their own neighborhoods. Bergh himself was not above advertising in the newspapers to communicate with the public and to encourage support for the work of the ASPCA. Here is a December 1870 advertisement:

> "Fowl" Play – Sports Contrary to Law
> ASPCA, No.696 Broadway at Fourth-street
> To the Editor of the New York Times: The holiday season being near for the "sport," as it is termed, of tying fowls to stones, and otherwise, the undersigned would kindly, and in the spirit of humanity, remind all persons that it is contrary to law, and that this Society has taken necessary measures to enforce the same, by the arrest and punishment of offenders discovered in the violation thereof.
> Henry Bergh, President[18]

Two problems that demanded Henry Bergh's attention and energy led him to seek professional legal counsel for the ASPCA. First, the judiciary became an obstacle when it often refused to recognize Mr. Bergh's right to appear in a case, refused to accept the recorded judgment of scientific authorities, and refused to hear the testimony of medical experts testifying for the ASPCA in court. The second problem was the need for money to fund the multitude of ASPCA activities and to pay the agents on the streets of New York City. Mr. Bergh had given public lectures throughout 1870 to raise financial support for the Society, while also explaining and publicizing the work of the ASPCA to the public. Both issues came to a head in February, 1871 when Henry Bergh's ASPCA was named the sole beneficiaries in Louis Bonard's Will, it also revoked any inheritance for the Bonard family. There were several grounds on which the will was contested. First that at the time of its execution the testator was not of sound mind, second, that it creates a trust which is in conflict with the statute prohibiting the creation of perpetuities, third, that the terms of the revocation clause are faulty. Finally, that the act of incorporating the *Society for the Prevention of Cruelty to Animals* does not authorize it to take real property. By March 1871 Mr. Bergh had identified Elbridge T. Gerry as the lawyer to defend the ASPCA.

About the same time on February 8, 1871 the *Bar Association of the City of New York* held its monthly meeting at 20 West Twenty-Seventh Street. The Executive Committee reported on the status of the organization for the year and announced the appointment of a Library Committee, consisting of James Emott, Aaron J. Vanderpoel, Elbridge T. Gerry, Charles A. Hunt and William R. Martin. On behalf of the Committee Mr. Gerry called attention to the fact that the Library Committee was in need of funds. He then invited bar members to contribute with a subscription fee of at least $50 for use of the library. Following the approval of the Library proposal the following motion was proposed and discussed for the remainder of the evening:

> *Mr. Sewell* moved that the Executive Committee be instructed to have the house of the association opened on Sunday as on other days.
>
> *Mr. Gerard* opposed the motion, and thought that six days and nights in the week were enough to work. He had felt the benefit of the rest of the Seventh day, and he urged young men to adhere to the principle, and particularly he hoped that his building would be closed on Sunday.
>
> *Mr. McDermott* called attention to the fact that there was a law forbidding work on Sunday; besides this, he saw with pain that there was a growing disposition among the people to violate the Sabbath. He thought it would be injurious to have the people learn that the *Bar Association* kept open their house on Sunday.
>
> *Judge Barrett* noted that this Club was a social affair, and not always a place for work. We have light literature here, and why should not members be permitted to come here on Sunday and read or meet his brother lawyers?
>
> *Mr. Codair* agreed and believed it should be left to the individual as to whether to come to the Bar's house or not on Sunday. This is our property, we have a right here.
>
> *Mr. Smith* urged that the character of the membership has already undergone close scrutiny, and each gentleman was known to be a moral man at least. If they see fit to work on Sunday they do not violate any law of the state. Contracts are void which are made on that day, but labor is permitted.[19]

The motion was passed with great applause and members soon after adjourned the meeting. At the next monthly meeting of the Bar Association on March 15, the President stated that a new subscription had been opened for a larger Library Fund of $3,000. He noted that the appeal had not as yet been circulated generally among the Association but $1,200 had been raised among those present when the matter was proposed. Elbridge T. Gerry reported from the *Library Committee* a request for any old volumes that any member might have, as useful both in filling up imperfect sets on hand and available for exchange. He also reported a gift from Judge Edmonds of 30 volumes of carefully selected cases and points. The meeting closed with a communication from the *Medico-Legal Society* that appointed the President of the Bar Association an honorary member of their Association during his term of office. As a Trustee of one Association and a member of the Executive Committee of the other, Elbridge T. Gerry was likely instrumental in the proposal to establish the honorary "joint membership" of the respective Association Presidents. Nurturing life-time collegial associations was considered a civic duty by Elbridge T. Gerry as seen in his leadership of the 1857 class of *Columbia College* alumni throughout his lifetime.

While working to establish and develop the *Bar Association Library* Elbridge T. Gerry was contacted by Henry Bergh who requested his legal representation of a significant case, the *Bonard Will* dispute. This was the test case for whether and under what "trusts and estates" law a non-profit association like the ASPCA was eligible for private funding through testamentary gifts that often result in revocation of a surviving family's inheritance.

The June 25, 1871 fifth *Annual Report of the ASPCA* noted that Elbridge T. Gerry had joined the Association and was the new, indeed the first, legal counsel representing the ASPCA and would take over the *Bonard Will* case. As a member and Trustee of the *Medico-Legal Society,* Elbridge T. Gerry was able to quickly identify and skillfully examine expert witnesses in the fields of insanity and trusts and estates for the Bonnard case. Additionally, both Bergh and Gerry recognized the need for expert witnesses in ASPCA cases relating to veterinary medicine, the humane standards of care and treatment for animals, and the health and sanitation codes of New York City governing animals. Like his father-in-law, Robert J. Livingston, who shared a dedication to charitable and civic duty through the New York Hospital Board, Elbridge T. Gerry had found his second friend and colleague in humanitarian endeavors, Henry Bergh and the ASPCA. His professional association with Henry Bergh was the genesis of a shift in the focus and time of thirty-four year old Elbridge, who in 1874, would initiate a new Society that became his sustaining and passionate purpose for the remainder of his public life.

Elbridge worked diligently through March and April of 1871 researching the Bonard case history and preparing for the initial hearing in early May. At the same time his wife Louisa was in her ninth month of a healthy pregnancy and due any day. The Bonard case excited Elbridge as did the anticipated birth of his second child who would join two-and-one half year old Margaret in the Gerry/Livingston household. The trial opened on May 6, and Angelica Livingston Gerry was born on May 9, 1871. She was named after Louisa's Aunt Angelica Livingston, Robert J. Livingston's sister. The next few months were spent in preparation for the trial, handling assorted transactional legal matters and enjoying time with family. Hearings in the Bonard case continued through October 14, 1871 when the trial opened with witness after witness testifying to Mr. Bonard's eccentricities and beliefs, all in an effort to determine his competency in the weeks before his death when he changed his will to benefit the ASPCA.

With Elbridge T. Gerry handling all legal issues for the ASPCA, Henry Bergh was free to lecture and write letters to the Editor of the *New York Times.* He did not shy from publicly naming New York businessmen who failed to protect their horses. Just as he had taken on P.T. Barnum in the press in the summer of 1871 Henry Bergh challenged Commodore Cornelius Vanderbilt. In a private letter Bergh enclosed an anonymous note to the ASPCA accusing Vanderbilt of animal cruelty. Not surprisingly though, Bergh also sent the letters to the *New York Times* on September 5 thereby making public the accusation against one of New York City's wealthiest and most well-respected business leaders. Commodore Vanderbilt responded in a private letter which again, Bergh sent to the *New York Times* for publication; here are the letter from Vanderbilt to Bergh followed by Bergh's published response:

> Dear Sir: Your kind note of the 30th enclosing an anonymous letter is this moment received. It went to Saratoga and missed me. I am much obliged for your kind attention. This morning I saw the Superintendent, and he informs me that it was an accident that occurred at midnight, in which the two horses were killed; I have two good men to attend to my horses and stables. My instructions are not to overwork the horses, and to be particular never to permit anyone to misuse in any way the animal whom we all love so much. I feel it the duty of every good citizen to render you all the aid in their power in your efforts to protect the animal from unkind treatment, and I assure you I highly appreciate your efforts to do this.
> Very respectfully yours,
> C. Vanderbilt[20]

Henry Bergh's reply was not just a description of Vanderbilt's specific wrongdoing but an open letter to all citizens about the value of horses to society and the duty to treat them humanely. It was carefully drafted, perhaps with advice from legal counsel, Elbridge T. Gerry, and was not published in the *New York Times* until three months later in December 1871:

> Dear Sir: It has been a privilege of few men to benefit the State and country in relations to progress and internal development more than yourself... Great wealth has resulted to you from these achievements, and one, if not the greatest, element of success, I venture to assert, has been the horse. To this silent, generous, plodding servant and agent of civilization, you owe, along with the rest of us, more than half the benefits resulting from your genius... (*Bergh describes the use of horses in mines, farming, delivery carts, and personal and public-drawn transportation*) Your course of three miles each way, (*Vanderbilt's New York City horse route*) making eighteen miles per day, a distance of strain which is dreadful cruelty to inflict, and exceeding by eight miles the established rate known in other countries... Your feed, which is nearly similar to that of other public stables is

> wholly inadequate. Entire oats and hay of the best quality are absolutely imperative, instead of the chopped and oft times acrid mess which is given them... These along with bad shoeing, form the principal abuses against your toiling dependents; and would you but issue orders for their immediate and total reform, I venture to affirm that enhanced profits, and a more profound approval of conscience would ensue. I have enjoyed your acquaintance since my boyhood, and I indulge the belief that you will attribute no other purpose to me than that which I profess and for which I have made and am making many personal sacrifices in my efforts to alleviate the miseries of those humble creatures confided by heaven to the care and compassion of mankind. Henry Bergh, President[21]

Open letters became an effective tool of the ASPCA, garnering public respect and the support of New York City's elite society as they headed toward the emerging *Progressive Era* of the 1890's.

In addition to legal work that included the continuing Goelet v Spofford rent dispute that appeared on the December 1871 court calendar, Elbridge T. Gerry was working with a committee of the *Medico-Legal Society* to review State Statutes preventing abortions. Abortions were designated as criminal and Gerry was to draft proposed legislation to reform the existing New York laws. His work as a delegate to the 1867 *Constitutional Convention* that revised the New York Constitution proved most valuable in this endeavor. On December 22, 1871 the *Committee* submitted the ten-page proposed legislation to the Society, which in turn submitted it to the General Assembly in Albany, New York and in just three months the revision was passed into law.

The year 1871 ended on a happy note for the extended Gerry-Gallatin family. Frederick and Almy Gerry Gallatin, who lost their first son in December 1869 welcomed a new baby boy, Rolaz Horace Gallatin, on New Year's Eve 1871 and joined his sister Almy, their mother's namesake, in the warm family circle. Sisters-in-law Louisa Gerry and Almy Gallatin now shared two toddlers each and looked forward to their children being playmates and friends for a lifetime.

The year 1872 began with new court cases for Elbridge T. Gerry. The first case was taken in January to represent an accused murderer, Edward S. Stokes, who shot James Fisk, Jr. With the advice of counsel at the first hearing on January 20, Stokes told the court that he was not ready to plead guilty or not guilty so the judge postponed the trial until February 15. Elbridge argued for the defense that it was not the bullet which Stokes had in fact fired that killed Fisk, but rather it was the surgery itself that killed him while doctors attempted to extract the bullet. Gerry also argued that the Jury was illegally constituted due to a failure to meet legal rules and that the jury had been influenced to the prejudice of his client Stokes by the persistent efforts to procure an indictment against Stokes for conspiracy. Gerry advised his client not to discuss the case with anyone and to not take the stand to testify. Gerry further warned that if Stokes did speak to anyone about the case that he would resign as his attorney. By late April Stokes could no longer contain himself and gave a rambling statement to the *New York Times* appealing for public understanding. Gerry kept his word and resigned from the case.[22]

Elbridge was also representing another case, a dispute between a husband and wife over payments for debts between their separate estates. The significant issue in this case was technical, how did the common law rule that husbands and wives cannot testify against one another apply, when as here, they were the only antagonistic parties in the case. It required an unusual application of the law where a spouse testifies on his or her own behalf and yet they are essentially testifying against their spouse. Elbridge won this case on behalf of the appellant wife, Louise C. Southwick, because the Judge refused to allow the husband to testify on his own behalf (against his wife) about information they discussed prior to 1867 when the old law protected their private conversations.[23] This case has been cited as precedent by fifty-five cases, in the *Harvard Law Review*, and by the *American Law Reports* a compilation of scholarly articles discussing major legal topics.

During the *Southwick* trial in April tragedy struck the Gerry family. Louisa Gerry was two months pregnant with their third child, perhaps not even aware of the pregnancy at such an early stage, when on April 25 their first child Margaret Louisa died at the tender age of three years and eight months. There is no record of her illness only a published *New York Evening Post* death notice. Louisa and Elbridge had mourned the loss of Almy Gerry Gallatin's baby son just three years earlier and now they would be consoled in their own loss by Almy and Frederick Gallatin. The pregnancy of Louisa and the joyful presence of one-year old Angelica helped the family during their period of grief. Several weeks later a summer holiday at the Livingston farm estate at Lake Delaware, New York provided a pleasant retreat for the family. There is no record of a voyage to Europe in 1871, which in future years became the family tradition.

Elbridge returned to the therapy of hard work on the ASPCA's *Bonard Will* case, which he argued at trial in late May defending his client against charges of insanity. The decision was announced on June 26, 1871 affirming that Bonard was sane at the time he revoked his earlier will and the ASPCA received the $20,000 gift. A paper written in 1940 for a course on historical method discussed the trial of John Brown who was convicted of treason and hanged. The start of the *Civil War* was attributed to that moment in history. During the trial sympathizers sent a telegram to Brown's lawyer stating that the defendant's mother was insane and they therefore entered a plea of insanity. Brown however, rose in court and overruled his attorneys and withdrew the plea. No convincing evidence was ever produced to prove Brown's insanity. The paper notes that Brown had the same beliefs as Bonard and quotes from the Bonard decision:

> The mere fact that he believed in the forcible abolition of slavery is certainly no proof; for one may believe in Spiritualism, or in the transmigration of souls after death into the bodies of animals; and these opinions are not evidence of insanity which legally consists of delusion of fact and object, not belief.[24]

In 2006 the *Harvard Law Review* referred to Bonard, among many other cases, to show how judges continue the struggle to draft opinions for insanity decisions that use clear yet simple language to refute insanity as the basis for challenging the probate of a will.

> Indeed one court approved the will of a believer in metempsychosis (*Bonard*), who left the bulk of his estate to the ASPCA, the judge opining that "it was a strangely self-interested, not insane, act.[25]

There are no other cases reported in 1872 for Elbridge T. Gerry except for a small real estate matter he handled on behalf of his uncle Peter Goelet, *Goelet v N.J. Burchell* that was settled in early June. After the death of little Margaret it was important for the Gerry family to ensure the health and well-being of Louisa Livingston during her pregnancy. On November 4, 1872 she gave birth to a healthy baby girl, Mabel Gerry, who joined her one and one-half year-old sister Angelica in the Gerry family. After five years of marriage, the births of three children, and the death of one and still living with Louisa's parents at 184 Fifth Avenue, Elbridge and Louisa decided it was time to find a home of their own. Fortunately, with a new baby and a toddler, the Gerrys were delighted to move to one of two adjacent townhouses on east Forty-Eighth Street where Louisa's parents moved-in next door to ensure that the close family ties and daily support of the household would not be interrupted. The growing Gerry family would now have privacy plus the much needed space for raising their girls. Elbridge continued to keep his growing personal library at the *Broadway Farm* mansion at Nineteenth and Broadway, where the collection grew over the next two decades.

January to June, 1873 was an intense period for Elbridge T. Gerry when he represented his second round of big cases on behalf of the ASPCA, known collectively as the *Stage Horse Cases*. The first case was brought by the *Broadway & East Side Stage Companies* on behalf of all New York City horse-drawn stage coach companies. The *Stage Companies* were seeking an injunction from the

Court to prevent Henry Bergh and the ASPCA agents from stopping their coaches to arrest the drivers for cruelty to their horses thereby disrupting the company's business and interfering with passengers. The court held that it could not enjoin the ASPCA from arresting drivers or servants of the companies for a clear violation of the law. However, the law itself prohibited or enjoined the ASPCA for taking custody of the horses or interfering with the passengers themselves. Simply stopping the coach to make an arrest was not itself an interference with passengers but rather an inconvenience. The second case in June of 1873 emerged from the first case when the same companies accused the ASPCA of violating the injunction against stopping a coach without a warrant to arrest the driver for an animal cruelty misdemeanor. The court held that the act of creating the ASPCA was designed to empower "agents of the court" to use their judgment and expertise to enforce the laws and this could be done without a warrant when the misdemeanor was done in the presence of the agent. The third case was a charge of false arrest against Henry Bergh by the driver of a coach who was personally stopped by Bergh, a private citizen. This case was a pivotal turning point in clarifying for the public, the Stage Companies, and the ASPCA, the power vested in the *Society* to enforce animal protection laws. Elbridge T. Gerry's clear understanding of the law, his meticulous framing of the issues, and his detailed legal arguments were singularly effective in confirming that the enactment of the Legislature was sufficient to confer on the ASPCA agent the status of an *ex officio* conservator of the peace equal to a constable at common law or a police officer, thereby empowering Henry Bergh and his agents to enforce the laws by making arrests for offenses against the animal protection act.[26] Thereafter ASPCA agents wore their signature badges on their coats when on duty to clearly identify their official capacity to enforce the law.

The legal community in America learned on May 9, 1873 that the Chief Justice of the Supreme Court of the United States, Salmon P. Chase had died. In the Court of General Sessions in New York City, as in many courts across the country, a motion was made to adjourn the court for the day out of respect for the Chief Justice. The motion was seconded by Elbridge T. Gerry who was present in the courtroom for a hearing:

> During the whole of his distinguished judicial career he had borne an unsullied reputation, and had always transmitted the ermine to his successors without blot or stain. It would be vain to attempt to eulogize the life and actions of the deceased, for his reputation had been so pure and spotless, and his conduct so dignified, that language failed to express the sorrow of the people at the loss sustained by the nation in the death of the distinguished jurist. Still, it was fitting

> that a court holding the important position of that I now address should participate in the general sorrow by adjourning.[27]

Judge Sutherland stated that he quite agreed with the remarks of Mr. Gerry and thought it eminently proper that the motion should be granted and adjourned court for the day.

After providing two years of ground-breaking legal counsel to the ASPCA, which clarified the *Society's* purpose in New York City and empowered its agents through a strong legal presence in the courtroom, Henry Bergh was more than ready to honor Elbridge T. Gerry. Not only was the Society in a stable and strong position, Bergh himself was grateful for the luxury of time to administer the enforcement program, to continue his lectures, and to engage in fund raising efforts, all made possible by Elbridge T. Gerry taking on the heavy mantle of legal counsel to the ASPCA. Henry Bergh presented Elbridge with a silver vase designed by Tiffany & Company, engraved with the words, "Presented by the American Society for the Prevention of Cruelty to Animals to Elbridge T. Gerry, Esq., in recognition of his zealous professional services in the cause of humanity." A presentation letter dated June 15 from Bergh to Gerry read:

> Dear Sir,
> At a meeting of the Executive Committee of this Society, the following resolution was offered and unanimously adopted: That the President be authorized to cause a suitable testimonial to be made, expressive of the grateful recognition on the part of this society of the able and meritorious professional services of Mr. Elbridge T. Gerry, in the cause to which it is devoted. In the performance of this agreeable duty I have endeavored, while carrying out the views of the committee, to illustrate through the medium of a silver vase the chronology and purposes of the society. One of its earliest efforts, as you may remember, was directed at amelioration of the treatment of a creature popularly regarded as one of the lowest in the order of animated nature, but which the learned Agassiz has declared to be among the most sensitive of animals, namely the turtle. Hence upon the backs of four of this race of beings the superstructure rests. Upon a quadrilateral pedestal are seen, in bas relief and otherwise, the several representative orders as classified by zoology: and as a crowning glory to the work, that paragon of animals, the horse, is shown in high artistic beauty on the basin. While thus attempting a brief description of the token offered, the committee would not withhold its commendation of the taste and skill, which the house of Tiffany & Co. has manifested in the execution of it. There but remains for me to ask you, in the name of the society I represent, to accept it as an expression of its appreciation of

> your eminent attainments and devotion to the humane and civilizing labor it has in charge. I save the honor to be yours,
>
> Henry Bergh, President

Gerry's response to the Society:

> Dear Sir,
> The slight professional aid I may have hitherto rendered this Society was to me a matter of pleasure rather than duty. The cause embodied in it, and impersonated by yourself, so commends itself to every right-thinking person in the community that its own humanity has always been its strongest plea. The numerous decisions in its favor in the legal tribunals are simply the result of just applications of the law in response to its claims for mercy to the defenseless brute. Indeed, they seem to illustrate the uprightness of the judiciary rather than the ability of counsel, for the weakest advocate becomes necessarily able when pleading for a cause so just and righteous. The superb gift of the society I shall ever prize and value. Its design, which so admirably illustrates the work of the institution, is a speaking tribute to the artistic mind which planned it, while its execution is certainly a marvel of art and beauty. I beg you will convey to the Executive Committee of the society my full appreciation of this elegant compliment, and of their flattering resolution which accompanied it.
>
> With great respect, Elbridge T. Gerry[28]

The summer of 1873 not only bestowed the well-deserved accolades of the ASPCA on Elbridge T. Gerry, but also the pleasing news that his wife Louisa was once again pregnant with a baby due in November. As in most years when Louisa was pregnant, Elbridge refrained from taking new cases of any import, indeed he is not listed on any of the New York court calendars for the remainder of 1873. The shared family life of the Gallatins and Gerrys was once again bound together with new babies. Frederick and Almy Gerry Gallatin welcomed a daughter, Jean Buchanan Gallatin in September 1873. Within two months, on November 10, 1873 Elbridge and Louisa welcomed another daughter, Lillian Gerry. Both families were in good health and they quietly closed out the year celebrating Elbridge T. Gerry's thirty-sixth birthday on December 25, 1873 a happy Christmas day.

Elbridge T. Gerry was a founding member of *The Bar Association of the City of New York* and was Chairman of the Library Committee to establish the library.

Henry Bergh
Founder of the Society for the Prevention of Cruelty to Animals

Elbridge T. Gerry was Counsel to the SPCA for decades and was awarded a loving cup by the Society for his life-long dedication.

Etching of Elbridge T. Gerry in court arguing in defense of Daniel McFarland who murdered his wife's lover, Albert Richardson, a writer for the Tribune newspaper and the employee of Horace Greeley and his partner, Whitelaw Reid, the uncle of Louisa Gerry.

The famous 1870 case was sensational and the use of the insanity defense was creatively used by Elbridge T. Gerry.

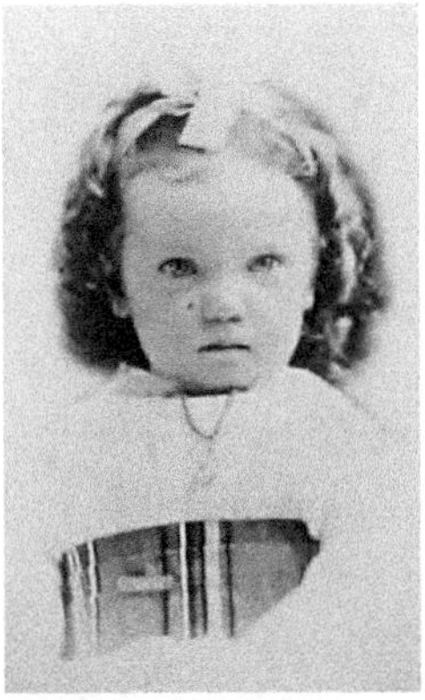

Margaret "Pearl" Gerry died unexpectedly at age 4

Margaret on a pony ride at Lake Delaware with her Nanny

Margaret in a stroller at Lake Delaware Farm with her Nanny.

Angelica Mabel

Elbridge and Louisa were blessed with two more daughters in 1871 and 1872.

5

GERRY'S SOCIETY

Childhood, who like an April morn appears,
sunshine and rain, hopes clouded o'er with fears.
C. Churchill, *Gotham, Book I*

The second half of the 1870's were the defining years in Elbridge T. Gerry's personal and professional life. He enjoyed the birth of his two sons, who happily joined three older sisters, Angelica, Mabel and Lillian. Elbridge became more selective about which cases to represent over the next few years and used his time judiciously. Gerry's financial security as a successful lawyer afforded him choices about the course of his life and that of his children and most notably, choices about his role in society at large.

His mother, Hannah Goelet Gerry, now fifty nine and his aunt Jean Buchanan Goelet seventy-two, along with Uncle Peter seventy-five, continued to be Elbridge's spiritual and philanthropic mentors, even as the elderly siblings lived quietly at the *Broadway Farm*. His mother and aunt actively participated in their Episcopal parish, Trinity Church, to support Indian tribes in the Dakotas with education and health care and paying for missionary expenses. Along with Sarah Goelet, their brother Robert Goelet's wife, the three ladies were members of the *Niobrara League* of New York in 1874, a branch of the *Women's Auxiliary* to the Board of Missions of the Episcopal Church. It held regular meetings on the second Thursday of each month from November to May in the Sunday-school room of the Church of the Transfiguration. All Episcopal Churches in New York City had their own League and all were collectively managed by an Executive Board. The President of the Board was Mrs. John Jacob Astor III (Charlotte), New York's up and coming social maven. Her ability to garner the financial support of New York's elite was critical to the success of the Indian Missions of the Episcopal Church. Mrs. Astor actively supported many charities including the *New York Hospital* during the years when Robert J. Livingston and Elbridge T. Gerry were on that *Hospital's* Board. Elbridge's philanthropic circles expanded over the coming decades as would his participation in the City's elite social life.

There are only two cases that are not related to the *American Society for the Prevention of Cruelty to Animals* reported for Elbridge T. Gerry in 1874, one in March and the other in November. Between January and March the *Wolfe v Burke* case was prepared, argued and decided, but then it was immediately appealed with a final decision on March 24. Elbridge represented the defendant Hudson G. Wolfe in an effort to enjoin D.H. Burke from trademark infringement. Wolfe lost in the lower court decision so Elbridge appealed the case for a review of the trademark issue and the court's injunction.

In 1871 plaintiff on appeal, D.H. Wolfe, sold gin under the family name started by his father Udolpho Wolfe in 1848 when he began selling old Holland gin under the name of "Wolfe's Aromatic Schiedam Schnapps." The words in the name were intended and used by the Wolfe family as their *trademark*. In 1871 Burke commenced the sale of an article of gin under the name of "Hudson G. Wolf's Bell Schnapps," the word *schnapps* being adopted with the intent to increase sales because of its use by Udolpho Wolfe. Mr. Burke's schnapps gin was sold in square bottles with labels recommending it as a medicine.

In 1872, Elbridge's client, Hudson G. Wolfe, circulated among the plaintiff Burke's customer's circulars claiming that Burke was infringing the Wolfe trademark and threatened to sue Burke to enjoin and restrain him from selling his gin under the name of *schnapps*, to the injury of Gerry's client. However, Burke managed to sue Wolfe first and won an injunction perpetually enjoining Wolfe "from interfering with Burke's business by threats, circulars, law suits, or injunctions in this State or elsewhere," and further, "that Burke's own trademark name, devices, circulars, bottles and packages" were properly and lawfully used and did not infringe Wolfe's rights, although the trade names were similar.[1]

Elbridge T. Gerry appealed the permanent injunction and sought recognition of Wolfe's trademark name, at least as to the use of the word *schnapps*. The judge was not sympathetic to either party. To Wolfe (Gerry's client) on the permanent injunction to sue, the Judge stated, "it is no ground for equitable interference (a court hearing) that the decision may result in determining the law in a way which will, or may, have the effect of preventing suits between parties. To Burke, the Judge stated, "A party who, while he has avoided liability for the infringement of another's trademark, yet has adopted a course calculated to secure a portion of the good-will of the other's business, will not be regarded with favor by a court of equity." And finally, to both Wolfe and Burke, the Judge stated, "It seems that a business which is, to a certain extent a fraud upon the public, such as the palming off of an alcoholic beverage in common use exclusively as a medicine for certain diseases under a name not generally understood by the community, is not entitled to the aid of a court of equity, and that name will not be protected by trademark."[2] This decision has been cited in subsequent litigation fifty times through the year 2009.

While Gerry was representing the Wolfe gin case in early 1874 the ASPCA was confronted with an unexpected case that required Elbridge T. Gerry's skills as a lawyer and his empathy as a father. Cruelty to a young girl was, for the first time, brought before civil authorities for help in a time when such cruelty was common place. In fact between 1820 and 1870 as the nation experienced the industrial revolution, the Civil War and the onset of a massive tide of immigration, the population of New York City increased to over a million people, half of whom were foreign born. Public and private service systems were overwhelmed, riots were frequent, crime was rampant and child cruelty and exploitation were as common as the sixteen-hour work day. In January 1874 in a New York City neighborhood called *Hell's Kitchen* a rooming-house janitress told Etta Wheeler, a church worker, about a case of child cruelty. Dedicated and compassionate, Mrs. Wheeler made discreet inquiries and determined to rescue the abused child, a little girl named Mary Ellen. When other charitable and service agencies declined to intervene, Wheeler approached Mr. Bergh's *Society for the Prevention of Cruelty to Animals.* She recognized that a *Society* sympathetic to cruelty to animals would surely understand and assist with protecting an abused child. Mr. Bergh turned immediately to Elbridge T. Gerry, his legal counsel, stating, "No time is to be lost – instruct me how to proceed."[3] After researching the law Elbridge T. Gerry made clever use of an obscure section of *habeas corpus* to secure the ASPCA's legal standing to intervene. Mary Ellen became the "model case" for the first child protective intervention at a time when interference with sacrosanct parental rights was frowned upon. Within forty-eight hours of Wheeler's initial report an investigation was conducted, a petition filed, a protective removal of the child successfully completed, a hearing commenced, a temporary placement arranged and a criminal prosecution was being prepared.

On April 9 Elbridge appeared in court along with little Mary Ellen, Henry Bergh, and the ASPCA agent who had taken the child into custody under authority of a special warrant. Elbridge described Mary Ellen to the court as a bright little girl with features indicating unusual mental capacity but with a care-worn, stunted, and prematurely old look. Her apparent condition of health as well as her scanty wardrobe indicated a need for a change of custody to improve her condition and safety. The couple who had been caring for the child, the Connellys, made no appearance at this first public court hearing. Mary Ellen made her own statement in court, as reported in the newspapers of the day:

> My name is Mary Ellen. I don't know how old I am; my mother and father are both dead; I call Mrs. C momma; I have never had but one pair of shoes or stockings this winter; I have never been allowed to go out... except in the night time, and only in the yard to use the outdoor privy; my bed at night is only a piece of carpet stretched on the floor underneath a window and I sleep in my little undergarment with a quilt over me; I am never allowed to play with other children; momma has been in the habit of whipping me almost every day; she used to whip me with a twisted whip of rawhide; the whip always left black and blue marks on my body; I have now on my head two black and blue marks which were made by momma with the whip, and a cut on the left side of my forehead which was made by a pair of scissors in momma's hand; she struck me with the scissors and cut me; I have no recollections of ever having been kissed by momma; I have never been taken on momma's lap or caressed or petted; I never dared speak to anybody, because if I did I would get whipped; I have never had any more clothing than I have on at present; I have seen stockings and other clothes in our room, but I am not allowed to put them on; whenever momma went out, I was locked up in the bedroom; I don't know for what I was whipped; momma never said anything when she whipped me; I do not want to go back to live with momma because she beats me so.[4]

Mary Ellen was determined by investigators to be eight-years old and to have been placed with a monetary stipend in the home of Francis and Mary Connelly when she was a toddler and was said to be the illegitimate child of Mrs. Connelly's former husband. The *Grand Jury* examined the Connellys, Mary Ellen, Etta Wheeler, members of the ASPCA, and all other witnesses involved in the case. On April 14 indictments were issued against Mary Connelly for assault and battery with intent to do bodily harm and she was sent to the *Tombs,* tried and sent to jail for one year. Mary Ellen was placed in a loving home and later married and raised a family of her own and died at age ninety-two in 1956.

Henry Bergh's statement to the *Grand Jury* was to make clear to everyone that his involvement in the Mary Ellen case was prompted by his duty as a humane citizen and that in no sense had he acted in his official capacity as President of the ASPCA, noting he was none-the-less determined to avail himself of such means as the law placed within his power to prevent the too frequent cruelties practiced on children.[5]

The Mary Ellen case prompted New York papers to expand coverage of the plight of the City's abused children. Indeed, by April 10 the City's *Ways and Means Committee* had a bill before it seeking a large appropriation of excise funds for fifty-five City charitable institutions. The papers reported that the funding requests totaled $362,000.00 and were initiated by the Mary Ellen case. This effort proved conclusively how inadequate some of New York's proud charitable institutions were at fulfilling their intended missions. The newspapers berated the charities for seeking money on the notoriety of Mary Ellen:

> Although the little waif Mary Ellen and her heartless and inhuman step-mother have been in court some seven or eight times, and the press have discussed the matter so well, it is a singular fact that not a single official connected with any of the city's charitable institutions, who so regularly apply to the people of the State for their annual stipend, have deemed it within their province to appear in court upon any single occasion while the case was being investigated; neither did they have the curiosity to ascertain why the ASPCA, the animal cruelty society, was participating in the case. Unlike the child services charities, the ASPCA had never asked for, nor received since its formation in 1866, a cent either from Federal or State governments. It not only accomplishes its own noble work in a thorough and effectual manner, but finds time and means to do the work of those who, instead of being invisible, should be the first to aid and assist in all cases of a similar character.[6]

In late May the ASPCA's involvement with the Mary Ellen case was successfully resolved just as the cool spring days slipped into hot, humid summer days. The Gerrys joined the annual exodus from the City seeking fresher air, relaxation, and relief from the social stresses. Elbridge T. Gerry's daughters were aged four, three and two, and not yet in school. Their mother, Louisa, cared for her active household with the help of her mother who lived next door; both women and children were no doubt ready to escape the approaching heat and smells of a nineteenth century summer in New York City. Sailing to Europe was out of the question with such young children so the Gerrys traveled up the Hudson River to Saratoga Springs north of Albany, New York for the summer. Two hotels in Saratoga drew the New York social set, one was the *Grand Union Hotel* and the other the *Broadway Hotel.* Lake Saratoga provided water sports and areas for family picnics. The Hudson River was just a carriage ride to the east where colleges competed in crew races. Traveling up the Hudson by train or steamboat from New York City were comfortable, reliable means of family travel which the Gerry's enjoyed.

At summers end, as was his habit, Elbridge was back at work in New York City by early fall to attend the October 10 meeting of the Executive Committee of the ASPCA. He was back in the courtroom November 10 for the decision of the *Wenzler v People* case, a defense against petit larceny that was tried before three police justices. Elbridge appealed the initial decision against his client for theft by challenging the constitutional law upon which the three police judges were appointed. Once again, Elbridge left no stone unturned in the defense of his client, he researched every aspect of procedural technicalities in addition to the substantive law relative to the original charges. The court ruled that the police judges were appointed within the meaning of the New York State Constitution and the lower court ruling was affirmed. The judge's majority opinion insightfully comments on the mind and temperament of Elbridge T. Gerry, both the intense, thorough man and the brilliant lawyer:

> The first of the questions presented has been discussed at length, and with infinite research, and much ability, carrying the inquiry as to the history of the office of justice of the peace, and to its nature and functions, back to the period of its origin in England, about the middle fourteenth century. Interesting as such inquiries are we are inclined to think that the meaning of the language employed by the people of the State in 1869, to express their will in respect to their judicial system, does not demand of us to follow this line of examination.[7]

Nonetheless, the Chief Judge and one other judge on the panel *dissented* from the majority opinion and agreed with Elbridge's historical argument. The dissent stated:

> An earlier case had declared a manifest conflict between the statute in question and the constitution. This case presents a far more marked and distinct departure from, and disregard of the Constitution than the earlier case. Here there can be hardly a pretext, certainly no plausible argument, in support of the claim that an act as general and radical as this, in changes effected in the law abolishing and dissolving the existing *Police Courts of Special Sessions of the Peace (among others)*... and providing for the appointment of ten police justices for the city at large (*among others*)... is expressed by or embraced within the terms of the title of the act. The court was not well constituted, and the act under which it was organized was void. Judgment should be reversed.[8]

This case has been cited in subsequent litigation nineteen times though 1953 and in a 1996 law review article about the quest by the Court of Appeals for principled decision-making.

On November 25, 1874 the final arguments in the continuing *Stage Horse Cases* litigation was held. During his examination of the horse vendor witnesses Elbridge T. Gerry, in an attempt to be facetious about their horse trade, described in detail the condition of maltreated horses used by the Stage companies:

> Although a horse might be sprung-kneed, spavined, foundered, hoof-cracked, swivel-eyed, sore-breasted, and in fact, afflicted with all the ills to which horse flesh is heir, it would be to the benefit of the animal thus endowed to make him

> drag a heavy, crowded stage through the City all day... *is that not what the Stage companies do... ?*[9]

At the December 5 monthly meeting of the ASPCA the decision "against" the *Stage Horse Companies* was announced to the membership. The fine of $450.00 imposed by the court and paid to the *Society* was shared with two out-of-state ASPCA's in Oregon and New Hampshire. Before the meeting adjourned three new members were elected to the ASPCA, one of whom was Frederic Gallatin, the nephew of an ASPCA co-founder, James Gallatin, and the brother-in-law of Elbridge T. Gerry with whom he valued sharing time in civic endeavors.

As the Christmas holiday approached Elbridge T. Gerry was haunted by the Mary Ellen *child cruelty* case, especially since he continued to battle *animal cruelty* as legal counsel to the ASPCA, a cause to which he remained dedicated. He had three daughters of his own and had lost little Margaret who would be six years old if she had lived, about the same age as little Mary Ellen. This quiet struggle over the cruel scourge of childhood abuse in New York City was most likely discussed by Elbridge with his wife Louisa and father-in-law Robert J. Livingston, a member of the Board of the *Children's Aid Society*. As a man with clearly defined principles, a deep religious faith, and with singularly relevant experience, Elbridge decided he had to act. On December 17, 1874 the most important turning point in the focus of Elbridge T. Gerry's professional and public life was announced in the *New York Times*:

> The apprehension and subsequent conviction of the persecutors of little Mary Ellen, some time since, suggested to Mr. Elbridge T. Gerry, the counsel engaged in the prosecution of the case, the necessity for the existence of an organized society for the prevention of similar acts and atrocities. Upon expressing his views among his friends, he found plenty of sympathizers with the movement, but no one sufficiently interested to attempt the formation of such a society. About this time Mr. Gerry met Mr. John D. Wright, to whom he stated his plan. The latter at once became warmly interested, and undertook the necessary steps toward effecting an organization. Invitations were extended to a large number of prominent citizens interested in the welfare of children to meet at *Association Hall* on Tuesday afternoon and many promptly responded. Mr. Gerry defined the object of the meeting, which he said, was to organize a *New York Society for the Prevention of Cruelty to Children*. There were in existence in this City and State, Mr. Gerry said, many excellent institutions, some as charitable corporations, and others as State reformatories and asylums, for receiving and caring for little children. Among these might be cited the *Children's Aid Society* and in addition, each religious denomination had one or more hospitals and similar institu-

> tions devoted to the moral and physical culture of helpless children. There societies however, only assumed the care of their inmates after they had been legally placed in their custody. **It was not in the province of these excellent institutions to seek out and rescue from the dens and slums of the city the little unfortunates whose lives were rendered miserable by the system of cruelty and abuse which was constantly practiced upon them by the human brutes who happened to possess the custody or control of them; and this was the defect which it was proposed to remedy by the formation of this society.** There were plenty of laws existing on the statute books of the State, which provided for all such cases as had been cited, but unfortunately no one had heretofore been responsible for their enforcement. The Police and prosecuting officers were engaged in the prosecution and conviction of offenses of a graver legal character, and although they were always ready to aid in enforcing laws when duly called upon to do so, they could not be expected to discover and prosecute those who claimed the right to ill-treat children over whom they had apparent legal control. **This society proposed to enforce legally, but energetically, the existing laws, and to secure the conviction and punishment of every violator of any of those laws. The society would not interfere with the numerous institutions already existing, but would aid them in their work. It did not propose to aid any single religious denomination, and would be kept entirely free from political influences. Its duty toward the children would be discharged when their future custody should be decided by the courts.** The counsel for the society, Elbridge T. Gerry, volunteers his gratuitous services in the prosecution of cases reported by its officers during the first year. The Secretary will be entitled to a moderate compensation, but no salary will be paid to the remaining officers.[10]

While the New *York Times* article was not reporting on the first official meeting of the new society, it was reporting on the "organization meeting" that created the *Society for the Prevention of Cruelty to Children.* To provide society leadership, the wealthy Mr. John D. Wright who orchestrated the meeting on behalf of Elbridge was appointed the first society President. There were ten Vice-Presidents named (more likely the executive board) that included powerful New Yorkers, Cornelius Vanderbilt, August Belmont, Theodore Roosevelt, Henry Bergh, and others. Elbridge T. Gerry was named Legal Counsel, John L. Griffin was named Secretary, and William L. Jenkins was named Treasurer. An office was temporarily made available at the ASPCA building at 100 East Twenty-Second Street.

On December 28, 1874 the *New York Society for Prevention of Cruelty to Children* held its first annual meeting. There was a large number in attendance three-fourths of whom were women. The President outlined the objectives of the society and noted that children have rights which parents and guardians must respect. Elbridge T. Gerry as counsel, gratefully acknowledged that the press in New York City had endeavored to do the new society justice. He then noted that the Society already had one case before it and they proposed to receive complaints from anyone discovering an abused child in need and that such complaints would be promptly investigated. Elbridge predicted that as soon as the habitual abusers of children learn that there is a hand of the law that can reach them, there would be very few cases like that of Mary Ellen. He concluded by hoping the various charitable institutions would give the society their aid and cooperation.

Henry Bergh then spoke at the meeting and took exception to his colleague and friend Mr. Gerry by objecting to him calling a father who ill-treated his child a "brute."

> While anxious to protect children from undue severity, Bergh said he was in favor of good wholesome flogging, which he often found most efficacious. He noted his connection with the new society was only a slender one, that Mr. Wright and Mr. Gerry being the active agents… He warned the society to avoid interfering in petty cases and only engage the atrociously bad cases… Mr. Bergh closed his extended remarks by saying that he hoped every man and woman would aid the new society's Christian and civilized work.[11]

The first meeting had been so well publicized and so well connected to New York leaders that the Consul-General of Italy, Mr. De Lucca, attended the next meeting where he stated that he was eager to cooperate with the society in its good work as similar problems with child cruelty existed in Italian cities.

The year 1875 was the beginning of decades of hard work for both cruelty societies, work well-suited to the skills and passionate interests of Elbridge T. Gerry. While Elbridge remained the dedicated Legal Counsel to the ASPCA for the remainder of his professional life, it was his role as founder and Legal Counsel of the *New York Society for the Prevention of Cruelty to Children* that became his legacy. It became affectionately known as *The Gerry Society* in New York City and throughout the world and he wore the NYSPCC badge on his coat for the rest of his life.

Family real estate cases continued to appear on Elbridge's calendar and on February 1, 1875 he represented the Goelet siblings, Peter, Robert, Hannah and Jean in a rent case where they actually owned the premises of several Police Precinct Headquarters, many of which were past due on their rent payments. The hearing was to allocate city funds to make good the debts owed the Goelets.

Between late February and March 1875 a more serious matter was occupying Elbridge's attention, the Henry Bergh contempt case. At the Grand Jury hearing on February 26 the following interrogatory was read to Mr. Bergh by the court:

> Did you write or cause to be written, and hand or cause to be handed or sent the accompanying letter to the Grand Jury of this court at this term, with the intention that the said letter should reach the said Grand Jury? If so, this was civil contempt. Appended to the question was the letter of Mr. Bergh to the Grand Jury reflecting on the conduct of that body for their action in the case of Jefferson Carpenter, charged by officers of the ASPCA with keeping a dog-fighting den.[12]

Mr. Bergh replied that he had addressed a communication to the Grand Jury in view of the facts and under the circumstances stated in the papers he submitted to the court. The hearing was then postponed to give the court time to read the papers. On Monday, March 2 the hearing resumed with the arguments limited to the question of what constituted "legal contempt." Elbridge then addressed the court and explained the difference between "physical contempt" such as refusing to answer questions on the witness stand, and "constructive contempt" which included speaking offensively in court or publishing comments in a newspaper. He then argued that if Mr. Bergh had been guilty of any offense it was that of an "attempted" constructive contempt at common law, which had been abolished by the Revised Statutes in 1830. Further, Elbridge argued that Mr. Bergh could not have been guilty of an attempt to influence the Grand Jury since the complaint before the jury had been dismissed on February 8 and the letter was not written until the tenth; and the letter itself contained no menace, threat, libel, or denunciation. Rather, the letter was a simple expression of opinion by a public officer on the action of the Grand Jury. In conclusion Elbridge said that in sending the letter to the Grand Jury Mr. Bergh simply desired that the civil power should be sustained. The court then concluded that Mr. Bergh stood exonerated under his explanatory oath from any intentional contempt.[13] The week after Bergh's exoneration the same case Bergh had written about in his letter was re-submitted to a new Grand Jury in which the prisoner declared that he was innocent of the offense of keeping a dog-fighting den for which the first Grand Jury had found him guilty. Both Bergh and Gerry could be quick with the pen to respond with editorials about perceived injustices like the re-submission of the dog fighting case, but they were also cautious because they were at the mercy of the press which continued to print cartoons about the city's "Great Meddlers."

Nineteenth century New York City commercial leases were negotiated in January and signed in February for annual occupancy with rent payments to begin on May 1 of each year. Therefore most of the big real estate cases involving the Goelets and represented by Elbridge T. Gerry were on the court calendar in the first two months of each year. Some cases were resolved by May while other controversies proceeded over many months or even years. On January 14, 1876 Elbridge filed seven foreclosure suits with the County Clerk on behalf of the Goelet siblings, Peter, Robert, Jean and Hannah against the *Third Avenue Savings Bank* for $59,500.00 in foreclosed mortgages. These proceedings were more procedural and less substantive and therefore demanded less of Elbridge's professional time. Determining the value of a lawyer's time can be found in the case law. An April 1875 case found Elbridge himself suing a client to recover $10,000.00 for his services in preparing the appeal of a contested will. Elbridge's client argued that the legal services provided were not worth more than $500.00. A number of lawyers testified as experts for both sides as to the value of Elbridge T. Gerry's services in appealing the will, and the jury awarded Elbridge $3,000.00.

By the end of 1875 Almy Gerry Gallatin and her husband Frederic, a successful lawyer in partnership with John J. Astor, were ready to build a suitable family home for their four children. One of Frederic's dear friends, James Renwick, Jr. was a successful architect who shared the Gallatins' vision for their home. The mansion was built on Fifth Avenue at Fifty-Third Street on the corner next to Saint Thomas Church. This block was on the leading edge of New York's most fashionable neighborhood. A few years later Frederic and Almy once again turned to their dear friend Renwick to design a summer home for the family on Long Island.

On February 15 Elbridge gave a lecture at Columbia Law School on behalf of the ASPCA and was joined by Henry Bergh. Elbridge lectured on the history of animal protection from ancient Egypt and Asia and their religious and civil regulations, to the common law of England and finally, the development of American law with a focus on New York. Bergh addressed how the ASPCA went about enforcing the laws. These lectures introduced law students to the new and emerging subject of animal protection law taught by the leading lawyer in both litigating the cases and in drafting the laws. Elbridge thereby mentored a new generation of specialist lawyers.

April and May 1876 were busy for the ASPCA. At the May meeting Elbridge T. Gerry reported on legislation before the State Assembly to prohibit cruelty to animals during inter-state transit. Elbridge read a letter from the *Committee on Agriculture* which regrettably informed the ASPCA that since the Governor had recently pardoned two convicted dog-fighters they did not see any hope of passage for the legislation under the current leadership in Albany. A letter from the ASPCA addressed to the *State Association for the Protection of Fish and Game* was read to the society. It urged them to aid the society in protest against the shooting of tame birds for competitive wagering. Sadly, the meeting also reported the death of a founding member of the ASPCA, James Gallatin, the uncle of Frederic Gallatin. James Gallatin died unexpectedly in Paris, France at the age of eighty. As a young man he served as personal Secretary to his father Albert Gallatin when he brokered the *Treaty of Ghent* ending the War of 1812 between the United States and Great Britain. James kept a colorful journal of his travels during this diplomatic trip which was published in *Scribner's Magazine* in 1914. The original journal is held in the Rare Books collection of the *New York Historical Society.* James Gallatin succeeded his father as President of the Gallatin National Bank in New York City in 1839. He retired to Paris in 1868 just two years after co-founding the ASPCA. Although James Gallatin lived the remainder of his life in Paris his body was returned to New York City for a funeral on May 28 at Trinity Church where the extended Gerry, Gallatin and Goelet families gathered to mourn his loss.

By the time of his uncle's death, Frederic Gallatin had become the Secretary of the ASPCA taking a more active role in society business. At the next meeting of the society in June, 1876, Frederic recorded in the minutes the status of a pending ASPCA case that challenged the way sea turtles were treated when unloaded from the ships and transported into New York City. The court found that sea turtles were not a protected species under the animal protection laws and, although the case was ultimately lost, it received tremendous publicity in the press, increasing both interest and support for the ASPCA.

From its first meeting in December 1875 under the leadership of Elbridge T. Gerry the *New York Society for the Prevention of Cruelty to Children* operated similarly to the ASPCA and its agents immediately began to rescue abused children. In the first year of operation the NYSPCC investigated hundreds of complaints, prosecuted sixty-eight criminal cases and rescued seventy-two children from abuse. The people of New York finally recognized that children had rights separate from their parents and saw that an issue they thought was private was not only immoral but had to be dealt with as a crime. After the Mary Ellen case was settled in mid-1875, Elbridge worked with the New York Legislature to draft a bill to protect children that performed in theatres and other entertainment venues from injury and exploitation. The legislation passed in 1876 was called *An Act to Prevent and Punish Wrongs to Children.* The act declared that, regarding the care, custody or control of any child under the age of sixteen years, it was unlawful to:

> Sell, apprentice, give away, let out, or otherwise dispose of any such child to any person, in or for the vocation, occupation service, or purpose of singing, playing on musical instruments, rope, or wire walking, dancing, begging, peddling, or as a gymnast, contortionist, rider or acrobat, in any place whatsoever; or for or in any obscene, indecent, or immoral purpose, exhibition, or practice whatsoever; of for or in any business, exhibition, or vocation injurious to the health or dangerous to the life or limb of such child.[14]

The new law created an official partnership among the police, the courts, and the NYSPCC Agents who had enforcement powers on behalf of the public. The agents proudly wore their official badges when they investigated complaints, removed children from abusive situations, and presented the children in court for a hearing to determine each child's placement in a safe environment. Gerry was initially careful, first focusing on children employed in obviously dangerous activity such as tight rope walking. In practice the NYSPCC did not interfere with the employment of children in all types of theatre, instead its efforts were focused on children working in harmful, lower-class entertainments. Contemporaries of Gerry and modern scholars acknowledge the existence of physical abuse in some situations, for example in November 1875 the NYSPCC rescued a child with the stage name Prince Leo from the *Tivoli Theatre* in New York City where he did a dangerous circus performance. The young child had been purchased from his parents by the acrobat Walla Leonard who was known to regularly beat Prince Leo as a way to force the boy to do tight-rope walking and other dangerous acrobatic feats. Two physicians testified to the effect that injuries had already resulted in weakening and partially destroying the walls of the boy's abdomen and unnaturally curving the spine. *Harper's Weekly* drew attention to the case in a story entitled "Little Infant Slaves of the Arena."[15] At their second anniversary celebration the officers of the Gerry Society triumphantly displayed six rescued children (all of whom had been gymnasts or circus performers) to the society membership. By 1879 the society had moved to stop the performances of children in what were called "miniature operas" or "pinafore troupes," an action which brought some public criticism, in part because of the popularity of these entertainments. By the early 1880's Elbridge T. Gerry was challenging P.T. Barnum's apparent abuse of circus children just as Henry Bergh had challenged the treatment of circus animals. However Elbridge did not find a friend in P.T. Barnum and for decades Gerry and those who sought to limit the labor of children on the stage and other dangerous entertainment venues were labeled as anti-theatre.[16]

Members of the Protestant Episcopal Church in New York City were also close friends and colleagues of the Gerry, Goelet and Livingston families. Elbridge

T. Gerry's spiritual and personal life was centered in the Episcopal community. He actively participated in the business life of the Episcopal Church where he demonstrated as much conviction and energy as he employed in his professional life. The first half of 1876 found Elbridge at regular church meetings and by early summer he was busy with preparations to participate in the annual *Episcopal Diocesan Convention* scheduled for September. The Gerry family spent the summer relaxing at Saratoga Springs, New York where Louisa and the three girls picnicked, visited with friends and family, and left Elbridge to his preparations for the *Episcopal Convention* and the *Gerry Society* legal work. While always on a "working vacation" Elbridge doted on his children and carved out time for them to read, to take playful walks, and to enjoy the outdoor music performances at the Saratoga Pavilion.

The summer holidays of the Gerry, Goelet, Livingston, and Gallatin families from the 1820's to the 1890's trace the changing popularity of holiday destinations for the socially elite. Nineteenth century families of every class preferred holiday locations at the seaside, on a lake front, or along a picturesque river; locations known popularly as "watering holes" or "watering places." Early nineteenth century watering places included the camp sites and hotels at *West Point* forty-five miles up the Hudson River from New York City. This was the annual holiday watering place for Uncle Peter Goelet, his brother Robert and sisters Jean and Hannah from 1820 to the 1840's. When Hannah married Thomas Russell Gerry in 1830 they joined the Goelets at *West Point* for a couple of years and stayed at the *Cozzens Hotel.* In the mid-1830's Thomas and Hannah began to stay closer to New York City at beach communities like Rockaway where hotels and cottages were accessible by stage coach and train. By 1844 Thomas and Hannah had two children and spent their summers at New Rochelle close to New York City which permitted Thomas Gerry to rush back if business called him while on holiday. However, after Thomas suddenly died at the *Neptune House Hotel* in New Rochelle during their 1845 family holiday, Hannah, Elbridge, Almy and Jean never returned to New Rochelle for another holiday. Hannah and her three children moved in with the Goelet family in New York City and began spending their summer holidays with the Goelets at the West Point *Cozzens Hotel* for the remainder of their childhood until each married. It was no surprise that twenty years later in 1865, the still single twenty-eight year old Elbridge T. Gerry coordinated a summer fancy dress ball at the *Cozzens Hotel* in West Point on the Hudson River where he had enjoyed many family vacations as a child.

The appeal of *Saratoga* and even *West Point* through the early 1890's was due to the ease of access via the Hudson River. Not only did steamers traverse the full length of the Hudson River from New York City to well above Albany, depositing vacationers at resorts along the way, but wealthier vacationers piloted their own yachts 181 miles up the Hudson to Saratoga. As yachting became famously popular from mid-1880 through the Gilded Age, the open water became more important for holiday yachting than the limitations imposed by inland waterways like the Hudson River. Watering places expanded to the upper eastern seacoast of Nova Scotia, Canada and off the mid-Atlantic coast to Newport, Rhode Island. Eventually, a *Gilded Age* holiday for the wealthy became an international "watering place" shared with European yachtsmen who joined the American yachtsmen on cruises to and from England, the Mediterranean, the United States, and exotic ports along the way. But that was another ten or fifteen years away for Elbridge T. Gerry. The hotels of the various summer resorts were open for the season in May when the exodus from the City began in earnest, although the climax of the season not until after the Fourth of July. Among the hundreds of hotels where summer boarders found accommodations, a few of the more prominent ones were mentioned in the *New York Times* which provided readers an overview of summer resorts easily accessible to residents of New York City. In 1876 four resorts particularly attracted the wealthy:

> **Saratoga Springs**, the most popular inland resort, furnishes unsurpassed hotel accommodations. The *Grand Union* is finely situated, the *Congress Hall* has been thoroughly renovated, and the *United States Hotel* is a favorite.
>
> **Newport**, distinguished as a resort for fashionable, refined people, offers first-class accommodations, the finest hotel being the *Ocean House* which offers an orchestra and free stages to and from the beach.
>
> **West Point** is a favorite resort for New Yorkers and one of the most picturesque places in America. It has two hotels, *Cozzens Hotel* and the *West Point Hotel*, both of which are first-class in every respect.
>
> **Catskills**, pure mountain air and imposing scenery are the chief attractions.[17]

By 1877 a small but select group of New York Society emerged who preferred Long Island for summer holidays. Frederic and Almy Gallatin were at the heart of this social circle that branched off from the New York Gerry/Goelet summer traditions. The Gallatins lived primarily in their New York City mansion and socialized in the City. A close mutual friend of Elbridge and Frederic was the architect James Renwick whom the Gallatins hired to build them a summer home in East Hampton, Long Island. East Hampton at the time was unpretentious and the small colony of summer people, which included a few socially prominent families, distinguished artists, and a number of clergymen, did not participate in customary social rituals. Instead the highlight of their day was assembling on the beach between 11:00 a.m. and 1:00 p.m. for picnics and conversation. The Gallatins and Renwicks were also avid yachtsmen and fishermen.

Renwick built the Gallatins a modest house by Newport, Rhode Island standards and they named it *Breezy Lawn*. The home had features reminiscent of an alpine chalet, possibly a symbolic reference to the Gallatin's Swiss heritage.[18] The Gallatin family were early settlers on Long Island so the choice to establish a summer residence in East Hampton made perfect sense. Golf courses, club houses and yacht landings were followed by summer mansions that appeared a decade later when the *Gilded Age* touched the summer watering place. Frederic Gallatin was a member of the East coast yachting circles and a member of the New York Yacht Club along with Elbridge and the Goelet brothers. Frederic named his first yacht *Bertie* in 1884 and his second yacht *Almy* after his wife in 1890.

When the Gerrys returned to New York City, Louisa discovered she was pregnant with their fourth child. With the kind support of her mother, who lived in the adjoining townhouse, Louisa Livingston focused on her health during her confinement and set aside her usual social activities through the winter. Elbridge joined the *Episcopal Diocesan Convention* in late September where each day opened with religious services followed by committee reports, a daily business meeting, and on September 29, the annual address of the Bishop. On that same day the *Report of the Committee on the Incorporation of Churches* was presented to the convention, which stated that the Church of the Holy Trinity of Highlands, had renewed its application for admission to the convention, but that the obstacle to the prior year's admission still existed: the Church had not declared in its certificate of incorporation that one of its main purpose was to remain forever a Protestant Episcopal Church, therefore under the 1872 Church canon, could not be admitted to the convention. Elbridge T. Gerry moved to disagree with the recommendation of the committee not to admit, noting that the certificate of incorporation held by Holy Trinity Church was granted prior to the 1872 law. He further stated that a new certificate (*required by the committee*) would make the Church give up its present one at great risk to church property. Elbridge offered a memorial in which the church set forth its intention to remain forever a Protestant Episcopal Church and asked the convention to admit Holy Trinity upon the memorial. For the next hour the convention debated the relevant canon law and Gerry's proposed memorial. When the vote was taken the recommendation to admit Holy Trinity was passed by a majority of the convention.[19] Elbridge T. Gerry's study and mastery of the canon law of the *Protestant Episcopal Church* began in earnest after this convention. He added books to his library at the

Broadway Farm mansion on canon law in which his own hand-written notes are still to be found on many of the pages. Eventually Elbridge would be an ex-officio legal counsel to the *Protestant Episcopal Church* of New York City.

The fall was dominated by a complicated case in which Elbridge T. Gerry represented Robert S. Kip against the *New York and Harlem Railroad Company*. Court hearings were held in 1876 and 1877 with a decision in 1878. The case involved leases to land with a defective title that limited its use. The lessee railroad sold the land without disclosing the defect. When that purchase fell through the land was re-sold with disclosure of the defect which diminished the value of the property. The railroad sought compensation for the loss in property value from the party who defaulted on the first sale, Mr. Kip. The issues focused on what disclosures or non-disclosures at a sale are *material* i.e. relevant and harmful, or *immaterial* i.e. would not have affected the sale. Also, whether after selling the land the condemnation of that same land by the railroad for public use was legal, and whether a release from the purchase agreement by Mr. Kip was legal under the circumstances. Although the court stated that the case presented hardship for both sides, it arose from the nature and condition of the property and not from any default or misconduct on the part of Elbridge's client, Mr. Kip. The railroad who was the mortgagee had suffered a loss in the defaulted first sale but the facts still did not show Mr. Kip liable.[20] This case has been cited thirty-three times by *cases* up to 2009, in the 2011 *New York Jurisprudence* encyclopedia and by articles in the 2011 *American Law Reports*.

Elbridge T. Gerry closed the year with a trip to Albany, New York for the founding meeting of the *New York State Bar Association* on November 21, 1876. The Association declared as its purpose, "to cultivate the science of jurisprudence, to promote reform in the law, to facilitate the administration of justice, to elevate the standard of integrity, honor and courtesy in the legal profession and to cherish a spirit of brotherhood in the members thereof."[21] Elbridge could not have drafted a better purpose for himself or his brethren; the words captured how he felt about all of his professional endeavors. Representatives from local bar associations attended the annual meetings as did individual members. The Bar Association occupied rooms on the first floor of the State Capitol Building where members and visitors entered through the Library.

In early 1877 Elbridge had to focus his attention on ASPCA business. In March he was negotiating a method to implement a City Ordinance, while also defending Henry Bergh in a law suit. On March 13 a conference was held in the Mayor's office between three Aldermen (Lewis, Cowing, and Morris) and the

ASPCA representatives, Mr. Gerry and Mr. Bergh. The Mayor joined the discussion about the new ordinance intended to control dogs in the City.

> Alderman Morris announced that he would submit amendments to the ordinance that would protect the public and the owners of dogs, and also the dogs themselves, in all the rights enjoyed by other animals that obeyed the corporation ordinances. His amendments would require a license to be taken out for each dog, the fee to be $2 for the first year, and $1 for every annual afterward. It also provides that all dog-catchers commissioned by the Mayor shall wear a badge in a conspicuous place, bearing the number of their license. This prohibits them from arresting any dog whose owner has complied with the License Law, under heavy penalty, ad also from giving away or selling any valuable dog after capture. They are to be appointed by the Mayor.
>
> Mr. Gerry, on behalf of Mr. Bergh and the society, then submitted the following:
>
> 1. The City appropriate a lot of ground on this island, and erect a small, inexpensive building in the center thereof, to be used for the temporary confinement and destruction of the dogs by a speedy, merciful, and noiseless process.
> 2. This building, of cheap material, shall be arranged so as to include a lodging place for the custodian, and separate kennels should be provided in a fenced lot. Wherein all dogs may be confined pending their recognition and removal by their owners; or, failing this, when valueless, their destruction.
> 3. To effect the removal from the streets of the vagrant dogs, men will go through the City early in the morning with the ambulance (horse / animal cart) of the Society, or a special vehicle for the purpose, the dogs to be captured by the aid of scoop-nets and carried to their place of destination or final disposition.
> 4. The Society will undertake to do the whole of this work and take entire charge of it, free of all remuneration, if the City will simply provide the premises mentioned and reimburse the Society in its actual expenses for employees, which will be estimated and agreed upon.
> 5. The foregoing is not a new plan, but is today in effect in Philadelphia. During the past year there, 3,212 dogs were taken of which 2,559 were destroyed, others redeemed or given away, for which the city received $1,154.50.

Mr. Bergh said the dog ordinance should also apply to cats. The ASPCA proposal was submitted to City Council with recommendations for approval.[22]

One week later, on March 16 the proprietors of a slaughter-house, Edward W. Davis, Isaac B. Atwood, and Monroe Crane, sued the ASPCA in an action to obtain a perpetual injunction against arrests of their employees on the ground that the ASPCA agents had threatened to interfere with their business by questioning their method of killing hogs. The method consisted of first hanging the animals up by the heels and then cutting their throats and bleeding them to death. The slaughter-house insisted that this method was a necessary and proper one in carrying out their business. Elbridge T. Gerry won the case on appeal when he argued that the grounds for the ASPCA interference was based on more detailed facts than the slaughter-house had described. In fact hogs were attached to a chain by their hind legs, then hauled up a 40-foot hoist-way, their throats cut, and then while still alive, were plunged into boiling water. While news coverage of this brutal treatment of hogs enlightened the general public, similar business enterprises saw the hand of the "Great Meddlers" at work once again.[23]

Unsettling news reached Elbridge T. Gerry on March 22 when he was summoned to the *Broadway Farm* mansion where his uncle Peter Goelet had taken ill. Two days later what had been a bad cold had become a serious case of acute pneumonia. At the age of 78, Peter Goelet was surrounded by family who had been told by physicians that he would not last more than a few days. Pneumonia was always feared in big cities and it had reached a near epidemic level in New York City the winter of 1877. Two days later the news was better, Peter Goelet's doctors reported that he had spent a comparatively comfortable day, which gave his family and friends some hope of recovery. While the doctors remained cautious Uncle Peter recovered, although he never regained his full strength.

Just one week later, after a long winter of confinement Louisa Gerry gave birth to the first of Elbridge's two sons. Robert Livingston Gerry was born on May, 31, 1877 into a home filled with three energetic sisters, Angelica 6, Lillian 4, and Mabel 5. The Gerrys spent April at home enjoying their first son and giving Louisa much needed time to recover her strength. With four young children, the Gerrys kept the summer holiday season simple, which meant finding fresh air and fun a little closer to home. It is likely they joined grandparents, Robert and Louisa Livingston at either their Lake Delaware, New York farm estate or their Highland Park, New Jersey estate, where Louisa Gerry had spent summers with her family as a young girl.

Louisa's sister-in-law Almy Gerry Gallatin had four children by this time and she and Frederic felt a need for a summer place of their own similar to the Gerrys' Lake Delaware farm. In the summer of 1877 they traveled over 100 miles by yacht off the Long Island coast and found farmland on the northern side near a sheltered cove just across from the Goelet family owned Gardiner's Island. The old Hedges Farm had been subdivided into four large properties of about twenty acres each and only one was left for purchase. These four estates were the first to establish East Hampton, Long Island as a resort community for wealthy New Yorkers. The Gallatins once again engaged architect and friend, James Renwick, Jr. to design a summer cottage. It was another year before the cottage was completed for the growing Gallatin family to enjoy.

Elbridge was in New York City in early summer for a June 22 case involving the appointment of a guardian for Richard F. Carman at the death of his father. Richard was a fourteen-year old boy who was entitled to over $300,000.00 on attaining his majority. There were two estates to which he was entitled, his fathers and his grandfathers. The court appointed the boy's mother his guardian as to his personal care, but appointed a Trust Bank to care for the wealth of the estate on behalf of the boy. His sister, Mrs. Cullman, was represented by Elbridge in a challenge to the personal guardianship of Richard. The claim was that his mother was an unfit person and should not have custody of her son. The final decision was not reported and likely was settled out of court to protect the under-age boy.[24]

On June 30 the convent school near the Gerry home, the *Academy of the Holy Cross* at Forty-Second Street between Eighth and Ninth Avenues, held their commencement exercises. The younger students provided entertainment with parades, music, and recitals. Angelica Gerry, then six years-old was likely the "Gerry" listed as one of eight young students playing the overture to "Zampa," and a second performance from "William Tell," as part of the entertainment. A second part of the program gathered the young students, including Angelica, into a choir for a musical performance of *Alia Paletrina*.[25] The convent school was only seven blocks from the Gerrys brownstone on West Forty-Eighth Street.

After a long, relaxing summer with family Elbridge attended the *Protestant Episcopal Convention* of the New York City Diocese in late September, where he was re-elected to the Missionary Committee. This archdiocesan committee work dove-tailed with the Indian missionary work of his mother, Hannah Gerry and his aunts, Jean Goelet and Sarah Goelet who participated through their local parish, Trinity Church. The convention also announced that the proposal from the prior year to establish reading-rooms for young men all over the City had been successfully accomplished. The Reading Rooms provided alternative activities to going to pubs to drink away hard earned paychecks. The convention adjourned on September 28.

In November Elbridge returned to Albany, New York for the second annual meeting of the New York State Bar Association. There were speeches, business meetings, and for the first time an award ceremony where $250.00 was presented for the best paper submitted by a law student. The winning student was Mr. Walter Howe of New York City whose paper was entitled *Relations of Master and Servant at Common Law as Affected by Legislation in England Prior to the Labor Inquiry Commission of 1876*. The proceedings were of great benefit to the profession as a source of continuing education and a means of networking with colleagues across the State.[26]

On January 4, 1878 funeral services were held for the President of the *Chemical National Bank*, John Quinton Jones, at Trinity Church. There was a large attendance comprising many prominent bankers, lawyers, and merchants including Robert Goelet as a member of the Board of the *Chemical Bank* and Elbridge T. Gerry as a Goelet relative and friend of the bank's inner circle. The pallbearers included Robert Goelet and James A. Roosevelt. The services were concluded in half an hour and the body borne to Saint Luke's Churchyard where it was placed in the family vault that held the remains of Mr. Jones' father, mother, brother, two sisters, and a nephew. Chemical Bank Board member Uncle Peter Goelet was too weak to attend the services, having never fully recovered from the earlier case of pneumonia.

Elbridge T. Gerry was back in Court on March 5 prosecuting a misdemeanor case on behalf of the ASPCA charging John McGill, an employee of the Bleecker-Street Railroad, with salting the tracks on that road. An officer of the Fourteenth Precinct swore that on the night of February 3 he saw a cart on the down track of Bleeker Street being driven by one man while another shoveled some substance in the space between the rail tracks where there was ice and snow for a distance of 175 feet. The officer found it to be a composition of salt, sufficiently mixed with sand to disguise the appearance. The salt would have been harmful to the horses pulling the carts along the tracks. A sample of the salt and sand mixture was presented to the jury for their inspection. Mr. McGill admitted there might be a little salt in the sand but there was no way to account for the mixture and in any case it was not intentional. The case went before the jury on March 6 with a verdict of not guilty.

On May 22 Elbridge T. Gerry joined his father-in-law for the annual meeting of the *Society of the New York Hospital* where both Robert J. Livingston and Elbridge were elected to the Board of Governors. The next day Elbridge was in Court defending an editor, James Gordon Bennett, of the *New York Herald* against a claim of libel by Louis Fleischmann, the owner of a bakery at the corner of Broadway and Tenth, the *Vienna Model Bakery*. The newspaper published an article stating that the bakery used milk from 800 diseased cows fed on distillery slops and produced 12,800 quarts of lacteal poison daily. Also, the milk and cream used in the bakery were impure and the bread made from the poisoned milk was unfit for human use and would cause death if eaten by children or sick people.[27] Gerry won the case exonerating the *New York Herald* and by the fall of 1878 an indictment was found against Fleishmann's Vienna Bakery and the *Blissville Dairy* one of the sources of the tainted milk. By November the New York State Legislature had voted on new laws to regulate milk production throughout the State due in large part to publicity from the Fleischman case.

On June 20 Elbridge T. Gerry represented the ASPCA in a case that involved cruelty to polo horses, a new issue even though he had represented horses for years under various fact patterns. However, Elbridge would later recall this case after fatherhood had mellowed his views on the sporting world and he had developed an appreciation for equestrian sports like polo and track racing. Elbridge, on behalf of the ASPCA sued James Fraser, the Manager of the *Polo Club Grounds* at Jerome Park for cruelty to a horse by "docking" the tail of Mr. Harry Oelrich's polo pony. The newspapers reported that among the attentive listeners at the trial were several members of the *Polo Club*, sportsmen, veterinary surgeons, and other horse lovers. The horse in question was known as "The Custer Mare" having once been the property of General Armstrong Custer, who was defeated by *Crazy Horse*, leader of the Sioux Indians in 1876. The horse was described as a beautiful 9-year-old light bay Indian pony, about $13^{1/2}$ hands high, very swift and symmetrical, and admirably adapted for the exciting game of polo. In fact, the pony was walked up and down Chambers Street outside the courthouse by a stable boy just in case the jury wanted to examine her; they did not and "The Custer Mare" was quietly returned to her stable that evening.[28]

The only witnesses for the prosecution were two veterinary surgeons who failed to show up to testify, whereupon the Assistant District Attorney and Elbridge T. Gerry endeavored to gain a verdict by a series of dramatic statements quoted from the *Horse Drivers Cyclopedia and* a display of horse tails, one of them dripping with blood and held under the nostrils of the jury. In summary the prosecution characterized the polo club members as a clique of snobs and would-be aristocrats who endeavored by importing the fashionable vices of England to give themselves airs of selectiveness. There was no address to the jury.

> The defense opened the case stating that:
> ... he would not a plain unvarnished tale deliver, because the tail (holding up the severed tip of the mutilated pony's tail which he held in his hand) was not plain, and it *was* varnished. He stated that the ASPCA knew that during the last gen-

> eration every horse had not only four joints cut off his tail, as is the case here, but ten joints. The custom had originated in consequence of the death of a nobleman and his wife in England from the entanglement of a horse's tail in the reins. The practice of "docking" was a common one in America and there were at the present moment, thousands of them on Long Island and in every other part of New York State. The practice of "docking" the defense contended was not cruelty or mutilating, and he denounced the prosecution as a "put up job" by Mr. Bergh against rich men of the Polo Club who did not invite him to their dinners. He further stated that Mr. Bergh had one hobby, the prevention of cruelty to animals, and like all men with a single hobby, he had ridden it to death, and become fanatical in spite of himself.

Witnesses for the defense were overwhelming in their testimony:

> George W. Bishop, who had been in the horse business for 50 years, testified that he had "docked" the tails of 20,000 horses, which took 20 seconds and was not painful.
>
> He further cited the content of the *Horse Driver's Cyclopedia* as dated and in error.
>
> James A. Going, a graduate of the Royal College of Veterinary Surgeons of Edinburgh, testified that "docking" was a well-recognized operation in Veterinary Science.

Even Mr. Henry Bergh was called as a witness by the defense;

> When questioned, Mr. Bergh admitted that he knew nothing of the facts in the case at issue.

The prosecution closed with:

> If the jury convicted the defendant, they would render 100,000 of their fellow-citizens liable to wear the convict's stripes.

The judge then charged the jury, and after deliberating an hour and a half, brought in a verdict of not guilty.[29]

The papers announced the decision as a triumph for the Polo Club, which confirmed that polo, the sport of the English gentry, was an American sport as well. Indeed, Elbridge T. Gerry's own sons, Robert and Peter, were destined to become *Harvard College's* and New York State's star polo players just fifteen years after the tail "docking" case was decided.

Around the Fourth of July, 1878 a *New York Times* article about the *West Point Military Academy* was published that included a description of summer holiday visitors at the nearby *Cozzens Hotel* and the appeal of the locale. The partial list of guests who had arrived before the Fourth of July holiday included Mr. Robert and Sarah Goelet, Mr. Peter Goelet, and Mrs. Gerry (may have been Hannah Goelet Gerry) and Ms. Gerry, Hannah's daughter Jean. Elbridge had just finished arguments in the polo case two weeks earlier and arrived late with Mrs. Gerry and the younger children to join the family already settled in at the *Cozzens Hotel.* The Hotel, then owned by J. P. Morgan, was described as sitting 200 feet above the river and one of the best known land-marks on the Hudson. It had always been a favorite resort of wealthy and exclusive New Yorkers to whom its broad, breezy piazzas with the most glorious views on the Hudson are to be obtained, offer opportunities for indulging in luxurious indolence hardly to be surpassed.[30]

While the Gerrys enjoyed their summer at West Point, the *Sag Harbor Express* newspaper reported on July 11, 1878 that the Frederic Gallatin family had moved into their nearly completed summer home, described as one of the finest houses in Suffolk County, New York. There were inlaid hard wood floors and stained glass windows, tiled hearths, and numerous fireplaces. There was a billiard room, parlor and dining room on the first floor with sets of French doors that provided access to the shaded veranda. The house was nearly 50 feet square, and in time, would be expanded even further. While the street frontage to the property was small, the frontage on the Hook Pond shoreline that extended to the ocean was beautiful and provided future anchorage points for visiting yachts. The Gallatins named their new summer home *Breezy Lawn* and spent every summer there for the next forty years. The plans for the house, long since demolished, were not discovered in the local East Hampton Library until the late twentieth century and only one postcard picture has been found of this early and significant James Renwick, Jr. summer cottage design.

Although the wealthy citizens of New York City and throughout the nation carried on life as usual, the Panic of 1873 and the subsequent five-year depression continued to affect the entire nation. The 1875 *Specie Resumption Act* scheduled the United States to return to the gold standard on January 1, 1879. Until the nation returned to the gold standard the economic depression continued through 1878 causing more bankruptcies and continued high unemployment.[31] A number of the Goelet real estate cases were initiated due to the bankruptcy or unemployment of their tenants, and more cases were on the horizon. On July 20, 1878 while the Gerrys were at *West Point* a major New York City builder, Andrew J. Kerwin, declared bankruptcy with a debt of $2,000,000.00. The declared cause was the depreciation in real estate values. Among Mr. Kerwin's principal creditors were: Peter Goelet claimed $263,000.00; Peter, Robert and Jean Goelet claimed $238,500.00; and Jean Goelet claimed $110,000.00. A meeting of the creditors to prove their debts and to choose an assignee was held on July 27, a meeting that likely called Elbridge back to New York City to represent the Goelets. One month later, on August 29 a voluntary petition of bankruptcy was filed for Hugh Blesson, a builder, whose principal secured creditor was Peter Goelet who claimed $122,000.00; Uncle Peter was also the un-secured creditor of Mr. Blesson, with a second claim for $30,000.00.[32]

By September the Gerry family was back in New York City and Elbridge T. Gerry was preparing to argue another complex case, almost identical to the 1876 *Kip v NY & Harlem Railroad* case that lasted for nearly two years and was finally being decided in mid-1878. As before, Elbridge represented purchasers at a foreclosure sale related to a re-sale of property with undisclosed title defects. Mr. Riggs refused to complete the purchase of the defective title so the plaintiff, Mr. Pursell sued asking the court to enjoin Mr. Riggs from canceling the purchase.[33] Elbridge T. Gerry won this case, and as with the Kip case it has withstood the test of time and has been cited by ninety cases through 2008 and was cited in articles in the 2011 *American Law Reports*.

Louisa Livingston received sad news in late September that her young cousin, thirty-one year old Maturin Livingston, Jr. had died. Although the son of Louisa's Uncle Morgan Livingston, her father James's brother, he took his name from his father's brother Maturin. He had been suffering from a serious abscess of the ear and took medications to relieve the pain and induce sleep. Upon his return from the Adirondacks, tan and healthy but complaining of the abscess, Maturin spent the day visiting family. Later in the evening he had a few drinks before he checked into the *Hoffman House* hotel where he appeared to be drunk. A chambermaid found him dead the next day fully clothed on his bed. The Coroner, Dr. Goldshmiedt, went to the hotel and decided that Mr. Livingston died from inhaling chloroform to relieve the ear pain. His mother was notified and she arrived the next night and arranged for a private funeral for Maturin's burial at St. James Church Cemetery in Hyde Park, New York, that was attended by Louisa and Elbridge T. Gerry.

In October high society news covered the Commodore Cornelius Vanderbilt Will challenge that had raged on since his death in early 1877. Visions of the *Mumler Spirit Photograph* case from 1869 must have run through Elbridge's mind as he read the newspaper accounts of the legal challenge to Vanderbilt's state of mind around the time of his death. Two of his estranged daughters, Ethelinda Allen and Mary Alicia La Bau, claimed that the Commodore's Will was obtained by fraud and undue influence by his son, William H. Vanderbilt. They also claimed that the Commodore was laboring under morbid mental delusion and mania at the time the Will was made and was influenced by the *Spiritualist Movement* of the 1850's. The contest over the Will captivated the public as accusations were made that witnesses were being tampered with and even disappearing. The names of witnesses were withheld from the court to protect them, which caused the proceedings to continue with no end in sight.[34]

In mid-November Elbridge T. Gerry and Henry Bergh traveled to Baltimore, Maryland for the *International Humane Society* meeting at the Barnum Hotel. Although they were long- time friends and colleagues, Gerry and Bergh did not always share the same opinions. The President of the society gave a welcoming speech and stated that less support had been received from the clergy than from other professions or persons for the work of humane societies. During the protracted discussion about the remark Mr. Gerry spoke in favor of the clergy while Mr. Bergh asserted that his experience led him to agree that the clergy did not generally support the humane societies. Later in the meeting the *Constitution and By-Laws Committee* recommended an amendment to include the words "and children" after the words "cruelty to animals." Mr. Bergh said that in every State there was provision made for children with institutions subsidized by the State for the protection of children but not for the protection of the lower animals. His experience made him suspicious of humanity and he found that cats and dogs were honorable in comparison. If animal and child protection were united the human would very soon absorb (dominate) the agent for the protection of the lower animals.[35] The proposition was rejected by the membership. While Gerry did not speak to the issue he likely agreed with the separation of the societies but may not have agreed on the reasoning. Henry Bergh never had children while Elbridge T. Gerry had four children at time which solidified his dedication to the *Gerry Society* (NYSPCC) and the enforcement of child protection laws in a City with rampant and mostly unreported child abuse.

There was one last court appearance in 1878, to hear the court decision on the appeal of the *ASPCA v Davis* case about the cruel method of killing hogs which Elbridge T. Gerry had won in the lower court in March, 1877. On appeal, Davis charged that his arrest before the cruelty to hogs was proven had harmed his business and reputation. Gerry again won with the judge stating, "Whether a person accused of a crime be guilty or innocent is to be determined in a common law court by a jury. An innocent person, upon an accusation of a crime, may be arrested and ruined in his character and property, and the damage thus sustains injury, unless, in such a case, he can maintain an action for malicious prosecution or false imprisonment. The innocent man is exposed to the risks of such damage by being a member of an organized society and his compensation for such risks may be found in the general welfare which society is organized to promote. Further, the administration of justice would be greatly paralyzed if no criminal could be arrested until it could be infallibly ascertained that he is guilty of the offense charged."[36] This case has been cited ninety-two times by cases through 2001, and by eight legal treatises and legal encyclopedias through 2011.

On his arrival home in New York City Elbridge learned of the birth of his nephew, Goelet Gallatin on November 18, 1878. He was the second son of his sister Almy Gerry Gallatin and her husband, Frederic Gallatin. Three weeks later, on December 12 as the Christmas holidays approached Elbridge's father-in-law Robert J. Livingston awarded his customary annual prize to each of three boys who had saved the most money in their banks at the *Newsboy's Lodging House* on Duane Street. One hundred and thirty-six boys saved $232.53. The successful competitors saved $15 each, the next boy had $12.25 in the bank, and the next $12.15. All of the boys received five percent interest on their deposits.

Unlike the past few years, 1879 found Elbridge T. Gerry focused on his growing family and Goelet family business. Athough he took no cases to trial Elbridge would not have neglected routine society business, both the ASPCA and the NYSPCC.

The *Windsor Hotel* on Fifth Avenue between Forty-Sixth and Forty-seventh Streets was put up for bid on February 6, 1879 at a Sheriff's sale to satisfy a judgment obtained by Peter Goelet and others who owned the ground upon which the hotel stood. The owner and builder of the *Windsor Hotel* was the late John T. Daly who had leased the ground from Peter Goelet for twenty-one years. The hotel sold for $353,000.00 to Mr. F. W. Barker who was compelled to pay $4,800 due Peter Goelet for back rent and the expenses of the sale. Mr. Barker left the Exchange-Sale room and returned within half an hour with a check for $39,400.00 and the transaction was closed. Unlike the intensity of trial work, these Goelet family business transactions were regularly managed by Elbridge even when he reduced his overall work load.

The *Massachusetts Society for the Prevention of Cruelty to Animals* was the second oldest society after Henry Bergh's society in New York City. In 1868 the Massachusetts society began publication of "Our Dumb Animals" a magazine intended to speak for those who cannot speak for themselves. The May 1879 monthly column "Doings of Kindred Societies" reported on Henry Bergh's remarks at the Thirteenth Annual Meeting of the ASPCA where he noted that it is the exceptional good fortune of this society, as compared with other societies, to be able to own real estate where rent can represent nearly half of all the New York ASPCA's expenses. In time, both Bergh's ASPCA and Gerry's NYSPCC owned their own buildings and rented ground-floor space as a means to generate regular income.

By late spring Louisa was pregnant with their fifth child and the Gerrys were ready for a summer holiday, one where the children would have their own rooms and be close to the ocean. The children ranged in age from 18 months to eight years old. Louisa Gerry had been raised in Highland Park, New Jersey and was no doubt familiar with the resort town *Long Branch,* known in earlier times as the summer capital. A new ocean ferry system had just opened between New York and Long Branch, New Jersey increasing the visitors from New York and made the resort a less exclusive holiday destination. While the Gerrys were ready for the family-oriented activities in the area they also wanted some of the privacy offered by West Point and Saratoga. They chose to rent an entire house, usually called a cottage, that was more exclusive than most of the hotels in the area. The Gerrys rented the former cottage of General Ulysses S. Grant. The verandas that surrounded the house provided fresh air and sunlight throughout the living quarters and provided an outdoor play area for the children. Most of the Gerrys' social circle would not have summered at Long Branch, New Jersey which ensured family privacy and low-key entertainments with less formality. This arrangement perfectly suited Louisa Gerry, who was six months pregnant and in need of relaxation.

The Gerrys returned to New York City in early September when Louisa was eight months pregnant and confined to her home until the October birth due date. In the midst of happy anticipation came sadness. On September 22, 1879 Robert Goelet, Uncle Peter's younger brother died at age seventy at his residence at 857 Broadway surrounded by family. He was the younger brother of Elbridge's mother Hannah Goelet Gerry, one of the four siblings who had spent their lives sharing holidays at *West Point* and jointly owning and managing their New York family real estate. The shared customs of the early Goelet family were slipping away. The body of Robert Goelet was taken from his residence at 10 a.m. on September 26 to *Saint Mark's Protestant Episcopal Church* where brief funeral services were held. The pall-bearers included Robert Goelet Jr., George H. Warren and James A. Roosevelt. In the pews assigned to the chief mourners were Sarah Goelet, Ogden Goelet, Elbridge T. Gerry, and Jonathan Ogden. Mr.

Goelet's four servants of many years were present and attired in mourning black. A choir of several voices sang and at the close of service the plain casket was borne on the shoulders of the undertaker's assistants through Second Avenue to the Marble Cemetery on Second Street with relatives and friends following on foot. Robert Goelet was laid to rest in his wife Sarah Ogden's family vault, rather than burial in the Goelet Vault in Saint Mark's church yard. In death the close brothers, Peter and Robert, were separated in their final resting places.

While Elbridge T. Gerry handled the estate of his uncle Robert Goelet in September, he also prepared and represented an unprecedented law suit on behalf of his uncle Peter Goelet. The suit was against the local government of Elizabeth City, New Jersey. The suit stated that the Charter of the City of Elizabeth was passed by the Legislature and that there was a restriction in the Charter that limited indebtedness for improvements to $20,000 per annum. The suit was to recover $6,000 interest on $129,000 worth of bonds held by Peter Goelet, plaintiff. It is alleged that tax money collected by the city was not applied for the purposes authorized by the Legislature, and that, by reason of extravagant outlays and gross carelessness in the management of the City's affairs the bonds deteriorated in value and were almost worthless. Further, tax-payers refused to pay their tax assessments and the City was alleged to be on the verge of financial ruin.[37]

The City attorney, Mr. R.E. Chetwood, argued that the clause limiting the amount of indebtedness had been abrogated by subsequent acts of the Legislature and that the debt had increased to the amount set forth in the newer legislation. Mr. Gerry insisted that the city needed a receiver appointed, both for the welfare of the citizens and for the security of its creditors. If ever there was a case of insolvency, he said, it was this of the City of Elizabeth.[38]

Mr. Gerry noted that his client did not want to interfere with the Executive Department, just the financial interests. There was no municipal property to satisfy the plaintiff's judgment and the application for a receiver was as much *pro bono publico* as to the individual creditors. If this was not done the City would, in time, be unable to carry on its governance. Gerry claimed that even if the amount to pay the debt or interest had been collected it would have been squandered by Ring extravagance. He concluded by saying that the time had come for the court to interpose its hand to prevent the whole city being involved in financial ruin.[39]

The defense opposed Mr. Gerry's motion and insisted there was no precedent for such a proceeding and that, although the United States courts have gone further than the State courts, he hoped the local courts would pause before they went too far. The State courts had decided that the condition of Elizabeth should be made an issue for a decision by the Federal Courts. When an injunction did more injury than the remedy sought, a court of equity would not grant it. The city expected to pay its debts, but if it was driven too hard financially it would work nothing but ruin. The defense insisted that a Receiver not be appointed and the city should be allowed to come to terms with its creditors.[40]

Elizabeth City was in no position to meet creditor demands and it was not until May 21, 1883 that a peremptory mandamus in the United States Circuit Court ordered the City to include in its next tax levy the amount of indebtedness to Robert Goelet Jr., heir to his father and Uncle Peter's property rights. Near bankruptcy, Elizabeth City avoided the demand when five out of the eight members of the Board of Assessors resigned before the order was served and the board, being without a quorum, was unable to carry out the Court's order. Again, in November 1884 the United States Circuit Court issued an order for the City to assess and levy taxes sufficient to pay the plaintiff Robert Goelet's judgment, by then amounting to $18,000. Many cities and counties were in financial distress across the country and in New Jersey, Elizabeth City was the most dire case at the end of the late 1870's depression.

Only a month after Robert Goelet's death on September 22 and the September 27 Elizabeth City bond case, Elbridge T. Gerry was home with his wife Louisa who gave birth to their sixth child and second son, Peter Goelet Gerry on October 30, 1879. He joined siblings Angelica 8, Mabel 7, Lillian 6, and 3-year old Robert. Just a few months earlier, Ogden Goelet and his wife, Mary Wilson, gave birth to their daughter, Mary (her mother's name sake), who was called "May," to distinguish mother from daughter. While the new babies were healthy, and the families were celebrating the new cousins, the joy would be tempered.

On November 20, 1879 just two months after his brother's death, eighty-year old Uncle Peter Goelet died at his residence at Nineteenth and Broadway. He had been quite ill for several weeks and he worsened about the time of Robert's death. In his old age uncle Peter was said to be about mid-height, somewhat bent by age with strongly marked features and a countenance expressive of unusual determination and much mental acuteness. His usual expression was of complete abstraction, bordering at times upon melancholy. The family from which Peter Goelet sprung was one of the oldest and most respected in New York City. For 160 years it had produced cautious, conservative, business men, frugal and industrious in their habits, and preferring the slow and steady accumulation of solid wealth to the glittering fantasies of speculation.[41] The next generation of Goelets, Robert and Sarah's sons Robert Jr. and Ogden, shifted the legacy of their introverted ancestors into the social whirl of the coming *Gilded Age*. The funeral for Peter Goelet was held at Saint Mark's Church on Stuyvesant Street near

Second Avenue on November 24. Few persons came to the viewing although many friends sent their cards to the family. A plain hearse, followed by less than half a dozen carriages, arrived at the Church at 10a.m. The Gallatins, Goelets and Gerrys were all in attendance at the service as were a large number of representatives of the old New York families that included John Jacob Astor, Robert B. Roosevelt, M.H. Field, Judge Peabody, Mr. Wilson, George DeWitt, and George Warren, among many others. When the services in the church had ended the coffin was borne through the front doorway down to the eastern side of Saint Mark's church yard to the Goelet Vault for burial. Among those who remained to see the vault covered were several mechanics who were employed by Peter Goelet for a number of years, and who it is said, were special favorites in his close circle of associates.[42] Peter's vault was just two blocks from his brother Robert's at the *Marble Cemetery* where the Ogden family was buried.

Only the Goelet sisters, Hannah and Jean Buchannan, remained at the old *Broadway Farm* townhouse along with Hannah's daughter, Jean. Elbridge was their closest companion as he made regular visits and continued to add to, and use his immense book collection that remained in the old house. On December 5 the Will of the Peter Goelet was admitted to probate. He left twenty million dollars in property to be divided equally among his siblings, Robert (deceased), Hannah and Jean. To Elbridge his beloved nephew, he left $500,000. Upon the death of Elbridge's mother Hannah in 1895, he would inherit the Goelet estate. Peter Goelet named Elbridge T. Gerry along with cousins Robert Goelet Jr. and Ogden Goelet as executors of the estate. The last sentence in Peter's Will read, "The will was executed on May 29, 1876 and is written on three pages of legal paper, fastened together with a piece of blue ribbon."[43]

An article in a Milwaukee, Wisconsin newspaper chastised New York City newspapers for complaining that their millionaires die without leaving anything to the City. The deaths of Peter Goelet, Alexander Stewart, William B. Astor and Cornelius Vanderbilt were discussed as examples of stinginess in a world of need[44] Many of these men did contribute generously to charities during their life-times, however they chose to bequeath the bulk of their wealth to their families. Peter Goelet, as an example, only gave anonymously as was the custom of earlier, more private generations. Philanthropy in Uncle Peter's old-fashioned world, the world of his father, was based on religious conviction and revolutionary civic duty. In fact, Peter was most generous in stressful times of need, like the *Civil War*, during which he paid for the aid and support of returning wounded soldiers and the families of deceased soldiers in his district of New York City. Elbridge T. Gerry often told his own children to give generously while they lived to the causes of the day, then leave your estate to your children to carry on the good work. Elbridge T. Gerry practiced what he learned from the life-long example of his reclusive Uncle Peter and his generous father-in-law, Robert James Livingston. Elbridge accomplished a great deal more through his Gerry Society which became a legacy that managed to continue his philanthropy long after his own death, while leaving a substantial estate to his own children to follow in his footsteps.

1879 closed with an international trial for the *New York Society for the Prevention of Cruelty to Children* and it was a federal rather than a state case. Elbridge T. Gerry had a world-wide reputation as the founder and leader of the first enforcement society for child protection, having worked with foreign countries, including England and China, to encourage their protection of the rights of children. In September 1879 the NYSPCC received from the government of Italy information that a *padrone* named Antonio Ancarola was about to illegally bring a number of children to America. For many years prior to 1880 there existed in Italy a class of adventurers called *padrone* who falsely "offered shelter," as opposed to the honest Italian meaning of *padrone* as an innkeeper. These unscrupulous men obtained children by a contract with poor or destitute parents who were paid a fixed sum for the services of their children and always with the understanding that the children would be fed, clothed, and taught to sing and dance. The children usually worked half the year in Italy after which the young children worked in England or France. Finally they sailed to a port in America, usually New Orleans or New York, where they remained for six months and stayed in the slums of the cities. By day the padroni forced the children to play and dance in the streets for pocket change and at night the children performed in the lowest dens and concert saloons. At the end of each day their earnings were given to the padroni with little more than squalid shelter and little food as payment to the children. The girls became prostitutes at an early age, the boys learned to steal, many of the children died young of exhaustion and illness. The children could not speak English and were threatened if they attempted to escape or seek help. It was extremely difficult to obtain correct information about their names or the circumstances under which they had entered the country.

The *English Society for Organizing Charitable Relief* and the *Italian Benevolent Society* had broken up the traffic through England with vigorous efforts. In 1873 the Italian government enacted a law to prevent the sale of children by their parents, similar to the legislative efforts of Elbridge T. Gerry after the *Shepard's Fold* scandal in New York City, where children were purchased from parents and state funds were used for personal gain while the children starved. In 1874 the Congress of the United States passed an Act making it a felony for anyone to knowingly and willfully bring into the country or the territories any person sold or forcibly kidnapped in any other country for involuntary service. Under that law, the NYSPCC had enforcement jurisdiction over the *padroni* and the children they brought into the United States, specifically into New York City. In the fall of 1879 the agents of the NYSPCC, in response to the notification by the Italian government that *padroni* Ancarola had left Italy with several children, kept a close watch on all steamers and vessels from Europe. In November, after the arrival of the steamer *Elysia* from Liverpool the agents found seven boys, ranging in age from nine to thirteen years, all of whom were taken into custody by the *Gerry Society*. After being assured of protection the children admitted to their false names, identified the padroni as Antonio Ancarola, and described how they were threatened with severe punishment if they disclosed that information.[45]

Elbridge T. Gerry represented the federal government and the NYSPCC and was joined by Count Mario Campagnoni Marefoschi who appeared on behalf of the Italian Government. Ancarola was apprehended by NYSPCC agents a week after fleeing from the ship *Elysia* and was indicted under the Federal statute, tried on December 10, 1879, found guilty by the jury and sentenced to five years imprisonment. This was the first prosecution under the United States statute that started nation-wide enforcement practices to protect children imported from foreign countries as well as efforts to prevent the importation in the first place. These coordinated world-wide efforts went a long way in the *Progressive Era* to reduce the number of children sold into a life of poverty and servitude. The reach and influence of the Gerry Society was international in scope and was a living legacy for Elbridge T. Gerry during his lifetime and to his credit, the *New York Society for the Prevention of Cruelty to Children* continues today as a leading organization that provides oversight and proactive education programs for at-risk families in New York City.

Elbridge T. Gerry at the November 1876 meeting of the *New York Bar Association* in the Great Hall.

Gerry founded the *New York Society for the Prevention of Cruelty to Children* in 1874
after rescuing and representing Little Mary Ellen and citizens of New York clamored for his help.

Elbridge T. Gerry wore his NYSPCC badge on most days. The NYSPCC later became known as the *Gerry Society*.

Little Mary Ellen

Mary Ellen with her own two daughters

Display of NYSPCC badges as they evolved

Carriage designed to rescue children and bring them to the *Gerry Society* for protection and care

Three Gerry children were born before the close of 1879.

Lillian Gerry
1873–1891

Robert L. Gerry
1877–1957

Senator Peter G. Gerry
1879–1957

Elbridge T. Gerry with Mabel, Lillian, Angelica and little Robert "Bobby" on stone wall at Lake Delaware in 1880 when Peter (*not shown*) was just a year old.

Robert J. Livingston still owned Lake Delaware in1880 when his daughter Louisa Livingston visited with her children and her husband, Elbridge T. Gerry.

This photograph was taken on the same day and at the same spot as the photo above. This is a rare photo of the children with their beloved grandfather who lived in the adjoining townhouse in New York City.

Bobby

Angelica

Peter

Lake Delaware dock

Sailing on Lake Delaware

Lake Delaware boat house

Servants gathered on the lawn at Lake Delaware estate and farm near Delhi, New York, 1890's

Renwick built a townhouse (first building to the left of the church) for Frederick and Amy Gallatin at 670 Fifth Avenue on the corner just across the street from St. Thomas Church. The townhouse has a second story bay window above a pillared front entry.

James Renwick, Jr., architect
1818–1895
A close friend of both Frederick Gallatin and Elbridge T. Gerry

Several years later, Renwick also designed and built the Gallatin's summer home *Breezy Lawn* at East Hampton, Long Island, NY.

Renwick designed St. Patrick's Cathedral, New York City.

Renwick Art Gallery
Washington, DC

General Ulysses S. Grant (*seated left*) with his family at Long Branch

Grant Cottage at Long Branch, New Jersey

The Gerry family rented the Grant Cottage for the summer of 1879 when Louisa was pregnant with their fifth child.

St. Mark's Church and cemetery where Uncle Peter and Hannah Goelet were buried in the Goelet vault.

St. Mark's Church today

The church plaque reads:

Saint Mark's-in-the-Bowery

This late Georgian 1799 church replaced the chapel Peter Stuyvesant built in 1660 on his Bouwerie farm, making this Manhattan's oldest site used for a place of worship. Not only is the last Dutch Governor-General buried here but also seven generations of his descendants as well as members of the Goelet, Schermerhorn and Lorillard families. The Greek Revival steeple added in 1823 and the Italianate cast-iron porch of 1854 harmonize remarkably well with the original church.

Large stone on Goelet vault

6

GILDED GOTHAM

THE 1880'S PART I

Give me your tired, your poor, your huddled masses yearning to breathe free, the wretched refuse of your teeming shore. Send these, the homeless, tempest-tossed to me, lift up my lamp beside the golden door.

Statue of Liberty, New York City, 1883

The period between the Civil War and World War I is generally described as the *Gilded Age*. While New York City epitomized the period the entire country benefited in some way from the new found riches of Reconstruction growth and the emerging Industrial Revolution. In 1873 at the very outset of the *Gilded Age* one of America's greatest authors, Mark Twain, observed the coming impact of rapid growth and the resulting riches in his novel *The Gilded Age: A Tale of Today* in which he coined the name for the period. Twain looked to Shakespeare for his inspired and prophetic title; the play *King John* written in 1595 read, "To gild refined gold, to paint the lily, to perfume the violet or add another hue to the rainbow... is wasteful and ridiculous excess." The *Gilded Age* is popularly viewed as a dark age for American cities when the contrast between the rich and poor was dramatic and obvious. Newspapers of the day were in the business of selling papers so the story was everything. The scourges of New York City were justifiably editorialized, but just as prominently, the glitzy social doings of the upper-class were a tried and true means of selling papers. Indeed, the *Gilded Age* is similar to contemporary movie stars and billionaires who are captured in photos and print on a daily basis to satisfy the publics insatiable desire to vicariously share in the glamor and excitement of the lives of the rich and famous, even while the scourges of unemployment, poverty and civil wars share the daily news. Historians looked beneath the gleaming excess that the newspapers of the *Gilded Age* focused on, to understand the more complex growth of society, industry, and the resulting era of progressive change. It was a time when unions emerged to secure improved wages and working conditions, monopolies led to efficiencies, and mechanical and electrical invention improved work and daily life. There was unprecedented wealth that spurred wide-spread philanthropy that often out-shone the superficial excesses of the *Gilded Age.*[1] The *Gerry Society* and the establishment of *Carnegie Libraries* are lasting examples in twenty-first century America.

Literary New Yorker, Washington Irving, published a satirical little periodical in 1807 called the *Salmagundi.* The articles had shared authorship among Washington Irving, his brother William Irving, seventeen years his senior and his best friend, James K. Paulding. Scholars have compared the little publication to the twentieth century *Mad Magazine.*[2] The nickname for New York City, *Gotham,* was coined in 1807 in the *Salmagundi* article entitled *The Chronicles of the Renowned and Ancient City of Gotham.* Washington Irving looked to a British collection of stories, the *Merry Tales of the Mad Men of Gotham* published in 1460 for inspiration. The *Merry Tales* was a collection of legendary stories of English villagers alternatively wise and foolish.[3] The article, while written in a quaint and antiquated style, still brought a smile to a New Yorker's face when reading about the *Hoppingtots* attacking the city with their fancy footwork (dancing) and fiddle music that captured the imagination of the ladies of *Gotham.*[4] This satire could easily have been written seventy years later to poke fun at the *Gilded Age* fancy dress balls and dance lessons of the City's upper class youth. The characters sketched in the pleasant articles were assumed to be drawn more or less from the notables in the City; a whole bevy of beaux and belles saw themselves reflected in the *Ding Dongs* and *Sophy Sparkles* characters. In the *Gilded Age* the dapper, upper-class young men were known as *Dudes,* reminiscent of the *Ding Dongs* of the Washington Irving musings. The *Salmagundi* was found at almost every tea-table in New York City between 1807 and 1808. Its popularity was resurrected in the years after 1860 when the articles were collected for publication in a one-volume book.

Elbridge T. Gerry lived his entire life in *Gilded Gotham,* from *Gerry's Folly* as the brilliant lawyer of the Goelet and Livingston estates, to *Gerry's Society* as the protector of the City's abused children. But he was also a prominent member of *high society* in New York City. The decade of the 1870's established Elbridge as a full-time, hard-working lawyer, with clients from every strata of society. Elbridge may have moved in elite social circles but his legal work lay in the chaotic daily life of Gotham, from children of the dark corners of the City to the hog slaughtering warehouses, from divorce court to corporate bankruptcy, and even murder. He was a leader on hospital boards, the lawyers' Bar Association, and the Episcopal Church. Elbridge T. Gerry was a rare and significant bridge between the rich and poor of *Gilded Gotham.*

Why was Elbridge T. Gerry so hard-working and idealistic when the *Gilded Age* offered increasing leisure time and frivolity to the upper class and the wealthy? First of all, Elbridge was raised by Uncle Peter Goelet and his mother Hannah Goelet Gerry. They were part of an older generation of the early New York founding families. The Goelets began as humble, immigrant merchants who, by 1800, had grown their hardware business into the largest, most profitable enterprise in New York City. Eventually, the Goelets co-founded the *Chemical Bank* on whose Board sat the son of every successive generation. Additionally, investing in real estate was the prudent and wise way to protect one's earnings in the early days and old habits die hard. Old line Goelets were never ostentatious in their behavior, their life-style, or their social activities. Money was saved because they knew what it was to have none. Time was industriously spent in honorable work and the family was close-knit and religious. Elbridge was raised in a large but plain house on the outskirts of town by a near miserly Uncle Peter Goelet and a reclusive mother, Hannah Goelet Gerry, the widow of Thomas Russell Gerry, himself low-key, brilliant, but of frail constitution. Elbridge's father Thomas led a very private life, very compatible with the Goelet family he married into. It was in his son Elbridge's upbringing and nature to work industriously in every pursuit of his life. He was thirty years old before he married and had spent money only on his education and books, happily living the principled, highly focused life of a scholar/lawyer in the old *Broadway Farm* for nearly 25 years.

Second, the Goelets and Gerrys were highly intelligent families, well-educated and often eccentric in their intellectual approach to life. Elbridge was more entertained by his books, extensive research, and courtroom elocution than he was by fancy dress balls. He was not a cold man, his warmth, humor and caring touch were found in his wife and five children, a close-knit family that exchanged gifts on special occasions that almost always included favorite books. He was not reclusive as was the prior generation of Goelets that raised Elbridge. He was a student leader at Columbia College and had a close, active life with his cousins, Robert Jr. and Ogden Goelet, and his brother-in-law, Frederic Gallatin, all of whom became expert, passionate yachtsmen, the sport of *Gilded Age* wealthy gentlemen.

Third, the Goelets, Gerrys, Gallatins and Livingstons were active in the Episcopal Church of New York City. Elbridge T. Gerry was a highly principled man, sometimes rigid but always willing to negotiate, indeed, he eagerly worked to understand every aspect of circumstances he encountered. Even within his church, Elbridge chaired committees, prepared church legislative documents, and eventually became an expert on canon law, attending the annual *Episcopal Diocesan Convention.* The most sincere gift he gave his children over the years was religious in nature, often beautiful little bibles. He and Louisa raised their children with one foot firmly planted in the world of the mind, with exceptional educations, and in the principled world of their church; the other foot was planted in the glamour of *Gilded Age* society in which the children enjoyed friendships, horsemanship, summer holidays and even romance.

Elbridge and Louisa, in contrast to their cousins, Robert and Ogden Goelet, had wealth that belonged not to them, but to their parents. Their wealth was that of "anticipated inheritance" and not of available, liquid assets. Elbridge was literally an elite working man who had to support his family on an earned income. The *Washington Post* in a December 20, 1880 page 2 column entitled *Personal*, made a one line statement, "Elbridge T. Gerry is the richest practicing lawyer in New York City." While he was a highly-paid and prominently successful lawyer, the Gerrys lived modestly in a brownstone townhouse adjacent to Louisa's parents for over twenty years until their youngest child was sixteen and their eldest twenty-two. In fact Elbridge was fifty-seven years old before he built his mansion on Fifth Avenue. By *Gilded Age* standards the Forty-Eighth Street townhouse was barely acceptable for entertaining elite society friends like the Astors, Gallatins, Vanderbilts, and the Goelet brothers, all of whom had built mansions along Fifth Avenue by 1884. Both Robert and Ogden chose architect Edward H. Kendall to design their modified *French Renaissance* style mansions on corners at the same intersection, located within two blocks of their cousin Elbridge's Forty-Eighth Street townhouse. The proximity of their homes sustained close-knit relationships among the three family units. The Goelet mansions accommodated glittering social events, hosting 200 guests for dinners, receptions and society balls for fifty years. The Goelets decorated with tapestries, antiques and artwork collected from around the globe by two successive generations through the 1930's.

The first inheritance for Elbridge and Louisa was the $500,000 left by Uncle Peter in November 1879, part of which Elbridge used to buy his first yacht. Robert Jr. and Ogden inherited multi-millions from their father, Robert Sr., and their Uncle Peter that same fall of 1879. The Goelet brothers knew how to manage their inheritance, but they also knew how to spend it, this was a new generation of Goelets. Elbridge's mother, Hannah, also inherited her share of the multi-millions from her brothers, Peter and Robert in the fall of 1879. But for Hannah it was income from the real estate holdings that continued to support her, her daughter, and her sister in the Nineteenth and Broadway house. Hannah's inherited "millions" were in the "value of the real estate," which was managed by her nephew, Robert Goelet Jr. and not her son Elbridge. It was not until 1891 when Louisa's father, Robert James Livingston died, and 1895, when Elbridge's mother, Hannah Goelet Gerry died, that Elbridge and Louisa Gerry inherited great wealth that, for the first time, they personally accessed and managed. The *Gilded Age* life-style of the Gerrys was on a smaller scale than that of their prominent Gotham social circle but it was active and glamorous nonetheless.

January 1880 opened with joyful news in the Gerrys' extended family. Frederic and Almy Gerry Gallatin welcomed the birth of Albert, their third son on January 8. He joined his sisters, Almy 12 and Jean 7, and older brothers, Rolaz 9 and Goelet 3 years old. All of the Gallatin children were the namesakes of Gerry, Goelet, and Gallatin family relatives. Thirty-five years after their father's untimely death, siblings Elbridge and Almy each had five children, a total of ten cousins to inaugurate the next generation of Gerrys in New York City.

In early January, just after the Gallatin baby was born, Elbridge T. Gerry as President of *New York Society for the Prevention of Cruelty to Children* (NYSPCC) was notified by *Saint Luke's Hospital* that a boy named Louis Victor, belonging to the *Shepherd's Fold* charitable institution for children run by Mr. and Mrs. Cowley, was in their hospital suffering from the effects of starvation. Elbridge visited the child in the hospital and had a photograph taken of him as evidence for the Court to support the rescue of other children from the charity house by the NYSPCC. Today the *NYSPCC Archives* hold hundreds of such photos in their case files going all the way back to the Mary Ellen case.

On January 14 the NYSPCC brought six carriages and several officers and Society Agents to the *Shepherd's Fold* tenement house, surrounded it and after peacefully entering, proceeded to search for children. Many were found on the third floor in two twenty-foot square bedrooms that housed thirteen beds each. All of the discovered children were placed in the waiting carriages and taken directly to the Supreme Court. As Judge Donohue was disposing of the routine business before him, Elbridge T. Gerry suddenly came into the courtroom and marshaled in a company of twenty-four children ranging in age from three years to thirteen years old. Accompanied by officers and agents of the NYSPCC the children were seated at the back of the court room. The judge immediately signed an order giving custody of the children to the NYSPCC until the *Shepherd's Fold* had time to present their defense in the case. A reporter for the *Herald* asked Mr. Gerry what he would do now and Elbridge replied, "I shall follow Dicken's example in *David Copperfield* and I shall first give them something to eat." The children were at once taken to a restaurant on Chatham Street where they were fed amid many onlookers. Proper precaution was taken to see that the children did not over-feed themselves. About an hour later lawyers for Mr. and Mrs.

Cowley of the *Shepherd's Fold,* almost out of breath, entered Judge Donohue's chamber and stated that they wished to interpose a defense. The judge adjourned the hearing for one week to provide time for a proper defense.[5] The papers followed the case through its conclusion with the safe placement of all the children. Subsequently, after further hearings, Mr. Cowley was sent to prison on *Blackwell's Island* and the *Shepherd's Fold* was closed. This highly publicized case led to state legislative proposals, City council testimony, and correspondence from prison through December 1880.

The NYSPCC, six years old in 1880, was the first of its kind in the world and its work was noticed in the foreign press. Elbridge T. Gerry understood the valuable knowledge that could be gained by taking an interest in the problems and solutions of child cruelty as practiced in other countries. He read several newspapers each day, including the international press to follow the world-wide status of children. Elbridge was never passive in his public response to known instances of cruelty, regardless of the country or the status of the culprit inflicting the harm. The 1880s initiated Elbridge's regular and broad-based presence in the public forum seeking to redress the scourge of child cruelty. A January 1880 internationally publicized incident in China prompted Elbridge to write on behalf of the mistreated Chinese children:

> Washington, Jan. 21, 1880, a few months ago the civilized world read with a feeling of horror and astonishment a graphic account of the treatment visited by the Chinese Government upon the person and family of Yakoob Bey, a distinguished and formidable rebel, who successfully defied the authority of the Imperial government for many months before he was vanquished and captured. Yakoob Bey and certain other members of his family were put to death with fearful tortures. Two of his boys, who were infants, were consigned to custody under an Imperial decree and will be confined until they are 11 years old, when they will be made eunuchs and given over to the soldiers as slaves. A few days before the meeting of the United States Congress, Mr. Elbridge T. Gerry, the President of the NYSPCC, addressed a letter to the President of the United States, requesting him to appeal to the Chinese Government to deliver up the children to the government of the United States, and offering on behalf of the society which he represents, to take care of them. The President, of course, could not undertake to comply with this request, and Mr. Gerry, through Senator Kernan, appealed to Congress.[6]

There is no record of any success with the appeal to Congress, but the gesture itself was a means of lobbying the federal government to take notice of a humanitarian issue that plagued cities throughout America and the world.

February and March were consumed with an appeal by Elbridge T. Gerry on behalf of David W. Bruce, a creditor of the *New York Republication Newspaper* whose trustees had abandoned the corporation because it had no means of procuring money and had ceased to carry on business. Elbridge argued that there was a sufficient organization of the company to hold the trustees liable for debts incurred before the corporate default, and that the trustees were obligated by law to produce an annual report, which would have notified investors and creditors of the impending collapse of the corporation. However, the Judge ruled that the corporation was uncertain from the point of its original incorporation and when it failed the suspension of business was not temporary but complete. Further, by the fact that the corporation was bankrupt and had ceased to do business relieved the trustees from the obligation of the statute to make and file a report.[7] Complex litigation win or lose was as ever Elbridge's specialty.

Late March offered the Gerrys a social antidote to the intensity of Elbridge's law practice. One of the most brilliant weddings on the list for Easter week was celebrated at 3 o'clock on March 30 at the Church of the Transfiguration, Twenty-Ninth Street and Fifth Avenue. The groom was ex-State Senator Alfred Wagstaff and the bride Miss Mary A. Barnard. At no recent occasion had the legal profession and the wealth and fashion of the City been more fully represented. The ceremony lasted but a few minutes followed by a reception at the residence of the late Judge George A. Barnard at 23 West Twenty-First Street. The bridal presents were displayed in an upper room where guests observed that they were the largest and most magnificent array of the season. The Gerrys' gift was a silver water pitcher. Being the *Gilded Age,* the groom's family presented a set of diamonds, and the bride's grandfather presented $10,000 in cash and a magnificent set of pearls worn at the ceremony. Guests joined the bride and groom for a lavish wedding breakfast served under the supervision of the fashionable *Pinard* restaurant, which was a most satisfying close to the celebration.[8] Adding to the extended Gerry family joy, just one year after their wedding, on March 19, 1880 Elbridge's cousin Robert Goelet and his wife, Harrietta Warren, welcomed their first child, a son, Robert Walton Goelet, a playmate for cousins 3 year-old Robert Gerry and 1 year-old Peter Gerry.

In April Elbridge once again put pen to paper to respond to a newspaper article that may have misconstrued the intentions of legislation that he had requested be introduced in the Assembly in response to the *Shepherd's Fold* case. His letter to the *New York Times,* read:

Permit me to correct some misapprehensions contained in your editorial entitled "Abuses of City Charity."

1. The bill introduced by Mr. Mitchell, at my request, is designed simply to prevent the committal of children by Civil Justices, by consent of their parents and that the instance of the latter, to institutions which derive thereby a per capita allowance from the City. Our Police magistrates are now chargeable by law with all commitments of children; and, so far as I can ascertain, they usually exercise both discrimination and judgment in their action. The bill in question does not attempt to limit their authority.
2. The bill in question is non-sectarian. In my judgment, the *Catholic Protectory* is one of the best governed institutions in this City.
3. The subject of per capita allowances does not necessarily depend on a question of faith. How to diminish the expense of caring for children who must be cared for somewhere, and who certainly are not well cared for in an absolutely public institution, is the problem which the committee appointed at the recent meeting of the *State Board of Charities* will consider. In the solution there are two things to be borne in view: First, the benefit of the children; and, second, possible diminution of expense to the tax-payer. Elbridge T. Gerry, President, NYSPCC[9]

This same month, his cousins Robert and Ogden Goelet were busy working on designs for their mansions. Robert's was built on Fifth Avenue over the next year and a half. The Goelet brothers also contributed to the cultural life of New York City in mid-April 1880 when they joined J.P. Morgan, Cornelius, William H. and William K. Vanderbilt and George Warren (Robert Goelet's brother-in-law), among other wealthy leaders, at the office of James A. Roosevelt on Pine Street, to inaugurate plans for a new opera house for New York City. By 3 o'clock subscriptions amounting to $250,000 were received on condition that the entire capital stock ($600,000) would be raised in the next ten months, otherwise the money would be refunded. The gentlemen had the enterprise in hand and had no doubt whatsoever that the entire stock would be bought at once and the work would begin by the end of the year. The intention was to build the most magnificent opera house on the continent. By the time it was finished the five-year lease at the *Academy of Music* on Fourteenth Street would expire and the *Academy* would go out of existence. The valuable property on which it stood was needed for office buildings.[10] Through the twenty-first century the Goelet family has been faithful in its generous support of opera and musical theatre in New York City. Robert Goelet Jr.'s daughter-in-law, Anne-Marie Gustier, and his grandson, Francis Goelet (1926-1998) joined together in 1966 to contribute to the construction of

Lincoln Center, the new home of the *New York Metropolitan Opera,* and where the *Grand Staircase* was gratefully named in honor of the Goelet family.

May and June were business as usual for New York's busiest lawyer. In May, Peter Goelets property was still in probate six months after his death. The size and complexity of property holdings required the expertise of Elbridge T. Gerry who, as Executor of the estate, had just completed the assignment of a Goelet mortgage on May 13.

The next week on May 18 the courts in New York City adjourned to honor the recently deceased Chief Justice of the Court of Appeals, Judge Church. A meeting of members of the Bar was held in the Supreme Court to give expression to the sadness at the sudden death of the Chief Justice. A series of resolutions declared that the Bar of the City of New York bore willing and grateful testimony to Judge Church's learning, ability, industry, and scrupulous fidelity in the discharge of his judicial functions. Judge Davis then appointed a committee to represent the Bar at the funeral to take place that afternoon. Elbridge T. Gerry was appointed to the distinguished committee.[11]

Another testimonial of a leading New Yorker was held June 19. An elegant gold badge set with diamonds was placed on exhibition at Tiffany's. It was presented to Mr. Henry Bergh, now sixty-seven years old, as a mark of the personal esteem and friendship of his colleagues. Accompanying the badge was a beautifully illuminated scroll signed by the Executive Committee of the *Society for the Prevention of Cruelty to Animals,* which included the following gentlemen: Frederic Gallatin, Elbridge T. Gerry, and Charles L. Tiffany, among several others.[12]

By June 22 the *New York Society for the Prevention of Cruelty to Children* was back on the front page of the City papers. A sixteen year old girl, Florence Mosby, had gone missing from her home and the City was helpless to find her. She was the daughter of General John Singleton Mosby (1833-1916), the famous Confederate soldier known as the *Grey Ghost* during the Civil War. General Mosby led a special cavalry battalion known as *Mosby's Rangers* famous for carrying out daring raids far inside Union lines and successfully disrupted supply lines and courier communications. Col. Mosby's classical college training at the University of Virginia was similar to Elbridge T. Gerry's at Columbia College. Mosby joined the *Literary Society* and the *Debating Union* and after the Civil War he became a lawyer and established a private practice. He married Pauline Clarke the daughter of a prominent attorney and they had six children, one of whom was Florence Mosby. Her mother died shortly after giving birth in 1875 when Florence was eleven years old. The children were placed with various care-givers for the remainder of their childhood. Col. Mosby had supported Gen. Ulysses S. Grant for President in 1872 and in 1879 President Rutherford B. Hayes appointed Col. Mosby the United States Consul to Hong Kong (1879-1885). Later he worked as an assistant attorney in the Department of Justice (1904-1910). The prominence of Col. Mosby was broad-based in the United States during his life-time. In fact, during Gen. George S. Patton's childhood one of the best friends of the Patton family was none other than Col. Mosby. Patton grew up hearing tales of daring raids and stunning cavalry attacks from the *Grey Ghost* himself. Gen. Mosby would play the role of himself and let young George Patton play the part of General Robert E. Lee when they re-enacted the battles of the Civil War astride their imaginary horses.[13]

In recent years while her father Col. Mosby was Consul to Hong Kong, Florence Mosby was living with Mrs. Camp and her two sons in Somers, New York. The Camps were not family relatives but rather had legally adopted Florence as a young child. She had not seen her father Col. Mosby for many years. On April 13, 1880 Florence ran away from the home of a friend, Mrs. Smith, at 67 Saint Mark's Place in New York City where she was visiting. After a week of searching the City, the police and detectives decided to place an advertisement in the *Herald* newspaper offering a reward to seek the public's help in finding the girl. Just after the advertisement was published, Mrs. Camp received a letter from Elbridge T. Gerry stating that Florence Mosby was in the hands of the *Society for the Prevention of Cruelty to Children* and he demanded to know by what right a reward was offered for her recovery. Mrs. Camp then went to the Society office for an interview with Mr. Gerry. Elbridge explained that Florence had left the Smith home and proceeded directly to the NYSPCC and asked for protection. The reasons given by the young girl for running away were very strong but of such character as to render their publication imprudent. Elbridge indicated that as a "voluntary charge" with the society, he would not force her to leave and indeed preferred to bring her before the court to sort out the girl's charges against the Camp family. The interview ended and Mrs. Camp left with a threat to commence a suit against the Society for the girl's return to the family. Mr. Gerry immediately notified the New York City police of Florence Mosby's whereabouts, and without apology, refused to disclose her precise location. In June a dedicated reporter discovered that Florence was living in the home of the *Children's Aid Society* at 27 Saint Mark's Place just four blocks from the house she fled. Elbridge's father-in-law Robert J. Livingston was on the Board of the *Children's Aid Society* and no doubt assisted in safely placing the girl in the care of the society home. The matron of the home described Florence:

> She could neither read nor write, and although sixteen years of age, her manner was unsophisticated and simple in her speech, as a child of ten years. She was very beautiful and wonderfully prepossessing, tall, of fair complexion, with light blue eyes and dark brown hair. Her features stamp her as an aristocrat, no matter where she came from. She is as guileless a girl as I have ever met, and while Mrs. Camp never sent her to school, she has learned the alphabet while staying here at the *Children's Aid Society* home.[14]

The authorities made attempts to contact Col. Mosby in Hong Kong but the difficulty in communicating such a distance proved a delay in the resolution of this case; the Mosby story was not further reported in the newspapers. Elbridge T. Gerry always strove to protect the privacy of his charges, particularly the older children like Florence Mosby. Ultimately, after appearing in court with Mr. Gerry she was returned to the care of the *Children's Aid Society* to be educated, protected, and prepared for emancipation at age eighteen in just two years. Then Florence, like most properly trained society charges, would be carefully placed in a service position to earn a wage and thereafter to support herself independently.

News reports from across the country at the start of the 1880 summer season had established Newport, Rhode Island as the nation's most prominent "watering place." The next generation of New York elites abandoned both Saratoga and West Point, the resorts of their childhood, for what became a *Gilded Age* extravagance that was exclusive and more formal by 1885. Although Newport was a small seaport town of twelve-thousand inhabitants in 1880, it was beautiful and had a glorious history as one of the first settlements in the Colonies, and in fact had been the commercial rival of Boston, New York, and Philadelphia. The *American Revolution* dealt a heavy blow to the town and reduced its population by half when the predominantly British population that was opposed to independence fled Newport and returned to England. After independence, Newport also lost its commercial ambition and became a thriving, yet small port town known to have a pleasant climate with many wealthy, often artistic and literary residents.[15] The historian, George Bancroft, spent his summers in Newport and as widely traveled as he was, he found Newport an admirable place for study and literary work. In 1878 he was in Newport writing the tenth and final volume of his famous *History of the United States, from the Discovery of the American Continent* published by Little Brown in Boston. George Bancroft was a regular guest at the balls, teas, and social affairs of Newport during the early *Gilded Age* summer holidays. Historically many Easterners had summered at Newport but usually at the hotels where there were dances called "hops," weekly musicals, and where charades was always a favorite game. By 1880 "new money" arrived in the sleepy town. Over the next seven years large farms skirting the cliffs that overlooked the ocean were subdivided and sold as estate land on which to build summer residences, known as "cottages" or "villas." Most newcomers prized locations along the Eastern and Southern rim of the Island which was edged by the *Cliff Walk*. Local historians suggest that the first established paths along the cliff shore line were outlined by deer, followed by the Narragansett Indians, and then the early colonists traveled the path to salvage from shipwrecks. Serious development of the *Cliff Walk* started about 1880 and then each successive estate owner improved their bit of the *Walk*, improving it piece-by-piece through 1929. Over the last 150 years the public and some of the wealthy estate owners have clashed over access rights. Owners at times have moved the pathway closer to more dangerous areas, erected walls or fences, and even placed boulders directly across the *Walk*. Some even planted shrubs and trees to block or discourage access to the *Walk* and a few posted dogs to scare people away. Legal challenges have opened the *Walk* for public use based on "Fisherman's Rights" granted by the *Colonial Charter* of King Charles II and a passage in the *Rhode Island Constitution* that granted the public "rights of fishery and the privilege of the shore to which they have heretofore been entitled."[16]

Bellevue Avenue was the main thoroughfare that connected the port town with the emerging area of exclusive mansions. What was known locally as *Bailey's Farm*, adjacent to the southern beach of Newport, was purchased for $150 an acre in 1865. Just ten years later parcels were being sold for $9,000 an acre to build summer residences. The southern beach became exclusive by subscription to the estate owners and was named *Bailey's Beach* in honor of the original farm designation. A few years later another farm of twenty-two acres, known as *Ochre Point* due to the color of the cliff, sold for $10,000. Within ten years just six acres of the total parcel was sold for $88,000.[17]

Elbridge T. Gerry's father-in-law, Robert J. Livingston, had several brothers and sisters, some of whom lived in or near New York City. His brother, Maturin Livingston, named after their father, was summering at a cottage in Newport, Rhode Island in 1880. He joined one of the early *Gilded Age* hostesses Mrs. Levi P. Morton at her villa *Fairlawn* where she entertained a hundred guests for dinner and dancing. Guests included John Jacob Astor and George Bancroft among others described as "brilliant" by the press.[18] Neither the Gerrys nor the Gallatins were at Newport; each had five children ranging in age from one year to nine and twelve respectively. Indeed, the Gallatins spent the summer of 1880 expanding their East Hampton, Long Island summer home Breezy Lawn. The house was expanded with the addition of turrets providing at least six bedrooms on the second floor and expanding the servant quarters on the fourth floor. The house was painted a deep red to complement the green of the natural surroundings. The remote country life during the hot summers suited the growing but very young Gallatin and Gerry families for several years. Not until their children were teenagers in the 1890's did the Gerrys join the Newport "watering place," although cousins Robert and his brother Ogden had long since purchased property along the *Cliff Walk*, part of the *Ochre Point Farm* on which they later built homes, Robert in 1882 and Ogden in 1885. While the cousins remained intimate friends the 1880's found a departure of life-style between the Goelet brothers and Elbridge T. Gerry. The Goelet inheritance initiated grand building projects, first their mansions on Fifth Avenue and then their mansions in Newport, Rhode Island, all built while they were in their late 30's and early 40's and when each only had one or two young children. Not for another ten years, when Elbridge was in his late fifties was he financially able to build a mansion home in New York City for his large family. Between 1881 and 1886 the Gerrys summered at the historic *Lake Delaware Farm* in the Catskills with Robert J. and Louisa Livingston. Between 1887 and 1894 the Gerrys rented a cottage in Newport and later bought a furnished cottage at the end of Bellevue Avenue, never choosing to build a villa of their own. This suited the Gerrys well. They were extremely involved with their children and took less interest in building villas outside of New York City than did their society peers. Indeed, Elbridge always took working vacations, which eventually included tutors for his children. Louisa was not shy about entertaining, she was well known for her large dinner parties, balls, and teas when the children were older and the opportunity to meet worthy suitors was essential. However, Louisa was a task-master and she was the envy of her peers for her ability to manage a household and orchestrate her large dinner parties flawlessly. Louisa was, after all, a Livingston, the daughter of a leading family in the history of New York State. She cherished both the Gerry and Livingston family histories and took personal responsibility for ensuring the continuity of their position and influence in contemporary New York social life, instilling the founding family pride and sense of duty in the next generation.

Sometime in 1880 Elbridge T. Gerry was socializing with two friends, both *Columbia College* alumni, Judge Monell and Mr. Hattendorf, Jr. who in later years was the Historian for the national *Chi Psi* Fraternity. During their conversation Elbridge happened to say that their fraternity had never surrendered its charter and that Elbridge would like to revive the fraternity. Later Mr. Hattendorf introduced Elbridge to other Chi Psi brothers who also shared his interest in reviving the fraternity. Elbridge sponsored a dinner at the Hotel Brunswick where a *Chi Psi Lodge* was opened and five members initiated and at a subsequent dinner another three Columbia alumni were initiated into the *Lodge*. This type of joint mentoring and socializing with *Columbia College* alumni was a special pleasure for Elbridge, as well as what he considered to be a civic duty of educated men of means. While the Lodge did not last more than a few years, Elbridge T. Gerry continued his personal college friendships and participated as a life member of *Chi Psi* through the Fraternity's national newsletter *The Purple and the Gold,* of which a few old copies are held in the manuscript collection of Columbia University's *Butler Library* Rare Book Room in the personal papers of Elbridge T. Gerry.

New York's prominent wedding of the summer season was held on August 12, 1880 at All Saints' Church in Newport, Rhode Island. It was the marriage of *Cambridge* graduate, Mr. George Cavendish-Bentinck, cousin of the Duke of Portland and Miss Bessie Livingston, the daughter of Maturin Livingston and the first cousin of Louisa Livingston Gerry. The Gerrys traveled with Robert J. and Louisa Livingston to Newport for the family wedding, one of several notable *Gilded Age* marriages between a British blue-blood and an American heiress. In this case the Cavendish-Bentinck family were in fact wealthy and came from a line of Prime Ministers with connections back to King William III , and later King George IV who personally stood as best man at the wedding of Mr. Bentinck's grandfather who was on the *Privy Council* in London. The newlyweds rented a cottage in Newport for the remainder of the season to get to know new family and friends before returning to the Cavendish-Bentinck estate in England which became their permanent residence.

The new year of 1880 welcomed the birth of Ogden and Mary Goelet's second child, Robert Wilson Goelet, who was called "Bertie" to distinguish him from his cousin, Robert Walton Goelet, who was also born in 1880 to Robert and Harrietta Goelet. The cousins "Robert" grew up as brothers, attended Harvard together and then studied for their masters degrees together. They looked very much alike. Both "Robert's" followed in the footsteps of their fathers, Bertie became the consummate businessman with the low-key life-style of his father Robert, and Robert III became a wealthy socializer like his father, Ogden, and sadly, would marry four times.

The Gallatin family spent their summers at the *Breezy Lawn* estate in East Hampton, Long Island. The growing children had lots of room to play and relax and Frederic and Almy avoided the glamour and formality of Newport. In fact, Almy Gerry Gallatin invited her mother, Hannah Goelet Gerry, her Aunt Jean Goelet, and her sister Jean Buchanan Gerry to spend summers at *Breezy Lawn* to rejuvenate in the fresh air and quiet respite away from the New York City noise surrounding the *Broadway Farm* mansion, their reclusive home of thirty-five years. The elderly sisters and thirty-eight year old Aunt Jean also found quality time to enjoy the five Gallatin children, who in turn got to know their grandmother Hannah, great-Aunt Jean Goelet, and Aunt Jean Gerry. Although Frederic Gallatin was an intimate friend of his brother-in-law Elbridge T. Gerry, and both were lawyers, Frederic was primarily a banker by profession. He was free to indulge in more secluded non-working holidays unlike his brother-in-law Elbridge who made his living as a practicing lawyer. Working vacations meant going on vacation where your clients, friends, and family (the Goelets) went on vacation, which meant Newport, Rhode Island instead of East Hampton, Long Island. In a couple of years, however, all of these social circles would add two new "seasons" to their annual calendar. First, they began traveling to Europe by steamship, and second, yacht clubs established regattas between America and Europe. In London the arrival of yachts and New Yorkers was called the American season where socializing on estates, attending opera, shopping, and of course, having English high tea was the norm. By the late 1880's the new seasonal activities created "traveling social circles" that stimulated a transcontinental life-style that introduced foreign art and culture to the *Gilded Age*, particularly exemplified in fashion, mansion architecture, and interior design using French, Italian, Spanish, or Asian influences. America's elite society was embarking on their Shakespearean period of "painting the lily, perfuming the violet, and adding a new hue to the rainbow," *gold*, the glitter of the *Gilded Age*.

Men of the gilded period were busy making deals, making money, joining the right clubs, and socializing with all the right people, essentially wielding power to make more millions. The wives of these wealthy, powerful men provided the social venues in which their husbands could do business while enjoying good food, lovely company, and accomplish the requisite match-making of their privileged children. These women had enormous power within their allotted sphere of influence and their daughters joined in the social rituals which included "visiting" friends on a regular basis, attending lectures at the lyceum, and participating in charity work. Women discovered that, beyond being pretty and hosting a lovely dance, they could think independently, discuss and struggle with social issues, and travel to countries beyond their own shore. While they would never press beyond their circumscribed social routines, women were emerging from the background, attending suffrage lectures and discussing women's rights during their afternoon round of visits among friends. In October, 1880 one of the leading society ladies, Mrs. Elisabeth Thompson, made a liberal contribution for the publication of the *History of Woman Suffrage in the United States*, which Miss Susan B. Anthony, Mrs. Cady Stanton, and Mrs. Gage were then compiling. In fact, both Ms. Anthony and Mrs. Stanton cancelled all of their lyceum lectures for the season to spend the winter together at Mrs. Stanton's home in rural Tenafly, New Jersey to complete the multi-volume publication. The Tenafly house is now on the *National Register of Historic Places* in America.[19] Mrs. Cady Stanton was the daughter of Margaret Livingston, who was the daughter of Col. James Livingston, an officer in the Continental Army during the American Revolution. He had fought at Saratoga and Quebec and had assisted in the capture of Major John Andre at West Point, where Andre and Benedict Arnold, who escaped aboard the HMS *Vulture,* were scheming to turn West Point over to the English. Col. James Livingston's mother was the sister of General Abraham Ten Broeck. James's father, John Livingston 1709-1791 was a prominent lawyer and the grandson of James Livingston, the brother of Robert Livingston, the First Lord of the *Livingston Manor* at Clermont. Elizabeth Cady Stanton was in the Livingston lineage just as Louisa M. Gerry was in that same historic family. In 1867 after presenting the keynote speech at the first anniversary of the *American Equal Rights Association* in New York City, Mrs. Stanton presented a signed copy of the proceedings to Elbridge T. Gerry, which remained in his library throughout his life among a collection of books on women's health and women's rights.[20]

November 1880 found Elbridge T. Gerry in City Hall testifying before a Senate Investigating Committee into the funding of state charity institutions. In his testimony Elbridge condemned the policy of paying to private institutions of charity a certain per capita amount toward the support of their inmates, and recommended passage of a law prohibiting such allowances. Further, he stated that the work of maintaining the really destitute, especially orphans or homeless children, and placing juvenile offenders under wholesome corrective influences, was an entirely proper one for private benevolent charities. But when private institutions became beneficiaries of the public they had to be subject to such supervision as would secure a proper application of the funds and prevent abuses that may otherwise creep in, such as the starvation of children at the *Shepherd's Fold* charity earlier that year.[21] A month later on December 3 Elbridge T. Gerry appeared once again before the Senate committee to refute charges that his earlier testimony was misleading as to the accounts of specific charities. Elbridge denied the interpretation of his earlier statements and offered to produce letters from the accusing charity and himself to clarify the matter. The committee agreed to have Mr. Gerry's letters entered into evidence, which finally resolved the dispute. Then, on December 9 the Senate Committee received another charge against Elbridge T. Gerry in a letter from the former Superintendent of the *Shepherd's Fold,* Mr. Edward Cowley. It was written from his prison cell on Blackwell's Island.

In it he said some misstatements had been made concerning him by Mr. Gerry and Mrs. Lowell, and he asked to be permitted to lay the facts before the committee. While the committee responded for the record that they would consider Mr. Cowley's request, the case had been decided in a court of law and letters from prison after conviction would not alter the verdict. Mr. Cowley's jailhouse complaints found neither pity nor justification.

Elbridge T. Gerry seemed to be on a letter-writing campaign in 1880. In the fall the *New York Opera* engaged several performances, of which two, *Mephistopheles* and *Aida,* included the performance of British children. A newspaper reporter found the manager of the opera, Col. Mapleson, at his desk very seriously studying a letter he had received from Elbridge T. Gerry.

> Just look at this," he said. "Did you ever hear anything like it? Anybody who knows me knows that I couldn't be cruel to anybody. Read that letter, it seems to me that everybody wants to bother me, as if a manager didn't have trouble enough on his hands without being pestered by all sorts of societies. I wonder what will be next.[22]

The letter notified Mr. Mapleson that employing children in a dance was in violation of the law and that unless he ceased to employ them, he would be proceeded against in a summary manner. Mr. Mapleson notified the press because he believed the children were all well and happy. In fact last winter when *Aida* was brought out the opera had obtained permission from the NYSPCC to employ the children. Mr. Mapleson had the *New York Times* publish his reply to Elbridge T. Gerry. In turn, Elbridge published his reply both to answer Mr. Mapleson's public inquiry and to explain to the general public how the law protected children using the case of the Italian opera on stage in New York City as a prime example. The assertion of Mr. Mapleson in your paper that this society ever consented to his violation of the law relating to using children for dancing purposes is simply untrue. I proceed to show briefly that the intention as well as the letter of the law, applies to the existing case of which he complains.

1. The *letter* of the law expressly prohibits dancing by children of the ages of those used in the opera.
2. The *spirit* of the law was intended to protect these children from physical exhaustion and to enable them to be educated rather than travel the world performing.

3. The law treats as infants all persons under a certain age without distinction. I see no reason why these children, because born of British parents, should not be protected while in the United States.
4. These theatrical performances by children work a permanent injury to them, because, in the first place, they deprive them of their natural rest, and subject them to unnecessary physical efforts.
5. It is idle to say that these children are lawfully earning their livelihood by this business. The law of England, as well of this State, contemplates that parents shall support their children during these tender years.
6. If the law is erroneous, the Legislature amends it.[23]

Elbridge told the papers that he was at a loss to understand the conduct of the *London School Board* in permitting the children to leave England for a purpose which the law of England declares to be illegal. He addressed a letter to the *Society for the Protection of Women and Children in England,* inviting their attention to the case of Mr. Mapleson's opera company to request that the society not allow this practice to be repeated. Three days later the papers described the disappointed audience at the opera when the children did not appear on stage as expected. Mr. Mapleson told the press, "Well, I'm sorry, but it couldn't be helped. Mr. Gerry secured a warrant for my arrest, and said that if the children were allowed to come upon the stage tonight, I should be arrested and dragged away somewhere to answer for my cruelty. I understand his officers are hanging about the house now. So I decided to avoid the annoyance and sent the children home. If Mr. Gerry's society insists that they should not dance, then I will send the children back to England, and lamented that one of the children had a gold medal presented to her by the Princess of Wales for her proficiency as a scholar, and for her graceful dancing in *Aida.*" [24]

Christmas heralded Elbridge's forty-third birthday and the newspapers happily printed two articles celebrating the family heritage of the Gerrys and the Livingstons. A lecture at Harvard College recalled several battles of the *Revolutionary War* and described how after the *Battle of Bunker Hill,* among others, wounded soldiers were taken to the abandoned *Elmwood* mansion in nearby Cambridge to be treated for their wounds. Many died in the make-shift hospital and were buried in the field fronting the confiscated mansion. After the war, Elbridge Gerry purchased the *Elmwood* estate and out of respect for the soldiers buried in his front yard, he never permitted a ploughshare to disturb the ashes of the revolutionary heroes. The Gerry family always considered it sacred ground for as long they lived in Cambridge.[25]

The second article described the annual holiday *Patriarchs' Ball,* held at the famous Delmonico's Restaurant on Christmas Day. There were forty-eight members of the association, which was founded ten years earlier by leaders of New York society. The *Patriarchs* were recognized as the oldest founding families of colonial New York City, and in several instances, founders of New York State, called *Patroons.* Included were the Astors, Fishs, Goelets, Roosevelts, Stewarts, Schermerhorns, Warrens and of course, the Livingstons among others. The Gerrys were not listed because they were patriarchs of Massachusetts, not New York. However, by way of Elbridge T. Gerry's marriage to Louisa M. Livingston and his mother being a Goelet, he was warmly welcomed as one of the New York Patriarchs.

On February 26, 1881 the Patriarchs sponsored the winter *Bachelors' Ball* by soliciting young men of the Clubs to each pay a tax to defray the expenses of the festivities. The ball was held at the *Metropolitan Concert Hall* and the dinner was provided by Delmonico's restaurant.

The Patronesses were Mrs. William Astor, Mrs. Hamilton Fish, Mrs. Adrian Iselin, Mrs. Maturin Livingston, Mrs. Francis Rives, and Mrs. William Schermerhorn. Maturin Livingston was five years older than his brother Robert James Livingston, Louisa Gerry's father, and Maturin was more active and prominent in New York and Newport society. Younger brother Robert J. Livingston was a private man, more often found at the charity balls rather than at the Patriarch balls. Indeed, in mid-career he had abandoned the stress and congestion of New York City to raise his children in Highland Park, New Jersey. Robert James Livingston returned to New York years later and dedicated his time to the *Children's Aid Society* and the *New York Hospital* Board. The historic Livingstons had more political tensions up and down the Hudson River Valley and across generations than did the quiet, close-knit Gerrys of Marblehead, Cambridge, and New Haven. It was Maturin Livingston who was among the dignitaries at the *Patriarchs' Ball* and the *Bachelors' Ball* and his wife was one of the glittering hostesses for the balls. The *Gilded Age* extravagance of the February 1881 *Bachelors' Ball* was enthusiastically described by a Philadelphia newspaper:

> Along the corridors on the ground floor, which opened to the ballroom, were placed orange and lemon trees and flower bushes in full bloom, interspersed with palms and ferns, and at their base long banks of hothouse flowers. At the west end of the ballroom large mirrors were placed, and before them two large palm trees. Every part of the wood-work was hung with draperies of cardinal velvet and cloth of gold, while on every post were placed suits of armor and shields, which reflected the light in prismatic hues. The boxes on the second story were filled with brilliantly dressed ladies and their escorts, and when the

> dancing was at its height, the scene, looking down from above was brilliant in the extreme. They danced from two until four o'clock.

The reporter closed his article with:

> Philadelphia must now yield the palm for your Assembly ball, it was said on all sides last night that is has been surpassed. The guests numbered all the best known names in New York society and the whole affair was the finest private entertainment ever given in the metropolis.[26]

The Goelet brothers, Robert, 48 and Ogden, 43 shared club memberships with their cousins Elbridge T. Gerry 43 and Frederic Gallatin, 40, which offered the men opportunities to share a drink, catch-up on what each was doing and perhaps do a little family business. By 1880 the close-knit group of friends had developed a shared interest in the sport of yachting. The first to own a yacht was Robert Goelet, five years older than Ogden his younger brother. Ogden usually followed his older brother's lead with the intent to "out-do" Robert in the size and expense of each endeavor. By 1881 Robert had owned two famous racing yachts, the *Cambria* and the *Magic* both built in 1870. Shortly after her launch the *Cambria* had won a memorable yacht race from Cork, Ireland to New York in July 1870 defeating the noble yacht *Dauntless.* By 1880 the four friends had no doubt sailed many times with Robert on the *Magic* from New York to Newport, R.I. discovering the appeal of owning one's own yacht. In 1881 Robert continued to race the yacht *Magic,* which was 80 feet in length. Ogden Goelets first yacht the *Norseman* was 131 feet in length and was built for him in 1881 by the C&R Pouillon Company in Brooklyn, New York. Ogden had managed to build a yacht fifty feet longer than his older brother Robert's yacht the *Magic.* Ogden's new yacht was spectacular. It was one of the largest keel schooner yachts in the world, built of white oak with a deck of white pine; the launch of the *Norseman* was covered by the press. The description of the *Norseman* captured *Gilded Age* imagination:

> The arrangements below are admirable. The saloon is 18 feet by 20 feet and has 6 ½ foot head room; It is lighted by a skylight 5 feet 9 inches by 3 feet 6 inches. The finish of the saloon is striking and elegant. The overhead woodwork is mahogany, covered with metal birds, scales, fish, etc. Forward, on the starboard side, is the owner's room, 20 feet by 10 feet, which connects with a toilet room. Sofas, cabinets, bookcases and sideboards will be in the cabin. There are three staterooms for guests, there is a pantry, galley and officer's mess room with hammocks for the crew.[27]

Ogden Goelet and his wife Mary Wilson made their inaugural cruise of the *Norseman* sailing from New York harbor to Newport, Rhode Island in early July 1881. Lying in Newport Harbor, the Goelets hosted a reception on their yacht for the fashionable people summering in Newport. Of such size and splendor was the new yacht that the *Norseman's* every move and every entertainment were reported as far away as Philadelphia.[28]

The next in the group of friends to own a yacht was Elbridge T. Gerry who purchased his first yacht the *Pastime* in 1881. This second-hand yacht was built around 1867 and was only intended to satisfy Elbridge's desire to immediately join his friends on cruises. In the meantime, Elbridge had an impressive yacht built to his own specifications between 1883 and 1884; he took notes from Ogden's *Norseman* and improved upon the luxury. Frederic Gallatin also had a steam yacht built to his specifications, the *Bertie* and again in 1890 the *Almy.* He joined the cruises with the Goelets and his brother-in-law Elbridge and even raced the *Bertie* in 1886. Yachting was a genteel sport that was enjoyed by family and friends who participated in all of the yacht cruises, even staying overnight on the well-appointed schooners. The four great friends enriched their yachting experiences by joining the relevant "gentleman's club" where like-minded sportsmen made plans for annual cruises, shared ideas for improved yacht design, and generally shared stories of sailing adventures, like the first *America's Cup* race between England and the United States in 1851.

This was the year that Elbridge and Frederic joined Robert and Ogden Goelet as members of the *New York Yacht Club,* established in 1844 by nine yachtsmen who wanted to develop the sport and to establish a meeting house. The first yacht club in America was short-lived, the *Boston Yacht Club* was organized in 1835 but lasted only two years. As early as 1775 England's kings and queens had yacht races on the rivers and inland waters. The *Cumberland Yacht Club* is said to be the earliest in Britain, established in 1775. However, Britain was almost continually at war between 1739 and 1815 and yacht building was replaced with revenue cutters, and boats designed for smuggling. While Britain was still the undisputed master of the seas the post-war British yachts were not of the superior design or style of American yachts. Still in a few short years the English designed competitive yachts that matched the quality of American designs. The greatest stimulus to improve yacht design was challenge racing rather than just pleasure cruises. The first *America's Cup* race in 1851 was actually a playful challenge during the celebration of the Queen's Jubilee. In the fall of 1850 preparations were also being made for the first *International World's Fair* to be held in London, England. The annual summer yacht races were planned for 1851 when many international visitors for the *World's Fair* were still in Britain. With such a large audience for the Queen's favorite pastime, and to honor her Jubilee, an invitation was sent to the *New York Yacht Club* in the United States to join the celebrations and show off the speed of their best yacht.[29] A private syndicate of investors, mostly NYYC members headed by Commodore John C. Stevens, accepted the friendly challenge in 1850. They had George Steers design the yacht *America* which was built over the next twelve months just in time to sail cross the Atlantic in the summer of 1851 for the August Jubilee yacht races at Cowes, England. The *America* was the first pleasure yacht in history to cross the Atlantic Ocean.

The queen had arranged for a special competition for the yacht *America* to race against the British Royal Squadron. The race was sailed around the *Isle of Wight* for a prize named the *100 Guineas Cup* or the *All Nations Cup*. When *America* won the race and passed the royal yacht *Victoria & Albert*, Commodore Stevens ordered the American flag dipped, and the entire crew took off their hats in courtesy. A popular saying in yacht-racing circles, "there is no second place" is said to have originated after this historic race. Still uncertain as to the saying's origin, it is believed to be a *London Times* quote from a spectator at the race who asked at the finish, who came in second and got the famous reply that "there is no second place" for such a brilliant race.[30]

The syndicate owners of the yacht *America* brought the prized British silver Cup home to New York City where the Cup was privately owned by the syndicate. Six years later in 1857 the four surviving members of the *America* syndicate wrote a letter to the *New York Yacht Club* deeding the silver Cup to the club with the understanding that it would be held as a permanent challenge trophy, it would be named after the first winner *America's Cup*, and also, that the race must be open to competition from any member of an organized foreign yacht club. However, another condition in the letter permitted any number of American yachts to join the race against any single foreign yacht, thus making it nearly impossible for a foreign yacht to win. The letter also allowed the NYYC to select and change the start dates which often confused or misled foreign yacht clubs. Few challenges were forthcoming. In 1887 the last surviving member of the original NYYC organizers and a member of the *America's* yacht syndicate, George Schuyler, requested his dear friend, both a lawyer and yachtsman, Elbridge T. Gerry to draft a new *Deed of Gift* for the *America's Cup*. The deed included the following remedial requirements:

> That, the challenging club would inform the defending club of the length, beam, and draft of the challenger; that the boats could not be shorter than 65 feet or

> longer than 90 feet; that the vessels must proceed on their own bottoms to the match; that centerboards or sliding keels would always be allowed and never be figured in as part of the boat for measurement purposes; all races would be made on ocean courses, free from headlands; the challenging club would only use one boat throughout the series; and, the ocean course would always be deep enough to accommodate vessels of 22-foot draft.[31]

The club fathers were once again operating under "a match well made" theory of sportsmanship and the new Deed was very well received internationally. It stayed in effect until 1956 when yacht design evolved beyond the outdated nineteenth century design rules.

In 1848 Congress enacted a law which gave yachts a certain status with several privileges but also required them to be registered. The principal privilege was that yachts could sail in and out of all ports of the United States without entering or clearing at a customs house. Yachts traveling to Europe could return with wine, specialty foods, and artifacts without passing customs, and in turn could take specialty items, usually gifts, to give their foreign friends during regattas and summers abroad. In 1849 another honor was bestowed upon the NYYC, the first enduring yacht club in the United States, when the United States government asked the Club to submit a design for a national yachting ensign or flag. The NYYC design was submitted and approved and has since been carried on all registered American yachts.

The *Model Room* at the *New York Yacht Club* to this day still holds the models gifted by Robert Goelet of his two *America's Cup* yacht competitors, the *Cambria* and the *Magic,* and also holds the model of *Electra,* Elbridge T. Gerry's famous steam yacht. The magnificent NYYC building on Forty-Fourth Street in New York City stands like a proud ship with architectural features reminiscent of the *Gilded Age* era. Today the *New York Yacht Club* remains the mecca of yachtsmen from around the world. Elbridge T. Gerry eventually became the *Commodore* of the *New York Yacht Club* where his portrait still proudly hangs as testimony to his leadership.

The *Gilded Age* growth of New York City was astounding to its citizens while also exciting as it generated enormous civic pride. The building boom was reported as far away as Chicago where it was said that "there had been 1,140 buildings started during the present year, 1881, in New York City, the cost of which was nearly $19,000,000. Large stores are being put up by the Goelet, White, Astor, Myer, Levy, and Sloan family businesses, among many others. Vanderbilt is putting up a depot on the site of the Manhattan Market; the Cornells are putting up a Church; there are new Theatres, an Orphan Asylum, additions to Columbia College, hotels, and Clubs are buying mansion homes for their meeting places.

Some of the most expensive private houses in the world are going up."[32] Indeed, Frederic and Almy Gerry Gallatin began their Fifth Avenue mansion in 1881, an Italianate townhouse at Fifty-Third Street designed and built by William W. Renwick, the Gallatins' dear friend and architect of their Long Island summer home, *Breezy Lawn.* Their new mansion was just three blocks north of the Goelet brothers' mansions at Forty-Ninth and Fifth Avenue. The four friends in yachting and by marriage created their own *Gilded Age* neighborhood between 1880 and 1887. The collective fourteen Gallatin, Goelet and Gerry children were within walking distance of their family homes, bonding them as playmates and classmates through their youth, and becoming the *Dudes* and *Sophy Sparkles* in their young adulthood as described by Washington Irving in his fanciful tales of *Gotham.*

The summer of 1881 found the Gallatin family at *Breezy Lawn* in East Hampton, Long Island enjoying their summer holiday with Grandma Hannah Goelet Gerry, Aunt Jean Goelet, and Aunt Jean B. Gerry. In the midst of their summer holiday on July 22, Elbridge T. Gerry's youngest sister Jean Buchanan Gerry died at age 39, surrounded by the women with whom she had spent her entire life. She had never married and left no will, having owned no property in her own right. She led a happy but reclusive life with her mother and Aunt Jean (her namesake), sharing holidays with her sister Almy Gallatin and now dying at *Breezy Lawn* happily surrounded by her five nieces and nephews.

Also in July 1881 a newspaper reported that a telegram from Quebec, Canada announced that through the instrumentality of the Governor-General of Canada, the sword which belonged to the gallant but ill-fated General Richard Montgomery who fell before Quebec on the last night of the year 1775, had been transferred to the Livingston family residing on the Hudson River, New York. The General had married into the family as the husband of Janet Livingston.[33] General Richard Montgomery, Louisa Livingston Gerry's great uncle, was born and raised in Ireland, studied at *Trinity College,* Dublin and two years later joined the British Army to fight in the French and Indian War. He served in the Caribbean after which he was stationed at *Fort Detroit* during *Pontiac's Rebellion,* followed by a return to England for health reasons. In 1773 Montgomery returned to the colonies to marry Janet Livingston, the sister of Gertrude Livingston who had married General Morgan Lewis. General Montgomery and his new wife settled on a small farm along the Hudson River on part of the Livingston Manor property. When the *Revolutionary War* broke out he took up the Patriot cause and was elected to the *New York Provincial Congress* and then commissioned as a Brigadier General in the Continental Army. After Phillip Schuyler, also a distant relative of Louisa M. Gerry, became too ill to lead the invasion of Canada, General Montgomery took over. He captured *Fort St. Johns* and then Montreal in November 1775 and then advanced to Quebec City where he joined another force under the command of Benedict Arnold. On December 31 he led an attack on Quebec but was killed during the battle. The British found his body and gave it an honorable burial. On January 25, 1776 Congress approved the establishment of a monument in memory of General Montgomery. His wife Janet Livingston always referred to him as "my general" or "my soldier" and always guarded his reputation. After his death Janet temporarily moved to the house in which her husband and she had lived before the war. Janet Livingston became a successful business woman and cultivated the mansion farm estate she built and named in honor of her husband. The estate was on the Hudson River not far from *Clermont* her childhood home that was often called *Livingston Manor*. Janet Livingston lived another fifty-three years, long enough to see in 1818 Governor of New York, Stephen van Rensselaer obtain permission for General Montgomery's remains to be moved from Quebec, Canada to America for re-burial in the Livingston Memorial Church and Burial Ground in Columbia County, New York.[34] Sixty-three years later his sword also returned home.

The great American families of the nineteenth century still recalled the Revolutionary days, and many of them lived long enough to also recall the Civil War in that same new republic. Opportunities to honor the leading families of the Revolutionary and Civil War era throughout the colonial states were alive and well in the *Gilded Age* as demonstrated by the *Patroons* and their annual *Patriarchs' Ball*, by the establishment of patriotic societies such as the *Daughters of the American Revolution*, and by the university dinners and lectures that regularly celebrated the anniversaries of battles, the inauguration of Presidents, and the signing of documents of Independence and proclamations of freedom. Elbridge T. Gerry did not know his grandfather, a signer of the Declaration of Independence, but he knew and was close to his grandmother and his aunts and uncles, all of whom lived through the Revolutionary period with their Founding Father, Vice President Elbridge Gerry. Family memories, treasured artifacts, and many stories were shared throughout Elbridge's lifetime, keeping his heritage tangible, and inspiring his civic duty within his community. Louisa Livingston Gerry also had the same tangible connection to those who experienced first-hand the Revolutionary period through the Livingston legacy in New York State. Louisa fully appreciated the symbolism of Canada's return of General Montgomery's sword to the Livingston family's *Clermont Manor* on the Hudson River, not far from her father Robert J. Livingston's boyhood home at Staatsburg on the Hudson. Louisa Gerry's great grandmother, Gertrude Livingston Lewis, was Janet Livingston

Montgomery's sister. Louisa's pride in the Livingston heritage matched well with Elbridge's pride in the Gerry heritage, their historic lineages happily joined together in their five children and the family's full and active life in Gilded Gotham.

The year 1881 closed with two legal cases for Elbridge T. Gerry; the first was related to a case he argued four years earlier in 1878, the *Swill Milk Case* where a bakery had sold products made from tainted milk. State legislation followed regulating dairies and the production of milk products. Elbridge was now defending a newspaper that had published six consecutive articles subsequent to the earlier case, which discussed the subject of businesses that use milk, cream or butter in their food products, and the importance of protecting the public from tainted dairy products. The owner of the *Vienna Model Bakery,* Mr. Louis Fleischmann, was suing for libel arguing that while his business was not specifically named in the articles, he was identified by innuendo and suggestion. The court found that innuendo is not a legal basis for libel, and that in fact, there was no harm done to Mr. Fleischmann's bakery business.[35] This case has been cited sixty-three times through 1996 by other cases on libel, and is referenced in the American Law Reports, 1987.

The second case was on behalf of the *New York Society for the Prevention of Cruelty to Children,* where Mrs. Jennie Flaherty, better known by the stage name Jennie Kimball, was charged with abducting her daughter, the child actress known as "Little Corinne" from the protection of the NYSPCC safe house. Mrs. Flaherty's counsel argued that bail should not be set and that she should not be charged with abduction but rather simply contempt of court because she took her child out of love and a desire to protect her. Elbridge T. Gerry argued to the contrary, stating that Mrs. Flaherty had committed an act of unparalleled audacity to remove a child from a house of protection. Judge Donohue agreed, noting that Mrs. Flaherty seemed to think she could do what pleased her and escape punishment. She had no right to prevent the court from trying the question raised as to her fitness to be the guardian of the child. It was assumed by Mrs. Flaherty's silence in court that she was the person who stole the child in defiance of the law and it was therefore proper to fix her bail at such a sum as would ensure her appearance for trial on the charge of abduction. The judge committed her to jail in default of the $10,000 bail he set. With parental rights came parental responsibilities, lessons learned by the public through press coverage of NYSPCC cases.[36]

January 18, 1882 found Elbridge T. Gerry appearing before the Board of Health on behalf of the NYSPCC, to complain that the *Catholic Asylum for Infants* on University Place was taking in new patients after those already there had been removed by the NYSPCC because of the dangerous and unhealthy condition of the building. The report of the physicians who had inspected the building showed that it would have to be completely reconstructed to make it a safe abode for children. Statistics showed that since the establishment of the institution 399 children had been received, that 64 remained, 156 had been discharged, and shockingly 179 had died. The Board of Health responded to Elbridge's plea and issued an order directing that the institution be closed within twenty-four hours.[37]

While Elbridge's case load dominated the first months of 1882, Ogden Goelet and his brother Robert had discovered the regular pleasure of sailing between New York Harbor and the society life of Newport, Rhode Island. On February 14 Ogden purchased a cottage from Mr. J. Fred Kernochan for $90,000, which had been built on a piece of subdivided land from the *Ochre Point Farm.* Ogden purchased the cottage as a temporary summer residence while he worked on designs for his own mansion to be built between 1886 and 1888 on another piece of the *Ochre Point Farm* situated along the *Cliff Walk,* which he had purchased earlier. The building lot was adjacent to a tract of land owned by his brother, Robert Goelet, who would in fact build his Newport mansion *Southside* between 1882 and 1883, six years before Ogden's designs were completed by Richard Morris Hunt for his 1888 *Ochre Court* mansion. Ultimately, Ogden's design resulted in the second largest mansion ever built in Newport. Only the *Breakers,* built for Cornelius Vanderbilt by Richard Morris Hunt between 1892 and 1895, was larger. Hunt clearly outdid even himself with the scale and elaborate décor of the *Breakers* by comparison to his first project, *Ochre Court.* The two mansions sat along the *Cliff Walk* with only one cottage separating them. In February 1882 the cottage Ogden purchased as a temporary summer home was known as *Edgewater* and had been built in 1864 on Bellevue Avenue for Mr. Frederick Kernochan. By the summer of 1882 Ogden Goelet had his own cottage and Robert was in the midst of building *Southside.* By the following summer in 1883 both men began their annual ritual of sailing between New York City and the *Gilded Age* watering place of high society Newport, Rhode Island.

The next month, in March 1882, the building progress of the Goelet brothers' mansions on Fifth Avenue was reported in the City papers. Their homes were under construction at the intersection of Fifth Avenue and Forty-Ninth Street, one of their modified French Renaissance townhouses on the southwest corner and the other on the northeast corner. Robert Goelet's townhouse was less grand than his competitive younger brother Ogden's and therefore the newspaper articles describe only the proposed interior design of Ogden Goelet's mansion:

> The interior decorations of the house are in every way more striking than the exterior. The entrance hall is of English weathered oak with carvings from old temples of India and a large Sienna marble fireplace, with a base of Champlain marble, of fifteenth century design. The reception room is Occidental to a bewildering degree, a combination of Japanese and Chinese, with lacquered panels and rich silk hangings on the walls. In the parlor, 20 by 30 feet in size, are applied with great elaboration the artist's ideas of Indian decoration. The ceiling is finished in heavy silks, with gold and silver bronze ornamentation of patterns adapted from studies made in India. The latticed windows will harmonize with their surroundings, and an Indian fireplace, which at first appears to be a paradox, will be a prominent feature of the room. The decoration of the hall and parlor alone will cost upward of $59,000, and the entire interior will present many new and striking features which will be studied with interest when the house is completed. [38]

While Elbridge T. Gerry was too busy with his law practice to keep up with the "mansion-building" of his much wealthier cousins, eventually Goelet projects would "inform" Elbridge and Louisa's ideas for the design and style of their own mansion in another ten years.

The *New York Society for the Prevention of Cruelty to Children* prided itself on not taking city or state funds, however that also meant that fund raising was a necessary part of the society's regular work. Elbridge T. Gerry was able in many instances to raise funds from his wealthy society friends, but he also believed that the community itself should endeavor to sustain the protection of its abused children. As today, news coverage of the Society's work was the best means of indirectly obtaining both the moral and financial support of the community. The press chose to publish articles that were clear solicitations for financial contributions to the NYSPCC. An editorial soliciting funds was published on March 4, 1882:

> A noble society is established in our midst, a society having for its aim and object, the protection of helpless little children from heartless cruelty. That there are brutes bearing the stamp of God's image who take fiendish pleasure in hearing the childish voice raised in terror, grief, or pain, is the pitilessly patent fact; wretches, whose pastime is to plant agony where there should be sunshine, to give blows instead of caresses, curses in place of gentle words. The unceasing effort of the *New York Society for the Prevention of Cruelty to Children* has done noble work. Its officers visit the slums and dens of the city, remove helpless and wronged children, and place them, by the aid of the courts, in the institutions which receive children, reform their vicious habits, give them moral and intellec-

> tual training, and procure comfortable homes for them. During the past seven years of the society's existence, its work has expanded, thus responding to the courts and magistrates official requests for investigations, having on its books, over 7,000 cases. The society relies on voluntary contributions for its resources. It still has a mortgage debt of $25,000 on its building. It has rendered a good account of its stewardship, and it deserves our support. *The article closed with the quote,* "Adversity may wither them, sickness may fade, a cold world may frown on them, but amidst all let memory carry them back to a home where the law of kindness reigned, where the mother's approving eye was moistened with a tear, and the father frowned, more in sorrow than in anger.[39]

Two weeks later on March 21 the decision in the estate case Elbridge T. Gerry had argued on behalf of a member of his Episcopal church, Ms. Catherine H. Marx, was decided. The case was complicated and the decision was only partially successful for Elbridge. Catherine and Mary Marx lost their sister Emma several years earlier and because Emma did not approve of Mary's life style, she cut her out of her will. Mary returned home to challenge Catherine for half of Emma's estate and won. The sisters thereafter had joint ownership of the property, after which Catherine and Mary became estranged. Mary had befriended an Episcopal priest over the course of several years, traveling and working with him and routinely contributing money to his church endeavors and to his personal expenses. When Mary died, Catherine challenged the will because it was drafted under the guidance of the priest and his associates, and in fact, left all of her personal property to the priest and a convent of Catholic sisters. Mary only left her sister Catherine $1,000. Elbridge argued four major points on behalf of Catherine in challenging the Will. First, the church witnesses were unqualified because they did not know Mary and could not, therefore, attest to her soundness of mind. The judge said that the statute did not require any particular qualifications for a witness to a will and the evidence alone did not show that the witnesses were unsatisfactory. The second argument was more serious, that the witnesses used undue influence to get Mary to sign the Will. The judge again refused Elbridge's argument and said that it was not sufficient for the purpose of establishing undue influence to show that the Will was the result of affection or gratitude, or the persuasion which a friend or relative may legitimately use. In fact the influence must be such as to overpower the free thought of the subject and to interfere with her own intentions for the Will. In this case, Mary herself edited and changed the drafts of the will until it suited her own purposes. The third argument Elbridge won was that the gift to the convent of sisters was not legal because they were an unincorporated entity and therefore not legally capable of taking title to real property. Then Elbridge lost on his fourth argument, which was that the priest was not legally entitled to accept the gift of all of Mary's personal property because he was not a citizen of the United States but rather a British citizen. The judge held that the priest had no real estate property whatever. What he received in the will was a personal "right to the income" of the real estate held in trust by a local citizen and when the money was distributed to the priest it was only *personal property,* not "real estate" that as a non-citizen he would otherwise not be permitted to inherit.[40] Through 1999 this complicated case has been cited one hundred times on one or more of the issues Elbridge T. Gerry argued.

The next month, on April 11 another *New York Society for the Prevention of Cruelty* to Children case was decided. The Society had made a complaint to the Supreme Court against a Mr. Davene for exhibiting a little child at Gilmore's theater in dangerous performances in violation of the law, and the court issued a warrant for his arrest. The NYSPCC officers proceeded to the theater to deliver the warrant and make the arrest, however, Edward Gilmore, the owner of the theater obstructed the officers, for which he was later convicted for criminal contempt of court, imprisoned and fined. Gilmore appealed the conviction for contempt and was exonerated and the NYSPCC was charged with the costs of the trial. Elbridge T. Gerry appealed the case and got a split decision. The Judge stated that he could not review the "exoneration" of the contempt charge, a final court decision; however, the judge found no authority in the statutes for charging the NYSPCC for the trial costs. Elbridge's NYSPCC had saved the child and saved some money, but lost the deterrent effect that *contempt charges* provided to those who obstructed the work of the society.

On June 12 a special car on the Harlem Railroad left *Grand Central Station* with a pleasant party of clergymen and laymen, including Robert J. Livingston, to attend the annual meeting and Sixteenth Anniversary reception of the *Home for the Incurables* at Fordham, New York. The Incurables' home was located just a few minutes' walk from the railroad station and was surrounded by handsome trees and a spacious lawn with walkways that led to the columned veranda of the main entrance. The annual meeting included several reports by members of the Hospital Board, as well as the President's address in which he announced the kind and generous contribution, indeed the largest gift of the year $25,000 from Robert J. Livingston. As a fellow member of the *New York Hospital Board,* it was likely that Elbridge T. Gerry attended the annual meeting and celebration that honored his father-in-law, Robert J. Livingston. The afternoon closed with a splendid reception before the group traveled back on the Harlem railroad car to Grand Central Station in the City.[41]

Spending time with his growing children, now ranging in age from 3 years to 11 years-old was important to Elbridge. In early June of 1881 he and Louisa took advantage of their yacht, the *Pastime*, and sailed up the Hudson River past the West Point resort to the *Rondout* dock on the western shore near *Kingston*, just below the Livingston Manor at *Clermont* located on the eastern shore of the Hudson River. Depending on their length of stay, the yacht *Pastime* was docked locally or its captain sailed back to New York City harbor until the Gerry family's return was scheduled. After leaving the yacht at Rondout the Gerry family traveled by train to Andes, New York then by carriage to the Livingstons' historic *Lake Delaware Farm,* the home of General Morgan Lewis and his wife Gertrude Livingston. This was land that was part of the historic *Hardenburgh Patent.* The farm belonged to Louisa's father, Robert J. Livingston. The original farm house was large enough to accommodate the Livingston grandparents, their five active grandchildren and Elbridge and Louisa. The Gerry children spent summers on the *Lake Delaware Farm* learning to swim, to ride horses, and to experience nature in the cultivation of the land and by exploring the surrounding Catskill Mountains. In 1872 Robert J. Livingston hired Mr. William Coulter, a prominent resident of the local village of Bovina, to manage the *Lake Delaware Farm* and all of the buildings. Mr. Coulter had from three to ten men working under him to keep 150 acres under cultivation. The property had twenty buildings that included the main dwelling-house, carriage house, gate house, tenant houses, boat-house, fowl house, laundry, dairy and horse barn. The farm had twenty-five to thirty full blooded Jersey cows, which produced about 275 pounds of butter each year for market. The lake covered sixty acres and was well-stocked with California salmon, trout, and other fish. For eighty-one years there stood a grist mill at the outlet of the lake, built by Gen. Morgan Lewis in 1796. After it burned a new mill was built in 1823 and after the death of Robert J. Livingston in 1891, Mr. Coulter oversaw the dismantling of the mill. Produce, meat, butter, milled grains, and poultry, were not only sold, but were shipped to New York City for the Livingston and Gerry family tables. Summers at *Lake Delaware* were a healthy antidote to the Gerrys' city life and also avoided the pomp of Newport's gilded summers. The children were young and in need of rigorous exercise and lots of fresh air. Not until 1887 when the children were ages 8 years to 16 years of age did the Gerrys begin to split their summers between *Lake Delaware* and a rented cottage in Newport, Rhode Island, where the Gerry daughters would eventually be introduced to society.

Later in the summer the mid-July newspapers covered an unusual out-break of major fires in four different parts of the City, all at nearly the same time. Large real estate holders were likely to be affected and the Goelets were no exception. At 6 o'clock on that hot and humid evening a fire broke out on the third floor of a five-story brick building embracing numbers 15 to 25 Whitehall Street and it stretched from Stone to Bridge Streets, and extended back 90 feet. It was rented out as a cotton, cheese, and hops storage warehouse where the loss of the contents was estimated to be $75,000. The building, worth $215,000, was owned by the *Goelet Brothers Estates.* the damage was estimated at $15,000. The other major fires were on Pearl Street and on Washington Street with other small fires scattered about the City. The smoke was so intense that the trains on the elevated rail track had to be stopped. Every fire company in the area was called to help fight the fires, which was made almost unbearable by the summer heat. Fortunately there were no deaths and only one fireman was injured by falling glass. The Goelets along with other property owners were fully insured and they immediately began to rebuild and re-stock the warehouses and stores.[42]

The following week Elbridge T. Gerry was back in New York City and went directly to City Hall for a one hour conference with Mayor Grace to plead against the performance on stage of certain young girls belonging to the *Boston Miniature Opera Company* at the City's *Wallack Theater.* The Mayor agreed and declared that he would not allow any children less than sixteen years of age to perform based on the current law. The theater company, like many others, was forced to adjust the performance and release the children to their parents' care.[43]

In August as President of the NYSPCC Elbridge T. Gerry traveled to Madison, Wisconsin to present a paper at the Annual Charities Conference entitled, *Societies for the Prevention of Cruelty to Children in Their Relation to Child-Saving Work.* The conference lasted six days and Elbridge's paper was presented on Wednesday when the audience was the largest of the week. The full-text of his speech was printed in the Milwaukee paper. The conference ended on Friday after a visit to the *Wisconsin Industrial School for Girls* and an evening address at the *Plymouth Church* to hear an address entitled *Charity Organization, a New Philosophy of Philanthropy* given by the President of the Wisconsin Humane Society. The conference closed with a late dinner and the next morning Elbridge left by train for New York.

The Gallatins, with Almy six-months pregnant, spent the summer of 1882 at *Breezy Lawn* in East Hampton, Long Island, their annual summer "watering place." They were joined as was now the tradition by Almy's mother, Hannah and Aunt Jean B. Goelet. Almy's sister Jean B. Gerry had died the summer before and her absence was surely felt at Breezy Lawn. With Almy pregnant it was nice to have her mother and Aunt available to help with her five energetic children.

Perhaps a blessing, although heart breaking, Aunt Jean Goelet, 80 died that summer at *Breezy Lawn* on September 2, 1882 surrounded by those she loved, in a beautiful and peaceful place that she found so refreshing during her annual summer holidays. The funeral was not listed in the papers but it was held at the family parish, Saint Mark's Church in New York City, followed by her burial in the Goelet family vault in Saint Mark's Cemetery, where her brother Peter Goelet was laid to rest just two years earlier. In October 1882 Jean Buchanan Goelet's Will was entered into probate. Jean bequeathed to her sister Hannah Gerry all the lands devised to her by her brothers, Peter and Robert, together with all real estate at any time purchased and held in common with her sister and nephews, Robert and Ogden Goelet. She also gave to her sister an equal half of the real estate she inherited under the will of their mother, and gave the other half to her nephews, Robert and Ogden. Jean left her household furniture, pictures, etc. to her sister, Hannah G. Gerry, also her pew in Trinity Church. To her niece Jean Buchanan Gerry (her namesake), Jean left $300,000 (having died the year before her share was inherited by her mother, Hannah) to Almy Gallatin's children and to Elbridge's son Peter, $100,000 each. Peter G. Gerry was only three years old and must have been a favorite of his great Aunt Jean, as he is the only child of five in Elbridge's household to whom Aunt Jean left money. The residue of the estate was left to be divided equally between Elbridge and his sisters, Almy Gallatin and Jean Buchanan Gerry. Hannah Goelet Gerry was the last of the four Goelet siblings and thus became the matriarch of the historic Goelet family in New York City. She continued to live in the old *Broadway Farm* mansion at Nineteenth and Broadway for another fourteen years with her faithful servants and was visited often by her devoted son and daughter, Elbridge T. Gerry and Almy Goelet (*Gerry*) Gallatin. Hannah Goelet Gerry continued to share Gerry family celebrations throughout the year as well as summer holidays with the Gallatins at *Breezy Lawn,* always happy to escape the metropolis that had swallowed up everything pastoral that once surrounded her *Broadway Farm* home so many years ago.

November 1882 welcomed the sixth and last child of Frederic and Almy Gerry Gallatin. Mary Gallatin was born on November 19 a healthy baby girl. The Gallatins had recently settled in to their new mansion at Fifth Avenue and Fifty-Third Street, just in time for a happy holiday season shared with their extended Gerry and Goelet families who were within walking distance down Fifth Avenue to the Forty-Eighth Street Gerry/Livingston twin townhouses.

The idea of establishing child protection societies had taken hold across the United States by the 1880's. Because the *New York Society* was the first in the world dedicated to protecting abused children, the work and words of Elbridge T.

Gerry were followed by the press from across the country. Elbridge had become the "father" and "role model" of the now national movement. On December 8, 1882 the *Cleveland Herald* sent a reporter to New York to find out how the NYSPCC was planning to enforce the new laws for child protection and safety. The reporter first met with Superintendent Jenkins at the society's headquarters but he immediately introduced the reporter to the President, Elbridge T. Gerry for an interview that focused on children employed in theaters. Elbridge responded with vigor to the inquiry and noted that under the old law children under sixteen were allowed to appear upon the stage under certain stated conditions, whereas under the new law, if it were literally interpreted, there was an absolute prohibition of their appearance. Elbridge gave examples of child abuse in theaters and even produced a scrapbook to verify his assertions. The society kept a very complete record of all those it had attempted to help. Elbridge closed the interview with:

> There is much discretion needed in the enforcement of such a law as this, and until I have examined the code more thoroughly I will not undertake to say just how far the society will look after the enforcement of the new provisions. This much I will say, wherever a child is used as an adjunct of a play in a respectable theater, and is not required to undergo physical exertions for which it is unfitted, this society will not interfere. But, whenever a child is employed in low saloons and dens of the kind in which this city abounds, wherever a child is employed in a way prejudicial to its moral or physical future, we will interfere and that, vigorously.[44]

The year 1882 closed with the annual *Patriarch's Ball* held at Delmonico's on December 26. The hostesses were Mrs. Robert Goelet, Mrs. Walter Gore, Mrs. W.K. Vanderbilt, Mrs. L.C. Hamersley and Mrs. DeLaney Kane. The dinner was at 12:30 a.m. with the cotillion dance at 1:00 a.m. The Saint Louis newspaper that covered the ball focused on the dresses worn by the patronesses, "to gratify the curiosity of readers as to how leaders of fashion dress." A few descriptions of *Gilded Age* gowns are worthy of note:

> **Mrs. Robert Goelet** wore a dress of white satin with a corsage waist, the front of colored brocaded satin on a white background, the under part of the waist and sleeves having brocade leaves, applique edged with beads and lace, while the train was bordered by fan-trimming, appliques and bead edging.

> **Mrs. William K. Vanderbilt** wore a dress with a peaked bodice and draped skirt of shrimp pink satin soleil and white lace. The bodice was cut square front and back, and half high on the shoulder, with sleeves made of lace ruffles, the skirt was bordered with plaited frills and a white lace scarf was draped across the front and around the back.
>
> **Mrs. DeLaney Kane** was clad in a brown cashmere, with a tunic and bodice of the same and a wide sash of crimson velvet draped over it. The underskirt was of crimson velvet, laid in wide, single box-plaits.[45]

A week later, at another formal holiday gala, the same newspaper happily reported the appearance of two society ladies wearing the same dress, surrounded by ladies wearing a variety of gowns of the highest fashion:

> **Lady Mandeville and Mrs. William K. Vanderbilt** were dressed exactly alike, in costumes of yellow satin, with trimmings of buttercups and diamond ornaments. They were both surrounded by friends and admirers during the whole evening.
>
> **Mrs. Ogden Goelet** wore blue tulle of a new and peculiar shape, the loopings of which were held in place, not by flowers and ribbons, but by large diamond buckles.
> **Mrs. Frederick Nelson** wore the richest dress in the room, which was of white satin, massed with pearls, and with a high Elizabethan collar thickly embroidered with the same pearls. She wore around her neck the string of Oriental pearls worth a fortune.[46]

Elbridge T. Gerry was a professional scholar who surrounded himself with books, not only to satisfy his endless quest for knowledge but also to serve as a comprehensive reference library in his areas of expertise, law, mental health, and theology. The enormous personal library that was growing at the old *Broadway Farm* mansion eventually compelled Elbridge to incorporate a magnificent library into his mansion design in 1894. One subject that Elbridge had mastered by the mid-1880's was canon law and the history of the Episcopal Church. His extensive book collection of theological resources included, among hundreds of others:

Ancient Liturgy of the Church of England, 1844
Anglican Orders and Jurisdictions, 1893
Church Vestments, Their Origin, Use and Ornament, 1868
The Ecclesiastical Law of the Church of England, vol. II, 1873

History and Antiquities of the Anglo-Saxon Church, 1845
Laws Affecting Parish Matters, 1821

The many books on religious topics included in his library at his death in 1927 are primarily scholarly in nature, certainly not considered casual or inspirational reading by the common man. Elbridge T. Gerry actively participated in his parish and the annual *Diocesan Convention* because he had achieved the level of expertise of a canonical lawyer. In his later years he was awarded an honorary *Doctorate of Divinity* degree in Theology, which he cherished as much as he cherished his *Juris Doctor* degree in Law. Elbridge T. Gerry had a general reputation in New York City as an expert in Episcopal matters and was interviewed by the press on January 31, 1883 for his opinion about an Episcopal priest who was being accused by some in New York's *Episcopal Diocese* of heresy. The Reverend Richard Newton was among the first students in the Philadelphia School of Divinity in 1858 and was ordained a Deacon in 1860, the same year Elbridge was admitted to the Bar. The Rev. Newton was one of the first advocates of the principles of "Higher Criticism" and introduced these views into his pulpit, indeed he became a very popular preacher in his parish, but at the same time, he offended "old time" clergy. In 1881 Rev. Newton received his *Doctorate of Divinity* from Union College and by 1883 he had published *Right and Wrong Uses of the Bible.* It was the discussion of this book that prompted the press to inquire of experts both priests and lay experts like Elbridge T. Gerry, as to their opinion on the accusations of heresy surrounding Rev. Newton's book. The controversy centered on a new intellectual approach to interpreting the Bible; essentially, theologians incorporate scientific methods in their interpretation of the Bible and look to history and fact for support. An example is the theory that the books of the *Old Testament* were written by several persons over a long period of time based on different styles of writing and changes in the use of language. When asked about Rev. Newton's Biblical interpretation, Elbridge replied: "I do not pretend to say whether the gentleman violated his ordination vows or not; but if he has, the Episcopal Church authorities are certainly afforded every facility by their canons to bring him to trial. " Elbridge then proceeded to discuss, in detail, the two relevant canons of the Church, then pulled a book out of his desk, read the guidelines for Church trials, and said, "You can see for yourself, the question of heresy is very indirectly alluded to, and as to Rev. Newton, his congregation show no signs of moving against him, nor does the Bishop, and therefore his arraignment and trial for heresy remains very much problematical." [47] Elbridge T. Gerry staunchly refused to express any opinion regarding Rev. Newton's criticisms of the Bible, although he acknowledged that the clergyman had as good as denied the inspiration of the Bible, even though the doctrine was one of the tenets of the church.

February 17, 1883 brought sad news to Elbridge T. Gerry; his Aunt Ann Gerry, one of the last two surviving children of the Founding Father, died in New Haven, Connecticut. Ann was ninety-one years old and her surviving sister Emily was eighty. For more than forty years the two maiden sisters had lived in their old-fashioned house at Temple and Wall Streets in New Haven. From that house their mother, three sisters, and sea-faring brother, James were buried. In May 1882 another sister, Elizabeth Gerry Townsend, had died in a small town near Boston, at age ninety-one. Ann Gerry always felt a special closeness to her father, Vice-President Elbridge Gerry, his constant companion when he was home. The archive of their life-long correspondence shows how much the Vice President relied on his daughter Ann to handle family business in his absence. By her father, Ann was led to take a deep interest in politics, literature, and the sciences, and was considered a most entertaining conversationalist up to the end. Elbridge T. Gerry had but one Massachusetts relative left with whom he had maintained a close relationship, Aunt Emily in New Haven. Elbridge's thoughts must have turned to his mother and Louisa's parents, as they were all now in their late seventies. Indeed, the very next year Louisa Gerry lost her mother, Louisa Storm Livingston, on May 29, 1883. Robert J. Livingston was left without the companion with whom he had shared a long, happy, but rather private life. The companionship of his son-in-law Elbridge and the love and care of his daughter, Louisa, and the joy of his five grandchildren provided the support and focus he needed to sustain him through his grief and to fill the remaining years of his life. The close and caring relationships of the Gerry and Gallatin families were their strength as one generation slipped seamlessly from one to another but never losing the ties that bind all great American families across time.

Louisa M. Livingston's will was drafted in 1866 the year before her daughter Louisa married Elbridge. All of her property was left in equal shares to her husband, Robert J. Livingston, and her daughter, Louisa Matilda Gerry. If however, they were to pre-decease her, Louisa directed that all of her property be sold and distributed equally among eighteen listed charities. Among those listed are the *Children's Aid Society*, the *Society of the New York Hospital*, the *Orphans Asylum*, and the *Association for the Benefit of Colored Orphans.*

In March of 1883 one year after appearing before the *Board of Health* to have an infants' asylum closed for dangerous and unhealthy building conditions, Elbridge T. Gerry sent a letter to William P. Esterbrook, the *Inspector of Buildings* for New York City. His letter called attention to the condition of a large number of school buildings in the city which were ill-adapted for children to escape fires. Accompanying Elbridge's letter was a list of fifty-three schools, some public and some Roman Catholic, some Protestant and some Hebrew. Each school was visited and problems specific to each school were described. The major problems included: street doors opened inward, no fire drills, main doors or escape doors kept locked, steep ladders not adapted to children, windows covered with wire mesh, crowded conditions, or no fire escape at all. The impact of Elbridge T. Gerry's personal work for the NYSPCC included the inspection of buildings, the oversight of child performers, and meetings with government officials. His work had a broad-based impact on the improvement of the care and protection of the City's children in every aspect of their young lives during the Gilded Age and beyond.[48]

Also in March, Elbridge was visited by a *Journal* reporter who asked why the NYSPCC was so eager to prevent the employment of children in theaters. In response to numerous questions Elbridge replied the law protects children under a certain age as a result of a long and careful medical investigation into the relative physical strength of children. The most critical period of a child's life is when it is about to become a man or a woman. Yet, it is just at this age that children are most attractive for the juvenile opera business. He went on to list, by name, the fate of numerous child actors; some had died. Elbridge noted the juvenile opera children learn only a few operas performed by the troupe and acquire but a flimsy knowledge of music and the stage business, and then he asked," what becomes of the troupe when it is disbanded? The only market for such talent is to be found in low concert saloons and dime museums." Elbridge reminded the reporter, "that day after day children are rescued by officers of the society from the vilest slums of this city, where they eke out a precarious livelihood by singing and dancing, often long after midnight, before audiences of the worst classes of the community." [49]

About the same time, P. T. Barnum brought a London circus family over from England to be special attractions at his circus performance at *Madison Avenue Garden*. The performers were clever unicycle riders, sweeping around the floor in graceful circles and a variety of astounding curves. Elbridge T. Gerry was invited to see the performance before rendering judgment on whether the performance was dangerous to the children, but not before one of Mr. Barnum's men stated, "If the society stops Barnum, I shall announce the facts of the case from the ring, and shall also announce that the children may be seen on the public square outside, after the performance. This seems to me the only proper and effective answer to Mr. Gerry's action, against what other children do for play every day." When

Elbridge arrived for the preview, he was introduced with, "Now, dance before the king."[50] Shortly after the preview, P.T. Barnum distributed five hundred free tickets to the performance in hopes of gaining public support for the harmlessness of the unicycles. Barnum was arrested, and for nearly a week after, newspapers printed letters from Barnum to Gerry, and from Gerry to Barnum, which only improved the paid attendance at the *Madison Avenue Garden.* This adverse publicity for Elbridge's theater crusade continued over the next few months. In May, Elbridge prevented the appearance of ten-year-old twin boys from performing in *Callender's Minstrels.* On stage before beginning the show the manager, Mr. Welch, addressed the audience in an attempt to gain public support in his fight to stop Mr. Gerry's interference with theaters:

> These boys are twins who were picked up by us in Alabama, their parents were poor and almost helpless. We contracted to feed, clothe and educate the youngsters until they attain the age of twenty-one. They do one dance that takes no more effort than hide and seek. The three larger boys were found in Michigan, homeless, fatherless and motherless, on the verge of starvation. The little three-year old mite is the child of two members of the company. If Mr. Gerry can do as well by these little fellows as they are doing with us; we are prepared to commit them to his charge and treasury, regardless of the preferences of the children themselves. The speech was received with applause.[51]

The challenge for Elbridge T. Gerry personally was balancing the public's moral support of the NYSPCC work to protect children from obvious cruelty and dangerous conditions, against not appearing to prevent the public from enjoying their circus and theater entertainments. Elbridge was held in extraordinarily high esteem through every strata of New York City society while also suffering the "wrist slaps" of mocking cartoons and letters published in newspapers from the likes of P.T. Barnum and theater managers. Even as the crusade to prevent child cruelty had successfully moved across the nation it was nowhere nearly as effective or broad-based as it was in New York City. The prevalence of child performer shows across the country made the New York public and the managers of child performers resent the legal oversight or in their view, interference with child performers in New York City.

After the death of his mother-in-law, Louisa Storm Livingston, Elbridge turned his attention to managing the probate of her will and supporting his wife, Louisa and father-in-law, Robert J. Livingston in their grief. The Gerrys spent the summer taking short family cruises on Elbridge's yacht the *Pastime,* no doubt they visited cousins Robert and Ogden in Newport, Rhode Island. There was no indication that the Gerrys rented a cottage anywhere and if they did need fresh air and respite from their sorrows, they would have traveled up the Hudson to spend time at the Livingstons' *Lake Delaware Farm* where the children rode horses and drove ox carts, as well as swimming and boating on the lake. Elbridge did not resume his busy schedule until mid-August when he was back in New York City.

Elbridge T. Gerry spent the fall writing an eight page article for the *North American Review,* entitled "Cruelty to Children." The article was a scholarly justification for the need of all people to understand the developmental needs of children, the nature of their physical growth, and the inflicted harm and illness that results from employment in dangerous working conditions at too early an age. Citing census statistics, the laws of England and France, and legislation in the United States, Elbridge supported the international recognition of child cruelty and the need to protect all children. His closing words were:

> A wise experience has shown the necessity of creating societies for the prevention of cruelty to children to enforce the laws. The records of these societies show that the humane and intelligent, in every city and State where the organizations exist, are unswerving in their efforts to secure to little children that consideration by the community which their future so imperatively demands. Until some better mode of reaching the evil is pointed out, the work of these child-saving societies deserves the support of every humane person. They are the dread of all who practice cruelty to children; they incur the resentment of those who are unable to control their action by political, pecuniary, or personal influences; but their work speaks for itself, and illustrates more strikingly than any other creation of the American people the crystallization of the humanity of the age in a most concise, compact, and efficacious form.[52]

Ogden Goelet

Robert Goelet

The Goelet brothers built their New York City mansions on opposite corners on Fifth Avenue at Forty-Ninth Street, just a few blocks from their cousin E. T. Gerry who lived on 48th Street. Ogden's townhouse (*left*) was bigger and more lavish than older brother Robert's townhouse (*right*).

The Goelet brothers also built their Newport, Rhode Island holiday mansions next door to each other on the cliffs.

Ochre Court

Ogden Goelet built Ochre Court in 1885. Richard Morris Hunt built Ogden the second largest mansion in Newport, twice the size of his older brother Robert's cottage.

Southside

Robert Goelet built Southside in 1882. Stanford White built Robert a very large stick style cottage suited to the seaside resort.

Newport Cliff Walk

Magic (*above*)
Older brother Robert was the first to buy a yacht among the Goelet, Gerry and Gallatin men. The Goelet brothers and E.T. Gerry owned the Newport Yacht Station used by the *New York Yacht Club* to this day.

Norseman (*right*)
Younger brother Ogden built a bigger yacht and was the leading society man in Newport. New York society followed Ogden to Newport to create the Gilded Age Resort.

Elbridge T. Gerry

Pastime

Louisa M. Gerry

The Gerrys had neither the great wealth to purchase a luxury steam yacht nor the desire to join the Gilded Age society in Newport, Rhode Island with their brood of six children. Elbridge Gerry had loved sailing since childhood and did purchase the "used yacht" the Pastime on which he transported his family up the Hudson River to Kingston and by carriage to the Lake Delaware estate for their summer holidays with Louisa Gerry's parents.

Aerial view of Lake Delaware and the estate

Lake Delaware estate mansion 1870's

Frederic Gallatin

Yacht *Riviera*, Frederic's 2nd yacht after the *Almy*

Almy Gerry Gallatin

Frederic Gallatin was a wealthy banker as well as a lawyer by profession. He joined his in-laws (and best pals) "yachting" with the *New York Yacht Club*. He and wife Almy Gerry had architect William Renwick, Jr. build their family summer home at East Hampton, Long Island. It was quieter than Newport and frequented by artists and writers, which suited their quiet, private temperaments.

Queen Victoria being welcomed by George Schuyler at Cowes, England in 1851 when the United States won the British yacht race that became the America's Cup race thereafter.

Madison Square Garden, 1910 (right)

Stanford White's grand Madison Garden was the center of entertainment in Gilded Age New York, from the Barnum circus and the annual horse show to musicals and society balls.

P.T. Barnum and Mr. Nutt

Suffragette Cady Stanton (*above*) was a proud member of the Hudson Valley Livingston family and was a distant cousin of Louisa Livingston Gerry. Stanton sent some of her pamphlets to Elbridge T. Gerry because of his interest in the movement and for inclusion in his famous law library; Cady often signed her pamphlets with affection to Elbridge.

Col. James Livingston, who fought in the American Revolution and assisted with the capture of Benedict Arnold was Cady Stanton's maternal grandfather.

Montgomery Hall

Louisa Gerry's great-grand mother, Gertrude Livingston, the wife of General Morgan Lewis, was the sister of Janet Livingston who married the famous General Montgomery for whom she named her estate on the Hudson River.

General Richard Montgomery died gallantly at the 1775 Battle of Quebec.

7

GILDED GOTHAM

THE 1880'S PART II

Have you got one or two men whom you are fond of, that you can depend on always to go off yachting with you? Because if you haven't, don't buy a yacht, as it will be the loneliest place in the world for you.
Commodore J. Pierpont Morgan

Summer gossip in Gotham was swirling in 1883. A claim to reclusive Uncle Peter Goelet's estate was made by lawyer Wilson S. Wolfe on behalf of a woman claiming to be the daughter of Peter Goelet. The newspapers told the story that early in his life when Peter Goelet lived in Parke County, Indiana from 1843 to 1847. Peter was in his mid-forties and by 1845 he had married a local woman who died shortly after giving birth to their daughter in 1847. Neither the mother's nor the child's first names were ever given in the news stories. Soon after the death of his wife Peter Goelet moved back to New York to explore reuniting with his family. He left the baby girl in the care of a friend, Mr. McElwee. However, shortly after his return to New York City, Peter was notified by Mr. McElwee that the baby girl had died. Not until the time of Peter Goelet's death thirty-two years later did Mr. McElwee explain that he had lied about the death of the child. He misled Peter because he wanted to the keep the baby and raise her as his own. Peter Goelet had accepted the truth of his daughter's death even as he mourned the loss of his wife. Peter's brother-in-law, Thomas Russell Gerry, had died in 1845 just two years before, leaving Peter's sister Hannah a widow with three young children. Hannah was then living in her parents' old mansion on Broadway where she had quietly married Thomas Gerry in 1830. It was in 1848, a year after his return home to the old Goelet mansion that Peter Goelet purchased the *Broadway Farm* at Nineteenth Street to care for his two sisters, Hannah and Jean, and to raise his nephew, Elbridge and two nieces Almy and Jean. This new family circle was just what Peter Goelet needed after the loss of his own small family which he never spoke of again.

However, Peter's child was not dead and, according to information in 1883, she grew to womanhood as part of the McElwee family in Indiana and then married George Meyers, a resident of Parke County. It was not until sometime after Peter Goelet's death around 1881 that Mrs. Meyers discovered the story of her birth and instituted inquiries through a legal firm in New York City. Then in July, 1883 she left Indiana to meet with Robert and Ogden Goelet's lawyers. Her lawyer Mr. Wolfe had satisfied himself that the evidence was genuine and worthy of a claim on the estate.[1] A *Tribune* reporter contacted the Goelet brothers' law firm on July 30 and was told that the story was "rot" and that in the lawyer's opinion it was an attempt at blackmail, and further, Peter Goelet was never in Indiana and that it was not worth anyone's time to run around and investigate such a report. On July 29 Mrs. Meyers and her lawyer were seen at the Goelet house in New York City but the Goelet lawyers refused to say anything about the meeting since the Goelet brothers were away on their yachts. After the meeting the *Tribune* reporter asked Mr. Wolfe if the published reports stated the facts of the case, and he responded that "they were in some particulars" clarifying that "it was not Parke County that Mr. Goelet had lived in and I will say nothing more until my detective returns from Indiana in about ten days." He went on to say, "Of course I have a strong case, I never present a case without good grounds for expecting to win it. I tell you it will be interesting reading when I tell all I know about this matter; interesting to the public as well as the Goelets. I have been investigating this case since 1880 and I have written several hundred letters about it. I wanted it kept quiet but it must have been leaked by the Goelets who had agents investigating out west. I guess they know of some of my movements. They say they have never heard of Peter having lived in Indiana. Well, I can say nothing more at present."[2] At the time of the alleged death of Peter Goelet's wife in 1847 Robert Goelet, Jr. was only six years old and his brother Ogden was just one year old. Unless their father or aunts had disclosed the story of Peter's brief time spent in Indiana, neither brother would have had first-hand knowledge of the incident. On the evening of July 30, 1883 Robert Goelet arrived home in New York City after a stop-over on his yacht in Newport, when the *Tribune* reporter saw him at the *Union Club*. "It's all new to me" Robert said, "I never knew my uncle was out there. I cannot say anything about it tonight but I may tomorrow in my office. I have just returned from a fishing excursion in Canada and Ogden is abroad cruising on his yacht."[3] There were no follow-up articles denying the claim which suggested the claim was settled quietly out of court. Uncle Peter's early and brief time in Indiana once again faded from memory, which poignantly moved Uncle Peter's long life from that of a *reclusive bachelor* to that of a *reclusive widower*. The

1883 summer gossip quickly turned to new stories that endlessly circulated in *Gilded Gotham,* not unlike contemporary Hollywood gossip.

Robert Goelet had stopped at Newport that night to see his new cottage, *Southside,* which had just been completed in July 1883 while he was on his Canadian fishing cruise. It was designed by the firm of McKim, Mead and White known, for their *Shingle Style* homes in Newport, Rhode Island. The newspapers reported on the opening of Robert Goelet's *Southside* cottage in Newport, calling it magnificent and describing it in detail for the vicarious pleasure of readers eager to visualize the lifestyle of the *Gilded Age* elites.

> Placed on a charming site with lawns running to the ocean cliffs, where, upon arrival at the house, one passes through a broad carriage-way that sweeps from the north side, comes past the house entrance, to the other end of the estate. Above the entrance, between two towers that project from the front of the edifice, are bronze scrolls, set in huge mosaic work. Through the massive oak door, studded with brass nails in fanciful patterns, one enters a long, two-story "great hall" that passes through the house to the ocean side veranda. There are stained glass windows in the front and rear of each story. A staircase runs from behind the massive fireplace and turns up a tower to an open balcony above that runs across the front and half of the two sides above the great hall. The dining room has large windows overlooking the Atlantic Ocean and is paneled with mahogany and cherry, contains a fireplace, and a magnificent sideboard occupies nearly the entire east wall. The music room is finished in redwood paneling and frescos, with doors opening to the billiard room, also paneled and decorated with frescos. The drawing room has woodwork painted ivory white, and the walls are covered with an embossed papier-mâché frieze. The library is paneled in woodwork painted in a terra cotta shade, and has large glass doors opening to a large veranda terrace, from which broad steps lead to the lawn. The house had electric "call bells" throughout, and a large porch on the top of the building provided an expansive view of Easton's Beach, the small islands and ocean beyond. The cottage is much larger than it first appears.[4]

For as beautiful and "oversize" as Robert Goelet's summer "cottage" was in 1883 his younger brother Ogden would "out-size" him in a few short years, with the second largest mansion ever built in Newport, Rhode Island. *Ochre Court* was built between 1888 and 1891 on a beautiful lot immediately adjacent to Robert's *Southside* property. The inseparable brothers built their homes at the same intersection in New York City and now, next door to each other in Newport.

The Goelet brothers led *Gilded Gotham's* social elite to spend time and money on their seasonal life style in Newport, Rhode Island. The homes the

Goelet's built in the 1880's were not just for a healthy and luxurious summer get-away from the scourges of the metropolis, they were also the social mecca of the island's wealthy yachtsmen, including the Gerry, Gould, Schuyler, and Vanderbilt families. It was Ogden Goelet who established Newport as the center of American yachting when, at the 1882 annual meeting of the *New York Yacht Club,* he advised the club of his intention to present two cups, one worth $1,000 for schooners and one worth $500 for sloops, to be raced off Newport during the annual cruise of the NYYC. The Goelet Cups, produced by Tiffany & Co. were valued by Americans just as the Queen's cups were appreciated by the British. The Goelet Cup was re-designed each year.

Ogden Goelet repeated his liberal donation of cups every year until his death in 1897 after which John Jacob Astor offered to continue the trophies during his lifetime and also to make provision for their maintenance in his will. After 1897 the cup was renamed the *Astor Cup* for Newport yacht races. Today the cup is simply known as the *Commodore's Cup.*[5] The race for the Goelet Cup in 1883 was held on August 6 with fifty-two yachts making their appearance in Newport Harbor. The arrival of Gotham's elite was announced by the press, for example the steam yacht *Atlanta,* with Jay Gould and family on board arrived on August 5.[6] Elbridge T. Gerry arrived with his family on his yacht *Pastime* which was entered in the competition for the Goelet Cup. During the day entertainments were held on-board the larger, more lavish yachts, and in the evening dinners, dancing and receptions were held at the homes of the Goelets, the Vanderbilts and other yachtsmen who owned mansions on the island. Experiencing this new social life on-board one's yacht influenced Elbridge's ideas for what he wanted in the design of his new yacht, which was in the process of being built for an 1884 delivery. Elbridge was not a competitive yachtsman, in fact he would never again compete in yacht racing. His passion was for lengthy cruises with friends and family and eventually, to have his yacht be the flagship for the *New York Yacht Club.* Elbridge T. Gerry put the "gentleman" in the pastime of yacht *cruising* while the Goelets put the "sportsman" into the pastime of yacht *racing.*

The Gerrys were back in New York City shortly after the *Goelet Cup* races in Newport and while Elbridge T. Gerry was in the thick of his legal work, he managed to incorporate his yacht into his leadership of the *New York Bar Association.* The Chief Justice of England's high court, Lord John Coleridge, had sailed from London with his son and other Parliamentary officials for a two month tour that began in New York City, then on to Boston, then to the White Mountains and then a lengthy round-trip to the west through Canada. The *New York Bar Association* was Lord Coleridge's host for his arrival in America as well as his official farewell when he departed for England in late October. The Bar Association committee appointed to receive Lord Coleridge cruised up and down the Hudson Bay on August 29, 1883 on Elbridge T. Gerry's yacht the *Pastime*, awaiting the arrival of the steamship *Celtic* which arrived at 5:30 a.m. at Sandy Hook for quarantine. The committee, led by Elbridge, transferred to a tug which proceeded to meet the *Celtic* for the formal but brief welcome of their distinguished visitor and avoided the usual examination of transatlantic passengers. The party descended from the steamer to the tug and in a few short minutes boarded the yacht *Pastime*. A sumptuous breakfast was immediately served as the yacht slowly steamed up the East River toward the City, stopping to admire the newly completed *Brooklyn Bridge*. The yacht then slowly proceeded to the Twenty-Third Street Landing where the *Pastime* docked about 11:15 that morning. Lord Coleridge and his son were immediately escorted to the home of their local host, Mr. Elliott F. Shepard at Two West Fifty-Fourth Street where they stayed for a day or two of receptions with New York City's political and legal leaders. The other English gentlemen went to the *Hotel Brunswick*. At a private dinner that evening cordial toasts were offered and welcoming speeches made and a dispatch from the *American Bar Association* was read aloud on behalf of the association which had convened for their annual meeting at Saratoga, New York.[7] Lord Coleridge's crossing from England was the hundredth voyage of the British steamer *Celtic* and the Lord Chief Justice celebrated the event that evening at dinner. Lord Coleridge made a splendid speech and his son Gilbert, fresh out of Oxford, sang a song about seasickness playing his own accompaniment on a banjo.[8]

Notwithstanding the fact that the bar committee took measures to prevent reporters from interviewing the Chief Justice, some of the newspaper representatives succeeded in seeing and talking to the great jurist. Lord Coleridge was shown a newspaper in which a statement was published to the effect that the Irish miners known as "dynamiters" had planned to give him a "warm reception." Lord Coleridge's face changed color as he read the paragraph and with an apparently forced smile he said, "Oh, I never pay attention to such reports, threatening letters and messages are very numerous in Ireland but they are not given any heed in England, and I presume nobody is frightened by them in this country."[9] The Chief Justice refused to be interviewed in regard to the recent trials of the "dynamiters" in England but said in conversation with one of the committee that the dynamite conspiracies had been a cause of great concern to the British Government and that they were determined to nip their plans in the bud at any sacrifice. After the celebrations in New York City, Lord Coleridge's party left for a short visit to

Newport, traveling on Elbridge T. Gerry's yacht the *Pastime* before heading to Boston on the steamer *Celtic.*[10]

On October 27, 1883 upon their return from the west, Lord Coleridge and his party stopped in New York's harbor for a farewell ceremony on board the steamer *Britannic* where the *New York Bar Association* committee, led by Elbridge T. Gerry, said their farewells. Although the Chief Justice's son, the Honorable Gilbert Coleridge, remained in America for a longer stay he joined Elbridge T. Gerry on board the steamer *Britannic* to say farewell to his father. During the voyage to Liverpool Lord Coleridge occupied the captain's cabin, a large salon on the upper deck. At two thirty in the afternoon the last warning bell was given and everyone not sailing for England left the transatlantic steamer to board the yacht *Pastime* for the short ride back to the city Landing. Ten minutes later the *Britannic* swung out to sea and the last sight of Lord Coleridge by his friends was his tall figure standing on the upper deck, hat in hand, his face wreathed in smiles.[11]

The same week that Lord Coleridge sailed for England the grand opening of New York City's first *Metropolitan Opera House* was celebrated on October 23, 1883. Three and half years earlier the Goelet brothers had met with Morgan, Vanderbilt and Warren at James A. Roosevelt's Pine Street office to pledge $250,000 to inaugurate plans for a magnificent new opera house. It was built on a plot of land bounded by Broadway and Seventh Avenue, and Thirty-Ninth and Fortieth Streets. At the time, April 1880, the investors estimated the total cost of the project at $600,000. The opera house was the largest theatre in America and cost more than a million dollars, no doubt due to inflation over the multi-year construction process and the elaborate design. The style of the exterior was Italian Renaissance constructed with light buff colored brick with ornaments and panels of molded clay of the same hue. The interior incorporated foyers, parlors, lobbies, supper rooms and numerous stairs; however, there was no monumental staircase. The construction of the whole building was fireproof, built primarily of brick and iron. At the stage end of the building the dressing rooms for the performers were conveniently located for access at ground level on each side of the stage, which occupied a five-story building for the stage, props, and dressing rooms on various levels. The opera house offered 3,064 seats, whereas the *Academy of Music* only sat 1,900 persons; also the old *Academy* had only twenty private box seats compared with seventy private box seats in the new opera house. The holders of the chief boxes in the new house included: Ogden Goelet, Robert Goelet, Elbridge T. Gerry, Cornelius Vanderbilt, William Rockefeller, Jay Gould, and other millionaire elites who each paid $20,000 for lifetime use of their private boxes. One concern of theatre critics was the location of public seats above the horse shoe tiers of private boxes. There were two remote tiers, one with 750 public seats, and high above that, another 900 public seats. The press described these seats as being "up in the skies" at the highest level and wondered who would pay $5 to sit so far from the stage. Even today, the cheap seats at sports stadiums are "high in the skies" and often nick-named the nose-bleed seats. The general public has always accepted the location of the "cheap seats" if it meant access to a great performance, whether music or sport. Ultimately, the *Metropolitan Opera House* was a great success and a model for similar projects across the nation. The wealthy investors of *Gilded Gotham* had the pleasure of seeing their contributions to the growth of New York City realized during their lifetimes.[12] The Goelet brothers also built the *Gorham Building* in 1883 at Nineteenth and Broadway across the street from the home of their Aunt, Hannah Goelet Gerry. The new office building rented commercial space on the ground floor with offices on the upper floors that included the new *Goelet Brothers, Inc.* offices that moved from their prior location at 9 West 17th Street. The building was described as having a prim precision and delicacy in the design by McKim, Mead, and White. The building stands today, having endured some redesign and facelifts over the decades.[13]

The personal life of the Gerrys was more difficult in the first half of 1883 when the boys, Robert 6 and Peter 4 both contracted scarlet fever and fortunately survived the illness. Indeed, nine-year old Lillian and her ten-year old sister Mabel began to keep diaries in 1883, which in most instances are the only intimate documentation of the family's personal life. Lillian's diary noted the death of her grandmother, Louisa Livingston on May 29 leaving her grandfather, Robert James Livingston, a grief-stricken widower. The family spent most of the summer of 1883 at the Goelets' traditional "watering place" at West Point on the Hudson, perhaps to distance themselves from the summer memories of family holidays at *Lake Delaware* (the Livingston estate) while the Gerrys mourned grandmother Louisa's death. The family boarded the yacht *Pastime* in July to join the *New York Yacht Club* for the Newport run of the annual *Goelet Cup* races, which provided fresh sea air and a distraction from their sorrow. By late August 1883 the Gerry family had returned to New York City and the routines of legal work, school, charity work and social engagements.

Elbridge T. Gerry and his father-in-law, Robert James Livingston, were in court together on March 11, 1884 to hear the decision on appeal of a real estate case that they had lost in the lower court. At issue were two pieces of land, each leased separately more than twenty years earlier to the same person, Russell Sage. When the time for renewal arrived, the lessor, Robert J. Livingston wanted to unite both pieces of land for a single assessed value and to renew the lease as one unified lease. The rationale was that one piece of the property faced Fifth Avenue at Forty-Second Street and the second piece of land was "interior" to the city block only accessible through the first piece of property on Fifth Avenue. The judge once again ruled against Robert J. Livingston, stating that:

> We find no warrant in the facts of the case for reforming or construing the leases. No fraud or mistake is shown. All the arbitrators have to do is to fairly appraise the value of each parcel as it stands. It does not follow that in making such separate valuations they will disregard the facts that the rear piece is in the same ownership and occupancy as the front piece. All the facts, relating to the situation and connections of the property and the facilities for its enjoyment, must necessarily be considered in determining its value, and the plaintiffs (Robert J. Livingston) are not entitled to relief in this action upon the mere apprehension, in advance of their determination, that the arbitrators, or an impartial umpire, may fail to consider the facts, or fail to reach a just conclusion.[14]

This is a case where the issue in dispute, the valuation of land, was "not ripe" for a court to decide. At the time of this appeal the assessment had not yet been accomplished so the judge had no "land value" to review for fairness or adequacy. Elbridge T. Gerry had jumped the gun on his argument by "presuming" the valuation would not be fair even before the assessment was done. Although Elbridge lost this appeal he retained the option to appeal a second time, but only after the arbitrator had finally completed an assessment of value, and only if Robert J. Livingston believed the amount of that valuation to be unfair. There was no further appeal.

Two days after leaving the courthouse Elbridge was on a train traveling to the state capitol in Albany, New York to lobby the State Assembly to pass two pending bills that the *New York Society for the Prevention of Cruelty to Children* had strongly supported. One was the whipping post bill, which was drafted to punish husbands who beat their wives, and to offer protection for women who suffered the brutal hand of their spouses. The second bill was drafted to restrict baby farming, where individuals took advantage of state funding for the care of abandoned and orphaned children, often mistreating or starving them and at times simply taking children given to them by their parents in exchange for money. For two years, Elbridge had met with the mayor of New York City and state senators, indeed, anyone in power who would listen, to press for the drafting of this legislation, and now he was in Albany to ensure it was passed.[15]

At the same time, Robert Goelet was traveling by train to Chicago, Illinois to attend the annual stockholders meeting of the *Illinois Central Railroad.* During the meeting Robert was elected to the railroad's *Board of Directors.* That week another forty railroad companies, interested in the freight business to interior towns in Illinois, Indiana, Ohio and Michigan, also met in Chicago and agreed on a basis for the maintenance of rates to these points.[16] Robert Goelet managed not just the real estate interests of the *Goelet Brothers Inc.,* but also their railroad and banking interests, primarily as a member of several Boards of Directors. While Ogden Goelet also participated in the business, it was his older brother Robert Goelet who had the leadership role on behalf of his brother in the routine management of the Goelet Empire.

While still in Albany, Elbridge T. Gerry joined a number of prominent laymen of the *Protestant Episcopal Church* on March 15, at the home of T. B. Coddington to advance the effort underway to build a cathedral in Albany. Among those participating from New York City were Cornelius Vanderbilt, Hamilton Fish, Bradley Martin, and E.H. Harriman, among others. The group was addressed by Bishop Doane describing the purpose of the project:

> All citizens of the State who are members of the Episcopal Church are concerned in having their church represented by a building that would represent the unity and strength in the capital of the State. Just as all citizens are represented at the State Capital, so all churchmen should be represented in a church building in Albany, one that is commensurate in dignity and beauty with the Episcopal Church.[17]

The design of the cathedral building was made by Robert W. Gibson, an English architect who was then living in Albany. The plans required an immediate outlay of $150,000 with the total cost to be $500,000. Similar to the private meeting held in New York City in 1880 to initiate the construction of the New York City *Metropolitan Opera* house, the wealthy of the *Gilded Age* met once again to contribute the "start-up funds" and they immediately raised $70,000 by subscriptions from the meeting participants. The land for the cathedral, valued at $80,000, had been donated by Erastus Corning, and by June, the committee planned to lay the cornerstone. The church hoped to have the entire foundation of the cathedral completed over the summer of 1884. So that work could proceed without delay, members of the lay community returned to their home cities across the state to work with local Episcopal parishes to raise the remainder of the construction funds over the next year.

Elbridge was back in New York City by the end of March as the Lenten Season of the Christian churches was well underway. Society activities in *Gilded Gotham* slowed down during the penitential weeks in advance of Easter, but it by no means stopped. The annual *Bachelors' Ball* was held after Easter in 1884, as were many of the private dinners and balls. The most anticipated party was that of Mrs. Ogden Goelet, known as one of the most tasteful ladies in society, and whether it was the decoration of her house or table, or in her dress, she was always considered perfect. Her balls, receptions and dinners were always delightful and invitations were eagerly sought after. With such a reputation it came as a surprise in late March 1884, when Mrs. Goelet invited a whole houseful of young people for a "fortune telling" party, at which she herself was the palm reader. One young girl was said to exclaim, "She tells awfully true, and I know everything she said will come out. What did she tell me? Oh, I shan't tell, but it was a lovely fortune." A movement or fad that was at once so novel and successful could not fail to be followed, and without doubt, many other fortune telling parties were inaugurated.[18] The article described other entertainments, including an amateur play hosted by Mrs. Bradley Martin, a private musical concert hosted by Mrs. Kellogg at the Clarendon, and a dinner dance for thirty guests hosted by Mrs. Cornelius Vanderbilt. The press noted that Mrs. Vanderbilt still lived in the once "almost sacred-to-society precincts of Washington Square," where old money avoided the new fad of building gilded mansions. Indeed, "old money" society preferred to remain in their rather plain, yet large brownstone houses to conserve their hard-earned wealth, while also hosting grand society entertainments. The Gerrys in fact, lived in just such a plain, yet large old brownstone on Forty-Eighth Street, next door to old-money Robert J. Livingston, just like Elbridge had done with old-money Uncle Peter Goelet at Nineteenth and Broadway.

Elbridge T. Gerry's first extravagance was a contract in 1883 with the *Harlan and Hollingsworth* ship building company in Wilmington, Delaware. He had bought his first yacht, the *Pastime,* with money inherited from Uncle Peter in 1879 and the sale of the *Pastime* would help finance a yacht even more luxurious than his cousin Ogden Goelet's yacht. While the Goelet brothers historically had their yachts built in Glasgow, Scotland, Elbridge chose a local, and by 1884, well-established American ship builder. Always attentive to detail, and perhaps a task-master at times, selecting a local builder allowed Elbridge to follow the progress of the building and suggest adjustments as needed during the design and building process.

Harlan and Hollingsworth & Company was initially established in 1821 by Mahlon Betts who partnered with the machinist, Samuel Pusey, and the master carpenter, Samuel Harlan, in 1836. They began manufacturing railroad cars, both passenger and freight. By 1841 Harlan's brother-in-law Elijah Hollingsworth joined the company and by 1843, they were building and repairing marine engines, which progressively led to ship building. Slow to evolve initially, the company only built nine ships between 1841 and 1851. The first two hulls built by the company were the earliest constructed of iron, and in 1844 they built the first seagoing iron propeller steamship in the United States. By the 1880's they were building ferryboats and luxury yachts. As the firm's reputation grew, orders for steamboats came in from across the country and by 1880 they had built over 75 vessels. One of the notable yachts built by *Harlan and Hollingsworth* was the *Mischief,* winner of the fourth America's Cup regatta in 1881. By the end of the nineteenth century the company was the largest employer in Wilmington, and in 1996 it was listed on the *National Register of Historic Places.*[19]

The introduction of steam power to yachts introduced the "fancy vessel" or "luxury yacht" to the sport. Yacht races continued to be powered under full sail, but yacht club annual cruises became ten-day excursions that required entertainments, lavish meals, and sleeping accommodations. Elbridge T. Gerry designed his yacht for comfortable, long cruises with friends and family, insisting on luxury finishes, conveniences, and equipment never before encountered on a private yacht, including an ice machine, porcelain bathtub, and electric call bells in every room. Working with Thomas Edison, he had the first electric lights installed on his yacht. A hundred lights illuminated the elegant outline of the rigging and masts, as well as lighting the interior rooms. The masthead light used at sea was an incandescent cluster lamp of 100-candle power, visible ten miles away. The port and starboard lights were also bright incandescent lamps. The formerly dark, overnight stays in harbors along the annual cruise routes became brilliant displays of floating society entertainments, with small launches moving guests among the yachts for visits. Elbridge fittingly named his illuminated yacht *Electra,* a model of which is displayed in the *New York Yacht Club* to this day.

On April 14, 1884 the official launch of Elbridge T. Gerry's new love, the yacht *Electra* at Wilmington, Delaware, was announced on page one of the *New York Times* newspaper:

> The handsome yacht Electra, built by the Harlan and Hollingsworth Company for Elbridge T. Gerry, of New York, was launched this afternoon. Among the persons who witnessed the launching were Mr. and Mrs. Gerry, Frederick Gallatin, Robert J. Livingston, J. Lawrence Aspinwall, Josiah M. Fiske, Mrs. Boyd, and George W. Hall, of New York. Lillian Gerry, daughter of the owner [*then twelve years old*] christened the vessel as it plunged into the water. The launch was successful in every particular. The hull was adorned with festoons of flags, the union jack at the bow and the national flag at the stern.[20]

Lilly Gerry noted the special occasion in her diary, "April 14 we went to Wilmington, Delaware to see our new steam yacht launched. She was built by Harlan & Hollingsworth Company. I named her *Electra* and we spent the night in Philadelphia and I went to the theatre."

Descriptions of the new yacht with its novel electricity and luxury interior were written by the foreign and local press over the years, whenever *Electra* docked and invited guests onboard to visit or join the Gerrys for dinner or a day of sailing. One of the more detailed descriptions of the yacht's interior design was published in 1891:

> The yacht's dimensions are 172' 6" overall, 161' 6" water line, 23' beam, and 9' 6"depth. Just abaft the forward bulkhead are the quarters of the crew known as the forecastle. The officer's mess is also located here. Abaft these rooms is the Commodore's private cabin, which is thirteen feet long, and occupies the entire width of the vessel. On the starboard side is a state-room nine feet long by eleven feet wide, with a bathroom leading off this cabin, and a separate stairway leading through the deckhouse to the forward deck. The boilers and engines occupy the space between the forward and main salon, which is seventeen feet long and also as wide as the yacht. There are two staterooms for guests abaft of this salon. The kitchen is situated just forward of the after cabin bulkhead and between that and the engine room. The cook's quarters are rather cramped, but it would astonish a good many hotel men to see the meals that Commodore Gerry's chef can furnish. The decorations, upholstering, and hangings in the *Electra's* cabins are of the most expensive kind and it is considered by many a privilege to be invited for a day's sail with the Commodore if only for the sake of inspecting the boat.[21]

The Columbia College Alumni magazine published the latest news in 1886 from Elbridge T. Gerry, an 1857 illustrious graduate of the college, focusing on his magnificent yacht. The article notes that "when one goes aboard the steam yacht Electra, he puts his foot in a floating palace. In beauty and luxury no yacht excels the *Electra* and in bountiful hospitality and considerate courtesy no yachtsman excels Elbridge T. Gerry. At dinner when the Commodore assembles his guests in the main saloon, the electric lights shed their radiance on a table laden with cut flowers, tropical fruits and rare porcelain and cut glass. An ice machine makes the champagne of the consistency of syrup. The game pates melt in one's mouth, the wines are of the best vintages and the cigars and cigarettes make one bless the memory of Sr. Walter Raleigh." The article closes declaring that "next to making others happy, Mr. Gerry likes to stand on the brass-railed bridge in command of his beautiful yacht, *Electra*."[22]

Elbridge T. Gerry spent part of every year on his yacht for the next thirty years, never replacing *Electra* with another, but rather, he had her overhauled and maintained with the care of a proud sea captain, not unlike his father, Captain Thomas R. Gerry, and his uncle, Captain James T. Gerry.

The next month, on May 5, 1884 Elbridge refocused on his work and put pen to paper and published a letter to the Editor of the *New York Times*, seeking assistance for the *New York Society for the Prevention of Cruelty to Children*:

> The New York Society for the Prevention of Cruelty to Children again is compelled to appeal to its members and to the charitable public for a supply of new and second-hand clothing, hats, and shoes for the little children rescued on a daily basis by the Society. The children range in age from two to sixteen years old. Since January 1, 1884 it has clothed, fed and sheltered in its reception-rooms 205 children, besides furnishing clothing in many deserving cases brought to its notice. This has exhausted its stock and compelled this appeal. Bundles may be sent to his office. No. 100 East Twenty-Third Street, or will be "called-by for" on notice by postal card.
>
> Elbridge T. Gerry, President[23]

The next month the *Saint Louis Globe-Democrat* published an article on Sunday, June 15 that applauded the work of what were called the "professional philanthropists," including Henry Bergh and Elbridge T. Gerry. The article first noted that there were hundreds of these "professors" across the nation, with as many doing harm in the name of charity as those who were doing good. The article remained skeptical of the good "professors" suggesting that some evil or swindle must be overlooked for the sake of the good they accomplish. Nonetheless, the praise for Bergh and Gerry far outweighed the criticisms, which simply highlighted their eccentricities. Of Henry Bergh, the article notes:

> Henry Bergh is a familiar figure in the streets of the metropolis and at nearly all public gatherings here. He is a "first-nighter" at every theater on the production of a new play, and it is to his credit that he pays for his seat. He is quite as Quixotic in his appearance as in ideas, and strange as it may seem, he is quite convinced in his own mind that his is a handsome figure and face. He dresses with the greatest care in the newest style and he is fully as dogmatic in clinging to his outer style of costume as to his peculiar ideas. He is a man of wealth and can therefore afford to be eccentric in both manners and ideas.

As to Elbridge T. Gerry, the article refers to him as a "so-called Crank," who is of one of the oldest families of the city, a lawyer by profession, a philanthropist by nature, and a millionaire by work and inheritance.

> Elbridge T. Gerry has many eccentricities of manner and speech and appearance. He is never seen, summer or winter, without a fur [seal skin] cap, but of his sincerity in behalf of little and helpless children nobody has any doubt. His liberal donations to the cause, his almost entire abandonment of every other work for this, and his great wealth, absolve him from any suspicions of mercenary motives. His modesty is so manifest that all acquit him of seeking notoriety by his efforts in behalf of children. Mr. Gerry even suppressed an amateur performance by children at a theater under the management of one of the life members of the NYSPCC. From this it was made quite evident that Mr. Gerry means to be just in his actions.[24]

Another article published in August of 1884 noted that women were also philanthropists in their own right. Miss Catherine L. Wolfe, equally well-known in New York for her generosity as for her lavish entertainment, was then considered the richest woman in New York City. Miss Wolfe was a close friend of Bishop Potter of Grace Church, and she gave with princely liberality to his church as well as all worthy charities. She was notable for her school and free day care nursery for children of working mothers; this was a case of women helping women in the period of women's rights, especially the right to vote.[25] That same week another newspaper published an article describing America's richest women and the source of their money, usually inherited from a father or husband; the Goelet women were included on the list. Further, it described how rich single women protected their wealth by either not re-marrying or surprisingly, they had antenuptial agreements prepared if they did marry. The article notes that these women knew the value of a dollar and the secret of increasing their wealth, and in comparison with men, the women lived longer. Perhaps written with a wry smile, the article noted that the hobbies of rich women might make an interesting chapter, but such a record would be an invasion of private life. However, the article suggested that the greater number of men who had gained large fortunes crowded a great deal of living into a few years, and the intensity of life made them old while they were comparatively young in years.[26] Elbridge T. Gerry may have crowded a lot of intense work into his life, but he also found time for warm camaraderie and socializing.

On the evening of February 17, 1885 members of the *New York Alumni Association of Chi Psi* made one of the banquet rooms of the Hotel Brunswick merry with laughter and song, when about thirty-five gentlemen sat down to the seventh annual dinner of their association. The table was decorated with emblems of the society set among flower displays. Elbridge T. Gerry presided, the honorable Hugh L. Cole spoke to the sentiment of "Lovely Woman," and Mr. Samuel P. Blagden spoke to "Chi Psi." Other toasts were responded to by General Albert Lee, the honorable Julius A. Skilton, United States Consul General in Mexico, among others. Before entering the banquet room the diners held a business meeting and elected officers for the ensuing year, selecting Elbridge T. Gerry as President.[27]

Elbridge spent more and more of his time working on behalf of the NYSPCC than representing legal cases, although his law practice remained active and substantive. Unlike former summers, work with the Society and his law firm took a back seat in late July through September of 1884 when Elbridge took his family and friends on a series of yacht cruises. The first season for Elbridge's yacht *Electra* was not only for personal enjoyment, but it was, more importantly, the yacht's trial run, to test her metal so to speak. The Goelet Cup races in August, at Newport, were the first stop on Elbridge's summer plans, where the *New York Yacht Club's* annual cruise was well underway. Newport held lavish entertainments for the yachting families at the residence of both Robert and Ogden Goelet. In one case, a dinner for nearly a 1,000 was hosted by Mrs. Ogden Goelet. The Gerrys joined their in-laws and friends for a night of entertainment before setting sail once again on *Electra.* The next month, *Electra* sailed from New York and arrived in Provincetown, Massachusetts on July 17, and after a brief stay, sailed up to Marblehead, the Gerry ancestral port town. By September 25, the *Electra* was heading for Bristol, Rhode Island to pick up a small boat called a "steam launch" that was just completed for loading onto *Electra.* Immediately after the stop in Bristol, the Gerrys left for *Gardiner's Bay* for a few days of fishing. In addition to cruises on *Electra,* the Gerrys continued summer fishing, swimming, and horseback-riding at the Lake Delaware estate throughout their lifetimes to ensure the health and well-being of their five children. In October, after several months of sailing the new yacht *Electra* was sent to the Harlan and Hollingsworth shipyard in Wilmington, Delaware for several weeks to have her machinery improved and to get the yacht ready for winter excursions.

In November, 1884 a lengthy article was published in a Massachusetts magazine that, like many other publications nationwide, described the origin and history of the ten-year old *New York Society for the Prevention of Cruelty to Children,* the well-established leader in a world-wide movement. The article opened with a quote from Elbridge T. Gerry that captured his philosophy of child care and protection.

> From a political point of view, the future of the nation depends on the physical and intellectual education of its children, whose numbers increase every year, and who will soon constitute the sovereign people. From the moral and social point of view, the welfare of society imperatively demands that the atmosphere in which they live, and the treatment they receive from those entrusted with their care or custody, shall be such as to establish in them habits of industry, sobriety, of honesty, and good conduct. For injurious treatment of a child, inasmuch as it results in the distortion of its physical and moral nature, constitutes an offence whose importance seriously affects the public order. Moreover, the complaint of the child, often directed against its parents or its legal guardians, involved the examination of a delicate situation, the interference between parents and children, and it would become ineffectual when the "child victim" has neither the energy nor the knowledge necessary to demonstrate that its claim was well-founded, at least not without help from someone in power. Child protective societies are the guardians of the rights of childhood from the repression of the offences from which it is liable to suffer. In its first nine years, the NYSPCC investigated 13,077 complaints, involving 52,308 children and it prosecuted cases that returned 3,637 convictions, and placed 7,555 children in safe homes or institutions.[28]

Elbridge T. Gerry spent October and November preparing and arguing a case that questioned the state's constitutional right, through specific legislation, to control the occupation of wharves on navigable rivers when owned by private persons. Of significance was the client, Elbridge's own mother, Hannah Goelet Gerry, who was the owner of the wharf property condemned by the state under eminent domain. The February 3, 1885 judgment was a loss for Elbridge and his mother; the opinion stated that the special legislation to provide additional ferry slips and facilities on New York City water front property was not in violation of either the state or federal constitutions since the property was not being given to a private person or company, but was *taken* by the state for "public use" and leased to a company to provide public access to, and use of, river transportation. The state legislature has the right to control the management and occupation of wharves in navigable rivers, even in the hands of private persons. Hannah G. Gerry was given "just compensation" from the state, payment for the assessed value of the property, which was usually much lower than the market value. The greater loss was the cumulative "rental income" value in future years, which was lost to the Gerry family for all time.[29] This case has been cited in fifty-five cases through 2005, as well as in *New York Jurisprudence*, 2nd 2011 and an October, 2003 *New York Law Journal* article.

The next month, the Mayor of New York City sent a letter to Elbridge on March 19 that appointed him a member of the *Committee of Arrangements* for the mass meeting of taxpayers of the City. The meeting was held at *Chickering Hall,* 437 Fifth Avenue at 18th Street on Monday evening March 23 to urge legislation relieving the city from the burdens imposed by the prior year's *Park Bill* that authorized parks in the 23rd and 24th Wards and Westchester County. *Chickering Hall,* considered one of the finest designs of architect George B. Post, was located near the Goelets' Broadway Farm townhouse in the entertainment district near Union Square. The venue held a large 1,400 seat concert hall used for many popular events. Both Oscar Wilde and Thomas H. Huxley lectured there and the first interstate telephone call, made by Alexander Graham Bell in 1877 to New Brunswick, New Jersey, was made in *Chickering Hall.* The committee met at the Mayor's Office in City Hall to discuss the legal issues and what course of action, if any, could be taken. While not participating in elective office, Elbridge was a civic leader through his role as advisor and counselor to the Mayor and many city and state officers. His influence was quietly exerted through his writings, including letters to the editor of newspapers, articles published in newspapers, magazines, and even the prestigious *North American Review.* Elbridge T. Gerry's speeches were quoted with some frequency as law-makers, academics, and social action groups relied upon his international expertise on the comparative legal aspects of child welfare and protection in the United States and throughout the world.

Robert Goelet was back in the New York City papers in July 1885 when he and the *Bank for Savings of the City of New York,* among others, as holders of $11,000,000 in city stocks and bonds, obtained a preliminary injunction to restrain the *sinking fund* of New York City from issuing $2,000,000 in Dock Department bonds. The City had a debt limit which could not be exceeded and in order to protect city departments from exceeding the limit a "sinking fund" was created under the *New York City Charter* that was funded by taxation and other assets. The "sinking fund" money was used for the payment of interest on bonds, stocks, indebtedness, or outstanding obligations for which the City was liable. The City's debt in July 1885 was $126,000,000, or about $14,000,000 in excess of the constitutional limitation of ten per cent of the assessable valuation of city property. Unless the City was allowed to deduct about $34,000,000 of city bonds held in the "sinking fund," the debt limit would be exceeded in violation of the *New York City Charter.* Robert Goelet and the Bank's investment in bonds was at stake should the City incur too much debt and face potential default. The appeal by Robert Goelet and others was not just to protect their private investments, but to protect the solvency of the City. A court opinion was not handed down until

December 14 in which Judge Daly rendered an elaborate decision continuing the injunction, noting that the City's indebtedness must not exceed the legal limits, and bonds must be issued only in anticipation of the amount of annual taxes as determined at the beginning of each year.[30]

While Robert Goelet was battling City Hall in July, 1885 Elbridge T. Gerry was off on a summer cruise with his family and friends on *Electra*. The Gerry children ranged in age from seven years to fourteen years old and all were capable of enjoying the entertainments of a sea voyage. The summer of 1885 found many New Yorkers sailing up to Bar Harbor, Maine, and the Gerrys were no exception. The Gerrys arrived at Bar Harbor in early July and hosted elaborate dinners on board *Electra* for friends, including Mr. and Mrs. De Grasse Fox of Philadelphia, J.W. and Miss Minturn, Hamilton L. Hoppin, Mrs. Bronson, Mr. J. L. Lawrence Lee, and Mr. J. L. Aspinwall, of New York. Later in the month Mr. and Mrs. DeGrasse Fox entertained the Gerrys at dinner at their house on the Duck Brook Road. The Gerrys joined the local holiday crowd trout fishing at Eagle Lake, which was also stocked with salmon, and rode the Green Mountain Railway for a day trip. Saturday "hops" or dances were held at the *Belmont* and *West End* hotels. Daily yacht cruises in the Bay or drives along the shore were popular as were picnics on the shoreline. The Gerry children had fresh air, room to frolic, swim, horseback ride, and the society of other children for their entertainment.[31] By July 23 the *Electra* had left Maine, and arrived in Provincetown, Massachusetts in the company of other yachting families sailing back to New York. The Gerrys arrived in Newport, Rhode Island by July 27 in time for the *New York Yacht Club* Goelet Cup races on August 3. The two leading contenders for the Cup were the *Priscilla* and the *Puritan*, the annual favorites. The *America's Cup* race was scheduled for early September by which time the Gerrys were home in New York City. In the fall of 1885 Lilly Gerry noted in her diary "In the autumn I had a cold so went up to Staatsburgh on the *Electra* with Papa and Grandpa." Indications of Lillian Gerry's fragile health, essentially asthma and weak lungs, were documented in her diary for years.

In October Elbridge took his yacht back up to Bristol, Rhode Island to pick up a small boat for *Electra*, to be used for quick errands when docked. The smaller boat was more efficient than having to lower the larger "steam launch" carried on *Electra* and used for passengers moving between the yacht and the docks. Upon its return to New York *Electra* was then sent off for seasonal refurbishing and mechanical maintenance.

Elbridge returned to New York City in the midst of *Gilded Gotham's* holiday bustle. The City's expansion required more trolley car lines to move the exploding population up and down the cities fashionable thoroughfares. On November 20 a number of wealthy city residents met to form an organization to oppose any railroad that might attempt to lay track on their residential stretch of Fifth Avenue. Among those present were Cornelius Vanderbilt, Robert and Ogden Goelet, August Belmont, W.W. Astor, Henry Bergh, and Clarence A. Seward who was chosen the group's President. Even the New York City *Parks' Department* supported the group's effort and pledged their involvement. The group agreed to start by asking for assistance from the Attorney General. Most of the wealthy members of this lobby group owned large mansions on Fifth Avenue and clearly did not want the beauty or the peace of the Avenue disturbed by trolley cars. Eventually, Elbridge T. Gerry built a mansion on Fifth Avenue and benefited from the efforts of his wealthy friends, who successfully protected the fashionable thoroughfare.[32]

Appearances before the Magistrate Court were routine for Elbridge T. Gerry, who represented hundreds of cases of cruelty to children each year, indeed Elbridge was in the courthouse every week except when on holiday. In October 1885 one of his cases was reversed, and he was involved for several weeks during the holiday festivities in preparation for his appeal of the *Van Heck* case which was scheduled for argument in late December.

On November 29, newspapers announced that the Astor and Vanderbilt families each had a debutante to introduce into society. While neither girl was an Astor or Vanderbilt by name, merely a close relative, they were fortunate to become foremost figures of the season, and occasioned a grand entertainment in *Gilded Gotham.* The press did not hesitate to comment upon the beauty, or lack thereof, in the debutantes.

> Miss Edith Minturn [the first debutante] is a niece of Mrs. William Astor. She is tall and very slender, but to compensate for a faulty form, her face is notably pretty, brightened by beautiful blue eyes, and shadowed by masses of dark brown hair. She is eighteen years old.
>
> Miss Annie Webb [the second debutante] is of approved blue blood all around. She is not yet eighteen, and has a fine figure, dark hair and eyes, and a bright complexion. Tennyson's lines may be applied to her, "Roses are her cheeks and a rose her mouth." Miss Webb is a superlative beauty.[33]

Another article published the same day described the antics of the actor, Joseph K. Emmet, who went on an insane week-long spree about the city, which included interrupting Elbridge T. Gerry while he was enjoying a performance from his box at the Opera House. The papers reported what was called a sadly humorous story:

> Emmet declared himself the dramatic critic of the *Sunday School Times* and was bound to reform the theatrical stage. He made the rounds of theaters to abolish "ticket speculation," including a visit to the *Eden Musee* of wax works where different modes of capital punishment were depicted in wax forms. While there he scared women and children into hysterics by emitting an echoing, blood-curdling yell in the dark, ghostly crypt in which these wax forms were situated. Emmet quickly left the *Musee* and started following the actor, Kyrle Bellew, down the streets to learn whether he was flirting with New York girls as he had been reported doing in London. Emmet was also obsessed with protecting young boys from theatrical exploitation, and so after stalking the actor Bellew, he headed to the Opera House where he knew the child protector, Elbridge T. Gerry was enjoying the evening performance. Emmet managed to get to the Gerry Box and drew Elbridge away from his family party into the corridor for an earnest conference, urging Mr. Gerry to remove the boys from the presence of scandalously costumed chorus girls and the back-stage beer-drinking. Police Captain William Conner arrived, and engaged Emmet in his continuing conversation about "rescuing boys" as he was taken to Bellevue Hospital, suffering from delirium tremens.[34]

Elbridge T. Gerry was on the Board of the *Hospital for the Insane* and had argued insanity defense cases, which prepared him to offer both a kind ear and the generosity of his time to a disturbed man while assistance was on the way. For the moment, the opera could wait.

There was happy holiday news for the extended Gerry-Goelet families. On December 11 the first and only daughter of Robert Goelet and his wife Harrietta was born. Their lovely daughter, Beatrice, born into great wealth was famously painted by the artist John Singer Sargent in 1890 when she was seven years old. Beatrice was much younger than the Gerry children at the time of her birth but she would have been adored by her cousins

On December 22 just three days before Elbridge T. Gerry's forty-eighth birthday he was in the Magistrates Court arguing the *Van Heck v New York Catholic Protectory* case, on behalf of the *Protectory*. A nine year old boy was committed to that institution for begging, and was to remain under its guardianship until discharged in a manner prescribed by law, but without notice to the father of the commitment of his child. Under a writ of habeas corpus the boy was eventually released. However, Elbridge T. Gerry argued that under the Penal Code, stating that *begging* is an arrestable offence, and under the Consolidation

Act, defining the authority of institutions like the *Protectory* to accept court-confined children, that the father had no right to discharge his son from the protection of the *New York Catholic Protectory*. The case was a challenge for the Judge because the Consolidation Act left the families and the courts to act based on the "confinement rules" of each institution into which a child was placed. In essence, the court has to "reconcile" and "read together" the enactments to ensure they do not conflict or clash in their intended meaning and outcome. The Judge determined in his January 19, 1886 decision that the Penal Code cannot stand alone and must be influenced by the modifying effect of the institution charters that are "authorized by law to receive and take charge of minors." The Judge stated finally that in every case the institution so authorized was "left to take and hold the child for the time and in the manner and under the regulations prescribed by its fundamental law," or charter. This was Elbridge's win on the technical interpretation of the law, his highest expertise, yet it meant that the nine year old boy, and others like him, could remain in a *Protectory* even where a poor but good parent wished to withdraw the child and take them home. The court and Elbridge looked for the ultimate welfare of the child in the "discretionary application" of the sound yet firm child protection regulations of each and every *Protectory* in the City. In this particular case the boy's mother was arrested with him, and this may have made the discretionary decision to release the boy to his family too much of a risk for his future well-being.[35] This case, while cited by eighteen cases through 1915, has been discussed in four major law journals between 1954 and 1997.

The *New York Times* greeted the new year of 1886 with an article praising New Yorkers for their inventiveness in dispensing with one fashion or custom and replacing it with another, pointing out two examples in high society. First, the custom of remaining in the city during the cold winter months was turned upside-down with New Yorkers following the customs of England by going on excursions out of town despite snow and sleet, to enjoy themselves in winter sport. The *Times* described the scene, "a great silence fell upon the fashionable portions of the city, a silence that was due to the absence of each and every person who could by any possibility get out of town."[36] Nonetheless, the same society column described fashionable weddings, dinners, dances and other entertainments planned for the next several weeks of winter in New York City.

The second new fashion the *Times* described was a chiefly juvenile entertainment that added to the merriment of the winter season for the entire family. It was Mrs. Elbridge T. Gerry's children's fancy dress ball which was not only the most brilliant affair of its kind ever given in New York, but with the exception of Mrs. Vanderbilt's dress ball, it brought out the most beautiful and striking costumes that had been seen in the metropolis. There was no limit as to age and dainty little maidens and youths, indeed, Washington Irving's *Sophy Sparkles* and little *Dudes* came to life. Not only Mrs. Gerry's beautiful townhouse, but that of her father, Mr. Robert J. Livingston, next door, was thrown open through connecting doors, and every possible arrangement made for entertaining the children. The costume that captured the attention of one and all was that of young Arthur Iselin who appeared as Mephistopheles, dressed in dark-red and black satin, high peaked hat, and face painted a dull copper color, with fierce black mustache; the sensation among the smaller children could better be imagined than described.[37] Two weeks later, the Gerrys hosted a debutante ball, the largest private ball of the season, for their eighteen-year old niece, Almy Gallatin, the eldest daughter of Elbridge's sister, Almy Gerry Gallatin. Once again, the adjoining Gerry and Livingston townhouses were opened through interior doors between the houses, and both were decorated with an abundance of flowers throughout by the popular florist *Klunder*. Supper was served by the famed restaurant *Pinard,* and favors for the young ladies were velvet sachets, while the young men received boutonnieres of hyacinths and lilies of the valley.[38]

The Gerry family clearly stayed in New York City the winter of 1886 rather than joining the new fad of "getting out of town" for winter sports and socializing. Nonetheless, Elbridge and Louisa had two more grand parties on their January calendar. The first was what the papers comically called the "carnival of the cops" that was actually the gathering of the "city guardians" at their annual dinner which was an all-male affair. Elbridge T. Gerry was a man's-man among gentlemen and policemen. His warmth as a civic leader and his generous encouragement of camaraderie was legendary. The opportunity to relax among friends in a boisterous yet classy dinner setting made this annual dinner one of Elbridge T. Gerry's favorite events.

With tongue-in-cheek gusto the all-male gathering was described by the *New York Times*:

> It is safe to say without libel that each one of the hosts was a man on whom every patrolman in this city keeps vigilant eye; that they singly and collectively have appeared in the criminal courts more than once, and most of them have been often in jail, and that their guests were men who are very well known to the police.

In fact it was the fourth annual dinner given by the Superintendent, Inspectors, and Captains of the Metropolitan Police, and Mayor Grace, Algernon S. Sullivan, Henry Bergh, Franklin Edson, Noah Davis, and "the rest of the boys" were present as guests. It was the yearly custom of the Titans to whose hands the city's welfare was entrusted to relax for a few bright January hours the stern discipline to which they were sworn.[39] The famous Delmonico's was described as ablaze with a medley of fiddles, fruits, flowers, ferns, and foaming champagne, ruby burgundy, and a maze of glowing lamps. There were brass buttons, service stripes and good fellowship among the bronzed veterans of many a gallant struggle for law and order against crime, who sat down to enjoy the good things of this mad world with their friends, men famous in politics, law, science, art, literature and commerce. The *Times* shared the teasing yet brotherly introductions of the speakers:

> **Chief Murray** was there, a man with a heart as big as his body, keen-eyed as a lynx, and genial as a May morning, young, with many years of service before and behind him. His hair is just beginning to silver. The chief illustrates that pluck and energy are three-fourths of the battle; he is jovial among friends with a sudden, bad left hand in a row. He smokes like *Vesuvius* but never drinks, and is a fisherman from way back.
>
> **Captain Williams** is present, all 210 pounds when dinner began, and 250 when it ended. His greatest talents in private life lie in the direction of boat building, ancient gunnery, and chewing taffy. He possesses *Daniel Boone's* rifle and more blood-stained gloves than the Smithsonian Institution could collect in a year. He never forgets anything, from a crook's face to a Japanese pronoun, having visited Japan in his early years and mastered the language.
>
> **Inspector Byrnes** is as much a boy as when he whooped things up with Hose 21 and Engine 53. It is due to his sagacity and sleepless vigilance that many a fine game of nasal checkers is now being played at Sing Sing or Auburn. For five years Inspector Byrnes has had the unfortunate habit of swearing-off smoking and betting a suit of clothes that no one could catch him with a cigar. The result has been that the inspector has made several tailors enormously wealthy, to the great detriment of his own pocket, and has finally made up his mind to either give up on swearing off or go naked.[40]

For two months before the great feast, there had been significant betting in police circles that Captain Theron R. Bennet, who had seven service stripes and had been known to eat four turkeys and a leg of mutton as an appetizer, would out-eat Judge Clancy at the Delmonico dinner. So there was a careful watch kept, and seven competent scorers were kept busy, with the result that while Captain Bennett was undoubtedly seven portions of canvas-back duck and thirteen helpings of fish ahead, his opponent had scored fourteen rolls, nine sorbets, and thirteen turtle soups more than his opponent. So the match was declared a tie, and the stakeholders resolved to hang on to their money until next year. The evening continued with merriment all around.

Inspector George Washington Dilks did a public service by presiding at a table of gentlemen whose riotous spirits he held in-check, while nearby all the police captains were united in preventing an uprising at the central table where sat such men as the Rev. Dr. Wilbur Watkins, Elbridge T. Gerry, John D. Hoffman (Elbridge's brother-in-law), Henry Bergh, and Fredric Coudert, who were having a grand time. Finally, when everybody was mellow and satisfied, the Mayor rapped the party to order, and amid a cyclone of applause, he proceeded to express his appreciation of the noble work done during his administration and then offered a toast to New York City, followed by toasts from various tables, including a toast by Elbridge T. Gerry to the press, "while its criticisms were often harsh, it was the ablest and best ally of the force which guarded the city. And finally, amid the clink of merry crystal the hours passed to midnight, "when the stern voice of duty called a truce to pleasure, and each Captain was again a soldier and wended his way to his watch over the peace and dignity of New York City."[41]

The next night, even though exhausted, Elbridge T. Gerry escorted his lovely wife Louisa to the second *Patriarchs' Ball* of the season. It was held at the *Metropolitan Opera House*, with dinner served in the Assembly Room, which adjoined the Ballroom. The floral decorations were by *Klunder* and the dinner served by *Pinards*. About 350 persons were present including Mr. and Mrs. J.P. Morgan, Mr. and Mrs. W. W. Astor, Mr. and Mrs. Robert Goelet, Mr. and Mrs. Ogden Goelet, Mr. and Mrs. Frederic Gallatin, Elbridge's sister, as well as Mr. and Mrs. Darius Ogden Mills, first cousin of Louisa Gerry. The cotillion, which embraced about 100 couples, was led by J. Ridgeway Moore.[42]

The cold winds of February 1886 swept in one of the brightest and proudest accomplishments of Elbridge T. Gerry's professional life. The *New York Yacht Club* membership began discussing possible nominees for the upcoming election of a new Commodore for the club. Two names were floating among the membership, ex-Commodore James D. Smith and Elbridge T. Gerry. The two gentlemen were warm personal friends, however, and were unwilling to run in opposition to each other for the candidacy. In order to come to an understanding on this point, Mr. Smith wrote to Mr. Gerry on January 30 that he had heard that the latter was willing to accept the position of Commodore. He then said:

> I desire to say to you, in compliance with pressing and urgent importunity of a number of friends, I very reluctantly said under some circumstances I might be induced to accept such nomination. It is so satisfactory to me to have you in that

> place, that if it is true that you will accept it, I shall positively decline to be a candidate, and you will have my cordial and heartfelt support.
>
> James D. Smith

Mr. Gerry sent the following reply:

> After receiving your very kind letter of this date I have no hesitation in saying that if elected Commodore of the New York Yacht Club for the ensuing year I will accept the position, which I regard as the highest compliment that can be paid by the club to any member. Should my name be presented for the office I shall value your support as an additional personal compliment.
>
> Elbridge T. Gerry[43]

The next week, on February 8 the *New York Times* reported on the results of the election, which were not without some controversy. Besides the regular ballot there was a fraudulent one printed, similarly headed and printed with red ink, but with the names of Charles A. Minton for Secretary and James O. Proudfit for Treasurer substituted for those of John H. Bird and F.W. Hurst among other name changes from the regular nominees. The name listed for Commodore that of Elbridge T. Gerry was included on both the fraudulent ballot and the original ballot. The fraudulent ballot was offered as a "substitute" by disgruntled members of the club who were upset that the prior administration had run up a debt and had not provided an explanation. In fact, the sweeping victory by the opposition ballot was a great surprise to the club membership, indicating the deficit bothered the entire club house.

Nonetheless, Elbridge T. Gerry was unanimously elected Commodore of the *New York Yacht Club*, and was celebrated as the brightest and most welcome outcome of the election by one and all. One of his first duties was to appoint a committee to arrange the details of the *America's Cup* races that summer. The Goelet Cup race between New York's yacht, *Atlantic*, and Boston's *Mayflower*, resulted in a strong win for the Mayflower, who would defend the America's Cup. A busy Yacht Club calendar lay before Commodore Gerry, which he handled with the same efficiency and enthusiasm he applied to the NYSPCC, his law practice, fraternal club memberships, and all the while never neglecting his personal life or family.[44]

A sporting club to which the ladies belonged was the *Knickerbocker Bowling Club* headquartered in the Tennis Building on Forty-First Street. The game of bowling at the club was an indoor sport with bowling alleys. There were also outdoor bowling greens where the British form of "lawn bowls" was still played in

America. The April issue of *Outing Magazine* announced that the *Knickerbocker Bowling Club* held it first spring reception on March 9 and the meeting brought out a large attendance of ladies, including Mrs. Frederic Gallatin, among 200 ladies and gentlemen. The thirteen alleys of the club were kept in constant use during the season.[45]

About the same time in early spring 1886, the Gerry family celebrated an Episcopal milestone for one of their daughters as noted in Lillian Gerry's diary, "Angelica was Confirmed by Bishop Potter at Trinity Chapel on May 2, 1886." Commodore Gerry would not have missed such an important religious event for one of his children, indeed it was the core of their family values.

The warm days of spring found Commodore Gerry and the NYSPCC in the papers once again when he was caught off-guard by a Grand Jury summons to appear as a witness in the investigation of the *Ramscar Unsectarian Home*. In response, Elbridge addressed a letter to the *Times* stating that the Society had not called for the Grand Jury, however, the Society had presented the *Home* with a copy of the law forbidding "baby farming," notifying Mr. Ramscar that the place was unfit for the proper care of children. Mr. Ramscar immediately made an application for a license to open a home for young children, and the Society promptly interposed a protest to granting the license. While the matter was still pending, the extraordinary step was taken to call a Grand Jury and Commodore Gerry sought to understand why, "it is for those who know to explain." He closed his letter with the words, "The Society is now continually in receipt of complaints from various persons in regard to the *Ramscar Unsectarian Home,* and it proposes to enforce the law to the letter if allowed to do so. If Mr. Ramscar's institution is to be permitted to take charge of children in the manner it proposes it is idle for this Society to attempt to stop baby farming cases of less pretentious arrangement."[46]

The summer of 1886 was the first *New York Yacht Club* cruise that was led by the flag ship *Electra* and Commodore Elbridge T. Gerry. The lengthy cruise encompassed stops in Newport for the *Goelet Cup* race and New York Bay for the *America's Cup* race. However, several days were spent sailing among the club ports such as Marblehead, Massachusetts and while cruising every craft bound in the same direction was at once made a contestant in an improvised race. Nothing proved more conclusively that yachting meant racing than the chief interest and pleasure of individual yachts to encounter en route a well-appointed fishing vessel for a spontaneous race. So regular were these impromptu races that in some instances, to avoid the distraction, the *New York Yacht Club* hired a tug to accompany the yachts for the whole cruise so that from the tug deck the time could be taken accurately at the start and finish of each day's sail.

Commodore Gerry had the regatta committee join him on the *Electra* where he made it a practice to keep a correct record of the daily runs. He then made copies of the daily results and sent each cruise yacht a copy almost as soon as her anchor was let down. This increased the interest in the entire cruise and Commodore Gerry was the only club leader who took the trouble to do this for his fleet.[47]

The annual regatta of the *New York Yacht Club* began its "sail" on Thursday, June 17 at 11 a.m. with the signal for starting given from Commodore Gerry's steamer *Electra*. The start consisted of a preparatory blast of the steam whistle, to be followed 30 minutes later by a second blast, when the time of each yacht was be taken as it crossed the start line. A third blast was blown 10 minutes later, and this time was recorded as that of any yacht starting in the race after this final signal. The iron steamboat *Taurus* furnished for the exclusive use of NYYC members and their guests, left the pier at the foot of Twenty-third Street, North River at 9:30 a.m., then Pier 1 North River at 10 a.m. and finally, the ferry landing at Stapleton, Staten Island at 10:30 a.m. The *Goelet Cup* races would take place three weeks later in early August at Newport, Rhode Island. That race was over a triangular course of forty-five miles and back to the starting point. The *Goelet Cup* race was open to the fleetest yacht that sails, of any shape, size or nationality, and was held as part of the NYYC annual cruise.

During a break in the Club's cruise in the last week of August 1886, a few weeks before the September regatta, the Gerry family boarded *Electra* for a private family holiday at the Lake Delaware Farm estate. They headed up the Hudson River and docked at Rondout near Kingston, where they boarded the local train of the *Delaware and Northern Railroad* to Andes, New York, built not far from the large estate. From the station a horse carriage took the Gerrys along dirt roads through beautiful forests, finally arriving at the Lake house. The history of the railroads in the Catskill Mountains is a curious one, where local spurs like the one to Andes, were needed to support the dairy market in Delaware County. These spurs were often financed by locals, like Robert James Livingston, who as the largest land-owner in the area, needed reliable access to transportation for his farm products. In December 1872 he purchased fifty shares of capitol stock at \$199 each in the *Delhi Middletown Rail Road Company* which had planned to build a line from the western side of Delaware County, beginning at Oneonta, passing through Delhi and on to Andes. A competing railroad, the *Delaware and Eastern Rail Road* (later the *Delaware and Northern*) managed to fund and construct the Andes spur from the eastern Hudson River side of *Delaware County* before the *Delhi & Middletown Rail Road Co.* could accomplish the task. The 1872 stock certificate still hangs on the wall in the Lake Delaware house to this day. The local rail lines changed names and ownership over the years; by 1912 the line from Kingston to Andes was the *Delaware & Northern Rail Road,* which was used by the next generation of Gerrys to move building materials, horses, farm products, furnishings as well as family, up from the Hudson River until 1925 when the Andes Station closed. Today, the town of Andes plans to restore the intact but abandoned original station as an historic site.[48]

While at Lake Delaware in 1886 Commodore Gerry engaged the Hilborne Roosevelt organ company to do a substantial re-build and enlargement of the *Opus 34* organ he had purchased in 1876 for his in-laws, Robert and Louisa Livingston, who owned the estate until 1891. Elbridge had married their daughter Louisa in 1867 and by 1869 they were regular summer visitors at the Livingstons' farm estate. The original Opus 34 organ was described in a 2008 conservation report as "the DeLorean" of the Victorian organ-building world. It was a trophy organ for the residence of the wealthy elite. The Gerry instrument bears all the typical Roosevelt trademarks: exceptionally high quality materials, all wood surfaces shellacked, action components of the first quality, and a particularly high degree of quality in the execution of the finish. The organ, like the great organs of Europe, can easily last for centuries. The organ remains on the Gerry estate in *Saint John's Chapel* at the Lake Delaware Boys Camp and is deemed unique for many reasons, not the least of which is its rarity as one of the few existing organs of world-class builder, Roosevelt Hilborne, as well as its unique unaltered condition even down to its hand-pumping system. Of the 350 historic instruments of note, the Lake Delaware instrument qualifies as one of the most historic intact residence pipe organs to have survived to modern times.[49] The organ was located in the parlor when first installed in 1876, but after the enlargement in 1886, the organ crossed the space of two rooms. On May 17, 1912 the *Andes Recorder* reported that the organ was relocated to St. John's Chapel at the *Lake Delaware Boys Camp,* which required a small addition at the side of the Chapel to accommodate its enormous size. In the 1920's and 1930's Clement Campbell was the organist and choir director, and was also the organist at the Church of the Resurrection in New York City. From 1940 to 1990 the organist and choir director was Charles Dodsley Walker who was a legendary figure in the world of organ and choral music. His career began when he entered the Choir School at the Cathedral of Saint John the Divine at age ten. His education continued at Trinity School, Trinity College in Hartford, Connecticut, and following service in the U.S. Navy, at Harvard University. He held positions at the American Cathedral in Paris, St. Thomas Chapel and the Church of the Heavenly Rest in New York, Union Theological Seminary School of Sacred Music, and New York

University. He is a Fellow of the *American Guild of Organists* and was a founding director of the *Canterbury Choral Society*. In an interview in 2009 Mr. Dodsley fondly recalled his days with the *Lake Delaware Boys Camp*:

> "The director of the camp asked Channing Lefebvre if he knew of an organist and he recommended me. I went and saw the Director and he said I appeared to be qualified but that they couldn't possibly use someone who was the same age as the campers. At that time the campers' age range went up to seventeen, so I tucked my tail between my legs and went off to college. After I graduated I went back and proclaimed, 'I am now twenty-one years old and how about putting me on your staff.' So they did... My son and nephew went to the camp. I played for Sunday masses and the Evensong and Benediction of the Blessed Sacrament. There were twenty-three boys in the choir and they loved to sing descants and of course, we did a lot of them and everyone loved that... The chapel was the most impressive building in the camp, there were two transcepts, one of them contained the organ and the other contained the sacristy so it was cruciform. The organ a two-manual tracker by Hilborne L. Roosevelt had a Bassoon (I think) a free reed. The thing that is most notable about the organ is that it has never been electrified. It has three large bellows that are attached to a crank shaft with a very large wheel, the rim of which has a handle that is eighteen inches long. You could put two boys alongside it. The effort required depends on how loudly the organist is playing – if the organist is playing loudly the thing has to be pumped quite vigorously, if it's being played for meditative music during Communion the kids found that they could sit right on the window sill by this big fly wheel and put their feet on the handle and just rock it back and forth. There's an air gauge which has a green light at the end of it, and an amber light part way down, and a red one further down, and the bottom of it has a huge skull and cross bones. That means the organist has no air at all and you are in trouble. Anyway it's a wonderful organ and I made a recording in 1960 that has a lot of solos on it and at least three or four different boys sang. I trained the kids and played, but I didn't select the music because they were still doing the music they did back in 1909 and that was *Caleb Simper's Mass* and Will C. McFarlane's *Magnificat*."[50]

The conversation with organist Charles Dodsley Walker took place just after the publication on Sunday, July 26, 2009 of an article in the *New York Times* describing the 100th Anniversary celebration of the *Lake Delaware Boys Camp*. Charles Dodsley Walker passed away in January 2015 just eight months after this author met him in New York City for a brief visit, he was a gentleman and a brilliant organist. The history of the Gerry organ continues to touch the lives of everyone who has encountered its magnificent sacred music or seen the grand design and physical beauty of the organ. Not unlike Commodore Gerry himself, as a cultural treasure of rare distinction, the 137 year-old Lake Delaware Boys Camp Opus 34 pipe organ, essentially 15 years old in terms of actual use, was completely restored in 2014. Indeed, the historic Gerry/Livingston *Lake Delaware Farm* is to this day an artifact-rich colonial estate. The Gerry family left Lake Delaware in early September 1886 and traveled by train back to Kingston where *Electra* was waiting for the Commodore's return trip down the Hudson River to New York City to rejoin the remainder of the NYYC cruise schedule. The first week the international races were held in New York Bay, where the sole topics of conversation were the relative merits of the English and American boats. Tuesday's inside race and perfect weather brought the largest outpouring of society. Many persons came from Lenox and Newport for the races while many others had hurried down from Bar Harbor and Narragansett. Boston sent the largest delegation, and a final delegation arrived from Chicago. Thursday's races were not as pleasant as were Tuesday's. Many ladies chose, rather imprudently, to brave the ocean swells and threatening weather and join their men on the Thursday outside ocean course race. It was an uncomfortable, dreary, and wretched day of anxiety, peril and suspense, both on the yachts and on shore. The cabins and staterooms were transformed into sick bays and upon landing, amid dense fog that evening, it was the sight of hundreds of seasick women and girls dragging themselves from their couches and chairs, lemon in hand, that gave the most excitement to the day.[51] On September 16 Commodore Gerry arrived at Newport on the flagship *Electra* to start, time, and oversee the *New York Yacht Club's* final races of the season. A lavish dinner on-board *Electra* was a fitting close to the Club's extended summer sailing cruise.

In the fall of 1886 in the midst of a public debate throughout the western world about capital punishment, the *New York State Legislature* passed a law of general interest to the public and the legal community. The law provided for a Commission to investigate and report to the legislature the most practical and humane method known to modern science of carrying into effect the sentence of death in capital cases. There was no public sentiment at the time in New York averse to the infliction of death as a punishment for murder, but hanging was repulsive for many reasons. Commodore Gerry, as a member of the *Medico Legal Society*, which had discussed the subject, was appointed Chairman of the three-man commission. The other two members were Dr. A.P. Southwick of Buffalo, and Matthew Hale, Esq. of Albany.

The old idea of "spectacle" either for the purpose of gratifying the public vengeance or striking terror in potential criminals, had been abandoned by 1886 and hanging was as decorous as anything so horrible could be and spectators were limited. Independently, the British government also appointed a Committee in 1886 to inquire into the existing practice of carrying out the death sentence and the causes that, in several cases, led to either failure to kill the criminal or to unseemly occurrences, like a beheading. They were to consider and report on what arrangements could be adopted (without altering the existing law) to ensure that all executions be carried out in a becoming manner without risk of miscarriage in any way. The Committee was not charged to look at alternative methods, such as the use of an electric chair rather than the gallows. England's *Capital Sentences Committee* worked for two years and ultimately produced an official table of gallows "drops" that took another four years to refine based on trial and error in calculating the foot pounds of energy required to effectively, and immediately, kill a criminal by hanging based on each individual's height and weight. The construction of the gallows was adjusted depending on how many individuals were to be hung, and sheriffs would choose from a list of trained hangmen and assistants approved by the *Prison Commissioners*. The Committee required that a detailed and uniform report be made after each hanging, in effect, it gave Britain its first execution protocol and paved the way for standardized executions using the Committee's recommendations up to 1964 when England abolished the death penalty.[52]

While the capital punishment committees in *New York* and *England* investigated, surveyed, interviewed and drafted their reports over the next two years, the general public continued to debate the issues, and author's, such as New York's own Herman Melville, wrote books that incorporated the challenging death penalty issue, particularly by hanging, into the central plot. In 1886 Melville began writing his novella, *Billy Budd* while living in New York, at about the same time the *Capital Punishment Commission* was appointed and started its work.

The plot follows Billy Budd, a seaman forced into service aboard the *HMS Bellipotent* from another British ship, *The Rights of Man*, a name not lost on Melville's readers. Billy had a natural innocence and charisma and was well-liked by the crew, but for unexplained reasons aroused the antagonism of the ship's Master-at-Arms, John Claggart, who falsely accused Billy of conspiracy to mutiny. When Claggart brought his charges to Captain Edward Vere, the Captain summoned both men to his cabin for a private confrontation. When Claggart made his false charges, Billy was unable to find the words to respond, and when Captain Vere taunted him to "speak up for yourself," Billy spontaneously struck and accidentally killed Claggart. Captain Vere immediately convened a shipboard court-martial, and acted as judge, prosecutor, defense counsel and sole witness (except for Billy himself). He claimed to be following the letter of the *Mutiny Act* and the *Articles of War*. The law stated that an enlisted man killing an officer during wartime (accidentally or not) must hang. Captain Vere spelled out the awful truth and explained his inability to be lenient, arguing that any appearance of weakness by an officer, or failure to enforce discipline, could stir the already turbulent waters of mutiny throughout the British fleet. Readers were meant to struggle with the issue of intentional versus unintentional killing, and when the punishment of death, particularly death by hanging, was right. Billy was condemned to be hanged from the ship's yardarm at dawn the morning after the killing which no one on board the ship, not even the Captain, believed was intentional.[53]

From the 1860's through the end of the nineteenth century, hanging became the focal point of abolitionist and reformist arguments, and New York State became the pivotal battle-ground. Herman Melville's most enthusiastic patron during the period of *Billy Budd's* composition was Edmund Clarence Stedman, who wrote an article entitled *The Gallows in America* in 1869. Law and literature were merging in an eloquent and articulate arena for popular discussion of the challenging issues facing the reformers of the *Gilded Age.*

With full knowledge of the world-wide debate about capital punishment, Commodore Elbridge T. Gerry led the New York *Commission on Capital Punishment* by first preparing a circular of inquiry that proposed the following questions to be sent to officials and others presumably capable of advising the Commission.

1. Do you consider the present method of inflicting capital punishment by hanging objectionable? Please give the reasons for your opinion.
2. Were you ever present at an execution, and if so, will you kindly state details of the occurrence bearing on the subject.
3. In your opinion which would carry into effect the death penalty in capital cases in a more humane manner than the present one of hanging? If so, what would you suggest?
4. The following substitutes for hanging have been suggested to the Commission. What are your views on each:
    - Electricity
    - Prussic Acid or other poison
    - The Guillotine
    - The Garrote
5. If a less painful method of execution than the present should be adopted, would any legal provision as to the disposition of the body of the executed criminal be expedient in your judgment in order that deterrent effect of capital punishment might not be lessened by the change? What do you suggest on this issue?[54]

The Committee received responses to their survey over the next several months and conducted interviews and held regular meetings to evaluate the information as it accumulated. Throughout 1887 more surveys were sent, followed by interviews and open meetings as additional experts and interested parties were identified. Indeed, the Commission became a part-time job for the Commodore, right along with his many other responsibilities and commitments. The topic of execution by electricity was controversial and so the Commission's work was followed by the press throughout the process.

An estate case, argued in mid-October, *In the Matter of the Final Accounting of Elbridge T. Gerry as Trustee,* was a challenge to the final distribution of a life-estate created in a *Trust Fund* established in 1828 by Grandfather Peter P. Goelet for his daughter, Jean Buchanan Goelet, in which she held a "life estate" and her brother, Uncle Peter Goelet was named the *Trustee* of his sister's *Trust Fund.* Upon the death of Jean, the *Trust* income was directed by the will to go to her children, and if no children, then the fund would be distributed equally among her siblings, and if they died, their lineal descendants. Fifty-two years later, in 1880, Jean B. Goelet and her nephews, Robert and Ogden Goelet, and her nephew Elbridge T. Gerry, met in a probate proceeding of the will of her brother Uncle Peter Goelet who had died in November 1879. The will passed the trustee responsibilities for Aunt Jean's *Trust Fund* from Uncle Peter to his three nephews since Jean's only other brother, Robert, was dead. They all agreed in the court that Elbridge T. Gerry should be appointed the sole *Trustee* of Aunt Jean's *Trust Fund,* relieving the Goelet brothers of the shared responsibility. At the same time, the court evaluated the *capital, securities, bonds* and *cash* in the corpus of the *Trust Fund* and issued an order defining and determining its value and status, noting that at some undetermined point, the prior *Trustee* had purchased securities, which while not in accord with the specifics of the will, nonetheless accomplished the intent of the will. All four Goelet-Gerry relatives agreed with the court's determination and therefore acquiesced to how the prior *Trustee,* Uncle Peter Goelet, had managed the fund over the past fifty-two years under the terms of his father, Peter P. Goelet's will. Two years later, in 1882, Jean B. Goelet died during her annual summer holiday at *Breezy Lawn,* the summer home in Long Island of her niece, Almy Gerry Gallatin. As the *Trustee,* Elbridge T. Gerry liquidated the *Trust Fund* through the sale of securities and bonds that were the corpus of its value, which resulted in a surplus of nearly $23,000 over the amount of the original investment. This unanticipated increase to the fund was considered part of the corpus under *Trustee* Gerry's final accounting for distribution. However, the "final accounting" was appealed in 1885 and again in 1886 by representatives of the "Life Estate" or "Life Tenant" against the remainder men, the Goelet brothers, among others. In November 1886, the appellate judge made the final determination and ruled that Peter P. Goelet's 1828 will specified and indeed limited, the *Trustee* to purchasing certain types of federal or state fixed, interest-bearing investment instruments with the $70,000 capital provided in the fund. The legatee for life, Jean B. Goelet, was limited to the annual interest, income and dividends, thereof, over her lifetime. All money beyond this must have been intended by the will to go to the remainder men. The sale of securities by the *Trustee* Gerry did not affect any change in the respective rights of the life-tenant and the remainder men in the *corpus* of the trust, and indeed, both the remainder men, and the life tenant in the fund, had acquiesced in the prior unauthorized stock purchase during their participation in the 1880 court determination. Of note, the action of *Trustee* Uncle Peter Goelet so many years ago in making the unauthorized investment was wise and inured to the benefit of all parties concerned, and the representatives of the "life-tenant" should not, after so long an acceptance of that stock purchase, be allowed to obtain an advantage by questioning its legality. Also, it seems that even if the investments in unauthorized securities had not been assented to they would have been subject to the same rules of distribution as though made in accordance with the terms of the will. The remainder men, including the Goelet brothers, received the $23,000 surplus as part of the distribution of the *Trust Fund* corpus under the correct accounting by *Trustee* Elbridge T. Gerry.[55] This case has been referenced in significant legal resources, including 76 *American Law Reports* second 162, the *Restatement of Trusts* 240, three *Harvard Law Review* articles, and articles in 28 *Virginia Tax Review* 477, and 45 *Yale law Journal* 156.

The holidays approached offering some social respite to Commodore Gerry's busy schedule. As a member of the *Sons of the Revolution,* Commodore Gerry joined a hundred other members on December 5, 1886 to celebrate the anniversary of George Washington's farewell to his officers. The meeting was held in the "long room" of *Fraunces Tavern* built in 1719 at Pearl and Broad Streets, where Washington had his headquarters. Very little had changed in the historic room and it was indeed, not a very attractive room and nothing had been done to modernize it. As the men sat at the tables and gazed at the two American flags crossed at the lower end of the room, and at the portrait of Washington and his framed *farewell address,* among other historic documents on the wall, their patriotism was aroused and many recalled stories of men and events of a hundred years ago. Commodore Gerry would have told some of the best stories, particularly of his grandfather, Vice-President Elbridge Gerry, who hid in the cornfield behind the *Black Horse Tavern* to avoid the British Militia in 1775 just after Paul

Revere had passed through Cambridge on his famous ride to Lexington. The gregarious men drank a toast to almost everything appropriate to the occasion. President of the group, Frederick S. Tallmadge, brought the men to order for elections, where Commodore Gerry was elected Vice-President, and Mr. Tallmadge was re-elected President. The members were encouraged not to be content with only meeting for the annual dinner. President Tallmadge hoped that in time they might be able to purchase either the old tavern property or some other historic building, where they could collect valuable relics and meet frequently to hear papers of interest and to have discussions. Cheers greeted these remarks, followed by a toast to the "Society of the Sons of the Revolution," made as the proud members stood and raised their glasses. After singing a heart-felt *Old Lang Syne* the Sons departed to meet again on George Washington's birthday early in the next year.[56] Today *Fraunces Tavern* is the oldest surviving structure on this historic New York City block.

Four days later, Commodore Gerry traveled south by train to represent the *New York Yacht Club* at a meeting on December 9 in Washington, D.C. at which the yacht clubs from across the country discussed the formation of a naval reserve corps on the model of the *National Guard.* A large number of yachtsmen wanted better recognition from the federal government, which would give them a certain rank and status as well as the honor of serving in time of need. The British yachtsmen were often members of the British naval reserve force, and often underwent training to hold certificates of their proficiency. Commodore Gerry spoke to the matter:

> Last year I tried to put a bill through Congress which provided for the examination, as masters, of any owners who cared to pass the examinations required, and that gave to them certain privileges which they do not now possess. The bill did not go through on account of the opposition of certain Western members who took no interest in such things. I will, however, bring it up again before Congress this year, and hope to get it through.

Rear Admiral Stephen B. Luce, then in command of the *Northern Atlantic Squadron* of the United States Navy, was not entirely confident of the success of such a plan. He noted:

> It is doubtful if the owners of yachts can be got to undergo the process of instruction which would be necessary to the formation of such a reserve corps. That such an organization would be of immense value there can be no doubt, and it certainly ought to be effected. There would be great value in time of war to

> have a number of steam craft able to render immediate service were it necessary to send an immediate dispatch to a distant part of the coast. One of these steam yachts could be put into commission in a matter of hours. An armament of machine guns could be put on board at once and a sufficient number of experienced men from the navy to handle the guns. She would be just the boat for such a commission, and if she met an enemy she would be able to defend herself if she were put in close quarters.[57]

Commodore Gerry's recommendation mirrored what his grandfather, Vice-President Elbridge Gerry, had put into place in the *Revolutionary War* at Marblehead, Massachusetts, when he used private Gerry merchant ships, mounted them with cannon, and moved arms and supplies for the colonial armies, among the West Indies, France and America. That endeavor was viewed as the first official, although secret, fleet that established the first navy for the new nation.[58] In fact it was during heated discussions in the United States Congress about the unprotected Eastern sea coast that Commodore Gerry had introduced the idea of steam yachts as part of a naval reserve. As early as 1884, newspapers had chastised Congress for their refusal to act.

> For a great and prosperous nation like this to refuse to supply itself with a navy, or to arm the forts in its harbors, is as preposterous as it would be for a rich man to insist on saving money by going without food or clothing. Yet this is precisely what the Democratic House of Representatives has insisted on doing. England has 500 steel guns of the largest size on suitable fortifications. We have not a single gun of the same caliber, and not a fortification that would sustain such a piece of ordinance if we had it.[59]

In his annual November 1884 report to the Secretary of War, Lieutenant-General Sheridan responded to the public outcry and urged the importance of giving immediate attention to the perfectly defenseless condition of seaboard cities and their harbors against foreign naval attacks.[60] The "Father of the Naval Reserve Movement" during the 1880's and a close friend of Commodore Gerry was Admiral Howard Patterson, who was born in Brooklyn, New York in 1856. His father, Thomas H. Patterson, was a naval officer as was his father before him. His mother was the daughter of William Durbrow, a *Knickerbocker* Patroon of New York City. Admiral Patterson had joined the merchant marine at age 15, and by special appointment, joined the United States Navy at 17 where he underwent a rigorous schooling in scientific navigation for the next two years. At 19 Patterson began a lengthy and demanding education in naval seamanship, gunnery and discipline. His years of special education and highly skilled experience at sea led to his appointment in 1889 as Admiral of the Haitian Navy for two years. However, Admiral Patterson was a teacher by nature, and while a seaman at heart, he resigned his commission and returned to New York to begin a distinguished career as a naval educator at the *New York Navigation School* in Brooklyn, which Admiral Patterson had himself established, finding no other institution adequate to the task.[61] Commodore Gerry met Admiral Patterson sometime in 1885 through the *New York Yacht Club* where the men shared ideas and concerns, no doubt comparing the naval history of their respective fathers and grandfathers. The men shared two endeavors over the next few years that bonded them as dear friends and colleagues until Patterson's death in 1916. Although nineteen years younger than the Commodore, the Admiral was known as a *bookworm* as was Commodore Gerry who had amassed a private law library of a quality and size unknown among his peers. They were both published writers, journal articles for one and navigation books for the other. Their first shared passion was the national debate over the need for protection of the eastern sea coast and both men agreed that a naval reserve would assist in resolving the problem. Commodore Gerry publicly acted in support of Admiral Patterson's lobbying for coastal protection when he traveled to Washington and offered steam yachts as a first step in establishing a naval reserve, which focused attention on the need to train yacht officers for official certification as *Masters* of United States coastal waters. Indeed, the comments by Rear Admiral Stephen B. Luce in Washington, that "while steam yachts in a naval reserve would be of immense use, it was doubtful that the owners of yachts could be led to undergo the process of instruction necessary to the formation of such a reserve corps," initiated the second shared endeavor by these fast friends. Shortly after Commodore Gerry returned to New York, Admiral Howard Patterson admitted him to his *New York Navigation School* acting as the Commodore's private tutor for the remainder of 1886 and into early 1887. While training for his *Masters License,* Commodore Gerry and Admiral Patterson developed a scientific, detailed, and highly successful training plan for yacht officers to qualify them for naval reserve service. Commodore Gerry's black tin box with small wooden boats, large nautical maneuvers map, and *Mariner's Compass Training Manual* are held in the Rare Book Room of the Supreme Court of the United States to this day. When Admiral Patterson published *The Yachtsman Guide* in 1887, the book was dedicated to Commodore Elbridge T. Gerry, who received his official "certificate" as a *Master Steam Pilot* on November 27, 1887. The strength of Commodore's Gerry's leadership of the *New York Yacht Club* was his "leadership by example" indeed over the next two years, 400 steamship and sailing ship officers graduated from the *New York Navigation School* in Brooklyn. In 1888, Admiral Patterson submitted a feasible plan for the eventual creation and organization of the State naval militia, thereby securing increased protection of the eastern seaboard and its major cities.[62]

Gilded Gotham closed the year 1886 with the same glamour and social activity with which it ushered in the year 1887. Late December opera nights captured the attention of the press who published teasing articles about the wealth displayed in cushioned, padded and silk-lined private opera boxes. Mr. Robert Goelet's box was walled with red satin and the heavy drapery was of the same costly fabric. Commodore Gerry's box was very similar to his cousin's, but the drapery was trimmed with heavy gold fringe. One observer estimated that nineteen million dollars was possessed by the men who owned the grand tier of private boxes. Another estimated that the jewels displayed on the ladies in the grand tier boxes were worth a million dollars.[63] However, the same article noted that the dresses the ladies wore to the opera were not particularly gorgeous or costly as a rule. They were often plain silks or satins, with low corsages, very full skirts, and either short sleeves or no sleeves at all. The young misses who had not "come out" were completely clad in every instance, and rarely displayed diamonds. It was the customary privilege that only married ladies wore jewels to denote their status. A typical evening in a private opera box was described thus:

> In all the boxes the ladies sit well forward and the gentlemen occupy the rear seats a foot higher than the front ones. The women are able to see and be seen, while the men are free to move from box to box, paying visits between acts. As a rule, the women received guests, and the men visit. Each box has a second room behind it, a reception or salon area, often with luxurious carpet, a chandelier, and walled with mirrors to give a sense of space. These usually dark red opera boxes were dubbed by irreverent youthful males of the day as "bath tubs" because of their size and shape. The *New York Sun* asked its readers, "On every grand opera night at the *Metropolitan Opera House*, it is a question, which is better worth seeing, the spectacle on the stage or the scene in the house itself as fashionable society transforms the theatre into a great reception room.[64]

While the Gerry family would normally have taken their place at the Opera during the last month of 1886, an illness in the family changed their plans as noted in Lilly Gerry's diary, "Grandpa had a bad cold so we sailed for Europe on the Cunard Steamship *Etruria* on December 4, 1886. We were in London, then went to Paris and then to Nice." This was a six-month trip for the Gerry family which demonstrated their independence of mind and their reputation as a close-knit family that would abandon New York's social whirl for the sake of the family.

Indeed, after setting sail, the first grand ball to welcome *Gilded Gotham's* 1887 New Year was the *Patriarchs' Ball* at *Delmonico's* restaurant. It is needless to say that the beauty and dress of the ladies of the ball splendidly matched the names and dollars of the men. The observant press offered comments for public reflection on *Gilded Gotham's* ways, noting that the Sunday before the ball the Reverend Heber Newton, apparently following the trail of Reverend Morgan Dix the Sunday before that, preached a sermon about social matters in which he said:

> While society resolves itself into a marriage market, in which paternal florists offer their ripening buds, duly reared for this human horticultural exhibition, we may expect social scandals.

The press then commented:

> The parental florists were present in force at the Patriarchs' Ball, and the ripening buds were there too, as fine an exhibition of them as eye could see. I dare say the ladies gave much more thought to the music and dance, and the delicious Delmonico supper, than to the Reverend's admonitions, which in all probability, were a mere waste of words. Society will have a fling, though all the preachers in the universe make the welkin ring with cries of woe, woe, woe! It is noted that none of the ripening buds were ticketed "for sale" though some persons were cynical enough to ask, "Why else were they there.[65]

After compiling the annual report of the NYSPCC in January 1887, Commodore Elbridge T. Gerry sent the document from Europe to New York City. The Commodore continued to represent, via trans-Atlantic legal memorandum, the endless flood of child abuse cases that the agents of the *New York Society for the Prevention of Cruelty to Children* investigated, and where warranted, removed the children from dangerous situations. The press regularly highlighted the most recent NYSPCC incidents, both to tell a chilling story and to honor the work of the society. In February 1887, Commodore Gerry wrote and sent from Europe for publication the *Twelfth Annual Report* of the NYSPCC, which the press summarized for the public and illustrated with examples of the Society's work in the recent weeks:

> The first incident was the recent rescue by an agent of the Society, of two children from a squalid tenement house in the *Putty Alley* neighborhood, opposite

> No. 149 Bank Street. On the top floor of a foul and wretched hive, were found Jimmy Murphy, aged four years, clothed in rags and smoking an old clay pipe. His sister Maggie, aged six, was watching over the insensible form of their mother, who lay drunk on the bed. "Pap's dead, and mam' will be soon," the children informed the agent, without apparent emotion. The little ones were taken to the Society's quarters, and the woman was encouraged to "straighten up.
>
> The second incident, at No. 456 West Twenty-Eighth Street, accomplished the rescue of two other poor children under circumstances similar to that in *Putty Alley*, a drunken mother, and two starving children, aged eleven and seven years. The boy and girl begged to be taken away, and the agent did his duty. The infuriated mother aroused the neighborhood with her shrieks, and a crowd of idle men and women ran after the officer down the avenue, threatening violence. It would have gone hard on the Society's agent, but for the timely police interference, which enabled him to conduct his young charges safely to the headquarters at East Twenty-Third Street.[66]

Commodore Gerry's *Twelfth Annual Report* showed that during the past year the Society investigated no less than 5,638 complaints, prosecuted 2,029 cases, and secured 1,958 convictions. The number of children relieved and placed in homes and institutions was 3,150 of whom 805 were cared for and clothed at the NYSPCC reception-rooms. The *Gerry Society,* as it was affectionately known in New York City, faithfully carried a bright lantern of hope into the shadows of *Gilded Gotham* every day of every year, and remained Commodore Gerry's first priority throughout his long and busy life.

Most New Yorkers outside the Gerry family and close circle of friends would not have realized that the family was in Europe for six months with the volume of work produced long distance by the workaholic Commodore Elbridge T. Gerry. Traveling in Europe was not easy with four children exposed to illness in winter months. Lilly Gerry notes in her diary the troubles of the 1887 family trip. "We had mumps at Nice so we went to Rome. Peter had Pneumonia at Nice. Some of us went traveling, I went to Naples and up Vesuvius." On March 19 while in Rome, Commodore Gerry purchased an original life-size marble sculpture of *Penelope* in a seated position, which was shipped directly to the *Lake Delaware* estate where it remains to this day, one of only three in American museums. The receipt dated March 19, 1887, signed by the artist, Franklin Simmons, 72 Via San Nicola da Tolentino, Rome, for the price of $4,800.00, is today, still tucked inside Elbridge T. Gerry's old pocket photo case at Lake Delaware. Lilly further noted in her diary that, "in both May and June Mabel had pleural-pneumonia," and that

"We sailed for home on the White Star steamship *Britannic* on May 13, 1887." At the time, Angelica was 16, Mabel 15, Lillian 14, Robert 10, and Peter was 8.

After his return to New York City in the spring of 1887 Commodore Gerry occupied every spare moment of his time spent on *Electra* with Admiral Patterson as his tutor to become a certified Master of a steam or sail yacht. Both men were rigorous in the detail and completeness of every instruction session. The coming summer cruise and regatta competitions of the *New York Yacht Club* would be the perfect training ground with the Admiral on board the flagship *Electra* for immediate and thorough guidance in the midst of Commodore Gerry's real-time coordination of an entire fleet of schooners, sloops, and steam yachts. By the late fall of 1887 he would be ready for the *Master's License* examination.

In anticipation of the early August start of the *New York Yacht Club* cruise and races, financier John Pierpont Morgan, who succeeded as the next Commodore of the NYYC in 1897, sent a letter to Commodore Gerry on August 1, with an offer to fund three cups, $1,000 cup for schooners, a $500 cup for sloops over 71 feet long, and one $500 cup for 71 feet or less at the water line. The race would follow the *Goelet Cup* and would be run 112 nautical miles from Newport to Marblehead in time for the *Eastern Club* races at that location. Morgan was prominent in steam yacht circles, but had not before demonstrated an interest in sailing yachts. Morgan's proposal was presented at the August third meeting of fleet captains on board *Electra* anchored at New London, Connecticut, and was accepted as a new regatta race in the Club's annual cruise.[67]

Electra left her New York anchorage off the foot of East Twenty-Sixth Street at 10 o'clock on Wednesday, August 3, 1887 heading to the harbor at New London, Connecticut where the fleet would gather for the annual cruise of the *New York Yacht Club,* scheduled to begin the next day. Commodore Gerry had on board the flagship yacht, George L. Schuyler, the oldest member of the club, the fleet surgeon, the club officers, and the Regatta Committee. Also on board was Admiral Patterson and members of the press, including A.G. McVey of the *Boston Herald,* who had the distinction of joining Commodore Gerry for 23 consecutive years as a guest to report on the *Goelet Races.* With her new wheel and new rudder, the flagship *Electra* steamed along easily at 14.5 knots, reaching 16 knots in the open sea. A more beautiful day for yachting could not have been imagined; the bracing breeze was a godsend to those who had been in the sweltering heat of New York. The fleet, when gathered, was composed of 41 schooners, 32 sloops, and 22 steamers. The Commodore and his guests arrived at New London at 5:30 pm, in time for a lovely meal on board *Electra,* followed by the captain's meeting, after which, as the sun set, the flagship was illuminated with electric lights running from the bow over the masts and down the stern. The deck was aglow with lights along the under-side edge of the awning and from the long row of windows emitting lamp light from the interior cabins.

The fleet started for Newport the morning of August 4 with the preparatory cannon shot at 9 o'clock from the Commodore's flagship. The start was at 9:30 o'clock from an imaginary line between the flagship *Electra* and the beacon on *Seaflower Reef*, a sand bar with a warning light off the coast of New London, and the finish at Newport was between the flagship *Electra* and the *Dumplings*, a large rock in Narragansett Bay. The fleet spent the night in Newport Harbor visiting among yachts, sharing lavish dinners or late night drinks and cigars. The *Goelet Cup* was recognized as the nautical derby for American yacht racing. Indeed, the sloop that won the cup was to be the NYYC's competitor in the *America's Cup Race* against England's *Thistle* that followed in just a few weeks. The winner at Newport in 1887 was out of Boston, the yacht *Volunteer*, which made the most successful "first appearance" in the *Goelet Cup* in its history. In fact, as an untried yacht, the *Volunteer* beat the "big four" of the previous year, the *Mayflower* by nine minutes, the *Atlantic* and the *Puritan* by nearly ten minutes, and the *Priscilla* by almost nineteen minutes. Although the *Volunteer* was conceded to be the fastest American yacht ever to sail in the *Goelet Cup*, the British yacht, the *Thistle* was the fastest yacht that had ever been produced by England. Looking then to the upcoming *America's Cup* race, observers suggested that if the *Thistle* beat the *Volunteer* it would be because the United States was unable to produce a boat fast enough to keep the *America's Cup*. With that kind of press, no other series of races for the trophy had approached the interest that the race of 1887 inspired.[68]

On Monday, August 8 the fleet set sail at 7:00 am at the sound of the flagship *Electra's* cannon shot, this being a one-gun start for the *J. P. Morgan Cup*. There were mishaps even before the fleet was out in open waters. The schooner *Gitana* was the first victim; the shackle of the bobstay broke from the bowsprit and put her out of commission. The cutter *Isealt* lost her topmast as did the *Puritan* later in the day. The 112 nautical mile race continued through the night, when the *Volunteer* arrived well ahead of the fleet at Marblehead on Tuesday morning, the winner of the *J.P. Morgan Cup* beating the second place *Mayflower* by over two hours.[69]

Marblehead welcomed the yachts as they progressively filled the harbor and anchored off the *Eastern Yacht Club* house. All day long throngs of spectators lined the wharves on both sides of the harbor and along the ocean side of the Neck, while others continued to arrive by train to see the display. The local papers described the scene as idyllic:

> The center of attraction was, of course, the magnificent yacht squadron with graceful hulls and long tapering masts arrayed from the deck to the masthead in gorgeous bunting, made a spectacle of rare beauty, to which a kaleidoscopic effect was given by the gently rocking, on long regular swells, of the close-lying craft. There was an immense flotilla of dories and sailboats that kept skimming about and among the yachts, laden with curious spectators in holiday dress, adding to the ever changing beauty of the scene and prevented anything like monotony in the grand ensemble.[70]

Commodore Gerry kept open house on the flagship *Electra,* as did all of the yachtsmen, and all were crowded by sight seers who inspected everything from truck to keel. On shore the yachtsmen had a pleasant time; some enjoyed entertainments at the *Eastern Yacht Club,* and some explored the sandy beach of the Neck, while others visited sleepy Marblehead, and still others traveled the fourteen miles to see Boston. Just before dusk every yacht took-in all the fancy bunting changing the effect as if by magic. At 7:15 in the evening a signal gun fired on the *Electra* to announce the hour of illumination, and in an instant the whole aspect changed. Like a flash of lightning, from stem to stern, over mainmast and foremast, there appeared an electric line of light from 200 incandescent lamps. At the same moment lines of lanterns swung from the rigging and the decks of all the other yachts and the scene seemed complete in its' particular beauty. The moon, which had now risen, cast a line of silver light across the harbor and its effect was as beautiful as the arrangement of artificial light was picturesque. The *Eastern Clubhouse* and the residences on *Marblehead Neck* contributed to the scene by general illuminations. The scene reached its point of greatest grandeur at this time with a general display of colorful fireworks. The evening was filled with receptions, dinners and a concert, and the illumination continued until midnight when the yachtsmen returned to their yachts to get much needed rest for the next round of sailing.[71]

The second great center of American yachting was Boston, where its two-hundred-square mile sailing area encompassed the rough-water Massachusetts Bay. Marblehead, fifteen miles north of Boston, was considered the best location for yacht racing. Isolated from New York influences by the barrier of Cape Cod, yachting in Massachusetts waters was shaped by the region's own environmental conditions and rich maritime heritage. Massachusetts yachts were more numerous and seaworthy than those around New York, and more of them were actually sailed by their owners. In 1891 there were 4,000 yacht club members among several club houses, who owned about 1,400 yachts.[72] It was from the proud and experienced *Boston Yacht Club* that the 1887 yacht *Volunteer* was entered in the annual *New York Yacht Club* cruise and racing regattas, of which she had won both the *Goelet Cup* at Newport in early August and the *J. P. Morgan Cup* at Marblehead in mid-August. One last round of races at Newport was scheduled to prepare the *Volunteer* to defend the *America's Cup* against Britain's challenge by the *Thistle* in late September. The annual fleet of the NYYC was a composite of yachts belonging to many other American clubs who joined together under the unified command of New York's flagship *Electra* for the annual cruise and races. Since the *America's Cup* trophy was held by the NYYC, and the rules required the defending yacht to be a member, then any yachtsman who wished to defend the trophy had to join the NYYC for the season. As a NYYC member, yachtsmen competed in the *Goelet Cup* race to decide which yacht would represent the United States in defense of the *America's Cup*. Boston's own, the *Volunteer,* earned the honor in 1887 with the Goelet Cup, and would hone her skills in one last round of races in Newport, Rhode Island, which followed the Marblehead regatta festivities.

Commodore Gerry sounded the cannon early on August 12, 1887 announcing the departure of the fleet from Marblehead, the Gerry ancestral home. Just three days later, on August 15, the sun rose bright and warm in Newport, where the well-rested crews of the fleet awoke to the 8 o'clock cannon fired from the flagship *Electra,* announcing the certainty of the start as the breezes were increasing to a favorable level. The fleet began active preparation for the start of the race and by 9:15 the *Electra* and the entire squadron were in position. Anxiously the yachts held their positions until the second cannon fire, starting the race at 9: 30 o'clock. A large steamer carried an excursion party of NYYC guests who earnestly waved to the crowds that lined the Newport shore line, gathered to cheer the yachts as they positioned themselves for the day's race. The Regatta Committee was onboard the *Electra* where Commodore Gerry extended every courtesy to his guests, provided refreshments, and all the while, timed and recorded the race from start to finish. The U.S. Navy yacht *Rena,* bound east, gave cheers for *Volunteer* as she passed, and exchanged salutes with the *Electra.* At 2 o'clock the cannon and whistle of *Electra* saluted the victor, the *Volunteer,* as she passed the flagship at the finish line. As soon as the yachts had dressed line they put into harbor and the crews were soon asleep, resting for the last race of the cruise in the morning. The yachts passed a quiet evening in the harbor while onboard the *Electra* the yacht captains passed a *Resolution of Thanks* to Commodore Elbridge T. Gerry for his efforts in making the cruise a success, and declared the 1887 cruise was the finest ever held by the *New York Yacht Club.* The meeting closed with a vote to disband the cruise after the next day's race. Those yachtsmen or clubs who planned to attend the *America's Cup* in one month's time, September 27-30, would do so under their own flags. The *New York Yacht Club,* as the defender of the Cup, would host the 1887 *America's*

Cup competition between the United States and the challenger, Scotland's *Royal Clyde Yacht Club,* in the waters off New York City.

In early September newspapers across the country reflected the emerging national interest in the *America's Cup* race. It was described as a new public sentiment, where interest in the race was no longer confined to a small circle, but prevailed wherever daily papers were read. The international character of the contest at first appealed to the patriotic impulse or spirit of the people, and with that came information as to yachting, yacht building, and indeed, promoted a wholesome liking for the sport. For the first time in its history, the *America's Cup* was the leading event of the day across the United States. The country saw it as more than a race for a trophy; it was a trial of two near perfect systems of yacht construction. One paper noted, "If the *Volunteer* wins, several points in dispute will be settled, and Americans will experience an old-fashioned glow of satisfaction and triumph."[73] One issue in dispute had to do with the size and construction of the *Thistle,* which was built in great secrecy during the 1886-87 winter. The yacht was designed in Glasgow, Scotland by George Lennox Watson, who had come to the United States the previous year, 1886, to watch the Cup races to understand the sea and wind conditions, and noted that the British challenger that year was under-canvassed. The *Thistle* was also the first *America's Cup* yacht to be launched with its hull hidden by huge canvas covers to keep it away from prying eyes. The media and the Americans were astonished and realized that the *Thistle*'s owner, Scotsman, James Bell, was determined to win. The skipper of the *Thistle* was John Barr who had raced 15 regattas before leaving Scotland for New York, and had won 11 of those races, and came in second in two of them. The reputation of the *Thistle* preceded her. When the yacht arrived in New York, it was measured based on the rules of the *Deed of Gift* for the *America's Cup,* and was found to be seven inches longer than declared in the challenge papers, and larger than the defender, *Volunteer.* The matter was referred to George L. Schuyler who deeded the trophy to the NYYC and was the last living organizer of the club. Schuyler with a sense of fair play recommended that the match go on, and it did.[74] The yacht race at New York excited but little interest in London, except in the city proper where a large crowd assembled early in the evening around the bulletins at the cable offices, disappearing however before the results were announced since British time was seven hours ahead of New York time. Nonetheless, the citizens of the *Thistle's* home port in Glasgow, Scotland engaged in lively betting on the race and had planned to give the owners and designers of the yacht a public banquet on their return.

The 1887 race was a match of the best two out of three runs, where two runs were "inside" the New York Harbor, and one run "outside" the Harbor in open water. What was unusual in the early days of yacht racing was the incursion on the "inside" course by spectator steamers and excursion boats. On this day thousands of boats covered an area of 50 acres on the water near the starting line, and were noisy throughout the race with incessant gun firing, steam whistling and cheering that inspired wild enthusiasm; the noise nearly interfered with the duties of Commodore Gerry's flagship that had to fire a cannon to start the race. The first of the three runs was "inside" the Harbor and was expected to take seven hours to cover start to finish over a course of 38 statute miles.[75] At the start line, while awaiting the start cannon, the *Thistle* moved about in a lively fashion taking pleasure in running past and around the *Volunteer* several times and met with loud applause from spectators at each pass. At the sound of the gun, the *Thistle* crossed the start line over a minute ahead of the *Volunteer,* but almost at once the *Volunteer* pulled ahead, even as the spectator boats began to interfere with the run. The *Thistle* was more than a little bothered by the excursion steamers that crossed her bow and kicked up the water, in fact, twice the crew hung from the yacht a large canvas sign which said KEEP ASTERN, but it did little to scatter the boats. Worse still, the wind varied in strength, shifting between southeast and southwest, and sometimes one boat had it and the other did not. But the average made things pretty nearly even. The *Volunteer,* beating, stretching and running with free sheets, except when excursion boats interfered and kept the wind from her, out-sailed her antagonist the *Thistle.* The first two races, one "inside" the Harbor, followed the next day by one "outside" in open waters, were soundly won by the *Volunteer* thereby ending the need for the third race. Despite the lingering dispute over the size of the *Thistle,* it was a decisive victory by the United States in her defense of the *America's Cup* in 1887, and the yacht *Volunteer* became the wonder of the yachting world.[76]

The win of the Cup was not just an American victory over an international rival, but was also like the historic baseball rivalry between the New York *Yankees* and the Boston *Red Sox.* The *New York Yacht Club* may have held the trophy in their club house and therefore hosted any challenger out of New York waters, but it was the *Boston Yacht Club's* own yacht, the *Volunteer,* built and skippered out of Massachusetts that won the race and defeated the *Thistle.* In the first week of October the Mayor of Boston held a meeting to arrange for a grand public celebration to honor the *Volunteer's* designer, Edward Burgess, and her owner General Paine. The enthusiastic Mayor's committee expanded the goals of their celebratory discussions and declared that:

> Boston was assuredly the yachting center of the country. Yet, in the international contests our yachts must go to New York Harbor, while Boston which supplies the boats to keep the *America's Cup* here, can only view the race from a distance. Filled with pride from yachting's greatest victory, the Mayor suggested that the citizens of Boston should proceed to establish a cup, open to the world, to be sailed for on the best yachting course in the world, the waters off Marblehead, which had expansive views from the coastline for spectators. Further the Mayor stated that a trophy be designed, the most beautiful in the world, one made in the United States as distinct from the *America's Cup* which was originally the Queen's cup won by New York in 1851 from England. The new Cup was not intended to supersede the *America's Cup*, but rather to extend international competition with a truly American trophy. The Mayor of Boston closed his remarks with "A movement for such a result would meet with an immediate response and be of direct and lasting benefit to our city. It should be set on foot without delay."[77]

Neither the city of Boston nor the *Boston Yacht Club* ever followed up on the grand suggestion. However, that did not dissuade Boston designers from continued production of yachts to participate in future *America's Cup* races. Boston hosted some of the most popular and competitive local cup races for years to come at Marblehead, Massachusetts. The *New York Yacht Club* continued its annual cruises up to Marblehead to compete in races and to enjoy the illuminated celebrations well into the twentieth century.

A month after the Cup race, the *New York Yacht Club* met to discuss and resolve lingering disputes. George L. Schuyler accepted the return of the Cup Trophy so that the Club could revise the *Deed of Gift* relating to the conditions under which future races should be sailed. One complaint from the *Thistle* was taken to heart, notably, the "inside" race in New York Harbor had disruptive tides, dangerous shoals, congestion and other hazardous conditions that made for a chaotic race, and was not enjoyed by even the most competitive yachtsman. The *America's Cup* was never again run on an "inside" course. Although the changes to the *Deed of Gift* improved many of the rules, it was not welcomed internationally. While the clause allowing a "time allowance" for uneven size boats was eliminated, the NYYC assumed the clause allowing "mutual agreement" as a resolution to such disputes would provide fair, sportsmanlike negotiations with the next challenger for the cup. However, England believed it unfair and the new *Deed of Gift* would lead to disputes rather than a resolution of disputes. There would not be another challenge to the *America's Cup* for six years, until 1893.

Commodore Gerry was ready for a change of pace. After *Electra* was sent to Wilmington, Delaware, for her winter maintenance and overhaul, he turned his attention to his law practice, with a major decision handed down October 4, 1887. A second case against the *New York Catholic Protectory* had been argued June 21 in the Court of Appeals. A fourteen-year old girl, Florence Van Riper, was brought before the Magistrate by an agent of the NYSPCC and charged with being found improperly exposed and neglected and wandering in *Union Square Park* without any proper guardianship, in the company of a known prostitute. After being found guilty, Florence was committed to the care of the *New York Catholic Protectory*. Under the law a parent must be notified of the arrest and be present at the trial, and in fact, Florence's mother, Mrs. Van Riper was present during the trial. After her commitment to the *Protectory*, Florence's father gained her release with proceedings for a writ of habeas corpus and certiorari, which stated that the law required that the father, not the mother be notified of the arrest, and that the facts of the case were not adequate to the arrest, specifically: *being without a guardian* - she was under the care of both parents; simply *found wandering in a park* - was for innocent reasons; and merely being in the *presence of a prostitute* - without further acts was not sufficient for an arrest warrant. The court agreed noting that when removing a child from the custody of a parent, the evidence presented must be precise and unequivocal. It is interesting to note that Commodore Gerry had tried, and won, the *Van Heck* case the previous year, which had nearly the same parental notification issue, and in fact, that 1886 decision triggered a change in the law that clarified the notification requirement. Based on that change in the law, Commodore Gerry lost this 1887 case because the Judge decided that it was a matter of "statutory interpretation" to decide what the new law meant when it stated that a "parent" must be notified. The question was whether the word "parent" being singular, meant mother and/or father, or only the father must be notified. The judge chose to interpret the singular form of the word "parent" in the statute to mean only the father, and further, it would mean "mother" only if the father was dead. It was the court's view that the father of a child was, in most cases, best able to provide for the proper defense and care of the child. The father was deemed by the law to have parental control and custody. It was a tough day in court when a lawyer lost his case based on a change in the law triggered by one of his own cases won just the year before. This case has been cited forty times in cases up to 1985 and in a 2006 law review article.[78] The remainder of 1887 found Commodore Gerry writing the final report for the *Commission on Capital Punishment*, which was due in early 1888. He celebrated his fiftieth birthday on December 25, surrounded by the holiday cheer of his wife and five children.

Harlan and Hollingsworth & Company Wilmington, Delaware

Steam yacht *Electra* built by Harlan & Hollingsworth (*below*)

Lillian "Lilly" Gerry (*left*)

April 14, 1884 The yacht *Electra* is christened with a champagne bottle by Elbridge T. Gerry's youngest daughter, Lilly.

Chief Justice, Lord Coleridge (*right*)

One of the first official guests on Commodore Gerry's magnificent new yacht was the Chief Justice of England, Lord Coleridge in August 1883, when they cruised up the Hudson River and past the newly finished Brooklyn Bridge. The new steam yacht was electrified by Thomas Edison and produced ice to cool Lord Coleridge's water.

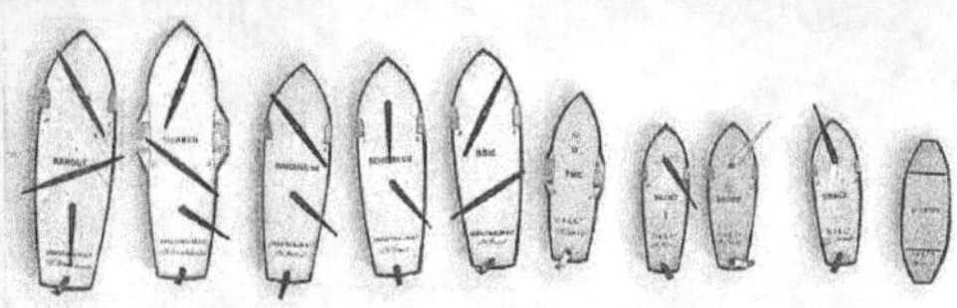

When Commodore Elbridge T. Gerry, elected 1886, led the New York Yacht Club's annual cruise and regatta, his yacht *Electra* was the Club's "Flagship" and was covered in bright flags. During the regatta races Commodore Gerry oversaw the races with his navigation tool kit which included small wooden models (*above*), a compass with tin spinners (*left*), a navigation map and manual with rules of sailing navigation and races. He had a Master's Certificate as a steam yacht pilot.

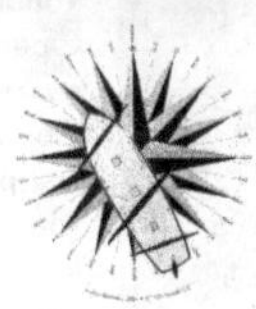

These navigation tools and manual (*below*) are held in the Rare Book Room of the United States Supreme Court as part of the Gerry Collection.

Artist's rendering of the famous 1887 America's Cup Race between the *Volunteer* and the British *Thistle*. Commodore Gerry's yacht *Electra* is the dark boat (*center*) between the *Volunteer* and the *Thistle* as the race crosses the finish line.

Silver water pitcher engraved *Electra*

The five Gerry children costumed for New York's first ever children's "Fancy Dress Ball" hosted by Mrs. Gerry in the winter of 1886 and reported by the *New York Times*

Lilly Mabel Angelica

Peter Robert

Penelope

Purchased in Rome in 1887, stands today at Lake Delaware

Organ pump wheel

Historic Organ
Hillborne Roosevelt Opus 34

Charles Dodsley Walker
Boys Camp organist
1940-1990

Interior of Old Metropolitan Opera House

The Goelet brothers organized James A. Roosevelt, J.P. Morgan and Cornelius Vanderbilt to financially sponsor the first Opera House in New York City, which replaced the old Academy of Music. Elbridge T. Gerry purchased one of the first private boxes along with the sponsors. The Goelet family has substantially contributed to the opera to this day, with the Lincoln Center's grand staircase as one of their major Twentieth Century gifts.

Metropolitan Opera House, opened 1900

The Goelet Office building incorporated elaborate metalwork that remains intact in the lobby.

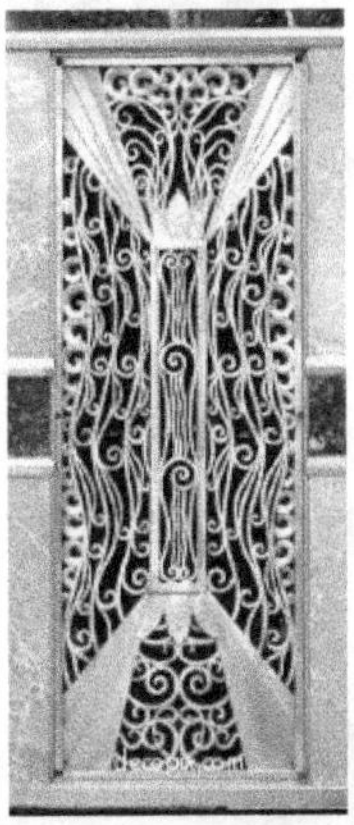

John Singer Sargent portrait of 7-year-old Beatrice Goelet, daughter of Robert and Harrietta Goelet

Two fine examples (*right*) of the Goelet Cup that was re-designed each year for the yacht races at Newport, Rhode Island and sponsored by Ogden Goelet during his entire life.

Spectators at the annual Newport Goelet Cup yacht race.

Fraunces Tavern

One of the oldest buildings in old New York City, Fraunces Tavern was George Washington's headquarters during the American Revolution and where Commodore Elbridge T. Gerry met annually with the *Sons of the American Revolution* in the Long Room at the table beneath the portrait of Washington.

The Long Room

Chickering Hall at the corner Fifth Avenue and 18th Street

Grand staircase entrance

Grand Auditorium

8

GILDED GOTHAM

THE 1880'S PART III

I hope I shall possess firmness and virtue enough to maintain what I consider the most enviable of all titles, the character of an honest man.
President George Washington, 1789

The New Year was welcomed on January 17, 1888 with the annual *Patriarch's Ball* held at Delmonico's and organized by Ward McAllister, the godfather of the social elite of *Gilded Gotham*. He published a list of what he believed to be the 400 elite families of New York City, which was actually closer to 300 if relatives were consolidated under one family name. The 1888 gala's most unique aspect was the first use of electric lighting at a *Patriarchs' Ball*. The novelty was not welcome at such elaborate gatherings since the bright glare was not flattering to a lady's face nor did it set a romantic, perhaps intimate mood to a gathering of 400 guests. Electric lights were described as having a cold and stony glare that had to be muted for the ball by the elaborate decorations orchestrated by *Klunder* florists. The glare was softened to a golden yellow tone by the use of delicate yellow silk draperies and porcelain shades. There were also hung between the lights bunches of yellow tulips so that wherever the rays of light touched they were transmuted to gold before they fell upon the youth and beauty beneath. Palms and evergreens formed the background everywhere and mirrors were draped with smilax and roses, while the walls were hung with plaques of pink lilies, violets, yellow tulips and hyacinths. The assemblage of first families included the Gerry, Goelet, Harriman, Kane, Mills, Roosevelt, Vanderbilt, Van Rensaelaers, and Wilson families among others. New York society could stand a great deal in the way of amusement as was proved by these same families who had attended a formal cotillion the previous evening hosted by Mr. and Mrs. Ogden Mills of the Staatsburg estate on the Hudson, the aunt and uncle of Louisa Gerry.[1]

Commodore Elbridge T. Gerry on behalf of the *Commission on Capital Punishment* submitted their 95-page report to the New York State Legislature in January 1888. The questionnaires distributed the year before had initiated substantial discussion and experimentation. Commodore Gerry chaired the commission which had two other members. One was Matthew Hale a prominent Albany lawyer and the grandson of American Revolutionary War hero, Nathaniel Hale, who famously said at his hanging by the British for treason, "I only regret that I have but one life to lose for my country." It seemed somehow appropriate for his grandson to advocate the elimination of hanging as a means of execution. Hale agreed with his colleagues that executions must be private and that the bodies of those executed should be either buried inside the prison or given to hospitals for medical research. The third member of the commission was Doctor Alfred P. Southwick of Buffalo, New York who took a decidedly scientific approach to his work on the commission. The returned surveys had favored hanging over electrocution as an unknown and untried method of killing. Dr. Southwick decided to research the actual effects of electrocution by experimenting on dogs. In the summer of 1887 he worked with the *Society for the Prevention of Cruelty to Animals* to organize a test center in Buffalo where stray dogs that were to be killed in any event were assigned to his testing laboratory. Over the course of the summer and fall the evidence was collected in scientific papers for the commission's consideration. Commodore Gerry was not easily convinced and proposed that before any electrocution a massive dose of morphine be injected to put the prisoner to sleep. However, doctors believed it went against their Hippocratic Oath, and indeed it might even scare the general public into refusing medical injections. While Dr. Southwick performed his scientific research in Buffalo two scientists were competing in the field of electricity, Thomas Edison and George Westinghouse. In the *Gilded Age* scientific advances translated into unprecedented profits for many companies and Edison already had financial interests to protect, in fact by 1886 he was focused on the distribution of electricity to homes and businesses. Unfortunately Edison was wedded to his idea of using DC (direct current) distribution and rejected his employee Nikola Tesla's discovery of the AC (alternating current) distribution. It was Westinghouse who understood the application of AC distribution and purchased Tesla's idea and patented it in 1886. Westinghouse built the first citywide AC power station in Buffalo, New York where Dr. Southwick was performing his dog experiments. Dr. Southwick first contacted Edison for his endorsement of electrocution as a method of capital punishment. While he was personally against capital punishment, Edison agreed electrocution was more humane than hanging. By this time Edison accepted AC distribution and referred Dr. Southwick back to Westinghouse's patented dynamo as the best method to employ in an electric chair. Swayed by the recommendations to the Commission by Thomas Edison,

Commodore Elbridge T. Gerry completed the report with the full approval of Matthew Hale and Dr. Alfred Southwick. On June 5, 1888 the *Electrical Execution Act* was passed that endorsed private electrocutions and established a veil of secrecy that surrounds United States executions to this day. The law went into effect several months later on January 1, 1889.

Commodore Elbridge T. Gerry received sad but not surprising news in mid-March with the announcement of the death of his life-long friend, Henry Bergh at the age of seventy-seven. For several months, in fact since the death of his wife in June 1887, Mr. Bergh had been gradually failing. He suffered from chronic bronchitis and an enlarged heart and had become very feeble. There were present at his bedside his three nephews, the sons of his brother, Edwin Bergh. His funeral was held at St. Marks Church, the same church where Uncle Peter Goelet's funeral was held. Henry Bergh's dear friend Commodore Gerry was a pallbearer. He believed that the *Society for the Prevention of Cruelty to Animals* would stand as the monument to his life. But that is an understatement; as a result of his endeavors all fifty states and many foreign countries established community SPCA's. Henry Bergh supported new ways of protecting animals, like encouraging the use of *clay pigeons* as an artificial substitute for live pigeons as "marks" for sport shooters. On March 24, 1888 acting-President Commodore Gerry called a meeting of the Board of Managers of the *American Society for the Prevention of Cruelty to Animals* to elect a new President, Henry Bergh, Jr., who then gave to the *Society* the handsome diamond-studded badge presented to his uncle in 1880 and said he wished it to be held for all future Presidents. The Board of Managers accepted the badge and then passed a resolution authorizing subscriptions for a monument to be erected in Central Park to honor Henry Bergh. The monument stands today with a loyal dog sitting happily at Mr. Bergh's feet.[2]

The warm days of late April welcomed the return of the steam yacht *Electra* to New York City after a winter of maintenance, refitting and surface refinishing in Wilmington, Delaware. However, the new finish gave a dark color to the deck houses that Commodore Gerry found to be too somber, so he had the varnish removed and the mahogany re-finished in a lighter tint. By mid-May *Electra* was out in the Harbor for trial excursions to get the crew in shape for the busy summer season. The month of May was also a time of religious celebration for the Gerry family. Lilly Gerry noted in her diary that "Mabel and I were Confirmed by Bishop Potter at Trinity Chapel on May 8 and made our First Communion on the following Sunday." Gifts of prayer books were received by the girls as was the family custom. Two months later, the Fourth of July holiday was celebrated with family and friends at Newport, followed by a cruise up the Hudson River to Kingston for a visit to the *Lake Delaware Farm* estate. Robert Gerry, then eleven years old, had suffered a bad case of Pneumonia in January, as noted by his older sister Lilly in her diary, but had recovered his robust health over the summer holidays. The Gerry children then ranged in age from 9 years to 17 years old and enjoyed the same ports-of-call as their parents and had well-established circles of their own friends which included their Goelet cousins at Newport, Rhode Island. Relaxed and rejuvenated the Gerry family boarded *Electra* at Kingston and returned home to New York City by the last day of July. The Gerrys enjoyed a short break at home to re-pack personal belongings and to purchase necessary supplies before embarking on *Electra's* last cruise of the summer with the fleet of the New York Yacht Club.

In early August the *New York Yacht Club* was ready to set sail for the 1888 annual cruise. Commodore Elbridge T. Gerry had communicated to all the Clubs interested in joining the cruise to rendezvous in the New London, Connecticut harbor on August 8. The flagship *Electra* with the Regatta Committee, the fleet Surgeon and the New York press corps on board, set sail at 10 o'clock from the foot of the East Twenty-Sixth Street dock. The press corps immediately gathered in the quarter deck smoking room to inspect a trophy cup on display that would be awarded at the end of the cruise. Although Commodore Gerry had his *Master's License,* he hired George Wicks to captain the *Electra* so he could oversee the cruise, time and record the many races, and entertain his guests along the way. The *Corsair,* the yacht owned by J.P. Morgan, followed the *Electra* out of New York Harbor. Other Schooners, Sloops, and steamers left ports from New York to Boston for the New London rendezvous that evening, which was met with cannon salutes from the shore, followed by the grand illumination of the yachts after dark and ended with dinner and dancing in the Pequot Hotel. There were two mishaps during the 1888 cruise. The first was the loss of *Electra's* flange off her propeller while cruising from New York to New London for the first day rendezvous. Commodore Gerry managed to telegraph ahead to get a new flange sent to New London for timely repairs. The second mishap was at Newport on the third day of the cruise and the annual *Goelet Cup* race had just started. Everything went smoothly until just after crossing the start line. The yacht *Mayflower* was directly behind the yacht *Grayling* and was sailing a trifle faster when suddenly the *Mayflower's* bowsprit caught the end of the *Grayling's* main boom. This of itself was nothing serious, however the sloop *Regina* a smaller boat, was right ahead of the *Grayling's* boom and the latter's stern was pushed to windward, her bow swung off and in a moment the *Graylings* big bowsprit struck the *Regina's* mainsail near the mast. The little sloop keeled over to starboard, her topmast snapped and the rigging came rattling down on her deck. Three guests on board became excited and jumped overboard. Lines were thrown from the *Grayling* and the *Electra's* gig boat arrived on the scene for the rescue. By the time the excitement had subsided all the yachts had crossed the start-line and the faster boats were rapidly moving to the front with the *Volunteer* from Boston in the lead. Throughout the ten-day cruise the *Volunteer* continued to dominate the races upholding her glorious reputation from the 1887 victory over Scotland's *Thistle* the year before. The successful cruise ended on Monday, August 20 on the yacht *Electra* when Commodore Gerry formally disbanded the fleet until the next year.

Robert James Livingston's brother, Maturin Livingston, died November 29, 1888 at his residence, 30 West Twenty-Fourth Street, at the age of seventy-three. *Gilded Gotham* knew the story of how Maturin stole the heart of his wife Ruth Baylies whom he married November 12, 1852. One of the richest men in New York, Edmund H. Schermerhorn, fell madly in love with Ruth when they were both young. He courted her and asked her to marry him, but she said no and broke his heart when she married Maturin Livingston. The sad story is that Edmund divorced himself from society and devoted himself to his library and music for the remainder of his life. He died a veritable recluse in 1891 in Newport where he had lived the last ten years of his life.[3]

Maturin and Ruth lived a full and happy life as one of the foremost representatives of the Livingston family in *Gilded Gotham.* Maturin's hospitality at his city mansion, at his manor house at Staatsburg on the Hudson, and at his villa in Newport made him a prince among hosts. His only children were twin daughters, Ruth, who married D. Ogden Mills, and Elizabeth, who married William Cavendish-Bentinck, the Duke of Portland in England. The funeral for Maturin Livingston was private and he was buried at *Saint James Church* in Hyde Park, New York. Less than two weeks later the annual *Patriarchs' Ball* was held December 11 at *Delmonico's* and as was the custom, guests assembled at a late hour, the ladies did not appear in the ballroom until midnight. Several of the Patriarchs were kept away through family bereavements or illness, which included Commodore Gerry and his wife Louisa who were in mourning for the loss of her Uncle Maturin Livingston, the brother of Robert J. Livingston, Louisa's father.

Just before Christmas the Mayor of New York City, Abram S. Hewitt (1822-1903) was completing his term of office. Mayor Hewitt was a lawyer and a wealthy industrialist who had graduated from *Columbia University* just a few years before Commodore Gerry. Mayor Hewitt had participated in the fall of *Tammany Hall,* helped to organize the *Democratic Party* of New York and served in the *United States House of Representatives* for five terms before being elected Mayor of *Gilded Gotham.* He married the daughter of industrialist Peter Cooper with whom he founded the educational institution *Cooper Union* for the advancement of science and art. Mayor Hewitt was known as the "Father of the New York Subway System" because he initiated the use of public funds for subway construction and leased the completed facility to a private company for day-to-day operation. This was a visionary approach that required fundamental changes in both law and policy.[4] To recognize their friend and the leader of their great metropolis, Commodore Gerry joined J. P. Morgan, John Jacob Astor, D. Ogden Mills, and James A. Roosevelt and invited Mayor Abraham Hewitt to a dinner at *Delmonico's* as a bi-partisan public "thank you" for his personal sacrifice and for the fearless and impartial manner in which he administered the affairs of the city. The letter noted that such public service deserved an appropriate acknowledgement by the people. Mayor Hewitt graciously replied that while he could not accept the invitation for a "public" banquet he was gratified by their appreciation for his service. The Mayor was content to leave his record to the impartial test of time and truth. He believed that his children were under an obligation to continue for another generation an unselfish and honest effort for the public good.[5] In fact his three daughters founded the *Cooper-Hewittt National Design Museum,* two of his sons were inventors and authors, and his third son became a lawyer and philanthropist in New York City just like his father. Beneath *Gilded Gotham's* glittering façade was an enduring commitment to civic duty by those in a position to make a difference, not just with their philanthropy, but by instilling a sense of public service in their children by their own example. Certainly not every high society family embraced the maxim that "with great wealth came great responsibility," but most did respond to opportunities to serve the great metropolis with a sense of civic pride during the late nineteenth century. Henry Bergh's nephew carried on his work with the *American Society for the Prevention of Cruelty to Animals* just as Commodore Elbridge T. Gerry's sons, grandsons, and great-grandchildren carried on the work of the *New York Society for the Prevention of Cruelty to Children* through the twenty-first Century.

The breadth of Commodore Elbridge T. Gerry's charity extended to assisting seamen, who like his father, Lieutenant Thomas Russell Gerry, and his uncle Captain James T. Gerry, spent decades of their lives serving in the United States navy. On January 8, 1889 Commodore Gerry joined the *American Seamen's Friend Society* which was established in 1833 to "improve the social and moral condition of seamen by promoting in every port, boarding houses of good character, savings banks, register offices, libraries, museums, reading rooms and schools; and also to minister to their spiritual needs."[6] Commodore Gerry had three primary interests in the Society. First, to provide for the welfare of homeless seamen, second, to provide for their spiritual and moral guidance, and third, to provide and support libraries for the seamen on land and sea. No one understood the value and power of the written word more than Commodore Gerry whose own library was a life-long passion, exceeding even his thirty year passion for his beloved yacht *Electra.* The *Society* used member donations to purchase between $10 and $25 worth of books which were placed in stout wooden cases with a hinged door which could be locked, and when opened gave the appearance of a small bookcase. Each library bore a plate giving the donor's name. They were placed on-board each ship by a *Society* representative who was well known along the waterfront as the *Ships Visitor.* Commodore Gerry donated $100 which would have provided between five and ten "book cases" to be delivered to that same number of ships. The Seaman Society faithfully kept a detailed list of all the libraries sent out to the ships and set-up in the club houses. The annual report of the *Society* for the year ending 1930 recorded that the whole number of libraries sent to sea since 1859 was 13,352 and that an additional 16,688 had been refitted and re-shipped. There was an aggregate of 30,040 libraries sent to sea from ports between Boston and New York City over a seventy year period. The full story is told in the *History of the American Seaman's Friend Society,* G. W. Blunt White Library, Manuscript Collections, Mystic Seaport Museum, Mystic, Connecticut. The Commodore's tendency to "join" societies and organizations had both charitable and personal motivations. He thoroughly enjoyed the company of male friends and jovial times shared in celebrations. Indeed on March 16, Commodore Gerry was a special guest of the *Society of the Friendly Sons of Saint Patrick* at *Delmonico's* where good food, good drink and a good time celebrated St. Patrick's Day 1889.

The Washington Inaugural Celebration

The centennial celebration of the inauguration of the first President of the United States, General George Washington, was set for April 1889 in *Gilded Gotham.* The plans were initiated two years earlier in 1887 when the location of the national celebration was debated in the United States Congress. In fact, because General George Washington was inaugurated on Wall Street in front of *Federal Hall,* just down the street from Trinity Church, it was decided that the national celebration would be held in New York City. This followed the precedent set in September 1887 when the *Centennial Celebration of the signing of the United Constitution* was held in Philadelphia, Pennsylvania where the document was signed by the nation's Founding Fathers. That celebration took place over a three-day period with great pomp and to great effect, serving as a model of how the nation might design a celebration of Washington's 1789 Inauguration. Indeed, in mid-1887 every state in the nation was invited to contribute ideas to the planning and to participate by sending representatives to the celebration. Between 1887 and 1888 local newspapers across the country began to cover the story of what appeared to be a potentially grand event:

> *St. Louis Globe-Democrat,* Missouri: A meeting of citizens of New York will be held on Thursday next to take preliminary steps looking to the centennial celebration in 1889 of the inauguration of George Washington as the first President of the United States. The call for the meeting embraces over a hundred names of the most prominent citizens of New York, and it is proposed to make this celebration the grandest of all the centennial events which have occurred. It will be national in character.[7]

> *Bismarck Daily Tribune,* North Dakota: George Washington, centennial of his inauguration as President will be celebrated in New York in 1889. *The article describes in detail Washington's journey from Mount Vernon to New York City and events of the day, ending with,* Congress and president entered at once upon their duties; the rest is historic, and its fruits the heritage of a great and free people.[8]

National celebrations offer opportunities to remind American citizens of their revolutionary history and the nation's awkward first steps in self-government. Looking back to the election of George Washington and his inauguration, we find a prophetic letter from founding father Elbridge Gerry to his dear friend, John Adams, the first Vice-President under Washington, sent on March 4, 1789, seven weeks before the inauguration in New York City, concerning the first Electoral College vote results.

> My dear friend,
>
> I find on inquiry that you are elected Vice-President, having three or four times the number of votes of any other candidate. Maryland threw away their votes on Colonel Harrison, and South Carolina on Governor Rutledge, being, with some other states which were not unanimous for you, apprehensive that this was a necessary step to prevent your election to the chair. On this point, they were mistaken, for the President, as I am informed from pretty good authority, has a unanimous vote. It is the universal wish of all that I have conferred with, and indeed their expectation, that both General Washington and yourself will accept; and should either refuse, it will have a very disagreeable effect. The members present met today in the City Hall, there being about eleven Senators

and thirteen Representatives, and not constituting a quorum in either house, they adjourned until tomorrow.

Mrs. Gerry and the ladies join me in sincere regards to yourself and your lady,

Elbridge Gerry[9]

No quorum of the House of Representatives had been formed until the first of April, nor had the Senate until the sixth of April. These bodies then counted the electoral vote, with the result predicted by Elbridge Gerry in his letter written a month before; but news of the election results were so slow that Washington would not leave for New York City until April 16, 1789; he wrote in his diary:

> About ten o'clock I bade adieu to Mount Vernon, to private life and to domestic felicity; and with a mind oppressed with more anxious and painful sensations than I have words to express, set out for New York.... with the best disposition to render service to my country in obedience to its call, but with less hope of answering its expectations. *He writes over the course of the journey to New York...* At my age, and in my circumstances, what prospects or advantages could I propose to myself, for embarking again on the tempestuous and uncertain ocean of public life. *Later...* The acclamations of the people filled my mind with sensations as painful as pleasing.[10]

The inauguration finally took place on April 30, 1789 and Chancellor Robert R. Livingston Jr. administered the oath. He was Louisa Livingston Gerry's great-uncle, the brother of Gertrude. General George Washington was described as agitated and embarrassed more than he ever was by the leveled cannon or pointed musket. He addressed the two houses in the Senate Chamber which was both touching and solemn, his expression was grave almost to sadness, he was modest and actually shaking, his voice deep, a little tremulous, and so low as to call for close attention to be heard. He had been a General of the first order who led his infant nation to revolutionary victory, and now must be the first President to lead his nation into statehood. No American had carried such a burden over the course of his lifetime, and George Washington felt the weight on his shoulders. Celebrating the centennial of his inauguration was a celebration of his success in leading the republic through infancy, ensuring its future as one of the greatest nations on earth just one hundred years later. *Gilded Gotham* was ready to lead the nation in celebration.

By January 1888 the committee structure for the celebration was in place and committee members appointed. The Executive Committee was charged with planning and organizing the celebration and Commodore Elbridge T. Gerry was given the distinct honor of being appointed the Chairman of the committee, and it was said that he was the controlling spirit of the monumental commemoration. The committee almost immediately sent a Bill to the New York legislature to make April 30, 1889 a legal holiday in the state. This would ensure maximum participation by citizens of the state and also assist with managing the crowds in New York City, already anticipating nearly a million people for the event.

By November 1888 the outline of the celebrations were in place; the committee recommended that services of praise and thanksgiving be held in the different churches, as they were 100 years before, with special services in *Saint Paul's Church,* which Washington attended. There would be literary exercises designed by Commodore Gerry on the steps of the sub-treasury, where *Federal Hall* stood when Washington was inaugurated. The suggested program included a prayer by Reverend Dr. Stoors, a poem by John Greenleaf Whittier (*a descendant of Elbridge Gerry's mother Ann Greenleaf*), and a benediction by Archbishop Corrigan. Foreign countries were invited to take part in a naval display as the President of the United States was expected to arrive from Washington with his Cabinet and Justices of the Supreme Court of the United States. They followed the precedent of General Washington and traveled to Philadelphia then to Trenton and arrived at Elizabeth port, New Jersey. They were immediately taken from there on a government boat that passed through a flotilla of United States and foreign war ships to the foot of Wall Street. At Wall Street the President was welcomed by the Mayor and other distinguished officers and guests.

In December 1888, Russell Harrison, son of the President, attended a meeting of the *Sub-Committee on Plan and Scope* of the centennial celebration. He informed the committee that the President would lend all the aid in his power to make the celebration successful. Commodore Gerry wanted to locate the original Bible upon which President Washington had taken the oath of office. The history of the Bible was connected with the early days of the Masonic fraternity in New York City. When General Washington was about to be inaugurated the committee of arrangements found, that in the excitement at *Federal Hall,* the necessity of a Bible had been overlooked and the hour for the Inauguration was rapidly approaching. The *City Hotel* was not far away and at the time was the place where both General Washington and Chancellor Livingston met with the *Free Mason's Saint John's Lodge* and therefore knew a Bible would be found there, a requirement for Masonic meetings. The Bible was secured and used for the first inauguration after which it was returned to the Lodge altar. An entry of the fact was made in the minutes of the next meeting of the Lodge. Years later, when it became necessary to replace the old Bible with a modern style Bible, the ancient volume was deposited in a place of security as a relic of the Lodge. According to the records of *Saint John's Lodge No 1* the authenticity of their old Bible was assured and was made available for display at the *Washington Centennial* in 1889.

At least 7,000 were expected to participate in the great *Banquet and Inaugural Ball* to be held on the night of April 29, 1889 and each lady at the ball was presented with a souvenir, as was done at the first *Inaugural Ball* of 100 years before. There was a vast array of distinguished guests in the boxes, balconies and galleries of the hall, as many watched as danced. *Landers* furnished the music for the ball and banquet with two orchestras of fifty musicians each. The programs of music and order of dancing were engraved by *Tiffany.* Dancing began with *Wiegand's Declaration quadrille* and concluded with *No. 24, Funkenstein's Dianelli polka.* The buffet was furnished by Hoffman House and included hors d'oeuvres, soup, salmon, filet of beef, aspics, sorbet, salads and an assortment of delicate desserts. The banquet, both in numbers and arrangements, was the most magnificent in the history of New York. The celebrations were compared to the 1860 celebration and ball in honor of the Prince of Wales, which paled by comparison to the 1889 Centennial Celebration that engulfed *Gilded Gotham* for three days and nights, including fireworks, private dinners, concerts, and endless speech-making. Each day there were magnificent parades with floats and bands trooping along Fifth Avenue in New York City with reviewing stands for hundreds of special guests. Patriotic banners and colorful bunting decorated the buildings and marching bands played rousing music for public entertainment.

While many photographs, newspaper and periodical articles remain accessible today documenting the magnificent centennial celebrations of President George Washington's inauguration, there are few intact artifacts to be found. Two of the most significant artifacts are the official memorial scrapbooks given to the leading organizers and the marble monument at New York City's *Washington Square.*

Commodore Elbridge T. Gerry, as the Chairman of the Executive Committee was presented with a large black memorial scrapbook, the cover engraved with gold lettering. The scrapbook remains in the Gerry family and includes all of the tickets, invitations, letters, and programs in pristine condition. Of note are replicas of every medal given to distinguished guests, Centennial officials, and Commodore Gerry and worn during the three-day event. The replica medals are embossed with gold and silver leaf. A beautiful *Certificate of Gratitude* to Commodore Elbridge T. Gerry as Chair of the *Executive Committee,* for the success of the Centennial is included in the Gerry family memorabilia.

The second artifact is a marble monument that stands in New York City's *Washington Square Park,* bounded by Fifth Avenue, Waverly Place, West Fourth Street, and MacDougal Street. While the park was named for General George Washington, it also reflects the evolution of lower Manhattan. The parkland was once a marsh fed by a riverlet called *Minetta Brook.* In 1797 the Common Council acquired the land for use as a *Potter's Field* or common burial ground. The field was also used for public executions, giving rise to the tale of the *Hangman's Elm* which stands in the northwest corner of the park. By 1826 the site was used as a *Military Parade Ground* and by then, was already named after General George Washington, which brought some prestige to the location. Indeed, a number of wealthy and prominent families, including the Vanderbilt's, moved to the area and built the distinguished Greek revival mansions that still line the square's north side. One of these mansions provided the setting for Henry James' 1880 novel, *Washington Square.* In 1835, the park also hosted the first public demonstration of the telegraph by Samuel F. B. Morse, a professor at *New York University,* which is adjacent to the park.[11] It is no surprise then, that the *Centennial* of Washington's inauguration would incorporate *Washington Square Park* as a focal point of the public celebrations.

Commodore Elbridge T. Gerry, Chairman of the Centennial Executive Committee, commissioned the building of four temporary grand Arches in New York City for the Centennial. The greatest success, and the Arch that remains today, was that of architect Stanford White, whom Commodore Gerry commissioned to design and construct a "triumphal Arch" on the north side of *Washington Square* at Fifth Avenue. Stanford White was a favored architect of Ogden and Robert Goelet, as well as other prominent New York families and commercial institutions. Stanford White designed the *Southside* summer mansion in Newport, Rhode Island for Robert Goelet, and redesigned the *Staatsburg* mansion of Ruth and Ogden Mills in 1890, first built by Louisa Gerry's grandparents, and the boyhood home of her father, Robert J. Livingston.

The *New York Times* wrote on April 28, 1889 that the most beautiful of the four temporary centennial arches was Stanford White's Washington triumphal arch. His idea was to carry out a type of architecture that prevailed during colonial and General Washington's own time and which belongs more naturally to America than any other country. The public loved it and there was an outcry for a permanent version of the wood and plaster arch. The plaster on the arch was painted a gleaming ivory-white and adorned with molded ornamentation of festoons and wreaths. Bunting hung from the arch and bunches of flags were arranged at the sides including foreign flags of countries from whom the population of America drew its immigrants. Two stuffed American bald eagles were mounted on either side of the keystone. The statue of George Washington was purchased from an antique shop and placed at the top of the Arch; it did not survive as part of the later, permanent redesign of the arch built of marble. The

Edison Company provided hundreds of electric lights that were powered by a noisy generator in a neighboring yard. Traffic passed under the arch, both by carriage and on foot for the next two years, until the arch was torn down to be replaced with a permanent monument.

A month after the celebration was over, Stanford White eagerly offered to design for free, the permanent arch, and suggested that the arch be re-constructed of marble rather than granite as had been suggested and decorated with sculptural groups. A design was started soon thereafter when the $150,000 budget for construction was raised by private donations.

A year later, on April 30, 1890 ground was broken in an understated ceremony. However, within two weeks laborers realized they were digging up skeletons, headstones, and coffins. Stanford White stopped work, and when two headstones inscribed 1803 were discovered, it confirmed that the workers had unearthed an old German cemetery. The bones were all carefully reinterred and the work went on for another four years. On May 4, 1895 the completed arch built of Tuckahoe marble was dedicated with great pomp and ceremony. Sculpture Frederick W. MacMonnies had designed the bulk of the ornamentation which was then carried out by the master Italian stone carvers of the *Piccirilli Studio*. MacMonnie used his own wife's face as the model for *Peace* and Stanford White's wife, Bessie, as the model for *War*. The massive marble eagles were designed by Philip Martiny.[12]

Commodore Elbridge T. Gerry did in fact take time out from his labors in connection with the Centennial to fight a proposal in the New York legislature. The *General Assembly* in Albany was debating a bill which would restrict the power of police magistrates to commit children to the care of benevolent institutions. The intent was to establish the right of appeal from such committal and enable unworthy and unfit parents or guardians to take back children who had been rescued from cruel and dangerous circumstances. The chief argument advanced by proponents of the bill was that the institutions to which children were committed were overanxious and overzealous in their intent to make a speculation of charity by receiving $104 a year for each child committed to their care. Commodore Gerry, on behalf of the *New York Society for the Prevention of Cruelty to Children* (NYSPCC), argued against the bill by noting that the organizations directly affected by the proposed legislation did not receive a dime from the city or state for the care of the children placed in their care, rather, funding was through institutional donations or by subscriptions to the NYSPCC. Further, all complaints against neglectful or criminal parents made in police courts were investigated by the NYSPCC at its own expense. The common endeavor was to find homes for the children beyond the reach of urban pitfalls, temptations and bad influences. Henry L. Hoguet, president of the

Catholic Protectory, the largest institution of its kind in the country, stated, "I should regard the passage of the bill as the severest blow our institution has received in its twenty-six years of existence. It would impede our work and tie our hands. We could not afford to contest the cases which would be brought and we should have to let the children go."[13]

Capital Punishment by Electrocution

While New York City prepared to lead the nation in the centennial celebration and Americans benefited from the bounty of the Progressive Era's expansion and invention, the uncertainty of daily life in the darker corners of society continued unabated. In March 1889 in upstate New York, the scourge of alcoholism led to a heinous murder that would test the state's recently passed law on capital punishment, which was based on the *Gerry Commission's* successful recommendation to stop the use of hanging as the death penalty and instead, use the *Electric Chair* as the least cruel or unusual form of punishment.

William Kemmler was born in Philadelphia, Pennsylvania to immigrant parents from Germany. His father died from an infection that he received after a drunken brawl; his mother also died of alcoholism. As a boy, William worked in his father's butcher shop after dropping out of school at age ten, learning neither how to read nor write. William was reportedly slender with dark brown hair and spoke both German and English. After his parents died he went into the peddling business and earned enough money to purchase a horse and cart to carry fruit, vegetables and other goods to sell on street corners, which was known as being a *huckster*, an honest way to make a living. He spent most of his life in drunken stupors and after moving to Buffalo, New York as a young man, he was known in the local saloons and to his friends as "Philadelphia Billy," for his drunken binges.[14] By 1889 Kemmler found enough success as a huckster that he was able to hire a few men to help him work the streets. He lived on Division Street in Buffalo with his wife, Tillie, and their daughter, six-year-old Ella. Tillie was known to rage at Kemmler about his daily drunkenness. Also living with them in the cramped four room apartment was another huckster named John De Bella, with whom Kemmler split the profits of the business. On March 28, 1889 Kemmler was out drinking late into the night, and finally passed out on the floor of the bar. Back at the apartment the following morning, Kemmler was shaking with delirium tremens and became irritated by what he perceived as the overly affectionate tone Tillie was using with De Bella. He noted that her traveling trunk was packed and appeared to have a lot of his money in it. Tillie protested that she had simply cleaned up the apartment and was straightening her things.

Kemmler went out to the small barn to prepare his cart for the day's work where he then picked up a small hatchet to make quick repairs to the barn door. De Bella went outside to express his concern to one of the workers that Kemmler was angry. About the same time Tillie went to the barn to ask Kemmler for some eggs, which he gave her. However, with the small hatchet still in hand, Kemmler followed Tillie back to the house. Kemmler struck Tillie 26 times in the head, neck and chest with the blunt end of the hatchet. Mary Reid, the landlord, was going about her morning in the front part of the house when Kemmler entered, his hands and shirt sleeves covered in blood. "I had to do it," he exclaimed, "There was no help for it. One of us had to die. I'll take the rope for it." Ella ran into the room terrified and screamed, "Papa has killed Mamma!"[15] Kemmler returned to the apartment and, after wiping his hands of the blood, he casually stepped over his wife's body and walked down to *Thomas Martin's Saloon* as he did every morning in search of a beer. It was not yet nine o'clock when he was apprehended in the bar and taken back to the scene of the crime where he learned that Tillie was still alive; she was taken to the *Fitch Accident Hospital* where she died 16 hours later after doctors tried desperately to save her. Tillie was just thirty-one years old.

When questioned by police William Kemmler refused to offer a motive aside from his quick temper and that he had been drinking heavily the night before in a local saloon. Five weeks after the murder jurors were selected and the case went to trial, prosecuted in Buffalo, New York by District Attorney George T. Quinby. Because William Kemmler had admitted to the gruesome act that was also witnessed by six–year-old Ella, there was no doubt of his guilt. The prosecution argued that it was a case of first degree murder, while the defense brought a colorful parade of characters to the witness stand, each with a more outrageous anecdote of Kemmler's drinking habits with laughter often flooding the courtroom. The Defense also called upon a medical witness to testify that excessive alcohol abuse caused brain defects and was a legitimate defense of insanity. However, the prosecution cross-examined the medical expert and asked if even small amounts of whiskey could cause brain defects. The expert said yes, that is true, which opinion implicitly accused mostly everyone in the courtroom of having a defective brain. On Monday, May 13, 1889 the sky grew steadily darker until the moment the jury was to pronounce its verdict. With a bright flash of lightning, a mighty thunderclap rattled the courtroom windows as William Kemmler was found guilty of first degree murder.

William Kemmler was sent to *Auburn State Prison* for solitary confinement until June 24, 1889 when the death penalty was scheduled to be delivered for the first time in history by the *Electric Chair*. Kemmler's attorney, Bourke Cockran, immediately filed an appeal of the sentence and received a stay of execution on July 9, 1889 to determine if death by *Electrocution* was cruel and unusual punishment. Although it was widely charged that Cockran had been hired by Westinghouse as a final attempt to block electrical executions using his company's dynamos, the respected litigator denied it with the explanation, "I believe the law to be unconstitutional and inhuman, and deem it due to the honor of the State and the welfare of justice that it should be tested. No electrical company has retained me, and I am doing this without hope of financial remuneration." Hearings were held in New York City, where Cockran's argument was that too many variables were at play to guarantee the electric chair would produce a quick and painless death for each person in exactly the same way, and was therefore cruel and unusual. One key witness was Commodore Elbridge T. Gerry, chairman of the *Death Penalty Commission*. He testified on July 18, 1889. He arrived at 10 o'clock and was warmly greeted by Mr. Cockran. Commodore Gerry was asked to summarize the *Death Penalty Commission's Report*, which included a brief description of commonly used methods of execution around the world. He explained that a circular had been sent out by the commission to judges, medical experts and others asking for their opinion as to whether some other method of execution should be substituted for hanging, and which of the four current methods they thought preferable. Mr. Cockran read from the commission's report extracts of letters opposing the electric method giving instances in which men had received heavy electric charges, such as lightning strikes, and had not been killed. Commodore Gerry then noted that he did not believe that such persons had received a charge sufficiently strong to kill and noted how an electrical execution would be scientifically designed to kill instantly and without pain, leading to the following exchange.

> Mr. Cockran then asked, "How do you account, then, for the great difference of opinion among experts as shown at this hearing?"
>
> In reply, Commodore Gerry stated, "I regard that as the best possible indication of their great knowledge. You never knew two physicians, however highly educated they might be in their profession, who could agree about any one case."
>
> Mr. Cockran then asked, "Then in the degree to which *Electricians* differ, they approximate the exactitude of *Physicians*? That is to say they reach the same height of ignorance!"
>
> Commodore Gerry slyly replied, "Oh, no. Mr. Cockran we all know that the law is the only exact profession."

After Commodore Gerry had been further examined about lightning and artificial currents, in which he took occasion to remark that in electricity Franklin had discovered the key and Edison the keyhole, the Commodore was permitted to retire after two and a half hours of testimony.[16] There was a long line of witnesses that included Thomas Edison. After collecting a thousand pages of evidence Judge Edwin Day punted, and cited a "diversity of opinion" among many experts, and the case was appealed. The *Supreme Court of the State of New York* heard William Kemmler's case next and upheld the sentence of death. In anticipation of an appeal to the federal courts, Commodore Gerry wrote an article for the *North American Review* entitled "Capital Punishment by Electricity," published in volume 149 in September 1889. This scholarly article would be available for the Justices in Washington to read during their review of the case, which indeed was appealed to the *Supreme Court of the United States.* After nearly a year, Chief Justice Melville Fuller ruled on July 12, 1890 that the Supreme Court could not overrule the highest court of the State of New York unless that court had made a big enough mistake as to constitute a denial of due process, which he ruled it had not done. In the meantime New York State Assemblyman Newton Curtis, a decorated Civil War veteran of the Union Army, introduced a bill to abolish capital punishment altogether, as he had for the previous seven years. It was now the hot topic of the day, and the Assembly approved the measure by a vote of 74 to 29. However, the Senate Judiciary Committee stepped-in and voted it down, 7 to 2. It could not be reintroduced for a vote again until the following legislative session. On July 12, with all appeals exhausted, Kemmler returned to solitary confinement at *Auburn State Prison* to await his execution on August 6, 1890. Commodore Elbridge T. Gerry was among twenty-seven witnesses to the first execution by the *Electric Chair* in history.

Within two weeks Commodore Gerry was preparing his yacht *Electra* to take his family away from the lengthy New York *celebrations*, the intensity of the *Death Penalty Commission* and the daily responsibility of the *New York Society for the Prevention of Cruelty to Children.* It was only August and it felt like one of the longest years of the Commodore's life; he needed some rest and recuperation. The Gerrys sailed up the Hudson River to the Livingstons' *Lake Delaware Estate* for a few weeks of horseback riding, cattle-drawn cart rides, swimming and catching up on correspondence. Lillian Gerry wrote in her diary for the summer of 1889 that she "received 30 letters over the summer" and that she "knitted charity clothes" which included "12 baby jackets, 12 pair of socks, and 4 caps" and that she "sent them to the *Garitt Dispensary,*" named after her grandmother's family, who were patrons of the charity. She also noted that the Gerry children "watched the Naval Parade off the Electra" during the Washington Centennial, and they "watched the processions from Mrs. Gallatin's" mansion at 670 Fifth Avenue, with window views facing the *Centennial Parade* route.

The Gerry family arrived at Newport, Rhode Island to lead the annual NYYC cruise in the regatta for the *Goelet Cup* challenge on August 23, 1889. The Gerrys returned to New York Harbor at 5:30 p.m. on September 5 where the entire family, including grandpa Robert J. Livingston and Almy Gerry Gallatin, remained onboard *Electra* for a relaxing dinner. They were in no hurry to return to city life and so they all slept overnight on the yacht. About 8 o'clock the next morning the steam yacht *Providence* came into the Harbor heading for the anchorage grounds where the *Electra* was anchored along with many other yachts. A dense fog settled in quickly and by some miscalculation or circumstance, the steamer *Providence* approached nearer the New York side of the river than usual. The tide was ebbing quickly and the commander of the *Providence* gave orders to starboard the helm to pass a schooner that was dead ahead. In swinging round the *Providence* drifted with the fast moving tide and although the officers on board saw the *Electra* they could not prevent a collision. The bowsprit of the anchored *Electra* caught the *Providence* just aft of the wheelhouse on the starboard side, tearing out the stanchions of the middle deck of the steamer and ripping open the fronts of several state rooms that fortunately were unoccupied. After ripping up things for fifteen feet the bowsprit broke and fell on the deck of the *Electra* startling all on board.

A lady from Baltimore was sitting on the deck bench by the *Providence's* rail and as she looked up she saw the bowsprit of the *Electra* coming toward her. She jumped up quickly enough to escape being crushed to death. Others on the steamer were unhurt but very frightened.

Commodore Elbridge T. Gerry went down to his office and penned a letter to the *Inspector of Steam Vessels* to lay out the facts, which noted that at the time of the collision the *Electra* was lying at anchor within the anchorage limits prescribed by the rules and regulations of the *Port of New York*. He described the damage to the *Electra:* the bowsprit had broken off at the foot, which tore up the steel shoe into which it fitted, and the jib and bobstays were carried away while the carved work of the figure head was seriously defaced. The shock of the collision also destroyed a quantity of china and glass causing a loss altogether of about $1,000. Commodore Gerry noted that when the fog became dense the *Providence,* instead of anchoring as she should have done, or steaming down the Brooklyn side, came to the New York side. This brought her into dangerous proximity to the vessels at anchorage where she nearly ran down the steam yacht *Adelaide,* and then veering toward the Astoria side to avoid that yacht, she drifted down with the fast moving tide and came upon the *Electra*. The official determination was that the collision was unavoidable due to the unanticipated density of the fog and the speed of the ebb tide; both occurred after the *Providence* was already too far into the anchorage area to turn back. It was determined that the captain of the *Providence* maneuvered his steamer in such a way as to avoid what would have been even more severe damage to the *Electra*. The *Providence* suffered $500 damage and the matter was settled out of court to the satisfaction of both parties.[17]

The Gerry family needed to extend their time away from New York City while the yacht *Electra* was sent to Wilmington, Delaware for repairs. Since Commodore Gerry was more than capable of handling his legal work with transatlantic cables and mail packets, the family sailed for Europe. Sixteen-year-old Lillian Gerry, affectionately known as *Lilly,* wrote in her diary that the family "sailed on the *La Gascogne* French Steamer" which left on September 28, 1889 bound for Havre, France. Lilly kept a detailed dairy of this trip and noted that both Mabel and Lillian celebrated their November birthdays in Europe. Her simple words tell the story of the Gerry family holiday in the fall of 1889 including Lilly's life-long battle with asthma. The diary also provides us with insight into how New Yorkers spent their time while in Europe.

> **Saturday, September 28:** We got up at about 4 o'clock this morning as the Gascogne sailed at 7:30. We have very nice state rooms in the middle of the boat. It is very smooth. A man plays the guitar and a girl plays the piano beautifully.
>
> **Sunday, September 29**: We made 437 miles since yesterday. It is still very smooth and rather stupid. (*Lilly may have been bored*)
>
> **Monday, September 30**: We made 385 miles since yesterday. Mr. Chamberlain is on board and is very nice.
>
> **Tuesday, October 1:** We have made 397 miles. It is still smooth and pleasant. The young one played a game of cricket which was amusing.
>
> **Thursday, October 3:** We made 401 miles. It is a little rougher today.
>
> **Friday, October 4:** We made 402 miles. It has rained nearly all day. We all went down to supper with Mr. Chamberlain. It was very gay.
>
> **Saturday, October 5:** We made 401 miles. We saw the Sailly Islands and Izzards Light. It was very pretty coming in tonight.

Arrive in France

> **Sunday, October 6:** We got into the dock about 9 o'clock this morning at Havre. It was very pretty and as I have never seen it before I enjoyed it very much and I have some photos. We rode the train to Paris and got here about four. We have some of our rooms in the hotel so we are going to change some of them tomorrow. This evening Papa took me for a walk. Paris is so pretty and the shops so bright.

Monday, October 7: This morning we went to Worth and Redfern. I have ordered two dresses at Redfern, a green, and a red & green plaid. I have also ordered a dress in white tulle dressed in gold.

Monday, October 8: We went to the Exposition this morning and saw a great many things and it is perfectly lovely and very, very large. There are 84 galleries of pictures. We went and saw Sarah Bernhardt in *Theodora*. It was very well acted but the last act of the play was disgusting.

Wednesday, October 9: I went to the exposition this morning with Grandpa and the boys. We went to all the columns but I didn't enjoy it very much as I was watching for a chair for Grandpa. This afternoon we went to the *Passage Paris* where Mama gave me a party fan.

Wednesday, October 10: This morning I went to Redfern where I ordered a red silk dinner gown. This afternoon I went to a bull fight. I took my camera with me and got a quantity of photographs. We saw 3 bulls fight and none were killed and only one badly hurt. This was very fierce and the bull's horns were wrapped-up but it nearly killed the horse. It was the last performance of *Mazzantini*. It was a disgusting performance. After, we came home and I went to *Madame March* for my corsets. We also went to the *Rue de Honori* where I ordered a card case. Will have one of the boys give it to me for my birthday, it has my monogram in silver. We also went to the *Passage Panorama*. Mama gave me a very pretty white fan.

Thursday, October 11: We went to the *Exposition*. Mama gave me a Bohemian glass cup and saucer. In the afternoon we went to *Madame Worth* and had our first fitting but as we are going to change our fitter, I guess we will have to have another first fitting. (*Lily's sisters, Angelica and Mabel, were also fitted for dresses, as was their annual practice*)

Saturday, October 12: This morning we went to the *Exposition*... we also went to Rue Le Louvre where I ordered a pink wrapper and a pair of bedroom slippers.

Sunday, October 13: We went to the 11 o'clock services. (*church*) Aunt Ruth (Livingston) Mills, came to see us after lunch. In the afternoon I took a drive with Papa in the Boulevard. For the evening we went to see the illuminations at the *Exposition Fountains*. The fountains were beautiful and they changed color very often. Red lights were only burned on the *Eiffel Tower*. Some said there were 25,000 people there.

Monday, October 14: Went shopping this morning, corsets not ready. I went to Redfern in the afternoon to order my note paper, pink and gold. I hope it won't be too gorgeous but I'm afraid the pink and gold is much too gay.

Tuesday, October 15: This morning I went wandering and shopping with Jane (*her nanny*). I got a quantity of things I wanted. I went to the theatre but won't write the name of the play.

Wednesday, October 16: This morning we went shopping and in the afternoon I tried on the gown. They are so slow here.

Thursday, October 17: Tried on hats... *describes dinner menu...* Aunt Ruth Mills who bye the bye is looking extremely well. Mr. Ogden Mills at one end for dinner and his father sat on the other side of us. We had a beautiful dinner but I was rather tired.

Friday, October 18: Shopping and Elena came to see us.

Saturday, October 19: Bought some hair bows. I went to the *Exposition* in the afternoon with Grandpa. He gave me a watch with a ruby and a diamond back. I have wanted one so long and now have it for my birthday present from him.

Sunday, October 20: This morning we went to the American Church and they had communion service so we received. This afternoon I went with Papa and we saw a great many little chapels.

Wednesday, October 30: Went up the Eiffel Tower this morning.

Thursday, October 31: In and out of bed with a cold.

Saturday, November 2: Left Paris at 10 o'clock. Arrived Bologne 2 p.m. There was a private car waiting. Passage across the Channel. Arrived London 6 p.m. Rooms. *Hotel Berkeley,* London.

Saturday, November 3: Have a cold and had asthma quite severely.

Monday, November 4: Mabel's birthday. She is seventeen today. Ordered my saddle this morning. Went to several silver shops. My cold was still annoying me so Mama stayed home while the girls went out.

Tuesday, November 5: Remained in bed all day but think better amused myself with *The Girl in the Brown Habit* and *Killed in the Opera.*

Wednesday, November 6: Stayed in bed all morning, rose after lunch. Received a letter from my devoted friend Margaret. I have a temperature of 101 and feel very poorly.

Thursday, November 7: Got up this morning but was taken ill and returned to bed in the afternoon. I am afraid I have a malaria. I have this attack every year but now not so severe.

Friday, November 8: Woke up this morning for six grains of quinine. No fever today. This hotel is wretched, so drafty.

Saturday, November 9: I coughed most of the night, am still in bed and took six grains of quinine at 7 o'clock. My family has gone to see the *Lord Mayor's* show.

Sunday, November 10: Today I am sixteen. Grandpa gave me a watch. Mama a sealing tray. Papa a gold bracelet. Angel a gold pin. Mabel a silver pencil and pen holder. Bobby a card case. Peter a pocket book. It was very foggy today.

Monday, November 11: Got up this morning and packed.

Tuesday, November 12: Left London this morning and arrived at Liverpool in the afternoon. Had lunch at *Rugby*. I was sick the entire time in London. I love London, and who knows, may make it my home.

Trans-Atlantic Ocean Steamer Travel

In the nineteenth century any traveler who wished to proceed from any point on the North American continent to any other part of the world, in order to go conveniently and comfortably, had to depart from New York City. As early as 1870 there were thirty to forty steam ships based in *New York Harbor* that carried both commercial cargo and passengers to different ports in England, Scotland, Germany, France, and down to South America. As many as ten ships would leave New York Harbor on the same day. The scene onboard a sea-going steam ship captured the imagination of passengers and writers of the period. The following description is a compressed version of a late nineteenth century article published in *Harper's New Monthly Magazine*, and includes some of the most charming and accurate sketches of life on a transatlantic sea voyage just like the trip Lilly Gerry described in her 1889 diary.

The scene an hour before departure had both romantic charm and an element of solemnity. The force with which a dozen heavy passenger trunks were held in a slip-noose, then run up by machinery into the air, and then rapidly lowered into the hold captivated passengers as they boarded the massive ship. The captain in his naval uniform accompanied by his friends and attendants inspired a feeling of awe among the passengers who toasted champagne as the ship prepared to depart the dock. Then the sound of the great bell and the call of "All ashore!" that brought the goodbyes, some given to laughter and others to tears. When the ponderous bridge connecting the steamer with the pier had been hauled back upon the dock, a bell signaled the engineer at his station far below deck to immediately start the engines into action. The water at the stern of the ship was thrown into a whirlpool of boiling surges as the massive ship, with hundreds of occupants gathered from all parts of the country into close companionship, slowly began to creep away from the dock. White handkerchiefs waved from the pier and the ship in silent farewells. As the ship picked up speed and glided out to sea the passengers turned their thoughts to themselves, some found comfortable seats on the promenade deck to view the scene of the fading New York skyline, while others needed some fresh air to avoid sea sickness. Many found a steward to assist with their parcels and luggage and sort which were to be sent to their cabins and which to send to the storage area. Most found their cabins and began to settle-in for the lengthy voyage.

Traveling, in all its nineteenth century forms, was a wonderful means of exposing the hidden traits of character, the bad as well as the good. A young man got a deeper insight into the disposition, character and mental constitution of the lady whom he was inclined to choose as his partner for life, if he made a voyage to Europe in company with her party. He would learn more on that voyage than by half a dozen seasons of association with her in the balls and concerts of New York City. One good woman, a middle-aged widow, gave sage advice on the topic while on a *Cunard Line* steamship. She told a lady passenger that, as a rule, one could always discover the true state of the case in respect to any couple seen together in the ship's saloon. If the gentleman is very attentive to the lady, then they are going to be married. If, on the other hand, the lady is very attentive to the gentleman, then they have just been married. Finally, if they do not seem to care anything about each other at all, then they have been married some time. Gossip throughout the ship was a constant source of entertainment.

Only passengers with a strong constitution were able to read or write for any length of time or else they were prone to sea sickness from the constant rolling of the ship, some days smoother and some rougher, as noted by Lilly Gerry. There is never an indication that members of the Gerry family, having descended from a long line of seamen, were ever seasick. Passengers in the midst of a vast ocean, where even the *horizon line* can be lost to sight by fog, rain or darkness, cannot see a fixed point in their sight-line to adjust their equilibrium. Many passengers would lie down in their cabin or on a *Promenade Deck* recliner chair, so the horizontal position could calm their equilibrium until they overcame the seasickness.

The Gerry family, comfortable in the elegant yet cramped quarters of a yacht, were easily pleased with the staterooms of the large steamship lines. Most cabins were simple and only intended as a place to sleep and to safely store one's things. Socializing took place in the common saloons, the ladies room, the gentlemen's smoking room, the dining room or outdoors on the promenade deck. The transatlantic voyage provided Americans, including the Gerrys, the wonder of being a vast distance from home, the adventure of rambles through Europe, the health benefits of ocean air, and ultimately, the pleasure of returning home, renewed in body and soul.

Based on Commodore Gerry's experience with the Presidential Bicentennial, he joined the *New York Bar Association* in the late fall and winter, as a member of the *Finance Committee* to organize a smaller celebration for the Centennial of the United States Supreme Court, which first held court in New York City in 1790. Since the Commodore was not chairing the committee, nor did he wish to contribute in any over-arching executive capacity, he was able to enjoy the holiday season with his family in New York City, and only attend meetings as needed, and began to refocus on his regular work with the *New York Society for the Prevention of Cruelty to Children,* as the full-time counsel and President.

Elbridge T. Gerry chaired the Washington Centennial Committee on celebration festivities that included military parades, floats and marching bands, plus a naval and yacht parade in New York Harbor in which the flag ship *Electra* participated with the Gerry family on board. A complete scrapbook of the entire planning and execution of the celebration compiled by Commodore Gerry is held in the Gerry family collections.

George Washington's inauguration

Stanford White designed the Washington Arch for the Centennial celebration

Reenactment of Washington's inauguration at Federal Hall on Wall Street

The Centennial Ball rivaled any Gilded Age society ball.

Commodore Elbridge T. Gerry chaired the Capital Punishment Commission that investigated every means of torture and execution throughout history and was advised by Thomas Edison and others on the use of electricity as a more humane method of execution. Their 95-page report ushered in the new era of the electric chair.

Contemporary artist's rendering of Kemmler execution

William Kemmler
First person executed in the electric chair in the United States

Tillie Kemmler
Murdered by her husband

Thomas Alva Edison advised the Gerry Commission on the use of electricity for execution.

New York state's Auburn Prison, the site of the first execution by the electric chair of William Kemmler on August 6, 1890

Gilded Age travelers boarded trans-Atlantic steamships bound for Europe at Chelsea Piers in New York City (*below*).

Steamship promenade

Ladies state room

Steamship dining room

American steamship landing in Liverpool, England

Lilly's diaries are kept at the Lake Delaware estate.

Lillian Gerry
1873-1891

Lillian Gerry, known as "Lilly," lost her life-long battle with asthma (consumption) very unexpectedly just a week after her 18th birthday.

Lilly's diary captured the private life of the Gerry family. Less than 2 years before her death she noted her last trip to Europe for the 1889 Paris World's Fair.

Paris Exhibition Hall of Art and Sculpture

Balloon flight was a highlight of the Paris Exhibition.

Although Bergh's work was mocked in many editorial cartoons, his work outlived the criticism and is respected world-wide.

Henry Bergh (1813–1888) founded the Society for the Prevention of Cruelty to Animals, known today as the SPCA, a world-wide society.

Elbridge T. Gerry was one of Henry Bergh's closest life-long friends. Both wore their respective Society badges with great pride.

Horse rescue carriage

Henry Bergh statue, Milwaukee Wisconsin

Henry Bergh had the rescue carriage designed and built to facilitate his agents in their work throughout the city, especially when horses were too weak to walk any distance without assistance.

9

GILDED GOTHAM

THE 1890'S PART I

The problem of our age is the proper administration of wealth; and the best means of benefiting the community is to place within its reach the ladders upon which the aspiring can rise – free libraries, public parks, public institutions and works of art... The millionaire will be but a trustee of the poor.

Andrew Carnegie, *The Gospel of Wealth,* 1889

The *Gilded Age,* in full bloom in the last decade of the nineteenth century, embraced an era of Anglo-American marriages between 1870 and 1914. The Gerry/Livingston/Goelet families were prominent among the elite marriages of American belles and British aristocracy, starting with Maturin Livingston's daughter, Elizabeth, who married the *Duke of Portland,* William George Cavendish-Bentnick, a Minister of Parliament and trustee of the British Museum in 1880. Her twin sister Ruth inherited the Staatsburg estate on the Hudson, and she married D. Ogden Mills, the gold mine millionaire from California. While Elizabeth lived her married life in England, she traveled to the United States regularly for the Newport social season and society weddings. Ruth and her husband, D. Ogden Mills, succeeded her parents as leaders in New York social circles and traveled to Europe in the great steamships for extended visits with her twin sister, the Duchess of Portland. Ruth and Elizabeth were Louisa Gerry's first cousins and shared the same intimate social circles on both sides of the Atlantic Ocean, as noted in Lilly's diary "Aunt Ruth Mills joined the Gerrys for a gay dinner" in Paris in 1889.

Born in the same year as Lillian Gerry, 1873, was Emily Price who became the first lady of etiquette under her married name, Emily Post. At the time of her birth in Baltimore, women were being jailed for promoting birth control for married couples. However by the time Emily post died in New York City in 1960, women and men, married or not, campaigned for legalized abortion. The youth of these women was shaped by the high *Victorian* era, corseted by the *Gilded Age,* and then tossed about by the restless years that culminated in World War I. Emily Post attended finishing school in New York City and met her husband at a ball held at one of the Fifth Avenue mansions. In her journals, Emily painstakingly documented the world of a wealthy young matron, a job involving everything from planning the day's menus to scheduling the servant's day off. Upper-class women of the *Gilded Age* no longer needed to contribute to the household's physical labor as in the past, though they had found another way to imbue their privileged lives with meaning; they directed the labor of others. The British television series *Downton Abbey* captures the essence of this daily routine, as well as the spirit of Anglo-American marriages like Elizabeth *Livingston* Cavendish-Bentnick, the Duchess of Portland. Just as Lady Grantham did at *Downton* or Lady Cavendish-Bentnick did in London, Emily Post established a routine whose morning ritual remained essentially the same throughout her life. She would be served toast and coffee in bed while she carefully reviewed her day's list of chores and prepared written assignments for her servants. Then she dressed for the requisite afternoon socializing. She often went shopping and after lunch at *Delmonico's,* Emily paid her social "at home" visits, directing her driver to deposit her calling card on the silver trays placed in the hallway entrances for acquaintances whose "visiting day" it was. Visitors who were close friends or who had been specially invited would be escorted into the study or parlor for tea. The ladies stuck to a fairly routine list of subjects: the weather, current fashion, new menu items at *Delmonico's,* recent (non-controversial) national or world news. By late afternoon, Emily Post was back at home where she used the remaining time before dinner to review her wardrobe for the next day. Dinner parties were given half of the week and the other half of the week Emily was a guest for dinner elsewhere.[1] Like Emily Post, Lilly Gerry received her silver monogrammed "card case" for her sixteenth birthday, yet, while the Gerry women respected and adhered to the routines of "visiting day," they lived a broader, more robust life. Beyond city socializing they relished summers at the *Lake Delaware Farm* where they pursued a passion for horses. They swam, fished, and sailed small boats on the lake with their brothers.

Emily Post divorced her husband, Edwin Main Post, in 1905 after years of enduring his famous affairs with show girls. She became what might be called a domestic anthropologist and turned to writing newspaper articles, light fiction, and humorous travel books to earn a living. Her life and work was influenced by the presence of millions of immigrants in Baltimore and New York City who sought to become real Americans. Emily Post observed the social interactions of all strata of society and believed in the art of treating people well in all circumstances. Emily Post's classic book, *Etiquette: In Society, Business, in Politics and at Home,* published in 1922, was called magisterial, impatient, collegial, and neighborly by readers and critics alike. The guidance it provided society in proper behavior outlasted the age it reflected and corrected. At its broadest the book was the measure of how we treat one another, and it reached across class, race, gender, and culture. For many women the book fashioned our country's ideal of what it was to pursue a gracious, possibly even a moral life.[2] Emily Post's book was on the desk of every lady in late *Gilded Age* society, as well as on the desk of every businessman's secretary. Her book was revised ten times, had 89 printings, and sold around the world. Emily's youth and adult life in *Gilded Gotham,* although with only "passing" experience in elite circles, was broad enough for her to attend the public balls and society teas with the wealthy young women of her generation.

The second *Assembly Ball* of the 1890 season was held at *Delmonico's* on January 9 to celebrate the New Year. It was hosted by and attended by the *Patroons* of New York, which did not include Emily Post, a Maryland girl by birth. Commodore and Mrs. Gerry attended as did their eldest daughter, Angelica then nineteen. There were a number of people from out of town, including guests from England. This social event was different from those of earlier years in that many of the guests in attendance were ill with colds. Most seemed unaware that some among them were contagious. The *New York Herald* described the ball as "dissolving itself into a painful sneezing match where limp little scented handkerchiefs fell on the floor like roses and the most classic noses were tinged with pink, and many of the silvery voices sounded off tune."[3] As noted in her diary two months before, Lilly Gerry had taken ill in Paris, followed by a stay in bed with a 101 degree fever while the family visited London. Whether Lilly alternately described her illness as a cold, asthma, or malaria, it was clear that the high fever was one of the greatest concerns of her doctor and family. Indeed, beginning in 1889 and ending in 1891, the earliest pandemic with recorded details was affecting the entire globe. Although it would not be as virulent as the 1918 *Spanish Flu* which killed over 50 million worldwide, this *Russian Flu* as it was known was first documented in France at precisely the time the Gerry family was in Paris and Lilly was at the *World Exposition* amid crowds from around the world. An article written in February 1892 documented the influenza outbreak in a collection of essays by specialists in the field. Some sufferers experienced the high fever, others had serious lung involvement, still others had a serious weakening of the heart, and some had a combination of symptoms.[4] In the Gerry family, young Peter had pneumonia in 1889, Lilly in 1889 and 1890, and Robert J. Livingston in 1891. There is a very good chance that the Gerrys were passing the influenza virus within the family, and those who were older or had weak lungs were most likely to suffer a severe case. Some of the *Patroons* at the January 1890 *Assembly Ball* may have had a simple cold, while others had the Influenza and were passing the virus among *Gilded Gotham's* elite families. Most did not die from this particular influenza but it nonetheless was a serious epidemic.

Lilly described her chronic illness over the years as consumption which is tuberculosis. As early as 1859 the first sanatorium was opened in Germany but not until around 1906 did the sanatorium movement take hold in the United States. By then Dr. Robert Koch, a German scientist in the field of epidemiology and a 1952 *Nobel Prize* winner for his work with tuberculosis had identified the cause as a bacteria. It was indeed contagious and Dr. Koch advocated isolation for the sick, enforced rest, and a proper diet in a well-regulated sanatorium to assist the healing process. Lilly did not have the benefit of the sanatorium in the 1880's and 1890's but her family did recognize that the fresh air of *Lake Delaware* and the transatlantic ocean crossings always helped her to recover. Lilly's 1890 diary noted that she "spent February, March and part of April at Augusta, Georgia as I had consumption. Peter got Pneumonia." She also noted that "Eva cost $340" which may have been a new horse or a pure bred dog. Lilly took a photograph of her mother mounting a horse in front of the Augusta, Georgia *Bon Air Hotel,* where the Gerry family stayed for over two months.

A letter written by Commodore Gerry in May, 1890 confirms that the entire family was in Georgia with Lilly, when he wrote to an autograph collector:

> My dear sir:
>
> Your request for an autograph letter from me was received last winter during my temporary absence from New York City caused by illness in my family. Upon my return home I send you this sheet, which may increase the number of your collection although I confess I fail to see how it possibly can add to the value thereof.
>
> I have the honor to remain,
>
> Elbridge T. Gerry, President NYSPCC[5]

Commodore Gerry was quite famous around the world by this time in his life yet he remained modest and unaltered by his notoriety. In fact, on February 4, 1890 just before leaving for Georgia with his family, he celebrated with the *New York Bar Association* the long planned *Centennial Celebration of the Founding of the United States Supreme Court.* The "Court founding" festivities held at the *Metropolitan Opera House* were lengthy in stark contrast to similar celebrations, indeed, one lady who attended the five-hour exercises commented, "It's awfully learned, but frightfully slow."[6]

The *New York Herald* proclaimed, "The amount of legal lore and racking secret knowledge that crammed the heads of the two thousand jurists who were present would suffice to fill a library that would stretch from City Hall to Yonkers." The *Opera House* walls were decorated with a display of the coat-of-arms of all the States, as well as with festoons and banners in the national colors. The stage was decorated with oil paintings of the Chief Justices of the Supreme Court. The grand symphony orchestra under the direction of Victor Herbert entertained the audience. At 11 a.m. the Chief Justice and Associate Justices were escorted to the stage by local bar officials, including Commodore Gerry. The Justices were in their robes, which were not considered "English costume" because they wore no wigs. However the *New York Herald* noted that "the drapery in the back radiated from a point between the shoulders and the plaiting of the folds reminded one of the mechanical workmanship on the side of a cloth-covered coffin. Each shoulder was enveloped in a cloud of silk as if to hide wings. The sleeves were the most curious feature of all, they were made fast at the wrist and between this point and the shoulder was a flowing billow of silk that could easily have concealed a few barrels of herring."

The speech that captured the spirit of the day for all assembled was that of former President Grover Cleveland:

> Today we have met to commemorate an event connected with our beginning as a people, which more than any other gave strength and a promise of perpetuity to the American plan of government, and which more than any other, happily illustrated the wisdom and the enlightened foresight of those who designed our national structure. It is fairly plain and palpable, both from reason and from a review of events in our history, that without an arbiter to determine (finally and conclusively) the rights and duties embraced in the language of the Constitution, the union of States and the life of the American nation would have been precarious and disappointing.[7]

The evening banquet was held at the *Lenox Lyceum*, which was made beautiful with floral arrangements by *Florist Le Moult*. The stage was converted into a miniature tropical rain forest. Palms and trailing vines were in such quantities that the great hall seemed to be a mass of white, gold and green. Each table had its dozens of candy miniatures of Justices as well as huge vases and baskets of flowers.

Of the eight hundred men at the dinner there was a profusion of white heads and gray beards in the assemblage. The toastmaster of the evening closed the celebrations with a series of toasts; the most touching was to honor the President of the United States who was absent due to the continuing struggle with recovery efforts after the catastrophic 1889 flood a few months before in *Johnstown, Pennsylvania,* where over 2,200 people were killed. The state and federal governments diligently worked together to establish flood control and flood relief assistance through emergency legislation. Commodore Gerry left immediately after the centennial celebrations for the family stay in Georgia to enable Lilly to recuperate and gain her strength from a terrible bout of tuberculosis. Two months later in mid-May, with warm weather arriving in New York and Lilly stronger, the Gerrys returned to New York City.

A well-established, elegant sport of *Gilded Age* society was known as "coaching." This colorful sport, or display, was held in *Central Park* each spring and captured the attention of all New Yorkers. Fashionable families were able to "show" their fine horses and elaborate coaches in a public parade. Each coach had a stylish driver called a "Whip" who was always one of the society men, often the bachelor dudes, behind whom sat four to six guests in their finest attire. The newspapers described the "coaching parade" held on May 25, 1890 in great detail.

> It seemed as though half the town turned out to witness the annual parade. At the Mall in Central Park where the start was made, the crowd was so great that it spread out over the grass in its eagerness to catch a glimpse of the "four-in-hands," *referring to the four horses managed by the whip.*

Each coach and whip was described:

> The third coach in line was that of Mr. Perry Belmont, which bore the colors, maroon and scarlet, which have been made so famous on the turf by his father. Mr. Belmont's team was made up of splendid bays, and altogether his was the coach most looked for and most closely scrutinized by the crowd of spectators. This was chiefly due to the fact that the box seat beside Mr. Belmont was occupied by Mrs. Grover Cleveland. Others of this party were Mr. and Mrs. Henry Sloane, **Miss Angelica Gerry,** and Mr. T. F. Cushing of Reston.

Mr. James Roosevelt's coach, with blue body came next.

> Mr. August Belmont, Jr.'s coach was the counterpart of that of his brother Perry, and he also held rein over a team of bays. Mrs. Belmont occupied the box seat.[8]

After the parade ended about 6 o'clock the participants returned home to dress for the annual dinner at the *Hotel Brunswick* at 8 o'clock. A table for sixty-six was arranged in the shape of a bridle-bit with two rings and a connecting bar. In the center of each of the two circular tables representing the rings was a mass of flowers made up of corsages for the ladies. The stunning center piece was a *four-in-hand* coach of sugar and nougat. Around the walls of the banquet hall were hung the shields and emblems of the coaching clubs. The dinner lasted until 10 o'clock when the ladies retired to one reception room for coffee, and the gentlemen to another for cigars. Meantime the table was cleared away to make room for dancing until midnight. This was an intimate affair because it was a circle of horse lovers who invested good money in both the animal and the coach. It is likely that 1890 was one of Angelica Gerrys first public coaching parades, but it would not be her last.

All of the Gerry children rode horses from a young age and appreciated quality stock. When traveling in Europe in 1887 Mabel Gerry, then only 15 years of age, inspected the royal stables in Rome with her Papa, Commodore Gerry, and commented in her diary on the size, color and quality of the animals. Indeed, over their life-times, Angelica, the eldest daughter, and Robert, the eldest son became passionate horse breeders and each was elected President of the women's and men's *Coaching Clubs* of New York City.

The summer of 1890 brought illness and death into Commodore Gerry's close circle of relatives. His sister-in-law, Mrs. Ogden Goelet, contracted typhoid fever, no doubt from the vast amount of time the Goelets spent on the water on their yacht. Her sister Miss Grace Wilson had typhoid while in Paris, France some time ago and was successfully treated. In an unusual move, Mr. Ogden Goelet contacted the same French doctor requesting that he provide the same care to Mrs. Goelet using the transatlantic communication cable to direct an American doctor in her treatment. The French doctor agreed and through his guidance every step of the way over the wireless, Mrs. Ogden Goelet was successfully treated, setting a new precedent for remote medical treatment.[9] The Goelets were healthy and eager to join the 1890 cruise of the *New York Yacht Club* by mid-summer and to entertain once again in Newport, Rhode Island.

Commodore Elbridge T. Gerry steamed his flagship *Electra* to New London, Connecticut on July 30 to rendezvous with all yachts wishing to join the NYYC for the start of the annual cruise. The fleet of billowing white sails that greeted the *Electra* was the largest ever assembled in the NYYC's forty-six years of existence. There were over a thousand crew and guests onboard the one-hundred and thirty-six yachts in the New London, Connecticut harbor. Commodore Gerry's oldest friend, and his wife's distant relative, George Schuyler, boarded the *Electra* in the afternoon to join the cruise as the honored guest of the flagship. After a jovial evening of dinner, fireworks, and the illumination of the fleet, George Schuyler retired to his cabin for the night at 11 o'clock. At 2 a.m. the *Electra's* steward passed through her cabin and saw Mr. Schuyler's stateroom door closed. At 6 a.m. the Superintendent of the NYYC who was onboard passed through the cabin and noticed the stateroom door ajar and glanced through the opening where he saw Mr. Schuyler lying on the floor. The fleet surgeon onboard, Dr. Morris J. Asch, was called immediately and after an examination he believed Mr. Schuyler had been dead several hours and pronounced the cause of death to be heart disease from which he had suffered for some time. His death came so suddenly that, when the *Electra*'s gun signaled for colors at 8 o'clock, and then again for colors to be "half-masted," no one outside of the *Electra's* company knew what had happened. In reflecting on the evening before, guests noted that Mr. Schuyler had chatted pleasantly with a number of gentlemen in the course of the evening, among them being Secretary Tracey and Mr. E.C. Benedict of the steam yacht *Oneida*. The latter recalled that Mr. Schuyler had remarked that although he had witnessed the annual cruise of the NYYC since its foundation, he thought this cruise would be his last. Commodore Gerry notified Mr. Schuyler's daughter and brought her to Newport on the *Electra*. The body of Mr. Schuyler was put into a coffin on the yacht by the medical examiner and when a brief ceremony had been conducted in the *Electra's* cabin, the body was carefully lowered away and brought ashore in the *Electra's* steam launch and prepared for shipment to New York City.

No one in the *New York Yacht Club* had been wider known in yachting circles than Mr. Schuyler, who was one of the original owners of the schooner yacht *America* that captured the famous *America Cup* in English waters in 1851. He had figured conspicuously in all the international races for this trophy and was the last donor of the *Deed of Trust* to the NYYC. That night at a yacht captains meeting on the *Electra* a committee was selected to draft an expression of condolence to the bereaved relatives of Mr. George Schuyler. Out of respect for his memory there were thoughts of postponing the cruise until after the funeral, but this would have disappointed so many thousands who had gone to Newport to see the races that the cruise proceeded. Friday and Saturday, August 1 and 2 the *Goelet Cup* races were held in Newport, Rhode Island. On Monday, August 4 the fleet sailed from Newport to Martha's Vineyard, on Tuesday they took a run to New Bedford, Massachusetts, and on Wednesday they returned to Newport, where the cruise was called to a successful close on Saturday at a captains meeting, followed by dinner onboard the *Electra*. Commodore Elbridge T. Gerry remained in Newport, Rhode Island for a few days to spend time with his cousins, Robert and Ogden Goelet, and to pay a visit to Louisa Gerry's cousin, Mrs. Ruth Livingston Mills, of Staatsburg on the Hudson River. He then sailed *Electra* up the Hudson River to dock at *Kingston* and from there, by train to the *Andes Station* to join his wife and children at Robert J. Livingston's *Lake Delaware Farm* estate where Lilly was continuing to regain her strength.

Lilly Gerry noted in her diary that she "spent the summer at Lake Delaware" and was busy reading and sewing. She was clearly proud of her efforts over the holiday with a list of the items that she made:

> Charity clothes, I dressed six dolls
> Each had a trunk which contained
> 2 extra dresses
> 1 change of underclothes
> 1 hair brush and comb
> 1 box of candy
> I gave them to poor children
> I also knitted 2 pair of socks for Mrs. Mason's baby.

The knitting, sewing and embroidery skills of the three Gerry daughters were nurtured as both practical and aesthetic pastimes. In addition to all the physical activity in the fresh outdoors, the children were active readers. Both Lilly and Mabel noted the books they read during their travels through Europe. The many book cases at the *Lake Delaware* house contain several of the books each of the Gerry children owned and read, as well as those owned and read by successive generations of the Gerry and Livingston families. The art of reading is a valued family tradition.

While the Gerrys relaxed in the Catskill Mountains, Frederic Gallatin was awaiting the completion of his yacht at *Harlan & Hollingsworth* in Wilmington, Delaware, the builders of the yacht *Electra.* Commodore Gerry's sister, Almy, grew up with boating along side her brother at *West Point* and *Saratoga.* She and her husband Frederic summered every year at their home on Long Island, *Breezy Lawn,* where boating was a daily pastime. The Gallatins were ready for a large and luxurious steam yacht for their growing family. Frederic named his new yacht the *Almy* after his beloved wife and soon to be shipmate.[10] The Gallatins new yacht was of comparable size to the *Electra* but was equipped with new and improved engineering. Unfortunately, in trial runs in the summer of 1890, the *Almy* was an initial disappointment. In fact the yacht was returned to the Wilmington shipyard of *Harlan & Hollingsworth* on September 16 for extensive alterations. The Gallatins did not take final possession of the *Almy* until late 1891, and did not enjoy their yacht in open water until the spring of 1892. In the meantime, Frederic and Almy continued to join her brother Elbridge for sails on *Electra,* which provided relaxing adventures for the sailing men, fun interactions among the cousins, and private time for Louisa and Almy to catch up on New York, Newport and Long Island gossip.

While the Gallatins prepared to leave *Breezy Lawn* at the end of the season, Frederic's younger brother, James Gallatin, Jr., and his family also prepared to leave their nearby East Hampton home to return to New York City. However, on September 18 James died unexpectedly of heart failure. He was only forty-four and left a wife and two daughters and four sons. James was born in 1846 and was educated by tutors and at the New York University Grammar School, after which he planned to enter the University. However, his frail health prevented him from attending college or engaging in regular business activity. James independently devoted his time to the study of mechanics and electricity and made and patented several inventions. He was an amateur musician who composed and published music. He also mastered the construction of the organ and built one for his own amusement. James contributed his time to community endeavors and between 1879 and 1882 he was the President of the *New York Sanitary Reform Society*. His greatest effort was to draft and secure passage of the *Tenement House Reform* bill of 1879, to require sanitary plumbing and proper air ventilation and light in tenement housing. The funeral of James Gallatin was held on September 19 at his summer home in East Hampton, Long Island. He was buried the following day in the Gallatin vault in Trinity Cemetery in New York City.

Commodore Elbridge T. Gerry was called upon in October 1890 to provide the services of his yacht to meet and escort a distinguished French visitor to New York City. At 10:15 o'clock on October 3 the *Count of Paris*, Philippe d'Orléans (1848–1894) and his distinguished group arrived on the White Star steamship *Germanic*. The steamship was due a day earlier but the fog was so thick as the vessel neared the coast, that the utmost care had to be used which slowed progress by several hours. The *Electra* went down the bay the night before and anchored off New York City's Quarantine. On board with Commodore Gerry were members of the *Loyal Legion* of Philadelphia, of which the *Count of Paris* was a member. Two revenue cutters also bore parties of friends and government officials who came to welcome the *Count*, who eagerly responded to the cheers which greeted him by lifting his hat and smiling broadly. After stepping onto the *Electra*, the *Count* said, "I am very glad to see you, and I think it was very kind of you to bring so many old faces from the *Army of the Potomac*." He spoke of his departure from America twenty-eight years ago and referred to the sad and trying times in the old days. A historian, journalist and outspoken democrat, the *Count of Paris* volunteered to serve as a Union Army officer in the *American Civil War* along with his younger brother, the Duke of Chartres. As Captain Philippe d'Orléans, the *Count of Paris* served on the staff of the commander of the *Army of the Potomac* under Major General George McClellan for nearly a year. He distinguished himself during the unsuccessful *Peninsular Campaign.*

In need of rest after the transatlantic voyage the *Count* of *Paris* steamed up the bay on the *Electra* with Commodore Gerry and landed at the City dock where he was escorted to the *Windsor Hotel.* The next night the *Count* dined at the *Union Club* with his fellow warriors, and on Monday, he traveled to Philadelphia for a reception and visits to area battle fields. Before embarking for France, joined by his son, the *Count* enjoyed a two-month tour of the United States.[11]

A *New York Society for the Prevention of Cruelty to Children* case that Commodore Gerry had appealed was finally decided on October 14 by the New York Court of Appeals. The case involved another challenge to the right of a parent to notice and hearing before being deprived of custody of a child. Commodore Gerry won the appeal which required the child, Annie Brown, to be returned to the care of the *New York Juvenile Asylum* for her care, education, and personal protection. The judge reversed the lower court's interpretation of "a parent" as only being the father, with the mother not permitted to attend a custody hearing as the sole parent. Now, under the new interpretation by a higher court, the presence of either parent would be sufficient at the examination before the court or magistrate when determining the custody of a child. Often, a father was derelict or alcoholic, and the mother was the only parent fit to make a court appearance. The interests of the child would be better served with both a parent and a charitable institution's representative able to testify.[12]

On November 7, 1890 Ogden Goelet purchased fishing grounds on the *Restigouche River* in Canada for the right to fish salmon. Ten years earlier in 1880, the *Privy Council of Canada* passed legislation to grant fishing rights to riparian owners (river bank property) on the *Restigouche River* in the Acadian wilderness of New Brunswick. At the time the area was a sportsman paradise, and in fact, in 1883 when old Uncle Peter Goelet's purported widow came to New York City to claim his estate, Robert Goelet was just returning on his yacht from salmon fishing on the *Restigouche River.* Canada granted the fishing rights for the cost of a ten year leasehold, most of which were renewed by the same club for decades. In 1880, thirty of *Gilded Gotham*'s wealthy businessmen formed the *Restigouche Salmon Club* and purchased a leasehold on 1,600 acres for $32,000, chiefly along the south bank of the river at its confluence with the *Matapediac River,* and only twelve miles from the tidewater. In 1880 the property included the Fraser homestead which was designated the "club-house" and capable of accommodating about 40 to 45 people. Included on the property was a store, a private cottage, a Post Office, quarters for Indian guides, and a storehouse for boats, canoes, and tools. The railway depot was just 100 yards from the club-house, and directly below the club-house ran the *Restigouche River*, 2,000 feet wide at that point with an island in the center of the river. To ensure privacy and to limit outside fishermen, the club purchased a strip of land running along the north bank of the river, which lies in the *Province of Quebec*. A few miles below the club grounds was the little town of Campbellton, where tons of salmon are cured, canned, and sent all across America and on to European markets.

The original club members subscribed the $32,000 within ten minutes, and within six weeks the club house was furnished, a staff of cooks and servants employed and sent up to Canada, and the club was open for use year-round, with winter hunting for caribou, moose or even bear. The *Restigouche Salmon Club* was 500 miles north of New York City and easily accessible by train or by yacht, which was the preferred method of travel for the Goelet brothers. Their close friend, architect Stanford White was a founding member of the club and he designed and built the new *Camp Harmony* club-house in 1896. Previous club houses had twice burned as reported in *A Sportsman's Paradise,* New York Times June 8, 1880. As late as 2003 the Goelet family in New York had renewed the leases on the *Restigouche River*, the fifth generation to maintain the hunting and fishing paradise in Canada. Francis Goelet (1926-1998) maintained the *Toad Brook club* on the *Restigouche River* as a family fishing lodge and in 1974 he acquired the *Tracadie* fishing lodge on the *Grand Cascapedia River* in Quebec. To ensure that future generations had the opportunity to enjoy Atlantic salmon, Francis Goelet founded the *Atlantic Salmon Foundation* in 1968. He was its first President and later served as Chairman and Treasurer. Francis helped fund the ASF's first building in St. Andrews, Scotland, which was dedicated to him as the *Francis Goelet Atlantic Salmon Research Center* on October 5, 1991. He served as Chairman Emeritus until his death in 1998.[13]

The *Children's Aid Society* held its thirty-eighth annual meeting on November 25 at the American Exchange National Bank, 128 Broadway. Robert J. Livingston and his son-in-law, Commodore Gerry were prominent Board members and participated in the meeting. At the meeting Robert J. Livingston was elected a Trustee, a position of honor for those longest associated with the Charity, and who were successful at courting benefactors to fund major projects. The Treasurer of the Society noted that one of those benefactors was Mrs. William Waldorf Astor, who had given a $5,000 endowment for one of the children's homes. The meeting placed particular stress on the value of the work done by ladies who volunteer their services. There was a woman from Boston who supported the cooking school as well as various other branches of the charity. The meeting closed with recognition of the *Cottage Place School* where the same group of women had labored for over twenty years.[14]

The holiday social season had arrived and Louisa Gerry opened up the adjoining brownstones at numbers 8 and 10 East Forty-Eighth Street for her first reception of the season on December 3 at 3 o'clock in the afternoon. Less than a week later the great ceremonial of New York society, the *Patriarchs' Ball* was held on December 8, the first of three balls organized by Mr. Ward McAllister between December and February. When asked by the press why these balls were so important to him, he responded that the idea of them was suggested by anecdotes told him by his father regarding the great balls given years ago at *Almack's Assembly Rooms* (1865-1871) on King Street in the St. James area of London. These extravagant balls were given by the leading ladies of London high society because they recognized that "union was strength" and exclusivity identified the powerful elite. Fondly recalling his father's stories, Mr. Ward McAllister looked to America's founding families for the elite of the new world. Of course, the self-made wealthy in *Gilded Gotham* were included because they were powerful and were already established within the elite social circles of New York City. The *Patriarchs' Ball* was in its eighteenth season in 1890 while the *Almack's Assembly Ball* had managed to survive only six years in London high society. Indeed, Mr. Ward McAllister would see the demise of the *Patriarchs' Ball* in 1892, the end of a nineteen year *Gilded* society tradition.[15]

Two days after the *Patriarchs' Ball,* on December 10, the Gerrys attended the wedding of Anna Ogden Pendleton to Mr. Duncan Clarkson Pell at *Christ Church,* New Brighton on Staten Island. Only the more intimate friends and relatives of the bride and groom were at the reception held at the residence of the bride's mother in New Brighton. During the ceremony the Gerrys sat with Mr. and Mrs. Robert Goelet and close friends Mr. and Mrs. Whitney, and Mr. and Mrs. Lorillard. A private train car transported the New York guests back to the City.

Christmas trees had become a new holiday tradition by 1890 and the welcome snowfall in the suburbs spurred an exodus of families for afternoons of ice skating, sledding, and tobogganing. Commodore Gerry celebrated his fifty-third birthday on Christmas Day with his family.

The winter season brought out the exquisite gowns designed by *Madame Worth* in Paris for American ladies while they traveled in Europe during the warmer months of the previous year. The Gerry girls, Angelica 19 and Mabel 18 were eager to wear their *Madame Worth* gowns at the January 19, 1891 ball given by Mrs. Cornelius Vanderbilt. The Vanderbilt mansion at Fifth Avenue and Fifty-Seventh

Street had a heavy tapestry curtain separating the entrance vestibule from the central hallway, which was lifted as each guest entered the hallway and passed into the drawing room and library where guests met to dance and socialize. A sumptuous dinner was served at 12 o'clock after which the dancing resumed until 2 o'clock.[16]

The Gerry girls saved their favorite gowns for the February 10 cotillion given in their honor by their parents, Commodore and Louisa Gerry, at their Forty-Eighth Street home. The newspapers reported the cotillion in all its festive detail, but only Angelica and Mabel were listed as the honored "daughters" in attendance. The past several months had been difficult for Lillian with her tuberculosis and it may have been a wise decision not to expose her to crowds of people during the winter flu season. Indeed, her grandfather Robert J. Livingston lived in the adjacent brownstone and was in bed upstairs during the Gerrys' cotillion with a serious case of pneumonia or the Russian Flu. Lillian kept him company as she knew all too well what it was like to be side-lined from fun excursions during family travels across Europe, when she was often confined to bed with a cold or consumption.

A week later, New York took Philadelphia by storm when 200 of the *Patriarchs'*, including Commodore and Mrs. Gerry, traveled by a special train to attend the wedding of *Gilded Gotham's* native son, John Jacob Astor IV, who was to marry Philadelphia's greatest belle, Ava L. Willing. All of the fashionable hotels were reserved as were all the local carriages. The ceremony and breakfast celebration were held in the bride's home at 511 South Broad Street, Philadelphia. The bride wore a *Madame Worth* dress of heavy, creamy duchesse satin with an immense train. The petticoat was edged with deep flowing point lace caught up in festoons by small clusters of orange blossoms. The gown was cut away at the neck and the bride wore a long lace veil. The six bridesmaids wore Marie Antoinette gowns of pink chiffon, the half-trained skirts edged with frills of lace, the sleeves had frills of similar lace, and a pink satin sash passed around the waist with a bow in the back.

The gifts were magnificent, costly, and beautiful and included diamonds from the Astor collection. The couple also received from the Astor family a furnished house on Fifth Avenue in New York City. Afterward, on the way back to the train station, many of the New Yorkers had to walk because there were not enough carriages to be had, and the elegant parade looked like a scene from Fifth Avenue in *Gilded Gotham.*[17]

Commodore Gerry was eager to get Louisa Gerry back to New York City to be with her father who was suffering from pleurisy, an acute and painful inflammation of the lining of the lungs, which may actually have been the Russian Flu. Robert J. Livingston took a turn for the worse just before the Gerrys arrived home. Louisa had lost her mother seven years before, her brother Warren in 1857, and her father, the last member of her immediate family, was now gravely ill. On February 22, 1891, Robert J. Livingston, the grandson of General Morgan Lewis, died of complications from pneumonia at the age of eighty surrounded by his five grandchildren, his daughter, and his son-in-law and best friend, Commodore Elbridge T. Gerry. His funeral was held at the *Church of the Heavenly Rest* and burial at the family vault at St. James Church, in Hyde Park, New York.[18]

Commodore Elbridge T. Gerry filed for probate February 27 as the executor of the will of Robert J. Livingston that had been drafted on February 2. His daughter Louisa M. Gerry received all of his real estate and personal property in Lake Delaware, New York; all the movable property in the brownstone at 10 East Forty-Eighth Street, and the stable at 19 East Fifty-Second Street near Fifth Avenue, and the farm estate at Raritan, New Jersey where she was raised with her brother Warren. She inherited all income and residue of the estate making her a millionaire property owner in her own right, adding to the property she had inherited from her mother in 1883, and also retained in her own name. The entire Gerry family was in mourning for several weeks; the loss was intimate and profound. Robert J. Livingston had been a constant companion in their lives, sharing the adjacent townhouse for over 21 years, participating in the daily lives of his five grandchildren, and joining in every family trip on the *Electra,* at the *Lake Delaware* estate and on family travels through Europe.

While the Gerry family was in mourning *Gilded Gotham's* leading men, particularly the well-established, middle-aged peers of Commodore Gerry, had become disgruntled with the *Union Club,* of which Elbridge was a member. Although highly respected among the gentlemen's clubs, it appeared to be progressively taken over by the next generation of wealthy dudes who started to "black ball' membership nominations by the older gentlemen, and when they turned down nominees of J.P. Morgan and Cornelius Vanderbilt, that was the last straw. The twenty-five senior *Union Club* members, including Goelet, Iselin, Morgan, Whitney, and Vanderbilt, met on February 20 with the intention of founding a new club. Commodore Gerry was at his father-in-law's death bed and was unable to participate in the establishment of the new club, but would have agreed with his long-time friends. Regular meetings of what was referred to by the press as the "millionaires club" were held in the Goelet Offices. On March 7 the group announced that the new *Metropolitan Club* had been formally named and organized, had elected officers, and would take a modern approach to the design and use of their new club. From the beginning the founders had decided to provide, for the first time in any gentleman's club, separate accommodations for ladies, including dining facilities, a library and social parlor.

The general move uptown of wealthy residences and the vast stretches of land fronting *Central Park* attracted the new club members to look at property above Fifty-Ninth Street, which set a new precedent for the location of gentlemen's clubs. By May 1891 a large tract of land on Fifth Avenue, known as the *Hamersley Estate,* between Sixtieth and Sixty-First Streets with over two hundred and fifty feet facing *Central Park,* was for sale. Also at this time, Commodore Gerry had settled his wife's inheritance from Robert J. Livingston, and Louisa had eased out of her deep mourning and needed to refocus her energy and concentrate on the future. Louisa was ready to leave the old brownstones on Forty-Eighth Street where she had lost her first child, Margaret, and both her parents, indeed she was eager for a new home for her family in the upscale neighborhood along *Central Park* where her near-adult children could conveniently pursue "coaching" and riding horses in the City. As a soon-to-be member of the newly organized *Metropolitan Club,* Commodore Elbridge T. Gerry was delighted to discover that both Louisa and the new club were looking at the *Hamersley Estate* on Fifth Avenue. Neither needed the full 250 foot Fifth Avenue frontage, so they split the property in two. The *Metropolitan Club* purchased the 100+ feet along Fifth Avenue to the corner at Sixtieth Street, extending 200 feet down East Sixtieth Street. Louisa Gerry purchased the 100 feet frontage on Fifth Avenue to the Sixty-First Street corner, and 200 feet down East Sixty-First Street. Several weeks later the club membership had secured financing for construction of the club and purchased the land through contributions of $5,000 by each of the twenty-five original members. By the end of May, 1891 the ground excavation began for the *Metropolitan Club* house.[19]

The Goelet brothers' good friend and fishing partner Stanford White and his firm, *McKim, Mead & White,* was selected as the architect for the building. The society men continued their seasonal travels and most left for Newport for the summer and Europe in the fall, so the design of the new *Metropolitan Club* was still unfinished as late as February 1892. In fact, Cornelius Vanderbilt was sending his own sketches to the architects from Europe. However, it was J.P. Morgan's suggestion of a courtyard entered from Sixtieth Street through tall and ornate iron gates that became the highlight of the building plan. This entrance would avoid disruption of the Fifth Avenue façade and permitted expansive views of *Central Park* from the west side public view of the building. The magnificent building was not occupied until 1894, but was well worth the wait.

Commodore and Louisa Gerry engaged architect *Richard Morris Hunt* to design their home at Fifth Avenue and Sixty-First Street. The entrance would be on the side street to provide privacy, to ease congestion on the Avenue, and to permit the architecture of the west façade to accommodate the broadest possible views of *Central Park.* The final design of the floor plan was not submitted for approval to the City until May 1892. Meanwhile, the Gerry family continued to live at numbers 8-10 Forty-Eighth Street until the house was completed in late 1894, when the children ranged in age from 15 to 23.

In April 1891 Angelica Gerry, the eldest daughter, was noted by the press as a guest at an Easter celebration when young people enjoyed the annual *Bachelors' Ball,* attending society teas and the warm-weather rounds of "at home visits" with the ladies dropping their cards on silver trays in the fashionable entry-halls of their many friends. The press also caught up with Louisa Gerry's cousin, Elizabeth, the twin sister of Ruth Livingston Mills of Staatsburg. Bessie, as she was known to the Gerrys when she was a young woman, had been the *Duchess of Portland* for ten years and was living in England. Elizabeth and her Duke, William C. Cavendish-Bentnick, were reported to be special art patrons in London and decorated their drawing rooms in strict accordance with the French taste of Louis the Sixteenth. They were said to entertain often and well with dinners and small dances on terraces that overlooked the Thames River in Richmond, just outside London. The press could not resist reminding their readers that the marriage ten years earlier had carried off Livingston millions to refresh the depleted coffers of the Duke of Portland, Mr. Bentnick. Nonetheless, it was a happy marriage and curiously by this marriage Mrs. Elizabeth Bentnick, the Duchess, became a cousin to Lady Randolph Churchill (Jennie Jerome), whose sister, Leonie Jerome married Jack Leslie the brother of Mr. Bentnick's mother.[20]

The sultry days of summer approached, and the Gerrys were not only in the early stages of planning a new mansion on Fifth Avenue, but they were making plans for extensive improvements on the *Lake Delaware* farm estate which now belonged to Louisa M. Gerry and was the childhood summer home of her five children. In May, Commodore Gerry had 6,000 trout placed in Lake Delaware from a private hatchery, and planned to add more fish, including salmon. The Gerry family arrived later in the summer on July 25 and found the fishing to be very good indeed. Over the summer all of the farm buildings, water supplies and the main house were reviewed for renovations and upgrades. In late August Commodore Gerry contributed \$200 toward completing the Episcopal Church at *Griffin's Corners,* now *Fleishman's* in Delaware County, New York just down the road from the Gerry's *Lake Delaware* estate. His generosity was well-known and was acknowledged in the area to be a natural inclination of the Livingston family for three generations and was happily continued with Louisa Livingston Gerry and her husband, Commodore Elbridge T. Gerry. In fact, the small town was also able to build the *Skene Memorial*

Library on Main Street in 1901 through another significant donation of $5,000 from Andrew Carnegie for a free public library. "Carnegie libraries" were built across the United States with donations by one of the nation's *Gilded Age* millionaires, who simply believed that his wealth was a trust for the poor and that the best means of benefiting a community was to place within reach the ladders upon which the aspiring could rise to success. Andrew Carnegie wrote the essay The *Gospel of Wealth* in 1889 when he and men like Commodore Gerry were practicing what they preached in small towns and major cities alike.

The summer of 1891 was very exciting for Ogden Goelet and his wife Mary Wilson Goelet because their summer cottage, *Ochre Court,* was finally finished. It was the first of four mansions in Newport designed by architect Richard Morris Hunt. During the construction of *Ochre Court* between 1889 and 1891, the Gerrys visited their cousin Ogden Goelet to learn about the design, building materials and mechanics of the great house under construction. In fact, the Gerry's came to know Richard M. Hunt as an intimate friend and it was not surprising that when the Gerrys were ready to build their mansion on Fifth Avenue they chose Hunt as their architect. However, Richard M. Hunt was in great demand and in 1891 he accepted both the Gerry commission in New York City and the George Vanderbilt commission in Asheville, North Carolina to build Biltmore, the largest home in America. *Ochre Court,* the second largest mansion in Newport, was built next door to the *Breakers,* the home of Cornelius Vanderbilt, the largest mansion ever built in Newport, Rhode Island. Although Hunt completed both the Gerry and Vanderbilt commissions in 1894, he was exhausted and died just one year later in 1895 at the age of sixty-eight.

Ochre Court was of such interest when completed that an article was published in *Architectural Record* in 1895 that described it as a distinct and triumphant success as a chateau. The article called Hunt's design a free and romantic architecture in which the modern designer had proceeded not by way of imitation, but by way of assimilation, taking the best European architecture had to teach. *Ochre Court* was a fifty-room limestone palace with design elements from French renaissance chateaus and churches. He created a three-story Great Hall, from which radiated impressive first floor reception rooms, a library, dining room, and a ballroom. Private upstairs family rooms were richly designed with imported antique fireplaces and lavish wall coverings. Hunt emphasized the Goelets' social position and their patronage of learning and the arts with exuberant decoration in classical ceiling paintings, royal heraldic devices, carved emblems and statues, and a rich collection of stained glass. Many of the furnishings were obtained through high-end dealers and many rare objects were brought back from world travels.[21]

Ochre Court was generally open just eight weeks a year for summer entertainment. During the season the mansion required twenty-seven house servants, eight coachmen and grooms, and twelve gardeners to maintain the formal gardens, walkways and expansive lawns running to the cliffs overlooking the Atlantic Ocean. When Grand Duke Boris Vladimirovich, brother-in-law of the Czarina of Russia, was a house guest of *Ochre Court* in the 1890's he exclaimed in wonder, "I have never dreamt of such luxury as I have seen in Newport." Nonetheless, this was the last time that Ogden Goelet would "out size" his older brother Robert, whose summer home *Southside* was dwarfed by the new *Ochre Court* next door. Ogden Goelet died just three years later in 1897 at age fifty-one. In 1947, Ogden and Mary's son, Robert Goelet who inherited the mansion, gave the estate to the *Religious Sisters of Mercy* who established *Salve Regina College*, where the mansion sits at the heart of the now sixty-acre campus in Newport.[22]

Commodore Elbridge T. Gerry continued full-time as President and Legal Counsel of the *New York Society for the Prevention of Cruelty to Children.* Since the courts had clarified the definition of parent as being either mother or father, the cases on appeal were shifting to whether the magistrate who placed a child in a protective institution had the jurisdiction, or legal authority to do so. One among many such challenges was decided on October 6, 1891 in which the *Protestant Episcopal House of Mercy* had legal authority to detain a female over the age of twelve years after writs of habeas corpus and certiorari were issued to obtain the discharge of the girl to her parents. Upon review the appellate court held that the order of the lower court judge was erroneous because the law forbids a judge to review the decision of a magistrate, and therefore the girl was ordered to be returned to the *Protectory.*[23] Two weeks later a suit for damages brought against the *NYSPCC* by Tillie Halpern was decided. The plaintiff was a ten year old girl arrested the previous January by officers of the Society for selling newspapers on the street. She resisted the officers and it was with some difficulty that Tillie was taken to the police station. She was afterward discharged and immediately brought suit through her guardian, declaring that she had been illegally arrested, falsely imprisoned, and that undue violence was used by the officers. A number of the officers testified that they had been instructed by President Gerry to stop the selling of newspapers on the streets by young girls, and other testimony was introduced to show that the girl had not been roughly treated. The jury brought in a verdict for the Society.[24] While the *NYSPCC* cases were numerous and seemed to "slice and dice" the legal issues associated with child custody, each time Commodore Gerry won a case, as he did here, that particular "slice of the issue" was settled for future child custody placement. Case by case, year by year, the law was making it clear that children were protected against cruel and harmful homes and that "parental rights" had limits which society neither articulated nor acknowledged before the late nineteenth century. Unfortunately, in November, the NYSPCC was embarrassed by the arrest of one of its agents. William A. Hunt had been an agent for the Society for over a year based on a recommendation by J. Edward Simmons, President of the *Fourth National Bank.* The circumstances of Hunt's arrest were peculiar. He had obtained clear evidence against Peter Breckerman, a liquor dealer on Sixth Avenue, of selling alcohol to minors. He called on Breckerman, and after telling him that he was one of Mr. Gerry's agents, said that he intended to arrest him. Breckerman, who was convinced that Hunt was nothing but a bogus agent, induced him to postpone the arrest until the following day, promising to pay him $50 to settle the case. A place of meeting was agreed, but Breckerman also notified the police who sent Detective Hayes to observe the meeting. He witnessed the NYSPCC agent, Hunt, receive from the saloon keeper, Breckerman, some marked bills. The arrest followed and agent Hunt was taken to police headquarters. However, Breckerman refused to press charges so Hunt was released. Hearing about the charge of blackmail, Commodore Gerry summoned his agent, William A. Hunt to his office and immediately dismissed him from his position with the NYSPCC.[25]

One of the few times that Commodore Elbridge T. Gerry was publicly associated with a political party was on October 9, 1891 when twenty-thousand New York Democrats met at *Cooper Union* to ratify the nominees and the platform of the State party. Ex-President Grover Cleveland was Chairman and Governor Hill was the keynote speaker. Had the big hall been five times as big as it was, it would have comfortably accommodated the crowd that tried to enter. When the doors were opened at 7 o'clock there was a mighty rush of men who did not wait to go down the aisles but jumped helter-skelter over the red leather seats. When the doors closed nearly ten thousand cheering spectators remained outside in the square. By 8 o'clock the stage was filled by leading representatives of the party and among those sitting closest to the speaker's table were Ex-Secretary of the Navy William C. Whitney, Commodore Elbridge T. Gerry, Mayor Grant, and Police Commissioner Voorhis. At 8:15 o'clock Ex-President Cleveland, escorted by Governor Hill, walked down the aisle to the stage and the crowd began to cheer wildly and wave their handkerchiefs. Finally the meeting was called to order for preliminary business, the election of the several *Democratic Party Vice-Presidents,* which included the election of Commodore Gerry. Speeches followed which addressed issues of honesty, war tariff reform, and discontent with the Republican Party. The *State Democratic Party* was committed to taking back the New York legislature in the November election and Commodore Gerry was now a political figurehead.[26]

The Gerry family was preparing for the holiday season of society balls, winter sport and family gatherings for the first time without Grandpapa Livingston who had died nine months earlier. But the family would face an unexpected and devastating loss at Thanksgiving. On November 27, 1891 came the unexpected death of Lillian Gerry, who had just celebrated her eighteenth birthday on November 10. The family was helpless when Lilly experienced an attack of tubercular asthma that quickly overcame her frail constitution. During the past several months Lilly had been taking one of the newest medications called *Koch's Lymph* because other remedies were no longer as effective for her deteriorating condition. Losing her grandfather may have weakened her spirit. Even while Lilly noted how ill she felt in her diary she also noted how she distracted herself by counting the eighty-one pearls on her necklace to listing the books she read, the things she knitted or sewed for the poor children, and most especially photography, her favorite hobby. Without Lilly's passion for capturing her family in photographs at *Lake Delaware,* on *Electra,* and on European travels, much of the visual history of the Gerry family would be lost. Louisa Gerry was inconsolable and Angelica and Mabel were broken-hearted to lose their sister. Robert 14 and Peter 12 were at an impressionable age and felt the loss as deeply as their parents and sisters. The family refrained from attending the holiday events swirling in *Gilded Gotham* and remained in mourning at home through Commodore Gerry's fifty-fourth birthday. Private funeral services were held at 10 a.m. on Monday, November 30, at *Trinity Chapel* on West Twenty-Fifth Street. A special *Hudson River Railroad* car carried Lilly's coffin, her family and friends from Grand Central Station to the *St. James Church* cemetery in Hyde Park, New York, for interment in the family vault. Lilly was placed near her grandfather, Robert J. Livingston, who was brought to St. James just a few months earlier. Perhaps it gave some comfort to Louisa to have her father and her daughter together just as they were in life. The Gerry family returned by train to Grand Central Station that night and retired to their quiet home on Forty-Eighth Street.[27] Commodore Gerry presented a pure gold ciborium to the Church of *St. Edward the Martyr* in Lilly's honor. The inscription read:

> *In memoriam. Lillian Goelet Gerry entered life eternal*
> *Nov. 27, 1891, aged eighteen years.*

Only Commodore Elbridge T. Gerry represented the family at the January 13, 1892 *Patriarchs' Ball* which was the first opportunity he had to allow the Gerrys' extended circle of family friends to share their personal condolences and to ask after the family. The arrangement of the dinner tables at *Delmonico's* for the dinner was a change from past tradition. Each *Patriarch* had a table of his own, which allowed Commodore Gerry to surround himself with his closest friends and his cousins, Robert and Ogden Goelet, for a more intimate meal after several weeks in mourning. The evening provided a transition that lifted his spirits.

The only way that Commodore Gerry could manage his grief was to throw himself into his work. On January 29, 1892 Mayor Grant appointed an advisory commission to investigate the condition of the pauper insane in New York City and determine whether their care should be transferred to the State. As soon as the Mayor called the meeting to order in his private office he withdrew and the gentlemen organized the commission and elected Commodore Gerry the Chairman. Mr. Porter of the *Department of Charities* met by invitation with the Commissioners and planned to advise them throughout their investigation. He provided the group with descriptions of the property owned by the city and used for the pauper insane, statistics bearing on the asylums, and other data that would be useful to the commission. The commission decided to visit the institutions beginning the next morning at 9:30, when they met at the foot of East Twenty-Sixth Street to take a boat to *Blackwell's Island.* The work of the commission proceeded over the next few months to investigate institutions and to prepare their final report to the Mayor.[28]

A week later on February 4 Commodore Elbridge T. Gerry traveled by train up to Albany, New York for a hearing on a bill presented by Mr. Stein. The bill permitted children to appear on the stage when such appearance was endorsed by their parents and by the certificate of an attending physician that it was not injurious to the health of the child. A second bill provided that nothing in the act was to be construed as allowing any child to appear in a place where liquor was sold. The second bill was presented to specifically overcome the objections of Commodore Gerry, on behalf of the NYSPCC, to the first bill. Those speaking in favor of the bill noted that the theater managers needed relief from the NYSPCC supervision when children were often on stage for no more than fifteen minutes and it did not interfere with their studies or harm their morals. Commodore Gerry testified that the Society aimed not only to release children from immoral bondage, but from physical injury during the tender and highly impressionable years of childhood. Dr. Stoddard of Rochester, New York supported the Commodore's position, while Judge Dittenhoffer of New York argued for the bill as counsel for the managers. The matter was put over for a future hearing and Commodore Gerry returned by train to New York City. Testifying before the state legislature was imperative because the votes were held in the Assembly, but pressure on representatives in Albany through public opinion was another means to influence votes. Commodore Gerry put pen to paper when necessary to broaden his voice. His article in the *North American Review* in 1890, entitled "Children of the Stage," was widely referenced during the debates in Albany in 1892.

While Commodore Gerry pursued the needs of the pauper insane and children of the stage, *Gilded Gotham* was looking for more novelty in their entertainment. In late March it was reported to the press that society men had proposed a scheme to build a first-class fireproof circus in New York City. The committee set to organize the proposal included Perry Belmont, Robert and Ogden Goelet, A. Iselin, Cornelius Vanderbilt, W. C. Whitney and other millionaires. The plan was to establish a permanent circus similar in general outlines to the *Noveau Cirque* in Paris, France which had a history of financial success and high class entertainment. While the details were not yet set, they proposed a one-ring circus in which the very best acrobats and the very best horsemen and women of the world would appear. The committee asked Mr. Hutchinson, formerly of *Barnum, Bailey and Hutchinson,* to take the management of the circus for half of the net profits after the payment of expenses, taxes and interest on the mortgage. P.T. Barnum had joined J.P. Morgan and others as investors in the 1890 construction of the second *Madison Square Garden,* but Barnum suffered a stroke that same year and died in April 1891 at the age of eighty. While the concept for a new venue dedicated to a world class one-ring circus never materialized in 1892, both the *Barnum & Bailey Circus* and the *Ringling Brothers Circus* performed for years at *Madison Square Garden* for the enjoyment of all New Yorkers.[29]

During the first few months of 1892 Louisa Gerry focused her mind and heart on the future with serious work on Richard M. Hunt's floor plans of the new family home to be constructed at Fifth Avenue and Sixty-First Street. By May the first set of plans had been submitted to the City for review and approval. The exterior design was to be a combination of French, Gothic, and Renaissance architecture. The building itself was 99 feet by 144 feet and stood three stories topped by a peaked roof. There was an expansive ground floor (semi-basement) and a modern basement for coal storage and a boiler system. The main entrance on Sixty-First Street was to have a covered carriage way, yet to be designed. Two great chimneys at the gable ascended forty feet from the nearest cornice. The first floor main hall ran through the center of the building where a central marble winding stairway and a passenger elevator were placed. Off of the central hall were the formal rooms, a large dining room, two grand parlors, a picture gallery, and most significantly, a library for Commodore Gerry's book collection, which had been growing for decades in the old *Broadway Farm* mansion at Nineteenth Street where he spent his youth, and where his elderly mother still resided. On the third floor, the architect added an "isolating room" for the care of any family member who might take ill in the future. While the floor plans continued to evolve over the next year the land was excavated for the foundation in April 1892 just as excavations started on the adjacent *Metropolitan Club* building project.[30]

A new slice of the law in child custody challenges was determined in favor of Commodore Gerry and the *NYSPCC* on April 26, 1892 in the New York Court of Appeals. The father of a girl placed in the custody of the *Protestant Episcopal House of Mercy* brought a writ of habeas corpus alleging that his daughter was nineteen, not seventeen years old at the time of her commitment and was now over twenty-one and should be released from the custodial institution. In the lower court the judge released her based on the testimony of the father and another witness as to the girl's actual age. The appellate judge however, looked deeper into the letter and spirit of the law and noted that a custodial institution should not be compelled to assume the risk of an unlawful detention if a magistrate hearing should incorrectly, but in good faith, determine the age of a child as stated in the warrant. That would place all such custodial institutions in a position of uncertainty which the law did not intend. Further, the managers of the institution have the authority to discharge an inmate at any time when it appears that a child is no longer a proper subject for their care. However, as to the actual fact of the girl's age in this case the father was then, a year later, attempting to show that she was nineteen on the date of commitment, a plain contradiction of the judgment of the police magistrate when the child had a parent present at the hearing. The Judge reversed the lower court's release of the daughter to her father and returned her to the custody of the *Protestant Episcopal House of Mercy*. The point here was that the law protected the judgment of the police magistrate at the time of commitment based on the facts known at that time and then "shifts the decision" from the courts to the child care institution as to when to safely release a child from its protective custody, regardless of their age.[31]

In July 1892, one of the only cases represented by Commodore Elbridge T. Gerry to reach the *United States Supreme Court* was decided at the lower state trial court in New York City. The case began with the arrest of Charlotte Ewer for permitting her seven-year old daughter, Mildred, to appear as a dancer on the stage. The first challenge to the decision in favor of the State, represented by Commodore Gerry, was to question the legality of Mrs. Ewer's commitment under the *Penal Code* as unconstitutional. The court determined that the legislature was vested with the entire police power possessed by the people of the state, and its determination through legislation that young girls should not be exhibited as dancers before they reach the age of fourteen was a final decision and not subject to review by the courts. The case was appealed in June 1893 to the state's highest court, and then in January 1894 was appealed to a federal court, alleging the *New York State Constitution* violated the *United States Constitution* because the state Legislature exceeded its sovereign power to regulate and control the legal relation of a parent and child. Four years after the 1892 case was appealed, the case was docketed for a hearing before the *United States Supreme Court* in Washington, D.C. However, the case was dismissed with costs and without a court opinion. It was noted that the case had abated, which meant that there was no longer a viable constitutional issue before the Court or perhaps the party to the case had since died rendering the controversy moot. That automatically left the *New York State* legislation in place and constitutionally valid.[32] This case is an excellent example of how long Commodore Elbridge T. Gerry was working on any one case, some for a few months, but many demanded his legal skills and attention over a period of years before finally being resolved. His law practice was always active in the background of his otherwise busy personal, social, and civic life.

In the late nineteenth century, the *United States Senate* commissioned sculptors to create a series of busts of the Vice-Presidents of the United States for permanent display in the Senate Chamber. The second round of commissions in 1891 included the bust for Vice-President Elbridge Gerry, almost eighty years after his death. The Sculptors were selected from the home state of each Vice-President and Herbert Adams, a Massachusetts sculptor, had just returned from five years of study and work in Paris under the accomplished sculptor Antonin Mercie. Adams immediately accepted the commission and created a plaster cast from a clay model. The cast was translated into marble in Paris, which the artist finished by hand in his studio. The sculptor requested to see the corner niche in the *Senate Chamber* where the bust would be placed. Adams used the location to his advantage by turning Gerry's head away from the corner in a natural, communicative pose, his head cocked slightly forward and to the side, his eyebrows raised as though listening to a pleasant companion. The finished bust was placed in the *Senate Chamber* in July 1892 where it can be seen today by visitors to the nation's Capital. In addition to the Gerry bust, Herbert Adams also designed the bronze doors of the *Jefferson Building* of the Library of Congress in Washington, D.C, and the statue of *William Cullen Bryant* that stands in *Bryant Park*, New York City.[33]

The summer of 1892 was an opportunity for the Gerry family to use *Electra* as their escape from the metropolis that was filled with the cold winter memories of sorrow. The open sea would invigorate the body and quality time spent with the Gallatins and Goelets, the closest family remaining to the Gerrys, would strengthen the soul. This was the first summer that the Gerry children did not spend most of their time at *Lake Delaware,* in fact it was the first summer that Commodore and Louisa Gerry rented *Lyndenhurst,* a Newport cottage, for their own family. It was on the corner of Bellevue Avenue and Webster Street, and was just two long blocks down Webster Street from the Goelets' summer cottages, *Southside* and the newly opened *Ochre Court.* The three families were within easy walking distance or a "coaching" ride away from each other. Neither Robert J. Livingston nor Lilly had ever stayed at *Lyndenhurst* and the Gerry family embraced the opportunity to create new memories as they healed from their loss. With the family based in Newport it would be a summer of celebration and reflection since this was the last cruise of the *New York Yacht Club* and the last *Goelet Cup Races* with Elbridge T. Gerry as Commodore, and the yacht *Electra* as the club's flagship. So famous was Commodore Gerry and his yacht, that the popular magazine *Harpers Weekly* published a sketch of the Commodore on the observation desk of *Electra,* timing and recording the NYYC races. His family and friends joined him in an accurate sketch which provided a lasting glimpse into Commodore Elbridge T. Gerry immersed in the joy of his favorite pastime.

Before the 1892 summer cruise of the NYYC, Robert Goelet proudly took possession of his new yacht, *Beatrice,* named after his only daughter who was then seven years old. This was perhaps the fourth yacht owned by Robert, and it would not be the last. In 1897 his largest and most luxurious yacht would be delivered from Glasgow, Scotland, along with a twin yacht for brother Ogden Goelet, who was not to be out-done by his older brother. This was the friendliest of competitions, but also one of the most expensive, even by *Gilded Gotham* standards. Commodore Gerry enjoyed sharing life with his Goelet cousins but he remained circumspect with his life-style and primarily focused on his work, even while on vacation. He would never have another yacht but *Electra,* even though she required considerable upkeep, which included repairs from accidents. In fact, not long after the Gerry family had settled in at *Lyndenhurst* for the summer in Newport, they set out on *Electra* July 15 to Vineyard Haven, then headed to Nantucket about 9 o'clock. The *Electra* almost immediately ran upon the foot of *Tuckernuck Shoal,* about four miles to the westward of *Cross Rip Lightship.* The yacht was running at her usual speed and landed her full length on the hidden sand. The steamer *Nantucket* answered Commodore Gerry's call for assistance, but the steamboat did not have sufficient power to haul the yacht off. *Electra* was firmly grounded in eleven feet of water on an ebb tide. Another towboat, the *Elise,* was sent for and after her arrival it took another hour to haul the yacht off the shoal. The *Electra* did not appear to be badly damaged but a diver would examine her plating after she proceeded back to Newport on her own steam. The accident was caused by an obstruction not shown on the latest charts. The buoy that should mark the shoal was missing from its position. Commodore Gerry promised to look into the issue and have the shoal identified on revised charts and the necessary buoy marker set in place.[34]

On August 3, 1892 Commodore Gerry steamed up the coast to New Haven, Connecticut to rendezvous in *Hempstead Harbor* off Glen Cove for the forty-eighth annual NYYC cruise. The *Electra's* cannon boomed as she dropped her big anchor and the roaring of cannon on all the yachts ushered in the cruise with the usual formality. Small boats went scooting for the starboard gangway of the *Electra,* gathering all of the yacht captains on the deck to talk over plans for the cruise. It was left to the discretion of Commodore Gerry to signal later in the day what the objective of the afternoon run would be, whether to *Black Rock* or to *Morris Cove.*

The evening was filled with sumptuous dinners and drinks on the yachts, some went ashore to the clubhouse, and after the grand illumination the evening closed with late night preparations for the 9 o'clock departure the next morning. The fleet arrived in *Marblehead,* Massachusetts on August 9 where Commodore Gerry expressed his pleasure at the success of the cruise thus far around *Cape Cod,* and said that if the wind held out until the next day, there would be a splendid race in *Massachusetts Bay.* The next day a hot westerly wind blew off the shore and owners, crew and guests kept under the awnings which were spread everywhere on the yachts. Promptly at eight bells a gun was fired on board the flagship *Electra,* the *Eastern Club's* signal (flag) was sent to the foretopmast head, and the *New York Yacht Club's* signal was sent up the main mast. Then two more guns from the *Electra* in salute of the *Eastern Club* were followed by a salute of one gun from all the yachts in the harbor. The firing began far down by the lighthouse and continued up through the fleet, until it seemed with the smoke rolling away to leeward, as if a regular bombardment was in progress. After a short interval the salute was returned by two guns from the yacht of the Commodore of the *Eastern Yacht Club.* But Commodore Gerry was not done with his cannon yet. Another shot rang out from the flagship, the signal to haul down the colors of the *Eastern Club* and then another shot as the order to "dress the ship." Flags of all colors and various shapes had been sent up in "stops" rolled up into little balls. When the signal was given a line was pulled, the "stops" were broken out and the flags fluttered in the breeze, presenting all the colors of the rainbow. In fact this mode of dressing ship is called "in rainbow fashion."[35] After a leisurely lunch, there were cutters, launches, and gigs flying about the water taking the yacht owners visiting among boats or to the clubhouse dock. Crowds of men, women and children viewed the beautiful scene from *Marblehead* beaches and many more people observed from their carriages. The colorful flags were not hauled down until sunset. The next day the fleet sailed for Newport, Rhode Island for the *Goelet Cup Races.* At 9:30 a.m. the following day Governor Russell and staff went onboard *Electra* as the guests of Commodore Gerry to watch the Newport races, including the *Gerry Cup* race between schooners and sloops. The prestigious *Goelet Cup* race was won by the yacht *Harpoon,* but some jovially argued it was a tie with the *Glorianna,* while others argued the *Wasp* had beaten the *Harpoon.* The 1892 NYYC annual cruise was blessed with perfect weather, worthy competitions and all around good fun. Commodore Gerry was ready to relinquish his glorious seven-year run as Commodore when he closed the annual cruise with a grand dinner for the captains onboard *Electra.* The *New York Yacht Club* itself did not celebrate and honor Commodore Gerry until the following summer when the newly elected Commodore would officially take office.

While *Gilded Gotham's* elite relaxed after the summer yacht cruises in Newport or sailed on the big steamers for a tour of Europe, a catastrophic fire destroyed the *Metropolitan Opera House* on Saturday morning, August 27. It had only been nine years since New York's leading millionaires built the greatest music venue in America, and were assured that it was a fireproof structure. A construction crew was in the midst of removing old sets and building and painting new sets early on Saturday morning when one of the workmen dropped a cigarette in the paint room under the stage, engulfing the stage and all the scenery. A fireproof curtain designed to protect the auditorium from just such a mishap was no longer in use, and the flames quickly spread throughout the opera house. The fire was discovered at 9 o'clock and was extinguished by noon, but the extent of the damage was catastrophic. The wealthy stockholders in their various summer retreats were incredulous and sentiment was divided on the question of rebuilding. Complicating the matter was the completion of *Carnegie Hall* the year before, in 1891, as a venue for New York's *Oratorio Society* and the *Symphonic Society,* on whose boards Andrew Carnegie sat and he therefore provided the funding to build the Hall named in his honor. The New York *Philharmonic Orchestra* concerts were the primary entertainment at *Carnegie Hall,* while the *Opera* was held at the *Metropolitan Opera House.* The opera season was cancelled for 1891/92 and the majority of stockholders in the *Company* decided not to rebuild and sold the land and the devastated building to a corporation of 35 stockholders, including Robert and Ogden Goelet, J.P. Morgan, Cornelius Vanderbilt II, John J. Astor IV, and a new sponsor, A. D. Julliard, whose fortune established the *Julliard Foundation,* which remains today, one of the major sponsors of New York opera. This new corporation, a core of the original elite stockholders who built the first opera house, incorporated as the *Metropolitan Opera and Real Estate Company* and the enterprise was as much a sponsorship of opera as it was a significant financial investment in the valuable real estate.[36] Once again a horseshoe tier of private boxes, the diamond tier, was incorporated in the new *Metropolitan Opera House* which was rebuilt in April 1893 and later refurbished and expanded in 1906 when electric elevators were added. The Opera Company went out of business in 1940 and sold the opera house to the *Metropolitan Opera Association.* The building was razed in 1967 after the opera moved to *Lincoln Center* in 1966 at which time the Goelet family provided a substantial part of the funding and in whose honor the grand staircase was dedicated. In 1883, Ogden Goelet, with a passion for the theatre as well as the opera, built the *Abbey Theatre,* later renamed the *Knickerbocker Theatre,* and in 1896 Ogden built the *Murray Hill Theatre* on Lexington Avenue. One can only speculate on the animated conversations Ogden Goelet might have had with his dear cousin, Commodore Gerry, about the enduring controversy over children on the stage. There is no record of any challenges by the NYSPCC to theatres owned by the Goelets, and perhaps they carefully selected their managers and which productions their theatre engaged, adhering to the letter and spirit of the child protection laws.

Fourteen months after Lillian Gerry's death, her mother Louisa M. Gerry attended her first social event in *Gilded Gotham's* winter season of 1893. On March 14 she attended a gala charity concert for *Saint Mary's Hospital for Children,* which was held as part of the grand opening of the new *Hotel Waldorf.* The concert was one of the best of the season with Walter Damrosch and his orchestra presenting a program of classical and modern music. The concert was over in time for those present to inspect the new *Hotel Waldorf* from cellar to mansard. It was brilliantly lit with electricity and decorated with potted plants throughout. Because it was still the Lenten season, there was no dancing, which gave Louisa Gerry a more subdued transition back into the social world; she took quiet opportunities to visit with close friends as they wandered through the new hotel after the concert. This was primarily an event sponsored by lady patronesses of the *Hospital* and therefore gentlemen did not attend this intimate yet glittering event.[37]

The summer of 1893 was a celebration of all things Newport. The Gerry family once again rented the *Lyndenhurst* cottage down the road from their Goelet cousins. During the Gallatins' summer holiday at *Breezy Lawn* Long Island, they traveled on their steam yacht *Almy* to visit family, anchoring at Newport Harbor along with Gerry's *Electra* and the Goelet brothers' yachts, the *Beatrice* and the *Norseman.* The extended families dined and partied between their various yachts and their summer cottages. Their children, cousins who were now young adults, shared pastimes like coaching, beach picnics, dances, and in 1893 to everyone's delight, a new *Gilded Age* sport was introduced to Newport which threatened to overshadow tennis.

Theodore Havemeyer, a wealthy sportsman whose family owned the *American Sugar Company,* played a new game while on a trip to France in 1889; it was called golf. He convinced his Newport friends, Robert Goelet, John Jacob Astor, Perry Belmont and the Vanderbilt brothers, to purchase the 140 acre *Rocky Farm* overlooking *Brenton Point* for $80,000 to establish a golf club in the summer of 1893. A nine-hole golf course was designed by William Davis, the club's first professional, and later expanded to eighteen holes in 1915. The nearby *Bateman Hotel* was rented as a clubhouse but the members wanted their own building for relaxing and entertaining friends. Whitney Warren, the son of a millionaire financier, just back from studying architecture in Paris, was commissioned by his brother-in-law Robert Goelet to design and build the *Newport Country Club.* When the Y-shaped, wood-and-shingle building was completed in 1895 the *New York Times* wrote that "it stood supreme in magnificence among golf clubs, not only in America, but in the world." Warren moved on to become one of the most decorated architects in history, partnering with Charles Wetmore to design New York's *Grand Central Terminal* and the *New York Yacht Club* in Manhattan.[38]

Ogden Goelet managed to take the spotlight in Newport twice over the course of the summer. First, while his yacht the *Norseman* was entered in regattas and races, Ogden Goelet leased the English steam yacht *Whyte Ladye* just after its nineteen day passage from Cowes, England to Newport. The owner of the *Whyte Ladye* was none other than Lillie Langtry, nicknamed the *Jersey Lilly* by the artist Sir John Everett Millais, who painted her portrait in 1878 in which she held a lily that grew on her native Channel Island, Jersey. She was painted and photographed often, described as the most beautiful woman in the world. She was high spirited with a kindness that disarmed hostility and almost dispelled jealousy. In the Victorian era "professional beauties" were honored in high society and sought after by artists who sold their likeness on postcards. She captured the attention of the royal household in England and became the most famous mistress of the *Prince of Wales,* Edward Albert, who was known to friends as "Bertie." The *Prince of Wales* was a close personal friend of Ogden Goelet and he knew both Robert

Goelet and Commodore Gerry. The Prince had dinner on the Goelet yacht when they were in port in Cowes, England, as well as at the Goelets' *Wimbourne House* in London. While the Gerrys met royalty, it was the Goelets who socialized with the Prince year-round, particularly on the *French Riviera* at Nice during the winter yacht season. Lillie Langtry's affair with Prince Bertie lasted three years from 1877 to 1880. Afterward they maintained a life-long friendship during which he and his wife Princess Alexandra encouraged and supported Lillie's theater career.[39] Over her lifetime Lillie had many affairs, two marriages and one child, a daughter who was raised as her niece to protect the father, the nephew of the Prince of Wales.

Lillie lived in America between 1882 and 1888 during which time she owned a California horse ranch, a winery, and a New York theatre until it burned down. Her American lover for several years was Frederic Gebhard who traveled with Lillie on her American theatre tours in her private Pullman railroad car. He even bought a ranch next to hers in California where they spent their happiest days together. Frederic Gebhard was a personal friend of the Gallatins, Goelets and Gerrys, and was a member of the same social clubs in *Gilded Gotham,* including the Tuxedo Club of New York where horse lovers shared their love of country life. Frederick brought Lillie Langtry to all the high society affairs when she was in New York City. She became an American citizen to obtain a divorce from her estranged husband, Edward Langtry, who adamantly refused to divorce her in England. Although she had promised to marry Gebhard after the divorce Lillie still refused to marry him. He broke off their relationship in 1890 which led Lillie to return to London to visit old friends and family.

Shortly after her return to England, she developed an interest in horse racing at *Newmarket* in Suffolk, sixty-five miles north of London, which is considered the birthplace of thoroughbred racing. While at *Newmarke*t, Lillie Langtry met the brash George Baird, a Scottish millionaire who owned a stable of thoroughbreds. He was an obsessively jealous and brutal man, who beat Lillie frequently, but would pay her 5,000 pounds in remorse money, with which she bought her own thoroughbreds. In the autumn of 1891, George Baird, known as "The Squire," went up to Scotland for the annual races at Ayr and the shooting season. Lillie returned to London and met up with Robert Peel who had fallen for her, just like every other man who met the international beauty. He persuaded her to go off to Paris with him which gave Lillie the opportunity to shop in the *Paris Fashion Houses* at Peel's expense. When "The Squire" got back to London and found Lillie had gone off to Paris, he immediately went in pursuit. He beat her so severely that she ended up in the hospital for two weeks. To the utter amazement of everyone, she refused to press charges and George was released from jail. He tried to make peace with Lillie Langtry with a promised inheritance and by spending 50,000 pounds to build her a yacht, which she named the *Whyte Ladye,* but to her friends it was known as the *Black Eye.*[40] The *Whyte Ladye* was thoroughly equipped, 204 feet in length and 693 tons, and built especially for long ocean cruises. She had a spacious deckhouse with saloon and chart room, with the principal accommodations below that included a drawing room, dining room, and several luxurious staterooms. The yacht was lighted by electricity and heated by a hot-water system in the winter. In the summer blowing machines kept rooms below deck cool by forcing air over tons of ice and pushing it through the yacht's ventilation system. The *Whyte Ladye* was operated by a crew of thirty.

Lillie sailed the Mediterranean for months on end when not touring with her theatre company. In the winter of 1893 she sailed to Nice for the yacht season on the *Riviera* where she socialized with the Ogden Goelets, the Perry Belmonts, and Lillie's intimate friend, Bertie, the Prince of Wales. While she was in Nice her lover, George Baird, a boxing enthusiast, went to America to contribute money to sponsor a fight between Gentleman Jim Corbett and John L. Sullivan. He also bet heavily on his own fighter, Jem Hall, who lost his fight to Bob Fitzsimmons. The loss sent George Baird into a rage and a round of drinking in all the New Orleans night spots. His constitution was already weakened by a life of debauchery and he was seized with a debilitating chill and was dead within two days; he was only thirty-one years old. Baird's estate was valued at almost a million pounds, none of which went to Lillie Langtry, the woman he professed to love. However, the *Whyte Ladye* was hers to keep. Her elite social circles on both sides of the Atlantic shared her passionate interest in horses and yachts, so after the death of her lover, George Baird, Lillie Langtry left Nice for America and steamed her schooner into Newport for the summer season, desperately in need of money.

In Newport Lillie was among friends and admirers including her friend and that of the Prince of Wales, Ogden Goelet. In mid-July Ogden offered to lease the *Whyte Ladye* from Lillie for a few months with an option to purchase if he found it suitable. Indeed, the yacht was considered one of the finest steam yachts to come over from England and after about six months, Ogden Goelet purchased the yacht and happily cruised the oceans of the world for the next five years. In 1897 he sold the *Whyte Ladye to* Mr. John L. Johnstone at Cowes, England when the grand yacht, the *Mayflower,* was launched from Glasgow, Scotland and delivered to Ogden Goelet at Cowes.[41] Coincidentally, Mr. John L. Johnstone had just purchased the Prince of Wales' yacht, *Britannia,* only to discover that the Prince would not allow her to ever be raced in England. It was then that Mr. John L.

Johnstone immediately sold the *Britannia* and replaced her with the *Whyte Ladye,* the yacht that had belonged to the Prince of Wales' mistress, Lillie Langtry.

The second spotlight on Ogden Goelet in the summer of 1893 was centered on the new fad of deep sea fishing which he decided to try. When the mackerel were running off Newport in a manner that made the professional fisherman excited, Ogden gave the Master of his newly leased yacht, the *Whyte Ladye,* an order to fit up the yacht for a fishing excursion. Newport's fishermen heard of Mr. Goelet's unusually large purchase of bait and tackle and through selfish motives became indignant, but the fish dealers were surprised when Ogden Goelet returned with several thousand big, fat mackerel aboard his yacht, all of which he divided among the fish mongers. It was an odd piece of charity which made Ogden immensely popular among Newport's working citizens.[42]

By late July, the Gallatin family, Elbridge's sister Almy and her husband Frederic, were preparing their yacht the *Almy* at Tebo's Yard for a trip north. On July 31 they steamed to Bay Ridge and anchored there until Mr. Gallatin and his guests went aboard. All six of the Gallatin children were along for the voyage, Almy 25, Rolaz 22, Jean 20, Goelet 16, Albert 14, and Mary 11 years old. The yacht *Almy* was issued her papers from the Custom House and steamed out of port on August 1. Her first stop was *Buzzard's Bay Head* where President Grover Cleveland, Secretary of War Lamont, and a number of capitalists boarded the yacht for a two-day cruise. During this private cruise the elite group of men spent hours discussing the nation's financial situation. In the last days of President Benjamin Harrison's administration, the *Reading Railroad,* a major eastern line, went into receivership due to overbuilding and under financing just as most other railroads had done. That collapse was followed by the failures of hundreds of banks and businesses dependent upon the railroads. The stock market reacted with a dramatic plunge, and fearing further economic collapse, European investors pulled their funds from the United States. Depression gripped the United States and more than four million people were left unemployed.[43] President Grover Cleveland was inaugurated just as the public panic to withdraw money from the banks exploded and the nation's gold reserve dropped below $100 million. The panic of 1893 forced President Cleveland to borrow $65 million from JP Morgan, not unlike bailouts in the world-wide financial meltdown in 2008, only it was the government bailing out the bankers in modern times. As a director of a major national bank in New York City, Frederic Gallatin was able to gather the *Gilded Gotham* financiers, men like JP Morgan, August Belmont and Henry Villard on his yacht *Almy,* to provide counsel and advice to President Cleveland. The economy did not begin to recover until 1897 when the *Klondike*

Gold Rush helped to restore confidence in the economy, which was followed by ten years of rapid growth. After the financiers departed the yacht *Almy* the Gallatin family proceeded to Montreal, Canada, for a one month cruise to St. John's, Newfoundland and along the coast of Greenland.[44]

On August 16, 1893 at the close of the *New York Yacht Club's* annual cruise a celebration and dinner was held in Newport, Rhode Island to honor Commodore Elbridge T. Gerry at the successful completion of his seven years as the glorious leader of the yacht Club. Of the many yachting trophies and cups of nautical design made by Tiffany & Company, none was thought more beautiful than the testimonial cup designed for Commodore Gerry. The inscription on the silver cup is the tribute:

THE NEW YORK YACHT CLUB
To
ELBRIDGE T. GERRY

In recognition of his services as Commodore from 1886 to 1892

The testimonial is in the form of a Roman loving cup, with two handles entwined with clinging sea urchins and seaweed. There is a cover upon which is surmounted in exquisite workmanship the figure of Victory, rising fully 8 inches above the lid, making the total height of the cup 24 inches. The figure is in a graceful pose with shapely limbs and stands balanced on her right foot, the left arm raised above her head, the right arm outstretched toward the laurel wreath held in her other hand. Upon the front body of the cup is an etching of Mr. Gerry's stream yacht *Electra*. For those not able to join in the celebration, and for the pleasure of New York Society, a picture of the *Gerry Cup* was printed in the New York Times along with the article describing the presentation ceremony.[45]

The next day on August 17 the summer tranquility at *Lyndenhurst* cottage was disrupted for the Gerry family when diamond jewelry was discovered missing from Angelica Gerry's bedroom. Miss Margaret Limbeck had been employed as the personal maid to the Commodore's eldest daughter while in Europe in June 1893, just two months earlier. Miss Limbeck had raised herself from the position of a cook to that of maid while serving with credit in aristocratic families in England. She had advertised for a position in America while employed with Lady Jane Douglass in London, England, which is where Mrs. Louisa Gerry reviewed Margaret Limbeck's references, interviewed her and offered her employment. Miss Limbeck returned on the steamship to America with the Gerrys. She had packed Angelica's things for the trip and specifically chose to hide the boxed diamond jewelry in the sleeves of Ms. Gerry's dresses. The family immediately went to Newport where Ms. Limbeck worked as Angelica's maid for the next two months. On the day of the robbery, Margaret Limbeck was noted to be away from the *Lyndenhurst* cottage between three and four o'clock and said she actually saw some of the little boxes that held the jewelry in the sleeves of the dresses after the robbery had been reported. When told of the robbery she denied emphatically that she had taken any of the jewels or had knowledge as to who stole them or when. Commodore Gerry observed at the time that silver and valuable items in the same bedroom had not been taken or disturbed and suggested that the police be notified. There were no accusations, only an investigation for the first week. On August 20 a policeman arrived at *Lyndenhurst* and was greeted by Commodore Gerry who asked if he could help, but the policeman simply asked for Miss Limbeck. The policeman overheard Miss Limbeck asking the Commodore who the man was because she did not wish to be kidnapped. He reassured her that he was a local policeman that he personally knew. Miss Limbeck then left by carriage for the police station in Newport where she was detained for a two hour interview and statement after which she was returned to the Gerry cottage by carriage. Although Miss Limbeck was not accused by Commodore Gerry of taking the jewels, nor did he press charges, she left his employ due to the humiliation of the circumstances. Shortly thereafter, Margaret Limbeck sued Commodore Gerry for false arrest and false imprisonment because she claimed that she did not want to go to the police station to testify but was made to believe she had to accompany the police officer. She asked for $50,000 damages in a two year courtroom drama that put the case on the front page of the papers in New York City and across the country. In February 1896 the jury finally returned a verdict that fully cleared Commodore Elbridge T. Gerry of any wrong-doing and, in fact, he was considered a gentleman to have not pressed charges in a robbery that was never solved while also paying Miss Limbeck double wages when she left Newport to assist her return to England.[46]

No sooner had Commodore Gerry completed the *NYYC* retirement celebration and endured robbery of his cottage in Newport than one of the worst storms in history tore apart much of the east coast of the United States, ravaging the cotton and tobacco interests of Georgia. People drowned in North Carolina, Maryland, and Virginia, where communications were disrupted. Trains running from Washington, D.C. to New York City were seven to twenty-four hours late. When the full force of the storm reached New York City boats were tossed about the Hudson River, trees fell throughout the city, a tornado swept across Coney

Island, piers were washed away and some houses were destroyed in Brooklyn. Clearly the NYYC was concerned about the fate of the various schooners in their yacht fleet. The yacht *Vigilant* was pushed so hard by the gale that she drug her anchors and came near going on the rocks at New Rochelle, but was pulled from harm's way with the assistance of two tugs and was not seriously damaged. Word was received that the yacht *Priscilla* had gone ashore in the fog near *Watch Hill.* The *Priscilla* was on her way from New Haven, Connecticut to Newport, Rhode Island. The yacht fired her guns in distress and life-saving boats arrived to carry the crew of seven to safety. The wrecking boat *Scott* left the next morning with tugs and derricks to assist the *Priscilla* which lay on the sand and would be difficult to put afloat. The great storm was expected to reach the *Priscilla* within twelve hours and they feared she would be torn to pieces. The storm blew across Newport while the Gerrys were still at the *Lyndenhurst* cottage. The wind first blew from the southeast and kicked up a very heavy sea that washed across the roadway by the beach and far up the rocky shores, which were lined with spectators. But the startling news circulating around the summer colony was that John Jacob Astor's huge steam yacht *Nourmahaul* was crashed against the *Blue Rocks* of Fort Greene, which is in the upper Newport Harbor. A reception and sail were to be given during the afternoon and evening aboard Astor's yacht, but the storm prevented guests from boarding and so an attempt was made to move the yacht to *Long Wharf.* Her anchor had been dropped but the wind was too powerful and she was soon upon the ragged rocks a distance from the *Wharf.* The harbor tug *Aquidneck* and two other tugs were soon to the rescue and in two and half hours the *Nourmahaul* was safely docked at *Long Wharf* and her guests were brought aboard for the planned evening entertainments. Numerous stories as to the yacht's injuries were circulating but ex-Commodore Gerry, who boarded her shortly after she went ashore, denied that any perceptible injury had been done. There was talk of nothing else until the summer colonists ended their leisurely holidays in Newport and returned to New York City. The great storm passed but left behind many sad stories and incalculable damage in all the harbors and cities along the entire eastern seaboard.[47]

The fall of 1893 welcomed some new excitement that helped the citizens of New York City look beyond the jarring close of their otherwise warm summer months. There would be a *World's Fair* held in the United States with every state in the country participating in some way. Mayor Gilroy appointed an *Executive Committee,* including Commodore Gerry, to oversee plans for New York City's participation in the *1893 Columbian Exposition* named for the 400th anniversary of Columbus' discovery of the New World, but popularly known as the *Chicago*

World's Fair. A meeting of the *Executive Committee* was called on October 13 to finalize plans that had William H. McDonough, the Mayor's confidential clerk, leaving immediately for Chicago with instructions to make the necessary on-site arrangements, and Mayor Gilroy was to follow in a week to greet New York delegations as they arrived in Chicago. At the meeting, the committee requested that bronze medals be ordered for members of the committee, and silk badges for excursionists who would travel to Chicago to celebrate *Manhattan Day.* Commodore Gerry had also issued fancy medals for committee members and special guests at the *Washington Centennial* in 1889. The committee was given the free use of *Festival Hall* in Chicago for the celebration. Each member of the Executive Committee contributed $100 toward the costs of decorating *Festival Hall* and purchasing the medals and ribbons. The Mayor's *Railroad Committee* issued a schedule giving the time of departure of the trains for which tickets cost $15 for the round trip, New York to Chicago and back, which left on October 21 and returned on October 23 or 24. Those who desired sleeping accommodations had to travel by regular trains. The Gerrys did not travel to Chicago for the *Exposition* but Commodore Gerry worked tirelessly to ensure the *Manhattan Day* celebrations were well planned and represented only the best of New York City.[48] Indeed, Mayor Gilroy and his wife and daughter returned from their trip to the *Chicago World's Fair* on October 27. The next morning, the Mayor was in his office by 10 o'clock and said that he had enjoyed his eight day trip immensely. "So far as *Manhattan Day* was concerned," said the Mayor, "I think that the people of New York have reason to feel proud of its observance at the *World's Fair.* The weather was perfect and everything went off without a hitch."[49] There were between 60,000 and 70,000 New Yorkers at the *Fair* and the Mayor expressed his gratitude that so many citizens made the trip. The committee had one last task to accomplish, which was to plan a few fund raisers to pay for the outstanding costs for *Manhattan Day.* The committee had raised $10,000 but the full cost of the excursion and the Chicago site expenses totaled $20,000. With Commodore Elbridge T. Gerry leading the charge, the money was raised within a reasonable time ensuring only happy memories of *Manhattan Day* at the 1893 *Chicago World's Fair.*

In 1891 sculptor Antonin Adams was commissioned by the United States Senate to create a marble bust of founding father, Vice President Elbridge Gerry. The bust was completed and installed in the chamber of the United States Senate In July 1892.

Old Supreme courtroom (*above*) on the second floor of the U.S. Capitol (*below*)

A MOST
EXCITING
PHASE OF
"THE AMERICAN MONTE CRISTO"
In Next Sunday's Journal.

NEW YORK
Morning Journal.
Largest Circulation of any Paper in New York and Vicinity.

"THE RUSSIAN WEDDING."
WITH NEXT SUNDAY'S JOURNAL.

WEDNESDAY, FEBRUARY 5, 1890. PRICE ONE CENT.

THE UNITED STATES "NINE."

Centennial Celebration of the Founding of the Supreme Court.

Judges Delivering Opinions Without Objections—Lawyers Talking Without Fee and Feeding at Their Own Expense—Other Marvels on Top Yesterday.

Commodore Elbridge T. Gerry celebrated the Centennial of the founding of the United States Supreme Court with the Bar of the City of New York at the Metropolitan Opera House. The Chief Justice and Associate Justices, in their robes, were honored with speeches and fine food. The day closed with an evening banquet at the Lenox Lyceum where former President Grover Cleveland presided over the festive dinner banquet.

Current Supreme courtroom (*above*) on the first floor of the Supreme Court building (*below*)

Captain Philippe d'Orleans

Emily Post

Richard Morris Hunt

Ochre Court in Newport

R. M. Hunt was Ogden Goelet's architect for his 50-room mansion, Ochre Court in Newport, Rhode Island which was completed in 1891. Hunt was then commissioned by Commodore and Louisa Gerry in 1892 to build them a mansion on Fifth Avenue in New York City at the same time George Vanderbilt commissioned Hunt to build his great estate, Biltmore, in North Carolina.

Entry gate

Great Hall (*left*)

Grand staircase

Ballroom

In 1891 Louisa Gerry purchased one half of the block on Fifth Avenue and the Metropolitan Club purchased the other half with the 60th Street corner lot going to the Club and the 61st corner lot going to the Gerrys.

Entry to the Metropolitan Club on 60th Street at Fifth Avenue

Metropolitan Club grand staircase

Metropolitan Club library

Lillie Langtry (1853-1929), mistress of Prince Edward Albert, sold her yacht *Whyte Ladye* to Robert Goelet.

Whyte Ladye

"Bertie"
Prince Edward Albert
King Edward VII

Bon Air Hotel
Augusta,
Georgia

The last holiday the Gerrys took with Lilly the year of her death was to Georgia for warmer air for Lilly's health.

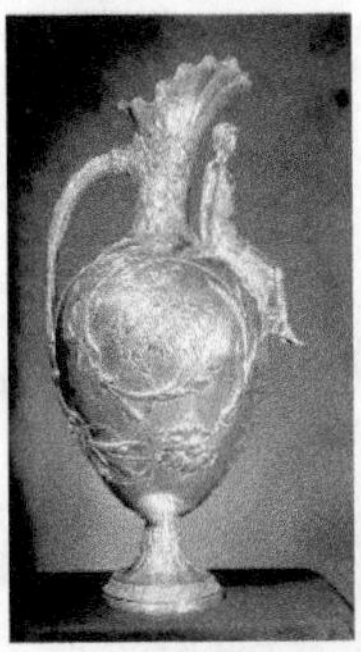

Gerry Cup
Awarded to New York Yacht Club race winners

(*Below*) Lyndenhurst Cottage Bellevue Avenue, Newport, Rhode Island

After Lilly's death the Gerry family decided to go to Newport for the first of many summers; they were near Robert and Ogden Goelet, their close extended family circle.

NYYC Commodore
1886-1892

The Gerry family found privacy for their mourning on board *Electra*, far away from New York. (*Below*) *Harper's Weekly* sketch of Commodore Gerry overseeing a yacht race from *Electra* platform

The Atlantic Salmon Federation

Francis Goelet, as the founder of the Federation in 1969, was admitted to the Joe Cullman Hall of Fame where fifty sculptures are hung to honor those who have made notable contributions to saving wild Atlantic salmon from extinction. The portrait sculptures are all hand-carved in South American mahogany.

In 1880 Robert Goelet in particular, but also Ogden Goelet, were founding members of the *Salmon Fishing Club* in Quebec, Canada called the *Restigouche Salmon Club*. The love of salmon fishing has been carried on through the generations, with Robert's grandson, Francis, the most passionate salmon fisherman in the Goelet family.

The estate of Francis Goelet continues as a major donor.

Francis Goelet
1926 – 1998

Stanford White (*above*)

A founding member of the *Salmon* club, he was also the architect of the *Restigouche* club house (*right*).

Fishing on the Restigouche River

Whitney Warren
1864-1943

Robert Goelet married Whitney Warren's sister, Harrietta, an artist in her own right.
The Goelets commissioned Whitney to design and build a golf club in Newport, Rhode Island.

Newport Golf Club

Grand Central Station

One of Whitney Warren's greatest architectural achievements in New York City

The adult Gerry children pursued sports and social entertainment with their own circle of friends; here Peter, Angelica and Robert enjoy their passion for horses.

Mabel seated in right rear of carriage behind smiling Angelica at the whip.

Above left, Robert, Peter, and Mabel entertain cousins May Goelet, Gladys Mills, Beatrice Mills and Ogden Mills at Lake Delaware on front veranda.

Above right, Robert and Peter have male pals visit at Lake Delaware in 1902.

10

GILDED GOTHAM

THE 1890'S PART II

Every great architect is, necessarily, a great poet. He must be a great original interpreter of his time, his day, his age.
Frank Lloyd Wright (1867–1959)

G*ilded Gotham* danced from 1893 into 1894 amid the glamour of the annual fancy balls. The grand ladies of society proudly hosted the *Matriarchs' Ball* on December 21 in the ballroom of the new *Sherry Hotel* where several dinners, each with its own hostess, were held before the late night dance. The ball room was decorated in floral Christmas displays and the midnight cotillion was led by a popular new bachelor, J. Wadsworth Ritchie. Just two weeks later in early 1894 he was once again honored when asked to lead the cotillion at the popular *Bachelors' Ball.* The young Mr. Ritchie even introduced new "figures" or dance steps to the eager debutantes, which included twenty-two year old Angelica Gerry. It was at these formal winter dances that she met the eligible bachelor and discovered they shared a passion for horses and coaching. Also in January the *Knickerbocker Riding Club* was organized and sponsored ten indoor rides with plans to find a permanent building for regular meets. Almy Gerry Gallatin's twenty-year old son, Horace was also a member of this riding club. Other groups of interest, the *Theatre Club* and the *Music Club,* were places where the now adult *dudes* and *Sophy Sparkles* could interact and get to know each other beyond the formal constraints of the ballroom. By now, the Gerry and Goelet parents often attended separate entertainments from their adult children, indeed, while *Gilded Gotham* danced in the New Year 1894, Ogden Goelet was in Nice, France on his yacht the *Whyte Ladye,* where he was soon joined by his brother-in-law Mr. Cornelius Vanderbilt III and his wife, Grace Wilson the sister of Mary Wilson, Mrs. Ogden Goelet. The social season on the Continent was in full swing where the usual suspects from across Europe like Prince Edward and Lilly Langtry enjoyed the *Riviera* galas and yacht cruises.

The Gerry family was the center of *Gilded Gotham* gossip during the entire month of March, made all the more fascinating since their mansion on Fifth Avenue was in the last few months of completion and everyone was eager to tour the interior. The three Gerry sisters had been introduced to society just months before Lilly's death and shortly before Robert J. Livingston's death. The family was thrown into such a deep and lengthy mourning, that Angelica and Mabel withdrew from society just as they had been introduced as debutantes in 1891. Their return to society in late 1893 was welcomed by eager bachelors since the Gerry girls were among the wealthiest single debutantes, highly educated, attractive and charming. One of Angelica's best friends, Edith Kip, shared the March spotlight with the Gerry family. Both young women were frequently rumored to be engaged but it was always denied. Then in March 1894 the formal announcement of both engagements were made by each family. Commodore and Mrs. Gerry released the announcement of Angelica's engagement to J. Wadsworth Ritchie, known as "Jack," on Sunday, March 24 and in the London papers on March 25. The Gerrys hosted at least one gala dinner per week in March. One gala was an engagement dinner for Edith Kipp, the daughter of Lorillard Kipp. The townhouse was decorated with an elaborate display of vases, candle sticks and dinnerware in sterling silver, strikingly offset with an abundance of red roses. Angelica was a private person even as she was an avid and well known horse woman, so Louisa held three smaller, more intimate dinners in March for Angelica and Jack to celebrate their engagement with close friends and family.

The society wedding of the season was celebrated on April 19, 1894 in which Angelica Gerry was a bridesmaid to her dear friend, Edith Kip, the only daughter of Col. and Mrs. Lawrence Kip. The groom was Richard McCreary of London, who was a well-known coaching whip in Paris, Hamburg, and New York City. Angelica's circle of friends was consistently filled with horse lovers. Like many brides of the season, Miss Kip choose a color theme for the wedding which was blue, so a profusion of blue flowers filled the chancel and draped the aisles of *Grace Church.* J. P. Morgan's daughter Mary was also a bridesmaid with Angelica; each wore blue and white gowns with hats of ecru straw, trimmed with black ostrich tips, and blue scarfs. They carried parasols presented to them by the bride, each finished with thin gold handles and bearing the monogram of the bridesmaid and the date of the wedding. The reception was held at the home of the bride's parents at which guests whispered about the unpleasant incident of Mr. Richard Dana, a guest whose pocket was picked while standing in the crowd outside *Grace*

Church. After the reception the newlyweds, Mr. and Mrs. McCreary, sailed for London, England, where they made their permanent home.[1]

Commodore and Mrs. Gerry had busy schedules the first few months of 1894 when Louisa Gerry was preoccupied with designs for the new house on Fifth Avenue. Commodore Gerry became a *Patron* of the *American Museum of Natural History* on February 7 with the payment of $1,000, giving him membership in perpetuity with the right to appoint a successor. Museum patrons could attend exclusive programs without charge, share behind-the-scenes tours, and attend advance previews of new exhibitions, educational pastimes that the entire Gerry family shared with friends while supporting a significant New York cultural institution.

On April 21 Commodore Gerry, as President of the *New York Society for the Prevention of Cruelty to Children,* was one of the honored guests and speakers at the unveiling of the Cushing bronze statue of Father John Drumgoole, known as the un-canonized saint of New York's nameless newsboys. He was born in Ireland in 1816 and came to America at age eight and worked for years as a cobbler's assistant to support his mother, later becoming the janitor and sexton at St. Mary's Church for twenty-one years during which time he sheltered the homeless in the basement. Not until age fifty-two, after his mother was settled with a family, was he able to enter the priesthood. He was assigned to his old parish in New York City where Father Drumgoole immediately took over the *Newsboys Shelter* that expanded over the next twenty years to become the ten-story *Mission of the Immaculate Virgin* at Lafayette Place and Great Jones Street, which cared for over 20,000 homeless children under Fr. Drumgoole's leadership. He died at age seventy-two in 1888, leaving such a legacy that an estimated 100,000 people paid their respects at the *Mission* and at *Saint Patrick's Cathedral* where his funeral was held on Easter Sunday. A dear friend of Father Drumgoole was sculptor Robert Cushing, one of America's earliest and most successful sculptors. Robert Cushing created the marble bust of President Millard Fillmore that stands in the *United States Capital* and that of Cardinal McCloskey which stands in *Saint Patrick's Cathedral* in New York City. Robert Cushing worked at a studio at 44 West Thirtieth Street just off Broadway, in a weather-beaten, old style three story wooden building with a café on the ground floor. In March 1896, just three years after completing his last large public work, the Drumgoole bronze, a sign was hung on the door of his studio, one flight up, with a hand written note saying "called away by an important engagement. Back at 3 p.m. tomorrow. Robert Cushing." Visitors did not call again, for Robert Cushing's engagement was with death. He had left his studio to go to *Saint Vincent's Hospital* expecting to be able to return the next day but heart trouble, combined with other ailments, quickly overcame Robert Cushing at age 55, who otherwise, was still vital and in a productive period of his life.[2] In his ten-foot tall bronze statue, Cushing depicted a group of three figures intended to portray the life and teachings of Father Drumgoole, the Priest in the middle, who trained the young child on his right side, who became the adult holding a book on his left side. At the time of the unveiling, Pope Leo XIII sent a letter to Father James J. Dougherty, the successor to Father Drumgoole, in which the Pontiff bestowed his benediction upon all those who resided in the *Mission of the Immaculate Virgin,* those present at the ceremony and all members of *Saint Joseph's Union* who commissioned the statue. In his remarks at the ceremony, Commodore Gerry said that Father Drumgoole continued to live among us on earth through his good works as certainly as he lives with Our Lord in Heaven. Commodore Gerry and Father Drumgoole were well acquainted through their shared endeavors to save the unprotected children on the streets of *Gilded Gotham.* Ten thousand people gathered for the tribute speech by Archbishop O'Brien and when he rose to speak one of the priests shouted, "Three cheers for the Archbishop," to which the great throng, the priests and Commodore Gerry rose and joined in loud applause. The crowd pressed forward to get a glimpse of the bronze statue of Father John Drumgoole the un-canonized patron saint of Gotham's homeless, orphans, and the poor.[3]

Most of the elite society women of the *Gilded Age* held wealth in their own right, primarily from inheritance from parents or a deceased husband. All of the Gerry, Gallatin and Goelet women held inherited wealth in their own right prior to marriage. Therefore, both before and after their marriages they were all involved in property transactions under their own name, even if handled by a lawyer, a father, or a husband on their behalf. Commodore Elbridge T. Gerry handled law suits on behalf of his mother, Hannah Goelet, and his mother-in-law, Louisa Livingston, during their lifetimes, which usually involved landlord-tenant controversies. When Louisa Livingston died she made it clear in her will that her daughter was to inherit and retain all property and income in her own right, even if she married. In turn, Louisa Gerry put the same restrictive language in her will to protect her daughters should they marry. Just as Louisa Livingston had purchased the New Jersey estate in Highland Park, and contracted to have the house built, so did her daughter Louisa purchase the Fifth Avenue at Sixty-First Street property and contract with Richard Morris Hunt to design and build her home. All signatures on the blue prints for the mansion read *Elbridge T. Gerry, Esq. on behalf of Louisa M. Gerry, owner.* The architectural correspondence between Louisa Gerry and Richard M. Hunt related to the placement of rooms and architectural details, while the mechanical decisions were left to Commodore Gerry and the architect. Elbridge and Louisa put to good use the advice and experience gained first-hand from their cousins, Robert and Ogden Goelet, who over the past several years had built their luxury townhouses in the City and their summer mansions in Newport and had incorporated the advanced electrical and mechanical systems of the day.

The local papers followed the Gerry property transactions with interest, not only the new mansion next to the *Metropolitan Club,* also under construction, but a second piece of property just two blocks south at the corner of Fifth Avenue and Fifty-Eighth Street. Louisa Gerry owned two adjoining lots, one 75 feet by 100 feet on Fifth Avenue, and the other 25 feet by 100 feet on Fifty-Eighth Street. In October 1893 Louisa had leased the land to architect Alfred Zucker, with the lease to begin November 1893. There was much speculation about the plans for this prime piece of real estate until February 1894 when Alfred Zucker spoke to the press. He indicated that he intended to improve the property with a six-story luxury apartment building, and his lease was $35,000 a year for twenty-one years.[4] This was not the last project that Louisa had with Alfred Zucker who had clearly earned her confidence in his abilities sufficient for Louisa Gerry to hire him the following year as her own architect.

The Gerry mansion was constructed between the May 1892 first turn of the shovel to excavate the large parcel of land and September 1894 when the Gerry family first occupied their new home. The correspondence and blue prints, called linens, drafted and exchanged between the Gerrys and their architect, Richard M. Hunt, document the progress of the construction. The steel and stone shell of the mansion had been enclosed by January 1893 and the time agreed to by architect Hunt with his contractors to complete the interior construction and finishes was ten months, by October 1893. Unfortunately, the contractors were unable to meet the deadline and on October 3, 1893 the contract had to be extended another six months with a new completion date of April 1894. The intense correspondence between the Gerrys and Hunt and his contractors document a project that was chronically behind schedule with work that was often unsatisfactory. Additionally, the Gerrys would change a design feature mid-stream by either adding something new or changing the finish color, although the requests were only minor delays in the work schedule. Because the Gerry family had planned to move in to the house in the fall of 1893 or no later than January 1894, the first six month delay was disruptive to their personal and business plans for the spring and summer of 1894. They were to sail for Europe on May 16 with plans to have already moved out of their Forty-Eighth Street townhouse and all the storage and wine closets of the new mansion waiting when they returned from Europe to store their new cases of *Madeira* wine, trunks of Paris gowns, and cases of furnishings and artwork for the new mansion. With the potential delay, everything shipped back from Europe would have to be sent to the old house and moved a second time to the new mansion. It was up to architect Richard M. Hunt to get his contractors to move more quickly. Commodore Gerry wrote to Hunt on April 18, 1894 (the capitalization is his own):

> I invite your attention to the fact that NOTHING YET HAS BEEN DONE towards the finish of the BUTLER'S PANTRY. You will observe that the original time to have completed this contract was October 3, 1893: and you will find that six months additional time was allowed to complete the contract by April 5, 1894, and the distinct understanding is that after that date there was to be deducted from the contract a sum of $50 for each and every day occupied in the completion of the work beyond the deadline. What have you to say in defence? Very little, I fear.

The next day April 19, 1894 Gerry wrote to Hunt:

> Will you kindly hurry up and have completed as soon as possible the shelving in my Madeira closet, and also the shelving in the Wine Closet off the Dining Room. I am extremely anxious, if possible, before sailing home from Europe, to transport all my Madeira into the new house and lock it up, in order for the longest possible time may be given it to settle before there is a possibility of its use in the Fall.

Bottles of Madeira did arrive that fall from Europe, but they were not the only valuable bottles that the Commodore placed in the locked wine closet. He owned bottles of bourbon, brandy, cognac and scotch that had labels dating from 1811, 1820, and 1830 that were likely imported through his Uncle Peter Goelet's family business and housed in the old Broadway brownstone until 1894 when he removed his library and historic possessions to the new mansion. Many of these bottles were never opened and remain in the Gerry family wine cellars; however at least one bottle was opened in 2004 by the Commodore's grandson, Henry Gerry, who shared the brandy with his grand-son while telling old family stories.

The Gerrys sailed for Europe on May 16 as scheduled and decided that they would move into the new home, finished or not on Saturday, September 1, 1894, following a second six month extension to the contract. The anxious correspondence with their architect, Richard Morris Hunt, continued through the summer and into September. The last letter in the Hunt archive for the *Gerry Project*, dated October 2, 1894 after the Gerrys had moved in, was sent to Mr. Hand the primary contractor whose slow work was the source of the delays from start to finish:

> In reply to your letter of September 27, 1894 enclosing a bill from Sarre & Lellacheur for finishing and filling dresser in kitchen pantry, I have to say, as this work was done in strict violation of Mr. Gerry's edict, you will have to stand the expense yourself. I return their bill herewith. Your bill of September 24th for scaffolding for stone carvers and setters has been forwarded to James Sinclair & Co. who are responsible for this charge. Note that on Monday the 8th, a certificate for $50 will be issued in your favor for drawers for third story hall closet and drawers to closet for Boudoir, and will mail same to you on that date.[5]

The Library of the *American Institute of Architects* in Washington, D.C., houses the complete Richard Morris Hunt architectural archive, which includes all the correspondence and linen blue prints for the New York Gerry mansion project. One of the most important aspects of the house design was the incorporation of a grand law library space on the first floor off the main hall with double door access to the adjacent Picture Gallery at one end and the formal Dining Room on the other end. There were French Doors to an exterior patio on the private, east side of the residence. By this time in Commodore Gerry's life, his personal library exceeded 20,000 volumes and was still housed in the old *Broadway Farm* mansion at Nineteenth and Broadway where his 89 year old mother continued to live. The new mansion library was designed not only to conveniently house the enormous collection and provide access and work space for Commodore Gerry, but also to create an elegant space for entertaining in the midst of a fascinating display of rare and unique books within his extensive law collection. The nearly complete mansion occupied four floors of living space plus a full basement, a full cellar, and attic storage space. Unfortunately, the law library was one of the rooms that remained unfinished at the close of the Richard Morris Hunt contract in the fall of 1894.

The following linen floor plans are in the Library Archives of the *American Institute of Architects* in Washington, D.C. A bound personal set of the final floor plans for the New York mansion are in the possession of the Gerry family.[6]

The Gerry Mansion Floor Plans

North side backing onto *Metropolitan Club*

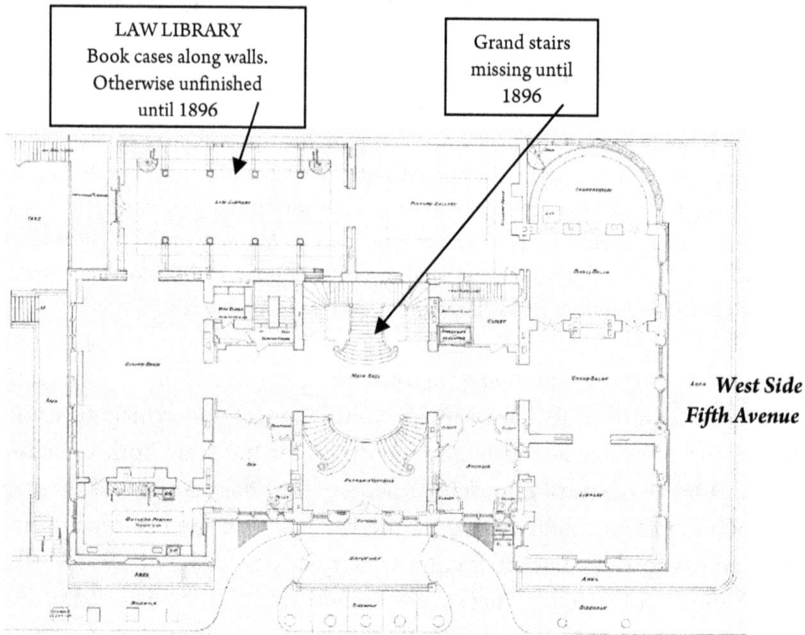

First Floor *Carriage way and formal entrance on Sixty-First Street*

South Side backed up to *Metropolitan Club*

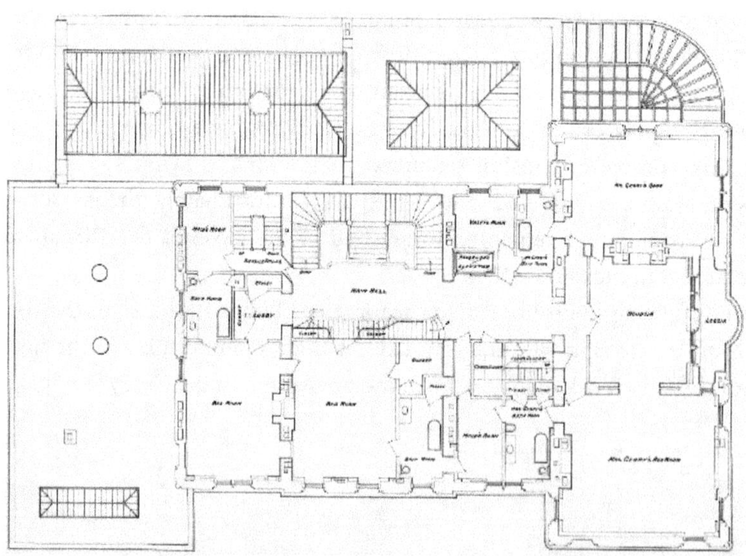

Second Floor *West end girls' bedrooms and parents' bedrooms which overlook Central Park across Fifth Ave.*

South Side backed up to *Metropolitan Club*

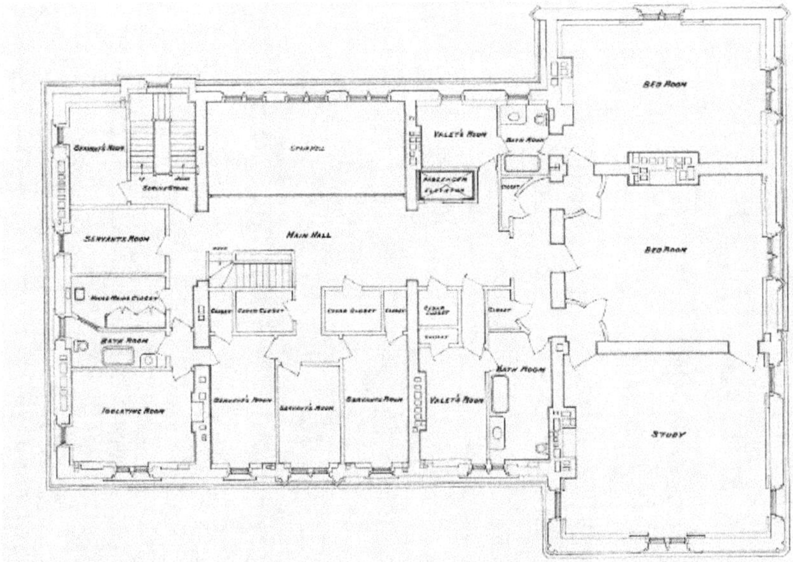

Central Park

Third Floor *West side facing Central Park, boys' bedrooms and study. On the east side is an innovative isolating room and nurse room. Servants' rooms off center hall.*

South Side backed up to *Metropolitan Club*

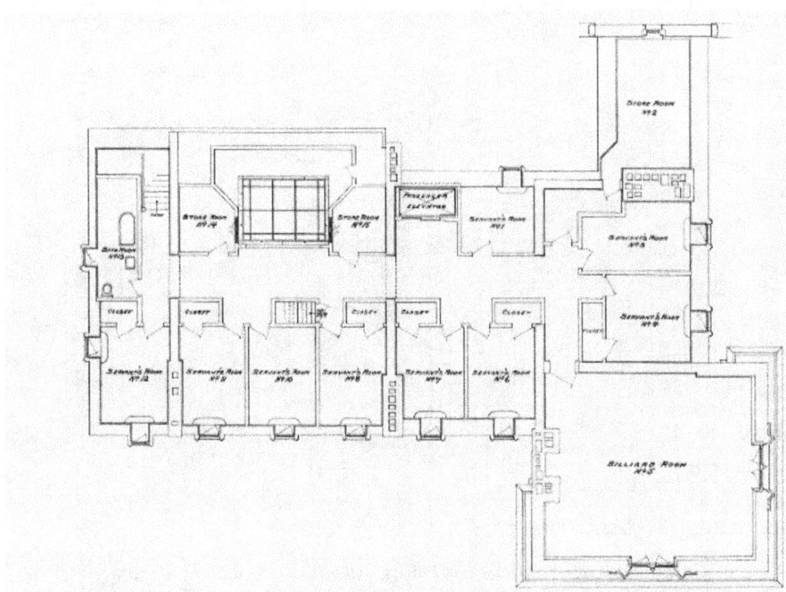

Fourth Floor *8 servants' bedrooms and bathroom and a corner family billiard room.*

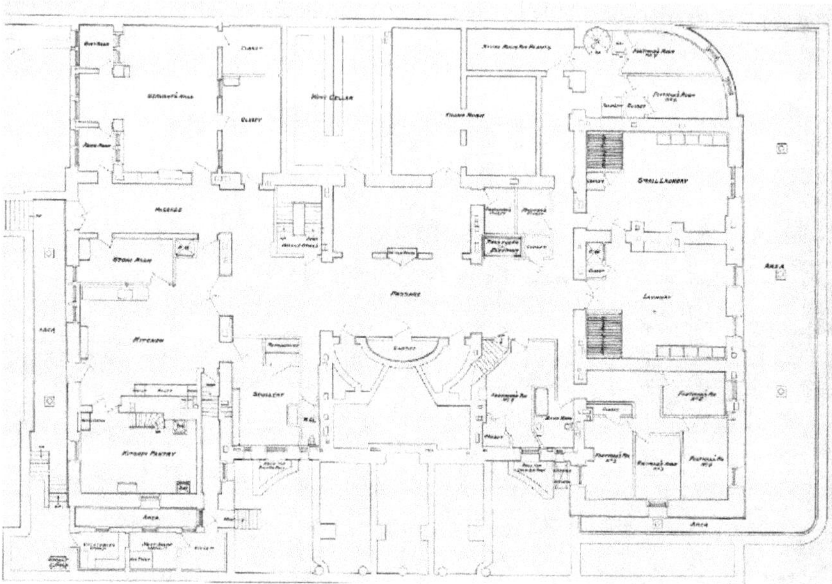

Basement *Servants congregating room, trunk storage room, wine cellar, kitchen and scullery, food storage, footman's bedrooms and bath, laundry, plant storage.*

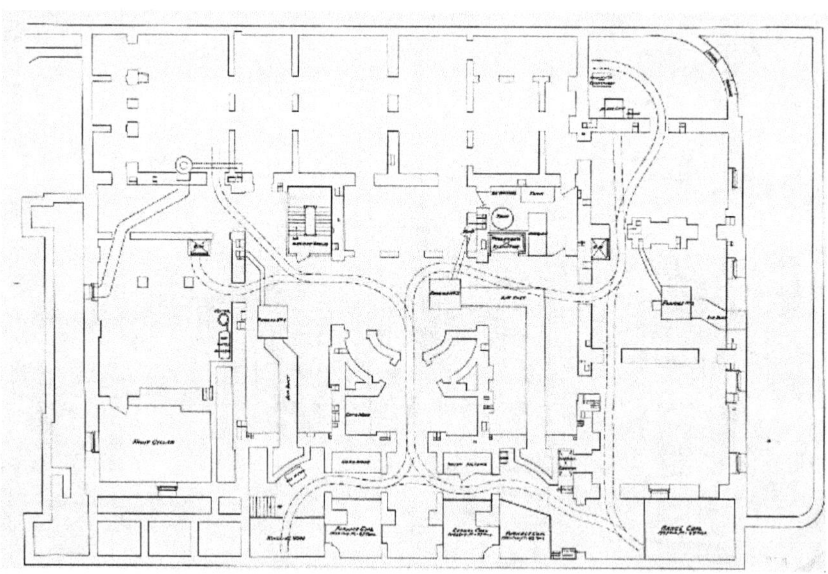

Cellar *Fruit cellar, furnace and boilers, water filter, wood and coal storage*

The plumbing in the Gerry mansion was so advanced that an article was published in 1894 by the *Engineering Record* illustrating the impressive system. The article read, in part, that the mansion was a large and costly building equipped with an ample provision of hot and cold water supply and abundant fixtures for the comforts and necessities of the domestic and toilet requirements. The pipe lines were all screw-connected and pressure-tested. The water supply was received through two 2-inch connections with street mains and was all filtered through a battery of four pressure filters, then pumped by electricity to a 4x6x8 foot attic tank which was intended to provide a day's storage and furnish uniform pressure. There was a complete system of trap and local ventilation and an abundant supply of hot water from several separate interchangeable attic and basement sources. The installation, which was executed by James Muir, Sons & Co., of New York City, comprised nine bathrooms, a butler's pantry, kitchen, scullery, and two laundries, together with metering, filtering, pumping, storing and heating apparatus, with its necessary machinery. The house had four water-closets, 10 washbowls, three slop sinks, one urinal, one sitz bath, two butler's sinks, a kitchen sink with special marble table, two sets of five earthenware wash trays, and two iron sinks for washing and drip drying. Most of the bathrooms had white tiled floors and walls with oak cabinet-work, but the boudoir bathroom was finished with rose-colored tiles, mosaic floor, and rosewood cabinet-work, the metal-work being of ornamental design, silver-plated, and the porcelain decorated in white. The bathtubs were of porcelain and enameled iron. Several switchboards located in each bathroom controlled the supply of hot and cold water to the different fixtures in the room. Offsets, intersections, and changes of direction were made by curving the plated brass pipe, so skillfully as to present a notably handsome and elegant appearance. Each double kitchen stove had a 60-gallon boiler that also supplied the radiator coil in the laundry room for five laundry tubs. The water consumed in this complex and extensive system was replaced by an automatic feed-water regulator furnished by the *Duparquet, Moneuse & Huot Company.*[7]

The Gerry mansion sat right on the sidewalk with one small yard on the east side of the house, accessible by stairs off an extended patio adjacent to the Dining Room and the Library, both of which had exterior French doors. The mansion's ornate masonry exterior was French Gothic in style and the entire structure was fireproof, built entirely with brick, marble and steel. Although a large townhouse and certainly a mansion, it was modest by comparison to the Gerrys' *Gilded Gotham* peers, like the Vanderbilt mansion a few blocks south on Fifth Avenue. The Gerrys lived here for over thirty years; both Elbridge and Louisa died in their family home.

Before the Gerry family set sail for Europe on May 16, 1894 Commodore Gerry had one more public celebration to attend. On Saturday, May 12 at 3 o'clock the much anticipated presentation by the citizens of New York of the bronze statue of *Christopher Columbus* was held at the Mall in *Central Park.* More than a decade had passed since an American, General James Grant Wilson, the *President of the New York Genealogical and Biographical Society,* strolling through the Plaza de Colon in Madrid, Spain came upon the superb marble statue of *Christopher Columbus.* He then and there resolved to have the same statue made in bronze for *Central Park.* After his return to America, General Wilson laid his plans before a number of prominent New Yorkers, including Mr. Cornelius Vanderbilt, Mr. August Belmont, Mr. William Waldorf Astor, and Mr. Elbridge T. Gerry, and enlisted their hearty interest as well as secured their money to initiate a drive to raise the fifteen thousand dollars to pay for the statue and pedestal. The statue was created by Spanish sculptor Jeronimo Sunol in commemoration of the *400th Anniversary of the Discovery of America.* The statue was placed at the edge of the Mall in *Central Park* opposite the statue of *Shakespeare,* and by having the pedestal designed in a similar size and material, the two statues harmonized. General Wilson presided over the ceremony which opened with a prayer by Dr. Henry C. Potter, Bishop of New York, followed by the unveiling of *Christopher Columbus* by the Vice President of the United States, Adlai Ewing Stevenson (1835-1914) and the acceptance of the statue on behalf of the citizens of New York, by Mayor Thomas F. Gilroy. A letter from the Duke of Veragua, the descendant of Christopher Columbus, was read by Cornelius Vanderbilt. The ceremony was capped by the reading of the poem, *A Mariner's Dream,* by Mrs. Julia Ward Howe, composed by her especially for the unveiling. Julia Ward Howe was born in New York City in 1819, the fourth child of banker Samuel Ward, and the granddaughter of William Greene (1731-1809) the Governor of Rhode Island. In 1843 she married Samuel G. Howe, a physician and reformer who founded the *Perkins School for the Blind* in Boston, MA. Her book of intensely personal poetry, *Passion Flowers,* was published in 1853 without her husband's knowledge. Julia Ward Howe was inspired to write *The Battle Hymn of the Republic* after she and her husband visited Washington, D.C. and met Abraham Lincoln at the White House in November 1861. During the trip a friend suggested she write new words to the Union Army's marching song *John Brown's Body,* written in 1856 by William Steffe, which Julia did within the month. Julia Ward Howe's version was first published in the *Atlantic Monthly* in February 1862 and quickly became the most popular song of the Union during the American Civil War. After the war she focused her activities on causes of pacifism and women's suffrage. In 1870 Howe established the tradition of celebrating *Mother's Day* with her *Mother's Day Proclamation.* After her husband's death in 1876, she focused more on her interests in reform. She was the founder and president of the *Association of American Women,* a group which advocated for women's education. After Julia Ward Howe's death at age 91 in 1910 at her home in Rhode Island, her children collaborated on a biography, published by Houghton Mifflin in 1916, *Julia Ward Howe,* which won the *Pulitzer Prize for Biography.*[8] The program committee for the unveiling ceremony of the *Christopher Columbus* statue selected Julia Ward Howe to write and present the poem, *A Mariner's Dream,* because she was the nation's poetess of the day, not unlike the twentieth century requests for Dr. Maya Angelou to write and present poetry at public ceremonies, like the inauguration of President William Jefferson Clinton in 1993. At the end of the *Christopher Columbus* ceremony the audience gathered at the base of the statue to admire its beauty. The celebrations came to a glittering close that evening at a dinner party given by ex-Mayor and Mrs. William H. Grace at their residence, 31 East Seventy-Ninth Street, at which the Vice President of the United States and the General Counsul of Spain, the Spanish Ambassador, and the Ambassador of Italy were honored guests.[9]

When the Gerry family returned from Europe they once again rented the *Lyndenhurst* house in Newport for the summer season, where the game of golf was now one of the most popular summer sports. The papers eagerly followed the lady golfers, the newest converts to the game. Mrs. Robert Goelet was the latest to play, and in July 1894 she joined the ranks of pupils at the Golf Club with the promise of becoming an expert. Mrs. Fulton Cutting, in her first season as a Newport cottager, also took her golf lessons with Mrs. Goelet. Within a few weeks they became friendly rival players and their contests attracted much attention at the Club. Other women who played golf well were Miss Winthrop, the best among the ladies, Louisa Gerry's cousin Mrs. Ogden Mills, the lovely Miss Tooker, as well as Mrs. Whitney. The Gerrys were never mentioned as golfers; rather, they preferred horses and joined in the coaching runs around the Island. The Newport Coaching Parade was held on August 18 with the handsome dudes as "Whip" and each coach carried three lovely ladies in their best summer attire. There were sixty-seven in the coaching party including Angelica Gerry who rode with "Whip" Perry Belmont. Mabel Gerry's best friend, Gertrude Vanderbilt, rode in the coach with "Whip," Dr. W. Seward Webb. The six mile run of the parade ended with lunch under a large red tent where they dined at a horseshoe-shaped table; afterward the party danced on the lawn until it was time to drive their coaches back to the polo grounds and a round of cheers.

The summer of 1894 was especially significant for the Gerry family. Angelica Gerry's engagement to the popular bachelor she had met at the winter balls, J. Wadsworth Ritchie, had blossomed into the most anticipated society wedding for the fall. Commodore and Mrs. Gerry invited Mr. Ritchie to join the family for the summer as a guest at *Lyndenhurst.*

Mr. Ritchie, known as "Jack" was born in 1861, in Genesco, New York. His mother was from Genesco and his father came from a prominent family in Boston. Mr. Ritchie's father died young from wounds suffered during the *Civil War* so his mother took her two small sons to France where she lived off and on in Paris for the rest of her life. After his brother died at a young age his mother re-married the wealthy Mr. John Adair of London. While on a trip to America for a tour of the west, the Adairs purchased the *JA Tule Ranch* in Texas, where cows were raised and horses were successfully bred. After completing his education in Europe, Jack returned to Texas to visit the ranch and was immediately attracted to the activities of ranching life. He eventually became the ranch manager and lived in a dugout like a real cowboy. However, his mother was now living a life of considerable social distinction on both sides of the Atlantic and was loathe to have her handsome son Jack punching cows in Texas. After Mrs. Adair ordered her son to leave the ranch, Jack took up residence in New York City for several years during which time he enjoyed his job purchasing horses for the *New York City Police,* all of which bore the respected *JA Tule Ranch* brand. He had no fortune of his own, but was hard working with prospects, and he came from a family well established in British society.

During his years in *Gilded Gotham,* J. Wadsworth Ritchie became the most eligible bachelor among the debutantes, but in the winter of 1894 he had stolen the heart of fellow horse lover, Angelica Gerry, who was ten years younger than Jack. She was an expert rider as well as President of the *Women's Coaching Club.* No doubt, Jack regaled Angelica and her family with stories of his ranch life in Texas, his life in Europe and his plans for the future during his summer stay at *Lyndenhurst.* Throughout the summer season at *Lyndenhurst*, Jack joined the Gerrys when they hosted summer luncheons, gourmet dinners and garden parties at their cottage. Indeed, large garden parties hosted on the sprawling grounds of Newport mansions had become the favorite summer entertainment. At one party the expansive green lawn was dotted with tents and Japanese umbrellas in assorted colors to provide shade for three hundred guests who enjoyed buffet lunches and strolls around the manicured grounds.

While enjoying this very special summer at *Lyndenhurst*, Commodore Gerry once again interspersed work with his holiday. The summer of 1894 offered an irresistible opportunity for him to spend a few days away in Albany, New York to briefly join the *1894 New York State Constitutional Convention.* Although he had been a delegate to the 1867 convention nearly thirty years earlier, this time he was only an observer. However, he was "sponsored" by an official Delegate which gave him "floor privileges" allowing Commodore Gerry to address the convention, which he did on July 11 before the *Joint Committees on Education, Taxation, Charities, and Legislative Powers.* Commodore Gerry's remarks were published in a twenty-nine page pamphlet in which he spoke to the amendment prohibiting the use of public money for sectarian institutions, proposed by the *National League for the Protection of American Institutions.* The *League* was incorporated in 1889 to prohibit the appropriation of public money for sectarian schools, although the *League* was not against the establishment of sectarian schools, essentially raising the issue of the separation of church and state. The social backdrop of this convention was the rapid change taking place in New York State due to industrialization, contentious views between town and country, and the widespread impact of railroads diffusing the population throughout the state where immigrants found industrial employment. Religious groups, particularly Catholics, established sectarian schools, and believed in state support for parochial schools because their taxes funded the public schools, which their children did not attend. An effective compromise was reached when supporters of parochial schools accepted constitutional restrictions foregoing aid to their schools while continuing support for sectarian charities, including child welfare institutions like orphan asylums, homes for dependent children, and funds for educating the deaf, dumb and the blind. This compromise was supported by Commodore Gerry's remarks before the *Committee* noting that the *Constitution* was a clear exposition of the great principles upon which the entire government of the State rested and the amendment had to be narrowly yet effectively tailored to serve the needs of the less fortunate.[10]

Commodore Gerry returned by train to Newport and joined his family for the remainder of the 1894 summer season. He spent his quiet time providing the *New York Society for the Prevention of Cruelty to Children* with legal advice through a steady stream of correspondence. He also advised the Newport elite on their real or perceived legal concerns about a right to privacy from an intrusive press corps. Just as scandals are reported today in the Hollywood rag magazines, the public in the *Gilded Age* was hungry for any whiff of scandal among the social elite. The 1894 summer cottagers were so incensed by reports published about the misdoings of the elite *Four Hundred* that they organized the *Society for the Suppression of Newspaper Notoriety.* Commodore Gerry was asked to chair the *Society* whose purpose was to prevent the publication in New York and Boston of matters that were purely personal to the *Four Hundred* and of no public interest. The Society believed that if, for example, Mrs. Smith's maid takes advantage of Mr. Jones' valet that is legitimate news, and no objection will be made to its publication. However, if Mrs. Smith herself should cast a longing eye at Mr. Jones, or if Mr. Jones should sue his wife for a divorce, these are matters that concern nobody but the culprits themselves and their most intimate friends. These private matters must not be published. The newspapers responded to this new *Society* demand with a grand sense of humor:

> It would be hard indeed if we could not get a laugh out of all these horrid scandals that sour society's face and it has come at last, broad, hearty and irrepressible. Dear, comical, old Elbridge T. Gerry is at the head of the new society, and it looks as if he would have time to attend to nothing else. Unfortunately, bad news sells better than good news."[11]

Just before the Gerrys were to leave on *Electra* for the annual *New York Yacht Club* cruise, Commodore Gerry learned on August 1, 1894 that State Committeeman, Edward T. Fitzpatrick of the Ninth District, a conservative leader of *Tammany Hall,* put forth the name of a Democrat as the best candidate for Mayor of New York City. He stated that while it would be a bitter pill to swallow to have to share political power in his district, he could not be deaf to reason, and urged unity for the sake of the Democratic Administration, the city and the state. He was ready for sacrifice and conciliation and would look outside *Tammany Hall* for a nominee. "Give me as a candidate for Mayor, Elbridge T. Gerry, a Democrat, a gentleman, a humanitarian, and a philanthropist. I have such faith in him that I would not inquire as to his program when elected. I could trust him with my life, and would most cheerfully welcome him as a candidate."[12] Although there is no record of any formal endorsement of the nomination in the Ninth District, it was a public acknowledgement of the City's high regard for Commodore Gerry's integrity and his ability to bring compromise out of conflict, whether in the legal or the political arena in the stratified society of *Gilded Gotham.*

Commodore Gerry's brother-in-law, Frederic Gallatin and his wife, Almy Gerry Gallatin, leisurely sailed their yacht the *Almy* off the Eastern seaboard for the month of June and did not return to their summer home *Breezy Lawn* on Long Island until July. The *Almy* was then anchored at *Gardiner's Bay* within sight of *Breezy Lawn* where entertainments onboard the luxury yacht were regularly hosted. The Gallatins enjoyed their Southampton summer friends at the local

Meadow Club, many of whom were taking an active interest in a community project to build a local library. The idea was encouraged by a benefactor who donated $10,000 to the *Club,* similar to the *Newport Casino,* to kick-off the project. The *Meadow Club* was also sponsoring the 1894 *Long Island Tennis Championship,* a favorite local sport, which would be a week-long tournament ending with a summer dinner dance. On August 5 Frederic and his family set out on the *Almy* to rendezvous at *Glen Cove* for the start of the annual cruise of the *New York Yacht Club,* joining Commodore Gerry and his family, also heading for *Glen Cove* on the *Electra,* as was Robert Goelet on his yacht the *Beatrice,* named after his daughter. *Glen Cove* had many associations of interest connected with the *New York Yacht Club,* particularly as the annual cruise start point. It was a pleasant sheet of water with picturesque scenery and landscapes, but truth be told, it was a spot shunned generally by the winds creating flat calms, thus it was ideal for steam yachts, but as a rendezvous for racing craft it had many drawbacks. Nonetheless, its easy accessibility and generous space made it a reliable location to begin the annual cruise. In fact on August 7 there was barely a puff of wind and the start of the cruise had to be delayed until late morning when at 10:30 the preparatory gun was fired just as a light breath of air stole over the water from west-southwest. The yachts bunched together so closely between the flagship of the Vice-Commodore and the buoy, that pleasant chats and cheery bantering were exchanged among the passing yachtsmen.[13] The cruise arrived at *Morris Cove* on August 8 and *New London* on August 9, and was back in *Newport* on August 10 for the *Goelet Cup* races. Indeed, 1894 was the *Fiftieth Anniversary* of the *New York Yacht Club* and the mood of the cruise was relaxed yet eager for the annual Cup races at Newport. After hosting the *Goelet Cup* competition for thirteen seasons this was the first year that Ogden Goelet was unable to attend because he was on the *Whyte Ladye* in the Mediterranean, where he now spent most of every year. The evening following the successful *Goelet Cup* race, Commodore Gerry and Frederic Gallatin joined a large fleet of pleasure craft on a cruise out to *Brenton's Reef.* On most of the sight-seeing yachts there were large parties of Newport's fashionable young ladies. Among the larger steam craft on the evening cruise were John J. Astor's *Nourmahal* and Fred W. Vanderbilt's *Conqueror.* Finally, on August 14 the Vice-Commodore hosted a meeting on his yacht at which congratulatory speeches were made and resolutions of gratitude were passed. After a pleasant dinner the fleet captains formally closed the *Fiftieth Anniversary* cruise of the *New York Yacht Club.* There was never a Commodore as masterful as Commodore Gerry and he never missed a cruise. He made every port of call a colorful event, in fact, in 1891 it was said that a couple became engaged after an incident on the *Electra* during that NYYC cruise. The two were guests of Commodore Gerry and when the yacht began to pitch and toss in heavy swells off the *Brenton Reef* lightship, the young lady remarked, "Oh Mr. B., I am afraid that I will never make much of a sailor," to which the young man wittily replied, "But you will make a perfect mate," and the next day he sent to *Tiffany* for the ring.[14] On this *Fiftieth Anniversary* cruise, the Commodore of the Club, E.D. Morgan was absent in England with the NYYC flagship *May,* leaving the Vice Commodore to lead what might have been a more colorful and brightly celebrated cruise. The *New York Yacht Club* found its way to a pleasant and successful cruise, although it was not one of the most memorable or exciting cruises in the club's history. Fifty years earlier in 1844 the Club squadron had 9 yachts, and fifty years later in 1894 there were 294 vessels flying the NYYC burgee. Also fifty years ago the Club had only 9 members and by 1894 there were over a thousand members. The 1890's were the golden age of yachting for the *New York Yacht Club.* Today the Club is thriving and sponsors festive regattas and exciting races, primarily off of Newport, Rhode Island. This historic Club continues to occupy the magnificent building on Forty-Fourth Street in New York City.

Yachting on the ocean was not confined to men, indeed, it was likely that a skipper in 1894 would heed the advice of a good yachtswoman. Several of the wives of members of the NYYC were, to varying degrees, gifted yachtswomen. Louisa Gerry, while known as a charming hostess in the gorgeous saloon of the *Electra,* was also known as an educated yachtswoman in her own right. Louisa had said on one occasion that "My taste for yachting is entirely a cultivated one, as I have had an opportunity for a liberal education in the science of navigation, for during the summer season I hear nothing else but yacht for breakfast, yacht for dinner, yacht, yacht, yacht. But I have grown to like it and during the races I become as enthusiastic as anybody."[15] There was no American woman more enthusiastic onboard a yacht than Mrs. C.O. Iselin. She was one of the practical yachtswomen who would rather be manning the wheel of her yacht *Titania* in a thrash to windward than sitting in a luxuriously appointed cabin. Mrs. George Gould once said of her yacht the *Hildegarde,* "I love every foot of her timber and every inch of her canvas, and if anything should ever happen to her I think I should wear mourning dress." Once, the *Hildegarde* was caught in a squall and for a while things looked rather bleak. Mrs. Gould displayed the bravery of a true sailor, she neither cried nor screamed, but stood fast, drenched to the skin and said, "Well, if she's got to go I'm glad we are here to go with her."[16] Mrs. E. D. Morgan who sails on the largest schooner-yacht, the *Constellation,* liked to sail outside of Sandy Hook in a September gale, with the foresail, mainsail, and one jib double reefed and with the topmast housed. She believed that women ought to have clubs, not the sort that lunch on dainty sandwiches and cambric tea, but "just like a man's club, you know, where they have a real good time." Mrs. Morgan and Mrs. Iselin were very much like the unsinkable Molly Brown who survived the sinking of the Titanic. Two British yachtswomen who sailed in American waters and were much loved and admired by the NYYC women were Lilly Langtry who sailed the oceans in her own yacht, the *Whyte Ladye,* which Ogden Goelet purchased in 1893, and Mrs. Henn, the charming wife of Lieut. Henn of the Royal Navy, who was on board the yacht *Galatea* when she lost the 1886 *America's Cup* to the *Mayflower.* Mrs. Henn never would admit that it was the superior speed of the *Mayflower* that defeated the *Galatea.* She was explaining to pretty Amy Bend one day after a race why her yacht was beaten. Although Miss Bend had been on many yachting excursions, she paid no attention to nautical terms and her blue eyes opened wide with wonder when Mrs. Henn proceeded to explain the *Galatea's* defeat:

> "Under water! Why what do you mean" gasped Miss Bend.
>
> "Oh," rattled on Mrs. Henn, "I mean that our lee scuppers were awash. But, don't you see, that was where the sloop gained about four points in the wind on us, and, coming leeward when we set our balloon jib topsail and boomed out our spinnaker."
>
> "Boomed your what?" cried Miss Bend.
>
> "Our spinnaker, don't you know what a spinnaker is?" replied Mrs. Henn
>
> "No, I don't." cried Miss Bend ruefully, "I don't know what any of those things are. I don't know what you are talking about. Can't you tell it to me in American?"[17]

At one point in their lives, the Henns lived on their yacht for eight years, cruising in the summer time among the fjords of Norway and the firths of Scotland, and in the winter months along the Mediterranean coast and the islands of the Indian Ocean.

After an eventful summer in Newport, the Gerrys boarded their yacht *Electra* the first week of September and sailed up the Hudson River to Kingston, where they traveled by train to Andes for a few days at the *Lake Delaware* farm estate. Mr. J. Wadsworth Ritchie remained in Newport staying with other family friends. The Gerrys were eager to return to New York City to take possession of their new home and to make plans for Angelica's wedding to Mr. Ritchie.

By the end of September the flurry of correspondence between the Gerrys and their architect, Richard M. Hunt, had ended and work on the interior finishes, while incomplete, also ceased. The Gerrys contracted with professional movers to pack, transport and unpack the entire household of furnishings and personal possessions from their brownstone on Forty-Eighth Street. Many of the Gerry possessions in the twin brownstones occupied by the Gerrys and the Livingstons were heirlooms from both sides of the family. An example of the priceless items that were moved was a series of Louis XVI Aubusson tapestry (circa 1780) originally brought from France by Chancellor Robert R. Livingston (1746–1813) who became minister to France in 1801 and enjoyed a personal friendship with Napoleon; his principal accomplishment was the negotiation of the *Louisiana Purchase.* The series of tapestries furnished the drawing-room at Clermont, the Livingston's ancestral manor in New York, and descended through Lewis Livingston, from whom they were acquired by Robert J. Livingston in 1889, the father of Louisa Gerry.[18]

The move into the mansion had to be carefully staged because new furnishings purchased during their early summer European tour had to be delivered even while the furnishings from the old townhouse were delivered. Louisa Gerry had complete oversight of the careful placement of all decorative items, artwork for the gallery, furniture and personal possessions of family members. The concern Commodore Gerry had expressed to Richard M. Hunt in early April about the completion of the house in time to receive the cases of Madeira wine and the ladies' trunks was justified. In mid-July when the cases of wine, the trunks, and fifty-four crates of furniture and decorative woodworks arrived in New York harbor under contract with *Allard & Sons*, with offices in Paris and New York, everything was detained by *Customs* officers. The itemized valuation invoice drafted by *Allard & Sons* was said to be grossly under-valued. When the *Customs House* unilaterally increased the invoice valuation *Allard & Sons* appealed the action. Commodore Gerry, like anyone who contracted with an importer, was not held liable for discrepancies on an invoice since the company agreed to accept full liability under their contract. The *Board of General Appraisers* was established to review the often challenged appraisals of Customs officers to protect the import company's reputation. The invoice for the fifty-four crates of furnishings listed finely carved panels for wainscoting, iron worked into filigree patterns, pilasters of artistic design, ornamental cornices, and rich upholstery fabric, among other items. The *Board* did a full and independent re-appraisal and determined the Gerry shipment had been correctly invoiced by *Allard & Sons*. By August, the *Custom House* had released the shipment. All the crates were stored in a warehouse at the dock until Commodore Gerry notified the movers of a delivery date.[19]

By the end of the 1890's many large elegant mansions had been erected on Fifth Avenue, which provided elite neighbors for the Gerry family. Caroline Schermerhorn Astor, one of the wealthiest families in *Gilded Gotham,* was at Fifth Avenue and Sixty-Fifth Street, the Josephine Schmid mansion was at Fifth Avenue and Sixty-Second Street, the Havemeyer mansion was at Fifth Avenue and Sixty-Sixth Street, and the Vanderbilt mansion, the largest on millionaire's row, was at Fifth Avenue and Fifty-Eighth Street, across from the *Plaza Hotel.* All of the mansions were within eight blocks of each other, perfect for social visits and weekend strolls along the Avenue and into *Central Park* located just across the street from the mansions.

The era of stately and opulent town houses associated with Fifth Avenue and the Upper Eastside was a brief one, lasting about 25 years. After World War I the cost of living in Manhattan, and the value of land, made it too expensive to maintain a mansion. Most wealthy New Yorkers sold their townhouses and moved into luxury apartments built on land where their mansions once stood. The apartments were designed with style, elegance and expansive floor plans equivalent to the townhouses. Although few of the townhouses remain to remind one of this fashionable period, some may still be seen on the side streets, particularly on the blocks between Fifth and Madison Avenues. In the twenty-first Century these luxury high rise apartments remain beautifully updated and are still owned and occupied by wealthy New Yorkers who continue the tradition of the *Upper East Side* as the elite area of Manhattan.[20]

The Gerry family had completed the move by October allowing Louisa time to prepare for Angelica's fall wedding to J. Wadsworth Ritchie. Commodore Gerry was busier than ever and continued to maintain his formal office at 261 Broadway facing *City Hall Park* and near the State and Federal Court Buildings; convenient for his participation in civic and legal affairs. Although his new residence was twenty blocks further north of his Broadway office, his work remained anchored in lower Manhattan and city transportation was convenient. Indeed, on October 5, 1894 Commodore Gerry was in the *Old Criminal Court Building,* at the time known as the *Tweed Courthouse,* to observe the New York State Senate hearings on police corruption in *Gilded Gotham.* The investigating committee, chaired by State Senator Clarence Lexow, examined evidence from the *City Vigilance League,* as well as evidence gathered by the Committee itself. Charles H. Parkhurst (1842–1933) pastor of the *Madison Square Presbyterian Church* and a social reformer, published *Our City Vigilance League* as a call to the citizens of New York to embrace the principle that municipal officials are hired public servants and as such, it is the people's civic responsibility to look after the Mayor, the Judiciary and the Police in order to keep them faithful to their duty and oaths of office. He inaugurated a campaign against the political and social corruption of *Tammany Hall* and the Police Department. The *Hall* had begun innocently as a social club, but had drifted over the years into politics and graft. It acquired a lock on elections in the city and its bosses protected crime and vice in Manhattan and the Boroughs. When the municipal grand jury asked Rev. Parkhurst for hard evidence, he hired a private detective and through his writing and preaching, he inspired private citizens to form the *City Vigilance League*. Members went undercover and gathered evidence that they carefully documented with written records, charts, and affidavits. The League had no political or sectarian views, its only ambition was to provide the evidence needed to prove municipal corruption so that it could be prosecuted.[21] During the hearings the chief counsel for the *Lexow Committee*; John W. Goff, was examining witnesses about the false conviction of a mother by corrupt police, which resulted in the placement of her children in the care of *the New York Society for the Prevention of Cruelty to Children*. Before the conviction was proven false, the agents for the *Society* acted lawfully and with the direction of the police magistrate. However, now that the conviction was proven corrupt, the committee's counsel, Mr. Goff, spoke about the NYSPCC. First he praised their work, then he questioned whether their authority was too absolute and arbitrary as demonstrated by how difficult it was to remove the children in the case under review, after a wrongful conviction of their mother. At that point in the proceedings, there was a bustle in the courtroom when Commodore Gerry walked briskly through the crowd to where Mr. Goff was standing in front of the Senate Committee. Mr. Goff looked at the Commodore in surprise and stepped to one side. Without looking to his right or left, Commodore Gerry unbuttoned his coat and removed a prepared statement from his pocket and straightened it out with a rapid movement. The following intense discussion ensued:

> Commodore Gerry, "With the consent of the committee I desire to read a statement setting forth the facts in relation to the commitment of the children to the care of the *NYSPCC* of which I have the honor to be President."
>
> Chairman Lexow stretched forth his hand, "The Committee has made it a rule not to allow any testimony given before this committee to be discredited by any unverified verbal or written statement."

> Mr. Goff in turn, "I object to Mr. Gerry's reading an unverified statement here, on any subject. Let Mr. Gerry be sworn, for I have not the slightest objection to his going on the stand, and I will be delighted to examine him on this case."
>
> Commodore Gerry paused, and the hand holding the statement fell to his side "This seems to me a bit strange that I am not to be permitted to defend the *Society* from the attacks made upon it before this Committee."
>
> Senator O'Connor interposed, "As I understand it, the *Society* has not been attacked. The remarks Mr. Goff made had reference to the law, and not to your *Society*."
>
> Commodore Gerry, "It has been stated here that our power is absolute and that there is no appeal, which is not true as my learned friend Mr. Goff knows. The placement of the children with the *Society* could easily have been appealed by their mother's counsel but was not.
>
> Senator Pound responded, "The *Society* is not on trial here and there can be no investigation of it because there are no charges against it."
>
> Commodore Gerry, "The *Society* has simply done its duty."

Unable to read his statement, Commodore Gerry took his seat. To everyone's surprise, Mr. Goff made the following statement mocking the status of the Commodore as a yachtsman/lawyer:

> "Mr. Chairman," said Mr. Goff, "Commodore Gerry has sailed in here with every foot of canvas spread to the breeze. The Commodore was affected by an imaginary puff of wind that yesterday crossed his course. But he has sailed in here without becoming at all familiar with the shoals and rocks. I would respectfully suggest to the Commodore that the next time he sails in here he bring with him a pilot who is acquainted with these shoals and rocks."

Mr. Goff followed with a lengthy statement that did in fact attack the *NYSPCC* knowing that Commodore Gerry was prevented from offering a reply before the committee. However, as Commodore Gerry rose from his seat to leave he managed to say,

> "Well I never knew that the *NYSPCC* possessed arbitrary or absolute or despotic power, unless you call our sheltering a few poor, homeless children despotic power."

As he passed Mr. Goff he smiled and said,

> "It has been wickedly suggested to me that you made your attack on the *Society* of which I have the honor to be President with the idea of increasing your chances for the Mayoralty and decreasing mine. If that be so, I hope it will succeed."

This is the only time that Commodore Gerry was quoted in the press as a possible candidate for Mayor of New York, other than the article he had read during his summer holiday in Newport when Committeeman Edward T. Fitzpatrick offered the Commodore's name for the nomination. The remark by Commodore Gerry to Mr. Goff clearly suggests that he would prefer not to run for mayor.[22] Based on all the evidence, the *Lexow Committee* uncovered police involvement in extortion, bribery, counterfeiting, voter intimidation, election fraud, brutality, and scams. The testimony collected during the hearings ran to over 10,000 pages and the resultant scandal played a major part in the defeat of *Tammany Hall* in the 1894 elections.

While the Gerry family was busy with the household move, wedding preparations, and the legal affairs of the Commodore in New York City, their future son-in-law J. Wadsworth Ritchie, "Jack" remained in Newport, Rhode Island. He was thirty-three and had a wide circle of friends. The newspapers kept an eye on all the bachelors and relished society intrigue. One article described "Jack" as a swaggering cowboy, very big and good looking, and perhaps for this reason no one had complained of his being a stranger. Of course, being a stranger to the elite *Four Hundred* of New York simply meant you were neither "born nor married into" one of the State's founding families. However, Jack was indeed relatively new to New York and his roots were in Boston and London, with a frustrated passion for the cowboy life in Texas. The article went on to say "Alas! Mr. Ritchie was to be married to a very wealthy young woman, Miss Gerry, and it may safely be predicted that his cotillion leading days were over because married women did not take kindly to having husbands dance with debutantes in ballrooms in New York society."[23] Another rag exclaimed, "So ex-Cowboy 'Jack' Ritchie has captured the Gerry heiress after all. No fellow could wish for a jollier old pa-in-law than the ex-Commodore. He is always the same, a trifle pompous and verbose, but a ripping, good, old sea dog at heart, and very solvent." It went on to note that Jack had been working in the street tramway business, working his way up gradually from car inspector to a high position in the financial bureau of the street railroad trust. The article advises, "It is this kind of adaptability and perseverance, old chappies, that usually wins the best girls in the end."[24] Angelica Gerry maintained a personal scrapbook in which she clipped newspaper articles that concerned the Gerry family, but most particularly those that described herself to the public. The primary publications from which she clipped but gave no, or incomplete citations, were: the *New York World,* the *New York Journal,* the *New York Herald,* the *New York Times,* the *Boston Globe* and the *Newport Daily News*.

While the Gerrys prepared for Angelica's wedding, Jack was in Newport involved in the festivities of another wedding, his good friend Mr. Victor Sorchan to Miss Charlotte Hunnewell of Newport. On September 23, Victor hosted a farewell bachelor dinner at the *Knickerbocker Club* in New York City. His guests were his friends and ushers, Jack Ritchie, Hamilton Cary, William Cutting, Jr. and Brockholst Cutting. The wedding was celebrated on October 6 at the *Chapel of All Saints* in Newport, Rhode Island. In retrospect, it might be noted that Jack Ritchie was the usher in the wedding party to Miss Emily Tooker, a bridesmaid in the party with whom he was acquainted and their friendship was rekindled. Within three weeks of this event, Commodore Elbridge Gerry announced on October 30 that his daughter, Angelica, had broken her engagement with J. Wadsworth Ritchie. When asked why, the Commodore responded that "Yes it is true, and it was by mutual consent, but I have nothing further to say."[25] Angelica wrote to her intimate friends to announce that her engagement to Mr. Ritchie was broken though no cause was given. The broken engagement came as a surprise to elite society, all of whom nursed their disappointment and invented a hundred reasons of its own to supply explanation. The wedding was to serve as a house-warming for the new mansion, and in fact, Commodore and Mrs. Gerry had already purchased another townhouse as a wedding gift for Angelica and Jack. It had been furnished by Louisa and Angelica over the previous weeks. The new home for Angelica and all the wedding preparations were complete. The Commodore also gave Angelica an income of her own, $100,000 a year after her marriage. Angelica had her Paris trousseau on hand for the ceremony and only the invitations were left to be sent. This was to be the most brilliant wedding of the year in *Gilded Gotham.*

Friends of the Gerry family would only say that the engagement was probably broken merely because of a lack of congeniality between the young people. However, Jack had spent the summer with the Gerry family at *Lyndenhurst* in Newport and was on intimate terms with not only Angelica but also her parents. The suddenness of the break suggests that Jack was perhaps indiscreet or had misled the Gerrys about his circumstances. Commodore Gerry knew everyone and was highly respected; his friends would have cautioned him if necessary for the protection of his family. Years later it was reported that Commodore Gerry was strenuously opposed to the marriage at the time, but there were no indications of such feelings until just before the wedding. Commodore Gerry had the entire summer to end the engagement if he thought it was in the best interests of his daughter. During the November 1894 press "feeding frenzy" Commodore Gerry's role as chairman of the *Society for the Suppression of Newspaper Notoriety* organized in Newport in the spring of 1894 would have served him well. In fact, the old society gossip, Mrs. Grundy, who was without gentlemanly scruples, asserted to the press that the cause of the broken engagement was Mr. Ritchie himself. The article entitled *Ritchie a Clubman, Wrecked in Sight of Port,* said that the last straw was a little dinner at the Waldorf, which lasted until morning, "when rosy fingers drew the curtain of the night from over a revel more roseate than the blushes of a bride." These and other outspoken articles were clipped by Angelica and pasted into her scrapbook. While society was shocked, it was neither the first nor the last time a debutante would break an engagement. Jack, the ever handsome and popular bachelor was not shunned by society. Indeed, at the December ball hosted by Perry Belmont, the cotillion was once again led by J. Wadsworth Ritchie, and both Angelica and Mabel danced, but perhaps not with Jack. The Commodore and Louisa Gerry were at the Belmont gala and life, as they say, had moved on in *Gilded Gotham.* Then again, the young woman Jack had met at the October wedding, when he was an usher and she, Emily Tooker, was a bridesmaid, became engaged to Jack Ritchie in June 1895, and they were married in a brilliant Newport wedding on August 24, 1895 at which the Astors, Belmonts, Goelets, and Vanderbilts were all guests. The Gerrys did not attend the wedding because Mrs. Hannah Gerry was seriously ill with pneumonia at the time. The gifts were said to fill a room and one gift was presented in a photograph. It was a saddle-horse from the Texas ranch that was to be shipped when the Ritchies returned from their honeymoon. Emily Tooker Ritchie was in fact a fine horsewoman, as was Angelica. The previous summer Emily was a leader in the cross-country movement and had brought over an English thoroughbred hunter that was a champion in France. She was hoping to encourage an interest in American fox hunting, in which Peter and Robert Gerry became actively involved. Also in the summer of 1894 while Angelica and Jack were socializing in Newport as an engaged couple, they attended an intimate surprise party hosted by Mrs. John Jacob Astor to which only forty elite guests were invited, and Miss Emily Tooker was one of them. Angelica and Emily knew each other and shared Jack's circle of intimate friends in Newport. After their 1895 wedding, Jack and Emily Ritchie permanently moved to Rutlandshire, England, Jack's boyhood home and still the home of his mother, Mrs. Adair. They had no children and Emily died suddenly in 1903 from blood poisoning. Jack did not remarry until 1907, and had three children with his second wife. Jack visited Newport between 1903 and 1904 and also the Texas ranch over the years. He joined the military and served in the Boer War, was wounded and became a semi-invalid in 1914 preventing him from ever again visiting America. Jack died in England in 1924. There is no doubt that Angelica Gerry suffered a broken heart over J. Wadsworth Ritchie. She even refused to take possession of the house Commodore Gerry had purchased for her as a wedding gift in 1894, as well as the $100,000 annual income. While there were rumors over the years of engagements, Angelica was never again engaged although she had many male friends and was the center of society her entire life. In 1921, twenty-seven years after her broken engagement, Angelica pasted into her scrapbook a clipping about Jack Ritchie. The article noted that he had been a widower who had later re-married, and then, surprisingly the article resurrected the story of the famous 1894 broken Gerry engagement, perhaps suggesting it was a turning point in Jack's life, maybe even one of his great mistakes.

The Christmas holidays brought sad and sobering news to the Gerry family. The last surviving family member of a signer of the *Declaration of Independence*, and the last surviving child of Vice President Elbridge Gerry, had died on December 29, 1894. Emily Gerry was the sister of Thomas Russell Gerry, the father of Commodore Gerry. As a child living in Cambridge, Massachusetts, she and her sisters received their primary training in the local schools and thereafter were tutored at home by professors from the nearby Harvard College, from which her three brothers graduated. After her father's death in 1814 her mother took the children first to Boston, where Emily's eldest brother, Elbridge, Jr. lived, as did her married sister Elizabeth. After several years the family moved to New London, Connecticut for a short time; finally in 1837 the family settled in a colonial style house at Church and Temple Streets in New Haven. Emily Gerry was a woman of extensive reading and well acquainted with political affairs. She was a fine botanist when the science was in its infancy, a passion she shared with her brother, Capt. James Gerry, who faithfully wrote to Emily whenever he discovered a new plant as he sailed about the world. In 1880 at age 75, she suffered a devastating illness, perhaps a stroke, which confined Emily to a wheelchair for the remainder of her life. Although her mind was clear until the end, she had lost her eyesight and her interest in favorite pastimes such as gardening, and she could no longer read. She was 90 years old and had lived most of her life in the quaint old-fashioned house in New Haven with her mother and sisters until each passed away. Commodore Gerry arranged for her funeral and acted as executor of her small estate. The New Haven *Mary Clap Wooster Chapter* of the Daughters of the American Revolution prepared and published a memoriam in honor of Emily Gerry who had been their revered first *Regent*. Many of the personal items from the Gerry home in New

Haven were donated to the DAR Chapter for their Museum and Library with the assistance of Emily Gerry's niece, Annie Townsend, the daughter of her sister Elizabeth Gerry Townsend.[26] The *Colonial Era* of the Gerry line had come to a close, but the family drive, intellect and civic patriotism was alive and well in the Gerrys of New York City.

Commodore Gerry and Louisa welcomed the New Year with a grand house warming reception on Wednesday, January 3, 1895. This was just what the Gerry family needed to put the sadness of Emily's death and the break-up of Angelica's engagement behind them. Over a thousand of *Gilded Gotham's* elite society arrived for the gala affair around 10 o'clock in the evening and most stayed until 1 o'clock in the morning. The Gerrys received their guests in the *Grand Salon* at the west end of the great hall, which was decorated in the Louis XIV Regency style, and the old Livingston tapestries, the finest in the country, were hung in this room. On the ceiling was a large circular painting of the goddess Flora and her nymphs. Mrs. Gerry was richly attired in purple velvet and brocade, with diamond ornaments. Angelica and Mabel, now 23 and 21 years old, wore lovely white satin gowns frilled with lace and chiffon.[27]

The reception was the first entertainment in the new mansion and the entire first floor was thrown open and flooded with electric light arranged in every conceivable new and artistic fashion. The immense first floor hall, reached by a few low, wide steps was still incomplete as was the library. On the left of the entrance hall was a small *Smoking Den* for the gentlemen, and beyond it at the east side of the first floor was the great *Dining Room*. It was decorated in the Flemish style with stone coats of arms emblazoned on the raftered ceiling. The long dinner table was set to one side of the room and was adorned with silver and red roses. Beyond this *Dining Room* at the southeastern corner of the first floor was the *Law Library*, which was plain and unfinished except for the book cases along the four walls. Commodore Gerry had finally removed his 20,000 volume collection from the old Nineteenth Street and Broadway mansion and had his book collection carefully arranged on the shelves. The immense library collection provided an interesting display for guests to peruse until the room could be completed over the next two years. The large room adjoining the Law Library and opposite the entrance hall was the *Picture Gallery* and it was used as a ballroom when needed. From the *Picture Gallery* guests wandered into the *Small Salon* decorated in Louis XV French Rococo in pale gray and ivory; on the ceiling was an oval mural. This Salon opened onto the *Conservatory* at the southwest corner of the first floor. It was decorated with palms and other greenery as well as statuary. It is possible that the life-size statue of *Penelope* purchased in Rome in 1887 was placed here as the centerpiece of the all-glass (walls and ceiling) atrium, and if not, the sculpture was at the Lake Delaware estate in Delhi, New York where it was first documented in 1929 by Angelica Gerry as part of an immense garden setting, where it stands today on the New York estate.

At the southwest corner of the mansion guests moved through the *Small Library* dramatically decorated in red and mahogany with a majestic ceiling mural. Between this smaller library and the main entrance hall was a small *Boudoir* for the ladies, decorated in pale blue in the Louis XVI Classic Revival style with a ceiling mural of the universe with floating cupids, painted by *Ignace Spiridon* (1860-1900). Spiridon was born and studied in Rome, Italy, then moved to Paris where he settled and opened a studio. He painted Mark Twain, who noted that *Spiridon* was a very quick painter and produced the best portrait of the writer, indeed, it was Twain's favorite.[28]

The newspaper account of this first grand reception noted that there were no stairs visible in the mansion because they were off to one side, enclosed behind a doorway. In fact, those were the servants' stairs; the grand staircase was yet to be designed and built. However, there was an elevator which was described as ornamental and comfortable. This would suggest that it had oak panel doors and had a mirrored and paneled interior.

In the afternoon before the Gerry reception another much talked-about reception was hosted by Mrs. Cornelius Vanderbilt II in honor of her daughter, Gertrude Vanderbilt. Throughout their youth and adulthood, Mabel Gerry and Gertrude Vanderbilt were best friends, as only girls can be. Mabel's photo album contains many photographs of the two young women together, not only in New York, but at the Lake Delaware estate and in Newport. When Mabel traveled to Europe she wrote to Gertrude almost daily, often collecting the letters and mailing them in bundles. One such bundle is with the Gerry family along with the photo album and Mabel's diary.[29]

Gertrude Vanderbilt was born in 1875 just two years after Mabel Gerry, and was the first cousin of Consuelo Vanderbilt who was born in 1877. As the wealthy daughters of Commodore Cornelius Vanderbilt's sons, William "Willie" Vanderbilt (1849-1920) and Cornelius Vanderbilt, II (1843-1899), Gertrude and Consuelo were women with one foot in the *Gilded Age* and the other in the *Progressive Era* of women rights, particularly the right to vote.

Gertrude Vanderbilt spent her summers in Newport at the family mansion, *The Breakers,* built by Richard Morris Hunt for Cornelius Vanderbilt II right next door to Ogden Goelet's *Ochre Court. The Breakers* was the largest mansion ever built in Newport. Mabel's cousin Consuelo also spent her summers in Newport at the family mansion called *Marble House* with her mother, Alva and father, William K. Vanderbilt. While an intimate of both women and best friends with one, Mabel Gerry summered in Newport but did not live in a mansion. The *Lyndenhurst* cottage was a handsome large house, and the home Commodore Gerry later bought in Newport, *Seaverge*, was also a very large, shingle style house. Unlike the Vanderbilt girls, Mabel did not marry until she was in her early fifties. She had many suitors but had neither the inclination nor the family pressure to marry. By contrast, Consuelo Vanderbilt, the daughter of Alva and Willie Vanderbilt, was not only pressured to marry, but was forced to marry a British aristocrat, the ninth Duke of Marlborough. She later wrote of her life at *Blenheim Castle* in England, "It seemed I was but to exchange one bondage for another. An English lady was hedged round with boring social restrictions," and she observed that her new husband, as well as his entire household, strictly adhered to matters of rank; so much so that the words "your Grace" were pronounced with such "reverent unction" that clergymen would ask, "May I say grace, Your Grace?" which highly amused Consuelo. After eleven years of marriage and two children, she separated from the Duke and embarked on a multitude of philanthropic activities. She was elected the first female member of the London County Council, which decided policies for the city and allowed her to push forward the platforms of the *Women's Municipal Party* of which she was a member. She made speeches on behalf of poor children and health care and was able to obtain a playground for the children of Southwark.[30]

Finally in 1921 after the war, it was possible for women to obtain a divorce which Consuelo's own mother Alva had done in America and then married Oliver Belmont, her husband's best friend. After her British divorce, Consuelo fell happily in love and married Lt. Col. Jacques Balsan, a record-breaking pioneer French balloon, airplane, and hydroplane pilot who once worked with the Wright Brothers. He was also a textile manufacturing heir. They lived in Paris where Consuelo continued her charity work, establishing a hospital for the middle-class and a sanatorium for children. The Balsans' private life was happy and enriched by friendships with artists, actors, and writers like Henry James, Edith Wharton, and Charlie Chaplin. Consuelo was a first cousin by marriage to Winston Churchill who was her life-long, intimate friend. He was a frequent visitor to her château in St. Georges Motel, a small commune near Dreux about 50 miles from Paris in the 1920s and 1930s, where he completed his last painting before the war. Consuelo Vanderbilt found happiness by escaping *Gilded Gotham*, the yoke of her mother in Newport, and the restrictive life of a British aristocrat. She basked in the French freedom that was both gay and cosmopolitan and attracted the famous ex-patriate crowd from America.[31] Local history records in Florida show that in 1932

Consuelo Vanderbilt Balsan built a home just south of Palm Beach called *Casa Alva,* in honor of her mother. Many believe that Winston Churchill polished his famous *Iron Curtain* Speech in that house as he visited his cousin on his way to Fulton, Missouri to deliver an address at Westminster College. After a long and happy life together, Jacques Balsan died in 1956 at the age of 88 and Consuelo died in 1964 at the age of 84.

Gertrude Vanderbilt, on the other hand, was the daughter of the more liberal-minded Alice Vanderbilt. Both Mabel Gerry and Gertrude Vanderbilt were creative by nature and understood themselves as artists. Mabel, and Angelica for that matter, were known for their beautiful voices, and entertained at musicals at the Gerry home. Mabel pursued voice lessons both in the United States and while in Europe, noting in her diary that she was friendly with famous opera stars and often attended their practice sessions to develop her knowledge of operatic singing. Gertrude Vanderbilt was both a painter and sculptor throughout her life. Gertrude had a love of sports and kept up with the boys during summers in Newport. She was educated by private tutors and at the exclusive Brearley School in New York City. In 1896 at age twenty-one, Gertrude Vanderbilt married Harry Payne Whitney (1872-1930), the extremely wealthy son of a banker and investor, and whose mother was a wealthy Standard Oil heiress. Gertrude and Harry had three children between 1897 and 1903, after which she discovered a flourishing art world while traveling in Europe. Her artistic drive was ignited and she studied to be a sculptor at the *Art Students League of New York* and then with Auguste Rodin in Paris, France. Eventually, Gertrude maintained art studios in Greenwich Village and in Passy, a fashionable neighborhood of Paris. Her works received critical acclaim both in Europe and the United States, and include *The Scout* commemorating Buffalo Bill in Cody, Wyoming; the *Fountain of El Dorado* for San Francisco, but now in Lima Peru; the *Women's Titanic Memorial* in Washington, D.C. and *The Three Graces* at McGill University in Montreal, Canada.

During World War I, Gertrude Vanderbilt Whitney dedicated a great deal of her time and money to various relief efforts, establishing and maintaining a hospital for wounded soldiers in Neuilly-sur-Seine, near Paris in France. Following the end of the War, she was involved in the creation of a number of commemorative sculptures. Harry Whitney built a magnificent studio for his wife at their Long Island estate where they were known for their gracious and sincere hospitality. In 1914 Gertrude Whitney established the *Whitney Studio Club* on West Eighth Street in Greenwich Village as a facility where young artists could exhibit their work. The studio evolved to become Gertrude's greatest legacy, the *Whitney Museum of American Art.* In 1934, Gertrude was at the center of a highly publicized court battle with her sister-in-law for the custody of her ten-year old niece, Gloria Vanderbilt, based on inadequate care and the squandering of the child's inheritance. Full custody was granted to Gertrude and Harry Payne, with visitation rights expanded in later years. Gloria Vanderbilt became a famous fashion designer. She is the mother of journalist Anderson Cooper and lives in New York City. Gertrude Whitney died in 1942 at age sixty-seven and was buried next to her husband in Woodlawn Cemetery in New York.[32]

The Gerrys hosted two gala affairs in mid and late January, a ball for several hundred guests and a cotillion for fifty couples of the younger set. Commodore and Mrs. Gerry also attended the opera with Angelica and Mabel, a passion the family shared. Sons Robert 18, and Peter 16, were both at Harvard College and were only home for holidays and summers in Newport. In March, Mrs. Gerry and her daughters inaugurated a new fad among society ladies with a sewing circle to make items for charity, similar to what the Gerry girls had done every summer of their youth. They hosted small groups once a week followed by afternoon tea. Other society ladies soon followed with their own sewing circles for charity.

Easter Sunday was always a day looked forward to with a great deal of anticipation and the 1895 Lenten Season had been an especially quiet one. The dudes and belles were looking forward to their walks on Fifth Avenue in their Sunday best. The Gerry family attended Easter services at Trinity Chapel, after which they were driven up the Avenue by coach, preferring not to walk the distance. While the Gerry ladies usually dressed modestly for Sunday services, on Easter they dressed-up for the festive holy day. Angelica wore a brown corded silk with a flourish of canary colored chiffon in the front, while Mabel wore a Paris gown of pale-purple cashmere. After arriving home and enjoying a family breakfast, the family joined their neighbors for a stroll on Fifth Avenue and through Central Park. As part of the Easter season, the Gerry ladies attended a recital and musical at the home of Mrs. Brockholst Cutting, at Madison Avenue and Twenty-Ninth Street, to provide support for the *Little Sisters of the Assumption* and their charitable work. Everyone in attendance contributed a donation which brought about $1,200 for the convent. Most of the private activities of *Gilded Gotham's* elite ladies, outside of social galas, were intended to benefit a wide variety of the City's charities.

Two years after initiating his lifetime membership with the *American Museum of Natural History*, Commodore Gerry was elected to the Board of Trustees in 1895. He joined trustees J. Pierpont Morgan, Cornelius Vanderbilt II, William C. Whitney and Theodore Havemeyer, among others, who had successfully led fund raising efforts and provided oversight for the enlargement of the Museum building. The new wing comprised six stories from cellar to roof, with a frontage on Seventy-Seventh Street of 157 feet and a width of 66 feet. The building was meant to be fire-proof, the floors were finished in tile and marble mosaic of bright and attractive patterns, and mahogany was used in the construction of display cases. The cellar was for storage and for unpacking materials, the ground floor contained the Jesup Collection of Woods, the first floor housed the large mammals and bison, the gallery floor was for insects, birds and small mammals, and the second floor provided exhibition space for the department of invertebrate paleontology. Study rooms, storage apartments, and space for keeping study materials were housed on the top floor. The construction of galleries in the curator's offices in the old wing of the Museum was doubled for the storage of specimens. Many other improvements were implemented throughout the old spaces in the Museum to great effect. The Board of Trustees announced at their March meeting that the Museum would re-open in the fall to the great benefit of the citizens of New York and the world.[33]

In February, Commodore Gerry traveled by train with Frank W. Hawley, a wealthy cattle breeder, to Albany to observe the Senate deliberations on the development of electricity at *Niagara Falls*, New York. Mr. Hawley spoke with the Governor and Mr. Aldridge, the Superintendent of Public Works, about the Senate's plans for the project. Upon their return to New York City, Mr. Hawley stated to the press that "work will commence in early spring to test the value of various devices submitted for the movement of canal traffic on the great waterways of New York."[34] Commodore Gerry brought quiet yet influential support for many causes to the *State General Assembly* simply by virtue of his presence at committee hearings that were open to the public.

On March 6 Commodore Gerry returned to Albany, only this time his quiet influence became a heated topic before the *General Assembly*. The Senate Judiciary Committee had reported favorably on the *Whipping Post Bill* instigated by Commodore Gerry, permitting corporal punishment on persons assaulting a female, or a child of either sex under the age of sixteen. An amendment to the bill exempted wife-beaters because the Committee believed it would be too hard to prove assault and battery when wives usually refused to testify against their husbands.[35] The bill was now before the House, and Commodore Gerry was aware of the controversy surrounding corporal punishment and the narrow edge by which the bill had passed the Senate. He had come to Albany to lobby the bill through to the final vote which was to take place in a week or two. The press had noted that Commodore Gerry in his characteristically nervous fashion had been doing some effective work for the bill since his arrival in Albany. However, on

March 7 while sitting in the House Chamber next to Mr. Foley, and just after the reading of committee reports, Assemblyman Alonzo Bell claimed the attention of the House by uttering the words, "Mr. Speaker, I wish that the presiding officer of this House would enforce the rule with reference to lobbying. I notice on the floor of the House a gentleman who is in favor of the *Whipping-Post Bill.*" Every eye in the Chamber glanced toward Commodore Gerry. "The Sergeant at Arms will enforce the rule," said Speaker Fish. No one stirred, and Mr. Gerry calmly looked up at the Speaker of the House. Throwing his voice several notes higher than usual, the Speaker repeated the order, whereupon the Chief Doorkeeper walked down to Mr. Gerry, touched him on the arm, and escorted him to the rear of the Chamber to the public viewing space.[36] Here Commodore Gerry stood and complacently listened to the debate that Mr. Bell's suggestion had precipitated. Mr. Foley, a Democrat, defended the Commodore, and said that it was his idea that Mr. Gerry was entitled to the privileges of the floor, and while he was not now, he had been a State officer, and was entitled to respect. He then made a formal motion to accord floor privileges to Commodore Gerry. Nonetheless, the Speaker of the House responded with "The Chair objects to any one remaining on the floor who is interested in the bill." The Speaker then said, "Calendar of the Day," and with that, Commodore Gerry walked out of the Chamber. Ten minutes later, in the Senate Chamber, on the motion of Democratic Senator Guy, Commodore Gerry was unanimously granted the freedom of the Senate floor, as a palliative for the wound to his sensibilities by the underserved action of the House Chamber. Commodore Gerry was then warmly congratulated by the twenty-eight Senators who had voted in favor of the *Whipping Post Bill* the day before.[37]

On March 14, the day of the final vote, one last Representative spoke to the House Chamber. John A. Hennessy, who was not more than five feet, three inches tall and weighed scarcely 135 pounds, was known as the "legislative wasp" due to his pugnacity and vitriolic speeches. On this day he stung the *Whipping Post Bill* to death. When Representative Hennessy rose to speak, the passage of the bill was all but assured. He used all of the abuse case statistics and the percentage of convictions to controvert some of the strongest arguments in the bill's favor. On the final vote there were only 53 affirmatives or twelve less than the majority, and fifty-seven negatives. The motion to reconsider the bill failed. After the legislature adjourned, over twenty members assured "the wasp" that but for his speech they would have voted for the bill.[38] Commodore Gerry published an article entitled "Must We Have the Cat-O-Nine Tails?" where he argued for the need of corporal punishment in cases of wife and child beating when incarceration routinely fails to deter or adequately punish a man prone to physical violence. He provides the historical context for his position and cited States that had passed legislation permitting corporal punishment in the same circumstances proposed by the *Whipping Post Bill*.[39]

Upon his return home to New York City, Commodore Gerry took a moment to breathe and went down to the *Tebo Yacht Basin* in Brooklyn, New York where his yacht *Electra* was being fitted-up for the summer season. His brother-in-law, Frederic Gallatin, also had his yacht the *Almy* at *Tebo Basin* being made ready for club and family cruises.

The *Society of the New York Hospital*, of which Commodore Gerry was a long-standing trustee, met in April to release their Annual Report. It had been a momentous year for the Board with its oversight of the historic move of the *Bloomingdale Asylum* from One Hundred and Seventeenth Street at Amsterdam, to the new location at White Plains, New York. The great majority of patients, who were quiet and well behaved, were transferred by special cars. The feeble patients and those liable to violent or disorderly impulses went in small parties by ambulance or carriage the distance of twenty miles. Patients found it an agreeable change with cheerful new buildings and beautiful grounds. Another important move was the *House of Relief* from Chambers Street to 67 and 69 Hudson Street, subsequently known as the *Hudson Street Hospital*. The *Society Board* was also in the midst of a fund-raising campaign to assist with the Hospital's work. The Annual Report was of particular interest in 1895 because it included numerous illustrations of the new hospital buildings and their beautiful interior rooms and exterior surroundings.[40] About the same time, another charitable institution, the *Home for the Incurables*, a charity supported by the Gerry and Livingston women, celebrated its 29th anniversary. The Reverend George McGrew addressed the celebration, noting how far charities had come:

> Twenty-nine years ago this home was founded, whose name "home" marks the period when New York City began to solve her own problems in her own way, and under the new order of things the "institution" is replaced with the "home." There is nothing more depressing to visitors and patients than the indefinable something called an institution, and it is not an easy thing to avoid it. The source from which it springs is the presence of paid officials and the distinction made between paying and non-paying patients. In this home the officers are the patient's friends, and in all these buildings there is but one person who knows who pays and who does not.[41]

The successful partnership of public and private charitable institutions during the *Gilded Age* was sustained by the personal effort and the private wealth of many of society's most elite families whose philanthropy was often overshadowed by their extravagant life-styles.

Mr. and Mrs. Ogden Goelet were back in the news in May 1895 with reports that they had invited Prince Edward Albert, "Bertie" for a visit to Newport for the summer and to enjoy the *America's Cup* race to be held in late summer. The Goelets were considered to be the warmest and most intimate personal friends the Prince had in America. Ogden Goelet was the recipient of the prince's hospitality more frequently than any other American when visiting England, indeed, on many occasions they spent several days hunting or several weeks yachting together.[42] In personal magnetism and charm of manner Mr. Goelet was without peer in New York society. He and his brother Robert Goelet were shorter men who dressed fashionably without being conspicuous. Their wives were beautiful and considered to be impeccable hostesses. Their circle of mutual friends with the Prince included the actress Lilly Langtry who was at the time, living in New York. She had participated in several charity events in March and April of 1895, but in mid-May Lilly joined most of the yachting set, including the Goelets, and set sail for the spring season in Europe. Those who went directly to London, especially the elite set, stayed at the *Hotel Bristol,* which included the Goelets, Vanderbilts, and Whitneys. The luggage of these wealthy Americans was said to fill the hotel lobby and the first floor corridors. The London press welcomed the invasion of Americans who spent money at the best shops, hired all the dressmakers, frequented the best restaurants, and in general gave an economic boost to the city. Almost immediately the Goelets were deluged with invitations to various aristocratic gatherings, which caused a renewal of rumors that there was a possibility that the Prince of Wales would accompany them back to the United States for the *America's Cup* race in September.[43]

The Gallatins and Gerrys remained in the United States, and the Gallatins entertained on their yacht the *Almy* for Decoration Day on May 14with a trip up the Sound. On June 2, clearly the start of the summer season, Commodore and Mrs. Gerry attended the wedding of Anne Cameron to Belmont Tiffany at St. John's Episcopal Church in Clifton, Staten Island. Cornelius Vanderbilt had owned most of the Clifton area in the early days when he established the ferry service between Long Island and Manhattan. Most of the wedding guests from New York City were brought to Clifton by special boat, whereas Commodore Gerry steamed over on the *Electra.* Back in New York, Peter Gerry, home for the summer, was participating in a coaching run in which Gertrude Vanderbilt joined the party. Also on June 2 the Gallatins again entertained family and a few friends on the *Almy* with an excursion to *Stoney Point.* The next day, June 3, the engagement of J. Wadsworth Ritchie to Miss Emily Tooker was announced in Newport and published in all the papers, none of which failed to mention the broken Gerry engagement just seven months earlier. Needless to say, society had moved forward with their lives and the engagement was enthusiastically welcomed in Newport. Fortunately for Angelica, the Ritchie engagement was quickly overshadowed on June 6 with rumors that the Prince of Wales would visit Newport in August as the private guest of Mr. and Mrs. Ogden Goelet. Although the Goelets were presently on a Mediterranean cruise, they already had contractors redecorating parts of their mansion, *Ochre Court*, with a suite to be especially furnished for the Prince. The only special request by the Prince should he visit, was that no fuss be made over him while in America, and that he be allowed to move about Newport and the Cup races strictly incognito. The Prince of Wales was not hard to recognize, nonetheless, society in Newport respected the privacy of their many famous neighbors and visitors, so the prince was assured a "no fuss" visit.[44] Later in June, while Ogden Goelet was at Cowes, England on his yacht the *Whyte Ladye*, he spent time with the Prince of Wales at the royal yacht races. They discussed the Prince's health and his schedule for the remainder of the summer and concluded that the visit to Newport was not feasible. His yacht *Britannia* was in dry dock at Southampton, and not available for a transatlantic voyage. The fifty-four year old Prince actually spent most of August and September in Homburg, Germany for his annual health spa treatments, and from there he traveled to Copenhagen to visit his wife's family and attend to state business.[45] The last visit the Prince of Wales had made to America was in 1860 at age nineteen when he attended the *Grand Ball* in New York City where Commodore Gerry first met his wife, Louisa Livingston. Indeed, the 1860 visit was the first by the royal family since before the *American Revolution.* By July 26 the steam yacht *Whyte Ladye* had returned from Europe and was anchored in Newport Harbor in anticipation of the *Goelet Cup* race the first week of August. Ogden Goelet remained in Newport for several weeks, which gave him an opportunity to socialize with his architect and dear friend, Richard M. Hunt, before leaving for the *America's Cup* race in early September.

Newport's tranquility was shaken on July 31, 1896 when architect Richard Morris Hunt died unexpectedly at his Newport home after a leisurely summer among his dearest friends. He was sixty-eight years old and weakened by numerous ailments and a brutal work schedule. His wife, two daughters and one of three sons were with him during his last days. He had been awarded the *Victoria Gold Medal* in 1893 by the *Royal Institute of British Architects,* the highest distinction that an architect can receive in England. He was a member of the *Architectural*

Institute of France, the *Society of Architects and Engineers* in Vienna, and a member of the *Academy of St. Luc* in Rome. Hunt was a founding member of the *American Institute of Architects* in Washington, D.C. and President of its New York *AIA Chapter* for many years.

In the last few years of his life Hunt's wife begged him to slow down, but Richard Morris Hunt knew only hard work. Between 1891 and his death in July 1895 he was simultaneously involved in the following historic projects:

> *Administration Building,* World's Columbian Exposition, Chicago, IL
> *Astor Mansion,* New York City for John Jacob Astor
> *Belcourt Castle,* Newport, RI for Oliver Belmont
> *Biltmore Estate,* Asheville, NC for George W. Vanderbilt (*largest residence in America*)
> *The Breakers,* Newport, RI for Cornelius Vanderbilt II
> *Fogg Art Museum,* Boston, MA
> *Gerry Mansion,* New York City, NY for Commodore Elbridge T. Gerry
> *Indian Springs,* Newport, RI for J. R. Busk
> *Marble House,* Newport, RI for William K. Vanderbilt
> *Ochre Court,* Newport, RI for Ogden Goelet

Richard Morris Hunt possessed the finest architectural library in America, and a peerless collection of casts, drawings, and photographs. Most of these materials are part of the *American Institute of Architects Library* and *Archives* in Washington, D.C. Among the pallbearers at his funeral at Trinity Church, Newport, RI, were Charles McKim and Henry Marquand. He was buried in Newport's *Island Cemetery* where his gravestone reads, *"Laborare Est Orare,"* labor is prayer.[46]

The Newport summer season was slowly winding down and the special guests of society were leaving for distant homes. The most illustrious summer guest in 1895 was the Duke of Marlborough, the special guest of the former Mrs. Willie Vanderbilt at *Marble House.* Alva's divorce from Willie Vanderbilt only increased her determination to find a suitable husband for her daughter, with or without love. After the *America's Cup* race the Duke returned to Newport with the Vanderbilts and in a private moment, he proposed marriage to Alva's twenty-year-old daughter Consuelo. There had been wild speculation all summer that the Duke was visiting for that very purpose, but Alva Vanderbilt repeatedly denied any engagement, even while she was frustrated that he had not proposed sooner. New York society enjoyed the momentary excitement of the beautiful Tooker-

Ritchie wedding in Newport on August 27, but it could not compare with the announcement of a Vanderbilt engagement and what became one of *Gilded Gotham's* grandest weddings on November 6, 1895. Alva Vanderbilt was so sure that the Duke would propose while in Newport, that she had ordered Consuelo's wedding gown from *Worth* in Paris the previous spring. The engagement involved signing dowry documents and sending out 4,000 invitations on both sides of the Atlantic. The wedding took place at Saint Thomas Church on Fifth Avenue and was of such public interest that 300 police were required to manage the thousands of spectators.[47]

The 1895 *America's Cup* race, held just two months before the Vanderbilt wedding, was of great interest to the Duke of Marlborough because the challenger was the British yacht the *Valkyrie III,* owned by the fourth Earl of Dunraven. This was one of the strangest *Cup* races in the history of the *New York Yacht Club.* Lord Dunraven had been racing yachts for almost ten years and had in fact first negotiated for an *America's Cup* challenge in 1889 but was unable to persuade the *Royal Yacht Squadron,* acting on his behalf, to come to an agreement. Finally, the 1895 challenge was accepted and Lord Dunraven's yacht, the *Valkyrie III,* raced against the *NYYC's* contender, the *Defender,* owned by Mr. C. Oliver Iselin. The design of yachts, sloops and schooners were constantly evolving and before every *Cup* race the competing yachts were measured and evaluated against the *America's Cup* Deed of Gift rules. The *Defender* had a water-line of 88 feet 5 ½ inches, and the sail area was 13,000 feet square, or 400 square feet less than that of the *Valkyrie III,* whose water-line was 88 feet 10 inches.[48] The *America's Cup* consisted of three races on three successive days. The first race, fifteen nautical miles outside of New York Harbor, was won by the yacht *Defender* when it crossed the finish line an amazing seven minutes ahead of the *Valkyrie III.* Immediately after the finish of the first race, Lord Dunraven made a complaint to the *Cup* committee that the yacht *Defender* was immersed below the officially measured water-line due to tampering with the ballast during the race. The regatta committee responded immediately to the charge of cheating and re-measured the *Defender* in the presence of Lord Dunraven and C. Oliver Iselin before the second race. The *Defender* was found to be of the correct length and the matter was apparently dropped.

Within a few seconds of the starting-gun being fired for the second Cup race, a foul occurred between the two yachts, the *Valkyrie III* being to windward and her boom end catching the starboard topmast-shroud of the *Defender,* which tore it from the broken end of the spreader. Although the *Defender* was crippled she continued the race a full minute behind. Lord Dunraven's yacht, *Valkyrie III,* won the second race by forty-seven seconds after the *Defender* pursued her challenger despite the accident, making for an exciting race. After the race C. Oliver Iselin filed a protest for the foul by the *Valkyrie III,* which was sustained by the regatta committee after a hearing of both sides. The cause of the foul began with crowding by the fleet of pleasure steamers, notably the *Yorktown,* which lay close to the course. All the evidence, including many important photographs, showed that the *Valkyrie III* took the active part in the preliminary maneuvers around the steamer *Yorktown* while the *Defender* held her course on the wind. As the two yachts came within view of the finish line the *Valkyrie III* found herself in very limited space near the steamer *Yorktown* and when she then came dangerously close to the *Defender,* she steered too far past the optimal windward trim and caused the foul. The owner of the *Defender,* C. Oliver Iselin offered to call the race off and re-sail it, but Lord Dunraven would not consent, apparently accepting the decision of the regatta committee to award the second race to the *Defender* because of the foul.[49]

Finally, the two yachts were at the starting line of the third and final Cup race when the signal shot to start was fired. The *Defender* was off with good speed but the *Valkyrie III* started slowly and then veered away and headed back to the New York Harbor, effectively canceling the *America's Cup* race for 1895. The Earl of Dunraven returned to England without explanation, but then, obviously dissatisfied with the regatta committee's decision on his charge that the *Defender's* ballast had been tampered with between the two water-line measurements taken before the first and second races he published a pamphlet that made public his charges of cheating, which resulted in a serious international quarrel.

The *New York Yacht Club* appointed J. Pierpont Morgan, William C. Whitney, and George L. Rives to an official Investigation Committee. They immediately asked a Navy captain and an ambassador to join them to ensure the investigation was thorough and would be respected by the international yachting community. At a meeting of the *NYYC* to discuss the matter, Ex-Commodore Elbridge T. Gerry addressed the Club, "The yacht club has acted in a dignified way and has done the only thing that could be done. I don't know of any reason why Lord Dunraven should come over, and he hasn't come yet. Mr. Iselin's letter was a fair presentation of his case. The committee has the three ablest men, two are noted lawyers and Mr. Morgan is well known here and in Europe as a business man. It is such a jury as will render an impartial verdict, which will be approved on both sides of the Atlantic."[50] Lord Dunraven and his lawyers returned to America in December to defend their charges before the committee, and to hear all the witnesses. The committee rendered its decision on February 6, 1896 and delivered copies to the press and to Lord Dunraven, who refused to be interviewed in London. The result was the complete exoneration of Mr. C. Oliver Iselin and all connected with the yacht *Defender*. Because Lord Dunraven refused to apologize for his unfounded public charges he was expelled from the *New York Yacht Club*, after which he abruptly withdrew from the sport of yachting on both sides of the Atlantic. The action of Lord Dunraven in issuing his pamphlet was never endorsed by British yachtsmen or the *Royal Yacht Squadron* at Cowes, England.[51]

The 1895 *America's Cup* race was held September 1 to 10 during a difficult time in the personal life of Commodore Elbridge T. Gerry. About the time of the Tooker-Ritchie wedding on August 27, Hannah Goelet Gerry, the Commodore's mother, had taken ill and the Gerry and Gallatin families congregated in New York City. Her last surviving children, Elbridge and Almy Gerry Gallatin, attended her bedside through her illness. On September 3, the press released a short notice stating that, "Mrs. Hannah G. Gerry, the widow of Thomas R. Gerry, is dangerously ill from pneumonia at her home in the Goelet mansion, and it is feared that she cannot recover."[52] Just two days later the paper reported on September 5 that, "The condition of Mrs. Gerry, who has been dangerously ill with pneumonia at her residence, was said last night to be greatly improved. Commodore Elbridge T. Gerry sent word that his mother was much better, and that he had strong hopes of her recovery."[53] Commodore Gerry and Frederic Gallatin were then able to attend the *America's Cup* between September 7 and 10, although the third race on the tenth was a default by Lord Dunraven. Back at Hannah's bedside on September 11, the Gerry and Gallatin families remained hopeful of their mother's recovery, however she took a turn for the worse and on Friday, September 13, Commodore Elbridge T. Gerry's beloved mother died at age ninety. She had lived in virtual retirement since moving into the old Broadway Farm mansion in 1848 with her brother, Peter Goelet, her sister Jean Buchanan Goelet, and her three small children, Elbridge, Almy, and Jean. Hannah survived all her siblings and remained the head of the Goelet family dynasty in New York City until her death in 1895. She left a simple will that gave all of her property, possessions and income to be shared equally between her two children, Elbridge and Almy, which had a shared inheritance value in the millions of dollars. The funeral for Hannah was held on September 17 at the family church, *Trinity Chapel* at Wall Street and West Twenty-Fifth Street. The services were of extreme simplicity and a request that floral tributes be omitted was honored. The casket was of antique oak and on the lid was a brass plate in the form of a Greek cross with the inscription, "Hannah G. Gerry, Born January 19, 1806. Died September 13, 1895." Among the relatives who followed the casket were Elbridge T. Gerry, Mr. and Mrs. Fredric Gallatin with three of their children, and Robert Goelet, General James R. Pearsall, and Clinton Roosevelt. Hannah was buried in the Goelet Vault in the cemetery at

Saint Mark's Church where her husband, Thomas Russell Gerry was interred 50 years earlier, and her brother, Peter Goelet was laid to rest in 1879, and her sister Jean in 1882. Hannah's nephews and Commodore Gerry's cousins, Robert and Ogden Goelet, were now the Goelet family patriarchs.[54]

The house at Nineteenth and Broadway was inherited by Commodore Gerry's sister Almy Gallatin. In partnership with her husband Frederic she had the ancient, empty and isolated townhouse razed in 1897 and erected a commercial building in its place. What was an expansive farm on the outskirts of New York City in 1835, with its exotic animals and a reclusive family, became in fifty years-time the location of the last occupied mansion on Broadway in lower Manhattan that was completely surrounded by skyscrapers and commercial buildings. The old Broadway Farm was the last remnant of Elbridge T. Gerry's childhood memories with Uncle Peter Goelet, his mother and sisters.

By the end of September Commodore Gerry had the yacht *Electra* anchored at the *Tebo Dock* in Brooklyn. In early October the *Electra* was sent down to the *Harlan & Hollingsworth* yard in Delaware where it would undergo a thorough overhaul and modernization over the winter months. Sometimes Commodore Gerry considered a replacement for the aging *Electra,* but he always preferred an upgrade, so this year he had her hull painted white which gave the appearance of a new yacht.

Although Hannah Gerry's will made an equal distribution between her two children, the estate itself was a complex mix of real estate, personal property, and income, some of which was derived from a trust. When Thomas R. Gerry died in 1845 his will created trusts for the benefit of his four sisters, the last of which, Emily, had just died a year ago. On the death of his sisters the trusts were to go to his wife, Hannah G. Gerry, to revert on her demise to the remaining heirs, her children, Elbridge and Almy. In January, 1896, six months after Hannah's death, the *Gerry Trust* account was settled in the General Session of the New York Supreme Court. At Hannah's death the trust funds were $34,898, for which the court had to appoint a new administrator. On January 2, 1896, Judge Beekman signed a judgment that appointed Commodore Elbridge T. Gerry the administrator of the remaining *Gerry Trust* funds and also released the funds for immediate division. Commodore Gerry gave public notice of the distribution in the *General Session Assignments* in the New York Times, January 3, 1896. The extended family of Gerrys, Gallatins Goelets and Livingstons remained in mourning over the holidays and did not attend the balls or dinners through December 1895.

The January 5, 1896 annual *Assembly Ball* held at the Waldorf Hotel was the first public affair that Commodore and Mrs. Gerry had attended since Hannah

Gerry's death. Mrs. Maturin Livingston, Louisa Gerry's widowed aunt, joined them at the ball, as did Ogden and Mary Goelet. Shortly after the ball, Ogden and Mary Goelet left New York City on their yacht the *Whyte Ladye* for a month in Paris, followed by their annual winter yacht cruises between their home in London and their home in Nice, and a leased residence in Cannes on the Mediterranean Sea.[55] During this extended cruise, Ogden Goelet was patiently awaiting the construction of a new yacht that was designed by George L. Watson in consultation with Ogden before he set sail in January. The twin screw and steel yacht was constructed in Glasgow, Scotland, and was described as unsurpassed in luxury appointments with the latest in mechanical upgrades, but it would not be ready for a trial run until the fall of 1896. Ogden Goelet was a gentleman yachtsman as was his cousin Commodore Gerry; although they cruised in their luxury yachts with family and friends, they were passionate observers of yacht club regatta races. Ogden Goelet not only sponsored the *Goelet Cup* in Newport every year, he did the same in Europe. In the 1890's many of the international large-class racing yachts competed in a series of regattas in the Mediterranean. These races were popular among the owners and spectators because they coincided with the fashionable winter season along the Riviera at Cannes, Nice, San Remo and other exclusive harbors. The regatta at Cannes was sponsored by Americans Ogden Goelet and James G. Bennett, and the *Union des Yachtsmen de Cannes*, which they founded together in 1893. After the winter season, the large class racers would return to their homeports to be re-fitted before the early summer regatta season started in England, followed by the American season in late summer. Both Ogden and his wife Mary were yachting enthusiasts and by 1896 lived most of the year on the *Whyte Ladye*. While anchored in Nice, France, their dear friend the Prince of Wales arrived on his yacht *Britannia* to compete in the regatta races. To everyone's delight, his mother, Queen Victoria, had accompanied the Prince to Nice for a holiday. On April 7, 1896 the Goelets had the honor of being presented to the Queen by the Prince on the yacht *Britannia*. This may have been the Prince's way of making up for his cancelled visit to Newport the previous summer.

From Nice, Ogden and Mary cruised to London for the *Royal Yacht Squadron* regatta in early summer. For these lengthy stays in London they purchased one of the most attractive mansions in London known as *Wimborne House*. It had a massive stone exterior that at times appeared gloomy. However, the interior was sumptuously decorated and many of the ceilings had enormous sky lights. During the American season in London, invitations to *Wimborne House* galas were highly sought after and the Goelets often hosted hundreds of guests.

In mid-March, Cornelius Vanderbilt sent a special train from New York City to Palm Beach, Florida to celebrate the completion of Henry M. Flagler's bridge extension to the *Royal Poinciana Hotel.* Flagler completed his first-class Hotel *Royal Poinciana* in 1884 but needed the train bridge to bring the wealthy to Palm Beach. The special Vanderbilt train was the first to cross the bridge and bring *Gilded Gotham's* finest to the *Royal Poinciana Hotel.* The train carried Mabel Gerry, her friend Gertrude Vanderbilt and Harry P. Whitney, and several other guests. Flagler eventually set his sights on Key West, and in 1912 saw construction completed of his Over-Sea Railroad linking the Keys. It would operate until 1935, when it was damaged by a hurricane. As early as the 1890's Palm Beach was the playground of the wealthy.

Meanwhile, back in New York City the first wedding of the next generation of Gerrys was celebrated on April 28, 1896 in *Trinity Chapel.* Almy Gerry Gallatin's son, twenty-five year old Rolaz Horace Gallatin married Emily Lorillard Morris. The decorations in the Chapel were unique. On either side of the entrance to the chancel stood two huge palms, and a little in front of them were two tree ferns, each eighteen feet high, which towered high over the alter. The trunks of the trees were covered with orchids and the Alter was almost hidden beneath a mass of American Beauty roses. More than 1,000 guests were present, representing the most fashionable people in society. The maid of honor was fourteen-year-old Miss Mary Gallatin, sister of the bridegroom, and one of the ushers was his brother, nineteen-year-old Goelet Gallatin. There was no reception after the ceremony, however a few guests and family enjoyed a lovely breakfast at the Gallatin home. The bride and groom sailed for Europe the next week for an extended honeymoon.[56]

In the midst of a busy New York social season Commodore Elbridge T. Gerry was involved in the appeal of a child commitment case on behalf of the *NYSPCC.* On March 11, 1896 Lucy Poly, a fifteen year old girl, was found in a reputed house of prostitution associating with dissolute persons, and was arrested at the instance of an agent of the *NYSPCC.* The next day Lucy was brought before a magistrate of the city of New York. An Agent representing the *Gerry Society* and the girl's aunt were present at the hearing. Lucy's aunt advised the magistrate that the girl and her parents were members of the Roman Catholic Church, yet the girl was committed to a Protestant institution instead of a Catholic institution. On appeal, the Magistrate admitted that he knew the girl and her parents were Catholic, but in his opinion, there was evidence of the impracticability of committing Lucy to the Catholic Institution. The judge cited both the *Penal Code* which required the arrest of Lucy Poly for associating with a house of prostitution, and the *Consolidated Acts,* which clearly stated that any commitment of a juvenile must be to an institution of the same religion unless there is clear evidence that it is not possible due to overcrowding or other impediment. While the arrest and commitment were upheld by the judge, he reversed the lower court, finding that the magistrate had no clear evidence that it was impractical to place Lucy in a Catholic home. The judge ordered the defendant, Lucy Poly, to be removed from the Protestant institution and placed in *the House of the Good Shepherd,* a Catholic institution.[57] This case was cited in the *Columbia Law Review* in 1954, a discussion of religion as a factor in adoption, guardianship, and custody.

Another NYSPCC case appeared in the summer papers next to another article about troublesome New York City children. The first involved a five-year old boy in the custody of the *Gerry Society* because he was accused of stabbing a two-year old boy by the two-year-old's mother. The five year old was brought before the magistrate where he said that he had no knife and that the little boy fell while they were playing and cut his head on a piece of glass. When the mother of the two-year old was questioned she said she did not see how it happened and was only told by two older boys whom she did not know. The magistrate found the mother vindictive and asked if she would like him to give the five-year old the electric chair, attempting to put the situation in perspective. She simply shrugged her shoulders and said, "Let the law take its course, I don't care what they do with him." Fortunately, the child was returned to the care of the *Gerry Society.* The second article noted that several boys were "scorching" on their bicycles, which meant they were racing on busy streets and sidewalks. The magistrate shouted at the boys, "Can you men read?" to which they answered yes, and the magistrate continued, "While you cannot believe more than one-tenth of what you see in the newspapers, you can at least rely upon enough to convince you that life and limb are being endangered every day by just such fellows as you. The law only allows me to fine you $10 each, but if it were in my power, I would make the fine very much more." A succession of boys were paraded before the magistrate, each being fined $5 or $10 for either reckless bicycle riding or "scorching," a new scourge in *Gilded Gotham.*[58]

Both Commodore Gerry and Ogden Goelet managed property transactions during 1896. Commodore Gerry handled adjustments to leases for property he owned, one at 88 West Broadway and another at 72 Warren Street. His lessee, Mr. Prial, sought an adjustment to his lease to permit alterations to his five-story brick factory that sat on one of the properties. By contrast, Ogden Goelet sought to support his cultural interests and built the *Murray Hill Theatre* on Lexington Avenue in 1896, no doubt with the oversight and business management of his brother Robert Goelet, who ran the extensive Goelet business holdings. Ogden built the *Murray Hill Theatre* on land owned by the Goelet Brothers Inc., and Frank B. Murtha was the theater's first manager. Later William Morris took over and converted the theatre to a vaudeville playhouse. In 1909 Marcus Loew bought the building and re-named it Loews 42nd Street. The original building was demolished in 1950, and the site is now home to the *Mobil Building.*[59]

The entire Gerry family set sail on the *White Star* steamship *Majestic* on June 3, 1896 for Liverpool, England. They remained in Europe through July, except for Robert who returned early to open their rented *Lyndenhurst* house for the summer season in Newport, Rhode Island. The Gerrys had an opportunity to visit with their cousins Ogden and Mary Goelet who were at Cowes, England in July for the royal yacht races. On July 15 a dispatch was received by the newspapers saying that despite denials, Ogden Goelet was seriously ill on board his yacht the *Whyte Ladye.* The report stated that Ogden had not left his cabin for three weeks. However, his brother Robert Goelet who was in New York City denied the reports by saying that when he first heard the rumors he sent a dispatch to his brother in England who responded that he was fine. Robert reassured the press that he was not at all worried and the message from his brother was convincing. Ogden Goelet's health had been in a weakened state for the last few years, a chest condition like asthma, and it was the advice of his physician that he should spend the winters abroad in warmer climates, which in fact had helped.

The Gerry family was reunited at *Lyndenhurs*t in Newport the first week of August, just in time to welcome the opening of the *Newport Country Club,* a superb new building for hosting society entertainments. It offered a handsome new ballroom, a large banquet hall and outdoor verandas for taking tea and light lunches. The club was adjacent to the golf course and the tennis courts, and nearly 200 new bicycles were delivered, exceeding the number of horses in Newport. The old *Casino* on Bellevue Avenue was available for smaller affairs and offered additional tennis courts for the ever popular sport. The new club was the perfect place to join in the summer gossip which was buzzing about the visit of the Duke of Manchester, known to be in search of a wealthy American belle to marry. The papers were touting Gertrude Vanderbilt, Mabel Gerry, Angelica Gerry and May Goelet as the most desirable belles in Newport. To everyone's delight it was announced that Mabel Gerry's best friend, Gertrude Vanderbilt was engaged to Harry P. Whitney; it was one of society's most successful matches. A gala dinner at the Vanderbilt mansion, *The Breakers,* was held in their honor on August 23 to which Angelica and Mabel were happily invited. Commodore and Louisa Gerry also joined the celebration.[60]

Frederic and Almy Gallatin did not visit Newport in 1896 but rather they cruised the Mediterranean and the European coast as far north as Denmark on their yacht *Almy*. On August 2 the shipping news reported seeing the *Almy* sailing southward past New York, perhaps heading for Palm Beach, Florida, the popular yacht destination that was publicized in March by the special Vanderbilt train ride to the *Royal Poinciana Hotel*. The cruise of the *Almy* covered an astonishing 17,000 miles from June until the first week of October. The Gallatins did take a break in Hamburg, Germany mid-way through the extended cruise, while the *Almy* proceeded to Queenstown, New Zealand to be supplied and repaired for the remainder of the cruise. The crew of the *Almy* encountered a hurricane en route but skillfully rode out the storm and then returned to Homburg to pick up the Gallatins and continue the cruise. Meanwhile, Commodore and Louisa Gerry closed their cottage and left Newport on September 7. They boarded *Electra*, and sailed up the Hudson River for Kingston to spend some quiet family time at the Lake Delaware estate in Delhi, New York. By October the Gerrys had returned to New York City and the *Electra* was sent to the *Tebo Dock* in Brooklyn to prepare for its annual maintenance and refurbishing. The Gallatins' yacht the *Almy* was also back at *Tebo Dock* by the end of September for its winter overhaul. The Gerry and Gallatin families settled in for the holidays in *Gilded Gotham*.

The luxury apartment building that Louisa Gerry had arranged for architect Alfred Zucker to build on a plot of land she owned at Fifth Avenue and Fifty-Eighth Street had been completed about the time the Gerrys moved into their new home in 1895. It was named the *Bolkenhayn Apartment House*, after Alfred Zucker's home town in Prussia. Each apartment was named after a Prussian king, emperor or premier, and a Majorca tile panel was imbedded in the door of each apartment entrance with a depiction of the leader. Finely painted Majorca tile panels were hung along the main public hallways depicting scenes of daily life in Prussian towns. There was no apartment house in *Gilded Gotham* that could compare with the ornate detail and design of the Tuckahoo marble and Pompeian brick building. In October 1896 Alfred Zucker filed plans for alterations to the apartment building with Louisa Gerry's approval. The first floor of the building was rented out as retail space while the upper floors each had two 4,000 square foot apartments. The annual rent was $8,000 for each apartment and only the very wealthy could afford such luxury. By 1905, millionaires like Isaac Guggenheim occupied the apartments. The changes that Alfred Zucker had planned in 1896 were just the first among many that he filed over the years. He added a roof-top garden for the pleasure of the renters, and progressively, he re-constructed apartments to suit their needs, like when he converted an entire floor to the use of a single wealthy family. Finally in 1926 the apartment house was annexed for use by the *Savoy-Plaza Hotel* next door. The hotel was then demolished in 1964 and the *General Motors Building* was built on the site.[61]

With the untimely death of Richard Morris Hunt just several months after the Gerrys had moved into their residence, the mansion remained unfinished. Eager to complete her home, and confident in his skills as an architect, Louisa Gerry engaged Alfred Zucker in early 1896 to prepare designs for remodeling and completing the mansion. The first architectural task was to design a *Grand Marble Staircase* centered on the main hallway, and facing the Sixty- First Street entrance to the mansion. As the project progressed, Louisa Gerry would review Zucker's sketches of designs for iron work, plaster, and wood panels, after which she would make a final selection. The *Grand Marble Stairs* ascended to the second floor, but from there Zucker used a modest, more functional stair design for access to the private upper floors. Wood panels, both carved and beveled, were added as needed to enrich the formal first floor areas, especially the great hallway that ran the full length of the house from east to west. Alfred Zucker had the grand staircase built first because it was a primary access point, and, because it was the first architectural feature encountered by guests upon entering the residence.

The second major task was to elaborate on the original design of the *Law Library* space which lacked ornamental wood work, symbolic artwork, stained glass, and the overall scholarly aesthetic that Commodore Elbridge T. Gerry sought to achieve. Zucker's idea for the library required significant structural alterations that raised the roof to incorporate enormous allegorical friezes at the third floor elevation of the grand space. The east wall incorporated an arched stained glass window above a wall frieze taken from the *Temple of Apollo in Phigalia* that was dedicated to Apollo Eipikourious, meaning "helper" or "succourer." This tied in nicely with Commodore Gerry's life-long work with the *Society for the Prevention of Cruelty to Children*.

The frieze depicted noble battles between the Greeks and the Amazons, like E. T. Gerry's legal and civic battles in New York.[62]

Alfred Zucker significantly increased the number of book shelves by adding four, 6 foot long book cases at 9 foot intervals along the north and south walls of the room. Each book case was anchored with a marble pillar with a marble bust of an historical figure sitting on top. This created intimate alcoves where books could be shelved by size to save space or by subject for ease of use. The collection, which is now part of the *United States Supreme Court Library*, included the statutes and case reporters of every state. It was a working law collection that reflected the cases he argued, e.g. books on the insanity defense, and books for his advisory roles, e.g. historic methods of torture and capital punishment, and books on canonical law for his work with the *Episcopal Church.* For his own personal pleasure as a bibliophile, Commodore Gerry collected extremely rare books such as the vellum bound *Doomsday Books,* a record of over 13,000 legal settlements commissioned by William the Conqueror in 1085, or *The Great Charter of the Forest,* the first publication of law in the English language in 1477. This was the largest private law library, both physically and by volume count, in America. It is striking how similar the architectural design is to that of the *United States Supreme Court Library,* designed by Cass Gilbert and completed in 1937, just ten years after the Commodore's death. Both have a nearly three-story cathedral ceiling with balconies along three sides with allegorical friezes.

The north wall of the Commodore's *Law Library* was anchored by a central marble fireplace and at the north-east corner there was a handsome set of sliding doors inset with stained glass panels that separated the library from the dining room. One could also enter the Library through a doorway located under the new *Grand Marble Staircase* or through the double sliding-doors leading into the *Picture Gallery* located at the west end of the library.

The third and final task for architect Alfred Zucker was to design and build a stable for Commodore Gerry on two adjoining lots he owned at numbers 39 and 41 on East Sixty-Second Street. The stable was conveniently located three blocks from the mansion, out of sight and away from any animal smells. The design was a handsome and innovative plan with a basement and three floors that incorporated a mechanical hoist to store carriages on the second floor.

Alfred Zucker created a completely self-contained stable complex within the constraints imposed by a mixed-use, yet upscale residential neighborhood. High maintenance functions like the delivery of hay and the removal of waste were serviced through the basement and the exterior, street-level elevator. The stable had electricity and modern plumbing with city water piped to all three floors. The four adult Gerry children were actively involved in horse shows and coaching clubs, so the new stable accommodated sixteen horses. The carriage loft held two or three coaches on the second floor, well out of the way of the daily activity on the first floor where horses were groomed, fed, and saddled. Immediately adjacent to this work area on the first floor were the sixteen horse stalls, which provided easy access to the street when a horse or carriage was called for by the Gerry family. Two expensive yet thoughtful features of Zucker's stable-design were the massive skylight and the comfortable staff apartments.

First was the large 30 foot by 13 foot third floor roof skylight, which provided natural light that passed down to the first floor horse stalls by means of a twin 30 x

13 foot "well" or floor cut-out on the second floor. The skylight added architectural beauty to the stable. The second floor hay loft completely surrounded the "light well" and, at the north end, it had a feed chute and a hay chute that were directly over the feed and hay troughs on the first floor. The stable was a model of efficiency in labor, storage, and light management. Electric lights edged the first floor ceiling around the "light well" to provide light in the stall area at night.

The second expensive yet thoughtful feature of the Zucker stable design was the provision of a beautiful apartment at the front half of the third floor, well away from the horses, and the space was enhanced with natural light from eight windows, four on each of the north and south walls. The apartment had five bedrooms, each could accommodate more than one man, and there was a shared kitchen, bath, and a large drawing room with a fire place. Working for Commodore Gerry was both demanding and comfortable. The family was known for keeping staff for many years at a time when unemployment was rampant. The Gerry horses and carriages had previously been housed at Robert J. Livingston's stables located a few blocks from the Forty-Eighth Street townhouses, which he shared with the Gerry family until his death in 1891. The Zucker plans for remodeling the mansion were "signed off" in March, 1896, and the plans for the new stable were signed in May 1896. The work on both projects proceeded uninterrupted for five months, between May and October while the Gerry family was away, first in Europe, then Newport, and finally a stay at Lake Delaware, returning to New York City the first week of October 1896.[63]

Commodore and Louisa Gerry were comfortably settled in their now completed mansion and for the first time in a few years, looked forward to the swirl of holiday entertainments. The *Metropolitan Opera House* opened its three-month season on November 16 with three performances each week. The Gerrys held box seats on the south side of the main tier with nearby boxes occupied by the Goelets, the Iselins, and the Morgans. Three weeks later the Christmas season was inaugurated with the first *Assembly Ball* held on December 11 in the new ballroom of the *Hotel Waldorf*. The "receiving ladies" were Mrs. Astor, Mrs. Taylor, Mrs. E.T. Gerry, and Mrs. Van Renselaer, and in the "march to supper" Mrs. Astor led with Commodore Gerry at her arm. The warm glow of *Gilded Gotham* had once again embraced the Gerrys. They hosted three Monday evening "house warming" dinner-dances during January 1897, co-hosted by 24 year old Angelica and 23 year old Mabel who, although no longer debutantes, were considered the most eligible women in society.

The winter season of high society gala balls reached a pinnacle of extravagance on February 10, 1897 with the *Bradley Martin Fancy Dress Ball*. This was one of the most prominent events that came to narrowly define the *Gilded Age* as self-indulgent, excessive, and indifferent to the contemporary scourges of poverty and unemployment. The Martins sparked unprecedented press coverage of their gala affair from start to finish. This was not the first fancy dress ball in elite society, indeed the first fancy dress ball was given by "old money" Commodore and Mrs. Cornelius Vanderbilt in 1883 at their *Washington Square* townhouse, before the days of over-sized and over-decorated mansions.

To understand why this particular fancy dress ball touched such a sensitive cord with the press, one had to know who Bradley Martin and his wife Cornelia Sherman were in the rarified world of *Gilded Gotham*. Bradley was born in Albany, New York; his father was a merchant of some means and his mother was a Townsend. His wife Cornelia Sherman was born in New York City, the daughter of a retired merchant of apparently modest means. Bradley and Cornelia met at the wedding of Emily Vanderbilt and immediately fell in love. They began life very modestly living with Cornelia's parents at West Twentieth Street in the winter, and spent their summers at Saratoga, north of Albany. They had three children, and before 1881 were not prominent in society, although Bradley was a member of the *Union Club*, and they attended a few of the winter dinners and balls. Everything changed in January 1881 when Cornelia's father died and she discovered that his will had left her almost six million dollars. The Martins made two significant decisions: first they planned an extended European holiday to break into British society, and second, while they were gone, they had their townhouse renovated and expanded by opening walls to the adjacent townhouse in which Cornelia's mother lived, just as the Livingstons and Gerrys had done. Upon their return from Europe, the Martins began to entertain more lavishly and Cornelia was determined to be accepted by *Gilded Gotham's* elite social circle. In the winter and spring of 1883, Mrs. Martin's name began to appear among the patronesses, and after working with Mrs. Astor on one of the early *Assembly Ball* committees, she was all but accepted in what became known as the *Four Hundred*. The Martins attended the 1883 Vanderbilt fancy dress ball, an occasion Cornelia Martin never forgot. About this time, in 1884, while on a European tour Bradley Martin secured a lease for the famous game preserve in Scotland known as *Bal Macaan*, which became the Martin family home with only occasional winter visits to New York City. The Prince of Wales often hunted on Bradley Martin's preserve and fished for salmon on the local rivers, as did many Americans during their London season. With the friendship of the Prince, "Bertie," the Martins had been accepted into the most elite circles of British society. Before the current excitement of the 1897 fancy ball, the Martins' last notable entertainment in New York was a two-month visit in 1893 for the wedding of their daughter to the Earl of Craven, adding nobility by marriage to Bradley and Cornelia Martin's pedigree.[64]

The Martins' heralded return in December 1896 for a gala visit to New York began with the Christmas holiday celebrated in Albany at the Bradley family home. In January they returned to *Gilded Gotham* for the brilliant social season, especially to fulfill two of Cornelia Martin's ambitions. First, she was determined to round-out her society career in New York with the most superb entertainment the city had ever seen, and second, it was her enduring desire to host a fancy dress ball that would completely surpass the famous 1883 Vanderbilt fancy dress ball. The Martins immediately secured the *Hotel Waldorf* for the ball and Cornelia had fifteen second floor rooms and the Astor Dining room set aside as dressing apartments, where hair dressers, costumers, maids, and all manner of attendants were waiting.

Each guest had to select an historic character from England, France or Germany during the Fifteenth to the Eighteenth centuries and have a costume made for the ball. Needless to say, everyone attempted to keep it a secret as to which character they would be, but the dressmakers, costume shops, and house maids all knew, and much was leaked to the press. Articles were written disclosing complaints about the inflated costs for renting or making a costume, to which both the tradesmen and the social elite took offense. Bradley Martin himself paid over $800 for his costume, a sum that shocked the public. When the Martins realized the publicity for their brilliant "swan song" society ball had become negative, they let it be known that the true purpose of the ball was to stimulate the economy by creating work for the florists, hair dressers, caterers, waiters, jewelers, and costumers. But that only drew the ire of the anarchists who threatened to blow up the Martins' home, causing Bradley Martin to board up the windows. Undeterred by public discontent the Martins issued 1,600 invitations and 1,200 attended, including guests from Boston, Philadelphia, Washington, New Orleans, San Francisco, and six braved a mid-winter ocean crossing from London. Not surprisingly, the London papers derided the Martins' ball as extravagant and ill-timed with so much unemployment, just as the American papers continued to assault the self-indulgence of the event, which reportedly cost over $300,000.[65] Although the extravagant *Bradley Martin Fancy Dress Ball* had indeed surpassed the 1883 Vanderbilt fancy ball, which by comparison was modest and elegant, Bradley and Cornelia Martin were shocked by the harsh judgment of the press and the public, and finally left *Gilded Gotham* for their Scotland home, never to return to New York society.[66]

During the winter social season, Commodore Elbridge T. Gerry represented a *New York Society for the Prevention of Cruelty to Children* case first decided in December 1896, then appealed in February, and again in March 1897. There were three issues that involved the manner, the duty, and the failure of a Magistrate to take and preserve the minutes of a commitment hearing. Two children were left without a caregiver when their mother was arrested and taken before the Court of Sessions, which resulted in the children's appearance before a Magistrate for commitment to a Protectory. The children were committed to the *NYSPCC* which was challenged by their mother after her release from jail. While she alleged that the Magistrate failed to take and preserve minutes of the hearing, she failed to allege any problems with the evidence presented at the hearing. The court used this case as an opportunity to clarify the law and stated that the children were properly committed under the evidence and therefore remained with the *NYSPCC*, but also that the Magistrate was required under the law to take and preserve the minutes in all future hearings. It was clear that even if the Magistrate had taken and preserved the hearing notes for just such an appeal by the mother, she still would not have gained custody of her children based on the evidence of her imprisonment. The judge upheld Commodore Gerry's technical argument.[67]

Early 1897 was a time of great anticipation for Robert and Ogden Goelet who had ordered new yachts in 1896 to be built by *Clydebank Engineering and Shipbuilding Company* in Glasgow, Scotland. The yachts were identical twins except for the personal preferences for interior designs, personal furnishings, and exterior color schemes. Ogden Goelet's yacht was the first to be launched from dry dock for initial trial runs in November 1896 but the interior remained unfinished and more work was to be done to fine-tune the mechanicals. The second to leave dry dock was Robert Goelet's yacht which he first saw during a test cruise on February 20, 1897 before it also returned to Scotland for several months of work on the interior finishes and engine adjustments. In the meantime, Ogden and Mary Goelet set sail for the Mediterranean on the *Whyte Ladye* in February 1897 for the regattas on the French Riviera. Then, in mid-May the Goelets headed to England for a stay at *Wimborne House,* their London mansion, before going down to Cowes, for the *Royal Yacht Squadron* races.

The Gerrys traveled to Europe always looking for those special objects of art and rare pieces of furniture that would further enhance their residence. Upon their return to New York on the steamer *St. Paul,* the Gerry crates, filled with their European purchases, were once again held by the *Customs Office* based on a challenge to the valuation. Commodore Gerry had imported, among other articles, some very old furniture that he classed as "antiques" of the Louis XV period. Under the *Wilson Tariff* antiques made before 1700 were admitted duty free, but under the recently enacted Dingley *Tariff* antiques made after 1700 were subject to a duty at the rate of 35 percent of value. The contention of the Custom House officials was that even under the *Wilson Tariff* the antiques would not have escaped duty if accepted as Louis XV period furniture because the monarch was not born until 1710, ten years after the limiting date. Commodore Gerry disagreed and asked for an appeal based on the fact, or fine line, that while the furniture was classed as Louis XV, such a designation was often applied to furniture made during the reign of Louis XIV, 1643 to 1715, so that more than half a century would be on the right side of the antique date limit not requiring a tax. Commodore Gerry was said to have presented the Customs House with a "puzzling conundrum" and the matter was left open for adjustment of the tariff while the crates were temporarily held as unclaimed goods. Commodore Gerry was never far from the courtroom in his exceptionally analytical mind.[68]

Frederic and Almy Gallatin had also embarked on their annual summer cruise of the Atlantic, but for a change, they stopped in Newport, Rhode Island to enjoy the *Goelet Cup* races with family and friends. On Thursday, August 12 while anchored in *Newport Harbor* the Gallatins' yacht was involved in an accident when another yacht, the *Wild Duck,* carelessly slammed into the *Almy.* The yacht's starboard bow was stove in, the main rail smashed to kindling wood, and the bridge fixtures entirely carried away on one side. One of the launches hung precariously off one side of the *Almy.* Although there was considerable damage to the steering gear the badly damaged yacht limped back to the *Tebo Dock* in Brooklyn, New York for repairs, disrupting an otherwise pleasant summer. The owner of the *Wild Duck* agreed to pay for the damage which amounted to about $1,000.[69]

A welcome new hobby in Newport of an attractive and useful nature was gardening, and not just landscaped estates, but greenhouse gardening. The gardening magazines of the *Gilded Age* followed the exploits of the nation's most accomplished gardeners, two of which were in Newport, Rhode Island. Patrick Carr was the gardener at *Southside,* the Robert Goelet estate and J. R. Johnson was the gardener at Ogden Goelet's estate *Ochre Court.* The Vanderbilt and Morgan estates in Newport also had professional gardeners. They competed in annual garden shows with new varieties of roses, azaleas and even exotic fruits.[70] Commodore and Louisa Gerry admired the creative work of Newport's master gardeners and realized just how much they enjoyed their annual holiday with family and friends in the summer colony. It was time to find a permanent summer home in Newport. In August 1897 they purchased *Seaverge,* a forty room, fully furnished shingle-style home located at the very end of Bellevue Avenue, a family retreat that remained in the Gerry family for thirty-five years. It was a perfect location, nestled modestly at the southern edge of Newport's mansion area, with private access to the *Cliff Walk* that meandered its way to the back lawns of Robert and Ogden Goelet's estates. This rough-hewn ocean trail suited the outdoor nature of the Gerrys who also found the same freedom at their *Lake Delaware* farm. Commodore Gerry immediately purchased a large plot of land 210 x 293 feet on Ledge Road, adjacent to Oliver Belmont's estate, *Belcourt Castle.* It was located around the corner, just a block away, a perfect spot to build a stable and greenhouse.

By mid-May, Ogden and Mary Goelet had opened their mansion in London, *Wimborne House,* to prepare for one of the most successful private dinners held in honor of Queen Victoria's *Diamond Jubilee.* Prince Albert Edward, "Bertie", was the guest of honor, representing his mother, to whom the Goelets had been formally "presented" the year before at Nice, France. Long rows of German kings and Russian princes filled the spacious halls of *Wimborne House* as they listened to prominent opera stars perform.[71]

After the spectacular success of the Goelets' jubilee dinner, Ogden Goelet was exhausted and eager to take possession of his long-awaited new yacht. He contacted the Clydebank, Scotland builders who informed him that the "test cruises" of his yacht were successful, and except for interior finishes, it was considered ready for delivery. Ogden was concerned that if he waited any longer the new yacht would not arrive at Cowes in time for the June 26 *Jubilee Naval Review,* where all the important yachts of Europe would gather. Without delay, he ordered that the yacht be delivered to Cowes, England with the interior unfinished. In fact much of the upholstery had yet to be installed and some of the paneling was also incomplete. Between late May and June 6 when the new yacht arrived in Cowes, Ogden Goelet realized that he was not well and remained onboard the *Whyte Ladye* to recuperate. The best medicine for Ogden Goelet was the arrival of his new yacht which he christened the *Mayflower* at Cowes, England on June 6, 1897. Ogden's 2,000 volume library, the Goelets' personal belongings, and their furnishings were immediately transferred from the *Whyte Ladye* to the *Mayflower.* The new yacht had electric lights and heaters throughout, the dining table could seat 24, and the yacht even had a bicycle rack for day-trips on land. The yacht was fitted up to be the Goelet family home for most of the year. After Ogden and Mary settled in, the *Whyte Ladye* was sent off to London where she was eventually sold. The *Mayflower* had a crew of 22 seamen and 13 officers. It was the eighth largest yacht in the world, only 378 tons smaller than William K. Vanderbilt's steam yacht the *Valiant,* which was the largest yacht in America.

Ogden and Mary Goelet steamed on the *Mayflower* to the waterway known as *Spithead* between the Isle of Wight and Portsmouth, east of Cowes, England where the Goelets happily joined the *Jubilee Naval Review* followed by dinner and celebrations with the *Prince of Wales*; this was the capstone event of their 1897 European tour. The *Mayflower* returned immediately to port at Cowes, England where she anchored. This was to provide an extended period of recuperation for Ogden Goelet. He remained on the yacht under the care of his personal physician, Dr. Dawson, who kept Ogden confined to his cabin for all of July and early August. In late August he took a turn for the worse. His doctor deemed it necessary to hold a consultation and summoned Sir William Henry Broadbent Physician in Ordinary to the Prince of Wales. Ogden's seventeen year old son, Robert W. Goelet, the namesake of his uncle, arrived with Doctor Broadbent on Sunday, August 24. Ogden's wife Mary, son Robert, and eighteen-year old daughter May, remained at his bedside until Ogden Goelet's death at the relatively young age of fifty-one on Wednesday, August 27, 1897. It was fitting that he died on board the *Mayflower* with his beloved wife Mary by his side, the one place he felt most at home and able to travel the world. Ogden had a frail constitution his entire life and could never keep up with the drive or energy of his brother Robert, who administered the day-to-day challenges of the complex Goelet business interests. Robert understood Ogden's health issues and was pleased to carry the lion's share of the management responsibilities. They lived next door to each other in New York City and in Newport. They shared a life-long, extravagant yet playful competition in their personal life, where younger brother Ogden always "out-sized" his big brother Robert. Ogden had the bigger townhouse, the bigger mansion, and the bigger yacht, until the end of his life, when their yachts were a perfect match, built as twins by the same Scotland shipyard. Ogden's death stunned his brother Robert, his cousin Commodore Elbridge T. Gerry, and his cousin Almy Gerry Gallatin, all of whom had grown up together since the days of Uncle Peter's *Broadway Farm* with its exotic peacocks and prized cow roaming about in the yard. Ogden Goelet's Will left everything to his wife and children. His valuable personal library was dispersed at a public sale in 1935 by the *Anderson Gallery* in New York. Ogden Goelet was buried in the *Goelet Memorial Vault* in Woodlawn Cemetery, in the Bronx, New York. The Gerrys remained in Newport through September 1897, no doubt to comfort Mary Goelet in her time of grief. Once again, the Gallatin, Gerry, and Goelet extended families spent the holidays in mourning, particularly avoiding the swirl of the early holiday balls and dinner parties.

Mary Goelet was broken hearted at the loss of her beloved husband, and could not bring herself to keep their yacht the *Mayflower*. She even told her intimate friends that it would always be the "funeral ship" to her. Neither she nor her son Robert Wilson Goelet or her daughter May ever again showed any interest in owning a yacht. In the future, Mary Goelet traveled by steam ship to Europe and continued to cruise the Mediterranean during the European season as a guest with the friends she had shared with Ogden for over twenty years of marriage. Mary Goelet loaned the *Mayflower* to the Navy during the *Spanish American War* and other military assignments until 1905 when the Navy purchased the *Mayflower* from the Goelet family and converted it for use as the official yacht of the *President of the United States.* The *Mayflower* was the scene of many diplomatic and social events for twenty-five years. President Theodore Roosevelt transported foreign diplomats on the *Mayflower* to the *Portsmouth Peace Conference* which ended the Russo-Japanese War. President Woodrow Wilson embarked on the *Mayflower* for much of his courtship of Mrs. Edith Galt and finally, President Hoover decided to dispense with the *Mayflower* as an economic measure during the *Depression Era* and decommissioned the yacht in 1929.[72]

In October, Commodore Elbridge T. Gerry traveled to Albany, New York for the annual *New York State Convention of Societies,* an affiliation of animal and child anti-cruelty organizations. He was elected President of the Convention where he led discussions about the differing positions of individual society leaders in an attempt to develop more cohesive perspectives and to find new ways to garner public support. The proceedings of the convention were published in the annual report and in many instances, the writings and speeches of Commodore Gerry were also published in *The Child's Guardian,* the London publication of the British protection society. Twenty years after the 1897 convention, when Commodore Gerry was eighty years old, that same *Convention of Societies* honored him for a lifetime of work in the protection of children and for two decades of work with the *Convention.*[73]

Almost two months to the day after Ogden Goelet's death, his brother's twin yacht was delivered to Newport Harbor after braving nasty weather on the crossing from Scotland. Robert Goelet christened his magnificent yacht the *Nahma,* an American Indian word that simply means *sturgeon,* a fish that can be found in either fresh or salt water. The eggs of the larger Atlantic and Baltic sturgeon are the source of the world's best caviar. Perhaps Robert named his yacht *Nahma* because, like the sturgeon, he cruised all the great waters of the world and his yacht was a luxury few could match just as excellent sturgeon caviar was a luxury few could afford. The *Nahma* had a handsome appearance with a white exterior, a green boot top, and a beautiful promenade deck that was 190 feet long. She had a crew of seventy-two, led by Captain Churchill, who had previously worked for the trans-Atlantic *Cunard Steamship Line.* The yacht was sumptuously furnished with gilded furniture, a marble fireplace, and oak paneled walls. French decorators had been employed to make each room as artistic as possible. There was a cabin for a doctor, two for the Goelet children, and several for guests. The Goelet family owned the *Nahma* until 1922, except for two years when the yacht was loaned to the *United States Navy* for engagement in World War I when it was equipped with guns and sailors. With several sealed bulkheads, the yacht was seaworthy for world travel and even for battle. Between 1923 and 1927 the yacht was sold three times and was finally scrapped in 1930 by *British Marine Products* at Southampton, England. Robert Goelet took his yacht the *Beatrice* for her last cruise to pick up the *Nahma* at Newport. Select furnishings and personal belongings, including Robert's personal library, were transferred between the yachts and then *Beatrice* was returned to New York and sold.[74]

In early November 1897 the Gerry family indulged their passion for horses by attending the annual auction of "box seats" at *Madison Square Garden* for the season of *Horse Shows.* The annual sale always aroused spirited competition for a choice location, and Commodore Gerry matched one of the highest bids at $400 and obtained Arena Box 27 for the year. The first show of the thirteenth season was held on November 16 during some bad weather, which kept many from venturing out. Nonetheless, Commodore and Louisa Gerry, joined by Angelica and Mabel, arrived for the evening show. The evening shows were more formal than the afternoon shows, and the ladies "dressed" for the social occasion. The newspapers took a fancy to the lovely Gerry women and described their outfits for their readers:

> Mrs. Gerry was in a beautiful gown of black and white silk, with the bodice trimmed with steel embroidery and black chiffon. Her bonnet was a gray velvet and steel embroidered barege with a small tuft of gray feathers. Miss Angelica Gerry was dressed in black cloth with dark blue silk front, with slashes of gold braid. She wore with this a small round hat, simply trimmed with two blue plumes. Miss Mabel Gerry was dressed in a gown of very dark red velvet and the bodice was plainly made, but was relieved by a full jabot of real lace. Her picture hat of dark red velvet with long red feathers was most becoming.[75]

The Gerry box was crowded all evening with visitors from other seats, very much like the opera house visits among the box holders. The *Horse Show* ended on November 21 after a week-long exhibition. There had been more or less complaining among the exhibitors about the work of the judges and the way the ribbons were awarded. Mr. C.F. Bate's horse was one of the top contenders but did not win a ribbon. He was so upset at his loss that he got out of his cart and plainly told the judges what he thought of the award and then stormed out of the *Show Ring*, noting that he would not compete again unless they had judges who knew what they were doing. After Mr. Bate's rude display of temper all of the spectators, including the Gerrys, remained at *Madison Square Garden* to enjoy the closing festivities of the first horse show of the season.[76]

Commodore Gerry continued to represent the NYSPCC in court every week, particularly appeals against the decision of the Magistrates that repeatedly questioned the validity of a child's commitment or the legitimacy of the evidence presented at the hearings. In December the Annie Lazarus commitment case against the *Protestant Episcopal House of Mercy* required his attention for the second appeal by the child's mother challenging the Magistrate's commitment order. Commodore Gerry gladly provided his time and attention as legal counsel for the unprotected children, especially during the holidays when the children most acutely felt the suffering.[77]

The January 1898 meeting of the *New York Yacht Club* was called to discuss a letter from John Jacob Astor to the *NYYC* Secretary concerning the death of Ogden Goelet and the continuation of the summer Cup races at Newport, Rhode Island:

> Dear Sir,
>
> I saw in last Saturday's paper that unless Ogden Goelet left provision in his will for continuing the Goelet Cups for the Newport races they may be discontinued. This would be a great pity, and very likely he has provided for them. If he has not, however, I should be glad to continue them, giving the same kind of prizes, to be called the Astor Cups, and to be called for at the same times and places. Please let me know what you think of this and refer it to the committee having charge of this matter.
>
> Yours very truly, John Jacob Astor[78]

A second letter followed in which J.J. Astor also indicated that he would incorporate his proposal into his will to provide permanent support of a *NYYC* annual regatta race in Newport. The *Club* accepted the offer and immediately drafted a resolution to honor Ogden Goelet's fifteen years of sponsoring the *Goelet Cup* and to express the *Club's* appreciation for Ogden's engaging personal qualities and his enthusiasm for yachting that made him one of their most popular and valued members. He was also recognized for his keen interest and active leadership in the development of the sport and in the advancement of yacht design, and finally, Ogden Goelet was honored for his dedicated support of the *New York Yacht Club*.

The Gerrys welcomed the *New Year* with their second annual winter cotillion and dinner in the new mansion. Two hundred and fifty invitations were sent and guests began to arrive at 10:30 o'clock for dancing and a gourmet dinner at midnight followed by a cotillion of sixty couples. Worthington Whitehouse and Mabel Gerry, along with Craig Wadsworth and Angelica Gerry, led the cotillion. The Gerry mansion was decorated throughout the entry and great hall with numerous palm and fern plants. The smaller "red library" had six-foot tall vases filled with red roses set dramatically about the room. The twenty-piece *Landers Orchestra* played from their station on the balcony on the west side of the *Picture Gallery* that doubled as the ballroom. The favors for the guests were not without a sense of humor, for the ladies a music director's wand tied with roses, and for the gentlemen, a novelty "court order" from Commodore Gerry that was most likely a cordial demand that the gentlemen have a jolly good time at the cotillion.[79]

Now that the Gerry family owned their own home in Newport, they had a year-round interest in the town and its activity. In mid-February the Gerry stable was well underway on the property they purchased on Ledge Road the previous summer. Commodore Gerry and Robert Goelet both believed they were residents of Newport because they owned property and paid taxes. However, the state of Rhode Island questioned their status as "legal residents" since they were also legal residents of New York City. Both men petitioned the Rhode Island Court for a hearing. Robert Goelet's petition was more easily accepted because he had voted in the Newport elections. However, Commodore Gerry had yet to vote in his first local election, so in March 1898 he testified before the court in Newport that he paid property tax on *Seaverge*, was now visiting Rhode Island almost every month, had registered his yacht in Newport, and was a member of the *Rhode Island Bar Association.* In October 1898 the court entered a decree declaring both Elbridge and Robert legal citizens of Newport, Rhode Island.[80]

In anticipation of the coming summer Commodore Gerry enrolled his sons, Robert and Peter, in the all-male *Newport Reading Room* across the street from the historic *Redwood Library.* The subscription was high enough to keep the club exclusive and catch the eye of the press who observed that the difference between the name and the practice of the club was an amusing illustration of the change that had taken place in public sentiment.

> When application for a charter was made the "hayseed" element in the General Assembly refused to incorporate a club, holding that it would be a danger to the good name of the State, but was willing to incorporate it as a means of advancing light and learning. The light however, is a very up-to-date substitute for midnight

> oil, and the learning is rather of golf and yachting than of philosophy. But the fact remains that within the walls of this cottage there may be found experts in every branch of human knowledge, such as to points of law, politics, finance and army and navy matters, or even pigeon shooting at Monte Carlo. However, what is said or done in a Club is purely a private matter. The echo of these discussions not only reaches the outside world but is assuming an influence on local affairs which is visibly felt.[81]

The *Newport Reading Room* was founded in 1854 by William Shepard Wetmore, a wealthy China trade merchant, and a few Southern planters who summered in Newport. Several of the managing stock holders were full time Rhode Island residents while others were summer residents. The *Reading Room* had a history of hosting charitable fundraisers, for example, the club's 1912 baseball game against the U.S. Navy officers of the *Atlantic Fleet* to raise funds for the *Newport Hospital.* The *Reading Room* was not just a center of Newport social interaction, it did in fact have a library for the "light and learning" of its members as envisioned by the *General Assembly* of Rhode Island in 1854.[82]

The first half of 1898 was overshadowed by the start of the first significant conflict for the United States since the Civil War. The 1898 *Spanish American War* was the result of American intervention to stop the atrocities by Spain in the ongoing *Cuban War of Independence.* The mysterious sinking of the American battleship, the *Maine,* in *Havana Harbor* on February 15, 1898, led the American people to encourage President McKinley to bow to political pressure and declare war on Spain. Despite crippling outbreaks of malaria, the joint American, Cuban, and Philippine forces obtained the surrender of Santiago and Manila owing to numerical superiority in most of the battles during the five month war from March to July 1898.[83] The Spanish troops put up a spirited defense as chronicled in the siege of *San Juan Hill* led by Theodore Roosevelt and his *Rough Riders,* a group of volunteers gathered from the southwest where men were used to hot weather similar to that of Cuba where they would be fighting. Roosevelt selected a diverse bunch of men consisting of cowboys, gold or mining prospectors, hunters, gamblers, Native Americans and college boys, all of whom were experts with horses and shooting. The men who had served in the normal army during campaigns against Indians or served in the Civil War were assigned to serve as higher ranking officers in the cavalry. The uniforms of the regiment were designed to set the unit apart; the *Rough Rider* uniform was a slouch hat, blue flannel shirt, brown trousers, leggings, and boots, with handkerchiefs knotted loosely around their necks. They looked exactly as a body of cowboy cavalry should look, a "rough and tumble" appearance and charisma that contributed to earning them the title of *The Rough Riders.*[84]

The *Spanish-American War* also gave the North and South a common enemy for the first time since the *Civil War* in 1865. Not only were many of the 1898 military men veterans of the Civil War, there were also African Americans who strongly supported the rebels in Cuba and supported America's entry into the war. The most influential black leader at the time, Booker T. Washington, was born into slavery in Franklin County, Virginia around 1858. After emancipation in 1865 he helped his poverty stricken parents by working in the salt mines and coal mines of West Virginia. He desperately wanted an education, so at age 16 Booker walked over 200 miles to attend school at the *Hampton Institute* in Hampton, Virginia. He became a teacher and in 1881, under Alabama House Bill 165, Booker T. Washington founded the all black *Tuskegee Institute.* In 1882 the college became an independent, private institution. Under Washington's leadership *Tuskegee* established the *Veteran's Administration Hospital,* the *School of Veterinary Medicine,* and the *Tuskegee Airmen Program* the all-black U.S. Air Force Squadrons that were highly decorated in World War II. In March 1898 as President of the *Tuskegee Institute,* Booker T. Washington promised the Secretary of the Navy that at least ten thousand loyal, brave, and strong black men in the south would lay down their lives for their country so that they might have the fullness of their freedoms and rights. The African American community did indeed fight with honor and showed both skill and bravery in their wartime performance in the Army of the *Spanish American War.*[85] Booker T. Washington remained President of the *Tuskegee Institute* until his death at age fifty-nine in 1915. He wrote his autobiography in 1901 in which he described his youth, the value of education, the dignity of work and that a man's character was built by obstacles overcome, that it was the process of achievement that was more important than the finished product. His book emphasized his optimism and belief that whites and blacks living together in harmony was not only possible, but probable despite the ghost of the institution of slavery.[86] The 1898 War reinforced his belief in America's future.

The fighting in the *Spanish American War* ended with the surrender of Spain in August 1898, but it did not officially end until the *Treaty of Paris* was signed on December 10, 1898. The treaty gave the United States the islands of Guam, the Philippines and Puerto Rico, plus a permanent presence at Guantanamo Bay, where Cuba had just declared its independence from Spain. The blow to Spain's political strength turned the nation inward and ushered in a bright cultural renaissance. This war also marked America's entry into world affairs and the beginning of a long and prosperous period of economic growth and technological innovation in the United States that lasted through the 1920's and did not slow down until the *Great Depression.*

Commodore Gerry's insightful recommendation that he and his colleague, Admiral Howard Patterson, made to the United States Navy in 1886 was put to the test in 1898 at the start of the *Spanish-American War.* They had prepared the plan for using private steam yachts as a *Naval Reserve* in time of war, and Commodore Gerry led the way for training 400 civilian yachtsmen to become certified *Master Steam Pilots* to meet the expectations of the navy. One of the first private steam yachts to be purchased and commissioned by the navy for the *Spanish American War* was Frederic Gallatin's *Almy,* which he sold to the Navy in February, 1898. The United States Navy renamed her the *Eagle.* Two other yachts purchased by the Navy were the *Alicia,* renamed the *Hornet,* and the yacht *Hermione,* renamed the *Wasp.* The Goelet yachts, the *Nahma* and the *Mayflower,* also served the Navy in times of need between 1898 and 1929 but curiously, were never "renamed" by the Navy. Of note, Commodore Gerry's yacht, the fifteen-year old *Electra,* was never commissioned by the military because she was not constructed for ocean travel with the fully-sealed, massive steel bulk heads that were the hallmark construction of the *Nahma* and the *Mayflower* in 1897, and therefore the *Electra* was not suitable for combat missions.[87]

The *Spanish American War* required substantial funding in 1898 which prompted the federal government to pass the *War Revenue Act* in June 1898 that authorized a tax on tea, tobacco, beer, liquor, amusements, and some business transactions, and also authorized a $200 million bond issue. Additionally, the transfer of wealth was, for the first time in American history, taxed by the *War Act,* which imposed a tax on legacies, referred to as the "death tax" or receipt of property by death.[88]

Taxation of property transfers at death can be traced back to ancient Egypt as early as 700 B.C. Nearly 2,000 years ago, Roman Emperor Caesar Augustus imposed the *Vices,* a tax on successions and legacies to all but close relatives. In the *Middle Ages,* taxes imposed at the death of a family member were quite common in feudal Europe, often amounting to a family's annual property rent. By the 18th century, stamp duties and registration fees on wills, inventories, and other documents related to property transfers at death had been adopted by many nations, including the newly formed *United States of America.* Despite strong opposition, the 1898 legacy tax was made law and, while short-lived, it taxed only personal property, and exempted both small estates and bequests to the surviving spouse from taxation. In 1901 additional gifts were exempted from tax, including gifts to charitable, religious, literary, and educational organizations and gifts to organizations dedicated to the encouragement of the arts and the prevention of cruelty to children. The years immediately following the repeal of the 1898 inheritance tax witnessed an unprecedented number of mergers in the manufacturing sector of the economy and the development of new forms of corporate ownership, which concentrated the nation's wealth, fueled fears over the rise of an American plutocracy and sparked the growth of the progressive movement. Progressives, including President Theodore Roosevelt, advocated both an inheritance tax and a graduated income tax as tools to address inequalities in wealth. This thinking eventually led to the passage of the *16th Amendment to the Constitution* and the enactment of the *Revenue Act of 1916* (39 Stat. 756), which created a tax on the transfer of wealth from an estate to its beneficiaries, and thus was levied on the estate, as opposed to an inheritance tax that is levied directly on beneficiaries.[89] One other tax imposed to pay for the *Spanish American War* was an excise tax on long-distance phone service. Telephones were a relatively new technology and since only the wealthy had access to the service they bore the brunt of the tax. Somehow, while the other war taxes were repealed, Congress neglected to repeal the long distance phone tax and it remained in place for over 100 years until August 1, 2006, when the *Treasury Department* announced that the IRS would no longer collect the tax.[90]

On Wednesday, May 4 a High Mass was celebrated at *Saint Patrick's Cathedral* on the silver anniversary of Archbishop Michael Augustine Corrigan's leadership of New York City's Catholic population. The Archbishop's influence was so broad-based that the City fathers also honored him the next evening at the *Metropolitan Opera House* where the Archbishop was presented with the "fully paid" mortgage of $250,000 for *Saint Joseph's Seminary*. The opera house was crowded when *Seidi's Orchestra* stuck up the *Zampa Overture* and the entry procession began, led by the Archbishop and followed immediately by the main speakers, including Commodore Elbridge T. Gerry. In his tribute to his dear friend, Archbishop Corrigan, Commodore Gerry also acknowledged the current state of war in America:

> The great characteristic of our American people is confidence, confidence in ourselves, confidence in our country, confidence in our Government, and last but not least, confidence in our God. In this trying state of War the confidence of the people that their cause is just, their Government wise and prudent, and their loyalty unlimited, challenges the admiration of the world. Yesterday, the Holy Roman Church, by grand and imposing ceremonies in its splendid Cathedral, proclaimed its confidence in their great Prelate. Tonight, irrespective of creed,

> politics or nationality, the people of the great city of New York in this assemblage reflect and repeat the confidence in the Archbishop's modest and unswerving loyalty to the Church. He presents a living example of what a good man can do who thinks nothing of himself, but everything of his people and of his God. To realize what has been accomplished you have today but to visit one of the great Catholic reformatories in this city and see the condition of the bright, well-cared for, well-educated children... who today lack only the age to enable them to achieve honor when they enter the world able to support themselves or to serve their country.[91]

At the 1898 *General Convention of the Protestant Episcopal Church,* Elbridge T. Gerry had become more deeply involved in church affairs than at any other period in his life. His representation of Episcopal Church affairs was formalized with an appointment to the *Commission on Ecclesiastical Relations* and his election to the Board of Trustees of the *General Theological Seminary*. Louisa Gerry's uncle was the Reverend Eugene A. Hoffman, the Dean of the Seminary and he too was a member of the *Ecclesiastical Commission* with Elbridge. There were few endeavors in Elbridge's church and humanitarian service that were not actively shared with his closest family and friends, in fact, *Gilded Gotham* must have felt like a small town community for the extended Gerry family.

Commodore Gerry also financially supported the Catholic *Mission of Our Lady of the Rosary,* established for the protection of immigrant girls who arrived at *Ellis Island,* and after a physical inspection, were sent by tug boat to disembark at the Battery at the tip of lower Manhattan. The girls walked to 7 State Street, an imposing rotund, orange-brick mansion with large windows, and a balcony supported by three-story Doric pillars. Located just across the street from the Battery, the *Mission* often housed up to 700 girls who were welcomed regardless of race, color or religion. The girls were cleaned, fed, and given shelter until positions were found for those desiring work. Railroad tickets were purchased for girls to join friends or family in distant cities. The *Mission* was supported by voluntary contributions, especially the regular financial contributions of Commodore Elbridge T. Gerry and his friend, John Jacob Astor.[92] Immediately next door to the Mission, at 5 State Street, was the original Goelet family home in New York City. This was where not only Uncle Peter Goelet was born, but also his niece and nephews, Hannah, Robert and Ogden Goelet. While the Goelet home was demolished decades ago and replaced by a modern glass and steel building, the original *Mission* house still stands at 7 State Street across from the Battery in lower Manhattan. The *Shrine of Mother Elizabeth Seton* now occupies the *Mission* house, which is still owned by the Catholic Church.

The Gerry family enjoyed their first full summer at *Seaverge,* their home in Newport. They now had a finished stable for their horses allowing Angelica, Mabel, Robert and Peter to participate in the coaching parades, and it also allowed Robert and Peter to engage in polo at the *Newport Country Club* polo grounds. On August 28 the *Newport Horse Show* was held at the Casino grounds on Bellevue Avenue. Angelica Gerry, age twenty-seven, entered her brown bay gelding, *Idle Boy* into the class 21 competition. Robert Gerry, age twenty-one, entered his four bay geldings named *Student, Suitor, School Master* and *Scholar* in the four-in hand coaching completion and his chestnut gelding, named *Spaniard,* in several class competitions. Younger brother Peter Gerry, age 19, entered his two brown mares, *Starlight* and *Twilight,* in class 37 and 38 competition. Sister, Mabel Gerry, age twenty-five was rarely associated with horses except as a passenger on a coach or a faithful spectator at the horse shows. The Goelet children competed right along with the Gerrys, Beatrice Goelet just thirteen years old entered her pony, *Ruby,* in the class 42 competition and her older brother Robert Walton Goelet, age eighteen, entered his horse, *Miss Woodline* in the competition. Casino box holders included the Perry Belmont, Commodore E. T. Gerry, Robert Goelet and the Vanderbilt families. With a permanent home in Newport the Gerrys had the flexibility to arrive earlier, stay longer, and indeed to socialize with friends in Newport throughout the year which also kept the yacht *Electra* in service year-round.

For the remainder of 1898 gossip ran wild about the "rumored engagements" for both the widow Mrs. Mary Goelet and her daughter, May. Of course none were true and the Goelet family learned to ignore the newspapers, and in fact, Mary Goelet spent more time in England during the winter introducing her daughter to society in London, rather than in New York City.

The 1899 New Year celebrations were reflective and happy as *Gilded Gotham* entered the last year of the nineteenth century. With the *Treaty of Paris* just signed a feeling of hope was the universal sentiment at the annual *Assembly Balls.* Commodore and Louisa Gerry held their annual dinner and Cotillion on February 5 with 150 guests arriving at 11 o'clock. This year the mansion had but a few palms and ferns at the entrance, and instead, relied on the additional elegant furnishings purchased while in Europe to provide tasteful decoration to the residence. Cut flowers were held in lovely small vases set throughout the house, more understated than the prior year when six-foot floor vases were used in the *Red Library*. Both Angelica, 28, and Mabel, 26, shared hostess duties with their parents, and for the first time, Robert Gerry, 22, joined his sisters as a host; this was his debut to society. Peter Gerry, 20, was not yet formally introduced to society. After the reception line many guests strolled through the first floor rooms to the ballroom *Picture Gallery* to enjoy dancing before supper, while other guests wandered into the beautiful *Law Library* where they chatted in the many nooks among the book cases. Supper was served on twenty-four small tables in the *Dining Room,* each table seating an intimate group of six to eight people. The supper was prepared under the supervision of Mrs. Gerry's own chef and was served by her own men servants who were assisted by a force of outside waiters. The cotillion began after supper and was danced by sixty couples who were led in the "figures" by Craig Wadsworth and Angelica Gerry. The favors included papier mache parrots on sticks, comic Japanese dolls, and silver trifles. The annual cotillions had become less a match-making opportunity for the Gerry daughters and more an opportunity to enjoy the unpressured company of friends and family.[93]

By March 1899 Commodore Gerry was almost famous in *Gilded Gotham* society for his latest hobby, or perhaps passion, for greenhouse gardening. In the eighteen months since he had purchased *Seaverge* and the Ledge Road property in Newport, he had four greenhouses built, one a palm house, one a nectarine house, and two grape vine houses. The latest greenhouse, said to be the only one of its kind in the country, was a melon house. He planned to grow tomatoes, asparagus, cucumbers, strawberries, and other fruits and vegetables throughout the year. Notwithstanding the fact that the structure was only recently completed, there were four sections planted with melons and the tomatoes were already in flower. The heating of each section of the greenhouse was controlled entirely by valves, which enabled heat to be turned on or off independently. The potting benches were made with iron frames and bench surfaces made with perforated clay tiles. The benches were three and one half feet wide and ran along the sides of the greenhouse with a wide concrete walk between. Each greenhouse contained two boilers located beneath the potting room or shed. Commodore Gerry also hired a professional gardener, Mr. Arthur Griffin, to maintain the greenhouses and the exterior landscape of *Seaverge* throughout the year.[94]

The 1899 *Saint Patrick's Day Parade* was held on Fifth Avenue on March 17 and the crowds lined the Avenue for a great distance. Many stood at the edge of Fifth Avenue between Forty-Sixth and Forty-Seventh Streets to watch the parade. They stood on the sidewalk in front of the *Windsor Hotel,* which had opened in 1873 and by the 1890's it was known as the most comfortable and home-like hotel in New York. The hotel was owned by Warren F. Leland and was built on land owned by Commodore Elbridge T. Gerry. About 3 p.m. as the *Saint Patrick's Parade* passed, the crowds in front of the hotel could smell smoke and began to hear cries for help. One of the worst fires in New York history started around 3 p.m. and spread so fast that the building had been reduced to rubble by 4:30 p.m. Many escaped, including the dancer Isadora Duncan and her mother and Alfred A. Pope who escaped with his Claude Monet paintings, *The Haystacks* and *Boats Leaving the Harbor.* Although the fire department made heroic efforts, many guests were trapped on the upper floors by smoke and flames. There were a few fire escapes which saved many and every room had a backup, a coiled rope that guests were meant to slide down from the window in their room. Some managed to escape by rope but others fell when the rope burned their hands. Many guests simply choose to jump rather than face the flames. While Warren F. Leland, the hotel's owner escaped, his twenty-year old daughter, Helen jumped to her death. Forty-five bodies were recovered but forty-one people remained missing. The cause of the fire was determined to be accidental. Many of the dead were buried at *Kensico Cemetery* in Westchester County paid for by Mr. Leland and Commodore Gerry, while others were buried privately by their families. Commodore Gerry worked with Warren Leland to assist families in any way they could, and the *New York Times* said the extraordinary work of the firemen was something New Yorkers would always remember with great pride.[95]

In February 1899 Robert and Harrietta Goelet left New York for their second annual Mediterranean cruise on the *Nahma,* their home away from home. They followed the same route that Ogden Goelet had taken in previous years stopping at the beautiful ports of the *French Riviera.* By March the *Nahma* had reached Italy where the cruise continued along the western coast from Genoa to Rome, and by April the Goelets had reached the beautiful port town of Naples. Although Robert and Harrietta were less involved in the elite social life of the *Riviera* than were Ogden and Mary, they had many friends in Europe with whom they visited during stops at favorite ports. While anchored at Naples on April 27 Robert Goelet suffered a sudden heart attack and died with no time to seek assistance. The news was received in New York with complete surprise and disbelief by family and friends who had been with Robert in recent weeks and found him to be in perfect health. Robert was only fifty-seven and his daughter Beatrice Goelet was thirteen and his son Robert Walton Goelet was nineteen. His wife Harrietta, devastated and in shock, had to endure the long voyage home with Robert's coffin which lay in state in his beautiful library on board the *Nahma,* surrounded by his rare first edition books and prints. The yacht left Naples on May 2 and made stops at Gibraltar and Bermuda. The *Nahma,* with its flag at half mast, arrived in Newport Harbor on May 25 with Harrietta's mother, Mrs. George H. Warren, waiting with Commodore Elbridge T. Gerry on the yacht *Electra.* The *Nahma* was boarded by the port Health Officers and Customs officials who transferred the remains of

Robert Goelet to a special casket brought from New York City on the *Electra.* Commodore Gerry brought Harrietta, her mother and Robert's casket back to New York City for funeral services at *Trinity Church.* Two representatives of the *New York Yacht Club* were pall bearers. Just twenty months after Ogden Goelet's death, his beloved brother Robert Goelet was interred with him in the *Goelet Memorial Vault* at Woodlawn Cemetery in the Bronx, New York.[96]

Robert Goelet had always asked Harrietta to keep their yacht the *Nahma* until her death, and unlike Mary Goelet, who could not bear to go on the "funeral ship" *Mayflower* after Ogden's death, the *Nahma* became Harrietta's second home until her death. For two years after Robert's death, Harrietta was practically a stranger to New York City, cruising in foreign waters most of the year. Robert and Harrietta's son Robert Walton Goelet was born in 1880, the same year as his cousin, Robert Wilson Goelet, the son of Ogden and Mary. The two Roberts were in college together, both without their fathers. They were said to look so much alike that they were often mistaken, one for the other, even though they were not brothers.[97]

Robert Goelet inherited an inclination and rare capacity for business, and devoted a large part of his time and energy to the care and development of the extensive property interests left to himself and his younger brother Ogden. Even when his brother Ogden was alive, Robert was the guiding influence in the management of their inherited estates. Although a lawyer, he did not practice law, but rather was regarded as an uncommonly sagacious businessman, who was clear-headed and keen-witted, and his judgment in financial and real estate matters invariably commanded the respect of New York businessmen. Robert was liberal in contributing in a quiet way to projects of a semi-public character, both in New York and in Newport. It was his aim to aid every worthy effort to improve the condition and beauty of the community in which he lived. He was one of the original founders of the *Metropolitan Opera House,* even contributing the land on which it was built after the first opera house was destroyed by fire.[98]

Robert was known as a man without a trace of arrogance or selfishness, yet he weighed his friendships carefully and once a person became his friend, they had his steadfast loyalty. He was a kindred spirit with Commodore Gerry. They graduated from Columbia College together in 1860 and shared the challenges of running extensive family real estate holdings, and often, Commodore Gerry acted as legal counsel to the *Goelet Estates.* The next generation, Robert Walton Goelet and Robert Livingston Gerry, followed in their fathers' footsteps as the brilliant business managers of the Goelet and Gerry family real estate enterprises. The name "Robert" seems to carry with it the "gifted businessman" gene in successive generations of these two close-knit families. The loss of Robert and Ogden Goelet was as painful as losing brothers for Commodore Gerry. Only his brother-in-law Frederic Gallatin was left as an intimate relative.

Commodore Gerry provided his children with the best educational opportunities available both in Ivy-league schools and with private tutors. By June 1899 Robert L. Gerry age, 22, had completed his third year of college at Harvard, and Peter, age 20, had completed his second year of college at Harvard. During the summer of 1899 a tutor was hired for Robert and Peter, who lived with the Gerry family at *Seaverge* over the summer in Newport. William Lyon Mackenzie King was born in Kitchener, Ontario, Canada in December 1874. He graduated with honors from the University of Toronto in 1895 and immediately began studying law while working as a journalist. After earning his law degree, William known as "Mackenzie" came to the United States to study for a Master's Degree at the *University of Chicago* as a Fellow in Political Economy, which he received in 1897. He continued to write journal articles and tutor students to earn a living and was admitted to Harvard University with a second Fellowship in 1898 which was renewed for the fall of 1899. During the summer of 1899, Commodore Elbridge T. Gerry hired Mackenzie King to tutor his sons. Mackenzie was twenty-five years old when he came to Newport, just three years older than Robert and five years older than Peter. This was a wise selection by Commodore Gerry because, while the youth of the tutor made him appealing to his sons, Mackenzie's brilliance made him an effective and skillful tutor. Mackenzie King began keeping a diary in 1893 that he faithfully maintained his entire life. The diary notes about his stay with the Gerrys were insightful. Mackenzie wrote that although he claimed to dislike the lifestyle of the very rich, he greatly enjoyed the summer, noting "I had my first swim in the ocean, enjoyed it very much and found it refreshing and exhilarating. Have felt like a lord all day."[99] He learned horse jumping, had one fall, but persevered and succeeded in jumping several walls. He wrote, "I never enjoyed a sport more and believe that nothing compares in the manliness of this sort of exercise." [Diary, September 12, 1899] He also enjoyed the social life of Newport and he tasted champagne for the first time. One of the people he met that summer was Julia Grant, granddaughter of the former American President, Ulysses S. Grant. He maintained a friendship and a detailed correspondence with July Grant for the rest of his life. The money Mackenzie earned as a tutor to the Gerry boys made it possible for him to take an extended trip to Europe in connection with his Fellowship at Harvard. From Newport, he traveled to Boston where he sailed on September 17, 1899 for Europe. He traveled and studied in England and Europe for the next year. Mackenzie King went on to a brilliant career in journalism and politics, becoming one of Canada's most heralded *Prime*

Ministers. He kept in touch with Peter and Robert Gerry over the years and when he traveled to Washington, D.C as the *Prime Minister* of Canada in 1939, Mackenzie presented then Senator and Mrs. Peter Gerry to King George VI and Queen Mary who were on a State visit to Washington, D.C.[100]

When the summer tutoring ended the last dance of the summer was held at the Newport Casino after an afternoon of motoring about the island, where even modern young ladies like Miss Daisy Post were seen driving automobiles. The dresses worn to the dance were described in the *New York Times,* including those of Angelica and Mabel Gerry. Mabel wore white spangled net over silk. A single white rose ornamented the left shoulder and the skirt was edged with a ruffle and roses at the left side. She wore diamonds. Angelica was dressed in pale blue silk, worn with a sash of flowered ribbon tied in a girlish knot at the back. The white silk tucked petticoat was revealed by the open skirt front. Cream lace was caught about the simple neckline and a velvet bow adorned her hair. Nearly fifty guests attended the last dance of the season with few ladies wearing white as compared with prior years.

When the Newport colonists abandoned their cottages for their city homes, the Gerry family briefly returned to their Fifth Avenue mansion before their September 5 departure from New York Harbor on a trans-Atlantic steamship for a holiday in Europe. The Gerrys' eldest son Robert, age 22, did not join the family but rather remained at *Seaverge* in Newport. Later that week he hosted a dinner and a moonlight coach ride for his friends around Newport. The Gerrys boarded a steamship filled with Americans, many of whom were headed to Scotland to hunt and fish on the Bradley Martin estate, *Balmacaan,* in Glen Urquhart, while others departed the dock in Liverpool, England and traveled to London, France, Germany, Spain, or even Italy. Already in England at this time was Mrs. Mary Goelet, the widow of Ogden who was hosting her first gala since her husband's death two years before. At the end of July, Mrs. Goelet hosted a dinner at Wimborne in honor of "Bertie" the Prince of Wales and his approved list of guests. Mrs. Goelet's daughter May attended as did the Duke and Duchess of Marlborough and Lady Randolph Churchill. After the London gala Mrs. Goelet and her daughter made several countryside visits and then left for a spa in Homburg, Germany. The Gerrys usually met Mrs. Goelet for lunch and dinner while in London before the families proceeded on their separate holidays. The Gerry "family" holidays became harder to schedule as the adult children branched out into their own social circles and pursued other interests, often traveling with their own friends. In fact, on October 15, Robert L. Gerry's best friend Alfred Vanderbilt was rushing home to Newport from Kobe, Japan through San Francisco to join the entire Vanderbilt clan for the probate of the late Cornelius Vanderbilt's will. Robert, Harry Payne Whitney and other friends met Alfred at the Newport train depot to help with his eight trunks. The group of friends went directly to the Breakers Villa where Alfred met his mother and sisters, Gertrude and Gladys. Alfred's brother Reginald arrived on the Wickford boat at 7 pm that evening just in time for a grand family dinner. The next day the Vanderbilt entourage proceeded to New York City for probate of the will, after which the family dispersed and Robert L. Gerry rejoined his family at the Sixty-First Street mansion upon their return from Europe.

The Gerrys closed out the nineteenth century as guests of Mrs. John Jacob Astor at her annual holiday dinner on December 22 which was shared with an intimate circle of friends and family. The Astor mansion was decorated with an abundance of red American beauty roses, perfect for the Christmas holiday dinner that also served as an early celebration of Commodore Elbridge T. Gerry's December 25 sixty-second birthday.

MacKenzie King, future
Prime Minister of Canada

Tutor to Robert and Peter Gerry when he was in college and they were teenagers

Queen Victoria

Ogden Goelet joined her Jubilee Celebration.

Booker T. Washington

Teddy Roosevelt in Rough Rider outfit

Childhood neighbor of Gerry, Goelet, and Gallatin families.

Bradley Martin at his infamous Fancy Dress Ball

Duke and Duchess of Marlborough

Consuelo Vanderbilt,
Duchess of Marlborough

Consuelo Vanderbilt's marriage to the Duke of Marlborough was one of the most unhappy Gilded Age matches.

After divorcing the Duke of Marlborough Consuelo Vanderbilt fell in love with Frenchman Jacques Balson and began a life of chari-table work and travel between America and Europe.

Gertrude Vanderbilt (*right*) was Mabel Gerry's (*left*) best girlfriend from childhood. Gertrude married Harry Payne Whitney who supported her career as a sculptor and artist. She established the Whitney Museum in New York City.

Jacques
Balsan

Gertrude V. Whitney

Gloria Vanderbilt with her guardian Gertrude Vanderbilt Whitney

Angelica Gerry

J. Wadsworth Ritchie

After a one-year engagement to Ritchie and just days before the wedding it was cancelled due to Ritchie's indiscretion. Angelica Gerry never married.

Mabel Gerry joined Gertrude Vanderbilt and friends for a train trip to the Poinciana Hotel in Florida. Mabel is center in dark suit.

Newport Reading Room

Coaching at the Newport Golf Club

Seaverge, Gerry estate in Newport, Rhode Island

Windsor Hotel before the fire

Rescue of Monet paintings, Windsor Hotel fire, 1899. The hotel was built on property owned by Elbridge T. Gerry.

In March 1946 Winston Churchill went to Casa Alva, the Florida mansion of his cousin Consuelo Vanderbilt Balsan to work on his famous "iron curtain" speech.

Winston Churchill gives his Iron Curtain speech March 5, 1946, Fulton, Missouri

Consuelo Vanderbilt and cousin Winston Churchill Blenheim Palace, England

Commodore Gerry spoke at the dedication of the Columbus statue along with Julia Howe, a poet who also wrote *The Battle Hymn of the Republic*.

Statue of Christopher Columbus, Central Park

Julia Ward Howe

Ogden Goelet
1846-1897

Robert Goelet
1841-1899

Mayflower, delivered for the Queen's Jubilee shortly before Ogden's death.

Nahma... was the twin to his brother's yacht, *Mayflower*. Robert died two years after his brother, and he too died on board his yacht.

The Mayflower was docked at Cowes, England when Ogden Goelet died on board after joining the regatta celebrating Queen Victoria's Jubilee.

The yacht *Mayflower* was sold to the United States Navy for use as the first Presidential Yacht.

Gerry Mansion
Fifth Avenue
at 61st Street

The mansion was completed in 1896 and demolished in 1928; it was replaced with the Pierre Hotel which stands on the site to this day.

Alfred Zucker
architectural drawings
of the grand staircase,
Central Park

New finished grand staircase, Central Park, 1894

The mansion was right across the street from Central Park where the adult Gerry children led coach whips and where family walks and outdoor sports were regular activities.

Commodore Elbridge T. Gerry's private law library

Just as Thomas Jefferson's private library was the foundation of the Library of Congress, Elbridge T. Gerry's private collection was the foundation for the first independent law library for the United States Supreme Court. Gerry's collection was moved into the first separate building for Supreme Court in 1935 and remains the core special collection on the fourth floor of the now historic building on First Street in Washington, D.C.

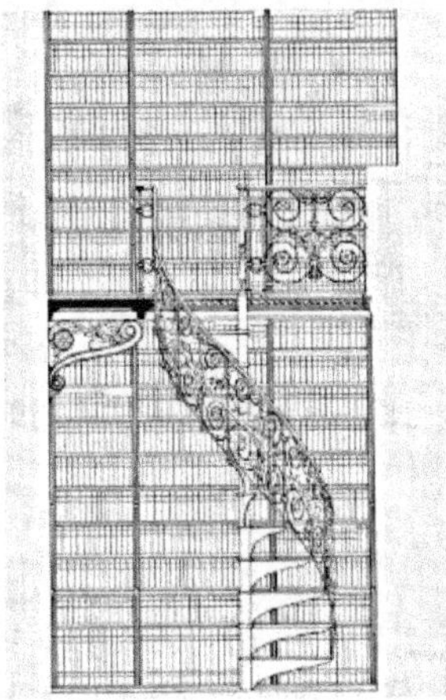

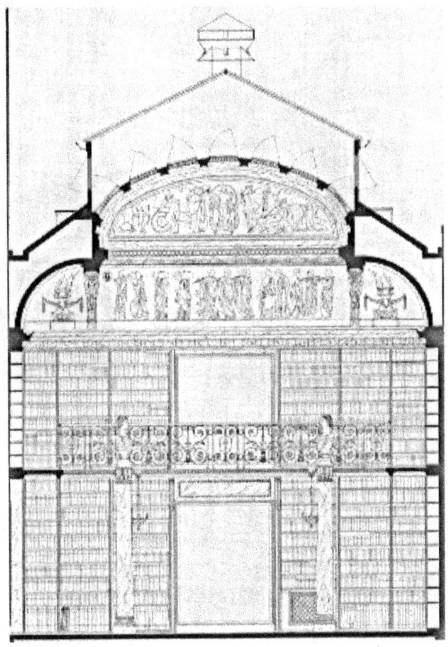

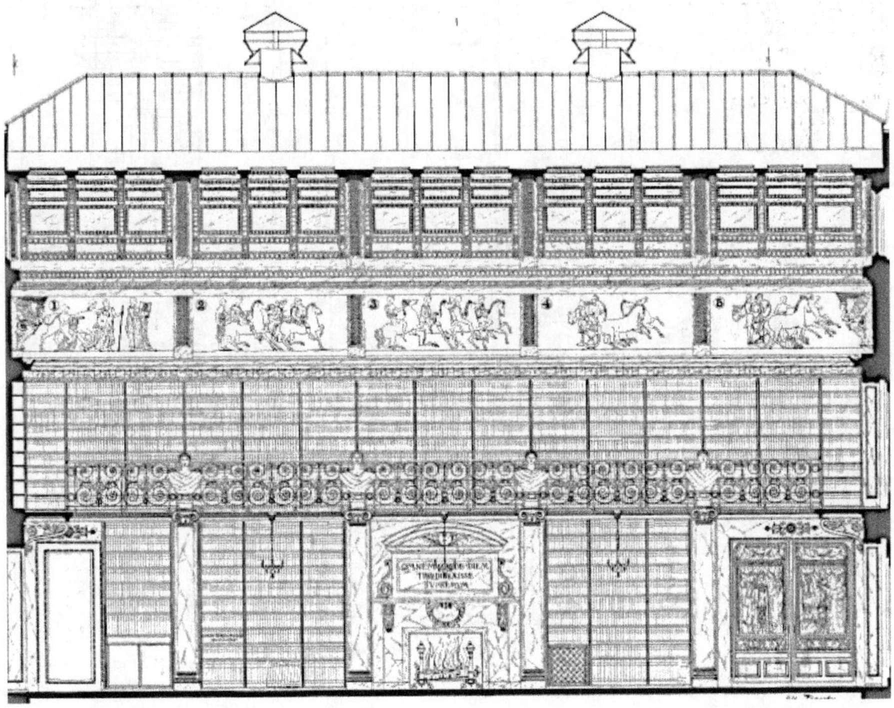

Door to entry hall

Doors to dining room

Alfred Zucker
1852-1915

Architect Zucker expanded Richard M. Hunt's unfinished library in the Gerry mansion and also designed and built the three story stables (*shown below*) on East 62nd Street with a unique "carriage lift" between the first and second floors.

Zucker's office in New York City

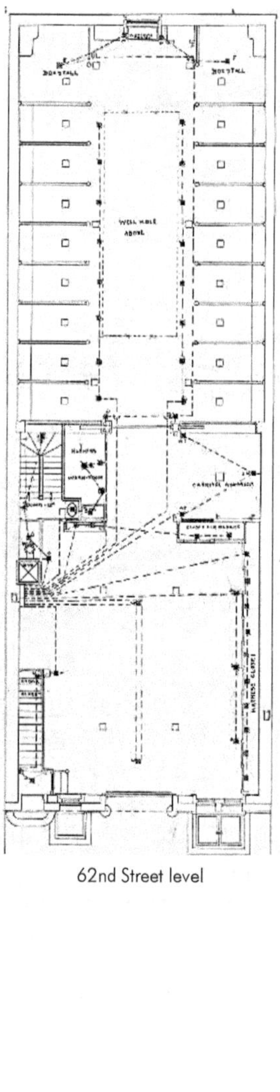

62nd Street level

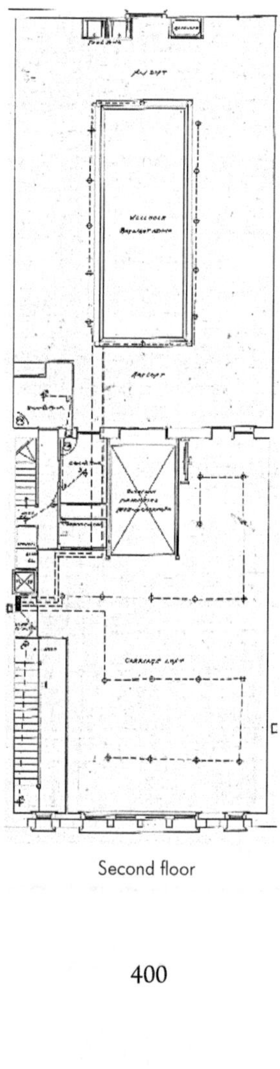

Second floor

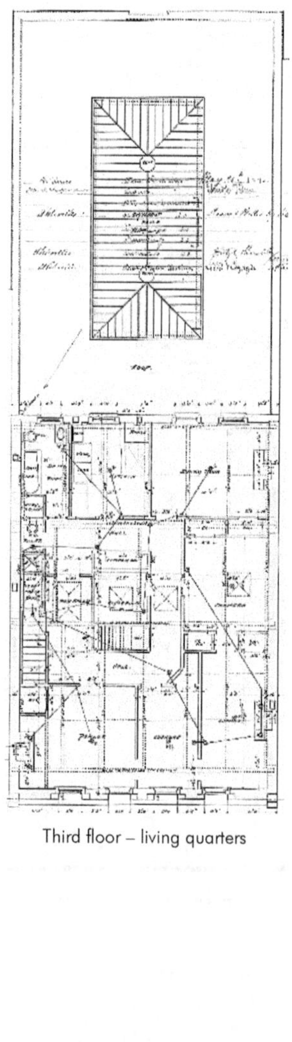

Third floor – living quarters

Madeira Wine
Bottle owned by
Elbridge T. Gerry

Gerry mansion second from left next to Metropolitan Club

View of Gerry home from Plaza on Fifth Avenue just south of Central Park at Fifty-Ninth Street

Elbridge T. Gerry supported the *Mission of Our Lady of the Rosary* for immigrant girls sent from Ellis Island.

Mother Seton Shrine in New York City, but as it looked when it was the Mission. Located at number 8 State Street just three doors from numbers 4 and 5 where the Goelet family first lived.

Onboard *Electra*

Gerry family photos of cruises with friends and family on *Electra*.

Mabel Gerry with big smile behind *left*
Mr. & Mrs. E.H. Harriman

Casual photo of "guests" onboard *Electra*

Electra staff

Cruise guests

Nanny with Peter Gerry

Electra staff with Commodore Gerry (*standing right*)

Jean Gerry, little Peter, and Grandpa R.J. Livingston

Louisa M. Gerry, qualified shipmate to husband Elbridge

Electra, dismantled, 1912

11

The Twentieth Century

Part I 1900 to 1909

A horse! A horse! My kingdom for a horse!
William Shakespeare, *King Richard III*

A driving rain the morning of February 14, 1900 kept New Yorkers cloistered indoors until noon when the sun came out and brightened up Valentine's Day. Carriages filled the streets and the sidewalks along Fifth Avenue quickly filled with the fashionable set who hurried to their afternoon engagements. Lilly Langtry, now Mrs. De Bathe, had returned to New York for the season and hosted a *Valentine Day Concert* at the Sherry Hotel for the benefit of the *Maine Hospital Ship Fund.* That evening, Commodore and Louisa Gerry hosted their annual dinner and dance, which for the first time, included musical entertainment with a touch of vaudeville. After dinner Mr. Maurice Farkoa, a musical comedy star, performed several songs and a monologue from his concert performed for the Lilly Langtry de Bathe benefit earlier that day. His earliest recognition as a singer was his appearance at London's *Prince of Wales Theater* in an 1895 performance of "Three Little Maids." Although he resided in Kensington, London, Maurice Farkoa traveled frequently to perform in New York City and Commodore Gerry would have paid a large amount for the private performance of such a famous entertainer.[1]

Across the Atlantic winter entertainment was offered to visiting American's and their European friends by John Jacob Astor. He sponsored winter sports at St. Moritz, Switzerland with the annual *Astor Challenge Cup* in the same way he funded the summer Newport *Astor Cup* yacht races. The winter sport competing for the Cup was the Bob Sled race in which both Mr. Astor and Mrs. Astor competed. Mrs. Astor's sled was called the *Wideawake* and came in second in the women's competition. Other popular winter sports at St. Moritz were ice skating, hockey, and skiing. Americans who fled the cold winter weather traveled to the French Riviera, Nice, Cannes and Monte Carlo, like the Vanderbilt family who went to Nice to join their daughter Consuelo, the Duchess of Marlborough. From

Nice the Vanderbilts cruised to Rome, Italy for a few weeks before they returned to Newport, Rhode Island for the summer season.[2]

The spring months in Newport were filled with projects under Commodore Gerry's direction in preparation for the family arrival at *Seaverge* around the first of June. The old landing and wharf for anchoring yachts in Newport Harbor, which Commodore Gerry owned in partnership with the Goelet family, were refurbished and upgraded over the winter with expanded docks for the steam launches and the station house was remodeled and given a fresh coat of paint. The upgrades at the wharf property, and the addition of Commodore Gerry's new stable and greenhouses, were improvements that triggered a tax reassessment of his property in Newport. All of the estates in the summer colony had been reassessed every year because taxation at the state level followed the federal trend to focus tax legislation on wealth that was concentrated in relatively few hands. Although the wealthy property owners were not pleased with the higher assessments they willingly paid the taxes that funded and, in fact, have sustained the city of Newport as a popular and thriving holiday community to this day.[3]

The spring of 1900 also brought a German measles epidemic in America that both Robert and Angelica Gerry contracted. The family remained at their New York City residence from late May through the first week of June, making good use of the "isolating room" that was a signature design of the new Fifth Avenue mansion. Adjacent to the sick room was a small apartment for a nurse, which insured that Robert and Angelica received the best of care. By June 5 both had sufficiently recovered for the Gerry's to travel on *Electra* to Newport where they continued their recovery surrounded by fresh ocean breezes and the warmth of the summer sun.[4]

Just eighteen months after the first round of plantings in Commodore Gerry's greenhouses in Newport, he entered his best plants in the annual flower show competition of the *Horticultural Society,* which had international affiliations. The Newport show was a local chapter of the national *Private Gardeners' Flower Shows* and the results were published in *American Gardening.* The Newport show was held June 26 and 27 in which participants presented their best specimens in a variety of plant categories. In Newport, it was a friendly competition of the *Edwardian Era* and in the rose categories, such as vase presentations and hybrid tea roses, "cut" or "scented," Mrs. Harrietta Goelet, Robert's wealthy widow, took most of the prizes. Harrietta's main competitor with rose specimens was Mrs. John Jacob Astor. However, for the first time, Commodore Gerry dominated the fruit category in which he won first prize for his strawberries, with Harrietta Goelet his closest competitor. He also won first prize for his tomatoes, second prize for his peas and first prize for his cucumbers. He did not win for his nectarines, peaches or grapes, but he would no doubt be more successful next year. The competition for best fern and palm plants were shared among Mrs. Astor, Mrs. Goelet, Mrs. Vanderbilt, and Commodore Gerry, who took first prize for his palm plant.[5] All of the greenhouse plants, especially the ferns and palms, supplied the decoration for the balls and dinners held at the New York City mansions of the greenhouse owners. Most of the Newport residences located their greenhouses and stables on property separate from the mansion, which was accessed by horse and carriage or by automobile when they came into fashion. Most of the greenhouses in Newport were built by E. J. Berwind who was listed by the *American Florist* magazine in their annual publication, the *National Directory* of horticultural specialists.[6]

On August 6 the *New York Yacht Club* gathered at Glen Cove in Hempstead Harbor to rendezvous for the annual club cruise. Commodore Lewis Cass Ledyard anchored early on his flagship schooner the *Corona.* Vice Admiral of the *NYYC* in 1900 was August Belmont Jr. in his schooner the *Mineola.* Joining the cruise were former commodores, J. Pierpont Morgan and Elbridge T. Gerry. The cruise started at 11 o'clock after the formal meeting of the yacht captains, a ceremonial gathering that Commodore Gerry loved and would never miss. The fleet arrived in Newport on August 12 for the *Astor Cup* regatta races, the third year under the new name. Newspapers used the annual race as an opportunity to reminisce about the great *America's Cup* race winners that had been nurtured by the highly competitive *Goelet Cup* in former years. After the annual cruise the *Electra* was anchored in Newport Harbor and taken out for leisurely cruises with family and friends for the remainder of the season.

The 1900 summer season was winding down when Mary Goelet hosted one of the most lavish dinner dances in Newport's history. It had been three years since her husband Ogden Goelet had died on his yacht the *Mayflower,* and the Goelet mansion, *Ochre Court,* had not been opened since his death. Mrs. Goelet returned with her daughter May to host what Newport considered both a housewarming for *Ochre Court* and a debut for Miss May Goelet, who had had her formal "coming out" the year before in London, rather than New York City. The 200 guests for the celebration began to arrive about 11 o'clock and were delighted as they entered the massive gates and passed the long drive lined with trees covered in multi-colored electric lights. Fringes of electric lights surrounded the marble fountain on the right, and there was a triple arch of the same lights over the fountain, whose waters were also illuminated from below by blue, crimson, and orange-hued electric lights set in the fountains base. The flower beds on the lawns sloping to the cliff walk on the other side of the mansion were outlined and interwoven with many colored miniature electric bulbs. Nearly 2,000 electric lights were used and these were fed by an independent dynamo, which took many electricians many weeks to install.

Entering *Ochre Court,* guests were received by Mrs. Goelet and her daughter May in the drawing room which, along with hallways and most other rooms, was decorated with banks of flowers as beautiful as the light display outdoors. The press reported that the east wall of the dining room had been expanded but architectural historians say there is no indication of disruption to the original design. Guests were seated for dinner on the terrace and in the dining room, all of whom had a view of the beautifully lit lawn and garden area. There were two suppers served by Sherry's hotel, one before the cotillion dancing, and one near dawn, after the ball. A huge lighted tent was set up on the back lawn as a smoking room for the gentlemen. A multitude of favors were offered throughout the ball, which Mrs. Goelet had personally selected while in Europe. The glow of the lights at *Ochre Court* and the sound of beautiful music performed by two orchestras drew the attention of many local people who gathered on the cliff walk creating a sea of spectators for most of the night.[7] The international press hailed Miss May Goelet as the richest and most eligible belle on either side of the Atlantic.

Frederic and Almy Gallatin were not part of the Newport "set" except for quiet visits to Almy Gallatin's brother Commodore Gerry and family. East Hampton, Long Island was their summer escape from New York City and happily, the press seemed to ignore most of the low-key society doings on Long Island. In fact, by 1903 the Gallatins were one of only three families in East Hampton that had a telephone and they were the first family to own a car in the village. The six Gallatin children were now between the ages of eighteen and thirty-two, with two already married. In the fall of 1900 Frederic and Almy began plans to introduce their daughter and youngest child, eighteen-year old Mary, to society. The Gallatins began the introduction with a simple, unpressured afternoon reception at their Fifth Avenue residence on December 1, 1900. Although low-key all of *Gilded Gotham* society came to the lovely reception where Miss Mary Gallatin greeted her guests assisted by several of her best girlfriends, all dressed in pink. Over the next few weeks three dinner-dances were held at the Gallatins' home which provided Mary the opportunity to meet eligible young men and develop her skills as a hostess.[8]

On January 13, 1901 Robert L. Gerry, then twenty-three, was an usher at one of his best friends' wedding, Alfred Vanderbilt who married Elsie French in Newport, Rhode Island. Robert and Alfred had been friends since childhood, when their homes were both on Forty-Eighth Street, and then both families moved up Fifth Avenue to within two blocks of each other near the Plaza at *Central Park.* In Newport, they spent summers together involved in polo matches and coaching parades; both were expert horsemen. The wedding gifts were magnificent and of such great value that they were placed in a bank vault as they arrived over a three-week period. Robert L. Gerry gave them a complete silver dessert service and his parents, Commodore and Louisa Gerry, gave the bride and groom a set of silver fruit dishes. Unfortunately, a few years later while Elsie and Alfred were in Newport celebrating their five-year anniversary with family, rumors began swirling that the marriage was in trouble. In 1908 Elsie filed for divorce. The evidence was taken in secret and the terms of the divorce were sealed. Alfred had inherited millions at his father's death and was considered one of the richest men in America. About the time of his divorce, Alfred was rumored to be involved with a Mrs. Ruiz who divorced her husband for Alfred and moved to London where she awaited his arrival after his divorce from Elsie. Alfred failed to keep his promise and did not meet Mrs. Ruiz in London. Now divorced and alone, she committed suicide in May 1909. Her companion and servant disclosed to the press the sad end to the affair. By 1911 after months of rumors of another trans-Atlantic affair, Alfred married Margaret Emerson, a Newport friend who was unhappily married. To avoid the press, they were married in Surrey, England, not long after Margaret's 1910 divorce in Reno, Nevada was final.[9]

Within a few weeks of Alfred Vanderbilt's 1901 wedding in Newport, Commodore Gerry joined his best gentlemen friends and members of the *New York Yacht Club* to celebrate the club's occupancy of its' new *Club House* on West Forty-Fourth Street. The house-warming was also a "thank you" to ex-Commodore J. Pierpont Morgan for his contributions to the *NYYC*, not the least of which was donating the land upon which the new House was built. Architect Whitney Warren, the brother of Mrs. Robert Goelet the former Harrietta Warren, designed the new *Club House* which incorporated many elements and features of ships. The *Model Room* was the focal point of the first floor with an enormous stained glass insert in the ceiling. The presentation of a three-foot tall silver loving cup to Commodore Morgan was made in the *Model Room* with 300 members of the *NYYC* in attendance. More than 200 cups and trophies were displayed especially for the celebration, along with the permanent models of the yachts of the club's membership. The *NYYC* celebration was followed the next day by a reception for the "ladies" to give them an opportunity to congratulate Commodore Morgan and to enjoy the display of trophies.[10]

The recent victory in the *Spanish American War* and a rebounding economy resulted in the re-election in November 1900 of Republican President William

McKinley. However his Vice-President, Garrett Hobart, had died of heart failure before the election and so the President asked Theodore Roosevelt to be his running mate. For this prominent New Yorker and intimate of high society, invitations to the March 1901 inauguration were liberally distributed in *Gilded Gotham*. The Gerrys were friends with Teddy Roosevelt and so their eldest daughters, Angelica and Mabel Gerry, went to Washington with Mabel's best friend, Gertrude Vanderbilt, and her family on the Vanderbilts' private Pullman car to attend the ceremony and the ball.

The Gerry family made an effort in June to spend time together in Newport at *Seaverge*, the family's third home. The forty-room residence had been purchased fully furnished and after six years Louisa decided to re-decorate, which was accomplished over the winter, and the family was eager to enjoy the results. While the summer colony slowly filled with the usual suspects, the Gerrys made time for short cruises on the *Electra* around the Island and the Narragansett Bay. In late July, shortly before their annual cruise, the *New York Yacht Club* gathered in Newport Harbor to honor the *North Atlantic Squadron* with a joint cruise followed by a celebration in Newport Harbor. The *Spanish American War* was a recent memory and the Squadron was the protector of east coast cities and harbor communities like Newport, so it was time for a "thank you." Of the many entertainments incident to the celebration were large parties held at homes that overlooked the harbor, as well as parties held onboard the yachts anchored off the wharf. Commodore and Mrs. Gerry hosted a party on the *Electra*, just as John Jacob Astor did on the *Noumahal* and Mr. and Mrs. Perry Belmont on the *Satanella*. One of the most beautiful features of the celebration was the parade of illuminated boats; every craft in the harbor was lighted from stem to stern and boats of every description took part.[11] During the celebration, Commodore Gerry invited C. Oliver Iselin and his family to join the Gerrys on the *Electra* to watch the *Astor Cup* races in Newport where the winner would defend the *America's Cup* race in late September. Sir Thomas Lipton of London, England challenged the *NYYC* with his yacht the *Shamrock* for the 1901 Cup race off New York Harbor. The winner of the *Astor Cup* was the *Columbia* and so she would defend the *America's Cup* against Britain's *Shamrock*.

The *NYYC* had finally taken seriously the complaints of past *America's Cup* races that the private boats, tourist steamers, and other vessels were obstructing the waters where the two racing yachts had to maneuver. The club organized a patrol fleet that was meant to prevent interference with the racing yachts. There were two divisions in the patrol line. The first division included the cutter *Gresham*, a government vessel and the *Erin*, Sir Thomas Lipton's steam yacht, plus several other cutters and steamers. The second division patrol line included J. Pierpont Morgan's yacht the *Corsair* and Cornelius Vanderbilt Jr.'s launch *Mirage,* among several other vessels. The lines were formed more than an hour before the race was to start. The two protecting divisions were so stationed that they formed an acute angle with each other, which was the starting point for the *Columbia* and the *Shamrock.* All viewing vessels had to remain behind the two patrol lines as they moved forward while the racing yachts started the race. By the time the racing yachts had turned and were headed back for the finish, the two patrol lines had the miscellaneous viewing craft in two parallel lines between which the rival yachts passed. It was a grand success with the *Columbia* winning, well ahead of the *Shamrock,* and without any kind of interference by passenger vessels. Although the race was exciting the sea was rolling and many spectators onboard the boats became sea sick. By night-fall the ocean had calmed and the harbor glowed with vessels covered in sparkling multicolor lights, the perfect setting for the Gerrys to host an intimate dinner party onboard *Electra.*[12]

The Gerry son's, now 22 and 24, were independent in their activities, both from one another and from the family. Robert had spent the summer in Europe and did not return until after the yacht season just in time to prepare for the fall horse shows. Peter, on the other hand, was in Newport with the family for the yacht season but left just as his older brother returned; he headed off for an extended hunting trip in the far northwest of the United States.

Fall was horse show season throughout the Eastern United States. Robert L. Gerry participated in two horse shows, one in October and one in November. The first show was the *Goshen Horse Show* north of New York City in Orange County, frequented by the Tuxedo crowd. The dominant horse show winners were almost always the Lorillard family and the Harriman family. In the next few years Robert Gerry would meet his future bride at the Goshen show, Cornelia Harriman, the daughter of E. H. Harriman and a fellow award-winning equestrian. The second show of the season was held in *Gilded Gotham* and the auction for the best box seats was held on November 7 at the Madison Square Garden Theater. A crowd of 200 appeared for the 3:30 o'clock auction when the best seats were offered first. Only two bids were considered excessive, one by C.K.G. Billings a wealthy industrialist who paid $500 for Box 29, and George J. Bascom, who paid $500 for box 38. Both were patrons of harness horses for "trotting" and road driving horses. Aside from these two bids, twenty-five of the total sixty-one box seats sold for $300 or less. A few other high bids were placed, one by young Alfred Vanderbilt who paid $415 for Box 13, one by twenty-four year-old Goelet Gallatin who paid $425 for Box 64, and one by Commodore Gerry who paid $400 for Box

Seat 11. The total receipts from the sale and attendance at the first *Horse Show* on November 18 indicated the exhibition season would be a success.[13]

After the lavish summer ball at *Ochre Court,* Mrs. Mary Goelet and her daughter May, had returned to Europe. While they were absent, Mary rented the Fifth Avenue *Goelet Mansion* to Mrs. Cornelius Vanderbilt, Jr. to use for entertaining during the winter season. When Prince Henry of Prussia made a state visit to the United States in 1902, the Vanderbilts gave a formal dinner party at the *Goelet Mansion* for the Prince during his stay in New York City. The dinner was described as elegant with a notable display of gold and silver plate and finger bowls filled with gardenias and jasmine. The gourmet dinner was catered by *Sherry's* and served by waiters dressed in handsome liveries. The guest list included the cream of New York society, the Astors, Belmonts, and the Assistant Secretary of State, David J. Hill. Also invited was Robert L. Gerry, now a well-connected young businessman working with his father at the *Gerry Estates* office on Broadway. After the Prince left the Vanderbilt dinner, he visited the *New York Yacht Club* where he had refreshments and toured the *Model Room.* The visit was documented in a booklet with photographs and an extensive narrative describing the Prince's activities; even the Vanderbilt dinner was described in great detail.[14]

The German measles epidemic that started in 1900 and had made Angelica and Robert Gerry quite ill in early summer had not yet ebbed and continued to claim more victims. A mild flu epidemic also kept many New Yorkers, like the millionaire Mrs. Schermerhorn, in bed and delayed many scheduled trips to Europe. In February 1902, Robert Goelet's widow Harrietta Goelet and her daughter Beatrice had made plans to sail shortly on a trans-Atlantic steamship for a journey to Alexandria, Egypt where their yacht the *Nahma* awaited their arrival for a summer Mediterranean cruise. Beatrice had not yet had her "coming out" cotillion, which would be in 1903 after her eighteenth birthday. Harrietta had not only lost her husband Robert in 1897, but also her mother, Mrs. George Henry Warren had died in the spring of 1901. The Goelets' winter cruise was to be their emergence from a lengthy period of mourning. A week before they were to sail, Beatrice Goelet contracted the measles, however she and her mother recalled how her cousins Angelica and Robert Gerry had recovered several months earlier, which gave Beatrice and her mother confidence. After a week of attendance by two family doctors, Beatrice developed a pernicious pneumonia that was feared could not be survived through the night. She lingered until 3 o'clock the next day when seventeen-year old Beatrice Goelet died with her mother and brother, Robert Walton Goelet, at her bedside. Her passing was regarded as acutely sad as she was the only daughter of Robert and Harrietta and was loved by family and friends alike. Beatrice was known world-wide as the beautiful seven-year girl in the portrait famously painted by John Singer Sargent in which Beatrice stood beside her pet parrot and wore a floor-length brocade dress. The Gerry family consoled their cousin Harrietta, which resurrected their own memory of the unexpected death of their daughter Lillian at about the same tender age. Beatrice's funeral was a private affair held at the Goelet mansion at 591 Fifth Avenue, just across the street from Ogden and Mary Goelet's mansion, which was then occupied by Mrs. Cornelius Vanderbilt, Jr. Beatrice was interred next to her father Robert Goelet in the Goelet Vault at *Woodlawn Cemetery*.[15]

Harrietta Goelet kept Beatrice's bedroom and that of her father, Robert Goelet, intact for the rest of her life. She also kept their staterooms on the *Nahma* as they were when last occupied by her beloved daughter and husband. Harrietta did not become a recluse by any means, in fact she sailed for Europe two weeks after the funeral and traveled to Egypt and from there, set sail for two years of cruising on the *Nahma*, rarely anchoring in New York Harbor.

The mid-February wedding of Miss Alice Morten and Winthrop Rutherfurd had to make last minute adjustments to the ceremony when Beatrice Goelet's uncle, Whitney Warren, a wedding usher, had to withdraw from the groom's party due to the death of his niece. Other social events also required adjustments including Harrietta Goelets planned visit by Prince Henry of Germany which had to be cancelled out of respect for the death of his hostess's daughter. Mrs. Vanderbilt discreetly offered to host the Prince, whom she had met through an introduction by Harrietta Goelet while entertaining the German Emperor on the *Nahma* during a cruise of the Baltic a few years before.[16]

On April 3, 1902 a judgment was entered in the New York Supreme Court disposing of the real and personal property of the estate of Robert Goelet due to the death of his daughter, Beatrice Goelet. The judgment was based on a *Referee Report* in a suit brought by Mrs. Harrietta Goelet and George De Witt, as executors of the estate, to have their accounts considered. Beatrice died while the suit was pending. The only other child involved was Robert Walton Goelet who had not long before attained his majority. The judgment declared the trust property left to Beatrice to now belong to her brother, Robert Walton Goelet, which made him one of the richest men in America.[17]

On April 20 Commodore and Louisa Gerry joined Louisa's aunt, Mrs. Hoffman, for a celebration of Dean and Mrs. Hoffman's golden wedding anniversary. Dean Hoffman was the venerable head of the *General Theological Seminary* of the Episcopal Church of New York City. The celebration was held at the Hoffman home at 1 Chelsea Square, Ninth Avenue and Twentieth Street. Escorted by her husband and followed by her children and grandchildren, Mrs. Hoffman wore the wedding gown she had worn fifty years ago as they formally entered the dining room. The entire house was transformed with golden blossoms of tulips and yellow roses. All of the gifts were made of gold and included loving cups, vases, trays and dishes. Commodore and Louisa Gerry gave them a large gold vase. This was a welcome and life-affirming celebration at a time of mourning for young Beatrice within the extended family.[18]

The summer exodus from New York City was well underway by June and Dean and Mrs. Hoffman left for Canada for a few weeks of fishing at the *Restigouche Salmon Club,* where they likely met other club members, like Robert W. Goelet, Stanford White, and the Vanderbilt men. Dean Hoffman was quite frail with a weak heart and the Canadian mountain air always improved his health. Toward the end of their second week at the fishing lodge, Dean Hoffman became quite ill and his doctor, who traveled with him, insisted that he return to New York. On the train ride home Dean Hoffman died with his wife by his side, just two weeks after celebrating their golden wedding anniversary. He left three married daughters and a son, Samuel Verplanck Hoffman, a *Fellow in Astronomy* at Johns Hopkins University in Baltimore, Maryland. Dean Hoffman's funeral was held at Trinity Church and was attended by the extended Gerry, Hoffman, and Livingston families.

Robert L. Gerry had already sailed for Europe on the same trans-Atlantic steamship with his life-long friend, Alfred Vanderbilt, and his wife Elsie. The horse exhibitions and the coaching and racing season were starting in England and France and both men wanted to enjoy and share their life-long passion for horses. The Gerry family went to Newport on *Electra,* where Robert would join them at *Seaverge* later in the summer. Whether or not he was on a holiday, one of the pleasures Commodore Gerry enjoyed with his yacht *Electra,* was the privilege of taking special guests to important destinations, particularly when it served as a civic duty. The first week of August he was honored to be invited to Oyster Bay, New York for lunch with President Theodore Roosevelt at *Sagamore Hill.* Commodore and Mrs. Gerry were joined by Ambassador and Mrs. Whitelaw Reid, also guests of the President, on the *Electra* for the trip to Oyster Bay. Mrs. Whitelaw Reid, Elizabeth Mills, was the sister-in-law of Ruth Livingston Mills, the daughter of Maturin Livingston, Louisa Gerry's uncle. The women were first cousins by marriage and had shared family gatherings for years at Staatsburg-on-Hudson, the Livingston family estate. Their daughter, Jane Reid, was a long-time close friend of the Gerrys' daughter, Mabel. At *Sagamore Hill* they joined the other guests, Archbishop Ryan of Philadelphia and Gifford Pinchot, the Chief of the Forestry Division of the U.S. Department of Agriculture. The lunch was a mixture of friendly chats, a little business and enjoying the outdoors. Ambassador Reid relayed the affairs of work in London as an American representative and the cordiality of the British officials. Archbishop Ryan spoke with the President about the reaction of Catholics in the Philippines to the replacement of Spanish priests with American priests since the *Spanish American War.* Commissioner Pinchot spoke with the President about his assignment in the Philippines to investigate and study the forests of the islands. Commodore Gerry was a personal friend of the Roosevelt family and spoke of less serious matters. After lunch Mr. Pinchot joined the President for a trek in the woods of the estate to cut away underbrush and dead timber. The two had a lively hour of exercise during which the President demonstrated he had the better hand with an axe. The Archbishop caught a local train at 4:15 for his return to Philadelphia, and around 5 o'clock the Gerrys and the Reids left Oyster Bay on the *Electra* for their return to Newport.[19] The Gerry family remained in Newport until early September when they closed *Seaverge* for the season and traveled up the Hudson River on *Electra* to Kingston, then by train to Andes for a quiet fall holiday at the *Lake Delaware* estate.[20]

Newport's most illustrious guest during the summer of 1902 was the Grand Duke, Boris Vladimirovich of Russia, the guest of Mrs. Ogden Goelet at *Ochre Court.* The Duke lived in his own palace in Saint Petersburg, built in 1895 in the style of an English country house. From early youth Boris was notorious for his restless life style. He was very social and liked to drink and have fun. By the time he was an adult he was known as the terror of jealous husbands, as well as, of watchful mothers. In 1901 the Grand Duke Boris left Russia for Cannes, France to enjoy the social season on the Riviera where he joined an elite circle of Americans, including Mrs. Ogden Goelet, John Jacob Astor, and the Vanderbilts. Before setting off on an "around the world" trip the Duke was extended an invitation by Mrs. Mary Goelet to visit her at *Ochre Court* to enjoy the summer season in Newport. In January 1902, accompanied by a large entourage on the German ship *Bremen,* he began several months of travel to visit Egypt, India, Ceylon, Siam, French Indochina, Japan, Honolulu, California, Chicago and finally New York City in late August. From there Duke Boris sailed to Newport, Rhode Island for the remainder of the summer where he was entertained at luncheons and dinners, thoroughly enjoying the attention.[21] On September 15 at the moment Mrs. Goelet and the Grand Duke, along with his escorts, were leaving *Ochre Court* they heard screams from inside the mansion and immediately returned. Mrs. Goelet's housekeeper, fifty-year old Margaret Blake, was caught by her clothing as she attempted to enter a descending elevator in the servants' quarters and was crushed to death. Those present were unable to render help because it happened so quickly. Mrs. Blake, a widow, came from England and had just been hired by Mrs. Goelet the month before.[22] It was a terrible tragedy to which the Duke extended his sincere condolences and was supportive of Mrs. Goelet's need to attend to her household. The Grand Duke left America much impressed, particularly by the beauty and strength of American women. He followed a military career as a Major General in the Russian Army and took part in the *Russo-Japanese War* and in *World War I.* Grand Duke Boris managed to escape revolutionary Russia into exile in France where he married his mistress and settled in Paris.[23]

The first week of October brought the Gallatin, Goelet and Gerry families together to celebrate the wedding of Goelet Gallatin to Edith Church Post at picturesque *St. Ann's Episcopal* Church in Bayport, Long Island. The wedding was of special interest because the decorations and details, reproduced as far as possible, the wedding eleven years before of the present bride's half-sister Miss Lina Post and Hamilton Fish Webster. The interior of the little stone church was decorated with garlands and wreaths of green, the font was filled with white and pink roses, and bunches of roses were tied at the end of each pew. Goelet Gallatin had his brother Albert stand as his best man. After the church service all of the guests were driven to *Strandhome,* the Post family mansion where the newlyweds received guests on the enclosed yet sun-filled veranda. Guests were served breakfast in a large tent on the mansion's sprawling lawn overlooking the *Great South Bay.* Guests could see the Post family yachts and those of other guests, like the Gerrys' *Electra,* anchored in the bay, many flying festive flags. Commodore and Mrs. Gerry gave their nephew and his bride a gold punchbowl, and Frederic and Almy gave their son and his bride a fully furnished house at 444 Madison Avenue in New York City. Guests who did not travel by private transport left Bay Port on a special train that arrived back in New York at 6 p.m. in time for dinner.[24]

Shortly after the Gallatin wedding on Long Island, Commodore Gerry was involved in the most publicized interventions of the *Society for the Prevention of Cruelty to Children* which began at the *Ellis Island Immigration Station* for the Port of New York. The Ward Line steamship *Orizaba* had a small group of children from Santiago de Cuba among the passengers that arrived on November 1, 1902. The eleven children, escorted by Dr. Gertrude Van Pelt, M.D., consisted of nine boys and two girls, who were between eight and twelve years of age. They were to be cared for and educated at the *Raja Yoga Academy* of the Universal Brotherhood, at Point Loma outside of San Diego, California. The school was founded by Katherine W. Tingley, a Theosophist, whose fundamental ideas were the development of character and an emphasis on individual responsibility. The children's escort, Dr. Van Pelt, herself a dedicated Theosophist of long standing, did not expect any problems at *Ellis Island* from immigration authorities since she had escorted 40 children from Cuba the previous year.

However, the docking of the steam ship was mentioned in the newspapers with a story about a demonstration in Santiago de Cuba that protested the children being sent to America. This article attracted the attention of the *NYSPCC*, the *Gerry Society* who immediately requested that immigration detain the children so the Society's agents could investigate the matter. To Dr. Van Pelt's chagrin the thinly clad and shivering little Cubans were herded off to detention. Devoted local New York followers of the Theosophist, Mrs. Tingley, hurried to request a hearing before the *Board of Special Inquiry* at Ellis Island, headed by Charles Semsey.[25]

At the hearing, Vernon M. Davis a lawyer working for the *Gerry Society* protested the entry of the Cuban children based on the financial irresponsibility of the Point Loma institution in California, and the detrimental atmosphere of the institution on the children. The hearing was publicized and drew the attention of one of the most strident supporters of the Theosophists, former baseball star, Albert G. Spalding, now a prominent businessman in sporting goods. He brought two reporters to Ellis Island to inspect the Cuban children and found them in a 6 by 12 foot cell with only a few cots and a watering trough. To avoid adverse publicity from the reporters the children were transferred to more spacious and livable quarters for the balance of the investigation. However, by now, the international press was following the story. Franco Ortiz, the acting mayor of Santiago de Cuba, sent a telegram to the *New York Tribune* in which he refuted the earlier story about protest demonstrations and stated that the children had left his community under the most pleasant circumstances. Frank P. Frary, the Mayor of San Diego, as well as Henry J. Baldwin, Superintendent of San Diego Schools, both cabled the Commissioner at *Ellis Island* demanding the release of the children at once, attesting to the stability and good atmosphere of the *Raja Yoga Academy*. Nevertheless, on November 3 the *Board of Special Inquiry* recommended to exclude the children on the basis that they were assisted immigrants and liable to become public charges. Considering the growing mobilization of elements favorable towards the Theosophists and Mrs. Tingley, the Commissioner at *Ellis Island* ordered a re-hearing on November 5.

At this turn of events the *NYSPCC* lawyer, Vernon M. Davis, called Commodore Gerry into the case. As the hearings dragged on, the *Gerry Society* marshaled an impressive array of witnesses. Late in November Governor Henry T. Gage of California sent representatives of the *State Board of Health* to inspect Point Loma and its school. Their report was favorable to Mrs. Tingley. Determined to buttress their position, Vernon David and Commodore Gerry traveled to Washington, D.C. to plead their case before the *Commissioner General of Immigration* and the *Assistant Secretary of the Treasury*. After a full review the *Gerry Society* was overturned and the Cuban children were ordered released from *Ellis Island* on December 6, 1902. However, the *Gerry Society* still had the power to seize the children upon their release when they entered New York City. To avoid this possibility, Albert G. Spalding hired a steam launch, loaded the children at *Ellis Island* and made a bee line for the New Jersey shore. From there the children were conveyed by train to Washington, D.C. and from there on to California. While the *NYSPCC* never took custody of the children, it did act as a private advocate on their behalf.[26]

While Commodore Gerry fought the *NYSPCC* battles in 1902 his sister was busy developing her real estate interests in New York City. Almy Gerry Gallatin inherited property from her mother on Twentieth Street between Broadway and Park Avenue in addition to the Nineteenth Street Goelet mansion on the next block over, which was demolished and replaced with a commercial building just before the turn of the century. In 1902 Almy Gallatin combined her lot on Twentieth Street with the adjacent lot that had belonged to her husband Frederic Gallatin's family since the 1830's and built a neo-Renaissance six-story store and loft building at numbers 16-18 and 20-24. The original Theodore Roosevelt townhouse, now reconstructed at 28 East 20 Street, occupied part of the same row of townhouses as the Gallatin family from the 1840's to the 1890's. Theodore Roosevelt Sr. was seven years older than Elbridge and ten years older than Frederic and would have known his young neighbors, indeed, he could see the old Goelet house on the next block from his back windows. His son Teddy Roosevelt was born in his father's house when Elbridge was twenty and Frederic was seventeen and they were still neighbors of the Roosevelt family. The asthmatic young Teddy Roosevelt took some joy in watching the exotic birds in old Peter Goelet's yard while wandering around the neighborhood doing his out-of-door breathing exercises.[27] The Gerry children lived with the Goelet family just around the corner at Nineteenth and Broadway in Uncle Peter's mansion, which provided the opportunity for young Frederic Gallatin to share his childhood with neighborhood playmates, Elbridge Gerry and his two sisters, and ultimately, to marry Almy Gerry the girl next door. Forty years later in 1902 Frederic and Almy merged the Gallatin and Goelet homestead properties to construct handsome new commercial structures on Twentieth Street. Both Louisa Gerry and Almy Gallatin held property in their own names and actively participated in land use decisions over their life-times and even endured law suits as landlords, which were represented in court by their lawyer husbands, Elbridge and Frederic.

Just as the Gerrys owned property at *Lake Delaware* and the Livingstons at *Staatsburg,* the Gallatin and Goelet families purchased property in upstate New York in a sleepy village called *Tuxedo.* They joined a group of *Gilded Gotham's* society who abandoned the city in the winter to spend the Christmas and New Year holidays in a growing but exclusive enclave at *Tuxedo Park.* In 1885 the area was a wilderness where Indians hunted elk, deer, bear and wild turkeys. The Indians named the area *Ptucksepo* which white settlers pronounced *Tuxedo.* The Continental Road that passed through the area was named after George Washington's march through this wilderness on what was then called the Corduroy Road during the *American Revolution.*[28] The Lorillard family had been interested in the Tuxedo locality since 1814, when Peter Lorillard foreclosed a mortgage on part of the territory. Three generations later, in 1867, the enlarged tract passed into the hands of the seven children of Peter Lorillard III. The oldest son, Pierre Lorillard, visited the rocky, tumbled hills and conceived the idea of using them for sport. In 1884-85 he set to work buying up the shares held by his siblings. Pierre and his architect, Bruce Price, made the forty mile journey north from New York City to inspect the land and immediately hired 1,800 men who were lodged in a small city of shanties built along regular dirt roads with such names as "Fifth Avenue" and "Broadway". The mess hall was called "Delmonico's" after the fashionable New York City restaurant whose architect, James Brown Lord, was to live in the new *Tuxedo Park.* By May 1886 the luxury sport club was ready for the opening celebration. Lorillard hired three special trains to carry 700 guests up from New York City. The run was supposed to take an hour and a half, but the exuberant engineers made it in forty minutes to the alarm of the passengers, many of whom were so frightened by the way the rickety old coaches careened on the narrow-gauge track that they refused to return until the engineers promised to go at the slow, normal speed. Despite their fears, they arrived safely at the *Tuxedo* station and were met by coaches and wagons painted brightly in the club colors of yellow and green. Between 1889 and 1902, lakes were stocked with fish, a golf course, tennis courts, and a swimming pool were built. Even a short horse racing track was installed. Winter sports included snowshoeing, ice skating and curling on the lake. When elite society built their mansions on lake property the area became known as *Tuxedo Park* and families could then come more often and stay longer. For seventy-five years, stating in 1886, an autumn dance was held at the *Tuxedo Club House,* which became a second venue for debutantes to host a formal ball to be presented to society. Also, a new fashion for men, a short version of the formal dinner jacket known around the world as a *Tuxedo,* originated in this elite enclave. The story of its origin is attributed to Mr. Grenville Kane, a founding member of the Club who told the story to his friend, J. Earle Stevens in 1929. In the summer of 1886, club members Mr. and Mrs. James Brown Potter, while on a visit to England, were invited by the Prince of Wales, "Bertie," to join him at his country estate, *Sandringham,* for the weekend. Prior to going Mr. Potter asked the Prince what he should wear for dinner to which the Prince replied that he had adopted a short jacket in the place of the tailcoat for dinner in the country and that if Mr. Potter went to his tailor in London he could get a similar jacket made. Mr. Potter did and when he returned to America his friends at the *Tuxedo Club* were impressed with the look of the jacket and its practicality. Club members had their own tailors make one for each of them and the jacket was thus adopted as the customary attire for formal dinners at the *Tuxedo Club.* One evening in New York City a group of Club members wore their new jackets to a bachelor's dinner at Delmonico's restaurant and it attracted so much attention that everyone called the short jacket a *Tuxedo,* as in "that's the jacket worn at the *Tuxedo Club.*" From that day forward the jacket was quickly adopted as the universal dinner jacket, leaving long tailcoats for weddings and the most formal of occasions.[29]

On December 31, 1902 the *Tuxedo Club* held their *New Year's Eve Ball.* Every guest room at the club house was occupied and most of the local estates were open for holiday parties, which included ice skating, tobogganing and coasting on *Tuxedo Lake.* Frederic and Almy Gallatin had gone to Tuxedo Park for the holidays as did Robert Walton Goelet. They all joined the large celebration at the club house to welcome the New Year. After dinner everyone assembled in the ballroom where dancing began at 10 o'clock and precisely at midnight, a large framed picture with numerous incandescent electric lights representing an American eagle wrapped in an American flag, was dropped from the stage inscribed with "A Happy New Year." Everyone joined hands in the center of the ballroom, the punch bowl was brought in, and all sang "Auld Lang Syne," and made a toast before resuming the dance. A second supper was served at 1 o'clock in the morning.[30]

The New Year began for the Gerry family with a short trip to Newport to accommodate a January 15 lecture Commodore Gerry gave to the Rhode Island *Society for the Prevention of Cruelty to Children.* The lecture was given in Providence and allowed the Gerrys to travel on *Electra* to Providence and then to Newport for a couple of nights before returning to New York City.

March and April were occupied with a legal action brought against Louisa Gerry by one of her tenants, Mrs. Anna Davidson. A twenty-one year lease made to Mrs. Davidson's husband, now deceased, was about to expire in April and as the new lessee, Mrs. Davidson notified Mrs. Gerry that she wished to renew the lease. The property was located at the corner of Seventh Avenue and Forty-Second Street, and was occupied by the *Victoria Theater.* The original lease required that upon renewal, each party to the lease would appoint an appraiser to determine the new rent for the twenty-one year renewal. Mrs. Davidson appointed Samuel Goldsticker as her appraiser, and Mrs. Gerry appointed Michael Coleman with the *Mutual Life Insurance Company* as her appraiser. The two arbitrators met and trouble ensued. Mr. Goldsticker said he believed the assessed valuation of the land by the city Tax Commissioners should be the basis for fixing the rent, which was recorded as $450,000. Mr. Coleman said that was ridiculous because the land was easily worth $1,000,000 and insisted that $40,000 a year rent was the proper figure. Mr. Goldsticker said that was exorbitant, a heated argument followed and Mr. Coleman ordered Mr. Goldsticker from his office. The primary claim on January 15 was that Mr. Coleman, as the paid manager of the Gerry real estate interests, was not an impartial arbitrator for the lease renewal. The matter was continued to the following week and a compromise was reached allowing Mrs. Davidson to renew the lease of the *Victoria Theater.* Leases held over many years for property that progressively escalated in value led to many disputes and negotiated compromises that both the *Gerry Estates* and the *Goelet Estates* routinely managed as New York City became a center of international business.[31]

Six years after Robert Goelet's death, his wife Harrietta and son Robert Walton Goelet wanted to build a memorial that would inspire future generations to work and succeed on behalf of New York City, the way Robert Goelet had throughout his life. They chose *Columbia University,* where Robert Goelet graduated in 1860 and where his business and social life had their start. They engaged Daniel Chester French to design a memorial that honored Robert by honoring the University. The sculpture was executed in bronze and placed on a marble pedestal. Daniel Chester French said he wanted to create a figure that would make a gracious impression with an attitude of welcome to the young people who chose Columbia as their college. He created an enormous yet elegant seated woman wearing an academic gown with a laurel crown on her head. The sculpture incorporates an owl for wisdom, a book representing knowledge, and one hand holding a staff with a *Kings College* crown at the top that represented the parent institution, *Oxford University* in England, from which *Columbia College* emerged after the *American Revolution.* Her other hand is outstretched in welcome to the students. The statue's base is emblazoned with the words "Alma Mater" by which she has been known for well over one hundred years.[32]

The spring of 1903 was especially beautiful in New York City and vicinity and the cottagers in Tuxedo Park and Newport would open their summer estates in just a few weeks. The usual rush to Europe from *Gilded Gotham* had begun to ebb ever so slightly as the next generation of New Yorkers embraced the seasonal entertainments it found from coast to coast in America. The Prince of Wales, Bertie, the primary social draw of Americans to England for a quarter century, was now King Edward VII and ushered in the Edwardian era from 1902-1910. He was no longer able to freely socialize with American friends which caused the many lavish parties to fade from their former glory. King Edward had to lead his country into a new century that heralded significant changes in technology and society, including powered flight and the rise of socialism. The new King encouraged the modernization of the *British Home Fleet,* the reform of the *Army Medical Services,* and the reorganization of the *British Army* after the Second Boer War. King Edward VII fostered good relations between Great Britain and other European countries, especially France, for which he was popularly called "Peacemaker," but his efforts before his death in 1910 were unable to prevent the outbreak of World War I.[33]

Spring was New York City's most glorious time of the year when everyone engaged in outdoor activities, especially walks in Central Park and the return of equestrian sports like polo and coaching. In early April 1903 the *Durland Riding Academy* held its annual horse show on West Sixty-Sixth Street within a few blocks of the Gerry and Vanderbilt homes and private carriage and horse stables. Alfred Vanderbilt and his childhood pal Robert Gerry entered their polo ponies in the challenge to ride between six posts arranged in a long, straight line, to show their ability to turn sharply and stop quickly. Alfred dominated the competition and Robert usually came in second or third. Small polo matches were performed to entertain the spectators including Robert Walton Goelet, the first cousin of Robert Gerry. The next generation of Gerry and Goelet men were less interested in yachts and the sea than they were in polo matches, fox hunting and horse breeding.

By May the elegant sport of coaching had become the most popular spring ritual in beautiful Central Park. May 9, 1903 was a perfect day for the annual *Coaching Club Parade* and brought out a large crowd of spectators, on horseback, in carriages, in automobiles and on foot, to witness the start at the Fifty-Ninth Street and Eighth Avenue entrance to Central Park. The President of the Coaching Club, Colonel William Jay, led the line of coaches to the circle at One-hundred-and-Fourth Street where the coaches or "drags" passed in review; afterward the coach line started off by way of Central Bridge for *Morris Park,* where lunch was served at the clubhouse. The four Gerry children all participated in the parade. Robert L. Gerry, then twenty-six years old, was whip on his own coach with a party that included Miss Cornelia Harriman, whom he was then courting, and Mrs. Louisa Gerry. On E. Victor Loew, Jr.'s red and blue coach was Mabel Gerry, now thirty years old. Also whip on his own black and maroon coach was Peter G. Gerry, now twenty-four years old. His party included Mrs. J. Borden Harriman and his older sister, Angelica Gerry, then thirty-two years old. Robert Gerry's best friend Alfred Vanderbilt was the whip on his coach with his wife Elsie at his side, and Mabel Gerry's best friend, Gertrude Vanderbilt Whitney, was beside her husband and whip, Harry Payne Whitney on his coach. The group of intimate friends and family shared an enjoyable luncheon after the parade in *Morris Park* at the private *Coaching Club House*.[34]

The following week Commodore and Mrs. Gerry, joined by Angelica and Mabel, sailed on a trans-Atlantic steamship for what was described as a "flying trip to London and Paris."[35] Like others in their circle, the entertainments in Newport held more interest than Europe which the family had toured many times over the past twenty-five years. The trip to London and Paris was to visit close friends and family, including Ambassador and Elizabeth Reid, Louisa's second cousin, at *Dorchester House*, and their niece, May Goelet, and her mother, Mary Goelet, who had spent most of the year in Europe. The Gerrys and Mary Goelet were also joined by sister-in-law Harrietta Goelet who was cruising off the Riviera on the *Nahma* after a humorous yet inconvenient detention by the Turkish government a few weeks before. On May 17 the State Department made public the account of how on April 27 Mrs. Robert Goelet's yacht *Nahma* with a party of New York friends entered the *Dardanelles* when sentinels on the Turkish fortresses caught the outlines of guns under the tarpaulin coverings of the deck. Signals were flashed back and forth and soon a shot plunged across the *Nahma's* bow and the yacht hove to and came to a stop. The Turkish officers boarded the *Nahma* and were polite but firm when they informed Harrietta Goelet that her vessel was a warship since it had two six-pound rapid-fire guns on deck. In fact, the guns only fired blank cartridges when used for salutes. Harrietta had a dinner engagement in Constantinople for which she had already broken all speed ordinances and she did not appreciate the interference with her plans. After two days of diligent telegraphing to Constantinople and the exercise of great persuasion, it was agreed that the detention was altogether accidental and that the *Nahma* was not a warship, and it was allowed to pass the *Dardanelles*. When Harrietta Goelet arrived at Constantinople the Sultan sent his grand master of ceremonies aboard the *Nahma* to pay the respects of the Turkish government and to welcome her to their country. While onboard, the Sultan's Master conferred on Mrs. Robert Goelet the *Grand Cordon of the Turkish Order of the Chefakat*, one of the most notable decorations the Sultan could award. Some said that the Sultan was not without a sense of humor, having many wives, and after all, Harrietta had done as a woman what great powers had been unable to do with all their armaments. Amends were made and the *Nahma* remained a few days at Constantinople, then proceeded on its cruise of the Mediterranean, and sailed northward to London where family and friends awaited her arrival.[36]

Summer rumors swirled around Newport in 1903, one of which even surprised the Gerry family. The small upstate New York newspaper, *Catskill Mountain News* reported on June 12 that Robert L. Gerry was to marry his cousin May Goelet, but of course they were like brother and sister and no doubt enjoyed the gossip. The broken engagement of Robert's sister Angelica to J. Wadsworth Ritchie was also resurrected when news of Mrs. Ritchie's untimely death reached America from England. She was Emily Tooker of Newport before her marriage and was well known and loved in the community. Her death was sudden and unexpected, reportedly from blood poisoning while traveling in Europe.[37] All of Newport society was saddened by the news.

Then, for the first time the summer papers focused on Peter G. Gerry, the Commodore's youngest child, and now an eligible bachelor. The article described Peter as quite a sedate young man, very fond of coaching and polo. He tried yachting in Delaware Lake with his brother Robert on some small boats and had inherited the love of salt water from his father. Like his brother Robert, twenty-four year old Peter was an excellent polo player and it was suggested that he and Robert form a Gerry brothers' team.[38] Peter followed his father's profession and attended Harvard Law School from 1903-1906, and may have been wistfully flattered by the attention. The Commodore's daughters were not ignored by the press when they hosted a summer subscription ball at the *Newport Casino.* Angelica and Mabel were said to have wonderful executive ability as demonstrated by their energetic organization of the ball for which they purchased the favors for the cotillion, selected the decorations, the music and the supper menu. Mrs. Gerry and her daughters always gave personal attention to all of their home entertainments and it was no surprise that the subscription ball was such a success. When Mabel Gerry was mentioned as a possible bridesmaid at an upcoming wedding, the press described her as tall and slim with an exquisite figure with dark hair and eyes, almost Parisian rather than American in her appearance. She was fond of all sports and within the last few years had developed a certain chic in how she dressed. Both Angelica and Mabel had worn the latest Paris fashions at summer entertainments like the hand-painted gowns done by famous artists with dainty festoons of ribbons, leaves, and flowers traced on the fabric. There was never an article about Angelica and Mabel that did not remind the reader that they were the wealthy and eligible daughters of Commodore Elbridge T. Gerry, and they had yet to show an interest in any of their many suitors.[39]

Comfortably settled in at *Seaverge* for the summer, Commodore Gerry again competed in the annual flower show in Newport, which was held at the Masonic Hall. Upon entering the hall the fruit exhibits were to the right and flower exhibits to the left. Commodore Gerry won first prize for the fancy "basket of roses" display and second prize for his "American beauty" roses. He also won either first or second prize for his fern and palms, and for the first time, he won a special premium award for his orchids. However, once again, he did not win in any fruit category which was dominated by Mrs. Harrietta Goelet with her winning strawberries and tomatoes and it was Perry Belmont who won for white and black grapes, difficult fruits to grow in the Rhode Island environment. The *Horticultural Society* competitions always encouraged Commodore Gerry to double his efforts for the next year.[40]

Mrs. Mary Goelet and her daughter May had a busy summer in London where they had been in the company of Henry Innes-Kerr for many social entertainments. In mid-August Mrs. Goelet, her daughter and Henry sailed on the trans-Atlantic steamship *Compania* for America and arrived in New York City on August 15 where they were met by Cornelius Vanderbilt, Jr. who had just arrived from Europe on his yacht the *North Star*. Mrs. Goelet and her party boarded the *North Star* where they joined her sister Mrs. Vanderbilt and her sister-in-law Mrs. Harrietta Goelet, who had recently returned from Europe on the *Nahma*. The group planned to live onboard the *North Star* during the *America's Cup* race and occasionally go ashore to dine at the fashionable restaurants in the city. After the races the *North Star* cruised to Newport, Rhode Island where the two Mrs. Goelets opened their neighboring residences, *Southside* and *Ochre Court* for a few weeks. Henry was the *Duke of Roxburghe* and during his stay at *Ochre Court* Mrs. Goelet hosted many small dinners for his entertainment. Henry and May spent a great deal of time together at the *Newport Casino* and the *Newport Country Club* watching the polo matches. The rumor of romance overshadowed all other Newport summer gossip, and finally, on September 1 Mrs. Goelet formally announced to society the engagement of her daughter May to Henry John Innes-Kerr, the *Eighth Duke of Roxburghe*, Scotland. The Duke's mother, Lady Anne Spencer Churchill, the great aunt of Consuelo Vanderbilt, the *Duchess of Marlborough*, announced the engagement in London about the same time it was announced in Newport.[41]

Friends of the engaged couple believed it was a true romance, a love match that was in the making for a few years. The Duke was twenty-seven and the bride twenty-three, both were modest and reticent, attractive and well educated. May Goelet had been presented at *Buckingham Palace* at age 17 and her parents were intimate friends with King Edward VII, as was the young Duke Henry who had carried the King's crown at his coronation ceremony in 1902. Henry had fought well in the Boer War and the king rewarded him by making him a *Knight of the Thistle.* The Duke lived at *Floors Castle* with an enormous estate. He was well respected and liked among his peers who described him as amiable and democratic in his manners, quiet and well read. At six feet tall, Henry was one of the best polo players on the famous team of the *Royal Horse Guard* to which he once belonged. May Goelet was described as petite and most attractive with dark hair and eyes and had an aristocratic bearing. She was clever and amusing and had been sought after by every eligible prince of Europe and bachelor in New York society. The Duke had been closely associated with May for a year before the engagement so they knew each other well and their wealthy families approved the match.[42]

The wedding was held at *Saint Thomas Episcopal Church* on Fifth Avenue in New York City on November 10, 1903. It was the second time in the history of the church that there had been married within its walls an American girl and a British duke. The ceremony was elegant, with an organ, a harp and a male choir of fifty voices. A reception followed the wedding at the Goelet mansion on Fifth Avenue, after which the bride and groom sailed for England. May and Henry Innes-Kerr, the Duke and Duchess of Roxburghe, lived a happy life together *at Floors Castle* where they had one son, George Innes-Kerr, the ninth duke. While they lived primarily in Scotland, they had a home in London and they returned quite often to Newport for holidays and New York for weddings of family and friends. Today their grandson, Guy David Innes-Kerr, the tenth Duke of Roxburghe lives at *Floors Castle* where he raised five children.[43] After her daughter moved to Scotland permanently, Mrs. Mary Goelet lived a trans-Atlantic life between her Newport and New York City homes which she shared with her son Robert Wilson Goelet, and her daughter's residences in Great Britain.

The following year, in January 1904, Mabel Gerry, then 32 years old, traveled to Washington, D.C. to visit her aunt and uncle, Ambassador and Mrs. Whitelaw Reid, and her younger second cousin, Jean Reid. Although single, Mabel traveled extensively with her intimate friends and family. The Ambassador had just returned from London, England for a short diplomatic visit. Elegant lunches and dinners were held throughout Washington society for the Ambassador and his family, which included Mabel who relished an evening at the Austrian Embassy and a diplomatic reception hosted by New Yorkers Mr. and Mrs. Oliver Cromwell who shared stories of their extended trip to Mexico.[44] Another young woman, nineteen year old Washington belle Mathilda Townsend, attended the diplomatic dinners and knew Mabel from her summer visits to Newport, Rhode Island and winter balls in New York City. Jean Reid and Mathilda Townsend, both wealthy and beautiful, were like younger sisters to Mabel and Angelica Gerry. Mathilda Townsend had been active in the equestrian world and the horticultural world since she was a young girl, winning prizes for her creamy white large chrysanthemums at age 11 and ribbons for her pony at the horse shows in Bar Harbor, Maine and Orange County, New York. It was no surprise that in just a few years Mabel's younger brother Peter Gerry would begin courting the beautiful Mathilda Townsend, the most eligible Washington heiress of her day.

One reception that Mabel did not attend was held at the White House, hosted by President Theodore Roosevelt, the mutual friend of Commodore Gerry and his wife's cousin, Elizabeth Reid and her husband, Ambassador Whitelaw Reid. Born on a farm near Xenia, Ohio in 1837 and an honors graduate of Ohio's Miami University in 1856, Whitelaw Reid was a peer of Elbridge T. Gerry. His grandparents were immigrants from Scotland just as Louisa Livingston Gerry's family was originally from Scotland. Shortly after college, Whitelaw purchased the local paper, the *Xenia News,* and was the editor for three years. As a vocal supporter of Abraham Lincoln in the 1860 election, he was elected a state delegate to the Republican National Convention. At the outbreak of the *Civil War* he accompanied General George B. McClellan as a war correspondent, and while in that position he began a military correspondence under the pseudonym of *Agate* for publication in the *Cincinnati Gazette* that provided one of the most authentic contemporary records of the war. In 1862 Whitelaw Reid moved to Washington, D.C. to report on the war from the nation's capital where he made influential friends and was soon appointed the Librarian of the House of Representatives. His later friendship with Commodore Gerry would find a deep kinship in their love of books and their approach to developing and organizing libraries. In 1868 his journalist work caught the attention of Horace Greeley who asked Reid to become associate editor of the *New York Tribune*; he became the managing-editor the following year. After the death of Horace Greeley, Reid became printer, publisher and circulation manager. His work on the *Tribune* influenced President Rutherford B. Hayes to ask him to be Minister to Germany, which he declined, and then President Garfield offered him the same position in 1881 which he again declined. Then, in 1889 President Harrison asked Reid to be Minister to France, which he accepted. After ten years of outstanding service Whitelaw Reid resigned and returned to New York, and was almost immediately nominated to run for Vice-President with Benjamin Harrison the Presidential nominee. The Republicans lost the election but Reid gave effective and passionate speeches, reinvigorating his reputation in the United States. In 1896 he was appointed Special Ambassador of the United States at the *Diamond Jubilee* of Queen Victoria. As members of the Gerry/Livingston family, Ambassador Reid and his wife Elizabeth were intimates of the Goelet family in New York City. Indeed, the Gallatin, Gerry, Goelet, Livingston and Reid families were part of the intimate core of subscribers to the *Patriarchs' Ball* and guests at the Astor, Vanderbilt, and other *Gilded Gotham* affairs during the 1890's. Whitelaw Reid joined Ogden Goelet at the *Diamond Jubilee* celebrations in London, both intimate friends with "Bertie," Prince Albert Edward. Ogden Goelet died at Cowes, England just as the *Jubilee* celebrations were winding down and his wife, Mary, welcomed the comfort and assistance of her dear friends, Whitelaw and Elizabeth Reid, whose presence in London at the time of Ogden's death in the summer of 1897 was a blessing.

At the beginning of President Teddy Roosevelt's second term he appointed Whitelaw Reid the permanent Ambassador to Great Britain and in 1909 he was retained by President Taft. He rented a stately mansion called *Dorchester House* on Park Lane in London which he occupied as the American Embassy during his seven-year tenure, where he died in 1912 at age seventy-five. A huge memorial service was held in Westminster Abby in London after which his body was brought home to the United States on a British war ship for his funeral in New York City. Whitelaw Reid was a Regent of the *University of the State of New York* with honorary degrees conferred upon him by Princeton University, Cambridge University, Oxford University and the University of Saint Andrews, Scotland. *Ophir Farm*, the Reid estate in Westchester County, New York, designed by architects McKim, Mead and White, and landscaped by Frederick Law Olmstead between 1888 and 1891, was purchased in 1949 as the new home of *Manhattanville College*. Whitelaw Reid's only son, Ogden Mills Reid, was a Yale Law School graduate and followed in his father's footsteps as Managing Editor of the *New York Tribune*.[45] His daughter Jean married Sir John Hubert Ward, the brother of the second Earl of Dudley, Staffordshire, England and lived primarily in London at *Dudley House* on Park Lane.

While Mabel Gerry spent January in Washington, D.C., her twenty-seven year old brother, Robert L. Gerry, was making plans for the spring and summer equestrian season, particularly fox hunting and polo playing followed by the horse shows. His participation in *Coaching Parades* as a whip of his own horse carriage was a leisurely activity that was less a sport than an opportunity to socialize with the ladies and display ones horses in Central Park. Robert and Peter Gerry began their polo playing at Harvard where they were star players on the team. Robert dropped out of Harvard before finishing his senior year and in 1902 he and his brother Peter went to work full-time with their father at 261 Broadway for a one-year apprenticeship; neither brother is listed in the *New York City Business Directory* again until after Robert married in 1908 and Peter married in 1910. So for Peter G. Gerry, 1904 was all about law school and for Robert L. Gerry, 1904 was the year of the horse.

As early as 1881 fox hunting and polo playing had become so popular that August Belmont Sr., the old business partner of Robert J. Livingston, and some friends established the oldest polo club in America in Old Westbury, Long Island, just twenty-four miles east of New York City. Robert and Peter Gerry and pal Alfred Vanderbilt joined the established polo set led by E. H. Harriman, John R. Townsend and August Belmont Jr. at the *Meadow Brook* hunt and polo club on Long Island beginning around 1902. Although polo remained the heart of Meadowbrook for years to come, by 1903 both Harriman and Townsend, who owned estates in Orange County north of New York City, moved their fox hunting to the country near the beautiful *Red Swan Inn* built in 1903 in the village of Warwick, near Harriman's 20,000 acres of undeveloped property. In early summer E. H. Harriman traveled to England and Ireland for the fox hunting season and managed to purchase a number of valuable hounds, increasing the Orange County pack to thirty-five pairs. Alfred Vanderbilt had purchased his own pack the year before, and not to be out-done, Robert L. Gerry asked E.H. Harriman to invest in land located between Warwick and the Harriman estate in a town called Goshen, to establish a new center for equestrian sports, especially the fox hunt and polo.[46] The land was near Tuxedo Park and *Glenmere Lake*, country that was rough but beautiful and perfect for hunting. With a gentleman's agreement in hand for the move to Goshen in 1904, the late summer 1903 fox hunt in Orange County was underway with the following description of the hunt:

> There is a flush upon the cheeks of the women and exultation depicted in every line of the faces of the men. It is hard to describe the fascinating spectacle as they pass down the lane, expectant and happy. Upon this rainy afternoon the men and women who brave the inclement weather include Mr. Townsend upon his horse *Sarah,* Peter Gerry upon *X-Ray,* Miss Mary Harriman upon *Solution,* Miss Cornelia Harriman upon *Burridge,* and Robert Gerry upon *Goshen.* First came the swift gallop to the center of the field, then after fording a small stream a mass of pink coats and the scarlet garb of the men disentangle in the broad green field. The once compact mass is soon strung out in the wake of the flying hounds. To

> the spectators standing at the first wall there is a "chug" and a "squash" as the horses lift themselves and land. To the layman, this spectacle is inspiring as the women are steady on the mounts they know so well. The hunt ended after a nine mile run from Warwick to Goshen.[47]

To celebrate the close of the hunt season in November, Mrs. Harriman hosted a ball at the *Red Swan Inn* which served as a social venue for her two daughters and celebration of the agreement to move the hunt to Goshen the next year. Mrs. Harriman asked "Bobby" Gerry, as he was known to family and friends, to coordinate the ball and he did so with the usual Gerry perfectionist attention to detail. Most of the invited guests came by special train from New York and Tuxedo Park, returning home the next morning. The dance began at 11 o'clock and the beautiful favors for guests included silver top riding crops, jockey caps and silk gowned jockey dolls. The cotillion was led by Bobby Gerry and Cornelia Harriman; the men wore their scarlet riding suits and the ladies their finest gowns which added to the picturesque scene.[48]

This was the beginning of a long and happy courtship between Robert L. Gerry and Cornelia Harriman. Moreover, it was the start of a business and personal relationship between Robert and his future father-in-law, railroad and business tycoon, Edward Henry Harriman. Born in 1848 in Hempstead, Nassau County, New York, E. H. Harriman was the son of an Episcopal minister. He left school at fourteen to work on Wall Street doing whatever chores or tasks were asked of him. As a teenager Edward shared the streets of New York with many other homeless youth struggling to find their way through the scourges of Gotham. He was sufficiently hard working and talented to be noticed and mentored on Wall Street, so much so that by the age of twenty he was the managing clerk in a brokerage house, and two years later he purchased a seat on the New York Stock Exchange. His days as a solitary boy on the streets were a recent memory that haunted Edward and led him to reach out in 1876 at the age of twenty-eight and establish the first *New York City Boys' Club*. His goal was to provide a safe place off the streets where the boys could learn manners and skills that would lead them into productive activities. During the first five years only 100 boys took advantage of the Club which gained financial and moral support from *Gilded Gotham's* philanthropists and by the twentieth century the Club had moved from being simply a refuge from the dangers of urban life to an organization that encouraged boys and young men to seek the highest standards of scholarship, moral development, and physical achievement. Today there are three full-service clubhouses in New York City that serve nearly 4,000 boys on the Lower East Side, East Harlem, and in Flushing, Queens.[49]

Three years after founding the Boys' Club, Edward H. Harriman married Mary W. Averell in 1879. Their daughter Cornelia was born in 1884 making her seven years younger than Robert Gerry, the man she eventually married. The work his father did with the *Gerry Society* to protect abused children in New York City resonated with Robert Gerry when he met E. H. Harriman, the founder of a Boys' Club, which solidified their mutual respect well beyond the love of horses and their developing business relationship. In 1885 Harriman purchased over 7,000 acres of land in the Ramapo Mountains in eastern Orange County, New York. By 1900 he had increased the estate to 20,000 acres or thirty square miles, the size of the 1749 Livingston share of the *Hardenburgh Patent* that was progressively reduced to the Gerrys' contemporary 1,600-acre *Lake Delaware* estate.

Harriman purchased his first railroad in 1883 and by 1901 he had gained control of the Southern Pacific Railroad and the Union Pacific Railroad. Harriman's success was the result of his great financial acumen and his passionate interest in the practical side of running a railroad. When he first became the leader of the Union Pacific Railroad he traveled over 5,000 miles to evaluate the entire rail system and then spent 174 million dollars in the next few years to improve every aspect of the railroad. As a result of his insistence upon excellence, the Union Pacific Railroad in 1909 carried 10 million more freight-tons than it had in 1901, but with a drop of 3 ½ million freight-train miles run to carry the freight.

The railroad magnet decided to build a mansion on his Orange County property near the end of his astounding career. Harriman's 20,000 acres was near the elite enclave of Tuxedo Park and not far from the village of Goshen where the new Hunt and Polo club was established, the perfect location to build his great stone house at the top of a 1,300-foot ridge that rose from the Ramapo River. Named *Arden House,* the Harriman mansion was started in 1905 and completed in the summer of 1909, but tragically, within a few weeks Edward Henry Harriman died on September 9, 1909 at the age of sixty-one, just one year after his daughter, Cornelia, married Robert L. Gerry. In 1950 *Arden House* was given to *Columbia University* as a public policy conference center and for weekend Business Classes until 2005 when the property was sold to a great-grandson of E. H. Harriman who later gave the property to New York's *Land Preservation Society.* Other intact buildings on the hilltop include a carriage shed and cable car storage and a waiting room. The track and cars were scrapped in 1941 when the cable car stopped running. The Harriman family still owns several acres that include the original two-story Tudor style *Arden Stables* and the two-story cable car Station.[50] *Arden*

Homestead Stables is the successor business started by E. Roland Harriman with Peter and Robert Gerry, which has remained in the Gerry family over four generations and is located at the Lake Delaware farm estate in New York.

Peter G. Gerry, a companion polo player with his brother Robert at Meadow Brook and Goshen, was also under the wing of Edward H. Harriman. Peter finished law school in May and after the late summer equestrian season, he joined Harriman for a hunting trip to the western United States, which he had done before in 1901. Peter had been described over the years as the least robust of the Gerry children, similar to his sister Lillian who had died years earlier just days after her eighteenth birthday. On the hunting trip out west, Peter contracted a serious case of typhoid fever and Harriman took him to Seattle, Washington for initial treatment, which was followed by months of recuperation in a hospital in San Francisco, California.[51] Peter did not return to New York for the winter holidays, indeed he did not return home until early 1904.

For many years Commodore Gerry had attended the *American Humane Association* annual meetings as the representative of *the New York Society for the Prevention of Cruelty to Children.* The November report of the 1903 meeting reflected the world-wide maturity of the movement and a new struggle that faced local societies, a legislative proposal in Washington, D.C. to create a trust that would oversee all state societies, which was to be called *The National Humane Association.* The report itself was a detailed international overview of the history and status of leading societies in Austria, Canada, England, France, Italy, Switzerland and the United States, some of the 314 humane societies world-wide in 1903. The report quoted Commodore Gerry's remarks given in his January 1903 Providence, Rhode Island speech to the state *Society for the Prevention of Cruelty to Children.* In reference to the proposed legislation, Commodore Gerry was against the bill for a national trust. He stated that the parent society of the whole world, the *New York Society for the Prevention of Cruelty to Children* had forcefully defined its opposition to the measure, which, if passed, would disrupt the whole association as then constituted. Trusts of any kind were not popular and their extension into the domain of philanthropy was to be dreaded. Commodore Gerry gave his audience a clear example of how these societies worked well without federal intervention.

> The great success of the society and its power depends upon its corporate existence. The three-fold cord, consisting of the legal right to appear and prosecute and be heard, the corporate right to apply the donations of the charitable, and the legacies of the dead, for that purpose, and the earnest zeal of private indi-

> viduals who give their time, their talent, and their money to carry out the views of the society is not easily broken. The question has been asked, 'Why is it that the regularly appointed officers of the law cannot be entrusted with the enforcement of this, as well as other branches of the criminal laws?' The answer is very simple. They are necessarily occupied with the protection of the entire community and their attention is given very properly to the duties of preserving the peace of the public, and in arresting and prosecuting cases of felony.[52]

Commodore Gerry then proceeded to explain the role of the Society's legally authorized agents, the structure of prosecution, and the method of child placement. He closed with a personal plea for public support of local societies, "A single child saved makes the expenditure of money worthwhile. Knowing that the work is bringing forth good, the society should be given the support of the public in the execution of its noble work."[53]

The national legislation was never passed but a journal called The *National Humane Review* was established which provided unifying discussions on law and policy among all of the societies across America.[54]

In December 1903, the press closed the year with reports of the latest fad in fashionable society, the health spas and clubs in London that offered a new treatment called "electric light baths." The fad began in London with "Bertie", then King Edward VII, who professed to be greatly benefited by the treatments. The principle was the same as sun bathing for vitamin D where various colors of electric light are shown upon the body as an invigorating tonic but was provided privately indoors. Other treatments were mineral water baths and needle treatments such as acupuncture. While most clubs did not have the space or equipment for these treatments, the New York Athletic Club, the University Club and the Racquet Club were creating the space to offer these popular new treatments for the rejuvenation of club members. The papers also touted Mrs. Louisa Gerry as starting a second health craze known as the "fashionable constitutional," or taking regular, vigorous walks for your physical wellbeing. It was noted that Fifth Avenue had never been so crowded with pedestrians who followed Mrs. Gerry's example of briskly walking up and down Fifth Avenue with her daughters.[55]

On January 3, 1904 the press reported that the entire Gerry family had traveled west by train on a private Pullman car to San Francisco to spend several weeks with Peter Gerry during his continued convalescence from typhoid fever contracted while hunting in the northwest three months earlier. He was described as a favorite in society, clever, amusing and an excellent whip and proficient in all out-of-door sports, Peter's absence, and that of his family, was felt in New York social circles. The Gerrys spent several weeks in California, eventually moving

Peter down to Santa Barbara for the fresh air and sunshine. During their stay Mrs. Louisa Gerry and her daughter Angelica took a day-trip by private train car on E. H. Harriman's Union Pacific Railroad from Santa Barbara to Los Angeles for some sight-seeing. They arrived at the Arcade Depot and immediately boarded a passing street car and rode about the city to discover the sights and sounds of Los Angeles. Later, Louisa and Angelica boarded a local trolley for a trip to an area near Pasadena known as Garvanza where the trolley crossed the highest bridge span on the rail system, high above the spectacular Arroyo Seco gorge. The destination of this picturesque train ride for Louisa and Angelica was the nine acre *Cawston Ostrich Farm.*[56] It was America's first ostrich farm, which sat on the east bank of the Arroyo Seco and opened in 1886. The birds were imported from Africa, and although many of them died, enough survived to produce chicks nurtured in incubators. There was a dye house and a factory that produced colorful feathers that were a mainstay of high fashion in the *Gilded Age.* The three-mile trolley ride from Los Angeles, which included the entry fee to the ostrich farm, was just twenty-five cents. Visitors were able to ride on the backs of ostriches, be taken for ostrich drawn carriage rides and buy ostrich feathered hats, boas, capes and fans at the farm shop that was connected to the factory. A large variety of ostrich feather products were shipped throughout the world. Most of the original brick structure of the factory and store remain today and it is a designated South Pasadena *Cultural Landmark.*[57] Louisa and Angelica returned that evening to Santa Barbara and the next morning the Gerry family boarded a private train car for their return trip to New York City, with a stop in New Orleans to experience the winter Carnival, a distraction Peter Gerry welcomed after his long convalescence.

Robert L. Gerry had arrived earlier in New York to join John R. Townsend to negotiate the purchase of a farm and stables in Goshen as a place to live during the annual Orange County Hunt season and also to purchase hounds and thoroughbred horses for their pack. Robert Gerry, Edward Harriman, and John Townsend's planning and charisma brought the enthusiastic participation of the Hempstead and the Meadow Brook Hunt clubs in the 1904 Orange County Hunt, held for the first time in the Goshen meadows and hills. Many of the New York City club members were also in Goshen in January to negotiate for houses to occupy for the late summer and early fall fox hunt season.[58]

By March 1904 the coaching season in New York's Central Park was in full swing with Angelica Gerry a member of two women's clubs. The first was the *Ladies' Four-in-Hand Driving Club* which held its annual parade on March 3. The second was the more *exclusive Dorcas Coaching Club,* which hired a professional coachman to train the ladies in driving four-horse coaches on public streets. This was the only woman's coaching club in America where the ladies drove on public roads. Guests on Angelica Gerry's coach in the Central Park Parade were her sister Mabel and her brother Peter who was finally recovered from typhoid fever. Also in the parade as whip of her own coach was Mary Harriman, who had her father, Edward H. Harriman, and her younger sister, Cornelia riding as her guests.[59] Observing the parade on their own mounts were Robert L. Gerry and his pal, Alfred Vanderbilt, members of the men's coaching club that participated in similar parades in Central Park.

In April, just after Mary Goelet announced the engagement of her son Robert Wilson Goelet, the Commodore and Mrs. Gerry, with Angelica and Mabel, sailed on a trans-Atlantic steamer for their annual round of visits with family and friends in England and France. As was now the custom, Peter remained home to finish law school and then joined Robert in the polo season with a break to rejoin the Gerry family in June for the wedding of their cousin, Robert Wilson Goelet, the only son of Ogden Goelet. Robert W. Goelet had just graduated from college and was considered one of the richest bachelors in America. His bride, Elsie Whelen, an acclaimed Philadelphia beauty, brought with her a comfortable fortune and great social standing. Both were twenty-four and were acquainted through summer holidays in Newport and winter balls in *Gilded Gotham*. Mrs. Ogden Goelet was extremely pleased with the prestigious match and more importantly she liked her new daughter-in-law, as did Robert's sister, May, the Duchess of Roxburghe. The wedding was celebrated in Wayne, Pennsylvania at Saint Mary's Episcopal Church. The bride's sister, Mrs. Craig Biddle, was her matron of honor and Alice Roosevelt was one of the bridesmaids. Robert Wilson Goelet's cousin Ogden Mills was his best man and Robert L. Gerry was one of seven ushers. The bride wore a simple, floor-length white satin gown with a chiffon overlay and touches of antique lace; the waist was accented with a long satin sash tied in a bow that fell loosely almost to the hemline. Her veil was short and crowned her head like a broad halo that was gently reflected in the style of the hats worn by the bridesmaids. The formal wedding photograph shows a very understated gown for such a wealthy debutante's wedding in *Gilded Age* high society. The seven bridesmaids wore rose pink taffeta gowns, very large straw hats covered with shaded pink plumes and each carried a pink silk parasol, the bride's gift. The four hundred guests arrived from across the country for the afternoon ceremony, and most left Philadelphia on special trains that evening, including the bride and groom who spent the first part of their honeymoon *at Ochre Court* in Newport, Rhode Island, while Mrs. Ogden Goelet returned to her Fifth Avenue home in

New York City. The couple planned to leave in late July for a European tour and Robert's mother would join them at *Ochre Court* for a warm and heartfelt bon voyage in mid-July. Robert and Elsie had two sons over the next fourteen years, Peter III and Ogden II, but the marriage would end in a highly publicized divorce that broke his mother's heart and, sadly, would not be the last divorce for Robert Wilson Goelet.

Not long after Robert and Elsie's wedding, summer gossip swirled around Ogden Goelet's widow, Mary Goelet. On the evening of June 20 Mary had returned to her Fifth Avenue home from a small function and removed her jewels, placing them in their case. Her maid then secured the case in the boudoir safe. Only Mary and her maid had the five keys necessary to access the safe and the jewelry cases. In July the maid removed the jewelry cases in preparation for Mary Goelet's move to *Ochre Court* in Newport for the summer season. While dressing for dinner on July 19 at *Ochre Court* Mary was startled to find the $200,000 worth of jewels missing. Tiffany & Company circulated fliers with illustrations of the jewelry and the Pinkerton Bureau was put on the case. Mary offered a reward of $10,000 for the recovery of her jewels. Within a few days it was announced that the jewels were found back in the safe in the Goelet mansion on Fifth Avenue in New York City. Although the search was called off, not everyone was content to believe that Mary had merely forgotten that she had left the jewel case at home. Many looked askance at the maid who, they believed, had stealthily replaced the stolen jewels in a panic.[60] This incident recalled the 1896 Limbeck case in Newport at the Gerrys' rented cottage, *Lyndenhurst*, when Angelica Gerry's jewels were stolen and her maid sued Commodore Gerry for false arrest. The maid was exonerated as was Commodore Gerry, but the jewels were never recovered.

After the late summer Orange County hunt season came to a successful conclusion in Goshen and Newport society had closed their villas and cottages, the fall entertainments began for society in New York City. While the old Patriarchs' balls were no longer in vogue, the private dinner and formal cotillion dance was still an important remnant of the fading *Gilded Age* in Gotham. In November and December at least two galas were held in the private homes of the Gerry, Reid, Astor, and Vanderbilt families. In addition to the formal dances, the latest fad in high society, although not as pervasive as past novelties, was to add a private theatre to the mansion. Some incorporated the theater into the ballroom space but more often it was constructed as a separate room. The out-of-town country mansion in places like Lakewood or Tuxedo Park was more likely to have a private theatre for additional winter entertainment than the New York City mansion.[61]

Commodore Gerry closed out 1904 with his life-long Columbia College friends at a rousing dinner and business meeting at the *Alpha Delta* fraternity Lodge on the Morningside Heights campus. Commodore Gerry, at the age of 68, had been the president of the *Chi Psi Alumni Society* of New York City for many years and cherished the role of leading his band of brothers. The 1905 Columbia College alumni magazine, *Purple and Gold,* reported on the December festivities of *Chi Psi* and specifically on the activity of their president. In his address to the gathering at Columbia he described in detail the insignia and initiation service of their shared fraternity and distributed copies of the requiem service he had prepared for the recent funeral of a fraternity brother. After his inspiring speech Commodore Gerry was honored with thanks from the fraternity, not only for newsy clippings he regularly sent to his brethren, but also for his very generous financial gift to repair the *Alpha Delta Lodge* building. The refurbishment required the chimneys to be rebuilt and the replacement of interior plaster. The work was completed in time to open the Lodge for the Columbia College's fall term 1905. The accolades for Commodore Gerry closed with "Brother Gerry is constantly doing us favors, and would that many might follow his example."[62]

For the first time in two years, since the illness of Peter, the Gerrys welcomed the New Year with two of the most celebrated galas in *Gilded Gotham.* The first was held in late January on an evening when the opera was not held, and the nearly 400 guests arrived earlier than usual. Mrs. Gerry, dressed in mauve velvet, and joined by Angelica in rose pink satin and Mabel in white satin, graciously received guests in the Louis XVI salon. The mansion was decorated with plants from the Newport greenhouse and the Gerrys' celebrated French chef used fruit from Newport and fowl and game from Lake Delaware to prepare his gourmet buffet dinner that included consommé en masse, huitres a la poulette, saumons froids sur socle de Neptune, boeuf roti a la gelee, gelatins d'inde a la Flora Dora, chaufraid re poulette a la Rousse, gois-gras a la Strasbourgeise, salade de volaille, sandwiches au jam bon café. After dinner guests danced in the spacious picture gallery and handsome law library, both of which were two stories high with balconies. In the picture gallery hung paintings by Gerome, Constant and Ball, and Church's painting of *Cotopaxi.* Music was provided by Lander's Orchestra and guests danced waltzes, lanciers and the two-step.[63] The ball was hosted for a broad range of Gerry friends and relatives of all ages, rather than for the younger set as was the norm with single adult children.

The second gala however, was hosted by Mrs. Louisa Gerry for her well educated and very socially active daughters, Angelica and Mabel, now in their early thirties and in no hurry to marry. The cotillion was held on February 12, 1905 and was especially for the younger set, less formal and, consequently, more lively and fun. Since this gala followed the opera, many guests arrived later, around 11 o'clock. The entire house was decorated in cut flowers and palms from Newport. The dinner was more intimate than the buffet served at the earlier gathering; guests were seated at small tables arranged throughout the dining room and the law library. After supper, the tables were removed from the library for dancing with the orchestra located on the balcony of the picture gallery. Cotillion favors for those who danced included silver vases and ash trays, and leather trays decorated with sport scenes or flowers. After the dancing a second supper was served to the three hundred guests. Personal guests of Commodore and Mrs. Gerry were Mrs. Robert Goelet, Mr. and Mrs. Cornelius Vanderbilt, Jr., Col. and Mrs. John J. Astor, Mr. and Mrs. Ogden Mills. Foreign guests included Prince Henri de Croy of Belgium, Captain Hugo Baring, son of the Baron of Revelstoke, England, French Ambassador Viscomte de Chambrun, Dutch diplomat Count Von Limburg-Strium, and Scotland diplomat, Lord Kelbourne.[64]

With the success of the winter galas in hand Commodore and Mrs. Gerry, with Angelica and Mabel, left on their yacht *Electra* the first week of March for a holiday in the warm Palm Beach, Florida sunshine. They stayed at the *Royal Poinciana Hotel,* made popular and famous years before by the extension of the Vanderbilt railroad to Palm Beach. In March 1905 the hotel was filled with New York society escaping the cold northern winter. Angelica and Mabel were entertained as guests of Mr. and Mrs. Howard Brokaw at a delightful luncheon on their houseboat where music was provided for the enjoyment of their guests.[65] By the end of March the special train cars left Florida filled with New Yorkers headed north back to their mansions and the beautiful spring season of *Gilded Gotham.* The Gerrys also left Palm Beach with a small party of friends on *Electra* and after a stop in Saint Augustine they headed north to New York City. Three weeks seemed to be as long as any northerner wanted to remain in the southern resorts as there was little to do, and most preferred Newport for the summer where they had their own cottages or villas for extended visits and the days were always filled with sports and a busy social life.[66]

The summer of 1905 was the first time in over ten years that the Commodore and Mrs. Gerry did not summer in Newport, and they did not join the *New York Yacht Club* for the annual cruise and *Astor Cup* races. The "changing of the guard" between generations, while subtle, was happening throughout *Gilded Gotham* society just as it was in the Gerry family. Robert and Peter Gerry rarely cruised with their father on the *Electra*; indeed the brothers were usually onboard only when the yacht was "family transportation" to the Lake Delaware estate up the

Hudson River. Elbridge and Louisa spent the entire summer in Europe as did their generation of the Goelet and Vanderbilt families. Angelica and Mabel spent more time with their parents' generation as their girlfriends, like Gertrude Vanderbilt, married and had children of their own. In Europe, "Bertie," King George VII, quietly socialized with his old American friends the Goelets and Gerrys, attended a party hosted by Consuelo Vanderbilt, the Duchess of Marlborough, and had dinner in Paris with William K. Vanderbilt.[67] The Gerrys were guests of Louisa's second cousin, Ambassador to England Whitelaw and Elizabeth Reid, for *Cowes Week,* the British equivalent to the *New York Yacht Club's* annual activities. They were joined in Cowes by Mrs. Robert Goelet on the yacht *Nahma,* Mrs. Ogden Mills and her daughters, as well as the Duchess of Marlborough, Consuelo Vanderbilt.[68] The royal British yacht races still excited the American visitors who relished the history and tradition of the *America's Cup* yacht race that started with a friendly challenge by Queen Victoria many years before at this very same annual event in Cowes, England in 1851.

The next generation of *Gilded Gotham* "dudes" and "sophy sparkles" were adults now and hosted their own parties at home in America, where Robert and Peter Gerry joined Alfred Vanderbilt on the spring and early summer horse show circuit, led the coaching season, enjoyed polo at Meadow Brook, and hosted the fox hunt at Goshen. The highlight of the equestrian season in 1905 was the grand opening of *Belmont Park* racetrack in Hempstead, New York on Long Island by August Belmont, Jr. an intimate friend of Robert, Peter, and Alfred. The opening event was the running of the prestigious *Belmont Stakes,* inaugurated in 1867 and named in honor of his father, August Belmont senior. Three times, horses from August Belmont Jr.'s stable won the *Belmont Stakes,* the first in 1902 when the race was run at the *old Morris Park Racecourse,* followed by wins in 1916 and 1917 at his own *Belmont Park.* August Belmont Jr. inherited *Nursery Stud,* a thoroughbred breeding operation established in 1867 by his father at his 1,100 acre Babylon, New York estate. Belmont junior raised polo ponies and played on a polo team with Harry Payne Whitney, Gertrude Vanderbilt's husband; their team was challenged by Robert and Peter Gerry and Alfred Vanderbilt's polo team among many other competitors. A second Belmont stud farm, *Kentucky Stud Nursery,* was opened by Belmont senior in the 1880s about three miles outside Lexington, Kentucky. Belmont junior transferred all of his breeding business to Kentucky where he bred 126 *American Stakes* winners, the greatest of which was *Man o' War,* born while he was serving in World War I. When the foal was born, Belmont junior's wife, Eleanor, named it "My Man o' War" in honor of her husband serving overseas in what was called the Great War. However, in 1917 shortly after

Belmont returned home, he felt unsettled by the continuing war, and to Eleanor's surprise, he began to reduce his stock of thoroughbred horses at the *Kentucky Stud Nursery*. When he sold his most valuable yearling, August Belmont dropped the "My" from the name and put "Man o' War" up for auction. By 1917 Robert L. Gerry owned his own breeding stables and his wife Cornelia wanted this promising horse in their stable. By the end of the auction, and to her disappointment, Cornelia was the under-bidder with an offer of $4,500 for *Man o' War* who was sold to the highest bidder, the *Glen Riddle Farm* in Maryland, for $5,000.[69]

The original *Belmont Park* race track featured racing in the "clockwise" direction in the English fashion, which allowed box seat holders to have the race finish in front of the clubhouse, just to the west of the grandstand at the top of the stretch. The original clubhouse was torn down in the 1950's, however the original "racing motif" iron railings on the south side of the old grandstand were salvaged and now partially border the walking ring. In addition to racing, *Belmont Park* made history in another industry, aviation. Over 150,000 gathered at the track on October 30, 1910 for one of the famous Wright Brothers international aerial tournaments.[70] Hosting non-equestrian events in the off season was a means of increasing the profits of the enormous race track establishment. The *Belmont Park* racetrack operates to this day as the largest thoroughbred racing facility in New York State and is known as the "Test of the Champion," the third leg of the Triple Crown in horse racing. The most famous winner of the Crown was the thirty-one length win by *Secretariat* in 1973; a handsome statue of the horse now stands in the center of the *Belmont Park* paddock in Hempstead, New York.

By 1905 the Gerry brothers had invested substantial time and money in various equestrian sports which had become an avocation, especially for Robert. At the conclusion of the spring and early summer equestrian season, Robert and Peter opened *Seaverge* in Newport to relax and host leisurely dinners, lunches, and coaching rides for their peers, which included married friends like Alfred and Elsie Vanderbilt and Harry and Gertrude Payne. When their parents returned from Europe in September, Commodore Gerry, Louisa, Angelica and Mabel boarded *Electra* for the nine-hour cruise to Newport, Rhode Island to join Robert and Peter for a short but restful stay at *Seaverge*. After the Gerrys closed their summer cottage for the season the entire family boarded *Electra* for a cruise up the Hudson River for an extended reunion at the Lake Delaware estate near Andes, New York. Even when the Gerry family was at their remote family estate the press reported on their activity, primarily because their holidays always involved their community, especially their charitable assistance and Episcopal mission work. Commodore Gerry often expressed his firm belief that religious education in the home was essential to prepare children to take their place in civilized society as mature and responsible adults. The adult Gerry children were highly disciplined individuals, almost perfectionists, with a sense of civic duty that found its basis in their Episcopal faith. From childhood, Angelica and Mabel joined their mother, Louisa, in mission work in all of the small towns and villages surrounding Lake Delaware whenever they visited for holidays. As a girl, Angelica and Mabel's sister Lillian had noted in her diary all the items they knitted for local needy families and the gift boxes the sisters put together for children around Lake Delaware. As adults the Gerry women continued their mission work with local individuals, families, and schools to offer assistance where needed and to help small communities establish Episcopal parish churches. In 1905 Angelica Gerry gave Saint Paul's Episcopal Church in Bloomville, about 20 miles from Lake Delaware, a handsome five-piece communion set made of silver and lined with gold and inscribed "In Loving Memory of Lillian S. Gerry." Mrs. Louisa Gerry made her own commitment to the little mission church, which had just opened in May, to provide a baptismal font, altar cross, candlesticks and vases for flowers.[71] The Gerry women also socialized with their community and joined in chestnut picking, local festivals and visiting the local schools to find out what assistance was needed. Over Angelica Gerry's lifetime, she quietly paid for the education of many local children living in the communities surrounding Lake Delaware, many of whom are active members of their local community today.

One story that remains part of local lore in the towns surrounding Lake Delaware that exemplifies what Commodore Gerry and his family meant to the community happened in October 1905 during the family's fall reunion at the estate. Just six miles from Lake Delaware in Andes, New York, two young men had just dropped off their dates after a dance at the local fire hall and were walking down the street at one o'clock in the morning when they interrupted a robber on the street just outside the bank. A shot rang out and Frank Graham, one of the most popular young men in Andes, was grievously wounded in the stomach. Frank struggled to his girlfriend's house just behind the bank (her father was a doctor), but it became obvious that delicate surgery was needed to save the man's life. Commodore Gerry was notified of the dire situation and he contacted his New York doctors summoning them to Andes. The eminent surgeons arrived the next day by train where Commodore Gerry's carriage met them at the station and took them directly to Andes. Louisa and Angelica Gerry immediately drove over to Andes to console the families and offer whatever assistance they could. While a posse searched the hills and towns for the criminals, the doctors performed the surgery on Frank Graham on Sunday. Commodore Gerry visited the young man every day that week until he died the following Friday. Commodore Gerry quietly paid for the surgery without a word to anyone because he believed such kindness was his spiritual and neighborly duty; he helped wherever and whenever he was needed. Although the criminals were not found and brought to justice, the generosity of Commodore Gerry and his family has never been forgotten.[72]

About the same time *Electra* cruised up the Hudson River to Lake Delaware, Frederic and Almy Gallatin were cruising off the Chatham, Massachusetts coast on the steam yacht *Riviera* that Frederic purchased in 1905. It was built in Glasgow, Scotland in 1898 by George L. Watson, weighed 400 tons and measured 196 feet overall. The Gallatins' son and his wife were on board when the *Riviera* went aground in the Chatham Bay. There was a crew of 27 on board headed by Captain O.A. Oakes and fortunately, there were no injuries. The *Monomoy Point Life Saving Station* team came to the rescue, pulled the yacht from the shallows and re-floated her without any damage. Immediately upon her release, the Gallatins continued their cruise on the *Riviera* from Long Island to Bar Harbor, Maine for a family holiday.[73]

The following winter, in February 1906, Peter Gerry spread his wings beyond the trend of recent years for New Yorkers to flee northern winters for the Florida sunshine. Peter ventured to Nassau in the Bahamas, a new and exotic winter resort easily accessed by boat from train destinations in Palm Beach or Miami Florida. Peter attended a ball to celebrate Washington's Birthday at the *Colonial Hotel* in Nassau which had opened in 1901 on the site of the *Old Fort Nassau.* A few New Yorkers like Governor and Mrs. Winthrop ventured to San Juan, Puerto Rico for their winter get-away, another exotic destination for *Gilded Gotham.*[74]

Harrietta Goelet, the widow of Robert Goelet, sailed on her yacht the *Nahma* for the Mediterranean in the winter of 1906 where she had the experience of a lifetime. In April, while cruising off the coast of Naples, Italy she and her guests watched in utter astonishment the eruption of Mount Vesuvius. The last big event had been in 1872 when an avalanche of hot rock killed twenty five tourists and instead of frightening tourists away it drew even more people to experience the great natural phenomenon. In Mabel Gerry's 1887 diary she writes of the family visit to the volcano, "Friday, March 25, Naples. This morning we went to Mount Vesuvius. Angel, Jane and I went on a carriage drawn by four white horses, while Lily and Pa went in one drawn by three brown ones. When we arrived there we went up in a sail-way car nearly strait up and down. We were then carried by guides in chaises up to the top, we did not go close as we smelled the sulfur but we saw a hole with smoke coming out, it was great fun."[75] Mabel was describing the fifteen-passenger cable cars or "sail way" cars that climbed 1,300 feet in a twelve minute trip to the upper station near the summit. The cable cars counter-balanced each other as they rose and descended and this was known as a funicular. The cable car ride had opened with such fanfare in 1878 that it was celebrated in the famous song "Funicular, Funiculi" written by songwriters, Luigi Denza and Peppino Turco.[76]

In 1905 new and suspicious rumblings from the active volcano had been reported worldwide and volcanologists from around the globe visited the active site for months. Harrietta Goelet was aware of the reports but knew it was a historically active volcano and she had cruised throughout the Mediterranean for years under similar reports without a problem. Indeed, seven years earlier her husband Robert Goelet died on the *Nahma* in the Bay of Naples in which Harrietta now confidently sailed. But this year was different and everyone was startled when the actual eruption of Vesuvius took place between April 4 and April 24. A *New York Times* reporter was in Palermo to cover the story and noted the arrival from Naples of American Harrietta Goelet who had witnessed Vesuvius erupt with friends on the yacht *Nahma,* even while war ships were evacuating people from the flowing lava and ash. The *Nahma* was never in harm's way but the earthquakes, glowing yellow lava, and the roar of the enormous plumb of brilliant red flames and smoke thrust to the heavens from Vesuvius were magnificent and terrifying to behold from the Bay of Naples.[77] While Harrietta Goelet would never forget the experience she nonetheless welcomed her arrival in Athens, Greece for her next memorable adventure. The 1906 *Olympic Games* were held in Athens the first week of May and the *Nahma* arrived in the port of Athens to join several other Americans, the Drexel, Gould and Havemeyer yachts which had large parties of friends on board. To add to the fun Sir Thomas Lipton had arrived from London and anchored his yacht *Erin* near his American friends. After leaving Athens, Harrietta cruised to Venice, Italy where an Italian war ship unceremoniously collided with the *Nahma* as it entered the harbor, startling all onboard. While no one was injured both ships were damaged, Harrietta had to leave the *Nahma* for repairs and travel by train to Paris for a much needed rest and visit with her niece May, the Duchess of Roxburghe.[78]

In New York City the coaching season began on Easter Sunday and lasted for seven weeks. The four-in-hand *Coaching Clubs* that were favored by the next generation of *Gilded Gotham* society expanded the annual challenge to their carriage teams with long distance runs. Some of the intermediate runs were connected with an event or destination like the rides that Robert L. Gerry, Alfred Vanderbilt and Angelica Gerry provided as individual whips on public coaches between New York City and the *Belmont Park* race track at Hempstead, Long

Island. Angelica Gerry, the leading women's whip, also joined the men in a rotation of whips on the long distance coach team that would travel for a period of days. She kept a meticulous scrapbook that documented one of the long distance runs that began in front of the Gerry mansion at Sixty-First and Fifth Avenue in New York City to Gerry's Lake Delaware estate and back, a 300 mile round trip coaching run. For several years beginning in 1905 the "Gerry Long Distance Run" was the highlight of the season. Angelica's scrapbook has photographs of the coaches as they made their designated stops to change horse teams and she inserted poems here and there that she had written to capture the spirit of the coaching run. The printed charts that were given to each of the participating whips noted the distance of each leg of the run, the proposed time versus the actual time of the run, the places where the coach would stop and "remarks" which often commented on the heat, the difficulty ascending a hill where everyone but the whip got off the coach and walked, the nature of each horse team (some were lazy), and the actual speed the coach was traveling. The chart indicates that the long distance run was a competition of the team with itself; in most cases there were only seconds or a few minutes difference between the anticipated time to run a leg of the distance and the actual time it took. Some of the stops had a symbol next to the place indicating that either a "change of horses" took place, a "meal was eaten," or where they slept overnight.[79] It took weeks for the Club to plan the logistics of the 300 mile run. On both the outbound trip and the return trip, the team had to cross the Hudson River. This was managed by having two overnight stays at the James Roosevelt estate at Hyde Park. The first stay was on the outbound trip "before" the team left the Hyde Park dock on *Electra* and crossed over to the west side Kingston dock from where the whip team picked up the coach and fresh horses and headed to the half-way point at Lake Delaware. The second stay at the Roosevelt estate was on the return trip "after" the team left the Kingston dock on *Electra* and crossed the Hudson River to the east side Hyde Park dock to rest overnight and pick up the coach and fresh horses for the run back to New York City. Eighteen teams of horses were used from New York City to Lake Delaware, with another eighteen teams for the return trip. Eighty horses were used in one combination or another for the thirty-eight total teams. The round trip took five days to complete and when the coach arrived back in New York City at dusk on the last day, the whips were all a little sun-tanned but in fine spirits and very proud of their accomplishment. It is interesting to note that on the City coach runs in *Central Park* or out to *Belmont Park,* Robert L. Gerry was the lead man, but for the long distance run to *Lake Delaware,* Peter Gerry was always the host which spoke to his genteel manner versus Robert's competitive nature when it came to horses. Nonetheless, their personalities were complementary when they shared personal interests and each was well-suited to the distinct choice each brother made in his professional life, one a businessman and one a lawyer and politician. The brothers' deepest and most lasting bond was the time they shared with their sisters on the historic family estate at Lake Delaware over their lifetimes.

In June 1905 Commodore and Louisa Gerry, with Angelica and Mabel, joined by their New York friends, Harry and Gertrude Whitney, Mr. and Mrs. J Pierpont Morgan and others, boarded a trans-Atlantic steamer for a few weeks in Europe. Frederic and Almy Gallatin had gone over earlier and were actually returning to America as the Gerrys were leaving.[80] Two of the Gallatins' adult married children had joined the Newport, Rhode Island cottagers for the summer, no doubt to enjoy the company of their Gerry and Goelet cousins who hosted their own affairs in Newport. It was time for the younger Gallatin generation to branch out beyond *Breezy Lawn* and East Hampton, Long Island to stretch their adult wings.

While most of architect Stanford White's friends were off in Europe he remained in New York City attending to his work. White had two reputations during his lifetime, one as a leading American architect, and unfortunately, the other as a womanizer which he did little to hide. White was the architect and impresario of *Madison Square Garden* where he had built a 315 foot tower that housed a rooftop garden dinner theatre and the lower floors housed apartments for artists and architectural offices. It was known to many that Stanford White kept one of the apartments as his meeting place with young women, and one was Evelyn Nesbit, a chorus girl and artist's model whom he met in 1901. After their affair ended Evelyn married millionaire Harry Thaw, a man with a cocaine habit and a mean jealous streak. He knew about Evelyn's past and while he and his wife were in New York City in June 1905, they stopped at the Café Martin where he saw his wife's former lover, Stanford White. While at the café Harry Thaw overheard that Stanford White planned to leave shortly for a show at the *Madison Square Rooftop Theatre*, the very place where his wife had her affair with the famous architect. Filled with jealousy, Thaw went back to his nearby hotel room where he put on an unseasonable overcoat in which he hid a gun, and immediately returned to escort Evelyn to the *Madison Square Rooftop Theatre Restaurant* for dinner, which Evelyn thought would be a lovely night out on such a warm evening. At the theater Harry Thaw refused to give his coat to the hat check girl and had to sit uncomfortably through his meal with Evelyn. After dinner and near the end of the theatre performance, Harry excused himself and wandered among the theatre crowd until he located where Stanford White was sitting. As a dramatic gesture Harry Thaw waited briefly for the finale song, "I Could Love A Million Girls," to draw his pistol and shoot Stanford White three times in the head at point blank range, killing him instantly. The crowd initially suspected the shooting might be part of the show, as elaborate practical jokes were popular in high society at the time. However it became clear that the famous architect was dead. Thaw walked away holding his gun in the air and met his wife at the elevator where Evelyn asked him what he had done, to which he responded, "probably saved your life."[81] Harry could have killed his wife or her lover; he chose to kill her lover. There were two trials; the first resulted in a deadlocked jury in April 1907, and at the second, where his wife testified that Stanford White abused her and her husband was just trying to protect her, Harry Thaw was found not guilty by reason of insanity. He was institutionalized for fifteen years and released when deemed sane, but Evelyn Nesbit had divorced him and gone back to vaudeville performances with little success.[82] Although the trial scandalized White's reputation at the time, he is remembered for an extraordinary architectural legacy, not the least of which is *Southside,* the Robert Goelet shingle-style cottage in Newport, Rhode Island, the only remaining Stanford White shingle-style home still owned and occupied by the original family, and faithfully preserved in its' original warm splendor.

In October of 1906 Ogden Goelet's widow, Mary, endured a small whirlwind of gossip when the whole of Newport's limited police force arrived with the patrol wagon at *Ochre Court.* House maids and kitchen maids were hanging out the upper floor windows uttering shrill appeals for help. The gardeners were standing in the yard at a safe distance with pitchforks and other handy weapons at the ready. The center of the hysteria was Mrs. Ogden Goelet's French chef, who stood amid a desolation of broken glass and crockery in the kitchen busily whetting a meat cleaver. His white cook's cap was poised at a rakish angle over his left ear, and he cast a bloodshot eye alternately upon a copper jelly mold and a porcelain fish dish set on the table beside him. "Les Americans sont des peegs!" he muttered angrily. He poised the cleaver in the air, hesitated a moment, then brought it down with all his might upon the copper mold, denting it out of shape beyond repair, and then smashed the dish with a wild laugh. Policeman Jack Tobin prided himself on his knowledge of French and was encouraged to go in and confront the crazed chef. Tobin didn't want to argue with the chef and he could recall no words in French appropriate to the present circumstance; he suggested that they raid the kitchen en masse and overwhelm the chef. But the police force was unanimous against him and he simply had to go in and negotiate. Tobin advanced boldly to the kitchen door and threw it open and said "Bon jour, mossieu," extended his hand in greeting and said in a friendly tone, "Parlez-voo Francaise?" With a smile the chef responded, "Mais oui, monsieur," and his wrath cooled at the policeman's polite manner. The chef asked what he wanted and invited him in to sit down. The chef put the cleaver down on the table so he could shake hands with the policeman, then, in an instant, Chief Tobin had him down on the floor and the whole police force rushed into the kitchen to overwhelm the crazed chef. The subdued chef spent the night in jail and was released the next morning. Although Mrs. Goelet refused to prosecute him she immediately set out to hire a new chef for *Ochre Court.*[83]

In November, Commodore Gerry was the center of *Gilded Gotham* gossip when it was discovered that he had given his daughter Angelica a townhouse of her own. What was worse, the gift of a townhouse with a free and clear title or that it was to be occupied by an unmarried woman of high society. It was a lovely four-story townhouse one door off the corner of Sixty-Third Street and Fifth Avenue. Angelica would be a block and a half from the Gerry stables and her beloved horses, and just two blocks down the Avenue from her parents' mansion at Sixty-First and Fifth Avenue. On the corner of Sixty-Second Street on the one block between Angelica and the Commodore's mansion, where Robert and Peter still lived while in the City, was the E.H. Harriman townhouse. Robert Gerry and Cornelia Harriman socialized as neighbors as well as at Goshen and Arden Farms during the equestrian season. In November, six years earlier, almost to the day that Commodore Gerry gave the townhouse to his daughter, Angelica had broken her engagement to J. Wadsworth Ritchie, and at that time Commodore Gerry had also purchased a townhouse for them as a wedding gift. *Gilded Gotham* had a long memory and so the press bombarded the Commodore with the question of the day, "Was this townhouse an engagement gift?" The Commodore was emphatic in his response, "No, it's not a wedding present, and, furthermore, my daughter is not engaged to be married to anyone. I guess a man can give his property to his children if he wishes to."[84] While he ended the engagement rumors, which he did every few months, society was still focused on the idea that a prominent single woman was to open her own house, furnish it to her own aesthetic tastes, and entertain on her own account. However, the press was more supportive and liberal with their take on the significance of Angelica Gerry becoming an independent woman in a new century. She was well educated, a leading whip in a male –dominated equestrian sport, independently wealthy, and after all, Angelica Gerry was thirty-five years old. The press called her a "girl bachelor" among other women in high society and artistic circles that did not wait for a wedding ring before owning and managing their own elaborate homes. Included in this high society "girl bachelor" crowd was Miss Helen Gould with her large *Irvington Estate* and a great Fifth Avenue house, Miss May Van Alen with a Newport cottage, Miss Norma Munro with her handsome apartments and, finally, the artistically prominent Miss Maud Adams with a townhouse and a country place on Long Island.[85] Society gossips turned their attention elsewhere as was in keeping with a more progressive age driven by the women's suffrage movement.

Although Angelica Gerry had her private residence she joined her mother Louisa and sister Mabel at the family mansion to host the January 1907 dinner and dance following the opera. Cholly Knickerbocker, the society column reporter for the *New York Times* attended the gala affair which had been the case for several years. Indeed, the name Cholly Knickerbocker was a pseudonym that each successive society reporter used for decades. During the gala affair on January 14 Cholly asked Commodore Gerry a few questions about his gala "ball" to which the Commodore responded, "Cholly, I object to this affair being called a ball, it's just a little dance you know, of some two hundred invited guests. The girls asked for an unpretentious cotillion for the younger married set and the debutantes."[86] Once again the "changing of the guard" between generations emerged in both the characterization of high society events and the new tastes and the less formal sensibilities of adult children. The *Gilded Age* would be replaced by the First World War in ten years and Washington Irving's idea of "dudes" and "sophy sparkles" would disappear along with the Worth gowns, the horse and buggy, and the formal ball and cotillion.

Commodore Gerry was seventy years old and his law practice was leisurely compared with earlier years of high profile cases. In February 1907 he was involved in a case representing the owner of Piers 19 and 20 on the East River where New York City had condemned the property under eminent domain to take it for public use. The issue was not the "taking of private property" but rather how to assess the value of the property to determine the compensation that had to be paid to the owner. Years before, the owner had obtained a license to build a shed on one of the piers, which he built and used for years until the shed burned down and was never rebuilt. Was the City to assess the pier on its value alone or must it also assess the value of a shed that an owner has a "right" to build but never does? Commodore Gerry was asked to represent the case because he had used the piers in the past to service his steam launches for his yacht *Electra* and the pier owners were his business associates. When there is no conflict of interest most lawyers will represent their friends, family, or business associates. In this case there was no conflict of interest, just a simple case of statutory interpretation for Commodore Gerry. He won the case arguing that the license issued by the City to build a shed on the pier, whether or not a shed stood on the site, had a value unto itself that a potential purchaser of the property would gladly pay and the City would gladly impose a tax on if the shed was built. The owner's "right to build" the shed was an "assessable value" that required compensation along with separate compensation for the assessed value of the pier.[87]

Angelica and Mabel were both bridesmaids at the spring wedding of their dear friend Miss Marguerite Loew, which was held in mid-March. The next month after Angelica's last coaching parade in April the sisters joined their parents, Commodore and Louisa Gerry, on a trans-Atlantic steamer for their annual trip to Europe. Their return trip from Europe to America on July 10, 1907 foreshadowed an historic event just five years later that they could not have imagined. For the first time in many years of trans-Atlantic travel to Europe, the North German Lloyd steam liner, *Kronprinz Wilhelm*, carrying thousands of passengers to New York City from Europe, including the Gerry family, crashed into an iceberg after traveling through dense fog for seven hours. Most of the passengers had been sitting in their state rooms or the main saloon trying to ignore the noisy fog horn that had been sounded repeatedly for hours to alert any ships in the area of the steamer's presence. Suddenly there came a deafening sound that sent a chill of terror through every passenger followed by a pounding blow that threw many of them to the floor. Immediately after the first noise there was an eerie crunching sound as the iceberg jammed itself against the side of the great steam liner. To everyone's astonishment the ship did not sustain any structural damage and was able to finish the ocean crossing and dock at the Hoboken, New Jersey pier.[88] Because no one was injured and the voyage had resumed in a normal manner the passengers found the experience exciting and were pleased to share the story with family and friends when back on solid ground. Safe and composed the Gerrys were transported to their yacht *Electra* for the nine-hour trip to Newport, Rhode Island where they joined Robert and Peter at *Seaverge* for a relaxed family reunion. It may have come as a surprise to some, but the very next month the Commodore and his wife and daughters boarded another trans-Atlantic steamer for a trip to Geneva and Paris. Perhaps they wanted to follow the old saying that if you fall off a horse you must immediately get back on to avoid a fear of horses. Indeed, after an uneventful ocean crossing the Gerrys were soon out and about in Paris. The French papers reported that while the Commodore and Louisa did their sight-seeing by automobile, their daughters walked everywhere in Paris and had introduced the people of Paris to the famous New York City "fashionable constitutional" made popular by their mother, Louisa Gerry.[89]

In November 1907 the artist John Singer Sargent who famously painted little Beatrice Goelet was engaged to paint the Washington beauty and friend of Mabel Gerry, twenty-two year old Mathilda Townsend. She was well-known in Europe as an eligible American beauty whose mother, Mrs. Richard Townsend, had been seeking a royal match for her daughter. Both women were presented at the Spanish court during the summer by the Duke de Alba of Spain, who had met Mathilda and her mother two years earlier at the Spanish Embassy in Paris. The courtship continued happily for two years after the Paris introductions and finally, during the summer of 1907 formal plans for the marriage began with negotiations over Mathilda's annual income when she moved to Spain. About the time John Singer Sargent was painting the full-scale portrait of Mathilda Townsend, the Duke de Alba notified Mrs. Townsend that the offered income from the Townsend estate was not adequate to due honor to his name and titles, and would not be enough to assist his encumbered estates.[90] With the engagement broken, Mathilda Townsend was available for young American bachelors to pursue her, which included Peter G. Gerry whom she later married in 1910.

Commodore and Louisa Gerry had one of the most brilliant dances of the New Year to celebrate the engagement of their son, thirty-one year old Robert L. Gerry to Ms. Cornelia Harriman after their long and happy courtship. Not long after a rollicking bachelor dinner Robert escorted Cornelia to City Hall the last week of February to get their marriage license. The wedding was March 3, 1908 at Grace Church where the crowd on Broadway was so great during and after the ceremony that thirty mounted police and fifty foot patrolmen had their hands full clearing a passageway for the bridal party. The church was simply decorated with the chancel surrounded with flowering peach and almond trees with palms as a background. Palms also lined the side aisles of the church. The musical program included a full choir, an orchestra and solos on harp and violin. The guests overflowed into the aisles, the entrance and out the front steps; many did not see the bridal party until they passed in the exit procession. Peter G. Gerry stood as best man for his brother, and while Cornelia's sister, Carol, was to be her maid of honor, she was too ill to attend the wedding and was replaced by another sister, Mary Harriman. Cornelia's brother Averell was an usher as was Robert Walton Goelet, first cousin of the groom. The brides-maids wore gowns of peach-colored chiffon trimmed with embroidered satin, topped with filet lace coats, and each wore a brown tulle hat with brown ostrich plumes. The bride wore a princess robe of pure white satin, with a yoke and panels down the sides of old point de Venise lace, and sleeves of the same lace over short ones of chiffon. Her veil was a large square of point lace edged with a pointed border caught with orange blossoms to form a soft edge over her golden brown coiffure.[91] The church ceremony was followed by a reception for relatives and intimate friends at the Harriman home at 874 Fifth Avenue. Mr. and Mrs. Gerry received congratulations in the center hall on the first floor, which had its electric chandeliers done in amber-color lights and quantities of forsythia and other yellow flowers arranged in masses and trailed across the walls to give the effect of sunshine. It is interesting to note that Robert L. Gerry's best pal, Alfred Vanderbilt, was not in the wedding party, although he was a guest at the wedding. By now, Alfred was having an affair and was in disfavor with his family and friends for the hurt he caused his wife Elsie, who was loved throughout their social community. It would have been unseemly for the proper and principled Robert L. Gerry to have his "womanizing" friend play a role in his wedding. After the reception the bride and groom sailed to Europe for an extended honeymoon. The press noted that the union of the Gerry and Harriman families had special interest because it was an essentially "American" marriage; there had been no foreign intermarriages in either family for over one hundred years.[92]

In 1908 the next generation of Goelet men began to focus on their philanthropic interests which often continued projects initiated by their fathers, Robert and Ogden. When Harvard University decided to establish a new *Graduate School of Business* around 1900 there was a gulf between academic life and the business world. The new model would focus on the administration of business rather than the traditional focus on the technical aspects of a business. Not until 1908 was the mission and curriculum formulated into a formal plan and presented for approval to the University Board of Governance. Once approved, raising money was the challenge. Both Robert Walton Goelet and his cousin Robert Wilson Goelet were part of a small group of alumni who contributed money that made the program a reality. The sum raised from this select group of alumni covered half of the funds needed to implement the new *Graduate Business School* at Harvard, which is now considered to be one of the top programs in the nation.[93] Another endeavor that Robert Walton Goelet pursued in the footsteps of his father was support for the *Metropolitan Opera* in New York City. The support was financial indeed, but even more, Robert Walton Goelet played a leadership role in the opera as did his son, Francis Goelet after him. In 1908 Robert Walton Goelet hosted an important meeting at his Fifth Avenue home for the Board of the opera where they decided to hire the three greatest opera talents in Europe, Toscanini as conductor of French and Italian music, Mahler for German music, and, as General Manager of the *Metropolitan Opera,* Giulio Gatti-Casazza. There was no opera house in the world able to afford such a superb triumvirate.[94]

One month after their wedding, Robert and Cornelia Gerry left Paris to meet Commodore and Louisa Gerry when they arrived in London from America in late April for a lengthy stay in London. The two events that brought them together were the 1908 Summer Olympics and the marriage of Louisa Gerry's niece, the daughter of the American ambassador, Jean Reid in June. The extended family stayed at the luxurious *Claridge's Hotel.* The hotel was established between 1812 and 1856 by the successive purchase of adjacent buildings on Brook and Davies Streets until 1894 when all the buildings were demolished and rebuilt as one magnificent hotel that reopened in November 1898 and began its life as the top class luxury hotel we know today. In 1908 the Commodore and his son Robert selected *Claridge's Hotel* for their stay in London because it rented full apartments by the month and was situated in the heart of the exclusive Mayfair area on the classy West end (side) of London.[95] Also Louisa, Angelica, Mabel and Cornelia could take their "fashionable constitutionals" while browsing the most exclusive shops on Bond Street for outfits for the royal wedding and their attendance at the Olympic Games.

The selection process for the *1908 Summer Olympics* consisted of four bids, and it was Rome that was chosen over Berlin, London and Milan. The selection was made in 1904 and after two years of preparation Italy opened the *1906 Olympic Games* in Athens with other cities in Italy hosting specific sports. While Athens opened the Olympics, and just when the games were ready to begin across Italy, Naples was devastated by the eruption of Mount Vesuvius the first week of April 1906. Because Italy had to immediately divert their Olympic funds and staff to the evacuation and reconstruction of Naples a new venue was required. The *International Olympic Committee* selected London and moved the games to 1908 to provide London time to prepare. A little known twist in the history of this event was that after Harrietta Goelet and others from around the world had stopped in Athens for the 1906 *Olympic Opening Ceremony,* the *1906 Rome Olympiad* was replaced by the *International Olympic Committee* with the *1908 London Games* which were deemed the new "start" of the *Fourth Olympiad* in keeping with the now-accepted four-year cycle. The official 1908 London games lasted 187 days, or 6 months and 4 days, the longest in modern Olympic history and featured athletes representing 22 nations competing in 24 sporting disciplines. There were a number of "firsts" at these games; one was the beginning of the four-year cycle of the Olympics, and another was the "distance" from the start of the Marathon run to the finish of the Marathon run in a stadium. The original distance of 25 miles was changed to 26 miles so the marathon could start at Windsor Castle at the request of Princess Mary; the "start line" would be beneath the windows of the Royal Nursery for viewing by the royal family. The change to the "finish location" was in response to shot putter and American flag carrier Ralph Rose's refusal to dip the American flag before the Royal Box during the opening ceremony. British officials felt compelled to restore the importance of the monarchy and moved the finish line of the most important event, the Marathon, into the stadium below the King's box which ensured that the race finished immediately in front of the King. As a result of these changes the Marathon covered a distance of 26 miles which became the standard length of all marathon runs beginning with the *1924 Summer Olympics*.[96]

A great crowd gathered June 23 in the *Square* in front of *Saint James Palace* to watch the arrival of England's King Edward VII and Queen Alexandra, followed by the bridal party of the American ambassador's daughter, Jean Reid. The American bride married the Honorable John Hubert Ward, equerry-in-waiting to the King, and brother of the Earl of Dudley, in the ancient *Saint James Palace Chapel* where Queen Victoria and her daughters were married. There was only a maid of honor and no bridesmaids with five little children, two boys and three girls, in quaint little costumes who followed behind the bride. The bride's gown was made of satin with overlays of old point rose lace given to her by her grandmother. The chapel was quite small and only 100 guests attended the ceremony, which likely included the Gerry family, relatives of the bride and old friends of "Bertie," the King of England. A large reception for over a thousand was held at *Dorchester House*, the American Embassy, where the King and Queen mixed freely with the guests. The bride and groom were known as avid collectors of rare old silver and many of the wedding gifts were antique silver serving pieces, vases and trays, and some were heirloom pieces from the groom's extended family, the Barons of Dudley. The King and Queen presented the couple with a splendid set of old silver sauce dishes recently secured at a sale of an historical collection.[97] The Honorable John and Jean Ward lived at *Dudley House* in Carlton House Terrace, London. After King Edward VII's death in 1910, John Ward stayed on as equerry to Queen Alexandra. John and Jean's son, Edward, was the godson of the King and became *Commander of the Household Cavalry* when Queen Elizabeth II was crowned in 1953; that same year Queen Elizabeth attended the debutante party of Jean Reid's daughter. Jean outlived her husband John Hubert Ward by twenty-four years. Jean Reid Ward was honored for her distinguished charity work during World War II and was made a Commander of the British Empire.[98]

As newlyweds this was the first spring that Robert L. Gerry and Cornelia Harriman Gerry did not lead the spring *Coaching Parade* in Central Park, ride the horse show circuit, or join the Orange County Hunt. They began their life together in New York City where Robert embarked on a regular leadership role in the *Gerry Estates* business at the historic Gerry office on Broadway and with Cornelia happily pregnant. Robert's boyhood friend Alfred Vanderbilt was absent more than usual with growing marital problems. The older generation looked to their own lives and left their adult children to take responsibility for theirs.

Commodore Gerry had returned to New York City immediately after the Reid wedding and on July 7 he boarded the yacht *Electra* with his wife and daughters for a stay at Newport, Rhode Island where they joined Peter who had opened Seaverge early in the summer. The family settled down for a summer of sport and leisurely socializing with their now pregnant daughter-in-law, Cornelia Gerry. In August the Gerrys and several friends enjoyed the *Astor Cup* yacht races on *Electra* in the waters off Newport, still the highlight of the *New York Yacht Club's* annual cruise. Frederic and Almy Gallatin, now 68 and 69 years old, also joined the yachting season but it was their custom to cruise up to New London, Connecticut, then on to popular Bar Harbor, Maine. In New London they enjoyed watching their adult children play baseball, the newest summer fad, where visiting cottagers and hotel guests formed a team and played baseball against the locals while their children enjoyed their latest fad, sidewalk roller skating. Most of the "locals" in holiday resorts had happy and long-standing friendships with their temporary summer neighbors. They not only enjoyed their company but also the annual revenue that wealthy vacationers contributed to the local economy.

The fall of 1908 was a momentous time for Commodore and Louisa Gerry who became grandparents for the first time. Nine months after the beautiful spring wedding of Robert and Cornelia Gerry the first of their four sons was born on November 22 just in time for Thanksgiving. Robert named his son Elbridge Thomas Gerry II, in honor of his own father. This handsome child was known as "Ebby" his entire life just as every namesake to follow was affectionately known as Ebby. The only known time that Commodore Gerry was himself called "Ebby" was by his uncle, Captain James T. Gerry, in a letter written to the Commodore when he was 17 years old. The extended family gathered for Ebby's baptism on Wednesday, December 23 just two days before the Commodore's seventy-first birthday. The godmother was Angelica Gerry with Robert Walton Goelet the co-godfather with W. Averell Harriman.

The week before his grandson was born Commodore Gerry was in New Orleans to give a speech about his life-long dedication to child-saving work. Perhaps the knowledge that he would be a grandfather within days influenced Commodore Gerry to choose as his topic the role that religion plays in the life of a child. He spoke of how from infancy religion is the central guiding light to the inculcation of a child's character and value system, indeed in their future ability to take their place as the "future sovereigns of the Republic, expected to live when they arrive at the age of maturity, knowing the truths about God, life and the hereafter. "[99] He had raised his children with a firm moral foundation, a deep faith, an educated mind and an abundance of unconditional love. Robert Gerry could not help but be a great father with such an exemplary role model.

In 1909 although healthy in his seventy-second year, Commodore Elbridge T. Gerry began to send more letters of regret than acceptance to the many requests for the pleasure of his company among his associates and old business friends. He was asked to be a Commissioner for the *Hudson Fulton Centennial Celebration* which he refused, and he no longer joined the New York Bar for their regular dinners to celebrate one thing or another. Commodore and Louisa Gerry seemed to enjoy more than ever the opportunity to be the guests of old friends and to host fewer entertainments than prior years. Trips to Europe began to offer them pleasant stays at *Dorchester House* where they enjoyed wonderful meals with Ambassador and Elizabeth Reid with whom they shared stories about their adult children and their new grandson. There was also excitement at the Embassy in 1909 when the *Fourth of July* was grandly celebrated with an "open house" for over 2,000 people who were both Londoner's and Americans. Everyone flocked to the great celebration of fireworks and food that Ambassador Reid had evolved into one of the most anticipated annual events of the summer in London.[100] Commodore Gerry, Louisa, Angelica and Mabel left for America shortly after *Independence Day* on the German steamer the *Kronprinzessin Cecilie*. When asked how his trip was Commodore Gerry replied, "The weather was cold and rainy in Paris and London, and the ocean passage was rough. We are glad to be home."[101] The Gerrys headed up the Hudson River in late summer not only to relax and enjoy their almost one-year old grandson Ebby, but also to take a look at how things were progressing on the family homestead. While in Europe they had been notified that several cows in the Gerry herd were found to have tuberculosis. The herd had a perfectly healthy appearance but in the course of routine examination the veterinarian discovered the disease in various stages among the cows. Twenty cows had to be killed which left only seven in the herd alive, plus a dozen young stock. By August the herd was completely healthy and new stock had been purchased to replenish the herd.[102]

While at Lake Delaware in 1909 the Gerry family visited local community friends and the small Episcopal churches they supported. The local papers reported on a new "mission" project that the Gerry family wanted to pursue in Delaware County. Louisa Gerry and her daughters leased some land on the old Armstrong farm between Bovina and Andes with the intention of creating a rustic tent camp for the poor children of New York City to provide a free summer outing. The first twenty-four boys were from the choirs of Episcopal Churches in Manhattan and Brooklyn and from the Big Brothers' program in New York City.[103] The site proved to be problematic with mosquitoes and other issues and it was not until Robert L. Gerry purchased property in 1911 on which to build a proper camp that the Gerry family idea blossomed into a successful summer camp.

The remainder of 1909 was dominated by one of the biggest real estate stories in New York City history. The local city government was investigating whether land owned by nearly every major patriarch of New York was actually owned by the city. The historic sixteenth and seventeenth century original Dutch and English charters, deeds, records and maps in both New York State and Europe were to be investigated. Included in the search were several very valuable properties currently in the Gallatin, Gerry, Goelet, and Livingston families. Millions of dollars in land value were at stake. All of the land involved was known as "made land" that was originally underwater and filled in over many decades to create the lower Manhattan waterfront that lies along the East River on one side and the Hudson River on the other side. Old documents often referred to property boundaries that started at a tree or a building or a pile of stones that no longer existed and could not be verified. The city admitted that the search had been quietly underway for several years and there was no way to anticipate the result, but it assured those affected that the investigation was being done thoroughly and systematically, and would take considerable time to resolve.[104]

Maurice Farkoa
British musical & comedy performer

President Theodore Roosevelt

Theodore Roosevelt's birthplace and home is on the same block on 20th Street as the Gallatin family and around the corner from the Goelet/Gerry brownstone at 19th and Broadway.

Sagamore Hill
Summer home of President Teddy Roosevelt at Oyster Bay, New York

Gents in Tuxedo Park 1886

Tuxedo Club House
Tuxedo Park, New York

A classic tuxedo from the original tailor
Henry Poole & Co., London

Whitelaw Reid
Ambassador to England

Reid memorial window in St. John the Divine Cathedral

Dorchester House, Mayfair, London

Grand staircase

Mrs. Elizabeth Mills Reid
Louisa Gerry's cousin

Grand salon

John was the brother of the Earl of Dudley and also the Equerry to the King.

Honorable John Hubert Ward

Queens Chapel, St. James Palace

Jane Reid

The King and Queen attended the wedding of John Hubert Ward and Jane Reid.

Saint James Palace, London, England

Edward Henry Harriman

Mary Averell Harriman

Commodore Gerry (*center*) and Peter Gerry (*white hat*) arrive at train station to attend E.H. Harriman's funeral in 1909.

Arden House

Surrounded on three sides by more than 110,000 acres of permanently protected state parkland, the Arden House mansion in Harriman, New York is a historic and architectural gem of the Hudson River Valley. For several years it served as the Columbia University Business School, it is now a conference center.

Boys Club Library

New York Boys Clubs were founded by E.H. Harriman.

Robert and Cornelia's wedding party March 1908

Robert Livingston Gerry
1879-1957

Cornelia Harriman Gerry
1884-1966

Cornelia Harriman Gerry
with sons Robert L. Gerry Jr. born 1911 and Ebby born 1909

Red Swan Tavern

Robert L. Gerry and Cornelia Harriman were neighbors in New York City who spent most of their courtship in Orange County at the horse stables, shows and fox hunts. Socializing was centered at the Red Swan Tavern in Warwick and the Harriman's Arden House estate.

Model of *Electra*

New York Yacht Club on 44th Street, 1917

New York Yacht Club model room

New York Yacht Club library

Newport, R.I. Yacht Station 6

Launch boat (left) hoisted up on *Electra*

After *Electra* was dismantled in 1912 Commodore Gerry used his *Electra* Launch at Newport for years.

Trolley crossed Arroyo Seco from L.A. to Pasadena

Ostrich farm in Pasadena, California

Angelica Gerry at the reins. "The whip" with her brother Robert beside her and sister Mabel in the back seat with friends.

Ostrich feather shop

Coaching parade in Central Park

Goelet family gave the statue ALMA MATER to Columbia University

May Goelet
Duchess of Roxburghe

Henry John Innes-Kerr
8th Duke of Roxburghe and son of
Lady Anne Spencer Churchill

Grand Duke Boris ladimirovich
Russian guest at Ochre Court,
Newport home of
Mrs. Ogden Goelet

Floors Castle – Duke of Roxburgh estate in Scotland

New York American

TO THE FRONT!

NEW YORK, TUESDAY, JUNE 26, 1906.—16 PAGES. PRICE ONE CENT

HARRY THAW KILLS STANFORD WHITE ON ROOF GARDEN!

GAS TRUST | MISS KATHERINE STRYKER | GIRL SLAIN IN | FIVE ICE TRUST | STANFORD WHITE | SHOOTS ARCHITECT

Contemporary dinner show at the Rooftop Garden Theatre at Madison Square Garden about the time of Stanford White's murder.

Harry Thaw

Evelyn Nesbit Thaw

Stanford White

Harry Thaw testifying in court

Evelyn Nesbit Thaw testifying in court

Harry Thaw heading for mental hospital

Mrs. Harrietta Goelet

1906 explosion of Mount Vesuvius

The *Nahma*

Harrietta Goelet witnessed the 1906 eruption from her yacht Nahma as she passed in the Bay of Naples.

The cable car that both Lillian and Mabel Gerry described in their 1889 diaries during the family tour of Italy. They rode in horse-drawn carts up to the Funicular Railway Etna cable cars that took them up to the top.

The girls called it the "sail away"

12

THE TWENTIETH CENTURY

Part II 1910 to 1930

To laugh often and much, to win the respect of intelligent people and the affection of children, to leave the world a better place, to know even one life has breathed easier because you have lived.... This is to have succeeded.

Ralph Waldo Emerson [1803–1882]

Peter Goelet Gerry at the age of thirty-one fell in love in 1909 with an accomplished equestrian just as his brother Robert had done two years earlier. The relationship was celebrated openly in society for the first time in February 1910 in Washington, D.C., at the home of his fiancée, Mathilde Townsend. For several weeks in January and February Peter was the guest of Mrs. Richard H. Townsend, Jr. at her mansion on fashionable Twenty-Fourth Street in northwest Washington. Mathilde's mother, Mrs. Mary Townsend, was the wealthy daughter of William L. Scott, a successful railroad man, a politician, a member of Congress, and a democratic delegate to four national conventions. He was also an avid horse breeder who established the *Algeria Stock Farm* in Erie, Pennsylvania and the *Hollywood Stud Farm* on the Chesapeake Bay, Maryland. He was a close associate of August Belmont, Jr. as a stockholder and member of the board of the racetracks owned by the *Coney Island Jockey Club* and the *Brooklyn Jockey Club*.[1] After William L. Scott's unexpected death of heart failure in 1891 his stud farms were closed and the stock sold. One of his most valuable horses, *Ryon D'Or* was purchased at auction by August Belmont, Jr. who stood him at his *Nursery Stud* in Kentucky.

His daughter Mary Scott married Richard H. Townsend, Jr. who was also a railroad man and a War Democrat, the same as Peter Gerry, who would become his son-in-law after Richard's death in 1902 from a fractured skull caused by a fall from his horse.[2] His death left Mrs. Townsend a wealthy widow with an estate valued at 15 million dollars. Mathilde was seventeen at the time of her father's death and not yet a debutante. A year later her mother presented the beautiful Mathilde to society where she soon became one of the most sought-after debutantes in Washington and Europe. Every summer they sailed for Europe in search of the perfect aristocrat for Mathilde and sure enough in 1907 she was tentatively engaged to the Duke of Alba of Spain who so famously spurned her because the Townsends' annual income was not worthy of the Duke, which in truth simply would not cover the debt of his estate. The search for a European match subsided for the next eighteen months and Mathilda enjoyed coaching at Newport and in *Central Park* in New York City where her cousin, Reginald Ronalds, was a leading whip with pal Robert Gerry. Both Peter and Robert fell in love with women who were accomplished horsewomen, were whips on their own carriages, and joined the Fox Hunt alongside the men. These genteel sports of the wealthy made it inevitable that while sharing their passion for equestrian pursuits these young men and women of the *Gilded Age* would find their love match in the great outdoors rather than at a fancy ball.

The noted veterinarian and one-time Dean of *the University of Pennsylvania School of Veterinary Medicine,* Dr. Rush S. Huidikoper and his wife were relatives of Mrs. Townsend's father, William L. Scott, and had treated Mathilde like a daughter for years. Every summer since her father's death in 1902, Mathilde went to Bar Harbor, Maine with Mrs. Huidikoper who had also lost her husband in 1901. Each year they stayed with wealthy friends and hosted dinners and dances at the local inn and Mathilde participated in the horse shows and coaching parades. By age twenty Mathilde had started a tradition in Bar Harbor that awarded silver cups to winners of the equestrian competitions. In the summer of 1909 Mathilde hosted a Friday afternoon buckboard party to *Jordan's Pond* at Seal Harbor, followed that night by supper at the local Inn.[3] Before closing out the season at Bar Harbor, Mathilde hosted a dinner at *Colonial Hall* on September 18 to say goodbye to her friends before her return home to Washington. Mrs. Huidikoper did not accompany Mathilde home, rather she boarded a trans-Atlantic steamship in New York City for an extended stay with her sister, Mrs. Scott, in Devon, England, after which she returned to Washington for the winter holidays.

In November of 1909 Mathilde Townsend, twenty-three, accompanied her friend Peter Gerry to the fall horse shows in New York City and Washington, D.C., after which they became inseparable and attended all of the early holiday dinners and dances as a couple. However, Mathilde and Peter decided to spend Christmas at home with their own families where they each announced their desire to be married. With his parents' blessing Peter Gerry traveled to Washington, D.C. in January to spend several weeks with Mathilde Townsend and her mother at their Twenty-Fourth Street mansion that had gardens designed by Frederick Law Olmstead who also designed *Central Park* in New York City. Peter escorted Mathilde to dinners, luncheons and dances throughout the New Year season, meeting her friends and family, and generally becoming part of Mathilde's social world. On January 9, 1910 Mrs. Richard Townsend hosted a gala ball for her daughter with Peter Gerry as Mathilde's escort for the evening.[4] It didn't take long for the papers in Washington and New York City to notice that the wealthiest and most eligible bachelor and belle of their two cities had spent the winter holidays out and about as a happy couple. February and March were filled with gossip columns speculating on when the engagement would be announced; all the while, the Gerry and Townsends denied the speculations. Then in early April Mathilde Townsend and her mother traveled to New York City for several days to spend time with Peter's family and returned home to Washington on April 15. The next day the formal engagement was announced simultaneously in New York City by Commodore Gerry and in Washington by Mrs. Townsend.

Immediately after the announcement and perhaps to avoid press inquiries, Commodore and Louisa Gerry and their daughters boarded a trans-Atlantic steamship for England where they rented a house in Mayfair for the remainder of April and into May. It was the height of the "American season" in London. Some of the Gerry friends and family who also rented houses in Mayfair included Mrs. Ogden Goelet, Mr. and Mrs. Ogden Mills, Mr. and Mrs. William K. Vanderbilt, and Mabel's best friend, Gertrude, now Mrs. Harry Payne Whitney. In March the royal friend of this set of New Yorkers, Bertie, King Edward VII, was at the palace of Napoleon III and Princess Eugenie in *Biarritz,* a seaside town in the Basque Territory of France, to recover from a serious case of bronchitis. The King usually smoked twenty cigarettes and twelve cigars each day and was increasingly suffering from chronic bronchitis. While in *Biarritz* the King collapsed and spent weeks in convalescence. He returned to *Buckingham Palace* in London on April 27 at the height of the social season. On May 5 his wife, Queen Alexandra, returned from *Corfu* where she had visited her brother, King George I of Greece. The following day the King suffered several heart attacks but refused to go to bed saying, "No, I shall not give in, I shall go on, I shall work to the end." Not only was the King's family at his side, but so was his favorite mistress, Alice Keppel, who was the great-grandmother of Camilla Parker Bowles, the mistress of Prince Charles until their marriage after the death of Princess Diana.[5] The King's mistress was tolerated by Queen Alexandra but she was escorted from the palace immediately after Bertie's death, never to return. Nonetheless it was the King's son who had Bertie's ear at the end; drawing near to the King as he was dying George told his father that his favorite horse, *Witch of the Air,* had won at *Kempton Park* that afternoon. The King replied to his son, "I am very glad" and those were

Bertie's last words after which he was finally placed in his bed where he lost consciousness and died fifteen minutes later.[6] Prince Edward Albert, "Bertie," was nineteen when he made his first visit to America, the first British royal to visit since *the American Revolution,* he was fifty-nine when he was crowned King, and sixty-three at his death. He was known as the "Uncle of Europe" because of his love of life and years of socializing with friends from around the world. The King lay in state at Westminster Abbey where his American friends passed by his casket, grief-stricken at the loss of a dear friend. His casket was solemnly marched to the train station where it was transported to Windsor Castle for King Edward VII's funeral in *St. George's Chapel* where "Bertie" was buried on May 20, 1910.[7]

The death of King Edward VII shrouded London in gloom. While the new King George V encouraged the tradespeople of London to support the social season to avoid serious financial loss, the Palace abandoned all royal balls, receptions and concerts, and did not attend *Ascot* that year.[8] Many Americans returned home early as did Commodore and Louisa Gerry to assist their son Peter with preparations for his marriage to Mathilde Townsend. Robert, Cornelia and little Ebby Gerry had joined Mrs. Harriman at *Arden House* in Orange County, New York for an extended visit in April and early May, but they too had returned to New York City for the wedding of Robert's younger brother, Peter.

While the wedding plans were handled primarily by Mrs. Townsend in Washington and coordinated with Louisa Gerry and Peter in New York, Commodore Gerry engaged in two significant real estate transactions. The first was a forty-year lease of Gerry property consisting of a corner plot where 100 feet fronted Fifth Avenue and 280 feet fronted on East Forty-Seventh Street. The property had a long and interesting family history. It was originally a cow pasture on common land that Uncle Peter Goelet had purchased decades ago. By the time he died in 1879 the land was occupied by the *Windsor Hotel* and it was inherited by Uncle Peter's sister, Hannah Gerry. When she died in 1895 Commodore Gerry inherited the property which was destroyed by a deadly fire in 1899. Between 1899 and 1900 Commodore Gerry had the landmark *Windsor Arcade* built on the site. It was modeled after the exclusive *Burlington Arcade* on Bond Street in fashionable Mayfair, London where the Gerry family often rented a house for holidays. Just ten years later the character of the surrounding blocks had changed and the value of the land demanded that in 1910 the *Windsor Arcade* be demolished to make way for more productive commercial use. The property was leased to the W. & J. Sloane Company which erected a building to house both business offices and street-level showrooms. A portion of the entire property, about 80 feet on Forty-Seventh Street, was leased to the Carlton House Company, owners of the adjacent *Ritz Carlton Hotel* which stood on land owned by the Goelet Estates. The W. & J. Sloane lease was valued at one million dollars a year.

The second lease was for a prime plot of land on the southwest corner of Sixth Avenue and Forty-First Street located opposite *Bryant Park.* The frontage on Forty-First Street was 125 feet and on Sixth Avenue the frontage was 100 feet. This property was in the trendy *Times Square* neighborhood and was leased to Lee Shubert for a term of sixty-three years. The old houses that stood on the corner had to be demolished before construction could begin the following spring. While the general plan of the new building was not definitely settled, Mr. Shubert planned to erect a commercial structure with offices for his extensive theatrical interests and the building would be adjacent to the new *Shubert Comedy Theatre.*[9] The sixty-three year lease was even more valuable than the earlier W.& J. Sloane agreement to the Gerry Estates, which like Old Uncle Peter Goelet, purchased but did not often sell their land.

Peter Goelet Gerry married Mathilde Townsend at noon on May 26, 1910 in Washington, D.C. at the Townsend mansion. The ceremony was performed in the ballroom, a mirror-lined apartment modeled after the *Salle de Glace* at Versailles, with its windows curtained in pink silk and the floral decorations an abundance of pink and white peonies. The maid of honor was Miss Katharine Elkins, a lifelong friend of the bride, who was her only attendant. Peter Gerry's best man was his older brother Robert L. Gerry, and the bride was escorted down the aisle by her uncle, Charles H. Strong of Erie, Pennsylvania.

Mathilde Townsend wore a *Worth* gown made in Paris that was a princess style of white satin over which was mounted a robe of rich point d'Alencon lace. The bodice had long, close-fitting sleeves of lace and satin with a V-shaped neck and back. The bride wore a single strand of pearls given to her by her father before he died in 1902. She wore a tulle veil with no lace adornment, held in place by a crown of orange blossoms, and she held a fragrant bouquet of elegant white orchids, accented with sweet orange blossoms.[10]

The small party of 100 guests included the President and Vice-President of the United States, Justice Oliver Wendell Holmes, the Secretary of the Treasury, the Attorney General, the Secretary of the Navy, and the German ambassador. Mrs. Townsend was prominent in Washington society through her father and her husband who had both been prominent Democrats in Congress, and now, Peter G. Gerry was officially introduced to the world of politics which he would join as a Congressman just two years later. The United States *Marine Orchestra* provided music during the wedding breakfast at which President Taft proposed a toast to "the most beautiful bride he had ever seen," after which Peter Gerry rose and thanked the President for his presence at the wedding and for the compliment to his bride. Peter also expressed surprise at himself for being neither nervous nor afraid as he had expected to be, and he attributed his serenity to the example of his beautiful bride, Mathilde.[11] Among the rich and tasteful wedding gifts was a diamond pin in the shape of a fox given to Mathilde by her maid of honor and best friend, Katharine, with whom she had fox hunted for years since their youth. Shortly after the wedding breakfast Mr. and Mrs. Peter Gerry traveled to New York with Commodore and Mrs. Gerry on board the yacht *Electra* and from there Peter and Mathilde went on a honeymoon tour of Europe.[12] When they returned to America the newlyweds made their home in New York City where Peter Goelet Gerry practiced law with his father, Commodore Elbridge T. Gerry, at the *Gerry Estates* office on Broadway.

After their bon voyage to Peter and Mathilda, Commodore Gerry , Louisa, Angelica and Mabel continued up the Hudson River on *Electra* for a three week visit to the Lake Delaware estate. While there, Commodore Gerry made arrangements for the second year of summer camp in Delaware County. He asked a local man and associate, Robert Doig, to oversee the camp now located on *Lake Tunis,* a small natural body of water on a local farm. They agreed that there should be one caretaker for every ten children using a combination of local people and the children's chaperones from New York City. The Gerry family paid for the costs of running the camp and transporting the children to and from New York City. The local papers in Delaware County began to call the campers the "fresh air children."

In mid-June the Gerrys left Lake Delaware on *Electra* and went directly to Newport, Rhode Island to open *Seaverge* for the season, and where Peter and Mathilde Gerry joined them on June 17 to continue their honeymoon among family and friends. Indeed, Louisa Gerry sent out invitations for a large dinner party followed by fireworks on the *Fourth of July* at *Seaverge.* This was an important family holiday because Commodore Gerry's grandfather had signed the *Declaration of Independence,* a legacy that was honored and celebrated. This was also a perfect welcome for Peter's new bride into the family circle at their summer home. But Mathilde also wanted to share her summer resort with Peter, so in mid-July they traveled north to spend August and September in Bar Harbor, Maine, where Mrs. Richard Townsend planned to join them in September upon her return from a summer in Europe.

Robert, Cornelia and little Ebby Gerry, almost two years old, also joined the family at *Seaverge* for the *Fourth of July*. On July 6 after a three-week visit, Robert drove his wife and young boy up to Lake Delaware for a quiet family holiday, starting a new tradition of boyhood fun on the farm with his own son. On July 20 during their return drive from Lake Delaware to New York City, Robert L. Gerry's automobile encountered a team of horses pulling a wagon that was headed in the opposite direction. Mr. John Sundlent and his wife and daughter, as well as Mr. Faulkner, his wife and two children were all on the wagon headed to Andes for a funeral. As the Gerry automobile drew closer to the wagon near the town of Kingston and they were about to pass each other, the horses became startled. Mrs. Sundlent waved her handbag wildly in the air to stop the car but it was too late. The wagon swerved off the road and over a twenty-foot embankment where the occupants were tossed to the ground. Robert immediately stopped the car at the scene of the accident and offered to take the injured to a doctor. Mrs. Sundlent pulled herself up and looked about the tumbled family and with great relief she said, "No one is injured, we're just scared silly."[13] Mr. Sundlent inspected the wagon and horses and found the animals were fine but a wagon wheel was broken, which Robert paid to have repaired. He assisted the group in getting to the funeral in Andes before proceeding with Cornelia and little Ebby on their trip home to New York City.

Commodore Gerry joined the *New York Yacht Club's* annual cruise when it arrived in Newport Harbor on August 8, no longer participating in the full ten-day cruise from New York to Boston and then to Newport. The Commodore stayed closer to home and his growing family. In fact, the summer of 1910 swirled with a new round of gossip that Mabel Gerry was engaged to any number of men on both sides of the Atlantic. Commodore Gerry became exasperated and emphatically denied all the rumors. Louisa Gerry, a publicity shy woman, told a *New York Times* reporter in Newport that "the report is absolutely without foundation, it is ridiculous."[14] The Gerry sisters, now in their mid-thirties, had a large peer group of life-long friends, many of whom were men and whose company they regularly enjoyed. While Angelica happily accepted her reputation as one of the wealthy "bachelor girls," her younger sister Mabel always enjoyed the attention of her suitors and her role as a belle of society. Mabel cultivated her fashionable style and her personal talents. She noted in her private diary over the course of several years that she was gifted with a lovely voice and that she desired to have some professional training. Mabel always noted what color dress she wore to each and every dinner or ball and the names of the men who paid attention to her, although it was written without guile in a day when keeping a journal was common practice for young ladies. Unlike Angelica's comprehensive scrapbook on her coaching trip, there were only two journal entries about horses in Mabel's diary where she described magnificent horses the family saw while on a trip to Europe. Until

Mabel Gerry married much later in life, she neither encouraged nor discouraged her many suitors, she simply enjoyed the pleasure of their company.

In late August 1910, Mrs. Ogden Goelet hosted one of her gala summer events in Newport. She gave a dinner and ball at *Ochre Court* to honor her summer guest, the Duke Franz Joseph of Bavaria. Special guests included Congressman Nicholas Longworth, Lord Rocksavage, and Count Wedel the German ambassador. Commodore and Louisa Gerry attended the gala of their cousin as did Mrs. Robert Goelet, of *Southside* next door, and Robert Wilson Goelet, the hostess's son. The grounds of *Ochre Court* were aglow with hundreds of electric lights that adorned the trees, fountains and also edged the veranda.[15] Mrs. Ogden Goelet, at age fifty, was still the mistress of Newport and the toast of Europe.

Commodore Gerry closed *Seaverge* on September 1 and returned with his family to New York City. Two days later he was at the Surrogates Court Building to join the Justices of the *Special Sessions* court for the presentation of the plans for a new Children's Courthouse. The property chosen for the new court was conveniently located on East Twenty-Second Street near the *United Charities Building* and just north of the *New York Society for the Prevention of Cruelty to Children* on Park Avenue. These were the primary houses for the care of children who would appear before magistrates in the new courthouse. The design for the new building was a Classical Revival four-story structure, faced with limestone and two-story Ionic columns. Today the building is occupied by *Baruch College,* but the façade is relatively unchanged. The new Children's Courthouse had two separate courtrooms, one to accommodate 200 people and the other quite small for private interviews with boys on parole who had to report to a magistrate. The hope was that the children would not be treated as criminals, as they had been in adult courtrooms, but rather as wards of the State who had guardianship responsibilities.[16] The Chief Judge told the reporters at the presentation of the plans that the idea for the new Courthouse originated thirty-six years earlier with the Mary Ellen child abuse case, the first brought by Commodore Gerry on behalf of the NYSPCC, the *Gerry Society*. There had been 250,000 children represented in the years since that first case caused a wave of indignation to sweep over *Gilded Gotham.*[17]

One month later Commodore Gerry traveled to Washington, D.C. to attend the sixth "International Humane Conference," the first ever to include child cruelty in addition to animal cruelty. The conference was held in the new *National Museum* building from October 10-15, 1910. President Taft was the "Honorary President" of the conference and the "Honorary Vice-President" was King George V, the son of Bertie, King Edward VII. Both Commodore Gerry and his son Peter Gerry were members of the New York City delegation, the Commodore as Counsel to the

NYSPCC and Peter as a Board member. The two major topics discussed relative to child cruelty were child labor laws and the disregard of laws that made it illegal to permit any child less than 16 years-old to enter a movie theater without an adult. The New York City delegation was prepared to support the exclusion of children altogether from moving picture shows because evidence showed that it corrupted a child's morals. Commodore Gerry remained the "father of child protection" around the world and his son, Peter, followed in his footsteps.[18]

In late November 1910 the 80 year-old father of Mrs. Ogden Goelet died at his home at 511 Fifth Avenue. Richard T. Wilson was head of the banking firm he had founded on Wall Street until just four years before his death, when he retired due to heart ailments. Since his wife had died six years earlier in 1904, his daughters were his constant companions. Mr. Wilson had five children and it was his eldest daughter, Mary Rita Wilson, who married the late Ogden Goelet. The second daughter, Lelia, married the late Lord Michael H. Herbert of *Milton House*, Salisbury, England who later became the British Ambassador to the United States. Mr. Wilson's third daughter, Grace, married Cornelius Vanderbilt, Jr. The three sisters were known in *Gilded Gotham* as the "marrying Wilsons" because they were beautiful and all married great wealth, if not nobility.[19] The funeral of Richard T. Wilson was simple and held at his Fifth Avenue residence. He was buried next to his wife in the family vault at *Woodlawn Cemetery*, New York City. The extended family of Goelets, Gerrys, and Gallatins all remained in mourning through the holidays, returning to society in the New Year.

After more than thirty years as founder and legal counsel to the *Gerry Society*, the NYSPCC, Commodore Elbridge T. Gerry remained passionate about the purpose and legacy of the work that had been the focus of his public life. On February 8, 1911, as Chairman of the *Conference on the Law and the Child* held in New York City, Commodore Gerry presented the keynote address to the conference. He opened with the statement, "Child rescue work differs materially from the popular idea in regard to child welfare institutions. It is literally the foundation upon which the whole superstructure of improving the welfare of the child necessarily rests."[20] He told the story of little Mary Ellen, the first rescue case in the world and how the *Gerry Society* was founded because the *Bergh Society* handled only animal cases, and Mary Ellen had triggered a flood of public calls for child rescues. The state legislature then passed a law to establish the *New York Society for the Prevention of Cruelty to Children*, the first of its kind in the world. Commodore Gerry emphasized that "the legislature created an Auxiliary Governmental Agency, not a charitable institution. The *Gerry Society* "rescues" the child by the hand of the law and reports only to the District Attorney of the

County in which it stands, and presents to him the facts when the offender is prosecuted."[21] Commodore Gerry continued in the tone of an advocate who recognized that the *Gerry Society's* work was often misunderstood and needed to be explained and defended every few years. He further stated that where the work of the NYSPCC ends the work of reformation starts in "welfare institutions" most suited to the care and education of the child. His final point, and one that was a core belief of the man, was that the agents of the NYSPCC had a legal mandate to identify the religion of each rescued child so the Court could place the child in a home or institution of that religious denomination. It was not a matter of converting the child to a new religion but a duty to nurture the child in the faith of the absent parent.[22] Commodore Gerry was essentially a lawyer who used his expertise and moral conviction to apply the power of the law to the scourges of *Gilded Gotham*. His rescue work was not charity, it was a moral and civic duty.

Madison Square Garden, home of the annual fall horse show, was also the winter exhibition hall for the annual dog show of the *Westminster Kennel Club*. Louisa, Angelica and Mabel Gerry were dog lovers and they attended the dog show every year, eager to learn which breed had won "best in show." Their cousin, Robert Wilson Goelet preferred to breed dogs rather than horses, and owned hundreds of acres in Orange County that included *Glenmere Lake* near the towns of Chester and Goshen where the Gerry brothers hosted their annual fox hunt. Robert Goelet had established the well-known *Glenmere Kennel* on his property about four miles from the town of Chester. He raised several breeds which included the Great Dane, but his special breed was the *West Highland White Terrier*. At the February 1911 dog show at Madison Square Garden, Robert W. Goelet won second place for his terrier "Kiltie" and first place for his Bull Terrier, "Channel Queen."[23] The success of the Kennel coupled with the amount of time Robert spent at nearby Tuxedo Park, convinced him to build a mansion on the hill that overlooked *Glenmere Lake* in Orange County. Building began in 1910 and the thirty-five room Tuscan style villa *Glenmere* was completed in the summer of 1911. On March 27 Robert Goelet had visited the building site and the *Glenmere Kennel* and was being driven by his chauffeur back to New York City in his six-cylinder, seventy-horse power Dietrich automobile. As they passed along the main thoroughfare of the village of Chester, there were half a dozen children standing on a corner after Sunday school. Marie Potter, 3 years-old, was among them. A boy on the opposite side of the street called to little Marie and she then toddled abruptly from the sidewalk just as the car came along. Though the chauffeur struggled to avoid the child, the front wheel struck her, knocked her down, and passed over her body, as did the rear wheel. Robert leaped from the car and picked up the unconscious little girl and carried her to her parents' home, but she died by the time she was placed in her mother's arms. Witnesses to the accident assured both the mother and Robert Goelet that the car was traveling slowly and there was no fault on the part of the driver. Robert remained in Chester until the coroner arrived and completed an investigation of the accident, which officially determined there was no fault, that it was a terrible accident. Robert Wilson Goelet, sad and shaken, returned to New York City.[24] The car of his cousin, Robert Gerry, had collided with a horse–drawn wagon the summer before, and it too had happened in a small country village where the automobile was still a novelty and sharing the roadway with horses had become increasingly dangerous.

Years before his death in 1907, E.H. Harriman, the father-in-law of Robert Gerry, along with Richard J. Townsend and August Belmont purchased land in Plains, Virginia where they built a hunting lodge and a kennel for their dog pack. The clubhouse was built a short distance from the small Plains train depot for easy access from New York City to Virginia's best fox hunting country. Mr. Townsend succeeded his friend Harriman as President of the Orange County Hunt Club. In April 1911 when the hunt club traveled to Virginia for a stay at the Plains Clubhouse, Robert and Cornelia Gerry, both members of the club, brought their toddler Ebby with them. However, when Cornelia arrived with the baby to settle in at the Club House she was told by Mr. Townsend that the rules of the club prohibited children in the house. Unable to locate a nearby place to rent, Cornelia asked Robert to build a very small "baby house" for the Nurse and the baby. Robert worked with local carpenters and plumbers and had a structure built near the entry porch to the adult Club House so Cornelia could stay with Robert but be near little Ebby at night. The house was designed to be very sturdy yet portable and able to be dismantled with little effort. The baby house was a little framed building with a nursery and kitchen on the ground floor and a bathroom and large nursery on the second floor where the nurse and baby slept. Large windows flooded the rooms with sunlight and opened to allow mountain breezes to cool the house. The front entry had a covered porch the width of the little house. The local plumber doubled his season's earnings by equipping the baby house with everything needed or desired. The townspeople felt that a young, wealthy, and fashionable woman, who loved her husband and baby too much to be separated from either of them, even for a few weeks at a time, was truly an old fashioned wife and mother who shared their traditional values. Where the farmers had been angry for years with the fox hunts on their land, they were now happy to have the Orange County hunt run freely throughout the county. Every Easter Cornelia

Gerry sent flowers from New York City to Plains, Virginia to decorate the village's Episcopal Church.[25]

While Mrs. Ogden Goelet, Mary, was still in Newport, the façade of her Fifth Avenue home in New York City was remodeled. She continued to spend winters at the 30-year old Goelet mansion even though most of society had moved north to the upper east side of *Central Park*. As a result, when Fifth Avenue was widened in September 1911, the dramatic front portico of the house had to be removed. The work site became like a scene from a silent movie comedy when a dense swarm of bees descended on a wooden soap box sitting on a sawhorse. Before long the box was covered with buzzing insects and passersby were gathering to see the curious sight. When one workman overturned the box, trapping most of the bees inside, those still free began to sting the crowd and everyone scattered. When one woman complained that the poor bees were suffocating, a workman thrust a stick under a corner of the box to admit air. Immediately the swarm again rushed out and flew into open taxi cab windows and startled passing horses. Mrs. Goelet's refined and cultured home was the scene of panic and chaos. When the bees finally swarmed and returned to the box, things came to a peaceful end until a policeman soaked the box with kerosene and lit a match. The press reported that most of the bees were not killed and "some sought refuge in chimneys and others wandered down side streets in quest of adventure. Some of the bees even visited the *Hotel Buckingham* at Fiftieth Street to the terror of guests." Despite all this, the newspaper added, "No arrests were made."[26]

The extended Gerry family traveled to Lake Delaware in the early summer of 1911 for a holiday reunion and to see how the "fresh air children" were doing at the Lake Tunis tent camp. By the second year there was a Chaplain who held regular services with the 96 boys in the temporary chapel/dining hall. The Gerrys had learned a great deal the first two years about what was really needed for a successful camp and it was apparent that the Lake Tunis site was not the right fit for a permanent camp. Robert L. Gerry took the lead and purchased the 250 acre James R. Wright farm on the other side of route 28 that was closer to the Lake Delaware estate. Robert worked with local builders and plumbers to design a camp with permanent structures and to dig a man-made lake for swimming. A construction crew from nearby Delhi built the pond for swimming and the Andes Hardware store owner, E.J. Turnbull, furnished the lumber and labor for the buildings.[27] The plan was to have a new camp up and running for the following season, and indeed, by the spring of 1912, the chapel was up and enclosed with a tin shingle roof. The 1876 Opus 34 pipe organ was removed from the historic Lake Delaware Gerry home and was installed in the new Chapel at the *Lake*

Delaware Boys Camp, as it was known after 1912. The chapel was also furnished with the rare chalice and paten used on Commodore Gerry's beloved yacht, *Electra,* for the celebration of Mass during extended family cruises. The yacht was dismantled in 1912 which facilitated the transfer of salvaged items to the *Lake Delaware Boys Camp* Chapel and for use in the interior construction of Robert and Cornelia Gerry's new *Aknusti* mansion on the hill above the camp. According to Robert L. Gerry the "establishment of the Church as a center from which all activities have ever radiated is owed to the advice of my father, for it was to him that we owe the building of the whole organization around the Chapel and the teaching of the Episcopal faith."[28] During their entire lives Robert and Cornelia Gerry were hands-on, dedicated supporters of the *Lake Delaware Boys Camp,* established by the Gerry family, as well as active supporters of the *Boys Clubs of New York City,* established by the Harriman family. The Gerry and Harriman children and heirs have carried on the leadership of both institutions to this day.

Robert and Cornelia Harriman loved the outdoors and in 1911 when they realized just how much time they spent with little Ebby at Lake Delaware and how much more time was needed to oversee the new camp, they decided to build their own place at Lake Delaware. Robert and Cornelia worked with architects *Walker and Gillette* to design a 20,000 square foot Georgian Colonial mansion on the top of a high hill that overlooked Lake Delaware and the family homestead below. Robert had purchased 2,000 acres from the remainder of his great-grandmother Gertrude Livingston's 22,000 acre 1749 sibling share of the early Livingston family's original assignment of the 1708 *Hardenburgh Patent.* Over the years Gertrude and Morgan Lewis sold off several farm lots as did their daughter Margaret Livingston and her son, Robert James Livingston, which reduced the original size of the land grant by the time Louisa L. Gerry inherited the estate in 1891. Robert hired Frederick Law Olmstead Jr. to design seven miles of access roads and stone bridges and the gardens surrounding the mansion. Robert and Cornelia designed a complete estate that included a Gate House, Carriage House, Manager's House, Game House, Stables, and a staff house. These were family homes with an office for each of the managers. The Game Keeper was responsible for the "fowl house" where state of the art incubators were installed to raise hundreds of game birds for the table and for hunting. The Stable Manager was responsible for a world-class multi-stall equestrian facility with a unique indoor covered riding track and outdoor exercise arena. The Tudor-style stables were handsome and the interior track walls were lined with subway tiles. Robert established the *Aknusti Stud* farm at Lake Delaware which motivated his wife, Cornelia to bid on "Man O' War" in 1917 but they were disappointed to be the under bidders. However, his greatest pride and joy would be his four sons who became the "Aknusti Team" of champion polo players in the 1930's. The estate was completed in 1913 and named *Aknusti,* the Indian word for "expensive proposition."[29]

In October 1911 on the twentieth anniversary of Lillian Gerry's death, her mother had a set of large gold candlesticks made for a church altar as a memorial to her daughter. Louisa traveled to Staatsburg-on-Hudson to stay with her cousin, Mrs. Ogden Mills, so she could personally give the beautiful candlesticks to the pastor at *Saint James Church* in Hyde Park, New York, where Lillian was laid to rest in the Gerry/Livingston Mausoleum. Lillian's books, diary and formal portrait remain in the Lake Delaware house to cherish her memory. Not long after her return to New York City from her stay at Staatsburg, Louisa and Commodore Gerry welcomed their second grandchild, Robert L. Gerry, Jr. who was born to Cornelia Harriman Gerry on December 5, 1911 in New York City. The new *Aknusti* estate would offer the perfect outdoor life style that Robert and Cornelia wanted for their growing family.

Winter fun in *Central Park* was in full swing in February 1912 when the press captured a photo of little Ebby Gerry, now 3 ½ years old, in his snow suit with bright rosy cheeks. The article was about the children of the rich who play and sled in the park, and it was noted that Ebby was there every day. The family lived in a lovely brownstone house just across the street at 816 Fifth Avenue at Sixty-Third Street where Ebby and his new baby brother had year-round exercise and fun with playmates in *Central Park.*[30] Robert and Cornelia lived here until 1926 when they moved six blocks north to 69 East Seventy-Ninth Street. They alternated family time between *Aknusti* at Lake Delaware and their New York City townhouse for the next forty-five years, where their grandchildren also shared the family love of horses and the outdoor life.

Frederick Gallatin, now aged seventy-one, watched with great pride, and not a little sadness, the negotiations for the amicable absorption of the *Gallatin National Bank* by the *Hanover National Bank.* The history of both banks was closely interwoven with the commercial and financial development of New York City. The two banks were among the oldest in the city, but the Hanover, though comparatively younger, had grown more rapidly in the past decade and was one of the largest banks in the United States. The *Gallatin National Bank* began business in 1831 under a special charter granted in 1829, but was not known as a "national" bank until 1865 when it entered the national banking system. Frederick's grandfather, Albert Gallatin was the first bank president after he served as Secretary of the Treasury under President Thomas Jefferson. In 1839 Albert's son, James Gallatin, succeeded him as president of the bank, remaining in office until 1868. Up to the time of the merger, the bank had paid dividends every year since 1832. *The Gallatin National Bank* had continuously occupied the premises at 36 Wall Street except for brief periods during the construction of three successive buildings on the site which it owned. The Gallatin Directors were added to the Hanover Board in the merger. The new *Hanover National Bank* inherited the full measure of good-will and influence created by the Gallatin Bank during its long and honorable career.[31]

The summer of 1912 marked one of the most emotional transitions in Commodore Elbridge T. Gerry's life. On June 1 the Gerry family, with sons Robert and Peter and their wives, boarded the yacht *Electra* for their last cruise to Newport, Rhode Island. Commodore Gerry wanted one last opportunity to entertain on *Electra* at the *New York Yacht Club's* station on the Wharf in Newport's beautiful Harbor. The yacht, built in 1884, was almost thirty-years old and its proud owner was now seventy-five years old, and Louisa was seventy-six. Their children had taken responsibility for their own busy lives which left no time for family cruises. It had become more convenient to drive non-stop from New York City to Lake Delaware than to cruise on *Electra* up to Kingston and then switch to a train or have a car come down from Lake Delaware to pick up family members. Many of the Gerrys' friends had died or retired from active lives and the NYYC had a new generation of members who were less interested in large luxury steam yachts and more interested in the streamlined competition yachts. Commodore Gerry had sold *Electra* to John W. Sullivan of New York City, who was contracted to dismantle the yacht and salvage most of its components. Mr. Sullivan had arranged to tow the yacht from Newport at the end of June after Commodore Gerry had finished his last round of summer entertainment on *Electra* in early June.[32] Both of the large steam launches on *Electra* were kept by Commodore Gerry at the Newport Wharf, which he used for several years to travel around the island and in Newport Harbor while vacationing at *Seaverge*.[33] The yacht was cherished by the family and to honor the role it played as a "home away from home" for the Gerry children, Robert L. Gerry had all of the teak wood planks and wall boards reused to line the walls of his new *Aknusti* library under construction at Lake Delaware. The silver serving pieces and flatware with *Electra* etched on each piece as well as other decorative items were incorporated into the furnishings of *Aknusti*. Many of the larger pieces, like the mast, were stored at the Lake Delaware Barn, which unfortunately burned down years later before the salvaged items could be used by the Gerry family. In fact, the timing was perfect for the family to accompany Robert L. Gerry up to Lake Delaware in mid-June to arrange for the salvaged items to be incorporated into the building project and for storage of other *Electra* items. Commodore and

Louisa Gerry looked after Cornelia Harriman and six-month old Robert Jr. and little Ebby who was walking and talking, all of which made both the Lake Delaware house and *Seaverge* vibrant family homes. The entire Gerry family returned to *Seaverge* just after *Electra* had been removed to New York City. There was no need for a melancholy send-off for the yacht because the grandchildren were the future for Commodore Gerry. He gathered his wife, four children, their wives, and his two grandchildren around him at *Seaverge* to celebrate the time honored *Fourth of July* with a gala dinner and fireworks, now the highlight of the Gerry summer reunions in Newport, Rhode Island.

Mrs. Robert Goelet, Harrietta, had her yacht the *Nahma* redecorated in the spring before setting off on her early summer cruise where she joined friends at ports in the Mediterranean and the Riviera. She arrived in Kiel, Germany in June for the annual European yacht week celebrations, where Mrs. Goelet entertained the Crown Princess of Germany aboard the *Nahma* before leaving for England. By late July the *Nahma* was anchored in the waters just off the Port of Southampton, England where Mrs. Goelet became ill. In early August she was so seriously ill that her son Robert Walton Goelet was cabled in America to come immediately. He sailed on the trans-Atlantic steamship *Cambria* and arrived on August 14 to join his mother on the *Nahma* at Southampton.[34] British doctors had determined that Harrietta had terminal stomach cancer. The *Nahma* immediately lifted anchor and headed to the port at Havre, France and then Harrietta was taken directly to a Paris hospital where she underwent emergency surgery. Harrietta was taken to her apartment in Paris to recuperate but after several weeks there was no improvement. Then suddenly on December 4 she took a critical turn for the worse and underwent another surgery that failed to save her life. Mrs. Robert Goelet, Harrietta, died at the age of fifty-eight in Paris on December 4, 1912 with her son Robert Walton Goelet at her side.[35] When Harrietta Goelet became ill in Southampton, she was onboard the *Nahma* just as her beloved husband Robert was ten years earlier in Naples, Italy where he died onboard. Harrietta's brother-in-law, Ogden Goelet, also died onboard his twin yacht the *Mayflower* and she knew the brothers would not have wanted it any other way. Mrs. Goelet's illness did not become known to her American friends in Europe or the United States until shortly before her death. Robert accompanied his mother's body home on a trans-Atlantic steamship for her funeral at *Saint Thomas Episcopal Church,* held on Monday, December 23, 1912. The private rite was attended by Mrs. Ogden Goelet and the Gerry and Gallatin families. Harrietta was buried beside her husband Robert and daughter Beatrice in the Goelet Mausoleum in *Woodlawn Cemetery,* in New York City. Robert continued to use the *Nahma* and loaned it to the United States Navy for use during the *First World War* from 1917-1919. Robert Walton Goelet was a 33 year-old bachelor, the last living member of his immediate family. Robert remained alone until he was forty-one, when he married Anne Marie Guestier in Paris, France.

The spring of 1913 was a busy time for Robert L. Gerry, splitting his time between New York City and Lake Delaware where a tent camp was established for several dozen workers from New York City to live while the fifty-room *Aknusti* mansion was built. Local men and boys were also hired to work for the massive project. The house was built of steel and concrete to make it as fireproof as possible. The twenty-five foot deep basement was blasted out of solid rock which took longer than expected to accomplish. The three-story house had elevators and steam heat, and fifteen rooms had fireplaces with fifteen-foot high ceilings. The mansion was 100 feet by 50 feet plus a 79-foot servant's wing with a special elevator for outside deliveries. A tennis court was laid out on a beautiful stone foundation and a small lake was excavated for the duck, pheasant and chickens raised for shooting parties and meals. The large barns accommodated wagons and farm implements, with carriages and automobiles parked in the multi-bay frame and stone garage. Robert Gerry treated his workers well and had kegs of beer shipped up for the men; he also established a commissary in the nearby town of *Andes* for the laborers to buy clothes and groceries. Roads in Delaware County were unpaved and could be impossible to pass in the rain, so Robert Gerry had most of the building materials for the project brought in on his own locomotive and freight cars from Albany and New York City.[36] Everything arrived at the *Andes* train depot, four miles from the building site. After *Aknusti* was finished in the fall of 1913, Robert had his locomotive pull stock cars to bring in his thoroughbred horses, polo ponies and other farm animals. He eventually added private baggage and passenger cars to transport his family from New York City to *Andes* throughout the year. Robert L. Gerry, now thirty-five years old, was not only on the boards of several banks, but also on the boards of several railroads and he knew the business well, which facilitated his use of the local train lines. Robert's grandfather, Robert J. Livingston, contributed to the first efforts to build a railway into Delaware County. A stock certificate dated 1872 and numbered 4 of 50 shares in the *Delhi and Middletown Rail Road Company* still hangs on the wall of the Gerrys' Lake Delaware house.

In February 1913 the local Delaware County newspapers reported on an accident at the Gerry estate, and Commodore Gerry was notified directly by his estate manager. In the days before artificial refrigeration it was a laborious effort on the Lake Delaware farm to produce and store the milk, butter and cheese produced at the Gerrys' dairy located on the estate. Prior to 1920, icehouses used in homes and grocery shops were supplied with block ice obtained from local ponds, rivers and lakes and transported by teams of horses pulling narrow bobsleds. Once at the icehouse the ice blocks would be packed tightly, several layers high and surrounded with sawdust, which acted as an insulator for weeks or even months. Numerous tools of the trade were used in harvesting the ice, particularly long-toothed saws that were pulled by hand or by a team of horses. Needless to say, ice cutting in Delaware County was carried on at the coldest times of the year. The work was physically demanding and dangerous and many unfortunate accidents occurred. One of the worst accidents involved Commodore Gerrys' horses when a team pulling an ice saw on Lake Delaware broke through the ice and all the horses drowned. The Gerrys were passionate about horses and each family member felt a personal loss from the lake accident in addition to the incidental financial loss to the estate.

While Robert L. Gerry was building his grand homestead, his thirty-three year old brother Peter G. Gerry ran for Congress in the 1912 Rhode Island election. Like his father and brother, the Gerry men claimed Rhode Island as their place of residence, even though the Commodore and Robert worked primarily in New York City. Mathilde Gerry was the daughter and granddaughter of politicians and was both eager and prepared to be the wife of a Congressman. Peter and Mathilde lived at *Seaverge* in Newport, Rhode Island during the 1912 campaign and were thrilled when the October election results sent Congressman Peter G. Gerry to Washington, D.C. in January 1913. Peter and Mathilde soon left for Washington and moved into the Townsend mansion on fashionable Twenty-Fourth Street, Mathilde's childhood home and the location of their wedding in 1910.[37] Peter and Mathilde would never again own a private home in New York, although Peter eventually inherited the historic Lake Delaware estate built by Governor Morgan Lewis and Gertrude Livingston.

Commodore and Louisa Gerry and their daughters sailed for Europe in March 1913 and made a special trip into Staffordshire, England to visit the famous potteries in the town of Stoke-on-Trent. While visiting the *Minton Pottery*, Louisa Gerry ordered a dinner service in raised gold with a chased pattern in Rose Du Barry. When they returned to London and were guests of Ambassador Whitelaw and Elizabeth Reid, Louisa's cousin, the King and Queen were also guests at *Dorchester House*, the American Embassy, and had an opportunity to discuss the Gerrys' trip to Stoke-on-Trent. The following month while on a scheduled official tour of England's six pottery factories in Staffordshire, King George V and Queen Mary, made a special stop at the *Minton Pottery* to examine the magnificent dinner service being made for Commodore and Louisa Gerry. The cost of the service was $150,000 or nearly $150 a plate and when finished was shipped directly to New York City from England.[38]

Also in England in March was Alfred Vanderbilt, Robert Gerry's life-long pal. He had divorced and was remarried in 1911 to *Bromo Seltzer* heiress, Margaret Emerson, with whom he had a baby son, Alfred, Jr. the first of their two boys. On March 22 the couple left their baby with friends in Surrey, England while they went on a ten-day business trip to America. On the second day of their return trip on the steam liner *France,* another ship, the *Companello,* made a sudden change of course in a heavy mist and cut across the bow of the *France,* which forced the steam liner to turn abruptly to avoid a collision. There were no injuries but passengers were terrified when they were thrown about their cabins and onto the decks. Alfred and Margaret landed safely at Havre, France where they boarded a ferry and crossed the channel to England, eager to reunite with their young son. The following year they had their second son, George W. Vanderbilt. A year later, the unthinkable happened. On May 1, 1915 Alfred G. Vanderbilt boarded the RMS *Lusitania* bound for Liverpool as a first class passenger. It was a business trip so he left his young family at home and traveled only with his valet, Ronald Denyer. On May 7, off the coast of Cork, Ireland, a German U-boat torpedoed the *Lusitania,* triggering a secondary explosion that sank the giant ocean liner within eighteen minutes. Alfred and his valet helped other passengers into the available lifeboats. Alfred noticed a young mother with a baby and told her he would find her a life-vest and finding none, he removed his own vest and tied it onto the young mother. Many considered his actions to be brave since he could not swim, he knew it was the last vest and there were no more life boats. Because of his fame, several people on the *Lusitania* who survived the tragedy had observed Alfred's heroic actions during the sinking. He and his valet were among 1198 passengers that died that day, and their bodies were never found. A memorial was erected on the A24 London highway to Holmwood, just south of Dorking with an inscription that read, "In memory of Alfred Gwynne Vanderbilt a gallant gentleman and a fine sportsman who perished in the *Lusitania* May 7th, 1915. This stone is erected on his favorite road by a few of his British coaching friends and admirers."[39] Another memorial to Alfred was built by the Vanderbilt family in a small park on Broadway in Newport, Rhode Island where the family shared happy summers throughout Alfred G. Vanderbilt's life. Robert and Cornelia Gerry were shocked and saddened at the loss of their dear friend, especially since both couples were now the parents of two young boys, which had brought their families closer together in recent years.

Mrs. Ogden Goelet, Mary, was also in England at the time of the *Lusitania* tragedy and was heartbroken at the loss of a dear friend and relative (her sister Grace married Cornelius Vanderbilt, Jr. and they were Alfred's aunts). This difficult time for Mary Goelet was eased by the news that her daughter, May, the Duchess of Roxburghe, was pregnant with her first child after ten years of marriage.[40] Mrs. Ogden Goelet remained in England through the New Year and did not open *Ochre Court* in Newport, Rhode Island where her summer galas were sorely missed. Commodore and Louisa Gerry returned from England to Newport at the end of June to open *Seaverge* in time for the *Fourth of July* celebration. Congressman Peter Gerry and his wife Mathilde had already arrived in Bar Harbor, Maine for the season where they were a leading couple in that summer colony. Angelica Gerry joined the women's *Four In Hand* for their annual run between New York City and Belmont Park on Long Island before joining the family at *Seaverge*. Robert and Cornelia Gerry spent most of the summer at the Lake Delaware estate where the work on *Aknusti* was progressing quickly and the *Lake Delaware Boys Camp* was opened in its new and permanent camp site to everyone's satisfaction. Particularly happy were the "fresh air children."

In August Commodore Gerry and his wife and daughters traveled by train from New York City to join Robert and Cornelia at Lake Delaware. This was the first year that they did not cruise up the Hudson on *Electra,* but all was well since Robert had sent his private luxury Pullman car to take his parents and sisters on a comfortable train ride. The tracks followed the banks of the Hudson River up to *Kingston* and on to *Andes* without a stop. The Gerry women were eager to join local efforts in Andes, Bovina and Delhi, the three towns that sat a few miles apart along the outer edge of the Lake Delaware estate and where they did their mission work.

The Gerrys' automobile trips in the area convinced them that residents in this part of New York State were not benefiting from adequate highway improvements. Louisa met with several supervisors of the local towns to discuss the state of the roads in the county that connected the three towns and provided access to Lake Delaware. The supervisors described how the towns could not afford the expense since the farmers had a difficult season and taxes were already high. Without further comment and with no solicitation, Mrs. Gerry sent a check for $5,000 to the supervisors of Andes, Bovina and Delhi to pay for 3.57 miles of paved highway through each of the three towns. Louisa Gerry gained the gratitude of the taxpayers in the local townships and encouraged a highway building boom in Delaware County.[41]

Angelica Gerry began a tradition in the local communities that she sponsored for the rest of her life and her efforts are remembered to this day. She entered many of the promising local children in special schools and paid their tuition so they and their community would have a better future. In September 1913, William and Harold, sons of Mr. and Mrs. Frank Johnson, began their studies at a trade school near New York City through the kind support of Angelica Gerry who paid their full tuition to complete the program. Angelica met the boys through the local Episcopal Church, *Saint Johns* in Delhi, where Harold was a member of the children's choir. The local paper noted that Angelica had not only provided for pleasure and spiritual uplift in the local communities but in many cases she helped alleviate suffering and want.[42] Mabel Gerry joined in the mission work with an interest in teaching catechism to the children and leading Bible study groups with the adults at the local Episcopal churches. The Gerry family did not believe in idle time and employed the courage of their convictions in every aspect of their lives. When the family gathered at Lake Delaware it was truly the "family homestead" where they relaxed, dressed down, and were close to nature. The farm was clearly unlike *Seaverge* in Newport which was always a holiday home where socializing with friends, yachting and restoring one's health were the objectives. More of the Gerry family time began to shift from *Seaverge* to Lake Delaware with the *Aknusti* home completed at the end of the year and yachting no longer a draw for an entire summer season in Newport. Robert and Cornelia Gerry spent the winter months furnishing *Aknusti* with plans to spend their first summer in the new mansion in 1914. *Seaverge* became more useful as an ideal summer location for Congressman Peter Gerry and his wife Mathilde to host dinners and lunches for their Newport and surrounding Rhode Island constituents.

The papers on both sides of the Atlantic announced on September 9, 1913 the birth of a healthy son and heir to the Duke and Duchess of Roxburghe at *Chesterfield House* on Curzon Street in Mayfair, London. Mrs. Ogden Goelet had not been so happy since before her late husband's death fifteen years before. The Duke received congratulations from King George V and Queen Mary who were godparents at the baby's christening. The boy was named George Victor Innes-Kerr and would be called the *Marquis of Bowmont* until he succeeded his father as the Ninth Duke. Bells rang throughout the town of Kelso in Roxburghshire, the location of *Floors Castle,* the family home. Although this was May Goelet's only child, she and the Duke would have five grandchildren who still live at *Floors Castle*. As a dear friend of Bertie, King Edward VII, for over thirty years before his death, Mrs. Ogden Goelet watched his son King George V grow to adulthood in the same social circle as her daughter May Goelet, and knew Queen Mary when she was betrothed to George. Now, as a close friend of May Goelet, the Duchess of Roxburghe, the King was often a guest at *Floors Castle* where he had said of the Duke's American wife, "she was one of the best-read women in English society."[43]

Eighteen months after the death of Harrietta Goelet in Paris, the *United States Supreme Court* handed down a decision on February 24, 1914 regarding the yacht *Nahma,* which was still owned by her son Robert Walton Goelet. There were actually two cases that had been initiated by the Internal Revenue Service, one in 1909 and the second in 1910. The issue was whether the United States had the right to tax the property of an American citizen, Harrietta Goelet, who lived abroad in Paris on a permanent basis during the taxable year, and, whether the property tax on an American registered yacht, the *Nahma,* cruising in foreign waters the entire taxable year, was constitutional. The two cases were heard by the Court as one and the opinion stated that if the first question, the right to tax Harrietta Goelet based on citizenship, was answered in the negative, then the second question was moot. Indeed, the Court decided that the citizenship of Harrietta was determined by her permanent domicile in Paris where she owned her apartment and where she lived when not on her yacht cruising in foreign waters. Therefore, Harrietta could not be taxed and it followed that her property could also not be taxed. The posthumous decision not only applied to past taxes on the *Nahma,* but also to all American citizens living abroad who by their actions, permanently living abroad, had in effect renounced their American citizenship and therefore could not be taxed by the United States on any of their foreign property.[44]

Between January and March of 1914 Robert Wilson Goelet's marriage to the Philadelphia belle, Elsie Whelan, unraveled. Elsie was a favorite of Mrs. Ogden Goelet and the marital troubles created a rift of silence between Robert and his mother. In late January the papers on both sides of the Atlantic disclosed the troubles in the Goelet marriage. There had been rumors among the Goelets' closest friends since August 1913 but to society in general they appeared to be happy. Elsie Whelan Goelet filed for divorce in Newport, Rhode Island on January 21, 1914 on grounds of extreme cruelty. The details of her suit were supported by the testimony of the couple's friends who were present when Robert verbally abused Elsie and he would not eat at the same table with her even when she had their friends for dinner. The allegations made reference to other women in Robert's life, and unfortunately, he gave no defense against any of the charges. In March the Judge granted the divorce that ended their ten-year marriage.[45] Elsie Whelan moved out of the Fifth Avenue mansion and took her two sons, 7 year old Ogden II and 3 year old Peter III, with her to stay with her brother. The decree gave" full custody" of the children to Elsie until each boy reached the age of ten, when the decree changed to "joint custody" shared with their father. Robert

Wilson Goelet moved to his *Glenmere* estate in Orange County, New York near his kennels in Chester. Ten months later, on December 19 Elsie Whelan married sculptor Henry Clews, Jr.at her townhouse at Washington Square North. The news of the wedding came as a great surprise to society. Elsie was devoted to art and music and while in Newport the previous two summers she had been tutored by Henry Clews, Jr in his studio to paint beach and marine scenes.[46] A year after the wedding they moved with Elsie's two young boys to a small town in France and Henry renamed his wife "Marie." She was only known as Elsie in America and to this day is remembered only as Marie Clews in France. They bought an abandoned fourteenth century castle that overlooked the Bay of Cannes, the *Chateau de la Napoule,* and restored it to its former glory, particularly the magnificent gardens which today are considered among the most beautiful in France. In 1951 Marie Elsie Clews founded *the La Napoule Art Foundation* and gave the castle to the foundation to serve as a cultural center in honor of her husband who died there on July 28, 1937. The castle is listed as a *Historic Landmark* on the Register of France.[47]

Robert and Elsie's son Peter Goelet III, named after the eighteenth century family patriarch, moved back to the United States from *Chateau de la Napoule* France as an adult, married, and lived a quiet life in Chester, New York, near his father's kennels. He established his own radio station WGNY in 1930 on a hill located on his father's *Glenmere* estate, although by the 1960's the station was relocated to Newburgh. In 1938 *Vassar College* in nearby Poughkeepsie, New York, arranged with Peter Goelet III to broadcast their first-ever college radio show. It ran on Tuesdays and Thursdays between 12:45 and 1:00 pm from a studio in Skinner Hall. The mission was to share the educational facilities of the college with the surrounding counties and to strengthen the relations with local communities.[48] Peter Goelet III had become a community leader himself and was a candidate for the New York state assembly from the second district in Orange County in 1940, but was unsuccessful. By the 1950's he had a studio in New York City near the Armory on Broadway. Peter never joined the "society life" in New York City and, unlike his father Robert Wilson Goelet who married three times, Peter remained happily married to his wife, Margaret Wheelock Wilson, a nurse, with whom he had no children. Peter Goelet III died in 1986 at the age of seventy-four.[49]

Robert and Elsie Goelet's son Ogden II would himself marry five times. With his third wife, Mimi Brown Cohane, a painter and photographer who lived in Paris, he had a son and namesake, Ogden III. He is a scholar whose quiet academic life, coupled with the quiet life of his Uncle Peter Goelet III in Chester, have together redeemed the Robert Wilson Goelet line of "often married men." Ogden Goelet III, a graduate of Phillips Exeter Academy and Harvard College, received a Ph.D. degree in Egyptian history from *Columbia University*. He served as a sergeant in the Marine Corps and in 1987 Ogden married Nancy Goeschel, a landmark preservation specialist in New York City. She graduated from Smith College and received a master's degree from the Institute of Fine Arts at *New York University*. Professor Ogden Goelet, a published author, teaches Egyptian language and culture at both *New York University*, co-founded by Albert Gallatin, and at *Columbia University*, the alma mater of both Elbridge T. Gerry and Robert Goelet.[50] The fabric of historic family ties in New York City is tightly woven.

On March 7, 1914 Commodore Gerry sold a large plot of land with a 100 foot frontage on East Forty-Fourth Street, and a 75 foot frontage on Forty-Fifth-Street that were connected by a 75 foot frontage on Lexington Avenue. The Bing & Bing Inc., two brothers who developed stately apartment buildings in the Art Deco style, had purchased the property. They had no immediate intentions to build and renewed the current leases for the next year.[51] A week after the real estate deal, a great northeastern storm hit Newport, Rhode Island on March 2, 1914 that caused substantial damage to the town and particularly to summer villas along the south eastern rim of the island. A two-hundred foot length of the stone seawall at *Bailey's Beach* was torn apart by tremendous waves and the wind and water tore off the doors and platforms of the bath house. The nearby estate of Henry Clews, Jr. was badly damaged, especially the front part where the studio was located and where Elsie Goelet had been tutored. Everything in the studio was lost. Seas washed up over the *Cliff Walk* in low areas tearing boards off of tea houses. The high cliffs in front of *Seaverge*, the Gerry estate, were damaged by substantial erosion; however the house was left unharmed. A large and ancient tree blew down on the lawn of Vincent Astor's estate and the large chimney of Mrs. Morgan's villa was blown over at the same time. A fifty-foot grapery greenhouse of Mr. Maher was blown down and completely destroyed.[52] Many years after *Seaverge* had been sold out of the Gerry family and converted into apartment units, it was so badly damaged by a savage northeastern storm that it had to be demolished in the late 1950's.

Within three weeks of the great storm Robert and Cornelia Gerry welcomed twin boys born on April 8, 1914. The boys were named after Cornelia's father, Edward Henry Harriman, one named Edward and the other Henry.[53] They joined their big brothers, Ebby II, now 6 years old and Robert Jr., now 4 years old. Cornelia gave birth at their home on Fifth Avenue between Sixty-Fourth and Sixty Fifth Streets, not far from Commodore and Louisa Gerry's home at Sixty-First and Fifth

Avenue. Angelica, now 43 years old, lived just off Fifth Avenue at Sixty-Second Street so visits among the three Gerry family homes were frequent and welcome.

While Commodore and Louisa Gerry and their daughters were on their annual visit to London and Paris in June, there were anxious discussions about the tensions among the imperialistic countries of Europe. To their great dismay, Archduke Franz Ferdinand of Austria was assassinated on June 28 putting an end to the "American season" in Europe. On July 16 Commodore Gerry and his family arrived in New York City on the ocean liner *Imperator* after an anxious crossing caused by a great deal of dense fog that engulfed the ocean liner for most of the voyage. This was the first year that the Commodore and Louisa traveled with a private family physician and two tubes of oxygen; their age had begun to affect their health. In deference to the cold, Commodore Gerry replaced his trademark seal skin cap for a straw hat that fully covered his head. It was wise to return to American soil because the long-feared conflict began on July 28, 1914 with the Austro-Hungarian invasion of Serbia followed by the German invasion of Belgium, Luxembourg and France, which triggered a Russian attack against Germany.[54] The *Great War* had begun and when the Gerrys arrived at *Seaverge* they found a somber summer colony with many galas and annual events canceled. The energy of the social set was now focused on the war effort with proceeds of bazaars donated to local families whose men were sent to war. Most of the chefs, chauffeurs and servants of the Newport villas were European citizens and departed immediately for New York City to report to their consuls, many of them seeking passage back to their homes in England, France and Germany.[55]

Commodore Elbridge T. Gerry, like his wife and daughters, practiced his faith as part of his daily life. He attended the annual conferences of the Episcopal Church, spoke at the funerals of both Protestant and Catholic bishops, and quietly assisted with drafts of religious works, such as the revision of Canons of the Church. One of his closest friends in the Episcopal Church with whom he had worked and corresponded for many years was Bishop Charles C. Grafton who had just died the year before in 1913. One of the greatest honors bestowed upon Commodore Gerry was by Bishop Charles C. Grafton in 1910 when he awarded the Commodore the *Honorary Degree of Doctor of Divinity* from the *Nashotah House Seminary* of the Episcopal Church in Wisconsin. Both men had spent their lives in service of the Episcopal Church, one as a clergyman and one as a layman, and from this shared commitment grew a deep and respectful friendship and mutual admiration. When the Bishop died Commodore Gerry wrote a letter to the Archdiocese of Fond du Lac, Wisconsin in August 1913 concerning the burial of the beloved Bishop in a local cemetery.

> To the Bishop and Chapter of the Cathedral Church of St. Paul, Fond du Lac, Wisconsin:
>
> I desire to present to the Cathedral, a Memorial Sarcophagus Tomb to receive and preserve the mortal remains of our beloved friend and late Bishop, the Right Reverend Charles Chapman Grafton, with the chief and express object of thereby forcibly and unmistakably emphasizing his splendid legacy to our Whole Church in his dying charge to your council in regard to the Blessed Sacrament of the Altar, that to believe in His Presence is a test of true faith.[56]
>
> Yours in the Catholic Faith,
> Commodore Elbridge T. Gerry

The new Bishop was both honored and delighted to accept Commodore Gerry's gift and immediately set to work to have an arch cut between the transept chapel and a small chapel that was formerly an organ chamber, so that the new tomb could be set under the new arch. One year later in September 1914 the memorial sarcophagus was delivered to Wisconsin. It was made of handsome red Numidian marble with a white marble base and carved Carrara marble top. On one end of the sarcophagus was the seal of the Diocese of Fond du Lac in brass, and on the reverse end the seal of the Confraternity of the Blessed Sacrament of which Bishop Grafton had been the Superior in the years up to his death. A recumbent figure of the late Bishop, which had been carved in Italy, was affixed to the top of the tomb. Commodore and Louisa Gerry traveled by train to Wisconsin for the September 3, 1914 ceremony. The service of re-entombment began with removal of the casket from the local cemetery and then it was opened at the Cathedral which revealed that only a glass plate had sealed the remains. To the surprise of everyone, the remains were found intact. The Bishop's features and hands were as natural as on the day he died. The mitre was somewhat discolored and the chalice which he grasped in his hand was tarnished, but the body itself showed no indications of decay. The open casket went in procession with a full choir and the diocesan clergy who were joined by several priests from across the country. A plaque had been attached to a wall near the new tomb which Commodore Gerry had made to describe the design of the handsome sarcophagus:

> The replica represents him as asleep in Jesus after celebrating his last Mass, indicated by his chasuble, and he blessed his people with the crozier in hand, and there is a simple prayer incised in the marble at the base which everyone utters who reads it:
>
> *Eternal rest grant unto him, O Lord, and let perpetual light shine upon him!*[57]

B. Talbot Rogers, a lay theologian who took an active part in all parochial affairs and ministered regularly in the Fond du Lac Cathedral from 1890 to 1914, worked with Commodore Gerry for over a year to collect and edit the works of Bishop Grafton. When the massive eight volume set was published in 1914, the editor, B. Talbot Rogers, honored Commodore Gerry with the following words:

> Let us here acknowledge the debt of sincere gratitude that we owe the Honorable Elbridge T. Gerry, LL.D., whose generous devotion has made this work possible. It is eminently fitting that his name should be associated with this enterprise. As a layman he stood before the world as an uncompromising Catholic, and has crystallized his faith in permanent foundations, and a life of service for the welfare of others, especially in arousing the American Conscience as to its duty toward children. It was he who made possible the manifestation of Catholic worship throughout the entire diocese, and laid enduring foundations that give promise of perpetuating the faith and service of Bishop Grafton for many generations.[58]

The mission work of the Gerry family was based on the Rule of Saint Benedict, "to work, study and pray." The Episcopal Church that the family attended was in the Anglican tradition that followed the *Oxford Movement* where Holy Scripture was the rule of faith but the church also reserved a place for Reason and Tradition in its theological discourse. The Episcopal Church's theology was "catholic" which meant "universal" and suited Commodore Gerry's very analytical and reflective mind even while it nurtured his deeply caring heart and soul. He was a centered and moral man who was driven by his convictions in his work, in his social life, and most important in his family life where his adult children were morally principled, happy and fulfilled.

During the Gerrys' fall stay at Lake Delaware, Bishop Nelson came to the nearby town of Bovina to bestow the sacrament of confirmation on seventeen new church members in a temporary chapel owned by Mr. William Mason which sat on property next to his house. The new congregation was initiated by Mabel and Angelica Gerry to better serve the local families in Bovina and Andes, and the surrounding farm communities that found the trek on dirt roads all the way to Delhi too difficult in most weather. The Gerry sisters had sought the permission of the Bishop six months earlier to establish a small parish but it also required the consent of the Pastor of Delhi's *Saint John's Church* within whose extensive parish boundaries the "new little parish" was located. Angelica and Mabel named the parish *Saint James Church* after the Hyde Park church where the Gerry and Livingston family mausoleum was located, and where Lillian Gerry was interred beside her grandfather, Robert James Livingston. General Morgan Lewis and his wife Gertrude were also buried in the *Saint James Cemetery* at Hyde Park.[59]

Shortly after the confirmation in Bovina Angelica Gerry visited the *Delhi High School* to learn more about the young people and their hopes and aspirations with the intent to identify students she might educate. The students were excited to meet her, having heard stories of her kind support of promising children in need. Angelica had visited the nearby Bloomfield School a few weeks earlier where she reached out to nine year old Iona Kelly, and with her parents' grateful permission, placed the young girl in *St. Christina's Episcopal Vocational School for Girls* in Saratoga, New York, an outstanding boarding school. Without Angelica Gerry's full financial support the Kellys could never have educated their bright and promising daughter in a girls boarding school.[60]

With the war in Europe drawing many of the young men away from family and work, it was not surprising that many people experienced difficult times in rural communities like Delaware County. Property theft was increasing and neighbors watched out for one another. However, the *Aknusti* and Lake Delaware estate were in a remote area with only the estate managers to oversee several main buildings scattered across hundreds of acres. Despite the generosity of the Gerry family to the area, it was widely known that a huge new mansion had been built at Lake Delaware and so the inevitable happened. On the night of December 14, 1914 both the *Lake House* and the *Aknusti* mansions were robbed. Commodore Gerry and his son Robert came up from New York to identify what was stolen.[61] No one was ever caught. Just like the bank robbery and murder in nearby *Andes* a few years before, the culprits vanished into the byways of the dark hills of Delaware County.

The Gerry family went on to celebrate the New Year of 1915 in New York City surrounded by family, completely content to enjoy their four boisterous grandsons. The continuing war kept *Gilded Gotham* society from venturing over to Europe, and so Commodore and Louisa Gerry opened *Seaverge* at Newport much earlier than usual. Angelica and Mabel joined the war effort in Newport to raise money for families whose men had gone to Europe to serve in the military. The festive bazaars that sold homemade food, crafts, and clothing were once again a big success and raised a substantial amount of money. It was also important to raise the morale of the military men as part of the war effort in Newport. Many of the summer socials for young people that were traditionally held at the *Newport Casino* were moved to the large barracks at the *Newport Naval Training Station* where the young ladies roller-skated with the young navy boys during the day and had informal dances in the evening. After the war the next generation embraced the informal dress and activities of the war effort and universally abandoned the excesses of *Gilded Gotham* for a new era of progressive simplicity.

Peter Gerry had lost his 1915 re-election bid for Congress, but undeterred, he used the loss as an opportunity to stand as a candidate for the 1916 United States Senate race in Rhode Island. Peter and Mathilde spent most of 1915 living at *Seaverge* to run a vigorous campaign among their local state constituency. Peter Gerry was a Democrat with an uphill battle in a very Republican state. He ran against his opponent's attitude toward labor legislation which Peter promoted on behalf of children and work-place safety; his position sat well with workingmen and women in Rhode Island.[62] His cousin Ogden Livingston Mills, a young Senator in New York State, was a staunch Republican which made for animated debates between the cousins when they shared family get-togethers at Staatsburg, the Mills estate on the Hudson River.

Robert and Peter Gerry reflected their father in two distinct ways. Although active and very successful in the business world of railroads, banks, and real estate, Robert L. Gerry was first and foremost a father. He had four children like his father, Commodore Gerry, and savored the time spent with them at summer homes and on travel adventures. On the other hand, Peter G. Gerry never had children. Yet, like his father, he was a lawyer and on the Board of the NYSPCC and was active in civic and political affairs. Indeed, also like his father before him, Peter was admitted to the Bar of the *United States Supreme Court* in 1909 and was most likely sponsored by his father, Commodore Gerry. After the successful 1916 Rhode Island race, Senator Peter G. Gerry and his wife Mathilde bought their own home in Warwick Neck, Rhode Island to be closer to the state Capitol in Providence, which also gave them access to the train depot for frequent trips to and from their home in Washington, D.C.

With four grandchildren ages seven, four and the twins, one and a half years old, activity at the two big houses, *Aknusti* and the *Lake House* at the Lake Delaware estate, grew to the point that the Gerrys decided to re-think the roads that traversed the estate. The automobiles of visitors and family, along with the trucks of delivery men, had substantially increased the traffic at the one main entrance near the town of *Andes*. So in the fall of 1915 Louisa Gerry presented a proposal to the Bovina Town Board for approval to close one road and extend another, which they gladly approved. The old entrance road that originally ran from the east end of the Lake along the northern shore and crossed just at the foot of the formal entry steps to the big house was closed permanently. A beautiful rolling lawn replaced it so that the family and guests would step down from the front veranda and wander all the way down to the shore of Lake Delaware with access to the boat house and wood-plank pier. The main drive that connected the farm buildings and the manager's house was widened and extended to run westward in a loop out to the highway to create a new main entrance to the *Lake House.* The same private road also ran eastward away from and past the *Lake House* and up the hill as it ran along the south side of the Lake and ended as a small lane near *Aknusti* at the top of the hill. Louisa Gerrys clever new road design provided an exclusive entrance on the eastern side of the Lake near the town of *Andes* for arrivals at *Aknusti,* and also provided an exclusive entrance on the western side of the Lake near the town of *Bovina* for arrivals at the *Lake House.*[63] The unpaved gravel roads remain in place today which retains the rustic natural beauty of the entire Lake Delaware estate. The two main houses are connected by a long, narrow, secluded road. Today if you sit on the covered veranda of either the *Lake House* or *Aknusti* you will enjoy a beautiful view of *Aknusti* on the hilltop above or the *Lake House* below on the shore of Lake Delaware.

The roadwork at Lake Delaware in the spring and summer of 1916 kept Commodore and Louisa Gerry and daughter Mabel at Newport for an extended summer stay. This extra time also gave Angelica Gerry an opportunity to spread her wings and take a road trip like she had done many times while in Europe but never in the United States. She was forty-five and owned her own automobile. With her maid and her chauffeur Angelica set off in June for a tour from the White Mountains on the border of Vermont to Bretton Woods in New Hampshire and south to the Berkshire Mountains in Massachusetts and Connecticut. A reporter who wrote about society people at exclusive resorts for the press recognized Angelica Gerry the day before she left the beautiful *Mount Pleasant Hotel* at Bretton Woods, New Hampshire. He wrote in his column, "Angelica passed the rainy Sunday in rigid seclusion, reading a book appropriately called *Exile,* and when she left the hotel the next morning he heard her heave a sigh that spoke volumes."[64] He further suggested that the hotel was full of honeymoon couples and that Angelica clearly felt out of place. On the other hand, Angelica may have thoroughly enjoyed the beautiful mountain hotel, a welcome retreat from city routines where she found time for leisure reading and quiet solitude. Her "great sigh," it might be suggested, was one of deep contentment as she headed off to yet another magnificent mountain resort in Massachusetts. As to the book, there was a book published in 1906 entitled *Hearts in Exile* which had as its main character a woman named Hope. It was set in Russia, one of the European countries in the midst of war just as Angelica read the book. The plot was about the isolation, death, and hope of soldiers in wartime as experienced by the women of Russia. Angelica was a woman of action and empathy, not a woman filled with self-pity or romantic notions of love. It was exactly the kind of insightful book that Angelica Gerry read to better understand the great *World War* raging in Europe in the countries she had explored and loved over so many years of travel with the Gerry family. Angelica knew from experience not to believe everything printed in the papers. The article was but a trifle of speculation and not a rumor in need of a response.

Indeed, when Angelica returned from her private exploration of the mountains of the northeastern United States, she immediately went to Lake Delaware to join a local war effort to help dependent children from all parts of the world. Angelica was the Delaware County representative on the Campaign Committee to raise money for the *Susan Fenimore Cooper Foundation* headquartered in Cooperstown, New York. The leading citizens of Cooperstown and representatives of surrounding counties were engaged in a growing endeavor to increase the capacity and therefore the beneficent work of the orphanage and vocational institution which was begun at Cooperstown by Miss Susan Fenimore Cooper (1813-1894) the daughter of naturalist and novelist, James Fenimore Cooper. During the later years of her father's life Susan became his secretary and began her own career as an author when she published her nature diary, *Rural Hours,* in 1850. She also wrote a novel, children's stories, short stories and published articles. In 1873 she founded an orphanage with five children in her home and in 1883 she garnered enough funds to construct a suitable building for the orphanage. By 1900, the orphanage housed ninety boys and girls who were fed, clothed and given a basic education. The successful and well-respected *Cooperstown Orphanage* survived Susan Fenimore Cooper's death in 1894 at the age of eighty-one.[65] In 1915 the orphanage combined with the *Saint Christina Episcopal Vocational School* of Saratoga and was re-named the *Susan Fenimore Cooper Foundation.* Angelica Gerry's Campaign Committee on behalf of the *Foundation* had set the fund raising goal at $250,000 to help restore the dilapidated buildings and equipment, despite which the orphanage school had been classed among the three best vocational schools in New York State. The great fundraiser that she was, Angelica sought her family's help and on August 20, 1916, Commodore and Louisa Gerry opened their mansion in New York City for a fund-raising meeting among "society's" wealthy citizens. After the fund-raising meeting hosted by Angelica, everyone gathered in the Gerrys' great dining room for a gourmet dinner to celebrate the twenty-five thousand dollars that was pledged in the course of the evening. There were other open-houses arranged by Angelica's committee in New York City from which there were sufficient pledges to assure the success of the $250,000 fund-raising campaign on behalf of the *Susan Fenimore Cooper Foundation* and the orphan school children.[66]

There had been an earlier fundraiser at the Gerry mansion in 1912 that Mabel Gerry had hosted, but she had designed a decidedly more upscale event specifically for society women. She hosted a bazaar and auction of rare and costly articles that included jewels worth thousands of dollars. Wealthy women donated items from their personal collections which were beautifully arranged on tables throughout the Library and Art Gallery of the mansion. The fundraiser was to benefit the Anglican *Sisters of Saint Mary* who ran a farm in Peekskill, New York. There were also religious articles made by the sisters on display for sale in the mansion's Reception rooms. One of the most admired items was a decorative panel entitled *Angels in Adoration.*[67] One of the most popular tables was filled with dolls of every kind. The highlight of the collection was a beautifully dressed bride doll that was placed on a pedestal near the grand staircase in the mansions great hall. She came with an adult-size trunk filled with accessories and outfits for the opera and for riding, indeed for every occasion in the life of a fashionable lady. She had an auction price of $300. There was also a "competition" table where guests paid $2 to vote on the best miniature replicas of city establishments like the Post Office building and the J P Morgan building among others; the Post Office was the blue ribbon winner. One special table offered plump fresh fruit from Commodore Gerry's Newport green-houses that included melons for $25 and Jerusalem cherries for $5 a quart. Honey and fresh eggs from the *Sisters of Saint Mary* farm were also on sale. The auction bazaar was an all-day affair with hundreds of society people passing in and out of the Gerry mansion. For an entertainment break, the mansion's dining room was converted to a theatre where a cinematograph flashed scenes of travel, fantasy, and melodrama on a large screen. The price of admission was $1 and a hefty $400 was collected. To assist Mabel with the flow of people was her best friend, Gertrude, Mrs. Harry Payne Whitney. Also managing the household logistics were Angelica Gerry, Mrs. Horace Gallatin, Mrs. Peter Gerry, Mrs. Robert Gerry, and her sister Miss Carol Harriman. The affair ran from 11 a.m. to 5 p.m. when the exhausted Mabel Gerry finally closed the doors of the Gerry mansion. She had successfully collected over $10,000 for the *Sisters of Saint Mary.*[68]

Commodore Gerry could not have been prouder in November 1916 when his younger son, Peter Gerry, was elected the Democratic Senator from Rhode Island. The Senator's wife, Mathilde Townsend Gerry, a dog lover, had become the President of the Washington, D.C. branch of the *Animal Rescue League* similar to Henry Bergh's Society, the SPCA. Together, they were the bright and rising couple of Providence, Rhode Island, where they had recently hosted the Vice President of the United States in their Warwick Neck home.

The same month however, Commodore Gerry learned of the death of a very old and dear friend, Captain Howard Patterson, the founder of the *New York Navigation School* where the Commodore had earned his Master's Certificate as a yachtsman. Captain Patterson was known as the "father of the Naval Reserve Movement" and was the author of *The Illustrated Nautical Encyclopedia.* He was just sixty-one when he died and was survived by his wife, a daughter and a son.[69] Commodore Gerry had been Captain Patterson's student as well as his mentor and co-author. His death was mourned by all yachtsmen of the Gilded Age.

Commodore Gerry was seventy-eight years old in March 1917 when news reached him of the death of his beloved sister Almy, the wife of Frederick Gallatin. She was seventy years old and died unexpectedly at the *St. Regis Hotel* in New York City. Her personal estate of over seven million dollars was distributed among her husband and their six children. Almy was also generous to her household staff and left $500 a year to the widow of her former coachman; $600 to her children's nurse; $250 to her grandchildren's nurse; and $1,500 to her secretary and clerk.[70] After Almy's death, her husband Frederic Gallatin never returned to their summer home, *Breezy Lawn* at East Hampton, Long Island. He sold the property two years later and lived at their Fifth Avenue home near his brother-in-law Commodore Gerry. The next generation of both families lived in the same neighborhood which provided Frederic Gallatin with the loving company of many playful grandchildren to fill his later years with great joy.

In October 1917 the Convention of the *American Humane Association* was held at Providence, Rhode Island. In the keynote speech, which reviewed the attitudes and efforts of the humane movement over the last fifty-years, the speaker highlighted how even men and women who prided themselves on their broad vision had time and again clashed with Commodore Gerry in his enforcement of the law that prevented the appearance of young children on the stage. Many times he was forced to endure vicious attacks in the columns of leading newspapers for his activities in cases which ran the whole gamut of crimes against children. The speaker reassured his audience that Commodore Gerry, who was in fact seated among them, had happily lived to see his theories accepted as fundamentally correct. Indeed, it was through his personal efforts that the right of a State to interfere between parent and child was well defined in model New York legislation against child cruelty. The speaker then recalled a little known anecdote that highlighted the quiet humanity of Commodore Gerry. Years ago in 1887 a child prodigy named Josef Hofmann, at the age of eleven, was on an American concert tour. He was barred from the New York stage by the *Gerry Society* because the boy was clearly in frail health and within a year the child returned to his home in

Poland and did not perform again until age eighteen. Nonetheless, without display or public knowledge, this gifted young boy was educated by the best masters of Europe in private lessons paid for by Commodore Elbridge T. Gerry.[71] He was also sponsored by Alfred Corning Clark to study science and mathematics. When Josef returned to America in manhood he had become both a world-famous pianist and an inventor with seventy patents to his name. After he married and had four children he became a citizen of the United States. He was acclaimed for his rare ability to play music from memory. In a 1912-1913 marathon performance he gave 21 consecutive concerts in St. Petersburg, Russia without repeating a single piece, playing 255 different works from memory. His wife wrote in her journal while on a 1909 tour that Josef had raised his eyebrows when he saw Brahms' Handel Variations on his program—a piece he had not played or even looked at for two and a half years. He sat down and played the Brahms work at the concert without hesitation and without a mistake. Although a poor sight reader, he was said to possess the ability of Franz Liszt to hear a composition once and play it back correctly without seeing the printed notes. His wife recalled that one time her husband heard a pianist play Franz Liszt's *Lorelei*, a piece Hofmann had neither heard nor seen before, and once again he played the piece perfectly as an encore at his own concert later the same day. During his lifetime Josef Hofmann performed world-wide in concert, composed over one hundred pieces of music, and taught piano throughout his life. He wrote the popular instruction book *Piano Playing with Piano Questions Answered* and in 1924 he was appointed the first head of the piano department at the *Curtis Institute of Music* in Philadelphia. He became the *Institute's* director in 1927 and remained so until 1938. Long after Josef Hofmann's death in 1957 his place in classical music was recognized in 1994 by the American Council for Polish Culture and the University of South Carolina who co-sponsored the annual *Josef Hofmann Piano Competition* in his honor.[72]

The *Society for the Prevention of Cruelty to Children* added another family member to the organization, W. Averell Harriman, the son of E. H. Harriman. He joined the Board of Directors where his sister, Mrs. Robert Gerry was on the Auxiliary Committee, Senator Peter Gerry was on the Executive Committee and Commodore Gerry was the Society Counsel. William Averell Harriman, known as Averell, was seven years younger than his sister, Cornelia Harriman Gerry, and only twenty-six when he joined the *New York Society for the Prevention of Cruelty to Children.* At the age of ten young Averell joined his family and twenty-five leading artists, naturalists, and scientists on the summer 1899 *Harriman Alaska Expedition* to survey the coasts of Alaska and Russia. Averell attended Groton School in Massachusetts before going on to Yale where he became the college's youngest crew coach. He graduated in 1913 and due to his father's death in 1909 was one of the wealthiest men in America. In 1915 he became the Director of the Illinois Pacific and the Illinois Central Railroads. In 1922 at the age of 31 he used his family wealth to establish *W.A. Harriman and Company,* a banking business. In 1927 his brother Roland joined the business and the name was changed to Harriman Brothers and Company, and then in 1931, they merged with Brown Brothers and Company to create the highly successful banking firm of today, *Brown Brothers Harriman and Company.*[73]

Following the death of August Belmont Jr. in 1924, Averell Harriman and two partners purchased much of Belmont's thoroughbred breeding stock and raced under the name of *Arden Farms,* the Harriman estate in Orange County, New York. Robert and Cornelia Gerry were close to her brother Averell through a shared passion for horses and breeding thoroughbreds, plus Robert and Averell were both involved in the railroad business. In 1936, to increase ridership on the Union Pacific line, Averell Harriman created a "new destination" out west, the famous *Sun Valley Ski Resort* in Idaho. It was modeled after *St. Moritz* in Switzerland and *Lake Placid,* New York where the 1932 Winter Olympics were held. The world's first chair-lifts were installed to replace the primitive rope tow to take skiers to the mountain tops. The resort soon became world famous when Ernst Hemingway wrote For *Whom the Bell Tolls* in suite 206 of the *Sun Valley Ski Lodge* in 1939. Averell Harriman invited Hemingway and other celebrities, primarily from Hollywood, to help promote the resort. Hemingway was a part-time resident over the next twenty years, eventually relocating to Ketchum, the nearest town where he died and was buried.[74]

William Averell Harriman began his political career as a Democrat in 1934 when he was appointed the Administrator of the *National Recovery Administration* with the endorsement of his brother-in-law Senator Peter Gerry. Although he was fourteen years younger than Senator Peter Gerry, they had a close political and personal relationship in Washington and New York, where they also shared an interest in the horses at the Harriman *Arden Farm* stables and the Gerry *Aknusti* stables of his sister Cornelia and her husband Robert Gerry. Averell Harriman went on to serve President Franklin D. Roosevelt as special envoy to Europe and then served as U.S. *Ambassador to the Soviet Union* and later as *Ambassador to Great Britain.* His third wife, Pamela Harriman, had been married to Winston Churchill's son Randolph. Averell Harriman was appointed *Secretary of Commerce* under President Harry S. Truman and later was later elected the 48th Governor of New York State. He was an unsuccessful candidate for President in the 1950's but went on to serve in numerous diplomatic assignments in the Kennedy and

Johnson administrations. He was a core member of the group of foreign policy elders known as "The Wise Men." In 1969 William Averell Harriman received the *Presidential Medal of Freedom,* the highest honor bestowed by the President of the United States on a citizen.[75]

Commodore and Louisa Gerry, with Angelica and Mabel, traveled to Newport, Rhode Island in October 1917 to attend a large fund-raising event for military and naval aviators. The meeting was held by the *National Special Aid Society* and was presided over by Mr. Alan R. Hawley, president of the *Aero Club of America.* The patrons and patronesses who made contributions to the fund raiser included the Gerry family, Mr. and Mrs. Ogden Mills of Staatsburg, Mrs. Whitney Warren and Mr. and Mrs. Harry Payne Whitney. The event included numerous speeches interspersed with patriot songs and hymns, and motion pictures of war planes in flight. The evening was a great success with a total of $3,000 in contributions.[76]

One year later on November 11, 1918 Germany agreed to a cease-fire which ended the *Great War* with a victory for the allies on *Armistice Day.* By the end of the war the major imperial powers, the German, Russian, Austro-Hungarian and Ottoman empires, ceased to exist. The successor states of the former two lost a great amount of territory, while the latter two were dismantled entirely. The map of central Europe was redrawn into several smaller states. The League of Nations was formed in the hope of preventing another world war. Six months later on June 28, 1919 the Treaty of Versailles was signed. The war had lasted four years and eleven months. American men returned home and families worked hard to re-establish their lives. The country spent the next year stabilizing the economy while Europe endeavored to restore peace and harmony and to rebuild the Continent's social and economic structure.

In February 1919 at the age of forty-seven, Mabel Gerry went to England on a benevolent mission to establish an orphanage for the sons of British soldiers killed in the War. The orphanage was the only one in Britain of the several that the *French Hero's Memorial Fund* was organizing in France. Mabel was reported to have worked constantly since her arrival in London to perfect the plans, form the proper committees and start the organizing work. United States Ambassador Davis accompanied Mabel on a special trip to *Sulgrave Manor* to inspect the site where the orphanage was to be situated. Mabel made a second trip alone to *Sulgrave* to personally visit every cottage in the village in an effort to gain the advice and support of the local community. She had learned how to do community work through her summer mission activities in Delaware County, New York. Mabel was indefatigable and she coordinated her efforts with New York City supporters of her special mission to England. While in London, Mabel also entertained a wide circle of friends and family whom she had known and visited her entire life. She was at her "home away from home" which made her mission all the more successful across the Atlantic.[77]

Back in America, five years after his divorce from Elsie Whelan, Robert Wilson Goelet decided to marry for the second time. It all started when Prince Riabouchinsky and his wife Fernanda came to the United States to purchase horses for the Russian government. Immediately there were rumors about Robert and Fernanda. The Princess had been involved with other flirtations and her husband had had enough with Robert Goelet, so he divorced his wife and returned to Russia. Robert and Fernanda were quietly married in Paris. Over the next five years, she found herself snubbed by both New York and Newport society. Even after she had a son, Mrs. Ogden Goelet would not receive her at *Ochre Court* or at the Goelets' Fifth Avenue mansion. Robert did nothing to remedy the situation and could not console his wife. Fernanda left Robert in despair in 1924 but happily fell in love with a middle-class man in Paris and then quietly divorced Robert Wilson Goelet.[78]

The end of the war not only allowed Robert and Fernanda to travel to Paris in 1919 but also stimulated many Americans to resume their seasonal trans-Atlantic voyages on the great ocean liners. The renewed tourist and family visits were a great stimulus to the European economy as well as a boost to the morale of a society struggling to find a sense of normalcy and vigor in their daily lives. The next decade was a unique era that became known as the "years between the wars," World War I and World War II.

The 1920 New Year swept in with a new political frenzy across America that had started the year before. Known as the *Red Scare,* it was a reaction to the Bolshevik Revolution in Russia in 1917 during the war with Germany. At the end of the *Great War* soldiers returned home to unemployment and the war industry had shut down which resulted in economic unrest. Two major unions that represented American workers, the *International Workers of the World* and the *Socialist Party,* had objected to the War and now anyone associated with them were suspected as being an unpatriotic communist "Red." The same phenomenon was happening in Canada in 1919, worker unrest after soldiers returned home to rampant unemployment. Significant labor strikes throughout 1919 in Canada and the United States were the result of failed labor negotiations. The *Winnipeg Strike* in Manitoba, Canada lasted six weeks between May and June 1919 and involved tens of thousands of citizens. The first major industry to strike in both Canada and the United States was the steel-workers, which led to a nationwide movement in both countries. In Winnipeg, the Strike Committee had 1000 members to ensure the strike was peaceful among a consolidation of local unions.[79] The *Winnipeg Trades and Labor Council,* the lead union, invited other Canadian union leaders, like William A. Pritchard from Vancouver, British Columbia to speak on behalf of the *One Big Union* movement whose aim was to have American unions join with the Canadians to form one big union. American union representatives were also invited, specifically the *International Workers of the World,* led by Bill Haywood, and the *Socialist Party* led by Eugene Debs. After weeks of failed negotiations the *Winnipeg Strike* was broken up on "Bloody Saturday" with an attack on the strikers. Seven men were arrested and convicted of conspiracy. During the trial William A. Pritchard, an invited speaker not on the strike committee, spoke before the court for two days in an eloquent self-defense for which he became known as the "boy orator." After the trials the leaders were imprisoned and collective bargaining was not permitted in Canada for the next two decades.

Similarly In America in May 1919 rallies were held throughout the country and in some instances the crowds resorted to rioting. Then on June 2 a multi-state bomb plot was uncovered and attributed to anarchists. The riots and bomb plot happened while the *Winnipeg Strikes* were in full force just across the border in Canada. The strikes in the United States were also massive with over 60,000 shipyard workers on strike in Seattle, Washington and 365,000 steel workers on strike nation-wide. Three quarters of Pittsburgh's steel mills were shut down, but in the end, not a single demand of the strikers was met. Although the unrest ended peacefully across America, the strikers were branded as "Reds" and unpatriotic. Both America and Canada feared that strikes would lead to a Communist revolution across the country which seduced citizens into the frenzy of "Red hunting." The national press reflected and played into the predominant mood of the country with articles about Justice Department arrests, raids, and deportations that filled the front pages for eager consumption by their readers. On January 10, 1920 there were thirty-three coordinated raids in major cities like New York, when 4,000 alleged radicals were arrested. The New York Legislature expelled five duly elected Socialist Assemblymen from its ranks. Fortunately America began to take a hard look at itself and at the toll the frenzy of fear had taken on the recovery efforts and on the civil liberties of its citizens. Newspapers realized that their industry was vulnerable to the sting of censorship and started to publish articles that ridiculed the "Red Hunters" as over-zealous. Business needed the economy to recover and the loss of skilled workers to deportation or strikes was not in their best interest.[80] Although the "Red Scare" quickly ran its course by the summer of 1920, the *Great War* had made America feel vulnerable as never before and it was time to unite for the sake of unemployed soldiers and a war industry that had to be re-tooled for economic growth. Senator Peter Gerry was in the midst of the government's struggle to stabilize the country as a strong supporter of President Woodrow Wilson who was war-weary in the last year of his second term in office.

New York City was bitter cold in January and another flu epidemic was running its course across the country. Commodore and Louisa Gerry celebrated the holidays with their daughter Angelica by the warm hearth of their Fifth Avenue home of twenty-five years. Now 83 and 84 years old, Elbridge and Louisa no longer held their annual winter galas which were too physically demanding, and in truth, their interest was focused on their four lively grandchildren, now 12, 10, and the twins, 6 years old. Mabel Gerry was not home for the New Year; she planned to remain in London for a few months to ensure the successful establishment of the war orphanage. Mabel was expected to join the family when they gathered for the summer at Lake Delaware. However, in February Louisa Gerry became ill, perhaps the flu which often was complicated with pneumonia. She was missed on the Avenue by those who joined her for a brisk daily walk, the "Louisa constitutional." By mid-March she had not improved and her doctors recommended that family members be asked to come in case her condition worsened. Senator Peter Gerry and Mathilde came immediately from Washington, and Robert and Cornelia were just down the block on Fifth Avenue. Much to Mabel Gerry's great distress, her mother quickly declined and died on Friday, March 26 before she could even pack for the trans-Atlantic voyage home. Louisa was surrounded by her loving family who shared her deep faith that the kingdom of God awaited her. Commodore Gerry, while devastated, was bound to Louisa in a deep faith that sustained him during his grief. They were in the fifty-third year of their happy and fruitful marriage. Their love of opera was a shared passion and Louisa was never happier than when she was hostess in Box 23, the Gerry box at the *Metropolitan Opera* that they held since it first opened. She often spoke in disagreement whenever Mrs. Astor commented to friends that "one hour of opera was quite enough." Louisa was born at *Staatsburg-on-Hudson,* the home of her great-grandparents, General Morgan Lewis and Gertrude Livingston, and she was one of the last leaders of the Livingston family in New York City. Her great-great-grandfather, Chancellor Robert R. Livingston, administered the oath of office to President George Washington on the steps of Old City Hall on Wall Street, now called Federal Hall. In the reports of Louisa Gerry's death, the press described her as a commanding figure with a distinguished presence, perfectly suited for her role as the kind and generous leader of New York society. Louisa Gerry was a patroness of numerous charitable enterprises in New York and Newport, but few of her many generous gifts to philanthropic projects became known to the public. She was said to have given away fortune after fortune with never a word to the press.[81]

Louisa Gerry's death plunged a good portion of New York society into mourning. Her funeral was held on Monday, March 29 at the *Church of the Transfiguration* at 11 o'clock. The most touching moment of the funeral rite was when a hymn written by Commodore Gerry and arranged by him to music from Mozart was played to honor his beloved wife. Immediately after the service Louisa's body was taken by special train to Hyde Park, New York for interment with her two daughters, Margaret and Lillian, and her father, Robert James Livingston, in the family mausoleum.[82] The press release of the *New York Times* was copied by wire to the Boston, Washington, London and Paris newspapers. Louisa Gerry's will was probated in early May 1920 in Newport, Rhode Island, her state of permanent residence. The three family homes in New York, Newport, and Lake Delaware were given to Commodore Gerry during his lifetime and to their children at his death. There were specific distributions of property and money to her four children and numerous distributions to a list of charitable institutions and hospitals.[83]

Commodore Gerry had lost his partner in life and spent most of his time thereafter with his daughters, Angelica and Mabel, who took care of his daily life at the mansion on Fifth Avenue, and hosted small dinners for his closest friends and family. It was a blessing and a pleasure for the Commodore to be right next door to the *Metropolitan Club* where he could take a short walk to spend leisure time or have lunch with his old male friends in the comfort of the beautiful surroundings that held memories of his long and active life. Commodore Gerry was in very good health. He continued as Legal Counsel to *New York Society for the Prevention of Cruelty to Children* and focused more time on his avocation of book collecting and managing his library.

The summer after her mother's death, Angelica Gerry went on another automobile tour with her chauffeur and maid, this time deep into upstate New York, all the way to Niagara Falls. She enjoyed her own company and a few good books while exploring new areas of the northeast. She had a large circle of friends who filled her days in New York City and she had her mission work, her mother's work, in Delaware County. Another story about the "bachelor girls" ran in the papers but this time it focused on how the times had changed for women who now lived in a democratic era of choice in their personal lives as well as in the public arena. The *Nineteenth Amendment* was formally ratified on August 19, 1920. The right to vote was a "family victory" for Angelica and Mabel because they were relatives of suffragette Elizabeth Cady Stanton who was a Livingston, the great granddaughter of Chancellor Robert R. Livingston, the same as their mother Louisa M. Livingston Gerry. The amendment had originally been written and proposed by Susan B. Anthony and had in fact, been voted on and defeated four times by the Senate in 1878, 1914, 1918, 1919, and finally approved and ratified in 1920. The victory ended a fight that really began during the *American Revolution* when women of several of the original Colonies had the vote, and all the others demanded a woman's right to vote be included in the Constitution. A close and dear friend of Elbridge and Ann Gerry in Massachusetts during the Founding period, Abigail Adams, wrote to her husband, John Adams, "If women are not represented in this new republic there will be a new revolution."[84] Abigail Adams' insightful comment predicted the *Women's Suffrage Movement* that followed one hundred years later. Democratic Senator Peter Gerry voted for the *Nineteenth Amendment,* not only because Rhode Island women, his constituents, already had the vote but his mother, sisters and wife were all well-educated, independent, and thoughtful women whom the Senator believed were like all women, fully competent to vote. Not long after women gained the right to vote in 1920 the *League of Women Voters* was founded in Chicago and the *Women's Bureau* was established in the United States Department of Labor; women were empowered with self-representation.

Senator Peter G. Gerry was a progressive Democrat who took Rhode Island by storm when he ran his election campaigns with a strong work ethic. He was the first state representative to do a "mail" campaign in which he personally signed most of the 30,000 letters to his constituents. He was also the first candidate to do an "automobile tour" of the towns in his district to meet the citizens and hear their ideas on the issues. He got the idea from a circular sent out by the state Tax Department that gave each District a notification of when and where the "tax collector" would be during an automobile tour to collect their taxes.

Senator Peter Gerry was raised on the Lake Delaware estate which was a full working farm and he understood the needs of the farm communities in his district. He decided to send a letter to every farmer to let them know that a variety of free seed packets were available from the Department of Agriculture and, if they would let him know which packets they wanted, he would take care of it. And he did, he sent seed packets by mail to every farmer in his district who asked for them. He also mailed the free *Farmer's Bulletin* to his constituents as a courtesy. These gestures made a tremendous personal impact on the voters of Rhode Island. The only break Senator Peter Gerry took from his campaign work was to have an operation to remove his appendix. In Washington, D.C. it was said that you could see his office light burning until 9 or 10 o'clock most nights. Everyone knew Senator Peter G. Gerry was a very wealthy man but his constituents often joked that "he forgot he was rich" because he worked like a poor man who didn't know where his next dime was coming from.[85] His wife Mathilde worked right alongside her husband and hosted lovely dinners for political colleagues as well as for constituents. They started *Woodrow Wilson Clubs* throughout the state to support President Wilson's earlier election bid, a grass roots effort to get out the vote. In November 1920 President Woodrow Wilson was awarded the *Nobel Peace Prize* for his leadership during and after the *Great War.* The same month that the President won the *Nobel,* the Presidential election results for 1920 were broadcast by radio from KDKA in Pittsburgh, Pennsylvania for the first time in history.[86]

When appropriate, Senator Peter Gerry incorporated charity work into his political life. The Christmas before his mother Louisa Gerry died, he and Mathilde hosted a holiday party for 130 poor children in Providence, Rhode Island. He played Santa and gave each girl a doll and each boy a drum or a baseball glove. He walked in his father's footsteps and it was immensely satisfying for Commodore Gerry to see his children become charitable, responsible, and successful adults in the post-war years of the early twentieth century.

As officers of the *New York Society for the Prevention of Cruelty to Children* Senator Peter Gerry, his sister-in-law Cornelia Gerry and her brother, Averell Harriman, were busy negotiating some controversy at the November 1920 annual meeting. The *Gerry Society* as it was popularly known experienced the "growing pains" of great success. There were now fifteen Directors on the *Board,* a President with nine Vice-Presidents, and a women's *Auxiliary Committee.* The work of the *Society* had been divided for many years between the legal and administrative duties of the *Board* and the non-legal duties of the *Auxiliary Committee* managing the NYSPCC *Children's Home* that cared for the rescued children until the court reviewed and decided their legal cases. Commodore Gerry advised the *Society* from a historical perspective on the two issues of contention that he believed could be resolved. The first issue was a four million dollar endowment that included a valuable plot of land which had been given to the *Gerry Society* by the Heckscher family. Some members of the *Board* took a conservative approach on how to use the gift and suggested the NYSPCC continue the status quo to grow the money for the long term and not be required to develop the plot of land. The majority of the *Board* was more progressive and voted to sell the old historic *Children's Home* on Fourth Avenue and build a new *Home* on Fifth Avenue between 104th and 105th Streets, the plot of land gifted to the *Gerry Society* as part of the Heckscher endowment. The second issue focused on a new administrative policy that was drafted when the NYSPCC installed its new President. The policy marginalized the role of the *Auxiliary Committee* after thirty years of responsibility for essential services in the Children's Home. In fact, seven women submitted their resignations in protest.[87] Their resignations were tabled until the end of the meeting when the Board unanimously passed a resolution that amended the new administrative policy to require consultation with the *Auxiliary Committee* before staff appointments or other essential duties of its membership were finalized. The resignations were rescinded by most of the committee members. The board also agreed by a great majority to review the fifteen plans already submitted for the construction of a new NYSPCC *Children's Home* and to continue discussions on how to both preserve the traditional success of the *Gerry Society* while also adapting to the new demands of post-war New York City.[88]

The quiet forty-one year old son of Robert and Harrietta Goelet fell in love for the first time while living near Paris at *Sandricourt Castle*, the chateau he inherited from his parents. Robert Walton Goelet's mother had made Paris her permanent residence for the last decade of her life and it was inevitable that Robert's social life became centered in Paris rather than New York or Newport. Indeed, during the *Great War* while living at *Sandricourt* Robert Walton Goelet donated $250,000 for the establishment and equipment of two ambulance sections of the Harjes-Norton, the *American Ambulance Corps* stationed in France.[89] The ambulance corps were assembled on the grounds of *Sandricourt* in preparation for their dispatch to the field. After the war effort and several seasons alone at his chateau in France, Robert finally found a companion with whom he would share the remainder of his life. Robert Walton Goelet's engagement to Anne Marie Guestier was announced by the *Paris Figaro* on November 9, 1920. Anne was the daughter of a large Bordeaux landowner and vintner who was the Director of the Orleans Railroad. Anne Marie Guestier was a Catholic and her strong faith was nurtured in her four children and their children's children. Today, the Robert Walton Goelet line is Catholic, while his cousin Robert Wilson Goelet's line is Protestant Episcopal. Robert and Anne Marie lived half the year in America where they occupied both the Fifth Avenue mansion and *Southside* in Newport, with the remainder of the year in France at *Sandricourt*. Today, both residences, *Southside* and *Sandricourt*, are family homes of Robert and Anne Marie's grandchildren and are holiday retreats for many of their great grandchildren.

Commodore Gerry continued to take an interest in the Gerry Estates Inc. although he left the day to day management to his son Robert L. Gerry. In July 1921 two important leases were negotiated on Gerry property in the upper Fifth Avenue business section of the city. At an aggregate rental of over seven million dollars, the northeast corner of Fifty-Eighth Street and Fifth Avenue was leased for a long term of years to Nicholas E. Partos, president of his own realty company. The Savoy Apartments built in 1895 occupied the 75 foot by 150 foot plot of land and under the terms of the new lease it was understood that substantial building improvements would be made within a stated period of time.[90] A second long-term lease with Commodore Gerry was for property purchased by Louisa Gerry's father in 1845 and inherited by her after his death. The old *Bristol Hotel,* a high-class rooming house, now sat on the land at the northwest corner of Forty-Second Street and Fifth Avenue and it was time to make better use of the property. The lease was originally signed in 1902 with Walter J. Salmon and required improvements to the property within three years. While Mr. Salmon's father guaranteed the lease, and the Gerrys advanced $100,000 toward renovations, he was still short of funds for the massive rehabilitation. A wealthy friend, Mr. Morton H. Meinhard, became interested in the project and agreed to fund 50% of the construction cost. The two men signed a partnership agreement separate from the Gerry lease. Significantly, the agreement was specific in that the co-investors would share the earnings 50/40 with Mr. Salmon, the hands-on manager, making more than Mr. Meinhard, however both would bear an equal share of the losses. Mr. Salmon was the sole proprietor and manager of the sub-leases of the commercial building, while Mr. Meinhard provided fifty percent of the total cash investment. Over the life of the twenty year lease each man received over half a million dollars on their $50,000 investment. By 1922 Commodore Gerry and his son Robert had accumulated property on both sides of the old *Bristol Hotel* and decided that the lease would be renewed for the original property plus all the adjacent property. Together this was the most valuable city property in the world in 1922 and the old lease of $45,000 annually would now be $350,000 for ten years and $450,000 for the remaining life of the lease. The trouble began when Mr. Salmon signed the new lease but intentionally kept it a secret from his partner, Mr. Meinhard. In fact, Mr. Salmon believed the new lease ended his co-investment with Mr. Meinhard because the property leased was larger than the 1902 plot originally agreed to be reconstructed by the partners. Meinhard sued Salmon, and the case was sent to a referee whose decision was sent to *New York Court of Appeals.*[91] The case was in the court system for several years with the final decision handed down in 1928. It is one of the most important business cases ever decided in which the "standard of loyalty" between fiduciary partners in a shared enterprise was unequivocally determined in the United States. The opinion in the case was written by Judge Benjamin Cardozo in which he placed Mr. Salmon's new lease with the Gerry Estates, Inc. in a "trust" to benefit both partners and ordered that the profits were to be shared equally while the stock was divided so as to give one extra stock to Mr. Salmon to allow him to continue to manage the enterprise without interference from Mr. Meinhard, who had accrued enormous financial benefits without any day-to-day effort during the life of the lease with the *Gerry Estates.*[92] The decision included an impassioned dissent which has caused the case to be debated in the scholarly journals of the American legal community to this day.

Commodore Gerry alternated summer months with his daughters Angelica and Mabel at *Seaverge* which enabled the women to have private time to carry on their own projects and social entertainments. However, in late summer and into the fall the three Gerrys always traveled up to the Lake Delaware House where they shared the historic family home in an intimate rural community of friends. The *Delaware County Sanatorium* was one of the local hospitals that Angelica Gerry visited while at the Lake House. Her sister Lilly had tuberculosis so Angelica had a good sense of what might make the patients stay happier, so she bought the Sanatorium a *Victrola* machine with a selection of records and accompanying pictures. The new machine encouraged others in the community to donate useful and entertaining items to the Sanatorium for years to come.[93]

However, in early October 1921, Angelica had to rush Mabel back to New York City when she suffered an acute attack of appendicitis. Her brother Senator Peter Gerry had had the same operation just a few years before while campaigning for office. Commodore Gerry also returned to New York City to open the Fifth Avenue mansion to prepare for Mabel's recuperation from surgery. Commodore Gerry remained in New York City to join his family, especially his grandsons, for the coming holiday season. By January Mabel had made a full recovery and to celebrate she hosted a large gala reminiscent of the old days with a late gourmet dinner and a whirl of new dances that brought renewed life to the Fifth Avenue mansion. It was the first large affair since Louisa's death two years before and it brought a twinkle to the eye of eighty-five year old Commodore Gerry. He and Mabel greeted their guests together without Angelica who had made her own plans for a private get-away from society. Mabel had invited her father's old friends like the Vanderbilts and Warrens, and she also had her brother Robert and his wife Cornelia share the role of host with the Commodore. Mabel's best friend Gertrude now Mrs. Harry Payne Whitney and other personal friends were prominent guests, but just for fun, Mabel also invited a few young debutantes of the season and some of the young bachelors.[94] Dinner was served shortly after midnight in the dining room after which Commodore Gerry retired to his room while the younger set resumed the dance. The next day the press raved about the "spice" that Mabel Gerry injected into stale New York society. One article made it clear, "Mabel Gerry is one of the few members of the inner circle who could have the leadership of the New York-Newport set for the asking, and can boast of an absolutely impregnable place in Vanity Fair."[95] However, in mid-life Mabel was less focused on New York City. She was drawn to London where she found satisfaction in her post-war charitable activities and where her social standing was well established. In time, London is where the "bachelor girl" Mabel would find love quite nicely on her own.

Shortly before the gala at the Gerry mansion, Angelica left New York City for what had become her annual automobile tour. In January 1922 it was too cold and snowy to venture north as she usually did, so she headed south to the warmth of sunny Florida. By February she was at the elegant *Clarendon Hotel* in Seabreeze, Florida near Daytona Beach. During her stay Angelica took a boat trip up the *Tomoka River* which had a *Manatee Sanctuary* and an *Aquatic Preserve* where she could see rare species such as the Wood Stork, the Bald Eagle and perhaps even the Atlantic Salt Marsh Snake.[96] Angelica arrived at the *Breakers Hotel* in Palm Beach the first week of March where she remained until early summer when she joined her father and sister at *Seaverge* in Newport. These wonderful trips created a happy and intimate relationship with her chauffeur and maid who stayed with Angelica through her lifetime.

Angelica joined her father at *Seaverge* in May and in late July Mabel returned from her London season to travel up to Lake Delaware with her family. The summer was focused on the plans of architects *Cram & Ferguson* for the new Saint James Church to honor Louisa Gerry. Angelica had signed a contract with New York builders, *Jacob & Young*, to construct the parish church, rectory, and a parish hall on land located just beyond "The Hook," a peculiar bend in the state highway between *Delhi* and *Andes* near the turn-off to *Bovina*. The wide and flat plot of land sat near the small bridge that crossed the *Little Delaware River* at the entrance road to Lake Delaware. The plot had to be enlarged by the removal of wild trees and shrubs to make room for the parish buildings that were constructed with imported stone. Although it would take a year to complete the Church, Angelica and Mabel took every opportunity to walk down the country lane from the Lake House to the building site to watch the work progress from paper to survey to excavation.[97]

While the Gerrys were at Lake Delaware, but away from the house, thieves broke in and robbed them of jewels and money. The exact amount of plunder taken and other details of the crime were scrupulously withheld. This was the second robbery in the last few years so Commodore Gerry hired a New York detective to investigate the case. The local papers had a humorous take on what was actually a rash of robberies in the area. "The stories of breaking and entering of Delhi houses during the week are also being hushed up, it being deemed unkind to hurt the feelings of the thieves by allowing their existence to become known."[98]

Commodore Gerry's children were now aged 44 to 51 and they realized that each of their four individual inheritances from their mother were complex real estate holdings that had become a burden for each sibling to manage separately. Their father was 85 years old and when he died, each of the four children would be burdened with even more responsibility for twice the complex holdings they currently held. Commodore Gerry and his sons decided to simplify the property management and protect the four children from individual liability from the normal but routine litigious nature of New York City real estate ownership. In May 1922 the plans filed by the Gerrys before the New York Supreme Court were approved which permitted the sale of Manhattan real estate owned by Commodore Gerry and his late wife, Louisa Gerry, valued at multi-millions of dollars, to the *Gerry Estates, Inc.*. This sale created one of the largest groups of family real estate under corporate control in New York City.[99] Each of the four Gerry children now held stock in the corporation, the *Gerry Estates, Inc.*, rather than having personal ownership of any property except a private residence.

The December holiday season at the Gerrys' New York mansion took on a more festive air than it had in recent years. Together Angelica and Mabel hosted a series of dinners that were eagerly anticipated by society who had coined the phrase "living like the Gerrys" and said it whenever they had an exceptionally wonderful gourmet dinner or a perfectly balanced wine. The Gerry wine cellar was famous as was the household selection of pickles, chutneys, and sauces. Some condiments were home-made but most were special orders from a well-known East India house in London. The reputation of the Gerry's French chef was widely acclaimed; one of his handwritten daily menu books, with notations by Commodore Gerry about who would be out that day or a suggestion about the menu, is in the *U.S. Supreme Court's* Rare Book Collection.

In the New Year of 1923 Mabel and Angelica, now in their early fifties, returned to their private pursuits, Angelica to Lake Delaware in March to oversee the building project of the new Saint James parish church, and Mabel to her work with *the League of Nations' Non-Partisan Association* in New York City where a dinner was held to honor Lord Robert Cecil, husband of Cornelia Vanderbilt, with whom Mabel also worked when she was in London in late spring. Society was familiar with Angelica's more reclusive nature as compared with her sister Mabel's more social and out-going nature. It made little difference to the sisters or to society because they were so highly respected and the pleasure of their company was always welcome. In Newport everyone knew that Mabel was driven by a chauffeur when she stepped out, whereas Angelica, like her mother, walked everywhere and was often seen walking her dog, an Irish Setter, down Bellevue

Avenue. Their parents, particularly Commodore Gerry, often spoke of the joy they took watching the personalities of their children emerge when left to their own pursuits. What the sisters did share was an unconditional love of family and a deep commitment to their charity work, which they both did regardless of which community they lived in from season to season. They were driven and passionate and very happy in the fullness of their "bachelor girl" lives, surrounded by a close-knit extended family.

In mid-September 1923 the Gerrys gathered at Lake Delaware to celebrate the completion of the Rectory for the new church which was already occupied by Reverend Edgelow and his family. The Church itself awaited a pipe organ and other interior finishes and would not be consecrated until the feast of Saint James the following July 25, 1924. The Parish Hall was finished and it was time for a festive celebration of the new parish buildings. Angelica Gerry hosted a party in the Parish Hall for nearly 400 parishioners, friends and neighbors. Angelica had four automobiles at Lake Delaware that she sent out to bring members of the parish to the celebration as well as to Mass every Sunday. Her generosity was boundless.

The holiday season in New York once again found the Gerry sisters hosting intimate dinners for their father and his friends. On one occasion in late December during a lovely seated dinner with fifteen guests, a burning log in the Commodore's picture gallery rolled out of the fireplace onto the floor. With everyone in the dining room "living like the Gerrys" the stray log went unnoticed and caught the carpet on fire. The flames burned their way toward nearby valuable tapestries and paintings until a passerby saw the glow of flames through a mansion window. The servants and fire department were notified just in time to avert a disaster.[100]

Senator Peter Gerry and his wife Mathilde took a well-deserved winter holiday to Europe before Congress re-convened in March. While in Paris Mathilde famously purchased Catherine the Great's *Black Pearls* from Pierre Cartier for $400,000. Described as "drops of liquid rose-beetle-colored darkness" the pearls had always had a sinister significance to superstitious minds.[101] Mathilde could not have been unaware of the pearls' recent history as part of the exiled Yusupov family jewels that Prince Felix Ysupov hid in his clothing when he fled Russia after the 1917 Revolution. The Yusupov family had acquired their wealth generations ago through extensive land grants in Serbia, extensive mineral mines, and the fur trade in Russia. There was a time when Prince Felix was the richest man in Russia after his brother was killed in a duel in 1908. He had a happy fifty-year marriage despite his flamboyant bi-sexual and self-admitted cross-dressing life-style. Prince Felix was best known for pariticipating in the murder of Rasputin with Grand Duke Dmitri and others in 1916. Grigori Yefimovich Rasputin (1869–1916) was a Russian Orthodox Christian and mystic who influenced the latter days of the Russian Emperor Nicholas II and his wife Alexandra even while he discredited the tsarist government which led to the fall of the Romanov dynasty in 1917. He was known historically as the "Mad Monk," and contemporary opinions say Rasputin was variously a saintly mystic, a visionary, a healer and prophet or simply a debauched religious charlatan. Needless to say, many Russians blamed him for the *Revolution*. Prince Felix Yusupov and his circle were no exception, and decided to murder Rasputin. Despite being poisoned, shot four times, and beaten with an iron bar, Rasputin refused to die. The conspirators finally had to tie him up and throw him into the icy Neva River in order to kill him. Following the murder Prince Felix Yusupov was placed under house arrest in his St. Petersburg palace for three months. After the *Revolution* he went into exile with the family jewels hidden in his clothing and also managed to take two of his Rembrandt paintings which helped sustain his family until his death in Paris in 1967. Prince Felix and his wife Irina successfully sued MGM Studios through the English courts for invasion of privacy and libel in connection with the 1932 film, *Rasputin and the Empress*. The alleged libel was not that the character based on Prince Felix had committed murder, but that the character based on his wife Princess Irina was portrayed as being seduced by the lecherous Rasputin. They won the case in 1934. The disclaimer that scrolls across the screen at the end of every American film, "The preceding was a work of fiction, any similarity to a living person is purely coincidental," first appeared as a result of the legal precedent set by the Yusupov case.[102]

In April 1924 the high Altar for *Saint James Church* at Lake Delaware was installed just in time for Easter. The Altar was one of the oldest in America and was imported by Angelica Gerry from Europe. It had been painted in 1320 by Venetian artist Pietro Lorenzetti almost two hundred years before the discovery of America. The symbolism employed was essentially female and included a pomegranate pattern that represented the Virgin Mary who was surrounded by a circle and quatrefoil, symbols of completeness and perfection. The complex triptych above the Altar had a portrait of the Virgin Mary as the central figure encircled by protecting angels bearing a shield charged with a sunburst.[103] With the beautiful Altar in place the new Church could now be consecrated on the feast of Saint James in late July.

Until then, the Gerry family gathered in Newport for a few weeks. Only Angelica and Mabel joined their father, Commodore Gerry at *Seaverge*. Robert and Cornelia Gerry had four boys and their servants and tutors, so they rented *Inchiquin* a large cottage across the street and three properties down from *Seaverge*. It was also just one cottage away from *Bailey's Beach* where Angelica had taken her daily walks with her mother for many years. The boys, Ebby Jr. 16, Robert Jr. 13, and the twins, Edward and Henry 10 years-old, could find their way safely to their grandfather Commodore Gerry's cottage or to *Bailey's Beach* without a car. The Gerry stables and greenhouses were even closer to Robert and Cornelia's cottage than they were to Commodore Gerry's cottage. Lots of fresh fruit and vegetables were available for the boys to pick and there were beautiful horses to ride throughout the summer. No doubt there were bicycles too. Senator Peter Gerry and his wife Mathilde rented *Ocean Lawn* the sprawling cottage of his uncle Ogden Mills. It sat on the cliffs with an ocean view and was located directly across the street from Cousin Robert Walton Goelet's *Southside* cottage. One could take a long stroll along the *Cliff Walk* between *Ocean Lawn* and *Seaverge* and never see an automobile. The big house was perfect for Senator Peter Gerry who had constituents to entertain and persuade. This year he and Mathilde needed their own cottage in Newport to accommodate the number and variety of guests who competed for the Senator's attention.

The social news of the summer in the Newport Colony was the engagement of Mabel Gerry, one of the wealthy "bachelor girls." For the second time in the Gerry and Livingston family history, an American was to marry a British aristocrat, Francis Saxon Drury whose ancient family had come to England with William the Conqueror. Louisa Gerry's cousin Elizabeth Mills of Staatsburg had married Duke George Cavendish-Bentnick of London. Francis Durry was a Knight of the Order of St. John. Mabel was fifty-two and Mr. Drury was a sixty-one year old widower with three adult children. They were married at *Trinity Chapel* where Commodore and Louisa Gerry were married in 1867. The wedding was celebrated on October 28 with over 1,000 guests, many overflowed out to the front steps. Robert L. Gerry escorted his sister down the aisle due to the advanced age of her father, Commodore Gerry. Mabel carried her mother, Louisa's ivory prayer book with a Lilly as a book mark in honor of her deceased sister Lillian. Mabel had her sister Angelica as her maid-of-honor and Mr. Drury had his son Vyvyan Drury as his best man. A reception and buffet breakfast were held at the Fifth Avenue mansion before the couple left for a honeymoon in Europe. When they returned to New York, Mabel purchased the beautiful Carharts' townhouse at 3 East 95th Street. It was twice the size of most townhouses and measured 50 feet wide. Today the beautiful townhouse has been divided into four luxury apartments, and has been designated a Historic Landmark building in New York City.

Senator Peter Gerry and Mathilde returned to Washington, D.C. in August after the Consecration Mass was celebrated at *Saint James Church* in Lake Delaware. Mathilde flew to Paris in early October to shop for her holiday wardrobe while Senator Gerry was back in the full swing of work in his Capitol Hill office. Mathilde returned to New York City just before Thanksgiving and took a room at the *Plaza Hotel* to spend time with relatives. However, her motivation for not returning to Washington was self-serving and cruel. The newspapers received word over the wires from Paris, that while there Mathilde Townsend Gerry had filed for divorce from her husband of fifteen years, Senator Peter Gerry. The shocking story was revealed to the utter disbelief of the Gerry family. Mathilde Townsend had been having a passionate affair with foreign diplomat, Sumner Wells, for almost a year. She had decided to leave Peter and marry her lover. Sumner Wells was seven years younger than Mathilde and had a history of womanizing for which his wife Esther had divorced him in 1923.[104] Mathilde's family in Washington, particularly her Aunt Mary Scott Townsend, was ashamed and angry at her behavior. She made Mathilde promise not to marry for a year out of respect for the Senator and her own family, but Sumner Wells did not want to wait and insisted on a June 1925 wedding. They were married in a quiet ceremony in upstate New York to avoid publicity. The shock was difficult for Senator Peter Gerry, and over the winter he moved to his own apartment on Twentieth Street in Washington while Mathilde remained in the Townsend mansion. They were seen together on walks and at meals in long conversation but there was no hope of reconciliation according to the Senator.

Peter and his sister Mabel were friends with Mr. George Cecil and his wife, Cornelia, the only daughter of George and Edith Vanderbilt. Mabel worked with the Cecils at the *League of Nations' Non-Partisan Association* and the Cecils had a friend in common with Senator Peter Gerry, the Spanish Ambassador and his wife, Mrs. Riano. In May just weeks before Mathilde and Sumner Wells' marriage, Mrs. Riano realized that Senator Peter Gerry was inconsolable and decided he needed to get away from Washington. He joined the Ambassador and Mrs. Riano for a trip to the Vanderbilt mansion in Asheville, North Carolina, *Biltmore House*, for a personal and business trip already planned with Mr. and Mrs. Cecil. In fact, George Vanderbilt had died in 1914 and left the mansion to his daughter, Cornelia Vanderbilt Cecil, who had a child of her own. George Vanderbilt's widow, Edith Dresser Vanderbilt, lived with her daughter at *Biltmore House.* Mrs. Riano would later admit that she was playing cupid between Peter and Edith, who had been widowed for over ten years. The visit to North Carolina was just what Senator Peter Gerry needed, and in fact, his courtship of Edith Vanderbilt was sparked during the friendly and reassuring visit to *Biltmore House.* Only seven months later they were married privately in London, England and remained together for the next thirty-two years until Peter's death. Senator Gerry continued his political career in Washington, D.C. while Sumner Wells retired to his Maryland estate for three years to write, and later became active for several years in Franklin D. Roosevelt's administration until it was discovered through a political rival that he had solicited homosexual acts and was asked to leave government service in 1943. Mathilde died in 1949 and Sumner Wells then married Harriet Post in 1952, a childhood friend with whom he lived until his death in 1961.[105]

Robert and Cornelia Gerry went to *Aknusti* in late summer 1925, and Commodore Gerry and his daughters went to the *Lake Delaware* house at the same time. Senator Peter Gerry joined his family with his fianceé, Edith Vanderbilt, to introduce her in a relaxed and private setting. While the family was together two announcements were made, first Angelica Gerry shared a set of plans for a 23-room home she was going to build on a low hill that was a long walk just up the lane from the *Lake House* and about 800 yards up the lane from Saint James Church. From the second floor of her Colonial Style house on the hill, Angelica would be able to see Lake Delaware. She was fifty-three years old and wanted her own place to entertain her friends for a few days' stay and a barn for her horses and dogs. After all, Robert had *Aknusti,* Peter stayed at the *Lake House,* and Mabel was the hostess of *Seaverge,* now Angelica would be the hostess of *Ancrum* named after the ancestral Livingston estate in Scotland. The second announcement was from Robert who had just pledged $100,000 to the *Cathedral of Saint John the Divine* in New York City for the erection of one of the great piers in the naïve. Commodore Gerry was a great patron of the Cathedral and in time, his funeral would be held at *Saint John the Divine.* The Gerrys were once again gathered as a happy family with the difficult times behind them. Indeed, it was clear that Senator Peter Gerry had found happiness with Edith and she with him, and Mabel too had found love in her second home, England. The Senator and Edith sailed immediately for England after the family reunion where they were married privately, away from Washington and New York social pressures. They joined Mabel and Francis Drury for dinner in London as both couples were on their honeymoons in Europe in October.

While the Gerry family rejoiced in the fall weddings of siblings Mabel and Peter, their cousin Robert Wilson Goelet was married for the third time on September 24, 1925 to Miss Roberta Willard. She was the daughter of an army colonel, of good stock, but of modest means. She was born in Newport, Rhode Island and was known as the "village girl" who played with summer colonists' children. Roberta was thirteen years younger than Robert and a Catholic. They had known each other for several years as members of the summer social circles but he had not paid much attention to the "village girl" until his second marriage to Fernanda Riabouchinsky began to fall apart. Robert had lost his mother's confidence when he married Fernanda and so he turned to his local friend, Roberta Willard, for consolation. After he divorced Fernanda his friendship with Roberta had blossomed into a stable and loving relationship. Their engagement was announced by the Willard family in mid-summer and they were married at the Willard home on September 24. Not only did Robert remain happily married to his third wife, but together they began a life of philanthropy that included giving the family mansion, *Ochre Court,* to the Sisters of Mercy in 1947 when they founded *Salve Regina College.* In the 1960's the *Roberta Willard Goelet Scholarship* for $50,000 was established by Robert in memory of his wife *at Salve Regina College.*[106]

In January 1926 a large force of men were steadily working on the excavation for Angelica Gerry's new home at Lake Delaware. Many local men found employment on the work site and neighbors came by to see the steam drill used to carve the foundation out of solid rock. Angelica worked with the landscape architect, Fletcher Steele, to design the grand entry drive called the "Gallop," the outdoor terraces and staircases, and a riding lane that ran between ornamental trees on either side of the entrance drive for exercising Angelica's horses. Of special importance was a magnificent garden that was suited to experimental and ornamental gardening and would provide small areas for reading, walkways for Angelica to stroll about her gardens, and play areas for her dogs. Fletcher Steele worked with Angelica to evolve and perfect the gardens for the next ten years, it was the largest and most impressive project of his career.[107]

Angelica took ill in January, the third of the four Gerry siblings to have appendicitis. She returned to New York City from Lake Delaware and had an appendectomy in the special "isolating room" at Commodore Gerry's Fifth Avenue mansion. Her recovery was so steady that her sister Mabel and her husband, Francis Drury, left on a planned trans-Atlantic voyage back to their London home, *Drury House,* 34-43 Russell Street. A special prayer and communion service was held by the parishioners of *Saint James Church* in Lake Delaware on Angelica's behalf. Their prayers were quickly answered and Angelica was back at Lake Delaware in late spring to manage the construction of her new home. In fact, by October 1926 she had purchased the adjacent farm known as the "Strangeway Place" both to ensure the privacy of her estate and to make use of the farm buildings for her horses and the house for her property manager.[108] Angelica joined the Delaware County community for an Independence Day picnic with a crowd of over 18,000 for the *Sesquicentennial Celebration* of the town of Delhi,

New York. She was "home again" and more than ready to see her home completed at Lake Delaware.

Angelica returned to New York City in the late fall to host small holiday dinners for her father Commodore Elbridge T. Gerry and to celebrate his 90th birthday on Christmas day, December 25, 1926. Robert and Cornelia and Senator Peter Gerry and his wife Edith were joined by Mabel and Francis Drury when they arrived from England to have a large family reunion at the Fifth Avenue mansion centered around the Commodore's birthday and the New Year. Mabel and Francis Drury were booked to return to England the first week of February 1927 when Commodore Gerry had a serious fall at the Fifth Avenue mansion in late January. Needless to say, they canceled their trip home and remained with Angelica at the Gerry mansion. His personal physicians indicated that while the Commodore would recover, he had suffered a broken hip and would never walk again. When out of danger he was able to sit in his chair to read and converse with his family and enjoy visits from his four grandsons, Ebby, Jr. 19 and in college, Robert, Jr. 16, and the twins, Edward and Henry now 13 years old. Fortunately his entire family remained with Commodore Gerry for a few weeks until February 27, 1918 when his heart began to fail after spending a few hours in his chair visiting with his children. After retiring to bed at his physician's insistence, Commodore Elbridge T. Gerry died peacefully in his sleep a few hours later at 6 a.m. surrounded by his family.[109]

Sometime before his wife's death in 1920, perhaps as early as 1906, Commodore Gerry placed a hand-written note addressed to his family in his personal papers that gave directions for his funeral. Nearly thirty years earlier in the 1870's he wrote and published *The Office for the Dead: Arranged with Appropriate Music* for use in small churches with limited resources and with a need for a simplified Anglo-Catholic funeral Mass. It was so popular that it was published in a third edition in 1906. It was this "Office" that Commodore Gerry mentions in the note to his family which read:

> My Dear Wife and Children,
>
> This note contains directions for my funeral. If possible I would like to have it at my own little Church of Saint Edward the Martyr. If not possible for any reason, then in such church elsewhere as the circumstances may require. I wish my own *Office for the Dead* used (printed copies in my large Den Closet) with a Solemn High Mass of Requiem for the repose of my soul, followed by absolution and committal in the church. I also desire my Rector of St. Edwards to be the celebrant and have so written him in a letter corresponding with this one.

> Bury me in the family Tomb in Saint James Churchyard, Hyde Park on the Hudson, in a plain casket of oak with a cross on the outside and this inscription on a metal plate: *Elbridge Thomas Gerry, Born Christmas 1837, Died, ..., 19.. .*
>
> And now my beloved Louisa and my beloved children I commend my soul to Almighty God in my firm belief in the Catholic Faith and absolute trust in Him through the merits of Our Blessed Lord Jesus Christ. It is my dying wish that none of you will ever cease to pray for me – especially at your Communions and in all offerings of the Hold Sacrifice at the Altar – that I may rest in Him.
>
> Ever Lovingly, Elbridge T. Gerry

His Requiem Mass, celebrated according to Elbridge T. Gerry's "Office of the Dead," was held at his "little" Church of Saint Edward the Martyr on East 109th Street, at 8:00 o'clock in the morning on February 21, 1927. He had been the senior warden at the little church for 40 years. The church was so small that only the immediate family and members of the parish attended the private Mass. Immediately afterward his casket was taken in procession to *Saint John the Divine Cathedral.* Although the largest Cathedral in America, it could not hold all who wished to pay their last respects to Commodore Elbridge Thomas Gerry at the public funeral ceremony. People stood on the streets and sidewalks during the service, even while another memorial service was held at *Trinity Chapel* where sixty years earlier he had married Louisa Livingston Gerry.

Commodore Elbridge T. Gerry's body was taken by special train to Hyde Park, New York for a private family ceremony and interment in the family mausoleum next to his beloved wife Louisa and daughters, Margaret and Lillian, and Louisa's parents Robert J. and Louisa Storm Livingston. Newspaper articles across the nation announced Commodore Gerry's death and paid tribute to his life. One Milwaukee newspaper wrote:

> Very many Churchmen will feel the death of Commodore Gerry as a personal loss, while to New Yorkers, regardless of religious affiliations, it is the loss of a "great giver." We dread to see this death described as that of a man of wealth. He was that, but he was so much more ... he was a model citizen, determined in whatever was of concern, giving much time and thought to the protection of children, the weak and suffering.

During his lifetime he paid the salary and expenses of two parish priests, the Rectors of *Saint James Church* at Lake Delaware, and the *Church of Saint Edward the Martyr* in New York City. He established trust funds that continued the support long after his death. Commodore Gerry furnished Saint Edward the

Martyr Church in the early 1890's, including a Chalice with the inscription: *In Memorium for Lillian Gerry, [died] Age Eighteen years, November 27, 1891.*

The $100,000 gift to *Saint John the Divine Cathedral,* made by the Commodore and his children in 1925 to pay for one of the mammoth pillars in the Nave as a memorial to the Gerry family, had been paid in annual installments of $20,000 while the Cathedral was constructed. When Commodore Gerry died, the pillar had not yet been erected but was finished the next year. When the architects asked the Gerry siblings what the memorial engraving at the base of the pillar should read, they chose to honor their parents rather than the family as a whole. The inscription reads:

In memory of Elbridge T. Gerry
and
Louisa M. Livingston, his wife
given by their children 1928

Commodore Gerry's estate was left to his four children with the immense property interests left to the *Gerry Estates, Inc.* and his law library was left to his son, Senator Peter Gerry. The family home on Fifth Avenue was left to Angelica Gerry and the Newport home, *Seaverge,* was left to Mabel Gerry. Angelica had her brother Robert L. Gerry take possession of the Fifth Avenue mansion as an investment for the family which meant the building had to be removed to derive any benefit from the prime location at Sixty-First Street and Fifth Avenue. Within a year the Gerry children had selected furnishings from the mansion that each wished to own and to keep for future generations, and Angelica had salvaged structural items from the mansion to incorporate into the design of her new home at Lake Delaware. When the mansion was finally demolished, it was a stunning symbol of the end of the *Gilded Age* in New York City. An investment group joined Robert L. Gerry in the construction of the exclusive *Pierre Hotel* on the site of the Gerry mansion, which opened to great fanfare in 1930 and today is one of New York City's famous luxury hotels located just across from *Central Park* and the *Plaza Hotel* a block away.[110]

Senator Peter Gerry also choose not to keep the great law library that he inherited, and in the spirit of his great grandfather, Vice-President Elbridge Gerry, who had placed a bill before Congress in 1789 to create a Library for the *Supreme Court,* but failed, contacted his friend at the Supreme Court, Chief Justice Howard Taft, who was at the Senator's first wedding as President of the United States. The Chief Justice was in the midst of finalizing plans for the first permanent home of the United States Supreme Court at 1 First Street, NE across from the Capitol, where the court stands today. The Court was still using books on loan from the Library of Congress in the basement of the Capitol and was in need of a Library for the new building. Senator Peter Gerry offered his father's historic 30,000 volume collection to Chief Justice Taft as the first independent *Law Library* of the *United States Supreme Court* since his great grandfather's attempt to establish it 150 years before. On May 1, 1928 President Coolidge signed a bill authorizing Chief Justice Taft to accept the gift from Senator Peter Gerry.[111] The books were boxed and sent to Washington, D.C. where they patiently sat in storage in the basement of the Capitol until the magnificent new Supreme Court building was completed in 1935. The architect of the building, Cass Gilbert, designed the Supreme Court Library to occupy the entire third floor of the building with special rooms to accommodate the Gerry collection

On September 8, 1927 just seven months after Commodore Gerry died, his brother-in-law Frederic Gallatin died at his New York home, ten years after his wife Almy Gerry Gallatin's death. He was survived by six children: one son lived in Big Horn, Wyoming, and the other five all lived on the upper east side of New York City between 54th Street and 71st Street. The Gallatin siblings were within walking distance from their Gerry cousins, Angelica, Mabel and Robert who all lived between 79th Street and 93rd Street off Fifth Avenue. Many of the Goelet cousins also continued to live in New York City and today, their paths cross through their business, philanthropic and church activities. The Gerry family descendants carryon the projects of their illustrious parents and grandparents and they have initiated or sponsored new projects that will be carried on by successive generations. These great American families are alive and well in twenty-first Century New York City and continue the historic legacy of family philanthropy. The *Lake Delaware Boys Camp*, the *Boys Club of New York City*, and the *New York Society for the Prevention of Cruelty to Children*, known as the "Gerry Society," all thrive in a modern day *Gilded Gotham.*

At the age of 12, young Josef Hofmann was probably the first pianist of note to record on Edison's phonograph in 1888. In 1937, the 50th anniversary of his debut performance was celebrated with a "Golden Jubilee" recital at the Metropolitan Opera, New York.

Josef Hoffman
1876-1957

Henry and Elsie Clews in France

Chateau de la Napoule

Justice Benjamin Cardozo
Salmon v Meinhard Case

Susan Fenimore
Cooper

Cooperstown Orphanage, NY

Electra in full illumination as she would have looked on her last cruise before dismantling in 1912.
Painting by Russ Kramer.

Commodore Gerry built the Windsor Arcade

Metropolitan Club was just next door for Commodore Gerry to visit old friends

Ice cutting on Lake Delaware

Edwardian period greenhouse

Gilded Age palm house

Edwardian flower, fruit and vegetable show

Senator Peter Gerry and wife Mathilde Townsend Gerry

Mathilde Townsend married Sumner Wells after a secret 1 year affair.

Mathilde Townsend mansion in Washington, D.C.

Townsend ballroom where Mathilda married Senator Peter Gerry

Senator Peter Gerry's home in Washington, D.C.

Senator Peter G. Gerry on Capitol Hill

Edith Vanderbilt Gerry at Lake Delaware

Senator Peter Gerry's yacht the *Owera*

Biltmore House, the Vanderbilt estate in North Carolina

Edith built the smaller Italianate Frith House in the forest of the estate for her and Peter.

Robert L. Gerry
1877-1957

Cornelia Harriman Gerry
1884-1966

The Baby House in Virginia

Ebby II and Robert Jr.

Ebby II and Robert Jr.

Ebby II and Robert Jr.

Robert Jr. and Ebby II

Ebby II Robert Jr.

Robert Jr. Edward and twin Henry Ebby II

Twins Edward and Henry Gerry

Twins

Edward and Henry around age twelve and as teenagers at the Aknusti estate

Lake Delaware Boys Camp

Camp chapel

Camp mess hall

GERRY SISTERS FINE SINGERS

Commodore's Daughters Surprise Friends With a New Accomplishment.

IN DEMAND AT MUSICALES

Newport, July 11.—Comodomre Elbridge T. Gerry's accomplished daughters, Angelica and Mabel, have surprised their friends by displaying vocal talent, for the possession of which their friends had not given them credit.

They made their debut this season as vocalists at a musicale given by Mrs. Stuyvesant Fish, when their well-trained and naturally pleasing voices were a revelation, as very few were awate that they were at all gifted in that line.

Since then they have been greatly in demand at the small musicales given at the cottages of the most exclusive.

Miss Angelica Gerry is an able whip, and is one of the very few young ladies here who are able to handle successfully a four-in-hand.

Mabel Gerry

Mabel and Francis Drury wedding photo

3-5 East 95th Street in NYC

Mabel Gerry Drury townhouse she shared with husband Francis and in which she died in 1930.

Angelica Gerry Bachelor girl

Ancrum House at Lake Delaware

Angelica's beloved horse

Angelica with a book on a motor car holiday

Almy Gerry Gallatin

Frederic Gallatin with grandson

Frederick lived the rest of his life at this townhouse on Fifth Avenue next to St. Thomas Episcopal Church near his extended family.

Frederic sold the Gallatins' Long Island summer home, Breezy Lawn, soon after Almy's death.

Saint Edward the Martyr 1887

Saint Edward the Martyr 2013

Gold Gerry candle sticks

Commodore Gerry financially supported his "little church" from 1887 through today with a Trust Fund. His private funeral Mass was held in this tiny church in February 1927 before the Burial Service at the massive gothic Cathedral of Saint John the Divine.

Cathedral of St. John the Divine

Silver sacristy lamp

Altar with Lillian's chalice at center

Comodore Elbridge T. Gerry honored his deceased daughter Lillian Gerry with altar gifts to his favorite little church on East 103rd Street near Park Ave., Church of St. Edward the Martyr.

Lillian Gerry memorial chalice

Gerry and Livingston family members buried in the St. James Cemetery Gerry Mausoleum

Commodore E. T. Gerry
1837-1927

Louisa Livingston Gerry
1836-1920

Louisa Storm Livingston
-1883

Robert J. Livingston
-1891

Lillian Gerry
1873-1891

Margaret Gerry
1868-1872

Mabel Gerry Drury
1872-1930

Francis Drury
d.1941

Gerry & Livingston family Mausoleum at Hyde Park

St. James Church and Cemetery at Hyde Park, New York

General Morgan Lewis and Gertrude Livingston Lewis are buried together at St. James close to the church and down the church lane from the Gerrys.

APPENDIX

A Goelet, Gerry, Livingston, Gallatin Family Tree

B New York City Locations

C Commodore Elbridge T. Gerry's Children

- C-1 Mabel Gerry Drury 1872–1930
- C-2 Angelica Livingston Gerry 1871–1960
- C-3 Senator Peter Goelet Gerry 1879–1957
- C-4 Robert Livingston Gerry 1877–1957

D Commodore Elbridge T. Gerry's Grandsons

E American Family Legacies

F European Family Origins

- F-1 Emigration Map
- F-2 Albert Gallatin and his Descendants
- F-3 The Gallatin Family Ancestry
- F-4 Goelet Family Tree
- F-5 The Goelet Family Ancestry
- F-6 Succession of Family Titles to Lake Delaware
- F-7 The Livingston Family Ancestry

APPENDIX A Goelet, Gerry, Livingston, Gallatin Family Tree

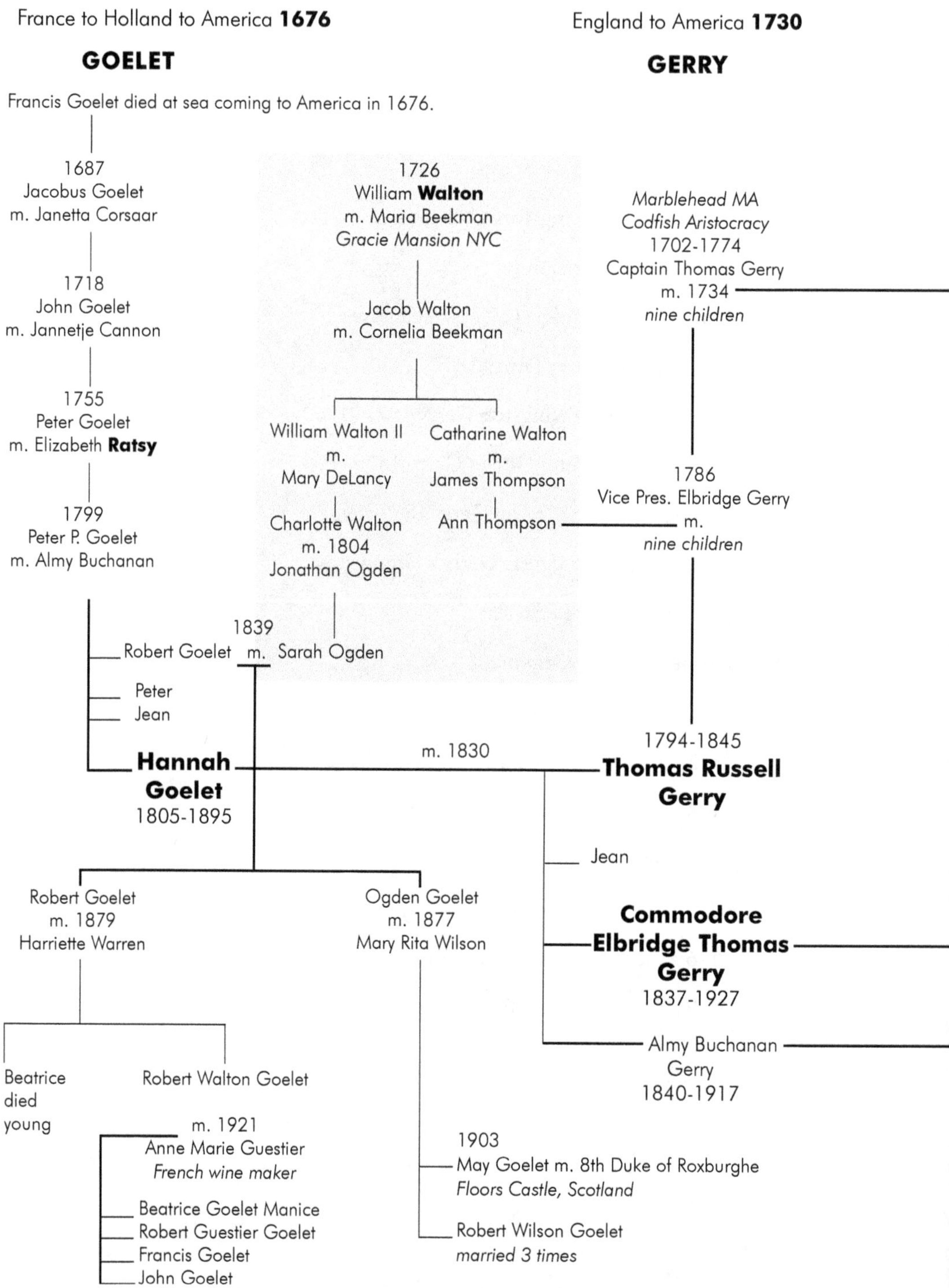

APPENDIX A Goelet, Gerry, Livingston, Gallatin Family Tree

Scotland to Holland to America **1672**

France to Holland to America **1780**

England 1690
Samuel Russell
m.
Elizabeth Elbridge
1715
Rebecca Russell
m.
Enoch Greenleaf
Rebecca Greenleaf

LIVINGSTON

Robert Livingston 1686
1st Lord of Clermont Manor
Hardenburgh Patent NY
m. 1679
Alida Van Rensslaer
Robert R. Livingston
m. 1736
Margaret Howerden

Robert Livingston Jr.
m. 1717
Margaret Beekman

Gertrude Livingston
m. 1779
General Morgan Lewis
Lake Delaware Homestead

Margaret Lewis
m. 1798
Maturin Livingston – 5th cousin

Robert James Livingston
m. 1833
Louisa M. Storm

GALLATIN

Came to America
sponsored by
Benjamin Franklin.

Founded
New York University
4th U.S. Secretary of Treasury
w/ Vice President Elbridge Gerry

Albert Gallatin
m. 1793
Hannah Nicholson

Gallatins opened
first federal bank
and co-founded
Chemical Bank NY

Albert Rolaz Gallatin Esq.
m. 1837
Mary Stevens

James Gallatin
Doctor

Albert Horatio
NYU Professor

Albert Eugene
Modern artist

1867
m.

Louisa Mathilda Livingston
1836-1920

1866
m.

Frederic Gallatin, Esq.
1841-1928 **Six children**

Margaret
died age 4

Angelica

Mabel
m. F S Drury
1930

Lillian
died age 18

Senator Peter G. Gerry
m. Mathilda Townsend
m. Edith Vanderbilt
1924

1909
m.
Robert L. Gerry
Cornelia Harriman

- Elbridge T. Gerry II *Ebby*
- Robert Gerry, Jr.
- Edward Gerry
- *twins*
- Henry Gerry

APPENDIX B New York City Locations

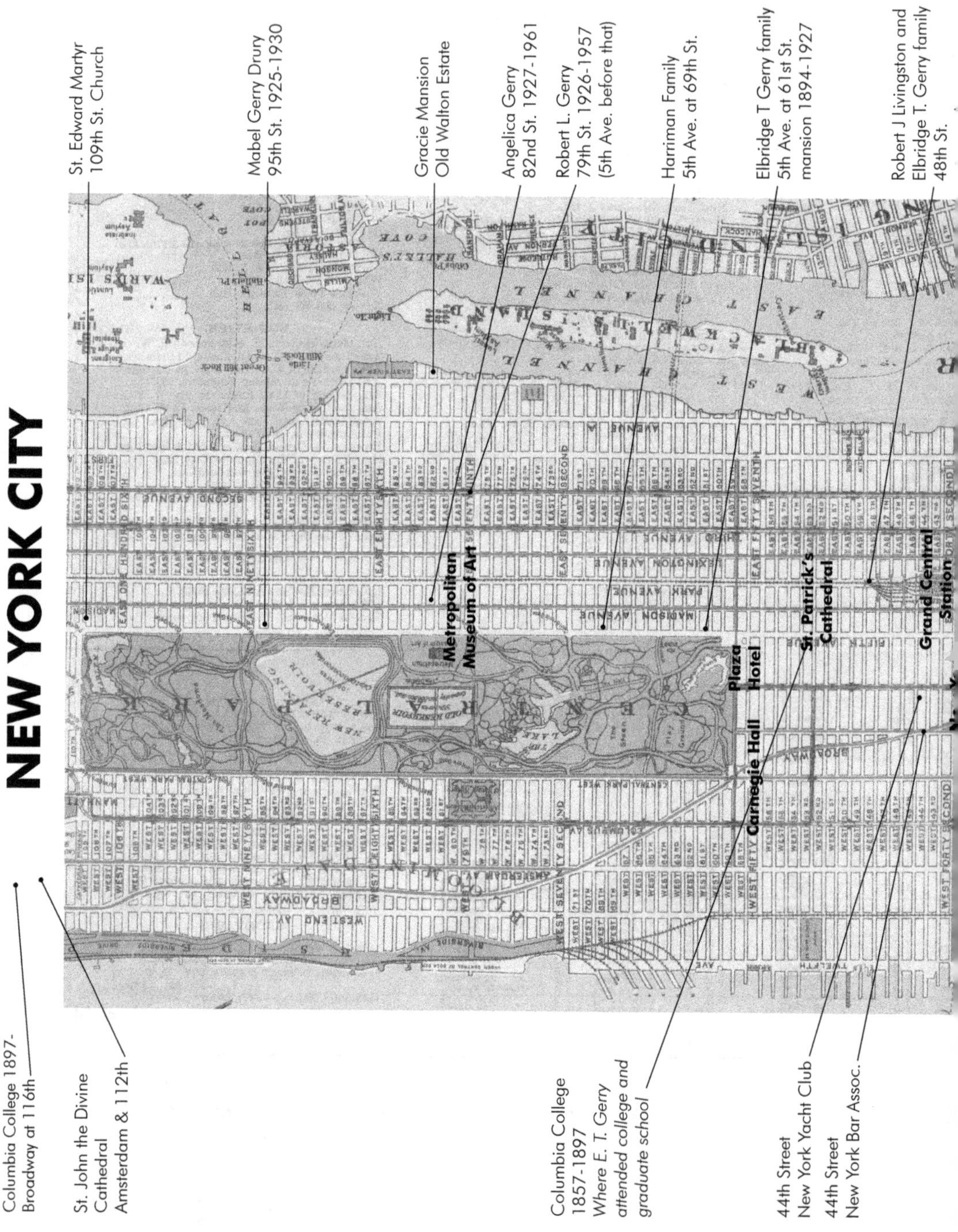

APPENDIX B New York City Locations

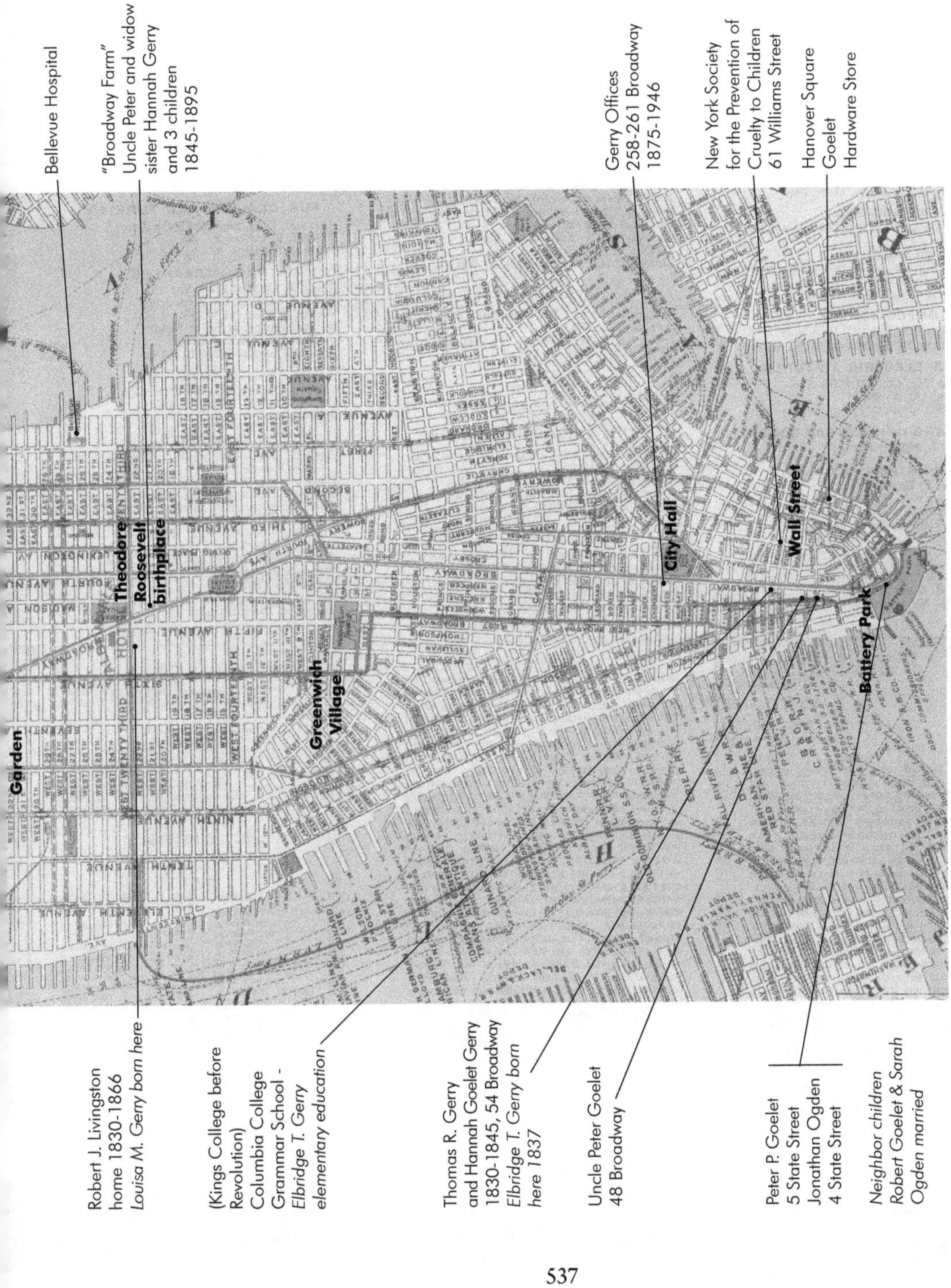

APPENDIX C

COMMODORE ELBRIDGE T. GERRY'S CHILDREN

> We live in a time of transition, an uneasy era which is likely to endure for the rest of this century. During the period we may be tempted to abandon some of the time-honored principles and commitments which have been proven during the difficult times of past generations. We must never yield to this temptation. Our American values are not luxuries, but necessities, not the salt in our bread, but the bread itself.
>
> President Jimmy Carter, Farewell Address

It is worthwhile to begin with a brief exploration of the twentieth century lives of the four Gerry siblings after the death of their father, Commodore Elbridge T. Gerry in 1927. The four Gerry children, Angelica, Mabel, Robert and Peter, cherished their family history and remained almost inseparable after the death of their father Commodore Gerry with whom they were all close. The Lake Delaware farm estate remained the center of family gatherings and summer holidays, and indeed, three of the four siblings owned or built their country homes on the Lake Delaware property. Robert Gerry had built his country mansion, *Aknusti* in 1912 followed by Angelica Gerry, who built her country mansion, *Ancrum House* in 1928. Senator Peter Gerry owned the enlarged and updated historic *Morgan Lewis House* on Lake Delaware after progressively buying his siblings' equal ¼ shares inherited in 1920 from their mother. Mabel Gerry Drury never built a home at Lake Delaware but stayed with one or the other of her siblings when she and husband, Francis, visited during summer holidays or special family gatherings. However, Mabel did inherit *Seaverge*, the Gerry family summer estate in Newport, Rhode Island, which made it available to the other siblings for a few years.

Three of the siblings lived primarily in townhouses in New York City in the same Upper East Side neighborhood as their first cousins, the children of Frederick and Almy Gerry Gallatin, which kept the extended family warmly connected into the second and third generations.

APPENDIX C-1

Mabel Gerry Drury 1872–1930

At the age of fifty-two, socially prominent Mabel Gerry married Francis Saxon Drury in 1925 two years before her father's death. Francis Drury's late father was the former Chaplain of the House of Commons in the British Parliament in London. Mabel's early life had focused on charitable work within the Protestant Episcopal Church in New York City and in the parishes surrounding the Lake Delaware estate. Both of the Gerry sisters lived an active life of charity instilled by the example of their parents and also inspired by some of their trips to Europe at a young age. In her 1887 *Diary* at the age of fourteen, Mabel humorously described the rare privilege of the Gerry family's presentation to Pope Leo XIII at the Vatican in Rome:

> "We were presented to the Pope. We were obliged to wear veils, no gloves and to dress in black. We passed through many beautiful rooms, at last we arrived where there were seats, we visited until they said the Pope was ready, then we went in the next room, my heart beat loud and fast as we stood waiting for him. Well, he came in at last and he blessed the room, he wore a red cloak. Just before the people went up one by one, the Cardinal presented him with some books from New York, then people began to be presented. They threw themselves on their knees and kissed his ring and he blessed them. Well, one lady, I think she was a Presbyterian and seeing these people kiss the ring, she got frightened, not knowing exactly what was expected of her, making a deep curtsey she ran out of the room, I felt like going with her... at last we were told to come around the throne or chair. First he handed Pa his ring, and Pa bent over it and made a cross and appeared to kiss it, well, I remained in a sitting curtsey, and one of the Cardinals standing behind me, pushed me and down I went on my knees, saying kiss his hand, kiss his ring. I paid no attention, the Pope suddenly caught hold of my wrist, well I nearly stumbled so I could hardly stand it, I saw the ring coming, but our interview was nearly over. Peter was handed the ring but he could not kiss it and said No, No, and straightened his head. Well then he stooped his head for the blessing that was all. The Pope was so pleased he laughed and blessed him a second time. We made a last reverence and left the room. Well when we were once more in the carriage I thanked heaven with all my heart." April 2, 1887 [*Peter was ten years old*]

Later, in the years before her marriage, Mabel had the distinction of being one of the first three women elected to the *Board of Managers* of the New York

City *Episcopal Mission Society*. She was also a life-long member of the *Altar Guild* of the Protestant Episcopal Church and a *Trustee* of *Saint Mary's Children's Hospital* and regularly contributed to a variety of charities. The Gerry family was the most well-known and respected members of the Episcopal Church throughout the New York Archdiocese. The family celebrated baptisms, confirmations, marriages, and funerals at *Trinity Chapel* even when they attended Sunday mass in other parishes. When Commodore and Louisa were first married in 1867 they were parishioners of the *Church of the Transfiguration* on East Twenty-Ninth Street where their first daughter, Margaret was baptized and where her funeral was held when she died at age four. In the 1890's when the family moved north to Sixty-First and Park Avenue, the Commodore, Louisa and Angelica Gerry attended mass regularly at the *Church of the Heavenly Rest* or *Trinity Chapel*, while Mabel continued to actively support the little *Church of the Transfiguration* on East Twenty-Ninth Street. After their mother's death in 1920, and before Mabel's marriage in 1925, the sisters lived with their father in the Gerry mansion at Sixty-First and Fifth Avenue. Each joined a new parish, Angelica at *Saint Thomas Episcopal Church* and later the *Church of the Resurrection* on East Seventy-Fourth Street. Mabel joined her sister at the *Church of the Resurrection* for services but she remained a committed and active member of her childhood parish, the *Church of the Transfiguration*, thirty blocks south of the Gerry mansion where her mother Louisa Gerry's funeral and her little sister Margaret's funeral were held years earlier.

The *Church of the Transfiguration*, known locally as the "Little Church Around the Corner" was where all the famous actors attended church, including Sir Laurence Olivier and Tallulah Bankhead, whom the Rector, Father J.H. Randolph Ray, called his "frivolous saints." Because of the close relationship established between the English and Americans while "Bertie" King Edward VII socialized for decades with New York's social elite, many British visitors attended services at the *Church of the Transfiguration* with their American friends and family. In fact, the church had a long tradition of holding memorial services whenever a British monarch died. In 1936 when King George V died, and sixteen years later when King George VI died, the Reverend Ray offered a Requiem Mass attended by many British actors and actresses. Indeed, when King George VI died Sir Laurence Olivier, the son of an Anglican clergyman who was just recently knighted by the King, was asked to give the eulogy. The service was tape-recorded and Sir Laurence Olivier's eulogy was flown to England where it was played as part of the King's funeral services at Windsor Castle. When the Queen Mother visited New York some months after the funeral she took tea with the Reverend Ray at the top of the Empire State Building, where she spoke of the success of the eulogy sent from his church, and noted that the royalties for its reproduction and sale were to be split between the New York Episcopal Actors' Guild and the English Guild in Britain, which looked after the welfare of the English clergy.

More importantly though, the Reverend Ray was the husband of Mabel Gerry's cousin and best friend, Mary Watson Ray. Mabel and Mary's maternal grandmothers were sisters, Louisa Storm Livingston and Glorvina Storm Hoffman, the mother of the famous Dean of the *General Theological Seminary*, Eugene Augustus Hoffman. Commodore Gerry was on the Board of Trustees of the seminary during the years that his uncle was the Dean. In 1957 the Reverend Ray published a lovely history of his parish entitled *My Little Church Around the Corner*, in which he described the friendship of his wife with her cousin Mabel and in which he offered an insightful description of Mabel:

> One of the three most influential women in our parish and a constant visitor at the Rectory was Mabel Gerry. Mabel herself was personally active in a great many charities. She kept a very strict accounting, right to the penny, of all the money she spent on herself in the course of the year, and then gave an exactly equal amount to the parish in addition to funding many other Philanthropies. I could not begin to estimate how much we owed, at the *Little Church*, to her open-handedness and natural generosity. When I took over, we needed all sorts of things, a new organ, a new roof and a lengthy list of expensive repairs. It was with Mabel's help that we made our improvements. As the Commodore got older, Mabel took over many of her father's functions with the *Gerry Society*. She was very fond of children, almost foolishly so. Also, she was fond of bangles and jewelry. She was always bringing classes of children down to me to be instructed for confirmation, and she would sit aside quietly while I went through the lessons. When she thought I had gone on long enough, however, she would begin to get restless and the dozens of bracelets she wore on her arms would set up a tinkling. I always knew when I heard that jingle-jangle that it was time to wind up the instruction and quit.
>
> As a life-long member of the Altar Guild, Mabel and a few devoted friends got together and provided suitable vestments and holy vessels for the prisons in New York. They then undertook to provide vestments and holy vessels for all of the ships crossing the Atlantic between England and America. The local Altar Society at each church was asked to choose its own contribution. Our little church was to raise money for the silver vessels, the chalice, the cruets, the paten and lavabo. All of the ships were supplied and I myself have many times celebrated mass while crossing the Atlantic, using the furnishings supplied by the Altar Society.

During World War I, Mabel Gerry converted *Seaverge,* the family's summer villa, into a temporary convalescent home for soldiers and sailors. After World War I she spent a few years working to establish a home and school for English war orphans outside of London, England, a period when her social life shifted away from New York City. It was in London's vibrant society that Mable finally met her husband, Francis Drury, a widower of high social standing in England, as a Knight of the Order of St. John who traced his family back to William the Conqueror. Fifteen hundred members of New York and London society attended the wedding in *Trinity Chapel* in New York City. She and Francis lived primarily in London at *Drury House,* built in the sixteenth century, which gave its name to the famous *Drury Lane Theatre.* In 1925 they decided to purchase a magnificent townhouse on 3-5 East 95th Street near the corner at Fifth Avenue which they used as their New York City residence when visiting family and friends. Because Mabel inherited *Seaverge* in Newport, Rhode Island they spent a few weeks at the large seaside villa during the first few summers after they were married. However, they were older and *Seaverge* was just too large for their needs so they decided to look for something smaller. Mabel donated the 44-room mansion to the Episcopal Church which briefly used it as a private convent school for girls. When the successful school needed larger quarters the Episcopal Church sold *Seaverge* to a private family. In the late 1950s *Seaverge* was irreparably damaged by a hurricane and was demolished.

In 1930, while Mabel and her husband were living in London, her dear friends the Reverend Ray and his wife, Mabel's cousin Mary, had routinely heard from them by letter. In late spring the letters stopped and they received an unexpected cablegram. Mabel had been checked by the best doctors in London but there was no doubt that she had terminal cancer and she wished to return home to New York City to die. She asked for prayers from her friends and the parish she loved so much, and that the Reverend Ray should be prepared to attend to her as soon as she returned. Angelica called Reverend Ray as soon as her sister Mabel was home. On his visit he found her in reasonable spirits considering the news, and after chatting for a short while they began the sad business of getting ready for death. She was concerned with making her will and thought it "unfair" to her husband, F.E. Saxon Drury, that they had been married for such a few short years. He grieved sincerely and was grateful that Mabel was solicitous of his welfare. Mr. Drury went one day to the Reverend Ray and said he would like to commission a memorial in Mabel's name, which resulted in the beautiful sculpture of the *Gerry Madonna.* To make room for the memorial the parish first removed one of the two baptismal fonts which stood in a beautiful rounded alcove at the end of the south transept, and masons then pierced the semicircular walls with tiny Gothic windows. In each arch was placed a cherub in stained glass to surround and give glory to the Madonna. In the center of the semicircular recess was placed the Madonna and Child, a slender and youthful conception backed by a golden screen of heavy filigree. Architects and artists often come to see the shrine which is well known in New York's Episcopal diocese.

In 1930, in anticipation of her death, Mabel purchased a smaller house in Newport called the *d'Hautville Cottage* from the estate of Frederic Grand d'Hautville of Vevey, Switzerland, which was just a few blocks down Bellevue Avenue from *Seaverge,* her childhood summer residence and where she still enjoyed the society of life-long friendships. Sadly, within several weeks of the purchase, Mabel Gerry Drury died suddenly at her 95th Street townhouse at the age of fifty-eight surrounded by family and friends, just three years after her father Commodore Gerry's death in 1927. Mabel's brothers, Robert and Peter, were the executors of her "will." She left a life-time interest in the Newport *d'Hautville Cottage* to her husband, and at his death the property went to the Episcopal Church. The furniture and linens of the cottage were left to the *Sisters of the Holy Nativity* of the same church. The servants of Mabel's household each received an allotment of money for each year they worked for her, and her secretary, Jean Russell, received a lump sum of $5,000. Her will made distributions to the *General Theological Seminary* of New York, the *Sisters of Saint Mary's of Peekskill,* three New York Episcopal parishes, $20,000 to Mrs. Julia W. West, and $5,000 each to Gertrude and Ann Gardener, her personal friends. Mabel also left $50,000 to the Reverend Ray and his wife Mary, her cousin and best friend, indeed the dearest people in Mabel's life within her beloved Episcopal Church.

Three years after Mabel Gerry's death, her husband Francis Saxon Drury built a second memorial to his beloved wife. He had a magnificent marble Altar designed and built in the *All Soul's Chapel* alcove in the *Cathedral of Saint John the Divine* in New York City in 1933 and had it located just a few yards from the great pillar that is engraved and dedicated to her parents Commodore and Louisa Gerry by their children. The communion rail of the marble altar was constructed of American walnut and the woodwork of the Altar Reredos was painted by Leo Cartwright of Boston. The chapel space and Altar was constructed between February and November when the *All Soul's Chapel* was dedicated to Mabel Gerry and consecrated on November 1, 1933 on the feast of All Souls. The inscription plaque reads:

Of your charity pray for the soul of Mabel
Daughter of Elbridge Thomas Gerry and Louisa Matilda Gerry
And beloved wife of Francis Saxham Elwes Drury
Knight of Grace of the Order of St. John of Jerusalem
She entered into the splendor of the gracious light
On the thirteenth day of October in the year
Of our Lord One Thousand Nine Hundred and Thirty
This altar dedicated to all souls
And to the glory of the ever Blessed Trinity
Is raised in her memory

A few months after his wife's death, Francis Drury sold the large New York townhouse to the *Lycee Francais de New York,* a nonprofit, private school approved by the French Minister of Education as a French school abroad.[1] In 2000 the school built a modern facility next door and sold the townhouse which was subsequently divided into four luxury apartments. Francis Drury did not sell the *d'Hautville Cottage* in Newport where he continued to spend summers and sometimes let his sister-in-law, Angelica Gerry, stay for a few weeks during her summer holidays. In 1941 Francis Drury died from pneumonia at the age of eighty-three at the d'Hautville cottage in Newport. At the time of his death his son, Captain Vyvyan Drury, was the aide de camp to the Duke of Windsor who had famously abdicated the throne for his mistress, Wallis Simpson. Francis Drury's funeral was held at *Saint James Church* at Lake Delaware. He was buried beside Mabel in the Gerry-Livingston Vault at *Saint James Cemetery* at Hyde Park.

Mabel noted in her diary the color of each dress she wore to special occasions.

Mabel Gerry about thirteen

Mabel's formal portrait

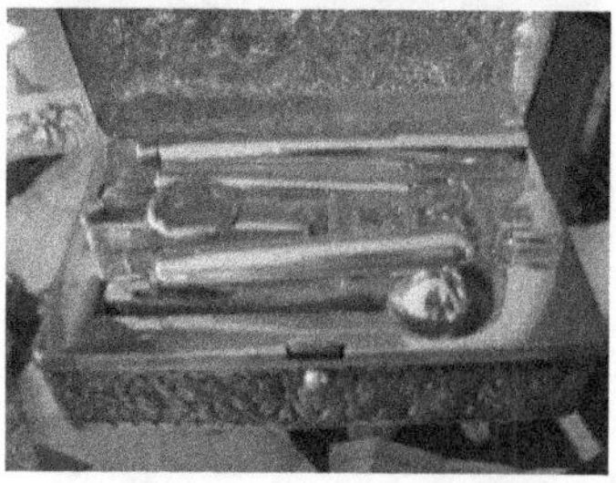

Mabel's silver boxed hair dressing set

Best friends from childhood through adulthood.
Above right Gertrude Vanderbilt (married H.P. Whitney).
Above left Mabel Gerry standing (married Francis S. Drury).

Church of the Transfiguration "little church around the corner"

Mabel Gerry

Reverend Ray
Mabel's close friend

His wife Mollie
Mabel's first cousin

Shrine to honor Mabel

Madonna and child in shrine (*left*)

Mabel Gerry Memorial Altar
in the Cathedral of Saint John the Divine

Altar Dedication on November 1, 1933

APPENDIX C-2

Angelica Livingston Gerry 1871–1960

Angelica Gerry, the oldest of the four siblings, was fifty-five when her father died and by then, a recognized bachelor lady in New York society. She inherited the Gerry mansion at Fifth Avenue and Sixty-First Street, which she immediately signed-over to the *Gerry Estates, Inc.* to be demolished for the development of what had become extremely valuable property in a time when the wealthy were down-sizing, usually to luxurious Fifth Avenue apartments. Angelica left the details to her brother Robert Gerry, the manager of the *Gerry Estates, Inc.*, to work with a syndicate of investors who built the *Pierre Hotel* on the Fifth Avenue property. Angelica then decided to move up Fifth Avenue to be closer to her sister Mabel. She bought a small but beautiful and exclusive townhouse on East Eighty-Second Street, where her block ended at Fifth Avenue across the street from the monumental steps at the entrance to the *Metropolitan Museum of Art.* In 1928 her brother Robert and his wife Cornelia Harriman Gerry, and their four boys had moved to a large townhouse just five blocks away on East Seventy-Ninth Street. Her sister Mabel and her husband, Francis Drury, were just eleven blocks north on East Ninety-Fifth Street. Of the four Gerry siblings, three were within walking distance of one another, just a beautiful stroll up or down Fifth Avenue for visits.

As a wealthy single woman, Angelica surrounded herself with family and friends, enjoyed attending the opera and theatre, and immersed herself in the country life of Lake Delaware. Because her brother Robert had built his own country mansion on a hill overlooking Lake Delaware and the historic lake house which was owned by her brother, Senator Peter Gerry, Angelica decided to build her own country mansion at Lake Delaware to be near her siblings and nephews on the farm where she had spent summers riding horses and swimming.

To furnish her new home and to develop her gardens at Lake Delaware, Angelica Gerry salvaged furniture and architectural pieces from the old Gerry mansion on Fifth Avenue before and during the demolition process. She had the furniture moved to either her townhouse in the City or to storage at Lake Delaware for use in the new mansion. Her three siblings also selected furnishings from the Gerry mansion to keep as treasured family mementos. Fine examples of these furnishings are shown in photographs in the catalogue of the auction for *Ancrum House* that was held by *Parke-Bernet Galleries* in March 1961, a year after Angelica Gerry's death at her 82nd Street town house.[2] Many special family artifacts were not auctioned and were moved to the historic Morgan Lewis house at Lake Delaware.

In the midst of her sophisticated life style in New York City, the most important focus of Angelica Gerry's regular activity was charity work. She developed a network of friends among caregivers and welfare agents at charitable institutions like the *Saint Mary's Hospital for Children* in New York City and the *New York Society for the Prevention of Cruelty to Children.* Angelica used every society function, like the opera and theatrical shows, as fundraising opportunities to benefit children aide societies. She was thoroughly defined by her Protestant Episcopal faith just like her father, Commodore Gerry, and both were perceived by some as stubborn when they stood their ground on decisions or positions that they believed were right, either morally or intellectually. Angelica, a highly intelligent woman with an excellent education, had a logical, pragmatic attitude toward the challenges of life. Although a bit stiff, both father and daughter shared a recognized and well-respected selflessness, indeed, an unconditional concern for others, especially underprivileged children. Just as her father had dedicated his entire adult life to the *New York Society for the Prevention of Cruelty to Children,* Angelica Gerry dedicated her life to the less fortunate children in the communities surrounding Lake Delaware, Andes, Bovina, and Delhi. Today, older adults in the community still recall her assistance from *Ancrum House* when they were children with both medical and educational support. One resident of Bovina recalled a night as a child when he was very ill and his mother called Angelica for help. She immediately roused her nurse and chauffeur and had them go with her to the Bovina family's home to attend to the sick child. [3]

The Gerry girls knitted hats and gloves for the neighborhood during childhood summers at Lake Delaware which was sweetly described in Lillian Gerry's diary written in the early 1880's. Angelica had embraced the spirit of giving and helping others during her teenage years when it became an integral part of her persona, and perhaps was another reason she never felt compelled to marry. When she was eighteen and a debutante in *Gilded Gotham,* the newspapers had already taken notice of her charitable disposition which they described rather than noting her youthful beauty, the usual focus of press coverage for the lovely debutantes. One article described a large trunk full of toys, books, dolls, and sweets that Angelica had put together and sent to the *Sheltering Arms Children's Home* in Augusta, Georgia. The Gerry family had traveled to Augusta for treatment when Lillian Gerry's tuberculosis became critical and while there the family visited and contributed to the children's shelter. The press interviewed Angelica to ask what she was giving up for Lent that year and she replied that she was giving her allowance, which she usually spent on chocolate and books, to the children's shelter to help make the children's lives a little happier.[4] In adulthood, with her own independent income and property, Angelica Gerry began an unpublicized assistance program that was quietly known throughout the local community and Episcopal parishes in Delaware County. She was thirty-five years old in the summer of 1906 and immersed with her mother and sister in their well-established parish charity work at Lake Delaware, when Angelica first made her decision to focus her life on the education of local children. She was proven correct in her belief that with the parents' permission, sending children to private high schools, industrial schools, and college, based on their abilities and interest, would provide them with a life of self-sufficiency, and ultimately encourage and uplift the entire community.

By the time Angelica had built her own home at Lake Delaware in 1928 she had already begun keeping formal records about the children she had helped since 1906, noting their name, birth date, family circumstances, and a chronological notation for each type of assistance provided and the amount of money expended. Each record continued to be updated over a period of years for each and every child. Eventually she had her secretary transcribe the records into a lovely black leather binder with the word *Protégés* embossed in gold letters on the cover. This is the first time that this record book has been seen outside the Gerry family and it traces Angelica's dedicated charitable support of 88 young men and 158 young women between 1906 and 1963. The children were privately recommended to Angelica by parish priests, child welfare agents, friends and local merchants, even the families themselves would contact her when in need. She was blind to the circumstances of the child's birth and helped many illegitimate children, mentally disturbed teenagers, and entire families left penniless at the death of one or both parents. She educated out of poverty at least one doctor at the Cornell University Medical School, countless nurses, a gifted music teacher at Skidmore College, and many business men. The doctor returned to become a general practitioner in the nearby town of Margaretville, thereby sharing the success with the entire community. The records show that Angelica was truly a "godmother" to these children; she paid for their health care, from eye exams and glasses, appendectomies, dental work, and surgery to remove a sixth toe, to mental health care, clothing and travel money. She did what it took to ensure that every child had the means and care to finish school, whether it was at an industrial school, a church school, or college and professional school; as long as the student progressed successfully, Angelica paid the bills through completion. Angelica gave each young person a watch when they had successfully graduated from their educational program, no doubt a symbol of "time well spent" and a future filled with promise. Those who attempted to repay her later in life were turned down because her assistance was the right thing to do and because it was a moral and community imperative she learned first-hand from Commodore and Louisa Gerry throughout her childhood. Some records note that Angelica corresponded with her young people throughout their adult lives, and sent her "favorites" wedding and baptismal gifts. It was not unusual for her to be asked to be godmother to their children when they were baptized. Several of the marriages were celebrated in Angelica's own *Saint James Church,* just a walk down the lane from her Lake Delaware home. While unmarried, Angelica had "her children" whom she raised with love and who in turn, both loved her and were grateful for their opportunity to succeed in life. When Angelica died in 1960 she left a valuable annuity in her will to continue paying the tuition for any of her young people who continued in school after her death.[5] Angelica Gerry sent so many students to the *Delhi Academy,* which became the *State University of New York* at Delhi, and contributed so much money to the institution, that two years after her death, the first Residence Hall built on the campus was named in her honor, *Gerry Hall.* Her nephew, Elbridge T. Gerry II, spoke at the dedication ceremony on June 8, 1963 on behalf of the Gerry family.[6]

While Angelica was a life-long philanthropist, she also used her wealth to hire the best architect available for her two major building projects, *Saint James Church* and her country mansion at Lake Delaware, *Ancrum House.* She hired Ralph Adams Cram, the great architect of cathedrals, churches and universities like *Saint John the Divine* in New York City and *Princeton University.* While working with Angelica the Gerry family took an interest in Cram's continuing work on the Episcopal cathedral in New York City, *Saint John the Divine,* and in 1925, through Robert L. Gerry, they pledged $100,000 toward its completion with a stipulation that $90,000 be used for the erection of one of the great piers in the nave. Ralph Cram rarely designed private homes, but Angelica was a friend and fellow member of the Anglo-Catholic wing of the Episcopal Church. Cram, the son of a minister, was such a dedicated believer that the Episcopal Church in the United States honored him, along with architect Richard Upjohn (who designed the home Senator Peter Gerry owned in Providence, Rhode Island) and the artist John LaFarge, with a feast day on December 16 on the liturgical calendar. The *New York Times* called him "one of the most prominent Episcopalian laymen in the country," and he was featured on the cover of *Time Magazine* December 13, 1926 for his body of work as an architect, an author, and for the seven years Ralph Adams Cram was the Head of the Architecture Department at the *Massachusetts Institute of Technology* .[7]

When Ralph Cram saw the 360 acres of rolling hills owned by Angelica Gerry at Lake Delaware, he suggested she hire landscape architect Fletcher Steele to design the gardens and property that surrounded the location of the house Cram had designed. The Georgian style architecture of the house was elegant and spacious but not heavy handed, and much of the salvaged mahogany and oak wood panels from the New York City Gerry mansion were used throughout the interior. Steele worked easily with Cram to create a grand public drive up to the entrance of the house called "the Gallop" which ran parallel to a service driveway that was hidden and separated by a lawn and a long row of mature beech trees. The same lawn and stand of trees separated the other side of "the Gallop," from another narrow lane that ran along the edge of the formal gardens. These side lanes protected the beautiful red stones that covered "the Gallop" the formal and impressive entrance road for guests who would be dropped off at the front door and the cars would disappear behind the beech trees. It was a brilliant design that later served another purpose for the *Aknusti Horse Farm* after Angelica Gerry's death. Her nephew converted the design of the driveway into an oval track that followed the lane on one side of "the Gallop" across to the lane that ran down the other side of "the Gallop" and around the far end that mimicked a race track for his standard bred horses.

After Ralph Adams Cram completed the 23-room country house, which included a dog "grooming room" with all white tile, except for the center tiles on the floor that formed the picture of a dog, Fletcher Steele continued to work on the gardens. In fact, he experimented with Angelica to creatively evolve the landscape for the next twenty-three years. He incorporated decorative balustrades salvaged from the Gerry mansion in New York City to use along the curved edge of a patio overlooking the horse meadow, and placed the ten-foot tall white marble statue of the seated *Penelope* as a central feature in the flower gardens. The marble statue is one of only four in the United States by sculptor Franklin Simons, which Commodore Elbridge T. Gerry purchased in Rome, Italy in 1887 during the trip when the Gerry family was presented to Pope Leo XIII. The receipt signed by the sculptor remains tucked into a small case, about the size of a deck of cards, that still holds the nineteenth century sepia colored "card stock" family photographs that Commodore Gerry had always carried with him since his college days at Columbia University.

The *Ancrum House* garden project was the largest commission of Fletcher Steele's career; the plant list alone ran in excess of one hundred pages. Angelica's summer holidays in Newport, Rhode Island, visiting her aunt's estate, *Ochre Court*, would have taught her much about flower specimens and how a formal garden might be designed. Of course her father, Commodore Gerry competed in the Newport Flower Shows and had a number of greenhouses that Angelica no doubt explored. Fletcher Steele was invited to Angelica's parties where her guests could join Steele for a stroll through the landscaped property to enjoy the expansive views and intimate corners with the personal guidance of the landscape architect. Fletcher Steele often obtained new commissions from these party guests through referrals. Angelica's brother, Senator Peter Gerry and his wife Edith, hired Steele in 1926 based on his *Ancrum* plans, to landscape the Mediterranean style holiday home on her *Biltmore* estate that Edith began building the year before she met Peter. Although *Ancrum House* was demolished in 1962 after Angelica Gerry's death, many features of Fletcher Steele's grand garden design remain in place although the property looks more like an archaeological site than a landscaped garden.

From 1930 to 1956 Angelica Gerry was also engaged in raising prize *Guernsey* cows at Lake Delaware and produced dairy products in her three-story *Ancrum House Creamery*. She had mentioned in passing to her local feed supplier that she liked the *Guernsey* because the calves looked so much like spotted fawns. Unfortunately, she lost the creamery and dairy barn in a raging fire in 1956 during a storm with hurricane force winds. All of the creamery equipment was destroyed and she lost twenty-four of her prize Guernsey cows along with tons of baled hay that went up in flames. Neither the barn nor the creamery were ever rebuilt.[8]

Angelica Gerry was 84 years old when the dairy enterprise was lost, but she still had her beloved dogs and horses to care for and enjoy in her old age. The following year, in 1957, she lost both of her brothers, Robert and Peter, on the same day and neither brother knew the other had died. Angelica lived just four more years as the last surviving child of Commodore Elbridge T. Gerry's six children. She died at the age of 89 in February, 1960 surrounded by her nephews after a long and meaningful life. She left large bequests to the local Episcopal parishes, favorite charities, and her four nephews, the sons of Robert L. Gerry. Her funeral was held at *Saint James Church* which she had built to honor her mother and she was buried on a hillside just up the lane from the church on the Lake Delaware estate. In fact, sometime after the death of her brother's Angelica consulted their widows, Cornelia and Edith, who agreed to have Robert and Peter re-interred in 1958 from the *Gerry-Livingston Vault* at Hyde Park to the pastoral cemetery created by Angelica just for the Gerry family at Lake Delaware. Angelica selected a low grassy hillside along the entrance lane to Lake Delaware midway between *Saint James Church* and *Ancrum House.* Both Cornelia and Edith were eventually buried next to their husbands Robert and Peter at Lake Delaware.

The Hyde Park vaults of the *Gerry-Livingston Mausoleum* hold the remains of Commodore and Louisa Gerry, their two youngest daughters, Margaret and Lillian, and also Louisa Gerry's parents, Robert James and Louisa Livingston. The last family members interred in the Gerry Vault were Mabel Gerry Drury and her husband, Francis Saxon Elwes Drury.

Angelica Gerry as teen

Angelica's formal portrait

Angelica in a Worth gown

Portrait of Angelica on her horse

Angelica's New York City townhouse, 11 East 82nd Street

Church of the Resurrection
Angelica's New York Parish

Photos of the beginning and mid-point of the famous annual Gerry 300 mile long coach run from New York City, up the Hudson Valley to Lake Delaware and back using 18 teams of horses.

Gerry siblings on coach in front of Park Avenue mansion

Gerry siblings arrive at Lake Delaware

Angelica Gerry

Saint James Church at entrance road to Lake Delaware

Ralph Adams Cram
Architect of
Ancrum House
and Saint James Church

Dedication of Saint James Church at Lake Delaware

Ancrum House at Lake Delaware designed by architect Ralph Cram

The Ancrum House landscape plan (*left*)

The initial plan was completed in a few short years but Angelica Gerry continued to work with Fletcher Steele to evolve the landscape and gardens with experimental plantings over two decades.

Fletcher Steele
Landscape architect
of Ancrum House

Various garden architecture and views at Ancrum House

Both the marble statue of Penelope (*above*) and the hooded wicker garden lounge (*left*) remain at the Gerry's Lake Delaware estate long after Angelica's Ancrum House was demolished over fifty years ago.

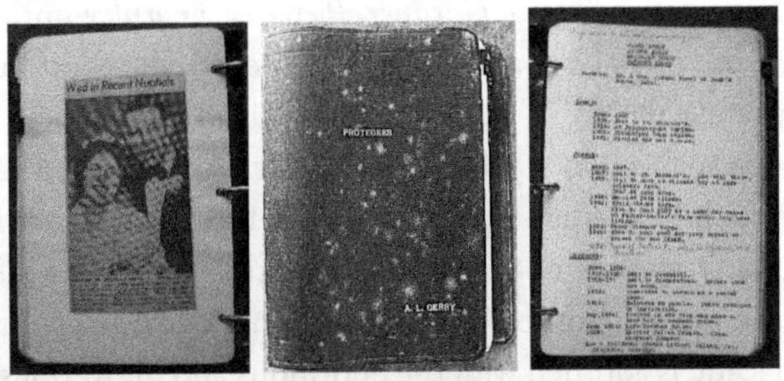

Angelica's Protégé book where she noted the progress of the 180 boys and girls she supported and educated until her death.

Angelica Gerry

Gerry Dormitory at Delhi University, New York named in honor of Angelica Gerry

APPENDIX C-3

Senator Peter Goelet Gerry 1879–1957

Senator Peter Goelet Gerry, the youngest of the siblings, was forty-eight years old when his father died and had been happily married to his second wife, Edith Vanderbilt Gerry for two years. At the time of their marriage, Peter had been a Senator from Rhode Island for nine years and well established in both Washington, D.C. and Providence, Rhode Island social and political circles. Before his political career, he practiced law immediately after Harvard Law School with the Providence firm of *Gardner, Pierce & Thornley* until he ran for Congress in 1912. Later, in 1917 at age 38, he became the youngest man ever elected to the United States Senate in Rhode Island history. While in the Senate, he bought two newspapers, in 1921 the *Providence News* and in 1929 the old *Providence Tribune,* which he merged and later sold in 1937. When not in Washington, Senator Peter Gerry worked out of his Providence office in the historic *Turk's Head Building* at the intersection of Westminster and Weybosset Street, a building whose corner façade is adorned with the enormous and mysterious stone head of a Turk.[9]

Edith Vanderbilt Gerry had lived with her daughter, Cornelia Vanderbilt Cecil, at *Biltmore House* in North Carolina since her first husband's death in 1914. She had a "life time" interest in the property which would then pass to her daughter and heirs. Edith's son-in-law was British aristocrat John F.A. Cecil, the descendant of William Cecil, Chief Advisor to Queen Elizabeth I. Coincidentally, Cecil also shared charitable projects with the Senator's sister, Mabel Gerry, in both London and New York and he no doubt knew Mabel's husband, Francis Drury, another British aristocrat from London. After marrying Edith's daughter, John Cecil moved to North Carolina and happily joined Edith in the management of the *Biltmore* estate in the manner George Vanderbilt had envisioned in 1889 – 1895 when he asked Richard Morris Hunt to build the Châteauesque style mansion. He also hired Frederick Law Olmsted to design the extensive gardens, roadways and panoramic landscape of the estate. *Biltmore House* itself had an unprecedented 4 acres of floor space, 250 rooms, 35 bedrooms, 43 bathrooms, and 65 fireplaces and 23,000 volume library. The basement housed a swimming pool, gymnasium and changing rooms, bowling alley, servants' quarters, and kitchens. During this massive building project in North Carolina, Richard M. Hunt simultaneously worked on the Gerrys' Fifth Avenue mansion in New York City. The two projects ultimately proved overwhelming and Hunt's health declined until he died in 1896 just as *Biltmore House* was completed and the Gerry mansion was near completion.

During her sixteen year marriage to George Vanderbilt and her ten years as a widow, Edith Gerry actively supported *Biltmore Farms'* progressive experiments in scientific farming, animal bloodline breeding, and forestry conservation with the goal of making *Biltmore* a self-sustaining estate. The estate was recognized as having the first professionally managed forest in the United States and had the first School of Forestry in North America, established in 1898 by Dr. Carl Schenck at the urging of Frederick Law Olmsted.[10] Today, Edith's grandson, George Cecil, is the owner and manager of the 8,000 acre *Biltmore* estate and the *Biltmore Farms Company.* Her second grandson, William Cecil, former Vice President of New York's *Chase Manhattan Bank,* now owns *Biltmore House* which is a designated Historic Landmark.[11]

When Edith's daughter became pregnant, she decided to build a smaller Mediterranean style home nearby on the *Biltmore* estate. Edith never found the enormous size of the Vanderbilt mansion appealing and she was excited to create a place of her own. In late 1924 she invited a group of friends to visit from Washington to see the progress of the building project. One of her guests asked if she might bring Senator Peter Gerry along to give him time to heal from his recent and highly publicized divorce from Mathilde Townsend who had been having an affair with Sumner Wells for over a year. The week-long visit to North Carolina was a great success for a number of reasons. One was that Senator Peter Gerry had graduated from Harvard with a bachelor's degree in science before he earned his law degree, and had been interested in agricultural science ever since his childhood on the Lake Delaware farm estate. Edith toured Peter through the experimental farming and forest conservation projects which stimulated endless discussion. The construction tour of Edith's new home, called the *Frith* which meant both "peace" and "open space in the woods," stimulated a conversation about the Senator's historic Morgan Lewis family home at Lake Delaware. Senator Peter Gerry found a wealth of shared interests with Edith and by the time he left *Biltmore* they were in the midst of a welcome and happy mid-life romance. They were married several months later in 1925 and after a leisurely post-honeymoon visit to Lake Delaware, the love of cows became a family hobby. Edith had an expert dairyman, Tom Wallis, at her *Biltmore Farms,* and since both Angelica and Peter Gerry raised prize cows, *Guernsey* and *Holstein,* she asked Tom to move to Lake Delaware in 1927 to manage the family dairy business. It became a great success and a happy family business. Edith was especially pleased that her husband represented Rhode Island as a Senator because she was born and raised in Newport where Peter had first been elected to office on the City Council in 1911 and where he spent many a happy summer holiday throughout his youth.

Edith was a good match as a political wife and soon formed a casual women voters club in Rhode Island that evolved into the *Women's Democratic Club,* and later she was repeatedly elected President of the *Congressional Wives Club* in Washington, D.C. from 1927 to 1929. Edith's long life was always full and busy as she supported her husband's career while she also pursued her passionate support of the *Biltmore* horticultural and farming enterprises. Her husband, Senator Peter Gerry, passionately supported his wife's progressive work at *Biltmore* and pursued his political career with both success and great personal satisfaction.

Senator Peter Gerry was also the Vice President of the *American Humane Association* just as his father, Commodore Gerry had been at one time, and both were Director and Counsel to the *New York Society for the Prevention of Cruelty to Children.* Senator Gerry was known as a conservative Democrat who opposed the New Deal policies of President Franklin D. Roosevelt, and, as a member of the *Senate Naval Affairs Committee,* he fought for a strong Navy and was instrumental in developing major naval installations in Rhode Island.[12] He passed legislation that permitted him to enter into a contract with the Secretary of the Navy on May 12, 1917 to lease his steam yacht the *Owera* for use by the Navy during World War I.[13] The steam yacht, built in 1907 in Leith, Scotland, retained its name as the *USS Owera* and operated out of Newport, Rhode Island in the experimental submarine zones off Long Island Sound and New London, Connecticut. Through most of the war the *USS Owera* towed torpedo targets for submarine target practice and acted as a patrol vessel along the East Coast. In January 1919 the steam yacht was "decommissioned" at the New York Navy Yard in Brooklyn and returned to Senator Gerry for his private use. Another piece of legislation that would have perplexed his father was a tax measure. Commodore Gerry had changed his residence to Newport, Rhode Island to avoid what he considered prohibitive income taxes in New York. Senator Peter Gerry worked to reduce the standard income tax while he also proposed an amendment to increase the federal surtax on large incomes, which passed. He followed in his great-grandfather Vice President Elbridge Gerry's footsteps, in that they both voted from a principled position rather than the prevailing party position. His great-grandfather had proposed the establishment of *a Supreme Court Library* in 1774 which was postponed by Congress for nearly one hundred years. The year that Commodore Gerry died, 1927, the Supreme Court began to build its first stand-alone building on Capitol Hill. Senator Peter Gerry revived his great-grandfather's proposal to establish a library for the Supreme Court of the United States with new legislation. The bill was signed by the President and authorized Chief Justice Howard Taft to accept as a gift from Senator Gerry the law library bequeathed to him by his father which included books from the Founding Father's eighteenth century private library.[14] Architect Cass Gilbert met with Senator Peter Gerry to design a magnificent library to occupy the entire fourth floor of the new historic Supreme Court building to house the 30,000 volume collection of Commodore Elbridge T. Gerry. The books were boxed in 1927 to allow for the demolition of the Gerry mansion on Fifth Avenue in New York City, and sent to the United States Capitol where they were stored in the basement until 1935 when they were moved into the new *Supreme Court Library* across the street. The *Gerry Collection,* as it is known within the Supreme Court, stimulated the research and writing of this historical biography of Commodore Elbridge T. Gerry by the author, then the Director of the Supreme Court Library. In fact, the Gerry collection that serves as the foundation of the *U.S. Supreme Court Library* is the historic equivalent to Thomas Jefferson's collection that serves as the foundation of the *Library of Congress,* a gift after the War of 1812.

Senator Peter Gerry was a leading member of the *Democratic National Committee* for several years and was the *Democratic Whip* of the United States Senate. The Senator was respected as a hard-working and astute politician and a generous philanthropist, who also just happened to be a society man, accomplished polo player and was a former coaching whip.

Senator and Mrs. Peter Gerry gave a great deal of personal energy to their public duties and special interests, and also managed to carve out quality time for shared projects like the annual *Children's Picnic* and the annual *Children's Christmas Party* that they personally hosted for the poor children of Providence, Rhode Island. They enjoyed some relief from the intensity of their public lives with quiet reclusive trips to *Frith House,* their modest Mediterranean style home nestled in the isolated forest of the *Biltmore* estate in North Carolina, or returned to their *Morgan Lewis House* at Lake Delaware. When they visited Senator Gerry's siblings in New York City they stayed at the *Pierre Hotel* built on the old Gerry mansion property on Fifth Avenue. They shared a full and happy marriage for over thirty years, and while they had no children of their own, they enjoyed Edith's daughter and two grandsons as their immediate family. Senator Peter Gerry died at his Providence home at the age of seventy-eight on October 30, 1957 after a long illness. He died just a few hours before his older brother, Robert who had also been ill for quite some time at his *Aknusti* estate. Senator Peter Gerry's funeral was held at *Saint James Church* and after his initial burial in the *Gerry-Livingston Mausoleum* at Hyde Park, he was re-interred at the lovely cemetery at Lake Delaware, where his wife Edith was buried beside him one year later in 1958. Senator Peter Gerry's home in Providence, Rhode Island, known as the *Woods-Gerry House,* is one of the most beautiful homes on Prospect Street near *Brown University*. The Italianate style house was built in 1860 by the famous architect, Richard Upjohn, was added to the National Register of Historic Places in 1971 and now houses the Admissions Office and Gallery for the *Rhode Island School of Design*.[15]

Senator Peter Goelet Gerry 1879-1957

Edith Dresser Vanderbilt Gerry 1873-1958

Peter Gerry was an expert horseman and a serious farmer since his youth.

Edith Gerry loved horses and farming.

Peter and Edith at an event. They shared a long and happy 30 year marriage.

Cornelia Vanderbilt Cecil with her husband John Cecil

ca. 1905

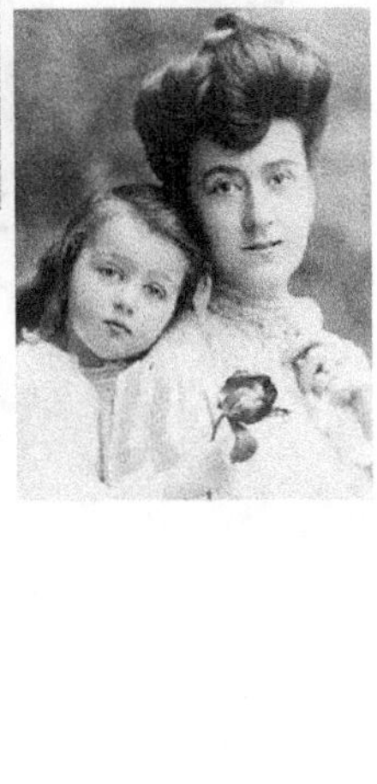

Edith Vanderbilt with daughter Cornellia before the death of her husband George Vanderbilt in 1914.

Senator Gerry with Senator Josiah Bailey

Senator Peter G. Gerry on Capitol Hill sitting in his chair in the Senate Chamber

Senator Peter G. Gerry walking on Capitol Hill in Washington, D.C.

Biltmore Industries in Asheville, N.C.

Edith Gerry wearing wool suit made of Biltmore "home-spun" made by Biltmore Industries, 1924

Biltmore Estate in Asheville, North Carolina

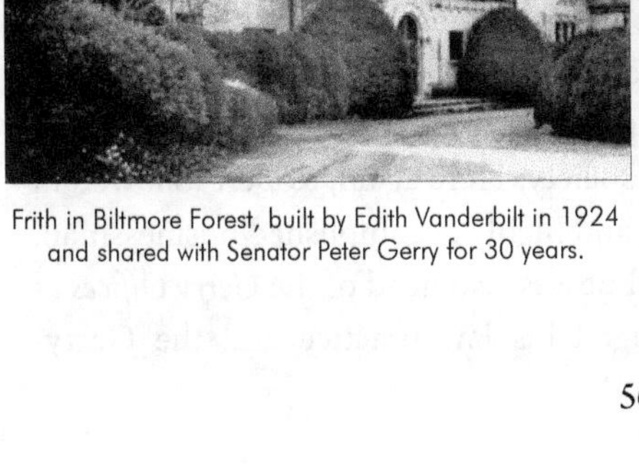

Frith in Biltmore Forest, built by Edith Vanderbilt in 1924 and shared with Senator Peter Gerry for 30 years.

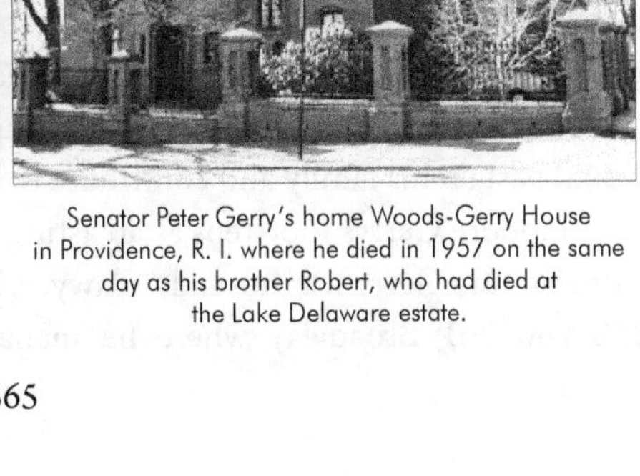

Senator Peter Gerry's home Woods-Gerry House in Providence, R. I. where he died in 1957 on the same day as his brother Robert, who had died at the Lake Delaware estate.

APPENDIX C-4

Robert Livingston Gerry 1877–1957

Robert Livingston Gerry, the third child and older son of Commodore Gerry, was fifty years old when his father died in 1927 and the only sibling who produced grandchildren for the Commodore and Louisa Gerry. Because Robert had married in 1908, his four sons enjoyed their grandparents during their entire youth. The boys ranged in age from six to twelve years old when Louisa died in 1920, and ages thirteen to nineteen years old when the Commodore died in 1927, the eldest in college and the younger three in high school.

Robert attended Harvard College from 1897 to 1900 but dropped out before completing his senior year. In 1900 he was listed as a member of the *Hasty Pudding Club*, a social club that put on full-costumed theatrical shows which suited Robert's fun-loving personality.[16] He and younger brother Peter were at Harvard for two overlapping years, 1898-1900, when they were both star polo players, having been raised on horses since childhood. Robert's own sons would also become star polo players at Harvard University. Not only were Robert and Peter both members of the *Spee Club* but so were Robert's sons Ebby II, Edward and Henry, as well as Ebby's sons Ebby III and Peter II, and a fourth generation, Christopher, Peter II's son.

Robert would not have dropped out his senior year without first discussing it with his father who was open-minded even while he held his own staunch views on most matters. It was up to Robert to convince Commodore Gerry of the wisdom of his decision and especially, what he would pursue instead. The Gerrys managed to remain a close-knit family across generations because they shared a core foundation in their Episcopal faith and despite their wealth, each individual had an unshakable personal work ethic coupled with good judgment and common sense. Of equal importance to the strength of the family bond was the freedom that Commodore and Louisa Gerry gave their four children to think for themselves. Peter was most like his father in his passion for the law and politics while Robert was most like his father in his thorough enjoyment of his family life and his children. It was less important that Robert finish college and pursue graduate work than it was that he passionately engaged in a career that suited him and would sustain his family and contribute to society. Here again, Robert followed in Commodore Gerrys footsteps as an astute and highly accomplished businessman. Commodore Gerry was not only a lawyer, but was also head of the *Gerry Offices* at 258 and 261 Broadway where he managed his law practice and the Gerry-

Livingston real estate holdings in New York City, and also advised the Goelet and Gallatin families in real estate litigation. He understood that Robert was the son most interested in the family business, so with his father's blessing, Robert L. Gerry dropped out of college and immediately joined *Strong, Sturgis and Company,* a brokerage firm at 20 Broad Street, as a clerk for six months of training. In the fall of 1901 he joined the real estate firm of *E.A. Cruikshank and Company* at 141 Broadway, just two blocks from his father's office, where he remained for nine years and rapidly advanced to become the Director of the company. In 1910 Commodore Gerry retired at the age of seventy-three from the *Gerry Offices* and proudly turned over the role of head of the enterprise to his son, Robert L. Gerry, then thirty-three years old and the father of a two year-old son, Elbridge T. Gerry the second, known as "Ebby." The firm's name changed to *Gerry Estates, Inc.* and in the 1930's Robert's own twin sons joined the firm. In 1946 the thriving business was renamed *Gerry Brothers, Inc.* and their father, Robert, happily retired in 1952 at the age of seventy-five.

Robert Gerry remained single until age thirty-two when he married in 1908. During his bachelor years, and employed at *Sturgis and Strong,* he indulged his passion for horses and participated in the annual coaching parades, the intermediate coaching runs between New York City and the *Belmont Race Track,* and the annual favorite "Gerry Long Run," a five day, 300 mile coach race from the Gerry mansion at Fifth Avenue in New York City to the Lake Delaware farm and back. The invention of the automobile put an end to these coaching events.

Robert Gerry was a fortunate young man in that he had two intimate mentors, his father, Commodore Gerry, and his future father-in-law, Edward Henry Harriman, the railroad executive of the *Gilded Age* who was a passionate conservator of the nation's natural landscape and a successful horse breeder at his *Arden Stables* in Orange County, New York. Harriman joined Robert and Peter Gerry in a horse breeding partnership in Arden Stables and the Aknusti Stud Farm that created Arden Homestead Stables at Lake Delaware.

Harriman, like Robert, had not graduated from college and as a teenager Harriman shared the streets of New York with many other struggling homeless boys while he worked hard every day to be noticed on Wall Street where he did whatever was asked of him as a messenger boy. Soon enough a brokerage house decided to train him as a clerk and Harriman quickly became the managing clerk by the age of twenty. His days as a solitary boy led Harriman in 1876 to establish the first *Boys' Club* in New York City. Today there are three full-service Clubhouses in New York City that serve over 4,000 boys. Harriman's great grandson, Elbridge T. Gerry III, also known as "Ebby" like his father, served as a Vice-

President and Trustee. Harriman's work with the *Boys' Club* resonated with Robert Gerry because his own father, Commodore Gerry, had founded the *New York Society for the Prevention of Cruelty to Children* in the 1870's. Their shared dedication to the welfare of young New York City boys created a great mutual respect between Harriman and Gerry that enriched their evolving relationship, not only in business, but also in their shared passion for horses.

Robert first met E.H. Harriman in 1902 when he and Peter Gerry joined the established polo set led by Harriman, John R. Townsend and August Belmont Jr. at the *Meadow Brook Club* on Long Island to play polo and fox hunt. In early 1903 Robert Gerry asked Harriman, his mentor, to invest with him in land located near the villages of Warwick and Goshen in Orange County, New York, to establish a new center for equestrian sports, especially the fox hunt and polo. With a gentleman's agreement in hand they moved their hunt club to Goshen in 1904 and used the beautiful *Red Swan Inn* built in 1903 in the nearby village of Warwick as their club house for socializing. Over the next few years, in the midst of the annual fox hunts and equestrian competitions, Robert Gerry socialized with Harriman's daughter, Cornelia, and they fell deeply in love. Although Cornelia was seven years younger than Robert she was a spirited young woman who gave Robert a "run for his money" as an accomplished and award-winning horsewoman. The wealthy Harriman family lived in a beautiful townhouse just a few blocks north of the Gerry mansion at Sixty-Ninth and Fifth Avenue in New York City which encouraged Robert and Cornelia to see each throughout the year. The Harriman townhouse was sold and replaced with a multi-story luxury apartment building in 1929 just two years after the Gerry mansion was demolished. Cornelia Harriman had two younger brothers who were a generation behind Robert Gerry. Brother W. Averell Harriman was Secretary of Commerce under Franklin D. Roosevelt and worked in the Truman administration as Ambassador to the Soviet Union 1943-46 and Ambassador to Great Britain 1946-48, and was then elected the Governor of New York from 1955-58. Cornelia's second brother, E. Roland Harriman, became a successful financier as Vice President of *W.A. Harriman & Co.* and eventually became a partner in *Brown Brothers Harriman* with Robert Al Lovett, former Secretary of War during WWII, and also Prescott Bush, his friend since their college days at Yale. In 1953 he was appointed *President of the American Red Cross* by President Dwight Eisenhower.[17] It was Cornelia's younger brother E. Roland Harriman who later invited her son "Ebby" to partner with him in the 1940's in the *Arden Homestead Stables* in Orange County which he had inherited from his father, E.H. Harriman, in 1909.

Edward Henry Harriman died at his country estate *Arden House* on September 9, 1909 at age sixty-one just a year after his daughter, Cornelia, married Robert L. Gerry. The next year E.H. Harriman's widow, Mary, carried on her husband's vision for the family's thousands of acres of pristine land and established a national park with the donation of ten thousand acres and one million dollars to safeguard the scenic beauty of *Bear Mountain* in New York. Since then, twenty-eight parks have been established and the Harriman family was presented the *Palisades Founders' Award* in 2010 by the New York State Conservancy that recognized 100 years of service and dedication by the family. Elbridge T. Gerry III, "Ebby," accepted the award on behalf of the extended Harriman family. In 1950 the Harriman family also donated the historic *Arden House* country estate to *Columbia University* for use as a conference center and for the Business School's weekend executive classes. The gift included some 400 acres. Arden House was resold to the Harriman family in 2011.

As newlyweds in 1909 it was the first spring that Robert L. Gerry and Cornelia Harriman Gerry did not lead the spring Coaching Parade in Central Park, ride the horse show circuit, or join the Orange County Hunt. They began their life together in New York City where Robert embarked on his new role as head of the *Gerry Estates, Inc.* at the historic family office on Broadway and Cornelia was soon pregnant with the first of their four sons. Her request to have a "baby house" built next to the "no children allowed" Hunt Club in rural Virginia in 1911 made headlines in the New York papers and endeared the well-known society couple to the locals as a "down-to-earth" family that couldn't bear to be parted from their children during their summer stay in rural hunt country.

That same year Robert L. Gerry purchased property adjacent to the Lake Delaware estate to build a proper summer camp for under privileged New York City boys, to replace the fledgling "tent camp" the Gerry family had initiated two years before which had no central buildings for a Chapel and dining hall. In 1940, Robert interviewed Charles Dodsley Walker at his father's Church of Saint Edward the Martyr on East 109th Street in New York City, to be the second organist at the boys camp. Charlie, as he is affectionately known to the Gerry family, became the camp organist for the next 50 years, until 1990. In 2014, at the age of 94, Charlie continue to conduct the Canterbury Choral Society in New York City until his death in 2015. He was always considered to be part of the Gerry's extended family. The *Lake Delaware Boys' Camp* became one of the most successful camps in New York State, a perfect complement to the Harriman *Boys' Clubs* in the City, and the *New York Society for the Prevention of Cruelty to Children.* All three endeavors occupied Robert and Cornelia's time and attention throughout their lifetimes, as well as considerable financial support and fund raising by the extended Gerry family that has continued without a break to the present day.

Robert and Cornelia lived in a large Fifth Avenue brownstone across from *Central Park* for the first twenty years of their marriage, then in 1926, they moved to the imposing 67-69 East 79th Street French Baroque-style double-townhouse designed by Carrere & Hastings, which was designated a *New York City Landmark* in 1981. In 1911 when their first child was a toddler and Cornelia was pregnant with their second child, they decided to hire the architectural firm of *Walker and Gillette* to design and build a country home along with their own stables at Lake Delaware to give their children the outdoor life that they had enjoyed in their youth. The location was near the *Lake Delaware Boys' Camp* which made it convenient for Robert and Cornelia to oversee the management and growth of the camp during their summer holidays.

They chose a spot at the top of a hill for the new country mansion on land Robert inherited from his mother plus adjacent farm properties he purchased to use as homes and work buildings for staff on the 2,000 acre estate. The hilltop location overlooked the Morgan Lewis farm on *Lake Delaware* below and was surrounded with miles of panoramic views of the Delaware County forests and hills. However, the location of the house sat on solid rock and the foundation had to be blasted out to a depth of twenty-five feet on which the 160 foot long by 50 foot wide house and the 79 foot long servants' wing and kitchen had to be built. The lengthy construction project brought welcome business to the area, including use of the D&N railroad that transported everything from construction materials and horses to the workers and supplies from Albany and the surrounding towns. The house had electric lights, steam heat, and a service elevator for deliveries to the servants' wing. A family elevator was added in the mid-1950's when it was rebuilt after the 1953 fire. There were at least 50 rooms, with fifteen fire places and one bathroom for every two bedrooms, except the master suites which had private baths. There was a wine cellar that held bottles of wine owned by Peter P. Goelet in the eighteenth century and Madeira bottles imported by Commodore Elbridge T. Gerry in the nineteenth century. There was a gymnasium for the boys and Robert had his large den decorated with a nautical theme that re-used mahogany wood panels on the walls and floor and displayed artifacts like the brass clock, brass bell, and silver serving items that were salvaged from the yacht *Electra*, owned by Commodore Elbridge T. Gerry who had it dismantled during the construction of *Aknusti* in 1912. Rare furniture and paintings inherited by Cornelia Harriman from her side of the family and selected items from the Fifth Avenue Gerry mansion in New York City were also used to decorate the remainder of the mansion.[18] *Aknusti* became the family homestead for Robert, Cornelia and their four sons.

The landscape was designed by Frederick Olmsted, Jr. who had assisted his father, Frederick Law Olmsted, with the *Biltmore House* estate in North Carolina, and who years before had designed *Central Park* in New York City. Olmsted, Jr. landscaped seven miles of access roads that led from the town of Andes up to the mansion's elegant circular entrance driveway. His landscape design included a small man-made lake, tennis court, and a beautiful stone bridge that is now overgrown as the property fell into disrepair after it was successively sold in 1977, 1989 and 1992 and still awaits the determination of its fate. There were nine additional structures on the estate that included a Gate House, Carriage House and multi-car garage, Estate Manager's House, Groundskeeper's House, Gamekeeper's Cottage, Carpenter's Shop, Black Smith Shop, and the Stable Manager's cottage, and two very special structures, the Fowl House and the Stable.

The *Fowl House* had state-of-the-art incubators for the breeding and hatching of thousands of game birds every year that could be released into the wild or used for the fall "shooting parties." It was not unusual for *Aknusti* shooting party guests to include Prescott and Dorothy Bush, George Herbert Walker Bush, and the Phipps, Vanderbilts and Whitneys.[19] In addition to ducks and pheasant, turkeys and chickens were raised for the Gerry family tables at Lake Delaware and for their New York City townhouses. The birds were prepared for consumption by a local butcher in the nearby town of Andes and then shipped by rail to New York City or delivered to the three Lake Delaware homes of Angelica, Robert and Peter when they were in residence for seasonal holidays.

The *Aknusti Stable* was carefully designed and was the most handsome structure on the estate except for the main Georgian style mansion. The stables were designed in the English Tudor style, perhaps reminiscent of Robert's bachelor days when he and pal Alfred Vanderbilt crossed the Atlantic to Liverpool for England's annual equestrian season and where they purchased hounds for fox hunting. The stable was a palace for horses that could be exercised indoors on an oval shaped track that was covered in tanbark. The walls of the stable were glazed brick made to look like cream color subway-tile and each of the thirty stalls had a Dutch door split midway to allow the upper half to be opened separately from the bottom half. Also there was an outdoor exercise courtyard where the ponies and horses were trained and exercised. The handsome stables were adjacent to scenic pastures enclosed with hurdle fences made onsite in the *Aknusti* Carpenter Shop out of rough cut wood beams that fit loosely into upright rough-cut wood poles anchored in the ground. The stable and pastures were a picturesque scene for the Gerry boys to grow up with and a healthy escape from city life.

After the four Gerry boys were born, the younger twins in 1914, and the *Aknusti* estate was completed, Robert and Cornelia returned to their love of horses and began to professionally breed ponies and thoroughbreds. By ten o'clock on most days they had their stableman saddle two favorite horses and after breakfast Robert and Cornelia would go riding along the bridle paths on the *Aknusti* estate. When their boys were older the pastures were used for polo practice to prepare them for both high school and college polo and, eventually, they played professional polo as the *Aknusti Team* and won major championships. Their son Ebby is in the *National Polo Hall of Fame*. By the 1930's the breeding enterprise was a profitable business for the Gerrys and the national breeders took notice when a stud named *Chance Play* sold for $65,000 in 1936 to the *Calmut Farms* in Kentucky.[20] Robert Gerry's friend, August Belmont, Jr., had transferred all of his breeding business from the east coast to Kentucky where he bred 126 American Stakes winners, the greatest of which was *Man o' War* born while he was serving in World War I. However, in 1917 after Belmont, Jr. returned home after serving overseas and put *Man o' War* up for auction. Robert Gerry had also just returned from the War where he served as assistant to the Supervisor of the Army Transport Service with the rank of Major. By then Robert Gerry's breeding enterprise was a continuing success and so he joined his friend, August Belmont, Jr. for the *Kentucky Stables* auction held at Saratoga Springs, New York. Cornelia wanted the promising *Man O' War* in her husband's *Aknusti Horse Farm* stable, and with Robert's encouragement, she was one of the last two high bidders. However, by the end of the Belmont auction, the disappointed Cornelia was the under-bidder and *Man o' War* was sold to the highest bidder, the *Glen Riddle Farm* in Maryland. Nonetheless, Robert eventually owned *Field Marshall* and *Ironside* sired by *Man O' War. Ironside* won the *Manhattan Handicap* at Belmont Park in 1929.

The official opening of the *Pierre Hotel* on the site of the Fifth Avenue Gerry mansion in New York City was held on October 15, 1930 with a luncheon program that officially opened the hotel, followed by a gala dinner dance in the hotel ballroom. Robert L. Gerry acted as host along with other members of the investment group, Walter Chrysler, Otto H. Kahn, Edward Hutton and Finley J. Shepard. Money raised from the all-day affair was donated to the general fund of the *New York Society for the Prevention of Cruelty to Children*, where Cornelia Gerry was a member of the Board of Directors. The benefit committee included Edith Vanderbilt Gerry along with the wives of the other investors in the *Pierre Hotel* project.[21] One philanthropic effort in 1930 that brought Robert L. Gerry together with his two cousins, Robert Walton Goelet and Robert Wilson Goelet, was the Harvard University *Hundredth Anniversary Fund* drive. Although Robert did not graduate senior year, his Harvard classmates always considered him to be a member of the class of 1900, so he gave generously and donated five thousand dollars to the anniversary fund.

Robert L. Gerry became a leading philanthropist and businessman during the 1930's and 1940's when he was appointed a Director of the *Oregon Railroad and Navigation Company* and the *Oregon Shortline Railroad Company* that his father-in-law E.H. Harriman had owned. He became a Trustee of three banks, the *Farmer's Loan and Trust Company* (now Citibank), the *Fulton Trust Company,* and the *Central Hanover Bank and Trust Company* that was originally the *Gallatin Bank* in its early years. Also like his father before him, he took a leading role in the Episcopal Church in New York City, was appointed a Trustee of the *General Theological Seminary* and is listed in the *Golden Book* honor roll of significant supporters of the *Cathedral of Saint John the Divine.* He was also a leading member of the growing *Big Brother Movement* in the United States, an outgrowth of his sponsorship of the *Lake Delaware Boys Camp* and his support of the Harriman's *Boys' Clubs of New York,* a model for similar clubs across the country.

Robert joined his brother Peter as members of the prominent and historic *Knickerbocker Club* and several sport clubs that included the *Jockey Club,* the *Tennis, Turf and Field Club* and the *Meadow Brook Club* in Westbury, Long Island, and the *Orange County Hunt Club* of which he was the co-founder with E.H. Harriman. Robert and Peter Gerry enjoyed active membership in the *Motor Club* which they joined after abandoning their horse-drawn coaches for handsome new automobiles and experienced the sense of power and freedom of a car. Even their sisters Angelica and Mabel learned to drive, although Mabel enjoyed it more than Angelica who preferred the company of her maid and chauffeur during her many road trips.

In the end Robert and Cornelia Gerry were happiest spending time with their four sons hunting and riding their horses. They hired a very successful trainer, George Odom, who with his son was responsible for many winning thoroughbred horses at the *Aknusti Horse Farm.* Some of the thirteen Gerry winners included: *Peanuts,* the family favorite, winner of three different stakes between 1925 and 1927, *Perpetuate* which won the Tremont Stakes in 1937, and *Young Peter* that won the prestigious Travers Stakes in 1947. Robert became a steward or judge at the *Saratoga Race Association* and with his extensive experience and knowledge he wrote the forward to a detailed book on breeding and racing thoroughbreds, titled

The Matriarchy of the American Turf, authored by Marguerite F. Bayliss which he privately published at his own expense in 1931.[22]

The greatest tragedy in Robert and Cornelia's later years was the 1953 fire that totally destroyed the *Aknusti* mansion. Similar to the 1956 fire that later destroyed Angelica's barn and creamery, the *Aknusti* blaze happened in February in the early morning hours during a hurricane-like winter storm. Only the night watchman was in the house and when he investigated what smelled like smoke he discovered Robert L. Gerry's den engulfed in flames. Because of the icy roads it took too long for all the local fire departments to get up the slippery seven miles of access roads to save the mansion. The only thing left standing was the servants' wing and an empty shell of the house. The basement wine cellar was spared as was the family safe because it was located in the kitchen of the servants' wing. The valuable library, priceless antique furnishings, photographs, and all of the artifacts from the yacht *Electra* were a complete loss. The mansion was too costly to fully rebuild so it was partially reconstructed without the grand staircase, the elegant two-story entrance portico, and without luxury interior finishes. It was simply made livable again. Four years after the fire, and five years after Robert L. Gerry retired from the *Gerry Estates, Inc.*, he became seriously ill in the fall of 1957. Cornelia moved Robert to their beloved but well-worn *Aknusti* country home at Lake Delaware where he died surrounded by his family on October 31, 1957 at the age of eighty, unaware that his brother Peter had died earlier that same day. His funeral was held at *Saint James Church* at Lake Delaware, one day after Senator Peter Gerry's funeral. He was buried in the *Gerry-Livingston Mausoleum* at Hyde Park and then re-interred beside his siblings in the new pastoral cemetery at Lake Delaware. Cornelia Gerry lived another nine years to enjoy her grandchildren and when she died in 1966 she was buried beside Robert at Lake Delaware, just five years after her sister-in-law, Angelica Gerry, was also laid to rest with her brothers.

Cornelia Harriman Gerry 1884-1966

Holiday gatherings of the extended family

Robert Livingston Gerry 1877-1957

Aknusti horse farm at Lake Delaware, built by Robert L. Gerry in 1912 and standing today.

Young foals frolicking at Aknusti Stables

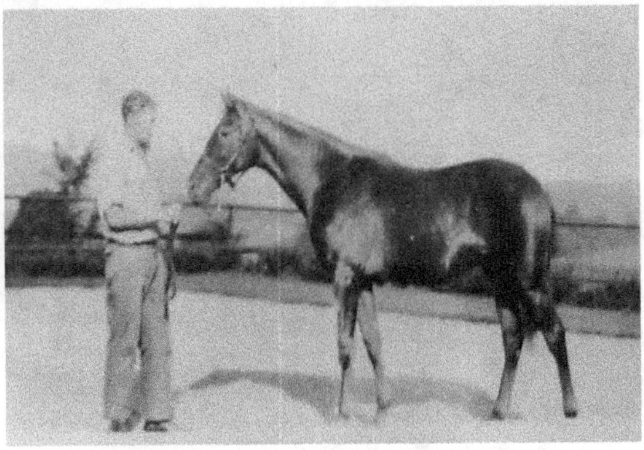

Robert and Cornelia Gerry's horse *Field Marshall* in 1926
Sired by the famous *Man O' War* and *Little Flower*

1910 air show at Belmont Park Race Track for off season

Edith Gerry and Cornelia Gerry
at the races

1913 Belmont Park Race Track

Cornelia and Robert Gerry's home
on East 79th Street in New York City

Robert and Cornelia Gerry were married for almost 60 years
before Robert died in 1957, the same day as his brother Peter.

Front of Aknusti before the fire 1912-1953

The shell of Aknusti after the fire

Aknusti front portico engulfed in flames

The mansion was rebuilt in a plain style with a 1950's interior. It was auctioned out of the family in 1977.

APPENDIX D

COMMODORE ELBRIDGE T. GERRY'S GRANDSONS

Robert and Cornelia Gerry's four sons were the only grandchildren of Commodore and Louisa Gerry. The four boys knew their grandfather well and were very familiar with their famous Gerry, Gallatin, Goelet and Livingston lineage back to the Founding Fathers. After all, their family homes at Lake Delaware were filled with historic artifacts, famous portraits, scrapbooks, and diaries, and there was endless story-telling on the veranda overlooking Lake Delaware.

All four Gerry boys attended *Saint Paul's School* in Concord, New Hampshire and spent part of each summer at the *Lake Delaware Boys' Camp,* both as young campers and then as teenage counselors. Three attended Harvard University and one graduated from the Columbia University School of Law. They were raised in a family of outdoor sportsmen and women where they were accomplished marksmen in game shooting, enjoyed the fox hunts, and most especially, they were star polo players. They played polo in its golden age from the mid 1930's until the outbreak of World War II, first in college and then professionally as the "red and yellow" team "Aknusti" (sometimes called the "four horsemen") who regularly played in the *Hempstead Cup Tournaments.* After the twins Edward and Henry were married, their older brothers, Ebby and Robert, Jr. were joined by two pals from the *Meadow Brook Club* on team "Aknusti." They were equally well known when they played together as the *Aiken Team* that played in the *Aiken Polo Club's* regional games in New York. The Club was located in Aiken, South Carolina where the famous health spas drew people from up and down the east coast during the *Gilded Age* and into the *Roaring Twenties.* Even today, the Gerry boys are listed in the *Aiken Polo Club's* history as some of the best players in America. The high point of the team's career was in 1940 when they defeated "Great Neck" in the *U.S. Polo Final* on the International Field in Westbury, Long Island. *The New York Times* wrote, "The *Aknusti* riders ruled the polo world tonight after one of the best finals in the 28-year history of the National Open. Ebby Gerry was Captain of the team that won a hard-fought thriller in front of a crowd of 15,000."[23] After the game Robert and Cornelia Gerry presented the *Silver Cup* to their own "team Aknusti" and were joined by twins Edward and Henry and their wives who cheered the team from the sidelines.

World War II called the Gerry brothers to service between 1942 and 1945. Captain Robert L. Gerry, Jr. and his brother, Captain Henry Gerry, were both sent to Italy with the Army Air Corps Intelligence Group, while Captain Edward Gerry was stationed in England also as part of the Army Intelligence service. The eldest son, Elbridge T. Gerry II, was first sent to Texas for training where he was made a Captain and assigned as an Intelligence Officer when he arrived in Germany in early 1945. During their wartime duty they were sometimes joined by their wives depending on where they were stationed, otherwise the wives stayed with family and often visited Robert and Cornelia at *Aknusti* or in the City.

After the war the four couples resumed their lives in New York City, but instead of building summer homes at Lake Delaware they began to settle on Long Island, in towns like Old Westbury, Mill Neck and Locust Valley, where their wives had family and friends, and where the polo and trotting tracks were located at Meadow Brook and Westbury. The Vanderbilts had constructed the first Long Island "motorway" to provide access to the booming summer community of the next generation and also to provide a place to race the latest automobiles. Newport was no longer "the resort" for New Yorkers; instead they were buying up the farms and rolling hills of Long Island out to Oyster Bay to build new summer estates. The Gallatin family had moved to Long Island decades before it was fashionable as did Harry Payne and Gertrude Whitney so she could have an isolated artists' colony with quiet entertainments and her own studio. By the 1920's the secret was out and New York's wealthy young men back from the war were eager to carve out their own space. By 1950 the Gerry brothers were no longer involved with competitive polo, a young man's sport, and while several continued to breed and race thoroughbred and Standardbred horses, their personal choices in sport were less dangerous than polo. One brother learned to play tennis and three of the brothers played competitive golf, all of whom contributed generously to the national *Golf Fund* to raise money for a building in New York State to house the first *United States Golf Association* museum, library and headquarter offices.

The four Gerry men were now successful businessmen in banking, oil, railroads, real estate, and horse breeding. They were also committed to support the Episcopal Church as leaders and active members of their congregations, and to support *the Lake Delaware Boys' Camp*, the *Boys' Clubs of New York City*, and the *New York Society for the Prevention of Cruelty to Children.*

Robert L. Gerry, Jr. married Marleigh Kramer, a Long Island girl, in 1934 at the *Episcopal Church of the Advent* in Westbury. Following the beautiful ceremony Robert Jr. and Marleigh joined 200 relatives and friends at a reception and lunch held at the bride's elegant family home known as *Picket Farm*. Marleigh was the daughter of Albert Ludlow Kramer, a lawyer and the Vice President of the *Equitable Trust Company* of New York. Following their marriage the couple lived in New York City and Westbury, Long Island for many years, which made it easy for Robert Jr. to continue playing polo and for his wife to see family and friends. Robert discovered the game of tennis, popular among Marleigh's family and friends. He became an accomplished player and a charter member of the United States Court Tennis Association. Robert won the *Tuxedo Gold Racquet Singles* championship in 1946, and then won the *U.S. Amateur Doubles Championship* in both 1949 and 1950 playing with Alastair Martin.[24] Robert and Marleigh had two children, their daughter Nancy born in 1936 and their son, Robert L. Gerry III, born in 1937. Nancy graduated from the all-girls *Foxcroft School* in Middleburg, Virginia in 1954 and Robert III graduated from the *Brooks School* in 1956, after which he served two years in the army. Even before the children were born, Marleigh Gerry was head of the *Girls' Service League,* Ebby II's wife Marjorie was one of the League Assistants, and a few years later, Edward Gerry was listed as a sponsor. Marleigh was active in the League as late as 1952 when her daughter Nancy was 15 years old and at boarding school in Virginia. The *Girls' Service League* was a non-sectarian group of women, almost like the Big Sisters of America, that provided guidance to girls between the ages of fourteen and twenty-one throughout New York City and Long Island.[25] Marleigh Gerry led the group in fundraising, sponsoring theatrical and concert benefits, teas and joint efforts with the Brooklyn League. In fact, in 1944, Marleigh was a guest on the WMCA radio show, *Greater New York Fund Drama,* where she spoke on the topic of "Adolescent Adventure" in her fifteen minute time slot. Of the four Gerry wives, Marjorie, Martha, and Nancy were all accomplished equestrians, but not Marleigh; she was the happy spectator who cheered her family on at the *Meadow Brook Club.* The four couples started a new tradition in 1941 when late summer evenings became popular times for night trotting races held at the *Roosevelt Raceway* in Westbury, Long Island. Dinners were held at the local clubs before the races, and Ebby T. Gerry II drove in many of the trotting races during the five-week program where eight races were run every night except Sunday.

Around 1956 when their children graduated from high school Marleigh and Robert Gerry, Jr. quietly divorced, and it may have been a long time coming. They were both forty-five years old and, happily for both, they eventually married again. Marleigh married Harry Payne Bingham, a seasonal resident of New York City and Palm Beach, Florida. He too was divorced with two adult children and was a quiet philanthropist who had given his Vermont home, *Stone Gate Farm,* to the *Ambula-*

tory Care Center Hospital in Bennington, which is named in his honor. Marleigh died in 1993 and Harry died in 2005; both were buried in Bennington, Vermont.

In 1957 after his divorce, Robert L. Gerry, Jr. inherited the *Aknusti* estate with his brother Edward when their father died. *Aknusti* had been only modestly rebuilt after the devastating 1953 fire and still had gutted spaces. Although neither Robert Jr. nor Edward ever remodeled or updated the mansion Robert still enjoyed the stables, and spent holidays at *Aknusti* for twenty years until he sold the entire estate fully furnished in 1977 to a syndicate of investors who used it as a horse farm. After the sale, no one ever occupied the mansion again, and it slowly deteriorated. *Aknusti* was sold once again in 1989 to a group of local Delaware County investors who held an auction to sell off the contents of the mansion. Three years later *Aknusti* was auctioned to the highest bidder for possible development into a private resort or sub-division into home plots. Since the last auction the mansion has stood empty in a state of utter disrepair. A few old books sit on empty shelves and the kitchen cupboards hold some dusty, long forgotten dishes and cooking pans. The *Aknusti Stables* are as handsome as ever and the overgrown *Fowl House* still contains the old incubators used for raising pheasants and ducks. *Aknusti* has become something of an archaeological site much like the *Ancrum House* gardens that hold memories of a vibrant by-gone *Gilded Age*.

In 1959 Robert Jr. married Harriett Wells Gardner, a widow who lived in New York City. Harriett's daughter, Penn Gardner, witnessed the marriage as did Robert III when they joined their parents for a private ceremony held at the New York City home of Harriett's mother. They moved to Houston, Texas where Robert pursued business interests in the petroleum industry. Over the years they made frequent visits to New York City and spent holidays at their *Aknusti* estate where Robert Jr. enjoyed watching his four grand-children grow-up. After twenty years of marriage Robert L. Gerry, Jr. died in December 1979 in New York City at the age of sixty-eight and was buried at the Lake Delaware hillside cemetery with his parents. His son Robert III is now a petroleum industry executive in Houston, Texas. He has been a Trustee of the *Texas Children's Hospital* since 1991 and is now on the Board of Directors of the newly formed *Integrity Bank* in Houston.[26] Robert L. Gerry Jr's daughter, Nancy, settled in Middleburg, Virginia where she had attended the Foxcroft School in her youth.

The twins, **Edward** and **Henry Gerry**, were both married a year apart in 1939 and 1940 when each joined their father at the *Gerry Estates, Inc.* on lower Broadway, the historic location of the business since the mid-nineteenth century. When the twins assumed the leadership role of the firm in 1946, they decided it was time for a change of name and location. The name change was subtle, just enough to retain the "good will" of the historic business yet clear enough to reflect the change in leadership: *Gerry Brothers, Inc.* However, it was a bigger challenge to move the business away from the financial center of New York City where the office had been located across from *Courthouse Square.* The twins started with a review of the inventory of property that *Gerry Brothers, Inc.* already owned to identify a location that could be adapted for their new offices. The original Fifth Avenue Gerry mansion at Sixty-First Street had a separate stable two blocks away at 39-41 east Sixty-Second Street. When the mansion was demolished in 1927 the stable was not, instead it continued to be used by the Gerry family or was leased. As businessmen responsible for the Gerry family's real estate investments, Edward and Henry had the ingenious idea in 1945 to reuse the four-story stable that had been so beautifully designed by architect Alfred Zucker in 1896. They converted the building into apartments to produce income but also added a large suite of offices on the second floor to use as the new *Gerry Brothers, Inc.* headquarters. The conversion was a success and the new location was on a side street rather than a noisy main thoroughfare, which lower Broadway had become in recent decades. Their oldest brother, Ebby II, was a banker who had joined his uncle E. Roland Harriman at *Brown Brothers Harriman* in 1936. Ten years after the twins moved to their new East Sixty-Second Street office their brother, Ebby II, then a partner in Brown Brothers Harriman, made them an offer in 1956 to have *Gerry Brothers, Inc.* become a limited partner of *Brown Brothers Harriman.* It was a marriage made in heaven that resulted in the three brothers working together in a partnership that ensured the growth and success of both firms.

The twins married well and happily. **Edward Harriman Gerry** married first in 1939 at the age of twenty-five. It was not surprising that he fell in love with an accomplished equestrian who loved thoroughbred horses as much as the Gerry family. Edward's wife, Martha, was the wealthy Vassar College educated daughter of William Stamps Farish, the founder of *Humble Oil* who merged his company with John D. Rockefeller's *Standard Oil* to become the new President and one of the wealthiest men in America. When William S. Farish retired in 1942 he moved to the historic *740 Park Avenue* apartment house in New York City where his daughter, Martha Farish Gerry, and her two children stayed while Edward H. Gerry served overseas during *World War II.* When Martha's father died suddenly in 1942 she inherited his thoroughbred horses and the family breeding stables. She went on to become the first woman member of the *Jockey Club* and the first woman to be honored as an *Exemplar in Racing* by the *National Museum of Racing.* Martha Farish Gerry was best known for breeding and racing *Forego,* named the horse of the year 1974-1976 when Willie Shoemaker was her famous jockey.[27]

Edward and Martha Gerry lived half the year in Mill Neck, New York and the other half in Monticello, Florida. Edward was always close to his twin brother, Henry, who lived on Long Island and spent winter holidays in Florida. Lake Delaware had become the summer home of their older brothers, Ebby II at the Morgan Lewis lake house, and Robert Jr. at the Aknusti mansion.

Edward and Martha had five children, Libby, Cornelia, Martha, William, and an infant son, Edward H. Gerry, Jr. who died in his first year and was buried in the cemetery at Lake Delaware. They were married sixty-three years and left eight grandchildren and three great grandchildren. Edward H. Gerry died at the age of eighty-eight at his Florida home in 2003 and his funeral was held at *Christ Episcopal Church* in Monticello, Florida. Martha Gerry died four years later in 2007 after heart surgery at New York's Presbyterian Hospital at the age of eighty-nine. Edward and Martha were buried in Florida where they had lived in their later years.

Henry Averell Gerry was twenty-six when he married Nancy Whitney in 1940 just a year after his twin married. She was educated at the *Brearley School* in New York City and the *Foxcroft School* for girls in Middleburg, Virginia. Nancy was the twenty-three-year-old daughter of the former president of the New York Stock Exchange. Like her sister-in-law Martha, she loved thoroughbred horses, but she preferred to race them in the steeplechase and joined in the summer fox hunts. Nancy Gerry owned *Flat Top,* one of the best horses that ran in the steeplechase. *Flat Top* won both the 1998 and the 2002 *Colonial Cup,* and also won the *Breeder's Cup* the same year.

Henry graduated from *Columbia Law School* in 1936 and handled the real estate litigation and legal side of the *Gerry Brothers, Inc.* until it joined Brown Brothers Harriman, where his skills and education were even more essential. He was a Treasurer and Trustee of the *Foxcroft School* and Vice-President of *The Gerry Foundation.* Henry and Nancy owned homes in Locust Valley, New York and in Boca Grande, Florida. Henry and Nancy and their children often joined the extended family for Christmas gatherings at Lake Delaware. They had five children, Sheldon, Ann, Nancy, Richard, and Henry Jr. who died at the young age of nineteen in an automobile accident and was buried in the hillside cemetery at Lake Delaware. Henry owned a townhouse in New York City on Fifth Avenue at Eighty-First Street, just around the corner from his Aunt Angelica who lived in her townhouse at 11 East Eighty-Second Street.

An article in the Massachusetts newspaper, the *Marblehead Reporter,* in March 2004, described a visit by Henry Gerry's grandson, Geoffrey Groat, the son of Nancy Gerry Groat, which described several bottles of very old liquor that were inherited from Commodore Gerry. Geoffrey noted that liquor ages beautifully when rocked by the wave action of the sea during transport from Europe to America and described the taste of his great, great grandfather's brandy with great relish, "I sipped the most magnificent, silken, smooth, outstanding, aged brandy ever to pass a human's lips." The article noted that:

> His mother, Nancy Gerry Groat, gave him six full and six empty liquor bottles from her collection of twenty for his thirtieth birthday in 2002. At least one label states the name of the ship on which it was imported, the *Old Bloodgood Yacht,* Brandy 1812. Other labels were dated 1811, 1820 and 1830. Henry Gerry regaled his grandson with stories about family liquor collection which included the *peach brandy* that he sipped with Geoffrey. Henry told him that when a small peach is on the tree, it is inserted into an empty brandy bottle suspended from the tree so the peach will grow inside the bottle with a glass neck the size of a silver dollar. The peach is picked with the bottle and the brandy is then poured into the bottle with the peach suspended inside. The peach in the Gerry brandy had been suspended in the aging liquor for almost two hundred years.

Henry and Nancy were happily married for sixty years until Henry's death at the age of eighty-six at his home in Florida in 2000, three years before his twin, Edward. Nancy lived twelve more years until she too died at their Florida home at the age of ninety-five, and left seven grandchildren and seven great-grandchildren. Henry and Nancy were buried at Fishers Island, New York across the bay from their Locust Valley home.

Elbridge T. Gerry II, called "Ebby" by family and friends, was the eldest of the four Gerry brothers and perhaps the most remarkable. From his business acumen and athletic skill to his philanthropic leadership and work with the Episcopal Church, he seems to embody the best of his parents and grandparents. His three brothers share many of the same accomplishments but none achieved so much in every aspect of his life. Ebby is in fact Commodore Elbridge T. Gerry's first true namesake. He is referred to in this book as the second, E. T. Gerry II, his son is E.T. Gerry III, and there are also E.T. Gerry IV and V. However, it is important to note that within the Gerry family today E.T. Gerry III is known as E.T. Gerry, Jr. which makes his successors III and IV. Birth years help to keep track of the five Elbridge Thomas Gerrys.

His skill as a polo player emerged while a star player on the Harvard team from 1928 to 1931. As Captain at Harvard he led the team to victory in the *Indoor Intercollegiate Championship* in 1929. After college he played professional polo and went to England with the American Team in 1936. He won the *U.S. Open*

Championship and the *Monty Waterbury Cup* three times each. As Captain of his family's *Aknusti* team he achieved a nine goal handicap in 1940. He later served as chairman of the U.S. Polo Association and was inducted into the *Polo Hall of Fame* in 1991. Ebby joined in a partnership with his uncle E. Roland Harriman to breed and raise standard bred horses at the Orange County *Arden Homestead Stables* and also made use of the *Aknusti Stables* as a secondary breeding farm.

In 1931, immediately after graduation from Harvard University, Ebby Gerry II joined the *Hanover Bank* in New York City where he worked for five years until joining his uncle E. Roland Harriman in the private banking firm of *Brown Brothers Harriman.* Ebby became a partner in the firm in 1956 at which time he invited his twin brothers, Edward and Henry, to join their business, *Gerry Brothers, Inc.* as a limited partnership with *Brown Brothers Harriman*, which they did with enormous success.

The year after Ebby Gerry II joined the *Hanover Bank* he married Marjorie Kane of Locust Valley, New York. She was the twenty-two-year-old daughter of John P. Kane, President and Director of a prominent holding company and known for his valuable book collection just as Commodore Elbridge T. Gerry was known for his private library collection. Marjorie attended *Miss Chapin's School* in New York City and graduated from *the Ethel Walker School*, a college preparatory boarding school in Simsbury, Connecticut. Marjorie was an accomplished equestrian who "trotted" horses as a young woman and was comfortable around the polo fields where her husband was the star player. Ebby II and Marjorie had an apartment in New York City most of the year and split their weekends and summers between their Locust Valley, Long Island home, and the *Arden Homestead Stables* in Goshen, about fifty miles north of New York City in Orange County. Marjorie's mother-in-law, Cornelia Harriman Gerry, still owned *Arden House* during the early years of Marjorie's marriage to Ebby II so they were able to stay there during weekends and holidays in Orange County. The women enjoyed horseback riding and watching the trainers with the young colts while at *Arden House* and the *Arden Homestead Stable.* On race days at the nearby *Goshen Historic Track*, the oldest harness racing track in America, the women usually sponsored festive social occasions that served as fundraising events. After Ebby II founded the *Horse Racing Museum and Hall of Fame* in 1949, hundreds of ladies volunteered for the annual *Hall of Fame Day* in Goshen. After the last race of the day, the women's auxiliary conducted the $1,000 *Road Apple Raffle.* A well-fed horse was placed in a fenced area that had been marked-off into squares with white chalk. For $10 each a person could buy a claim to one or more numbered squares and then wait until the end of day when the person who owned the square where the horse "left its' calling card" road apple was the winner.[28]

Over the years, the breeding and racing business that Ebby II shared with his Uncle E. Roland Harriman occupied his time more than the *Meadow Brook Club* on Long Island. Ebby II and Harriman bred many champions including their trotter *Titan Hanover* who won the 1945 *Hambletonian Stake.* Other winners were Florican, Tassel Hanover, Florlis, Flirth, Matastar, and Sharpshooter. Ebby II was president and director of the *Standardbred Owners Association,* Vice-President of the *Orange County Driving Park Association,* and Director of the *Hambletonian Society.* Elbridge T. Gerry II became so influential in the harness racing industry that he was appointed to serve as the first chairman of the New York State Harness Racing Commission, formed after pari-mutual betting was legalized in 1940. From 1976-1992 he was the President of the *Harness Racing Museum and Hall of Fame* in Goshen, New York. Ebby II brought as much passion in his later years to his leadership in the harness racing industry as he did in his youth when he was captain of the championship Harvard polo team. He had the rare distinction of being a member of two *Halls of Fame:* in 1975 he was elected to the *Harness Racing Living Hall of Fame* and in 1982 he was elected to the *Polo Hall of Fame.*

Ebby II and Marjorie Gerry had three children, Elbridge T. Gerry III (or Jr.), Peter G. Gerry, and Marjorie G. Ryland. Ebby III and Peter are as passionate about harness racing as their parents, and both sons spent summers at the Lake *Delaware Boys' Camp* as young campers and as teenage counselors. Elbridge T. Gerry II became the president of the non-profit *Lake Delaware Boys' Camp* when his father and founder, Robert L. Gerry, Sr. retired.

His philanthropy followed in his grandmother Louisa Gerry's footsteps when he carried on the work of his Aunts Angelica and Mabel as a member of the Committee on Trust Funds for the *Domestic and Foreign Missionary Society* of the Protestant Episcopal Church. Ebby II was like his grandfather in that he rarely said "no" when asked to serve. He first became a member of the Board of Trustees of the *American Museum of Natural History* in 1958, was the Treasurer from 1964-1972, and was elected an Honorary Trustee in 1988 after more than thirty years of service. Ebby II was also proud to be the Trustee of his grandmother's legacy, the *Mary W. Harriman Foundation,* a long and loyal supporter of the *American Red Cross* in Greater New York City. He also followed in the Gerry family tradition as the President and Director of the *New York Society for the Prevention of Cruelty to Children,* founded by his grandfather, Commodore Elbridge T. Gerry.

In the last years of their lives together, Ebby II and Marjorie lived at Lake Delaware in the historic Morgan Lewis farm house where they died in 1999 within a few days of each other after a vibrant sixty-seven-year marriage. Their funerals were held at *Saint James Church* at Lake Delaware and they were buried together just up the lane behind the church in the hillside family cemetery. A memorial service was held in New York City at *Trinity Church* at the foot of Wall Street which was attended by crowds of friends, colleagues and admirers. Their daughter Marjorie Ryland lives in Beverly, Massachusetts. Their son Elbridge T. Gerry III (Jr.) lives in Locust Valley, Long Island and their son Peter G. Gerry, a founder and partner in Sycamore Ventures, a successful venture capital investor, lives in Hopewell, New Jersey. There are eleven grandchildren and seven great-grandchildren with some "namesake" Roberts, Peters, and Ebbys for the next generation. These children often celebrate weddings, birthdays, and summer holidays at the Morgan Lewis house on Lake Delaware, boating, horseback riding and exploring the history of the estate.

Gerry brothers Ebby III (Jr.) and Peter are now owners of the *Arden Homestead Stables* which came into the Gerry family after their great Uncle Roland Harriman's death in 1978. Both brothers are directors in the *Hambletonian Society* and both are on the Board of Trustees of the *Harness Racing Museum and Hall of Fame*; Ebby III (Jr.) is President and Peter is Treasurer. They both drove in the amateur harness races wearing the *Arden Homestead Stable* royal blue and orange silks. Peter is also a member of the *New Jersey Sire Stakes* Board of Trustees and the Chairman of the Board of *Rensselaerville Institute*. Like his father, Ebby III (Jr.) was elected to the *Harness Racing Living Hall of Fame* in Goshen, New York.

Ebby III (Jr.) is a partner in Brown Brother Harriman like his father before him, and like his grandfather, he takes a leading role in the *Lake Delaware Boys' Camp* and the *Boys' Clubs of New York City*. He has been a tireless leader and supporter of the *New York Society for the Prevention of Cruelty to Children* founded in 1877 by his great-grandfather, Commodore Elbridge T. Gerry. Ebby III (Jr.) has worked with the *Society* for more than forty years beginning in 1959 as a Board member after his great Uncle Senator Peter G. Gerry's death, and then as President from 1972 until 2003 when the next generation of Gerrys took on the mantle of leadership that has continued for almost 140 years.

Elbridge Thomas Gerry III (Jr.) has been my advisor for three years, and more recently, Robert Livingston Gerry III, on behalf of the Gerry family, reading manuscript chapters as they were completed. It has been an honor to work with them and a privilege to be given access to the family papers, scrapbooks, diaries, photos and the Lake Delaware home of General Morgan Lewis and his wife, Gertrude Livingston. The simple question, "Who was Commodore Elbridge T. Gerry?" led to revealing the untold epic story about one of America's great Founding families and their substantial living legacy.

Commodore Elbridge Thomas Gerry's four grandsons

Elbridge Thomas Gerry II (Ebby)

Robert Livingston Gerry, Jr.

Henry Averell Gerry

Edward Harriman Gerry

TWINS

Robert and Cornelia Gerry's four sons at the champion Aknusti Polo Team. Family life was centered around the Lake Delaware Aknusti horse farm for over 70 years and three generations of Robert L. Gerry's family.

Gerry brothers as champion polo team AKNUSTI from left Edward, Robert, Elbridge and Henry

Ebby on Harvard team

Ebby was inducted into the Polo Hall of Fame for 9 goals.

Marjorie Kane
married

Martha Farish
married

Marleigh Kramer
married

Nancy Whitney
married

Elbridge T. Gerry II

Edward Harriman Gerry

Robert Livingston Gerry II

Henry Averell Gerry

Flat Top's owner, Nancy Whitney Gerry with jockey, Colvin Ryan, South Carolina 1998
(married to twin Henry Gerry)

Martha Farish Gerry with Forego
entering the winner's circle
(married to twin Edward Gerry)

Flat Top flew to victory in the 2002 Breeders' Cup Steeplechase en route to earning a second Eclipse Award. *Flat Top* is a dark bay/brown 5-year old gelding.

Three time Horse of the Year,
Forego with famous jockey,
Johnny Shoemaker

Elbridge Thomas Gerry, II (Ebby) married Marjorie Kane of Locust Valley, Long Island.

Their sons, Peter (*above and below left*) and Ebby, III (*above right and below right*)

Peter and Ebby III jointly own and run the Arden Homestead Stables established by their great Uncle Harriman.

Robert L. Gerry, III

Trotter in a harness race

Peter Gerry, II and Ebby, III

The original Morgan Lewis and wife, Gertrude Livingston's estate at Lake Delaware, New York as it looks today. The farm house and lake property have remained in the Gerry family for four generations since Louisa Livingston Gerry inherited the property in 1891 from her father, Robert James Livingston, the grandson of General Morgan Lewis.

Recent family photograph of the extended Gerry family on the front steps of the Lake Delaware family estate in Delaware County, New York

APPENDIX E

AMERICAN FAMILY LEGACIES

Let us develop the resources of our land, call forth our powers, build up its institutions, promote all its great interests, and see whether we also, in our day and generation, may not perform something worthy to be remembered.

Daniel Webster (1782–1852)

Interwoven throughout this historical biography of Elbridge T. Gerry are the lasting contributions of four closely knit great American families. They left us with the written legacy of our nation's early history by preserving and depositing their respective family papers in libraries and museums for scholarly research. In addition to written documents, interesting and valuable historic artifacts of the Gerry, Gallatin, Goelet and Livingston families have been carefully and happily preserved in their private homes and in extraordinary institutions like the *New York Historical Society* and the *Museum of the City of New York* among several others institutions noted in the acknowledgments at the front of this book. Many of the family artifacts and manuscripts pre-date the founding of America with origins in England, France, Holland, Scotland and Switzerland. These efforts have sustained not only the continuity of their families across successive generations but also the very fabric of American social history.

The most remarkable contributions are their contemporary "living legacies" that affect our lives today, whether financial, cultural, social or scientific institutions and foundations. A few of the notable ones may have been enjoyed by many of you reading this biography without realizing it. On the purely cultural and social level, there is the *New York Opera* at Lincoln Center which was first organized as the *Metropolitan Opera* in 1880 by a small group of *Gilded Age* families of which the Goelet family took the lead and donated the land on which the opera house was built. Every generation of Goelets has sustained the *New York Opera,* underwriting major opera productions for decades. They commissioned world famous composers and in 1966, funded the "Grand Staircase" in the current *Lincoln Center Opera House.* Indeed, Francis Goelet received the *National Medal of Arts* in 1988 from the President of the United States at the White House for his support and leadership of the *New York Opera.* The Goelet family also produced some of the greatest wines in the world through five wineries: *Taltarni Winery* in Australia, *Domaine De Nizas Winery* in France, the *Lalla Gully Vineyard* and the *Clover Hill Winery,* both in Tasmania, and the *Clos Du Val Winery* in Napa Valley,

California. Goelet winemaking has family ties dating back to 1725 with the *Barton & Guestier* wine label (known today as B&G), which Anne-Marie Guestier Goelet brought into the family. She herself a French woman who lived at *Sandricourt Castle* was named an Officer of the *French Legion of Honor* for her family's use of the castle as a staging area for the military Ambulance Corps and for medical assistance provided to servicemen and local citizens during World War II.

Some of the family legacies are quietly circulated throughout America with *postage stamps* that are used to honor our nation's leaders, social movements, and other American milestones. Three of our related families have been honored with a postage stamp: first, Robert R. Livingston was honored with a stamp in 1904 for negotiating the *Louisiana Purchase* with France; then Albert Gallatin was honored with a stamp in 1967 for his leadership as Secretary of the Treasury under Presidents Jefferson and Madison; the Harriman family (married and in business with the Gerry family) was honored with the "Boys' Clubs of America Movement" stamp in 1960. Edward Henry Harriman established the first *Boys' Club* in America in New York City around 1870, and today three active clubs continue to serve boys throughout the city. There is a movement in Marblehead, Massachusetts that began in 2011 to have a postage stamp made to honor the 100th anniversary of the death in November 1814 of their native son, Vice President Elbridge Gerry. The town has dedicated a school, a park and a fire engine to Elbridge Gerry. He is of course, the only Vice President whose name has become part of the nation's political lexicon with the word "Gerrymander" or "Gerrymandering," used to describe the strategic drawing of boundaries to create cohesive voting districts.

Often overlooked in America's art world is Commodore Elbridge T. Gerry's nephew, Albert Eugene Gallatin (A.E. Gallatin) who established the *Gallery of Living Art* at New York University in 1927 to display the first original work of the modern cubist movement in the United States. Gallatin made frequent trips to Paris, where he visited Picasso, Georges Braque, Henri Matisse, and other avant-garde artists in their studios and purchased works directly from them. He was the first to exhibit the abstract and cubist work of Pablo Picasso, Joan Miro, Paul Klee, Max Jacob, and Man Ray among other contemporary artists, primarily between 1926 and 1943. A. E. Gallatin was himself a cubist artist, an author and a critic; in his own words his *Gallery of Living Art* was a laboratory for exploration and experimentation and a forum for intellectual exchange.

Living legacies of substantial value to the American educational system are among the great contributions of these philanthropic families. In 1831 Albert Gallatin founded *New York University* which is one of the leading schools of higher education in the United States that draws students from around the globe.

Albert's son was a Professor of Chemistry and his grandson, Frederic (married to Almy Gerry) graduated from *New York University* and its School of Law. Similarly, the Goelet family donated their *Gilded Age* home *Ochre Court* in Newport, Rhode Island, to establish the Catholic college of *Salve Regina,* which continues to be supported by a *Goelet Scholarship* that provides a college education to students in need of assistance. The Goelet family has been involved for decades in higher education as Professors at Harvard, Columbia, and New York University. Indeed, if you walk into the grand plaza of *Columbia University* you will see the great statue *Alma Mater,* a gift of the Goelet family to "welcome" new students and to honor Robert Goelet who graduated in 1860, the same year his cousin Elbridge T. Gerry completed his Master's Degree at Columbia.

There are three living legacies of the Gerry family that stand out among their many accomplishments. One is related to the Harriman *Boys' Clubs* in New York City, the *Lake Delaware Boys' Camp* at the Gerry estate in Delhi, New York. Established in 1909 and expanded in 1911 with permanent buildings, the summer camp was attended free-of-charge by boys from poor families who came from the Manhattan and Brooklyn *Big Brothers* program and from the city's Episcopal Churches. Many of the campers return as camp counselors in later years and alumni banquets are held to celebrate milestone anniversaries. In fact, the camp is as successful and active today after 115 years and it is still managed by the Gerry family. Of note, the historic 1876 Hilborne Roosevelt Opus 34 organ at the Lake Delaware Boys' Camp was completely restored by the Gerry family in 2014 and it is considered to be one of the only early residential pipe organs to have survived intact to the present day. Charles Dodsley Walker, "Charlie," who was the camp organist from 1940-1990, is the current conductor, and creator, of the *Canterbury Choral Society* at the Church of the Heavenly Rest in New York City. When Charlie spoke with the author in May 2014, he described the beautiful sound of the historic organ and noted that the lack of air conditioning and heating in the boys' camp chapel actually preserved the Opus 34 organ for nearly 150 years.

The second living legacy of the Gerry family started the world-wide movement in child protection through the *New York Society for the Prevention of Cruelty to Children* that Commodore Elbridge T. Gerry initiated after handling the little Mary Ellen abuse case in 1875. It was a pragmatic blend of religious faith, humane concern, private initiative and public partnership that transcended political, sectarian and economic differences. The *Gerry Society* as it is known in New York City continues its work today with an emphasis on "prevention" rather than trial work. The classic story of "A Tale of Two Cities" opens with a line that could just as easily have been referencing New York City in the *Gilded Age,* "It was the best of times, it was the worst of times," The Gerry family led society in the crusade to rid itself of the scourge of child abuse and abandonment. In the one hundred and forty years since its incorporation as the first child protection agency in the world, the *Gerry Society* has investigated more than 650,000 cases on behalf of over 2 million children, and the work continues in our twenty-first century *Gilded Gotham.*

The Gerry legacy that inspired the research and writing of this historical biography is the *Gerry Library* that was donated in 1928 by Senator Peter G. Gerry as the "founding collection" of the *Library of the Supreme Court of the United States.* Like Thomas Jefferson's donation of his personal library to the *Library of Congress,* the Gerry donation made an unprecedented contribution to the breadth, depth and quality of legal research at the Supreme Court. The collection will sustain the rigorous legal analysis and decision-making of the Court throughout history, protecting the rights and freedoms of American citizens. Commodore Elbridge T. Gerry was a highly respected, well-known, brilliant lawyer in his day in New York City. Although his legal work is reflected in the Table of Cases in this book, hundreds of court hearings on behalf of the *New York Society for the Prevention of Cruelty to Children* are not listed. His work with the *New York State Legislature* and his participation in state *Constitutional Conventions* and *Commissions* were widely followed across the nation while he lived. A book collector or "bibliophile" since childhood, Commodore Gerry's private library grew exponentially with his legal career and his civic and humanitarian endeavors. The 30,000 volume collection reflected books purchased to support case law research and legal history, plus a wide variety of special and unique subjects like: canon law, insanity, torture, dreams and scrapbooks tracking his career and issues of the day.

The Supreme Court Library continues to grow and build on its founding collection and is one of Commodore Elbridge T. Gerry's most vibrant and substantial living legacies. The Court attracts high ranking visitors from courts and legal communities from around the globe. A brief history of the *Supreme Court Library* closes this epic story with the hope that it will inspire readers as much as it inspired the author during her years as the Librarian of the Court.

History of the Supreme Court Library

President George Washington signed the Judiciary Act into law on September 24, 1789, thereby establishing the Supreme Court of the United States. The President advised the newly appointed Justices in a letter in which he wrote:

> I have always been persuaded that the stability and success of the National Government, and consequently, the happiness of the people of the United States would depend in a considerable degree on the interpretation and execution of its laws. In my opinion therefore, it is important that the Judicial System should not only be independent in its operation, but as perfect as possible in its formation.[1]

The first session of the Court was held in the *New York Royal Exchange Building* on February 1, 1790. The first session was consumed with organizing the Court and its business, hiring a clerk, setting criteria for bar membership, and the admission of the first attorneys to practice before the Court. The first session recessed on February 10 and did not meet again until August 2-3, 1790 when the first session with all seven Justices present was held. The early caseload was small as the Court was discovering its emerging role. The Constitution restricts the Supreme Court's jurisdiction to deciding only actual cases and controversies; therefore, the justices must "await" an appeal of an existing and properly framed lawsuit. Denied the power of both the purse and the sword, the Court's enforcement power depends on the cooperation of the coequal branches of government and ultimately, on public acceptance of its authority as promulgated through its published decisions.

In the early years the Justices were required to travel through the country to preside over federal court sessions held throughout the three regional Circuits, the Eastern, Middle, and Southern, which had been created by the Judiciary Act of 1789. New federal cases were heard in each district within the three Circuits in the spring and fall of each year. The Justices themselves divided up the Circuit assignments based on residence, which in theory would draw on the local and regional knowledge each Justice had about the local laws and customs, as well as personal knowledge about the skills and character of individuals applying for admission to practice before the Supreme Court. On April 12, 1790, one of the first Circuit sessions was presided over by Chief Justice John Jay. His charge to the grand jury captured the purpose of "circuit riding" both to establish the new law of the land and to introduce the new federal judiciary to the people of the infant nation.

> We had become a nation, as such we were responsible to others for the observance of the laws of nations; and as our national concerns were to be regulated by national laws, national tribunals became necessary for the Interpretation and execution of them both. No tribunals of like kind and extent had heretofore existed in any country, from such, therefore, no light of experience, nor facilities of usage or habit, were to be derived. Our Jurisprudence varied in almost every State, and was accommodated to local not general convenience; to partial not

> national policy. A Judicial control, general and final, was indispensable. The manner of establishing it, with powers neither too extensive, nor too limited, rendering it properly independent, and yet properly amendable, involved questions of no little intricacy. The expediency of carrying justice as it were to every man's door, was obvious; but how to do it in an expedient manner was far from being apparent. [2]

The records of the early cases and charges of the early Justices to the juries are often found in their manuscript docket books. In addition to the docket books, the letters of early Justices describe in detail the personal hardships of riding circuit for many months each year, the costs of which were paid out of pocket. They traveled by carriage or horseback as a general rule, over dangerously rough roads and trails, and when these became impassable they resorted to traveling via rivers and waterways. Whether hot and humid or wet and freezing, the Justices continued their travels, often becoming ill by exposure to epidemics or injured in accidents and falls, all of which required these gentlemen to turn to the kindness of strangers for assistance.

The early years of the infant government were clearly fragmented by the various moves of the seat of government, the war debts and the whole evolutionary process of self-government. Public libraries were a relatively new idea and providing a private library for itself was a luxury the young federal government could not easily afford.

In 1774, several years before the first sessions of Congress or the establishment of the Supreme Court, the need for a collection of books for use by the leaders of the revolutionary government meeting as the *Continental Congress* in Philadelphia was recognized by the director of the *Philadelphia Company Library* who made the library available to the Congress. The Library was about half a century old at the time, and except for Harvard and Yale, was the largest library in America. Elbridge Gerry, John Adams and Thomas Jefferson all had comprehensive personal libraries at that time from which to draw, and their home collections compared well to the significant titles in the *Philadelphia Company Library.* All of these private libraries exist today, including the *Philadelphia Company Library* with books containing the "sign out slip" with the signatures of some of the Founding Fathers. Commodore Elbridge Thomas Gerry inherited the law and history books from his grandfather Vice-President Elbridge Gerry's rare Founding-period private collection. He expanded the collection for 60 years to create a collection that eclipsed both Jefferson's private library when it was donated to the *Library of Congress* after the War of 1812 and the *Philadelphia Company Library's* law collection.

The most important legal treatises that were progressively collected by the young federal government for use by Congress and were duplicated in the nineteenth century collection of Commodore Gerry included such older writings as Sir John Fortescue (1394-1476), *De Laudibuis Legum Angliae* (London, 1616). Not only did the educated Founding Fathers read Greek and Latin, so did Commodore Gerry, who had a classical education at Columbia University in New York City, and also earned a Master's Degree in the German language.

The Gerry library contained the best common law tradition in America which was fully elaborated during the early seventeenth century in a series of works by several of the most prominent judges and legal thinkers of the era. The most important figure in this effort was Chief Justice Sir Edward Coke (1552-1643), author of the *Institutes of the Laws of England,* which became the principal foundation for the English jurisprudential tradition when it reached the American revolutionary generation. Several other judges among Coke's contemporaries also made important contributions to the literature, among them Sir John Davies (1569-1626) in the *Report of Cases and Matters in Law, Resolved and Adjudged in the King's Court in Ireland* (London, 1615), and Nathaniel Bacon (1593-1660) in *An Historical Discourse of the Uniformity of the Government of England* (London, 1647-51). Another significant title was Scottish philosopher and historian David Hume's (1711-1776) widely read *History of England* (London, 1754-62). Equally popular in American libraries was John Locke's *Essay Concerning Human Understanding,* and the second-most commonly cited work in the American Revolution, William Blackstone's *Commentaries on the Laws of England* (17 editions published) which is the very title, in four small volumes, that initiated the writing of this historical biography that followed the leather-bound book from the Founding Father to the *Supreme Court Library* through generations of the Gerry family.

There is no class of persons, professional or otherwise, so dependent upon books as the lawyer and judge. Indeed, there is no library of any kind which so directly pertains to the interests which it is designed to serve as the law library. The Supreme Court's successful performance of its judicial functions from 1789 until it was granted permission to use a small loan of books from the Library of Congress in the late nineteenth century was possible only because the Justices also owned extensive personal book collections. Prior to 1935, when the Justices heard arguments on the second floor of the Capitol, they were provided neither office nor storage space. Each Justice worked out of his residence, which oftentimes was a rooming house. While "riding circuit" the Justices relied on personal volumes of miniature-size books they could manage to carry with them in saddle bags. They also used books found at the district courthouses where they held court sessions, which often were meager at best.

In the late nineteenth century when Justice Stephen Field occupied one of the Trumbull Row houses that stood on the ground now occupied by the Supreme Court Building, he built an addition to the row house he occupied to provide a second floor room for his 3,000 volume library. Justice Field was able to work in his library every day because his row house was located directly across the street from the Capitol where the Supreme Court Chamber was situated in the basement. In 1899 Justice Field died in his library at the age of 82.

Similarly Justice Louis Brandeis, appointed in 1916 nearly 20 years before the new Court building opened in 1935, rented a two-bedroom apartment above the one he lived in and used it as his office. The apartment office was overflowing with papers and books, even the bathtub was filled with research folders. The kitchenette was piled with manuscripts and corrected proofs. In 1926 when the Justices reviewed a case that needed research back to the fifteenth century they simply turned to Justice Oliver Wendell Holmes who had his own set of ancient vellum *Year Books* from which the Justice himself translated the Norman-French text for the Justices. Books were the laboratory of the *Supreme Court* in which to do the research that supported their analysis and interpretation of the laws of the nation.

Books that explain the procedural steps required in every court are essential for all lawyers and judges in all periods of history, and for that reason, it is not surprising that in 1794 William Wyche published his *Treatise on the Practice of the Supreme Court of Judicature of the State of New York Civil Actions.* The British texts on pleading and practice were not immediately displaced by the works of American authors. Eventually law books based on the emerging law of the new American republic were published in both England and America. The book most widely used in America was *A Practical Treatise on Pleading and of Parties to Actions, Forms of Action,* first published in 1809 by Joseph Chitty. These are just examples of historic titles found in the Gerry collection. When commodore Gerry prepared a case with a defense of insanity, he purchased every relevant book on the subject, both legal and medical. When he prepared the report on *Execution by the Electric Chair,* he purchased every book, ancient and contemporary, on torture and forms of execution throughout history to educate the commission and himself. His book collection encompasses not only the history of law in America and England, it is enriched with every subject matter related to each and every case he was involved with over his fifty-year career as a prominent New York City lawyer.

Commodore Elbridge T. Gerry was a brilliant lawyer and a passionate bibliophile who studied the book collecting habits of the Founding Fathers, the book collections of the Courts, and the private collections of his fellow lawyers. He worked with New York City book shops, Rare Book experts, and book specialists in England and Europe to identify and obtain every historically relevant rare and contemporary law book available to purchase. He was a man of immense wealth which enabled him to collect broadly and at the highest level of rarity and relevance in the field of legal scholarship. In *Gilded Age* New York City, Commodore Gerry was known to have the best and most extensive private law library in America. It is of great historic significance to the country and to the Founding Gerry family that his collection was not broken up at his death in 1927 or sold at auction; rather the collection remains part of our country's history as the practicing law library of Supreme Court of the United States.

Just as the gift of Thomas Jefferson's private home library to the Library of Congress in 1814 after the British burned the Capitol was the foundation of that great national library's collection, so was the gift of Commodore Elbridge T. Gerry's private home library to the United States Supreme Court the foundation of the first independent library in the new Court building in 1935.

Library of the Supreme Court of the United States

APPENDIX F

EUROPEAN FAMILY ORIGINS

Chapter 1 of this biography provides the European origin of the Gerry family who emigrated from England in 1730 with the arrival of Captain Thomas Gerry in Boston, Massachusetts. The three significant American families allied by marriage with the Gerrys were the Gallatins, Goelets and Livingstons. Each of those families also has a rich and historic beginning in Europe, especially the Gallatins and Livingstons who were leaders in their homeland, often during tumultuous times.

The story of their origins is appended here to reveal the era of exploration, revolution and enlightenment in Europe that inspired, even compelled, the educated and adventurous sons of exceptional families to seek opportunities in America. Two came from England and France by way of Holland, and the third from Switzerland. All had heard inspiring discussions in the Salons of Europe, often from royalty or from revolutionaries like Benjamin Franklin or John Adams while they served in Europe as American representatives.

The inter-marriage of such adventurous families with long and storied histories sheds great light on why they were destined to interact in the new world of America where their educations, religion, passionate interests and boundless energy brought them together in politics and business. This is how great American families evolve over time to leave lasting legacies for their posterity and for the nation as a whole.

APPENDIX F-1 Emigration Map

Arrival in America	Family	From
1672	Livingston	Ancrum, Scotland via Holland Exile
1676	Goelet	New Rochelle, France via Holland Exile
1730	Gerry	Newton Abbot, Devonshire, England
1780	Gallatin	Geneva, Switzerland (originated in France)

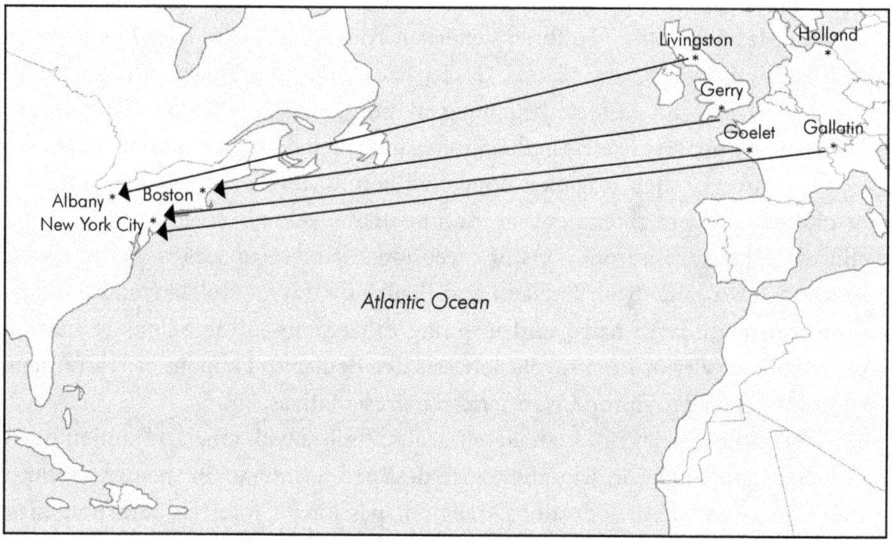

APPENDIX F-2 Albert Gallatin and his Descendants

Nov. 1, 1703
Albert Gallatin married Hannah Nicholson

- Albert Gallatin: b. Geneva, Switzerland, Jan. 20, 1761; d. New York, Aug. 12, 1849
- Hannah Nicholson: b. Sept. 11, 1766; d. May, 1849

Children:

1824
James m I.G. Pascault
- James: b. 1796; d. 1876
- I.G. Pascault: b. 1880; d. 1893

  1849
  Albert m Harriet D. Robinson
  - Albert: b. 1825; d. 1859
  - Harriet D. Robinson: b. 1828; d. 1893

    1876
    - Albert Louis m Zephita Heyward
      - Albert Louis: b. 1850; d. 1880, s.p.
      - Zephita Heyward: d. 1896
    - James Francis, b. 1853; d. 1915, unm.

1837
Albert Rolaz m Mary L. Stevens
- Albert Rolaz: b. 1800; d. 1890
- Mary L. Stevens: b. 1817; d. 1892

  1876
  Albert Horatio m Louise Belfort Ewing
  - Albert Horatio: b. 1830; d. 1902
    - Louise
    - Albert Eugene
    - Cornelia Lansdale

  1866
  Frederic m Almy Goelet Gerry
  - Frederic: b. 1841
    - Amy Goelet
    - Rolaz Horace
    - Jean Buchanan
    - Amy Goelet
    - Rolaz Horace
    - Jean Buchanan

  James m Elizabeth Hill Dawson
  - James: b. 1846; d. 1890
    - Albert Rolaz
    - Frances Dawson
    - Elizabeth Maud
    - Helen Dawson
    - James Nicholson
    - Frederic

1830
Frances m Byam K. Stevens
- Frances: b. 1803; d. 1877
- Byam K. Stevens: b. 1702; d. 1870
  - Albert G. Stevens, b. 1831; d. 1904
  - Frances M. Stevens, b. 1832; d. 1893
  - Alexander H. Stevens, b. 1834
  - Byam K. Stevens, b. 1836; d. 1911
  - Eugene R. Stevens, b. 1837; d. 1905
  - Frederic W. Stevens, b. 1839
  - Josephine L. Stevens, b. 1842

APPENDIX F-3

THE GALLATIN FAMILY ANCESTRY

The surname Gallatin is a derivative of the old Roman Gallatini and both spellings are used in this brief family history. The Gallatin family, like most leading families of their day, named their children with the proud but often repeated "given names" of their ancestors from the thirteenth through the twentieth Century. The most often used names were Abraham, Albert, Jean (both men and women), Frances, James, Pierre, and Almy. It should be noted that the names Goelet and Rolaz were maternal surnames that were later used as "given names" to preserve their historic connections with the Gallatin family.

The eighteenth century oral history of the Gallatin family suggested that the earliest ancestor was A. Atilius Callatinus, a local consul to Rome in the years 494 A.D. and 498 A.D.[1] Historians consider this to be unlikely because no further trace of the family appeared for over a thousand years. Nonetheless, Jean De Gallatin, second in command of the regiment of Chateauvieux in the service of King Louis XVI in the Swiss Guard, so strongly believed in the story that he fought a saber duel on horseback with the Baron de Pappenheim, and although he survived, he carried a life-long scar from a sabre-cut across his face as a mark of his belief in the antiquity of the Gallatin family.[2]

The first official record of the Gallatin family is an archived receipt dated 1258 that documented a transfer of property called *quindedim libras Viennenses* to the Abbess of Bellacomba for use by her convent. The property was bequeathed by one Faulcher Gallantini, who lived in the Savoy region of France.[3] Sixty years later in 1319, Guillanume Gallatini, "Chevalier" (a French nobleman), with his son Humbert Gallatini, "Damoiseau" (Master or Lord) appeared as minor figures in legal documents. Humbert's grandson was Henri Gallatini, Seigneur de Granges, Lord of the *Bugey Estate* in Savoy, who married Agnes de Lenthenay. When Agnes died in 1397 her will documented the transfer of the *Bugey Estate* to her son and heir, Jean Gallatini, the patriarch of the Gallatin family in Geneva and America. The estate was near Chambery, the capital of Savoy and lay along the Rhone River about thirty miles from Geneva and the same distance from Lyons. Jean Gallatini became the Equerry of Duke Philibert de Savoy and a man of importance in the region.[4] The *New York Historical Society* has in its collection the *Mazer,* a rare 15th century drinking cup made of maple wood, that Duke Philibert presented to Jean Gallitini in 1498. The cup has an engraved silver medallion inside the bowl which bears the arms of the Gallatin family surrounded by an inscription from the Duke. The cup was mentioned in a Gallatin letter in 1680 and again appeared in France in 1819 when it was owned by Pierre Gallatin, the Minister of Wurtemberg in Paris. The cup was gifted to the *Society* in 1908 by Albert Eugene Gallatin, the great-grandson of Albert Gallatin, Secretary of the Treasury under Thomas Jefferson and James Madison.[5]

His namesake son, Jean Gallatini II, succeeded his father to the *Bugey Estate* as well as the Equerry of the Duke of Savoy. His serious temperament and his conscientious opinions and acts held him in high esteem with Pope Leo X who appointed him an Apostolic Judge in 1522, with the power to create one hundred and fifty notaries and public judges. In time, Duke Philibert made him his secretary with the title of Vice Comtes. However, in 1530, Jean Gallatini II renounced both the Lordship of his estate and his obedience to the Catholic Church. Although there is no record of what caused such a radical change of heart and loyalty, that same year the French theologian, John Calvin, also renounced the Catholic Church. Gallatini then departed from France and went to Switzerland, thirty miles across the Jura Mountains, where he was made a citizen of Geneva and where he demonstrated his loyalty to Geneva by joining the powerful City Council in 1535, the same year that Geneva was declared a sovereign republic. He supported the Council's action to decree that the Pope had no power in Switzerland and they deposed the local Catholic Bishop of Geneva. Jean died the following year in 1536 just months after meeting John Calvin who had moved to Geneva from France to live and preach. From that time forward the Gallatins were among the closest allies of the great reformer and Calvin's extensive correspondence with the family was preserved until 1794 when the revolutionary armies of France invaded Geneva and burned the archive.[6] As one of eleven historically aristocratic families in Geneva, the Gallatin men always held high positions as civil leaders. They were consistently appointed chief magistrates, university rectors and professors, and sometimes even rectors of the Reformed Church. Only one Gallatin lost favor in Geneva when he was criminally charged as the leader of an attempt to make popular reforms to the Constitution. Nonetheless, he was considered a political martyr by the family after his twenty-one year imprisonment from 1698-1719.[7]

After Jean Gallatini II's death in 1536, his eldest son Pierre was the source of four distinct branches of the family that migrated across Europe and even returned to France near the end of the eighteenth century. However, the male lines of descent eventually died out except for the Geneva lineage of Abraham Gallatin (1706-1791) who lived at the *Pregny Estate* in Geneva. This line bore distinguished Gallatin men that included a celebrated physician in Paris who became the chief of a hospital, another was Minister of Foreign Affairs to the Duke of Brunswick, and yet another was made a Count in 1819 by the King of Wurtemberg.[8] Indeed, over the centuries many Gallatin men were military leaders who fought, and even died, on great battlefields from the 1602 battle at the Escalade in Geneva and the 1797 Battle of the Rhine, to the American siege of Yorktown, where the first brigade of General Rochambeau's *Grenadier Company* was led by Baron Gaspard de Gallatin in September 1781. As an officer of the Swiss Guard of Louis XVI and a leader in the French army allied with America, Baron Gallatin kept a military journal of his time in the colonies, and in fact, an early translation of his original manuscript journal entitled *Journal of the Siege of Yorktown* is held in the Rare Books Department of the *College of William and Mary* in Williamsburg, Virginia, just a few miles from the historic Yorktown Battlefield.[9]

The most accurate biographer of the Gallatin family was Henry Adams, the great-grandson of President John Adams, who described the family temperament in his 1878 biography of Albert Gallatin, the grandson of Abraham Gallatin of the *Pregny Estate* in Geneva. Adams noted that the main stock of Gallatins were always Genevan to the core and pre-eminently distinguished in civil life. In any other European country a family like this would have had a feudal organization, a recognized head, great entailed estates and all the titles worthy of their status in society. Instead, the Gallatins emerged as the product of Geneva, a city that stood by itself with an aristocratic and republican government in which the parade of rank or wealth was not one of its chief characteristics. After the Gallatins abandoned all "hereditary titles" in France and moved to Switzerland, they became prominent aristocrats in Geneva and enjoyed the honorary title of Noble. Although they had no great family estate to inherit and were not guided by a recognized leader, Henry Adams' book attributes their high social esteem to the Gallatins' courage, energy, integrity and intelligence, which were the only "family inheritance" of the Gallatin aristocracy. The qualities of a family's character were wealth enough to make the little city of Geneva the most intelligent and perhaps the purest society in Europe.[10] Henry Adams' apt description of the Gallatins reflected the contemporary view of Geneva as a near utopian society that drew the British moral philosopher, economist and lawyer, Adam Smith, to Geneva in 1765 to experience the republic first-hand. He published his book *The Wealth of Nations* in 1776 which incorporated the struggle for economic, religious and political freedom in the American Colonies. When he was in France as a tutor to the son of an English Lord, Adam Smith stayed with the Duchesse d' Enville, Marie-Louise de la Rochefoucauld and her son, the young Duc de la Rochefoucauld at her *Chateau La Roche-Guyon* on the Rhine River, just outside Paris. Adam

Smith also stayed with the Duchess in Geneva for two months in the early 1770's where her young son, the Duc, was a student and where the Duchess practiced the "natural hygiene" of Doctor Theodore Tronchin that stressed fresh air, diet, exercise and minimal sleep. Trochin was elected a foreign member of the *Royal Swedish Academy of Sciences* in 1779 and was a good friend to illustrious men such as Voltaire, a friend and neighbor of the Gallatins in Geneva.[11]

Abraham Gallatin, 1706-1791, married Susanne Vaudenet in 1732 in Geneva. They made their home on the small *Pregny Estate* on Lake Geneva at the edge of the city. The property was adjacent to the *Ferney Estate* of Voltaire, a pen-name for Francois-Marie d'Auret (1694-1778). The two households were part of a distinguished circle of European intellectuals who gathered in the salons of the estates to discuss economics, philosophy, science, religion and the arts.[12] The wives of these aristocratic families were highly educated and were, in fact, the leaders of the great salons of Geneva, Paris, and London. The friendship between the Gallatins and Voltaire was not limited to intellectual subjects. Most of the wealthy estates cultivated gardens, both for a variety of healthy food and to provide impressive, beautiful gardens for their cosmopolitan visitors to admire and to wander through while chatting, reading or enjoying private contemplation. Notes and messages were constantly passed between the neighboring estates and often included requests for seeds and cuttings from their gardens. Voltaire sought fig trees and asparagus plants from Madame Gallatin and she in turn asked Voltaire to write poetry for her friends to thank them for favors.[13] The Duchess of Enville shared the love of horticulture with her salon friends while staying in Geneva. She was known as a *Physiocrate,* who sought to stabilize France by liberalizing markets and maximizing agricultural output through the broad application of the scientific method. Voltaire's Enlightenment philosophy was a perfect fit for the Duchess, and she shared her ideas with two other great friends, Thomas Jefferson and Benjamin Franklin. Both the Duchess and Jefferson used their estates as veritable laboratories for agricultural experimentation. Jefferson took cuttings home to Monticello in America, and he in turn sent the seeds of maple and oak trees to the Duchess at her *Chateaux La Roche-Guyon* near Paris.[14] Benjamin Franklin lived at Passy for nine years (1777-1785) just a few miles down the Rhine River from the Duchess while he negotiated peace with England and France after the *American Revolution.* Franklin immersed himself in the intellectual and cultural life of the great salons of Paris and Geneva, and knew all the great minds of the day. As early as 1759, Franklin and his son visited Edinburgh, Scotland where he and Adam Smith became life-long friends and in fact, Franklin hired Smith's boyhood friend and colleague, David Hull, as a partner in his printing enterprise in America. Nearly fifteen years later, Adam Smith and Benjamin Franklin enjoyed extended visits with the Duchess d' Enville at her salon outside Paris, and at times was joined by John Adams and his young son, John Quincy Adams. The exchange of ideas was so rich and exhaustive among the intellectuals of the Enlightenment period that it was not unusual for Adam Smith to send every manuscript draft of each chapter of his book, *The Wealth of Nations*, to Benjamin Franklin for his review during the entire writing process.[15] The ideas, opinions and knowledge exchanged at one salon was soon shared with the other salons, particularly between the Gallatin/Voltaire salons in Geneva and the Duchess d'Enville salon in Paris.

Abraham and Susanne Gallatin's son Jean was born at the *Pregny Estate.* He was raised in an enlightened household and married a local girl, the well-educated Genevan, Sophie Rolaz in 1755. Their son Albert Gallatin was born in 1761 and when their only daughter became seriously ill, four-year-old Albert was placed in the home of a friend and neighbor of Sophie Gallatin so she could care for her daughter. Young Albert lost his father at age four and his mother and sister by age nine. As an orphan still living with a family friend Albert became very close to his grandparents, Abraham and Susanne Gallatin, and spent most of his time at their *Pregny Estate* when he was not in school. His education was paid for by the *Bourse Gallatin,* a family trust established by the 1699 Will of Francois Gallatin for the aid or relief of family members. Young Albert Gallatin could not help but be impressed by the many illustrious visitors to his grandparents salon and by his visits with Voltaire at the *Ferney Estate* next door. Albert Gallatin, though a few years older, was a childhood friend of the Duc de la Rochefoucauld and visited at his Paris home, the Chateaux of the Duchess d'Enville, where he and John Quincy Adams were sometimes mentored by Benjamin Franklin, a frequent visitor of the Duchess. The boys moved about freely in social gatherings filled with the vibrant discourse of historic characters who visited Geneva and Paris and whose liberal ideas and vision ultimately inspired Albert Gallatin to go to America at age nineteen in 1780.

Albert Gallatin's academic education in Geneva was enriched when he sometimes shared the local classroom with the sons of visiting intellectuals that included Benjamin Franklin's grandson, *Benjamin Franklin Bache,* John Adams' son, *John Quincy Adams,* and the Duchess d'Enville's son, *Duc de La Rochefoucauld.* These young men were mentored by the leaders of the *American Revolution* and the European Enlightenment, and each in his own way, became a leader in post-Revolutionary America, except the Duc de La Rochefoucauld who was murdered after the *French Revolution,* 1789-1799.

Albert Gallatin finished college in 1779 and was first in his class in mathematics, natural philosophy and Latin translation. He spent his first year as a tutor in Geneva but also spent time with a circle of friends that Henry Adams described as visionaries, inspired by the *Declaration of Independence* in America and dissatisfied with the conservative order of things in Geneva. He was advised from all sides about which career to pursue, especially by his grandparents. His family was closely connected with the Baron de Gallatin of the King's *Swiss Guard* which made a military career an obvious choice, while his grandmother wanted him to consider a legal career. Although Albert was not interested in the suggestions of his grandparents, Abraham and Susanne Gallatin, he also did not want to hurt them, so he quietly contacted the Duchess d'Enville for assistance with his plan to join a college friend and sail for America. The Duchess wrote to Benjamin Franklin to ask for a "letter of introduction" for Albert Gallatin to take with him to America. Franklin was only too happy to assist nineteen year-old Albert and supplied him with the necessary letter. On April 1, 1780, after making secret preparations and carrying with him minimal resources and a few personal belongings, Albert Gallatin, along with his friend Henri Serre, quietly left Geneva, boarded the American ship the *Katy* at the French port of Nantes, and sailed across the Atlantic Ocean to the port of Boston, Massachusetts. The first few years were spent learning English, exploring the Indian wilderness in Maine and teaching French at Harvard. After three years he used his savings to purchase land in western Virginia, now Pennsylvania, and became a land surveyor and in 1785 an American citizen. In 1786 he bought a 400 acre farm and established a permanent home he called *Friendship Hill.* The geography was reminiscent of Switzerland and no better spot could have been found in America for a man who had passed his youth on Lake Geneva. Nevertheless, Albert Gallatin was not yet firmly established in his American life. Henry Adams further wrote, that the business of store-keeping and land-clearing in a remote mountain valley had drawbacks, and the death of his friend Henri Serre was a severe blow, which made Gallatin reflect on the home he had deserted in Geneva. Forty years later, after his lands were bequeathed to his sons, Albert Gallatin remarked that the property had plagued him all his life, and it was his pursuit of a political and business life in New York City that ultimately gave him fulfillment.[16] In May 1789 Albert was married for the first time but within five short months his bride died, which left him so devastated that he never spoke of her again. His second marriage was not until 1793 when he married Hannah Nicholson with whom he had six children, three of whom survived childhood. His son James (1796-1876) served as his father's Secretary from 1813-1823 during peace negotiations in France following the *War of 1812* with Britain. The *Diary of James Gallatin* kept during those years was published in 1915 by his grandson, with an Introduction by the historian James Bryce, and is in the manuscripts collection of the *New York Historical Society*.

Albert Gallatin's political career began when he opposed the federal *Constitution* when it was placed before the state of Pennsylvania for ratification. A group of leading Pennsylvania citizens called a conference in Harrisburg in September 1788 to make one last effort to proclaim their reasons for the state to not ratify the document. Thirty-three men attended the conference and Albert Gallatin took the lead in drafting the conference "declaration of opinion" which he edited in response to the debate over the language and meaning of their declaration. Despite their best efforts Pennsylvania ratified the federal Constitution. The following year, in 1789, at the age of twenty-eight and without any effort on his part, Albert Gallatin was elected by the people of his local county to be a member of the state Convention to amend the Constitution of Pennsylvania. He was re-elected without opposition every year until he was elected to the United States Congress in 1795, and continued in that seat for three Congresses, until President Thomas Jefferson appointed him the Secretary of the Treasury 1800-1813.[17] Henry Adams writes that "there is no reason to suppose that Albert Gallatin's career was more brilliant or more successful in America than with the same efforts and with equal sacrifices it might have been in Europe; for his character and abilities must have insured pre-eminence in whatever path he chose."[18]

APPENDIX F-4 Goelet Family Tree

Francis Goelet – widower, died at sea in 1676 immediately after leaving 10-year old son, Jacobus in New York
Jacobus Goelet married Janette Coesaar 1687 (Jacobus raised by Frederick Phillipse)
John Goelet married Jannettie Cannon 1718
Peter Goelet married Elizabeth Ratze 1755
Peter P. Goelet married Almy Buchanan

- Jean
  unmarried
- Robert married Sara Ogden
  - Robert (1841-1899)
    married Harriette Warren
    - Robert Walton Goelet (1880-1941)
      - Married 1921 Ann Marie Guestier (1899-1988) (famous French wine family)
      - Beatrice married Hayward F. Manice
        (1922-2015) (1917-1989) (NY Architect)
        - John
        - Anne
        - Robert
        - Amelia
        - Pamela
      - Robert Guestier Goelet (1923-) (ornithologist)
        1976 m. Alexandra Gardiner Creel
        (Gardiner's Island)
        Trustee, Carnegie Institution
        Trustee, World Conservation Society
        Trustee Emeritus, National History Museum
        Sutton Place, NYC
        2 children
        - Alexandra
        - Robert
      - Francis Goelet (1926-1998)
        Bachelor – Riverside, CT
        Mary Eleanor Goelet
        National Medal of the Arts bestowed
        by Ronald Reagan
        NYC Metropolitan Opera sponsor
      - John Goelet (1927 -)
        Harvard art donations, Harvard Book Fund
        Clos du Val Winery, California, among others worldwide
        - Phillip
        - Thomas (d.1988)
        - Christopher
    - Daughter Beatrice
      (Dec. 1885- Feb. 1902)
  - Ogden (1846-1897) married Mary Wilson
    - Robert Wilson Goelet
      (1880-1966)
      Married 3 times
      - 1904-1914
        Elise Whelan
        - Peter Goelet married Margaret Wheelock Wilson
          (1911-1986) Chester, Orange County, NY
        - Ogden Goelet II (1907-1969)
          married 5 times
          - 1933 Enid Confeld
          - 1938 Maria Zimbalist
          - 1941 Mimi Brown
            - Ogden Goelet III
              (1942-)
              married 1987
              Nancy Goeschel
          - 4th?
          - 5th Sara Sherburne
      - 1919-1924
        Duchess Donna
        Fernanda Di Villarosa
        - One son
          - Robert Goelet, Jr. (1921-1989)
            married: 1942-1948 Jane Monroe
            1949-1956 Lynn Merrick
      - 1925-1949
        Roberta Willard
        (1895-1949)
        - Daughter
          Mary Eleanor Goelet
    - Daughter (1878-1937)
      May Goelet
      Duchess of 8th Roxburghe
      Innes-Kerr Family
      Floors Castle, England
      King George V godfather to son
- Peter
  unmarried
  Helped widowed sister Hannah
  raise her 3 children
  Elbridge, Almy & Jean
- Hannah
  1833 married
  Thomas Russell Gerry
  - Elbridge T. Gerry
    (1837-1927)

APPENDIX F-5

THE GOELET FAMILY ANCESTRY

The Goelet family ancestors are from La Rochelle, a beautiful town on the west coast of France. The region was first occupied by the Romans 2000 years ago to produce and export salt from the well-protected harbor of La Rochelle. By the tenth century salt production was overshadowed by the fishing industry and by the fifteenth century La Rochelle was a bustling city with active trade routes to England, Spain, and Africa.[1]

France had been predominantly Catholic since the *Concordat of Bologna* signed in 1516 created an alliance between the French monarchy and the Pope in Rome. By the middle of the sixteenth century followers of John Calvin's Protestant teachings, known as Huguenots, were rapidly growing throughout French society, from poor shopkeepers, artisans, and farmers, to businessmen, lawyers and the bourgeoisie.[2] One of the Huguenot strongholds was La Rochelle, considered to be the center of its organization. Tensions between King Louis XIV and the Protestants led Cardinal Richelieu, the monarch's chief advisor, to condemn the Huguenots as a "state within a state" and embarked on a crusade to dismantle La Rochelle, the Protestant stronghold. Richelieu's army blockaded the harbor with a make-shift dam to eliminate any hope of British rescue and to starve the 17,000 citizens of La Rochelle into submission. By October 1628 nearly 10,000 Huguenots were dead and the town surrendered followed in 1629 by the surrender of all Protestant towns in France.[3] Most of the devout Huguenot French families began to emigrate even before the siege of La Rochelle. In fact, one Protestant branch of the extended Goelet family left in 1621 for Amsterdam, Holland, the most tolerant city in Europe for religious exiles. The Goelets successfully re-established their merchant life in Holland and within fifty years the next generation was looking to America where a large number of La Rochelle exiles planned to establish a colonial Huguenot town called *New Rochelle* near New York City.

Francis Goelet, the youngest son of the family, had just lost his wife and was the father of a young son, ten-year-old Jacobus. Although he was born in Holland, Francis knew it was not the ancestral home of the Goelet family and he felt compelled to follow other adventurous Huguenots to America. He left Holland in 1676 and sailed to the port of New York City to explore the possibility of a permanent stay. Francis found the Huguenot community welcoming and supportive so he left his ten-year-old son, Jacobus, in the care of Frederick

Phillipse, a successful Dutch businessman, while he returned to Holland to collect his belongings for a permanent move. Francis Goelet sailed for Europe but did not arrive, neither the ship nor its occupants were ever heard from again and his family was notified that Francis and Jacobus were lost at sea. Some say that Jacobus returned to Amsterdam to find his father but to no avail, while others believe that Francis returned safely to Holland and remarried, never to return to America to rejoin his son, Jacobus.

The Phillipse family that mentored young Jacobus after the death of his father in 1676 had also originated in Holland where Frederick, Sr. and his wife, Margaret (Dacres), an English woman, raised and educated their son, Frederick Phillipse, Jr. who was born in 1626. That same year, Peter Minuit was appointed the first Director General of the West India Company's new colony on Manhattan Island which he named "New Amsterdam," considered to be the first permanent settlement in New York City. When Fredrick Phillipse, Jr. was twenty-one his parents financed his emigration to New Amsterdam where he soon established himself as a trusted local leader and was appointed the arbitrator of property valuation in real estate disputes. After six years he became the West India Company's local architect and builder through which he began to amass a great fortune. After the British conquered New Amsterdam in 1664 and renamed it New York, Frederick Phillipse Jr. became the City Surveyor and ten years later in 1674 he was appointed the City Alderman by the Duke of York in England. With a number of business enterprises and various properties to manage, he began to hire immigrants and hired as apprentices local orphan boys. When Francis Goelet arrived in 1676, he was assured by Alderman Frederick Phillipse that plenty of work was readily available so he left his ten-year old son Jacobus with the Alderman while Francis left on his fateful sea voyage to Holland. Left an orphan after losing his father at sea young Jacobus Goelet was hired by Alderman Frederick Phillipse as an apprentice along with several other orphans he hired, housed, fed, and most importantly, educated at the local Dutch Church School.

After several years Jacobus Goelet learned the skills of a merchant and a property manager from the best mentor in the colony. He also excelled in all of his academic studies and eventually became one of the few local school masters. By the time he was twenty-two the colony of New York came to respect Jacobus Goelet as a highly intelligent and trusted young leader, which encouraged him to marry Jannettie Coesaar in 1687, the daughter of a successful Huguenot family that had immigrated from La Rochelle, France, the Goelet ancestral home. During their happy marriage they had six children all of whom were assured a good education by their schoolmaster father. Jacobus became a familiar face in the New

York Huguenot community and was appointed the Clerk of the Dutch Church where he, and later his son John, became the official Dutch translators for the community. Like his surrogate father and mentor, Frederick Phillipse, a Lord of his own Manor by 1693, Jacobus Goelet purchased land and engaged in multiple occupations as a school master, clerk, and then a successful stationer and book seller. In 1920, one of his descendants, Robert Goelet, had the only known copy of the 1697 *Almanack* written by John Clap, in his private New York City library. It was just the type of book that was regularly sold in Jacobus Goelet's shop two hundred years earlier. An inventory of the library of the Master of the Dutch School from 1686 to 1702 lists the school books that were printed for Jacobus Goelet for sale in his shop. The inventory included history books, song books, arithmetic or cipher books, and catechisms. In fact, one of the earliest known imprints of a New York book seller was the small 1706 vellum-bound, *Heidelberg Catechism* with a publication note on the title page that read "printed for Jacobus Goelet."

Phillipsus Goelet, the namesake of his father's adopted family, became a prominent goldsmith and married Catharina Boelen. In 1718 Jacobus Goelet's third son, Johannes (John) Goelet married Jannettie Cannon, the daughter of a prosperous New York merchant family. John Goelet continued in the family business as a school master and shop keeper under the sign of the "Bible." Of John's several children it was his fourth son, Peter Goelet, born in 1727, who became the most eminent and opulent merchant in New York. He first went into business with Peter T. Curtenius who had married Catherine Goelet in 1755, his partner's sister. Eventually, Peter Goelet amicably dissolved the partnership when Peter Curtenius was made the Commissary-General of the Continental Army in 1776 and was opposed to the importation of British goods. Curtenius opened his own store under the sign of the "Golden Anvil" but soon after sold it for cash to help supply the army. Peter Goelet continued his hardware store at 48 Hanover Square (*today 113 & 115 Pearl St*) under the sign of the "Golden Key" as by custom, a symbol of one's business was selected and prominently showcased. He was the first in the city to import violins, guitars, flutes, and other musical instruments. He was a member of the first "Committee of Fifty" in 1774 to resist British oppression, and a member of the 1775 "Committee of One Hundred" put in charge of the city as the colonies entered the *Revolutionary War*.[4]

In 1755 Peter married Elizabeth Ratse the daughter of another prominent businessman. They lived at 63 Water Street until they bought a townhouse at No.5 State Street across from the Battery. He was enrolled among the *Sons of Liberty* during the troubled times of the Stamp Act. In 1774 their son Peter P. Goelet was born. Over his life time he added greatly to the wealth he inherited, and married Almy Buchanan, daughter of Thomas Buchanan, a well-educated Scotsman from Glasgow, and one of the leading merchants and leaders of the city during the Revolutionary Period. His shop was on Queen Street opposite the upper end of the Fly Market.[5] Peter's brother Robert Goelet married Almy's sister, Margaret Buchanan. When Thomas Buchanan died he left no male heirs thereby passing the Buchanan fortunes in New York City to the Goelet family through his daughters, Almy and Margaret.[6] This began generations of extensive land ownership and acquisition in the Goelet family, known for purchasing but never selling their valuable property.

Peter P. and Almy had four children, Peter, Jean, Hannah and Robert. At the death of their father in 1828 the four children inherited jointly, with no division of the extensive property and commercial investments in New York City. The Goelet brothers, Peter and Robert, continued the historic family policy of investing in real estate located in the path of the city's growth and improvement to become owners, with their sisters, of the largest and most valuable properties in New York City. The brothers were founders of the famous New York financial institution the *Chemical Bank* and the next generation of brothers, Robert Goelet II and Ogden Goelet, were also associated with the bank and managed the family investments.

The eldest of the four siblings, Peter Goelet (3rd namesake) was born in 1800, never married, and lived in his home at the corner of 19th and Broadway his entire adult life from 1848-1879. His unmarried sister Jean Buchannan Goelet and his widowed sister, Hannah Greene Goelet Gerry, lived with Peter until each of their successive deaths over a 50-year period. He was retiring in is habits but was charitable and contributed generously to aid the sick and wounded soldiers of the Civil War. He was one of the largest stockholders when the *Chemical Bank of New York* was re-chartered in 1844. For more than thirty-five years he worked as an invaluable advisor and voluntary helper in its business needs. It was said that if he could not be found in his old-fashioned house at Broadway and Nineteenth Street, he was sure to be in the *Chemical Bank* directors' room. Peter Goelet kept pheasants from India, storks from Egypt and guinea pigs, hens, cows, peacocks in the large yard of the Goelet mansion; it was often referred to as his "Broadway Farm." By never selling this prime piece of real estate, even when it became the last remaining private residence among rising business buildings, Peter Goelet essentially blocked the old Boss Tweed from extending Madison Avenue through to Broadway.

His younger brother, Robert Goelet, was born in 1809 and married Sarah Ogden, daughter of Jonathan Ogden who owned *Ogden, Ferguson & Company* at the old Bridge Street store until 1836 when it was moved to No.51 Williams Street and in 1843 the firm was renamed for his son, *Johattan Ogden & Company*. Sarah Ogden was raised at No.4 State Street on the Battery with her brother Johattan, where they were neighbors of the Goelet family at No.5 State Street. Robert Goelet married the "girl next door" and they had two sons, Ogden and Robert. Robert and Sarah continued to live at his family home on 5 State Street facing the green park of the Battery where Sarah had the company and support of her Ogden family just next door.

Their son, Robert Goelet II, was born in 1841 at 5 State Street and graduated from Columbia College in 1860 just two years after Elbridge T. Gerry completed his Master's Degree in German at Columbia. Robert Goelet was admitted to the Bar but relinquished the practice of law for the management of the vast Goelet estates, including the estate of his brother Ogden, which he inherited at his brother's death in 1897. While declining public office, he was on the board of directors of some of the largest financial institutions and railroads in the country.

Ogden Goelet, the younger son of Robert and Sarah (Ogden) Goelet, was also born at the family residence, 5 State Street, across from the Battery, in 1846. In his early years he devoted himself to the family real estate interests and married Mary R. Wilson of New York City. They had two children, Robert Goelet III and Mary Goelet. While a member of several clubs he was most noted for his devotion to yachting until his death in 1897.

After several decades, upon the successive deaths of the siblings, Peter Goelet's wealth was inherited by his sole-surviving sister Hannah Goelet Gerry, thus moving half of the Goelet fortune into the Gerry family upon Hannah's death in 1895. Hannah had married Capt. Thomas Russell Gerry from Massachusetts, the son of Vice-President Elbridge Gerry under James Madison. Hannah's son was Commodore Elbridge Thomas Gerry, a New York City lawyer, humanitarian and bibliophile. Nineteenth century New York newspapers often wrote that the entire Gerry/Goelet family were closely and affectionately united across generations.

The twentieth-century Goelets are a family of cautious, conservative, frugal and industrious businessmen who have traditionally avoided publicity and therefore remain one of New York's best kept secrets. Contemporary Goelets are more likely to be found in universities and scientific foundations as professors and scientists, while other members of the family are artists. The Goelets have been known to travel the world to explore insects and birds, while others married into French wine-making, becoming connoisseurs. The Goelets have historically participated in philanthropic efforts for the Museum of Natural History, the New York Historical Society, the New York Zoo, and the Lincoln Center for the Performing Arts.[7]

The New York Goelet descendants once again living in France at least part of each year, the country of their origins before 1621 and the Huguenot exodus. Some Goelets live in Paris and in two historic French landmark chateaus. The first is *Saint Aubin d'Ecrosville,* a chateau built around 1640 by the great Norman Leroux family. Since the nineteenth century the chateau has been owned by the Jousselin family who, in each generation, have restored and improved the land and buildings to achieve recognition as a *Cultural Heritage* designated chateau. Robert Walton Goelet's granddaughter, Anne Marie Guestier Manice, married Edmond de La Haye Jousselin and the chateau is now their country estate. The second chateau in the Goelet family today is *Sandricourt* which was a 16th century chateau purchased by Robert Walton Goelet in 1908 and rebuilt in the nineteenth century.during his years as a bachelor when his mother lived in Paris. The property includes nearly 10,500 acres and has always been considered some of the finest hunting grounds in France. *Sandricourt* was a vital location for allied forces in both World War I and II. During World War I the chateau's quadrangle of dairy barns, grain storage buildings, carriage and horse stables were converted by the Red Cross as a training and staging area for the Ambulance Corp that sent vehicles to the front lines each month. The Goelet family evacuated *Sandricourt* during the war, and left the army corps to repair, paint, and rehabilitate the chateau's quadrangle into useful living quarters and vehicle preparation stations. One soldier stationed at *Sandricourt* published the book *Red Poppies* in 1918 which includes detailed descriptions of his time at the chateau, especially the spontaneous bloom of expansive fields of red poppies in areas where soldiers had died. As far back as 1693 when William III of England fought the French army in the Netherlands, there are records of the spontaneous bloom of red poppies on the field of battle where 20,000 men were left unburied, symbolic of the field of blood. Today in London, when the military airplanes fly over Buckingham Palace to salute the Queen on *Trafalgar Day,* thousands of red paper poppies are released on the castle and the Mall. In World War II, Robert Walton Goelet's wife, Anne-Marie Goelet, was named an officer of the *French Legion of Honor* for her services in aiding French-American wives during the war and for providing medical services to inhabitants around her *Sandricourt* estate after the liberation of Paris in August 1944. Robert had married Anne Marie Guestier between the great wars in 1921. She was the heiress of the centuries old *Barton & Guestier* winery at the *Chateau Magnol* in Bordeaux where Thomas Barton established the winery in 1725, the first international "shipper" to also produce wine. In 1802 the French wine trader Daniel Guestier joined Hugh Barton to establish *Barton & Guestier (B&G label),* which today is the oldest and most famous wine merchant in

Bordeaux, France. Robert and Anne Goelet's son John Goelet, has established wineries worldwide, following in the footsteps of his mother's historic family calling. The extended Goelet family continues to spend part of the year in New York City and Newport, Rhode Island at the family homestead, *Southside,* built by architects McKim, Mead, and White in 1882, and known today as *Ochre Point.*

The Goelet family also owns the historic *Gardiner's Island* the oldest family owned property in America dating back to England's King Charles the First's original grant to Lyon Gardiner in 1639. It was settled almost 400 years ago and the first manor house, built in 1774, burned down and was replaced by a new mansion around 1938. About the same time other historic out-buildings on the island were restored including a carpentry shed built in 1639, the oldest standing wood structure in New York State. *Gardiner's Island* has never been developed although visitors came to hunt deer, turkey or fish and stayed in the old manor house before it burned down.

The privateer William Kidd buried treasure on the island in June, 1699, having stopped there while sailing to Boston to answer charges of piracy. With the permission of the island's proprietor, Kidd buried a chest of treasure and two boxes containing gold and silver, in a ravine between Bostwick's Point and the Manor House, and he told Gardiner that the box of gold was intended for Lord Bellomont. For Mrs. Gardiner's trouble he gave her a length of gold cloth (a piece of which is now at the East Hampton library) captured from a Moorish ship off Madagascar, and a sack of sugar. Kidd was tried in Boston, and Gardiner was ordered by Governor Bellomont to deliver the treasure as evidence. The booty included gold dust, bars of silver, Spanish dollars, rubies, diamonds, candlesticks, and porringers. Gardiner kept one of the diamonds which he later gave to his daughter. A plaque on the private island marks the spot where the treasure was buried so long ago.[8]

Gardiner's Island is 6 miles long and 3 miles wide with 27 miles of coastline. It has the largest stand of white oak in the Northeast, part of 1,000 acres of old growth forest and 1,000 acres of meadowlands. The town of East Hampton, Long Island granted a conservation easement on the Island until 2025 to ensure its natural state. The largest colony of osprey in North America line the shores with their nests because they have no natural enemies on the island. The isolated island is now entrusted to Alexandra and Robert Goelet who use it as a family retreat. Alexandra is a descendant of the Lyon Gardiner family of which there were sixteen Lords of the Manor on the island. She is a graduate of Yale University with a degree in Forestry which makes Alexandra Goelet the perfect "Lady of the Manor" in the twenty-first century.[9]

APPENDIX F-6 Succession of Family Titles to Lake Delaware

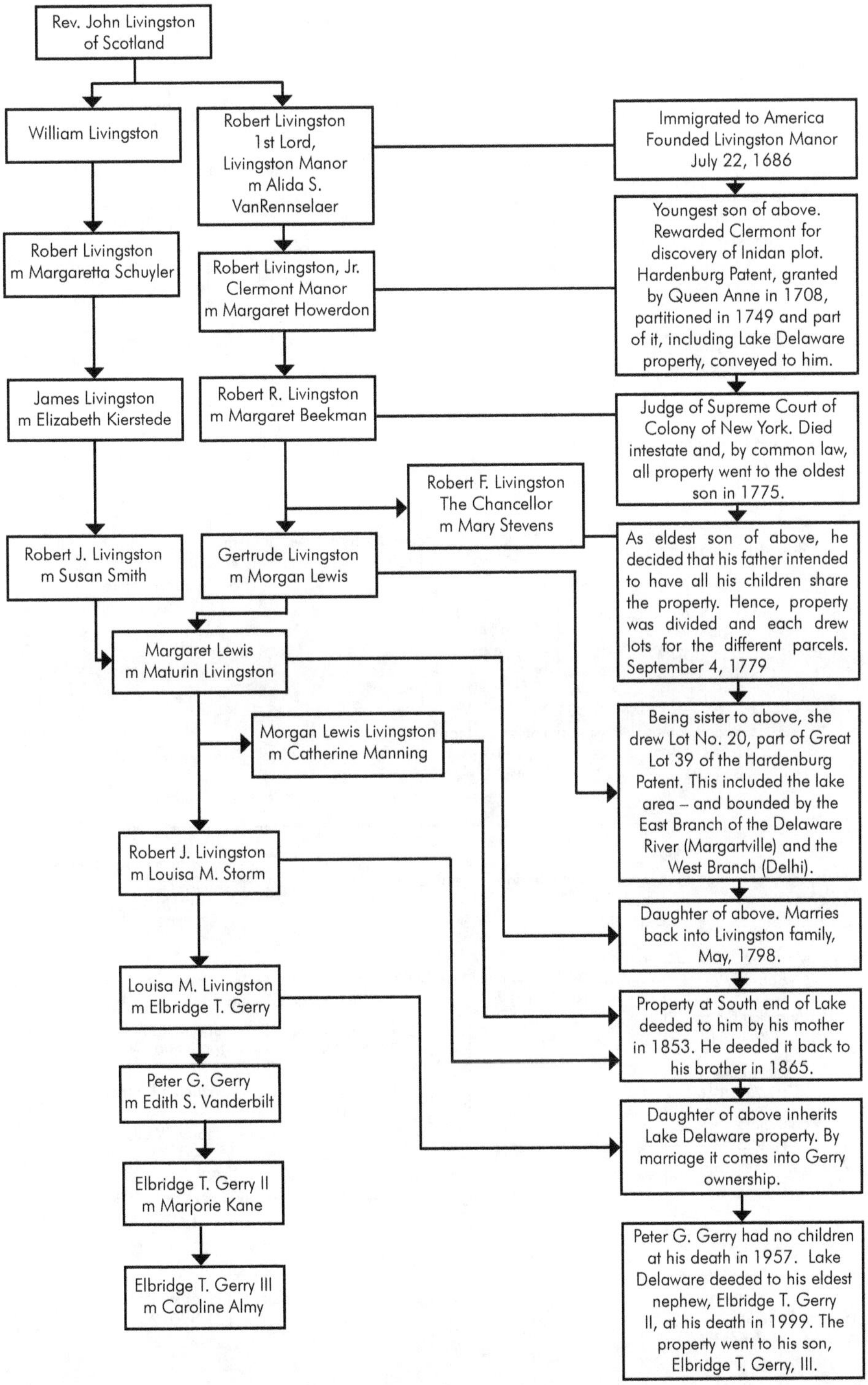

APPENDIX F-7 Livingston Family Tree

1635
Rev John Livingston married Janet Fleming
Kilsyth, Sterlingshire, Scotland
1663 exiled to Holland
b. 1603-1672 | 1613-1694
14 children born in Scotland

remained in Scotland
William Livingston
1638-1663

Robert Livingston (nephew)
1663-1725
1697 m Margarita Schuyler
1682-1725

James Livingston
1701-1763

Robert J. Livingston
1725-1771

Maturin Livingston
b. 1769
d. 1847

emigrated to New York 1672 Robert Livingston m Alida Schuyler – 9 children
1st Lord of Clermont Manor b. 1654 d. 1728 | b. 1656 Albany NY d. 1729

Robert Livingston, Jr.
1718-1775

Robert R. Livingston
1746-1813

5th cousins
1798

Gen. Morgan Lewis m Gertrude Livingston (1 child)
1754-1844 | 1743-1833
Lake Delaware Estate

m Margaret Livingston
b.1780
d.1860
6 children

1833
Robert James Livingston m Louisa M. Storm
b. 1811 | b. 1810
d. 1891 | d. 1883

1867
Louisa Matilda Livingston m Commodore Elbridge Thomas Gerry
b. 1836 | b. 1837
d. 1920 | d. 1927

Warren Livingston
b.1835
d. 1857

Margaret Gerry
1868-1872

1909
Robert L. Gerry m Cornelia Harriman
1877 - 1957

1932
Elbridge T. Gerry II m Marjorie Kane
1908-1999 | 1909-1999

Robert L. Gerry II m 1– Marleigh Kramer
1911-1979
m 2 – Harriet Wells

1939
Edward Harriman Gerry m Martha Farish
1941-2003 | 1918-2007
Twins

1940
Henry Averell Gerry m Nancy Whitney
1941-1960 | 1917-2012

Angelica Gerry
1872-1961

Lillian Gerry
1873-1891

Mabel Gerry
1874-1935
1930 m F. Saxon Drury

Senator Peter Gerry
1879-1957
1912 m 1 – Mathilda Townsend
1924 m 2 – Edith Vanderbilt

APPENDIX F-8

THE LIVINGSTON FAMILY ANCESTRY

It must be noted that given names are so often repeated by the Livingstons that confusion among generations is very common. In fact, the given names most often repeated in the Livingston line of succession in Scotland are Alexander, James and William. In America the most often repeated given names are Robert, Phillip and Peter. Therefore this summary of Livingston family ancestry is very narrowly tailored to not only avoid confusion, but most importantly, to shed light on the rich and tumultuous history of the clan, its critical role in the history of Scotland, and the clan's proud lineage to the Livingston family in New York.

The Livingston heritage dates back to twelfth century Scotland where the earliest documents record a Baron Leving de Levingston whose surname had slightly variant spellings throughout the course of the family's history. The first Livingston was a Saxon immigrant living in Lanark, Scotland, a village southwest of Edinburgh near the *Antonine Wall,* the old Roman wall built in 144 AD twenty years after *Hadrian's Wall* was built 99 miles south near the English border. Baron Leving's son, Thurston Levingston, witnessed a land charter in 1187 with his two sons, William and Alexander, who inherited the chartered property. The lands reached north from Lanark to Falkirk in the counties of Linlithgowshire and Stirlingshire.[1] Today the location of the ancient Leving Manor is the site of the town of Livingston in Linlithgowshire named in honor of the family. A later record of the earliest family line in Stirlingshire appeared in 1296 when Andrew Livingston became the Sheriff of Lanark, followed in 1301 by his brother, Archibald Livingston's appointment as the Sheriff of Linlithgow, near Falkirk to the north, due west of Edinburgh. Andrew Livingston died in 1297 at the famous *Battle of Sterling Bridge* trying to suppress the rebellion of William Wallace, known as "Braveheart" who was later appointed the *Guardian of Scotland,* and knighted by Scotland's disputed King John Balliol. William Wallace was ultimately defeated by King Edward I of England. After his capture in 1305 he was taken to London and tried for treason. Speaking at Westminster Hall after he was condemned to death, William Wallace spoke on behalf of freedom-loving Scotland when he said, "I could not be a traitor to King Edward, for I was never his subject."[2] Every generation of the extended Livingston Clan was involved in the tug-of-war between Scotland and England, even feuding with other Clan nobles like the powerful Douglas Clan and the Crichton Clan, often shifting sides when the monarchies made and broke alliances through the centuries.

In 1345 Archibald Livingston's son William was rewarded by King David II of Scotland for his support during the re-ignited wars for independence with a gift of the "confiscated " lands of Callendar in Stirlingshire, whose proprietor had been disloyal. One year later William Livingston married the lovely Christian de Callendar, the daughter and benefactor of the former proprietor of the *Callendar House* estate.[3] This assured the Livingstons a legal title to the lands of Callendar rather than an uncertain royal charter that could be revoked by a future monarch's political expediency. William and Christian lived their life in *Callendar House* as did successive generations who eventually consolidated all of the estates accumulated by the Livingstons from 1100 to 1400. During this time the Livingston Clan became a powerful influence in Scotland. In 1424 King James I returned to Scotland after eighteen years of house arrest in England, during which time he was educated and had married the daughter of the Earl of Somerset. The King endeavored in the first several years of his reign to reform and improve the legal system and to begin dismantling the feudal land system. The nobles of Scotland became jealous of the power that had been restored to the King which caused the royal family to live in fear and suspicion. In 1437 the King and Queen went on a holiday retreat to the Dominican Monastery in Perth, but shortly after settling-in for the night the monastery was invaded by a band of conspirators hired by a few angry and jealous nobles. The King ripped up the floor boards and climbed down into a narrow sewer canal that ran beneath the monastery and out to a river. The Queen replaced the floor boards before the door was broken down and managed to escape to Edinburgh with her guards while the intruders searched for the King. Huddled in the sewer the King was astonished to discover that he had blocked his own escape. The summer before he had played tennis on a grass court next to the Monastery but was frustrated when he kept losing tennis balls to the sewer drainage ditch. He had a permanent grate installed to prevent the loss of tennis balls, a grate that sadly also foiled his escape. The assassins found the King beneath the damaged floor boards, shivering in the drainage and promptly removed him and stabbed him to death.[4] In the midst of medieval mayhem the genteel games of tennis and golf were played, and even King Henry VIII had a tennis court installed at Hampton Court in 1530. Just twenty miles east of the Monastery where the King was murdered, the first game of golf was played at Saint Andrews, Scotland around 1400. Mary Queen of Scotland was rebuked for "disrespectfully" playing golf soon after the murder of her husband, Lord Darnley in 1567.[5]

After the sudden death of King James I the Queen and her young son, the infant king, were held hostage by Lord Crichton, the Keeper of the Royal Household, who proceeded to dissipate the royal revenues of Edinburgh Castle. During a rare visit with her son, the Queen tucked her baby in a garment chest and with the aid of her loyal guards, escaped Edinburgh Castle to Sterling Castle which was under the Governorship of the Livingston Clan. The Scottish Parliament determined in 1438 that Lord Crichton had treasonously held the royals as prisoners and therefore appointed Sir Alexander Livingston the guardian and protector of King James II during his childhood, thereby effectively acting as Regent during the King's minority. Years later he was rewarded with a Lordship of Parliament and was made Knight of Callendar. Between 1400 and 1500 a few branches of the Livingston family had moved northeast to Aberdeen and southwest to Kirkland, Scotland. However, most of the extended family remained in the Falkirk area of Scotland, where the direct ancestor of the American Livingstons was born in the village of Kilsyth, near Falkirk in Stirlingshire, Scotland.

In 1542, when King James V of Scotland died while temporarily living in France, Sir Alexander Livingston, Fifth Lord of Callendar, and seven other noblemen, were once again entrusted with the care of a King's heir, the infant , Mary, who was returned to Scotland.

King Henry VIII of England felt a continuous threat from his northern neighbors and hoped to win the crown of Scotland for his own infant son, Edward, by arranging a marriage with the infant Mary. The King's proposal was rejected by Scotland's nobles, who once again entrusted the guardianship and protection of Mary to the Livingstons of *Callendar House* and Keeper of Sterling Castle. Angered, King Henry VIII invaded Scotland followed in 1548 by the evacuation of young Queen Mary to France by her protector Sir Alexander Livingston. The little queen lived for the next twelve years of her minority exiled in France. Sir Alexander Livingston's own daughter, named Mary after the queen, became one of the four "ladies in waiting" to the Queen, known collectively as the "four Marys."[6] Sir Alexander Livingston of Callendar died five years after his arrival in France with little Queen Mary, and it was his son and heir, Sir William Livingston, a follower of the Protestant Reformation, who then became the protector of the Catholic Queen during the remainder of her minority. In 1561, Queen Mary returned to Scotland to begin her reign, and she often visited the Livingstons at *Callendar House,* her childhood family, and attended weddings and stood as godmother to one of their children.[7]

By the end of the sixteenth century the Livingston family support for the Stewarts brought Alexander, the Seventh Lord of Callendar, to prominence once again as part of the court of Mary's son, King James VI. The King's daughter Elizabeth, the first of the Hanoverian succession to the British throne, had been placed in the trusted care of the Livingstons at *Callendar House,* just as her grandmother, Mary, had been years before. Out of gratitude the King created the first Earl of Linlithgow and elevated Callendar to a free burgh or a Barony. Sir Alexander became the Earl of Calendar and his brother, the Earl of Linlithgow.[8] Sir Alexander Livingston lost his brother, James, and his own son, John, both of *Callendar House*, in a 1547 battle with English soldiers. To assist his deceased brother Jame's heir, also named Alexander, Sir Alexander Livingston appointed his nephew to be Rector of the Reformed Church in Kilsyth adjacent to Monyabroch, just west of *Callendar House* in Falkirk. While the successive Lords of of the Livingston clan were serving as Protectors of Scotland royalty, the sons of *Callendar House* began a long line of highly revered ministers across Scotland.

During these tumultuous decades in Scotland, from Queen Mary to King James VI to Charles II, the ministry was not without suspicion or scandals that often led to obstruction, parish transfers, and even excommunications. In fact, the wife of the seventh Lord Alexander Livingston of Callendar was called before the Glasgow Presbytery around 1580 to give a confession of her faith to dispel misgivings about her beliefs. After three years of pressure, Lady Livingston, the Countess of Linlithgow, appealed to then King James VI, the son of Queen Mary, for protection since the King's daughter, Elizabeth, was in the care of the *House of Callendar*. One charge against her ladyship was "having dealings with midsummer fairies," no doubt both hard to prove or defend against. However, the King avoided interfering by stating that his daughter was under the care of Lord Alexander Livingston and not his wife, and therefore her ladyship must face the church elders. She was excommunicated, and her cousin and counsel, Reverend Alexander Livingston of Kilsyth, was temporarily removed from his parish for an inability to discipline his congregation.[9] Nonetheless, Reverend Alexander's son, William also became a minister, the first in the parish of Monyabroch, just down the road from his father in Kilsyth, as did his own namesake son, Reverend William Livingston II. Of significance, the second Reverend William Livingston of Monyabroch and *Callendar House* became the grandfather of Robert Livingston, the first Lord of the Manor on the Hudson River in the colony of New York. Years later, in 1695 the two Earldoms of Callendar and Linlithgow were combined under the fourth and last Earl of Callendar, Sir James Livingston, who was exiled around 1715 for taking the wrong side in a fight against the Stewarts. Livingston lands under the Earldoms of Callendar and Linlithgow were forfeited and the titles extinguished, after which the light of the Livingston clan faded in Scotland. Today, *Callendar House* is the principal museum in Falkirk, Scotland for art and local history. The official *Falkirk Archives* are stored in the Research Center in the beautiful oak-paneled library of the fully restored *Callendar House*.

Of course, the American line of Livingstons had emerged in 1600 when the Reverend William Livingston of Monyabroch, Kilsyth, married his fifth cousin, Agnes Livingston who was the daughter of Alexander and Marion Livingston of *Airth Castle* in western Falkirk, near Edinburgh. *Airth Castle* became the successor family estate to the historic, but forfeited, *Callendar House.* Although William and Agnes inherited *Airth Castle,* the Reverend continued to preach in Kilsyth and to live in the parish house. Their son, John Livingston, was born in 1602 and after attending the Latin School in Sterling, he entered the University of Glasgow in 1618 where he earned a Master of Arts in 1622.[10] He followed in his father's calling to the ministry and in 1625 was the fourth generation to obtain a license to preach. However, from the start he had an aversion to Church rituals and therefore the Bishop of St. Andrews refused to ordain him in the Church of Scotland. During the next few years he preached a non-conformist theology and converted many across Scotland with his inspired sermons, some of which were famous at the time. In 1630 he grew impatient and crossed the narrow channel at Stranrear to Belfast, Ireland where he was ordained by an Irish Protestant Bishop. The church in Scotland responded quickly and excommunicated him which resulted in his first attempt to cross the Atlantic to America in early 1634. Reverend John Livingston, joined by his friend and teacher, William Wallace (not the *Braveheart*), boarded a ship in London for the long Atlantic crossing. To their dismay a terrible and lengthy storm forced the captain to dock in Plymouth for ten days where Livingston's travel companion, William Wallace, took seriously ill. The Reverend Livingston would not leave his friend behind and so disembarked and returned with Wallace to Scotland. Early in 1635 he married Janet Fleming in a ceremony officiated by his father at the West Church in Edinburgh, Scotland. Janet was a member of a successful merchant family who had been life-long friends of the Livingstons but whose father had died and her mother had remarried an Irishman. As an excommunicated, non-conformist minister, they immediately fled to Milton, Ireland near Belfast, where they lived with Janet's mother which allowed Reverend John Livingston to preach in local parishes. While on a short return visit to Scotland, he received a letter from the Massachusetts Governor, John Winthrop, a Puritan who had immigrated to America five years before in 1630 and established the *Massachusetts Bay Colony* where he became its first colonial Governor. It was a letter of invitation for the Reverend John Livingston and his "non-conformist" followers to join the Puritan colony in America where he would be their Minister. Indeed, the Governor's eldest son, also Mr. John Winthrop, Jr. visited Reverend Livingston in Scotland to deliver the letter of invitation in person. While there, the Reverend Livingston provided the young American with letters of introduction for use in his travel throughout

Scotland.[11] The non-conformist group accepted the invitation and, over the next several months, managed to have their own ship built and hired a captain. By the time they set sail, Janet Livingston had given birth to their first child. On his second attempt to cross the Atlantic Reverend John Livingston was once again thwarted when the ship encountered a violent hurricane that battered the ship on the New Foundland coast and left it in no shape to complete the voyage to America. This was taken as a sign from God that he should not go to America and so returned to Ireland. It was his youngest son, Robert Livingston, who successfully crossed the Atlantic to America sixty years later.[12]

In time, Reverend Livingston's sermons gained him a widespread reputation as a gifted preacher that belied his modest and somewhat introverted nature. In the midst of the historic tensions between Scotland and England, particularly between the Protestant and Catholic factions, the Reverend John Livingston was re-admitted to the Church of Scotland ministry and was often called upon by the Presbytery to serve on commissions. Once, in 1649, he offered private counsel to King Charles II about taking an Oath to keep his covenant with the Church of Scotland, which the Reverend John Livingston subsequently administered to the King in Edinburgh. Even Oliver Cromwell knew and respected the Reverend John Livingston, and in a letter sent in 1650 to the English Parliament, he described him as "a man as highly esteemed as any for piety and learning."[13] Cromwell invited him to London to preach at Whitehall which he did only once and with great reluctance. Although he was always under great suspicion in Scotland as a non-conformist minister, the Reverend John Livingston was welcomed by the Church hierarchy to join and lead important commissions as their most articulate spokesperson. His insightful and reflective mind, plus his preaching ability, gave the Church a persuasive voice.

During the Scottish Reformation, the Reverend John Livingston refused to adapt to the changes and after two failed attempts to leave for America to seek religious freedom, he moved briefly to Lanark, Scotland to seek his father's advice and where his second child was born. Within a year the Reverend John Livingston decided to live quietly in the small village of Stranraer, on the far west coast of Scotland at one of the shortest crossing points to Belfast, Ireland, which allowed him to regularly minister to the non-conformist faithful in both countries. Seven of his children were born in Stranraer and three of them died there before the age of four. After ten years as minister in Stranrear, the Presbytery of the Church decided to transfer Reverend John Livingston to a parish 100 miles southeast near the border with England to a small village called Ancrum, near Kelso in Roxburghshire, Scotland where John became the local minister. In the early days of rebellion, William Wallace the "Braveheart" had fought the English at Ancrum, where the historic town was always a vital part of Scotland's border skirmishes with England. In time, Reverend John Livingston built a beautiful estate called *Ancrum House* that sits on the River Teviot, even to this day. His youngest five children, out of fourteen births, were born at Ancrum, where two also died and five were married. The Livingston family thrived in Ancrum and Reverend John Livingston's ministry flourished.

Of note, just seven miles to the east of Ancrum, Roxburghshire, was the town of Kelso where the ancient and famous *Roxburghe Castle* stood, the residence of the Earl of Northumberland in 1107. It became a residence for Scottish Kings over the next two hundred years. Around 1300 it was captured by Edward I of England, then changed hands frequently. In 1460 it was recaptured by England who held the castle for 100 years until it was finally destroyed in 1550. The ancient castle sat on the lands of the Duke of Roxburghe who built *Floors Castle* in 1720 just across the Teviot River from the castle ruins, still visible in the distance. This castle estate became the home of an American Livingston relative, May Goelet, of *Gilded Age* New York City, when she wed the British Duke of Roxburghe some 250 years later, and where the current generation resides under the Tenth Duke of Roxburghe.

The coronation of Charles II of Scotland on May 29, 1662 was used by the Scottish Parliament to prove their loyalty to the King when they declared the date of the King's coronation May 29 a new holy day on the church calendar. Further, and more devastating, the usually jealous nobles of Parliament placed the supreme power in all matters civil and ecclesiastical in the King's hands. This meant that the Episcopal Church would be the new Church of Scotland and all the efforts of the Reformation from 1638 to 1650, and the safety of non-conformists were in peril. The parliament and church council required all ministers to either acknowledge the bishops council and honor the holy day or leave the church.[14] The new declarations were quickly followed by trials and in some instances, banishment. Like Thomas More with King Henry VIII, the Reverend John Livingston had the trust and respect of his king, Charles II, to whom he had personally administered the oath to the Reformed Church of Scotland thirteen years before, and yet like Thomas More, he could not act against his conscience. With the full knowledge that his non-conformist colleagues were going to trial in Edinburgh, Reverend John Livingston preached a sermon in his Ancrum church in which he openly refused to recognize the Bishops and refused to accept the "coronation date" of the King as a church "holy day." He closed his sermon with the words, "there are times and seasons wherein a man's silence may bring a curse upon his head."[15] Within six weeks of his sermon he was summoned to appear in Edinburgh where he was sentenced to banishment from Scotland and was ordered to leave the country within two months, providing just enough time to say his farewells and settle affairs.

The Reverend John Livingston was exiled to Rotterdam, Holland in 1663 and took with him his wife and two youngest children, Robert, nine, and six-year old Elizabeth, who died three years later. They left behind their six older children who ranged in age from 15 to 25. All but 18-year old Agnes were married. The extended Livingston clan in Scotland remained in contact with their exiled family and visited Rotterdam over the years. Two of Reverend John Livingston's sons, James (1646-1700) who had remained in Scotland, and Robert (1654-1728) who went to Holland, were the first generation connection between the "old world" Livingston family of Scotland and the "new world" Livingston family of New York State in America.

The younger of the two Livingston brothers, Robert, chose not to remain in Holland after completing his education, rather, he immigrated to Albany, New York in 1672 just a few years before his nephew, and namesake, followed him from Scotland. Although the older Livingston brother, James, remained in Scotland for the remainder of his life, his son Robert, known as "the nephew" followed his "uncle Robert" to New York. Not only did the two Robert Livingstons, uncle and nephew, both immigrate to Albany, they married the prominent Schuyler sisters, Alida and Margaretta, whose brother, Pieter Schuyler, was the first Mayor of Albany, New York. The older of the two sisters, Alida, was the widow of Nicholas Van Rensselaer with whom she had no children, but with whom she shared elite status in the Albany community. Her marriage to Robert Livingston renewed the old era of the Lords of Scotland with Robert as the first *Lord of the Manor* on the Hudson River in New York.

The American branch of the Livingston family that left Scotland for Rotterdam arrived in Holland about forty years after the Goelet family arrived in Amsterdam in 1621 following their exile from France to Holland.[16] Both families arrived in America just four years apart, the Livingstons in 1672 and the Goelets in 1676, and in time, the families were joined by business and marriage in New York City. The Livingstons of the Hudson Valley and New York City were no less tumultuous than their cousins in Scotland. There were family feuds, political in-fighting, and property disputes over massive land grants, across every generation. Nonetheless, their role as colonial leaders, founding fathers, and shrewd businessmen has ensured their status as the most historic leading family in the state of New York.

List of Illustrations

Most of the illustrations in the chapter "picture collages" are taken from the Gerry family collections and are included with the permission of the family, therefore no citations are provided for Gerry family illustrations. Some illustrations, for example family trees, were compiled by the author and each original illustration will be so noted with **AC** (author created). Author's own photographs are cited with **AP** (author's photograph).

All other illustrations have either an indication that the copyright has expired and are in the public domain or there is a source credit or reprint permission noted where appropriate. Many Internet illustrations are made available for public reuse or re-distribution with attribution and are licensed under these free-media repositories, http: //commons.wikimedia.org with *GNU Free Documentation License* (cited as *GNU License*); http:// creativecommons.org/ user license to freely copy and redistribute for any purpose with attribution (cited as Creative Commons License); and http://www. gutenberg.org/ (cited as Gutenberg) to share and reuse illustrations with expired copyrights.

1: THE EARLY YEARS

Page 33 Collage

Captain Thomas Gerry 1702–1774

Rebecca Russell Greenleaf 1720–1771 (married Thomas Gerry)

Gerry 1730 house, Marblehead, MA. Source: 2010 photograph by Fletcher posted on Wikimedia Commons and used here under The *GNU License*

Historic Town Hall, Marblehead, MA. Source: 2010 photograph by Z and used here under the *GNU License*

Wall Street, New York City in 1798. Source: Archibald Robinson (1765-1835) www.senate.gov/artandhistory/comm/image/Federal_Hall.htm

Ann Thompson 1763–1849 (*married Elbridge Gerry*).

Elbridge Gerry 1744–1814

Elmwood, Gerry home in Cambridge, now Harvard University's President's House. Source: 1900 chromograph published by the Detroit Company, used here under the *GNU License*

Gerry-Mander District *Cartoon.* Source: Reprint of Elkanah Tisdale cartoon published in the Boston Gazette, March 26, 1812 and used here under the Wikipedia Commons License, http://www.wikipedia.org/wiki/File: The Gerry-Mander

Page 34 Collage

Widow Gerry House – New Haven, CT. Source: Pre-1897 photograph, Chapter Sketches, Connecticut Daughters of the American Revolution: Patriot's Daughters, published in 1904, New Haven Connecticut, page 8

Elbridge Gerry, Jr. 1793–1848

James Thompson Gerry, 1797–1854

Thomas Russell Gerry, 1794–1845

Sloop of War Albany. Source: Library of Congress, Prints and Photographs Division,

Lithograph published by N. Currier between 1835 and 1856, http://www.loc.gov/pictures/item/2002698108

Emily, Helen and Ann

Hannah Goelet Gerry

2: EDUCATION AND APPRENTICESHIP

Page 61 Collage

Almy, Elbridge, and Jean Gerry (siblings around 1847)

Elbridge Gerry – Miniature *Blackstone's Commentaries* inherited by Elbridge T Gerry, **AP**

Uncle Peter Goelet's Broadway Farm at 19th & Broadway NYC

Goelet Doll House, *made by Uncle Peter Goelet in New York City for nieces Almy and Jean.* Source: Museum of the City of New York, Toy Collection, Object ID: 47.41. Four floors furnished in period style

Elbridge T. Gerry. Columbia Graduation Photo, *either BA 1857 or MA 1860*

Elbridge T. Gerry, Illuminated Class Notes at Columbia College 1856. Source: Columbia University, Butler Library, Rare Book Room, Elbridge T. Gerry Collection, Box 5, Notes on History for Professor John McVickar

Columbia College, NYC 1865. Source: New York Public Library, Miriam and Ira D. Wallach Division of Art, Prints and Photographs. Digital ID 54235 Record ID 118289, Engraved by artist J. Anderson, issued in the May 1790 *New-York Magazine*

Train & River Scene – Davenport, Iowa, Great Western Expedition. Source: Rock Island Post Card Company 1914, from the Mississippi Valley Digital Image Archive: digital file name: ripTautenPostcard243.tif

Page 62 Collage

William Curtis Noyes, 1805–1864. Source: Mathew Brady photograph taken between 1855 and 1865. Library of Congress, Brady-Handy Photograph Collection.http://hdl.loc.gov/loc.gov/loc-pnp/cwpbh.02586

Elbridge T. Gerry, Bar Membership Certificate – U.S. Supreme Court. Source: Hartwick College Archives, Oneonta, New York, Gerry Family Archives, Courtesy of Curator, Shelley Wiate

West Washington Market in New York City. Source: 1890's postcard. http://ebay.com/itm/T152-NY- NYC-West-Washington-Market

Uncle Peter Goelet and blended Gerry/Goelet family on holiday at Saratoga, New York, 1858

Metropolitan Ball for Prince Albert Edward, wood cut 1860 NYC. Source: *Harper's Weekly,* Oct. 20, 1860. New York Public Library Digital Gallery. http://theebonyswan.blogspot.com

Page 63 Collage

Gertrude Livingston (*married General Morgan Lewis*)

General Morgan Lewis 1754–1844 (*grandfather of Louisa M. Livingston Gerry*)

Margaret Lewis Livingston

Maturin Livingston

Louisa Mathilde Storm, 1807–1883, married Robert James Livingston

Robert James Livingston, 1811–1891, son of Margaret and Maturin Livingston, at Staatsburg, New York

Louisa Mathilda Livingston (married Elbridge T. Gerry)

Lake Delaware Farm 1840 and 2011 photographs

Staatsburg-on-Hudson 1815, inherited from Morgan & Gertrude, 1840 and 2000 photographs

Livingston Lewis by their daughter Margaret Lewis Livingston 1780-1860 and husband, Maturin Livingston Sr. 1769-1847 her 5th cousin

Albany Bridge, Highland Park, NJ, built by Robert J. Livingston & his brother-in-law Samuel V. Hoffman). Source: http://www.ebay.com/itm/NewBrunswick-NJ-BOAT-CLUB-ALBANY-STREET-BRIDGE-Postcard

Page 64 Collage

Orphan Train, photo about 1875 – children sent from NYC to the West. Source: New York Historical Society, Prints and Photographs Division, Records of the Children's Aid Society, Bulk 1853-1947, MS 111

Elbridge T. Gerry

New York City Street Boys. Source: New York Historical Society, Prints & Photographs Division, Records of the Children's Aid Society, Bulk 1853–1947, MS 111

Bloomingdale Hospital 1848. Source: *History, Descrip-tion and Statistics of the Bloomingdale Asylum for the Insane.* Pliny Earle, M.D., Egbert, Hovey & King, New York, 1848, front plate

Page 65 Collage
Gerry Family Tree, **AC**

3: PASSING THE TORCH

Page 87 Collage
Jean and Almy Gerry
Frederic Gallatin and Albert Gallatin
Elbridge T. Gerry (married Louisa M. Livingston)
Louisa M. Livingston (married Elbridge T. Gerry)
Margaret "Pearl" Gerry 1868–1872 on Louisa's lap (mother)
Anonymous spirit photograph, man with spirit just behind him. Source: Melvin Willin, *The Earliest Images, Ghosts Caught on Film, Photographs of the Paranormal*, Published by David and Charles, Newton Abbot, England, 2007, p. 22
William Howard Mumler 1832–1884 – spirit photographer. Source: *Harpers Weekly*, May 4, 1869, also in his memoirs, *The Personal Experiences of William Mumler*, 1875
Mary Todd Lincoln – Mumler spirit photograph with Abraham Lincoln spirit behind Mary, sometime after his death. Source: Melvin Willin, *The Earliest Images, Ghosts Caught on Film: Photographs of the Paranormal*, Published by David and Charles, Newton Abbot, England, 2007, p. 22

Page 88 Collage
Elbridge T. Gerry with his sisters, Almy and Jean 1879
West Point, New York – Goelet summer holidays – early 1860's poster Print. Source: Vintage Prints at http://www.ebay.com/sch/i.html
Hudson from Cozzens Hotel. Source: L. Prang and Co. Publishers, Boston, 1871 postcard out of copyright

Page 89 Collage
New York State Capitol in Albany. Source: Wikimedia Commons, used here under the *GNU Free Documentation License*
Assembly Chamber in Old New York State Capitol
Assembly Room Seating Chart. Source: Gerry Collection and also ttp://www.nysl.nysed.gov

4: FATHER, LAWYER, LEADER

Page 112 Collage
Interior of the Bar of the City of New York Margaret "Pearl" Gerry, about age 4 near the time of her deathin1872
Entrance to the Bar of the City of New York
Henry Bergh, established first SPCA
Tiffany Silver Vase – 1873 honor to Elbridge T. Gerry from SPCA. Angelica and Mabel Gerry around 1874
Daniel McFarland Trial – newspaper sketch of Elbridge T. Gerry, Henry Bergh 1813–1888 founder of the *American Society for the Protection of Animals* ASPCA

Page 113 Collage
Margaret "Pearl" Gerry the year she died, age 4
Margaret Gerry 1868 – 1872 in carriage
Margaret Gerry on horse with nanny
Angelica and Mabel Gerry aged 3 and 2

5: GERRY'S SOCIETY

Page 148 Collage
Founding Meeting, New York State Bar Association, Albany 1876
Elbridge T. Gerry – wearing NYSPCC badge
Mary Ellen NYSPCC was established based on documented abuse of Mary using this photograph and her testimony. Source: Archives of the New York Society for the Prevention of Cruelty to Children, 61 Williams Street, New York City, Courtesy of Joseph Gleason, Archivist
Mary Ellen as an adult with her two daughters. Source: Archives of the New York Society for the Prevention of Cruelty to Children, 61 Williams Street, New York City. Courtesy of Joseph Gleason, Archivist
NYSPCC Agent Badges – Display Case. Source: Archives of the New York Society for the Prevention of Cruelty to Children, 61Williams Street, New York City. Courtesy of Joseph Gleason, Archives
Rescue Carriage for children owned by the Gerry Society 1870–1890. Source: Archives of the New York Society for the Prevention of Cruelty to Children, 61 Williams Street, New York City. Courtesy of Joseph Gleason, Archives

Page 149 Collage
Lillian Gerry in childhood portrait
Robert L. Gerry in childhood portrait
Senator Peter G. Gerry in childhood portrait
Gerry children (baby Peter absent) with father Elbridge T. Gerry –1880 at Lake Delaware Estate

Gerry children (baby Peter absent) with grandfather (sitting) Robert J. Livingston –at Lake Delaware Estate

Page 150 Collage

Robert "Bobby" Gerry with small cow at Lake Delaware Farm estate
Angelica "Angel" Gerry on horse at Lake Delaware estate
Senator Peter Gerry on cow-drawn trotter wagon at Lake Delaware Estate
Sail boat on Lake Delaware
Dock on Lake Delaware
Boat House on edge of Lake Delaware
Aerial view of Lake Delaware Estate with inset photo of servants and butlers

Page 151 Collage

Gallatin townhouse in New York City. Source: Museum of the City of New York ID X2010.11.4755, H.N. Tiemann & Company, 1898 http://mcnyblog.org
James Renwick, Jr. Architect. Source: Columbia University, Avery Architectural and Fine Arts Library, Special Collections, James Renwick and James Renwick, Jr. architectural drawings and papers. Call Number D&A
Breezy Lawn, East Hampton, L.I., Gallatin summer home. Source: Columbia University, Avery Architectural and Fine Arts Library, Special Collections, Box 02, Selma Rattner Research Papers on James Renwick 2005.006, Plate: 1889 photograph of Gallatin summer cottage
Saint Patrick's Cathedral. Source: Smithsonian American Art Museum, The Renwick Gallery. Source: http://americanart.si.edu/renwick/
Renwick. Renwick Gallery in Washington, D.C. Source: Columbia University, Avery Architectural and Fine Arts Library, Special Collections, James Renwick and James Renwick, Jr. architectural drawings and papers. Call Number D&A Renwick

Page 152 Collage

General Grant and family at Long Branch. Source: 1870 Pach Brothers Photograph posted by Imperial Cabinet Card on Wikimedia Commons and used under *GNU License*
Grant Cottage, Long Branch, N.J., Gerry family summer rental
Saint Mark's Cemetery, NYC. Source: Church brochure, *Saint Mark's in the Bowery, A Comprehensive Guide to the Church Historical Site*, 1999. See also http://nycemetery.wordpress.com/
Saint Mark's Church, NYC 2013, **AP**
Goelet Vault Stone, early Goelet family vault in Saint Mark's Cemetery, **AP**

6: GILDED GOTHAM: THE 1880'S PART I

Page 193 Collage

Ogden Goelet Mansion NYC. Source: Salve Regina College, Killop Library Archives, 1887 Laram engraving
No. 608 5th Avenue, *Mr. Ogden Goelet's House*
Elbridge Thomas Gerry 1880
Ogden Goelet portrait. Source: Salve Regina College, Killop Library Archives, **AP** of portrait
Robert Goelet old photograph. Source: Salve Regina College, Killop Library Archives
Robert Goelet Mansion NYC. Source: New York Public Library, Prints and Photographs Department, Digital Catalogue Image ID:708882f dated 1931
Ochre Court – Newport estate of Ogden Goelet (now Salve Regina College). Source: Salve Regina College, Killop Library Archives, **AP** of original.
Southside – Newport estate of Robert Goelet (next door to Ochre Court). Source: Salve Regina College, Killop Library Archives, **AP** of original.
Newport Cliff Walk aerial view. Source: Flickr photograph used under the *Creative Commons License* to freely copy and redistribute for any purpose with attribution: *Cliff Walk Shore and Bank Protection page,* http://www.flickr.com/photos/corsnewengland/
Ogden Goelet's yacht – the *Norseman.* Source: New York Public Library, Prints and Photographs Department, Digital Catalogue, Image ID:403662 dated 1888
Robert Goelet's yacht – the *Magic.* Source: 1888 photograph in The Library of Congress Prints and Photographs collection and added to Wiki Commons under Digital ID: det.4a16297

Page 194 Collage

Elbridge Thomas Gerry 1880.
Elbridge T. Gerry's first yacht – the Pastime
Louisa M. Livingston (married Elbridge T. Gerry)
Lake Delaware Estate, Delhi, NY aerial view

Lake Delaware, view from the Lake House
Frederic Gallatin
Frederic Gallatin's 2nd yacht – the *Riviera* 1912 vintage postcard, used here under the Creative Commons license. http://www.navsource.org/
Almy Gerry Gallatin

Page 195 Collage
Queen Victoria Onboard the America. Source: 1902 heliotype print by C. Chase Ewersen. Printed by the Heliograph Company, Boston, MA originally published in T*he Lawson History of the America's Cup* by Winfield M. Thompson and Thomas W. Lawson, Boston, MA 1902
Madison Square Garden. Source: Museum of the City of New York, vintage 1910 callotype print, Wurts Brothers, New York. Item X2010.11.14115
P.T. Barnum with famous dwarf, Mr. Nutt. Source: undated Photograph by Charles DeForest Fredricks, New York Public Library, Prints and Photographs Department, Digital Catalogue, Image ID:120357
Elizabeth Cady Stanton: Stanton was Livingston relative. Source: 1880 photograph added to Wikimedia Commons and used here under *GNU License* http://www.freeschoolpress.com/us history/ElizabethadyStanton.jpg
Col. James Livingston 1774–1781. Source: Painting by Archibald Robertson, Metropolitan Museum of Art, Gift of Mr. and Mrs. Samuel Schwartz 1965, Digital Media Department, New York City. http://www.met museum.org
Montgomery Place-on-Hudson. Source: Photograph added by Photographer Daniel Case to Wikimedia Commons and used here under the *GNU License*
General Richard Montgomery 1738–1775. Source: Project Gutenberg eBook, Old Quebec by Sir Gilbert Parker and Claude Glennon Bryan. Engraving was made freely available at gutenberg.org

7: GILDED GOTHAM: THE 1880'S PART II
Page 245 Collage
Harlan & Hollingsworth Ship Building, Wilmington, Delaware. Source: Vintage 1890's postcard found at http://yorkship.us/html /otheryards.htm
Lillian Gerry, age 12 when she christened the yacht *Electra* 1884
Electra 1890 photograph of Elbridge T. Gerry's yacht
Chief Justice of England, Lord John Coleridge, 1820–1894. Source: 1920 engraving of a painting by Eden Upton Edds. A reproduction of the engraving is used under *GNU License*
Elbridge T. Gerry's navigation training set of tiny wooden boats, **AP**
1887 America's Cup Race – *Volunteer*, the flagship *Electra*, and the British challenger *Thistle.* Source: *Harper's Weekly*, August 1887 Engraving by J.O. Davidson http://www.ebay.com/itm/AMERICAS-CUP-VOLUNTEER-THISTLE-ELECTRA-1887-Print-Matted Item1e86f1e087
Elbridge T. Gerry's navigation training set chart folder, **AP**
Silver water pitcher etched with *Electra* and salvaged from yacht at demolition. Current owner of the silver Pitcher is Andy Woo, Andes, New York, **AP**

Page 246 Collage
Elbridge T. Gerry children Lilly, Mabel and Angelica dressed for fancy ball 1886 hosted by Louisa Gerry
Elbridge T. Gerry children Peter and Robert dressed for fancy ball 1886 hosted by Louisa Gerry
Penelope Sculpture at Lake Delaware, New York, **AP**
Rare Pipe Organ "bellows crank wheel" Lake Delaware, NY, **AP**
Rare 19th Pipe Organ, Lake Delaware Estate, NY, **AP**
Charles Dodsley Walker 1920 – Organist & choir director at the Lake Delaware Boys Camp 1940-1990. Source: Conversations with Charles Dodsley Walker, Part 1, March 2011 issue of the *The Diapason*, by Neal Campbell, photo of Charles Dodsley at the console of the new Aeolian-Skinner organ in Christ Church, Cambridge, 1941. Permission granted by Charles Dodsley to use his photo from http://nealcamp bell.wordpress.com/
Metropolitan Opera House – first in New York City. Source: Museum of the City of New York, Archives, 1905-1915 Illustrated Postal Card Company, Item Number X2011.34.44

Metropolitan Opera House interior. Source: Vintage 1880's Postcard shared on http://thegildedageera. blogspot.com, used here under the Creative Commons license

Page 247 Collage

Art deco design closeup photo of entrance to Goelet Building, **AP**

Goelet Building at 9 West 17th Street, NYC Built in 1887. Source: 1887 Public domain photograph, in Salve Regina College, Goelet Archives **See also** http://www.nyc-architecture.com/ CHE/CHE027-Goelet Building.htm

Art deco design closeup photo of air vent grate in Goelet Building, **AP**

Art deco design Entrance Doors to Goelet Building, **AP**

Beatrice Goelet, age 7 painted by John Singer Sargent. Source: *Harper's Weekly* magazine, May 1891, engraving for the 13th Annual Exhibition of the Society of American Artists, p.346. Copyright expired

Goelet Cups – designed by Tiffany for yacht races in 1882, 1884, 1892

Newport Regatta (Castle Hill shoreline spectators). Source: Mystic Seaport Museum Archives, Mystic CT, unidentified photographer Wharton Collection, 1895 gelatin glass negative, Accession Number: 1982.84.13

Page 248 Collage

Fraunces Tavern. Source: 1908 postcard published by George P. Hall & Sons, New York City, expired copyright. http://www.ebay.com

Fraunces Tavern Long Room, **AP**

Chickering Hall – exterior. Source: Amos F. Eno 1888 halftone print, New York Public Library, Stephen A. Schwarzman Building, Print Collection, Mariam and Ira D. Wallach Division of Art, Prints and Photographs, Catalog Number: MEZN Eno 438 and Digitital ID:1659325

Chickering Hall – Auditorium. Source: 1875 halftone print, New York Public Library, Stephen A. Schwarzman Building, Print Collection, Mariam and Ira D. Wallach Division of Art, Prints and Photographs, Call Number: PC NEW YC-Aud and Digitital ID 800330

Chickering Hall – Grand entry stairs. Source: 1875 halftone print, New York Public Library, Stephen A. Schwarzman Building, Print Collection, Mariam and Ira D. Wallach Division of Art, Prints and Photographs, Call Number: G-New York City – Auditoriums

8: GILDED GOTHAM: THE 1880'S PART III

Page 272 Collage

1889 Centennial Parade Passing Union Square. Source: Reproduction of 1889 photograph from E. Benjamin Andrews, *History of the United States, Vol. V,* Charles Schribner and Sons, New York, 1912. Used here under the Wikimedia Commons *GNU License.*

George Washington's hand on Bible – painting of Swearing-In. Source: Contemporary painting April 1789, by William Williams, National Archives ID: 148-CCD-92C used here under the Wikimedia Commons *GNU License*

1890 Washington Square Arch – by Stanford White – Gerry Scrapbook, **AP**

Federal Hall, NYC - 1889 Centennial of President George Washington's Inauguration. Source: *Harpers Weekly,* May 21, 1889, p.369 used here under the Wikimedia Commons *GNU License*

1889 Centennial Badges – Gerry Scrapbook, **AP**

Washington Centennial Ball. Source: Karal Ann Marling, *George Washington Slept Here: Colonial Revivals and American Culture, 1876-1986,* Harvard University Press, Cambridge, MA 1988, p. 113. Acknowledgement by Adrianna Rissetto 1997 from http://xroads.virginia.edu

Page 273 Collage

William Kemmler – *First execution by means of the Electric Chair.* Source: New York Herald, August 7, 1890, "In the Death Chair", p. 1 (expired copyright)

William Kemler cartoon portrayal, *First execution by means of the Electric Chair.* Source: New York Herald, August 7, 1890, "In the Death Chair", p. 1 (expired copyright)

Tillie Kemmler – murdered by her husband. Source: *New York Herald,* August 7, 1890, In the Death Chair, p. 1. (expired copyright)

Thomas Alva Edison. Source: 1922 Photographic print by Louis Bachrach, restored by Michel Vuijsteke and available from the Library of

Congress, Prints and Photographs Division under the digital ID:cph.3c50139
Auburn State Prison – Location of Kemmler Execution in 1889. Source: Vintage 1906 postcard, Printed in Germany, L.G. 142. Uploaded at http://www.ebay.com/itm/Postcard-905615-AuburnPrison-NY (ex-pired copyright)

Page 274 Collage
Chelsea Piers, New York City. Source: Vintage 1914 postcard, Published by the American Art Post Card Co., New York, NY Stock #270875 copyright expired http://www.cardcow.com/270875/chelsea-piers-new-york-city/
Trans-Atlantic Steamship shuffle board on deck. Source: *Harper's Magazine* archive of vintage magazine sketches from 1879 (copyright expired) article "The Ocean Steamer Crossing Atlantic in Early Steamships." http://www.gjenvick.com/SteamshipArticles/TransAtlanticShips and Voyages/1870-08-TheOceanSteamer-HarpersMagazine.html
Trans-Atlantic Steamship Ladies Room. Source: *Harper's Magazine* archive of vintage magazine sketches from 1879 Article (copyright expired), "The Ocean Steamer Crossing the Atlantic in Early Steamships" http://www.gjenvick.com/SteamshipAr ticles/TransAtlanticShips and Voyages/1870-08-TheOceanSteamer-HarpersMagazine.html
Trans-Atlantic steamship dining room on board. Source: *Harper's Magazine* archive of vintage magazine sketches from 1879 (copyright expired) article, "The Ocean Steamer Crossing the Atlantic in Early Steamships" http://www.gjenvick.com/Steam shipArticles/TransAtlanticShips and Voy-ages/1870-08-TheOceanSteamer-HarpersMagazine.html
Steamship docking at Liverpool, England. Source: Vintage postcard from the file: Inspection of Emigrants, with the Special Consular Reports, Department of Commerce and Labor, Bureau of Statistics, Volume XXX, GPO, Washington, D.C. 1904, p. 149.

Page 275 Collage
Lillian Gerry's diary
Lillian Gerry in ruffled blouse, age 16
1889 World Exposition in Paris, France Eiffel Tower vintage 1889 postcards with expired copyright used here under the Wikimedia Commons *GNU License*
1889 World Exposition in Paris, France Chrystal Palace vintage 1889 postcards with expired copyright used here under the Wikimedia Commons *GNU License*
1889 World Exposition in Paris, France Air Balloon Release vintage 1889. Postcards with expired copyright used here under the Wikimedia Commons *GNU License*

Page 276 Collage
Cartoon of Henry Bergh being flogged, Gerry scrapbook in U.S. Supreme Court collections, **AP**
Henry Bergh, photograph. Source: Archives of the New York Society for the Prevention of Cruelty to Children, 61 Williams Street, New York City. Courtesy of Joseph Gleason, Archivist.
Horse rescue carriage ASPCA. Source: Photo from the blog page http://www.ephemeralnewyork.wordpress.com and used here under Creative Commons License at http://en.wordpress.com/tos/
Henry Bergh Statue – Central Park, NYC. Source: Statue by James H. Mahoney, created in 1891, photographed by Gerald D. Tang and up-loaded to and licensed on Creative Commons for free use via "Save Public Art" at http://www.flickr.com/photos/wsavepublicart/

9: GILDED GOTHAM: THE 1890'S PART I
Page 314 Collage
Vice President Elbridge Gerry 1744-1814 – Bust in U.S. Capital, **AP**
First Courtroom of U.S. Supreme Court in Capitol Building, AP
Centennial of the U.S. Supreme Court – Cartoon. Source: The United States Nine, *New York Morning Journal*, February 5, 1890, p. 1 Gerry Scrapbook
United States Capitol Building, vintage postcards with expired copyright used here under the Wikimedia Commons *GNU License*
Courtroom of the U.S. Supreme Court today. Source: Office of the Curator, Supreme Court of the United States, Item # 1998-134-4 Courtroom, photographed by Franz Jantzen, Court Photographer

Captain Philippe d'Orleans, Duke of Chartres. Source: Library of Congress, Prints and Photographs Division, 1862 Mathew Brady Photograph with digital ID cph.3b03119

Emily Post 1890. Source: Used by permission of the Emily Post Institute, Inc. at http://www.emily post.com

United States Supreme Court Building, aerial view

Page 315 Collage

Richard Morris Hunt 1827–1895, Architect to Gerry and Goelet. Source: Late 1880's photograph on http://www.xroadsvirginia.edu/ Used here under the Wikimedia Commons *GNU License*

Ochre Court Aerial View. Source: Salve Regina College, McKillop Library Archives, Photograph collections. Courtesy of the Goelet family

Ochre Court Gates, Newport, RI. Source: Vintage postcard, copyright expired, http://www.ebay.com

Ochre Court Mezzanine view. Source: Salve Regina College, McKillop Library Archives, Photograph collections. Courtesy of the Goelet family

Ochre Court Grand Staircase view. Source: Salve Regina College, McKillop Library Archives, Photograph collections. Courtesy of the Goelet family

Ochre Court Ballroom view. Source: Salve Regina College, McKillop Library Archives, Photograph collections. Courtesy of the Goelet family

Page 316 Collage

Metropolitan Club to the right of Gerry Mansion, Fifth Ave. at 60th Street, NYC. Source: Museum of the City of New York, Byron Collection,1898 Photograph ID 93.1.1.2911

Metropolitan Club Entry Gates on East 60th Street, NYC. Source: Museum of the City of New York, Wurts Brothers 1915 gelatin dry plate negative ID X2010.7.1.1939

Metropolitan Club Grand Staircase. Source: Museum of the City of New York, 1895 gelatin silver print, ID 90.44.4.3

Metropolitan Club Library. Source: Museum of the City of New York, 1895 Bound Portfolio of vintage prints, ID90.44.4.

Lilly Langtry, British actress and mistress of the Prince of Wales. Source: 1885 photograph by William Downey in the National Archives of England and in the public domain.

Langtry yacht – the *Whyte Ladye* – sold to Ogden Goelet. Source: Vintage 1900 postcard (copyright expired). Posted by Andy Fitzgibbon online at: http://www.banjohang out.org/archive/251017

Prince Albert Edward "Bertie" 1841-1910, friend of Ogden Goelet. Source: Vintage cabinet card around 1868 by Sergie Levitsky. Used here *GNU License.* http://en.wikipedia.org /wiki/File: Prince Albert Edward

Page 317 Collage

Bon Air Hotel, Augusta, Georgia 1890. Source: Vintage 1890 postcard, copyright expired, http://www.ebay.com

Gerry Cup awarded at NYYC Regattas. Source: Silver cup designed by Whiting Manufacturing Co. Silversmiths, Union Square, New York. Photograph in Gerry collection

Lyndenhurst home rented by Gerry family in Newport, R.I., **AP**

Commodore Elbridge T. Gerry, portrait at Gerry Lake Delaware estate, **AP**

Commodore Elbridge T. Gerry recording yacht race on *Electra.* Source: Vintage 1887 engraving, *Harper's Weekly,* NY p708 http://www.museumsyndicate.com /item.php?item+67640

Page 318 Collage

Sculpted mahogany portrait head in the Federation's Cullmans Hall of Fame. http://www.asf.ca

Francis Goelet. Source: Out of copyright photograph courtesy of the archives of the Atlantic Salmon Fishing Federation, which he founded in 1919

Stanford White, Architect. Source: 1892 photograph by George Cox, loaded 2006 by Richard A. Norton, used here under theWikimedia Commons *GNU License,* http://en.wikip edia.org/wiki/File:StanfordWhite

Camp Harmony Fishing Club 1896, Restigouche River, Canada. Source: 1898 photograph, Notman Photographic Archives, McCord Museum of Canadian History, Montreal, Quebec, View-2844. http://www.history museum.ca5

Camp Harmony Fishing canoe, 1898, Restigouche River, Canada. Source: cropped detail from 1898 photograph, Notman Photographic Archives, McCord Museum of Canadian History, Montreal, Quebec, View-2844. http://www.historymuseum.ca5

Page 319 Collage
Whitney Warren, Architect. Source: Library of Congress, Prints and Photographs Collection, George Grantham Bain Collection, Stock Photo ID SF4704
Whitney Warren, Architect. Source: Library of Congress, Prints and Photographs Collection, George Grantham Bain Collection, Stock Photo
Newport, Rhode Island Golf Club. Source: Vintage 1890's postcard APC 52 in The Newport Postcard Museum (copyright expired) online: http://www.drawrmcom/mansions.htm
Grand Central Station, New York City. Source: 1900 vintage postcard, copyright expired. The Kubrick Theme Blog at WordPress.com, used here under Creative Commons License

Page 320 Collage
Peter Gerry dressed for the hunt at Lake Delaware, photo taken early 1890's
Robert Gerry dressed for the hunt at Lake Delaware, photo taken early 1890's
Angelica Gerry the "whip" on the Gerry coach.
Gerry siblings with Mills cousins on front porch of Lake Delaware estate around 1895
Robert Gerry and Peter Gerry entertain pals at Lake Delaware estate in 1902

10: GILDED GOTHAM: THE 1890'S PART II
Pages 328 - 330
Digital Gerry mansion plans purchased by the author from University of Texas- Austin Archives, **AP**

Page 393 Collage
MacKenzie King (Tutor of Gerry sons and future Prime Minister of Canada). Source: Library and Archives of Canada under Reproduction Number C-014191 and under MIKAN ID 3217536, Wikipedia image of MacKenzie King in 1899, used here under Wikimedia Commons *GNU* License. http://en.wikipedia.org/wi ki/File:King1899.jpg
Teddy Roosevelt – leader of the Rough Riders, *Spanish American War.* Source: Library of Congress, Prints and Photographs Division, 1898 photograph Reproduction Number: LC-USZ62-39935and Digital ID cph 3a40275
Queen Victoria on her Diamond Jubilee celebrated in 1897. Source: Reproduction of 1887 photograph by Alexander Bassano, National Portrait Gallery, London, England, Digital ID NPG x95802. Used here under the Wikimedia Commons *GNU License.* http://en.wikipedia.org/wiki/File: Queen Victoria_1887.jpg
Booker T. Washington 1856–1915. Source: Library of Congress, Prints and Photographs Division, 1903 photograh by Cheynes Studio, Hampton VA, Reproduction number LC-USZ62-49668 (b&w film copy neg.) Digital ID cph 3a49671 http://hdl.loc.gov.pnp/
Bradley Martin dressed for 1897 lavish Fancy Dress Ball. Source: New York Historical Society, Photographs and Prints Department, Portraits Box 86 PRO 52, Balls – Gilded Age, Folder: 1883 Vanderbilt fancy dress ball, photograph of Bradley Martin

Page 394 Collage
Duchess Consuelo Vanderbilt, John Singer Sargent portrait of Family. Source: 1905 print from the original painting, currently at Blenheim Palace, UK. The reprint is made available through the John Singer Sargent Virtual Gallery and used here under the Wikimedia Commons *GNU License*
Consuelo Vanderbilt after divorcing the Duke of Marlborough. Source: New York Public Library, Stephen A. Schwarzman Building, Manuscripts and Archives Division, Schwimmer-Lloyd Collection, Digital ID 1536818, Catalog Call Number MssCol 2703. http://www.nypl.org
Jacques Balsan, married divorced Consuelo Vanderbilt. Source: 1922 Photograph of aviator Jacques Balsan, Library of Congress, Prints and Photographs Division, Digital ID ggbain.33556. Used here under the Wikimedia Commons *GNU License*
Mabel Gerry *standing* with Gertrude Vanderbilt Whitney (best friends)
Gertrude Vanderbilt Whitney, first cousin to Consuelo, best friend of Mabel Gerry. Source: 1910? Jean de Strelecki photograph of Gertrude with her sculpture "Despair" from Gertrude Vanderbilt Whitney Papers, Archives

of AmericanArt, Smithsonian Institution, Digital ID 8699

Gertrude Vanderbilt, with son Harry P Whitney and niece Gloria Vanderbilt. Source: Archives of American Art, Smithsonian Institution, Gertrude Vanderbilt Whitney Papers, gift of Flora Miller Irving, photo taken in 1930's in the Adirondacks, Digital ID 11665

Page 395 Collage

Angelica Gerry

J. Wadsworth Ritchie 1861–1924, fiancé of Angelica Gerry. From scrapbook of Angelica Gerry

Special Vanderbilt Train to Florida, group included Mabel Gerry, Gertrude Vanderbilt, Harry Payne Whitney

Angelica Gerry

Newport Reading Room 1890's. Source: Vintage 1905? Postcard, http://en.wikipedia.org /wiki/Newport_Reading_Room. Used here under the Wikimedia Commons, *GNU License*

Coaching at Newport Golf Club in Newport, Rhode Island

Seaverge (aerial view of Gerry cottage in Newport, RI) Newport Golf Club 1893 and coaching parade

Page 396 Collage

Windsor Hotel before 1899 fire. Source: Office of Metropolitan History, *New York Times*, 1880 stereoscopic picture, copyright expired. Used here courtesy of the web site's royalty-free images under Creative Commons License

Windsor Hotel during fire of 1899. Source: Hillstead Museum, Farmington, CT, 1899 photograph, copyright expired. Used here courtesy of the web site's royalty-free images under Creative Commons License

Winston Churchill preparing a speech. Source: Telegraph Media Group, London, License to reprint "freelance image" by Bertrand Park, with article "Mr.Churchill's Profession," by Peter Clarke in the *Daily Telegraph* July 18, 2012, London, United Kingdom

Winston Churchill – Iron Curtain Speech 1946. Source: History Webpage https://bobhistory.wikispaces.com/ Who+Caused+the+Cold+War Used here under the Creative Commons License

Winston Churchill with his cousin Consuelo Vanderbilt at Blenheim. Source: 1902 photograph, with Wikimedia Commons *GNU License* http://www.en.wikipedia.org/wiki /File:Consuelo_Vanderbilt_mit_Winston Churchill.jpg

Christopher Columbus Statue, Central Park NYC. Source: New York City images made available http://www.new-york-pictures.org/ christopher_columbus_statue.html. Used here courtesy of the web site's royalty-free images under Creative Commons License

Julia Ward Howe, poet. Source: 1887 photograph, *History of Woman Suffrage*, volume 2, page 793, published in 1887, copyright expired. Used here under the Wikimedia Commons *GNU License*

Page 397 Collage

Ogden Goelet. Source: Portrait, Salve Regina College, Newport, RI, McKillop Library Archives, Courtesy of the Goelet and Manice family, **AP**

Robert Goelet, old photograph. Source: Salve Regina College, Killop Library Archives

Ogden Goelet's yacht *Mayflower* on which he died in 1897. Source: Library of Congress, Prints and Photographs Division, 1917 photograph from the Harris and Ewing Collection, ID 2368283455 online: http://www.flickr.com/ photos/library_of_congress /2368283455/

Nahma, Robert Goelet's 1897 yacht. Source: Department of the Navy, United States Naval Historical Center, Photo Number: NH 102049 Original print in the National Archives Record Group 19-LCM

Cowes, England, Yacht Station for Royal Yacht Club. Source: Vintage 1900 postcard printed in England, used here under Creative Commons License. http://www.ebay.co.uk/itm/ks498

Mayflower, Ogden Goelet's yacht became the United States Presidential Yacht. Source: Library of Congress, Prints and Photographs Division, 1912 Bains News Service Photo from glass negative, George Grantham Bain Collection, Call Number LC-B2-2450-8 and Digital ID ggbain.10887 Used here under the Wikimedia Commons *GNU License*

Page 398 Collage

Gerry Mansion exterior. Source: Byron Company (New York, N.Y.) Museum of the City of New York, Street Scene, 1899, 5th Ave. & 61st St.

(Gerry House), 93.1.1.18049, licensed for book publishing.
Gerry Mansion Interior Stairs. Source: University of Texas Library, Architecture and Planning Library, Alexander Architectural Archive, File: Alfred Zucker drawings, 1880-1904, Elbridge T. Gerry mansion, Sixty-First Street, New York City. Courtesy of Nancy Sparrow, Curatorial Assistant. (Complete digital copies of Gerry mansion plans purchased by the author)
Central Park, NYC, Mall Stairs to Bethesda Terrace. Source: Vintage 1894 photograph by J.S. Johnston, used here under Creative Commons License. Shared in 2011 by http://blog.thunderbaybooks.com

Page 399 Collage
Gerry Mansion Library Spiral Staircase from Floor Plans – 1894-96 (61st Street at Fifth Avenue, New York City). Source: University of Texas Library, Architecture and Planning Library, Alexander Architectural Archive, File: Alfred Zucker drawings, 1880-1904, Elbridge T. Gerry mansion, Sixty-First Street, New York City. Courtesy, Nancy Sparrow, Curatorial Assistant, plans purchased in digital format by author. **AP**
Gerry Mansion Library frieze on 2-story end wall. Source: University of Texas Library, Architecture and Planning Library, Alexander Architectural Archive, File: Alfred Zucker drawings, 1880-1904, Elbridge T. Gerry mansion, Sixty-First Street, New York City. Courtesy of Nancy Sparrow, Curatorial Assistant, plans purchased in digital format by author, **AP**
Gerry Mansion Library full length wall with fireplace, doors and upper story giant plaster reliefs. Source: University of Texas Library, Architecture and Planning Library, Alexander Architectural Archive, File: Alfred Zucker drawings, 1880-1904, Elbridge T. Gerry mansion, Sixty-First Street, New York City. Courtesy of Nancy Sparrow, Curatorial Assistant, plans purchased in digital format by author, **AP**

Page 400 Collage
Alfred Zucker, Architect. Source: New York Historical Society, Prints and Photographs Department, Winston Weisman Collection of Architectural Photographs, Box 27, Folder 518 Mixed Material, Portraits, PR-073.
Alfred Zucker, Office. Source: New York Historical Society, Prints and Photographs Department, William E. Wight Collection, Box 1, Folders 2-7, PR-37
Gerry Mansion Stable, 3-story floor plans. Source: University of Texas Library, Architecture and Planning Library, Alexander Architectural Archive, File: Alfred Zucker drawings, 1880-1904, Elbridge T. Gerry mansion, Sixty-First Street, New York City. Courtesy of Nancy Sparrow, Curatorial Assistant. (Complete digital copies of Gerry mansion plans purchased by the author), **AP**

Page 401 Collage
Bottle of Madiera Wine imported by Elbridge T. Gerry, **AP**
Grand Army Plaza with Gerry mansion at far left. Source: New York Historical Society, Portraits and Photographs, Winston Weisman Collection, Box 25, Folder 498, Mixed Material, view of East 58th to West 59th streets on Fifth Avenue, New York City
Ellis Island, New York City. Source: Vintage 1905 postcard by Coeffler, Thompkins LCC, New York. *http*://en.wikipedia.org/wiki/File:Ellis_Island_in_1905.jpg, Used here under *GNU License*
Mission of Our Lady of the Holy Rosary (*now Shrine of Elizabeth Seton*) 1870's photograph, architect James McComb, Jr., originally the James Watson house, 7 State Street, New York City. Copyright expired. Online at: http://nyc-architecture.com/LM/LM019-SHRINE
Page 402 Collage
Mabel Gerry with Mr. & Mrs. Edward Henry Harriman on board Elbridge T. Gerry's yacht *Electra*
Guests pose sitting on deck of Elbridge T. Gerry's yacht *Electra*
Staff & crew of Elbridge T. Gerry's yacht *Electra.*
Guests standing onboard Elbridge T. Gerry's yacht *Electra*
Peter Gerry with his nanny on deck of Elbridge T. Gerry's yacht *Electra.*
Commodore Elbridge T. Gerry on yacht *Electra* with his senior crew members
Jean Gerry, youngest sister Elbridge T. Gerry with Robert J. Livingston (Louisa Gerry's father) on *Electra*
Louisa M. Gerry on the deck of yacht *Electra* in sailing suit

One of the last photos of *Electra* before the yacht was dismantled in 1912

11: THE TWENTIETH CENTURY: PART I 1900 TO 1909

Page 455 Collage

Maurice Farkoa 1900 (entertained at Gerry mansion). Source: 1867 vintage postcard or cabinet photo by Alfred Ellis, Upper Baker Street, London. Used here under Creative Commons License. Sold on Ebay by bandj.images.http://www.ebay.com/itm/MAURICE-FARKOA

Theodore Roosevelt. Source: Library of Congress, Prints and Photographs Division, 1904 Pach Brothers photograph, Digital ID cph.3a53299

Teddy Roosevelt's childhood row house in New York City. Source: National Park Service, Washington, D.C. Birth place of Theodore Roosevelt, a designated National Historic Site, http://www.nps.gov

Oyster Bay home of President Teddy Roosevelt. Source: Courtesy of the National Park Service, summer home of President Theodore Roosevelt, designated National Historic Site http://www.nps.gov

Tuxedo Suits. Source: Tuxedo Historical Society, 1886 engraving of "Gents In Tuxedo Park" and the classic Tuxedo designed by Henry Poole & Co. in London. http://www.tpfyi.com/tuxedo-historical-society.html

Tuxedo Park Club House. Source: Vintage 1890's postcard (copyright expired) Tuxedo Historical Society, http://www.tpfyi.com/tuxedo-historical-soci
ety.html

Page 456 Collage

Ambassador Whitelaw Reid. Souces: Library of Congress, Print and Photographs Division, Reproduction No: LC-DIG-ewpbh- 03729 http://lcweb2.loc.gov/service/pnp/cwpbh/03700 /03729r.jpg

Reid Memorial Window. Source: Cathedral of St. John the Divine, the great east window by James Powell & Sons, London, entitled "Christ the Light of the World," 1913 gift of Mrs. Whitelaw Reid to honor her husband. Letters and reprint of photo courtesy of Archivist, Mr. Wayne Kempton, Saint John the Divine Cathedral, New York City

Dorchester House, Park Lane, London – *American Ambassador's Residence.* Source: The Sketch, June 26, 1895, p. 457, expired copyright, used here under Wikipedia Commons *GNU License*, from online: http://www.ebay.co.uk/itm/1895-Dorchester-House-Park-Lane

Mrs. Elizabeth Mills Reid (Louisa Gerry's cousin). Source: New York Public Library, Stephen A. Schwarzman Building, Miriam and Ira D. Wallach Division of Art, Prints, and Photographs, Digital ID 2004229 and Record ID 1937795

Dorchester House Grand Salon. Source: 1900 vintage photograph from J. Kleinwart Benson Wake, *The History of Two Families in Banking*, Oxford University Press, p.255, used here under Wikimedia Commons *GNU License*

Dorchester House Grand Staircase. Source: 1900 vintage photograph, reprinted from *Fred Cumberland: Building the Victorian Dream*, University of Toronto Press, p.176. Used here under Wikimedia Commons *GNU License*, http://en.wikiedia.org/File: Staircase_Dorchester_House.jpg

Honorable John Hubert Ward, (married Jane Reid at St. James Palace) Source: *A Genealogical Survey of the Peerage of Britain*, page 282, http://www.thepeerage.com/p282.htm

Queens Chapel in Saint James Palace (also known as the German Chapel). Source: Photographic reproduction by W.H. Pyne of the 1919 Aquatint print by Daniel Harvell, used here under the Wikimedia Commons *GNU License.* http://www.en.wikipedia.org/wiki/File: German_Chapel_St_James

Jane Reid, daughter of Whitelaw and Mary Reid. Source: Library of Congress, Prints and Photographs, vintage photograph between 1909 and 1914, Record Loc B.00898 http://www.loc.org/

Saint James Palace, London. Source: 1905 vintage postcard used here under Creative Commons License, retrieved from http://www.ebay.com /itm/London-England

Page 457 Collage

Edward Henry Harriman and wife, Mary Averell Harriman. Source: Vintage 1905 photograph, copyright expired and used here under Creative Commons License. Retrieved at http://www.ebay.com/itm/ART__PRINT-Poster-Portrait

Commodore E.T. Gerry and Peter Gerry and others arriving for E.H. Harriman funeral in 1909
Arden Homestead mansion (Harriman mountaintop estate in Orange County, New York). Source: Open Space Conservancy, New York, http://www.osiny.org Boys Club Library – founded by the Edward H. Harriman. Source: 1890 vintage photograph, copyright expired, used here under Creative Commons License. http://www.thirteen.org/edonline/
New York Boys Club Library, founded by E.H. Harriman, scrapbook

Page 458 Collage
Robert L. Gerry and Cornelia Harriman wedding party photo, 1908
Robert L. Gerry
Cornelia Harriman
Cornelia Harriman with sons Robert L. Gerry II (on lap) and Ebby Gerry II
Red Swann Tavern, Orange County, New York. Source: Vintage 1906 postcard from the Warrick, New York Historical Society (copyright expired). http://warwick newyorklocalhistory.blogspot.com/archiv

Page 459 Collage
Model of Electra in the New York Yacht Club Model Room. Source: Museum of the City of New York, Archives, Wurts Brothers Collection, 1917 Photograph ID X2010.7.1.2178 http://collections.mcny. org
New York Yacht Club Model Room. Source: Museum of the City of New York, Archives, Wurts Brothers Collection, 1917 Photograph ID X2010.7.1.2178 http://collections. mcny.org
New York Yacht Club Exterior. Source: Museum of the City of New York, Archives, Wurts Brothers Collection, 1917 Photograph ID X2010.7.1.2183 http://collections.mcny.org
New York Yacht Club Library. Source: Museum of the City of New York, Archives, Wurts Brothers Collection, 1917 Photograph ID X2010.7.1.2176 http://collections.mcny.org
Launch boat attached to yacht *Electra* with Peter Gerry and his nanny
Yacht Club Station in Newport Harbor, Rhode Island. Source: Vintage 1907 postcard by A.C. Bosselman & Co., Germany. Used under *GNU Free Documentation License.* http://www.cardcow.com/
Commodore Gerry and friends in Launch moving from land station to board *Electra*

Page 460 Collage
Arroyo Seco Trolley, CA. Source: University of Southern California, C.C. Pierce Photography Collection, 1885 photograph copyright expired, included in *A Brief History of Bridges in Los Angeles County,* by Nathan Masters. Used here under Creative Commons License
Ostrich Farm, CA. Source: Vintage 1890's postcard (copyright expired) http://www.cardcow.com/viewall
Peter and Mabel Gerry siblings on coach with Angelica with whip (also a male friend)
Ostrich Feather Shop, CA. Source: Vintage 1890's postcard (copyright expired) http://www.image-archeology.com
Coaching in Central Park in 1903

Page 461 Collage
Alma Mater Statue – Columbia University (Goelet Gift), **AP**
May Goelet, daughter of Ogden and Mary Goelet. Source: Library of Congress, Prints and Photographs Division, 1913 photograph by Lallie Charles. Glass negative number ggb2004004819
Henry Innes-Kerr, Duke of Roxburghe, married May Goelet in 1903. Source: Library of Congress Prints and Photographs Division, Bain Collection Digital ID ggb20055013742
Grand Duke Boris Vladimirovich of Russia, 1902 visit to Goelets. Source: 1900 photograph, Library of Congress, Prints and Photographs Division, Bain Collection, Digital ID ggbain.07517 Press photograph used under Creative Commons License
Floors Castle, Kelso, Scotland, May Goelet's home as Duchess of Roxburghe. Source: Found Photographs Shop, vintage postcard of Floors Castle used here under Creative Commons License, posted as royalty and copyright-free items. ttp://www.etsy.com/shop /foundphotogallery

Page 462 Collage
"Harry Thaw Murdered Stanford White,"*New York American,* page 1 headline June 26, 1906 Broadsheet, used under Creative Commons License, https://en.wikipedia.org/wiki/New _York_Journal-American

Roof Garden, Madison Square Garden Theatre. Source: Museum of the City of New York, Byron Company Collection, 1900 gelatin silver print, Item number 93.1.1.1084

Harry Thaw. Source: 1905 photograph *GNU License* https://commons.wikimedia.org/wiki/File%3AHarry_Kendall_Thaw_c.1905.jpg

Evelyn Nesbit (love triangle leads to murder). Source: Library of Congress, Prints and Photographs Division, 1906 photograph by the Sarony Studio, Digital ID cph.3c13758. Used here under the Wikimedia Commons *GNU License*

Stanford White, Architect. Source: 1892 photograph by George Cox uploaded 2006 by Richard A. Norton, used here under the Wikimedia Commons *GNU License*, http://en.wikipedia.org/wiki/File: Stanford_White

Headline for Stanford White Murder. Source: *New York American* June 26, 1906, page 1. Copyright expired.

Harry Thaw testifying. Source: 1906 photograph (copyright expired) online at: http://murderpedia.org/male.T/t/thaw-harry-photos.htm

Evelyn Nesbit testifying. Source: 1906 photograph (copyright expired) online at: http://keithyorkcity.wordpress.com

Harry Thaw taken to mental institution. Source: 1906 Photograph (copyright expired), online at: http://murderpedia.org/male.T/t/thaw-harry-photos. htm

Page 463 Collage

Mrs. Harrietta Goelet (wife of Robert)

Mount Vesuvius exploding, Naples Italy. Source: Private collection, uploaded to http://www.vesuvius.tomgidwitz.com Used here under Creative Commons License

Yacht *Nahma* (Robert & Harrietta Goelet)

Cable car and horse carriage on slope of Mount Vesuvius. Source: 1894 albumen photograph (copyright expired) http://www.ebay.com

Cable car lift up Mount Vesuvius. Source: 1894 albumen photograph (copyright expired) http://www.ebay.com

12: THE TWENTIETH CENTURY: PART II 1910 TO 1930

Page 522 Collage

Joseph Hofmann as an adult. Source: Library of Congress, Prints and Photographs Division, Bain Collection, Digital ID ggbain 23410 Used here under the Wikimedia Commons *GNU Free Documentation License*

Joseph Hofmann as a child prodigy. Source: 1888 photograph by Benjamin J. Falk, 949 Broadway, New York. (copyright expired) Found on http://www.ebay.com

Henry and Elsie Clews in France. Source: Courtesy of Chateau de la Napoule Archives LNAF. Online at: http://www.chateau-lanapoule.com

Chateau de la Napoule from the ocean. Source: Photograph by Sebastian Bertrand, uploaded by Sir Gawain from the French Wikipedia and the Ministry of Culture in France. Used here under the Wikimedia Commons *GNU Free Documentation License.* http://upload.wikimedia.org/wikipedia/commons/c/c1/Castle

Justice Benjamin Cardozo. Source: Library of Congress Prints and Photographs Division, Harris & Ewing Collection, Call Number: LC-132981-CD(P&PO), Digital ID hec 21519

Susan Fenimore Cooper. Source: Mid-1850's photograph by W.G. Smith, Cooperstown, New York, from *Pages and Pictures from the Writings of James Fenimore Cooper*, W.A. Townsend and Company, New York, 1861 in the James Fenimore Cooper Society Collection (copyright expired) http://external.oneonta.edu/cooper//susan.html

Cooperstown Orphanage, New York. Source: Vintage 1890's postcard (copyright expired) http://www.ebay.com

Yacht Electra – Oil painting. Source: "Annual Cruise of the New York Yacht Club, 1911" by Russ Kramer, (artist used *Electra* as the flag ship) www.russkramer.com (email permission to use by Russ Kramer).

Windsor Arcade, New York City (built by Elbridge T. Gerry) vintage 1906 postcard A 167 by the RotoGraph Company, New York City (copyright expired) http://www.ebay.com

Page 523 Collage

Gerry Mansion next to Metropolitan Club on Park Avenue NYC. Source: Museum of the City of New York, Byron Collection, 1898 Photograph ID 93.1.1.2911

Metropolitan Club Lounge. Source: Museum of the City of New York, Carbon Studio, Bound

portfolio of vintage prints, 1895 Photograph ID 90.44.4.4
Ice Cutting at Lake Delaware
Edwardian Period Greenhouse. Source: 1867 photograph of Durfee Plant House (copyright expired) from University of Massachusetts, Amherst MA, online at: http://www.library.umass.edu
Gilded Age Palm House. Source: 1915 photograph from donated Schmidt family album (no copyright) uploaded to "Images of Old Saint Louis," http://www.usgennet.org/usa/mo/county/stlouis/scenes.htm
Edwardian flower, fruit and vegetable show. Source: 1894 illustration by Arthur Hopkins (1848–1930) copyright expired. http://19thcenturybritpaint.blogspot.com

Page 524 Collage
Senator Peter G. Gerry and first wife, Mathilde *Townsend* Gerry
Mathilde Townsend. Source: Library of Congress Prints and Photographs Division, George Grantham Bain Collection, 19. 10 press Photograph Digital ID ggbain 04815
Sumner Wells. Source: Library of Congress, Prints and Photographs Division, Underwood & Underwood Collection, 1924 photograph, Digital ID cph.3b.12340. Used here under the Wikimedia Commons *GNU License.* http://en.wikipedia.org/wiki/File:Sumner_Welles_cph.3b12340.jpg
Mathilde Townsend mansion in Washington, D.C. Source: Library of Congress, Prints and Photographs Collection, Digital ID cph.3a43296
Townsend Mansion Ballroom. Source: Library of Congress, Prints and Photographs Collection, Frances B. Johnston photographer Collection, 1910 picture Lot Number11727
Page 525 Collage
Senator Peter Gerry's home in Washington, D.C. Source: Photograph Uses online attribution name Agnostic Preachers Kid. 2010 released without copyright and available for unrestricted use. *GNU License*
Senator Peter Gerry walking on Capitol Hill
Edith Vanderbilt Gerry on tractor
Senator Peter Gerry's yacht – the *Owera*
Biltmore House, North Carolina – Edith Vanderbilt Gerry's Estate. Source: Library of Congress, Prints and Photographs Division, Reproduction Number: LC-DIG-det-4a16855(digital file from original) and Digital ID: (digital file from original) det 4a16855 and online at: http://hdl.loc.gov/loc.pnp/det.4a16855

Page 526 Collage
Robert L. Gerry
Cornelia Harriman Gerry
Baby House in Plains, VA fox hunting lodge addition
Ebby II and Robert Jr. sitting on porch at Lake Delaware estate home
Robert Jr. twins Edward and Henry, and Ebby II dressed as little Indians at *Aknusti*, Lake Delaware
Ebby II and Robert II on white horses at *Aknusti* estate
Twins Edward and Henry on horseback together
Teenage twins Edward and Henry on car running board at *Aknusti* estate, Lake Delaware

Page 527 Collage
Four grandsons of Elbridge T. Gerry at *Aknusti*, Lake Delaware: Robert, Edward, Henry and Ebby
Gerry twins, Edward and Henry as babies
Gerry twins, Edward and Henry around five years old at the *Aknusti* estate, Lake Delaware
Gerry twins, Edward and Henry in early teens on rumble seat of car at *Aknusti*, Lake Delaware
Gerry twins, Edward and Henry in mid-teens driving country road at *Aknusti* with hunting rifle

Page 528 Collage
Lake Delaware Boys Camp, New York with tent shelters
Camp swimming hole
Camp Chapel where pipe organ is located to the front right hand side
Camp Mess Hall

Page 529 Collage
Gerry sisters sing – newspaper article from family scrapbook
Mabel Gerry with dog
Mabel Gerry wedding to Francis Drury in 1925
Angelica Gerry in teen portrait
Mabel Gerry Drury double-townhouse at 3-5 95th Street. Now on Historic Register

Ancrum House built by Angelica Gerry on property at Lake Delaware estate
Angelica on horseback
Angelica on car tour with her books

Page 530 Collage
Almy Gerry Gallatin
Frederic Gallatin in old age. Source: New York Historical Society, Manuscripts Division, Gallatin Family Papers, Box 76, 1925 photograph of Frederic Gallatin with grandson, Howland P. Rogers, at Breezy Lawn in Southampton, Long Island
Gallatin Home on Fifth Avenue, New York. Source: Library of Congress, Prints and Photographs Divison, Reproduction Number LC-USZ62-55956 (b&w film copy neg. of half stereo) 1903 Stereograph Card, Digital ID: (digital file from b&w film copy neg.) cph 3b03834 http://hdl.loc.gov/loc.pnp/cph.3b03834
Gallatins' Breezy Lawn summer home at East Hampton, L.I. Source: Columbia University, Avery Architectural and Fine Arts Library, Drawings and Archives, Selma Rattner Research Papers on James Renwick, 2005

Page 531 Collage
Saint Edward the Martyr Church 1887
Saint Edward the Martyr Church 2013, **AP**
Lillian Gerry memorial candlesticks, **AP**
Cathedral of Saint John Divine, New York City
Lillian Gerry memorial sacristy lamp, **AP**
Saint Edward the Martyr Church interior altar & sacristy lamp. 2013, **AP**
Lillian Gerry memorial chalice at Saint Edward the Martyr Church NYC, **AP**

Page 532 Collage
Gerry and Livingston family members buried in family Mausoleum, **AP**
Gerry Mausoleum at Saint James Church, Hyde Park, New York, **AP**
Family Vault at St. James Church set back within a little forest, Hyde Park, New York, **AP**
Saint James Church, Hyde Park, **AP**
Gen. Morgan Lewis and Gertrude Livingston Lewis, **AP**

APPENDIX

Except as noted below, all photographs are from the Gerry family collection.

APPENDIX A
GOELET, GERRY, LIVINGSTON, GALLATIN FAMILY TREE

APPENDIX A *pages 534 –535*
Two-page integrated FAMILY TREE of Gallatin, Gerry, Goelet and Livingston families, **AC**

APPENDIX B
NEW YORK CITY LOCATIONS

APPENDIX B *pages 536 –537*
Two-page New York City MAP annotated with family locations over time, **AC**

APPENDIX C
COMMODORE ELBRIDGE T. GERRY'S CHILDREN

APPENDIX C-1 Mabel Gerry Drury
Page 546 Collage
Mabel Gerry Drury in Worth gown in 1890's
Mabel Gerry about 13 years old
Mabel Gerry formal portrait in early twenties
Mabel Gerry silver hairdressing set
Mabel Gerry with best friend Gertrude Vanderbilt in their twenties

Page 547 Collage
Church of the Transfiguration. Source: Museum of the City of New York, 1950 postcard by Alfred Mainzer, Item Number F2011.33.2137N
Mabel Gerry portrait with dog in her thirties
Reverend Randolph Ray portrait at the church with permission of the parish archives, **AP**
Mollie Ray, first cousin of Mabel Gerry and dear friend, used with permission of the parish archives, **AP**
Shrine to Mabel Gerry by her husband Francis Drury, **AP**
Close-up of Madonna in Mabel's shrine at Church of the Transfiguration, **AP**
Memorial Altar to Mabel Gerry in the Cathedral of Saint John the Divine, **AP**
Memorial Altar to Mabel Gerry, dedication mass in 1933, newspaper clipping courtesy of Archivist, Wayne Kempton, Saint John the Divine Cathedral, New York City, **AP**

Page 554 Collage
Angelica Gerry as a teenager
Angelica Gerry formal portrait at Lake Delaware estate, **AP**
Portrait of Angelica Gerry on her horse at Lake Delaware estate, **AP**
Angelica Gerry's townhouse on 82nd Street in New York City where she died in 1960, **AP**
Church of the Resurrection in New York City. Angelica Gerry's parish, **AP**
Gerry siblings set off from Fifth Avenue Gerry mansion for a coaching run to Lake Delaware
Gerry siblings arrive at Lake Delaware destination of 5 day, round-trip coaching run

APPENDIX C-2 Angelica Livingston Gerry
Page 555 Collage
Angelica Gerry at dedication of Saint James Church at the Lake Delaware estate
Aerial view of Saint James Church at entrance to the Lake Delaware estate, New York
Ralph Adams Cram, architect. Source: Library of Congress, Prints and Photographs Division, 1911 photograph by Theodore C. Marceau, Digital ID cph.3b34921. Used here under the Wikimedia Commons *GNU License*
Saint James Church dedication formal portrait of Bishop, priests, altar boys and Gerry family members
Angelica Gerry's home at Lake Delaware estate, *Ancrum House*, built by Ralph Adams Cram, family archives

Page 556 Collage
Angelica Gerry's landscape plan for *Ancrum House* designed by Fletcher Steele, family archives
Fletcher Steele, landscape architect. Source: Library of American Landscape History Inc. Private Collection, with permission of Library of American Landscape History http://www.lalh.org. **See also** Secondary source: American Horticultural Society
Garden arbor at *Ancrum House* designed by Fletcher Steele
Garden stairs at *Ancrum House* designed by Fletcher Steele
Garden view of horse meadow at *Ancrum House* designed by Fletcher Steele
Ancrum House grand garden staircase into the gardens, Fletcher Steele's largest landscape project
View from grand garden stairs to overlook patio, designed by Fletcher Steele for *Ancrum House*

Page 557 Collage
Garden lounge with umbrella-hood in the *Ancrum House* gardens. (Lounge is now on porch of Lake Delaware estate historic home
Garden walk with long view to museum quality Italian sculpture, Penelope in the *Ancrum House* gardens.
Cover and pages from Angelica Gerry's *Protégé Book* documenting those she educated and mentored, **AP**
Angelica Gerry portrait that hangs in the Saint James Church parish hall, **AP**
Gerry dormitory at Delhi University in Delhi, New York, named after Angelica Gerry, **AP**

APPENDIX C-3 Senator Peter Goelet Gerry
Page 563 Collage
Senator Peter G. Gerry, family portrait as a young man
Edith Vanderbilt Gerry. Source: Biltmore Estate Archives, cover Photo for book, *Biltmore Village*, by Bill Alexander, Arcadia Publishing, Charleston, S.C. 2008
Peter Gerry as a teenager honing his equestrian skills
Edith Vanderbilt with dog and horse. Source: Used with permission from The Biltmore Company, Asheville, North Carolina
Edith Vanderbilt Gerry, President of State Fair N.C. Source: 1920's press photograph, reprinted in the *Citizen-Times* newspaper, North Carolina, article by Bruce C. Steele, "Downton Abbey: Lady Edith and Edith Vanderbilt." (copyright expired) http://www. citizen-times.com/article/20130122/LIVING
Peter Gerry arriving for funeral of E.H. Harriman in 1909
Cornelia Vanderbilt and husband, John Cecil. Source: 1928 photograph used with permission from The Biltmore Company, Asheville, N.C.
Edith Vanderbilt with daughter Cornelia. Source: 1902 photograph with expired copyright. Used here under the Wikimedia Commons *GNU License*

Page 564 Collage
Senator Peter Gerry with Senator Josiah Bailey. Source: Mr. Ray Hill contributed photograph

to knoxfocus.com. Permission granted by Mr. Ray Hill
Senator Peter Gerry sitting in Senate Chamber on Capitol Hill
Senator Peter Gerry walking on Capitol Hill in Washington, D.C.

Page 565 Collage
Weaving Shop of Biltmore Industries. Source: 1950's photograph of weaving machines of Biltmore homespun, courtesy of the Grovewood Gallery, Inc. Asheville, NC and the D.H. Ramsey Library, Special Collections, University of North Carolina at Asheville. http://www.grovewood.com
Edith Vanderbilt Gerry in Biltmore Industries Wool Suit. Source: 1924 photograph courtesy of Biltmore Industries. Used with permission from The Biltmore Company, Asheville, N.C.
Biltmore House, Asheville N.C. Source: Library of Congress, Prints and Photographs Division, Reproduction Number: LC-DIG-det-4a16855 (digital file from original) and Digital ID: det 4a16855 (digital file from original) http://hdl.loc.gov/loc.pnp/det.4a16855
Frith House, Biltmore Estate N.C. Source: Biltmore Estates Archives, photo published in *Biltmore Village,* by Bill Alexander, Arcadia Publishing, Charleston, S.C. 2008. Used with permission from The Biltmore Company, Asheville, N.C.
Gerry-Woods House, Providence R.I. Source: Photo taken by Kenneth C. Zirkel of the Gerry House on the Register of Historic Places, Reference number 71000003. Used here under the *Creative Commons License* http://en.wikipedia.org/wiki/File:Woods-Gerry_House

APPENDIX C-4 Robert Livingston Gerry
Page 565 Collage
Cornelia Harriman Gerry, wife of Robert L. Gerry and daughter of E.H. Harriman
Christmas at *Aknusti* with Robert L. Gerry and his four sons and grandchildren
Robert Livingston Gerry in his thirties
Aknusti Stables and stud farm on hill above Lake Delaware estate
Rare photo of *Aknusti*-bred foals at play in the stable courtyard
Robert and Cornelia Gerry's prize horse *Field Marshall* in 1926, son of famous *Man O' War*

Page 576 Collage
Air Show at Belmont Park, N.Y. Source: Library of Congress, Prints and Photographs Division, Ernest L. Jones Collection, 1910 Photograph, Call Number: LOT 6131 [item] [P&P] Digital ID cph.3a45232 http://www.loc.gov/Library
Belmont Park Stands (Edith Gerry and Cornelia Gerry). Source: Library of Congress, Prints and Photograph Division, 1913 photograph, *George Grantham Bain Collection,* Digital ID ggbain13115 http://www.loc.gov/Library
Belmont Park race track, vintage postcard. Source: F... -Date Created/Published: 1913 June 2. - Library of Congress, Prints and Photographs Division, Bain Collection - Reproduction number: LC-DIG-ggbain-13108 (digital file from original negative)
Robert and Cornelia Gerry's townhouse on East 79th Street, New York City, **AP**
Robert Gerry as older man, married to Cornelia for 60 years
Cornelia Gerry in her thirties

Page 577 Collage
Aknusti, home built in 1912 by Robert and Cornelia Gerry on a hill at the Lake Delaware estate
Aknusti in flames during the inferno that destroyed most of the mansion
Shell of *Aknusti* after the 1953 fire before it was rebuilt in a less grand reconstruction
Front entrance of *Aknusti* after rebuild without portico and without interior entry grand staircase

APPENDIX D
COMMODORE ELBRIDGE T. GERRY'S GRANDCHILDREN

Page 589 Collage
Military Portraits of Robert L. Gerry's sons and the grandsons of Commodore Elbridge T. Gerry:
Elbridge Thomas Gerry II (Ebby)
Robert Livingston Gerry II (known as Jr.)
Henry Averell Gerry (twin)
Edward Harriman Gerry (twin)
Page 590 Collage
Aknusti Polo Team, the four Gerry brothers, Edward, Robert, Ebby, and Henry
Ebby Gerry as captain of the championship Harvard College Polo Team
Ebby Gerry inducted into the Polo Hall of Fame for 9 goals

Page 591 Collage
Wives of the four Gerry brothers:
Majorie Kane married Elbridge T. Gerry, II
Martha Farish married Edward Henry Gerry
Marleigh Kramer married Henry Averell Gerry
Nancy Whitney married Robert L. Gerry
Portraits of the four brothers in military uniform:
Elbridge Thomas Gerry II (Ebby)
Robert Livingston Gerry II (known as Jr.)
Henry Averell Gerry (twin)
Edward Harriman Gerry (twin)

Page 592 Collage
Nancy Whitney Gerry with winning horse *Flat Top*, South Carolina newspaper *The State*, 1998 (scrapbook)
Martha Farish with champion horse *Forego*. Source: Courtesy of Adam Coglianese through Kevin Thompson at Blood-Horse Publications, Lexington, KY. NYRA.com http://www.nyra.com/
Flat Top wins 2002 Breeder's Cup Steeplechase, photo by Skip Dickstein, Mid-Atantic Thoroughbred, http.//midatlantictb.com/cms/index.php/19-pensioners/102-june-pensioner-on-parade-flat-top
Forego, Marlboro Cup 1976, Champions Gallery photos, used un GNU License. http://www.championsgallery.com/racephoto/fi/00000010.htm

Page 593 Collage
Marjoie Kane wedding to Elbridge T. Gerry, II.
Elbridge T. Gerry II (middle) with sons Peter Gerry II (left) and Elbridge T. Gerry III, (right)
Robert L. Gerry III, lives in Texas
Trotter in Harness Race. Source: Library of Congress, Prints and Photographs Division, Trotting mare "American Girl" driven by M. Roden, Reproduction Number: LC-USZ62-111320 and Digital ID (b&w film copy neg.) cph 3c11320 http://hdl.loc.gov/loc.pnp/cph.3c11320
Peter Gerry II and Ebby Gerry III
Page 594 Collage
Contemporary photo of Lake Delaware Estate, original home Gen. Morgan Lewis and Gertrude Livingston, **AP**
Contemporary photo of the extended Gerry family gathered at the Lake Delaware ancestral home

APPENDIX E
AMERICAN FAMILY LEGACIES
Page 603
Library of the U.S. Supreme Court. Source: Office of the Curator, Supreme Court of the United States, Item # 1995-139-3 Library Reading Room, photographed by Franz Jantzen, Court Photographer

APPENDIX F
EUROPEAN FAMILY ORIGINS
APPENDIX F-1 *page 606*
Emigration Map, **AC**

APPENDIX F-2 *page 607*
Albert Gallatin and His Descendants tree, **AC**

APPENDIX F-4 *page 615*
Goelet family tree, **AC**

APPENDIX F-6 *page 623*
Succession of Title to Lake Delaware, original in Lake Delaware estate home, **AP**

APPENDIX F-7 *page 624*
Livingston family tree, **AC**

NOTES

1: THE EARLY YEARS

1. "Edward King, Log of Ship Silas Richards, July 3, 1835," in Edward King Papers, Proceedings of the Massachusetts Historical Society, Katherine H. Griffin, 1993, n. p.
2. Christopher P. Magra, The New England Cod Fishing Industry and Maritime Dimensions of the American Revolution, (unpublished University of Pittsburgh Doctoral Dissertation, 2006), p. 27.
3. George Athan Billias, *Elbridge Gerry: Founding Father and Republican Statesman,* (New York: McGraw-Hill Book Co., 1976).
4. Samuel Roads, Jr., *The History and Traditions of Marblehead* (Boston: Houghton, Osgood and Company, 1880) p. 347.
5. *Supra* Magra, p. 161.
6. *Supra* Billias, p. 6.
7. *Id.,* Billias, vol. 2.
8. Della Gray Barthelmas, *Jefferson, The Signers of the Declaration of Independence: a Biographical and Genealogical Reference* (North Carolina: McFarland & Co., 1997) p. 80.
9. Austin, James Trecothick Gerry, *The Life of Elbridge Gerry: with Contemporary Letters,* (New York: McGraw Hill 1976 reprint of 1829 edition) p. 6.
10. http://www.colonialhall.com/Gerry/Gerry .php Elbridge.Gerry pp. 2-3.
11. Bill Oles, interview anecdote (Delhi, New York, October, 2010.
12. Samuel Roads, Jr., *The History and Traditions of Marblehead* (Boston: Houghton, Osgood Company, 1880) p. 119.
13. *Supra* Trecothick, vol. 2, p. 70.
14. "Our National Anniversary," *Harper's New Monthly Magazine* 11, number xiv, (1851) p. 157.
15. *Ibid.,* p. 70.
16. Harry Clinton Green and Mary Wolcott Green, *Wives of the Signers: The Women Behind the Declaration of Independence,* Aledo. (Texas: Wallbuilder Press 1997) p. 83. http://colonialhall.com/gerry/gerryAnn
17. Elbridge Gerry Papers1706-1895, (Boston: Massachusetts Historical Society,) Reel 3, p.362.
18. *Ibid.,* Gerry Papers Reel 3, p. 362.
19. *Supra* Billias, Foreword.
20. Benson John Lossing, "Sketches of the Signers of the Declaration of American Independence, 1800," in *The Spirit of Seventy-Six: The Story of the American Revolution As Told by Its Participants,* edited by Henry S. Commager and Richard B. Morris (Lebanon, Indiana: De Capo Press, 1995) p. 275.
21. *Supra* Billias, p 153-184.
22. "Gerry Library Put in Supreme Court," *New York Times,* September 9, 1935, p. 21.
23. *Supra* Gerry Papers, Reel 4, Elbridge Gerry to daughter Eleanor, Nov. 10, 1814.
24. http://colonialhall.com/gerry/gerry.php [p7].
25. "Biographical Memoir of Elbridge Gerry, Late Vice President of the United States" *The National Intelligencer,* Dec. 1, 1814, from http://bytesofhistory.org/Cemeteries/DC_Congressionl/Obits/G/G_PDF/Gerry_Elbridge.pdf.
26. Eugene F. Kramer, "Some New Light on the XYZ Affair: Elbridge Gerry's Reasons for Opposing War with France," *The New England Quarterly,* 29, No.4, 1956: 509.
27. *Supra* Gerry Papers, Reel 3.
28. *Ibid.*
29. *Supra* Billias, pp. 287-325.
30. Norman K. Risjord, "Election of 1812," in *History of American Presidential Elections, 1789-1968* edited by Arthur M. Schlesinger, Jr. and Fred L. Isreal, vol. 1, (New York: McGraw Hill, 1971) p. 252.
31. Norman K. Risjord, "Election of 1812," in *History of American Presidential Elections, 1789-1968,* edited. by Arthur M. Schlesinger, Jr., vol. 1, New York, 1789-1896, (New York: Simon & Schuster,1994) pp. 67-72.
32. "The Diary of Elbridge Gerry, Jr.," Foreword, Annette Townsend, Preface, Claude G.

Bowers, (Washington: Brentano's Publisher, 1927), p. vii.

33. *Supra* Gerry Papers, Reel 5.
34. *Supra* Gerry Papers, Reel 4.
35. Robert Allen Rutland, *The Presidency of James Madison*, (Lawrence: University Press of Kansas, 1990) p. 151.
36. http//:colonialhall.com/gerry Ann Thompson Gerry, pp. 1-2.
37. *Supra* Gerry Papers, Letter from E.T. Gerry to Eleanor Gerry, Nov. 10, 1814, Reel 4.
38. *Id.*, Letter from James Monroe to Elbridge Gerry, Jr., Dec. 21, 1814, Letter to Elbridge Gerry, Dec. 21, 1814, Cadet appointments, and a Certificate of Appointment to Inspector of Revenue 1817 Elbridge Gerry, Jr., Reel 4.
39. *Id.*, Letter to Mrs. Ann Gerry, October 7, 1814, Massachusetts Historical Society, Reel 4.
40. *Id.*, Letter from Elbridge Gerry, Jr. to his sister Eleanor, dated Nov. 10, 1814, Reel 4.
41. Letter found in Blackstone's Commentaries, hand-written by Elbridge Gerry, Jr., gifting the miniature 4 volume title to Elbridge T. Gerry, Dec. 25th, 1857 as a birthday gift. The note states that the book belonged to E.T. Gerry's grandfather, Supreme Court Library, Rare Book Room, Washington, D.C.
42. News, *Boston Courier*, Issue 426, column D, January 25, 1830, p. 1.
43. News, *Boston Courier*, Thursday, April 22, 1830, Issue 451, col. C, p. 1.
44. *Supra* Gerry Papers, Letter from Elbridge Gerry, Jr. to his sister Emily, dated Dec. 1839, Reel 4.
45. Lot 26337 *Commodore James T. Gerry Collection of Interesting Letters*, 2006 Dallas Books, Autographs and Manuscripts Auction, New York City, #626 (16 letters); http://historical.ha.co/common/view.
46. *Supra* Gerry Papers, Letter from James T. Gerry to his family, Sept. 1830, Reel 5.
47. Collections of the New Haven Colony Historical Society, New Haven, Connecticut, File 201.
48. "Transactions of Learned Societies," *American Monthly Magazine and Critical Review*1 (1817) p. 449.
49. News, *New York Morning Herald*, Issue 155 Friday, July 2 (1830) Column F, n. p.
50. *Supra* Gerry Papers, Reel 5.
51. Supra *New York Morning Herald* n. p.
52. The Gerry Family Papers, Letter from James T. Gerry to his family, Sept. 1830, Massachusetts Historical Society, Reel 5.
53. News, *Boston Courier*, Issue 725, December 10, (1832) Column B, n. p.
54. *Supra* Gerry Papers, Reel 3.
55. *Supra* Gerry Papers, Letter from Thomas R. Gerry to his sister Elizabeth, May 22, 1834, Reel 5.
56. *Supra* Gerry Papers, Letter from Jacob Thompson to his sister Ann Thompson Gerry, October 18, 1821, Reel 4.
57. *Supra* Gerry Papers, Letter from Thomas R. Gerry to his sister Elizabeth, May 31, 1834, Reel 5.
58. "The Death of a Venerable Lady Gives the Veteran a Theme," *Philadelphia Inquirer*, 133, issue 77 (September 1895) p. 6.
59. "The Election," *New York Spectator*, column E, (April 15, 1839) p. 1.
60. "Resort on Sound, Famous and Popular," Westchester County Historical Society Library, vertical file: New Rochelle – Hotels, Inns, restaurants, Advertisement, July 1842.
61. "An Apple of Gold in a Picture of Silver," *New Haven Herald*, 11 Issue 146 (1845), p. 2.

2: EDUCATION AND APPRENTICESHIP

1. "Broadway Farm Going," *Boston Daily Advisor*, Issue 76, Column F, (1896) p. 1.
2. Exhibit: "Stettheimer Dollhouse the Goelet Brownstone House" at the Museum of the City of New York, 2009.
3. "Peter Goelet," *America's Successful Men of Affairs: and Encyclopedia of Contemporaneous Biography*, edited by Henry Hall, volume I, 1891 (New York: Tribune Association, 1898) p. 259.
4. Geoffry T. Hellman, "You've Simply Got to Go Out and Raise the Scratch," *The New Yorker*, Profiles: October 18(1976) p. 46.
5. *Supra* America's Successful Men p. 259.
6. *Supra* "Broadway Farm Going," p. 1.
7. Sam Roberts, Grand Central: How a Train Station Transformed America, Grand Central Publishing, 2013, p. 50.
8. Columbia Grammar and Prep School, 5. West 93rd Street, New York, NY: http://www.gps.org/
9. Elbridge T Gerry (1837-1927) Columbia College Notebooks, Columbia College Memorabilia (printed items) Box 4.

10. Elbridge T Gerry 1837-1927, Columbia College Notebooks, Columbia College Memorabilia (printed items) Box 4.
11. Allen Johnson and Dumas Malone, eds., *Dictionary of American Biography*, volume VII, (New York: Charles Scribner's Sons, 1931) p. 227.
12. Wayne Craven, *Gilded Mansions: Grand Architecture and High Society*, (Verona, Italy: Mondadori Printing, 2009) p. 159.
13. William J. Petersen, *The Rock Island Railroad Excursion of 1854*, (Iowa City: State Historical Society of Iowa, 1934) p. 405.
14. Elbridge T Gerry (1837-1927) Columbia College Notebooks, Columbia College Memorabilia (printed items) Boxes 1-2, 4-5.
15. Elbridge T Gerry (1837-1927) Columbia College Notebooks, Columbia College Memorabilia (printed items) Box 1.
16. Julius Goebel, Jr., ed., *A History of the School of Law: Columbia University*, (New York: Foundation for Research in Legal History, 1955) p. 7.
17. John Fiske and James Grant Wilson, eds., "William Curtis Noyes," *Appleton's Cyclopedia of American Biography* (New York: D. Appleton Company, 1889). http://en.wikipedia.org, 4 KB.
18. John M. Murrin, et al., eds., *Liberty Equality Power: A History of the American People*, 2nd ed., vol. 1 (Fort Worth: Harcourt Brace, 1999), p. 488.
19. "Fifty Years in One Bank," *New York Times*, May 14, 1899, p. 12.
20. John A. Haddock, *The Growth of a Century: as Illustrated in the History of Jefferson County*, (Philadelphia: Sherman & Co., 1894).
21. "Wall Street-Commercial," *The Herald*, Friday, January 6, 1837, Issue 255, column A.
22. "Peter G. Gerry, Ex-Senator, Dies Hours Before His Brother Robert," special to *New York Times*, Nov. 1, 1957, p. 26.
23. Mark Simonson, "Politics to Philanthropy," *Daily Star*, Saturday, January 18, 2003.
24. Manuscript letter and 4 volume set, *Blackstone's Commentaries*, 6th edition, (Dublin: Printed for the Company of Booksellers, 1765), held in Rare Book Room, United States Supreme Court Library, Washington, D.C., 1 leaf.
25. "West Washington Market," *New York Times*, vol. May 1, 1860, p. 1.
26. "When a Prince of Wales Came to America," *The New York Times*, vol. section: NYT Magazine, June 15, 1919, p. 85.
27. *Ibid.*
28. Class Secretary, ed., *Biographical Memoranda Respecting All Who Were Members of the Class of 1832*, (New Haven: Yale College Press, 1886).
29. White, James T., ed. "Ferdinand Rudolph Hassler." *Appleton's Cyclopedia of American Biography*, http://www.famousamericans.net/.
30. *The Rebirth of the Survey*, NOAA Central Library, http://www.lib.noaa.gov/noaainfo/heritage/.
31. Fritz Redlich, "Banking 1840-1910," *Investment Banking, History of American Business Leaders: a Series of Studies*, volume 2, Part 2, (Buffalo: Heinonline, 2013) p. 353.
32. "Commencement at Burlington College," *New York Daily Times*, October 1, 1852, n. p.
33. Jeanne Kolea and Joanne Pisciotta, *Highland Park Borough Homes*, (Chicago: Arcadia Publications, 2005) p. 51.
34. "Children's Aid Society is in Touch with Poverty," *The New York Times*, Nov. 29, 1899.
35. "Children's Aid Society – Seventh Annual Meeting," *New York Times*, March 1, 1860, p. 8.
36. Stephen O'Connor, *The Story of Charles Loring Brace and the Children He Saved and Failed*, (Chicago: University of Chicago Press, 2002) prologue, xiv-xv.
37. *Supra* Children's Aid Society, p. 8.
38. http://en.wikipedia.org/wiki/Bloomingdale _Insane_Asylumbloomingdale.
39. "The New York Hospital, Removal of Bloomingdale Asylum," *New York Times*, April 25, 1895, n. p.
40. "The Home for Incurables," *New York Times*, June 13, 1882, p. 8.

3: PASSING THE TORCH

1. "Elbridge T. Gerry Papers," Butler Library, Rare Book Room, Columbia University, New York, Box 3.
2. Letter to the Board of Enrollment, Eighth District of New York, from President Abraham Lincoln, August 10, 1863, National Archives and Records Administration, New York, Southern Division, 8th District Letters, Box 13.
3. *Minute Book*, Provost Marshal, 8th Congressional District, New York, 1864, page 162, National Archives and Records Administration, New York, Southern Division, Box 13.

4. "Churchill's World," http://historymoment.blogspot.com/2010_05_01_archive.html.
5. Edward Robb Ellis, *The Epic of New York City*, (New York: Kodansha America, Inc., 1966), p. 306.
6. Obituary, *The New York Times*, May 18, 1864, p. 5.
7. "Special Services Commemorating the Transfer of the Old Cornerstone and the Noyes Tablet," *The New York Times*, December 17, 1894.
8. "Opening of Sealed Doors," *Law Library Journal*, volume XII, number 3, (Chicago: American Association of Law Libraries, 1920) p.69.
9. "Faithless Wives and Lazy Husbands: Gender Norms in Nineteenth Century Divorce Laws," *University of Illinois Law Review*, 2002, p.651.
10. "Visit to West Point," *Mr. Lincoln and New York*: www.mrlincolnandnewyork.org, 2011.
11. "A Fancy Dress Ball at West Point," *The New York Times*, September 9, 1865, Correspondence.
12. "Albert Gallatin Biographical Sketch," James Madison Research Library and Information Center: http://www.madisonbrigade.com/index.htm.
13. *The United States Army and Navy Journal & Gazette of the Regular and Volunteer Forces*, Volume III, 1865-1866, p. 385.
14. William v Newell 36 N.Y. 24 1867.
15. "The Charity Ball," *New York Times*, March 1, 1867, p. 7.
16. "Under Five Constitutions," *The New York Times*, May 7, 1894, p. 1.
17. *Ibid.*
18. Revising Constitution in 1867, *The New York Times*, July 11, 1915, p. SM11.
19. *Supra* Gerry Papers, Reel 5.
20. *Id.*, Gerry Papers, Reel 5.
21. "Expensive Matrimony," *Harper's Bazaar*, Novem-ber 2, 1867, p. 2.
22. "Museum's 1846 Doll House Recalls a More Bucolic Yuletide in New York," *The New York Times*, Dec. 17, 1956, p. 26.
23. *Journal of the American Geographical Society*, volume XII (New York: American Geographical Society, 1880), pp. i, xxvi.
24. Reade v Sweetzer, 6 Abb.Pr.N.S. 9.
25. Crista Cloutier, *The Perfect Medium*, New Haven: Yale University Press, 2005) p. 20.
26. *Ibid.*
27. Michael Leja, *Looking Askance: Skepticism and American Art from Eakins to Duchamp*, Michael Leja, (Berkeley: University of California Press, 2004), p. 29.
28. *Id.*, p. 31.
29. *Supra The Perfect Medium*, 23
30. George Martin, *Causes and Conflicts: the Centennial History of the Association of the Bar of the City of New York*, (New York: Fordham University Press, 1997), p. 45.

4: FATHER, LAWYER, LEADER

1. "Classified Ad 2," *New York Times*, February 2, 1870, p. 6.
2. "Real Estate Transactions," *New York Times*, February 3, 1870, p. 6.
3. "McFarland's Trial to Take Place in March," *The New York Times*, February 8, 1870, p. 2.
4. "From New York – Criminal," *Cincinnati Daily Gazette*, March 5, 1870, p. 3.
5. Edward Van Emery, "The Most Beautiful Illicit Love Tragedy," in *The Sins of New York as Exposed by the Police Gazette*, Part I, Chapter 8, (New York: Frederick A. Stokes Company, 1930), various pages.
6. "Trial of Daniel McFarland – Counsel Reading Letters," *Frank Leslie's Illustrated Newspaper*, Issue 761, 1870, column A, p. 101.
7. *Supra* Edward *The New York Times*, May 19, 1870, p. 3.
9. "Desecration of Mr. Goelet's Retirement – the Nineteenth Street and Broadway House to Come Down," *The New York Times*, June 19, 1870, p. 8.
10. "Another Street Job, the Madison Avenue Extension Swindle," *New York Times*, March 4, 1871, p. 2.
11. "Local Debt and Local Improvements," *New York Times*, April 5, 1874, p. 6.
12. Peter Goelet v Paul N. Spofford, 55 N.Y. Court of Appeals 647, Dec. 9, 1873.
13. W.F. Vanden Houten, *Papers Read Before the Medico-Legal Society of New York*, 2d series, revised edition, (New York: New York Medico-Legal Society, 1882), pp. 1-13.
14. "The Fall of Hecker's Bakery," *The New York Times*, November26, 1870, p. 2.
15. Smith v Miller 43 NY 171, 1870.
16. *Henry Bergh*, M. Lane and S. Heritage Zawistowski, ASPCA Science Advisors, (Westport CT: Praeger Publishers, 2007).http://learingtogive.org/papers/

paper357.
17. "Kit Burn's Gang Held for Trial," *The New York Times*, November 23, 1870, p. 1.
18. ""Fowl Play – Sports Contrary to Law," *The New York Times*, November 25, 1870, p. 3.
19. "The Bar Association," *The New York Times*, February 8, 1871, p. 8.
20. "Commodore Vanderbilt's Reply to Henry Bergh," *The New York Times*, Sept. 10, 1871, p. 8.
21. "Henry Bergh and the Car Horses – Letter to Commodore Vanderbilt," *The New York Times*, Dec. 6, 1871, p. 4.
22. "Edward S. Stokes – Two of his Counsel Positively Withdraw from his Defense," *The New York Times*, May 2, 1872, p. 8.
23. Southwick v Southwick, 49 N.Y. 510, 1872.
24. Daniel C. Draper, *Legal Phrases of the Trial of John Brown*, (Wheeling: West Virginia University, 1940), p. 87.
25. Susanna L. Blumenthal, The Deviance of the Will: Policing the Bounds of Testamentary Freedom in Nineteenth-Century America, 119 *Harvard Law Review* 959.
26. Broadway & East Side Stage Co. v. ASPCA, 15 Abbott 51, 1873.
27. "Action of the Courts," *The New York Times*, May 9, 1873, p. 5.
28. "A Splendid Testimonial to Elbridge T. Gerry," Esq., *The New York Times*, June 17, 1873, p. 8.

5: GERRY'S SOCIETY

1. Wolfe v Burke, 56 N.Y. 115.
2. *Ibid.*
3. *NYSPCC 125th Anniversary 1875-2000*, (New York: RPM Printing Corp., 2000).
4. *Ibid.*
5. "Mr. Bergh Enlarging his Sphere of Usefulness," *The New York Times*, April 10, 1874, p. 8.
6. "Our City Charities Versus the Case of Mary Ellen," *The New York Times*, April 16, 1874, p. 4.
7. Wenzler v People, 58 N.Y.516, 1874.
8. *Ibid.*
9. "The Courts," *The New York Times*, November 5, 1874, p. 2.
10. "Protection for Children: Organization of the Society for the Prevention of Cruelty to Children," *The New York Times*, December 17, 1874, p. 3.
11. Prevention of Cruelty to Children: Meeting of the Society Yesterday, New York Times, December 29, 1874, p. 2.
12. "The Bergh Contempt Case," *The New York Times*, February 27, 1875, p. 2.
13. *Ibid.*
14. *Laws of the State of New York, 99th Session of the Legislature*, chapter 122, (New York: Municipal Archives of the New York, City Department of Records and Information Services, 1876) pp. 95-96.
15. Shauna Vey, "Good Intentions and Fearsome Prejudice: New York's 1876 Act to Prevent and Punish Wrongs to Children," *Theatre Survey*, volume 42, number 1, 2001, p. 68.
16. Peter Stevens and Marian Eide, "The First Chapter of Children's Rights, (*American Heritage Magazine* 1990) (http://www.american heritage.com/articles/magazine, 1990.
17. The Watering-Place and Mountain Hotels About New York Where Health, Comfort, and Pleasure Can be Secured, *The New York Times*, June 18, 1876, p. 10.
18. Robert B. MacKay, Anthony Baker, and Carol A. Traynor, eds., *Long Island Country Houses and Their Architects, 1860-1940*, for the Society for the Preservation of Long Island Antiquities, (Long Island: Palace Press, Ltd. 1997), pp. 172-174.
19. "The Episcopal Church: New York Diocesan Convention," *The New York Times*, September 29, 1876, p. 2.
20. Kip v NY & Harlem Railroad Co., 74 N.Y. 370, 1878.
21. New York State Bar – A Sketch of the Association from its Organization, The Albany Law Journal, volume 49 no.3, 1894, p. 50.
22. "Legislating for the Dogs," *The New York Times*, March 14, 1877, pg. 2.
23. "Method of Killing Hogs, the Law Reports," *The New York Times*, March 16, 1877, p. 3.
24. "Mother Against Daughter, an Incident in the Settlement of the Carman Estate," *The New York Times*, June 22, 1877, p. 3.
25. "Academy of the Holy Cross: Seventeenth Annual Exhibition of the Pupils," *The New York Times*, June 30, 1877, p. 6.
26. *Supra* New York State Bar, p. 50.
27. "Swill Milk and Vienna Bread," *The New York Herald*, volume XLIII, issue 143, May 23, 1878, p. 8.
28. "The Polo Cubs Triumph," *The New York Times*, June 20, 1878, p. 8.
29. *Ibid.*

30. "Midsummer at West Point," *The New York Times,* July 7, 1878, p. 7.
31. Robert C. Kennedy, *Keeping the Money Where It Will Do the Most Good,* http://www.harpers.com/09cartoon.
32. "Taking the Last Chance," *The New York Times,* August 29, 1878, p. 3.
33. Riggs v Pursell, 74 N.Y. 370, 1878.
34. "The Vanderbilt Will Case," *The New York Times,* October 23, 1878, p. 3.
35. "Protecting the Animals," *The New York Times,* November 15, p. 5.
36. Davis v ASPCA, 75 N.Y.362, 1878.
37. "Suing a City for Debt," *The New York Times,* September 30, 1879, p. 2.
38. *Ibid.*
39. *Ibid.*
40. *Ibid.*
41. "An Eccentric Man Gone," *The New York Times,* November 1, 1879, p. 1.
42. "Peter Goelet's Funeral," *The New York Times,* November 5, 1879, p. 8.
43. "Peter Goelet's Will," *The New York Times,* December 6, 1879, p. 8.
44. "New York has Commenced to Whine," *Milwaukee Daily Sentinel,* December 11, 1879, column C, p. 4.
45. John D. Lawson, ed., "The Trial of Antonio Ancarola for Kidnapping," *American State Trials,* volume III, (Saint Louis: F.H. Thomas Law Book Co., 1915), pp. 868-876.

6: GILDED GOTHAM: THE 1880'S PART I

1. Gilded Age in a Nutshell, http://www.shmoop .com/gilded-age/.
2. William Irving, James Kirke Paulding, and Washington Irving, *Salmagundi; or the Whimwhams and Opinions of Launcelot Langstaff, Esq., and Others,* (Philadelphia: J.B. Lippincott & Co., 1860).
3. *Etymology Dictionary* 2010, http://www.etymonline.com/
4. *Supra* Salmagundi, Preface.
5. "Charity Disgraced: a Shocking Revelation in the Shepherd's Fold," *New York Herald,* issue 18, January 18, 1880, p 8.
6. "Chinese Cruelty, the Family of Yakoob Bey," *The Daily Inter Ocean,* issue 251 Thursday, January 22, 1880, col. C.
7. Bruce v Platt, 80 N.Y. 379, 1880.
8. "Easter Week Marriage Bells," *The New York Times,* March 31, 1880, p. 2.
9. "Commitments of Children, Letter to the Editor," *The New York Times,* April 5, 1880.
10. A New Opera House in New York, *Daily Evening Bulletin San Francisco,* issue 18, April 28, 1880, p.4, col. A.
11. "The Late Chief Justice," *The New York Times,* May 18, 1880, p. 8.
12. "Testimonial to Mr. Bergh," *Frank Leslie's Illustrated Newspaper,* issue 1, Saturday, June 19, 1880, p. 269, 290, col. A
13. http://en.wikipdia.org/wiki/John_S._Mosby, August 2011.
14. "Florence Mosby's Flight," *Saint Louis Globe-Democrat,* June 22, 1880, p. 3.
15. "Newport, One of America's Favorite Summer Haunts," *Saint Louis Globe-Democrat,* August 10, 1879, p. 4.
16. *Cliff Walk History,* brochure (Newport RI: Friends of the Waterfront, 2009).
17. "Newport, Rhode Island," *Harper's Weekly,* August 30, 1873, supplement.
18. "Midsummer Festivities," *North American,* Philadelphia, July 2, 1880, col. B, n. p.
19. "Personalities," *Daily Graphic: an Illustrated Evening Newspaper,* October 28, 1880, p. 898, column C.
20. *Proceedings of the First Anniversary of the American Equal Rights Association,* signed copy, Rare Books Collection, Library, Supreme Court of the United States, Washington, D.C.
21. "A Subject for Investigation," *The New York Times,* November 24, 1880, Editorial.
22. "Trouble for Col. Mapleson: Directed to Withdraw His Juvenile Dancers," *The New York Times,* Decem-ber 7, 1880, p. 12.
23. "The Children of the Opera," *The New York Times,* December 9, 1880, p. 5.
24. "The Babes of the Ballet," *Daily Inter-Ocean,* Chicago, December 11, 1880, p. 9, col. D.
25. "Colonel Higginson's Allusion at Cambridge to the Estate of Lt-Gov. Oliver," *Boston Daily Advertiser,* Issue 157, December 30, 1880, col. C, n. p.
26. "The Bachelors: An Event That Eclipsed all Previous Society Efforts," *North American,* Philadelphia, February 26, 1881, col. B, n. p.
27. *Frank Leslie's Illustrated Newspaper,* Issue 1,336, May 7, 1881, p. 174, col. A.
28. "Notes from Pleasure Seekers and Those Resorts," *North American Review,* Philadelphia, July 11, 1881, col. A, n. p.

29. Geoffrey F. Hammond, *Showdown at Newport: The Race for the America's Cup*, (New York: Walden Publications, 1974) p. 11.
30. *Id.*, Showdown at Newport, p. 20.
31. *Id.*, Showdown at Newport, p. 38.
32. "Building in New York," *Daily Inter Ocean*, Chicago, Issue 55, May 28, 1881, col D, p. 4.
33. "News," *Bangor Daily Whig & Courier*, Maine, Issue 172, July 22, 1881, col. A., n. p.
34. *Richard Montgomery*, Wikipedia, http://en.wikipedia.org/wiki/Richard_Montgomery
35. Fleischmann v Bennett, 87 N.Y. 231, 1881.
36. "Little Corrine Case," *Boston Daily Advertiser*, Issue 131, December 2, 1881, col. B.
37. "Slaughter of Infants," *Daily Inter Ocean*, Chicago, January 18, 1882, p. 3, col. E.
38. "Decoration of Grand Homes in New York," *Daily Evening Bulletin*, San Francisco, Issue 141, March 28, 1882, p. 4.
39. "The Prevention of Cruelty to Children," *Frank Leslie's Illustrated Newspaper*, Issue 1,380, March 4, 1882, p. 23.
40. Marx v McGlynn, 88 N.Y. 357, 188.
41. "Home for the Incurables," *The New York Times*, June 13, 1882, p. 8.
42. "New York the Scene of a Number of Large Conflagrations," *Daily Republican-Sentinel*, Milwaukee, July 15, 1882, p. 4.
43. "Cruelty to Children, New York Movement," *The Daily Inter Ocean*, Chicago, July 29, 1882, p. 6.
44. "Children in Theaters," *Cleveland Herald*, December 8, 1882, col. A, n. p.
45. "The Patriarch's Ball," *St. Louis Globe-Democrat*, December 26, 1882, p. 2, col. D.
46. "Two Splendid Dresses," *Saint Louis Globe-Democrat*, December 30, 1882, p. 3.
47. "Dr. Newton's Heresies," *Saint Louis Globe-Democrat*, Issue 255, January 31, 1883, p. 4.
48. "Unsafe School Buildings, Mr. Gerry Calls Inspector Esterbrook," *The New York Times*, March 3, 1883, n. p.
49. "Children in Theaters," *Washington Post*, March 11, 1883, p. 3.
50. "Objections to Juvenile Performers," *Milwaukee Sentinel*, March 22, 1883, col. C.
51. "The Drama Review," *Milwaukee Sentinel*, May 20, 1883, p. 6.
52. "Cruelty to Children," *North American Review*, volume CXXXVII, 1883, pp. 68-75.

7: GILDED GOTHAM: THE 1880'S PART II

1. "Claiming the Goelet Estate," *The New York Times*, July 30, 1883, p. 1.
2. "An Alleged Heir of Peter Goelet," *The New York Daily Tribune*, July 31, 1883, p. 8.
3. "An Alleged Heir of Peter Goelet," *The New York Daily Tribune*, July 31, 1883, p. 8.
4. "A Palatial Residence in Which One of New York's Millionaires Will Pass the Summer," *Bangor Daily Whig & Courier*, July 26, 1883, col. D, n. p.
5. "Yachting," *Outing: An Illustrated Monthly Magazine of Sport, Travel and Recreation*, volume 32, April 1898, p. 81.
6. "The Sail for the Goelet Cup," *Boston Daily Advertiser*, August 6, 1883, col. A, n. p.
7. "Lord Coleridge's Arrival," *Milwaukee Sentinel*, August 25, 1883, col. B, p. 3.
8. *Ibid.*
9. *Ibid.*
10. "Coleridge," *Daily Arkansas Gazette*, August 30, 1883, col. A.
11. "Departure of Lord Coleridge," *Boston Daily Advertiser*, Issue 103, October 29, 1883, col. F.
12. "New York's Operatic Speculation," *Daily Evening Bulletin*, San Francisco, October 24, 1883, p. 3.
13. Christopher Gray, "Streetscapes, the Goelet Building," *The New York Times*, March 19, 2000, http://www.nytimes.com.
14. Livingston v Sage, 95 N.Y. 289, 1884.
15. "Elbridge T. Gerry is in Albany," *Kingston Daily Freeman*, NY, January 23, 1884, p. 1.
16. "Railway Affairs," *Milwaukee Sentinel* March 13, 1884, p. 5.
17. "An Episcopal Cathedral," *The New York Times*, March 16, 1884, p. 9.
18. "Gossip of New York Society," *Saint Louis Globe-Democrat*, March 23, 1884, p. 20.
19. *The History of Harlan and Hollingsworth*, http://en.wiki pedia.org/wiki/Harlan_and_Hollingsworth
20. "Mr. Gerry's Yacht Launched," *The New York Times*, April 15, 1884, p. 1.
21. J.H. Mandigo, "American Sporting on the Seas," *Chautauquan Monthly Magazine*, vol. XIII (new series vol. IV) April 1891-Sept 1891, pp. 611-614.
22. "Alumniana, Alpha Zeta: Columbia College," *The Purple and the Gold*, volume IV, No. 1, November, 1886, n. p.

23. "Mr. Gerry Asks for Contributions," *The New York Times*, May 5, 1884, p. 2.
24. "Professional Philanthropists," *St. Louis Globe-Democrat*, Issue 25, June 15, 1884, p. 20.
25. "Newport Notions," *Saint Louis Globe-Dispatch*, August 31, 1884, issue 101, p. 11, col. D.
26. "About Rich Women," *Daily Evening Bulletin*, San Francisco, issue 127, September 3, 1885, p. 2, col. B.
27. "The New York Chi Psi," *The New York Times*, February 18, 1885, p. 2.
28. "The Protection of Children," *Bay State Monthly: a Massachusetts Magazine*, vol. II, No. 2, November 1884, pp. 89-96.
29. Matter of Union Ferry Co. of Brooklyn, 98 N.Y. 139, 1884.
30. "New York's Bonded Debt Restricted," *Daily Evening Bulletin*, San Francisco, issue 58, December 14, 1885, col. 1.
31. "Society at Bar Harbor," *The New York Times*, July 19, 1885, p. 3.
32. "Don't Want Cars on Fifth Avenue," *North American*, Philadelphia, PA, November 21, 1885, col. B, n. p.
33. "A Stir in Society," *Milwaukee Sentinel*, November 29, 1885, Issue 48, p. 10.
34. "A Sadly Humorous Story," *Washington Post*, November 29, 1885, p. 5.
35. People ex rel. Van Heck v New York Catholic Protectory, 101 N.Y. 195, 1886.
36. "Society Topics of the Week," *The New York Times*, January 3, 1886, n. p.
37. *Ibid.*
38." Stepping into Society," *The New York Times*, January 19, 1886, p. 4.
39. "The Carnival of Cops," *The New York Times*, January 26, 1886, p. 2.
40. *Ibid.*
41. *Ibid.*
42. "The Patriarchs Dancing," *The New York Times*, January 27, 1886, p. 4.
43. "New York Yacht Club Election," *The New York Times*, February 2, 1886, p. 2.
44. "Yachtsmen and Yachting," *The New York Times*, February 8, 1886, p. 8.
45. "Yachts," *Outing Magazine*, April – September 1886, p. 105.
46. "The Eulogy of Mr. Ramscar," *The New York Times*, April 7, 1886, p. 8.
47. Captain R. F. Coffin, "Memories of Yacht Cruises," *Outing Magazine*, vol. IV, 1888, p. 517.
48. Gertrude Fitch Horton, *The Delaware & Northern and the Towns It Served*, Fleischmans, NY: Purple Mountain Press, 1989) Ch. 3.
49. *Condition Report, Hilborne Roosevelt, New York City, Opus 34 1876/1886*, by S. L. Huntington & Co., Stonington, CT 2008, Gerry family business files.
50. "Conversations with Charles Dodsley Walker, Part I," *The Diapason*, March 2010.http://nealf campbell.wordpress.com
51. "Society Topics of the Week," *The New York Times*, September 12, 1886 p. 3.
52. *Capital Punishment*, http://www.capitalpunish mentuk.org/.
53. Herman Melville, Billy Budd, http://en.wiki pedia.org/wiki/Billy_Budd, 2011
54. "The Death Penalty," *Weekly Detroit Press*, Issue 52, December 25, 1886, p. 4, Col. B.
55. Matter of Gerry, 103 N.Y. 445 1886.
56. "Sons of the Revolution," *The New York Times*, December 5, 1886, p. 4.
57. "A Naval Militia," *Daily Evening Bulletin*, San Francisco, Issue 54, December 9, 1886 p. 4.
58. *Ibid.*
59. "No Means of Defense," *Frank Leslie's Illustrated Newspaper*, July 12, 1884, p. 322, col. A.
60. "In His Annual Report…," *Frank Leslie's Illustrated Newspaper*, November 22, 1884, p. 211, col. C.
61. "Admiral Howard Patterson," *Brooklyn Daily Eagle*, December 4, 1889, p. 1.
62. *Ibid.*
63. "The Rich at the Opera," *Milwaukee Sentinel*, December 19, 1886, p. 11.
64. *Ibid.*
65. "The First Grand Ball," *Weekly Detroit Free Press*, MI, January 1, 1887, p. 4.
66. "The Rescue of Children," *Frank Leslie's Illustrated Newspaper*, February 26, 1887, p. 27.
67. "New York Yacht Fleet Gathers," *The New York Times*, August 1887, p. 8.
68. "The Goelet Cup Race," *The New York Times*, August 6, 1887, n. p.
69. "At Marblehead," *Boston Daily Advisor*, Issue 36, August 10, 1887, p. 8, col. A.
70. *Ibid.*
71. *Ibid.*

72. Ed Holm, ed., *Yachting's Golden Age: 1880-1905*, (New York: Knopf, 1999), p. 17.
73. "The Volunteer and the Thistle," *Daily Inter Ocean*, Chicago, September 28, 1887, p. 4, col. C.
74. Geoffrey F. Hammond, *Showdown at Newport: the Race for the America's Cup*, (New York: Walden Publications, 1974) p. 36.
75. "The Volunteer Victorious," *Saint Louis Globe-Democrat*, Issue 126, September 28, 1887, p. 7, Col. A.
76. "Left the Thistle," *Milwaukee Sentinel*, September 28, 1887, p. 1.
77. "Honoring the Yachtsmen," *Boston Daily Advertiser*, October 5, 1887, p. 4.
78. People ex rel. Van Riper v New York Catholic Protectory 106 N.Y.604.

8: GILDED GOTHAM: THE 1880'S PART III

1. "The Patriarch's Ball: A Brilliant Scene at Delmonicos," *The New York Times*, January 18, 1888, p. 5.
2. "In Mr. Bergh's Place," *The New York Times*, March 24, 1888, n. p.
3. "He Had Millions," *Saint Paul Daily News*, October 8, 1891, p. 3, col. C.
4. Brian J. Cudahy, introduction, *The New York Subway: Its Construction and Equipment*, (New York: Inter-borough Rapid Transit Co., 1904), p .13.
5. "The Mayor Declines," *The New York Times*, December 21, 1888, p. 5.
6. *History of the American Seaman's Friend Society*, G. W. Blunt White Library, Manuscript Collections, Mystic Seaport Museum, Mystic, CT.
7. *St. Louis Globe Democrat*, Nov. 6, 1887, p. 4, col. B.
8. *Bismarck Daily Tribune*, Dec. 3, 1887, col. A.
9. *Supra* Gerry Papers, Reel 2.
10. Edward Everett Hale, "George Washington," in *Illustrious Americans: Their Lives and Achievements*, (Philadelphia: International Publishing Company, 1896) pp. 52-53.
11. Historical Sign (text) in Washington Square Park, New York City, 2012.
12. *Stanford White's Washington Square Arch*, http://daytoninmanhattan.blogspot.com/2011
13. "A Conspicuous Figure in the Great Metropolis," *Daily Picayune*, LA, April 14, 1889, p 12, col. A.
14. *William Francis Kemmler Biography*, http://en.wikipedia.org/wiki/Kemmler.
15. Buck Quiqley, *The Shocking Truth*, http://artvoice.com/issues/v6n43/shocking truth.
16. "Mr. Gerry on the Stand He Talks About Death by Electricity," *The New York Times*, July 19, 1889, p. 8.
17. "The Electra in Collision," *The New York Times*, September 6, 1889, p. 1.

9: GILDED GOTHAM: THE 1890'S PART I

1. Laura P. Claridge, *Emily Post: Daughter of the Gilded Age*, (New York: Random House, 2008), p. i, xii.
2. *Id.*, p. 100.
3. "The Second Assembly Ball at Delmonico's," *New York Herald*, January 10, 1890, p. 1.
4. Roland G. Curtin, M.D. and Edward W. Watson, M.D., "Epidemiology of Influenza and Its Relations to Catarrial Fever," *Climatologist*, February 1892, pp. 1-7.
5. *Supra* Gerry Papers, Reel 7.
6. "The United States Nine," *New York Morning Journal*, no. 2,620, February 5, 1890, p. 2.
7. *Id.*, pp. 3-4.
8. "Coaching Club Parade," *The New York Times*, May 25, 1890, p. 2.
9. "News," *Bangor Daily Whig & Courier*, June 13, 1890, col. C, n. p.
10. "Steam Yachting's Growth," *The New York Times*, September 25, 1890, p. 9.
11. "The Count Arrives," *North American*, PA, October 4, 1890, p. 4, col. C.
12. People ex rell. Annie Brown v Carpenter, New York Juvenile Asylum, 123 N.Y. 640, 1890.
13. http://www.asf.ca/about.php
14. "Children's Aid Society," *The New York Times*, Nov-ember 26, 1890, p.4.
15. "How the 400 Dance," *Bismarck Daily Tribune*, Dec-ember 30, 1890, p. 4, col A.
16. "The Vanderbilts Entertain," *The New York Times*, January 20, 1891, n. p.
17. "A Magnificent Wedding," *The New York Times*, February 18, 1891.
18. "Obituary – Robert J. Livingston," *The New York Times*, February 23, 1891, p. 1.
19. Ruth Selden-Sturgill, *Historic Landmark Designation: Metropolitan Club Building Report*, September 11, 1979, Designated LP-1020, (New York: Landmarks Preservation Commission, 1979).

20. "A Gotham Aristocrat," *Daily Inter-Ocean*, March 22, 1891, p. 31, col. A.
21. "The Works of the Late Richard Morris Hunt," *The Architectural Record*, vol. V, No. 2, 1895, p. 97.
22. *The Goelet Family Papers*, Archives, Salve Regina College, Newport, Rhode, Island.
23. People ex rel. Danziger v Protestant Episcopal House of Mercy of N.Y., 128 N.Y. 180, 1891.
24. "Mr. Gerry's Society Upheld," *New York Herald*, October 29, 1891, p. 4.
25. "A Gerry Society Agent Goes Wrong," *The New York Times*, November 13, 1891, p. 8.
26. "For Flower and Victory," *The New York Times*, October 9, 1891, p. 1.
27. "Entered Into Rest," *The New York Times*, November 28, 1891, Obituaries.
28. "The City's Pauper Insane," *The New York Times*, January 29, 1892, p. 6.
29. "A Circus in New York," *Boston Daily Advisor*, March 21, 1892, p. 2 col B.
30. "Mr. E. T. Gerry's New Mansion," *The New York Times*, May 15, 1892, p. 16.
31. People ex rel. Kuhn v. Protestant Episcopal House of Mercy, 133 N.Y. 207, 1892.
32. Ewer v. People of State of New York, 17 S.Ct. 993, 196.
33. *United States Senate: Art and History*, http://www.sen ate.gov/sculpture 22-0005.
34. "An Accident to the Electra," *The New York Times*, July 16, 1892.
35. "Not Settled Yet, Merits of the Wasp, Gloriana and Harpoon," *Boston Daily Advertiser*, issue 35, August 10, 1892, col. C, n. p.
36. "Metropolitan Opera House," *Illustrated American*, vol.12, no. 4, 1892, n. p.
37. "To Be a Noble Social Event," *The New York Times*, March 12, 1893, p. 8.
38. Kevin McNamara, *Newport Country Club has a Legendary History*, June 27, 2006, http://golf clubatlas.com.
39. http://www.lillielangtry.com/Society.htm
40. "Lillie Langtry and George Baird," *The Stichill Millenium Project*, http://www.bairdnet.com.
41. "Langtry Rents Her Yacht," *Milwaukee Journal*, July 21, 1893, p. 6, col. D.
42. "What Society Talks Of," *Milwaukee Journal*, September 29, 1893, p. 4, col. F.
43. *The Panic of 1893*, http://en.wikipedia.org/wiki
44. "The Almy Off for Greenland," *The New York Times*, August 1, 1893, n. p.
45. "The Gerry Cup: A Testimonial that is Much Admired by the Cruising Yachtsmen," *The New York Times*, August 17, 1893, n. p.
46. Limbeck v Gerry, 15 Misc. 663, 1896.
47. "Storms Havoc, Terrific Gale Along the Coast," *Boston Daily Advertiser*, Issue 51, August 30, 1893, Col. B, n. p.
48. "Subscriptions Poured in Fast," *The New York Times*, October 13, 1893, n. p.
49. "Mayor Gilroy Returns from the Fair," *New York Daily Tribune*, October 28, 1893, p. 1.

10: GILDED GOTHAM: THE 1890'S PART II

1. "Married in Grace Church," *The New York Times*, April 19, 1894, p. 4.
2. "Robert Cushing's Art," *The New York Times*, March 2, 1896, n. p.
3. "A Statue of Father Drumgoole," *New York Daily Tribune*, April 13, 1894, p. 12.
4. "In the Real Estate Field," *The New York Times*, February 1, 1894, p. 12.
5. *Gerry-Hunt Correspondence*, Richard Morris Hunt Archive, American Institute of Architects Library, Washington, D.C.
6. Richard Morris Hunt, *Gerry Mansion Floor Plans*, Richard Morris Hunt Archive, American Institute of Architects Library, Washington, D.C.
7. "Plumbing in the Residence of Mr. Elbridge T. Gerry," *American Plumbing Practice*, illustrated, (New York: The Engineering Record, 1894).
8. *Julia Ward Howe*, http://www.juliawardhowe.org/bio.htm.
9. "Presentation by Citizens of New York," *The New York Times*, May 12, 1894.
10. Richard Glotzer, "The Felton Decision in Perspective," *Educational Change*, spring 1999, p. 101-103.
11. "Society and Vice," *Bangor Daily Whig & Courier*, Issue 232, September 29, 1894, col. D.
12. "Favors an Unbroken Front," *The New York Times*, August 1, 1894, p. 2.
13. "Yachting: Cruise of the New York Yacht Club," *Outing Magazine*, vol. 24, no. 6, September 1894, p. 154.
14. "A New York Yacht Club Pun," *Rocky Mountain News*, Colorado, November 15, 1891, column E, n. p.
15. "Women Who Sail," *Milwaukee Sentinel*, April 27, 1890, col. E, n. p.
16. *Ibid.*
17. *Ibid.*

18. *Auction Catalogue - Angelica Livingston Gerry,* sale conducted by Louis J. Marion, Parke-Bernet Galleries, Inc. New York, NY, Item No. 413, p. 76.
19. "Imported Woodwork Detained," *The New York Times,* February 19, 1895, p. 15.
20. Marjorie Peason, ed., *Upper East Side Historic District Designation Report,* (New York: Research Department of the Landmarks Preservation Commission, New York, 1981).
21. "Our City Vigilance," *North American Review,* vol.156, 1893, pp.98-104.
22. "Paid the Police Thousands," *The New York Times,* October 5, 1894, n. p.
23. "What's Going on In Society," *New York Record,* June 3, 1894, n. p.
24. Contemporary newspaper clipping from Angelica Gerry's personal scrapbook, no attribution.
25. *Ibid.*
26. Lydia Bolles Newcomb, "Emily Louise Gerry," in *Daughters of the American Revolution: Patriot's Daughters,* edited by Mary P. Root, (New Haven CT: Edward P. Judd Company, 1904), pp. 3-10.
27. "Great Houses Opened," *The World,* New York, January 3, 1895, p. 1.
28. *Ibid.*
29. "Social World," *The New York Times,* January 2, 1895, p. 11.
30. "Consuelo Vanderbilt Balsan," in *The Glitter and the Gold,* by Dan Fang, (New York: Harper Publishers, 1952).
31. *Ibid.*
32. *Gertrude Vanderbilt Whitney* http://www.nnp.org
33. Annual Report of the President, American Museum of Natural History, (New York: Museum of Natural History, 1895).
34. "Electricity on the Canals," *The New York Times,* February 27, 1895.
35. "The Senate Judiciary Committee," *Morning Oregonian,* February 22, 1895.
36. "An Affront to Gerry," *The New York Times,* March 8, 1895, p. 1.
37. *Ibid.*
38. "The Legislative Wasp," *The New York Times,* March 14, 1895, p. 3.
39. "Must We Have a Cat-O-Nine Tails?" *North American Review,* volume CLX, 1895, pp.318-324.
40. "The New York Hospital: Its 124th Annual Report," *The New York Times,* April 25, 1895.
41. "Cares for the Incurables," *The New York Times,* June 12, 1895, n. p.
42. Gossip in Gotham, *Rocky Mountain News,* Colorado, Issue 126, May 6, 1895, p. 3.
43. "In the Swagger Set: Noted Americans Who Are in the English Swim," *San Francisco Call,* May 26, 1895, p. 4.
44. "Much Time Will be Spent on the Goelet Yacht," *Morning Record,* Connecticut, June 7, 1895, p. 1.
45. "American Tourists in Town," *Brooklyn Daily Eagle,* September 7, 1895, p. 1.
46. "Death of Richard Morris Hunt," *The New York Times,* August 1, 1895, p. 1.
47. Gail MacColl and Carol McD. Wallace, *To Marry an English Lord,* (New York: Work-man Publishing, 1989), pp. 168-179.
48. W. P. Stephens, *American Yachting,* (New York: The Macmillan Company, 1904), pp. 238-239.
49. *Id.,* pp. 242-243.
50. "The Committee Praised," *The New York Times,* November 20, 1895, p. 8.
51. *Supra* American Yachting, p. 246.
52. "Mrs. T.R. Gerry Dangerously Ill," *The New York Times,* September 3, 1895, p. 1.
53. "Mrs. Gerry Much Improved," *The New York Times,* September 5, 1895, p.1.
54. "Funeral of Mrs. Hannah G. Gerry," *The New York Times,* September 18, 1895, p. 9.
55. "Patriarch," *The New York Times,* January 5, 1896, p. 10.
56. "A Day's Weddings," *The New York Times,* April 29, 1896, p. 4.
57. The People ex rel. Teresa Plot v Lucy Poly, 40 N.Y.S. 990, 1896.
58. "Scorchers Come to Grief," *The New York Times,* July 14, 1896, p. 8.
59. *Murray Hill Theatre,* http://library.gc.cuny.edu/murrayhill/items/show/168.
60. "Dinner to the Bridal Couple," *The New York Times,* August 24, 1896, p. 4.
61. "The Bolkenhayn Apartment House," *The New York Times,* April 2, 1895.
62. Bassae Frieze at the Temple of Apollo, http://en.wikipidia.org/.
63. *Alfred Zucker: An Inventory of His Drawings,* Alex-ander Architectural Archive, University of Texas Libraries, Austin, Texas, identification: ZUCK Accession number 1979002.

64. "The Bradley Martin Ball," *The New York Times*, February 7, 1897, p. 1.
65. "Society Events of the Week," *The New York Times*, January 31, 1897, p. 10.
66. *Supra* Marry an English Lord, p. 267.
67. People v Giles, 152 N.Y. 136, March 1897.
68. "Personal Paragraphs," *The Milwaukee Journal*, August 6, 1897, p. 4, col. D.
69. "The Steam Yacht Amy," *The Traveler*, New York, August 13, 1897, n. p.
70. "Fruits of Experience," *American Gardening*, August 1897.
71. Thomas W. Handford, *Queen Victoria, Her Glorious Life and Illustrious Reign*, (London: Franklin Printing & Publishing, 1901), p. 356.
72. "The Mayflower II," in *Dictionary of American Naval Fighting Ships*, James L. Mooney, volume 4, (Washington: Naval History Center, Defense Department, 1969), pp. 281-283.
73. "The Advancement of Anti-Cruelty," *Humane Advocate*, November 1917, vol. XIII, p 1.
74. "Robert Goelet's New Yacht," *The New York Times*, October 28, 1897, n. p.
75. "Horse Show Here Again," *The New York Times*, November 16, 1897, p. 1.
76. *Ibid.*
77. People ex rel. Lazarus v House of Mercy, 23 A.D. 383, December 1897.
78. "Yachting," *Outing's Monthly Review*, January 1898, p. 82.
79. "Cotillion at the Gerrys," *The New York Times*, February 3, 1898, p. 7.
80. "Are Citizens of Rhode Island," *The New York Times*, October 1, 1898, n. p.
81. "Winter Days at Newport," *The New York Times*, February 20, 1898, p. 15.
82. "A Reception at the Reading Room, "*The New York Times*, January 12, 1890, n. p.
83. *The Spanish American War*, Wikipedia . http: //en.wikipedia.org/.
84. V.C. Jones, "Before the Colors Fade: Last of the Rough Riders," *American Heritage Magazine*, Vol. 20, August 1969, p. 26.
85. Willard B. Gate-wood, *Black Americans and the White Man's Burden, 1898–1903*, (Urbana: University of Illinois Press, 1975).
86. Booker T. Washington, *Up From Slavery*, (New York: Penguin Books, 1901).
87. "Three War Vessels Sail," *The New York Times*, April 19, 1898, p. 1.
88. D. B. Jacobson, B. G. Raub, and B. W. Johnson, *The Estate Tax: Ninety Years and Counting*, (Washington: Internal Revenue Service), pp. 119-121. http://www.irs.gov/pub/irssoi/ninetyestate.pdf.
89. *Ibid.*
90. *The Spanish American War*, Wikipedia. http://en.wikipedia.org/.
91. "The Archbishop Eulogized," *Irish World & American Industrial Liberator*, New York, May 14, 1898, p. 3, col. A.
92. "A Unique Charity," *Irish World & American Industrial Liberator*, New York City, August 24, 1895, p. 8 col. A.
93. "A Dance at Mrs. Gerry's," *The New York Times*, February 6, 1899, p. 7.
94. "What is Doing in Society," *The New York Times*, February 26, 1899, n. p.
95. "Ruins of Windsor Hotel," *The World*, March 19, 1899, p. 1.
96. "Death of Robert Goelet," *The New York Times*, April 27, 1899.
97. "Trouble Log of the Goelet Yacht," *Salt Lake Tribune*, magazine section, January 12, 1913, p. 1.
98. "Career of the Millionaire," *The New York Times*, April 28, 1899, n. p.
99. Mackenzie King Diary, August 16, 1899, http://www.lac-bac.gc.ca/king.
100. *Id.*, June 8, 1939.

11: THE TWENTIETH CENTURY: PART I 1900 TO 1909

1. "The Playgoer," *Society Illustrated*, volume 9, no. 49, 1913, p. 19.
2. "What's Doing in Society," *The New York Times*, May 22, 1900.
3. "Newport Raises Taxes of the Millionaires," *The New York Times*, May 18, 1905, p. 1.
4. "Gerry's Illness," *The New York Times*, June 5, 1900, p. 9.
5. "Private Gardeners – Newport, R.I.," *American Gardening*, July 7, 1900, p. 458.
6. "Greenhouse Building," *The American Florist*, August 18, 1900, p. 68.
7. "Mrs. Ogden Goelet's Ball," *The New York Times*, August 29, 1900, p. 7.
8. "Gallatin Reception," *The New York Times*, December 2, 1900, p. 18.
9. "Bride Cables Her Parents," *The New York Times*, December 18, 1911, p. 1.
10. "New York Yacht Club Honors J.P. Morgan," *The New York Times*, January 30, 1901.
11. "Expressions of Social Activity," *The Evening Telegram – New York*, July 31, 1901, p. 4.

12. "Patrol of the Course," *The New York Times,* September 27, 1901, p. 2.
13. "Horse Show Boxes Sold," *The New York Times,* November 8, 1901, p. 9.
14. *National Souvenir of Prince Henry's Visit to the United States,* (New York: J. Klingenbeck Publishers, 1902), pp. 102-103.
15. "Miss Beatrice Goelet Dead," *The New York Times,* February 11, 1902, p. 1.
16. "Emperor's Cable to Mrs. Vanderbilt," *The New York Times,* February 27, 1902, p. 1.
17. "Goelet Estate Judgment," *The New York Times,* April 4, 1902, p. 6.
18. "The Golden Wedding of Dean and Mrs. Hoffman," *The New York Times,* April 20, 1902.
19. "Guests of the President," *The New York Times,* August 5, 1902.
20. "The News of Newport," *The New York Times,* September 7, 1902, p. 9.
21. David Chavchavadze, *The Grand Dukes,* (New York: Atlantic Publishing, 1989), pp. 230-235.
22. "Killed in an Elevator," *The New York Times,* September 16, 1902, p. 1.
23. *Supra* Grand Dukes, pp. 230-235.
24. "Gallatin-Post Wedding," *The New York Times,* October 2, 1902.
25. *Charles Semsey,* by Stephen Beszedits, http://www.sk-sziged.hu/szolgaltatas, 2007.
26. *Ibid.*
27. Mosette Broderick, *Triumvirate: McKim, Mead & White: Art, Architecture, Scandal, and Class in Amer-ica's Gilded Society,* (New York: Alfred A. Knopf Publishers, 2010).
28. *East Twentieth Street, Ladies Mile Historic District,* (New York: Landmarks Preservation Commission, 1989), pp. 685-686.
29. *The Tuxedo Club History,* www.thetuxedo club.org/
30. *Ibid.*
31. "New Year's Eve Ball," *The New York Times,* Decem-ber 31, 1902, p. 6.
32. "Dispute Over Ground Lease," *The New York Times,* April 3, 1903, p. 16.
33. *Alma Mater Statue,* Butler Library, Columbia University, New York City, 2011.
34. *Official website of the British Monarchy,* http://www.royal.gov.uk/HistoryoftheMonar chy/- Retrieved May 2012.
35. "The Coaching Parade," *New York Daily Tribune,* May 10, 1903, p. 10.
36. *Ibid.*
37. "Mrs. Goelet Triumphed," *The New York Times,* May 19, 1903, p. 1.
38. "What is Doing in Society," *The New York Times,* June 30, 1903, p. 2.
39. "Talked About at the Clubs," *The New York Times,* July 26, 1903, p. 13.
40. "Told in Her Boudoir," *The New York Times,* September 13, 1903, n. p.
41. "Summer Flowers at Newport," *American Gardening,* Volume 24, July 4, 1903, p. 322.
42. "Announcement from London," *The New York Times,* September 2, 1903, p. 1.
43. "Miss Goelet to Marry Duke of Roxburghe," *Saint John Daily Sun,* London, September 7, 1903, n. p.
44. "Duke of Roxburghe Marries Miss Goelet," *The New York Times,* November 11, 1903, n. p.
45. "Russian Embassy Christmas," *New York Herald,* January 8, 1904, p. 7.
46. *Whitelaw Reid.,* http:www.electricscotland .com/history/descendants/chap125.htm
47. "Clubs and Clubmen," *The New York Times,* January 31, 1904, n. p.
48. "The Chase in Earnest," *New York Herald,* November 8, 1903, n. p.
49. "The Hunt in America," *New York Herald,* November 8, 1903.
50. *Gerry Clubhouse,* BCNY History, http:/www. bcny.org/.
51. Richard Greenwood, *Arden, the E.H. Harriman Estate,* Landmark Review Taskforce, National Historic Landmark, (Washington: United States Department of the Interior, 1975).
52. "Report of the Department of Philanthropy, Charities and Social Problems: Annals of the American Academy of Political and Social Science," *Business Management,* vol. 22, November 1903, pp. 123-126. http://www.jstor.org/.
53. *Ibid.*
54. *Id.,* p. 134.
55. "Gossip Between Games," *The New York Times,* December 20, 1903, p. SM14.
56. *Id.,* p. SM15.
57. "Distinguished Easterners Enjoy the Many Sights," *Los Angeles Times,* January 26, 1904, p. 1.
58. *Cawston Ostrich Farm,* http://southpasadena. patch.com/articles/the-cawston-ostrich-farm.
59. "Hunt Plans for Goshen," *The New York Times,* January 24, 1904, n. p.
60. "Women the Whips in Parade of Coaches," *New York Herald,* March 4, 1904, n. p.

61. "What Is Doing in Society," *The New York Times*, October, 1904, n. p.
62. "Sixty-Fifth Convention of the Chi Psi Fraternity," *The Purple and Gold*, Columbia University, New York, p. 207.
63. "The Gerry Ball," *The New York Times*, January 22, 1905, p. 44.
64. "Mrs. Gerry Gives a Ball for Young Dancing Set," *New York Journal*, March 1905, n. p.
65. "Society in Palm Beach," *Palm Beach Daily News*, March 14, 1905, n. p.
66. "What's Doing in Society," *New York Daily Tribune*, March 19, 1905, p. 8.
67. "What's Doing In Society," *The New York Times*, May 14, 1905, p. 33.
68. "Society At Home and Abroad," *The New York Times*, August 6, 1905, p. 32.
69. *Biography of August Belmont Jr.*, http://en.wikipedia.org/wiki/August_Belmont,_Jr.
70. *Belmont Park: More Than Just Horses*, http://www.belmontstakes.com/history/belmontparkmorethanjusthorses.aspx
71. "Gerry Gifts," *Delaware Gazette*, April 1905 and October 23, 1905, n. p.
72. "Burglar's Shot Kills Youth," *The New York Times*, November 4, 1905, p. 1.
73. "Gallatin Yacht Ashore," *New York Tribune*, September 25, 1905, p. 1.
74. "Society at Home and Abroad," *The New York Times*, February 28, 1906, p. 1.
75. *Mabel Gerry Diary*, March 25, 1887, Naples, Italy, manuscript at Lake Delaware estate, New York, 2011.
76. "The Grand Eruption," *The Journal of Geology*, volume 14, number 7, October-November 1906, pp. 636-655.
77. "The Nahma Collision," *New York Tribune*, May 10, 1906, p. 1.
78. *New York to Goshen to Lake Delaware and Kingston*, Scrapbook of Angelica Gerry, Lake Delaware Farm House, Delaware County, New York, 1905.
79. "Society at Home and Abroad," *The New York Times*, June 3, 1906, n. p.
80. *The Murder of Stanford White*, http://en.wikipedia.org/wiki/Stanford_White
81. "Murder at Madison Square Garden 1906," in *Lost New York* by Marcia Reiss, (London: Pavilion Books, 2011), p. 41.
82. "Captured the Goelet Chef," *The New York Times*, October 5, 1906, p. 9.
83. "My Daughter Not Engaged," *The New York Times*, November 10, 1906, p. 28.
84. "New York Bachelor Girls," *Kansas City Star*, November 25, 1906, p. 1.
85. "The E. T. Gerry Mansion, Dancing in the Art Gallery," *The New York Times*, January 15, 1907, p. 7.
86. In Re Piers, Old Nos 19, 20 East River in the City of New York, 102 N.Y.S.667 (1907).
87. "Big Liner Hits Ice Berg," *Los Angeles Times*, Los Angeles, CA, July 11, 1907, p. 12.
88. "Departures," *Paris Herald*, France, August 27, 1907, n. p.
89. "Fiancé's Finances Displease De Alba," *The New York Times*, November 2, 1907, p. 1.
90. "Society at Home and Abroad," *The New York Times*, March 4, 1908, n. p.
91. "Miss Harriman Bride of Robert L. Gerry," *The New York Times*, March 4, 1908, n. p.
92. Melvin T. Copeland, *The Story of the Harvard Business School*, (Boston: Little, Brown and Company, 1958), p. 9.
93. *Mahler in New York*, (New York: The Philharmonic Symphony Society, 1958), p.90.
94. *History of Claridge's Hotel in London*, http://www.milesfaster.co.uk/london-hotels/claridges-hotel-london.htm.
95. *1908 Summer Olympics*, http://en.wikipedia.org/wiki/1908_Summer_Olympics.
96. "Marriage of American Girl, Pandex of the Press," series II, volume 8, no.2, August 1908, p. 195.
97. *Supra* Marry an English Lord, p. 346.
98. "Religion in the Life of a Child," *Humane Advocate*, Volume 4, 1909, p. 20-21.
99. "Independence Day," *The Times*, London, July 6, 1909, p.8.
100. "Summering at New London," *The New York Times*, July 12, 1908, p. 45.
101. "Commodore Gerry Home from Europe," *The New York Times*, July 7, 1909, p. 16.
102. "Twenty Cows Slaughtered," *The Way We Were*, from the Andes Reporter, http://andesgazette.net/2009/05/01.
103. "Bovina Correspondent," *Delaware Gazette*, June 7, 1909, n. p.
104. "City May Make Claim to Waterfront Land," *The New York Times*, August 30, 1909, p. 11.

12: THE TWENTIETH CENTURY: PART II 1910 TO 1930

1. "William L. Scott Dead," *The New York Times*, September 21, 1891, p. 5.
2. "Obituary: Richard H. Townsend," *Evening Star*, November 28, 1902, p. 7.
3. "Society at Bar Harbor Engaged in Its Usual Round of Pleasure," *The New York Times*, August 1, 1909, p. 50.
4. "Dinners and Luncheons," *Washington Herald*, January 9, 1910, p. 2.
5. *Camilla Duchess of Cornwall and Edward VII's Favorite Mistress*, http://news.bbc.co.uk/news
6. *Funeral of King Edward VII*, http://www.thames web.co.uk/Windsor.
7. *Ibid.*
8. "Society At Home and Abroad," *The New York Times*, May 15, 1910, p. XI.
9. "New Shubert Building," *The New York Times*, May 24, 1910, p. 5.
10. "P.G. Gerry's Bride Toasted by Taft," *The New York Times*, May 27, 1910, p. 9.
11. *Id.*, p.10.
12. "Miss Townsend Married," *New York Daily Tribune*, May 27, 1910, p. 1.
13. "Tipped Over Bank Horses Scared by Automobile," Gerry Clipping File, Kingston Public Library, Kingston, New York, July 20, 1910.
14. "Denies Miss Gerry is Engaged to Wed," the *New York Times*, August 5, 1910, p. 9.
15. "Duke Franz Joseph Feted," *The New York Times*, August 21, 1910. p. 7.
16. "Children's Court to be Less Formal," *The New York Times*, September 4, 1910, p. 20.
17. *Ibid.*
18. "Foreigners Coming to Humane Congress," *The New York Times*, October 2, 1910, p. 8.
19. "Wilson Death Puts Many in Mourning," *The New York Times*, November 27, 1910, p. 13.
20. "Address of Hon. Elbridge T. Gerry," Gerry Folder, photocopy February 8, 1911, p.2. New York Genealogical and Biographical Library, New York Historical Society, New York City, New York.
21. *Id.*, p. 5.
22. Id., pp. 6-7.
23. "American Dogs Win at Garden," *The New York Times*, February 16, 1911, p. 8.
24. "Killed by Goelet's Auto," *The New York Times*, March 27, 1911, p. 1.
25. "Club Rule Broken for the Gerry Baby," *The New York Times*, May 1, 1911, p. 11.
26. "The Goelet Mansion Demolished," *The New Times*, March 2, 1930, n. p.
27. "Lake Delaware Camp," *The Andes Recorder*, September 8, 1911, n. p.
28. "Progress of the Boys Camp at Lake Delaware," *The Andes Recorder*, May 17, 1912, n. p.
29. *Robert L. Gerry*,http://en.wikipedia.org/wiki/Robert_L._Gerry
30. "Rich Children Enjoy Rare Sport in Central Park Snow," *New York Evening Journal*, February, 1912.
31. "Hanover Absorbs Gallatin National," *The New York Times*, April 26, 1912, p. 16.
32. "Warmest Day at Newport," *The New York Times*, June 30, 1912, p. X4.
33. "Newport Season Both Early and Gay," *The New York Times*, July 6, 1913, p. X2.
34. "Mrs. Goelet Dying," *The New York Times*, August 23, 1912, p. 2.
35. "Mrs. Robert Goelet Dies in Paris Home," *The New York Times*, December 5, 1912, p. 11.
36. Gertrude Fitch Horton, *The Delaware and Northern and the Towns It Served*, (Fleishmanns NY: Purple Mountain Press, 1945).
37. "Peter Gerry for Congress," *The New York Times*, October 11, 1912, p. 10.
38. "$150,000 Plate for Gerry," *The New York Times*, April 23, 1913, p. 1.
39. *Alfred G. Vanderbilt*, http://www.wikipedia.com/Alfred_G._Vanderbilt.
40. "Son and Heir Born to the Roxburghes," *The New York Times*, September 9, 1913, p. 3.
41. "Mrs. Gerry to Build Roads," *The New York Times*, November 17, 1913, p. 1.
42. "She is a Benefactor," *Delaware Express*, September 12, 1913, n. p.
43. "Son and Heir Born to the Roxburghes," *The New York Times*, September 9, 1913, p. 1.
44. United States v Harrieta Goelet, Nos 631 and 632, 1232 U.S. 293, February 24, 1914.
45. "Troubles of the Goelets," *The New York Times*, January 22, 1914, p. 1.
46. "Mrs. Robert Goelet Weds H. Clews Jr," *The New York Times*, December 20, 1914, p. 2.
47. Chateau de la Napoule, http://en.wikipedia .org/wiki/Ch%C3%A2teau_de_la_Napoule.

48. Mookie Singerman "06 At The Mic," http://encyclopedia.vassar.edu/organizations.
49. WGNY AM Early Roots, Radio Discussions.com.
50. "Nancy Goeschel and Ogden Goelet Wed," *The New York Times,* November 12, 1987, n. p.
51. "The Real Estate Field, Elbridge Gerry Sells Big Plot," *The New York Times,* March 7, 1914, p.18.
52. "Newport Hit Hard," *The New York Times,* March 3, 1914, p. 3.
53. "Twin Sons to R.L. Gerrys," *The New York Times,* April 9, 1914, p. 11.
54. *World War I, The Causes,* http://en.wikipedia.org/wiki/World_War_I.
55. "War Has Halted Newport Gayeties," *The New York Times,* August 7, 1914, p. 11.
56. "A Journey Godward," volume 4, in *The Works of the Right Reverend Charles C. Grafton,* edited by B. Tal-bot Rogers, (New York: Longmans, 1914), p. 317.
57. *Id.,* Preface, pp. v-x.
58. *Ibid.*
59. "Confirmed at Chapel," *Delaware Express,* November 27, 1914, scrapbook clipping at Gerry estate at Lake Delaware.
60. "To Educate Bloomfield Girl," *Delaware Express,* September 26, 1914, scrapbook clipping at Gerry estate at Lake Delaware.
61. "E.T. Gerry's Home Robbed," *The New York Times,* December 16, 1914, p. 6.
62. "Young Men Socially Conspicuous Achieve Success in Public Life," *Washington Post,* November 19, 1916, p. 13.
63. "Gerrys to Change Highway," *Catskill Mountain News,* September 10, 1915, n. p.
64. "Town Topics," *New York Tribune,* June 29, 1916, n. p.
65. *Susan Fenimore Cooper,* http://en.wikipedia.org/wiki/Susan_Fenimore_Cooper.
66. "Gerrys Ask Aid for School," *The New York Times,* September 3, 1916, n. p.
67. "Society Women Bid on Jewels at Fair," *The New York Times,* December 6, 1912, n. p.
68. *Ibid.*
69. "Captain Patterson Dead," *The New York Times,* November 2, 1916, p. 13.
70. "Estate of Mrs. Gallatin," *The New York Times,* April 4, 1917, p. 20.
71. "The Advancement of the Anti-Cruelty Sentiment" *Humane Advocate,* vol.XIII, no.1, November 1917, p. 1.
72. *Josef Hofmann.* http://en.wikipedia.org/wiki/Josef_Hofmann.
73. *W. Averell Harriman,* http://en.wikipedia.org./wiki/W._Averell_Harriman.
74. *Ibid.*
75. *Ibid.*
76. "National Special Aid Meeting at Newport," *Flying,* vol.6, October, 1917, p. 785.
77. "Miss Gerry on a Special Mission," *Town and Country,* vols. 75-76, February 20, 1919, p. 38.
78. "Fashionable Mr. Goelet and His Wife Number Three," *Pittsburgh Press,* September 20, 1925, n. p.
79. Susan Munroe, *Massive General Strike Paralyzes Winnipeg,* http://canadaonline.about.com.
80. Paul Burnett, *The Red Scare in America,* http://law2.umkc.edu/faculty/projects/ftrials.
81. "Mrs. Elbridge T. Gerry Dies," *The New York Times,* March 27, 1920, n. p.
82. "Many Pay Tribute to Mrs. E.T. Gerry," *New York Herald,* March 27, 1920, p. 15.
83. *Last Will and Testament of Louisa M. Gerry,* original manuscript, Hartwick College Archives, Oneonta, New York.
84. "Colby Proclaims Women's Suffrage," *The New York Times,* August 1919, p. 1.
85. "Gerry Shows 'Em Some Real Ideas," *The New York Times,* November 26, 1916, n. p.
86. Timeline, Part II 1920, http://washingtonart.com/beltway/timeline2.html.
87. "Seven Women Quit Gerry Society in Angry Protest," *The New York Times,* November 10, 1920, p. 1.
88. *Id.,* p.2.
89. "Robert W. Goelet May Wed Mlle. Guestier," *The New York Times,* November 9, 1920, n. p.
90. "Fifth Avenue Corner in $7,500,000 Deal," *The New York Times,* July 15, 1921, p. 23.
91. Meinhard v Salmon, 249 N.Y.458, 1928.
92. Geoffrey P. Miller, *Meinhard v Salmon,* New York University Law and Economics Working Paper 105, (New York: New York University School of Law, 2007).
93. "Delaware County Sanatorium News," *Delaware Record,* October 16, 1921, n. p.
94. "Mabel Gerry is Hostess," *The New York Times,* January 28, 1922, p. 13.

95. "Mabel Gerry Not to Stay Abroad All Summer," *The New York Times*, May 3, 1922, n. p.
96. "Guests at Seabreeze See Automobile Races,' *New York Herald*, January 22, 1922.
97. "New Church Buildings for Lake Delaware," *The New York Times*, 1922 clipping, scrapbook Gerry estate, Lake Delaware, New York.
98. "Gerry Home Robbed," September 29, 1922 clip-ping, Gerry Lake House, Lake Delaware, New York.
99. "Gerrys May Sell $18,000,000 Realty," *The New York Times*, May 23, 1922, p. 1.
100. "Tapestries Threatened by Fire in Gerry Home," *The New York Times*, December 19, 1923, n. p.
101. Hans Nadelhoffer, *Cartier*, (London: Thames & Hudson, Ltd., 2007).
102. "Any Resemblance to Persons Living or Dead, N. Z. Davis, Film and the Challenge of Authenticity," *The Yale Review*, vol. 86, 1987, pp. 457-82.
103. *High Altar*, typed sheet in scrapbook of Angelica Gerry, no date, Lake Delaware House, New York.
104. "Senator Gerry Sued for Divorce," *San Antonio Express*, November 22, 1924, n. p.
105. Christopher D. O'Sullivan, *Sumner Wells, Postwar Planning, and the Quest for a New World Order*, http://www.gutenberg-e.org/osc01/index.html.
106. "Robert Willard Goelet Scholarship," *Annual Report*, (Newport RI: Salve Regina College, 1969).
107. "Angelica Gerry's New Home," *Delaware Republic*, January 16, 1926, n. p.
108. Robin Karson, *Fletcher Steele, Landscape Architect*, (New York: Random House, Inc., 1989).
109. "Commodore E. T. Gerry Dead," *Catskill Mountain News*, February 28, 1927, p. 1.
110. *The Pierre Hotel- History and Heritage*, http://www.tajhotels.com/Luxury/Grand-Palaces-And-. Iconic-Hotels/The-Pierre-New-York/History-And-Heritage.html.
111. "Allows Chief Justice Taft to Accept Gerry Library," *The New York Times*, May 2, 1928, p.25.

APPENDIX B
NEW YORK CITY LOCATIONS

Lionel Pincus and Princess Firyal Map Division, The New York Public Library. "The Albemarle Hotel map of Manhattan, New York City : with index of streets and strangers' directory to business houses, public buildings, principal churches, places of amusement, etc. etc." New York Public Library Digital Collections. Accessed April 25, 2017. http://digitalcollections.nypl.org/items/510d47e4-736d-a3d9-e040-e00a18064a99

APPENDICES C- D
COMMODORE ELBRIDGE T. GERRY'S CHILDREN
COMMODORE ELBRIDGE T. GERRY'S GRANDSONS

1. "Streetscapes: A Garden Fence on E 95th Street," *The New York Times*, September 3, 2000, p. 5.
2. *Auction Catalog of Ancrum House Furnishings*, March, 1961, Parke-Bernet Galleries, Inc., New York, in the Gerry family collection at Lake Delaware, 2011.
3. Personal interviews with residents of Bovina Center, Shelley L. Dowling, New York, October, 2011.
4. Angelica Gerry Scrapbook, New York newspaper clipping without citation, Lake Delaware Farm House, Delhi, New York, 2011.
5. Letter of Advisement from Angelica's lawyer, advising her to add a codicil to her will, letter dated 1953 in the Gerry Family Papers, Hartwick College, Rare Books Room, One-onta, New York, 2010.
6. "Miss Gerry Deeply Loved Delhi Tech," *The Oneonta Star*, June 8, 1963, p. 1.
7. *Ralph Adams Cram*, http://en.wikipedia.org/wiki/Ralph_Adams_Cram.
8. "Angelica Livingston Gerry" (1871-1961), untitled and unsigned type-written manuscript in the *Gerry Family Papers*, Lake Delaware, New York, written sometime after 1996.
9. *Turk's Head Building*, http://en.wikipedia.org/wiki/Turk's_Head_Building.
10. *Biltmore House History*, http://www.biltmore.com/our_story/our_history/.
11. *Ibid.*
12. "Peter G. Gerry, Ex-Senator, Dies Hours Before His Brother," *The New York Times*, November 1, 1957, p. 26.

13. *Private Laws of the Sixty-Fifth Congress of the United States,* volume 38, chapter 14, p. 1109.
14. "Allows Chief Justice Taft to Accept Gerry Library," the *New York Times,* May 2, 1928, p. 25.
15. *Woods-Gerry House,* http://en.wikipedia.org/wiki/Woods-Gerry_House.
16. *Twelfth Catalogue of the Officers and Members of the Hasty Pudding Club,* Containing a Brief Sketch of the Club and an Index of Names, Harvard University Press, 1902, p. 173.
17. *Edward Roland Harriman,* en.wikipedia.org/wiki/E._Ro-land_Harriman.
18. Gerry Family Scrapbook Clippings and unpublished Gerry Family Reminisces essay by Betty Oles 1984, wife of Wilbur Oles, *Aknusti estate manager 1950's-1989,* examined at the Lake Delaware house and used with the permission of the Gerry family, 2010-2013.
19. Mark Simonson, The "Politics to Philanthropy," *Daily Star,* Delaware County, New York, January 18, 2003, p. 1.
20. "Andes Horse Brings $65,000," newspaper clipping, Gerry Scrapbook, Lake Delaware Farm, New York.
21. "Children's Society to Have Benefit," *The New York Times,* September 28, 1930, p. N6.
22. *Robert L. Livingston, Sr. Biography,* http://en.wikipedia.org/wiki/Main_Page.
23. *Gerry Family Reminisces* unpublished essay by Betty Oles 1984, wife of Wilbur Oles, Aknusti estate manager 1950's-1989, p. 31, examined at the Lake Delaware house and used with the permission of the Gerry family, 2010-2013.
24. *Id.,* Main Page.
25. Robert L. Gerry III, http://en.allexperts.com and http://en.wiipedia.org/wiki/Robert_L_Gerry_III.
26. "Girls League to be Beneficiary," *New York Sun,* January 19, 1947, p. 23.
27. *Martha Farrish Gerry,* http://www.thoroughbredtimes.com/national-news.
28. "Hall of Fame Day in Goshen Brings Crowd," *Times Herald-Record,* July 7, 2002, n. p.

APPENDIX E AMERICAN FAMILY LEGACIES

1. Maeva Marcus, *Documentary History of the Supreme Court,* 1789-1800, Volume 1, page xli Columbia University Press, New York, NY (1885).
2. *Id.,* page 27.

APPENDIX F EUROPEAN FAMILY ORIGINS

GALLATIN FAMILY ANCESTRY

1. Henry Adams, Life of Albert Gallatin, J.B. Lippincott & Co., Philadelphia, PA., 1879, p. 1.
2. *Ibid.,* Adams, p. 1.
3. *Ibid.,* Adams, p. 1.
4. *Id.,* Adams, p. 2.
5. Albert E. Gallatin A Fifteenth Century Mazer, , reprinted from *Art and Progress,* May 1914, DeVinne Press, New York, 40 copies printed on Roman parchment.
6. *Supra,* Adams, p. 2.
7. *Id.,* Adams, p. 3.
8. *Ibid.,* Adams, p. 3.
9. Gaspard de Gallatin, Journal of the Siege of Yorktown, translated from the original French manuscript by William A. R. Goodwin, United States Government Printing Office, 1931.
10. *Supra* Adams, pp. 4-5.
11. Theodore Tronchin 1709-1781, http://en.wikipdia.or/org/wiki/ThC3A90dore_Tronchin.
12. *Supra,* Adams, , pp.761-762.
13. *Ibid.,* Adams, 1879, p. 7-8.
14. The Prom en dates of the Chateau of La Roche-Guyon: Reflections on the Restoration of an Eighteenth Century Wilderness, *Historic Gardens Review,* Winter 2011, p. 3.
15. John Rae, *The Life of Adam Smith,* Chapter VII , 1895, pp. 4-5.
16. *Supra,* Adams, pp. 66-67.
17. "Biographical Memoir of Albert Gallatin," *The Democratic Review,* New York, June 1843, pp. 4, 6.
18. *Supra,* Adams, p.18.

F-5 THE GOELET FAMILY ANCESTRY

1. Discover La Rochelle History, http://www.francethisway.com/places.
2. Cardinal Richelieu's Conquest of La Rochelle: the Fall of the Huguenots and France's Subsequent Decline, http://www.huguenot-md.om/commentaries/.
3. *Ibid.,* Cardinal Richelieu.
4. Joseph Arthur Cossart, *The Cossart Family,* typed manuscript, New York: New York Historical Society 1936, p. 15.

5. "The Goelet's a Landmark New York Family," *Quest Magazine*, March 1989, pp.40-45. http://www.netprop.com/quest.htm.
6. John Austin Stevens, Colonial Record of the New York Chamber of Commerce, 1768-1784, p. 126-128. http://www.books.google.com/books.
7. Geoffrey T. Hellman, "You've Simply Got to Go Out and Raise the Scratch," *The New Yorker*, October 18, 1976, p. 46.
8. Richard Zacks, The Pirate Hunter, the True Story of Captain Kidd, pp.241,260, http://en.wikipedia.org/wiki/Gardiners _Island.
9. Gardiner's Island, Long Island, http://www.hamptonluxuryliner.com.

F-8 THE LIVINGSTON FAMILY ANCESTRY

1. Family Chart of Scottish Livingstons, http://www.hto-livingston.com/scotchart.html 2. William Wallace, http://en.wikipedia.org/wiki/William_ Wallace, p. 4.
3. Edwin Brockholst Livingston, The Livingstons of Callendar, http://www.falkirklocal historysociety. co.uk./home.
4. *Ibid.*, Livingston, p. xxiv.
5. Malcolm Campbell, Battles Lost but a Game Won, the Illustrious History of Scottish Golf, http://www.worldgolf.com.
6. Supra, Livingston, p. xxvi.
7. *Ibid.*, Livingston, p. xxvi.
8. *Ibid.*, Livingston, p. x xvii.
9. Edwin Brockholst Livingston, The Livingstons of Livingston Manor, 1910, pp.1-2.
10. *Ibid.*, Livingston, p. 20.
11. *Ibid.*, Livingston, p. 29.
12. *Ibid.*, Livingston p. 29.
13. *Id.*, Livingston p. 41.
14. *Id.*, Livingston, p. 46.
15. *Id.*, Livingston, p. 47.
16. Clare Brandt, *An American Aristocracy: The Livingstons*, (New York: Black Dome Press, 1986) p. 16.

TABLE OF CASES

This is a list of cases represented by Elbridge T. Gerry that were officially "reported" and published. Many cases that he argued simply were not reported at the discretion of the court. The cases below are grouped by year and listed alphabetically by case name.

Some cases in the text of the book were actually "hearings," for example the *Washington Square Market* case, and therefore were not true "cases" and not officially reported.

Elbridge T. Gerry represented hundreds of "hearings" before the Magistrate's Court as Legal Counsel to the *New York Society for the Prevention of Cruelty to Children*; these were never officially reported for publication unless they were appealed as a legal case in controversy. The most significant and representative *Magistrate Hearings* are discussed in the text of the book.

DATE	NAME & CITATION
1860	*Townsend v. Goelet*, 11 Abb. Pr. 187, 1860 WL 7751, N.Y. Supp., 1860
1861	*Fassett v. Tallmadge*, 13 Abb.Pr. 12, 1861 WL 5473, N.Y. Supp., 1861
1861	*Joyce v. City of New York*, 20 How. Pr. 439, 12 Abb.Pr. 309, 1861 WL4882, N.Y. Com. Pl., 1861
1861	*Martin v. The Mayor, & City of New York*, 12 Abb.Pr.242, 1861 WL 6325, N.Y., March Term 1861
1861	*In re Seventy-Sixth St.*, 12 Abb.Pr. 317, 1861 WL 5448, N.Y. Supp., 1861
1862	*Chauncy v. Arnold*, 10 E.P. Smith 330, 24 N.Y. 330, 1862 WL 4694, N.Y., 1862
1862	*Davenport v. Ruckman*, 23 N.Y. Super.Crt. 20, 16 Abb.Pr. 341, 1862 WL 4208, 10 Bosw. 20, N.Y. Super., 1862
1862	*In re Dwight's Case*, 15 Abb.Pr. 159, 1862 WL 4352, N.Y. Supp. Gen. Term, 1862
1862	*Fassett v. Tallmadge*, 23 How.Pr. 244, 14 Abb.Pr. 188, 37 Barb. 436, 1862 WL 4266, N.Y. Supp. Gen. Term, 1862

1862 *Fassett v. Tallmadge*, 15 Abb.Pr. 105, 1862, WL 4342, N.Y. Sup. Gen. Term,1862

1862 *Goelet v. Ross*, 15 Abb.Pr. 251, 1862, WL 4350, N.Y. Super., 1862

1863 *Fassett v. Tallmadge*, 18 Abb.Pr. 48, 1863 WL4055, N.Y. Supp. Gen. Ter., 1863

1863 *Johnston v. Johnston*, 16 Abb.Pr. 43, 1863 WL 5083, N.Y. Sup., May Term 1863

1863 *Johnston v. Johnston*, 25 How. Pr. 181, 1863 WL 5074, N.Y. June Term 1863

1863 *Pacific Mutual Insurance Co. v. Machado*, 16 Abb.Pr. 451, 1863 WL 4017, N.Y. Supp. Gen. Term, 1863

1863 *White v. Jones*, 24 N.Y. Super. Ct. 321, 1 Abb.Pr. N.S. 328, 1863 WL 3840, 1 Rob. NY) 321, N.Y. Super., 1863

1864 NO REPORTED CASES

1865 *Dunlevy v. Tallmadge*, 5 Tiffany 457, 32 N.Y. 457, 29 How. Pr. 397, 1865 WL 3976, N.Y., 1865

1865 *Rigney v. Tallmadge*, 19 Abb. Pr. 16, 1865 WL 3594, N.Y. Sup. Gen. Term, 1865

1865 *Walsh v. Washington Marine Insurance Co.*, 5 Tiffany 427, 32 N.Y. 427, 1865 WL 3326, N.Y.

1866 *Newall v. Wheeler*, 27 N.Y. Super.Ct. 190, 2 Abb.Pr.N.S. 134, 1866 WL 5172, 4 Rob. (NY) 190, N.Y. Super., 1866

1866 *People ex rel. Ritterman v. Kelly*, 1 Abb.Pr.N.S. 432, 1866 WL 5266, N.Y. Super. 1866

1866 *Strong v. Strong*, 28 N.Y.Super.Ct. 612, 1 Abb.Pr.N.S. 358, 1866 WL 5205, 5 Rob. (NY) 612, N.Y. Super., 1866

1866 *Right v. Ritterman*, 27 N.Y. Super.Ct. 704, 1 Abb.Pr.N.S. 428, 1866 WL5189, 4 Rob (NY) 704, N.Y. Super., 1866

1867 *Matsell v. Flanagan*, 2 Abb.Pr.N.S. 459, 1867 WL7862, N.Y.Com.Pl., 1867
1867 *Nash v. People of New York*, 36 N.Y. 607, June 1867

1867 *Osgood v. Laytin*, 3 Abb.Dec. 418, 3 Keyes 521, 37 How.Pr. 63, 5 Abb.Pr.N.S. 1,1867 WL 5776, 3 Transc.App. 124, N.Y., 1867

1867 *William Newell v. Ezra Wheeler, et al*, 9 Tiffany 244, 36 N.Y. 244, 1867 WL 7863, N.Y., March 1867

1868 *Burke v. Valentine,* 5 Abb.Pr.N.S. 164, 52 Barb. 412, 1868 WL 6029, N.Y. Sup. Gen. Term, 1868

1868 *Sowarby v. Russell,* 29 N.Y. Super.Ct. 322, 4 Abb.Pr.N.S. 238, 1868 WL 5781, 6 Rob. (NY) 322, N.Y. Super., 1868.

1868 *Ward v. Ward,* 5 Abb.Pr.N.S. 145, 1868 WL 5906, N.Y. Sup., 1868.

1869 *Knickerbocker Life Insurance* v. *Ecclesine,* 6 Abb.Pr.N.S. 9, Feb. 1869

1869 *Rockwell v. Merwin,* 31 N.Y.Super.Ct. 484, 8 Abb.Pr.N.S. 330, 1869 WL 6147, 1 Sweeny 484, N.Y.Super., 1869

1870 *In re McFarland,* 7 Abb.Pr.N.S. 348, 1870 WL 7393, N.Y.Gen.Sess. 1870

1870 *In re McFarland's Trial,* 8 Abb.Pr.N.S. 57, 1870 WL 7898, N.Y.Gen.Sess., 1870

1870 *Smith v. Miller,* 4 Hand 171, 43 N.Y. 171, 1870 WL 7765, 3 Am.Rep. 690, N.Y. 1870

1870 *Southwick v. Southwick,* 32 N.Y.Super.Ct. 234, 9 Abb.Pr.N.S. 109, 1870 WL 7337, 2 Sweeny 234, N.Y.Super., 1870

1871 *In re New York & H.R. Co.,* 11 Abb.Pr.N.S. 90, 1871 WL 9295, N.Y. Sup. Gen. Term, 1871

1871 *Price v. Price,* 9 Abb.Pr.N.S. 291, 1871 WL 9266, N.Y.Sup.Gen.Term, 1871

1872 *In re Bonard,* 16 Abb.Pr.N.S. 128, 1872 WL 9494, N.Y.Sup., 1872

1872 *Southwick v. Southwick,* 4 Sickles 510, 49 N.Y. 510, 1872 WL 9941, N.Y., 1872

1873 *Broadway & E.S. Storage Co. v. American Soc. for the Prevention of Cruelty to Animals,* 15 Abb.Pr.N.S. 51, 1873 WL 9871, N.Y. Com. Pl., 1873

1873 *Coulter v. Murray,* 4 Daly 506, 15 Abb.Pr.N.S.129, 1873 WL 9878, N.Y.Com.Pl., 1873

1874 *Davis v. Society for Prevention of Cruelty to Animals,* 16 Abb.Pr.N.S., 1874 WL 10867, NY.Com.Pl., 1874

1874 *People v. Brunell,* 48 How.Pr. 435, 1874 WL 9922, N.Y.Gen.Sess., 1874

1874 *People v .Morgan,* 13 Sickels 679, 58 N.Y. 679, 1874 WL 13544, N.Y., Nov. 1874

1874 *Smith v. City of New York,* 1 Hun. 56, 3 Thomp. & Co. 160, 47 How. Pr. 277, 1874 WL 10557, N.Y.Sup.Gen.Term, 1874

1874 *Wenzler v. People,* 2 Cow.Cr.Rep., 13 Sicklesl 516, 58 N.Y. 516, 1874 WL 11313, N.Y., 1874

1874 *Wolfe v. Burke*, 11 Sickels 115, 56 N.Y. 115, 1874 WL 9747, N.Y. 1874

1875 NO REPORTED CASES

1876 *Kip v. New York & H.R. Co.*, 22 Sickels 227, 67 N.Y. 227, 1876 WL 12745, N.Y. 1876

1877 NO REPORTED CASES

1878 *Davis v. American Society for the Prevention of Cruelty to Animals*, 30 Sickels 362, 75 N.Y. 362, 1878 WL 12754, N.Y. 1878

1878 *In re Lockman*, 4 Abb.N.Cas. 173, 1878 WL 11155, N.Y. Surr., 1878

1878 *Riggs v. Pursell*, 29 Sickels 370, 74 N.Y. 74, 1878 WL 12666, N.Y., 1878

1879 *Goelet v. Farley*, 57 How.Pr. 174, 1879 WL 9560, N.Y.Sup., 1879.

1879 *Goelet v. Hagan*, 31 Sickels 628, 76 N.Y. 628, 1879 WL 12281, N.Y. April 1, 1879

1879 *United States v Ancarola*, NY Circuit Court, Dec. 10, 1879, unreported

1880 *Bruce v. Platt*, 35 Sickels 379, 80 N.Y. 379, 1880 WL 12402, N.Y. 1880

1881 *Fleischmann v. Bennett*, 42 Sickels 231, 87 N.Y. 231, 1881 WL 13070, N.Y. 1881

1882 *Marx v. McGlynn*, 43 Sickels 357, 88 N.Y. 357, 1882 WL 12613, N.Y. 1882

1882 *People ex rel. New York Society for the Prevention of Cruelty to Children v. Gilmore*, 43 Sickels 626, 88 N.Y. 626, 1882 WL 12645, N.Y. 1882

1882 *In re Ramscar*, 1 N.Y.Crim.R. 33, 10 Abb.N.Cas. 442, 63 How.Pr. 255, 1882 WL 11425, N.Y. Sup., 1882

1883 *In re Moses*, 31 Hun. 45, 1 N.Y. Crim.R. 508, 13 Abb.N.Cas. 189, 66 How.Pr. 296, 1883 WL 12790, N.Y. Sup.Gen.Term, 1883

1884 *Livingston v. Sage*, 50 Sickel 289, 95 N.Y. 289, 1884 WL 12297, N.Y., 1884

1884 *Livingston, Executor v. Webb*, Not reported in N.E., 50 Sickels 658, 95 N.Y. 658, 1884 WL 14164, N.Y. March 11, 1884

1885 *In re application of Union Ferry Co. of Brooklyn*, 53 Sickels 139, 98 N.Y. 139,1885 WL 10540, N.Y., 1885

1886 *Matter of Gerry*, the Final Accounting of Elbridge T. Gerry as Trustee, Court of Appeals of New York, Nov. 23, 1886

1886 *People ex rel. Van Heck v. New York Catholic Protectory*, 56 Sickels 195, 01 N.Y. 195, 4 N.E. 177, 3 How.Pr. (n.s.) 343, N.Y. Jan. 19, 1886

1887 *People ex rel. Van Riper v. New York Catholic Protectory*, 61 Sickels 604, 106 N.Y. 604, 13 N.E. 435, N.Y. Oct. 4, 1887

1888 NO REPORTED CASES

1889 *In re Bennett*, 5 N.Y.S. 373, N.Y. Sup., January 22, 1889

1889 *In re Diss Debar*, 3 N.Y.S. 667, N.Y. Sup., January 7, 1889

1890 *Carpenter v. People ex rel. Brown*, 78 Sickels 640, 123 N.Y. 640, 25 N.E. 1044, N.Y., October 1890

1890 *People ex rel. Brown v. Carpenter*, 57 Hun. 588, 32 N.Y. St Rep. 822, 11 N.Y.S. 852, N.Y. Sup. Gen. Term, June 6, 1890

1891 *People ex rel. Cohen v. Protestant Episcopal House of Mercy*, 83 Sickels 625, 128 N.Y. 625, 28 N.E. 477, N.Y. October 6, 1891

1892 *Kuhn v Protestant Episcopal House of Mercy*, 88 Sickles 207, 133 N.Y. 207, 30 N.E. 853, Apr 26, 1892

1893 *In re Ewer*, 70 Hun 239, 54 N.Y. St. Rep. 348, 24 N.Y.S. 500, N.Y. Sup. Gen. Term, June 30, 1893

1893 *Sanders v. Grant*, 70 Hun. 233, 54 N.Y.St.Rep. 349, 24 N.Y.St. 776, N.Y. Sup. Gen. Term, June 30, 1893

1893 *Whitehead v. Halsey*, 3 Misc.378, 52 N.Y. St.Rep. 263, 22 N.Y.S. 923, April 1893

1894 *People v. Ewer*, 25 L.R.A. 794, 9 N.Y.Crim.R. 1, 96 Sickels 129, 141 N.Y. 129, 36 N.E. 4, 56 N.Y.St.Rep. 668, 38 Am.St.Rep. 788, N.Y., January 30, 1894

1895 NO REPORTED CASES

1896 *Dept. of Buildings v. Richard Field*, 9 A.D. 500, 41 N.Y.S. 1112, October 1896

1896 *Limbeck v. Gerry*, 15 Misc.663, Feb. 1896 (false imprisonment)

1896 *People v. Giles*, 12 A.D. 495, 42 N.Y.S. 749, N.Y.A.D. 1 Dept., December 22, 1896

1896 *Plot v. Poly*, 17 Misc. 162, 11 N.Y.Crim.R. 346, 40 N.Y.S. 990, N.Y.Gen.Sess., May 1896

1897 *People v. Giles,* 12 N.Y.Crim.R. 103, 6 E.H. Smith 136, 152 N.Y. 136, 46 N.E. 326, N.Y. March 2, 1897

1897 *People ex rel. James v. Society for the Prevention of Cruelty to Children,* 19 Misc. 677, 44 N.Y.S. 1100, N.Y.Sup., March 1897

1897 *People ex rel. Lazarus v. Protestant Episcopal House of Mercy,* 23 A.D. 383, 38 N.Y.S. 217, N.Y.A.D. 1 Dept., December 10, 1897

1898 *People ex rel. State Board of Charities v. New York Society for the Prevention of Cruelty to Children,* 25 Misc. 53, 53 N.Y.S. 1017, N.Y.Sup., October 1898

1899 – 1906 NO REPORTED CASES

1907 *In Re Piers, Old NOS 19, 20, East River,* 117 A.D.553, 102 N.Y.S.667, Feb. 8, 1907

1908-1914 NO REPORTED CASES

1915 *Fulton v. Ingalls,* 170 A.D. 904, 155 N.Y.S. 788, N.Y.A.D. 2 Dept., July 30, 1915

1928 *Meinhard v Salmon,* 249 N.Y. 458, 164 N.E. 545 (1928)
Decided after Elbridge T. Gerry's death in 1927

INDEX

Bold text is used for significant names or important subjects.
Italic used for illustrations and quotations.

A

Abbott, Francis, 5, 77
Academy of Music NYC, 38, 41
  Ball, Prince Albert Edward, 51
  Replaced by, 160, 202
Academy of Science, Berlin, 52
Academy of the Holy Cross NYC
  Angelica Gerry, 134
Adams,
  Abigail, xvii, 18, 505
  Henry, x, xvii, 14, 15, 18
  John, iv
  John Quincy, 612, 98 *quotation*
  John Quincy, Jr., 134
  Samuel, 7
Adams, Herbert, Sculptor 301
  Bryant, William Cullen, statue in Central Park NYC, 301
  Gerry marble bust, *314*
  Library of Congress doors, 301
Aiken Polo Team, 579
Airth Castle, Scotland, 629
Aknusti, 2,000 acre estate at Lake Delaware, Robert L. Gerry, 9, 517
  Architects, Walker & Gillette, 477
  Description, detailed, 570
    Buildings and staff homes, 477, 571
      Carriage house, 477, 571
      Fowl house, 477, 571
      Game keeper, 477, 571
      Gate house, 477, 571
      Manager, 477, 571
      Mansion, fifty rooms, 477, 577
      Stable, indoor track, 571, 575
  Landscape, Frederick Law Olmsted, Jr., 571
Albany Bridge, New Brunswick, N.J., 55
Albany Cathedral, Bldg. Committee, 205
Albany, New York, 632
Alma Mater statue, Columbia, 419, *461*
American Equal Rights Association, 168
American Philosophical Society, 53
American Revolution, 3, 6
  Committee on Correspondence, 7
  Committee on Supplies, 7
  Continental Congress, 8, 10, 13, 14
  Paul Revere, 8
  Provincial Congress, Elbridge Gerry, 7
  Trade ships become war ships, 9
  Traded goods for arms, 6, 9-12
  Wetherby Black Horse Tavern, 8
American Seamen's Friend Society, 254-255
  Book collections for ships, 255
  Elbridge T. Gerry, donor and Society member, 255
  Ship's visitor, 255
  Thirty thousand libraries sent, 255
American Society for the Prevention of Cruelty to Animals, 100+
  Agent badges, 109
  Animal ambulance, 101
  Bergh badge, diamonds, 161
  Bergh and Gerry disagree, 123, 140
  Bergh Contempt case, 124
  Board members:
    James T. Gallatin, 121
    Frederic Gallatin, 121,161
    Gerry, Elbridge T., 161
    Tiffany, Charles, 161
  Bonard Will case, 102, 104, 107

Building owned, 142
Connelly, Mary, child abuser, 118
Elbridge T. Gerry, legal counsel, 102
Elbridge T. Gerry, Service Cup, 110
"Great Meddlars," 101
International Humane Soc., 46, 170
Legislation, 131
Mary Ellen case, 117-119
Mary Ellen's Statement, 118
America's Cup, 174-175
Deed of Gift, NYYC, 174, 243
Elbridge T. Gerry, 174
First race, 174
Amsterdam, Holland, 617-618, 632
Ancrum, Lake Delaware,
Angelica Gerry mansion, 551-552
Dairy business, 553
Gardens designed by Fletcher Steele over two decades, 552
Penelope, white marble sculpture by Franklin Simons, purchased in Rome in 1867 by E.T. Gerry, 236, 552
Ancrum, Scotland, 630-631
Anne, Queen 1708 Hardenburgh Patent,
Antonine Wall, 625
Architects
Cram, Ralph, 551-552
See also
St. James Church, Bovina, 551
Builders, Jacob & Young,
St. John the Divine, 551
MIT, Head Architecture Dept., 551
New York Times, prominent Episcopal layman, 551
Time Magazine body of work, 551
Hunt, Richard Morris,
Gerry, Elbridge T., 292, 294, 324
Goelet, Ogden, 294
Vanderbilt, George, 294, 515
Gibson, Robert W. *British,* 205
Albany Cathedral, NY, 205
Gilbert, Cass, designed U.S. Court building with a library to hold the Elbridge T. Gerry gift collection, xvi, 598, 602
Kendall, Edward H., architect, 156
Goelet, Ogden, 156
Goelet, Robert, 156
McKim, Mead, White, 46, 200
Madison Garden, 443
Renwick, James Jr., 125
Breezy Lawn, L.I., 129, 134, 138, *151*
Fifth Ave, Gallatins, 125
Warren, Whitney,
Grand Central Terminal, 306
New York Yacht Club, 407, *459*
Newport Golf Club, 306, *319*
White, Stanford,
Southside, Newport, 180, *193*
Washington Square Arch, 260+, *272*
Zucker, Alfred, Gerry, 325, 367-371, *400*
Arden Homestead Stables, 430, 445, *457*
Aknusti Stud, 499, 586
Arden House, Orange County, NY, 430, 468, 567, 588
Edward Henry Harriman, 428+, 569, *457*
Astor, John Jacob, father of William B., 45
Astor, John Jacob III, 115
Married Charlotte Gibbes, 115
Mrs. John J. Astor, 115
Partner - Frederic Gallatin, 125
Peter Goelet funeral, 146
Astor, John Jacob IV, 290, 305
Astor Cup fun winter sports held in St. Moritz, France, 403
Continued Goelet Cup, yachts, 200, 379
Guests travel from NYC to Philadelphia by train, 290
Married Ava Willing, 290
Astor, William Backhouse, married Margaret Alida Rebecca Armstrong, 45, 57
Astor, William Backholst II,
Children's Aid Society, 57, 288
Auburn State Prison, New York, 219
First execution by electric chair 264+, 273
Austin, James Trecothick., 95
Death, 95
Married Catharine Gerry, 95
Automobiles, new hazard, 405, 471, 474, 494, 573
Gallatins, first in East Hampton, L.I .to own a car, 406
Gerry, Angelica, touring, 494, 504, 510
Gerry, Louisa M. paid local towns to pave local roads, 484, 491

Gerry, Robert L. collided with horse drawn carriage, 471
Goelet, Robert Wilson, riding with chauffeur kills child, 474
Racing, Vanderbilt track, 580

B

Bache, Benjamin Franklin, 613
Balliol, King John, 625
Balsan, Consuelo Vanderbilt, 350
Balsan, Jacques, 350
Bancroft, George, historian, 164
Banking. *See also* Panic of…
Chemical Bank, Goelet, xviii, 36, 43, 91, 135, 154, 619
Gallatin National Bank, 75, 126, 478
Absorbed by Hanover National Bank, 478, 573, 586
Gold Standard, 138
Bar Harbor, Maine, holidays, 214, 226, 425, 440, 452, 466, 470, 484
Belmont Hotel, 214
West End Hotel, xviii, 10, 53414
Bar of the City of New York,
Book donation plea, 75, *112*, 271
Creation, 85
Death of Chief Justice, 161
Elbridge T. Gerry, 45, 49, 72, 155, 453
Library Committee, E.T. Gerry, 103
Lord Coleridge, Britain, visit, 200
Arrived on the Celtic, 201
Departed on Britannic, 202
Interview, dynamiters, 201
Port transfer on Gerry yacht, the Pastime, 200-201
Son, Gilbert, sang, 201
Bar of the State of New York, 131,134, *148*
Bar of the U.S. Supreme Court, 43, 161, 188
Certificate, Elbridge T. Gerry, *62*
Robert Goelet, 620
Barnum, P.T., 83, 84, 101, 105. 127, 190, *195*
Death, 299
Baseball, 242, 381, 415, 506
Gallatin family, 452
Bachelor Girls, 472, 504, 510, 512, 514
Bear Mountain National Historic Park, Harriman family gift, 569
Palisades Founder's Award from the N.Y. State Conservancy, 569
Bee incident on Fifth Avenue, 476
Beekman, Margaret, 535, 623
Bellomont, Lord, 622
Bellevue Hospital, 216
Bloomingdale Asylum, 356
Bloomingdale Hospital, NYC, 59, *64*
Belmont, August *banker*, 54, 122, 309, 332
Fox hunt, 475
Horse breeding, 427, 438
Horse racing, 437, 475
Belmont, August Jr., 568
Horse breeding, 572, 465, 499
Polo, 568
Racing, 437
Yachting, 405
Bellevue Mansion,
Bentnick, George Cavendish, MP of the British Museum, married Elizabeth Livingston, twin of Ruth, 46, 514
Churchill relation by marriage, 293
Duke of Portland, 277, 278
Lived in Richmond on the Thames outside London, 293
Bergh, Henry, 100, *276*
ASPCA, 100,101, 110
Animals not children, 156
Badge, gold with diamonds, 161
Given to ASPCA, 251
Bonard's will dispute, 102, 104
Central Park monument, 251
Clay pigeon decoys, 251
Contempt case, 124
Death, succeeded by son, 251, 254
Description, 100, 209
Disagrees with E.T. Gerry, 123, 140
Funeral, St. Mark's Church, 251
Gerry, E.T., legal counsel, 104, Tiffany Cup 110, *112*
Great meddler, 124
Horse ambulance cart, 102,*276*
Horse cruelty, 109
Mary Ellen case, 117-123

Vanderbilt, Cornelius, 105
William Seward, 100
"Bertie," nickname Prince Albert Edward 306, *316*
Lillie Langtry, 306, *316*
Metropolitan Ball, 60, 66
Bicycles, 366, 514
Scorching, 365
Billias, George, biographer, 9, 12
"Billy Budd," Herman Melville, 227-228
Explored death penalty, 228
Biltmore Estate, North Carolina, 358, 515, *525*, 553, 558, 560, *565*
Blackstone's Commentaries, xv, 21, *42*, 61, 601
Blackwell's Island Prison, 158, 168, 298
Bloomingdale Mental Hospital, 356
Boston, MA, 3-5, 10, 14, 16+, 49, 52, 70, 79, 82, 84, 95, 163, 175, 189, 200, 237, 240, 242, 332, 334, 605, 613, 522
Boston Committee on Correspondence in American in the Revolution, 3-5
Bostwicks Point, 622
Bourse Gallatin Trust, 612
Boys Clubs, 428, *457*, 477, 521, 567, 569, 573, 580, 588, 591
Box list, Gerry library gift, xvi
Brace, Charles L., 57+
Children's Aid Society, 58
Orphan trains, 58
"Braveheart," William Wallace, 625, 629
Breezy Lawn, Gallatin cottage, 130, *151*
East Hampton, 166, 336+
Completed, 158
Demolished, 138
Expanded, 164
Renwick, James Jr., 166
Summers, Jean and Hannah, 176, 185
Broadway Farm, 32, *61*, 96, 619
Almy Goelet Gallatin inherited the property, 362
Book collection, 38, 86, 108, 155, 187
Demolished, 362
Developed the property, 362
Doll house, 30, *81*
Hannah alone, 185, 361
Jean and Hannah alone, 115, 145
Neighbors as children:
Frederic Gallatin, 416
Teddy Roosevelt, 416
Peacocks, 70
Street Widening, 96
Brown Brothers Harriman, 499, 568, 583+, 586
Bryce, James, 614
Buchanan, xviii, 115, 534,
Almy, 26, 31, 35, 619
Margaret, 619
Thomas, 619
Business School, Harvard, 449

C

Callendar House, *Scotland*, 626-629
Calvin, John, 609, 616
Cannon, Jannettie, 534, 618
Capital punishment, history
England, 216
Beheading to end, 216, 227
Death Penalty ends, 227
Gallows Drop rules, 227
Billy Budd, Herman Melville, 227
Explored death penalty, 228
Capital Punishment, New York State Commission, 228
Chairman, Elbridge T Gerry, 228
Electrical Execution Act, 251
Gerry, Elbridge T. article in "North American Review," 265
Kemmler, William, first execution by Electric chair, 264-265
Auburn State Prison, 264, *273*
"Report of Commission," 251
Spectacle abandoned, 216
Capitol of the U.S. xvi, 13, 18, 19, 78, *314*, 515, 521, 561, 601
Carnegie, Andrew, *quotation*, 277
Carnegie public libraries, xvii, 294
"Gospel of Wealth," 277, 304
Carnival of Cops, dinner, 218-220
Cars. *See* Automobiles
Carter, President Jimmy, *quotation*, 539
Cases. *See* Law, cases.

Catharine the Great's black pearls purchased
by Mathilde Gerry, 512
Background of Yusupov family that had to sell the pearls, 512-513
Cecil, Lord Robert, husband of Cornelia Vanderbilt, the daughter of George and Edith, 515, 558, 559
Charles, King 1639 manor, 622
Charles II, King Scotland, 628-630
Chateaux La Roche-Guyon, 611, 613
Cecil, John F.A., descendant of William Cecil, advised Queen Elizabeth I, 559
Married Cornelia Vanderbilt, 558
Daughter of Edith Gerry, 515
Chemical Bank, NYC, 36, 43, 91, 135, 154, 619
Chi Psi Fraternity, 165, 210, 435
Chicago World's Fair, 312
Festival Hall in Chicago incorporated Manhattan Day, 313
Fund Raising by E. T. Gerry, 313
New York City, Mayor's Executive Committee, 313
Gerry, Elbridge T. member, 313
Chickering Hall *248*
Bell, Alexander G. made first telephone call from New Brunswick New Jersey to Chickering Hall audience, 213
Gerry, Elbridge T. Parks Bill, 213
Huxley, Thomas H. lecture, 213
Post, George B., Architect, 213
Wilde, Oscar, lecture, 213
Children of New York,
Age of release, case, 300
Catholic Asylum for Infants, 217
Catholic Protectory, 244
Children's Aid Society, 57-58
Astor, Mrs. William B., 57
Charles L. Brace, 58
Orphan trains, 58
Cottage Place School, 289
Episcopal House of Mercy, 295, 300, 379
Gerry Society, 121+, 365, 415, 429
New York Juvenile Asylum, 287
New York Society for the Prevention of Cruelty to Children, 117-119,121-123
Mary Ellen Case, 117-123, 472
Mosby case, 161-163
New York Times, 133-134
Parental notification, 244
Parental rights case, 217, 261
Shepherd's Fold, 157, 168
Ramscar Unsectarian Home, 222
Christopher Columbus statue, 333, *396*
Benediction, Bishop Potter, 332
Dedication in Central Park, 332
Guests, 332
Julia Ward Howe poem, 333, *396*
Sculptor, Jeronimo Sunol, 333
Gerry, Elbridge T. donor, 333
Churches
Cathedral of Saint John the Divine, 516, 519
Drury, Mabel Gerry, memorial altar, 544, *547*
Gerry, Elbridge T. funeral mass, 578
Gerry, memorial column for Elbridge & Louisa Gerry, 520, 544, 551
Gerry, Robert L., 573
Church of the Heavenly Rest, 224, 541 597
Robert J Livingston funeral, 291
Church of the Resurrection, 224, 541
Gerry, Angelica member, 541
Church of the Transfiguration, 115, 159, 504, 541, *547*
British visitors made the church well known to royalty, 541-542
Gerry, Louisa M., funeral, 504
Gerry, Mabel, active in, 541
Gerry, Margaret, baptized, 541
Funeral, 4 years old, 541
"Little Church around the Corner," nickname, 541
Actors who attended:
Sir Laurence Olivier, 541
Tallulah Bankhead, 541
"frivolous saint," 541
Memorial to Mabel, 543
Ray, Rev. Randolph, pastor:
Married Mary Watson, cousin of Mabel Gerry, 543
Queen Mary has tea, 543

Grace Church, Bishop Potter, 210
Gerry, Robert L. married Cornelia Harriman, 448
Saint Edward the Martyr,
Funeral, 297
Lillian Gerry, 520, *531*
Saint James, Hyde Park,
Burials:
Elbridge Thomas Gerry 519
Francis Drury, 545, 553
General Morgan Lewis, 510
Gertrude Livingston Lewis 510
Lillian Gerry, 478
Louisa M. Gerry, 504
Louisa M. Storm Livingston, 189, 291, 492
Mabel Gerry Drury, 545, 553
Margaret Pearl Gerry, 108
Maturin Livingston 253
Robert J. Livingston, 291, 492
Saint James, Lake Delaware, 555
Altar painted in 1320 in Venice and imported, 513
Anglo Catholic, 518, 551
Established, 510
Parish Hall and rectory completed, 512
Saint Luke's, NYC, 135
Saint Mary's Church, 323
Father John Drumgoole, 323
Saint Patrick's Cathedral,
Archbishop Corrigan's Silver Anniversary, 384
Gerry speech, 323, 384
Saint Thomas, NYC,
Gerry, Angelica, 575
Trinity Chapel, NYC,
Gallatin, Rolaz married, 364
Gerry:
Angelica confirmed by Bishop Potter, 222, 541
Elbridge & Louisa married, 80
Lillian confirmed by Bishop Potter, 251, funeral, 297
Mabel confirmed by Bishop Potter, 251, married, 514
Trinity Church, NYC,
Gallatin, James, funeral 126
Gerry, Almy, married 75
Goelet, Robert Jr funeral, 389
Hoffman, Rev. Eugene A. funeral, 412
Hunt, Richard Morris, funeral 358
Indian Charities, 115
Niobrara League, 115
Women's Auxiliary, 115
Churchill, Sir Winston, 293, *396*
Cousin and friend of:
Consuelo Vanderbilt, Duchess of Marlborough, divorced, 350, *394*
Consuelo Vanderbilt Balsan, 293, 350,
Iron Curtain speech, 351,*396*
Leonard Jerome, 69
Pamela Harriman, daughter-in-law, 499
Quotation, 115
Circus. *See also* Barnum, P.T.
One ring circus proposal, 299
Madison Square Garden, 190
Nouveau Cirque, Paris, 299
Civic duty, 41, 103, 145, 166, 177, 254, 412, 439, 474,
Quotation, 1
Civil War,
Draft riots, longshoremen, 69
Leonard Jerome, 69
Draft suspended in NYC, 70
Emancipation Proclamation, 69
Enrollment Act, 68
Gallatin, Frederic, Vice-Judge Advocate, Army, 75
Gallatin, James, brother of Frederic 87
Gerry, Elbridge T.,
Draft substitution, 69
Riots - Broadway Farm, 70
Goelet, draft substitution, 69
Lincoln, Abraham, 69
Roosevelt, substitution, 69
Clans of Scotland, 626
Crichton, 626
Douglas, 626
Livingston, 626
Clap, John, "1697 Almanak," 618
Clermont Manor, NY, xviii, 177, 535
Cleveland, President Grover, 281, 296
Financial crisis meeting on Gallatin yacht Almy, 309-310

Cliff Walk, Newport RI, *193*, 375, 405, 488, 514
Clinton, De Witt, *defeat,* 16
Clinton, George, death, 16
Clubs, NYC,
Bachelors Ball sponsored by Clubs, 171
Century Club, 54
Knickerbocker Club, 54
Metropolitan Club,
Architect, McKim, Mead & White, gated entry, 292
Members were old money: 292
Gerry, Elbridge T. 292
Goelet brothers, 292
Morgan, JP, 292
Whitney, 292
Vanderbilt, 292
Next door to Gerrys, 292
Split off Union Club, 291
Women, space provided, 292
Union Club,
Divided members, 291
Break-away club called Millionaires Club, 291
Coaching, sport, 282
Central Park, 282, 292
Coaching Club House, 283
Four-in-Hands, 282
Carriage runs from NYC to Belmont Park, 333, 437
Gerry, Angelica scrapbook, 442
300 mile round trip long-distance run to Lake Delaware, 442, 567
Gerry annual long-distance carriage run from NYC to Lake Delaware, with guests on carriages, 442
Dinner, 283
Parade:
Belmont, August, 282, 437
Belmont, Perry, 282
Gerry, Angelica, 282
Club membership, 432
Roosevelt, James, 282
Whip, carriage driver, 282
Gerry, Angelica, 283
Gerry, Robert L., 283
Harriman, Mary, 433
Vanderbilt, Alfred, 437
Whitney, Harry Payne, 437
Women's Coaching Clubs:
Dorcas Coaching Club, 432
Four-in-Hand Driving Club, 432
For public streets, 432
Gerry, Angelica, President, 283
See also Horse culture.
Codfish Aristocracy, 3
Coenties Slip, No. 9, inherited grocery Louisa M. Gerry, 51, 53
Coesaar, Janettie, 615, 617
Columbia College,
Kings College, xiv, 46
Butler Library, 46
Elbridge Thomas Gerry, 45
Chi Psi Alumni Society, 478
Law school lecture, 138
Paid for repairs to Alpha Delta Lodge,
Rare Book Room, 46
Robert Jr., 39
Memorial in his name, 419
Seated *Alma Mater* marble statue at Columbia University, 419, *461*
Columbian Exposition, *See* Chicago World's Fair
Commission on Capital Punishment
Chairman, Elbridge T Gerry, 226
Process used, 227
Report of Commission, 249
Committee of One Hundred, 618
Company, Colonial venture, 4
Concordat of Bologna, 616
Constitution, New York State 1867
Convention to Revise, 77
Constitution of the United States,
Elbridge Gerry won't sign, 12
Elbridge Gerry proposals:
Bills of Attainder, 12
Bill of Rights, 12
Cooper, Susan Fennimore, 495
Father, James Fennimore Cooper, 495
Rural Hours, author, 495
Susan Fennimore Cooper Foundation, 495
Cooperstown Orphanage, 495

Gerry, Angelica, fund raiser for the orphanage, 495
Gerry mansion dinner, 495
Cooper Union, New York City,
Democrats meeting, 296
Founders, 254
Gerry, E.T. elected a vice chair, 296
Cornfield anecdote, 8
Cotillion, dance led by bachelor, 186, 220, 290, 321
Cozzens Hotel, West Point NY, 74, *88*
Gerry & Goelet families, 128, 138
J.P. Morgan, 138
Crichton, Lord, Scotland, 626
Cromwell, Oliver, 630
Cushing, Robert, sculptor, 323
Death in studio, 324
Father Drumgoole statue in Central Park, 323
Curtenius, Peter T., 618

D

D'Auret, Francois-Marie (*Voltaire*), 6, 611+
D'Enville, Duchess, France, 610-613
D'Hautville Cottage, Newport, 544, 546
D'Orleans, Count Philippe, Paris, 286, *314*
Army of the Potomac, 286
Staff member to General George McClellan, 286
Gerry, E.T., escort on *Electra,* 286
Loyal Legion, Philadelphia, 286
Dacres, Margaret, 617
Dallas, Alexander Report USSC, 20
Darnsley, Lord, 626
Daughters of the American Revolution,
Emily Gerry, 347
Mary Clap Wooster Chapter, 347
David II, King of Scotland, 626
Death penalty,
"Billy Budd," by Melville, 227
Commission on Capital Punishment, New York, 228
Commission methodology, 228
Electric Chair alternative, 237, 250
Electrical Execution Act, 264
Gerry, Elbridge T. Chairman of Commission, 265
Gallows in America, 228
New York State debate, 226+
Report of Commission, 264
Deaths of Gerry and Goelet brothers, 36
Debutantes, described, 215-216
Declaration of Independence, 9, 18, 20, 32, 48, 51, 177, 347
Delmonico Restaurant, NYC, 218
See also Restaurants
Carnival of Cops dinner, 218
Devonshire, England, 1-2
DeWitt, George, 145
Diary of Elbridge Gerry, Jr., 16
Diary of Francis Goelet, 26
Diary of James Gallatin, 614
Dog Show, Madison Square Garden, 474
Goelet, Robert Wilson, 474
Glenmere Kennels, 474
Doll house, Goelet brownstone, 36, *61*, 80
Dominican Monastery, Perth, 626
Dorchester House, London, 421, *456*
Ambassador Reid residence, 421, 426, 451, 482
Fourth of July celebrations, 451
Drumgoole, Father John, funeral, St. Patrick's Cathedral, 323
Gerry, Elbridge T., speaker, 323
Mission of the Immaculate Virgin, 324
Newsboys Shelter, 323
Statue in Central Park, 323
Dedication ceremony, 353+
Pope Leo XIII letter, 324
Drury, Francis Saxon Knight of the *Order of Saint John*, 540, 543, 544
Married Mabel Gerry, 514
Sold 95th Street Townhouse to the Lycee Francais for a French school in New York City, 545
Son, Captain Vyvyan Drury, the *Aide de Camp* to the Duke of Windsor at his abdication, 545
Drury House, London, 517, 543
Duchess of Roxburghe, 422+, *461*
May Goelet, daughter of Ogden and Mary Wilson Goelet, 423, 424

Duke of Alba, Spain, courted Mathilde Townsend, 448
Duke of Brunswick, 610
Duke Franz Joseph, Goelet guest, 472
Duke of Marlborough, *394*
Newport visits Consuelo Vanderbilt, 350
Duke of Roxburghe, *461*
Carried the crown at King Edward VII coronation, 424
Children - only one,
George Victor Innes-Kerr, 424
Godparents, King George V and Queen Mary, 424
Son of Lady Ann Spencer Churchill, 423
Floors Castle, Scotland, 424, *461*
Innes-Kerr, Henry John, 8th Duke 423, *461*
Knight of Thistle, by King Edward VII, 424
Married May Goelet, 424
Description of couple, 424
Saint Thomas Church, NYC, 424
Ochre Court visit to announce engagement of May Goelet, daughter of Ogden, 423
Royal Horse Guard, best player on polo team, 424
Wimborne House dinner for "Bertie"
Prince Albert host, Mary Goelet, 307
Duke of Savoy, 608
Duke Boris Vladimirovich, Russia, 295
Goelet, Mrs. Ogden, hosts the Grand Duke at *Ochre Court*, 413
Accidental death of maid during visit, 413

E

Earl of Dudley, Sir John Hubert Ward, Second Earl of Dudley, 451, *456*
Commander Household Cavalry, Queen Elizabeth II, 451
Equerry-in-Waiting to the King, 498, 451
Married Jean Reid at Queen's Chapel, in Saint James Palace, London, *456*
King and Queen attend, 451
Children: Edward Ward,
Godson of King Edward VII, 451
Live at Dudley House, London, 451
Earl of Somerset, 626
East Hampton, Long Island, 129
Gallatin, Frederic and Almy
Breezy Lawn, 130, 138, 369
Gallatin, James, brother of Frederic
Death, 286 at East Hampton
East Hampton home, 286
East River, NYC, 11
Ebby, succession of Gerry "nickname," 452, 468, 477, 518, 566
Edinburgh, Scotland, 611, 625-631
Edinburgh Castle, 627
Edison, Thomas Alva, *273*
Electric chair, 250
Yacht lights for Electra, 39
Edward I, King, 625
Edward VII, King, 51, *316*
Called "Bertie" when a Prince, 420
Ball in NYC 1860, 51
Biarritz, France for health, 467
Bunker Hill - Mr. Farnham, 51
Death, Buckingham Palace, 467
Bronchitis and cigars, 467
Last words, his race horse, 467
Mistress at death bed, 467
Camilla Parker Bowles, 467
Successor, his son crowned King George V, 468
Uncle of Europe, 420
Queen Alexandra, 451
Edwardian Era, 420, 431
Electric Light Baths, 431
Goelet, Ogden, friendship 426
Cowes, England, 375, 426
Invite to Newport, 356
Preparations, 356
King of England, 459-460
Accomplishments, 420
Coronation, 424
Peacemaker, 420
Lilly Langtry, mistress, 307+
Visits America in youth, 51
Wimborne House, London,
Guest at Goelet dinner, 307, 375, 391
Elbridge, Rebecca, 4

Electra, steam yacht Elbridge T. Gerry, *317*
207-208, 237, *245, 402*
Collision, 266
Dismantled, 310, *317,* 479
Flag Ship, NYYC, 207, 214, 222, 226, 239
Salvaged by Robert L. Gerry for Aknusti, Chalice & Paten sent to Lake Delaware Boys Camp Chapel, 477
Steam Launch kept by E. T. Gerry, 479
Electric Chair, New York State Commission, Commission's Methodology, 228
Edison, Thomas Alva, 251
Elbridge T. Gerry, Chairman, 228
Electrical Execution Act, NY, 264
Kemmler execution, 219
Report of the Commission, 251
Elizabeth I, Queen, 558
Elizabeth City, NJ bankrupt,
Gerry sues for Goelets, 143
Elmwood, Cambridge, MA, 11, 13, 22, 33, 70
Emerson, Ralph Waldo, 51
Quotation, 465
Episcopal Church, Scotland, 631
Episcopal Church, NYC,
Albany Cathedral, 205
Bishop Grafton Sarcophagus, Fond duLac WI, 489+
Funded by Gerry, E.T., 489
Bishop Potter, 222, 332
Bishop William Doane, 55
Cram, Ralph, architect, Time Magazine named most influential laymen, 551
Christopher Columbus statue dedication, 332
Diocesan Convention, 128, 130, 155
Gerry, Elbridge T., 385
Commission on Ecclesiastical Relations, board member, 385
Doctorate of Divinity, Honorary, bestowed by Nashotah House Seminary, 189, 490
General Theological Seminary, Board of Trustees, 385
Gerry family religious worship was Anglo-Catholic, 518, 551, 491
Gerry, Angelica and Mabel, 439, 551
Establish St. James parish in Bovina, NY next to Lake Delaware estate, 439, 551
Grace Church, 210
Heresy, Rev. Newton, 188
Hoffman, Rev. Eugene A., Dean, General Theological Seminary, 385, 411
Married Glovinia Storm, 411
Uncle of Louisa M Gerry, 411
Home for Incurables, 60
Newton, Rev., heresy, 188
Oxford movement of the Anglican Church, 491
Eustis, William *Gerry family letter,* 15
Exeter, England, 1
Exile to Holland, *Livingston,* 605, 632

F

Fads
Christmas trees, 289
Deep sea fishing, 309
Electric light baths, vitamin D, 431
Fortune telling, 206
Mansion building, 206
Roller skating, 452
Scorching, bicycles, 365
Sewing circles, 352
Walking, called the "constitutional" started by Louisa M. Gerry, 431
Walking, Paris, France, 447
Winter sports, 218
Fairs (cattle, cheese, onion) England, 2
Falkirk, Scotland, 625-629
Farkoa, Maurice, singer, 455
Gerry Party, 403
Langtry, Lillie, charity, 403
Ferney Estate, Geneva, 611
Fire in Fifth Avenue Gerry mansion while entertaining, 512
Fifth Avenue, residents oppose trolley, 214
Fillmore, President Millard Western Train Excursion, 40, 324
First Congregational Church, Marblehead, MA, 5

Fleming, Janet, *Scotland*, 629
Married John Livingston, 629
Floors Castle, 424, *461*
Florists, for New York society,
Florist Le Moult, 281
Klunder, 218, 220, 249
Fly Market, 619
Fort Sewell, Marblehead, 3
Fox hunts,
Gerry, Robert L. built Hunt Club Baby House, Ebby II, 475
Cornelia Gerry, 475
Harriman, E.H. Fox Hunt Club, Goshen NY, 432
Partner, Gerry, Robert L., 420, 427
Red Swan Inn, Warwick, NY, 427, 568
Ball after the hunt, Robert "Bobby" Gerry was host, 428
Description of a hunt, 427
Goshen land purchase, 427, 432, 568
Hounds purchased in England and Ireland, 427
Orange County Hunt, NY, 427
Plains, Virginia Club House, 475
Franklin, Benjamin, 9, 605, 611-613
Fraunces Tavern, New York, 230
Society of the Sons of the Revolution Meeting, 230
French Revolution, 612
Frith House, 561
Fulton, Robert's Steam Boat, 24, 45, 453

G

Gadsby's Tavern, Alexandria VA, 17
Gallatin Ancestry, 608
Abraham, 609, 611
Albert, 16, 20, 52, 75, 613
Gallatin National Bank, absorbed by Hanover National Bank, 478
Minister to France, 75
Treaty of Ghent, 126
New York University, 75
Secretary of Treasury, 55
Sponsor of Hassler, 52
"Views of the Public Debt," 75
Albert Eugene II, 596
Albert Rolaz III, 157, 608
Almy Gerry Gallatin, 30, 75, 80, *194*
Bar Harbor, 452
Breezy Lawn, 129, 134, *151*
Children born:
Albert, 157, 414
Almy namesake, 80
Goelet, 141, 414
Jean, 111
Mary, 185, 406
Rolaz, "Horace," 106, 321, 364
Death, 497
Doll house, 36, 81
Property development on old Gallatin & Goelet NYC home sites, 125, 362, 416
Sports club member, 337, 417, 222
Tuxedo Park, 418
Will, 497
Frederic, nephew of James Sr., *87*, 91
ASPCA Secretary, 126
Bar of the City of NY, 75
Breezy Lawn, 129, 134, *151*
Business partner, John J. Astor III, 125
Children born:
Albert, 157
Almy, 80
Goelet, 141, 414
Jean, 111
Mary, 185, 406
Rolaz, "Horace," 106, 321, 364
Civil War, Judge Advocate, 75
Death, seven months after brother-in-law Elbridge T. Gerry, 572
Legal cases with brother-in-law Elbridge T. Gerry as co-counsel, 81
Six cent jury award, 82
Married Almy Goelet Gerry, 75
Childhood neighbors, 416
NYSPCC Board, 161
New York Yacht Club, 75, 172
President, Gallatin National Bank, NYC, 75
Absorbed by Hanover National Bank, 75, 478

Property development - old Gallatin & Goelet NYC home sites, 362, 416
Renwick, James Jr., 125, 129, 138, *151*, 176
Yacht Berti, 130, 173
Yacht Almy, 173, 285
Pres. Grover Cleveland met with capitalists for 2 days on Gallatin yacht, US financial Crisis, 309+
James Gallatin Jr., brother of Frederic, *87*
Death, 286, buried in Gallatin vault,
East Hampton home, 286
Inventor, 286
Musician and composer, 286
Organ, built one himself, 286
New York Sanitary Reform Society, President, 286
Goelet Gallatin,
Born, 141
Married Edith Church Post, 414
Horace, 106
Knickerbocker Riding Club, 321
James Gallatin, son of Albert,
Banker, 478
Death, 139
Diary, 614
NYSPCC, 126
Jean, 608
Johannes, 618
Mary,
Born, 185
Debut parties, 406
Pierre, 608, 609
Rolaz "Horace,"
Born, 106
Married, 364
Gallatin homes,
Breezy Lawn, L.I., 130, *151*
Fifth Avenue, NY, 166
Friendship Hill, PA, 613
Geneva, Pregny, 609-610
Gardiner's Island, Long Island, 134, 622
Gardiner's Bay, Gerry cruise, 211, 336
Gardens and Greenhouses:
Aknusti, 477
Ancrum, 517, *536*, 548, 551
Chateau de la Napoule, 486
Geneva estates, 611
Newport, 404
Townsend Mansion DC, 466
Geneva, Switzerland, 609-610
Gerry family, nature of, 188, 196, 574
Almy Goelet Gerry, 70
See also Gallatin, Almy
Death, 497
Engaged to Frederic Gallatin, 75
Childhood neighbors, 416
Temperament, 166-167
Will, 497
See also Gallatin, Almy.
Angelica *395*, *529*, 539
Academy of Holy Cross School, 134
Ancrum Mansion, 516, *555*
Architect Ralph Cram 516, 551, *555*
Demolished, 553
Landscape architect, F. Steele, 517
Plans, 517, *556*
Salvaged - Fifth Ave Gerry mansion when demolished, 520, 548, 552
Appendicitis, 517
Automobile holiday touring with maid and chauffer:
Florida, Clarendon Hotel in Seabreeze, FL, 510
Aquatic Preserve, 510
Manatee Sanctuary, 510
Tomoka River, 510
Palm Beach, Florida, 436
Niagara Falls, 504
White Mountains, 504
"great sigh" incident, 504
Bachelor girl, walking distance from siblings, NYC, 471, 521
Best friends:
Edith Kipp, 322
Born, 104
Brothers Robert and Peter die on same day, 553
California train trip, 432
Ostrich farm, 432, *460*
Visits ill brother Peter, 432
Cemetery at Lake Delaware
Created for her siblings, 553
Charitable endeavors, 453, 504

Children's Aid fund raising, 439
Cooperstown Orphanage, 495
Gerry Hall, memorial to Angelica's support of the college, 551, *557*
Gerry Society, 549
God-mother to many local children, 550
Lake Delaware:
Educated 250 local children over her lifetime, 550
Nurse sent to local homes, 549
St. James Church (built), 491, 510, 512, 513, 515, 551, *555*
Visits local schools & festivals, 439, 485
Coaching whip 282, 333, 386, *460, 554*
Club President, 283
Confirmation, 222
Dairy, Guernsey cows, 553
Destroyed by fire, 553
Death, 89 years old, 551
Burial, Lake Delaware Gerry cemetery, 553
Funeral Saint James Church, 553
Will, 553
Ancrum demolished, 553
Auction catalogue, 548
Education annuity, 551
Dog lover, 474,552
Education of local children,
Record Book of Protégés, 550, *557*
St. Christina's Episcopal Vocational School for Girls, 492
Engagement, 322
Breaks engagement, 344-345
Fundraising, charity, 495
Girl bachelor, 445, 471, 504
Townhouse ownership, 445
Homes:
Ancrum, Lake Delaware, 349, 516+, 529, *551*, 553
Townhouse, East 82nd St., New York City, 548, *554*
Horse breeding, 283, 378, 386, 517
Horse carriage whip, *320*, 432, 441
Horse meadow at *Ancrum,* 552
Jewelry theft, Newport, 310+, 434
Ritchie, J Wadsworth, 334, *395*, 422
Ritchie with Gerry family at Newport, 322, 334
Ritchie bad behavior, 344
Society gossip excited, 344
Reading, 495, 504
Scrapbook, 344, 346, 442
Social life, 352, 366, 370, 387, 391, 422, 435, 446
Steele, Fletcher, landscape, 349, 517, 551, 553, *556*
Temperament, 347, 511, 549
Townhouse, 62nd St NYC, 345, 347, 445, 489, *554*
Wedding canceled, 344-345
Gift of townhouse, 345
Trousseau, 345
Worth ball gown, 289
Ann, daughter and namesake of mother Ann Thompson Gerry, 189
Advised her father, 189
Death, New Haven CT, 189
Ann Thompson *married* Elbridge Gerry,
Death, 14, 33
Educated, 10
Temperament, 11
Catharine, daughter of Ann Thompson, and Elbridge Gerry, 11, 19
Death, 80
Married James T. Austin, 95
Cornelia *Harriman* Gerry75, *458, 575*
Baby house at hunt club *526*
Born, 429
Children: *589*
Ebby, Elbridge T. Gerry II, 569,
Bobby, Robert Livingston Jr., 570
Twins:
Edward, 572
Henry, 572
Death nine years after Robert, 574
Buried in Gerry Cemetery at Bovina, Lake Delaware, 574
Equestrian award winning, 568
Courtship, met 409, 421, 428, *458*
Married Robert L. Gerry, 448, *458*
Homes:
Aknusti, 577

New York townhouse, *576*
Daniel, Devonshire, 1
Daniel, Jr., 1
Ebby *nickname. See* Ebby
Edith *Vanderbilt* Gerry, 37, *563*, *565*
Biltmore estate, 558, *565*
Children's Christmas party and children's picnic, 561
Congressional Wives Club President, 560
Dairy interests, 559
Death, 562
Burial, Gerry Cemetery at Lake Delaware, 562
Equestrian, *563*
Farming, scientific, *525*, 558, 559, 562
Frith House, *565*
Introduced to Peter, 515, 525
Introduced to Gerrys, 516
Married Senator Peter Gerry in London, 516
School of Forestry, 559
Widow of George Vanderbilt, 515
Women's Democratic Club, 560
Edward, Harriman, twin of Henry, 583-585, *591*
Aknusti Polo Team, 579, 582, *590*
Born, 572
Childhood photos, *527*
Children: 584
Death, 88 years old, 584
Burial in Florida, 584
Gerry Brothers, Inc., 583
Homes:
Mill Neck, NY, 584
Monticello, FL, 584
Married Martha Farish, *591*
Exemplar in Racing award, National Racing Museum, 583
Jockey for her race horses, Willie Shoemaker, 583, *592*
Jockey Club, first woman member,
Race horses, *Forego*, 583, *592*
Standard Oil heiress, 583
Military service, Captain, Army Intelligence, England, 580, *589*
Eleanor, daughter of Vice President, 18, 19, 23, 70, 80
Elbridge, xvii, xviii, 1, 5, 6
Adams, John, friend, 9, 14
Bust in U.S. Senate, 301, *314*
Cambridge home, 11, 14, 22, 33
Children, 19-20, *34*
Citizens Duty Speech, 14
Quotation, 1
Constitutional Convention, 12
Bill of Rights, 12
Continental Congress, 8
Cornfield, 8
Death, 19
Declaration of Independence, 9, 12, 18
Fortune spent on war, 19-20
Gerrymander, 16
Gerrys Folly, 14
Governor, Massachusetts, 16
Horses, 13
Letters to family, 11, 15, 17, 20
Lewis, Col. Morgan, 18
Married Ann Thompson, 9
Monument, 19
Stammering speech, 12
Supreme Court Library 13
Theatre, 13
Vice-President, 16
XYZ Affair, 14
Elbridge, Jr., 20, *34*, 35
Diary, 16
Death, 79
Legal studies, 20
Inspector of Revenue, 21-22
Liberty Square shop, 22, 29, 71
President Jackson spat, 21, 26
Elbridge Thomas, *Commodore*,
Aging and slows down, 509, 511
Travel is difficult, 489
Allen & Abbott law firm joined, 72
American Geographical Society, 81
America's Cup Deed, 174, 243
ASPCA legal counsel, 102
Cases, 120
Disagree with Henry Bergh 123, 140
Ball for Prince Albert in NYC, 51
Bar of the City of New York Committee, 49, 72, 85

Bar of New York State, 131, *198*
  Committee, 134
Bishop Grafton Sarcophagus, Fond du Lac, WI, 489
Blackstone's gift, 21, 49, *61*
Cap, seal skin, trademark, 210
Capital Punishment
  Article, 265
  Commission Chair, 228
  Commission Report, 251
  Kemmler execution, 264
Carnival of Cops, 218-220
Charity Ball, annual, 76
Children born:
  Margaret "Pearl," 90, death, 107
  Angelica "Angel," 104
  Mabel, 108
  Lillian "Lilly," 111
  Robert "Bobby," 133
  Peter, 144
Columbia Grammar School, New York City, 39
Columbia College BA, 40
  Chi Psi Fraternity, 165, 210, 435
    Purple & Gold, 165
  Class secretary, 41
  Master's degree, 40
Committee arrangements,
  Mayor appointed, 213
  Chickering Hall, 213
  Parks Bill, 213
Commission on Condition of Pauper Insane, appointed Chairman by Mayor, 298
Commodore, 175 *See* New York Yacht Club.
Constitutional Convention,
  1860 delegate, 77
  1894 sponsors guest, 335
  Committee address for compromise on aid to parochial schools, 335
Crank, newspaper characterization 210
Death, age ninety, 518
  Burial, St James Cemetery, Gerry Vault, Hyde Park, NY, 579
  Funeral, letter, 518
  Funeral masses:
    Family at Church of St. Edward the Martyr, 519
    Public, Saint John the Divine Cathedral, 519
    Tributes, 519
    Will, 520
Democratic Party, one of the Vice Chairmen, 296
Doctorate in Divinity, 189, 490
Ebby, nickname only used once in a letter from his uncle Capt. James Gerry, 452, 469, 625-631
Episcopal Church
  Canon law, 187
  Diocesan Convention 128, 130,155
  Saint Edward the Martyr Church, Trust Fund, established, 519
  Heresy, Bible uses, 188
  Higher criticism, 188
  Missionary Committee, 134
  Newton, Reverend, 188
  Reading rooms, 188
Examiner NY Supreme Court Bar Exam, 71
Gardening, greenhouses, 374, 387, 404
Grand Train Excursion, 40
"Great Meddler," 102, 124, 133
Harriman, E.H. met, 74
King Edward VII, friend, 426
Law books, 38, 86, 108, 155, 187
Lawyer temperament, 98, 125, 131
Legal apprenticeship with William C. Noyes, 42, 44, 50, *62*
Legal Cases. *See* Table of cases.
  See also Law cases.
Legal cases with brother-in-law
    Frederic Gallatin Co-Counsel 81
  Six cent jury award, 82
Legal Counsel to family. *See* Law cases.
Lectures and speeches:
  Annual Charities Conference, 184
  Christopher Columbus statue in Central Park, 333
  Dedication speech, 333
  Drumgoole, Father, statue in Central Park, 323
    Dedication speech, 323

Religion in the Life of a Child, New Orleans, 452
Rhode Island Child Protection Society, 497
St. Patrick Society, 255
Legislative proposals:
Cruelty to animals, 131
Dairy products, 136
NYC Ordinance, 132
Aid to parochial schools, 335
Library. *See also* Libraries.
Bibliophile, xv, 13, 38, 42, 155, 255, 598
Broadway Farm home, stored 208
Canon law books, 131, 187, 251, 369
Collection donated U.S. Supreme Court, xv, 21, 598-603
Columbia University, Butler Library Rare Book Room, 39-41
Mansion library, 327, 368
Description, 71, 327, 368, 369
Law books, 42, 102-103, 369
Womens issues, 168
Life style, 155-156
Married Louisa Livingston, 80
Master Steam License, 233
Mayor, considered in the 1894 Democrats Nominee pool, 336, 344
Newspaper mention, 344
Medico-Legal Society, 98, 104, 106, 226
Memorial column in Saint John the Divine Cathedral NYC, 516
New York Hospital Society, 115, 135
New York Society for the Prevention of Cruelty to Children (NYSPCC):
Agents, 123, 126, 127 powers
Creation, 123
First meeting, 123
Legal counsel, 295
Mary Ellen case, 117-123
Newspapers, 119
New York Yacht Club, 175
Commodore, election, 175, 220
Deed of Gift, 174, 293
Member, 173
Philolexian Society President, 41, 51, 68
Publications:
Milwaukee newspaper prints convention speech, 184
North American Review, 192, 213, 265, 299
Robert J. Livingston mentor 77, 80, 96
Roosevelt, President Teddy, childhood neighbor, 416
Sagamore Hill visit, 412, *455*
School notebooks, 39
Society for the Suppression of News paper Notoriety, 335
Society of the Friend of the Seamen, member, 254
Society of the New York Hospital, 115, 135
Society of the Sons of the Revolution,
Elected Vice President, 230
Fraunces Tavern, 230, *248*
Stanton, Cady, suffrage, 168, *195*
Supreme Court Bar, 43, *62*
Wealth, 155-156
Goelet inheritance, 156-157
Livingston inheritance, 156-157
Widower, 503-518
Yacht Pastime, 173, 183, *194*, 203, 206,
Yacht Electra dismantled, 477
See also Yachts.
Youth with Uncle Peter, 36-39
Elbridge Thomas **II**, nickname Ebby, 518, *569*, *590*, *591*, *593*
Aknusti Polo Team, captain, 579, *590*
American Museum of Natural History, Trustee, 587
Arden Homestead Stables, partner with E. Roland Harriman, 586
Baby House, Plains, VA, 475, *526*
Born, 452
Baptism:
Godmother, Angelica Gerry, 452
Godfathers:
Robert Walton Goelet, 452
W. Averell Harriman, 452

Brown Brothers Harriman, Limited partnership, 586
Children: 587
Elbridge T. Gerry III, 587
Marjorie (Ryland), 587
Peter G. Gerry II, 587
Death within days of his wife Marjorie at Lake Delaware homestead, 587
Buried in Gerry Cemetery at Lake Delaware, 588
Funeral, Saint James Church, Bovina, Lake Delaware, 587
Memorial service in NYC at Trinity Church, Wall St., 588
Founder Horse Racing Museum and Hall of Fame, 588
Goshen Historic Track, Harness racing, 587-588
Hambletonian Society, President, 588
Harriman Foundation, Trustee 587
Harvard University, 585
Polo team, captain, 585
Won championship, 585
Hanover Bank, five years, 586
Harness racing, horses, 587
Homes:
Arden House, Orange County, NY, 586
Lake Delaware Homestead, 587, 588
Locust Valley, LI, 588
Inducted into the:
Polo Hall of Fame, 572
Harness Racing Hall of Fame, 587
Lake Delaware summer, 566
Lake Delaware Boys Camp, 587, 588
Married Marjorie Kane, 586, 593
Equestrian who trotted horses, 586
Miss Chapin's School NYC and the Ethel Walker School in CT, 586
New York Society for the Prevention of Cruelty to Children, President, 587
Polo professional, 572
Polo Hall of Fame, 572
Standardbred Owners Association, President, 587
United States Polo Association Chairman, 572
Elbridge Thomas III, 593
Arden Homestead's Stables, 588
Boys Club NYC Vice-President and Trustee, 588
Brown Brothers Harriman, Partner, 588
NYC Hambletonian Society, Board of Directors, 588
Harness Racing Museum & Hall of
Lake Delaware Boys Camp, active leadership, 587
New York Society for the Prevention of Cruelty to Children, 587
Elizabeth, 29, 80, 189, 348,
Married David Townsend, 80
Death, 189
Letter from brother Thomas R., 29
Emily, *34*
Daughters of the American Revolution, member, 347
Life in New London, 347
Death, 347
Hannah *Goelet* Gerry, *34*
Buried in Goelet vault, 361+
Children born: *61*
Almy, 31
Elbridge Thomas, 31
Jean, 30
Peter, 28 death, 30
Death, 90 years old, 361
Funeral, St. Marks Church, 400
Married Thomas R Gerry, 27
Summers spent at:
Breezy Lawn, L.I., 166, 185
Cozzens, West Point N.Y., 138
Wealth, 156
Widowed, 32
Will and inheritance, 20, 361
Helen, *34*, *70*
Henry Averell, twin of Edward, *590*, *591*
Born, 532
Children: 584
Ann, 584
Henry, Jr. died young, 584
Nancy, 584

Sheldon, 584
Richard, 584
Columbia Law School, 584
Death at 86 in Florida, 585
Buried in New York, 585
Fox Croft School, Trustee and Treasurer, 584
Gerry Brothers Inc., also Brown Brothers Harriman, 583
Gerry Foundation, Vice President, 611
Homes:
Boca Grande, FL, 584
Eighty-second Street townhouse, NYC, 584
Locust Valley, NY, 584
Married Nancy Whitney, 584, *591*
Military Service, Captain Army Air Corps, Italy, 580, *590*
Raced thoroughbreds in the Steeplechase, 584, *592*
Race horse winner, Flat Top in Breeder's Cup and Colonial Cup, 584, *592*
Wine from old Gerry cellar, 588 (Example, 1812 Brandy)
James Thomas, 11, *34*
Death at sea, 1854, 25
Gifts, favors for siblings, 23
Letter about Goelets, 23
Letter about Slave Ship, 24
Letter – love of the sea, 25
Letter – brother's marriage, 23
Jean, Elbridge T.'s sister, 70, *61, 65, 402*
Death, 176
Spinster, 36
Summers spent at:
Breezy Lawn, L.I. 166-167
Cozzens, West Point, 138
John, 5
Libby Farish, 583 *See also* Edward Gerry
Lillian nicknamed "Lilly,"
Birth, 111
Burial, St. James Church Cemetery, Gerry Vault, Hyde Park, NY, 297, 491, 504,
Confirmation, 252
Death, age eighteen, 297
Funeral, Trinity Chapel, 297
Memorials:
Gold Altar set, church near Lake Delaware, 439
Gold candle sticks, Saint James Church, Hyde Park, NY, 478
Gold chalice, St. Edward the Martyr Church, 297, *531*
Diary – Began at age ten: 203, *275*, 277
Angelica confirmed, 222
Augusta, GA health, 308
Christened yacht Electra, 207, *245*
Death of Grandmother Louisa S. Livingston, 203
Dolls for charity, 297
Grandfather ill, 235, 290
Knitted charity clothes for Garrit Dispensary, 265
Lake Delaware holiday, 296
Lilly sick at Staatsburg, 214
Mabel confirmed, 252
Reading, 297, 285
Trip to Europe, 267-269
Children ill, mumps and pneumonia, 236
Watched naval parade from yacht *Electra*, 266
Watched street parades from Frederic Gallatin home, 266
Illness, tuberculosis, 290
Georgia, Augusta, 280
Bon Air Hotel, 317
Koch, Dr. Robert, 297
Nobel Prize, 280
London, 265
Paris, 235, 265, 275
Staatsburg, NY, 214
Photography, 297
Louisa Mathilda nee Livingston
California train trip:
Los Angeles, 432
Ostrich Farm, 432, *460*
Peter has typhoid, 432
San Francisco, 432
Children: *246*
Angelica "Angel," 104

Lillian "Lilly," 111 death, 297
Mabel,
Margaret "Pearl," 80, death, 108
Peter, 144
Robert "Bobby," 133
Children's fancy ball, 217
Courtship, 50, 67
Death 84 years old, 503
Burial, Saint James Church Cemetery, Gerry vault, 504
Funeral, Church of the Transfiguration, 504
Description, 503
Florist used, Klunder, 218
Grandchildren, 452, 488
Married E T Gerry, 46 63
Memorial pillar in Saint John the Divine Cathedral, NYC, 520
Move into Fifth Avenue mansion, 340
Family heirlooms, 340, *398*
Property development, 292, 325
Fifth Ave. Mansion, 324, *316*, *398*
Phase I:
Richard M. Hunt, architect, *315* 292, 299-300, 324
Floor Plans, *328-330*
Phase II:
Zucker, Alfred, architect, *400*
Grand staircase, 325+, *398*
Library, 325+, 368, *399*
Stable 62nd Street, 368, Floor plans *400*
Apartment House 58th Street at 5th Avenue lots, 325, 367
Lake Delaware and Aknusti access roads are redesigned, 484, 493+
Restaurant caterer used for parties, Pinard, 218
St. James Church memorial, 510, *555*
Staffordshire, England, china made just for Gerrys, 482
Tenements sue Louisa, 418, 508
Wealth, 157
Property, 50, 54
Lake Delaware estate, *194*, 294, 623
Livingston inheritance, 157, 190, 291
Storm inheritance, 50-51, 54
Walking for health, 431, 447, 503
Will distributions, 325, 504, 511
Yachtswoman, 339, *402*
Lydia, Newton Abbot, UK, 1-3
Mabel
Appendicitis attack, 509
Best friend, Gertrude Vanderbilt, 333, 349, 351, 364, 366, *394*, 395, 408, 437, 496
Born, 108
Death, cancer, 543
Memorial altar, in St. John the Divine Cathedral description, 544
Memorial sculpture, Madonna, 543
Will, 544
Diary: 285, 349
Began at age nine, 203
Dresses she wore, 289, 348, 352, 379, 391, 422, 436, 471
Horses, Europe visit, 386, 471
Pope, presented to, 540
Vesuvius, 440, *463*
Engagement rumors, 350, 471
Episcopal Church, active parish member, Church of the Transfiguration, Memorial Madonna, 541
Altar Guild, lifetime, 541
Bible classes, 541
Chalices for ships, 542
Prominent member, 542
Vestments for ships, 542
Episcopal Mission Society, 439, 485
Gerry Society work, 542
Homes:
Carhart Townhouse, 514, 544
East 95th Street, 514, *529*
D'Hautville Cottage, Newport, R.I., 544
Drury House, London built in 16th Century, 514, 516, 518
Seaverge, Newport RI, Mabel inherited the house 1927, 520, 539, 395
Converted it to a Convalescent hospital in WWII, 492, 500

Donated house to the Episcopal Church, 544
Married Francis Saxon Drury, 514, 518, 529
Knight of the Order of Saint John, at Trinity Chapel, 514, 540
Orphanage established in Sulgrave, England, 500, 503
Photo album, 349
Reading, 285
Sewing, 439
Social life shifts to London, 500, 501, 510, 516
Temperament, 411, 496, 509, 511
Trustee, St. Mary's Children's Hospital, 541
Voice, singer & lessons, 351, 471, 529
Worth Ball gown, 289, 446, *546*
Margaret Louisa, "Pearl," *113, 532*
85, 96, 104, 109, 121, 292, 504, 519
Birth, 81
Death, 107
Marjorie Kane, *591, 593*
Birth, 81
Education:
Miss Chapin's School NYC and the Ethel Walker School in CT, 586
Hall of Fame Day, Goshen *Road Apple Raffle*, 586
Harness races, trotted horses, 586
Homes:
Arden House, Orange County, NY, 586
Locust Valley, L.I., 586
New York City apartment, 586
Married Elbridge T. II, called *Ebby*, 586, 593
Martha Farish, *591, 592*
See also Edward Harriman Gerry
Children, 584
Death 89 years old, Florida, 584
Exemplar in racing award, 583
Jockey for her race horses was Willie Shoemaker, 583, 592
Jockey Club, first woman, 592
Married twin, Edward Harriman Gerry, 583
Race horses, *Forego*, 583, *592*
Standard Oil heiress, 583
Vassar College, 583
Mathilde Townsend, 465
Affair with Sumner Wells, 515
Divorced Senator Gerry, 515
Married Peter G. Gerry,
Description 469
Guest, President William Howard Taft, 469
Marine Corps Orchestra, 469
Married Sumner Wells, 515
President Washington Chapter Animal Rescue League, 496
Purchased Catharine the Great's black pearls, 512
Nancy Whitney, *591, 592*
See also Henry Averell Gerry (twin)
Children, 584
Death at 95 in Florida, 584
Buried in New York, 584
Flat Top, champion horse, 584
Fox Croft School, VA, 584
Married, Henry A. Gerry (twin) 584
Raced thoroughbreds in the Steeplechase, 584
Race horse winner, *Flat Top* in Breeder's Cup and Colonial Cup, 584
Peter Goelet, *Senator*, xvi, *149, 524, 564*
American Humane Society President, 560
Appendicitis attack, 509
Arden Homestead Stables, 430
Bahamas holiday, 440
Best man for brother Robert, 448
Born, 144
Coaching, 386, 421, 433
Death, Providence R.I., 561
Died within hours of his brother Robert L. Gerry 561
Buried in Gerry Cemetery at Lake Delaware, 553, 561
Funeral at St. James Church, Bovina, Lake Delaware, 561
Divorce, 515
Engagement, 465

Fox hunting, 346, 427, 437
Harvard University, B.A. and J.D. 352
Law School, 423
Polo team, 423, 427, 437
Spee Club, 566
Homes:
Frith House Asheville, N.C. 553, 559, *565*
Lake Delaware estate home, inherited, 482, 505, 539, *594*
Ocean Lawn, rental across the street from Southside, his cousin, Robert Walton Goelet's home, 514
Pierre Hotel, home while in New York City, 593
Seaverge, Residency home R.I., 482, 485
Townsend Mansion in Washington, DC, 482, *524* until divorce.
Woods-Gerry mansion Providence RI, 561, 551, *565*
International Humane Association, 472
Law library inherited from father, E.T. Gerry, 520
Donated collection to United States Supreme Court, xvi, 520-521, *603*
Law practice,
New York City, Gerry Estates, 427
Providence, R.I.:
Gardner, Pierce& Thornley, 558
Turks Head Building Offices, 558
Marriages:
Townsend, Mathilde, 465, 515
Description 469
Guest President William Howard Taft, 469
Marine Corps Orchestra, 469
Divorce, 515
Vanderbilt, Edith Dresser, *525*
Biltmore estate, 515, *525*, 558
Dairy interests, 559
Introduced and engaged, 515
Married, 515-516
Gerry in London, 516-518
Widow of George Vanderbilt, 515
Congressional Wives Club, 560
Women's Democratic Club, 560
New York Society for the Prevention of Cruelty to Children, Director and Legal Counsel, 473, 493, 498, 506, 560
Newspapers he bought:
Providence News, 558
Providence Tribune, 558
Northwest America, sportsman trip with E.H. Harriman, 409, 430
Politics:
Christmas parties for poor children in Providence, 506, 561
Congress 1912 elected, 482
Democratic National Com., 561
Introduced to Washington, DC political society, 469
King George VI, 391
Naval Affairs Committee, 560
Nineteenth Amendment, 505
Providence, RI Turks Head Building offices, 558
Red Scare, communism, 503
Senate race 1916, 493
Democrat, supports issues on child protection and labor rights, 493
Elected, 496, *525*
Senate race 1920, 505-506, *564*
First automobile tour, 505
First "mail" campaign, 505
Farmer's Bulletin packet of Seeds, 505
"forgot he was rich," 505-506
Seaverge, R.I. residency, 482, 485
Taxation, supporter, 592
Woodrow Wilson Clubs, started by Senator and Mrs. Gerry, 506
Polo player, 386, 427
Pope, visit as child, 540
Supreme Court of the United States Library *See also* Appendix E, 598
Bar member, 493
Book Collection, donated the founding collection, 520, 560+
Temperament, 442, 493, 566
Tutor, McKenzie King, 390, 393

Typhoid Fever, 430-432
Yacht, the Owera, *525*, 560

Peter Goelet, II *593*
Hambletonian Society, Board of Directors, 588
Harness Racing Museum & Hall of Fame, New Jersey Sire Stakes Trustee, 588
Rensselaerville Institute, Chairman of the Board, 588

Robert Livingston, *149*, 539, 575-577
Aknusti estate, 481
Access roads redesigned, 571
Descriptions, 481, 570-571
Fire and rebuild, 571, 574
Gerry train cars carried supplies and horses, 481, 570
Guests over the years, 571
Landscape, Frederick Law Olmstead, Jr., 571
Library incorporated paneling from Electra, 479
Robbed, 492
Stables, 499, 571
Wine cellar, 570
Arden Homestead Stables, 499, 568
Automobile hits horse drawn carriage, Kingston, N.Y., 475
Bank trustee for:
Central Hanover Bank & Trust *Formerly* Gallatin Bank, 573
Farmer's Loan & Trust Co. *Now* Citibank, 573
Fulton Trust Company, 573
Birth, 133
Best man at Alfred Vanderbilt wedding to Elsie French, 443
Big Brothers Movement, leading member, 573
Board member age 35 of Banks and Railroads, 570
Brokerage firm, Strong, Sturgis and Company, 567
Cathedral of Saint John the Divine, in the Golden Book, 573
Childhood, *149*, 159, 289
Nickname Bobby, 428
Tutor, McKenzie King, 390
Children: *589, 590, 591*
Ebby, Elbridge T. Gerry II, 452, 569
Bobby, Robert Livingston Jr., 570, 478
Twins: *527, 591*
Edward, 572, 488
Henry, 572, 488
Club memberships, Gilded Age, 574
Coaching, 420, 567
Coaching Club, President, 283
Death at Aknusti estate on same day as brother Peter, 48
Buried in Gerry Cemetery at Lake Delaware NY, 574
Funeral at Saint James Church, Bovina, Lake Delaware, 574
Director, Oregon Railroad & Navigation Company, 573
Director, Shortline Railroad Company, 573
Fox Hunt Club Plains, VA
Baby House, 475, *526*
NY State Conservancy, 569
Fox hunts, Goshen NY, 420, 430
General Theological Seminary, Trustee, 573
Gerry Brothers, Inc. renamed from Gerry Estates, Inc., 546, 569
Harriman, Cornelia, *526*
Born, 429, 575
Courted Red Swan Inn, 428, 448, *458*
Equestrian award winning, 409
Married, 448, *458*
Harriman, E.H., *457*
Arden Stables, 30
Death, 569
Elbridge T. Gerry met, 75
Harriman, E. Roland, 568
Arden Homestead Stables, 430
Harvard University, 3 years only,
Fund drive donor, 573
Hasty Pudding Club, 566
Polo team star, 566
Spee Club, 566
Homes:

Aknusti, Lake Delaware, 481, *577*
Fifth Ave & 62nd Street, NYC, 568
Fifth Ave & 69th Street, NYC, 568
Inchiquin House rented for his wife and four children, near *Seaverge* and his father Elbridge T., 513+
Seventy-Ninth Street double baroque townhouse, 570,*576*
Horse breeding, 420
Aknusti Stables, 571, *575*
Arden Stables and Aknusti Stud, 567, 568
Fox hunting, 346, 427, 432
Polo ponies, 420
Polo team, 572, *590*
Horse racing,
Belmont, 567
Bid loss, Man O' War, 572
Owned sons of Man O' War:
Field Marshall, 573
Ironside, 573
Gerry family's favorite horse was Peanuts, 573
Meadowbrook, 568
Saratoga, 573
Horse show:
Goshen, NY, 409
Madison Square, NYC, 409
Newport, 386
Horse season in Europe, 571
Illness, 252, 410
Lake Delaware Boys Camp: *528*
Buildings constructed, 569
Land acquired, 569
Organist, *Charlie,* Charles Dodsley Walker, 569, death 225
Anniversary, 225, *528*
Meadowbrook Polo Club, 568
Military service, Major, Army Transport Service, 420
New York Society for the Prevention of Cruelty to Children, Board, 498, 568
Pierre Hotel, opening, 548
Real Estate, early position with E.A. Cruikshank & Co., 567
Temperament, 442, 493, 5666
Debut to society, 3
Robert Livingston, Jr., *590*
Born, 478
Champion tennis player, 581
Death in New York City, 582
Buried in Gerry Family Cemetery at Bovina, Lake Delaware, 582
Homes:
Aknusti, sold, *577*, 582
Houston, Texas, 582
Westbury, Long Island, 580
Married Marleigh Kramer, 580, *591*
Children:
Nancy, 581
Lives in Virginia, 582
Robert L. III, 581
Lived in Texas, 582
Divorced, 581
Lived in Westbury, LI, 580
Married Harriett W. Gardner, 582
Lived in Houston, Texas, 582
Military service WWII, Captain, Army Corps, Italy, 580, *589*
Texas Children's Hospital Board, 582
Samuel Russell Gerry, 5-6, 26
Born, 5
Death, 15
Samuel R. Gerry, Jr., a Letter 79
Thomas, Captain, 33
Children, 5
Cod Fish Aristocracy, 3
Gerry Island small pox isolation, 7
Gerry's Wharf, Marblehead, 3
Married Rebecca Russell Greenleaf, 4
Merchant ships, 3
Newton Abbot, UK, 1-2
Thomas Jr., 5
Thomas Russell, *34*
Alderman NYC Council, 38
Children: *61, 87, 88*
Almy, 31
Elbridge Thomas, 30
Jean, 31
Peter, 28, death, 30
Death at New Rochelle, 30
Letters to family, 27, 28, 29, 30
Married Hannah Goelet, 25

Master's Degree, Harvard University, 28
Mansfield MA wool mill, 29
Naval appointment, 25
Gerry balls and dinners:
Children's dress ball, 27
Cholly Knickerbocker reports, 446
Debutante, Almy Gallatin coming out ball, 218
Housewarming ball, 348
Description of mansion, 348
Winter cotillion, 380, 386
Description, 352, 387
Gerry brothers Robert and Peter die same day in 1957, 561
Personalities, 442, 493
Temperaments, 566
Gerry Brothers, Inc., 567
Convert Gerry Stables in NYC into upper east side offices, 583
Formerly Gerry Estates Inc., 507, 546
Gerry chefs, 489, 435, 208, 387
Menu book held in Rare Book Collection of U.S. Supreme Court Library, 511
Staffordshire china set, 482
Gerry Elementary School, 5
Gerry European Travel (annual)
London, Mayfair rental, 450
Death of King Edward VII, 451, 467
Trans-Atlantic Steamers: 270, 274, 286
Cunard Line to London, Paris, Nice, 271
White Star to France, Naples, Mt. Vesuvius, 440-441
Purchased *Penelope*, 348
Gerry family changes between generations, 440, 446
Gerry family charity at Lake Delaware
Lake Delaware Boys Camp, 569, 528
Lake Tunis, Robert Doig, 476
started as tent camp, 470
Mission work in local towns, 439, 485
Gift boxes to local poor children, 439
Gold communion set for church, 439
Visit local schools and festivals, 439
Gerry community assistance:
Andes bank robber shot local boy, 439
Angelica consoled family, 439
Elbridge engaged a doctor, 439
Elbridge paid hospital bills, 439
Gerry Estates, Inc. *renamed* Gerry Brothers, Inc., 546
Gerry family illness:
Isolating Room in mansion, 300, 329
Appendicitis,
Angelica, 517
Mabel, 509
Peter, 509
Measles,
Angelica, 404
Robert, 404
Mumps, All 4 children, 236
Pneumonia,
Angelica, 410
Louisa, serious, 503
Lilly, 269
Mabel, 236
Peter, 236, 280
Robert, 410, 252
Scarlet fever,
Peter, 203
Robert, 203
Tuberculosis,
Letter, E.T. Gerry, 280
Lillian, 290, 280, 549
Death, age eighteen, 297
Serious illness not specific, 280, 509
Typhoid fever,
Mary Goelet, 283
Peter G. Gerry, California, 430
Family travels on Harriman's Pullman car to visit Peter in California, 431
Peter returns to New York, 433
Gerry family papers, 32
Gerry fire engine, 5, 596
Gerry family fundraisers:
Bazaar and auction hosted by Mabel Gerry at mansion, 496
Dinner for high society to raise Money for Cooperstown Orphanage, 495

War Effort, 492
Gerry Island, 7
Gerry holidays:
Christmas, 30, 49, 111, 121, 141, 171, 290, 321, 370, 372, 392, 417, 466, 506, 518, 562, 584
Easter, 205-206
Fourth of July, 129, 138, 251, 293, 352, 453, 470, 480
Gerry homes:
Elmwood, Cambridge, MA, 11, 13, 22, *23*, 170
Hardenburgh Patent, xviii, 18, 44, 183, 429, 477
Lake Delaware, NY, 45-47, 52, *63*
Buildings refurbished, 293
Cows get TB, 453
Dairy uses lake ice, 184, 553, 559
Horse culture, 192
Ice cutting accident on Lake Delaware, 482
Local philanthropy, 512, 549
Robbed, 492, 510
Summers, 149-150, 166, 184
Water system upgrade, 293
Marblehead, MA, 3-10
New Haven, CT, *34*, 11, 20, 22, 30, 35, 70, 79-80, 189, 303, 312, 347
Newport, Rhode Island,
Lyndenhurst, *rented*, 302
Seaverge,
Greenhouse, 374, 380, 387
Stable, 380
New York City. *See also* Appendix B
Mansion, Fifth Avenue at 61st St.:
Décor for parties, 348, 352
Demolished, 553
Floor plans, 328-330
Isolating room, nurse, 300, 329
Mansion description, 299-300
Mansion furnishings, 348
Stable, 368, *400*
Gerry Offices, New York City,
19th Century, 507
20th Century, 546
Gerry opera box, 234
Gerry property in New York City,
Beautification, 48
Bristol Hotel, land, 508
Inherited brownstones, 340
Savoy Apartments, land, 508
Schubert Comedy Theatre land, 469
Windsor Arcade, 468
Windsor Hotel, land, fire, 468, *396*
Gerry Sewing circle, 285, 297, 352
Gerry Society NYSPCC, 117-123, 127
Gerry Wealth, consolidated and protected in Gerry Estates, Inc. Angelica, Mabel, Peter and Robert held stock rather than individual title, 511, 520
Gerrymandering, 596, *33*
Gerry's Folly, 15, 47-49, 154
Gerry's Wharf, Marblehead, MA, 3, 5, 7
Gibson, Walter W., British architect
Albany Cathedral, N.Y., 205
Gilbert, Cass architect, xvi
Gilbert, Humphrey, 2
Gilded Age, 1, 57, 153-155, 167
See also philanthropy.
Assembly Ball, 172, 289, 372
Bachelors Ball, 171
Children's Fancy Dress Ball, Louisa Gerry hosts, 431
Christmas tree, new fashion, 289
Cholly Knickerbocker, society column reporter 446
Civic duty alive, 19, 145, 166, 177, 254, 412, 474, 439
Debutantes, 215-216
Cotillion, bachelor led dance, 220, 321
Matriarchs Ball, 321
Patriarchs Ball, 220
Ding Dongs, 154
Dresses:
Gerry women, 289, 348, 352, 379, 391, 422, 436
Diary record, Mabel, 471
Patriarchs Ball, 220
Worth, Paris, 289, 446, *546*
Dudes, 154, 176, 218, 282, 321
Come of age, 321, 437
Engagement gossip, 271, 346, 445, 471
Gerry to Goelet, 422
Era ends, 436-437

Etiquette, Emily Post, 277-279
European season, 403
  Astor Cup fun winter sports held in St. Moritz, France, 403
  European tours ebbing, 377, 489
  Yacht cruises, to the Riviera and the Mediterranean, 373
Florists, 249, 374, 404
Society families, 249
Girl bachelors: 445
  Adams, Maud, 446
  Gerry, Angelica, 445
  Gould, Helen, 446
  Munro, Norma, 446
  Van Alen, May, 446
Goelet, Mrs. Ogden (Mary)
  Fortune telling party, 206
Golden Age of Yachting, 338
Hoppingtots, 154
Irving, Washington, 154
McAllister, Ward,
  Elite families list, 249
Mansions. *See* family names.
Mansions, end of era, 520, 548
Marrying Wilsons, sisters, 473
Martin, Bradley, 205, 370
  Amateur Play Party, 206
  Anarchist's threats, 372
  Fancy Dress Ball, 370-372
  Retreat to Scotland, 372
Marriage, foreign, 305
  Duke of Marlborough, 350, 358+, 394, 437
  Duke of Portland, 166, 253, 277, 293
  Duke of Roxburgh, 424, *461*, 631
  Earl of Dudley, 426, 451, *456*
Matriarchs Ball, 321
Millionaires, 145, 292, 294, 299, 304, 367
Old money, 371
Opera, 370
  Boxes, private, 370
  Opera House, 304-305
  Socializing at the opera, 234
Origin of term Gilded Age, 153
Patroons, NY, 171
  Patriarchs Ball, 186, 249
    Electric lights, 249
    Flowers, 249
    Last ball of era, 289
    McAllister, Ward, 249
  State founders, New York, 171
Philanthropy, 153, 254, 355
Private balls and dinners:
  Church admonition, 235
  Astor, 370
  Gallatin, Almy debutante, 218
  Gerry:
    Children's dress ball, 217
    Housewarming ball, 348
    Winter cotillion, 380,386
  Goelet:
    Duke Franz Joseph, 472
    1000 Guests Newport, 211
    2000 lights, 406
    Wimborne House, 306-307
  Party favors, 218
    Sachet & flowers,
Salmagundi, 154
Seasons, social, 373, 403
  Changing tastes, 432-437
  Christian observance, 205-2-6
  Inventive activities,
Shakespeare, William, 153
Sophy Sparkles, 154, 176, 218, 321, 437, 446, 612
  Come of age, 437
Twain, Mark, 153, 349
Washington Square old money,
  Cornelius Vanderbilt, 206, 371
Watering holes/places, 31, 35, 97, 128-130, 163, 165, 179, 184, 203
Wealth and responsibility, 153, 254, 355
Wealthy women, 51, 81, 404, 446, 465, 521, 583
Wedding news:
  Kipp, Edith, 322
  Gallatin, Goelet, 864
  Gerry, Peter G., 469, 516
  Gerry, Robert L., 448
  Goelet, Robert Wilson, 433
  Reid, Jean, Queens Chapel, 450
  Townsend, Mathilde, 469, 515
Women, daily routine, 278
Women philanthropists, 167, 496

Women and sports:
Bowling, 221
Coaching, 282+, 292, 321, 333, 369, 386, 407, 412, 420, 432, 437, 442
Golf, 306, 333, 366, 418, 581,
Tennis, 221, 306, 337, 366, 481, 571, 580, 626,
Yachting, 169, 190
Women's suffrage, 167, 332-333, 446, 504, 505,
Gilded Gotham, 153-154
Glenmere Lake, Orange County, 427, 474, 487
Glenmere Mansion, Goelet, Robert Wilson built, 427
Glenmere Kennels, Goelet, 474
Goelet Ancestry, 616-622, 205
Alexandra, 622
Almy Buchannan death, 35
Anne Marie, 160
B&G Winery, 596
Children: *615* family tree
French Legion of Honor, 596
Married Robert Walton Goelet, 481
Sandricourt Castle, 508
Beatrice daughter of Robert Jr., *247*
Born, 216
Burial at Woodlawn Cemetery in the Goelet vault, 411
Death age seventeen, 410
Funeral was private at the Fifth Ave mansion, 410
Inheritance passes to her brother Robert Walton, 411
Mother Harrietta - Beatrice's Bedroom left intact, 411
Pernicious pneumonia, 410
Portrait age 7 by artist John Singer Sargent, 411
Elsie Whelen, *522*
Children, 486
Ogden, II,
Peter, III,
Divorced, 486
Married Henry Clews, 487
Married Robert Wilson Goelet, 433
Description of gowns, 434
Maid of Honor, Alice Roosevelt 434
St. Mary's Church in Philadelphia, PA, 433
Francis Goelet Diary, 27
Frederick Phillipse, 617
Francis, 288, *318*
Atlantic Salmon Foundation, 288
Toad Brook Club, 288
Tracadie Club, 288
Metropolitan Opera House at Lincoln Center, NYC, 305, 595
National Medal of Arts, 595
Hannah Greene Goelet. *See also* Gerry, Hannah 27
Death, 90 years old, 361
Hannah *Goelet* Gerry, 27, 156
Married Thomas R Gerry, 27
Summers, 166, 185
Widow, 32
Harrietta Warren, 408, *463*
Children:
Beatrice, 216
Robert Walton, 166
Death in Paris, cancer, 480
Burial, Woodlawn Cemetery in Goelet vault, 480
Funeral St. Thomas Church, 480
Married Robert Goelet Jr., 159
Jacobus, 616-618
Jean Buchannan, spinster, 115
Burial in Goelet vault, 185
Death, *Breezy Lawn*, 185
Funeral St. Mark Church, 185
Will leaves large estate, 185
Mary Wilson,
Bees on Fifth Avenue, 476
Children born:
Mary (May), 144
Robert Walton, 166
Fortune-telling party, 206
Married Ogden Goelet, 620
Mayflower yacht sold after Ogden's death, 418
Newport parties,
1000 guests, 211
Re-opens Ochre Court, 405
Two dinners by Sherry's, 405

2000 electric lights, 405
Rented 5th Ave Mansion to Mrs. Vanderbilt, 410
Typhoid fever, 283
Doctors use trans-Atlantic cable communication, 283
May (Mary) 206, *461*
Born, 144
Children:
George Victor Innes-Kerr, 485
God-parents, King George V and Queen Mary, 486
Debut at Newport, 405-406
Floors Castle, Scotland, *461*
Married Duke of Roxburghe *461*
Henry Innes-Kerr, 423-424
Description of couple, 424
St. Thomas Church, NYC, 424
Ochre Court announced engagement of May and Ogden Goelet, 423
Ogden, 125, *397*
Bigger house and yacht than older brother, 172, 179, 295
Children:
Mary "May," 144
Robert Walton, "Bertie," 166
Death on new Mayflower yacht at Cowes England attended by the Prince of Wales' doctor, 376
Burial, Woodlawn Cemetery Goelet vault, 376
Description, 91, 356
Edgewater House, Newport, Rhode Island, 179
Edward VII, King, friends, 306+, 363
Invitation to Newport, 356
Fifth Avenue townhouse, 180
Description, 180
Goelet Cup, created, 200, *247*
John Jacob Jr. continued Cup, 200
Greenhouse, 374
Illness, asthma, 366
Married Mary Wilson, 620
Mayflower yacht became Presidents Yacht, United States, 377, *397*
Next door to brother in NYC and Newport, 179
Ochre Court, R M Hunt, 294+, 349, 375, *315*
Salmon fishing, 287, *318*
Salve Regina University, 295
Theatres he built:
Abbey Theatre, 305
Knickerbocker Theatre, 305
Metropolitan Opera, 304-305
Murray Hill Theatre, 305, 365
Will disposed of library, 375
Wimbourne House, London
Prince Albert "Bertie," 363, 374
Yacht. *See* Yachts (by name)
Yachting established, 163-164
Newport center in America, 173, 179
Ogden II, married 5 times, 487
Ogden III,
Harvard College, 488
Columbia University PhD, 488
Professor and author, New York University, 488
Peter, "Uncle Peter," xviii, 32
Books and library, 38, 44
Born, 35
Broadway Farm, 36+, *61*, 96, 362, 468
Roosevelts neighbor, 416, 468, *455*
Guardian of Gerry orphans, 36, *61-62*, *88*
Chemical Bank, 36, 37, 43
Charitable and reclusive, 37
Civil War Soldiers, care, 37, 46, 68, 70
Death 144, 198
Burial Goelet vault, 145, 185, 362
Funeral St. Mark's Church, 144, 198
Description of Peter, 36-37, 144
Doll house, 36, *61*, 81,
Episcopal Church, 38
Grand Central Station spat, 37
Horses, 37
Illness and old age, 133, 135
Iron Monger basement, 37, 81
Metropolitan Opera, 36, 38
Property, 37, 39, 96+, 139, 143, 161
Saratoga Springs holiday, *62*
Trust and Trustee, 229
West Point, 35, *88*, 28-129,

Will read, 145
Challenged, 192, 287
Daughter question, 197-199
Death, 26
Executor, E T Gerry, 145, 229
Probate, lengthy, 161
Windsor Hotel, 141
Wine, 326
Peter P.,
Born, 618
Broadway home, 35
Chemical Bank, xviii, 36
Colonial business, 26
Death, 26
Dutch, xviii
Married Almy Buchanan, 534
Trust fund, 229
Will, terms of, 230
Wine, 570
Robert, Peter's brother
Born, 35
Chemical Bank, 36
Death, 142
Marble Cemetery, 143
Married Sara Ogden, 36
New York Yacht Club founder, 38
Ogden family vault, 143
Property, 85
Railroads, 40
Saint Mark's Church, 142
State Street home, 36
West Point holidays, 142, *88*
Robert, Jr., xiv Ogden's brother,
Banking, 213
Burial Woodlawn Cemetery in the Goelet vault, 389
Chemical Bank Board, 36
Children born:
Beatrice, 160, 216, *247*
Robert Walton, 166
Civil War, 69
Columbia University BA, 50
Death on yacht Nahma, 388
Harrietta kept his library & bedroom on the yacht intact, 378
Description of Robert, 91, 356
Fifth Ave townhouse, 160, 179
Goelet Brothers, Inc., 205
Funeral, Trinity Church, 389
Homes next door to brother, 173, 179
Married Harrietta Warren, 159, *463*
Metropolitan Opera, 36, 160, 202
Newport residency, 380
Property, 44, 67, 91-92
Railroads, 202
Salmon fishing Canada, 287, *318*
Southside, Newport RI, 179, *193*, 199, 260, 374
Yachts, 172, 302, 373, 378
Robert Walton, Robert Jr.'s son
Alma Mater statue, Columbia U., 419
Catholic, 507
Children, *615* family tree
Columbia University, sculpture, 419
Description, 166, 389
Harvard College, 166, 449
Homes:
Fifth Ave mansion, inherited, 507
Sandricourt Castle, France, 507
Southside, Newport, *193*, 507
Inherited sister Beatrice's trust, one of richest men, 411
Married Anne Marie Guestier, 481, 507
Metropolitan Opera support, 449
Paris, 480, 507
Polo, 420
Tuxedo Park, 419
Yacht tax I U.S. Supreme Court 486
Robert Wilson, Ogden's son
Automobile kills child, 474
Bedside of father in Cowes, 376
Born, 166
England at his death,
Children, 7
Ogden II, married 5 times
son Ogden III,
Peter III, radio stations
Newberg and NYC,
Engaged to Elsie Whelen, 433
Glenmere Lake, Orange County near Tuxedo Park, 474
Glenmere Mansion 474
Tuscan style, 4

Glenmere Kennels white terriers, 475
Harvard College, 166, 499
Married Elsie Whelen, 434
Description of gowns, 434
Maid of Honor, Alice Roosevelt, 434
St. Mary's Church in Philadelphia, PA, 434
Divorced, cause cruelty, 486
Married Fernanda Riabouchinsky, wife of Russian Prince, 501
Divorced after four years, 501
Goelet *Broadway Farm* NYC, 32, 96, *61*
Goelet Brothers, Inc., 205
Banks. See Chemical Bank.
Gorham Building, Goelet offices, 203
McKim, Mean & White, 205
Property. *See* Goelet property.
Railroads, 202
Goelet brothers, Ogden and Robert Jr.,
Died twenty months apart, 376, 388
Great loss for cousin Elbridge, 390
Goelet brothers, Peter and Robert Sr. died just weeks apart, 142,144
Goelet cousins, Robert and Robert W.,
Born on same day, 166, 389
Looked identical, 166, 389
Nicknamed *Bertie* to distinguish, 166
Goelet Cups – yacht races, 200, *247*
Goelet doll house, 36, *61*, 81
Goelet, Chemical Bank of NYC, 1857 Panic, 43
Goelet fortune inherited, 411, 185
Goelet homes,
Broadway Farm 19th St., 36, 362, 468
Chateau Magnal, France, 621
Edgewater, Newport, RI, 179
Fifth Avenue Townhouses, NYC, at Forty-Ninth Street, 180
Bees on Fifth Avenue, 476
Description, 180
Portico removed, 476
Rented to Vanderbilt, 410
Prince Henry of Prussia visit & formal dinner, 410
Floors Castle, Scotland, *461*
Gardiner's Island, NY, 622
Ochre Court, Newport, 294+, *315*
Built 1885, R M Hunt, 179
Saint Aubin d' Ecrosville, France, 621
Sandricourt Castle, France, 621
Southside, Newport, R.I., *193*
Built in 1882, 622
Description, 199
White, Stanford architect, 622
Wimborne House, London, 363, 374
Prince Albert, Bertie, guest of honor at dinner, 375-376
Queen Victoria Jubilee hosts Naval Review at Cowes, 375, *397*
Goelet *impression of* in Gerry letter,
Goelet and Metropolitan Opera, NYC, 36, 38, 160, 202, 304, 449, 595,
Goelet property in New York City 56, 98-99
Beautification, 48
Litigation, 37, 96, 97, 139, 143, 161
See also Law cases.
Windsor Hotel ground, 141
Goelet Trust Fund, trustee 229
Elbridge T. Gerry Trustee, 229
Goelet Wineries: 595-596
B&G – Barton & Guestier, 596
Clos Du Val Winery, CA, 595
Clover Hill Winery, Tasmania, 595
Domaine De Nizas, France, 595
Lalla Gully Vineyard, Tasmania, 595
Taltarni Winery, Australia, 595
Goelet Yachts:
Robert
Cambria, 172, 175
Magic, 172, 175, *193*
Beatrice, 302, 306, 337, 378
Nahma, 377, 383, 388, *397*, 410-411, 422, 424, 437, 441, *463*, 480,
Property tax on foreign yachts 486
Ogden
Mayflower, 308, 375, 376, 383,
Funeral ship 389
Presidential Yacht, 377, 397
Norseman, 172, *193*, 306,
Whyte Ladye, 306, 308, 309, *316*, 321, 357, 363, 366, 373,
Sold, 375
Golden Anvil (sign), 618

Golden Key (sign), 618
Gotham, 15, 47, 115, 154, 157
Gracie Mansion, New York City, xviii, 10
Grant Cottage, Long Branch NJ:
  E.T. Gerry rents cottage, 142
  Ulysses S. Grant Cottage, *152*
Grey Ghost, John Singleton Mosby,
  Florence Mosby case, 161-163
  Mosby's Rangers, Civil War, 161
Greeley, Horace, 92, 94, 425
Greenleaf family, 3-5
  Edmond, 3
  Enoch, 3
  Rebecca Russell, 4-5
  John Greenleaf Whittier, 4
  Joseph, 4
Greenhouses. *See* Newport, RI.
Guardian of Scotland, 625
Guestier, *French wine family*
  Anne Marie, 507
    Married Robert W. Goelet, 481, 597+
  Daniel, 621
Guestier Winery, 597

H

Hadrian's Wall, 625
Hampton Court tennis, 626
Hancock, John Colonel, 8
Hanover Square, NYC, 37, 618
Hanoverian lineage, 627
Hardenburgh, Johannes, xviii, 18, 183, 429, 477
Hardenburgh Patent NY, xviii, 44
Harlan and Hollingsworth, 206, *245*
  Navy ships, 383
  Register of Historic Places, 207
  Steam yachts 383
    Almy, 306
    Electra, 208
    Mischief, 208
Harriman
  Albany Cathedral, 205
  Arden House, 429
  Cornelia. See *also* Gerry, Cornelia.
    Born, 429
  Children:
    Ebby, Elbridge T. Gerry II, 452, 569
    Bobby, Robert Livingston Jr., 478, 570
    Twins:
    Edward, 488, 572
    Henry, 488, 572
  Baby House at Fox Club, 475, *526*
  Equestrian award-winning, 568
  Courtship, 409, 421, 428
  Married Robert L. Gerry, 448, *458*
    Homes:
      Aknusti, Lake Delaware, 481,577
      Fifth Ave & 62nd St., NYC, 568
      Fifth Ave & 69th St., NYC, 568
Edward Henry,
  Bear Mountain National Historic Park, Harriman family gift, 569
  Boys Club, New York City, 567-569
  Children: 448, 567-568
    Cornelia Harriman Gerry, 448
    Carol A. Harriman, 448
    E. Roland Noel Harriman, 568
    Mary Harriman Rumsey, 448
    W. Averell Harriman, 568
  Death, 569
  Fox Hunt Club, Goshen NY, 420, 430
    Gerry, Robert L. Partner, 420
  Palisades Founder's Award from the New York State Conservancy, 569
  Red Swan Inn, Warwick, NY, 428, 468, *458*
    Ball after the hunt, Robert *Bobby* Gerry was host, 428
    Description of a hunt, 428
    Goshen land purchase, 432
    Hounds purchased in England and Ireland, 427, 432
    Orange County Hunt, NY, land purchases, 432
  Married Mary W. Averell, 428, 457
    Bear Mountain National Historic Park, 569
  Elbridge T. Gerry met Harriman, 74
    Robert L. Gerry, 429
  Railroads
    Southern Pacific, 429
    Union Pacific, 429

Wall Street, 428
E. Roland Harriman,
Arden Homestead Stables, 430, 568
(a partnership with Gerrys)
Brown Brothers Harriman, 568, 499
Harriman, W. Averell,
Ambassador, 568
Arden Homestead Farm, horse breeding, with Peter and Robert Gerry, 499
Board of Directors, NYSPCC, 498
Brown Brothers Harriman, 499, 568, 583, 586
Gerry Brothers, Inc. subsidiary of Brown Brothers, 583
Governor of New York, 568
Harriman Alaska Expedition, 498
Presidential Medal of Freedom, 500
Red Cross President, 568
Secretary of Commerce, 568
Sun Valley Ski Resort, 499
Ernest Hemmingway, 499
Illinois Pacific RR, President, 499
Harriman Homes
Arden House, on a high ridge in Orange County, NY, 457, 471
Fifth Ave at 62nd St, NYC, one block north of Elbridge T. Gerry, 568
One block south of Robert L Gerry and wife Cornelia Harriman, 568
Harvard College/University,
Gerry, Elbridge B.A. M.A., 6
Gerry, Elbridge Jr. B.A., 20
Gerry Peter G. B.A. Law JD, 352, 422
Gerry, Robert L. 3 years, 390
Gerry, Thomas R., B.A. M.A., 25
Goelet, Ogden, B.A., 39, 166
Goelet, Robert Jr., B.A., 39, 166
Lecture, E. Gerry, respect for soldiers Buried in yard, 170
Philanthropy, 449
President's House, Elmwood, 13, 33
Hassler, Ferdinand Rudolph, engineer, 52
Albert Gallatin, Secretary of State, 52
American Philosophical Society, 52
President Andrew Jackson, 53
President Thomas Jefferson, 52
Robert James Livingston hired, 53
Triangulate east coast, 52
Heidelberg Catechism, 618
Henry VIII, King, 626, 627, 631
Hewitt, Abram S., Mayor, NYC, 253
Daughters founded Cooper-Hewitt National Design Museum, 254
Refused award, public service a duty, 254
Subway constructed, 254
Highland Park, NJ, 54-57, 324, 63
Hilborne Roosevelt Organ Opus 34 model, 224, 597
Enlarged, 226
Lake Delaware, 224-226
Historic landmark designations:
Biltmore estate, NC, 559
Carhart townhouse, Mabel Gerry, 514
Gerry Home, Marblehead, 6
Clews home in France, 487
Woods-Gerry House, RI, 562
History of the American Revolution, by Mercy Otis Warren, 15
Hoffman, Rev. Eugene, Dean, General Theological Seminary 385
Death on train, 412
Funeral at Trinity Church, 412
Glorvina Storm's son and cousin of Louisa M. Gerry, 56
Golden anniversary, 411-412
Hoffman, Glorvina Storm, 542
Great grandmother of Mary Watson Ray,
Hoffman, Samuel Verplanck, 412
Son, Rev. Eugene Hoffman, 56
Fellow in Astronomy, Johns Hopkins University, 412
Hofmann, Josef, child prodigy on world tour from home in Poland, 522, 497
Director, Curtis Institute of Music, Philadelphia, as adult, 498
Gerry, Elbridge T. paid for private lessons after NYSPCC barred 11-year old Josef from NYC stage, too young, 497
Played from memory, heard a piece once and played it perfectly, 498
Holland, 595, 605, 616, 616, 617
Home for Incurables, NYC, 60, 182, 355
Horn's Hook, Gracie Mansion, 10
Horse sports. See *also* Coaching

Competitions:
Durland Riding Academy, 420
Competition of polo ponies:
Robert L. Gerry, 420
Alfred Vanderbilt, 420
Fox hunting, 346, 420, 427
Red Swan Inn, Warwick, NY, *458*
Ball after the hunt, Robert *Bobby* Gerry was host, 428
Description of a hunt, 428
Goshen land purchase, 432
Hounds purchased in England and Ireland, 427
Orange County Hunt, NY, 427
Polo,
Aiken team, 579
Aknusti team, 478, 572, 586,
Harvard polo team, 427
Gerry, Ebby II, 587
Gerry, Peter 137, 427
Gerry, Robert L., 137, 427
Meadowbrook, Westbury, LI, 427
Members , 427:
Belmont, August Sr., 427
Belmont, August Jr., 427
Gerry, Peter, 427
Gerry, Robert L., 427
Harriman, Edward H., 427
Townsend, John R., 427
Vanderbilt, Alfred, 427
Polo Hall of Fame, 572
Horse culture. *See also* Coaching.
Brooklyn Jockey Club, 503
Coney Island Jockey Club, 503
Fox hunt, 427-428
Gerry, Robert L. polo pony, *320*
Goelet, 43, 430
Harriman, 447
Roosevelt, 311
Vanderbilt, Alfred polo pony, 460
Horse breeding,
Aknusti Stables, 481, 552, 571
Belmont, August Jr.,
Kentucky Stud Nursery, in Lexington, KY, 437
126 American Stakes winners, 437
Man O' War, 437, 572
Cornelia Gerry bid on the champion for her husband but lost, 438
Ryon D'Or purchased from William L. Scott, 465
Nursery Stud, Babylon, NY, 481
Merged with Kentucky Stud, 481,
Gerry, Arden Homestead Farms, Harriman partnership, 499
Scott, William L., Politician, 465
Algeria Stock Farm, PA, 465
Hollywood Stud Farm MD, 465
Horse cruelty. *See also* Bergh.
ASPCA, 100
Ambulance horse cart, 101, *276*
Horse Racing, 15, 16
Belmont, August Jr., 437
Belmont Park Race Track, 437
Wright Brothers Air Show, 438
Belmont Stakes, 437
Secretariat statue, 438
Triple Crown track, 438
Brooklyn Jockey Club, 465
Coney Island Jockey Club, 465
Gerry, Martha Farish, 583, 592
Jockey Club, first woman,
Jockey, Willie Shoemaker, 584
Rode *Forego,* 584, 592
Harness Racing, 409
Morris Park Race Course, 481
Horse season in Europe
Gerry, Robert L., 412
Vanderbilt, Alfred, 412
Horse shows
Madison Square Garden:
Gerry family, 378
1901 Show description, 378
Newport Horse Show, 386
Names of horses entered
Dudes & *Sophy Sparkles,* 386, 437
Hospitals:
Bellevue, 216
Bloomingdale Hospital for Insane, 59, *64*
Home for the Incurables, 60, 182, 355
Robert J. Livingston gift, 60
Hudson Street Hospital, 55
New York Hospital, 59, 104, 171, 182
Saint Luke's, 157

- Saint Mary's Hospital for Children, 305, 541, 549
- Small Pox Hospital, Marblehead, RI, 7-8

Hotels, Europe,
- Bristol Hotel, London, 356
- Claridge's Hotel, London, 450

Hotels, east coast,
- Bon Air Hotel, Augusta, GA, 280, *317*
- Hotel Brunswick, 165, 201, 210, 282
- Pierre Hotel, stands on the site of Fifth Avenue Gerry mansion, 520, 548, 561, 572
- Royal Poinciana Hotel, in Palm Beach Florida, 364, 367, 436
  - Vanderbilt train group: 364, 367
    - Gertrude Whitney, 364
    - Harry Payne Whitney, 364
    - Mabel Gerry, 364
  - Gerry winter visit, 436
- Sherry Hotel, 140, 321, 403, 406,
  - Matriarchs Ball, 321
- Waldorf Hotel, 288, 305, 372, 370, 346
  - Assembly Ball, 362
- Windsor Hotel, 141, 287, *396*, 469
  - Fire, 387-388, *396*

Howe, Julia Ward, background, 332-333
- Battle Hymn of the Republic, 332
- Biography by her children won Pulitzer Prize, 333
- Christopher Columbus Statue dedication, wrote A Mariner's Dream, 333
- Mother's Day creator, 333

Hudson Valley NY, 59, 128, 632,
- Gerry, 119, 128, 176, 284, 339, 440, 453, 470, 484, 493
- Goelets, 74, *88*, 97
- Livingston, 171, 177, 183, 632
- Roosevelt, 171, 442
- Vanderbilt, 249

Huguenots, 616

Hunt, Richard Morris, architect, *315*
- American Institute of Architects, 327, 358
  - Hunt papers & blueprints, 358
  - Founding member, AIA, 358
- Biltmore, North Carolina, 358, 558
- Breakers, Newport, 358, 349
- British Institute of Architects,
  - Victoria Gold Medal, 357
- Death, 357
  - Gerry Mansion, NYC, Central Park across street, 292
  - Delays, letters back & forth, 325- 327
  - Elbridge T. Gerry anger, 326
  - Description, 299-300, 325, 331
  - Finished 1894, last letter, 327
  - Floor plans, *328-330*
  - French Gothic style, 331
  - Hunt, Richard M. architect,292
  - Isolating room and nurse, 300
  - Land purchased, East 61st Street at Fifth Ave., Hamersley Estate, 292
  - Law library, 327
  - Louisa M. Gerry, owner and consultant to Hunt, 324
  - Madeira Wine, 326, *401*
  - Metropolitan Club, adjacent property,
    - Move-in, complex, 292
    - Customs holds furniture shipped from Europe, 340+
  - Plumbing, description, 331
- Ochre Court, Newport, 179
  - Description, 294, *315*
  - Personal architecture library, 358

Hunter's Island, New Rochelle, NY, 31

I

Ice Cutting, Lake Delaware,

Innes-Kerr, Henry, Scotland, *461*
- Duke of Roxburghe, 423-424
- Married May Goelet, Ogden's daughter, *Ochre Court*, Newport, 424

International Humane Conference,
- National Building Museum in Washington, DC, 472
- Honorary President, President W. H. Taft, 472
- Honorary Vice President, King George V,
- New York delegation, 473
  - Gerry, Elbridge T., 140, 472
  - Gerry, Peter G., 472
- Topic, child labor laws, 473

Ireland, Milton, 629

J

Jackson, President Andrew, 21-22, 26, 53, 83
James V, King, Scotland, 627
James VI, King Scotland, 627-628
Jerome Park, polo field, 136
Johnstown Flood, PA, 282
Jousselin family (Goelet), 621

K

Kemmler, William, murderer, 262, 273
  Article by Elbridge T. Gerry, 265
  Auburn Prison, NY, 264, 273
  Background, 262
  Capital Punishment by electric chair, first case, 264, 273
  Commission Report, 264
  Trial, 263-264
  Verdict of guilty appealed, 265
    Cruel and Unusual test, 264-265
    Upheld guilty verdict, 265
    U.S. Supreme Court refused to hear the case, 265
  Witnesses on appeal:
    Elbridge T Gerry, 265
    Thomas Alva Edison, 265, 273
  Westinghouse, George hires Attorney for Kemmler, 263-264
  Wife Tillie murdered, 263, 273
Kendall, Edward H. architect, Goelets, 156
  French Renaissance townhouses on Fifth Avenue, 156
Kernochan cottage, Newport R.I. called Edgewater, 179
Kidd, William Pirate, 622
King, Edward author, 2
King, Mackenzie 390, 393
  Canadian Prime Minister, 391
  Diary notes time at Gerrys, 39
  Harvard Fellowship, 390
  Tutor to Robert and Peter Gerry at Newport, 390-391
King, Rufus, 14
Kings College (British parent) *now* Columbia University, 39-40
Kingston, New York, 183, 224, 442, 471, 479, 484, 494
  Rondout, 183, 223, 252
Klondike Gold Rush, 309-310
Klunder, *Gilded Age* Florist, 218, 220, 249
Knickerbocker Bowling Club, 222
Knickerbocker, Cholly, society *column New York Times*, 446
Koch, Dr. Robert, Nobel Prize 297, 280

L

La Rochelle, France, 616
  1629 Siege, 616
Lake Delaware Farm, 46, *63*, *149*, 183, 226, 302, 443, 478, 482, 503
  Aknusti, Robert L. Gerry, 477
  Ancrum, Angelica Gerry 516
  Andes murder 439-440
  Andes train depot, 226
  Atmosphere is relaxed, 107, 183
  Buildings, 183
  Coaching run, 441-442
  Coulter, William, manager, 183
  Electra salvaged items sent to Lake Delaware, 480
  Farm tenants, 183
  Fishing (trout stocked), 183, 293
  Gerry Pullman car, train replaces yacht transport to Andes, 479
  Hardenburgh Patent, xviii, 18, 183, 429
  Horses, *150*
  Ice cutting on lake, 482,523
  Jersey Cow Dairy, 183
  Mode of travel, 479
    Carriage, 226
    Train, 226
    Yacht, 226
  Penelope sculpture, 236, *246*, 348, 557
  Pipe organ, Hilborne Roosevelt Opus 34 model, 224, *246*
  Products produced, sold, 183, 435
  Robbery, jewels and money, 492, 510
  Renovations to buildings, 293
  Road work, 484, 493
  Summer family activities, 266, *320*, 443

Animals on farm, 192, 441, 442
Charity work, 266, 285, 293, 438-439
Educated local children, 453, 485
Angelica, 439, 492
Bible classes, Mabel, 485
Sanatorium, 509
Reading, 285
Sailing, *150*
Water supplies upgraded, 293
Lake Delaware Boys Camp, *528*
Anniversary, one hundred years, 225
Buildings, 569
"Fresh air children," 476, 484
Lake Tunis, Robert Doig, 453-454
Organist, Charles D. Walker, 597
Robert L. Gerry,
Construction crews from Andes and Delhi, land purchased for 250 acre permanent camp, 477
Saint John's Chapel furnished,
Chalice & Paten from Electra, 477
Opus 34 pipe organ from the Morgan Lewis house, 597
Supplies - Andes Hardware, 476
Swimming pond crew from Delhi, 476
Landscape Architects
Olmsted, Frederick Law, 477
Steele, Fletcher, 517
Langtry, Lillie, mistress of Bertie, King Edward VII, 306
Life in America, 307
New York Society, 307
Gerry family friend, 307
Newport friends, 308
Race horses, 307
Suitors in England, 308
Whyte Ladye yacht, 306
Description of yacht, 308
Goelet, Ogden buys yacht from Lillie Langtry, 306-307
Latin School, Sterling, Scotland, 629
Law, cases represented by E.T. Gerry, *See also* Table of Cases
Gerry family cases:
Compensation for wharf water rights, Hannah, 212
Salmon v Meinhard, 507-508
Tenants sue Louisa, 508
Goelet family:
Depression foreclosures, 125
Elizabeth City, NJ, 143
Real estate matters, 48, 67, 68, 85, 92, 97, 108, 123, 125, 138, 141, 143, 144, 161, 229+, 365, 380, 404, 419, 454, 468, 486, 507
Trust Fund, Elbridge made Trustee, Accounting case, 229
Windsor Hotel, 141
Livingston family, interior property value, Robert J. Livingston, 203+
Landmark or significant cases:
ASPCA right to arrest, 108-109
Chauncey v Arnold, 67-68
Kemmler execution, Electric Chair, 262+
McFarland insanity defense, 92
Mary Ellen, child abuse, 117+
Marx Will case, 181+
Mumler spirit photograph, 82+
Salmon v Meinhard, business relationship, standard of loyalty, 507-509
Strong v Strong divorce, 72
Southwick, Spouses testify against one another, 107
Swill Milk Case, libel by innuendo, 178
Walsh v Washington Marine Insurance, seaworthiness, 72-73
Wolfe, public fraud, Schnapps Liquor 116
Legacies, family, 595-598
Alma Mater Statue, Columbia University Quad, 419, *461*, 597
Art collections and movements, Gallery of Living Art NYU, 596
Big Brothers Movement, 488, 597
Boys Clubs of New York City, 596
Gerry Fire Engine and fire house, 596
Gerrymander, 596
Goelet Scholarship, 597
Lake Delaware Boys Camp, 597
New York Society for the Prevention of Cruelty to Children, 597
New York University, founder, 597
Opera House, NYC, 595
Postage stamps, 596
Salve Regina College, 597

- Supreme Court of the United States Library, 598-603
- Wineries, 595

Lemon River, England, 1-2

Lewis family:
- Gertrude *See also* Livingston. 18, 45, 46, 63
- Morgan, General, 18
  - Daughter Margaret, 46
  - Judge and lawyer, 45
  - Governor New York State, 18
  - Lake Delaware Farm, 46
  - Married Gertrude Livingston, 45
  - Military service, 45
  - Princeton University, BA, 45
  - Schools, public, 45
  - Staatsburg Mansion, 46
  - War veterans, cared for 45-46

Libraries:
- Bar of the City of New York, 85, 102-103, *112*
- Elbridge Gerry, 6, 561
  - Books in personal collection, 102-103
- Elbridge T. Gerry, xv, 13, 38, 42, 155, 255, 598
  - Bibliophile, xv, 13, 38, 42, 155, 255, 598
  - Broadway Farm home, stored 208
  - Canon law books, 131, 187, 251, 369
  - Columbia University, Butler Library Rare Book Room, 39-41
  - Mansion library, 327, 368
    - Description, 71, 327, 368, 369
    - Law books, 42, 102-103, 369
    - U.S. Supreme Court gift, xv, 21, 598-603
    - Women's issues, 168
- George Vanderbilt, 558
- Harvard University, 6
- Lake Delaware house, 285, 297, 478, 504, 511, 549, 579, 582, 588
- Library of Congress, xvii, 13, 521
  - Thomas Jefferson donor, xvii
- New York Historical Society, 126
- New York Yacht Club library, *459*
- Newport Reading Room, 380
- Philadelphia Company Library Benjamin Franklin, 600
- Redwood Library, Newport, RI, 380
- Ship & yacht libraries, 255, 388, 376, 378
  - *Mayflower* yacht 2000 volumes, 207
- Skene Memorial, a Carnegie Public Library, 293-294
- Thomas Jefferson, xvii, 301, 561, 598, 600, 603,
- U.S. Supreme Court Library:
  - Gerry collection, xv, 560-561, 602, *603*
  - History, 598-603
  - Justices' books, 599-500, 602

Lincoln, Abraham:
- Emancipation Proclamation, 69
- Mary Todd, 84
- Spirit photograph, 84
- West Point, 74

Livingston Ancestry, xxiii-xxxii
- Agnes, 629
- Alexander, 625, 627-629
- Alida Livingston Armstrong, married William Brockholst Astor, 67
- Alida Schuyler, 632
- Andrew, 625
- Angelica sister of Robert James, *f*ather of Louisa Gerry, 104
- Archibald, 625
- Christina de Callendar, 626
- Cromwell, 630
- Elizabeth, "Bessie," twin of Ruth, 93, *456*
  - Cousin, Louisa M Gerry, 93
  - Daughter of Maturin Livingston, 412
  - Home in Richmond-on-Thames, outside London, 421, 426
  - Married Bentnick, George Cavendish, Duke of Portland, MP, British Museum, 515
- Gertrude, of Clermont Manor:
  - Children, Margaret, 52, 59, *63*
  - Lake Delaware Farm her share of Hardenburgh Patent, *594*
  - Married Gen. Morgan Lewis, 18, 45, 46, 54, 176, 183, 477, 483, 503, 588
- James, Col. Continental Army, *195*
  - Son of John Livingston, 168

Grandfather of Cady Stanton, suffragette, 168
Janet, Clermont Manor farm, 177
Sister, Gertrude Livingston Lewis, 176
Great Aunt of Louisa Livingston Gerry, *87*, 176,
Married General Richard Montgomery, 176, *195*
Re-buried husband, 177
Sword returned, by England, 177
Janet Fleming, Scotland, 629
Married Rev. John Livingston, 630
John Livingston, Reverend, 629-631
Married Janet Fleming, 630
Leving, Baron, 625
Louisa Storm Livingston, 53, *532*
Death, 189
Mother of Louisa M. Gerry, 519
Married Robert James Livingston, 54
Louisa Mathilda. *See also* Gerry, Louisa
Courtship, 50, 67
Death, 503, 504
Inheritance, 157
Married E T Gerry, 46
Margaret, daughter of Col. James Livingston, 168
Mother of Cady Stanton, suffragette, 168
Margaret, Daughter of Gertrude Livingston and Gen. Morgan Lewis, 52, 59, *63*
Death, 59
Margaretta Schuyler, 632
Maturin, brother of Robert James, 46, 172
Children: twin girls,
Elizabeth married a Duke, W. Cavendish Bentnick, 166
Ruth, married Ogden Mills, 253
Death, 253
Buried in Saint James Church, Hyde Park, NY, 253
Home, Staatsburg, 46, *63*
Married Ruth Baylies, 253
Newport holiday visit, 164
Maturin, Jr., son of Morgan Livingston
Death 139-140
Robert, Lord of Clermont, 168, 629-632
Robert, the nephew, 632
Robert C., brother of Gertrude, 44-45
Robert James, *63*
Albany Bridge built, 55, *63*
Birth at Staatsburg, NY, 52, *63*, 177, 260
Bloomingdale Hospital, 59
Buried, St. James Cemetery, Hyde Park, NY, 291
Children's Aid Society, 56, 121, 162, 288
Children Louisa & Warren, 55-56
Coast Guard Survey Team, 53
Apprentice to Hassler, 53
Daughter met E. T. Gerry, 56
Death, 56, 291
Death of wife, 189
Elbridge T. Gerry first met, 44, 51
Funeral, Church of Heavenly Rest, 291
Homes:
Lake Delaware estate, 183
New York townhouse, 206, 218, 290
Married Louisa Storm, 54, 189
New Jersey Farm Estate, 54
New York Home for the Incurables, 60, 182
News Boys Lodging House, 141
Partner, August Belmont, 54
Pneumonia, 279
Pleurisy, 290
Real estate, 203
Society of the New York Hospital, 60, 96, 115, 135
Temperament, 171
Wall Street banker, 54
Will, 291
Yale College, 52
Ruth, twin of Elizabeth, 249, 269, 277, 293, 437, 467, 478, 500
Daughter of Maturin, 46
Married Ogden Mills, son of Darrius Ogden Mills, 46, 59
Thurston, 625
Warren, 54
Burlington College B.A., 54
Oxford University M.A., 55
Death, early, 55

William, 626-629
Livingston homes:
Airth Castle, Scotland, 629
Albany, New York, 632
Ancrum, Scotland, 630+, 516
Callendar House, Scotland, 627-629
Clermont Manor, New York, xviii, 45, 46, 168, 177, 183, 340
Falkirk, 625
Highland Park, New Jersey, 54, 97, 133, 142, 171, 322
Kilsyth, Scotland, 627
Lake Delaware, Gertrude, 52
Leving Manor, Scotland, 625
Staatsburg, New York, 55, *63*
Rotterdam, Holland, 632
Sterling Castle, Scotland, 627
Stranrear, 629+
Livingston ministers:
John, 629-632
William, 626-629
Livingston temperament, 171
Locke, John *quotation,* 35, 601, 621, 624, 629, 630
London, 601, 611
Lord of the Manor, Clermont, 44, 628, 632
Louis, King, 608, 616

M

McKim, Mead & White,
Arch at Washington Square, Stanford White 260, *272, 318*
Camp Harmony, Canadian salmon, Stanford White, 288, *318*
Goelet Brothers Building, 203
Madison Avenue Garden 190, *195*
See also Madison Square Garden
Murder of Stanford White, 443+, *462*
Metropolitan Club, 292, *316*
Southside, Robert L Goelet cottage Newport R.I., *193*, 622
Staatsburg enlarged, *63*
Madison, Dolly, Gerry friend, 17
Madison, James President, 6, 15, 16, 48, 75, 609, 620
Madison Square Garden, *195*
Barnum, P.T dispute with Elbridge T. Gerry, 299
Dog shows, 474
Goelet, Robert Wilson, Great Dane and white terriers, 474
Horse shows, 378, 409
Malden, England, 4
Man o' War (*race horse*), 437
Manice family (Goelet), 621
Marblehead, MA, 3-10, 15, 22, 26, 33, 171, 211, 222, 237, 240, 303, 584, 596
Mary, Queen of Scotland, 627-628
Marshall, John, 14
Masons:
Elbridge Gerry, Master, 7
Philanthropic Lodge, MA, 7
Massachusetts, 4
Newbury, 4
Massachusetts Bay Colony, 629
Massachusetts Historical Society, 11
Mazer, Gallatin Cup, 608
Mayflower yacht, Boston, 221, 238, 254, 339
Mayflower yacht, Goelet, 308, 375-377, 383, 389, *397*, 405, 480
McAllister, Ward:
Almack's Assembly Room balls in London, 249, 289
Patriarchs Ball, 243
Gilded Society's Four Hundred, 289
McKinley, William, President, 381, 407-408
Medico-Legal Society NYC, 98, 103, 106
Capital Punishment, 226
Melville, Herman, Billy Budd, 227
Articles of War, 228
Mutiny Act, 228
Merchant mariners, shipping, 1, 4
Metropolitan Club. *See* clubs.
Metropolitan Ball, 1860 New York City, Prince Albert, 56
Metropolitan Opera House, NYC, 202, *246*
Box seats, 234
Gerry box, description, 234
Gerry incident, 215-216
J.K. Emmet, insane spree, 215
Built by, 202
Burned to the ground, 304

Rebuilt by original core investors, 305
Astor, John J. IV,
Goelet brothers,
Julliard, A.D.,
Morgan, J.P.,
Vanderbilt, Cornelius II,
Demolished in 1967, 305
Opera season canceled, 304
Private boxes, 339
Description, 202-203
Julliard, 305
Largest American theatre, 202
Lincoln Center, Goelets, 595
Opening nights, 202
General seats, 203
Goelet, Francis and Robert W., patron of:
Gustav Mahler hired, 449
Arturo Toscanini hired, 449
Milk Production, NY legislation, 136
Mill, Wool Spinning – Gerry family, 29
Millionaires Club, 291, 299
Mills, Darius Ogden, 320
Mills, Elizabeth, daughter of Ogden Mills
Married Whitelaw Reid, 412
Mills, Ogden married Ruth Livingston, 46
(twin of Elizabeth Livingston)
Mills, Ogden Livingston, Senator, 493
Milton, Ireland, 629
Mission of Our Lady of the Rosary, now
Mother Seton Shrine at 7 State Street, the
Battery, NYC, 385, *401*
Monroe, James President, 11, 20-21
Montgomery, General Richard, 45, *195*
Born Ireland, 176
Married, Janet Livingston, 45
sister Gertrude Livingston Lewis 176
Great-uncle of Louisa Mathilda
Livingston Gerry, 176
Pontiac's Rebellion, 176
Revolutionary War, 176
Benedict Arnold, 177
Continental Army, 177
Died Battle of Quebec, 177
Re-buried in America, 177
Trinity College, 176
Sword returned to family, 176
Montgomery, Janet Livingston, 45, 177-178,
More, St. Thomas, 631
Morgan, J.P. Commodore:
Cozzens Hotel owner, 138
Madison Square Garden, 299
Metropolitan Club, 292
Metropolitan Opera House, 160
Quotation, 197
Yacht Club:
Donated land, 407
Morgan Cup, 238, 240
Yacht named Corsair, 252
Mosby, John Singleton:
Florence Mosby case, 161
Grey Ghost, Civil War, 161
Mosby's Rangers, 161
Patton, Gen. George S., 162
Mount Vesuvius:
Cable car inspired the song Funicula,
Funiculi, 441
Eruption described, 440-441
Gerry family visit, 236
Goelet, Harrietta witness on her yacht
Nahma yacht in Bay of Naples, 440
Olympic Games in Athens canceled,
rescheduled for 1908 London, 441
Mumler, William Howard, 82
Barnum, P.T., 83
Mary Todd Lincoln, 84
National Photographic Assoc., 83
Spirit photography, 82
Spiritualist Movement, 82
Murder, Stanford White, 443-444, *462*
Museum of Natural History, 323
Expansion & renovation, 353
Gerry, Elbridge T., Trustee, 352, 587
Museum of the City of New York
Doll house, Goelet, 36, *61*, 80-81

N

Nahma, Goelet yacht *See* Yachts
National Guard created when Commodore
Elbridge T. Gerry suggested private
yachts be used by the U.S. Navy, 231
Rear Admiral Stephen B. Luce, 231
Secretary of War, Sheridan, 232

Unprotected East Coast, 232
National Medal of Arts, Francis Goelet awarded at White House, 595
National Photographic Association, 83
Abraham Bogardus, Rep., 83
National Register of Historic Places:
Cady Stanton home, NJ, 168
Harlan and Hollingsworth, NJ, 207
Staatsburg-on-Hudson, 46
Woods-Gerry house, Providence, 561+
Navy, origin with Elbridge Gerry, 9
Navy Service, Gerry brothers, 20
Neptune Hotel, New Rochelle NY, 31, 128
New Amsterdam, 617
New Rochelle, New York, 31, 35, 38, 128, 312, 606, 616
New York City Courts:
Children's courthouse, 472
Gerry, Elbridge T. advisor, 472
Proposed plans, 472
Today is *Baruch College,* 472
Magistrates Court, 216
Surrogates Court, 472
Tweed Courthouse, 342
New York City Hall:
Gerry testimony, charities, 168
ASPCA Ordinance, 131
Board of Health, Infant Asylum, Elbridge T. Gerry Letter, 178
Buildings Inspector Infant Asylum Elbridge T. Gerry Letter, 189-190
Challenge to ownership of "made land" owned by patriarch families since the 17th century, 454
Civil War, 68
Fires, Goelet losses, 183-184
Growth in the Gilded Age, 175, 203
Property investments, 175
Madison Ave. extension, 37-38, 96
The Tombs, Hall of Justice, 101, 118
New York City Department of Charities Commission on Pauper Insane, 298+
Gerry, Elbridge T., Chair, 298
New York City early business network, xviii
Goelet, Ogden, Thompson, and Walton,
New York City Mayor:
Commission on the Pauper Insane Gerry, Elbridge T., Chair, 298
Gerry, Elbridge T., name placed in 1894 pool of nominees for Mayor, as a Democrat, 336, 344
New York City, Parks Department supports Fifth Avenue residents in opposition to trolley, 215
New York City Police, annual dinner, Carnival of Cops, 218-220
New York City Police Corruption City Vigilance League, 341
Lexow Committee Hearings, 342
Gerry, Elbridge T. defends NYSPCC case used to show Police corruption, 342
Lexow Committee report, 344
Parkhurst, Charles H. Pastor published, Our City Vigilance League, 342
Tammany Hall graft, 342
New York City Sinking Fund, Robert Goelet sought injunction, 214
New York Historical Society, 26, 595
New York Hospital Soc., 59, 135, 187, 355
Board of Governors, 60, 96, 171, 182
Mrs. John J. Astor III, 115
New York Society for the Prevention of Cruelty to Children,
Agent Badges, 123, 126, *148*
Agent duties, 127, 473
Act to Prevent and Punish Wrongs to Children, 126
Annual Charities Conference, 561-562
Annual Reports, 235, 236
Articles by E.T. Gerry, 184, 192, 377
Auxiliary Committee, women Board members, resign in protest, 506-507
Bergh, Henry, 123
Blackwell Island prison, 158
Building owned, 158
Cartoons, 191, *276*
Case statistics, 236
Children's Court, 472
Consul General, Italy, 123, 146
Copperfield, David, referenced by Elbridge T, Gerry, 157
Corruption, 342
Courtroom insults, 342-344
Creation of Gerry Society, 122-123, 473

David Copperfield quote, 157
Elbridge T. Gerry, "father of child protection" 206
Endowment disagreement on Board of Directors, 506+
Gerry mocked at hearing, 342
Fundraising editorial, 180
Great Meddlers, 101, 191
International Humane Conference, 472
American Delegates:
President William H. Taft, 472
Commodore Elbridge T. Gerry 472
Senator Peter G. Gerry 472
U.K. Delegate, King Edward V, 472
International Leader, 123, 146,147,472
China case, 146
Gerry appeal to the U.S. President and Congress, 158
Cuba, Ellis Island children, 414-416
Raja Yoga Academy, 414
Theosophists, 414-415
England Theosophists, 146, 170
Gerry represents USA with Italian Representative, 146
Italian child trafficking, 123, 146
Illegal in America, child traffic, 146
Society jurisdiction, 165
Legal Counsel, 123, 271
Legislation:
Act to Prevent and Punish Wrongs to Children, 126
Baby farming ban, 204
Child protection, 126, 192
Model Legislation, 497
Opposed bill for a national trust to oversee all charitable societies, 472+
Opposed bill limiting right of Magistrates to commit children, 291
Parental consent children on stage, 331
Whipping Post Bill , spousal abuse, 204
Gerry asked to leave the General Assembly Chamber, 390
Magistrate's authority, 295, 373
Magistrates must preserve hearing notes and record, 414
Mary Ellen case, 117-123, 472
Girl's statement in Court, 118
Etta Wheeler, 117
Mosby, Florence case, Grey Ghost, 161+
National Humane Association, 430
National Humane Review, 473
New York State Convention of Soc., 377
New York Times, 1874 Gerry pleas, 169
Parental rights, 261, 287, 295
Opposition to bill to give parental consent, 231
Partnership with Police, 127, 473
Police corruption case, 342
Purpose and goals NYSPCC, 121-122, 192, 209-210, 212, 430-431
Presidents:
Elbridge T. Gerry, 157, 271
John D. Wright, first, 122
Protective Society, 117, 121-122
Religious affiliation of child must guide placement, 364-365
Shepherd's Fold, 157
Gerry marches children into court, 157
Theatre monitoring, 127
Callender's Minstrels, 191
Col. Mapleson, 169
Gilmore's Theatre, 182
Interview about, 182
Interview, damage to children, 182
Madison Avenue Garden,
P.T. Barnum show, 191
Letters published between Barnum and Gerry, 191
New York Opera with children actors,
Aida, 169
Mephistopheles, 169
New York Times, 121, 169, 209
Stage Children, 140, 169, 178, 182, 497
Tivoli Theatre, 127
Wallack Theatre case - under age sixteen,127
Wheeler, Etta in Mary Ellen case, 117
New York State
Bar Association founding, *148*, 202, 280, 271
Commission on Capital Punishment, 226
Advisor, Thomas A. Edison, 250, 265
Article by E.T. Gerry, 265

"Capital Punishment by Electricity"
Chair, Elbridge E. Gerry, 226, *273*
Electrical Execution Act, members:
Hale, Matthew, lawyer, 226
Southwick, A.P. doctor, 226
Methodology, 226,
Books, 369
Questionnaire, 228
Report of Commission, 264
Convention of Societies, 377
Gerry, Elbridge T. President, 377
Convention to Revise State Constitution,
Fifth Convention, Gerry, 77, *89*
Delegate, 77
Gerry motions, 78
Judiciary changes, 78
Legislation initiated by Gerry:
Child Protection, 118
Milk Production, 136
General Assembly, Albany, NY,
Gerry asked to leave the House Chamber, 353-354
Legislative Wasp, 354
Whipping Post Bill debate, 53-54, 204, 353
New York University, Albert Gallatin,
Founder, Albert Gallatin 75
Frederic Gallatin, graduate, 75
New York Yacht Club, *See also* Yachts.
1, 38, 47, 131, 173, 203, 205
America's Cup, 173, 243
"a match well made," 175
Annual cruise, 173, 207
Fleet size, 283
Illumination, 303
Boston Yacht Club, 243
Building dedication:
Ladies reception, 407
Model Room, 407
Morgan, JP donated land, 407
3 foot Silver Loving Cup, 407
Whitney Warren architect, 407
Commodore Elbridge T. Gerry,
Ballot fraud, 221
Boston Herald reporter on Electra, 237
Electra, first cruise, 252
Loss of flange, 252
Cruises, annual:
Harbor, 242
Night lights, 303
Marblehead, 238-239
Eastern Club, 237
Seasick ladies, 226
Socializing, 239
Start signal, 238
Deed of Gift, 243
Dinner on *Electra*, 200, 208, 226, 238, 266, 303+, 310, 337, 338, 409
Election, 220
Flag ship, *Electra*, 222, 226
George Schuyler, 178, 283, 254
Fleet Surgeon, Dr. Morris J. Asch, 284
Harper's Weekly sketch, 302, *317*
Last cruise as Commodore, 302
Cannon salutes extended, 252, 240
Dinner on Electra, 337
Eastern Yacht Club, Marblehead, 238
Golden age of yachting, 338
Grand Illumination, 207, 252, 254, 303
Marblehead overnight, 303
Master Steam License, 233, 252
National Guard formed, 231
New York Navigation School
Certified 400 yacht officers to Naval Standards, 233
Record keeper, cruises, 223, 240, 252, 302,
Signal flags, unfurled, 303
Socializing in port, 173, 179, *193*, 199, 200, 238, 303
Commodore J.P. Morgan
Morgan Cup Regatta, 238
Newport RI to Marblehead MA
Yacht Club Building, 175, 207, 407
Commodore's Cup, 310, *317*
Fiftieth Anniversary Cruise, 337
Founding Group, 173
Goelet Cup, Newport Regatta
Established, 200
$500 Sloop Cup, 200
$1,000 Schooner Cup, 200
Tiffany and Co., 38, 200
Newport, Regatta, 219-220

Model room, 175, 410
Cambria model, Robert L. Gerry
Electra model, Elbridge T. Gerry
Magic model, Robert L. Gerry
Organization,
George Schuyler, 173
America's Cup, 173
Club condolences, 283
Death on *Electra*, 283
Prince Henry of Prussia visit, 410
Steamboat, guest use, 223
Stevens, Com. John C., 174
"There is no second place," 175
Testimonial silver cup, 310
Yacht registration privileges, 175
Newbury, MA, 4
Newfoundland, 2, 310
Newport, Rhode Island, 163-164
Baileys Beach, 164
Bancroft, George, historian, 163
Bellevue Avenue, 164, 302, *317*
Breakers, Cornelius Vanderbilt, 179
Siblings:
Alfred Vanderbilt, 392
Gertrude Vanderbilt 349
Casino, bicycles, dances, tennis,
Coaching, 333, 386
Angelica Gerry, *320*
Cliff Walk, history, 164, 179
D'Hautville Cottage, Mabel Gerry, 544
Edgewater, Ogden Goelet 179
Engagement gossip, 347, 386, 445
Gerry to Goelet, 422
Fairlawn, Levi Morton, 164
Fashion, 422
Garden show, 404, *523*
Astor, Mrs. John J., 404
Belmont, Perry, 423
Gerry Garden, 404, 423
Goelet, Harrietta, 295, 404, 423
Vanderbilt, Mrs., 405
Gardeners, *523*
American Florist magazine, 404
National Directory of Gardeners, 405
Ochre Court, 374
Private Gardeners' Flower Shows, 404
Seaverge, Arthur Griffin, 387
Southside, 374
Greenhouses, *523*
Builder, E.J. Berwind,
Gerry, Elbridge T., 387, 404, 514
Palms and Ferns used for private balls in NYC, 405
Horticultural Society, 404, 423
Golf Club at Brenton Point, 306, *319*
Architect, Whitney Warren, *319*
Ladies Golf, 333, *319*
Inchiquin House, rented by Robert Gerry for his wife and four children, located 3-doors down from Seaverge, 513-514
Lyndenhurst, Gerry rental, 302, 305, *317*, 334, 350, 366
Jewelry theft, 310
Ritchie, J. Wadsworth, 334, 345
Marble House, Consuelo Vanderbilt 349
Newport Reading Room, men's Club, Gerry men members, 380
Ocean Lawn, rented by Senator Peter G. Gerry, located across the street from Southside, his cousin Robert Walton Goelet's summer home, 514
Ochre Court, Ogden Goelet
Close to Gerry rental, 302
Description, 295
Jewelry theft reported, 434
1000 guests, 211
Redwood Library, 380
Gerry family members, 380
Salve Regina College, 517
Seaverge, 40 room cottage, 350, *395*
Base for Peter G. Gerry's run for Congress in RI, 470, 482, 493
Bellevue Ave on the Cliff Walk, 375
Fourth of July celebration, 470, 480, 484
Greenhouses, 387, 409, *523*
Inherited by Mabel Gerry Drury, 520
Purchased fully furnished by Elbridge T Gerry, 374
Redecorate cottage, 408
Stables, 386,
Taxes, Gerrys are Rhode Island residents, 380

Society for the Suppression of Newspaper Notoriety, 335
Gerry Elbridge T., President, 336
Newspapers' response, 336
Southside, Robert Goelet cottage near
Gerry rental, 179, 199, 260, 374
Storm causes major damage, 311
Tax assessment on property 380
Visits, Gerry & Mills, 514
War effort, 492
Yacht Club Station, *459*
Owned by Gerry, E.T. and Goelet brothers, 404
Newsboys Lodging House, 57, 141
Robert J Livingston Prize, 323
Newspapers, 56
Boston Globe, Electra, 345
Boston Courier, 28
Boston Herald, 237
The Express, 50, 345
Harpers Weekly, 84, 302
Herald Tribune, merged title, 69
New York Evening Post, 107
New York Herald, 135, 279, 281, 345
New York Sun, opera fashion, 234
New York Tribune, 50, 92
New York Times, 50, articles:
ASPCA, 102, 104
Charity stories, 56, 60, 76, 159, 174
Cholly Knickerbocker, 446
Deaths, 362, 551
Draft Riots, 92, 96
Gerry cases, 106
Washington Market case, 50
Lake Delaware Boys Camp 100th Anniversary, 225
Theatre letters, 191
NYSPCC, 121-122, 169
Real estate, 92, 96
Round table, 91
Society page, 74, 129, 138, 217, 241
Vesuvius erupts, 441
Washington Square Arch, 260, 310
Windsor Hotel Fire, 387
Yachts, 208, 221, 346
Washington Post, 156
Society for the Suppression of Newspaper Notoriety, 335, 421
Gerry Elbridge T., President, 335
Newspapers' response, 336
Newton Abbot, England, 2, 6
Newton Bushel, England, 2
Nicholson, Hannah, 613
Non-Conformist, Scotland, 629
Noyes, William Curtis, lawyer, *62*
Death, 42-50,
Gerry apprenticeship, 42
Hamilton College gift, 71

O

Ochre Court, Newport, 295
now Salve Regina College
Description, 295, 517, 597
Chef goes crazy, 444-445
Hunt, Richard M. architect, *315*, 327, 358
Party extravagance, 211
Party favors from Europe, 406
2000 lights, 406
Two dinners by Sherry's, 406
Vladimirovich, Grand Duke Boris visits Goelet mansion, 413-414, *461*
Ogden family:
Johattan, 619
Sarah, 619-620
Oles, Bill, 9
Olmsted, Frederick Law, landscape Architect,
Biltmore estate, NC, 558
Central Park, NYC, 466
Olmsted, Frederick Law, Jr., Landscape Architect for roads at Aknusti, Lake Delaware, 477
Olympic Games 1906 closed due to Eruption of Mount Vesuvius, 450
Olympic Games 1908, London, 450
International Olympic Committee
Initiated 4-year cycle of games, 450
Marathon set at 26 miles in London due to American runner refusing to "dip the flag" to King's Box, 451
Opera boxes, 234

Ophir Farm, 497
Orange County Hunt Club, 409, 427, 432, 434, 451, 475, 499, 567+, 573, 586
Organ, Opus 34 by Hilborne Roosevelt – Located at Lake Delaware, NY, 224+
Orne, Azor Colonel, 8
Orphan Asylum, 59, 175, 189, 335
Orphan trains, 57-58, *64*
  Charles L. Brace, 57
  Children's Aid Society, 57
O'Shaughnessy, Arthur W. *quote, 67*
Ostrich Farm, Los Angeles, CA,
  Gerry family visit, 432, *460*
Our Dumb Animals magazine, 141

P

Panic of 1837, 54
Panic of 1857, depression, 43, 47, 76
Panic of 1873, depression, 138
Paris, 1889 World Exposition, 309, 275
Parliament, Scotland, 627, 630-631
Passy, France, Benjamin Franklin, 351
Patterson, Admiral Howard
  Author, Yachtsman Guide, 233
  Dedicated to E.T. Gerry, 233
  Death, 542
  Father of Naval Reserve, 232
    Certified Yachtsmen for National Guard or Naval Reserve Duty, 232
  Friend and tutor, E.T. Gerry, 233
  Gerry, E.T., Masters License, 233
    Navigation set at Supreme Court 233
  NY Navigation School, 233
Patton, Gen. George S. as a child, 162
Patriarchs Ball, 171, 253, 290, 298, 426, 434
  Church admonition, 235
  McAllister, Ward, 249
"Pearl," Margaret Gerry, *113*, died as child
Pearl Street, NYC, 184, 230, 618
Pearls:
  Ball gown adorned in pearls, 187
  Black Pearls, Catharine the Great, 512
  Gerry, Lillie's 81 pearl necklace, 297
  Gift from father, worn at wedding, 469
  Townsend, Mathilde pearl strands:
    Wedding gift for Barnard bride, 159
Penelope, 1867 white marble sculpture by Franklin Simons, purchased in Rome by E.T. Gerry, 236+, *246*, 348, 552, *557*
Philanthropy in the Gilded Age. *See also* family names. 48, 57, 145, 153-154, 254, 355-56, 430, 517, 520, 587
  Albany Cathedral Fund contributors: 205
    Fish, Hamilton, 205
    Gerry, Elbridge T., 205
    Harriman, E.H., 205
    Martin, Bradley, 205
    Vanderbilt, Cornelius, 205
  Bloomingdale Hospital, 59, *64*, 355
  Boys Clubs, NYC, 428
  Charity Ball, 76, 171
  Concert for St. Mary's Hospital for Children, 305
  Harvard Business School, 166, 449
  Home for Incurables, 60, 182, 355
  House of Relief, 59, 355
  Lilly Langtry Charity, 322, 356, 403
  Maine Hospital Ship Fund, 403
  "Professors" a newspaper nickname, 209
  Sisters of Saint Mary, Bazaar and auction host - Mabel Gerry at mansion, 495+
  Women philanthropists, 210
Philibert, Duke, 608
Phillipse Manor, 616-617
Pierre Hotel stands on 1927 site of Fifth Avenue Gerry Mansion, demolished 520
Pipe organ, Hilborne Roosevelt Opus 34 Model, 224+
Photographers:
  Bogardus, Abraham, 83
  Gerry, Lillian, 297
  Mumler, William H., 82
Photography case, 82
Physiocrate, 611
  D'Enville, Duchess, 610+
Pinard, caterers to Society, 159
  Patriarchs' Ball, 220
  Gerry family caterer, 218
Pinckney, Charles, 14
Pirate, William Kidd, 622
Plymouth, England, 629
Plymouth Colony, 629

Polo horses – cruelty, 13, 136
Polo teams. *See also* horse sports.
  Aiken Team, 579
  Aknusti Team, 478-479
  Hall of Fame, 572, 586, 587
  Harvard University, 587
Portraits,
  Ann Thompson Gerry, 19, 33
  Angelica Gerry, *554*
  Beatrice Goelet, 216, *247*
  Elbridge Gerry, 33
  Elbridge Gerry, Jr., *34*
  Elbridge Thomas Gerry, *frontispiece*
  Hannah Goelet Gerry, *34*
  James Gerry, Captain, *34*
  Lillian Gerry, *478*
  Louisa M Gerry, *194*, *402*
  Mabel Gerry, *546*
  Mathilde Townsend, *448*
  Ogden Goelet, 397
  Rebecca Russell Greenleaf Gerry, 5, 33
  Thomas Gerry, Captain, 33
Post, Emily, etiquette, 277+
  Author, 278
  Divorce, 278
Potter, Bishop:
  Gerry family, 222, 251
  Grace Church, 210
  Christopher Columbus statue
    dedication ceremony, 332
Presbytery, Scotland, 628
Prince Albert Edward, *Bertie*. *See* Edward
  VII, King.
Prince Henry of Prussia, 410
  Vanderbilt lavish dinner, 410
Pritchard, William A., boy orator, 502
  See also Red Scare.
Progressive Era, 57, 106, 147, 349, 362
  American plutocracy, 384
  Revenue Act, income and Inheritance tax
    began, 384
Puritan colony, 629

Q

Queen Street, NYC, 619
Queen Victoria, 393
  Diamond Jubilee, 363
  Holiday, 375, 426, 437

R

Railroads
  Delaware and Eastern RR, 223
    Kingston to Andes, NY, 223
    Andes Depot closed 1925, 223
  Delhi Middletown RR, 223
    R.J. Livingston stock, 223
  Grand Central Terminal, 37, 60, 182
  Harlem RR 60, 95, 131
  Illinois Central RR,
    Board of Directors,
    Robert Goelet,
  Oregon RR, & Navigation Co., 573
  Orleans RR, 507
  Reading RR, 309
  Southern Pacific, 429
  Union Pacific, 429
Railroad overexpansion, 47
Rasputin, the Mad Monk, 562
  Ancestor Prince Felix sued MGM Studios
    for libel in movie Rasputin and the
    Empress, 512-513
Ratze, Elisabeth, 618
Red poppies, 621
Red Scare, 501
  Labor unions, 501-502
  Pritchard, William A., boy orator 502
  Red hunting, 502
  Russian Revolution, Bolshevik, 501
  Seattle shipyard strike, 502
  Senator Peter Gerry, 503
  Socialist Party, 501
  Unemployed soldiers, WWI, 501
  Winnipeg Strikes, Canada, 501-502
Reformed Church of Scotland, 628, 631
Reformation, Scotland, 631
Reid, Elizabeth Mills, 93
First cousin of Louisa M. Gerry, 93

Married Whitelaw Reid, 93
Reid, Jean, 424, 450-451
Children, two sons:
Edward, godson of King Edward VII, 451
Commander of Household Cavalry for Queen Elizabeth II, 451
Commander of the British Empire for WWII charity work, 451
Daughter of Whitelaw Reid, 424
Friends with:
Gerry, Mabel, cousin, 424
Townsend, Mathilde, a Washington DC belle, 425
Married Sir John Hubert Ward, Second Earl of Dudley at Queen's Chapel, in Saint James Palace London, 450-451
Reception, Dorchester House, 451
Wedding guests:
Gerry, Elbridge T. & Louisa, 450+
King Edward VII and Queen Alexandra, 451
Reid, Whitelaw:
Ambassador to England, 412, 425
Background, 93+, 425
Civil War correspondent, 93
Minister to France, 425
New York Tribune, Associate Editor to Horace Greeley, 93, 425
Children:
Ogden Mills Reid, Managing editor, New York Tribune, 426
Jean Reid, married Sir John Hubert Ward, Second Earl of Dudley, 451
Died at Dorchester House, London while Ambassador, 426
Dorchester House, London, 421, 426
Fourth of July celebrations, 500
Gerry, Elbridge T. joins, 421
Gerry, Mabel visits Aunt and Uncle in Washington, 424
Gerry yacht to Oyster Bay to meet with President Teddy Roosevelt, Sagamore Hill, 412
Goelet, Ogden, joined him for Queens Jubilee in London when Ogden died on his yacht, 426
Home, Ophir Farm, Westchester, NY,
McKim, Mead, and White, designed the mansion, 426
Frederick Law Olmsted, landscaped the estate, 426
Married Elizabeth Mills, first cousin of Louisa M. Gerry, 93
Renwick, James Jr. *151*
Architect, 125
Gallatin friend, 125
Gallatin NYC home, 125
Gallatin East Hampton home, 129, 134
Restaurants and caterers, NYC:
Delmonico's, 298
Assembly Ball, 279, 417, 418
Carnival of Cops dinner, 219
Patriarchs' Ball, 171, 186, 235
Pinard, 159, 218, 220
Patriarch's Ball, 235
Restigouche River, Canada:
Goelet, Francis, 288
Atlantic Salmon Foundation, 288
Toad Brook Club, 288
Tracadie Club, 288
Goelet, Ogden, land purchase, 287
Leasehold for ten years, 287
Matapediac River confluence, 287
Quebec Province, 288
Restigouche Salmon Club, 288
Camp Harmony site, 288
Club house, by Stanford White, 318
Hoffman, Rev. Eugene,
Salmon processed, 288
Revenue Act, taxation, 384
Richard III, King, *quotation*, 403
Richelieu, Cardinal, France, 616
Ritchie, J. Wadsworth, suitor, 321, 334
Angelica broke engagement, 345
Gossip excited in NYC, 334, 346
Bachelor Dude, 321
Death, Boer War injury, 347
Gerry, Angelica, engaged, 322
Moved to England, 346
Newport, Gerry family visit, 334
Nickname Jack, 334
Horse breeder, 334
JA Tule Ranch, Texas, 334

Tooker, Emily 345, 346
Angelica Gerry's friend, 381
Death, 346
Engagement announced, 346
Married Jack Ritchie, 346
Road Apple raffle game, 586
Rochambeau Grenadier 1781, 610
Rochefoucauld, Duc de la, 610+
Rockaway Beach, NY, Thomas Gerry summer, 30, 31, 128
Rolaz, Sophie, 612
Roman walls in England:
Antoine Wall, 625
Hadrian's Wall, 625
Roosevelt, James A., 282, 442
Roosevelt, Robert B., 145
Roosevelt, Theodore, Teddy, 69, 416
Childhood neighbor of Gallatins, Gerrys, Goelets, 416
Mayflower yacht, Presidents yacht, 377
Rough Riders, 381, 393
Spanish American War, 381
Sagamore Hill, home, 412, 455
President, 425, 426
Vice President, 408
Angelica and Mabel Gerry attend inauguration, 425
Rotterdam, Holland, Livingston, 632
Roxburghe Castle, 631
Floors Castle, Scotland, 424, *461*, 485
Royal Swedish Academy, 611
Rush, Benjamin, 12
Russell, Samuel, 5-6
Russian Flu, 279

S

Sabbath Day law broken, 5
Saint Aubin d'Ecrosville, 621
Salmon Fishing, Canada, 287
Restigouche River, 287
Goelet, Francis 288
Atlantic Salmon Foundation, 288
Saint Andrews, Scotland, 288
Goelet Research Center, 288
Toad Brook Club, 288
Tracadie Club, 288
Goelet, Ogden, 287
Leasehold for ten years, 287
Restigouche Salmon Club, 287
Salmon processed, 288
Stanford White, 388
Salve Regina College, Newport, 295, 597
Formerly Ochre Court, 517
Saratoga Springs, NY, 35
1858 Goelet/Gerry holiday, 49, *62*, *88*
1874 Gerry holiday, 119
1876 Gerry holiday, 128
Sargent, John Singer, portrait painter 216
Beatrice Goelet, age seven, 216, *247*, 411
Mathilde Townsend, 448
Schermerhorn, Edmund, recluse after Ruth Baylies married Maturin Livingston, 253
Mrs. Schemerhorn ill with flu, 410
Schorching – bicycles, 365
Schuyler, Alida Albany, 410
Schuyler, George, grandson of Peter Schuyler, Albany 46-47, 283
America's Cup yacht race, 174
Deed of gift, Gerry, 174
Reviewed, 243
Revised & disputed, 243
Death on yacht Electra, 284
New York Yacht Club, 47
Schuyler, Margaretta Albany, 632
Schuyler, Peter, Albany Leader father of Alida and Margaret, 632
Scottish Reformation, 631
Scotland, Bradley Martin estate, Balmacaan, Glen Urquhart, 391
Scottish Clans:
Crichton, 625
Douglas, 625
Livingston, 625
Scotland locations:
Aberdeen, 627
Ancrum, 630
Edinburgh, 625
Falkirk, 625, 627
Hero, Prince Albert, 61
Kilsyth, 627-629
Kirkland, 627
Lanark, 625

Linlithgow, 625, 628
Linlithgowshire, 625
Monyabroch, 628
Perth, 626
Sterling, 625, 627, 629
Stranrear, 629-630
Scotland, Parliament, 627, 631
Scott, William L., 465
Child, Mary Scott Townsend, wealthy heiress at her father's death, 515
Congressman, Washington, 465
Death, 465
Horse breeder:
Algeria Stock Farm in PA, 465
Hollywood stud farm in MD, 465
Sculpture:
Alma Mater Columbia University, Goelet, 419, *461*
Sculptor, Daniel C. French, 419
Penelope, Ancrum Garden, Lake Delaware, Angelica Gerry, 552
Sculptor, Franklin Simons, 552
Sea voyage hazards, 2
Seaverge, Newport Gerry home, 395
Bellevue Ave on the Cliff Walk, 416
Fourth of July celebration, 510
Purchased fully furnished by Elbridge T Gerry, 350, 374
Stables, 387
Redecorated, 408
Tax, Gerry a Rhode Island resident, 404
Serre, Henri, 613-614
Seven Years War, 9
Shepherds Fold, NYSPCC, 157+, 168, 365
Ships and schooners. *See also* Trans-Atlantic steamers:
Achilles, 9
Bellipotent, Billy Budd, 227
Britannic, England, 202
Celtic, England, 202
U.S.S. Albany – death of Captain James T. Gerry at sea, 23
U.S.S. Concord, Gerry brothers together, 28
U.S.S. Constitution, Old Ironsides, 25
U.S.S. Constellation, 23
U.S.S. Franklin, 23
U.S.S. Warren, 23
John Adams, 25
Katy, 613
Lafayette, steamship, 96
Makepeace, 3
Pretty Betsy, 3
Rights of Man, (Billy Budd), 227
Rockingham, 4
Success, 3
Ship consignments, 3
Small Pox Hospital, Marblehead, 7-8
Smith, Adam, 610
Society of the New York Hospital, 59-60, 96, 115, 135, 189, 355
Board of Governors, 59, 96
Society of the Sons of the Revolution, 230
Elected Vice President, 231
Fraunces Tavern, 230-231
Sons of Liberty, 691
Southside, Newport, Goelet, 179, *193*, 194, 260, 295, 302, 374, 424, 444, 472, 507, 514, 622
Spanish American War, 69
Booker T. Washington, 382
Economic rebound, 382-383
Naval Reserve used private ocean-ready yachts for war:
Almy, Gallatin yacht, 383
Maine sunk, 382
Mayflower, O. Goelet yacht, 377, 383
Nahma, R. Goelet yacht, 383
North Atlantic Squadron honored in Newport, 383
Rough Riders, 69, 381
Treaty of Paris, ends Spanish American War, Guam, Philippines, and Puerto Rico given to United States, 382
Tuskegee Airmen, 382
War Act created "death tax" to fund the war, 383
Spirit photography, Mumler Case, 83
Spiritualist movement, 82-83
Staatsburg-on-Hudson 52, *63*
Built by Morgan Lewis, 46
Enlarged by McKim Mead, 260
State Street at the Battery, NYC: *401*

No. 4, Ogden family, 620
No. 5, Goelet family, 620
No. 8, Our Lady of Rosary Mission today
Seton Hall Mission, 385
Steele, Fletcher (landscape), *556*
Ancrum, Lake Delaware:
The Gallop, 517, 551
Penelope sculpture center of gardens, 552
Plant list was 100 pages, 552
Salvage from NYC mansion:
Balustrades for patio, 552
Sculpture, 553
Frith House, Biltmore estate, *565*
Senator Peter Gerry and Edith Vanderbilt Gerry, 553
Sterling Castle, Scotland, 625, *627*, *629*,
Stewarts, lineage England, 628
Stranrear, Scotland, 629-630
Storm family:
Garritt, wealthy grocer and father of Glorvinia and Louisa, 51
Glorvinia, married Rev. Eugene A. Hoffman, 55, 542
Death of husband, 412
Golden anniversary, 411
Louisa, mother of Louisa M. Gerry, 53, *63*
Married Robert James Livingston, 54
Death, note in diary, 109
Thomas, Lt. Governor under Governor Morgan Lewis, 54
Suffrage movement, 167, 505
Adams, Abigale, 505
Anthony, Susan B., 167
Elbridge T. Gerry, 168
Howe, Julia Ward, President of Association of American Women, 332-333
Mother's Day creator, 333
League of Women Voters, 505
Nineteenth Amendment, 505
Anthony, Susan B. wrote, 167
Gerry, Senator Peter, 505
Stanton, Elizabeth Cady, daughter of Margaret Livingston, 168, *195*, 504
Supreme Court of the United States, 15, *314*
Case decided, Harrietta Goelet IRS property tax on yacht Nahma sailed and docked in foreign ports and waters most of every year, Goelets won decision, 486
Centennial Celebration, NYC, 281
Banquet, Lenox Lyceum, 281
Chief Justice, absent, flood, 281+
Gerry, Elbridge T. 281
Justices candy miniatures, 281
Justice's robes, 281
Justices of the Court arrive, 281
Opera House venue, 280
Orchestra, Victor Herbert, 281
President Grover Cleveland, 281
Press coverage, 281
Chief Justice Salmon P. Chase, 109
Circuit riding to hear cases, 599
Establishment of Court, 598-*603*,
Gerry case dismissed, 301
Library history, 598-*603*
See also libraries, Supreme Court.
Swiss Guard (Gallatins), 608, 610, 613

T

Taft, William Howard, Chief Justice,
Gerry, Elbridge T. private library donated to Supreme Court facilitated through legislation, xvi, 21, 520-521
Gerry, Peter G. wedding, 469
Talleyrand, Charles M. de, XYZ Affair, 14
Tammany Hall:
Broadway Farm, 96
Civil War, 69
Corruption, 96-97
Tax Act, 384
Teign River, England, 1
Teignmouth Port, England, 1
Telephone, Gallatins one of three phones in East Hampton, 213, 384, 406
Tennis, 16th century, 626
Theft of Gerry jewels, 310+
Theosophists, 415
Cuba, Ellis Island children, 415
Gerry, Elbridge T. protest in Washington, DC, 414
Katharine W. Tingley, 415

Raja Yoga Academy, CA, 415
Mayor of San Diego, 415
Spalding, Albert G., 416
Thompson, Ann 9-11, 31, 33
Death, 32
Married Elbridge Gerry, 10
Nine children, 18
Thompson, Catharine Walton, 10
Thompson, Charles, 9
Thompson, Jacob, 1845 died England, 31+
Thompson, James Ann's father, 9
Tiffany Studios, NYC commissions:
ASPCA Badge, diamonds, 110, 161
ASPCA Silver Cup, E.T. Gerry, 110, 310
Engraved invitations, 259
Goelet Silver Cups, yachting, 38, 200
Ring, engagement on yacht, 338
Stolen Tiffany jewelry, 434
Townsend, David,
Married Elizabeth Gerry, 27
Townsend, George J., 79
Townsend, John, 433
Townsend, Mathilde, *524*
Bar Harbor, Maine holidays, 466
Daughter of Richard and Mary Townsend, 465
Duke of Alba, Spain, courts Mathilde, 466
Equestrian, award winning, 466
Friends with Jean Reid, niece of Louisa M. Gerry, 425
Garden hobbyist, 425
Horses, society circle, 466
Marriage, Senator Peter Gerry,
Description, 469, *524*
Guest, President Wm. H. Taft, 469
Music, Marine Corps Orchestra, 469
Marriage, Sumner Wells,
Affair, 515
Wedding, 515
Portrait, John Singer Sargent, 448
Senator Peter Gerry,
Courtship, 466-467
Divorce, 515
Engagement at Christmas, 467
Peter introduced to political Society in Washington, DC, 469
Summers in Bar Harbor, Maine, 466
Coaching events, 466
Horse shows, 466
Sumner Wells, 515, *524*
Townsend, Richard H.,
Children, Mathilde, 465
Death, fell off horse, 465
Home, 24th Street mansion on DuPont Circle, DC, 465
Married Mary Scott, 465
Wealthy heiress, 465
Trade with Enemy Prohibited, 9
Trains, Vanderbilt train group: 364,
Royal Poinciana Hotel, 364
Gertrude Whitney, 364
Harry Payne Whitney, 364
Mabel Gerry, 364
Trans-Atlantic Cable,
Wireless medical treatment, 283
Trans-Atlantic steamers, 270+
Customs held Gerry furniture shipped from Europe, disputed valuation, 340
Dingley Tariff, date of antique determined value, 374
Delays move to mansion, 340
Diary about crossing the Atlantic by Lillian Gerry, 267-269
Gerrys to London, Paris, Nice, 234
Gerrys to France on La Gascogne Steamer, 267
Diary of trip by Lillian Gerry:
1899 Paris Exposition, 268, 275
Birthday gifts, 269
Bull fight, 268
Eiffel Tower, 268-269, 275
Liverpool, steamer home, 269
London, 269
Mills family joins them, 268
Paris, Worth fitting, 268
Sarah Bernhardt play, 268
Tuberculosis attack of Lillian, 269
Gerrys return from Europe on Kronprinz Whilhelm steamer and crash into Iceberg, 447
Steamer Lines: *274*
Cunard Line, 234, 271
Description: 270
Boarding, 270

Cabins, 270
Promenade Deck, 271
Saloons, 271
Sea sickness, 271
Socializing, 271
White Star Line, Germanic, 286
World War I stops European travel for over four years, 489, 492
Trans-Atlantic trade, 2
Traonchin, Theodore Doctor, 611
Treaty of Ghent, Albert Gallatin, 75
Treaty of Paris, Spanish American War, 82
Guam, Philippines, and Puerto Rico given to United States, 382
Trinity Church, NYC, 39, 75
Trinity Chapel, NYC, 80, 222, 251, 297, 352, 361, 364, 514
Trolley opposed on Fifth Ave., 215
Tuberculosis, 280, 549
Delaware County Sanatorium established 1920 long after Lillian Gerry's died, 509
Gerry, Angelica assists, 509
Gerry, Lillian, her doctor,
Koch, Dr. Robert, *Nobel Prize*, 280
Sanatoriums, 280
Turks Head Bldg. Providence RI, 558
Tuxedo jacket, origin, 418, 455
Tuxedo Park, New York, 417, 455
Architect, Bruce Price, 417
Land owner/developer, Lorillard, 417
Club house and socializing, 417, 455
Construction:
Tent city for workers, 417
Mess hall called Delmonico's, 417
Streets humorously called Broadway & Fifth Ave., 417
Debutante balls, 417
Homes at Tuxedo:
Gallatin, 417
Goelet, 417
Lorillard, 417
Lake and boating, 417
Lorillard III, Pierre, developer, 417
Tweed, Boss:
Broadway Farm, 37, 97, 619
Corruption, 97

V

Vanderbilt family:
Alfred Gwynne,
Death on Lusitania, 483
Memorial in England, 483
Memorial in Newport, RI, 483
Gerry, Robert L.,
Best Man at wedding, 406
Life-long friend, 483, 437
Married Elsie French, 406
Divorced, Alfred's affair with Mrs. Ruiz and her suicide, 407
Married Margaret Emerson, divorcee and heiress, 483
Children:
Alfred Jr., 483
George, W., 483
Alva Smith Vanderbilt, social climber,
Daughter, Consuelo, Duchess of Marlborough, 350, *394*
Married William Kissam then Divorced, 350
Married Perry Belmont, 350
Consuelo, *394, 396*
London City Council, 350
Married Duke of Marlborough under pressure, 350, *394*
Lived at Blenheim Castle in England, divorced, 350, *396*
Married Col. Jacques Balsan in Paris, very happy, 350, *394*
Winston Churchill her friend and cousin, 350, *394*
Cornelia Vanderbilt Cecil, *563*
Daughter of George and Edith Vanderbilt, 511
Home, Biltmore House, NC, 511, 525
Married Lord Robert Cecil, whom she divorced, 515, *563*
Cornelius, Commodore, 37, 87, 105, 122, 139
Cornelius II, 305
Breakers, Newport, RI, 349
Children:
Alfred, Gwynn Vanderbilt, best friend of Robert L. Gerry, 391

Gertrude Vanderbilt Whitney, best friend of Mabel Gerry, 349
Married Alice Gwynne, 351
Cornelius, III,
Married Grace Wilson, 351
Edith Dresser Vanderbilt, 563
Biltmore Farms Company, 559, *565*
Congressional Wives Club, 560
Married George Vanderbilt, 558
Children, 558
Cornelia Vanderbilt Cecil, *563*
Married Senator Peter Gerry 516, 559
Homes together:
Frith House, Biltmore estate *565*
Woods-Gerry House, R.I., *565*
Women's Democratic Club, 560
George,
Biltmore, Ashville, NC, 515, *565*
Hunt, Richard Morris, architect 515
Daughter Cornelia Cecil Hunt, 516
Death, 515
Married Edith Dresser, 515 widow
Gertrude, *394*
Gerry, Mabel, best friend 349, 546, *394*
Guardian of Gloria Vanderbilt, 351+
Married Harry Payne Whitney, 351
Metropolitan Opera House, 175
Painter and Sculptor, 351
Whitney Museum NYC, founded 351
Gloria, niece of Gertrude Payne who was Appointed her guardian, 351-352, *394*
William Henry, 140
William Kissam
Daughter, Consuelo, 350
Divorced, Alva who then married Perry Belmont, 350
Married Alva Smith, 350
Newport, Marble House, 349
Van Rensselaer, Nicholas Albany, 632
Views of the Public Debt, Albert Gallatin, 75
Voltaire, Francois-Marie D'Auret, 611-612
Gallatin neighbor, Geneva, 611, 612, 629

W

Walker, Charles Dodsley, organist, 224-226, *246*
Lake Delaware Boys Camp, 569
Wallace, William, the Braveheart, 625
Walton,
Catharine, 10-11
Married James Thompson, 11, 13
Mother of Ann Thompson Gerry, 9
Jacob, xix
Sarah Walton,
Daughter namesake Sarah Ogden
Married Robert Goelet Sr., 619
Married Jonathan Ogden, 10
William Sr., Ann Thompson Gerry's uncle (mother's brother) in NYC, 10
War of 1812, 1, 12, 25, 45, 75, 125, 561, 601
Warren, George, 145, 161
Children:
Harrietta, married Robert Goelet Jr., 407
Metropolitan Opera House, 161
Warren, Mercy Otis author, History of the American Revolution, 6-7
Angers John Adams, 15
Warren, Whitney, architect, *319*
Grand Central Terminal, 306, *319*
New York Yacht Club architect, 407
Model room, 407
Morgan JP donated land, 407
Stained glass ceiling, 407
Newport Country Club, 306, *319*
Washington, Booker T., 425+, *393*
Tuskegee Institute, 425
Tuskegee Airmen, 425
Spanish American War, 382
Veterans' Hospital, 382
Washington, DC, 13, 16-17, 21, 29, 43
Capitol burned, 18
Patent Office, temp. Capitol, 18
Washington, George, President, 13, 230, 218, 272
Quotation, 249
Washington Inaugural Celebration, 272
Ball, 7,000 guests, 259
Banquet by Hoffman, 259
Bible used by Washington, 258+, 272

Diary entry, George Washington, 257
  Dignitaries:
    Cabinet of the President, 258
    Foreign guests, 258
    President of the United States, 258
    Supreme Court of the U.S., 258
  Executive Committee, 257
    Chairman, Elbridge T. Gerry, 257
    Bill for State holiday, 258
    Certificate of Gratitude, 259
  Founding Father Elbridge Gerry, 257
  Founding Father John Adams, 257
  Gerry children join celebration:
    Watch street parades from Gallatin 5th Ave. home, 266
    Watch naval parade yacht Electra, 265
  Invitations engraved by Tiffany, 259
  Literary recitations, Federal Hall, 258
  Location chosen by Congress, Federal Hall, Wall St. NYC, 255-258, 272
  Memorial scrapbook, E.T. Gerry, 259
  Newspaper coverage examples:
    Bismarck Daily Tribune, 256
    St. Louis Globe Dem., 256
  Oath administered to Washington by Relative of Louisa L. Gerry, Chancellor Robert Livingston, 257, 272
  Parades and Floats, 259, 272
  St. Paul Church service, 258,
Washington Square Arch, 259-260, 272
  Architect, Stanford White, 260, *318*
  Sculptors, Piccirilli Studio, 261
Washington Market controversy, 59, *62*
  Gerry, Elbridge T. first case, 59
  Coenties Slip, No. 9, inherited grocery Louisa M. Gerry, 63
Washington Square Park, history, 260-261
Watering holes (resorts) history, 141-143
  Bar Harbor, Maine, 214, 440, 452
    Gerry, Senator Peter, 470, 484
    Townsend, Mathilde 425, 452, 470
  Hotels:
    Catskill Mountains, N.Y., 29
    East Hampton, Long Island, 129
    Long Branch, New Jersey, 142
    Nassau, Bahamas, Peter Gerry, 440
    Newport, RI. *See* Newport.
  New Rochelle, NYC:
    Neptune House Hotel, 31
    Oyster Bay, New Rochelle, 31
  Palm Beach, Florida, 351
    Royal Poinciana Hotel, 364
      Vanderbilt train group: 364,
        Gertrude Whitney, 364
        Harry Payne Whitney, 364
        Mabel Gerry, 364
  Rockaway Beach, NY, 30-31, 128
  Sag Harbor, Long Island, Maine, 130
  San Juan, Puerto Rico, 485
  Saratoga Springs, NY, 129
  West Point NY, 31, 128-129, *88*
Wealth and responsibility, 210, 304
  Gospel of Wealth, Carnegie, 277
Wealth of Nations, 610, 612
Wealthy women:
    Adams, Maud, 446
    Gerry, Angelica, 445
    Gould, Helen, 446
    Munro, Norma, 446
    Van Alen, May, 446
Webster, Daniel, *quotation*, 595
Wells, Sumner, *524*
  Affair with Mathilde Gerry, 515
  Career, 516
  Married Mathilde, 515, *524*
West India Company, 617
West Point, NY, *88*
  Abraham Lincoln, 74
  Cozzens Hotel, 74, 129, 138
  Goelet and Gerry families, 128, 138
  Harriman, E.H. met E.T. Gerry, 74
  J. P. Morgan, owned hotel, 138
Westinghouse, George, 264
  Buys Tesla application, 250
  Competes with Edison, 250
  Electrical Execution Act, 250
Westminster Abby, London, 426, 468
Whelen, Elsie, *522*
  Children, 477
    Ogden II, married 5 times,
      Ogden III, 486-488, 531
    Peter III, 166, 389
      Radio stations Newburgh and New York City, 486, 487

Divorced, Robert Wilson Goelet,
Cruelty disclosed, 486
Custody decree, 529
Married Robert Wilson Goelet,
Description of gowns, 434
Maid of Honor, Alice Roosevelt, 434
St. Mary's Church in Philadelphia, PA,
Married Henry Clews Jr., a sculptor, *522*
Art Foundation, 487
Chateau de la Napoule, home in Cannes, France, 487 *522*
Wheeler, Etta,
ASPCA, 117
NYSPCC, 117-118
Mary Ellen case, 117-123
White, Stanford, *318*
Madison Square Garden, 443 *195*
Architect of, *462*
Apartment for ladies, 443
Evelyn Nesbit affair, 443-444
Harry Thaw, jealous husband of Evelyn Nesbit, 443-444, *462*
Murder of Stanford White, 443-444
Offices for work, 443
Rooftop Garden Theatre, 443 *462*
Southside, architect for Robert Goelet, Jr., Newport, 260, *193*
Washington Square Arch, 260, *318*
Whitehall, London, 631
Gertrude Vanderbilt Whitney *394*
Artist, 351
Born, 349
Brearley School, NYC, 351
Best friend, Mabel Gerry, 349, 546, *394*
Home childhood, Breakers, Newport 349
Hospital for wounded soldiers, established near Paris, 351
Gloria Vanderbilt, guardian, 351+
Married Harry P. Whitney, 351
Private studio, Long Island, 351
Rodin, Auguste, tutor in Paris, 351
Sculptor, Art Students League in New York City, 351
Acclaimed works, 351
Whitney Museum of Art, NYC, 351
Whitney, Harry Payne, financier,
Married Gertrude Vanderbilt, 351
Whittier, John Greenleaf, poet, 4
Willard, Roberta, 516,
Married Robert Wilson Goelet, 517
Salve Regina College, Newport, 517
Wilson, Richard, T., 473
Children, "the marrying Wilsons," 473
Grace (Mrs. Cornelius Vanderbilt III) 473
Lelia (wife of Lord Michael H. Herbert) 473
Mary Rita (Mrs. Ogden Goelet) 473
Death, 473
Wilson sisters, "the marrying Wilsons," 473
Wimborne House, London, 307
Windsor Arcade, 468
Gerry, Elbridge T. built, 468
Windsor Hotel, 141, 287, 288, *396*
Hotel Fire:
Claude Monet art saved, 388
Escaped, Isadora Duncan, 388
Gerry, Elbridge T. owned land, 387
Leland, Warren F., owner, 388
Paid for burial of the dead, 388
St. Patrick's Day Parade, 387
Wine, Madeira, *401*
Gerry, Elbridge T. shipments to new mansion, 326, 340, 570
Bourbon, brandy, cognac and Scotch, old bottles, 326
Wineries, Goelet 595, 596
Barton & Guestier in France 596
Clos Du Val Winery in Napa Valley 595
Clover Hill Winery, in Tasmania 595
Domaine De Nizas Winery in France 595
Lalla Gully Vineyard in Tasmania 595
Taltarni Winery in Australia 595
Winthrop, John, 629
Winthrop Jr., John, 629
Wolfe, Catherine L., philanthropy, 210
Women and society:
Daily routine of a lady, 278
Calling cards and visiting, 278
Etiquette, 278 *See also* Emily Post
Women and sports:
Bowling, 221
Coaching, 282+, 369, 407, 442
Golf, 306, 333, 366, 418, 581

Tennis, 221, 306, 366, 481, 571, 626
Yachting, 169, 190
Women's suffrage, 167, 332-333, 446, 504+
Women philanthropists, 167, 496
Women property holders:
Adams, Maud, 446
Gerry, Angelica, 445
Gould, Helen, 446
Munro, Norma, 446
Van Alen, May, 446
World Exposition 1889, 267-270, *275*
World War I, definitive end to the Gilded Age, 277, 341
Chefs and chauffeurs of society families Leave for Europe, 489
End of the Great War, 500
Armistice Day, 500
League of Nations, 500
Treaty of Versailles, 500
"Years Between the Wars," 501
Fashions simplify, 492-493
European holidays fade, 377, 489
Fund raising for the war effort, 489, 492
National Special Aid Society, Donors, 500
Gerry, Elbridge T.,
Mills II, Mrs. Ogden,
Warren, Mrs. Whitney,
Whitney, Harry Payne,
Newport roller skating at Naval Training Station, 492
Post-War orphanages of the French Hero's Memorial Fund, 543
Mabel Gerry, established orphanage Sulgrave Manor, England, 500+
Worth gowns, Paris 268, 289+, 359, 446, 469
Angelica Gerry, *554*
Mabel Gerry, *546*
Wright, Frank Lloyd, *quotation*, 321
Wright, John D. Pres. NYSPCC, 121-122
Wurtemberg, Minister of, 609-610

X

XYZ Affair peach mission to France, American commission members: 14
Gerry, Elbridge
Marshall, John
Pinckney, Charles
French foreign minister:
Charles Maurice de Talleyrand, 14

Y

Yacht races. *See also* New York Yacht Club.
America's Cup, history, 47, 173, *195*
Deed of Gift, Gerry, 174, 241
Reviewed, 243
Revised & disputed, 243
Flag ship, 222, 226
Golden Age of Yachting, 338
"Match well made," 175
National popularity, 226, 241
Race defenders:
1851 America, 47, 174
1886 Mayflower, 221
1887 Volunteer v Thistle, 240
Boston Yacht Club owns the Volunteer, 242
Spectator incursions, 242
1895 Defender v Valkyrie, 359
Race 1 - Lord Dunraven 359
Water line challenge Defender
Race 2 – Oliver Iselin 359
Challenges foul against Valkyrie III.
Race 3 – Valkyrie III forfeit, 260
Left the race and sailed back to Scotland.
International quarrel, 260-261
Investigation & expulsion of Lord Dunraven.
1902 *Columbia* v *Shamrock*, 408
Patrol line control incursions by spectator vessels.
Schuyler, George, 174, 237, 283+
"There is no second place," 174
Astor Cup continued the Goelet Cup after Ogden's death, 200
Cannes Regatta in France, 363
Race founded by Ogden Goelet and James G. Bennett, 363

Riviera Season for yachts, 363
Commodore's Cup, 200
Damage to yachts cruise and races, 252, 266, 312
Eastern Yacht Club, 237, 238, 303
Gerry, E.T. last race as Commodore,
Goelet Cup, Newport Regatta, 219-220
Astor Cup continued Goelet Cup.
Established, 200
$500 Sloop Cup,
$1,000 Schooner Cup,
Tiffany and Co., 38
Morgan Cup, 237
Record keeper Elbridge T. Gerry, *193*, 199, 200, 211, 223, 238, 240, 252, 302
Newport, Regatta (Goelet Cup):
Atlantic v Mayflower, 221
Priscilla v Puritan, 214
Volunteer v Mayflower, 221
Yachting, America. *See also* New York Yacht Club, America's Cup, history.
Bar Harbor, 200, 214
Boston Club, 243
Volunteer first America's Cup 243, *245*
Cruises, annual NYYC, 222, 237, 239, 242, 266, 303
See also New York Yacht Club.
Record keeping, Gerry, *193*
Social life, 173, 179, 208, 226, 239, 266, 303, 338, 409.
Cruises, the Riviera, 363
Fleet Surgeon, 284
Gerry, Elbridge T. made yachting the "gentleman's sport,"
Goelet's made it the "racing sport"
Gilded Age sport, 306
Goelets order new yachts, Glasgow, Scotland, 302
Golden Age of Yachting, 338
Holiday yachting in Europe, 363
National Guard and Navy, use yachts to patrol coastline in wartime, 383, 560
New York Yacht Club, 47, 138, 173, 203, 205, 284
North Atlantic Squadron honored Spanish American War effort, 408
Rainbow fashion, yacht dressed with colorful flags up the lines, 303, 304
Registration privileges for yachts, 175
Schuyler, George, 47, 174, 237, 283-284
Seasick, 226
Stevens, John C., 174
Storm ravages yachts, 311-312
Women yachtsmen, i.e. yachtswomen:
Gerry, Louisa M. yacht the Electra, 338
Gould, Mrs., yacht the Hildegarde, 338
Henn, Mrs., British, yacht Galatea, 339
Iselin, Mrs., yacht Titania, 338
Langtry, Lillie, yacht Whyte Ladye, 308, 339
Morgan, Mrs. J.P., yacht Constellation, 338
Yacht Club, *See* New York Yacht Club
Yacht Registration gives owners Customs inspection privileges, 175
Yachting, Europe
Astor Cup fun winter sports held in St. Moritz, France, 403
Cannes Regatta organized by Ogden Goelet, 363
Clydebank Engineering & Ship Building, Glasgow, Scotland, 302
Yachts for Goelets, 302
Goelet, Ogden and British royalty, 357, 366, 373, 375+, 397, 426
Queen Victoria on yacht Britannia joined Ogden Goelet in Cannes and Nice, *195*, 363
Prince Edward Albert, "Bertie" joins Ogden Goelet in Nice, 363
Cumberland Yacht Club, 173
Cowes Yacht Club, 174, 306, 308, 357, 361, 366, 375+, *397*, 426, 437
One hundred Guineas Cup became America's Cup, 174
Riviera to Mediterranean Cruise ocean-worthy yachts, 174, 207, 339, 388
Royal Yacht Victoria & Albert challenge:
Guinea's Cup Race, 174
Queen's Cup, 174
Turkish detention, *Nahma* en route to Constantinople, 421

Sultan awards Harrietta Goelet Grand Cordon of the Turkish Order of the Chefakat, 421-422
Yachts - alphabetical by name:
Almy, Frederic Gallatin, 306
Damaged in port, 374
Family cruise to Greenland and Newfoundland, 310
Family cruise Mediterranean, then to New Zealand, 367
Decoration Day, 356
Sold to navy for use in the Spanish American War, 383
America, America's Cup, 47, 173, *195*, 241, 243
Atlanta, Jay Gould, 200
Atlantic, America's Cup, 221
Beatrice, Robert Goelet, Jr.,
Built in Glasgow, Scotland, 302
Sold when Nahma arrived, 378
Berti, Frederic Gallatin, 130
Cambria, Robert Goelet Jr.130
Conqueror, Fred W. Vanderbilt, 337
Corsair, Com. J. P. Morgan, 252
Defender, America's Cup, 359
Electra, Elbridge T. Gerry, 208
Anchored at East 26th Street NYC,
Built Harlan & Hollingsworth, 207
Description as a palace, 207-208
Dismantled, 1912, 477
Salvaged by Robert L. Gerry, 477
Chalice & paten sent to Lake Delaware boys Camp Chapel, 477
Wood panels use in Aknusti Mansion library, 479
Steam launch (small boat) 211, 214
Kept by E.T. Gerry in Newport for casual cruising, 479
Edison, Thomas A, installed first lights on a yacht in *Electra*, 207
Engagement of guest anecdote, 338
Providence crashed into *Electra* in the morning fog, 266
Flag ship for Yacht Club, 222, 226
Florida cruise, Palm Beach, 436
Lunch ceremony for *Electra* at Harlan & Hollingsworth 207-208
Lillian Gerry christens Electra, *245*
Louisa M. Gerry talks about her skill and interest as yachtswoman, 371
Machinery on Electra improved, 234
NYYC Cruise, last for Gerry as the Commodore, 302
Refurbishing, 214, 367
Annual, 214, 367
Complete overhaul, 362
Painted, 362
Rudder replaced, 237
Tebo basin, 367
Varnished, 251
Wheel, 237
Wilmington, Del., 214
Roosevelt, Pres. Teddy, cruise to Oyster Bay to visit Sagamore Hill, 412
Runs ashore, 302
Schuyler, George, died on board on cruise, 284
Small boat for errands, 214
Steam launch, 211, 214, 479
Galatea, British, America's Cup, 339
Glorianna, in Goelet Cup race, 304
Grayling, Latham A. Fish,
hit by Mayflower, 252-253
Harpoon, Goelet Cup winner, 304
Magic, Robert Goelet Jr., 175
Mayflower, Charles J. Paine, Boston
Collides with Grayling, 252-253
Electra rescued passengers from the water,
Mayflower, Ogden Goelet, 308, 397
Anchor in Cowes, UK, 376
Death of Ogden on his yacht, 376
Delivery of yacht, 375
Description:
Electric heaters, 375
2000 volume library, 375
Table for 24, 375
Mayflower yacht became the Presidential Yacht of the United States, 377, 397
Mischief, 207
Nahma, Robert Goelet, Jr., 397, *463*
Death on board, 388
Description, 377-378

Delivered to Newport, 377
Library on yacht, 378
Mount Vesuvius erupts, 440-444, *463*
Navy, 383
Southampton, England doctor found Harrietta seriously ill, 480
Redecorated by Harrietta, 480
Sold and scrapped, 378
Supreme Court of the United States, case IRS property tax on yacht *Nahma* which sailed and docked in foreign ports & waters most of every year, Goelets won, 486
Turkish Incident, Harrietta, 422
Goelet detained as a threat, 421
Sultan awards Harrietta Grand Cordon of the Turkish Order of the Chefakat, 422
Twin yacht to Mayflower, 378
Norseman, Ogden Goelet, 172
Description, 172-173
Nourmahal, John J. Astor, IV, 337
Oneida, E.C. Benedict, 284
Owera, Senator Peter Gerry, *525*, 560
Pastime, Elbridge T. Gerry, 173, 183, 191, *194*, 200
Priscilla, ran aground in fog near Watch Hill, 215, 238, 312
Puritan, 214, lost top mast, 238
Riviera, Frederic Gallatin, yacht ran aground in Chatham Bay, *194*, 440
Shamrock, Sir Thomas Lipton, 408
Thistle, Scotland, America's Cup, 240
Hull hidden before race, 241
America's Cup rules reviewed 242
Volunteer, America's Cup, *245*
Boston Yacht Club, 242-243
Boston Mayor wanted own America's Cup, 242
Burgess, Ed, designer, 242
Wasp, competed for Goelet Cup, 304
Commissioned by Navy, 383
Whyte Ladye, Ogden Goelet, *316*, 308, 337, 357, 363, 363, 366
Description, 308
Lilly Langtry, 307
Last tour on yacht to Cowes, England for Royal Squadron Races, 373-375
Sold, 308+, 375
Touring cruise, 308
Yorktown, VA 1781Siege of Yorktown 610

Z

Zucker, Alfred, *architect, 400*
Bolkenhayn Apartments, 367
Isaac Guggenheim rented apartment for $8,000 mo. 367
Gerry, Louisa M., owned land on which apartment building sat, 325
Mansion not finished by Hunt, so Zucker was hired and drew-up plans:
Grand staircase, 368, *398*
Law library, 368-369, *328*, *399*
Stables on 62nd Street, 369-370, *400*

www.ingramcontent.com/pod-product-compliance
Lightning Source LLC
LaVergne TN
LVHW060727210926
848485LV00006B/1399
* 9 7 8 1 6 1 6 1 9 3 8 7 4 *